Handbook of Software Reliability Engineering

Michael R. Lyu Editor in Chief

IEEE Computer Society Press
Los Alamitos, California
Washington Brussels Tokyo

McGraw-Hill
New York San Francisco Washington, D.C. Auckland Bogotá
Caracas Lisbon London Madrid Mexico City Milan
Montreal New Delhi San Juan Singapore
Sydney Tokyo Toronto

Library of Congress Cataloging-in-Publication Data

Handbook of software reliability engineering / Michael R. Lyu, editor in chief.
p. cm.
Includes index.
ISBN 0-07-039400-8 (alk. paper)
1. Computer software—Reliability—Handbooks, manuals, etc.
I. Lyu, Michael R.
QA76.76.R44H36 1995
005.1—dc20 95-46468
CIP

McGraw-Hill

A Division of The ***McGraw-Hill*** *Companies*

1 2 3 4 5 6 7 8 9 0 BKP/BKP 9 0 0 9 8 7 6

P/N 039401-6
PART OF
ISBN 0-07-039400-8

The sponsoring editor for this book was Marjorie Spencer, the editing supervisor was Christine H. Furry, and the production supervisor was Suzanne W. B. Rapcavage. This book was set in Century Schoolbook by North Market Street Graphics.

Printed and bound by Quebecor/Book Press.

This book is printed on acid-free paper.

To my wife C. Felicia Lyu,
for her love, understanding, and
support throughout this project

This book is also available from

IEEE Computer Society Press
10662 Los Vaqueros Circle
P.O. Box 3014
Los Alamitos CA 90720-1314
(714) 821-8380

Catalog #RS00030

Contents

Part 2 Practices and Experiences

Contributors

Sarah Brocklehurst *City University, London* (CHAP. 4)

Ram Chillarege *IBM Watson Research* (CHAP. 9)

Mary Donnelly *AT&T Bell Laboratories* (CHAP. 6)

Joanne Bechta Dugan *University of Virginia* (CHAP. 15)

Bill Everett *AT&T Bell Laboratories* (CHAP. 6)

William Farr *Naval Surface Warfare Center* (CHAP. 3)

Gene Fuoco *AT&T Bell Laboratories* (CHAP. 5)

Joseph R. Horgan *Bellcore* (CHAP. 13)

Nancy Irving *AT&T Bell Laboratories* (CHAP. 5)

Ravi K. Iyer *University of Illinois* (CHAP. 8)

Wendell Jones *BNR Incorporated* (CHAP. 11)

Bruce Juhlin *U S West* (CHAP. 5)

Karama Kanoun *LAAS-CNRS, Toulouse, France* (CHAPS. 2, 10)

Nachimuthu Karunanithi *Bellcore* (CHAP. 17)

Taghi Khoshgoftaar *Florida Atlantic University* (CHAP. 12)

Diane Kropfl *AT&T Bell Laboratories* (CHAP. 5)

Jean-Claude Laprie *LAAS-CNRS, Toulouse, France* (CHAPS. 2, 10)

Inhwan Lee *Tandem Computers, Inc.* (CHAP. 8)

Bev Littlewood *City University, London* (CHAP. 4)

Michael R. Lyu *AT&T Bell Laboratories, Editor* (CHAPS. 1, 7, 16, APP. B)

Yashwant Malaiya *Colorado State University* (CHAP. 17)

Aditya P. Mathur *Purdue University* (CHAP. 13)

David McAllister *North Carolina State University* (CHAP. 14)

John Munson *University of Idaho* (CHAP. 12)

John Musa *AT&T Bell Laboratories* (CHAPS. 5, 6)

Allen Nikora *Jet Propulsion Laboratory* (CHAP. 7)

George Stark *Mitre Corporation* (APP. A)

Robert Tausworthe *Jet Propulsion Laboratory* (CHAP. 16)
Mladen Vouk *North Carolina State University* (CHAPS. 11, 14)
Geoff Wilson *AT&T Bell Laboratories* (CHAP. 6)

Foreword

Alfred V. Aho
Columbia University

In complex software systems, reliability is the most important aspect of software quality, but one that has often been the most elusive to achieve. Since more and more of the world's activities and systems are dependent on software, achieving the appropriate level of software reliability consistently and economically is crucial. Software failures make newspaper headlines because at best they inconvenience people and in extreme cases kill them.

It is refreshing to see a book that has the potential to make a significant improvement to software reliability. The *Handbook of Software Reliability Engineering* is an important milestone in the history of software reliability engineering. Michael R. Lyu has assembled a team of leading experts to document the best current practices in the field. The coverage is comprehensive, including material on fault prevention, fault removal, fault tolerance, and failure forecasting. Theory, models, metrics, measurements, processes, analysis, and estimation techniques are presented. The book is filled with proven methods, illustrative examples, and representative test results from working systems in the field. An important component of the book is a set of reliability tools that can be used to apply the techniques presented.

The subject is treated with the rigor that is characteristic of a mature engineering discipline. The book stresses mathematical models for evaluating reliability trade-offs, and shows how these models can be applied to the development of software systems.

With the publication of this Handbook, the field of software reliability engineering has come of age. This book is must reading for all software engineers concerned with software reliability.

Alfred V. Aho

Foreword

Richard A. DeMillo
Purdue University and Bellcore

Early in this exhaustive treatment of what may be the single most critical aspect of modern software development, the editor says "Mature engineering fields classify and organize proven solutions in handbooks so that most engineers can consistently handle complicated but routine designs." The reliability engineering of software has become mature with the appearance of this Handbook.

In my graduate software engineering course, I motivate the importance of early test planning with reliability requirement setting examples. It is, in my experience, an issue about which success or failure of major systems projects revolve. In the early 1980s I led the DOD's software testing and reliability analysis team for the final operational tests of the now-famous Patriot Missile System. The questions? What was the required system reliability? Was the operational test data consistent with these requirements? Not many people know how close Patriot came to being rejected as a viable weapons system—not because the system itself was bad, but rather because the reliability engineering was so flawed that developers could not determine how reliable it really was. This crisis could have been avoided had software reliability engineering practice been systematized and applied in the manner advocated by this Handbook.

Reliability theory and engineering statistics textbooks ignore software, for the most part. Software engineering textbooks generally ignore reliability theory. Classroom teachers of the subject are forced to the kind of anecdotal material mentioned above, perhaps augmented by special-purpose supplementary readings. Even worse, software reliability theory has a reputation for facileness that has been encouraged by the many contributors who try to apply hardware reliability models mutatis mutandis to the very different (and more difficult) problems of software reliability.

So, when I was asked by the editor to review this Handbook, I agreed eagerly. On the one hand, a "real" handbook would be of inestimable help to practitioners, decision makers, teachers, and students. On the other hand, a spotty or imbalanced treatment would only make matters worse. I said I would offer my comments only after reading the entire book.

The first thing I did when I received the manuscript was to check it against my classroom "staples." There for the first time in book form was a coherent approach to developing reliability requirements. There also was a discussion of the relationship between software test and reliability estimation, the impact of software architecture on reliability, error studies and software fault classification, tools and methods extracted from best-practice benchmarks of the best reliability labs in the world, actual data. It was all there—and in pretty much the same form in which I would have presented it myself. The editor even included exercises to make it suitable for classroom use.

Encouraged, I read the manuscript front to back. This is a book that will be the standard by which the field is measured for years to come. It is thorough, correct, readable, and so current that it actually anticipates results that have not appeared in archival journals yet. It contains the best work of many of the founders of the field. It contains innovations by some of the rising stars. It is, however, more than anything else a Handbook in the tradition of the classic handbooks of mathematics, physics, and engineering. It does not present software reliability as a silver bullet. It does not attempt to proscribe the complex system usages that would require skill and training on the part of software developers. Rather it seeks to "... classify and organize proven solutions ... so that most engineers can consistently handle complicated but routine designs." In this it succeeds, far beyond my expectations. It clearly establishes software reliability engineering as a mature engineering discipline.

Richard A. DeMillo

Preface

Ever since I entered the field of software reliability engineering some years ago, I have been looking for a book that exclusively and comprehensively deals with software reliability subjects that interest me, as both a researcher and a practitioner. I wasn't able to find one. So I started this project by inviting the leading experts in this field to contribute chapters for this book. I laid out the framework of the book, identified its essential components, and integrated them by maintaining completeness and avoiding redundancies. As an editor, my duty is to ensure breadth, while the chapter authors treat the subjects of their delegated chapters in depth.

This is a handbook on software reliability engineering. The theme underlying the book is the formulation, application, and evaluation of software reliability engineering techniques in practice. Reliability is obviously related to many characteristics of the software product and development process. This *Handbook* intends to address all its aspects in a quantitative way.

The book is designed for practitioners or researchers at all levels of competency, from novice to expert. It is targeted for several large, general groups of people who need information on software reliability engineering. They include:

1. People who need a general understanding of software reliability. These are high-level managers, professional engineers who use software or whose designs interface with software, and people who acquire, purchase, lease, or use software.
2. Software developers, testers, and quality assurance personnel who use and apply software reliability engineering techniques. This also includes practitioners in related disciplines such as system engineering, reliability management, risk analysis, management-decision sciences, and software maintenance.

3. Researchers and students in software engineering, reliability analysis, applied statistics, operations research, and related disciplines, and anyone who wants a deeper understanding of software reliability and its engineering techniques.

Each of the book's individual topics (i.e., chapters) could be considered as a compact, self-contained minibook. However, these topics are presented in relation to the basic principles and practices of software reliability engineering. The approach is to provide a framework and a set of techniques for evaluating and improving the engineering of software reliability. It presents specific solutions, obtained mostly from real-world projects and experimental studies, for routine applications. It further highlights promising emerging techniques for research and exploration opportunities.

The book has been thoroughly indexed for your convenience, so that it can serve as a true handbook, and a comprehensive list of references is provided for the purpose of literature search. As a unique value-added feature, this book includes a CD-ROM, which contains 40 published and unpublished software project failure data sets and some of the most advanced software reliability tools for ready application of software reliability techniques and a jump-start on software reliability engineering programs.

This book is also designed to be used as a textbook by students of software engineering or system reliability, either in a classroom or for self-study. Examples, case studies, and problems have been provided throughout the book to illustrate the concepts and to walk through the techniques. A *Solution Manual* is available from the editor with solutions to some of the exercises.

What is finally presented here is the work of celebrated international experts contributing their most advanced knowledge and practices on specific reliability-related topics. The development team of this book wants to thank our colleagues who provided continuous encouragement and thorough review of the chapters of the book. They are Jean Arlat, Phillip Babcock, Farokh B. Bastani, Brian Beckman, Justin Biddle, James Bieman, Harry S. Burns, Sid Dalal, Chris Dale, Adrian Dolinsky, George Finelli, Amrit Goel, Jack Goldberg, Myron Hecht, Walter Heimerdinger, Yu-Yun Ho, Yennun Huang, Robert Jackson, Mohamed Kaaniche, Kalai Kalaichelvan, Rick Karcich, Ted Keller, Elaine Keramidas, Chandra Kintala, Sy-Yen Kuo, Ming Y. Lai, Alice Lee, Haim Levendel, Yi-Bing Lin, Peng Lu, Richard E. Machol, Suku Nair, Mits Ohba, Gardner Patton, Hoang Pham, Francesca Saglietti, Norm Schneidewind, Robert Sherman, David Siefert, Pradip Srimani, Mark Sullivan, Robert Swarz, K.C. Tai, Yoshi Tohma, Randy Van Buren, C.W. Vowell, Anneliese von Mayrhauser, Chris J. Walter, Yi-Ming Wang, Pramod Warty, Chuck Weinstock, Min Xie, and Jinsong Yu.

We are most appreciative of the organizations and projects that provided funding for the work conducted in some of the book chapters. They are the Advanced Research Projects Agency, the ESPRIT Basic Research Action on Predictably Dependable Computing Systems, the ESPRIT programme as part of the PDCS1 and PDCS2 projects, the EU Environment programme as part of the SHIP project, IBM at Poughkeepsie, New York, the Illinois Computer Laboratory for Aerospace Systems and Software (ICLASS), National Aeronautics and Space Administration (NASA), NASA AMES Research Center, Office of Naval Research, Tandem Computers Incorporated, the U.K. EPSRC as part of the DATUM project, and the U.S. Air Force Operational Test and Evaluation Center (AFOTEC).

I also want to particularly thank Al Aho and Rich DeMillo for writing forewords to this book. Their comments are helpful and rewarding. I am greatly thankful to Karen Newcomb of NASA COSMIC and Liliam Valdez-Diaz of AT&T for permission to include CASRE, SoftRel, and AT&T SRE Toolkit in this book. My appreciation goes to Jean Glasser, Marjorie Spencer, John Wyzalek, and Suzanne Rapcavage, editing and production supervisors at McGraw-Hill during different stages of this book. Midge Haramis's assistance is also acknowledged. The invaluable guidance and help of Christine Furry at North Market Street Graphics during many revision, editing, and production cycles have also made this book project much easier than it would have been.

Finally, I want to thank my wife Felicia, to whom this book is dedicated.

Michael R. Lyu
Murray Hill, New Jersey

Part

1

Technical Foundations

Chapter

1

Introduction

Michael R. Lyu
AT&T Bell Laboratories

1.1 The Need for Reliable Software

With the advent of the electronic digital computer 50 years ago [Burk46], we have become dependent on computers in our daily lives. The computer revolution is fueled by an ever more rapid technological advancement. Today, computer hardware and software permeates our modern society. Computers are embedded in wristwatches, telephones, home appliances, buildings, automobiles, and aircraft. Science and technology demand high-performance hardware and high-quality software for making improvements and breakthroughs. We can look at virtually any industry—automotive, avionics, oil, telecommunications, banking, semiconductors, pharmaceuticals—all these industries are highly dependent on computers for their basic functioning.

The size and complexity of computer-intensive systems has grown dramatically during the past decade, and the trend will certainly continue in the future. Contemporary examples of highly complex hardware/software systems can be found in projects undertaken by NASA, the Department of Defense, the Federal Aviation Administration, the telecommunications industry, and a variety of other industries. For instance, the NASA Space Shuttle flies with approximately 500,000 lines of software code on board and approximately 3.5 million lines of code in ground control and processing. After being scaled down significantly from its original plan, the International Space Station Alpha is still projected to have millions of lines of software to operate innumerable hardware pieces for its navigation, communication, and experimentation. In the telecommunications industry, operations for phone carriers are supported by hundreds of software systems, with hundreds of millions of lines of source code. In the avionics industry, almost all new payload instruments contain their own microprocessor system with extensive embedded software. A massive amount of hardware and complicated software also exists in the Federal Aviation Administration's Advanced Automation System, the new generation air traffic control system. In our offices and homes, personal computers cannot function without complex operating systems (e.g., Windows) ranging from 1 to 5 million lines of code, and many other shrink-wrapped software packages of similar size provide a variety of applications for our daily use of these computers.

The demand for complex hardware/software systems has increased more rapidly than the ability to design, implement, test, and maintain them. When the requirements for and dependencies on computers increase, the possibility of crises from computer failures also increases. The impact of these failures ranges from inconvenience (e.g., malfunctions of home appliances) to economic damage (e.g., interruptions of banking systems) to loss of life (e.g., failures of flight systems or medical software). Needless to say, the reliability of computer systems has become a major concern for our society.

Within the computer revolution, progress has been uneven: software assumes a larger burden, while based on a less firm foundation, than hardware. It is the integrating potential of software that has allowed designers to contemplate more ambitious systems encompassing a broader and more multidisciplinary scope, and it is the growth in utilization of software components that is largely responsible for the high overall complexity of many system designs. However, in stark contrast with the rapid advancement of hardware technology, proper development of software technology has failed to keep pace in all measures, including quality, productivity, cost, and performance. With the last decade of the 20th century, computer software has already become the major source of reported outages in many systems [Gray90]. Consequently, recent literature is replete with horror stories of projects gone awry, generally as a result of problems traced to software.

Software failures have impaired several high-visibility programs. In the NASA Voyager project, the Uranus encounter was in jeopardy because of late software deliveries and reduced capability in the Deep Space Network. Several Space Shuttle missions have been delayed due to hardware/software interaction problems. In one DoD project, software problems caused the first flight of the AFTI/F-16 jet fighter to be delayed over a year, and none of the advanced modes originally planned could be used. Critical software failures have also affected numerous civil and scientific applications. The ozone hole over Antarctica would have received attention sooner from the scientific community if a data analysis program had not suppressed the anomalous data because it was "out of range." Software glitches in an automated baggage-handling system forced Denver International Airport to sit empty more than a year after airplanes were to fill its gates and runways [Gibb94].

Unfortunately, software can also kill people. The massive Therac-25 radiation therapy machine had enjoyed a perfect safety record until software errors in its sophisticated control systems malfunctioned and claimed several patients' lives in 1985 and 1986 [Lee92]. On October 26, 1992, the Computer Aided Dispatch system of the London Ambulance Service broke down right after its installation, paralyzing the capability of the world's largest ambulance service, which handles 5000 daily requests to transport patients in emergency situations [SWTR93]. In the highly automated aviation industry, misunderstandings between computers and pilots have been implicated in several airline crashes in the past few years [Swee95], and in some cases experts hold software control responsible because of inappropriate reaction of the aircraft to the pilots' desperate inquiries during an abnormal flight.

Software failures also have led to serious consequences in business. On January 15, 1990, a fault in a switching system's newly released software caused massive disruption of a major carrier's long-distance network, and another series of local phone outages traced to software problems occurred during the summer of 1991 [Lee92]. These critical failures caused enormous revenue losses to thousands of companies relying on telecommunications companies to support their businesses.

Many software systems and packages are distributed and installed in identical or similar copies, all of which are vulnerable to the same software failure. This is why even the most powerful software companies such as Microsoft are fearful of "killer bugs" which can easily wipe out all the profits of a glorious product if a recall is required on the tens of millions of copies they have sold [Cusu95]. To this end, many software companies see a major share of project development costs identified with the design, implementation, and assurance of reliable software, and they recognize a tremendous need for systematic approaches using *software reliability engineering* techniques. Clearly, developing the required techniques for software reliability engineering is a major challenge to computer engineers, software engineers, and engineers of various disciplines now and for decades to come.

1.2 Software Reliability Engineering Concepts

Software reliability engineering is centered around a very important software attribute: *reliability*. Software reliability is defined as *the probability of failure-free software operation for a specified period of time in a specified environment* [ANSI91]. It is one of the attributes of software quality, a multidimensional property including other customer satisfaction factors such as functionality, usability, performance, serviceability, capability, installability, maintainability, and documentation [Grad87, Grad92]. Software reliability, however, is generally accepted as the key factor in software quality since it quantifies software failures—which can make a powerful system inoperative or, as with the Therac-25, deadly. As a result, reliability is an essential ingredient in customer satisfaction. In fact, ISO 9000-3 specifies measurement of field failures as the only required quality metric: ". . . at a minimum, some metrics should be used which represent reported field failures and/or defects from the customer's viewpoint. . . . The supplier of software products should collect and act on quantitative measures of the quality of these software products." (See sec. 6.4.1 of [ISO91].)

Example 1.1 shows the impact of high-severity failures to customer satisfaction.

Example 1.1 A survey of nine large software projects was taken in [Merc94] to study the factors contributing to customer satisfaction. These projects were telecommunications systems responsible for day-to-day operations in the U.S. local telephone business. The survey requested telephone customers to assess a quality score between 0 and 100 for each system. The average size of these projects was 1 million lines of source code.

Trouble Reports (i.e., failure reports in the field) were collected from these projects. Figure 1.1 shows the overall quality score from the survey of these projects, plotted against the number of high-severity Trouble Reports.

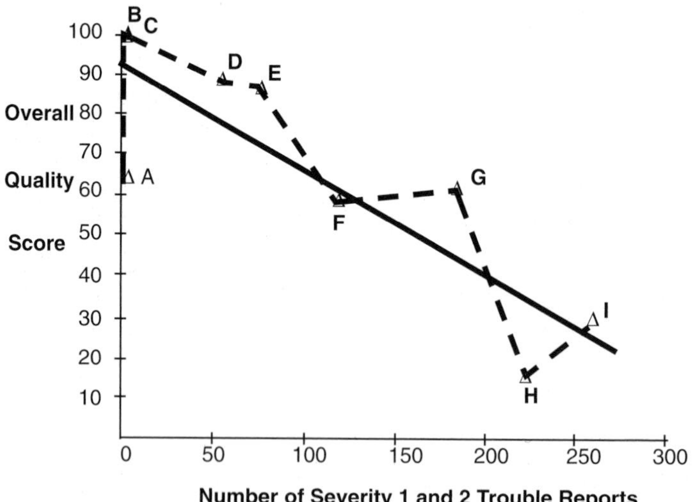

Figure 1.1 Correlations between software quality and high-severity failures.

From Fig. 1.1 we can observe a high negative correlation (–0.86) between the overall quality score and the number of high-severity failures for each project. This example illustrates that in the telecommunications industry, the number of critical software failures promptly indicates negative customer perception on overall software quality. This quality indicator is also generally applicable to many other industries.

Software reliability is also one of the system dependability concepts that are discussed in detail in Chap. 2. Example 1.2 demonstrates the impact of software reliability to system reliability.

Example 1.2 A military distributed processing system has an MTTF (mean time to failure, see definition in Sec. 1.4) requirement of 100 hours and an availability requirement of 0.99. The overall architecture of the system is shown in Fig. 1.2, indicating that the system consists of three subsystems, SYS1, SYS2, SYS3, a local area network, LAN, and a 10-kW power generator GEN. In order for the system to work, all the components (except SYS2) have to work. In the early phase of system testing, hardware reliability parameters are predicted according to the MIL-HDBK-217 and shown for each system component. Namely, above each component block in Fig. 1.2, two numbers appear. The upper number represents the predicted MTTF for that component, and the lower number represents its MTTR (mean time to repair, see Sec. 1.4). The units are hours. For example, SYS1 has 280 hours for MTTF and 0.53 hours for MTTR, while SYS2 and SYS3 have 387 hours for MTTF and 0.50 hours for MTTR. Note that SYS2 is configured as a triple-module redundant system, shown in the dotted-line block, where the subsystem will work as long as two or more modules work. Due to this fault-tolerant capability, its MTTF improves to 5.01×10^4 hours and MTTR becomes 0.25 hours.

To calculate the overall system reliability, all the components in the system have to be considered. If we assume the software does not fail (a mistake often made by system reliability engineers!), the resulting system MTTF would be 125.9

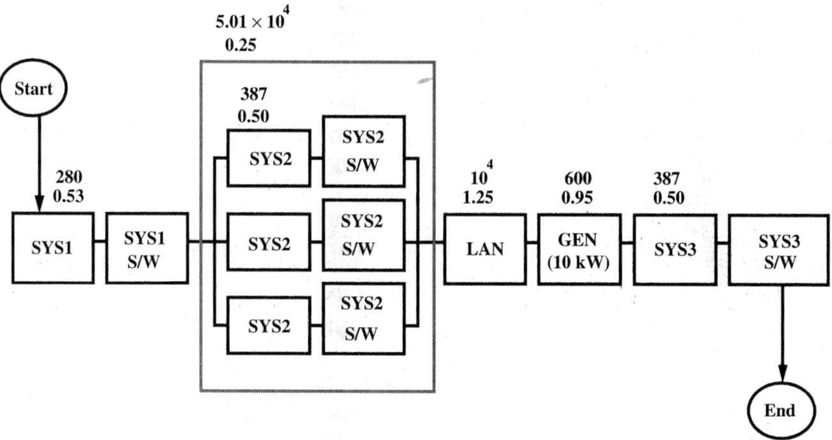

Figure 1.2 An example of predicting system reliability.

hours and MTTR would be 0.62 hours, achieving system availability of 0.995. It looks as if the system already meets its original requirements.

But the software does fail. Both SYS2 and SYS3 software contain 300,000 lines of source code, and following the prediction model described in Chap. 3 (Sec. 3.8.3) and [RADC87], the predicted initial failure rates for SYS2 and SYS3 software are both 2.52 failures per execution hour. (Note the three SYS2 S/W are identical software copies and not fault-tolerant.) Even without considering SYS1 software failures, the system MTTF would have become 11.9 CPU minutes! Assuming MTTR is still 0.62 hours (although it should be higher since it generally takes longer to reinitialize the software) and CPU time and calendar time are close to each other (which is true for this distribution system), the system availability becomes 0.24—far less than predicted!

Note that the system presented in Example 1.2 was a real-world example, and the estimated reliability parameters were actual practices following military handbooks [Lyu89]. This example is not an extreme case. In fact, many existing large systems face the same situation: software reliability is the bottleneck of system reliability, and the maturity of software always lags behind that of hardware. Accurately modeling software reliability and predicting its trend have become critical, since this effort provides crucial information for decision making and reliability engineering for most projects.

Reliability engineering is a daily practiced technique in many engineering disciplines. Civil engineers use it to build bridges and computer hardware engineers use it to design chips and computers. Using a similar concept in these disciplines, we define *software reliability engineering* (SRE) as *the quantitative study of the operational behavior of software-based systems with respect to user requirements concerning reliability* [IEEE95]. SRE therefore includes:

1. Software reliability measurement, which includes estimation and prediction, with the help of software reliability models established in the literature
2. The attributes and metrics of product design, development process, system architecture, software operational environment, and their implications on reliability
3. The application of this knowledge in specifying and guiding system software architecture, development, testing, acquisition, use, and maintenance

Based on the above definitions, this book details current SRE techniques and practices.

1.3 Book Overview

Mature engineering fields classify and organize proven solutions in handbooks so that most engineers can consistently handle complicated but routine designs. Unfortunately, handbooks of software engineering practice are unknown. Software development has been treated as an art. Although we understand a very large part of this art, it is still not a practiced engineering discipline. Consequently, mistakes in software development are repeated project after project, year after year, and the software crises of 25 years ago are still with us today [Gibb94].

Fortunately, the reliability component of software engineering is evolving from an art to a practical engineering discipline. It is time to begin to codify our knowledge in SRE and make it available—this is the main purpose of this handbook. This handbook provides information on the key methods and methodologies used in SRE, covering its state-of-the-art techniques and state-of-practice approaches. The book is divided into three parts and 17 chapters. Each chapter is written by SRE experts, including researchers and practitioners. These chapters cover the theory, design, methodology, modeling, evaluation, experience, and assessment of SRE techniques and applications.

Part 1 of the book, composed of five chapters, sets up the *technical foundations* for software reliability modeling techniques, in which system-level dependability and reliability concepts, software reliability prediction and estimation models, model evaluation and recalibration techniques, and operational profile techniques are presented. In particular,

1. Chapter 1 gives an *introduction* of the book, where its framework is outlined and the main contents of each chapter are surveyed. Basic ideas, terminology, and techniques in SRE are presented.
2. Chapter 2 provides a general overview of the *system dependability* concept, and shows that the classical reliability theory can be extended in order to be interpreted from both hardware and software viewpoint.
3. Chapter 3 reviews the major software *reliability models* that appear in the literature, from both historical and applications perspectives. Each model is presented with its motivation, model assumptions, data requirements, model form, estimation procedure, and general comments about its usage.
4. Chapter 4 presents a systematic framework to conduct *model evaluation* of several competing reliability models, using advanced statistical criteria. Recalibration techniques which can greatly improve model performance are also introduced.
5. Chapter 5 details a technique that is essential to SRE: the *operational profile.* The operational profile shows you how to increase productivity and reliability and speed development by allocating project resources to functions on the basis of how a system will be used.

Part 2 contains SRE *practices and experiences* in six chapters. This part of the book consists of practical experiences from major organizations such as AT&T, JPL, Bellcore, Tandem, IBM, NASA, Nortel, ALCATEL, and other international organizations. Various SRE procedures are implemented for particular requirements under different environments. The authors of each chapter in Part 2 describe the practical procedures that work for them, and convey to you their experiences and lessons learned. Specifically,

1. Chapter 6 describes the best *current practice* in SRE adopted by over 70 projects at AT&T. This practice allows you to analyze, manage, and improve the reliability of software products, to balance customer needs in terms of cost, schedule, and quality, and to minimize the risks of releasing software with serious problems.
2. Chapter 7 conveys the *measurement experience* in applying software reliability models to several large-scale projects at JPL and Bellcore. We discuss the SRE procedures, data collection efforts, modeling approaches, data analysis methods, reliability measurement results, lessons learned, and future directions. A practical scheme to improve measurement accuracy by linear combination models is also presented.
3. Chapter 8 shows *measurement-based analysis* techniques which directly measure software reliability through monitoring and recording failure occurrences in a running system under various user workloads. Experiences with Tandem GUARDIAN, IBM MVS, and VAX VMS operating systems are explored.
4. Chapter 9 proposes a *defect classification* scheme which extracts semantic information from software defects such that it provides a measurement on the software development process. This chapter explains the framework, procedure, and advantage of this scheme and its successful application and deployment in many projects at IBM.
5. Chapter 10 addresses software reliability *trend analysis,* which can help project managers control the progress of the development activities and determine the efficiency of the test programs. Application results from a number of studies including switching systems and avionic applications are reported.
6. Chapter 11 provides insight into the process of collecting and analyzing software reliability *field data* through a discussion of the underlying principles and case study illustrations. Included in the field data analysis are projects from IBM, Hitachi, Nortel, and space shuttle onboard flight software.

Emerging techniques which have been used to advance SRE research field are addressed by the six chapters in Part 3. These techniques include software metrics, testing schemes, fault-tolerant software, fault tree analysis, simulation, and neural networks. After explicitly explaining these techniques in concrete terms, authors of the chapters in Part 3 establish the relationships between these techniques and software reliability. Potential research topics and their directions are also addressed in detail. In summary,

1. Chapter 12 presents the technique to incorporate software *metrics* for reliability assessment. This chapter makes the connection between software complexity and software reliability, in which both functional complexity and operational complexity of a program are examined for the development and maintenance of reliable software.
2. Chapter 13 explores the relationship between software *testing* and reliability. In addressing the impact of testing to reliability, this chapter applies program structure metrics and code coverage data for the estimation of software reliability and the assessment of the risk associated with software.
3. Chapter 14 focuses on the software *fault tolerance* approach as a potential technique to improve software reliability. Issues regarding the architecture, design, implementation, modeling, failure behavior, and cost of fault tolerant systems are discussed.
4. Chapter 15 introduces the *fault tree* technique for the reliability analysis of software systems. This technique helps you to analyze the impact of software failures on a system, to combine off-line and on-line tests to prevent or detect software failures, and to compare different design alternatives for fault tolerance with respect to both reliability and safety.
5. Chapter 16 demonstrates how several *simulation* techniques can be applied to a typical software reliability engineering process, in which many simplifying assumptions in reliability modeling could be lifted. This chapter shows the power, flexibility, and potential benefits that the simulation techniques offer, together with methods for representing artifacts, activities, and events of the reliability process.
6. Chapter 17 elaborates how the *neural networks* technology can be used in software reliability engineering applications, including its usage as a general reliability growth model for better predictive accuracy, and its exercise as a classifier to identify fault-prone software modules.

In addition to these book chapters, two appendixes and an MS/DOS diskette are enclosed in the book. Appendix A surveys the currently available tools which encapsulate software reliability models and techniques. These tools include AT&T Toolkit, SMERFS, SRMP, SoRel, CASRE, and SoftRel. Appendix B reviews the analytical modeling techniques, statistical techniques, and reliability theory commonly used in the SRE studies. The MS/DOS disk, called *Data and Tool Disk* (or *Data Disk*), includes two directories: the DATA directory and the TOOL directory. The DATA directory contains more than 40 published and unpublished software failure data sets used in the book chapters, and the TOOL directory contains the AT&T SRE Toolkit, SMERFS, CASRE, and SoftRel software reliability tools.

Finally, at the end of each book chapter are problems which provide practice exercises for the reader.

1.4 Basic Definitions

We notice three major components in the definition of software reliability: *failure, time,* and *operational environment.* We now define these terms and other related SRE terminology. We begin with the notions of a software system and its expected service.

Software systems. A *software system* is an interacting set of software subsystems that is embedded in a computing environment that provides inputs to the software system and accepts service (outputs) from the software. A software subsystem itself is composed of other subsystems, and so on, to a desired level of decomposition into the smallest meaningful elements (e.g., modules or files).

Service. Expected *service* (or "behavior") of a software system is a time-dependent sequence of outputs that agrees with the initial specification from which the software implementation has been derived (for the verification purpose), or which agrees with what system users have perceived the correct values to be (for the validation purpose).

Now we observe the following situation: a software system named *program* is delivering an *expected service* to an environment or a person named *user.*

Failures. A *failure* occurs when the user perceives that the program ceases to deliver the expected service.

The user may choose to identify several *severity* levels of failures, such as: catastrophic, major, and minor, depending on their impacts to the system service. The definitions of these severity levels vary from system to system.

Outages. An *outage* is a special case of a failure that is defined as a loss or degradation of service to a customer for a period of time (called *outage duration*). In general, outages can be caused by hardware or software failures, human errors, and environmental variables (e.g., lightning, power failures, fire). A failure resulting in the loss of functionality of the entire system is called a *system outage.* An example to quantify a system outage in the telecommunications industry is to define the outage duration of telephone switching systems to be "greater than 3 seconds (due to failures that results in loss of stable calls) or greater than 30 seconds (for failures that do not result in loss of stable calls)." [BELL90c]

Faults. A fault is uncovered when either a failure of the program occurs or an internal error (e.g., an incorrect state) is detected within the program. The cause of the failure or the internal error is said to be a *fault.* It is also referred as a *bug.*

In most cases the fault can be identified and removed; in some cases it remains a hypothesis that cannot be adequately verified (e.g., timing faults in distributed systems).

In summary, a software failure is an incorrect result with respect to the specification or an unexpected software behavior perceived by the user at the boundary of the software system, while a software fault is the identified or hypothesized cause of the software failure.

Defects. When the distinction between fault and failure is not critical, *defect* can be used as a generic term to refer to either a fault (cause) or a failure (effect). Chapter 9 provides a complete and practical classification of software defects from various perspectives.

Errors. The term *error* has two different meanings:

1. A discrepancy between a computed, observed, or measured value or condition and the true, specified, or theoretically correct value or condition. Errors occur when some part of the computer software produces an undesired state. Examples include exceptional conditions raised by the activation of existing software faults, and incorrect computer status due to an unexpected external interference. This term is especially useful in fault-tolerant computing to describe an intermediate stage in between faults and failures.
2. A human action that results in software containing a fault. Examples include omission or misinterpretation of user requirements in a software specification, and incorrect translation or omission of a requirement in the design specification. However, this is not a preferred usage, and the term *mistake* is used instead to avoid the confusion.

Time. Reliability quantities are defined with respect to time, although it is possible to define them with respect to other bases such as program runs. We are concerned with three types of time: the *execution time* for a software system is the CPU time that is actually spent by the computer in executing the software; the *calendar time* is the time people normally experience in terms of years, months, weeks, days, etc.; and the *clock time* is the elapsed time from start to end of computer execution in running the software. In measuring clock time, the periods during which the computer is shut down are not counted.

It is generally accepted that execution time is more adequate than calendar time for software reliability measurement and modeling. However, reliability quantities must ultimately be related back to calendar time for easy human interpretation, particularly when managers, engineers, and customers want to compare them across different systems. As a result, translations between calendar time and execution time are required. The technique for such translations is described in [Musa87]. If execution time is not readily available, approximations such as clock time, weighted clock time, staff working time, or units that are natural to the application (such as transactions or test cases executed) may be used.

Failure functions. When a time basis is determined, failures can be expressed in several ways: the cumulative failure function, the failure intensity function, the failure rate function, and the mean time to failure function. The *cumulative failure function* (also called the *mean value function*) denotes the average cumulative failures associated with each point of time. The *failure intensity function* represents the rate of change of the cumulative failure function. The *failure rate function* (also called the *rate of occurrence of failures*) is defined as the probability that a failure per unit time occurs in the interval $[t, t + \Delta t]$, given that a failure has not occurred before t. The *mean time to failure* (MTTF) function represents the expected time that the next failure will be observed. (MTTF is also known as MTBF, mean time between failures.) Note that the above four measures are closely related and could be transposed with one another. Appendix B provides the mathematics of these functions in detail.

Mean time to repair and availability. Another quantity related to time is *mean time to repair* (MTTR), which represents the expected time until a system will be repaired after a failure is observed. When the MTTF and MTTR for a system are measured, its availability can be obtained. *Availability* is the probability that a system is available when needed. Typically, it is measured by

$$\text{Availability} = \frac{\text{MTTF}}{\text{MTTF} + \text{MTTR}}$$

Chapter 2 (Sec. 2.4.4) gives a theoretical model for availability, while Chap. 11 (Sec. 11.8) provides some practical examples of this measure.

Operational profile. The *operational profile* of a system is defined as the set of operations that the software can execute along with the probability with which they will occur. An operation is a group of runs which typically involve similar processing. A sample operational profile is illustrated in Fig. 1.3. Note that, without loss of generality, the operations can be located on the x axis in order of the probabilities of their occurrence.

Chapter 5 provides a detailed description on the structure, development, illustration, and project application of the operational profile. In general, the number of possible software operations is quite large. When it is not practical to determine all the operations and their probabilities in complete detail, operations based on grouping or partitioning of input states (or system states) into domains are determined. In the situations where an operational profile is not available or only an approximation can be obtained, you may make use of code coverage data generated during reliability growth testing to obtain reliability estimates. Chapter 13 describes some methods for doing so.

Failure data collection. Two types of failure data, namely *failure-count data* and *time-between-failures data,* can be collected for the purpose of software reliability measurement.

Failure-count (or failures per time period) data. This type of data tracks the number of failures detected per unit of time. Typical failure-count data are shown in Table 1.1.

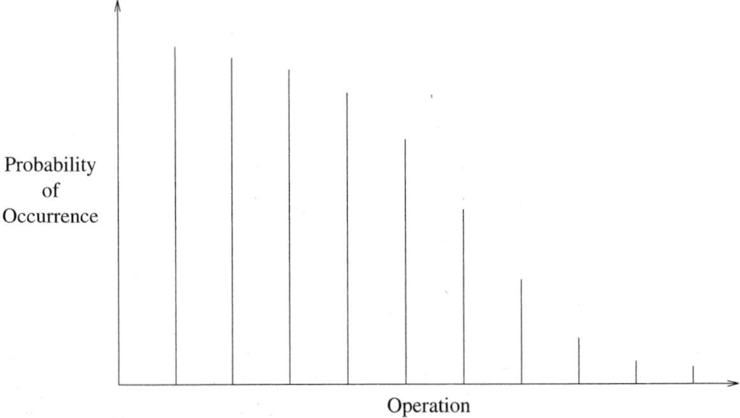

Figure 1.3 Operational profile.

TABLE 1.1 Failure-Count Data

Time (hours)	Failures in the period	Cumulative failures
8	4	4
16	4	8
24	3	11
32	5	16
40	3	19
48	2	21
56	1	22
64	1	23
72	1	24

Time-between-failures (or interfailure times) data. This type of data tracks the intervals between consecutive failures. Typical time-between-failures data can be seen in Table 1.2.

Many reliability modeling programs have the capability to estimate model parameters from either failure-count or time-between-failures data, as statistical modeling techniques can be applied to both. However, if a program accommodates only one type of data, it may be required to transform the other type.

TABLE 1.2 Time-Between-Failures Data

Failure number	Failure interval (hours)	Failure times (hours)
1	0.5	0.5
2	1.2	1.7
3	2.8	4.5
4	2.7	7.2
5	2.8	10.0
6	3.0	13.0
7	1.8	14.8
8	0.9	15.7
9	1.4	17.1
10	3.5	20.6
11	3.4	24.0
12	1.2	25.2
13	0.9	26.1
14	1.7	27.8
15	1.4	29.2
16	2.7	31.9
17	3.2	35.1
18	2.5	37.6
19	2.0	39.6
20	4.5	44.1
21	3.5	47.6
22	5.2	52.8
23	7.2	60.0
24	10.7	70.7

Transformations between data types. If the expected input is failure-count data, it may be obtained by transforming time-between-failures data to cumulative failure times and then simply counting the number of failures whose cumulative times occur within a specified time period. If the expected input is time-between-failures data, converting the failure-count data can be achieved by either *randomly* or *uniformly* allocating the failures for the specified time intervals, and then by calculating the time periods between adjacent failures. Some software reliability tools surveyed in App. A (e.g., SMERFS and CASRE) incorporate the capability to perform these data transformations.

Software reliability measurement. Measurement of software reliability includes two types of activities: reliability *estimation* and reliability *prediction.*

Estimation. This activity determines *current* software reliability by applying statistical inference techniques to failure data obtained during system test or during system operation. This is a measure regarding the achieved reliability from the past until the current point. Its main purpose is to assess the current reliability and determine whether a reliability model is a good fit in retrospect.

Prediction. This activity determines *future* software reliability based upon available software metrics and measures. Depending on the software development stage, prediction involves different techniques:

1. When failure data are available (e.g., software is in system test or operation stage), the estimation techniques can be used to parameterize and verify software reliability models, which can perform future reliability prediction.
2. When failure data are not available (e.g., software is in the design or coding stage), the metrics obtained from the software development process and the characteristics of the resulting product can be used to determine reliability of the software upon testing or delivery.

The first definition is also referred to as *reliability prediction* and the second definition as *early prediction.* When there is no ambiguity in the text, only the word *prediction* will be used.

Most current software reliability models fall in the estimation category to do reliability prediction. Nevertheless, a few early prediction models were proposed and described in the literature. A survey of existing estimation models and some early prediction models can be found in Chap. 3. Chapter 12 provides some product complexity metrics which can be used for early prediction purposes.

Software reliability models. A software reliability *model* specifies the general form of the dependence of the failure process on the principal factors that affect it: fault introduction, fault removal, and the operational environment. Figure 1.4 shows the basic ideas of software reliability modeling.

In Fig. 1.4, the failure rate of a software system is generally decreasing due to the discovery and removal of software failures. At any particular time (say, the point marked "present time"), it is possible to observe a history of the failure rate of the software. Software reliability modeling forecasts the curve of the failure rate by statistical evidence. The purpose of this measure is twofold: (1) to predict the extra time needed to test the software to achieve a specified objective; (2) to predict the expected reliability of the software when the testing is finished.

Software reliability is similar to hardware reliability in that both are stochastic processes and can be described by probability distributions. However, software reliability is different from hardware reliability in the sense that software does not wear out, burn out, or deteriorate, i.e., its reliability does not decrease with time. Moreover, software generally enjoys reliability growth during testing and operation since software faults can be detected and removed when software failures occur. On the other hand, software may experience reliability decrease due to abrupt changes of its operational usage or incorrect modifications to the software. Software is also continuously modified throughout its life cycle. The malleability of software makes it inevitable for us to consider variable failure rates.

Unlike hardware faults which are mostly *physical faults,* software faults are *design faults,* which are harder to visualize, classify, detect,

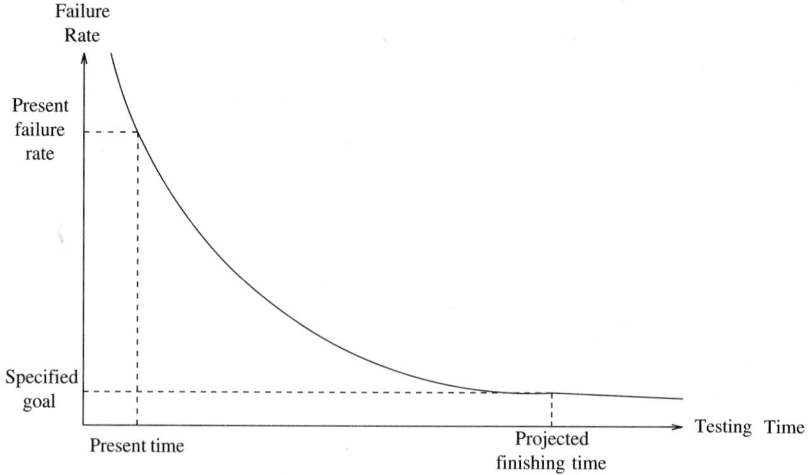

Figure 1.4 Basic ideas on software reliability modeling.

and correct. As a result, software reliability is a much more difficult measure to obtain and analyze than hardware reliability. Usually, hardware reliability theory relies on the analysis of stationary processes, because only physical faults are considered. However, with the increase of systems complexity and the introduction of design faults in software, reliability theory based on stationary process becomes unsuitable to address nonstationary phenomena, such as reliability growth or reliability decrease, experienced in software. This makes software reliability a challenging problem that requires employing several methods of attack.

1.5 Technical Areas Related to the Book

Achieving highly reliable software from the customer's perspective is a demanding job to all software engineers and reliability engineers. Adopting a similar notation from [Lapr85, Aviz86] for system dependability, four technical methods are applicable for you to achieve reliable software systems:

1. *Fault prevention.* To avoid, *by construction,* fault occurrences.
2. *Fault removal.* To detect, *by verification and validation,* the existence of faults and eliminate them.
3. *Fault tolerance.* To provide, *by redundancy,* service complying with the specification in spite of faults having occurred or occurring.
4. *Fault/failure forecasting.* To estimate, *by evaluation,* the presence of faults and the occurrence and consequences of failures. This has been the main focus of software reliability modeling.

Detailed discussions regarding these technical areas are provided in the following sections. You can also refer to Chap. 2 (Sec. 2.2) for a complete list of dependability- and reliability-related concepts.

1.5.1 Fault prevention

The interactive refinement of the user's system requirement, the engineering of the software specification process, the use of good software design methods, the enforcement of a structured programming discipline, and the encouragement of writing clear code are the general approaches to prevent faults in the software. These guidelines have been, and will continue to be, the fundamental techniques in preventing software faults from being created.

Recently, *formal methods* have been attempted in the research community to attack the software quality problem. In formal-methods approaches, requirement specifications are developed and maintained using mathematically trackable languages and tools. Current studies in this area have been focused on language issues and environmental supports, which include at least the following goals: (1) executable specifications for systematic and precise evaluation, (2) proof mechanisms for software verification and validation, (3) development procedures that follow incremental refinement for step-by-step verification, and (4) every work item, be it a specification or a test case, is subject to mathematical verification for correctness and appropriateness.

Another fault-prevention technique, particularly popular in the software development community, is *software reuse*. The crucial measure of success in this area is the capability to prototype and evaluate reusable synthesis techniques. This is why *object-oriented paradigms* and techniques are receiving much attention nowadays—largely due to their inherent properties in enforcing software reuse.

1.5.2 Fault removal

When formal methods are in full swing, *formal design proofs* might be available to achieve mathematical proof of correctness for programs. Also, *fault-monitoring assertions* could be employed through executable specifications, and test cases could be automatically generated to achieve efficient software verification. However, before this happens, practitioners will have to rely mostly on *software testing* techniques to remove existing faults. Microsoft, for example, allocates as many software testers as software developers, and employs a buddy system which binds the developer of every software component to its tester for their daily work [Cusu95]. The key question to reliability engineers, then, is how to derive testing-quality measures (e.g., test-coverage factors) and establish their relationships to reliability.

Another practical fault removal scheme which has been widely implemented in industry is *formal inspection* [Faga76]. A formal inspection is a rigorous process focused on finding faults, correcting faults, and verifying the corrections. Formal inspection is carried out by a small group of peers with a vested interest in the work product during pretest phases of the life cycle. Many companies have acclaimed its success [Grad92].

1.5.3 Fault tolerance

Fault tolerance is the survival attribute of computing systems or software in their ability to deliver continuous service to their users in the presence of faults [Aviz78]. Software fault tolerance is concerned with all the techniques necessary to enable a system to tolerate software faults remaining in the system after its development. These software faults may or may not manifest themselves during system operations, but when they do, software fault tolerance techniques should provide the necessary mechanisms to the software system to prevent system failure from occurring.

In a single-version software environment, the techniques for partially tolerating software design faults include monitoring techniques, atomicity of actions, decision verification, and exception handling. In order to fully recover from activated design faults, multiple versions of software developed via *design diversity* [Aviz86] are introduced in which functionally equivalent yet independently developed software versions are applied in the system to provide ultimate tolerance to software design faults. The main approaches include the recovery blocks technique [Rand75], the N-version programming technique [Aviz77], and the N self-checking programming technique [Lapr87]. These approaches have found a wide range of applications in the aerospace industry, the nuclear power industry, the health care industry, the telecommunications industry, and the ground transportation industry.

1.5.4 Fault/failure forecasting

Fault/failure forecasting involves formulation of the fault/failure relationship, an understanding of the operational environment, the establishment of reliability models, the collection of failure data, the application of reliability models by tools, the selection of appropriate models, the analysis and interpretation of results, and the guidance for management decisions. The concepts and techniques laid out in [Musa87] have provided an excellent foundation for this area. Other reference texts include [Xie91, Neuf93]. Besides, the July 1992 issue of *IEEE Software,* the November 1993 issue of *IEEE Transactions on Software Engineering,* and the December 1994 issue of *IEEE Transactions on Reliability* are all devoted to this aspect of SRE. This handbook provides a comprehensive treatment of this subject.

1.5.5 Scope of this handbook

Due to the intrinsic complexity of modern software systems, software reliability engineers must apply a combination of the above methods for the delivery of reliable software systems. These four areas are also the main theme of the state of the art for software engineering, covering a wide range of disciplines. In addition to focusing on the fault/failure forecasting area, this book attempts to address the other three technical areas as well. However, instead of incorporating all possible techniques available in software engineering, this book examines and emphasizes mature as well as emerging techniques that could be *quantitatively* related to software reliability.

As a general guideline, most chapters of the book are concerned with fault/failure forecasting, in which Chaps. 1 to 5 provide technical foundations, while Chaps. 6, 7, 10, and 11 present project practices and experiences, and Chaps. 16 and 17 describe two emerging techniques. In addition, Chaps. 9 and 12 are related to fault prevention, and Chaps. 8 and 13 address fault removal techniques. (Fault prevention and removal techniques are the subject of discussion in many software engineering texts.) Finally, Chaps. 14 and 15 cover fault tolerance techniques and the associated modeling work. For a detailed treatment on software fault tolerance, interested readers are referred to [Lyu95].

The scope of the handbook is summarized in Table 1.3, which provides a guideline for using this book according to various subjects of interest, including the four technical areas we have discussed, and some special topics that you may want to study in depth. For example, if you are interested in the topic of software reliability modeling theory (topic 1), reading Chaps. 1, 2, 3, 4, 9, 10, 12, 14, and 16 is recommended. Note that topics 1 and 2 in Table 1.3 are mutually exclusive. So are topics 3 and 4, topics 5 and 6. Please note that the classification of the book chapters into various topics in Table 1.3 is for your reading convenience only. This classification is approximate and subjective.

1.6 Summary

The growing trend of software criticality and the unacceptable consequences of software failures force us to plead urgently for better software reliability engineering. This book codifies our knowledge of SRE and puts together a comprehensive and organized repository for our daily practice in software reliability. The structure of the book and key contents of each chapter are described. The definitions of major terms in SRE are provided, and fundamental concepts in software reliability modeling and measurement are discussed. Finally, the related technical areas in software engineering and some reading guidelines are provided for your convenience.

Problems

1.1 Some hardware faults are not physical faults and have a similar nature to software faults. What are they?

1.2 What are the main differences between software failures and hardware failures?

1.3 Give several examples of software faults and software failures.

1.4 Some people argue that the modeling technique for software reliability is similar to that of hardware reliability, while other people disagree. List the commonalities and differences between them.

TABLE 1.3 Reading Guideline for Various Technical Areas and Topics

	Technical Foundations					Practices and Experiences						Emerging Techniques					
Chapter	1	2	3	4	5	6	7	8	9	10	11	12	13	14	15	16	17
Area 1									X			X					
Area 2								X					X				
Area 3														X	X		
Area 4	X	X	X	X	X	X	X			X	X					X	X
Topic 1	X	X	X	X					X	X		X		X		X	
Topic 2					X	X	X	X			X		X		X		X
Topic 3	X	X	X		X	X			X			X	X	X		X	
Topic 4				X			X	X		X	X				X		X
Topic 5	X	X			X	X			X				X	X	X	X	
Topic 6			X	X			X	X		X	X	X					X
Topic 7				X	X	X	X	X		X	X	X			X	X	X
Topic 8		X		X				X	X	X	X		X	X	X		X

NOTE:

Area 1—Fault prevention
Area 2—Fault removal
Area 3—Fault tolerance
Area 4—Fault/failure forecasting

Topic 1—Modeling theory
Topic 2—Modeling experience
Topic 3—Metrics
Topic 4—Measurement
Topic 5—Process issues
Topic 6—Product issues
Topic 7—Reliability data
Topic 8—Analysis techniques

1.5 Give a couple of examples for each of the definitions of failure severity levels. One is qualitative and one is quantitative.

1.6 What is the mapping relationship between faults and failures? Is it one-to-one mapping (one fault leading to one failure), one-to-many, many-to-one, or many-to-many? Discuss the mapping relationship in different conditions. What is the preferred mapping relationship? Why? How is it achieved?

1.7 The term *ultrareliability* has been used to denote highly reliable systems. This could be expressed, for example, as R (10 hour) = 0.9999999. That is, the probability that a system will fail in a 10-hour operation is 10^{-7}. Some people have proposed making this a reliability requirement for software. Discuss the implications of this kind of reliability requirement and its practicality.

1.8 What are the difficulties and issues involved in the data collection of failure-count data and time-between-failures data?

1.9 Regarding the failure data collection process, consider the following situations:

a. How do you adjust the failure times for an evolving program, i.e., a software program which changes over time through various releases?

b. How do you handle multiple sites or versions of the software?

1.10 Show that the time-between-failures data in Table 1.2 can be transformed to failure-count data in Table 1.1. Assuming random distribution, transform the failure-count data in Table 1.1 to time-between-failures data. Compare your results with Table 1.2.

1.11 For the data in Tables 1.1 and 1.2:

a. Calculate failure intensity at the end of each time period (for Table 1.1) or failure interval (for Table 1.2).

b. Plot the failure intensity quantities along with the time axis.

c. Try to fit a curve on the plots manually.

d. What are your estimates on (1) the failure rate of the next time period after observing the data in Table 1.1 and (2) the time to next failure after observing the data in Table 1.2?

e. What should be the relationship between the two estimates you obtained in *d?* Verify it.

1.12 Compare the MTTR measure for hardware and software and discuss the difference.

1.13 Refer to Example 1.2 and Fig. 1.2:

a. What is the failure rate of each component in Fig. 1.2? What is the reliability function of each component?

b. What assumption is made to calculate the MTTF for SYS2 in the triple-module redundant configuration? If the reliability function for SYS2 is $R_2(t)$, what is the reliability function for SYS2 in the triple-module redundant configuration? How is its MTTF calculated? How is its MTTR calculated?

c. How is the overall system MTTF calculated? Verify that it is 125.9 hours when software failures are not considered, and that it is 11.9 minutes when software failures are considered.

d. How is the system MTTR calculated? Verify that it is 0.62 hours.

e. Does the triplication of SYS2 software help to improve its software MTTF? Why? If not, what techniques could be employed to improve the software MTTF?

1.14 *a.* What is the difference between reliability estimation and reliability prediction? Draw the application range of each technique in Fig. 1.4.

b. What is the difference between reliability prediction and early prediction? Summarize their differences in a comparison table.

1.15 Section 1.4 describes the concepts and constructions for software reliability models. It is important to identify which models are better than the others. Make a list of evaluation criteria for software reliability models.

Chapter

2

Software Reliability and System Reliability

Jean-Claude Laprie and Karama Kanoun
LAAS-CNRS, Toulouse, France

2.1 Introduction

This chapter is mainly aimed at showing that, by using deliberately simple mathematics, *the classical reliability theory can be extended in order to be interpreted from both hardware and software viewpoints.* This is referred to as *X-ware* [Lapr89, Lapr92b] throughout this chapter. It will be shown that, even though the action mechanisms of the various classes of faults may be different from a physical viewpoint according to their causes, a single formulation can be used from the reliability modeling and statistical estimation viewpoints. A single formulation has several advantages, both theoretical and practical, such as (1) easier and more consistent modeling of hardware-software systems and of hardware–software interactions, (2) adaptability of models for hardware dependability to software systems and vice versa, and (3) mathematical tractability.

Section 2.2 gives a general overview of the dependability concepts. Section 2.3 is devoted to the failure behavior of an X-ware system, disregarding the effect of restoration actions (the quantities of interest are thus the time to the next failure or the associated failure rate), considering in turn atomic systems and systems made up of components. In Sec. 2.4, we deal with the behavior of an X-ware system with service restoration, focusing on the characterization of the sequence of the times to failure (i.e., the failure process); the measures of interest are thus the failure intensity, reliability, and availability. Section 2.5 outlines the state of art in dependability evaluation and specification. Finally, Sec. 2.6 summarizes the results obtained.

2.2 The Dependability Concept

2.2.1 Basic definitions

The basic definitions for dependability impairments, means, and attributes are given in Fig. 2.1, and the main characteristics of dependability are summarized in the form of a tree as shown in Fig. 2.2 [Lapr92a, Lapr93].

2.2.2 On the impairments to dependability

Of primary importance are the impairments to dependability, as we have to know what we are faced with. The creation and manifestation mechanisms of *faults, errors,* and *failures* may be summarized as follows:

1. A fault is *active* when it produces an error. An active fault is either an internal fault previously *dormant* and activated by the computation process or an external fault. Most internal faults cycle between their dormant and active states. Physical faults can directly affect the hardware components only, whereas human-made faults may affect any component.
2. An error may be latent or detected. An error is *latent* when it has not been recognized as such; an error is *detected* by a detection algorithm or mechanism. An error may disappear before being detected. An error may, and in general does, propagate; by propagating, an error creates other—new—error(s). During operation, the presence of active faults is determined only by the detection of errors.
3. A failure occurs when an error passes through the system-user interface and affects the service delivered by the system. A component failure results in a fault (1) for the system which contains the component and (2) as viewed by the other component(s) with which it interacts; the failure modes of the failed component then become fault types for the components interacting with it.

Some examples illustrative of fault pathology:

- The result of a programmer's *error* is a *(dormant) fault* in the written software (faulty instruction(s) or data); upon activation (invoking the component where the fault resides and triggering the faulty instruction, instruction sequence, or data by an appropriate input pattern) the fault becomes *active* and produces an error; if and when the erroneous data affect the delivered service (in value and/or in the timing of their delivery), a *failure* occurs.
- A short circuit occurring in an integrated circuit is a *failure.* The consequence (connection stuck at a boolean value, modification of the

Dependability is defined as the trustworthiness of a computer system such that *reliance can justifiably be placed on the service it delivers.* The service delivered by a system is its behavior *as it is perceptible* by its user(s); a user is another system (human or physical) *interacting* with the former.

Depending on the application(s) intended for the system, a different emphasis may be put on the various facets of dependability, that is, dependability may be viewed according to different, but complementary, *properties,* which enable the *attributes* of dependability to be defined:

- The *readiness for usage* leads to **availability.**
- The *continuity of service* leads to **reliability.**
- The *nonoccurrence of catastrophic consequences on the environment* leads to **safety.**
- The *nonoccurrence of the unauthorized disclosure of information* leads to **confidentiality.**
- The *nonoccurrence of improper alterations of information* leads to **integrity.**
- The *ability to undergo repairs and evolutions* leads to **maintainability.**

Associating availability and integrity with respect to authorized actions, together with confidentiality, leads to **security.**

A system **failure** occurs when the delivered service deviates from fulfilling the system's **function,** the latter being what the system *is intended for.* An **error** is that part of the system state which is *liable to lead to subsequent failure:* an error affecting the service is an indication that a failure occurs or has occurred. The *adjudged or hypothesized cause* of an error is a **fault.**

The development of a dependable computing system calls for the *combined* utilization of a set of methods and techniques which can be classed into:

- **Fault prevention:** how to prevent fault occurrence or introduction.
- **Fault removal:** how to reduce the presence (number, seriousness) of faults.
- **Fault tolerance:** how to ensure a service capable of fulfilling the system's function in the presence of faults.
- **Fault forecasting:** how to estimate the present number, future incidence, and consequences of faults.

The notions introduced can be grouped into three classes:

- The **impairments** to dependability: faults, errors, failures; they are undesired—but not in principle unexpected—circumstances causing or resulting from undependability (whose definition is very simply derived from the definition of dependability: reliance cannot or will no longer be placed on the service).
- The **means** for dependability: fault prevention, fault removal, fault tolerance, fault forecasting; these are the methods and techniques enabling one (1) to provide the ability to deliver a service on which reliance can be placed and (2) to reach confidence in this ability.
- The **attributes** of dependability: availability, reliability, safety, confidentiality, integrity, maintainability; these attributes (1) enable the properties which are expected from the system to be expressed and (2) allow the system quality resulting from the impairments and the means opposing them to be assessed.

Figure 2.1 Dependability basic definitions.

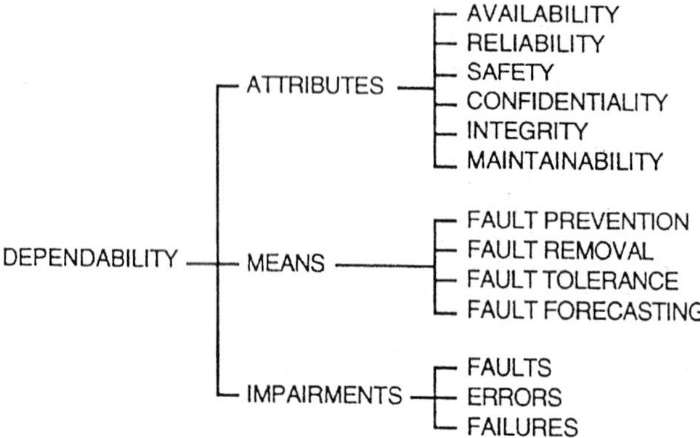

Figure 2.2 The dependability tree.

circuit function, etc.) is a *fault* which will remain dormant as long as it has not been activated, the continuation of the process being identical to that of the previous example.

- An inappropriate human–machine interaction performed by an operator during the operation of the system is a *fault* (from the system viewpoint); the resulting altered processed data is an *error*.
- A maintenance or operating manual writer's *error* may result in a *fault* in the corresponding manual (faulty directives) which will remain dormant as long as the directives are not acted upon in order to deal with a given situation.

Figure 2.3 summarizes the fault classification; the upper part indicates the viewpoint according to which they are classified, and the lower part gives the likely combinations according to these viewpoints, as well as the usual labeling of these combinations—*not their definition.*

It is noteworthy that the very notion of fault is *arbitrary,* and in fact a facility provided for stopping the recursion induced by the causal relationship between faults, errors, and failures—hence the definition given: *adjudged or hypothesized* cause of an error. This cause may vary depending upon the viewpoint chosen: fault tolerance mechanisms, maintenance engineers, repair shop, developer, semiconductor physicist, etc. In fact, *a fault is nothing other than the consequence of a failure of some other system* (including the developer) *that has delivered or is now delivering a service to the given system.* A computing system is a human artifact and, as such, any fault in it or affecting it is ultimately human-made since it represents the human inability to master all the phenomena which govern the behavior of a system. Going further, *any fault can be viewed as a permanent design fault.* This is indeed true in

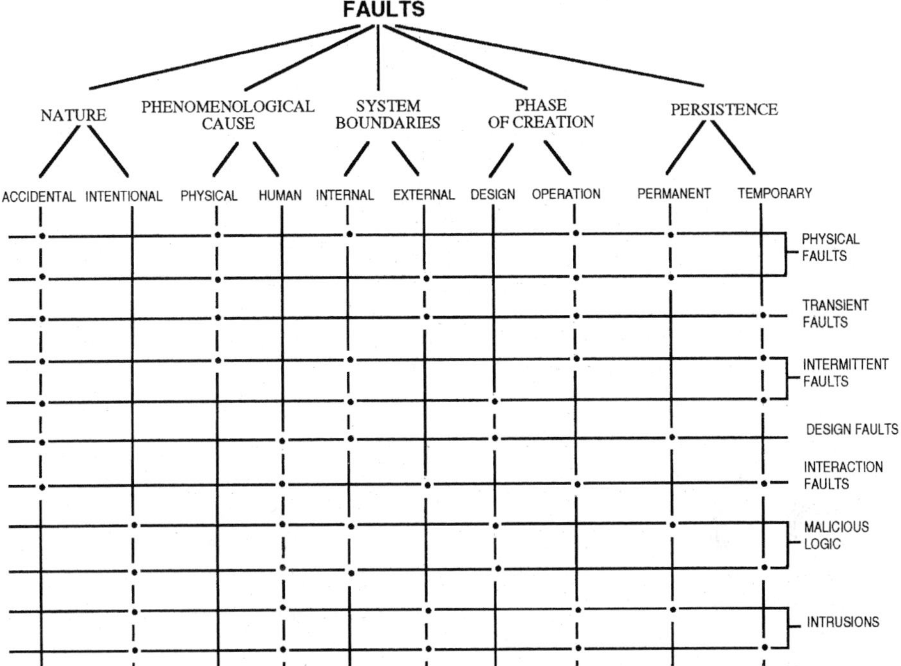

Figure 2.3 Fault classes.

an absolute sense, but not very helpful for system developers and assessors; hence the usefulness of the various fault classes when considering the (current) methods and techniques for procuring and validating dependability.

A system may not, and generally does not, always fail in the same way. The ways a system can fail are its *failure modes*. These can be characterized according to three viewpoints as shown in Fig. 2.4.

Given below are two additional comments regarding the words, or labels, *fault, error,* and *failure:*

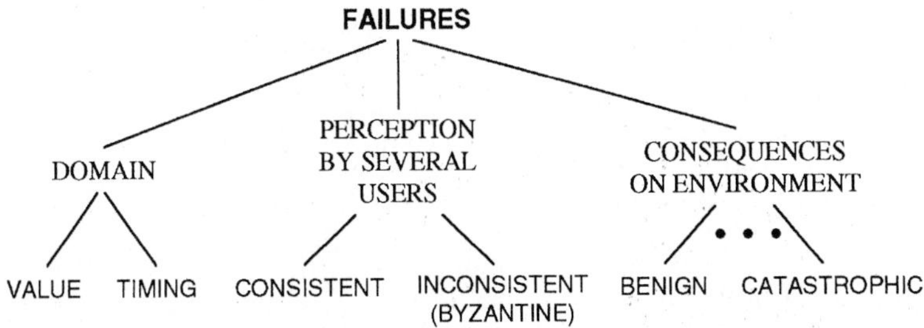

Figure 2.4 Failure classification.

1. Their exclusive use in this book (except Chap. 9) does not preclude the use in special situations of words which designate, briefly and unambiguously, a specific class of impairment; this is especially applicable to faults (e.g., bug, defect, deficiency, flaw) and to failures (e.g., breakdown, malfunction, denial of service).
2. The assignment of the particular terms *fault, error,* and *failure* simply takes into account current usage: (1) fault prevention, tolerance, and diagnosis, (2) error detection and correction, and (3) failure rate.

2.2.3 On the attributes of dependability

The definition given for *integrity*—the avoidance of improper alterations of information—generalizes the usual definitions (e.g., prevention of unauthorized amendment or deletion of information [EEC91] or ensuring approved alteration of data [Jaco91]) which are directly related to a specific class of faults, that is, intentional faults (deliberately malevolent actions). Our definition encompasses accidental faults as well (i.e., faults appearing or created fortuitously), and the use of the word *information* is intended to avoid being limited strictly to data: integrity of programs is also an essential concern; regarding accidental faults, error recovery is indeed aimed at restoring the system's integrity.

Confidentiality, not security, has been introduced as a basic attribute of dependability. Security is usually defined (see e.g., [EEC91]) as the combination of confidentiality, integrity, and availability, where the three notions are understood with respect to unauthorized actions. A definition of security encompassing the three aspects of [EEC91] is: the prevention of unauthorized access and/or handling of information; security issues are indeed dominated by intentional faults, but not restricted to them: an accidental (e.g., physical) fault can cause an unexpected leakage of information.

The definition given for *maintainability*—ability to undergo repairs and evolutions—deliberately goes beyond *corrective* maintenance, which relates to repairability only. Evolvability clearly relates to the two other forms of maintenance, that is, (1) *adaptive* maintenance, which adjusts the system to environmental changes and (2) *perfective* maintenance, which improves the system's function by responding to customer- and designer-defined changes. The frontier between repairability and evolvability is not always clear, however (for instance, if the requested change is aimed at fixing a specification fault [Ghez91]). Maintainability actually *conditions* dependability when considering the whole operational life of a system: systems which do not undergo adaptive or perfective maintenance are likely to be exceptions.

The properties allowing the dependability attributes to be defined may be emphasized to a greater or lesser extent depending on the application intended for the computer system concerned. For instance, availability is always required (although to a varying degree, depending on the application), whereas reliability, safety, and confidentiality may or may not be required according to the application. The variations in the emphasis to be put on the attributes of dependability have a direct influence on the appropriate balance of the means to be employed for the resulting system to be dependable. This problem is all the more difficult to address because certain attributes are antagonistic (e.g., availability and safety, availability and confidentiality), and call for tradeoffs. Given the three main design dimensions of a computer system (i.e., cost, performance and dependability), the problem is further exacerbated by the fact that the dependability dimension is not so well mastered as the cost-performance design space [Siew92].

2.2.4 On the means for dependability

All the how-tos which appear in the basic definitions given in Fig. 2.1 are in fact goals which cannot be fully reached, as all the corresponding activities are carried out by humans and therefore are prone to imperfections. These imperfections bring in *dependencies* which explain why it is only the *combined* utilization of the above methods—preferably at each step in the design and implementation process—that can best lead to a dependable computing system. These dependencies can be sketched as follows: despite fault prevention by means of design methodologies and construction rules (imperfect so as to be workable), faults are created—hence the need for fault removal. Fault removal itself is imperfect, just like all of the off-the-shelf system components—hardware or software—hence the importance of fault forecasting. Our increasing dependence on computing systems brings in the requirement for fault tolerance, which in turn is based on construction rules—hence fault removal, fault forecasting, etc. It must be noted that the process is even more recursive than it appears from the above: current computer systems are so complex that their design and implementation need computerized tools in order to be cost-effective (in a broad sense, including the capability of succeeding within an acceptable time scale). In turn, these tools themselves have to be dependable.

The preceding reasoning illustrates the close interactions between fault removal and fault forecasting and supports their gathering into the single term *validation*. This is despite the fact that validation is often limited to fault removal and associated with one of the main activities involved in fault removal: *verification* (e.g., in "V and V" [Boeh79]). In such a case the distinction is related to the difference between "building the system right" related to verification and "building the right system" related to validation.* What is proposed here is simply an extension of this concept: the answer to the question "am I building the right system?" (fault removal) being complemented by the additional question "how long will it be right?" (fault forecasting). In addition, fault removal is usually closely associated with fault prevention, together forming *fault avoidance,* that is, how to *aim* at a fault-free system. Besides highlighting the need for validating the procedures and mechanisms of fault tolerance, considering fault removal and fault forecasting as two constituents of the same activity—validation—is of great interest, as it leads to a better understanding of the notion of coverage, and thus of the important problem introduced by the above recursion: *the validation of the validation,* or how to reach confidence in the methods and tools used in building confidence in the system. Here *coverage* refers to a measure of the representativity of the situations to which the system is submitted during its validation compared to the actual situations it will be confronted with during its operational life.† Imperfect coverage strengthens the relation between fault removal and fault forecasting, as it can be considered that the need for fault forecasting stems from an imperfect coverage of fault removal.

The life of a system is perceived by its user(s) as an alternation between two states of the delivered service with respect to the specification:

- *Correct service,* where the delivered service fulfills the system function‡
- *Incorrect service,* where the delivered service does not fulfill the system function

A failure is thus a transition from a correct to an incorrect service, while the transition from an incorrect service to a correct one is a *restoration.* Quantifying the correct-incorrect service alternation

* It is noteworthy that these assignments are sometimes reversed, as in the field of communication protocols (see, for example, [Rudi85]).

† The notion of coverage as defined here is very general; it may be made more precise by indicating its field of application; e.g.,

- Coverage of a software test with respect to its text, control graph, etc.
- Coverage of an integrated circuit test with respect to a fault model
- Coverage of fault tolerance with respect to a class of faults
- Coverage of a design assumption with respect to reality

‡ We deliberately restrict the use of *correct* to the service delivered by a system, and do not use it for the system itself: in our opinion, nonfaulty systems hardly ever exist, there are only systems which have not yet failed.

enables reliability and availability to be defined as *measures* of dependability:

- *Reliability.* A measure of the *continuous* delivery of the correct service—or, equivalently, of the *time* to failure.
- *Availability.* A measure of the delivery of correct service *with respect to the alternation* of correct and incorrect service.

As a measure, safety can be viewed as an extension of reliability. Let us group together the state of a correct service with that of an incorrect service subsequent to benign failures into a safe state (in the sense of being free from catastrophic damage, not from danger); *safety* is then a measure of continuous safeness, or equivalently, of the time to catastrophic failure. Safety can thus be considered as reliability with respect to the catastrophic failures

For multiperforming systems, several services can be distinguished, together with several modes of service delivery, ranging from full capacity to complete disruption, which can be seen as distinguishing less and less correct service deliveries. The performance-related measures of dependability for such systems are usually referred to as *performability* [Meye78, Smit88].

2.3 Failure Behavior of an X-ware System

Section 2.3.1 characterizes the behavior of atomic systems: discrete- and continuous-time reliability expressions are derived. The behavior of systems made up of components is addressed in Sec. 2.3.2, where structural models of a system according to different types of relations are first derived, enabling a precise definition of the notion of *interpreter;* behavior of single-interpreter and of multi-interpreter systems are then successively considered.

2.3.1 Atomic systems

The simplest functional model of a system is regarded as performing a mapping of its input domain I into its output space O.

An execution run of the system consists of selecting a sequence of input points. A trajectory in the input domain—not necessarily composed of contiguous points—can be associated with such a sequence. Thus, each element in I is mapped to a unique element in O if it is assumed that the state variables are considered as part of I and/or O.

According to Sec. 2.2.2, a system failure may result from:

- The *activation* of a fault internal to the system, previously *dormant;* an internal fault may be a physical or design fault.

- The *occurrence* of an external fault, originating from either the physical or the human environment of the system.

Two subspaces in the input space can thus be identified:

- I_{fi}, subspace of the faulty inputs
- I_{af}, subspace of the inputs activating internal faults

The *failure domain* of the system is $I_F = I_{fi} \cup I_{af}$. When the input trajectory meets I_F, an error occurs which leads to failure.

Thus, at each selection of an input point, there is a nonzero probability for the system to fail. Let p be this probability, assumed identical for the time being whatever the input point selected:

$$p = P\{\text{system failure at an input point selection} \mid \text{no failure at the previous input point selections}\}$$

Let $R_d(k)$ be the probability of no system failure during an execution run comprising k input point selections. We then have

$$R_d(k) = (1 - p)^k \tag{2.1}$$

where $R_d(k)$ is the *discrete-time system reliability.*

Let t_e be the execution duration associated with an input selection; t_e is supposed for the moment to be identical irrespective of the input point selected. Let t denote the time elapsed since the start of execution: $t = kt_e$.

The notion of (isolated) input points is not very well suited for a number of situations, such as control systems, executive software, and hardware. Thus, let us assume that there exists a finite limit for p/t_e when t_e becomes vanishingly small. Let λ be this limit:

$$\lambda = \lim_{t_e \to 0} \frac{p}{t_e}$$

It turns out that the distribution becomes the exponential distribution:

$$R(t) = \lim_{t_e \to 0} R_d(k) = \exp(-\lambda t) \tag{2.2}$$

where $R(t)$ is the *continuous-time system reliability,* and λ is its failure rate.

Let us now relax the identity assumption of p and t_e with respect to the input point selections; let the following be defined

$p(j) = P\{\text{system failure at the } j\text{th input point selection} \mid \text{no failure at the previous input point selections}\}$

$t_e(j) =$ execution duration associated with the jth input selection

We then obtain

$$R_d(k) = \prod_{j=1}^{k} [1 - p(j)] \qquad t = \sum_{j=1}^{k} t_e(j) \qquad \lambda(j) = \lim_{\forall j\, t_e(j) \to 0} \frac{p(j)}{t_e(j)}$$

$$R_d(k) = \prod_{j=1}^{k} \{1 - \lambda(j)\, t_e(j) + o[t_e(j)]\} \tag{2.3}$$

$$R(t) = \lim_{\forall j\, t_e(j) \to 0} R_d(k) = \exp\left(-\int_0^t \lambda(\tau)\, d\tau\right)$$

Equation (2.3) is nothing other than the general expression of a system's reliability: see App. B (Sec. B.2), which describes the reliability theory in detail.

It could be argued that the preceding formulations are in fact better suited to design faults or to external faults than to physical faults, since they are based on the existence of a failure domain, which may be nonexistent with respect to physical faults as long as no hardware component fails. It should be remembered that, from the point of view of physics reliability, there is no sudden, unpredictable failure. In fact, a hardware failure is due to anomalies (errors) at the electronic level, caused by physicochemical defects (faults). Or to put it differently, there are no fault-free systems—either hardware or software—there are only systems which have not yet failed. However, the notion of operational fault (i.e., which develops during system operation, and thus did not exist at the start of operational life) is—although arbitrarily [Lapr92a]—a convenient and usual notion. Incorporating the notion of operational fault in the previous formulation can be done as follows. Let j_0 be the number of input point selections such that $p(j) = 0$ for $j < j_0$, $p(j) = p$ for $j \geq j_0$, and $u(j_0)$ the associated probability, i.e., $u(j_0) = P\{p(j) = 0, j < j_0; p(j) = p, j \geq j_0\}$.

The expression of discrete-time reliability becomes:

$$R_d(k) = \sum_{j_0=0}^{k} (1-p)^{k-j_0}\, u(j_0), \text{ with } \sum_{j_0=0}^{k} u(j_0) = 1$$

Going through the same steps as before, we get: $R(t) = \lim_{t_e \to 0} R_d(k) = \exp(-\lambda t)$.

What precedes shows that, although the action mechanisms of the various classes of faults may be different from a physical viewpoint according to their causes, a single formulation can be used from a probability modeling perspective. This formulation applies whatever the fault class considered, either internal or external, physical or design-induced. In the case of software, randomness results, at least from the trajectory in the input space that will activate the fault(s). In addition, it is now known that most of the software faults still present in operation, after validation, are "soft" faults, in the sense that their activation conditions are extremely difficult to reproduce, hence the difficulty of diagnosing and removing them,* which adds to the randomness.

The constancy of the conditional failure probability at execution with respect to the execution sequence is directly related to the constancy of the failure rate with respect to time, as evidenced by Eqs. (2.1) to (2.3). In other words, the points of an input trajectory are not correlated *with respect to the failure process.* This statement is all the more likely to be true if the failure probability is low, i.e., if the quality of the system is high, and thus applies more to systems in operational life than to those under development and validation. It is an abstraction, however, thus immediately raising the question of how well this abstraction reflects reality.

As far as hardware is concerned, it has been long shown that (see, for example, [Cart70]) the failure rates of electronic components as estimated from experimental data actually decrease with time—even after the period of infant mortality. However, the decrease is generally low enough to be neglected. Going further, the interpretation of the failure data for satellites, as described in [Hech87], establishes a distinction between (1) stable operating conditions where the failure rate is slowly decreasing (namely, a constant failure rate is a satisfactory assumption) and (2) varying operating conditions leading to failure rates significantly decreasing with time.

Similar phenomena have been noticed concerning software: (1) constant failure rates for given, stable, operating conditions [Nage82] and (2) high influence of system load [Cast81]. Also, a series of experimental studies conducted on computing systems have confirmed the significant influence of the system load on both hardware and software failure processes [Iyer82].

The influence of varying operating conditions can be introduced by considering that *both the input trajectory and the failure domain* I_F

* By way of example, a large survey was conducted on Tandem systems [Gray86]. From the examination of several dozens of spooler error logs, it was concluded that only one software fault out of 132 was not a soft fault.

may be subject to variations. The variation of the failure domain deserves some comments. It may be due to two phenomena [Iyer82b]:

1. Accumulation of physical faults which remain dormant under low load conditions and are progressively activated as the load increases [Meye88].
2. Creation of temporary faults resulting from the presence of seldom-occurring combinations of conditions. Examples are (1) pattern-sensitive faults in semiconductor memories, change in parameters of a hardware component (effect of temperature variation, delay in timing due to parasitic capacitance, etc.) or (2) situations occurring when system load rises beyond a certain threshold, such as marginal timing and synchronization. The latter situation may affect software as well as hardware: the notion of temporary faults—especially intermittent faults—also applies to software [Gray86]. Experimental work [McCo79] has shown that the failure rates relative to temporary faults decrease significantly with time.

From a probabilistic viewpoint, the failure probability at execution in discrete time, or the failure rate in continuous time, may be considered as random variables. The system reliability then results from the mixture of two distributions:

1. *In discrete time,* the distribution of the number of nonfailed executions in given operating conditions, thus with a given, constant, failure probability at execution, and the distribution of the probability of failure at execution.
2. *In continuous time,* the distribution of the time to failure with a given, constant, failure rate, and the distribution of the failure rate.

Let $g_d(p)$ and $g_d(\lambda)$ be the probability density functions of the distributions of the probability of failure at execution and of the failure rate, which may take G values relative to the realizations p_i, $i = 1, \ldots, G$, of p, and λ_i, $i = 1, \ldots, G$, of λ. The expression of discrete-time reliability becomes

$$R_d(k) = \sum_{i=1}^{G} (1 - p_i)^k \, g_d(p_i)$$

Going through similar steps as before, we obtain

$$t = k \sum_{i=1}^{G} t_{ei} \, g_d(p_i) \qquad \lambda_i = \lim_{t_{ei} \to 0} \frac{p_i}{t_{ei}}, \, i = 1, \ldots, G$$

where t_{ei} and λ_i are the execution time and the failure rate, respectively, for executions carried out under operating condition i, $i = 1, \ldots, G$. Finally we get

$$R(t) = \lim_{\forall i \, t_{ei} \to 0} R_d(k) = \sum_{i=1}^{G} g_d(\lambda_i) \exp(-\lambda_i t)$$

This is the mixed exponential distribution.

When p is a continuous random variable with density function $g_c(p)$, or λ is a continuous random variable with density function $g_c(\lambda)$, we get

$$R_d(k) = \int_0^1 (1-p)^k g_c(p)\, dp \qquad R(t) = \int_0^\infty \exp(-\lambda t)\, g_c(\lambda)\, d\lambda$$

From the properties of the mixture of distributions (see, for example, [Barl75]), the system failure rate is nonincreasing with time, whatever the distributions g_d and g_c.

A model is of no use without data. This is where statistics come into play. Let M instances of the system be considered, executed independently. The term *independently* is a keyword in the following. This is a conventional assumption with respect to physical faults when several sets of hardware are run in parallel, supplied with the same input pattern sequences. Of course, this approach cannot be transposed to software. The independence of the executions of several systems means that they are supplied with *independent input sequences.* This reflects operational conditions when considering a base of deployed systems; for instance, the input sequences supplied to the same text-processing software by users in different places performing completely different activities are likely to exhibit independence with respect to residual fault activation.

Let $M(k)$ and $M(t)$ be the number of nonfailed instances after k executions of each instance, and after an elapsed time of t, respectively, since the start of the experiment ($M(0) = M$); an instance failing at the jth execution, $j = 1, \ldots, k$, or at time τ, $\tau \in [0, t]$, is no longer executed. The independency of execution of the various instances enable these executions to be considered as Bernoulli trials, and the discrete-time reliability is thus $R_d(k) = E[M(k)]/M(0)$, and the continuous-time reliability is $R(t) = E[M(t)]/M(0)$. These equations are none other than the basic equations for the statistical interpretation of reliability as stated in the general systems reliability theory (e.g., [Shoo73, Kozl70]). Statistical estimators of $R_d(k)$ and $R(t)$ are then: $\hat{R}_d(k) = M(k)/M(0)$ and $\hat{R}(t) = M(t)/M(0)$.

The preceding shows that the equations forming the core of the statistical estimation of reliability for a set of hardware systems apply equally to software systems, *provided the experimental conditions are in agreement with the underlying assumptions.*

2.3.2 Systems made up of components

2.3.2.1 System models. Adopting the spirit of [Ande81], a system may be viewed from a structural viewpoint as a set of components bound together in order to interact; a component itself is a system, decomposed (again) into components, etc. The recursion ends when a system is considered *atomic:* no further internal structure can be discerned or is of interest, and can be ignored. The model corresponding to the relation "is composed of" is a tree, whose nodes are the components; the levels of a tree obviously constitute a hierarchy. Such a model does not enable the interactions between the components to be represented: the presence of arcs in a graphic representation would present only the relation "is composed of" existing between a node and the set of its immediate successors. The set of the elements of a level of the tree gives only the list of the system components, with more or less *detail* according to the tree level considered: the lower the level, the more detailed the list becomes. To obtain a more representative view of the system, the relations existing between the components have to be presented. This is achieved through interaction diagrams where the nodes are the system components and the arcs represent a common interface. An arc exists when two elements *can* interact. Although the relation "interacts with" is an essential relation when describing a system, it obviously does not infer any hierarchy.

The use of the relations in modeling a system is given in Fig. 2.5 for an intentionally simple system, where the components S_1, S_2, and S_3 can, for instance, be the application software, the executive software, and the hardware.

The respective roles of a system and of its user(s) with respect to the notion of service are fixed: the system is the producer of the service, and the user is the consumer. Therefore, there exists a natural hierarchy between the system and its user: the user *uses the service of* (or *delivered by*) the system.

With respect to the set of components of one given level of the decomposition tree, the relation "uses the service of"—a special form of the relation "interacts with"—allows for an accurate definition of a special class of components: if and only if *all* the components of the level may be hierarchically situated through the relation "uses the service," then they are *layers.* Or equivalently, components of a given detail level are layers (1) if any two components of that level play a fixed role with respect to this relation, i.e., either consumer or producer; similarly, (2) if the graph of the relation is a single branch tree. Conversely, if their

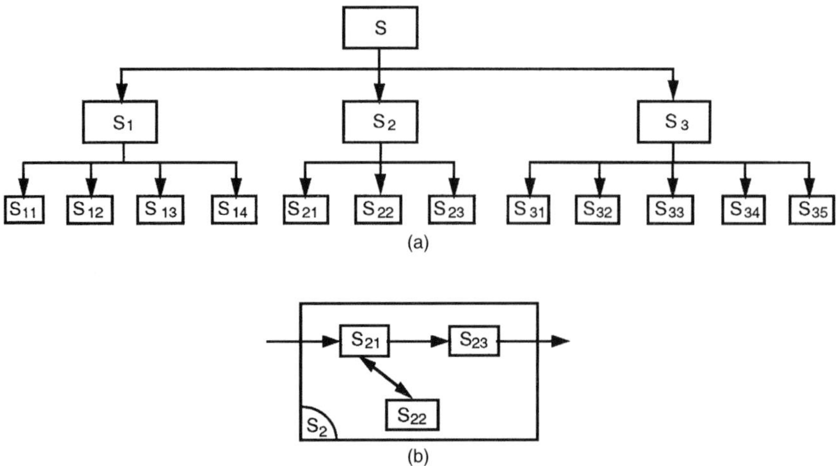

Figure 2.5 Components of a system. (*a*) System model according to the relation "is composed of." (*b*) System model according to the relation "interacts with."

respective consumer and producer roles can change, or if their interactions are not governed by such a relation, they are simply components. It is noteworthy that the notion of service has naturally—and implicitly—been generalized with respect to the layers: the service delivered by a given layer is its behavior as perceived by the upper layer, where the term *upper* has to be understood with respect to the relation "uses the service of." Also worth noting is the fact that the relation "uses the service of" induces an ordering of the time scales of the various layers: time granularity usually does not decrease with increasing layers. Considering the previous example in Fig. 2.5 leads to the model in Fig. 2.6.

Structuring into many layers may be considered for design purposes. Their actual relationship at execution is generally different: compilation removes—at least partially—the structuring, and several layers may, and generally are, executed on a single one. A third type of rela-

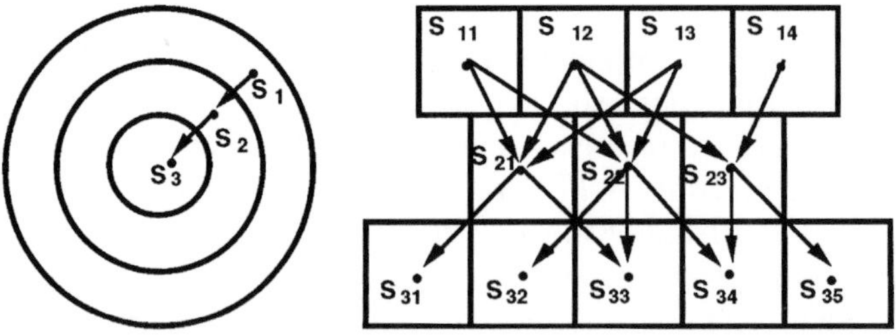

Figure 2.6 Layers of a system.

tion thus has to be considered: "is interpreted by." The *interpretive interface* [Ande81] between two layers or sets of layers is characterized by the provision of objects and operations to manipulate those objects. A system may then be viewed as a hierarchy of *interpreters,* where a given interpreter may be viewed as providing a concrete representation of abstract objects in the above interpreter; this concrete representation is itself an abstract object for the interpreter beneath the considered one.

Considering again the previous example, the hardware layer interprets the application as well as the executive software layers. However, the executive software may be viewed as an *extension* of the hardware interpreter—e.g., through (1) the provision of "supervisor call" instructions or (2) the prevention of invoking certain "privileged" instructions. This leads to the system model depicted in Fig. 2.7.

Finally, note that the expression "abstraction level" has not been used so as to avoid any confusion: all the hierarchies defined are, strictly speaking, abstractions.

2.3.2.2 Behavior of a single-interpreter system. A system is assumed to be composed of C components, of respective failure rates λ_i, $i = 1, \ldots, C$. The system behavior with respect to the execution process is modeled through a Markov chain with the following parameters:

- S: number of the states of the chain, a state being defined by the components under execution
- $1/\gamma_j$: mean sojourn time in state j, $j = 1, \ldots, S$
- $q_{jk} = P\{\text{system makes a transition from state } j \text{ to state } k \mid \text{start or end of execution of one or several components}\}$, $j = 1, \ldots, S$, $k = 1, \ldots, S$, $\sum_{k=1}^{S} q_{jk} = 1$

A system failure is caused by the failure of any of its components. The system failure rate ξ_j in state j is thus the sum of the failure rates of the components under execution in this state, denoted by

$$\xi_j = \sum_{i=1}^{C} \delta_{i,j}\, \lambda_i, j = 1, \ldots, S \tag{2.4}$$

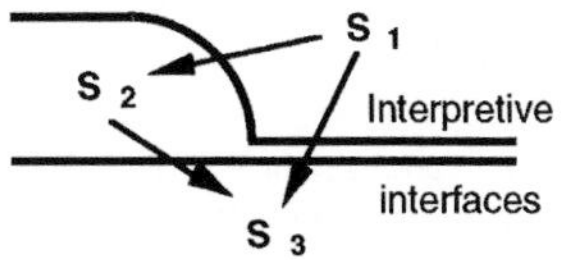

System model according to the relation «is interpreted by»

Figure 2.7 System interpreters.

where $\delta_{i,j}$ is equal to 1 if component i is under execution in state j, or else it is equal to 0.

The system failure behavior may be modeled by a Markov chain with $S + 1$ states, where the system delivers correct service in the first S states (components are under execution without failure occurrence); state $S + 1$ is the failure state, which is an absorbing state. Let $\mathbf{A} = [a_{jk}]$, $j = 1, \ldots, S$, $k = 1, \ldots, S$ be the transition matrix associated with the nonfailed states. This matrix is such that its diagonal terms a_{jj} are equal to $-(\gamma_j + \xi_j)$, and its nondiagonal terms a_{jk}, $j \neq k$, are equal to $q_{jk}\,\gamma_j$. The matrix $\mathbf{A}$ may be viewed as the sum of two matrices $\mathbf{A}'$ and $\mathbf{A}''$ such that: (1) the diagonal terms of $\mathbf{A}'$ are equal to $-\gamma_j$, its nondiagonal terms being equal to $q_{jk}\,\gamma_j$, and (2) the diagonal terms of $\mathbf{A}''$ are equal to $-\xi_j$, its nondiagonal terms being equal to 0.

The system behavior can thus be viewed as resulting from the superimposition of two processes: the execution process, of parameters γ_j and q_{jk} (transition matrix $\mathbf{A}'$), and the failure process, governed by the failure rates ξ_j (transition matrix $\mathbf{A}''$).

A natural assumption is that the failure rates are small with respect to the rates governing the transitions from the execution process or, equivalently, that a large number of transitions resulting from the execution process will take place before the occurrence of a failure—a system that would not satisfy this assumption would be of little interest in practice. This assumption is expressed as follows: $\gamma_j >> \xi_j$.

Adopting a Markov approach for modeling the system behavior resulting from the compound execution-failure process is based on this assumption. Similar models have been proposed in the past for software systems [Litt81, Cheu80, Lapr84], with less generality than here, however, since those models assumed a sequential execution (one component only executed at a time).*

By definition, the system failure rate $\lambda(t)$ is given by

$$\lambda(t) = \lim_{dt \to 0} \frac{1}{dt} P\{\text{failure between } t \text{ and } t + dt \mid \text{no failure between initial instant and } t\}$$

* In these references, the Markov approach was justified:

- Heuristically in [Cheu80, Lapr84], by analogy with performance models in the first reference, and with availability models in the second,
- From a weaker assumption, semi-Markov, in [Litt81]. It is shown there that the compound process of execution and failure converges toward a Poisson process, and that the contribution of the distribution functions of the component execution times is limited to their first moments.

Let *Pj*(t) denote the probability for the system to be in state j. It follows that

$$\lambda(t) = \frac{\left(\sum_{j=1}^{S} \xi_j P_j(t)\right)}{\left(\sum_{j=1}^{S} P_j(t)\right)} \tag{2.5}$$

The consequence of the assumption $\gamma_j >> \xi_j$ is that the execution process converges toward equilibrium before failure occurrence. The vector $\boldsymbol{\alpha} = [\alpha_j]$ of the equilibrium probabilities is the solution of $\boldsymbol{\alpha} \cdot \mathbf{A}' = \mathbf{0}$, with $\sum_{j=1}^{S} \alpha_j = 1$. Thus, $P_j(t)$ converges towards α_j before failure occurs, and Eq. (2.5) becomes*:

$$\lambda = \sum_{j=1}^{S} \alpha_j \xi_j \tag{2.6}$$

Equation (2.6) may be rewritten as follows, to account for Eq. (2.4):

$$\lambda = \sum_{j=1}^{S} \alpha_j \sum_{i=1}^{C} \delta_{i,j} \lambda_i = \sum_{i=1}^{C} \lambda_i \sum_{j=1}^{S} \delta_{i,j} \alpha_j \tag{2.7}$$

Let

$$\pi_i = \sum_{j=1}^{S} \delta_{i,j} \alpha_j$$

Equation (2.6) becomes

$$\lambda = \sum_{i=1}^{C} \pi_i \lambda_i \tag{2.8}$$

This equation has a simple physical interpretation:

- α_j represents the average proportion of time spent in state j in the absence of failure; thus π_i is the average proportion of time when

* Another approach to this result is as follows. A given system component will be executed; thus the transition graph between the nonfailed states is strongly connected. As a result, the matrix **A** is irreducible and has one real negative eigenvalue whose absolute value σ is lower than the absolute values of the real parts of the other eigenvalues [Page80]. Asymptotically, the system failure behavior is then a Poisson process of rate σ. In our case, the asymptotic behavior is relative to the execution process; therefore, (1) it is reached rapidly and (2) $\sigma = \lambda$, thus system reliability is: $R(t) = \exp(-\lambda t)$.

component i is under execution in the absence of failure. It is noteworthy that the sum of the π_i's can be larger than 1:

$$0 \leq \sum_{i=1}^{C} \pi_i \leq C$$

- λ_i is the failure rate of component i assuming a continuous execution.

The term $\pi_i \lambda_i$ can therefore be considered as the *equivalent* failure rate of component i.

Equation (2.8) deserves a few comments. First let us consider hardware systems. It is generally considered that all components are continuously active. This corresponds to making all the π_i's equal to 1, leading to the usual equation

$$\lambda = \sum_{i=1}^{C} \lambda_i$$

Consider software systems. The key question is how to estimate the component failure rates. There are two basic—and opposite—approaches: (1) exploiting results of repetitive-run experiments without experiencing failures (i.e., through statistical testing [Curr86, Thev91]) and (2) exploiting failure data using a reliability growth model, the latter being applied to each software component, as performed in [Kano87, Kano91a, Kano93b]. It is important to stress the data representativeness in either approach; a condition is that the data are collected in a representative environment (i.e., being relative to components in interaction, real or simulated, with the other system components). If this condition is not fulfilled, a distinction has to be made between the interface failure rates (characterizing the failures occurring during interactions with other components) and the internal component failure rates, as in [Litt81], where the expression of a component failure rate has the form

$$\lambda_i = \zeta_i + \gamma_i \sum_{j} q_{ij}\, \rho_{ij}$$

the ζ_i being the internal component failure rates and ρ_{ij} the interface failure probabilities. This leads to a complexity in the estimation of the order of C^2 instead of C.

An important question is how to account for different environments. If this question is interpreted as estimating the reliability of a software system of a base of deployed software systems, then the approach indicated in Sec. 2.3.1 where the failure rate was considered as a random variable can be extended here; the π_i's being considered as random variables as well. Another interpretation of the previous question is: knowing the reliability in a given environment, how can the reliability be estimated in another environment? Let us consider sequential software systems. The parameters characterizing the execution process are then defined as follows:

- $1/\gamma_i$: mean execution time of component i, $i = 1, \ldots, C$.
- $q_{ij} = P\{$ component j starts execution | end of execution of component $i\}$, $i = 1, \ldots, C$, $j = 1, \ldots, C$, $\sum_{j=1}^{C} q_{ij} = 1$

The Markov chain modeling the compound execution-failure process is a $(C + 1)$ state chain, state i being defined by the execution of component i, and the π_i's reduce to the α_i's (in the case of sequential software, $\delta_{ii} = 1$ and all others are zeros). We have $\lambda_i = p_i \, \gamma_i$, $i = 1, \ldots, C$, where p_i is the failure probability at execution of component i; hence

$$\lambda = \sum_{i=1}^{C} \pi_i \, \gamma_i \, p_i = \sum_{i=1}^{C} \eta_i \, p_i \tag{2.9}$$

where $\eta_i = \pi_i \, \gamma_i$ is the visit rate of state i at equilibrium. The η_i's have a simple physical interpretation, as $1/\eta_i$ is the mean recurrence time of state i (i.e., the mean time duration between two executions of component i in the absence of failure). Equation (2.9) is of interest as it enables a distinction to be made between (1) continuous time–execution process and (2) discrete time–failure process conditioned upon execution. If the p_i's are intrinsic to the considered software and independent of the execution process, then it is possible to infer the software failure rate for a given environment from the knowledge of the η_i's for this environment and the knowledge of the p_i's. The condition for this assumption to be verified in practice is that it is possible to find a suitable decomposition into components: the notion of component for a software is highly arbitrary, and the higher the number of components considered for a given software, the smaller the state space of each component, so the higher the likelihood of providing a satisfactory coverage of the input space for the component. A limit to such an approach is that the higher the number of components, the more difficult the estimation of the η_i's becomes. Also, time granularity (and near decomposability [Cour77]) can offer criteria to find suitable decompositions.

2.3.2.3 Behavior of a multi-interpreter system. When a system is viewed as a hierarchy of interpreters, as defined in Sec. 2.3.2.1, the execution relative to the selection of an input point for the highest interpreter (which directly interprets the requests originating from the system user) is supported by a sequence of input point selections in the next lower interpreter, and so on up to the lowest considered interpreter. Assume the system is composed of I interpreters, the first interpreter being the top of the hierarchy and the Ith interpreter its base.

Each interpreter may be faulty and submitted to erroneous inputs. Failure of any interpreter during the computations relative to the input point selection of the next higher interpreter will lead to the failure of the latter, and thus by propagation to the top interpreter's failure (i.e., to system failure). Adopting the terminology of the conventional system reliability theory, the hierarchy interpreters constitute a series system. Intuitively, it may be deduced that the system failure rate is equal to the sum of the failure rates of interpreters of the hierarchy. If $\lambda_i(t)$, $i = 1, \ldots, I$ denotes the failure rate of interpreter i, we then have (the demonstration is left as an exercise to you):

$$\lambda(t) = \sum_{i=1}^{I} \lambda_i(t) \tag{2.10}$$

Now consider that each interpreter is composed of C_i components, $i = 1, \ldots, I$. At execution, a component of interpreter i will use services of one or more components of interpreter $i + 1$, and so on. We may therefore define trees of utilization of services provided by components of interpreter $i + 1$ by the components of interpreter i, as indicated in Fig. 2.8.

Thus, with each pair of adjacent interpreters, it is possible to associate a service utilization matrix $\mathbf{U}_{i,i+1} = [\mathbf{U}_{jk}], j = 1, \ldots, C_i, k = 1,., C_{i+1}$. $\mathbf{U}_{i,i+1}$ is a connectivity matrix whose terms U_{jk} are such that $U_{jk} = 1$ if, during execution, component j of interpreter i utilizes the services of component k of interpreter $i + 1$, or else $U_{jk} = 0$.

Let us define the following failure rate vectors:

- $\mathbf{\Lambda}_i = [\lambda_{i,j}], i = 1, \ldots, I, j = 1, \ldots, C_i$, where λ_{ij} is the failure rate of component j of interpreter i.
- $\mathbf{\Omega}_i = [\omega_{i,j}], i = 1, \ldots, I, j = 1, \ldots, C_i$; $\omega_{i,j}$ is the aggregated failure rate of component j of interpreter i; the term *aggregated* means that the failure rates of components of interpreters $i + 1, \ldots, I$ needed for execution are accounted for.

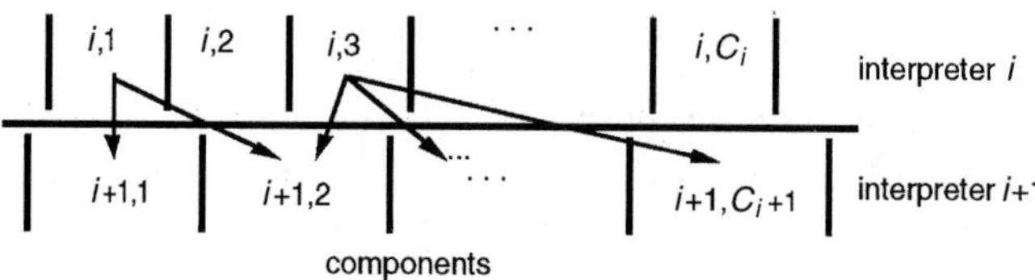

Figure 2.8 Utilization trees between components of interpreters.

The vectors $\mathbf{\Omega}_i$ are solutions of the following matrix equation:

$$\mathbf{\Omega}_i = \mathbf{\Lambda}_i + \mathbf{U}_{i,i+1}\,\mathbf{\Omega}_{i+1},\ i = 1, \ldots, I-1,\ \mathbf{\Omega}_I = \mathbf{\Lambda}_I$$

It then follows that:

$$\mathbf{\Omega}_1 = \sum_{k=1}^{I} \mathbf{V}_k\,\mathbf{\Lambda}_k$$

$\mathbf{V}_k$ is the accessibility matrix of the top interpreter to interpreter k: $\mathbf{V}_1$ is the identity matrix of dimensions $(C_1 \times C_1)$, $\mathbf{V}_k = \mathbf{U}_{1,2} \otimes \mathbf{U}_{2,3}, \ldots, \otimes \mathbf{U}_{k-1,k}$, $k = 2, \ldots, I$; where the symbol $\otimes$ denotes the boolean product of matrices (a given component can contribute only once through its failure rate).

When applying Eq. (2.8) to the components of the upper interpreter in the hierarchy, we obtain the following system failure rate:

$$\lambda = \sum_{j=1}^{C_1} \pi_{1,j}\,\omega_{1,j}$$

where $\pi_{1,j}$ is the proportion of time during which component j of the top interpreter is being executed, with an idle component period being characterized by $\omega_{1,j} = 0$.

Consider the important case in practice of a system composed of two interpreters: a software interpreter and a hardware interpreter. It is assumed that the software components are executed sequentially, and that all hardware components are together involved in the execution; it is further assumed that the system is in stable operating conditions. In the following, indices S and H relate to software and hardware, respectively. Applying the above approach leads to the following equations:

$$\omega_{S,j} = \lambda_{S,j} + \sum_{k=1}^{C_H} \lambda_{H,k}$$

$$\lambda = \sum_{j=1}^{C_S} \pi_{S,j}\,\omega_{S,j} = \sum_{j=1}^{C_S} \pi_{S,j}\,\lambda_{S,j} + \sum_{k=1}^{C_H} \lambda_{H,k} \tag{2.11}$$

The intuitive result expressed in Eq. (2.11) has thus been obtained through use of a rigorous approach.

2.4 Failure Behavior of an X-ware System with Service Restoration

In Sec. 2.3, the behavior of atomic and multicomponent systems was characterized without taking into account the effects of service restoration, thereby allowing expressions of the failure rate of such systems and of the reliability to be derived. In this section, service restoration is taken into account, thus allowing the system behavior resulting from the compound action of failure and restoration processes to be modeled. Restoration activities may consist of a pure restart (supplying the system with an input pattern different from the one which led to failure) or they can be performed after introduction of modifications (corrections only or/and specification changes).

System behavior is first characterized by the evolution of its failure intensity in Sec. 2.4.1. Section 2.4.2 introduces the various maintenance policies that can be carried out. Sections 2.4.3 and 2.4.4 address reliability and availability modeling, respectively.

2.4.1 Characterization of system behavior

The nature of the operations to be performed in order for the service to be restored (i.e., delivered again to its user(s)) after a failure has occurred enables stable reliability or reliability growth to be identified. This may be defined as follows:

- *Stable reliability.* The system's ability to deliver a proper service is *preserved* (stochastic identity of the successive times to failure).
- *Reliability growth.* The system's ability to deliver proper service is *improved* (stochastic increase of the successive times to failure).

Practical interpretations are as follows:

- *Stable reliability.* At a given restoration, the system is identical to what it was at the previous restoration. This corresponds to the following situations: (1) in the case of a hardware failure, the failed part is substituted for another one, identical and nonfailed; (2) in the case of a software failure, the system is restarted with an input pattern that differs from the one having led to failure.
- *Reliability growth.* The fault whose activation has led to failure is diagnosed as a design fault (in software or hardware) and removed.

Reliability *decrease* (stochastic decrease of the successive times to failure) is both theoretically and practically possible. In this case, it is hoped that the decrease is limited in time and that reliability is globally growing over a long observation time.

Reliability decrease may originate from (1) introduction of new faults during corrective actions, whose probability of activation is greater than that of the removed fault(s); (2) introduction of a new version with modified functionalities; (3) change in the operating conditions (e.g., an intensive testing period; see [Kano87], where such a situation is depicted); (4) dependencies between faults: some software faults can be masked by others, that is, they cannot be activated as long as the latter are not removed [Ohba84]; removal of the masking faults will lead to an increase in the failure intensity.

The reliability of a system is conveniently illustrated by the failure intensity, as it is a measure of the frequency of the system failures as noticed by its user(s). Failure intensity is typically first decreasing (reliability growth) due to the removal of residual design faults either in the software or hardware. It may become stable (stable reliability) after a certain period of operation; the failures due to internal faults occurring in this period are due either to physical faults or to unremoved design faults. Failure intensity generally exhibits an increase (reliability decrease) upon the introduction of new versions incorporating modified functionalities; then it tends toward an asymptote again, and so on. It is noteworthy that such a behavior is not restricted to the operational life of a system but also applies to situations occurring during the development phase of a system—for example, (1) during incremental development [Curr86] or (2) during system integration [Leve89, Tohm89].

Typical variations of the failure intensity may be represented as indicated in Fig. 2.9, curve a. Such a curve depends on the granularity of the observations, and may be felt as resulting from the smoothing of more noticeable variations (curve *b*); in turn, it may be smoothed into a continuously decreasing curve *c*. Although such a representation is very general and covers many practical situations (see, for example, [Kenn92]), there are situations which exhibit discontinuities important enough that the smoothing process cannot be considered as reasonable (e.g., upon introduction of a new system generation).

2.4.2 Maintenance policies

The rate of reliability growth (i.e., failure intensity decrease) is closely related to the correction and maintenance policies retained for the sys-

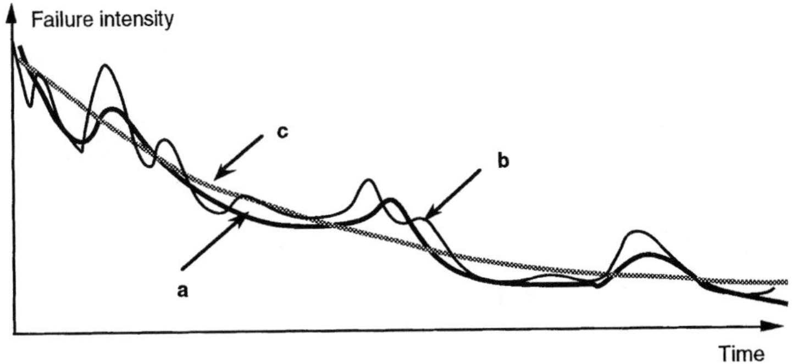

Figure 2.9 Typical variations of a system's failure intensity.

tem [Kano89]. These policies may consist of either (1) system modification after each failure, or (2) system modification after a given number of failures, or even (3) preventive maintenance (i.e., introduction of modifications without any failure observed on the system considered). The status of a system between two modifications will be called a *version*.

A policy that accepts as special cases the specific cases mentioned above is as follows: the jth system modification takes place after a_j failures have occurred since the $(j - 1)$th system modification, which means that version j experiences a_j failures.

Concerning the times to failure:

- Let $X_{j,i}$ denote the time between service restoration following the $(i - 1)$th failure and the ith failure of version j.
- Let Z_j denote the time between service restoration following the a_jth failure of version j and service interruption for the introduction of the jth modification, that is, for the introduction of version $(j + 1)$.

Considering now the times to restoration, two types of service restoration are to be distinguished: service restoration due to system restart after failure and service restoration after introduction of a new version. Let $Y_{j,i}$ denote the restart duration after the ith failure of version j, and W_j denote the duration necessary for the introduction of the jth modification; the modification itself may have been performed offline. Finally, let T_j denote the time between two version introductions. We have:

$$T_j = \sum_{i=1}^{a_j} (X_{j,i} + Y_{j,i}) + Z_j + W_j, \; j = 1,2, \ldots$$

The relationship between the various time intervals is given in Fig. 2.10.

The number of failures between two modifications (a_j) characterize the policy for maintenance and service restoration. It depends on sev-

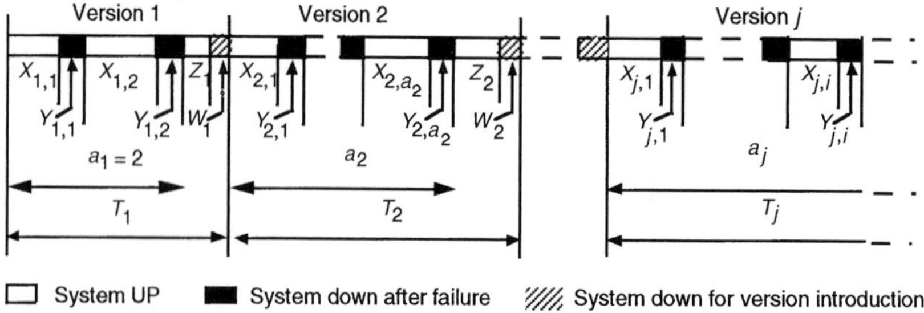

Figure 2.10 Relationship between the various time intervals.

eral factors such as (1) the failure rate of the system, (2) the nature of the faults (e.g., time needed to diagnose the fault and the consequence of the failure due to the activation of this fault), (3) the considered phase in the life cycle (the policy may vary for a given system within the same phase), and (4) the availability of the maintenance team.

Three (extreme) special cases of this general policy are noteworthy:

1. $a_j = 1$ and $Z_j = 0\ \forall j$. Service is restored only after a system modification has been performed. This case relates to (1) a usual hypothesis for several software reliability (growth) models or (2) the case of critical systems after a (potentially) dangerous failure occurrence.
2. $a_1 = \infty$ and $Z_j = 0\ \forall j$. Service is restored without any system modification ever being performed (stable reliability). This case relates to (1) hardware, when maintenance consists of replacing a failed part with an identical (new) one and (2) software, when no maintenance is performed; service restoration always corresponds to a restart with an input pattern different from the one having led to failure.
3. $a_j = 0$. The $(j + 1)$th version is introduced before any failure occurrence since the last modification. This case corresponds to preventive maintenance, either corrective, adaptive, or perfective.

Although this policy is more general than those usually considered, it is a simplification of real life, and does not explicitly model such phenomena as interweaving of failures and corrections [Kano88] and failure rediscoveries [Adam84].

2.4.3 Reliability modeling

We focus here on the failure process and therefore do not consider the times to restoration or the (possible) time interval between a failure and the introduction of a modification (i.e., we assume the $Y_{j,i}$'s, W_j's, and Z_j's are zero, which means that the failure instants are also restoration instants). Let:

- $t_0 = 0$ denote the considered initial instant (the system is assumed nonfailed).
- $n = 1,2, \ldots$ denote the number of failures. As the nth system failure is in fact the ith failure of version j, the relationship between n, i, and j is

$$n = \left(\sum_{k=1}^{j} a_{k-1} \right) + i, j = 1,2, \ldots, i = 1, \ldots a_j,\ a_0 = 0$$

- t_n, $n = 1,2, \ldots$ denote the instant of failure occurrence.

- $f_{\chi_j}(t), j = 1, 2, \ldots$ denote the probability density functions (pdf) of the times to failure X*j,i* and $sf_{\chi_j}(t)$ denote their survival function (the one's complement of its distribution function). The $X_{j,i}$'s are assumed stochastically identical for a given version.
- $\phi_n(t)$ and $\Phi_n(t)$ denote, respectively, the pdf and the distribution function of the instants of failure occurrence, $n = 1,2,\ldots$.
- $N(t)$ denote the number of failures having occurred in $[0,t]$ and $H(t)$ denote its expectation: $H(t) = E[N(t)]$.

Performing derivations adapted from the renewal theory (see, for example, [Gned69]) is relatively straightforward, provided that the $X_{j,i}$'s are assumed stochastically independent. This assumption, although usual in both hardware and software models, is again a simplification of real life. The T_j's can reasonably be considered as stochastically independent, as resuming execution after the introduction of a modification generally involves a so-called cold restart; however, it must be stated that imperfect maintenance, the consequences of which were noticed a long time ago [Lewi64], is also a source of stochastic dependency. The stochastic independence of the $X_{j,i}$'s for a given j depends on (1) the extent to which the internal state of the system has been affected and (2) the nature of operations undertaken for execution resumption (i.e., whether or not they involve state cleaning).

The following is then obtained under the stochastic independence assumption

$$\phi_n(t) = \left(\underset{k=1}{\overset{j-1}{\circledast}} f_{\chi_k}(t)^{*a_k} \right) * (f_{\chi_j}(t)^{*i}), j = 1,2,\ldots, i = 1,\ldots,a_j,\ a_0 = 0 \qquad (2.12)$$

where $*$ stands for the convolution operation, $f_{\chi_k}(t)^{*a_k}$, the a_k-fold convolution of $f_{\chi_k}(t)$ by itself, and $\circledast_{k=1}^{j} f_{\chi_k}(t)$, the convolution of $f_{\chi_1}(t), \ldots, f_{\chi_j}(t)$. In Eq. (2.12) the first term covers $j - 1$ versions and the second term covers the i failures of version j. We have

$$P\{N(t) \geq n\} = P\{t_n < t\} = \Phi_n(t)$$

$$P\{N(t) = n\} = P\{t_n < t < t_{n+1}\} = \Phi_n(t) - \Phi_{n+1}(t)$$

$$H(t) = \sum_{n=1}^{\infty} n\, P\{N(t) = n\} = \sum_{n=1}^{\infty} n\, [\Phi_n(t) - \Phi_{n+1}(t)]$$

$$H(t) = \sum_{n=1}^{\infty} n\, \Phi_n(t) - \sum_{n=1}^{\infty} (n-1)\, \Phi_n(t) = \sum_{n=1}^{\infty} \Phi_n(t)$$

Let $h(t)$ denote the rate of occurrence of failure [Asch84], or ROCOF, $h(t) = dH(t)/dt$, whence

$$h(t) = \sum_{n=1}^{\infty} \phi_n(t) = \sum_{j=1}^{\infty} \sum_{i=1}^{a_j} \left(\bigodot_{k=1}^{j-1} (f_{\chi_k}(t)^{*a_k}) * (f_{\chi_j}(t)^{*i}) \right) \tag{2.13}$$

As we do not consider simultaneous occurrences of failure, the failure process is regular or orderly, and the ROCOF is then the *failure intensity* [Asch84].

When considering reliability growth, a usual measure of reliability is *conditional reliability* [Goel79, Musa84]; since the system has experienced $n - 1$ failures, conditional reliability is the survival function associated with failure n. It is defined as follows:

$$\begin{aligned} R_n(\tau) &= P\{Xj,i + 1 > \tau \mid t_{n-1}\} = sf_{\chi_j}(\tau), \text{ for } i < a_j \\ R_n(\tau) &= P\{Xj + 1,1 > \tau \mid t_{n-1}\} = sf_{\chi_{j+1}}(\tau), \text{ for } i = a_j \end{aligned} \tag{2.14}$$

This measure is mainly of interest when considering a system in its development phase, as we are then concerned with the time to next failure. However, when dealing with a system in operational life, the interest is in failure-free time intervals τ whose starting instants are not necessarily conditioned on system failures; that is, they are likely to occur at any time t. In this case, we are concerned with the reliability over a given time interval independently of the number of failures experienced, that is, *interval reliability.* Interval reliability is then the probability for the system to experience no failure during the time interval $[t, t + \tau]$.

Consider the following exclusive events:

$$E_0 = \{t + \tau < t_1\} \qquad E_n = \{t_n < t < t + \tau < t_{n+1}\}, n = 1,2, \ldots$$

Event E_n means that exactly n failures occurred prior to instant t, and that no failure occurs during the interval $[t, t + \tau]$. The absence of failure during $[t, t + \tau]$ is the union of all events E_n, $n = 0,1,2, \ldots$ The interval reliability, owing to the exclusivity of the events E_n, is then

$$R(t, t + \tau) = \sum_{n=0}^{\infty} P\{E_n\}$$

The probability of event E_n is shown as

$$P\{E_n\} = P\{t_n < t < t + \tau < t_n + Xj,i + 1\}$$

$$P\{E_n\} = \int_0^t P\{x < t_n < x + dx\}\, P\{Xj,i + 1 > t + \tau - x\} = \int_0^t sf_{\chi_j}(t + \tau - x)\, \phi_n(x)\, dx$$

The reliability thus has the expression

$$R(t,t+\tau) = sf_{\chi_1}(t+\tau) + \sum_{j=1}^{\infty}\sum_{i=0}^{a_j-1}\int_0^t sf_{\chi_j}(t+\tau-x)\,\phi_{\left(\sum_{k=1}^{j} a_{k-1}\right)+i}(x)\,dx$$

which can be written as

$$R(t,t+\tau) = sf_{\chi_1}(t+\tau) + \sum_{j=1}^{\infty}\sum_{i=0}^{a_j-1} sf_{\chi_j}(t+\tau) * \phi_{\left(\sum_{k=1}^{j} a_{k-1}\right)+i}(t) \qquad (2.15)$$

This equation is obviously not easy to use. However, it is not difficult to derive, for $\tau << t$, the following equation from Eqs. (2.13) and (2.15):

$$R(t,t+\tau) = 1 - h(t)\,\tau + o(\tau) \qquad (2.16)$$

Besides its simplicity, Eq. (2.16) is highly important in practice, as it applies to systems for which the mission time τ is small with respect to the system lifetime t (e.g., systems on board airplanes).

The above derivation is a (simple) generalization of the renewal theory and of the notion of renewal process to nonstationary processes; in the classical theory (stationary processes), (1) the $X_{j,i}$'s are stochastically identical, that is, $f_{\chi_j}(t) = f_\chi(t)\ \forall j$ (the case where the first time to failure has a distribution different from the subsequent ones is referred to as *modified renewal* process in [Cox62, Biro74]) and (2) $H(t)$ and $h(t)$ are the renewal function and the renewal density, respectively.

Consider the case where the $X_{j,i}$'s are exponentially distributed: $f_{\chi_j}(t) = \lambda_j \exp(-\lambda_j t)$. The interfailure occurrence times in such a case constitute a piecewise Poisson process. No assumption is made here on the sequence of magnitude of the λ_j's. However, it is assumed that the failure process is converging toward a Poisson process after r modifications have taken place. This assumption means that either (1) no more modifications are performed or (2) if some modifications are still being performed, they do not significantly affect the failure behavior of the system. Let $\{\lambda_1, \lambda_2, \ldots, \lambda_r\}$ be the sequence of these failure rates (Fig. 2.11).

The Laplace transform $\tilde{h}(s)$ of the failure intensity $h(t)$ (Eq. (2.13)) is:

$$\tilde{h}(s) = \sum_{j=1}^{r-1}\prod_{k=0}^{j-1}\left(\frac{\lambda_k}{\lambda_k+s}\right)^{a_k}\sum_{i=1}^{a_j}\left(\frac{\lambda_j}{\lambda_j+s}\right)^{i} + \frac{\lambda_r}{s}\prod_{k=1}^{r-1}\left(\frac{\lambda_k}{\lambda_k+s}\right)^{a_k}$$

Derivation of $h(t)$ is very tedious (see Prob. 2.6). Thus our study will be limited to summarizing the properties of the failure intensity $h(t)$ that can be derived:

- $h(t)$ is a continuous function of time, with $h(0) = \lambda_1$ and $h(\infty) = \lambda_r$.

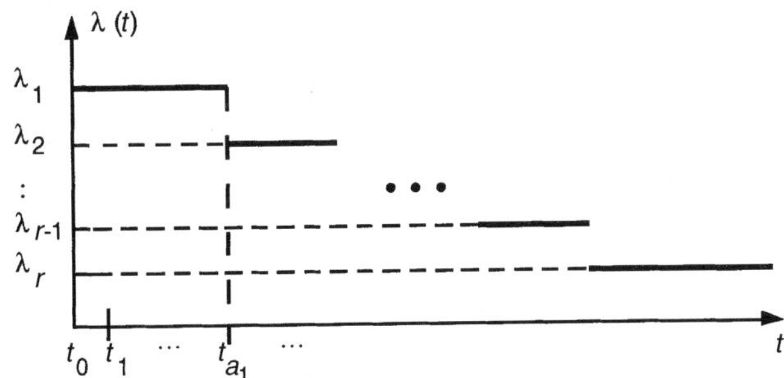

Figure 2.11 Sequence of failure rates.

- When the a_j's are finite,
  - —A condition for $h(t)$ to be a nonincreasing function of time (i.e., a condition for *reliability growth*) is $\lambda_1 \geq \lambda_2 \geq \ldots \geq \lambda_j \geq \ldots \geq \lambda_r$.
  - —The smaller the a_j's, the faster the reliability growth becomes.
  - —If a (local) increase in the failure rates occurs, then the failure intensity correspondingly (locally) increases.
- When $a_1 = \infty$, no correction takes place and we are faced with a classical renewal process; then $h(t) = \lambda_1 \ \forall \ t \in [0, \infty]$, which is the formulation of *stable reliability.*

These results are shown in Fig. 2.12, where the failure intensity is plotted for $a_j = a \ \forall j$.

Typical variations of conditional reliability $R_n(\tau)$ (Eq. (2.14)) are given by Fig. 2.13. When stable reliability is assumed, the underlying process is a classical renewal process with $R_n(\tau) = R_1(\tau)$, $n = 2, 3, \ldots$. For a so-called modified renewal process (the case where the first time to failure has a distribution different from the subsequent ones [Cox62, Biro74]), we usually have $R_n(\tau) < R_1(\tau)$, $n = 2, 3, \ldots$, with $R_n(\tau) = R_2(\tau)$, $n \geq 3$.

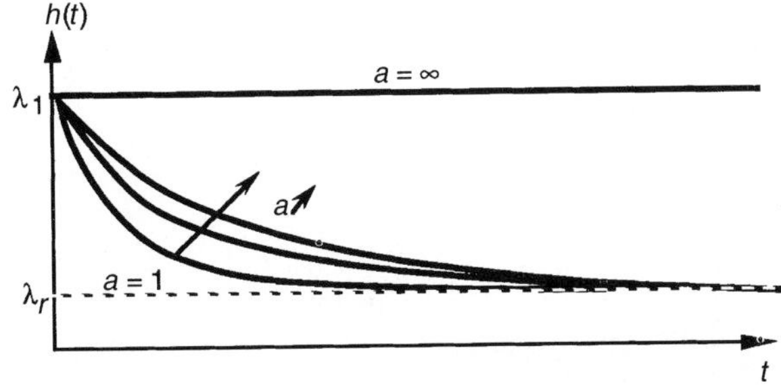

Figure 2.12 Failure intensity.

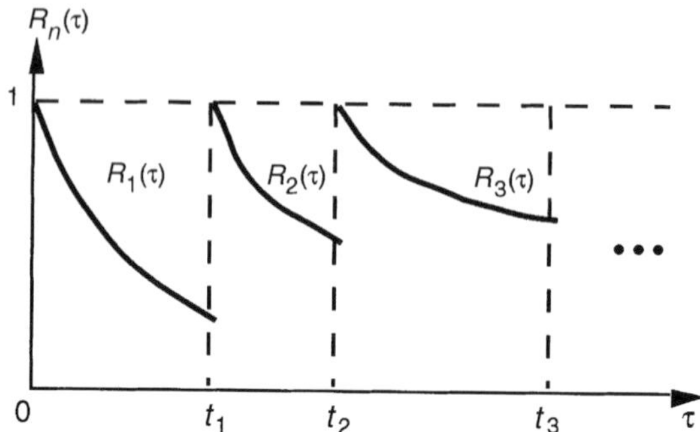

Figure 2.13 Conditional reliability.

Interval reliability $R(t,t+\tau)$ for a given, finite, a (which corresponds to a given curve of Fig. 2.12) can then be derived from Eq. (2.16) for $\tau << t$. Figure 2.14 indicates typical variations of $R(t,t+\tau)$: reliability over mission time τ increases with system lifetime t. In case of stable reliability (i.e., a classical renewal process), interval reliability is independent of the time origin t: the curves of Fig. 2.14 are thus not distinguishable; however, for a modified renewal process, depending on the granularity of time representation versus the mean time to failures, two groups of curves may be distinguished depending on the values of t compared to the mean time to failures.

Although still suffering from some limitations such as the assumed independency between the times to failure necessary for performing the renewal theory derivations, the derivations conducted in this section are more general than what has been previously published. The resulting model can be termed a *knowledge model* [Lapr91] with respect to the reliability growth models which have appeared in the literature, which can be termed *action models*. Support for this terminology, adapted from the Automatic Control theory, lies in the following remarks:

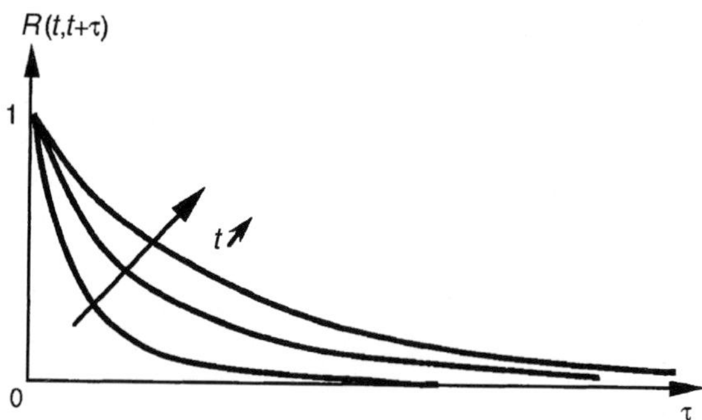

Figure 2.14 Interval reliability.

- The knowledge model allows the various phenomena to be taken into account explicitly and enables a number of properties to be derived; nevertheless, it is too complex in practice and not suitable for predictions.
- The action models, although based on more restrictive assumptions, are simplified models suitable for practical purposes.

The results obtained from the knowledge model thus derived in this section enable the action models reported in the literature to be classified as follows:

1. Models based on the relation between successive failure rates, which can be referred to as *failure rate models;* these models describe the behavior between two failures. Two categories of failure rate models can be distinguished according to the nature of the relationship between the successive failure rates: (1) deterministic relationship, which is the case for most failure rate models; see, for example, [Jeli72, Shoo73, Musa75]; (2) stochastic relationship [Keil83, Litt88]; the corresponding models are known as doubly stochastic reliability growth models in [Mill86].
2. Models based on the failure intensity, thus called *failure intensity models;* these models describe the failure process, and are usually expressed as nonhomogeneous Poisson processes; see, for example, [Crow77, Goel79, Yama83, Musa84, Lapr91].

Most reliability growth models consider reliability growth stricto sensu, without taking into account possible stable reliability or reliability decrease periods: they assume that the failure rate and/or the failure intensity decrease monotically and become asymptotically zero with time. Note, however, that the S-shaped models [Yama83, Tohm89] relate to initial reliability decrease followed by reliability growth, and that the hyperexponential model [Lapr84, Kano87, Lapr91] relates to reliability growth converging toward stable reliability. Finally, it is noteworthy that the models referenced above have been established specifically for software; however, there is no impairment to apply them to hardware [Litt81]; conversely, the Duane's model [Duan64], derived for hardware has been successfully applied to software [Keil83]. Chapter 3 provides a comprehensive survey of these reliability models.

Of prime importance when considering the practical use of the above models is the question of their application to real systems. Failure data can be collected under two forms: (1) times between failures or (2) number of failures per unit of time (failure-count data). Failure rate models are more naturally suited to data in the form of times between failures whereas failure intensity models are more naturally suited to data in the form of number of failures per unit of time. However, some models accommodate both forms of failure data, such as the logarithmic Poisson model [Musa84] or the hyperexponential model. The collection of data under the form "number of failures per unit of time" is less constraining than the other form, since one does not have to record all failure times; the definition of the unit of time can be varied throughout the life cycle of the system according to the amount of failures experienced, e.g., from a few days to weeks during the development phase, and from a few weeks to months during the operational life.

As action models are based on precise hypotheses (particularly with respect to the reliability trends they can accommodate, as discussed above), it is helpful to process failure data before model application, in order to (1) determine the reliability trend exhibited by the data and (2) select the model(s) whose assumptions are in agreement with the evidenced trend [Kano91b]. Trend tests are given detailed treatment in Chap. 10.

2.4.4 Availability modeling

All the time intervals defined in Sec. 2.4.2 are now considered, i.e., the times to failure and the times to restoration: the $Y_{j,i}$'s, Z_j's, and W_j's are no longer assumed to be zero. For simplicity, it is assumed that the times to restoration after failure are stochastically identical for a given version, i.e., $Y_{j,i} = Y_j$. Let:

- $t''_0 = 0$ denote the considered initial instant (the system is assumed nonfailed).
- n stand for the number of service restorations that took place before instant t.
- t'_n and t''_n, $n = 1,2, \ldots$ be the instants when correct service is no longer delivered and when service is restored, respectively, either:
  - —Upon (respectively after) failure, with $n = \sum_{k=1}^{j} (a_{k-1} + 1) + i$, $j = 1,2, \ldots, i = 1, \ldots a_j$, $a_0 = 0$
  - —Upon (respectively after) stopping the operation of system in order to introduce a modification, with $n = \sum_{k=1}^{j+1} (a_{k-1} + 1)$, $j = 1,2, \ldots,$ $a_0 = 0$
- $f_{Y_j}(t)$, $f_{Z_j}(t)$, $f_{W_j}(t)$, $j = 1,2, \ldots$ denote the probability density functions (pdf's) of the Y_j's, Z_j's, and W_j's, respectively, and $sf_{Z_j}(t)$ the survival function of the Z_j's.
- $\psi_n(t)$ be the pdf of the instants of service restoration, $n = 1,2, \ldots$

Derivation of availability is performed as in the case of reliability, with the pdf of the instants of service restoration $\psi_n(t)$ replacing the pdf of the instants of failure occurrence $\phi_n(t)$. As in Sec. 2.4.3, we assume that the various time intervals under consideration are stochastically independent, which leads to:

- For $n = \sum_{k=1}^{j} (a_{k-1} + 1) + i$

$$\psi_n(t) = \left(\bigotimes_{k=1}^{j-1} (f_{X_k}(t) * f_{Y_k}(t))^{*a_k} * (f_{Z_k}(t) * f_{W_k}(t)) \right) * (f_{X_j}(t) * f_{Y_j}(t))^{*i}$$

- For $n = \sum_{k=1}^{j+1} (a_{k-1} + 1)$

$$\psi_n(t) = \bigotimes_{k=1}^{j} (f_{X_k}(t) * f_{Y_k}(t))^{*a_k} * (f_{Z_k}(t) * f_{W_k}(t))$$

Let us consider the event $E_n = \{t''_n < t < t'_{n+1}\}, n = 0,1,2,\ldots$. The event E_n means that exactly n service restorations took place before instant t, and that the system is nonfailed at instant t. The pointwise availability $A(t)$, denoted simply by availability in the following, is then, due to the exclusivity of events E_n:

$$A(t) = \sum_{n=0}^{\infty} P\{E_n\}$$

The probability of event E_n is:

- For $n = \sum_{k=1}^{j} (a_{k-1} + 1) + i : P\{E_n\} = P\{t''_n < t < t + \tau < t''_n + Xj,i + 1\}$

$$P\{E_n\} = \int_0^t P\{x < t''_n < x + dx\}\ P\{Xj,i + 1 > t - x\} = \int_0^t sf_{X_j}(t - x)\ \psi_n(x)\ dx$$

- For $n = \sum_{k=1}^{j+1} (a_{k-1} + 1)$

$$P\{E_n\} = P\{t''_n < t < t + \tau < t''_n + Z_j\} = \int_0^t sf_{Z_j}(t - x)\ \psi_n(x)\ dx$$

The expression of $A(t)$ is then

$$A(t) = sf_{X_1}(t) + \sum_{j=1}^{\infty} \times$$

$$\left(sf_{X_j}(t) * \sum_{i=0}^{a_j - 1} \psi_{\left(\sum_{k=1}^{j} (a_{k-1}+1)+i\right)}(t) + sf_{Z_j}(t) * \psi_{\left(\sum_{k=1}^{j+1} (a_{k-1}+1)\right)}(t) \right)$$

Statistical estimation of the availability of a set of systems is given by the ratio of nonfailed systems at time t to the total number of systems in the set. When field data are related to times to failure and to times to restoration, considering the average availability rather than availability facilitates the estimation process, as the average availability is the expected proportion of time a system is nonfailed (see, for example, [Barl75]). The average availability over $[0,t]$ is defined by

$$A_{\text{av}}(t) = \frac{1}{t}\int_0^t A(\tau)\, d\tau$$

Denoting respectively UT_i the observed times where the system is operational, a statistical estimator of $A_{\text{av}}(t)$ is given by the following analytical expression

$$\hat{A}_{\text{av}}(t) = \frac{1}{t}\sum_{i=1}^{n} UT_i$$

So far, no assumption has been made on the pdf's of the various times considered. To derive properties of the availability, consider the case where:

- A modification takes place after each failure, i.e., $a_j = 1, Z_j = W_j = 0\ \forall\, j$,
- The $X_{j,i}$'s and the Y_j's are exponentially distributed: $f_{X_j}(t) = \lambda_j \exp(-\lambda_j t)$, $f_{\mathcal{Y}_j}(t) = \mu_j \exp(-\mu_j t)$, and that both corresponding piecewise Poisson processes converge toward Poisson processes after r modifications have taken place.

Then the Laplace transform $\tilde{A}(s)$ of availability is

$$\tilde{A}(s) = \sum_{j=1}^{r-1}\left(\frac{1}{\lambda_{j+s}}\right)\prod_{k=1}^{j-1}\left(\frac{\lambda_k}{\lambda_{k+s}}\right)\left(\frac{\mu_k}{\mu_{k+s}}\right) + \frac{1}{s}\,\frac{\mu_r\,\lambda_r}{\lambda_r+\mu_r+s}\left(\frac{1}{\lambda_{r+s}}\right)\prod_{k=1}^{r-1}\left(\frac{\mu_k}{\mu_{k+s}}\right)\left(\frac{\lambda_k}{\lambda_{k+s}}\right)$$

The times to failure are large with respect to the times to restoration, i.e., $\lambda_j/\mu_j << 1$. Performing an asymptotic development with respect to λ_j/μ_j for the unavailability $\overline{A}(t) = 1 - A(t)$ leads to

$$\overline{A}(t) = \frac{\lambda_r}{\mu_r} + \sum_{j=1}^{r-1}\alpha_j \exp(-\lambda_j t) - \frac{\lambda_1}{\mu_1}\exp(-\mu_1 t) \qquad (2.17)$$

with
$$\alpha_j = \sum_{k=j}^{r-1}\frac{\lambda_k}{\mu_k}\,\frac{\prod_{i=1}^{k-1}\lambda_i}{\prod_{i=1,i\neq j}^{k}(\lambda_i-\lambda_j)} - \frac{\lambda_r}{\mu_r}\prod_{k=1,k\neq j}^{r-1}\frac{\lambda_k}{\lambda_k-\lambda_j}$$

The α_j is linked by the following equation:

$$\sum_{j=1}^{r-1} \alpha_j = \frac{\lambda_1}{\mu_1} - \frac{\lambda_r}{\mu_r}$$

The following properties can be derived from Eq. (2.17), thus confirming and generalizing what had previously been established in [Cost78, Lapr84] through modeling via multistate Markov and semi-Markov chains:

P1. When reliability becomes stable, unavailability becomes constant: $\overline{A}(\infty) \approx \lambda_r/\mu_r$.

P2. If $(\lambda_1/\mu_1) \geq (\lambda_r/\mu_r)$, then there is an overshoot of unavailability in comparison with the asymptotic value (λ_r/μ_r).

P3. There is a single unavailability maximum (availability minimum) if $(\lambda_{j+1}/\mu_{j+1}) \leq (\lambda_j/\mu_j)$, for $j = 1, \ldots$; conversely, local maxima (minima) occur.

P4. If the piecewise Poisson process of the interfailure occurrence times is continuously nonincreasing from λ_1 to λ_r, and if the times to failure are large with respect to the times to restoration, then $\overline{A}_{\max} \approx (\lambda_1/\mu_1)$.

P5. The time to reach the maximum unavailability (minimum availability) is of the order of magnitude of the mean time to restoration $(1/\mu_1)$.

P6. The changes in availability are significantly more influenced by the stochastic changes in the times to failure than by the stochastic changes in the times to restoration, which can thus be assumed as stochastically identical over the system's life.

Figure 2.15 gives the typical shape of system unavailability in the presence of reliability growth.

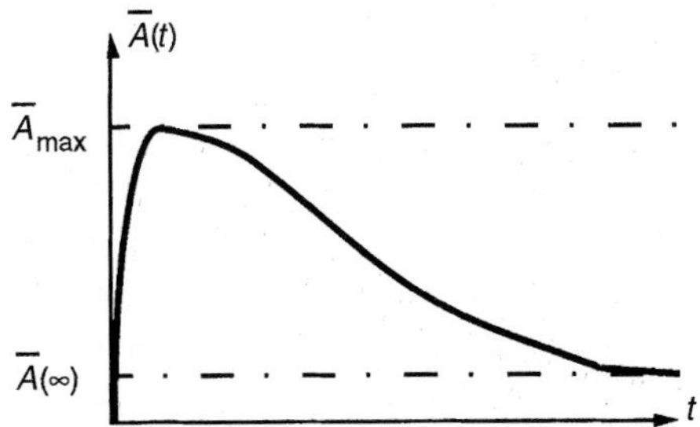

Figure 2.15 Typical system unavailability.

In case of stable reliability, ($\lambda_j = \lambda_1, j = 1, \ldots, r$), assuming $\mu_j = \mu_1$, $j = 1, \ldots, r$, the maximum corresponds to the asymptotic unavailability. Thus we have $\overline{A}(\infty) = \overline{A}_{\max}$.

Although the availability of operational computing systems is usually significantly influenced in the field by reliability growth (for instance, the data displayed in [Wall84] for AT&T's ESS-4 show that unavailability is decreased by a factor of 250 during 3.5 years of operation), the only published *action* model for availability in the presence of reliability growth is the hyperexponential model [Lapr91].

2.5 Situation with Respect to the State of the Art in Reliability Evaluation

Hardware evaluation and software evaluation have followed courses which could hardly have been more distant from each other.

Hardware evaluation has focused on the operational life, placing the emphasis on the influence of the system structure on dependability. A number of significant results have been derived with respect to (1) the role and influence of the coverage of the fault-tolerance strategies and mechanisms [Bour69, Arno73]; (2) the construction [Beya81] and processing [Gros84, Bobb86, Cour77] of large, stiff, Markov models; (3) the definition and evaluation of performance-related measures of dependability, which are usually gathered in the concept of performability [Meye78, Smit88]. These results have been integrated into software packages, such as ARIES, HARP, SAVE, and SURF. As far as elementary data are concerned, reliance has generally been placed on databases such as the MIL-HDBK-217, which are limited to permanent faults, whereas it is currently agreed that temporary faults constitute a major source of failure [Siew92]. In addition, it has largely been ignored that the reliability of hardware parts grows significantly during the whole system's life, as shown, for example, in the experimental data displayed in [Baue85].

Software evaluation has mainly focused on the development phase, and especially on the reliability growth of single-component (black-box) systems. Many models have been proposed (see surveys such as [Rama82, Yama85] and Chap. 3). Less attention has been paid to accounting for the structure of a software system, where most of the corresponding work has been restricted to the failure process, either for non-fault-tolerant [Litt81, Lapr84] or for fault-tolerant software systems [Hech79, Grna80, Lapr84, Arla88]; only our recent work [Lapr91, Kano93a] deals with the evaluation of the reliability growth of a system from the reliability growth of its components. In [Lapr91] a so-called transformation approach based on a Markov interpretation of the hyperexponential reliability growth model is derived: the hyperexponential model is regarded as resulting from the transformation of a traditional Markov model (stable reliability) into another Markov model, which, through a suitable addition of states, enables reliability growth phenomena to be accounted for. This stable reliability–reliability growth transformation—is shown to be applicable to the Markov models of systems made up of components. In particular, it enables the reliability and the availability of systems to be evaluated from the reliability growth of their components. This approach has been applied to model the reliability growth of fault-tolerant software systems (recovery blocks, N-version programming and N self-checking programming; see Chap. 14) in [Kano93a].

From the practical utilization viewpoint, the situation can be summarized as follows:

- Hardware evaluation is fairly well included in the design process; although the estimations are usually carried out more as an adjunct to the design methodology than an integral part of producing an optimized design, predictive evaluations of operational dependability are routinely performed during the design of a system.
- In the vast majority of software developments, evaluation (if any) is extremely limited, and most of the published work devoted to applications on real data is in fact post mortem work.

However, when dealing with the assessment of dependability, the users of computing systems are interested in figures resulting from modeling and evaluation of *systems,* composed of hardware and software, with respect to both *physical and design faults.* This statement may be supported by considering:

1. The requirements for systems in terms of dependability; an example is provided by the requirements for electronic switching systems [Clem87] (Fig. 2.16), in which it is explicitly stated that they apply to both hardware and software, especially in terms of reliability and availability.
2. The sources of failure of computing systems; an example of sources of failures is given in Fig. 2.17, showing results of a survey on the sources of unavailability for electronic switching systems and transaction processing systems [Toy85]. Clearly, an evaluation which would be performed with respect to hardware failures only would not be representative of the actual behavior of the considered systems, and this situation is exacerbated even more when considering (hardware) fault-tolerant systems, where software is the dependability bottleneck, as it contributes to more than half the system failures [Gray90].

The hardware and software for switching systems must be designed to meet the requirements shown in the table below.

Operation	• Continuous (20 years)
Time shared channels	• Thousands
Recovery time	• Critical
Value of reliability	• High 1 call per 100,000 call cut off
Downtime	• <3 minutes/year
Synchronization	• Network sync
System growth Database changes Program changes Maintenance	All must be done with the system on-line and operational

Figure 2.16 Requirements for ESSs.

Faced with these user requirements, the evaluations of the system's dependability in terms of hardware and software are not common practice compared to the large amount of evaluations considering only hardware. Hardware and software evaluations generally address stable reliability [Rohn72, Avey80, Angu82, Star87, Pign88, Duga94], with a few exceptions accounting for reliability growth [Cost78, Lapr91]. Evaluations dedicated to reliability growth are based on either multistate Markov modeling [Cost78] or on Markov modeling combined with the above-mentioned transformation approach [Lapr91]. For evaluations related to stable reliability, various modeling techniques are used: semi-Markov modeling [Star87] or Markov modeling used either (1) alone [Rohn72, Avey80, Angu82] or (2) together with other techniques such as fault tree analysis [Duga94b] or block diagrams [Pign88].

In addition, standardization bodies and regulating agencies are increasingly aware of the need to perform evaluations encompassing

<table>
<tr><th>Unavailability sources</th><th>Electronic switching</th><th>Transaction processing</th></tr>
<tr><td>Hardware failures</td><td rowspan="2">20%</td><td>40%</td></tr>
<tr><td>Environment</td><td>5%</td></tr>
<tr><td>Software failures</td><td>15%</td><td rowspan="2">30%</td></tr>
<tr><td>Recovery deficiencies</td><td>35%</td></tr>
<tr><td>Incorrect procedures</td><td rowspan="2">30%</td><td>20%</td></tr>
<tr><td>Others, such as updating</td><td>5%</td></tr>
</table>

Figure 2.17 Sources of failures.

Studies have been conducted for ESA into software reliability requirements for ESA Space programmes. These studies, conducted in 1986, concluded:

a) Software failure is a process that appears to the observer to be "random", therefore the term "reliability" is meaningful when applied to a system which includes software, and the process can be modeled as stochastic.
b) The definition of "Reliability" is identical for a system which includes software as it is for a purely hardware system. It is the classical definition: "the probability of successful operation for a given period under given conditions".
c) The specification of numerical levels of reliability for a complete system is meaningless unless the reliability of the software which it contains is similarly quantified and the level of reliability achieved by that software is verified.

Figure 2.18 Statement from ESA.

both hardware and software. Two such examples are given in Figs. 2.18 and 2.19. The example in Fig. 2.18 is extracted from an invitation to tender from ESA, the European Space Agency [ESA88], and reports the conclusions derived from the studies conducted for ESA in 1986. The example in Fig. 2.19, extracted from the British Standard [BStd86] (Part 4) is more general since it addresses all types of systems containing software. Unfortunately, despite the existence of such recommendations made several years ago, the specification of software reliability is far from being a common activity.

Clearly, the results presented in this chapter show that the current limitation to the practicality of dependability evaluations of hardware

Specification of reliability for systems containing software (Section 3.1.7)

The mechanisms for the specification of reliability requirements, from the point of view of the failure of an item to perform its function, should be no different for systems containing software than for any other. It is imperative that there should be no discrimination between failures due to logical faults in the system from those due to physical breakdown. The following areas, however, require special consideration:

a) In the prediction of reliability, allowance should be made for the contribution made by logical errors to the overall unreliability of the system. At the moment, prediction of such a contribution, particularly before testing begins, is neither accurate nor well understood. Experience from similar systems is the most likely source of such data.
b) The contribution of logical errors to system unavailability should be considered. Although there is no 'repair' in the strict sense, depending upon the design, considerable time may elapse after a after a failure before operation restart.
c) The principal area in which failures due to logical errors differ from physical failure is that such failures do not require spares, routine maintenance, and repair resources generally required for hardware. However, the inclusion of software in the system may indicate the need for a software facility and requirement for this facility should be separately considered.

Figure 2.19 Recommendations from British Standards.

and software systems is not due to theoretical impediments. The lack of credibility of *predictive* software reliability evaluations lies therefore in the capabilities of the current reliability growth models—the action models in our terminology—with regard to the failure data upon which their predictions are based. When the predictions and failure data are homogeneous, they apply to the same phase of the system life (either development or operation) and are commensurate; then the application of those models is greatly facilitated, and the evaluations done are meaningful. The problem lies in heterogeneous situations, typically predicting operational dependability from failure data collected during development. The current models, which are fundamentally performing extrapolations, then fall out (a typical situation is that the software will exhibit a reliability in operation that is hopefully much better than predicted from failure data collected during its development), and new approaches are needed, such as those proposed in (1) [Lapr92c] via the so-called product-in-a-process approach, aimed at enhancing the reliability prediction for a given software when exploiting field data collected for former, similar software or (2) [Haml93] via the amplification of software reliability testing.

2.6 Summary

In this chapter, we addressed the problem of software reliability and system reliability. Following our discussion of the dependability concept, we dealt with system behavior up to the (next) failure. We also focused on the sequence of failures when considering restoration actions consecutive to various forms of maintenance. The assumptions made for derivation purposes were carefully stated and analyzed, and we commented at length on the results obtained in order to relate them to the existing body of results. Furthermore, we described a generalization of the classical, hardware-oriented, reliability theory in order to incorporate software as well. This chapter is then concerned with reliability growth phenomena; since most published material on reliability growth is software-oriented, this chapter can be regarded as a generalization to include hardware as well. Finally, we were devoted to position the results obtained with respect to the state of art in dependability evaluation, considering both hardware and software.

Problems

2.1 Some illustrative examples of sequences fault–error–failure are given in Sec. 2.2.2. Considering physical and design faults, give similarities and differences with respect to fault creation mode and manifestation mode.

2.2 Give other examples of the sequence fault–error–failure.

2.3 In Sec. 2.3.1, a general formulation of the reliability $R(t)$ as a function of the distribution of the failure rate λ ($g_c(\lambda)$) is given. It is stated that a gamma distribution for λ leads to a Pareto distribution for $R(t)$. Demonstrate this result.

2.4 Considering a multi-interpreter system viewed as a hierarchy of interpreters, Eq. (2.10) gives the relationship between the failure rate of the system and the failure rates of its interpreters. Demonstrate this result.

2.5 The results of this chapter show that the same approaches can be applied to hardware and software systems; for those who are familiar with Markov modeling, construct the Markov chain of a multi-interpreter system with a hardware and a software interpreters. The hardware interpreter is made of two hardware redundant components (failure rate of a component λ_h, repair rate μ) and the software interpreter is made of one component (failure rate λ_s, restart rate δ). Derive the reliability of the system.

2.6 Section 2.4.3 gives the expression of the Laplace transform of the failure intensity, $\tilde{h}(s)$, related to the sequence of failure rates presented in Fig. 2.11. Assuming operation restart after correction only ($a_j = 1\ \forall\, j$), derive the equation given the temporal expression of the failure intensity function $h(t)$.

2.7 As in the previous exercise, assuming operation restart after correction only ($a_j = 1\ \forall\, j$), derive the expression of the conditional reliability, $R_n(t)$ from Eq. (2.14), and derive the plot of $R(t)$ (Fig. 13).

2.8 As in the previous exercises, assuming operation restart after correction only ($a_j = 1\ \forall\, j$), derive the expression of the interval reliability, $R(t, t + \tau)$ (Eq. (2.16) and Fig. 14).

2.9 Considering the following sequence of failure rates,

$$\lambda_0 = \lambda,\ \lambda_1 = [(n-1)/n]\ \lambda,\ \lambda_2 = [(n-2)/n]\ \lambda \ldots \lambda_{n-1} = [1/n]\ \lambda,\ \lambda_n = 0$$

derive the expressions of the failure intensity, the conditional reliability and the interval reliability.

Chapter

3

Software Reliability Modeling Survey

William Farr
Naval Surface Warfare Center

3.1 Introduction

With the ever-increasing role that software is playing in our systems, concern has steadily grown over the quality of the software component. Since the most important facet of quality is reliability, software reliability engineering (SRE) has generated quite a bit of interest and research in the software community. One particular aspect of SRE that has received the most attention is software reliability modeling. This chapter will present some of the more important models that have appeared in the recent literature, from both a historical and applications perspective. Not all of the models are considered because of space limitation (e.g., only time series models are considered). For additional models and further elaboration on the models considered in this chapter, you are referred to some other books on the subject of software reliability modeling [Musa87, Xie91a].

For each model that we do consider, we'll provide some motivation for it, present its assumptions and data required for implementation, show the model form and the resulting estimates, and conclude with some general comments about the model's implementation and provide an example in some cases of the estimation process. The derived estimates will be based upon the maximum likelihood procedure. In some cases, least-squares estimation will also be considered if the likelihood function is difficult to solve analytically. Other estimation procedures are also applicable (e.g., method-of-moments), but in this chapter we'll primarily concentrate on maximum likelihood estimates because of their many desirable properties, (e.g., asymptotic normality, asymptotic efficiency, and invariance).

Before considering the models we'll first provide a historical perspective of the development of this field and some needed theoretical results from reliability theory, which we'll use in each model development. We'll then go into the models. We'll first consider the exponential class of models, as that is the most important. Other distributional forms for the failure data, including Weibull and gamma, will then be considered. We'll also discuss some models based upon a Bayesian perspective and compare and contrast this approach with the more traditional one. The models that are presented were selected based upon a number of criteria. Important models in the historical development of this field were considered. In addition, the models that have been applied the most, based upon a literature review, were included. Another consideration was to select a model that was fairly typical of the class that it represents. Some important models may still have been left out in this review, but you are provided an extensive reference list for additional readings. Finally, we present some current research in generalizing the models and in extending them to the early phases of the life cycle.

This chapter will only consider models for reliability based on the time domain, i.e., models using either the elapsed time between software failures or the number of failures occurring over a specified time period.

3.2 Historical Perspective and Implementation

3.2.1 Historical background

Software reliability modeling has, surprisingly to many, been around since the early 1970s, with pioneering works by [Mora72, Mora75a, Shoo72, Shoo73, Shoo76, Shoo77a, Shoo77b, Cout73]. The basic approach is to model past failure data to predict future behavior. This approach employs either the observed number of failures discovered per time period or the observed time (actual wall clock or some measures of computer execution time) between failures of the software. The models therefore fall into two basic classes, depending upon the types of data the model uses:

1. Failures per time period
2. Time between failures

These classes are, however, not mutually disjoint. There are models that can handle either data type. Moreover, many of the models for one data type can still be applied even if the user has data of the other type, as explained by the two data transformation procedures in Chap. 1.

Either of these data transformation procedures requires that you test the applied model to determine the adequacy of the resulting fit. In the following sections the models will be introduced with the data class in which they first appeared in the literature.

These classes can themselves be considered part of the larger *time domain* approach to software reliability modeling, in contrast to the *error seeding and tagging* approach and the *data domain* approach. You are referred to [Farr83] and [Xie91a], among others, where these alternative approaches are described.

Since the development of these models was based upon concepts adapted from hardware reliability theory, you may want to review some reliability functions and concepts that show the relationships among these different functions. This is provided in App. B, Sec. B.2. We will make extensive use of these relationships in the development of the models throughout this chapter.

3.2.2 Model classification scheme

To aid in our development of the models in the ensuing sections, we'll need to discuss a model classification scheme that was proposed by Musa and Okumoto [Musa83]. It allows relationships to be established for models within the same classification groups and shows where model development has occurred. For this scheme Musa and Okumoto classified models in terms of five different attributes. They are:

1. *Time domain.* Wall clock versus execution time.
2. *Category.* The total number of failures that can be experienced in infinite time. This is either *finite* or *infinite,* the two subgroups.
3. *Type.* The distribution of the number of the failures experienced by time t. Two important types that we will consider are the Poisson and binomial.
4. *Class.* (Finite failure category only.) Functional form of the failure intensity expressed in terms of time.
5. *Family.* (Infinite failure category only.) Functional form of the failure intensity function expressed in terms of the expected number of failures experienced.

We will be especially concerned in the following sections with the category and type groupings. For the category group, suppose we let $M(t)$ be the random number of failures (faults) that are experienced by time t with mean value function $\mu(t)$, i.e., $\mu(t) = E[M(t)]$. If $\lim_{t\to\infty} \mu(t) < \infty$ (i.e., is finite), we have a finite failure model; otherwise we have a model of the infinite failure subgroup. In Secs. 3.3 and 3.4, we'll deal with the former group (finite failure models), while in Sec. 3.5 we'll specifically look at the latter group. Note that in this chapter we do not distinguish *faults* and *failures* exclusively. We assume there is a one-to-one relationship between them.

For the type consideration we will now relate some important properties of the Poisson and binomial groups. We will make use of these relationships for specific classes of models in subsequent sections.

First for the Poisson type, we consider that we have a Poisson process over time. By this we mean that if we let $t_0 = 0, t_1, \ldots, t_{i-1}, t_i, \ldots, t_n = t$ be a partition of our time interval 0 to t and $\mu(t)$ is as defined as above, then we have a Poisson process if each f_i, $i = 1, \ldots, n$ (the number of faults detected in the ith interval, t_{i-1} to t_i), are independent Poisson random variables with means, $E[f_i] = \mu(t_i) - \mu(t_{i-1})$. Thus for each of the random variables f_i's, $i = 1, \ldots, n$, the probability density function is:

$$P(f_i = x) = e^{-(\mu(t_i) - \mu(t_{i-1}))}[(\mu(t_i) - \mu(t_{i-1}))]^x/x! \qquad \text{for } x = 0, 1, \ldots$$

Note: If $\mu(t)$ is a linear function of time, i.e., $\mu(t) = \alpha t$ for some constant $\alpha > 0$, we say the Poisson process, $M(t)$, is a homogeneous Poisson process (HPP). If, however, it is nonlinear we refer to the process as being a nonhomogeneous Poisson process (NHPP).

If we have a Poisson process model, we can show a relationship between the failure intensity function and the reliability function (hence the hazard rate and the probability density function using the relationships established in App. B, Sec. B.2). Suppose we denote $R(t + \Delta t \mid t)$ as the conditional reliability function that the software will still operate after $t + \Delta t$ given that it has not failed after time t. Let $\mu(t)$ be the mean value function for the cumulative number of failures and $\lambda(t)$ be the failure intensity function, then

$R(t + \Delta t \mid t) = P(f_t = 0 \mid t)$ where f_t is a Poisson random variable over the interval t to $t + \Delta t$

$= \exp(-(\mu(t + \Delta t) - \mu(t)))$

$= \exp(-\lambda(t')\Delta t)$, t' is a point in the interval t to $t + \Delta t$ and using the definition of $\lambda(t)$

$= \exp\left(-\int_t^{t+\Delta t} \lambda(x)\, dx\right)$ using the mean value theorem of integrals

The relationship between the failure intensity function and the hazard rate for a Poisson process can also be derived. It can be shown (see Prob. 3.1) that

$$z(\Delta t \mid t_{i-1}) = \lambda(t_{i-1} + \Delta t) \tag{3.1}$$

where t_{i-1} is the time of the $(i-1)$st failure and Δt is any point such that $t_{i-1} \le t_{i-1} + \Delta t < t_i$. This shows that the conditional hazard rate and the failure intensity function are the same if the failure intensity function is evaluated at the current time $t_{i-1} + \Delta t$.

Another relationship that one can establish for the Poisson type of models is [Musa87]

$$\mu(t) = \alpha F_a(t) \tag{3.2}$$

where α is some constant and $F_a(t)$ is the cumulative distribution function of the time to failure of an individual fault a. From this, if we consider also distributions that belong to the finite failure category (i.e., $\lim_{t \to \infty} \mu(t) < \infty$), we have that $\lim_{t \to \infty} \mu(t) = \alpha$, since $\lim_{t \to \infty} F_a(t) = 1$. Thus α represents the eventual number of faults detected in the system if it could have been observed over an infinite amount of time. Using Eq. (3.2) and the relationship between the mean value function and the failure intensity function, we have also for the Poisson type of models

$$\lambda(t) = \mu'(t) = \alpha f_a(t) \tag{3.3}$$

where $f_a(t)$ is the probability density function of the time to failure of the individual fault a.

For the binomial type of models, we have the following assumptions:

1. There is a fixed number of faults (N) in the software at the beginning of the time in which the software is observed.
2. When a fault is detected it is removed immediately.
3. Using the notation of [Musa87], if T_a is the random variable denoting the time to failure of fault a, then the T_a's, $a = 1, \ldots, n$ are independently and identically distributed random variables as $F_a(t)$ for all remaining faults.

The cumulative distribution function, $F_a(t)$, density function, $f_a(t)$, and hazard rate function, $z_a(t)$, are the same for all faults for this class. Moreover, for this class no new faults are introduced into the software in the fault detection/correction process. [Musa87] shows for this class that the failure intensity function is obtained from the probability density function for a single fault as:

$$\lambda(t) = N f_a(t) \tag{3.4}$$

The mean value function is in turn related to the cumulative distribution function, $F_a(t)$, as

$$\mu(t) = N F_a(t) \tag{3.5}$$

Notice the similarity between Eqs. (3.4) and (3.3) as well as between (3.5) and (3.2). For the binomial we have a fixed number of faults at start, N, while for the Poisson type, α is the eventual number of faults that could be discovered over an infinite amount of time.

3.2.3 Model limitations and implementation issues

In fitting any model to a given data set, you are cautioned about some limitations for this type of analysis. First, you must be aware of a given model's assumptions. For example, if a selected model makes the assumption that the time intervals over which the software is observed or tested are all of the same magnitude (e.g., Schneidewind's model), don't attempt to use this model if this is not the case for your data. There are other assumptions that may not hold, but the model may be fairly robust with respect to violations. One such assumption is the distributional one about the number of failures per unit time or the time between failures. One can still do a credible job in fitting the data for a selected model even if its distributional assumption is violated. The only way to tell is to ask just how well the model is doing in tracking and predicting the data. The procedures discussed in Chap. 4 will help considerably in answering this question.

A second model limitation and implementation issue concerns future predictions. If the environment in which the software is being tested or observed changes considerably from the one in which the data have been collected, you can't expect to do well in predicting future behavior. If the software is being operated in a different manner (i.e., new capabilities are being exercised that were not used before, or a different testing methodology is employed), the failure history of the past will not reflect these changes, and poor predictions may result. Too many times model users tend to extrapolate either too far into the future or make reliability predictions for an environment in which little if any data have been gathered. Developing operational profiles is very important if one wants to predict future reliability in the user's environment (see Chap. 5).

For both violations of assumptions and considerations for predictions, one option that may be available to the practitioner is to use the most recent data if sufficient current data are available. Recent data may be more representative of the environment in which the software is employed than data collected in the distant past. This same reasoning applies to violations of assumptions. Current data may be more stable and reflective of the assumptions than past data. This is the basic idea behind Schneidewind's model 2 (see Sec. 3.3.3). It appears to us that there is nothing to preclude this approach on other models. Model validation should be the final word.

A final comment on implementation: this modeling approach is primarily applicable from integrated testing onward. The software must have matured to the point that *extensive changes are not being routinely made.* The models can't have a credible performance if the software is changing so fast that gathering data on one day is not the same as gathering data on another day. Different approaches and models need to be considered if that is the case. At the conclusion of this chapter some approaches for the earlier phases are presented.

3.3 Exponential Failure Time Class of Models

In the literature on software reliability, this class has the most articles written on it. Using Musa and Okumoto's classification scheme, this group consists of all finite failure models with the functional form of the failure intensity function being exponential. The binomial types in this class are all characterized by a per-fault constant hazard rate (i.e., $z(t) = \phi$); the hazard rate function before the ith fault that has been detected is a function of the remaining number of faults (i.e., $N - (i - 1)$); and the failure intensity function is exponential in form (i.e., $\lambda(t) = N\phi \exp(-\phi t)$). The Poisson types in this class are all characterized by a per-fault constant hazard rate (i.e., $z(t) = \phi$) and an exponential time to failure of an individual fault (i.e., $f_X(x) = \phi \exp(-\phi x)$). Since we have either a homogeneous or nonhomogeneous Poisson process, the number of faults that occur over any fixed period of time is a Poisson random variable. For the time-between-failures models, the distribution is exponential.

3.3.1 Jelinski-Moranda de-eutrophication model

3.3.1.1 Overview of the model. One of the earliest models proposed, which is still being applied today, is the de-eutrophication model developed by Jelinski and Moranda [Mora72], while working on some Navy projects for McDonnell Douglas. The elapsed time between failures is taken to follow an exponential distribution with a parameter that is proportional to the number of remaining faults in the software, i.e., the mean time between failures at time t is $1/\phi(N - (i - 1))$. Here t is any point in time between the occurrence of the $(i - 1)$st and the ith fault occurrence. The quantity ϕ is the proportionality constant and N is the total number of faults in the software from the initial point in time at which the software is observed. Figure 3.1 illustrates the impact that finding a fault has on the hazard rate. One can see as each fault is discovered that the hazard rate is reduced by the proportionality constant

ϕ. This indicates that the impact of each fault removal is the same. In Musa and Okumoto's classification scheme, this is a binomial type model.

3.3.1.2 Assumptions and data requirements. The *basic assumptions* are:

1. The rate of fault detection is proportional to the current fault content of the software.
2. The fault detection rate remains constant over the intervals between fault occurrence.
3. A fault is corrected instantaneously without introducing new faults into the software.
4. The software is operated in a similar manner as that in which reliability predictions are to be made.
5. Every fault has the same chance of being encountered within a severity class as any other fault in that class.
6. The failures, when the faults are detected, are independent.

Note: The numbered assumptions 4 through 6 are fairly standard as we consider other models in this chapter. Assumption 4 is to ensure that the model estimates that are derived using data collected in one particular environment are applicable to the environment in which the reliability projections are to be made. The fifth assumption is to ensure that the various failures all have the same distributional properties. One severity class might have a different failure rate than the others, requiring a separate reliability analysis be done. The last assumption allows simplicity in deriving the maximum likelihood estimates. Since assumptions 4 through 6 will appear often in the models that follow, we'll refer to them as the *Standard Assumptions* for reliability modeling rather than repeat them in each model development.

The *data requirements* to implement this model are: the elapsed time between failures $x_1, x_2, \ldots, x_n$ or the actual times that the software failed $t_1, t_2, \ldots, t_n$, where $x_i = t_i - t_{i-1}$, $i = 1, \ldots, n$ with $t_0 = 0$.

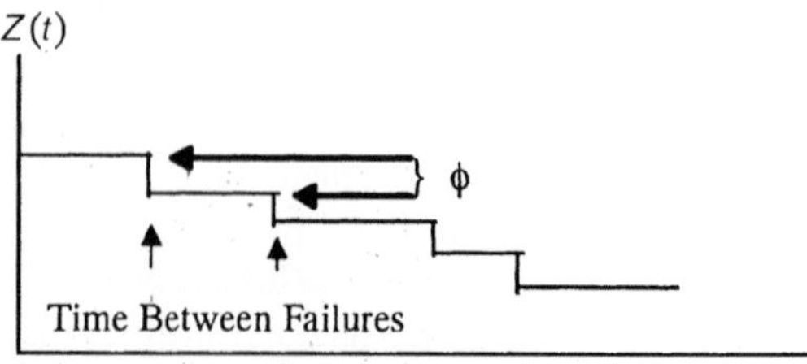

Figure 3.1 De-eutrophication process.

3.3.1.3 Model form. From the overview of the model and the assumptions from the previous section, we can determine that if the time-between-failure occurrences are $X_i = T_i - T_{i-1}, i = 1, \ldots, n$, then the X_i's are independent exponentially distributed random variables with mean $= 1/\phi(N - (i-1)) = 1/z(X_i \mid T_{i-1})$. That is

$$f(X_i \mid T_{i-1}) = z(X_i \mid T_{i-1})\exp(-z(X_i \mid T_{i-1})X_i)$$

$$= \phi[N - (i-1)]\exp(-\phi[N - (i-1)]X_i)$$

Since this exponential model belongs to the binomial type, using Eqs. (3.2) and (3.3), we have specifically:

$$\mu(t) = N(1 - \exp(-\phi t)) \qquad \text{and} \qquad \lambda(t) = N\phi\exp(-\phi t)$$

for the mean value function and the failure intensity function. It is clearly a finite failures type model as $\lim_{t\to\infty} \mu(t) = \lim_{t\to\infty} (N(1 - \exp(-\phi t))) = N$.

3.3.1.4 Model estimation and reliability prediction. The maximum likelihood estimates, MLEs, calculated from the joint density of the X_i's, are the solutions to the following equations:

$$\hat{\phi} = \frac{n}{\hat{N}\left(\sum_{i=1}^{n} X_i\right) - \sum_{i=1}^{n}(i-1)X_i} \qquad \text{and}$$

$$\sum_{i=1}^{n} \frac{1}{\hat{N} - (i-1)} = \frac{n}{\hat{N} - \left(1\Big/\sum_{i=1}^{n} X_I\right)\left(\sum_{i=1}^{n}(i-1)X_i\right)}$$

The second equation is solved by numerical techniques for the MLE of N, and then the solution is put into the first equation to find the MLE of ϕ. Using the MLEs, various reliability measures can then be derived by replacing the quantities N and ϕ in the reliability function of interest by the corresponding MLEs $\hat{N}$ and $\hat{\phi}$. An example is the estimated MTTF after n faults have been detected. The expression for this is MTTF for the $(n+1)$st fault $= 1/z(x_{n+1} \mid t_n)$, so the MLE is $M\hat{T}TF = 1/\hat{z}(x_{n+1} \mid t_n) = 1/\hat{\phi}(\hat{N} - n)$.

Example 3.1 To illustrate the above results, suppose we have observed the following elapsed-time-between-failure occurrences as

$x_1 = 7, x_2 = 11, x_3 = 8, x_4 = 10, x_5 = 15, x_6 = 22, x_7 = 20, x_8 = 25, x_9 = 28$, and $x_{10} = 35$

Using the SMERFS reliability program (see [Farr93a, Farr93b] and App. A), the MLE estimates for N and ϕ are respectively $\hat{N} = 11.6$ and $\hat{\phi} = 0.0096$. Thus the estimated MTTF to the next failure is

$$MTTF = 1/\hat{\phi}(\hat{N} - n) = 1/0.0096(11.6 - 10) = 65.1.$$

3.3.1.5 Comments. Much has been written in the literature on this model and many variations of it have been proposed. Farr [Farr83] has in his survey a discussion of many of these variations as well as alternative ways of deriving estimates of the reliability measures, e.g., least-squares estimation. This model, however, has largely been replaced by some of the more recent models that will be discussed. Its importance is largely in setting the framework for future work in this modeling area.

3.3.2 Nonhomogeneous Poisson process (NHPP) model

3.3.2.1 Overview of the model. The nonhomogeneous Poisson process (NHPP) model is a Poisson type model that takes the number of faults per unit of time as independent Poisson random variables. The model was first proposed in 1979 by Amrit Goel and Kazu Okumoto [Goel79] and has formed the basis for the models using the observed number of faults per unit time group. A number of others are spin-offs from it, e.g., the S-shaped model of Yamada, [Yama83] which we'll consider later (see Sec. 3.4.2).

3.3.2.2 Assumptions and data requirements. Including the Standard Assumptions (see Sec. 3.3.1.2), the *basic assumptions* are:

1. The cumulative number of failures by time t, $M(t)$, follows a Poisson process with mean value function $\mu(t)$. The mean value function is such that the expected number of fault occurrences for any time t to $t + \Delta t$ is proportional to the expected number of undetected faults at time t. It is also assumed to be a bounded, nondecreasing function of time with $\lim_{t \to \infty} \mu(t) = N < \infty$, that is, it is a finite failure model.
2. The number of faults $(f_1, f_2, \ldots, f_n)$ detected in each of the respective intervals $[(t_0 = 0, t_1), (t_1, t_2), \ldots, (t_{i-1}, t_i), \ldots, (t_{n-1}, t_n)]$ is independent for any finite collection of times, $t_1 < t_2 < \cdots < t_n$.

The *data requirements* to implement this fault count model are:

1. The fault counts in each of the testing intervals, i.e., the f_i's.
2. The completion time of each period that the software is under observation, i.e., the t_i's.

3.3.2.3 Model form. From the assumptions it can be shown [Goel79] that the mean value function must be of the form

$$\mu(t) = N(1 - e^{-bt})$$

for some constants $b > 0$ and $N > 0$. N is the expected total number of faults to be eventually detected. (*Note:* N is not required to be an integer since it is the *expected number* of faults that will eventually be detected.) Since the failure intensity function is the derivative of $\mu(t)$ we have, therefore

$$\lambda(t) = Nbe^{-bt}$$

Notice that the failure intensity function is strictly decreasing for $t > 0$. Because it belongs to the exponential class, we have the distribution of a single individual fault, X:

$$f_X(x) = be^{-bx}$$

We thus have for the failure intensity function

$$\lambda(t) = Nbe^{-bt} = Nf_X(t)$$

which shows the relationship between the failure intensity function and probability density function for a single fault.

From the assumptions, we also have that each f_i, the fault count in the ith interval, is an independent Poisson random variable with mean $= \mu(t_i) - \mu(t_{i-1})$. Therefore the joint density of the f_i's, $i = 1, \ldots, n$, is

$$\prod_{i=1}^{n} \frac{[\mu(t_i) - \mu(t_{i-1})]^{f_i} \exp\{\mu(t_i) - \mu(t_{i-1})\}}{f_i!}$$

3.3.2.4 Model estimation and reliability prediction. Using the joint density given above, the maximum likelihood estimates (MLEs) of N and b can be obtained as the solutions for the following pair of equations:

$$\hat{N} = \frac{\sum_{i=1}^{n} f_i}{(1 - e^{-\hat{b}t_n})} \quad \text{and} \quad \frac{t_n e^{-\hat{b}t_n} \sum_{i=1}^{n} f_i}{(1 - e^{-\hat{b}t_n})} = \sum_{i=1}^{n} \frac{f_i(t_i e^{-\hat{b}t_i} - t_{i-1}e^{-\hat{b}t_{i-1}})}{e^{-\hat{b}t_{i-1}} - e^{-\hat{b}t_i}}$$

The second equation is solved for $\hat{b}$ by numerical methods, and the solution is then substituted into the first equation to find $\hat{N}$. MLEs are then obtained for other reliability measures by substituting the MLEs for N

and b in the expressions of the measures of interest. For example, the MLEs of the mean value function and the failure intensity function are

$$\hat{\mu}(t) = \hat{N}(1 - e^{-\hat{b}t}) \qquad \text{and} \qquad \hat{\lambda}(t) = \hat{N}\hat{b}e^{-\hat{b}t}$$

The MLE of the expected number of faults to be detected in the $(n + 1)$st observation period is similarly determined as

$$\text{Estimated expected number of faults in } (n + 1)\text{st} = \hat{N}(e^{-\hat{b}t_n} - e^{-\hat{b}t_{n+1}})$$

3.3.2.5 Comments. Goel and Okumoto [Goel79] have also adapted this model to use the time of fault occurrences instead of the fault counts. Within this framework, [Okum80] have also determined an optimal release time for a software system. If the desired reliability is R for a specified operational time of O, then to achieve the desired result, the required amount of time that the software must be observed is

$$\text{Required time} = \frac{1}{b}\left[\ln(a(1 - e^{-bO})) - \left(\ln\left(\ln\left(\frac{1}{R}\right)\right)\right)\right]$$

In the paper [Okum80], they also determine the optimal release time based upon cost (cost of testing and of finding and fixing a fault in the testing environment versus the operational). You are referred to that article for the details or to [Farr83].

This model is equivalent to the model considered in Sec. 3.3.3 (type 1 model) if each of the periods that the software is observed are all of the same length, that is, $t_i = iL$, $i = 1, \ldots, n$ for some constant $L > 0$ and $N = \alpha/\beta$ where α and β are the parameters of Schneidewind's model.

3.3.3 Schneidewind's model

3.3.3.1 Overview of the model. The idea behind Schneidewind's model [Schn75] is that the current fault rate might be a better predicator of the future behavior than the observed rates in the distant past. The failure rate process may be changing over time so the current data may better model the present reliability. To reflect this idea, Schneidewind has three forms of the model that reflect the analyst's view of the importance of the data as functions of time. The data used are the number of faults per unit of time where all the time periods are of the same length. Suppose there are n units of time, all of some fixed length; then the three forms of the model are:

Model 1 Utilize all of the fault counts from the n periods. This reflects the view that all of the data points are of equal importance.

Model 2 Ignore the fault counts completely from the first through the $s - 1$ time periods, i.e., only use the data from periods s through n. This reflects the view that the early time periods contribute little if anything in predicting future behavior. For example, one can eliminate a learning curve effect by ignoring the first few time periods.

Model 3 Use the cumulative fault counts from the intervals 1 to $s - 1$ as the first data point and the individual fault counts for periods s through n as the additional data points. This is an approach, intermediate between the other two, that reflects the belief that a combination of the first $s - 1$ period is indicative of the failure rate process during the later stages.

Schneidewind [Schn93a, Schn93b, Schn93c, Schn93d] has recently developed criteria for the optimal selection of the s value. (We note that if $s = 1$, then models 2 and 3 become model 1.) This will be discussed further in Sec. 3.3.3.4.

3.3.3.2 Assumptions and data requirements. Including the Standard Assumptions (see Sec. 3.3.1.2), the *basic assumptions* are:

1. The cumulative number of failures by time t, $M(t)$, follows a Poisson process with mean value function $\mu(t)$. The mean value function is such that the expected number of fault occurrences for any time period is proportional to the expected number of undetected faults at that time. It is also assumed to be a bounded, nondecreasing function of time with $\lim_{t \to \infty} \mu(t) = \alpha/\beta < \infty$; for some constants $\alpha, \beta > 0$ (i.e., it is a finite failure model).
2. The failure intensity function is assumed to be an exponentially decreasing function of time. The failure intensity function $\lambda(t)$ is taken to be of the form $\lambda(t) = \alpha \exp(-\beta t)$. Therefore, large β implies a small failure rate, small β implies a large one. Moreover, we see α is the initial failure rate at time $t = 0$.
3. The number of faults (f_i) detected in each of the respective intervals are independent.
4. The fault correction rate is proportional to the number of faults to be corrected.
5. The intervals over which the software is observed are all taken to be of the same length, that is, $t_i = il$, for $i = 1, \ldots, n$ and l being some positive constant. (Note, without loss of generality, we can take $l = 1$ so that $t_i = i$.)

The *data requirements* to implement this fault count model are: the fault counts in each of the testing intervals, i.e., the f_i for $i = 1, \ldots, n$.

3.3.3.3 Model form. From the assumptions, the cumulative mean number of faults by the ith time period is

$$D_i = \mu(t_i) = \frac{\alpha}{\beta}[1 - \exp(-\beta i)].$$

Thus the expected number of faults in the ith period is

$$m_i = D_i - D_{i-1} = \mu(t_i) - \mu(t_{i-1}) = \frac{\alpha}{\beta}[\exp(-\beta(i-1)) - \exp(-\beta i)]$$

Using the assumptions again pertaining to the f_i's being independent nonhomogeneous Poisson random variables and incorporating the concept of the different model types, we have the joint density

$$\frac{M_{s-1}^{F_{s-1}} \exp(-M_{s-1})}{F_{s-1}} \prod_{i=s}^{n} \frac{m_i^{f_i} \exp(-m_i)}{f_i!}$$

where s is some integer value chosen in the range 1 to n, M_{s-1} is the cumulative mean number of faults in the intervals up to $s - 1$, and F_{s-1} is the cumulative number of faults detected up through interval $s - 1$.

3.3.3.4 Model estimation and reliability prediction. [Schn75] derived the MLEs for α and β. They can also be found in [Farr83], [Geph78], and the AIAA *Recommended Practice for Software Reliability* [AIAA93]. Three different sets of equations are derived for each of the three models.

Model 1 estimates

$$\hat{\alpha} = \frac{\hat{\beta} F_n}{1 - \exp(-\hat{\beta} n)} \quad \text{and} \quad \frac{1}{\exp(\hat{\beta}) - 1} - \frac{n}{\exp(\hat{\beta} n) - 1} = \sum_{k=0}^{n-1} k \frac{f_{k+1}}{F_n}$$

where $F_n = \sum_{i=1}^{n} f_i$ and the f_i's are the fault counts in intervals 1 to n.

Model 2 estimates

$$\hat{\alpha} = \frac{\hat{\beta} F_{s,n}}{1 - \exp(-\hat{\beta}(n - s + 1))} \quad \text{and}$$

$$\frac{1}{\exp(\hat{\beta}) - 1} - \frac{n - s + 1}{\exp(\hat{\beta}(n - s + 1)) - 1} = \sum_{k=0}^{n-s} k \frac{f_{s+k}}{F_{s,n}}$$

where $F_{s,n} = \sum_{k=s}^{n} f_k$. Notice if we let $s = 1$, model 2 estimates become equivalent to model 1.

Model 3 estimates

$$\hat{\alpha} = \frac{\beta F_n}{1 - \exp(-\hat{\beta} n)} \qquad \text{and}$$

$$\frac{(s-1)F_{s-1}}{\exp(\hat{\beta}(s-1)) - 1} + \frac{F_{s,n}}{\exp(\hat{\beta}) - 1} - \frac{nF_n}{\exp(\hat{\beta} n) - 1} = \sum_{k=0}^{n-s} (s+k-1) f_{s+k}$$

where $F_{s-1} = \sum_{k=1}^{s-1} f_k$. We note again that if $s = 1$ is substituted into the above equations we obtain the equivalent estimates for model 1.

Recent work by [Schn93a, Schn93b, Schn93c] has been identifying the optimal s in model types 2 and 3. Three criteria have been developed, (1) the weighted least-squares criterion, (2) the mean square criterion for time to next failure(s), and (3) the mean square error criterion for cumulative failures. Each criterion is handled the same for the selection of s. The analyst seeks the value of s that minimizes the respective criterion. The procedure is as follows. For a given value of s and a selected model type (2 or 3) the corresponding MLEs of α and β are derived, and then the criterion is evaluated. This is done over a range of s values. The optimal s is the one that globally minimizes the chosen criterion. Schneidewind has proposed that if the global minimum of the criteria cannot be determined because of the computational complexity involved, the analyst can use the first value of s, starting from $s = 1$, in which the selection criteria have achieved a local minimum. This is illustrated in the example that follows. The formulas for these criteria are, respectively:

Weighted least-squares criterion

$$\text{WLS} = \frac{\sum_{k=s}^{n} \exp(\beta(k-s+1))[\alpha/\beta(\exp(-\beta(k-s+1)))(\exp(\beta) - 1) - f_i]^2}{(n-s+1)}$$

Mean square criterion for time to next failure(s)

$$\text{MSE}_{\text{T}}(s) = \frac{\sum_{k=s}^{J-1} [[\log[\alpha/(\alpha - \beta(F_{s,k} + f_{j\,|\,k}))]/\beta - (k-s+1)] - (j-k)]^2}{(J-s)}$$

$$\text{for } \frac{\alpha}{\beta} > (F_{s,k} + f_{j\,|\,k})$$

where $f_{j\,|\,k}$ = number of faults detected during time interval j since k; k is the index variable and j is the next interval index beyond k (that is, $j > k$) for which $f_j > 0$ and J is the maximum $j \le n$ such that $f_{j\,|\,k} > 0$.

Mean square error criterion for cumulative failures

$$\mathrm{MSE_F}(s) = \frac{\sum_{k=s}^{n} [\alpha/(\beta(1 - \exp(-\beta(k - s + 1)))) - F_{s,k}]^2}{n - s + 1}$$

The $\mathrm{MSE_T}$ and the $\mathrm{MSE_F}$ are the preferred criteria. $\mathrm{MSE_T}$ looks at the squared error difference between the predicted number of periods required to generate a specified number of fault detections and the actual number it took. $\mathrm{MSE_F}$ compares the squared error difference between the predicted model cumulative fault counts and the actual values observed. The later is preferred if a failure count prediction is to be made, the former if a time to next failure prediction is of interest.

Example 3.2 To illustrate this model, suppose we have the following number of faults detected per unit of time (day, week, etc.): $f_1 = 20, f_2 = 18, f_3 = 25, f_4 = 30, f_5 = 35, f_6 = 36, f_7 = 31$ and $f_8 = 32, f_9 = 29, f_{10} = 26, f_{11} = 24, f_{12} = 21, f_{13} = 18, f_{14} = 20$. From the first few data points it appears that a learning curve effect may be present, so a model 2 might be appropriate with candidate s values of 4, 5, or 6. Using SMERFS, Table 3.1 was generated for model 2 to determine the optimal s.

The WLS and the $\mathrm{MSE_F}$ indicate an $s = 6$ may be appropriate. The $\mathrm{MSE_T}$ indicates the optimal s has not yet been reached. Since two of the three criteria indicate an s of 6 is appropriate, this was the model tried. Using the data points from 6 on, the MLEs are obtained as:

$$\hat{\beta} = 0.08305 \quad \text{and} \quad \hat{\alpha} = \frac{\hat{\beta}F_{6,14}}{1 - \exp(-\hat{\beta}(14 - 6 + 1))} = \frac{0.08305 \times 237}{1 - \exp(-0.08305 \times 9)} = 37.37$$

From this, various estimates of reliability measures can be calculated, such as

$$\text{Estimated total number of faults} = \frac{\hat{\alpha}}{\hat{\beta}} = 450$$

3.3.3.5 Comments. As was previously stated in the NHPP model, Schneidewind's model 1 is a special case of the NHPP model if all the

TABLE 3.1 SMERFS Output for the Optimal "s"

S	BETA	ALPHA	WLS	MSE-F	MSE-T
1	0.12061E–01	0.28334E+02	0.36602E+02	0.15082E+03	0.22780E+00
2	0.23640E–01	0.30825E+02	0.33908E+02	0.10539E+03	0.14059E+00
3	0.43698E–01	0.35016E+02	0.19540E+02	0.42996E+02	0.51981E–01
4	0.61054E–01	0.37698E+02	0.96338E+01	0.13589E+02	0.14931E–01
5	0.76042E–01	0.38840E+02	0.35426E+01	0.24855E+01	0.34200E–02
6	0.83051E–01	0.37390E+02	0.27012E+01	0.10740E+01	0.20634E–02
7	0.82575E–01	0.34331E+02	0.27868E+01	0.12602E+01	0.18962E–02

observation periods are the same length and we let $\alpha/\beta = N$ and $\beta = b$ be the correspondence between the parameters of the two models.

This model has been used extensively on IBM's Flight Control software for the Space Shuttle [Schn92b] with very good success, especially employing the procedure for determining the optimal s to obtain better fits to the data. This model is also one of the four selected models to start an initial attempt at model fitting as proposed in the AIAA's Recommended Practice for Software Reliability [AIAA93].

3.3.4 Musa's basic execution time model

3.3.4.1 Overview of the model. This model has had the widest distribution among the software reliability models and was developed by John Musa of AT&T Bell Laboratories [Musa75, Musa78, Musa79a, Musa79b, Musa80, Musa87]. Musa has been a leading contributor in this field and has been a major proponent of using models to aid in determining the reliability of software. As such, it is natural that his models (the basic execution and the logarithmic Poisson, see Sec. 3.5.3) have been applied in many diverse fields.

This model was one of the first to use the actual execution time of the software component on a computer for the modeling process. The times between failures are expressed in terms of computational processing units (CPU) rather than elapsed wall-clock time. Musa feels that execution time is more reflective of the actual stress induced on the software system than the amount of calendar time that has elapsed. The model does, however, have a feature to convert the execution time results to calendar time. This is accomplished by a second component of the model that functionally relates human and computer resources utilization with the execution time.

3.3.4.2 Assumptions and data requirements. Including the Standard Assumptions (see Sec. 3.3.1.2), the *basic assumptions* are:

1. The cumulative number of failures by time t, $M(t)$, follows a Poisson process with mean value function $\mu(t) = \beta_0[1 - \exp(-\beta_1 t)]$, where β_0, $\beta_1 > 0$. The mean value function is such that the expected number of failure occurrences for any time period is proportional to the expected number of undetected faults at that time. Since $\lim_{t\to\infty} \mu(t) = \lim_{t\to\infty}(\beta_0[1 - \exp(-\beta_1 t)]) = \beta_0$, it is a finite failure model. The parameter β_0 is the total number of faults that would be detected in the limit.
2. The execution times between the failures are piecewise exponentially distributed, i.e., the hazard rate for a single fault is constant. This is why this model belongs to the exponential class.

3. The quantities of the resources (number of fault-identification, -correction personnel and computer times) that are available are constant over a segment for which the software is observed.
4. Resource expenditures for the kth resource, $\Delta\chi_k$, associated with a change in MTTF from T_1 to T_2 can be approximated by $\Delta\chi_k \approx \theta_k\Delta t + \mu_\kappa \Delta m$, where Δt is the increment of execution time, Δm is the increment of failures experienced, θ_k is an execution time coefficient of resource expenditure, and μ_κ is a failure coefficient of resource expenditure.
5. Fault-identification personnel can be fully utilized and computer utilization is constant.
6. Fault-correction personnel utilization is established by the limitation of fault queue length for any fault-correction person. Fault queue is determined by assuming that fault correction is a Poisson process and that servers are randomly assigned in time.

Assumptions 3 through 6 are needed only if the second component of the basic execution model linking execution time and calendar time is desired.

The *data requirements* to implement this fault count model are:

- *For the basic execution time component.* Either the actual times that the software failed, $t_1, t_2, \ldots, t_n$ or the elapsed time between failures $x_1, x_2, \ldots, x_n$, where $x_i = t_i - t_{i-1}$.
- *For the basic calendar time component*
  1. The available resources for both identification and correction personnel and the number of computer shifts. We'll denote them as P_I, P_F, and P_C, respectively.
  2. The utilization factor for each resource, that is, ρ_I (=1), ρ_F, and ρ_C.
  3. The execution time coefficient of resource expenditure for each resource, that is, θ_I, θ_F (=0 usually), and θ_C.
  4. The failure coefficient of resource expenditure for each resource, that is, μ_1, μ_F, and μ_C.
  5. The maximum fault queue length Q for a fault correction personnel.
  6. The probability P that the fault queue length is no larger than Q.

3.3.4.3 Model form. Since $\mu(t) = \beta_0(1 - \exp(-\beta_1 t))$, the failure intensity function for this model is

$$\lambda(t) = \mu'(t) = \beta_0\beta_1\exp(-\beta_1 t)$$

We notice that for large β_1 the failure intensity function will decrease rapidly, while for a small one it will decrease slowly. In either case, the function decreases exponentially to 0. This is illustrated in Fig. 3.2.

By making the correspondence that $\beta_1 = B\phi$ and $\beta_0 = \nu_0$, where B is defined as the fault reduction factor (the proportionality constant relating the fault correction rate to the hazard rate) and ϕ is the constant hazard rate per individual fault, the preceding formulation can be put into the framework in which Musa originally introduced this model. (See [Musa87], p. 285, for this correspondence.)

Using the result of Sec. 3.2.2 and the above expressions for the mean value and failure intensity function, one can show (see Prob. 3.2) that the reliability function after $(i-1)$ failures have occurred is $R(\Delta t \mid t_{i-1}) = \exp(-[\beta_0 \exp(-\beta_1 t_{i-1})][1 - \exp(-\beta_1 \Delta t)])$ for $0 \leq \Delta t$, and the conditional hazard rate is $z(\Delta t \mid t_{i-1}) = \beta_0 \beta_1 \exp(-\beta_1 t_{i-1}) \exp(-\beta_1 \Delta t)$ for $0 \leq \Delta t$.

For the development of the calendar time component of this model you are referred to [Musa87].

3.3.4.4 Model estimation and reliability prediction. Suppose we have observed n failures of the software system at times $t_1, t_2, \ldots, t_n$, and from the last failure time t_n an additional time of x ($x \geq 0$) has elapsed without failure (that is, $t_n + x$ is therefore the total time the software component has been observed since the start). Using the model assumptions, the likelihood function for this class is obtained as

$$L(\beta_0, \beta_1) = \beta_0^n \beta_1^n \left[\prod_{i=1}^{n} \exp(-\beta_1 t_i) \right] \exp(-\beta_0 [1 - \exp(-\beta_1 (t_n + x))])$$

so the MLEs of β_0 and β_1 are obtained as the solutions to the following pair of equations:

$$\hat{\beta}_0 = \frac{n}{1 - \exp(-\hat{\beta}_1 (t_n + x))} \quad \text{and} \quad \frac{n}{\hat{\beta}_1} - \frac{n(t_n + x)}{\exp(\hat{\beta}_1 (t_n + x)) - 1} - \sum_{i=1}^{n} t_i = 0$$

Once the estimates of β_0 and β_1 are obtained, we can use the invariance property of the MLEs to estimate other reliability measures. These

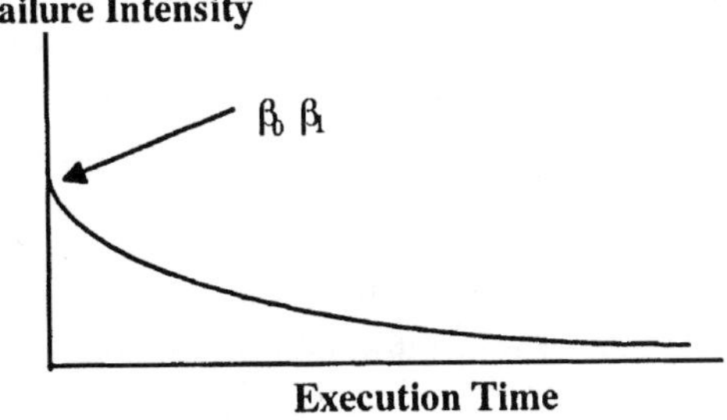

Figure 3.2 Failure intensity function for Musa's basic execution model.

include the reliability function, hazard rate, failure intensity function, etc. An example is the estimate of the failure intensity function. Since the function is $\lambda(t; \beta_0, \beta_1) = \beta_0\beta_1\exp(-\beta_1 t)$, the MLE of this function is $\hat{\lambda}(t; \hat{\beta}_0, \hat{\beta}_1) = \hat{\beta}_0\hat{\beta}_1\exp(-\hat{\beta}_1 t)$.

Example 3.3 Suppose the observed times of failures are $t_1 = 10$, $t_2 = 18$, $t_3 = 32$, $t_4 = 49$, $t_5 = 64$, $t_6 = 86$, $t_7 = 105$, $t_8 = 132$, $t_9 = 167$, $t_{10} = 207$, with an additional 15 CPU hours of no failure after the last one. All the units are taken to be in hours and are all measured in execution time. Using the above equations, the MLEs of β_0 and β_1 are the solution of the following equations:

$$\hat{\beta}_0 = \frac{10}{1 - \exp(-222\hat{\beta}_1)} \quad \text{and} \quad \frac{10}{\hat{\beta}_1} - \frac{2220}{\exp(222\hat{\beta}_1) - 1} - 870 = 0$$

The solutions to these equations are found to be: $\hat{\beta}_0 = 13.6$ and $\hat{\beta}_1 = 0.006$. Estimates of other reliability measures can then be calculated.

3.3.4.5 Comments. [Musa87] recommends this model in contrast to his logarithmic Poisson (see Sec. 3.5.3) if you wish to predict early reliability before program execution is initiated and failure data observed; if the program is substantially changing over time as the failure data are observed; and if you are interested in seeing the impact of a new software engineering technology on the development process.

3.3.5 Hyperexponential model

3.3.5.1 Overview of the model. This model is an extension of the classical exponential models considered by Musa and Goel (see Secs. 3.3.4 and 3.3.2). The hyperexponential model was first considered by Ohba [Ohba84] and has been addressed in variations by others (e.g., [Yama85] and [Lapr91]). The basic idea is that the different sections (or classes) of the software experience an exponential failure rate; however, the rates vary over these sections to reflect their different natures. This could be due to different programming groups doing the different parts, old versus new code, sections written in different languages, etc. The basic idea is that different failure behaviors are represented in the different sections. We thus reflect the sum of these different exponential growth curves, not by another exponential, but by a hyperexponential growth curve. If in observing a software system, you notice that different clusters of that software appeared to behave differently in their failure rates, the hyperexponential model may be more appropriate than the classical exponential model that assumes a similar failure rate.

3.3.5.2 Assumptions and data requirements. The *basic assumptions* are as follows. Suppose there are K sections (classes of the software) such that *within each class:*

1. The rate of fault detection is proportional to the current fault content within that section of the software.
2. The fault detection rate remains constant over the intervals between fault occurrence.
3. A fault is corrected instantaneously without introducing new faults into the software.

And for the software system as a whole:

4. The cumulative number of failures by time t, $M(t)$, follows a Poisson process with mean value function $\mu(t) = N \sum_{i=1}^{K} p_i[1 - \exp(-\beta_i t)]$ where $0 < \beta_i < 1$, $\sum_{i=1}^{K} p_i = 1$, $0 < p_i < 1$ and N is finite. (Notice it is a finite failure model.)

The Standard Assumptions of Sec. 3.3.1.2 are again assumed to hold.

The *data requirements* to implement this fault count model are:

1. The fault counts in each of the testing intervals, i.e., the f_i's.
2. The completion time of each period that the software is under observation, i.e., the t_i's.

3.3.5.3 Model form. Notice that if $K = 1$ we have the NHPP model of Sec. 3.3.2. Also, $\lim_{t \to \infty} \mu(t) = N$; so, as before, N represents the expected total number of faults to be eventually detected. (*Note:* N is not required to be an integer since it is the *expected number* of faults that will eventually be detected.) For the ith class, we also note that Np_i is the expected number of faults within that class. Since the failure intensity function is the derivative of $\mu(t)$, we therefore have

$$\lambda(t) = N \sum_{i=1}^{K} p_i \beta_i \exp(-\beta_i t)$$

Notice that the failure intensity function is strictly decreasing for $t > 0$.

3.3.5.4 Model estimation and reliability prediction. By letting $N_i^* = Np_i$, that is, N_i^* is the number of faults in the ith class, one can obtain the MLE estimates for each class as the MLE estimates given in the NHPP model (see Sec. 3.3.2.4). The MLE estimate of N is then found as the sum of the MLEs over the classes.

3.3.5.5 Comments. If there are only two classes (e.g., new versus old code; easy versus difficult to detect faults), this model is called the *modified exponential software reliability growth model* [Yama85].

Laprie et al. [Lapr91] considered a variation of this model for the situation where $K = 2$. They considered a hyperexponential model with failure rate function

$$\lambda(t) = \frac{p_1\zeta_1\exp(-\zeta_1 t) + p_2\zeta_2\exp(-\zeta_2 t)}{p_1\exp(-\zeta_1 t) + p_2\exp(-\zeta_2 t)}$$

From this they derived an expression for the unavailability of a system including both hardware and software components and then showed how the techniques could be extended. As discussed in Chap. 2, this is a significant step in helping bridge the gap between hardware and software models.

3.3.6 Others

We'll briefly describe some additional exponential models and variations of some of the models considered in this section. The first is the inflection S-shaped software reliability growth model proposed by Ohba [Ohba84], which has a mean value function of the form:

$$\mu(t) = N\left(\frac{1 - \exp(-\beta t)}{1 + \psi(r)\exp(-\beta t)}\right) \qquad \text{where } \psi(r) = \frac{1-r}{r},\ r > 0$$

The parameter r is the inflection rate that indicates the ratio of detectable faults to the total number of faults in the software. This model basically assumes that the error discovery rate increases throughout a test period. If r equals 1 we have the basic exponential growth curve considered in this section.

Everett [Ever92] proposed an extension of Musa's basic execution model, which he referred to as the *extended execution time* model. The mean value function for this model is of the form:

$$\mu(t) = \beta_0\left[1 - \int_0^1 \exp(-((a+1)\beta_1 t)x^a)\, dx\right] \qquad \text{where } a \geq 0$$

While the basic execution model was a function of two parameters, this one has an additional one, a. This parameter reflects the nonuniformity of instruction execution. The larger it gets the more nonuniform the execution is. If $a = 0$, this becomes the basic execution model, while as a gets large, this model tracks the logarithmic Poisson considered in Sec. 3.5.

Brooks and Motley [Broo80] and [AIAA93] formulated models of the Poisson and binomial type that are finite failures models. Each use the fault count per unit interval for model parameter estimation. These two models are especially mentioned because they are among the few that treat the situation where not all of the code is being tested equally, and/or not all of the software is complete at the time of testing. Some of the modules are under test while others are still to be written. These models specifically factor in those components that are under test at both the system or module level. You are referred to the references for details.

3.4 Weibull and Gamma Failure Time Class of Models

For Weibull and gamma failure time classes, we take the per-fault failure distribution to be the traditional Weibull and gamma distributions, respectively, rather than the exponential distribution considered in the previous section. These are important distributions because of the great flexibility given for failure modeling because of the shape and scale parameters that define them. Many hardware failure processes are modeled using these distributions. As such they were naturally one of the first groups to be applied in the software arena.

3.4.1 Weibull model

3.4.1.1 Overview of the model. One of the most widely used models for hardware reliability modeling is the Weibull distribution. It can accommodate increasing, decreasing, or constant failure rates because of the great flexibility expressed through the model's parameters. This model belongs to the finite failures category and is of the binomial type using the [Musa83] classification scheme of Sec. 3.2.2.

3.4.1.2 Assumptions and data requirements. Including the Standard Assumptions of Sec. 3.3.1.2, the *basic assumptions* are:

1. There is a fixed number of faults (N) in the software at the beginning of the time in which the software is observed.
2. The time to failure of fault a, denoted as T_a, is distributed as a Weibull distribution with parameters α and β (that is, the density function of T_a is $f_a(t) = \alpha\beta t^{\alpha-1}\exp(-\beta t^{\alpha})$), with $\alpha, \beta > 0$ and $t \geq 0$. (Since the per-fault distribution is $f_a(t)$, the per-fault hazard rate is $z_a(t) = \alpha\beta t^{\alpha-1}$.)
3. The number of faults $(f_1, f_2, \ldots, f_n)$ detected in each of the respective intervals $[(t_0 = 0, t_1), (t_1, t_2), \ldots, (t_{i-1}, t_i), \ldots, (t_{n-1}, t_n)]$ are independent for any finite collection of times.

The *data requirements* to implement this fault count model are:

1. The fault counts in each of the testing intervals, i.e., the f_i's.
2. The completion time of each period that the software is under observation, i.e., the t_i's.

3.4.1.3 Model form. Since this model belongs to the binomial type, from Eqs. (3.2), (3.3), and the cumulative distribution function for a Weibull, we have for the failure intensity function and the mean value function:

$$\lambda(t) = Nf_a(t) = N\alpha\beta t^{\alpha - 1}\exp(-\beta t^{\alpha}) \qquad \text{and}$$

$$\mu(t) = NF_a(t) = N(1 - \exp(-\beta t^{\alpha}))$$

Notice that $\lim_{t \to \infty} \mu(t) = N$, the total number of faults in the system at the start. Also, from the assumptions we have that if $\alpha = 1$, the distribution f_a becomes the exponential, and if it equals 2 we have the Rayleigh distribution, another important failure model in hardware reliability theory. We also note for the case $\alpha = 2$ that this becomes the early model considered by Schick-Wolverton [Schi73]. You can also see that if $0 < \alpha < 1$, the per-fault hazard rate is decreasing with respect to time; if α equals 1 (exponential) it is constant; and if $\alpha > 1$, it increases.

The form of the conditional hazard rate is shown to be (see Prob. 3.3):

$$z(t \mid t_{i-1}) = (N - i + 1)\alpha\beta(t + t_{i-1})^{\alpha - 1} \qquad \text{for } t_{i-1} \le t + t_{i-1} < t_i$$

This function is plotted in Fig. 3.3 for $0 < \alpha < 1$ to contrast its behavior with the exponential class illustrated in Fig. 3.1. In that figure, the change occurred at each fault detection and it was a constant change. For the Weibull distribution, the change occurs at a fault detection, but the change is not constant. The effect on the hazard rate decreases with time because of the power function component.

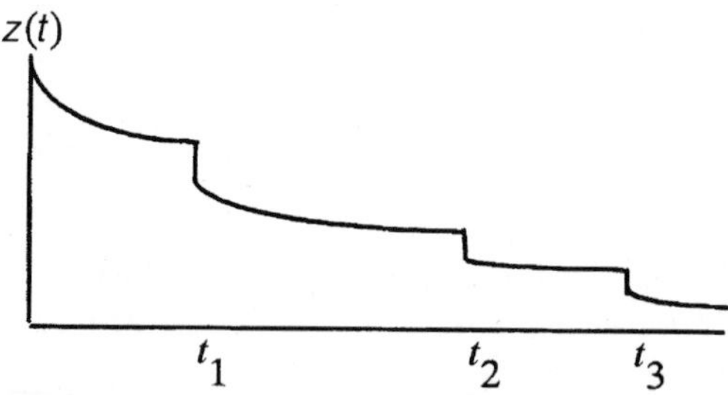

Figure 3.3 Program hazard rate function for Weibull.

The reliability function is obtained from the cumulative distribution function as $R(t) = 1 - F(t) = \exp(-\beta t^{\alpha})$ and, hence, from Eq. B.28 the MTTF is

$$\text{MTTF} = \int_0^\infty R(t)\,dt = \Gamma\left(\frac{1}{\alpha} + 1\right) \Big/ \beta^{\frac{1}{\alpha}}$$

where $\Gamma(\bullet)$ is the gamma function.

3.4.1.4 Model estimation and reliability prediction. [Cout73] shows that the parameters α and β can be estimated using method of moments, least squares, MLE, or even graphical procedures. For the case of the least squares estimates, suppose we let $b = \ln(\beta)$, $Y_i = \ln\,[\ln[1/(1 - F(i))]]$, with $F(i) = \sum_{j=1}^{i} f_j / \sum_{j=1}^{n} f_j$, the normalized cumulative number of faults found up through the ith time period, and $X_i = \ln(t_i)$. Starting with the cumulative distribution function, you can obtain the equation for a straight line of the form $Y = \alpha X + b$. Using the points (X_i, Y_i) calculated from the data, the usual least squares estimates (LSEs) for the slope and intercept are easily obtained. The estimates of α and β are then obtained as the slope estimate and $\hat{\beta} = \exp(\hat{b})$, respectively. Corresponding estimates of the reliability measures are obtained by substituting the associated LSEs for α and β in the measures expressions. [Wago73] also addresses the issues of parameter estimation for this distribution class.

3.4.2 S-shaped reliability growth model

3.4.2.1 Overview of the model. The S-shaped (or delayed S-shaped) reliability growth model ([Yama83], [Ohba84]) will be illustrative of the gamma distribution class. Here the per-fault failure distribution is gamma. The number of failures per time period, however, is a Poisson type model using the classification scheme of Musa and Okumoto [Musa83] rather than the binomial considered in the previous section. It, like the Weibull, is a finite failures model, i.e., $\lim_{t \to \infty} \mu(t) < \infty$. It is patterned after the Goel-Okumoto model considered in Sec. 3.3.2. Yamada, Ohba, and Osaki felt that the mean value function $\mu(t)$ is often a characteristic S-shaped curve rather than the exponential growth of the Goel-Okumoto model. The software error detection process can be described as an S-shaped growth curve to reflect the initial learning curve at the beginning, as test team members become familiar with the software, followed by growth and then leveling off as the residual faults become more difficult to uncover.

3.4.2.2 Assumptions and data requirements. Including the Standard Assumptions of Sec. 3.3.1.2, the *basic assumptions* are:

1. The cumulative number of failures by time t, $M(t)$, follows a Poisson process with mean value function $\mu(t)$. The mean value function is of the form $\mu(t) = \alpha[1 - (1 + \beta t)e^{-\beta t}]$ for $\alpha, \beta > 0$. This is a bounded, nondecreasing function of time with $\lim_{t \to \infty} \mu(t) = \alpha < \infty$, that is, it is a finite failure model.
2. The time between failures of the $(i - 1)$st and the ith depends on the time to failure of the $(i - 1)$st.
3. When a failure occurs, the fault which caused it is immediately removed and no other faults are introduced.

The *data requirements* to implement this model are:

1. The failure times, t_i's, of the software system, or
2. The number of faults detected, f_i, in each period of observation of the software along with the associated lengths l_i of those periods, $i = 1, \ldots, n$.

If data of type 1 are available, the data of the second type can be constructed by first forming a partition of the time period over which the software is observed and then counting up the number of faults that fall in each respective period of the partition. As a consequence, this model can be used for either the time-between-failures data or the number of faults per time period.

3.4.2.3 Model form. Suppose we have a partition of the time interval over which the software is observed. This partition could represent the testing intervals of the software. Let T^* denote this partition, that is, $t_0^* = 0 < t_1^* < \cdots < t_n^*$. Suppose $f_1, f_2, \ldots, f_n$ are the number of software faults detected in each interval of the partition, that is, f_i is the number of faults occurring in the interval of length $l_i = t_i^* - t_{i-1}^*$. From the assumptions we have, each f_i is an independent Poisson random variable with mean

$$\mu(t_i^*) - \mu(t_{i-1}^*) = \alpha[1 - (1 + \beta t_i^*)e^{-\beta t_i^*}] - \alpha[1 - (1 + \beta t_{i-1}^*)e^{-\beta t_{i-1}^*}]$$

$$= \alpha[(1 + \beta t_{i-1}^*)e^{-\beta t_{i-1}^*} - (1 + \beta t_i^*)e^{-\beta t_i^*}]$$

Also, from the mean value function $\mu(t) = \alpha[1 - (1 + \beta t)e^{-\beta t}]$, we have the failure intensity function $\lambda(t) = \mu'(t) = \alpha\beta^2 t e^{-\beta t}$. The model gets its S-shaped form because of the mean value function. Moreover, you can see that $\lim_{t \to \infty} \mu(t) = \alpha < \infty$, so we indeed have a finite failures model with α being the total number of faults in the system. If you were to plot the failure intensity function, you would see that it increases up to time $t = 1/\beta$ and then begins to decrease asymptotically approaching the time axis. Since we have a Poisson type as well as a finite failures model, using Eq. (3.3), the per-fault time distribution between failures is $f_a(t) = \beta^2 t e^{-\beta t}$, as $\lambda(t) = \alpha f_a(t)$. This is the gamma distribution.

Using the above relationships one can also establish (See Prob. 3.4) the following reliability measures for this model:

The reliability of the function at time $t_i + \Delta t$ given a failure at time

$$t_i = \exp(-\alpha[(1 + \beta t_i)e^{-\beta t_i} - (1 + \beta(t_i + \Delta t))e^{-\beta(t_i + \Delta t)}])$$

The hazard rate function at time $t_i + \Delta t$ given a failure at time

$$t_i = \alpha\beta^2(t_i + \Delta t)\exp(-\beta(t_i + \Delta t))$$

The expected number of faults in the ith period of length

$$l = \alpha\left[\left(1 + \beta\sum_{j=i}^{i-1} l_j\right)e^{-\beta\sum_{j=i}^{i-1} l_j} - \left(1 + \beta\left(l + \sum_{j=i}^{i-1} l_j\right)\right)e^{-\beta\left(l + \sum_{j=i}^{i-1} l_j\right)}\right]$$

3.4.2.4 Model estimation and reliability prediction. The joint density of the fault counts over the given partition is

$$\prod_{i=1}^{n} \frac{[\mu(t_i^*) - \mu(t_{i-1}^*)]^{f_i}}{f_i!} \exp(-(\mu(t_i^*) - \mu(t_{i-1}^*)))$$

using the assumptions from the previous section. The MLEs of α and β are then shown to be (see Prob. 3.5) the solutions of the following pair of equations:

$$\sum_{i=1}^{n} f_i = \hat{\alpha}(1 - (1 + \hat{\beta}t_n^*)e^{-\hat{\beta}t_n^*}) \qquad \text{and}$$

$$\hat{\alpha}(t_n^*)^2 e^{-\hat{\beta}t_n^*} = \sum_{i=1}^{n}\left(\frac{\left(\sum_{j=1}^{i} f_j - \sum_{j=1}^{i-1} f_j\right)((t_i^*)^2 e^{-\hat{\beta}t_i^*} - (t_{i-1}^*)^2 e^{-\hat{\beta}t_{i-1}^*})}{((1 + \hat{\beta}t_{i-1})e^{-\hat{\beta}t_{i-1}} - (1 + \hat{\beta}t_i)e^{-\hat{\beta}t_i})}\right)$$

For implementation purposes, if you have the observed failure times (t_i's), you could let the $\sum_{j=1}^{i} f_i$'s be the cumulative number of failures up to time t_i and let the partition correspond to the failure time points (i.e., let $t_i^* = t_i$); on the other hand, if you have the number of faults detected per period (the f_i's), with the associated period lengths (the l_i's), you would let $t_i^* = \sum_{j=1}^{i} l_j$ in the above equations. These equations are solved through standard numerical analysis techniques. Such an implementation is incorporated into the SMERFS [Farr93a, Farr93b] software package.

MLEs of the associated reliability metrics are derived, as in past sections, by replacing the respective parameters α and β according to their corresponding MLE estimates.

3.4.2.5 Comments. For many applications at our facility, this model has been successfully applied. Many times this model was able to successfully fit a given data set when others couldn't. Excellent fits and predictions can be obtained when the S-shaped behavior is present in your data set. Trend analysis (see Chap. 10) can help to detect this.

3.5 Infinite Failure Category Models

Using Musa and Okumoto's classification scheme [Musa83] for this category of models, the $\lim_{t\to\infty} \mu(t) = \infty$ for the mean value function of the process. This means that the software will never be completely fault free. This could be caused by additional faults being introduced in the software through the error correction process.

3.5.1 Duane's model

3.5.1.1 Overview of the model. Originally proposed for hardware reliability, one of the earliest models was Duane's model [Duan64]. While at General Electric, Duane noticed that if the cumulative failure rate versus the cumulative testing time was plotted on *ln-ln* paper, it tended to follow a straight line. Crow [Crow74] observed that this behavior could be represented as a Weibull process. This process is a nonhomogeneous Poisson process in which the failure intensity function has the same form as the hazard rate for a Weibull distribution. This same behavior has been observed for software systems and has been used to develop various reliability estimates based upon this result. This model is sometimes referred to as the *power model* since the mean value function for the cumulative number of failures by time t is taken as a power of t, that is, $\mu(t) = \alpha t^{\beta}$ for some $\beta > 0$ and $\alpha > 0$. (For the case where $\beta = 1$, we have the homogeneous Poisson process model.) This model is an infinite failures model since $\lim_{t\to\infty} \mu(t) = \infty$.

3.5.1.2 Assumptions and data requirements. Including the Standard Assumptions of Sec. 3.3.1.2, the *basic assumption* is:

1. The cumulative number of failures by time t, $M(t)$, follows a Poisson process with mean value function $\mu(t) = \alpha t^{\beta}$ for some $\beta > 0$ and $\alpha > 0$.

The *data requirement* to implement this model is: either the actual times that the software failed, $t_1, t_2, \ldots, t_n$, or the elapsed time between failures $x_1, x_2, \ldots, x_n$, where $x_i = t_i - t_{i-1}$ and $t_0 = 0$.

3.5.1.3 Model form. From assumption 1 we have a Poisson process with a mean value function of $\mu(t) = \alpha t^{\beta}$. If T is the total time the software is observed, then we have

$$\frac{\mu(T)}{T} = \frac{\alpha T^{\beta}}{T} = \frac{\text{expected number of failures by time } T}{\text{total testing time}}$$

so that if we take the natural log of both sides of the equations we have

$$Y = \ln\left(\frac{(\mu(t))}{T}\right) = \ln\left(\frac{\alpha T^{\beta}}{T}\right) = \ln(\alpha) + (\beta - 1)\ln(T)$$

We can thus see if the first equation is plotted on *ln-ln* paper versus observed time T, or the second equation is plotted on regular paper versus $\ln(T)$ we will obtain a straight line. It is this form that is fitted to a given data set.

The failure intensity function is obtained by taking the derivative of the mean value function, that is, $\lambda(t) = d\mu(t)/dt = \alpha\beta t^{\beta-1}$. From this function we see that the failure intensity function is strictly increasing for $\beta > 1$, a constant for the case of a homogeneous Poisson process ($\beta = 1$), and strictly decreasing for $1 > \beta > 0$ only. For $\beta > 1$, there can be no reliability growth!

3.5.1.4 Model estimation and reliability prediction. Crow [Crow74] derived the maximum likelihood estimates as:

$$\hat{\alpha} = \frac{n}{t_n^{\hat{\beta}}} \qquad \text{and} \qquad \hat{\beta} = \frac{n}{\sum_{i=1}^{n-1} \ln(t_n/t_i)}$$

Maximum likelihood estimates are then derived for the mean value and failure intensity function, $\mu(t)$ and $\lambda(t)$, by replacing the parameters α and β according to their maximum likelihood estimates (MLEs). In his paper Crow also shows that the MLE for the mean time to failure (MTTF) is $M\hat{T}TF = t_n/n\hat{\beta}$ for the $(n + 1)$st failure, and he provides tables that can be used to construct confidence intervals for this reliability measure.

3.5.2 Geometric model

3.5.2.1 Overview of the model. The geometric model was proposed by Moranda [Mora75b, Mora79] and is a variation of the Jelinski-Moranda model considered in Sec. 3.3.1. The time between failures is taken to be an exponential distribution whose mean decreases in a geometric fashion. The discovery of the earlier faults is taken to have a larger impact on reducing the hazard rate than the later ones. As failures occur the hazard rate decreases in a geometric progression. Figure 3.4 illustrates this behavior. The function is initially a constant, D, but it decreases geometrically ($0 < \phi < 1$) as each failure occurs. The change in the reduction of the function is seen to get smaller as more failures occur, reflecting the smaller impact of the later-occurring faults.

3.5.2.2 Assumptions and data requirements. Including ths Standard Assumptions of Sec. 3.3.1.2, the *basic assumptions* are:

1. The fault detection rate forms a geometric progression and is constant between fault detections, that is, $z(t) = D\phi^{i-1}$, where $0 < \phi < 1$ and $t_{i-1} \le t < t_i$, with t_{i-1} being the time of the $(i-1)$st failure.
2. There is an infinite number of total faults in the system, i.e., $\lim_{t\to\infty} \mu(t) = \infty$, where $\mu(t)$ is the mean value function of the process.
3. The time between fault detection follows an exponential distribution.

The *data requirement* to implement this model is: either the actual times that the software failed, $t_1, t_2, \ldots, t_n$, or the elapsed time between failures $x_1, x_2, \ldots, x_n$, where $x_i = t_i - t_{i-1}$ and $t_0 = 0$.

3.5.2.3 Model form. Using assumptions 1 and 3, we have the density for the time between failures of the ith and $(i-1)$st is exponential of the form: $f(X_i) = D\phi^{i-1}\exp(-D\phi^{i-1}X_i) = z(t_{i-1})\exp(-z(t_{i-1})X_i)$. Thus the expected time between failures is

$$E(X_i) = \frac{1}{z(t_{i-1})} = \frac{1}{D\phi^{i-1}} \qquad \text{for } i = 1, \ldots, n$$

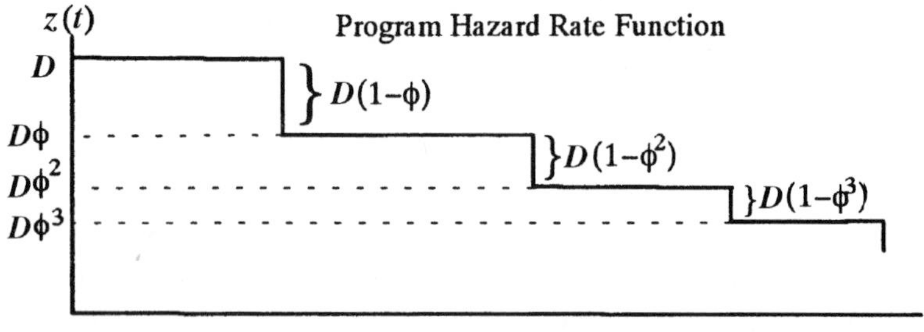

Figure 3.4 Geometric model hazard rate function.

Using the fact that $E(X_i) \approx 1/\lambda(t)$ and $i \approx \mu(t)$ (see [Musa87]), it follows (see Prob. 3.6) that

$$\mu(t) = \frac{1}{\beta}\ln([D\beta\exp(\beta)]t + 1) \qquad \text{and}$$

$$\lambda(t) = \frac{D\exp(\beta)}{[D\beta\exp(\beta)]t + 1} \qquad \text{where } \beta = -\ln(\phi) \text{ for } 0 < \phi < 1$$

Clearly, $\lim_{t\to\infty}\mu(t) = \infty$, so we indeed have an infinite failures category model.

3.5.2.4 Model estimation and reliability prediction. From the previous section and the assumptions, the joint density function for the X_i's is

$$\prod_{i=1}^{n} f(X_i) = D^n \prod_{i=1}^{n} \phi^{i-1}\exp\left(-D\sum_{i=1}^{n}\phi^{i-1}X_i\right)$$

Taking the natural log of this function and taking the partials with respect to ϕ and D, the maximum likelihood estimates are the solutions of the following pair of equations:

$$\hat{D} = \frac{\hat{\phi}n}{\sum_{i=1}^{n}\hat{\phi}^i X_i} \qquad \text{and} \qquad \frac{\sum_{i=1}^{n} i\hat{\phi}^i X_i}{\sum_{i=1}^{n}\hat{\phi}^i X_i} = \frac{n+1}{2}$$

Again, the MLE of the various reliability measures can be obtained using the invariance property of the MLE estimates. For example, the MLE of the failure intensity function is $\hat{\lambda}(t) = \hat{D}\exp(\hat{\beta})/\{[\hat{D}\hat{\beta}\exp(\hat{\beta})]t + 1\}$ where $\hat{\beta} = -\ln(\hat{\phi})$.

It is left as an exercise to you (Prob. 3.7) to show that the least squares estimates based upon the X_i's are the solutions to the following pair of equations:

$$\hat{D}_{\text{LS}} = \frac{\sum_{i=1}^{n}\frac{1}{\hat{\phi}_{\text{LS}}^{2(i-1)}}}{\sum_{i=1}^{n}\frac{x_i}{\hat{\phi}_{\text{LS}}^{i-1}}} \qquad \text{and}$$

$$\left(\sum_{i=1}^{n}\frac{1}{\hat{\phi}_{\text{LS}}^{2(i-1)}}\right)\left(\sum_{i=1}^{n}\frac{X_i(i-1)}{\hat{\phi}_{\text{LS}}^{i-1}}\right) = \left(\sum_{i=1}^{n}\frac{X_i}{\hat{\phi}_{\text{LS}}^{i-1}}\right)\left(\sum_{i=1}^{n}\frac{(i-1)}{\hat{\phi}_{\text{LS}}^{2(i-1)}}\right)$$

3.5.2.5 Comments. An extension of this model was proposed by Lipow and is discussed in [Suke76]. Lipow relaxed the assumption of an infinite number of faults being present in the code. For his model, the hazard rate is taken to be of the form $z(t) = D\phi^{n_{i-1}}$ for $t_{i-1} \le t < t_i$. The term n_{i-1} is the cumulative number of faults found up to the ith interval that the software is being observed. D and ϕ are as defined in the geometric model. Another variation proposed by Moranda [Mora75b] was the geometric Poisson. This takes the number of failures during specified time intervals as being independent Poisson random variables with the mean for the ith interval to be $D\phi^{i-1}$. Again we see the geometric progression of the mean starting as we progress from an initial value of D.

3.5.3 Musa-Okumoto logarithmic Poisson

3.5.3.1 Overview of the model. The logarithmic Poisson proposed by Musa and Okumoto [Musa84] is another model that has been extensively applied. It is also a nonhomogeneous Poisson process with an intensity function that decreases exponentially as failures occur. The exponential rate of decrease reflects the view that the earlier discovered failures have a greater impact on reducing the failure intensity function than those encountered later. It is called *logarithmic* because the expected number of failures over time is a logarithmic function.

3.5.3.2 Assumptions and data requirements. Including the Standard Assumptions of Sec. 3.3.1.2, the *basic assumptions* are:

1. The failure intensity decreases exponentially with the expected number of failures experienced, that is, $\lambda(t) = \lambda_0 \exp(-\theta\mu(t))$, where $\mu(t)$ is the mean value function, $\theta > 0$ is the failure rate decay parameter, and $\lambda_0 > 0$ is the initial failure rate.
2. The cumulative number of failures by time t, $M(t)$, follows a Poisson process.

Because of assumption 1, it follows that $\mu(t) = \ln(\lambda_0\theta t + 1)/\theta$ (Prob. 3.8), and therefore $\lambda(t) = \lambda_0/(\lambda_0\theta t + 1)$. Clearly this is an infinite failure model.

The *data requirements* are: either the actual times that the software failed, $t_1, t_2, \ldots, t_n$, or the elapsed time between failures $x_1, x_2, \ldots, x_n$, where $x_i = t_i - t_{i-1}$.

3.5.3.3 Model form. The plot of the failure intensity function versus time is illustrated in Fig. 3.5. This illustrates the exponential type decay and the fact that the earlier encountered failures have a more dramatic impact than the later ones. The parameter θ controls the shape of the curve.

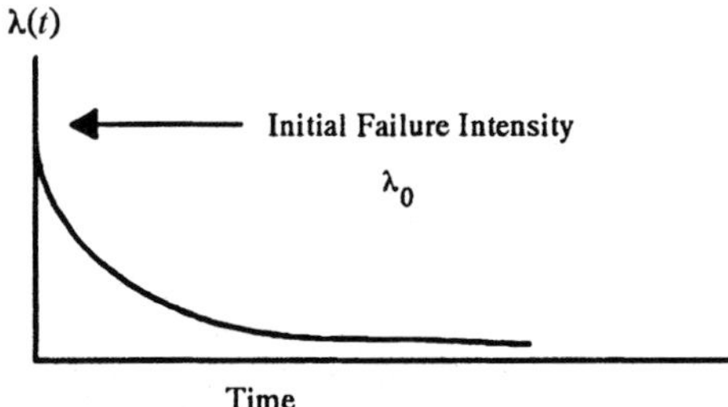

Figure 3.5 Failure intensity function for logarithmic poisson model.

A second expression of the logarithmic Poisson model to aid in obtaining the maximum likelihood estimates is through a reparameterization of the model. We let $\beta_0 = \theta^{-1}$ and $\beta_1 = \lambda_0\theta$. The intensity and mean value functions become in this case: $\lambda(t) = \beta_0\beta_1/(\beta_1 t + 1)$ and $\mu(t) = \beta_0 \ln(\beta_1 t + 1)$.

[Musa87] derives the program reliability and the hazard rate functions after the $(i - 1)$st failure, respectively, as:

$$R(\Delta t \mid t_{i-1}) = \left[\frac{\beta_1 t_{i-1} + 1}{\beta_1(t_{i-1} + \Delta t) + 1}\right]^{\beta_0} \qquad \text{for } \Delta t \geq 0$$

and

$$z(\Delta t \mid t_{i-1}) = \beta_0\beta_1/(\beta_1(t_{i-1} + \Delta t) + 1) \qquad \text{for } \Delta t \geq 0$$

3.5.3.4 Model estimation and reliability prediction. Using the reparameterized model, the maximum likelihood estimates of β_0 and β_1 are shown in [Musa87] to be the solutions of the following pair of equations:

$$\hat{\beta}_0 = \frac{n}{\ln(1 + \hat{\beta}_1 t_n)} \qquad \text{and} \qquad \frac{1}{\hat{\beta}_1}\sum_{i=1}^{n}\frac{1}{1 + \hat{\beta}_1 t_i} = \frac{n t_n}{(1 + \hat{\beta}_1 t_n)\ln(1 + \hat{\beta}_1 t_n)}$$

As in the previous sections, estimates of various reliability measures are then obtained by using the invariance property of the MLE, i.e., substituting in an expression the MLEs $\hat{\beta}_0$ and $\hat{\beta}_1$ for the corresponding parameters β_0 and β_1. For example, from the above the MLE of the failure rate function is $\hat{\lambda}(t) = \hat{\beta}_0\hat{\beta}_1/(\hat{\beta}_1 t + 1)$.

Example 3.4 Suppose we use the same data as in Example 3.3, i.e.,

$$t_1 = 10, t_2 = 18, t_3 = 32, t_4 = 49, t_5 = 64, t_6 = 86, t_7 = 105, t_8 = 132, t_9 = 167, t_{10} = 207$$

and there is an additional 15 CPU hours of no failure after the last one. All the units are taken to be in hours and are measured in execution time. Using the SMERFS software package, the solutions to the MLE equations of the previous section are found to be: $\hat{\beta}_0 = 7.93$ and $\hat{\beta}_1 = 0.01139$. Various reliability estimates can then be obtained using the invariance property of the MLE. For example, the hazard rate function is

$$\hat{\lambda}(t;\ \hat{\beta}_0, \hat{\beta}_1) = \hat{\lambda}(t;\ 7.933, 0.01139) = \hat{\beta}_0\hat{\beta}_1/(\hat{\beta}_1 t + 1) = 0.0903/(0.011385t + 1)$$

The estimate of the initial hazard rate is therefore $\hat{\lambda}(0;\ \hat{\beta}_0, \hat{\beta}_1) = 0.0903$, and the estimate of the hazard rate from the time of the last failure is $\hat{\lambda}(207;\ \hat{\beta}_0, \hat{\beta}_1) = 0.0269$, that is, a little less than three failures per 100 hours of CPU operation.

3.5.3.5 Comments. This model is especially applicable when it is anticipated that the program's operational use will be decidedly nonuniform. The nonuniformity tends to make the failures encountered earlier have more of an impact than later ones. It is this impact that this model is especially good at capturing. This model was also one of the selected models in the AIAA Recommended Practice Standard [AIAA93] as a good candidate to try initially for fitting your reliability data set.

3.6 Bayesian Models

This group of models views reliability growth and prediction in a Bayesian framework rather than the traditional one considered in the previous sections. The previous models allow change in the reliability only when an error occurs. Most of them also look at the impact of each fault as being of the same magnitude. A Bayesian model takes a subjective viewpoint in that if no failures occur while the software is observed then the reliability should increase, reflecting the growing confidence in the software by the user. The reliability is therefore a reflection of both the number of faults that have been detected and the amount of failure-free operation. This reflection is expressed in terms of a prior distribution representing the view from past data and a posterior distribution that incorporates past and current data.

The Bayesian models also reflect the belief that different faults have different impacts on the reliability of the program. The number of faults is not as important as their impacts. If we have a program that has a number of faults in seldomly used code, is that program less reliable than one that has only one fault in the part of the code that is used often? The Bayesian would say no! The Bayesian modeler says that it is more important to look at the behavior of the software than to estimate the number of faults in it. The mean time to failure would therefore be a very important statistic in this framework.

The prior distribution reflecting the view of the model parameters from past data is an essential part of this methodology. It reflects the viewpoint that one should incorporate past information, say projects of similar nature, etc., in estimating reliability statistics for the present and future. This distribution is simultaneously one of the Bayesian's framework strengths and weaknesses. One should incorporate the past, but *how* is the question.

The basic idea on the mathematics behind this theory is as follows. Suppose we have a distribution for our reliability data that depends upon some unknown parameters, ξ, that is, $f_T(\mathbf{t} \mid \xi)$ and a prior $g(\xi; \phi)$ that reflects our views on those parameters, ξ, from historical data. Once additional data have been gathered through the vector **t** (note that boldfacing of a component denotes a possible vector of subcomponents to allow for multidimensionality, that is, $\xi = (\xi_1, \xi_2, \ldots, \xi_K)$), our view of the parameter ξ changes. That change is reflected in the posterior distribution which is calculated as

$$h(\xi \mid \mathbf{t}; \phi) = \frac{f_T(\mathbf{t} \mid \xi) g(\xi; \phi)}{\int \cdots \int f_T(\mathbf{t} \mid \xi) g(\xi; \phi)\, d\xi} = \frac{f_T(\mathbf{t} \mid \xi) g(\xi; \phi)}{f_T(\mathbf{t}; \phi)}$$

Using the posterior distribution, various estimates of ξ can then be obtained leading to reliability estimates involving ξ. A common Bayesian procedure is to define a loss function, $l(\hat{\xi}(\mathbf{t}), \xi)$, where $\hat{\xi}(\mathbf{t})$ is an estimate of ξ, and then choose the estimate of ξ that minimizes the expected loss using the posterior distribution. For a squared-error function or quadratic loss function, that is, $l(\hat{\xi}(\mathbf{t}), \xi) = (\hat{\xi}(\mathbf{t}) - \xi)^2$, the estimate is the mean of the posterior distribution, that is, $E\{\xi \mid \mathbf{t}\}$. You are referred to any mathematical statistics book for further details, e.g., [Mood74].

3.6.1 Littlewood-Verrall reliability growth model

3.6.1.1 Overview of the model. The Littlewood-Verrall model [Litt73, Litt78, Litt80a] is probably the best example of this class of models. It is also the one recommended in the AIAA Recommended Practice Standard [AIAA93] if you are looking for an initial candidate Bayesian model for fitting your data. The model tries to account for fault generation in the fault correction process by allowing for the probability that the software program could become less reliable than before. With each fault correction, a sequence of software programs is generated. Each is obtained from its predecessor by attempting to fix the fault. Because of uncertainty, the new version could be better or worse than its predecessor; thus another source of variation is introduced. This is reflected in the parameters that define the failure time distributions, which are taken to be random. The distribution of failure times is, as in the earlier models, assumed to be exponential with a certain failure rate, but it is that rate that is assumed to be random rather than constant as before. The distribution of this rate, as reflected by the prior, is assumed to be a gamma distribution.

3.6.1.2 Assumptions and data requirements. The *basic assumptions* are:

1. Successive execution times between failures, that is, X_i's, are assumed to be independent exponential random variables with parameter ξ_i, $i = 1, \ldots, n$.
2. The ξ_i's form a sequence of independent random variables, each with a gamma distribution of parameters α and $\psi(i)$. The function $\psi(i)$ is taken to be an increasing function of i that describes the quality of the programmer and the difficulty of the task. A good programmer would have a more rapidly increasing function than a poorer one.
3. The software is operated in a manner similar to the anticipated operational usage.

By requiring the function ψ to be increasing, the condition $P\{\xi_j < L\} \geq P\{\xi_{j-1} < L\}$ for all j is satisfied. This reflects the intention to make the program better after a fault is discovered and corrected, but it cannot be assured that the goal is achieved.

The *data requirements* are: the time-between-failure occurrences, i.e., the x_i's.

3.6.1.3 Model form. To calculate the posterior distribution we first need the marginal distribution of the x_i's. The prior distribution is of the form:

$$g(\xi_i;\, \psi(i),\alpha) = \frac{[\psi(i)]^{\alpha}\xi_i^{\alpha-1}\exp(-\psi(i)\xi_i)}{\Gamma(\alpha)}, \quad \xi_i > 0$$

Using this prior and the following conditional exponential distribution for the x_i's: $f_{X_i}(x_i \mid \xi_i) = \xi_i \exp(-\xi_i x_i)$ for $x_i > 0$, the marginal distribution of the x_i (Prob. 3.9) can be shown to be:

$$f(x_i \mid \alpha, \psi(i)) = \frac{\alpha[\psi(i)]^{\alpha}}{[x_i + \psi(i)]^{\alpha+1}} \qquad \text{for } x_i > 0$$

that is, a Pareto distribution, so that the joint density is

$$f(x_1, x_2, \ldots, x_n) = \frac{\alpha^n \prod_{i=1}^{n} [\psi(i)]^{\alpha}}{\prod_{i=1}^{n} [x_i + \psi(i)]^{\alpha+1}} \qquad \text{for } x_i > 0,\ i = 1, \ldots, n$$

The posterior distribution for the ξ_i's is therefore obtained as (see Prob. 3.10):

$$h(\xi_1, \xi_2, \ldots, \xi_n) = \frac{\prod_{i=1}^{n} \xi_i^{\alpha} \exp\left(-\sum_{i=1}^{n} \xi_i(x_i + \psi(i))\right)}{[\Gamma(\alpha+1)]^n \prod_{i=1}^{n} (x_i + \psi(i))^{\alpha+1}} \quad \text{for } \xi_i > 0, i = 1, \ldots, n$$

Each ξ_i is an independent gamma distribution with parameters $\alpha + 1$ and $1/(x_i + \psi(i))$. Therefore, if you use a quadratic loss function, the Bayesian estimate of ξ_i is the mean; namely, $(\alpha + 1)/(x_i + \psi(i))$.

Littlewood and Verrall suggest a linear and quadratic form for the $\psi(i)$ function, that is, $\psi(i) = \beta_0 + \beta_1 i$ (the linear form) and $\psi(i) = \beta_0 + \beta_1 i^2$ (the quadratic form).

The failure intensity functions for the linear and quadratic forms can be shown (see [Musa87]) to be

$$\lambda_{\text{linear}}(t) = \frac{\alpha - 1}{\sqrt{\beta_0^2 + 2\beta_1 t(\alpha - 1)}} \quad \text{and}$$

$$\lambda_{\text{quadratic}}(t) = \frac{\upsilon_1}{\sqrt{t^2 + \upsilon_2}}((t + (t^2 + \upsilon_2)^{1/2})^{1/3} - (t - (t^2 + \upsilon_2)^{1/2})^{1/3})$$

where $\upsilon_1 = (\alpha - 1)^{1/3}/(18\beta_1)^{1/3}$ and $\upsilon_2 = 4\beta_0^3/(9(\alpha - 1)^2\beta_1)$.

3.6.1.4 Model estimation and reliability prediction. Using the marginal distribution function for the x_i's, the maximum likelihood estimates of α, β_0, and β_1 can be found as the solutions to the following system of equations:

$$\frac{n}{\hat{\alpha}} + \sum_{i=1}^{n} \ln(\hat{\psi}(i)) - \sum_{i=1}^{n} \ln(x_i + \hat{\psi}(i)) = 0$$

$$\hat{\alpha} \sum_{i=1}^{n} \frac{1}{\hat{\psi}(i)} - (\hat{\alpha} + 1) \sum_{i=1}^{n} \frac{1}{x_i + \hat{\psi}(i)} = 0$$

$$\hat{\alpha} \sum_{i=1}^{n} \frac{i'}{\hat{\psi}(i)} - (\hat{\alpha} + 1) \sum_{i=1}^{n} \frac{i'}{x_i + \hat{\psi}(i)} = 0$$

where $\psi(i) = \beta_0 + \beta_1 i'$ and i' is either i or i^2. Using a uniform prior for α, Littlewood and Verrall [Litt73] obtain the marginal distribution of the x_i's as a function of β_0 and β_1 only. The MLEs of these two parameters are then obtained. You are referred to that reference for further discussions.

A third procedure is to derive the least squares estimates. Using the fact that

$$E\{X_i\} = \int_0^\infty \frac{\alpha x_i [\psi(i)]^\alpha}{[x_i + \psi(i)]^{\alpha+1}} \, dx_i = \frac{[\psi(i)]}{\alpha - 1}$$

the least squares estimates are those parameters that minimize:

$$S(\alpha, \beta_0, \beta_1) = \sum_{i=1}^{n} \left(x_i - \frac{[\psi(i)]}{\alpha - 1} \right)^2$$

You are referred to [Farr83] for further details.

Estimates of various reliability measures are then obtained accordingly, using any of the estimates derived from above. For example, the estimate of the mean time to failure for the ith failure is:

$$\text{MTTF} = \frac{[\hat{\psi}(i')]}{\hat{\alpha} - 1}$$

where i' is the linear or quadratic term for i.

Example 3.5 Suppose we use the data set that we have considered before, i.e., the following elapsed time between failures where the units of time are CPU hours:

$$x_1 = 10, x_2 = 8, x_3 = 14, x_4 = 17, x_5 = 15, x_6 = 22, x_7 = 19, x_8 = 27, x_9 = 35, x_{10} = 40$$

Using the SMERFS program and the linear form, the MLE estimates for α, β_0, and β_1 are obtained as $\hat{\alpha} = 10415$, $\hat{\beta}_0 = 57269$, and $\hat{\beta}_1 = 28162$. The estimate of the failure intensity function is thus

$$\text{Failure intensity function (linear) at time } t = \hat{\lambda}(t; \hat{\alpha}, \hat{\beta}_0, \hat{\beta}_1) = \frac{(\hat{\alpha} - 1)}{\sqrt{\hat{\beta}_0^2 + 2\hat{\beta}_1 t(\hat{\alpha} - 1)}}$$

so the estimated current failure intensity is with $t = 207$, $\hat{\lambda}(207) = 0.02949$. An estimate of the mean time to failure is obtained as $\text{MTTF} = [\hat{\beta}_0 + \hat{\beta}_1(11)]/(\hat{\alpha} - 1) =$ 35.25 CPU hours.

3.6.1.5 Comments. A paper by Mazzuchi and Soyer [Mazz88] considers a variation of this model by assuming all of the parameters α, β_0, and β_1 are random variables with appropriate priors. Employing some approximations because of computational difficulties, they then obtain some corresponding results.

Musa [Musa84a] considered the use of a rational function for $\psi(i)$. He felt that this parameter should be inversely related to the number of failures remaining. The form of this function was expressed as:

$$\psi(i) = \frac{N(\alpha + 1)}{\lambda_0(N - i)}$$

Here N is the expected number of faults within the software as time becomes infinite, λ_0 is the initial failure intensity function, and α is the parameter of the gamma distribution considered earlier. The index i is the failure index. You can see that as the number of remaining failures decreases, the scale parameter, $\psi(i)$, increases.

Another variation of this model is the one considered by Keiller et al. [Keil83]. Again, successive failures follow an exponential distribution with an associated gamma prior. However for this case, the reliability growth is induced by the shape parameter α rather than the scale parameter $\psi(i)$. See [Keil83] for additional details.

3.6.2 Other Bayesian models

A Bayesian formulation of the Jelinski-Moranda model was considered by [Lang88] and [Litt80c]. The Jelinski-Moranda model [Lang88] assumes that the time between failures is an exponential distribution. In addition, the parameters that define the distribution are themselves random variables. [Litt80c] uses a similar approach to derive the additional testing time required to achieve a specified reliability for a given operational time. Others who have taken this same Bayesian approach with this model are: Jewell [Jewe85], who allows the parameter, λ, of the Poisson distribution for N to itself be a random variable; Littlewood and Sofer [Litt87], who consider a reparameterized version; and Csenki [Csen90], who uses this Bayesian approach to derive the distribution for the time to next failure.

Other Bayesian approaches include: Kyparisi and Singpurwalla's [Kypa84] Bayesian nonhomogeneous Poisson process model; Liu's [Liu87] Bayesian geometric model; Becker and Camarinopoulos' [Beck90] Bayesian approach for a program that may be error free; and Thompson and Chelson's [Thom80] Bayesian model. [Xie91a] provides additional details on these models as well as other pertinent references.

3.7 Model Relationships

This section will provide an overall structure for software reliability modeling.

3.7.1 Generalized exponential model class

The generalized exponential model first appeared in the AIAA's *Recommended Practice for Software Reliability* [AIAA93] standard as one of the recommended models because of its generality. It reflects work by Shooman and Musa to simplify the modeling process by having a single set of equations to represent a number of important models having the exponential hazard rate function considered in Sec. 3.3. The overall idea is that the failure occurrence rate is proportional to the number of faults remaining, and the failure rate remains constant between failures while it is reduced by the same amount when a fault is removed. Besides the Standard Assumptions of Sec. 3.3.1.2, the other assumptions of the model are:

1. The failure rate is proportional to the current fault content of the software.
2. The faults that caused a failure are corrected instantaneously without additional faults being introduced by the correction process.

The data required are the usual time between failures, x_i's, or the time of the failures, the t_i's.

The model form is expressed as:

$$z(t) = K[E_0 - E_c(t)]$$

where $z(\bullet)$ is the software hazard rate function; t is a time or resource variable for measuring the progress of the project; K is a constant of proportionality denoting the failures per unit of t; E_0 is the initial number of faults in the software; and E_c is the number of faults in the software which have been found and corrected after t units have been expended. Table 3.2 reflects how this model is related to some of the models considered in Sec. 3.3.

TABLE 3.2 Generalized Exponential Model Relationships

Model	Original hazard rate function	Parameter equivalences
Generalized form	$K[E_0 - E_c(t)]$	
Shooman model	$K'[E_0/I_T - \varepsilon_c(t)]$	$\varepsilon_c = E_c/I_T$ where I_T is the number of instructions $K' = KI_T$
Jelinski-Moranda	$\phi(N - (i - 1))$	$\phi = K, N = E_0, (i - 1) = E_c(t)$
Basic execution model	$\beta_1\beta_0[1 - \mu(t)/\beta_0]$ where $\mu(t) = \beta_0[1 - \exp(-\beta_1 t)]$	$\beta_0 = E_0, \beta_1 = K, \mu(t) = E_c(t)$
Logarithmic Poisson	$\beta_1\beta_0\exp(-\mu(t)/\beta_0)$ where $\mu(t) = \beta_0\ln(\beta_1 t + 1)$	$\beta_1\beta_0 = KE_0$, $E_0 - E_c(t) = E_0\exp(-\mu(t)/\beta_0)$

3.7.2 Exponential order statistic model class

For this model the failure times of a software reliability growth process are modeled as order statistics of independent and nonidentically distributed exponential random variables. Miller [Mill86] developed this generalization and showed that the Jelinski-Moranda, Goel's NHPP, the logarithmic Poisson, and the power law models (e.g., Duane's model), among others, are special cases of this class. Miller lets a set of random variables, X_i, $i = 1, \ldots, n$, be independent random variables with respective rates λ_i. He then defines a stochastic process, $N(t)$, that is the number of failures that have occurred by time t and an associated process $\{T_i, i = 1, \ldots\}$ that is the times of the failures, that is, $T_i = \min\{t: N(t) \geq i\}$. The $N(t)$ and the T_i are the counting and the occurrence-time processes of an exponential order statistic model with parameter set $\underset{\sim}{\lambda} = \{\lambda_1, \lambda_2, \ldots, \lambda_n\}$. The exponential order statistic model is characterized by this parameter set. The only restriction on it is that $\lambda_i \geq 0$, $i = 1, 2, \ldots$, and $\sum_{i=1}^{\infty} \lambda_i < \infty$. Miller shows some special cases of the class by letting the λ_i's be various functions (e.g., constant, geometric, logarithmic, etc.). He then goes on to prove various results concerning this general class, including showing how a wide variety of known models are obtained as special cases. Estimation of the parameters is not considered in this paper. You are referred to his paper for additional details.

3.8 Software Reliability Prediction in Early Phases of the Life Cycle

All of the approaches considered so far in this chapter attempt to predict the reliability of the software in the later stages of the life cycle (integrated test and beyond). What is lacking are models that are applicable in the earlier phases, when less costly changes can be made. This section will briefly describe some approaches in this area. More research is, however, greatly needed.

3.8.1 Phase-based model

Gaffney and Davis [Gaff88, Gaff90] of the Software Productivity Consortium developed the phase-based model. It makes use of fault statistics obtained during the technical review of requirements, design, and the implementation to predict the reliability during test and operation.

The assumptions for this model are:

1. The development effort's current staffing level is directly related to the number of faults discovered during the development phase.

2. The fault discovery curve is monomodal.
3. Code size estimates are available during the early phases of a development effort. The model expects that fault densities will be expressed in terms of the number of faults per thousand lines of source code, which means that faults found during the requirements analysis and software design will have to be normalized by the code size estimates.

Their model is then expressed as:

$$\Delta V_t = \text{number of discovered faults per KLOC from time } t-1 \text{ to } t$$

$$= E[\exp(-B(t-1)^2 - \exp(-Bt^2)]$$

where E = total lifetime fault rate expressed in faults per thousand source lines of code (KLOC)

t = fault discovery index, with $t = 1$ means *requirements analysis*, $t = 2$ means *software design*, $t = 3$ means *implementation*, $t = 4$ means *unit test*, $t = 5$ means *software integration* $t = 6$ means *system test*, $t = 7$ means *acceptance test* (note t is not treated in the traditional sense that we have used it previously)

and

$$B = \frac{1}{2\tau_p^2}$$

where τ_p is the defect discovery phase constant, the peak of a continuous curve fit to the failure data. This is the point at which 39 percent of the faults have been discovered.

The cumulative form of the model is $V_t = E[1 - \exp(-Bt^2)]$, where V_t is the number of faults per KLOC that have been discovered through phase t. As data become available B and E can be estimated. This quantity can also be used to estimate the number of remaining faults at stage t by multiplying $E\exp(-Bt^2)$ by the number of source line statements at that point.

3.8.2 Predicting software defects from Ada designs

This section, unlike the others that consider prediction in the early phases, addresses one particular language, Ada. Agresti and Evanco [Agre92] attempted to develop models for predicting defect density based on product and process characteristics for Ada development efforts. The model they considered was:

$$\log(DD) = a_0 + \sum_{i=1}^{m} a_i * \log(X_i)$$

that is, a multivariate linear regression with the dependent variable being the log of the defect density (DD), and the independent variables being the log of various product characteristics of the Ada design and process characteristics. Among the variables considered were:

- *Content coupling measures* of the external or architectural complexity of the design
  1. Number of exported declarations per library unit
  2. The ratio of the number of import declarations to export declarations
  3. Number of content couples per library unit
- *Volatility*
  1. Number of modifications per library unit
  2. The number of nondefect modifications per unit library
- *Reuse*
  1. Fraction of the total compilation units that were new or extensively modified
- *Complexity*
  1. The ratio of imports from within a subsystem to the total imports

Using data from various projects, the multivariate regression analyses were conducted with resulting models explaining 63 to 74 percent of the variation in the dependent variable. Content coupling emerged as a consistently significant variable in these models. We plan to apply this approach on additional data sets. The results appear encouraging for this phase of the life cycle and this particular language.

3.8.3 Rome Laboratory work

One of the earliest and most well known efforts to predict software reliability in the earlier phases of the life cycle was the work initiated by the Air Force's Rome Laboratory [RL92] (see updates in this reference). For their model, they developed predictions of fault density which they could then transform into other reliability measures such as failure rates. To do this the researchers selected a number of factors that they felt could be related to fault density at the earlier phases. Included in the list were:

A *Application type* (e.g., real-time control systems, scientific, information management).

D *Development environment* (characterized by development methodology and available tools). The types of development environments considered are organic, semidetached, and embedded modes.

Requirements and design representation metrics

SA Anomaly management
ST Traceability
SQ Incorporation of quality review results into the software

Software implementation metrics

SL Language type (assembly, high-order, etc.)
SS Program size
SM Modularity
SU Extent of reuse
SX Complexity
SR Incorporation of standards review results into the software

The initial fault density prediction is then:

$$\delta_0 = A * D * (SA * ST * SQ) * (SL * SS * SM * SU * SX * SR)$$

Once the initial fault density has been found, a prediction of the initial failure rate is made as [Musa87]

$$\lambda_0 = F * K * (\delta_0 * \text{number of lines of source code}) = F * K * W_0$$

The number of inherent faults = W_0 = (δ_0 * number of lines of source code); F is the linear execution frequency of the program; and K is the fault expose ratio ($1.4 * 10^{-7} \leq K \leq 10.6 * 10^{-7}$). By letting $F = R/I$, where R is the average instruction rate and I is the number of object instructions in the program, and then further rewriting I as $I_s * Q_x$, where I_s is the number of source instructions and Q_x is the code expansion ratio (the ratio of machine instructions to source instructions—an average value of 4 is indicated), the initial failure rate can be expressed as

$$\lambda_0 = \left(R * \frac{K}{Q_X}\right) * \left(\frac{W_0}{I_s}\right)$$

3.9 Summary

This chapter has presented an overview of the classes of models that have appeared most often in the literature on software reliability modeling. We clearly have not covered the myriad of models that have appeared to date—to do so would require a large book unto itself. We have tried to give an overview of the important classes of these models along with important examples within those classes. You should not be dismayed by the number of classes and the associated models. This should drive home two important points. First, that the field has matured to the point that it can be applied in practical situations and give meaningful results and, second, that there is no one model that is best in all situations. We firmly believe that to successfully apply software reliability modeling, you need to select the model that is most appropriate for the data set and the environment in which the data were collected.

We also must warn you to exercise care in applying the results of this chapter. As can be seen from the results presented, the mathematics can be quite complex. This cautionary statement is not made to discourage the application of these results, but to warn you that the results cannot be blindly applied. You don't need a detailed understanding of the mathematical derivations to apply it. You must, however, have an understanding of what software reliability models can and cannot do. A little time spent in learning this can be the difference between a successful program and one that isn't. Data collection, quality, and monitoring, as well as what has been emphasized for model selection and validation are all essential if these models are to be successfully applied.

This field will continue to evolve as newer models are developed. As this occurs, new ideas will no doubt emerge to improve the prediction and estimation process. This is especially true for software reliability prediction in the earlier phases of the life cycle (e.g., the requirements and the design phase).

Many challenges yet await the researcher and practitioner: distributed and parallel-based software systems, high-integrity software systems, and fault tolerance are just a few. The field of software engineering is continuously evolving. The software development process is changing, which, in turn, will present new problems for the software reliability engineer. We have made and will continue to make great strides in providing quantitative answers to the question, "Just how good is the software?"

Problems

3.1 Show for a Poisson process that the conditional hazard rate function, $z(t \mid t_i)$, with t_i being the time of the ith failure, and the failure intensity function, $\lambda(t)$ are the same if the failure intensity function is evaluated at the current time $t_i + t$ with $t \geq 0$, that is,

$$z(t \mid t_i) = \lambda(t_i + t) \qquad \text{for } t \geq 0$$

For this case, what can we then conclude about the relationship between the mean value function, $\mu(t)$, and the hazard rate?

3.2 Using the expressions for the mean value and failure intensity functions for the Musa basic execution model of Sec. 3.3, show that the reliability function and the hazard rate function after $(i-1)$ failures have occurred are

$$R(\Delta t \mid t_{i-1}) = \exp(-[\beta_0 \exp(-\beta_1 t_{i-1})][1 - \exp(-\beta_1 \Delta t)]) \qquad \text{for } \Delta t \geq 0,$$

and
$$z(\Delta t \mid t_{i-1}) = \beta_0 \beta_1 \exp(-\beta_1 t_{i-1}) \exp(-\beta_1 \Delta t) \qquad \text{for } \Delta t \geq 0$$

3.3 Show for the Weibull model considered in Sec. 3.4 that the conditional hazard rate after $(i-1)$ failures have occurred is:

$$z(\Delta t \mid t_{i-1}) = (N - i + 1)\alpha\beta(t_{i-1} + \Delta t)^{\alpha - 1} \qquad \text{for } \Delta t \geq 0 \text{ and } 0 < \alpha < 1$$

What happens to this function as α approaches 1?

3.4 Derive the conditional reliability function and the hazard rate function after a failure has occurred at time t_i for the S-shaped model in Sec. 3.4. Derive also the expected number of faults to be detected in the ith interval of testing assuming it is of length l.

3.5 Derive the maximum likelihood estimates of α and β of the S-shaped model considered in Sec. 3.4. What are the resulting estimates for the data set considered in Example 3.2? Using the results from Prob. 3.4, what is the expected number of faults in the next testing period where all periods have been normalized to length 1?

3.6 Show that the mean value and failure rate function for the geometric model of Sec. 3.5 are

$$\mu(t) = \frac{1}{\beta}\ln([D\beta \exp(\beta)]t + 1) \qquad \text{and} \qquad \lambda(t) = \frac{D\exp(\beta)}{[D\beta\exp(\beta)] + 1}$$

where $\beta = -\ln(\phi)$ for $0 < \phi < 1$. (*Hint:* See Sec. 3.5.2.3.)

3.7 Using the formula for the expected time between failures and the actual times $(X_1, X_2, \ldots, X_n)$, derive the least squares estimates for D and β of the geometric model considered in Sec. 3.5. Using the data from Example 3.3, calculate the least squares estimates for D and β, and then the corresponding estimates for $\mu(t)$ and $\lambda(t)$ using the results from Prob. 3.6.

3.8 Show that the mean value and failure intensity function for the logarithmic Poisson in Sec. 3.5.3 are $\mu(t) = \ln(\lambda_0\theta t + 1)/\theta$ and $\lambda(t) = \lambda_0/(\lambda_0\theta t + 1)$, respectively.

3.9 For the Littlewood-Verrall model in Sec. 3.6, taking the conditional distribution of the time between failures, (x_i) to be exponential with parameter ξ_i, and the prior distribution to be a gamma distribution with parameters $\psi(i)$ and α, show that the marginal distribution of x_i is

$$f(x_i \mid \alpha, \psi(i)) = \frac{\alpha[\psi(i)]^{\alpha}}{[x_i + \psi(i)]^{\alpha+1}} \qquad \text{for } x_i > 0$$

3.10 Using the results from Prob. 3.9 and Sec. 3.6.1.3, show the resulting posterior distribution of the ξ_i's for the Littlewood-Verrall model is

$$h(\xi_1, \xi_2, \ldots, \xi_n) = \frac{\prod_{i=1}^{n} \xi_i^{\alpha} \exp\left(-\sum_{i=1}^{n} \xi_i(x_i + \psi(i))\right)}{[\Gamma(\alpha+1)]^n \prod_{i=1}^{n} (x_i + \psi(i))^{\alpha+1}} \qquad \text{for } \xi_i > 0, i = 1, \ldots, n$$

Chapter

4

Techniques for Prediction Analysis and Recalibration

Sarah Brocklehurst and Bev Littlewood
City University, London

4.1 Introduction

The previous chapter gives a comprehensive summary of many software reliability models that have appeared in the literature. Unfortunately, no single model has emerged that can be universally recommended to a potential user. In fact, the accuracy of the reliability measures arising from the models tends to vary quite dramatically: some models sometimes give good results, some models often perform inadequately, but no model can be trusted to be accurate in all circumstances. Worse than this, it does not seem possible to identify a priori those data sets for which a particular model will be appropriate [Abde86b].

This unsatisfactory position has undoubtedly been the major factor in the poor take-up of these techniques. Users who have experienced poor results adopt a once-bitten-twice-shy approach, and are unwilling to try new techniques. It is with some trepidation that we claim that the approach presented in this chapter has largely eliminated these difficulties. It might be as well, therefore, before giving some details of the techniques and examples of their use, to declare our credo. We believe that it *is* now possible *in most cases* to obtain *reasonably accurate* reliability measures for software and *to have reasonable confidence that this is the case* in a particular situation, as long as the reliability levels required are *relatively modest.* The italicized caveats here are important, because there are some limitations to what can currently be achieved, but they should not be so restrictive as to deter you from attempting to measure and predict software reliability in industrial contexts.

We begin by recalling briefly the nature of the software reliability problem. In the form in which it has been most studied, this is a problem of dynamic assessment and prediction of reliability in the presence of the reliability growth which stems from fault removal. A program is executing in a test (or real) operating environment, and attempts are made to fix faults when these are found as a result of the observation of software failures. There is therefore reliability growth, at least in the long term, although there may be local reversals as a result of poor fixes causing the introduction of new faults. The reliability growth models utilize the data collected here, usually in the form of successive execution times between failures (or, sometimes, numbers of failures in successive fixed time intervals; see Chap. 1 for details), to estimate the current reliability and predict the future development of the growth in reliability.

It is important to realize that all questions of practical interest involve *prediction.* Thus, even if we want to know the *current reliability* at a particular point in this process, we are asking a question about the *future:* in this case about the random variable, T, representing the time to the next failure. However we care to express our questions concerning the current reliability—as a rate of occurrence of failures, as a probability of surviving a specified mission time without failure, as a mean time to next failure, or in any other convenient way—we are attempting to predict the future. Longer-term prediction might involve attempting to estimate the (distribution of) time needed to achieve some target reliability, or the reliability that might be expected to be achieved after a certain duration of further testing.

The important point here is that when we ask, rather informally, whether a model is giving accurate reliability measures, we are really asking whether it is *predicting* accurately. This is something that is sometimes overlooked even in the technical literature; there are several examples of authors "validating" a model by showing that it can accurately explain past failure behavior and claiming thereby that it is "accurate." It is a simple matter to demonstrate that such ability to accurately capture the past does not necessarily imply an ability to predict accurately. The point is nicely expressed in a quotation of Niels Bohr, one of the greatest physicists of the 20th century: "Prediction is difficult, especially of the future."

4.2 Examples of Model Disagreement and Inaccuracy

4.2.1 Simple short-term predictions

Perhaps the simplest prediction arises when we ask what is the *current* reliability of a system. This will be a statement about the distribution of the time to the next failure and it could be expressed in several ways, as discussed earlier: the current *mean* or *median time to next failure* (MTTF), the *hazard rate function* of the distribution, or the *reliability function.*

It is as well to start rather informally with some examples that show how seriously the models can disagree in the answers they give to this most simple of all questions: namely, how reliable is the system now? We shall first show this disagreement between models, and then show how some of the results are also clearly *objectively* wrong.

Figure 4.1 shows plots of the successive current median times to next failure for a set of data, SYS1 from [Musa79], as calculated by some of the popular models: Jelinski-Moranda (JM) [Jeli72], Littlewood (LM) [Litt81], and Littlewood-Verrall (LV) [Litt73]. Thus, in this plot at stage j the predicted median of T_j is calculated for each model based upon all the data that has been observed prior to this stage, i.e., interfailure times, $t_1, t_2, \ldots, t_{j-1}$. We chose medians here for no particular reason

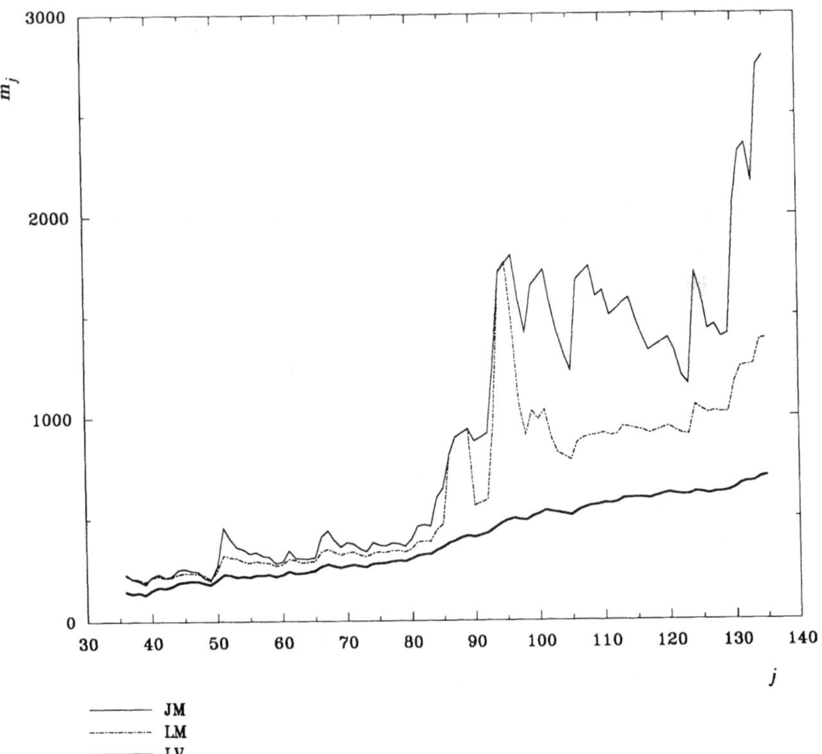

Figure 4.1 Successive one-step-ahead median predictions from models JM, LM, and LV of the time to next failure, T_j, plotted against j for $j = 36, \ldots, 136$, for data set SYS1. Notice the disagreement in these median predictions in the later part of the data.

other than convenience—the conclusions we draw will apply to other measures such as MTTF or *hazard rate.*

In the early stages of the plot there is reasonably close agreement between the three different models in how they predict the medians. This agreement disappears after about stage 85, when the medians begin to disagree. The first point to make, then, is that for this data the different models are giving quite markedly different numerical predictions in this very simple case of one-step-ahead median prediction. The fact of disagreement does not, of course, mean that all the predictions on this plot are inaccurate; on the contrary, it may be the case that one of the models is approximately correct and the other two are wrong (or even that some more complex reversals of fortune among the models are occurring as the data vector grows larger).

We can conduct quite crude investigations to examine this question of *absolute* accuracy. Figure 4.2 shows the actual data superimposed upon the median predictions of Fig. 4.1. At each stage j we can thus compare the three median predictions of T_j with the actual observed time to failure t_j. A very crude test of a certain type of accuracy would be to count the proportion of times the predicted median exceeded the later-observed time to failure. For accurate median predictions this proportion should be about one-half, and any significant departure from this would be evidence of some kind of bias in that sequence of predictions. If we look at the median predictions for JM, m_j^{JM}, we can see that from about $j = 90$ the proportion of times $m_j^{JM} > t_j$ is about 0.8. This suggests that the later predictions arising from the JM model are too large—i.e., in some sense the results from this model are too *optimistic* for this data set. Applying the same test to the LV predictions, there is evidence that the medians are too *pessimistic.* The LM model, on the other hand, passes this test quite well, with $m_j^{LM} > t_j$ about 57 percent of the time between stage 90 and the end of the data set.

Figure 4.3 shows a similar analysis using eight different models, JM, LM, and LV, as before, and Goel-Okumoto (GO) [Goel79], Musa-Okumoto (MO) [Musa84], Duane (DU) [Crow77, Duan64], Littlewood nonhomogeneous Poisson process (LNHPP) [Mill86], and Keiller-Littlewood (KL) [Keil83] models, on the data set SS3 from [Musa79], with once again the actual interfailure times superimposed. Again there is great disagreement between the eight different models, but, interestingly, they fall into two different groups of six and two models, respectively, with quite close agreement *within* each group. You might naively hope that the group of six models that agree with one another might be closer to the truth than the other pair. In fact, a comparison (as above) between the plots and the observed data shows that *none* of the eight models is getting close to the truth. The group of six are grossly optimistic in their median predictions, with a very high proportion of median predictions exceeding the later-observed times between failures; the other pair are grossly pessimistic.

4.2.2 Longer-term predictions

If these results were not discouraging enough, the problems of prediction inaccuracy become even more serious when we consider further-ahead prediction. In Fig. 4.4 we return to the SYS1 data to show median predictions 20 steps ahead, i.e., using only the data $t_1, t_2, \ldots, t_{j-20}$ to predict T_j. The performance of the JM model is extremely poor, with occasional excursions to infinity where it

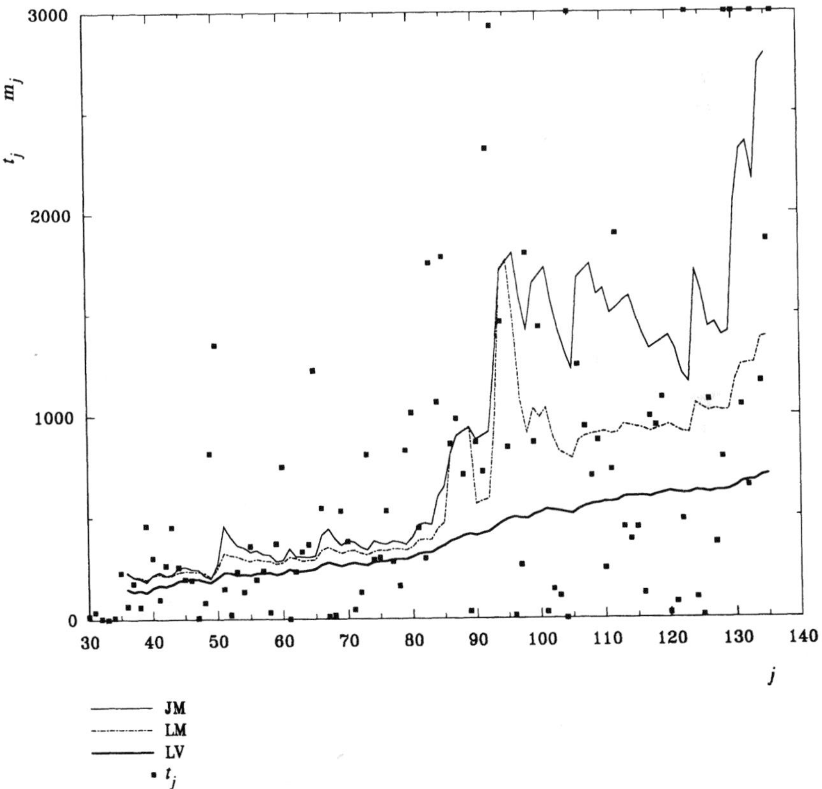

Figure 4.2 Observed times between failures, t_j, and successive one-step-ahead median predictions (as in Fig. 4.1) from models JM, LM, and LV of the time to next failure, T_j, plotted against j for $j = 36, \ldots, 136$, for data set SYS1. Comparison of the median predictions at each stage with the actual times between failures indicates the bias in these predictions; those from the JM model are too optimistic and those from the LV model too pessimistic, whereas those from the LM model would appear to be, on average, unbiased.

"believes" that the program under investigation will *never* fail again! This result can arise here because an intermediate parameter in this model is the number of remaining faults, which can be estimated to be zero. Clearly, the behavior shown by JM in this figure is very far from the truth. For example, each time the software is declared perfect it in fact disgraces itself by promptly failing again! Worse, the model does not even agree with the results that it produces itself when more data (the intervening 20 data points) are available (see Fig. 4.1).

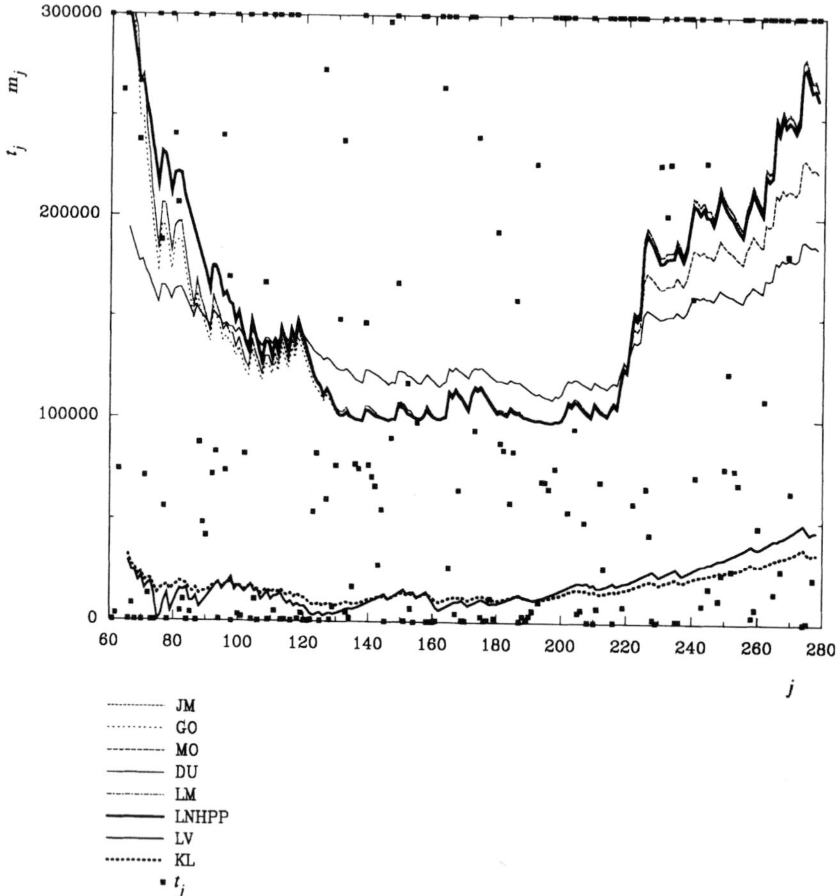

Figure 4.3 Observed times between failures, t_j, and successive one-step-ahead median predictions from eight models of the time to next failure, T_j, plotted against j for j = 66, . . . , 278, for data set SS3. These median predictions fall into two distinct groups, and the disagreement in the predictions for these two groups is great throughout the data set. The median test indicates that the predictions from LV and KL are grossly pessimistic, while the remaining median predictions are grossly optimistic.

The LV model performs better in this simple example of longer-term prediction. In Fig. 4.4 we show the 20-step-ahead median predictions with, for purposes of comparison, the one-step-ahead predictions of the same medians made at a later stage—these latter are the same as those shown earlier in Fig. 4.1. While we know from our earlier analysis that these are somewhat pessimistic, at least this model is exhibiting a reasonable self-consistency inasmuch as the predictions made earlier on a smaller data set are in good agreement with those made later. The JM model cannot even satisfy this minimal condition.

The results here are worrisome partly because they concern a very simple longer-term prediction. If we wished to predict much further into the future or to make more complex predictions of a different

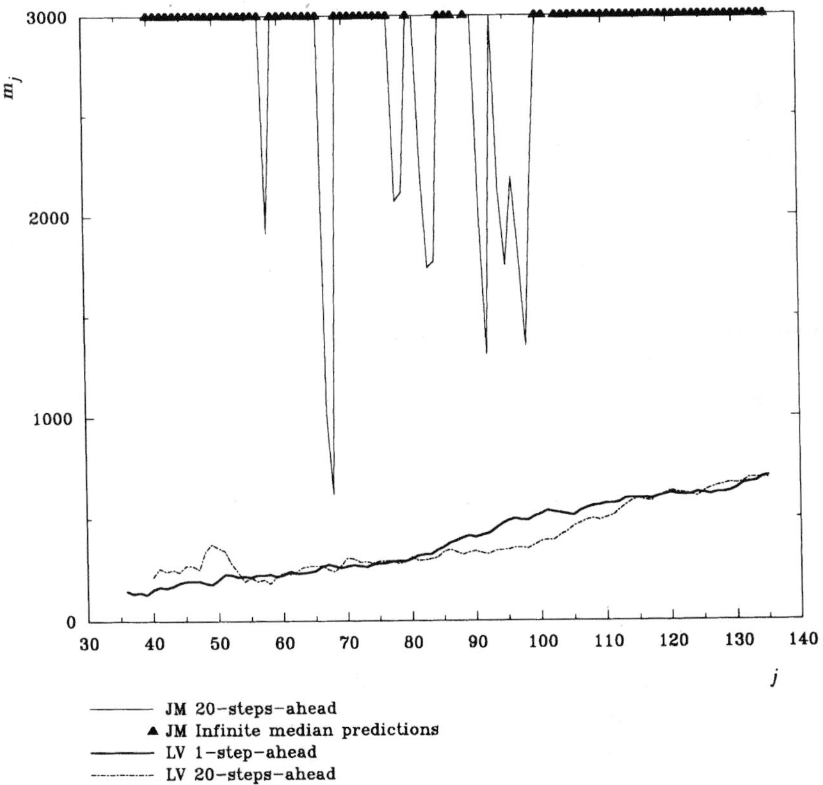

Figure 4.4 Successive 20-step-ahead median predictions from the JM model and successive one-step-ahead (as in Fig. 4.1) and 20-step-ahead median predictions from the LV model, of T_j, plotted against j for $j = 36, \ldots, 136$, for data set SYS1. The 20-step-ahead predictions from the JM are far too optimistic (compare with the times between failures in Fig. 4.2) and are much more optimistic than the one-step-ahead predictions from the same model (compare with Fig. 4.1). For LV, the one-step-ahead and 20-step-ahead median predictions are only marginally different.

nature (for example, predicting the time at which a prespecified reliability target will be reached), then it would be rash to assume that even *good* performance on some easier predictive task would allow us to conclude that other predictions would also be accurate. In fact, this observation can be made more generally: the fact that a model can give accurate predictions of one type for a particular data source does not allow us to conclude that predictions of a different type will also be accurate, even on the same data.

4.2.3 Model accuracy varies from data source to data source

Even in the results that we have shown already, which only concern two data sets, it is clear that the accuracy of some of the models varies considerably. For example, on the SYS1 data, the median predictions for the LM model pass the simple test of being in some sense "unbiased"—about 50 percent of the predicted medians exceed the later-observed times to failure, as should be the case—but on the SS3 data the same model gives grossly optimistic predictions.

The results of the more detailed analysis on the SYS1 and SS3 data sets in Sec. 4.3 will reveal even more serious differences between the behavior of a model on different data sources. In all the analyses that we have carried out over many data sets, we have found that the accuracy of the different models varies greatly from one data set to another [Abde86b].

It is certainly true that some models seem to be able to produce accurate predictions more consistently than others. The JM model, for example, appears to be fairly consistently *inaccurate,* and there are reasons for this in its unreasonable assumption that there are a finite number of faults contributing to the overall unreliability *and that these are all equal in their effect.* But even other, more plausible, models cannot be guaranteed to produce accurate results.

The conclusion seems to be that, even for a model which has given good results on a number of previous data sets, it would be unwise simply to *assume* that it will give good results on a novel data source.

4.2.4 Why we cannot select the best model a priori

Faced with this impasse—that models cannot be trusted to give accurate answers on all data sources—we might try to identify those characteristics of data sources that allow particular models to be accurate.

Unfortunately this does not seem to be possible. There is clearly great variation from one program to another: in the problem being solved, in the development practices, in the architecture, in the operational environment. No one has succeeded in identifying a priori those characteristics of a program that will ensure that a particular model can be trusted to produce accurate reliability predictions. In fact, this is not surprising, since the models involve rather crude assumptions about what may be a quite complex underlying failure process. There are many things that might impact upon the properties of the failure process that are simply ignored by the models. Examples include the nature of the operational environment, the internal fault-handling procedure (e.g., whether the software is fault-tolerant), etc. Such factors represent a source of uncontrolled variability in the properties of the failure process that is not treated by any of the models. In the absence of specific ways of taking account of such factors, we can expect the models to vary in their performance as the factors vary from one data source to another.

4.2.5 Discussion: a possible way forward

The results here are presented only to show that great disagreement between model predictions can and does exist and that we can show objectively that some very simple predictions can be extremely poor. It is worrisome that a model sometimes cannot even make one-step-ahead median predictions accurately, particularly if a potential user wishes to use the model for much more ambitious purposes. In fact, there is a sense in which results like this are only the tip of the iceberg. Models can go wrong in many different ways which might not be detected by the crude techniques used above. Even if a model were to pass our simple one-step-ahead median test, for example, this would not be a reason to trust its ability to produce accurate one-step-ahead predictions of a different nature—hazard rates, say, or reliability functions.

These observations show how important it is to devise more general ways in which the predictive accuracy of these models can be evaluated. We have shown that it is not possible to trust a particular model to give accurate results all the time or to select a model a priori that will give accurate results for a hitherto unseen data set. We therefore seem to have no alternative but to try to evaluate each model's predictive accuracy upon each new data set that is analyzed. The principle will be the same as the one that has been illustrated by the simple examples above: we must compare a prediction with the actual observation (when this is later made), and recursively build up a sequence of such prediction/observation comparisons. From this sequence we should be able to gain information about the accuracy of past predictions, and so make decisions about the current prediction (i.e., which model to trust, if any).

4.3 Methods of Analyzing Predictive Accuracy

4.3.1 Basic ideas: recursive comparison of predictions with eventual outcomes

Consider again, for simplicity, the simplest prediction problem of all: that of estimating the current reliability. Let us assume that we have observed the successive times between failures $t_1, t_2, \ldots, t_{j-1}$, and we want to predict the next time to failure T_j. We shall do this by using one of the models to obtain an estimate, $\hat{F}_j(t)$, of the true (but unknown) distribution function $F_j(t) \equiv P(T_j < t)$. Notice that if we knew the true distribution function then we could calculate any of the measures of current reliability, q_j, mean or median time to next failure or the rate of occurrence of failures (ROCOF), and so on, that may be appropriate for a particular application.

We now start the program running again, and wait until it next fails; this allows us to observe a realization t_j of the random variable T_j. We shall repeat this operation of *prediction* and *observation* for some range of values of j. In this way we can generate a *sequence*, $\hat{q}_j, j = s, \ldots, i$, say, of one-step-ahead predictions of interest. Table 4.1 shows an example of some times between failures and two prediction sequences, which we shall use to illustrate some of the techniques described in this chapter.

There are a number of ways suggested in the literature in which the accuracy of such a sequence of point predictions may be investigated. For example, the *variability* [Abde86b] may be examined,

$$\text{Variability}\{\hat{q}_j; j = s, \ldots, i\} = \sum_{j=s+1}^{i} \left| \frac{\hat{q}_j - \hat{q}_{j-1}}{\hat{q}_{j-1}} \right|$$

TABLE 4.1 Time Between Failures Data, $t_{12}, t_{13}, \ldots, t_{20}$ and Two Sequences, *A* and *B*, of Rate Predictions, $\hat{\lambda}_j^A$ and $\hat{\lambda}_j^B$, of T_j, $j = 12, \ldots, 20$

For illustrative purposes we shall assume that each prediction of T_j is based on previous data $t_1, \ldots, t_{j-1}$, and that the predictive distributions are exponential, with the predicted rates shown, for example, $\hat{F}_j(t) = 1 - e^{-\hat{\lambda}_j t}$ and $\hat{f}_j(t) = \hat{\lambda}_j e^{-\hat{\lambda}_j t}$. Predictions of mean time to failure $\hat{\text{MTTF}}_j = 1/\hat{\lambda}_j$ and median $\hat{m}_j = \ln(2)/\hat{\lambda}_j$ for these two prediction sequences are also shown.

j	t_j	$\hat{\lambda}_j^A$	$\hat{\text{MTTF}}_j^A$	$\hat{m}_j^A$	$\hat{\lambda}_j^B$	$\hat{\text{MTTF}}_j^B$	$\hat{m}_j^B$
12	105	0.010	100	69	0.0028	357	248
13	137	0.0077	130	90	0.023	43	30
14	125	0.0048	208	144	0.0071	141	98
15	161	0.0044	225	156	0.0020	500	347
16	162	0.0031	323	234	0.018	56	39
17	153	0.0029	345	239	0.0021	476	330
18	179	0.0028	357	248	0.0022	455	315
19	201	0.0017	603	418	0.0070	143	99
20	220	0.0013	769	533	0.0010	1000	693

This measure will detect whether a sequence of predictions is unduly *noisy.* Returning to our example earlier where we counted the proportion of the actual t_j exceeded by their predicted medians, $\hat{m}_j$, and asked if this proportion were very different from ½, it is clear that a sequence of predictions may pass this test, but still be very inaccurate. In other words, the predictions may *on average* be good but the *individual* median predictions may still be inaccurate. Using the above variability measure we might compare sequences of predictions from different models and reject one in favor of another on the basis that the predictions from the latter are more smooth, indicated by a smaller value of this variability measure. The obvious shortfall of such a measure is that reality may *itself* be noisy, and so we should not necessarily favor a predictor with a smaller variability measure.

It is clear that what we really need to examine, in order to assess the accuracy of a sequence of predictions, is the departure between the predictions and the truth. We would say, informally, that a model was giving good results if what we *observed* tended to be in close agreement with what we had earlier *predicted.* The approach we shall describe is based upon formal ways of comparing prediction with observation.

Of course, our problem would be easier if we could observe the true $F_j(t)$ so as to compare it with the prediction, $\hat{F}_j(t)$. Since this is not possible, we must somehow use the t_j, which is all the information that we have. Clearly this is not a simple problem, and it is compounded by its being nonstationary: we are interested in the accuracy of a sequence of *different* distributions, for each of which we see only one observation. However, it is possible to think of simple comparisons we can make such as the crude median test we discussed earlier. Other ways of comparing point predictions with observations are suggested in the literature. For example, in [Musa87], the *relative error* is used,

$$\text{Relative error} = \frac{\hat{\mu}(\tau_n) - n}{n}$$

Here, n failures have been observed by the total elapsed time τ_n, and $\hat{\mu}(\tau_n)$, the expected total number of failures by time τ_n, is a prediction made at an earlier time, $\tau(\tau < \tau_n)$, say. Plots of the relative error for different values of τ and for different values of τ_n may be examined, and these plots indicate the nature of the inaccuracy in the predictions of the expected number of failures, i.e., whether they are optimistic or pessimistic. They may also be used to *compare* two predictions or prediction systems, since the smaller the relative error the more accurate the predictions. Examination of the relative error, however, does not provide an *absolute* measure of accuracy of a single prediction system since tests to decide whether the error is significantly large do not exist.

A number of measures for which there are significance tests have been proposed. For example, the Braun statistic [Abde86b] may be used to see how accurate MTTF predictions are for those models for which the MTTF exists.

$$\text{Braun statistic}\{\hat{\text{MTTF}}_j; j = s, \ldots, i\} = \frac{\sum_{j=s}^{i} (t_j - \hat{\text{MTTF}}_j)^2}{\sum_{j=s}^{i} (t_j - \bar{t})^2} \left(\frac{i - s}{i - s - 1} \right)$$

This statistic may also be calculated when the available data is *failure-count data* [Abde86a] as opposed to time-between-failures data. This is where the observations are numbers of failures, n_k, within successive time intervals, x_k, $k = 1, \ldots, r$, say.

$$\text{Braun statistic}\{\hat{E}[N_k]; k = s, \ldots, r\} = \frac{\sum_{k=s}^{r} (n_k - \hat{E}[N_k])^2 x_k}{\sum_{k=s}^{r} (n_k - \bar{n})^2 x_k}$$

Another statistic which can be used to investigate the accuracy of predictions of the expected number of failures within successive time intervals is the χ^2 statistic,

$$\chi^2 \text{ statistic}\{\hat{E}[N_k]; k = s, \ldots, r\} = \sum_{k=s}^{r} \left(\frac{(n_k - \hat{E}[N_k])^2}{\hat{E}[N_k]} \right)$$

Unfortunately the analyses of the accuracy of point predictions such as those described above, regardless of whether they provide absolute measures of accuracy or merely comparative measures of one prediction system versus another, do not tell us a great deal. Even if a series of point predictions was found to be accurate based on these various criteria we would only acquire confidence in these point predictions. This would not tell us whether other reliability measures were accurate. What we really need is to be able to detect *any* kind of departure between prediction, $\hat{F}_j(t)$, and truth, $F_j(t)$. We shall proceed with a discussion of various techniques which can be used to assess the accuracy of predictive *distributions,* $\hat{F}_j(t)$, by comparing them with the (later) observed times between failures, t_j. Although the discussion of these techniques in this chapter is limited to time-between-failures data, extensions to failure-count data exist.

4.3.2 The prequential likelihood ratio (PLR)

The first technique we consider is a very general means of *comparing* sequences of predictions for accuracy. It will show (at least asymptotically) which of a pair of predictions is most accurate in a very general sense. It does not, however, provide direct evidence of *absolute* accuracy.

An intuitive and informal explanation of the prequential likelihood ratio approach is shown in Fig. 4.5, where there are two ways, A and B, of making a prediction at stage j. Here we see the *true* distribution (in fact the probability density function, pdf, $f_j(t) \equiv F_j'(t)$) of the next time to failure, T_j, together with estimates of this (i.e., predictions, $\hat{f}_j^A(t)$ and $\hat{f}_j^B(t)$) coming from two different models, A and B. In practice, of course, we shall not be able to see the true distribution, which is unknown. If we could see it, as here, we might be able to decide readily which is the best of the two predictions: clearly, here A is better than B.

After making these two predictions, which are based only upon the data we have seen prior to stage j, we wait and eventually see the next failure occur after a time t_j. Since this is a realization of a random variable whose distribution is the true one, we would expect t_j to lie in the main body of this true distribution, as it does here: that is, it is more likely to occur where $f_j(t)$ is larger. If we evaluate the two predictive pdf's at this value of t, there will be a tendency for $\hat{f}_j^A(t_j)$ to be larger than $\hat{f}_j^B(t_j)$. This is because the A pdf tends to have more large values close to the large values of the true distribution than does the B pdf. In fact, this is what we mean when we say informally that "the A predictions are closer to the truth than the B predictions"—that the value of the A pdf tends to be everywhere closer to that of the true pdf than is the value of the B pdf.

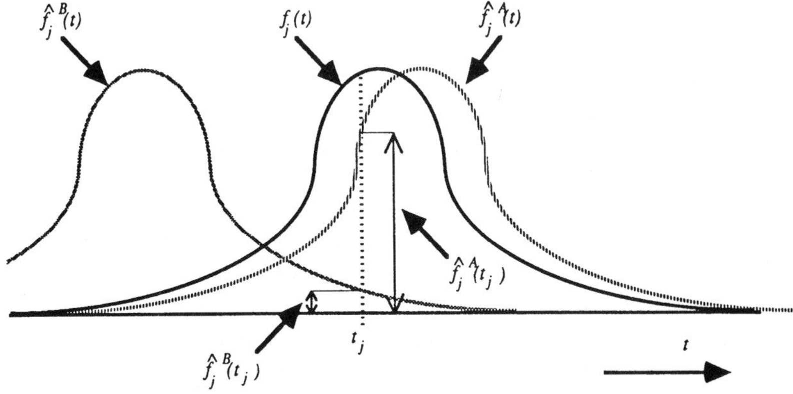

Figure 4.5 *True* predictive pdf, $f_j(t)$, of the next time to failure, T_j, together with estimates of this pdf, $\hat{f}_j^A(t_j)$ and $\hat{f}_j^B(t_j)$, from two models, A and B. A is clearly a better predictor of the truth than is B.

Thus if the predictions from A are more accurate than those from B, $\hat{f}_j^A(t_j)/\hat{f}_j^B(t_j)$ will tend to be larger than 1. The PLR is merely a running product of such terms over many successive predictions:

$$\mathrm{PLR}_i^{AB} = \prod_{j=s}^{j=i} \frac{\hat{f}_j^A(t_j)}{\hat{f}_j^B(t_j)}$$

and this should tend to increase with i if the A predictions are better than the B predictions. Conversely, superiority of B over A will be indicated if this product shows a decreasing trend.

You should note that, even if A is performing consistently more accurately than B, we cannot guarantee that $\hat{f}_j^A(t_j)/\hat{f}_j^B(t_j)$ will always be greater than 1. Thus, typically in a case where A is better than B, we would expect the plot of PLR_i^{AB} (or, more usually for convenience, the *log* of this) to exhibit overall increase, but with some local random fluctuations. We are looking for consistent upward or downward *trend* in the PLR_i^{AB} as we make successive predictions.

Table 4.2 shows how to do this PLR analysis for the simple predictors, A and B, mentioned earlier in Sec. 4.3.1. The corresponding plot of the $\log(\mathrm{PLR}^{AB})$ for model A versus model B is shown in Fig. 4.6. The fairly steady upward slope in this plot indicates that prediction sequence A is generally better than B over the range of predictions examined, although toward the end of this range, performance between the two prediction sequences would seem to be leveling out.

We are usually interested in comparing the accuracy of more than two sequences of predictions. To do this we select one, quite arbitrarily, as a reference and conduct pairwise comparisons of all others against this, as above. As an example, in Fig. 4.7 we show a PLR analysis of the SS3 data. Recall that, in Sec. 4.2.1, we saw an analysis of the one-step-ahead *median* predictions for this data, and established via a simple informal analysis that none of these models could be trusted to give accurate medians for this data. Nevertheless, six of

TABLE 4.2 $\hat{f}_j^A(t_j)$ **and** $\hat{f}_j^B(t_j)$ ($\hat{f}_j(t_j) = \hat{\lambda}_j e^{-\hat{\lambda}_j t_j}$) **for Prediction Sequences** ***A*** **and** ***B*** **Shown in Table 4.1, Together with the** $\log(\mathrm{PLR}_i^{AB}) = \sum_{j=12}^{j=i} \log(\hat{f}_j^A(t_j)/\hat{f}_j^B(t_j))$ **Evaluated for Prediction Sequence** ***A*** **versus Prediction Sequence** ***B*****.**

j	t_j	$\hat{f}_j^A(t_j)$	$\hat{f}_j^B(t_j)$	$\log(\hat{f}_j^A(t_j)/\hat{f}_j^B(t_j))$	$\log(PLR_i^{AB})$
12	105	0.00350	0.00209	0.516	0.516
13	137	0.00268	0.000985	1.00	1.52
14	125	0.00263	0.00292	–0.105	1.41
15	161	0.00236	0.00145	0.487	1.90
16	162	0.00187	0.000975	0.651	2.55
17	153	0.00186	0.00152	0.202	2.75
18	179	0.00170	0.00148	0.139	2.89
19	201	0.00121	0.00171	–0.346	2.54
20	220	0.000977	0.000803	0.196	2.74

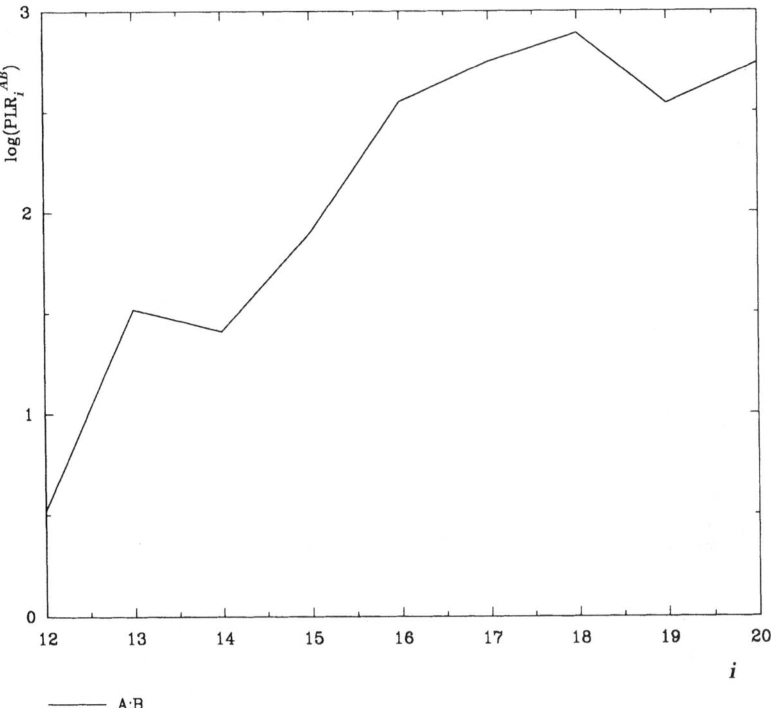

Figure 4.6 Log(PLR) plot for the prediction sequences shown in Table 4.1, that is, log(PLR$_i^{AB}$) versus i for prediction sequence A versus prediction sequence B as calculated in Table 4.2. The increase in the slope of this plot indicates that prediction sequence A is generally better than prediction sequence B.

the models gave median predictions that were in close agreement, and it might be thought that these would at least be *more* accurate than the other two. In fact this is not the case, and on the contrary the other two models (KL and LV) perform very much better on the PLR criterion.

In the figure, the DU model has been chosen as the reference model, so that all comparisons are pairwise with respect to this. It can be seen that for the LV and KL models the PLR plots against DU exhibit a clear upward trend (notice that the plots are of the log of PLR here), indicating their superiority over DU. The plots of the other models are similar to one another, exhibiting neither upward or downward trend and thus no superiority over DU. The evidence here, then, is that the six models that were in agreement on the earlier median plots are shown by the PLR analysis to be giving *general* one-step-ahead predictions that are of similar accuracy, and that this accuracy is much less than that given by LV and KL, which are themselves similar to one another in their accuracy.

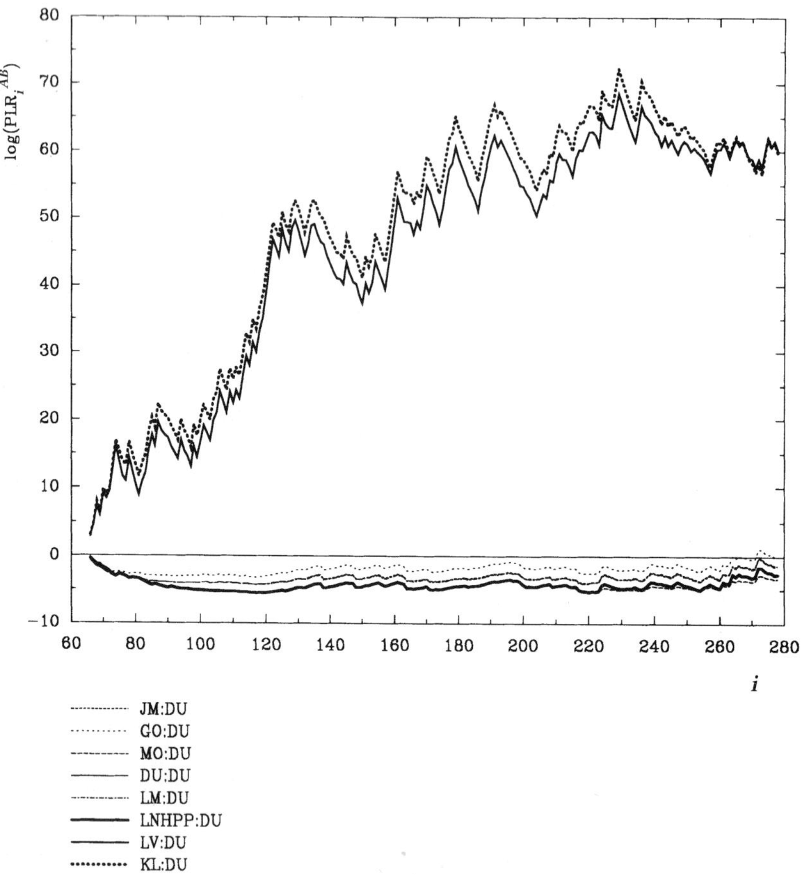

Figure 4.7 Log(PLR) plots for one-step-ahead predictions of T_i, $i = 66, \ldots, 278$, from eight models with the DU model chosen as the reference model against which to compare, for data set SS3. These plots indicate that, within the two groups of models which were previously identified as giving similar median predictions, there is indeed similar accuracy in the predictions and that the LV and KL groups are giving much more accurate predictions than the remaining six models.

The justification we have given here for the PLR is informal and intuitive. There is, however, a more formal asymptotic theory. If, as $i \to \infty$, the PLR_i^{AB} above tends to infinity, it can be shown that "we shall be . . . justified in regarding B as discredited, in favor of A . . ." [Dawi84]. If the ratio tends to neither infinity nor zero, then we cannot make a choice between A and B and *they will deliver indistinguishable predictions.* These results are completely general and concern circumstances (admittedly asymptotic) where we can be sure that A is a "completely better" predictor than B. In other words, they relate to any predictions, however expressed.

4.3.3 The *u*-plot

The PLR is a completely general technique for making *comparisons* of the accuracy of different competing predictions. It does not, however, allow us to say whether any of the predictions are *objectively* accurate. Our first general technique for detecting systematic objective differences between predicted and observed failure behavior is called the *u-plot,* and it is based on a generalization of the simple median check described above.

The purpose of the *u*-plot is to determine whether the predictions, $\hat{F}_j(t)$, are on average close to the true distributions, $F_j(t)$. It can be shown that, if the random variable T_j truly had the distribution $\hat{F}_j(t)$—in other words, if the prediction and the truth were *identical*—then the random variable $U_j = \hat{F}_j(T_j)$ will be uniformly distributed on (0,1). This is called the *probability integral transform* in statistics [DeGr86]. If we were to observe the realization t_j of T_j, and calculate $u_j = \hat{F}_j(t_j)$, the number u_j will be a realization of a uniform random variable. When we do this for a sequence of predictions, we get a sequence $\{u_j\}$, which should look like a random sample from a uniform distribution. Any departure from such uniformity will indicate some kind of deviation between the sequence of predictions, $\{\hat{F}_j(t)\}$, and the truth $\{F_j(t)\}$. Table 4.3 shows $\{u_j\}$ sequences for the simple predictors *A* and *B* mentioned earlier.

One way of looking for departure from uniformity is by plotting the *sample distribution function* of the $\{u_j\}$ sequence. This is a step function constructed as follows: for a sequence of predictions $\hat{F}_j(t)$, $j = s, \ldots, i$ on the interval (0,1), place the points $u_s, u_{s+1}, \ldots, u_i$ (each of these is a number between 0 and 1); then from left to right plot an increasing step function, with each step of height $^1/_{(i-s+2)}$ at each u on the abscissa, as shown in Fig. 4.8. The range of the resulting monotonically increasing function is (0,1), and we call it the *u*-plot. Figure 4.9 shows the *u*-plots based on the $\{u_j\}$ sequences shown in Table 4.3 for the two predictors *A* and *B*.

TABLE 4.3 u_j^A **and** u_j^B **(**$u_j = \hat{F}_j(t_j) = 1 - e^{-\hat{\lambda}_j t_j}$**) for Prediction Sequences *A* and *B* Shown in Table 4.1**

j	t_j	u_j^A	$u_{(j)}^A$	u_j^B	$u_{(j)}^B$
12	105	0.650	0.249	0.255	0.197
13	137	0.652	0.289	0.957	0.255
14	125	0.451	0.358	0.588	0.275
15	161	0.518	0.394	0.275	0.275
16	162	0.395	0.395	0.946	0.326
17	153	0.358	0.451	0.275	0.588
18	179	0.394	0.518	0.326	0.755
19	201	0.289	0.650	0.755	0.946
20	220	0.249	0.652	0.197	0.957

$u_{(j)}^A$ and $u_{(j)}^B$ are these same u sequences reordered in ascending order of magnitude.

If the $\{u_j\}$ sequence were truly uniform, this plot should be close to the line of unit slope. Any serious departure of the plot from this line is indicative of nonuniformity, and thus of a certain type of inaccuracy in the predictions. A common way of testing whether the departure is significant is via the Kolmogorov-Smirnov (KS) distance, which is the maximum vertical deviation between the plot and the line of unit slope (see, for example, Fig. 4.9) [DeGr86]; there are readily available tables for this. However, a formal test is often unnecessary: for many of the examples in this chapter it is clear merely from an informal perusal of the plots that the predictions are poor.

Figure 4.10 shows a u-plot analysis of predictions from the previous eight models on the SS3 data. Remember that the informal median analysis showed that none of the eight could be trusted. Recall that the group of six models was very optimistic (i.e., the models were underestimating the chance of the next failure occurring before t), while the other two were pessimistic, although PLR analysis showed that these latter two were in fact less inaccurate than the six. From Fig. 4.10 we can now see the reason for these results: all the models have extremely bad u-plots, with *KS* distances so large that they are well beyond the values that are tabulated. However, while very bad, the LV and KL pair have *KS* distances that are smaller (and so, less bad) than those of the other six—which confirms the PLR analysis.

What is so striking about Fig. 4.10 is that there is such a marked difference in *shape* in the two groups of plots. In fact, informal inspections of u-plots can tell us quite a lot about the *nature* of the prediction errors. The number u_j is the estimate we would have made, before the event, of the probability that the next failure will occur before t_j, the

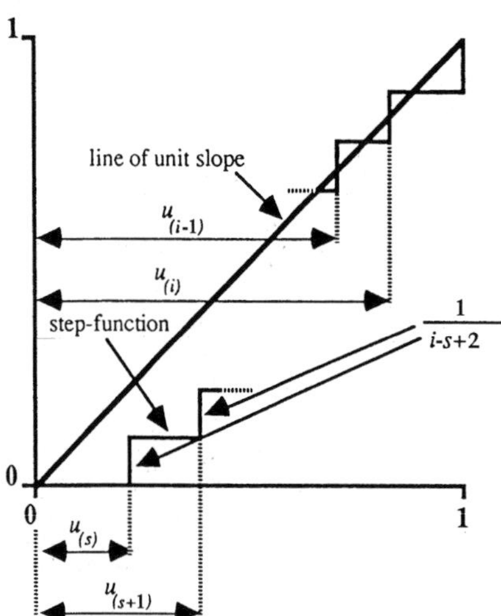

Figure 4.8 How to draw the u-plot, for predictions of $T_s, \ldots, T_i$. Here, $\{u_{(s)}, u_{(s+1)}, \ldots, u_{(i)}\}$ are the original set of u's $\{u_s, u_{s+1}, \ldots, u_i\}$ reordered in ascending order of magnitude.

time when it *actually does* eventually occur. In the case of consistently too optimistic predictions, this number would therefore tend to be smaller than it would be if the predictions were accurate. That means the u_js will tend to bunch too far to the left in the (0,1) interval, and the resulting u-plot will tend to be *above* the line of unit slope. A similar argument shows that a u-plot which is entirely below the line of unit slope indicates that the predictions are too pessimistic. In Fig. 4.10 the plots for LV and KL are almost everywhere below the line of unit slope, indicating that these predictions are objectively too pessimistic; similarly the other six are generally too optimistic. It is sometimes even possible to explain u-plot shapes in terms of inaccuracies more general than simple optimism and pessimism. In Fig. 4.10, for example, there is evidence that the optimism/pessimism argument is a slight oversimplification. Thus, the six models which are generally optimistic seem to be *pessimistic* for predictions associated with the right-hand tail of the

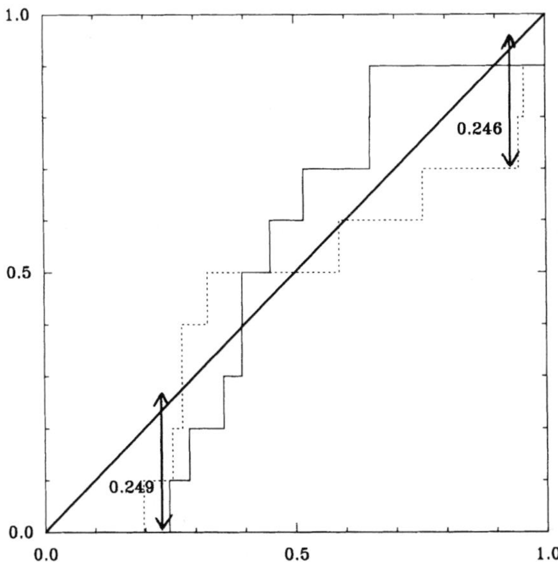

—— A 0.249 (insignificant at 20% level)
········ B 0.246 (insignificant at 20% level)

Figure 4.9 u-plots as calculated in Table 4.3 for prediction sequences A and B in Table 4.1. These plots are step functions with step size 1/10. The *KS* distances, indicated on the plots by the arrows, are 0.249 for prediction sequence A, and 0.246 for prediction sequence B, and these values are statistically insignificant at the 20 percent level, indicating that neither prediction sequence is significantly biased.

distribution of time to next failure (i.e., predictions associated with *high* reliability) as evidenced by the plots' crossing of the line of unit slope on the right. The LV and KL predictions, on the other hand, can be seen to be pessimistic in general, but slightly optimistic for predictions of high and low reliability.

Figure 4.11 shows a u-plot analysis of the JM, LM, and LV models on the SYS1 data. The plot for JM is everywhere above the line of unit slope, and its KS distance is highly statistically significant. This confirms that the predictions from this model are too optimistic, as we suspected from the earlier simple median analysis. Similarly, LV is too pessimistic, but less dramatically so. The plot of LM is not statistically significant: it thus passes this test, but may, of course, be deficient in some other way.

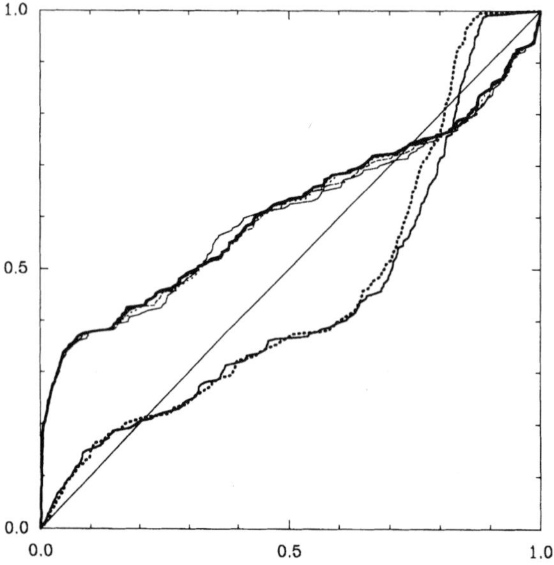

JM 0.294 (significant at 1% level)
GO 0.293 (significant at 1% level)
MO 0.290 (significant at 1% level)
DU 0.287 (significant at 1% level)
LM 0.294 (significant at 1% level)
LNHPP 0.293 (significant at 1% level)
LV 0.230 (significant at 1% level)
KL 0.215 (significant at 1% level)

Figure 4.10 u-plots and KS distances and significance levels for predictions of T_i, $i = 66, \ldots, 278$, from eight models for data set SS3. The departure of these plots from the line of unit slope indicates that predictions from all eight models are significantly inaccurate for this data set, with LV and KL giving generally pessimistic predictions and the remaining six models giving generally optimistic predictions.

These results for SYS1 and SS3 confirm and explain the earlier results dealing with the medians alone. But it must be emphasized that the u-plot approach is much more general than the analysis we conducted earlier; it relates to the whole shape of the predictive distribution rather than merely to one point (the median) on this distribution. The u-plot can be thought of as detecting a *systematic* difference between the predictions and the truth. This is very similar to the notion of *bias* in statistics: there we use the data to calculate an *estimator* of a population parameter, and this estimator is called *unbiased* if its average value is equal to the (unknown) parameter. Of course, our case is more complex since at each stage we wish to estimate a *function,* rather than merely a number; furthermore, we can only detect prediction error over a *sequence* of *different* predictions because of the inherent nonstationarity of the problem.

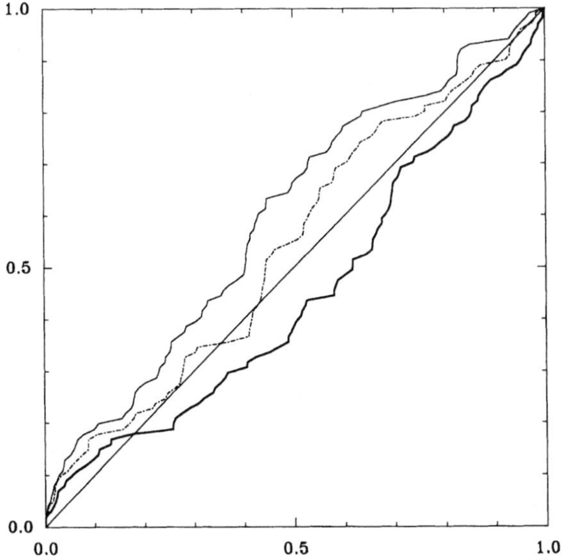

——— JM 0.181 (significant at 1% level)
- - - - - LM 0.103 (insignificant at 20% level)
——— LV 0.148 (2%–5%)

Figure 4.11 u-plots and KS distances and significance levels, for predictions of T_i, $i = 36, \ldots, 136$, from the JM, LM, and LV models for data set SYS1. These plots indicate that the JM model is giving significantly optimistic predictions, the LV model is giving significantly pessimistic predictions, and the LM predictions have, on average, no significant bias. (Note that 2%–5% means that the u-plot for the LM model is significant at the 5 percent level and insignificant at the 2 percent level.)

An interesting special case arises when the prediction errors are completely stationary, i.e., the nature of the error is the same at all stages. There will then be a constant (functional) relationship between $\hat{F}_j(t)$ and $F_j(t)$, and the u-plot is an estimate of this functional relationship. It turns out, in fact, that there is often *approximate* stationarity of errors of this kind. We shall show later in Sec. 4.4 that in such cases it is possible to recalibrate the model—essentially allowing it to "learn" from past mistakes—and obtain more accurate predictions.

4.3.4 The *y*-plot

The u-plot treats one type of departure of the predictors from reality—namely, a kind of reasonably consistent bias. There are other departures from reality which cannot be detected by the u-plot. For example, in one of our investigations we found a data set for which a particular prediction system had the property of optimism in the early predictions and pessimism in the later predictions. These deviations were averaged out in the u-plot, in which the temporal ordering of the u_j's disappears, so that a small *KS* distance was observed. It is necessary, then, to examine the u_j's for *trend.*

There is no obvious standard statistical test for this situation. One way to proceed is as follows, and has the advantage that it results in a plot that is visually similar, and is interpreted similarly, to the u-plot. Remember that the u_j sequence should look like a sequence of independent, identically distributed uniform random variables on (0,1). Since the range, (0,1), remains constant, any trend will be difficult to detect in the u_j sequence, which will look very regular. If, however, we make the transformation $x_j = -\ln(1 - u_j)$, we produce a sequence of numbers that should look like realizations of independent, identically distributed unit *exponential* random variables. That is, the sequence should look like the realization of the successive interevent times of a homogeneous Poisson process; any trend in the u_j's will show itself as a nonconstant rate for this process. There are many tests for trend in a Poisson process. We begin, as in [Cox66], by normalizing the whole transformed sequence onto (0,1). That is, for a sequence of predictions from stage s through stage i, we define

$$y_k = \frac{\sum_{j=s}^{k} x_j}{\sum_{j=s}^{i} x_j} \qquad \text{where } k = s, \ldots, i-1$$

A step function with steps of size $1/(i-s+1)$ at the points $y_s, y_{s+1}, \ldots, y_{i-1}$ is drawn from the left on the interval (0,1), exactly as in the case of the

u-plot. Table 4.4 and Fig. 4.12 show how to construct the y-plot for the two predictors, A and B, considered earlier.

Figure 4.13 shows an example using the same range of predictions as before from the same eight models on the SS3 data. Again, the results divide into the same two groups of six and two models, respectively. The six models have highly significant KS distances, so there is evidence that there is trend in the errors being made in the predictions; the results from LV and KL, the other two models, are not statistically significant. This means that the LV and KL predictions, while clearly shown to be in error by our previous analyses, are producing errors that are in some sense stationary. In a case like this, when the error being made remains constant, there arises the possibility of estimating its nature and using this to correct for the error in future predictions (on the assumption that its nature will continue unchanged into the future). This idea will form the basis of our recalibration technique described below.

4.3.5 Discussion: the likely nature of prediction errors, and how we can detect inaccuracy

With the techniques described above we have the beginnings of a framework for making decisions about which model to use within a particular context, and whether the predictions should be trusted to be accurate. It is important to emphasize the differences between, on the one hand, the PLR approach and, on the other, devices such as the u-plot and y-plot. PLR will only tell us about *relative* performance among competing models, but it will do this in the most *general* way possible, with the underlying theory [Dawi84] providing an assurance that all deficiencies have been taken into account. The u-plot and y-plot, on the other hand, give us some *absolute* information, but only about certain *specific* ways in which predictions can differ from the truth.

TABLE 4.4 x_j^A, y_j^A, x_j^B **and** y_j^B, $x_j = -\ln(1 - u_j)$ **and** $y_k = \sum_{j=12}^{k} x_j / \sum_{j=12}^{20} x_j$ **for Prediction Sequences** A **and** B **shown in Table 4.1.**

j	t_j	x_j^A	y_j^A	x_j^B	y_j^B
12	105	1.05	0.191	0.294	0.297
13	137	1.06	0.382	3.15	0.347
14	125	0.600	0.491	0.887	0.437
15	161	0.730	0.624	0.322	0.469
16	162	0.503	0.714	2.92	0.764
17	153	0.443	0.795	0.322	0.796
18	179	0.501	0.886	0.395	0.836
19	201	0.341	0.948	1.41	0.978
20	220	0.286	1.00	0.219	1.00

What this means is that, if we want to ask which of a set of alternative models should be preferred in the analysis of a particular set of data, we should use the PLR. When this gives dramatic evidence of an increasing trend for a pairwise comparison, then we should strongly believe that one model is giving more accurate results than the other. For example, Fig. 4.7 indicates that LV is clearly superior to DU for the SS3 data. However, even when a particular model is clearly superior to others for a particular set of data, it is not necessarily the case that it is giving accurate results: in the case of the SS3 data, according to the u-plots in Fig. 4.10, *all* models were giving results which were inaccurate.

It is important, therefore, after picking out the one (or more) model that performs best on the PLR, to investigate further via u-plot and y-plot analysis. A good u-plot (accompanied by a good y-plot) will tell us that a particular type of consistent bias is absent in the predictions (the good y-plot being needed to ensure that the errors in prediction are at least approximately stationary, so that the u-plot result can be trusted).

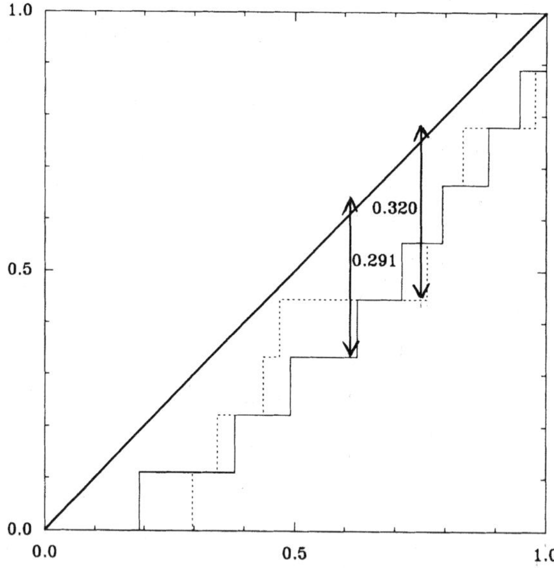

——— A 0.291 (insignificant at 20% level)
.... B 0.320 (insignificant at 20% level)

Figure 4.12 y-plots as calculated in Table 4.4 for prediction sequences A and B in Table 4.1. These plots are step functions with step size 1/9. The *KS* distances, again marked by the arrows, indicate that both prediction sequences A and B are capturing the trend in the failure data.

Of course, predictions can be in error in ways other than the bias that the u-plot detects. Consider the analogy of estimating a population parameter from a random sample in statistics. Even if we have an estimator that is unbiased we may still prefer on other grounds to use a biased one. For example, the unbiased estimator may have a large variance, so that although its expected value is equal to the unknown parameter, any particular calculated value of the estimator may be very far from this. This is the difference between what happens *on average* and what happens at *a particular instance.* Similar argu-

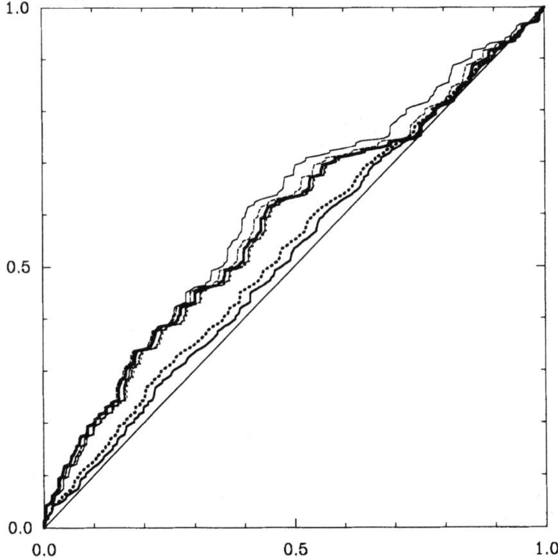

JM 0.157 (significant at 1% level)
GO 0.155 (significant at 1% level)
MO 0.180 (significant at 1% level)
DU 0.205 (significant at 1% level)
LM 0.158 (significant at 1% level)
LNHPP 0.166 (significant at 1% level)
LV 0.044 (insignificant at 20% level)
KL 0.064 (insignificant at 20% level)

Figure 4.13 y-plots and *KS* distances and significance levels for predictions of T_i, $i = 66, \ldots, 278$, from eight models for data set SS3. The y-plots for LV and KL show no significant departure from the line of unit slope, indicating that the prediction errors, which we know to be present from the u-plots in Fig. 4.10, are stationary, while for the remaining six models, significant departure in the y-plots is shown, indicating that for these models the prediction errors are not stationary.

ments apply to a good u-plot, which also tells us something about average behavior, but which can mask large inaccuracies on particular predictions. The analogy with variance in our case is a kind of unwarranted noisiness in a sequence of predictions, e.g., predictions that are randomly alternatively too optimistic and too pessimistic, but whose average is close to the truth. Such predictions might exhibit a good u-plot, but any individual prediction could be very inaccurate and hence useless.

It has not been possible to find a way of testing for this kind of inappropriate noisiness in predictions. The problem is that we are considering a much more complicated problem than the simple statistical estimation of a constant parameter from a random sample—in our case we *know* that what we are estimating is nonstationary. Indeed, it is precisely the nonstationarity (the reliability growth) that is of interest to us. It may be the case, then, that this nonstationarity is of a complex form. In particular, there may be genuine reversals of fortune within a general picture of average reliability growth: there may be bad fixes among the good ones. In other words, apparently invalid noisiness in a sequence of prediction may simply be reflecting the *true behavior* of the reliability. The difficult trick is to distinguish noisiness that is merely an artifact of the prediction technique from such real noisiness.

Although there is no direct method of detecting unwarranted noisiness in predictions, this may not be a serious problem. In the first place, it seems unlikely that the evolution of the true reliability will be very noisy in practice. Second, we can get some indirect evidence of inappropriate noisiness from the PLR analysis, since this is sensitive to *all* departures from predictive accuracy. For example, if a model appeared to differ from others in analysis of a particular data set only in its noisiness, *and* its PLR was inferior to others, it would be reasonable to infer that its noisiness was the cause of this poor performance and was therefore unwarranted.

In the next section, where we show how it is possible in some cases to remove the bias errors that are detected by the u-plot, we shall see that the nonstationarity in the prediction errors indicated by a poor y-plot does not in fact appear to be a problem in many cases.

Our own experience, then, is that the PLR and the u-plot alone can be quite powerful tools in deciding whether particular competing predictions should be trusted to be accurate. Certainly their use cannot guarantee that there are no subtle departures between predicted and actual failure behavior, but we believe that the most important and most likely problems are *bias* and *noise,* and that these are usually handled adequately. In Sec. 4.5 we shall work through some examples completely to show how all the different facets of our analytical approach fit together; before that, we complete our description of these new techniques by introducing the idea of recalibration.

4.4 Recalibration

4.4.1 The *u*-plot as a means of detecting bias

We now need to describe carefully what we mean by the notion of *bias* that has so far been discussed quite informally. One way of expressing the notion of *prediction error* more formally is to say that at stage i there is some function G_i which relates the predicted to the true distribution of the time-to-next-failure random variable, i.e., $F_i(t) = G_i[\hat{F}_i(t)]$. Such a function, if we knew it, would tell us everything there is to know about the error in the predictions being made at a particular stage. In particular, if we knew G_i we could recover the true distribution, $F_i(t)$, from the inaccurate prediction, $\hat{F}_i(t)$. In practice, of course, we do not know this function.

However, if we say that a model is *merely* biased in its predictions, then we are asserting not only that there is a difference between what is predicted and the underlying truth, *but that this relationship is constant* so that the sequence G_i is (approximately) stationary, i.e., $G_i \cong G$, say, for all i. In such a case, when there is only a single G function for the whole sequence of predictions, we might try to estimate it and thus provide a means of recalibrating future inaccurate predictions to produce better ones.

The point here is that there is always an unknown function that will transform the predicted distribution into the true distribution, but it is only *sometimes* the case that this function is approximately the same for all i. When this occurs, we have the opportunity of *estimating* this error function from the earlier predictions we have made by comparing these with the observed outcomes. In fact, it can be shown that the u-plot based upon these earlier predictions is a suitable estimator of G [Broc90].

You might reasonably ask whether the condition of stationary errors described above ever applies in real life. In fact such complete stationarity does seem rather implausible. However, as we shall show, this appears not to be critical for our recalibration technique to provide predictions with improved accuracy. And of course, it is not necessary to trust such an approach to be effective, since any recalibrated predictions can be evaluated for accuracy just like any other set of predictions.

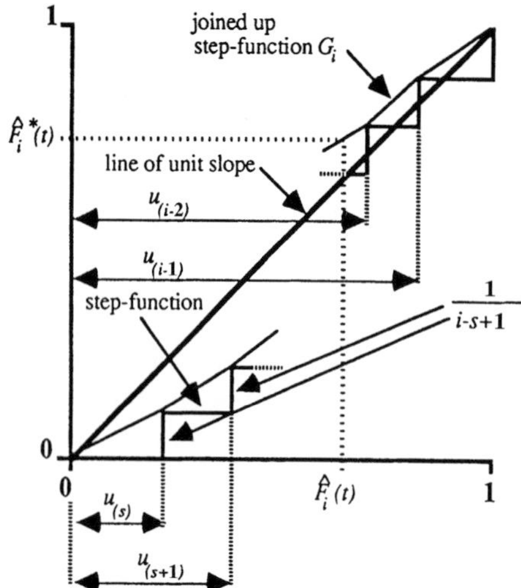

Figure 4.14 The joined-up step function, G_i, of the u-plot of predictions of $T_s, \ldots, T_{i-1}$. Again, $\{u_{(s)}, u_{(s+1)}, \ldots, u_{(i-1)}\}$ are the original set of u's, $\{u_s, u_{s+1}, \ldots, u_{i-1}\}$, reordered in ascending order of magnitude. In fact it is a smoothed version of this step function, G_i^*, which we shall be using to recalibrate predictions, and not simply the joined-up step function, as shown here.

4.4.2 The recalibration technique

The steps of the recalibration procedure are as follows:

1. Obtain the u-plot, say G_i^* based upon the raw[†] predictions, $\hat{F}_s(t), \ldots, \hat{F}_{i-1}(t)$, that have been made before stage i[‡] (see Fig. 4.14). This can be thought of as an estimate of the function G which is assumed to represent the (approximately) constant relationship between prediction and truth.
2. Obtain $\hat{F}_i(t)$, the raw prediction at stage i.
3. Calculate the recalibrated prediction, $\hat{F}_i^*(t) \equiv G_i^*[\hat{F}_i(t)]$ (see Fig. 4.14).
4. Repeat this at each stage i. In this way a sequence of recalibrated predictions will result.

The most important point to note about this procedure is that it is truly predictive, inasmuch as only the past is used to predict the future. This means that it is not necessary to believe a priori that the recalibrated predictions will be better than the raw ones, since the various techniques for comparing and analyzing predictive accuracy can

---

[†] We use *raw* here to indicate the predictions before recalibration has taken place. Although we usually think of these predictions as coming directly from a reliability model, this is not obligatory; it is possible, for example, that the initial raw prediction sequence is *itself* the result of recalibration.

[‡] For technical reasons, which do not detract from the general explanation given here, it is desirable for G_i^* to be a *smoothed* version of the joined-up step-function u-plot, G_i, shown in Fig. 4.14; a spline-smoothed version, see [Broc90], has been used in the examples that follow.

be used. In particular, the PLR will tell us whether recalibration has produced better results than a simple use of the raw model.

This is a particularly important point in view of the apparently strong assumption of stationarity of errors that underlies the recalibration idea. However, we can obtain some idea of whether there is nonstationarity here by examination of the y-plot. In fact, and quite surprisingly, it turns out that *even in those cases where the y-plot gives evidence of nonstationarity* the recalibration procedure can be shown to give significantly improved accuracy over the raw model. We shall see this in the following examples.

4.4.3 Examples of the power of recalibration

We have already seen that when we apply any of our eight models to the SS3 data, we obtain results that are extremely inaccurate. The u-plots (see Fig. 4.10) are highly statistically significant in all cases. Analysis of the y-plots (see Fig. 4.13) shows that for LV and KL these errors might be stationary, and thus these models are possible candidates for recalibration; the other six have highly significant y-plots and would not at first be thought able to benefit from recalibration. In fact we have applied the recalibration procedure to all eight models and Figs. 4.15 to 4.17 show the results.

Figure 4.15 shows the plots of recalibrated medians, i.e., the medians of the recalibrated versions of the successive predictive distributions.* Comparing this with the plots of the medians from the raw models (Fig. 4.3), we can see that the eight models are now producing median predictions that are in much closer agreement. In fact, the six models that were shown in the earlier u-plots (Fig. 4.10) to be grossly optimistic in their predictions now have much smaller predicted medians; similarly, LV and KL, which were grossly pessimistic, now have larger predicted medians. This might indicate that there is some objective sense in which the recalibrated predictions really are better than the raw ones, and in fact this is shown to be the case in the u-plots of the recalibrated predictions (Fig. 4.16). In comparison with the raw u-plots, the improvement is dramatic in all eight cases, as shown by the *KS* distances, but this is obvious even from a cursory glance.

What is surprising is that the improvement is so marked in the cases of those six models for which the y-plots tell us that the errors are not stationary. Since stationarity of the underlying sequence of errors is needed to justify the assumption that a single G function can be used

* An S appended to a model name is used to denote the recalibrated version of the model, so JMS is the recalibrated version of the JM model, and so on.

for the recalibration, this is very surprising. We can, however, confirm that there has been objective improvement in all eight sets of predictions by examining Fig. 4.17, which shows plots of the PLR, comparing for each model the recalibrated predictions with the raw predictions. In fact these plots show that there has been *greater* improvement for the six models than for LV and KL—but of course it must be remembered that there was more *room* for improvement in these cases, as shown in the original PLR plots of Fig. 4.7.

In fact, in other analyses we have carried out [Broc87] we have found that in general it does not seem to be necessary to pass the y-plot test in order for recalibration to be effective. In any case, since we have the general procedures of the previous section for analyzing the accuracy of any

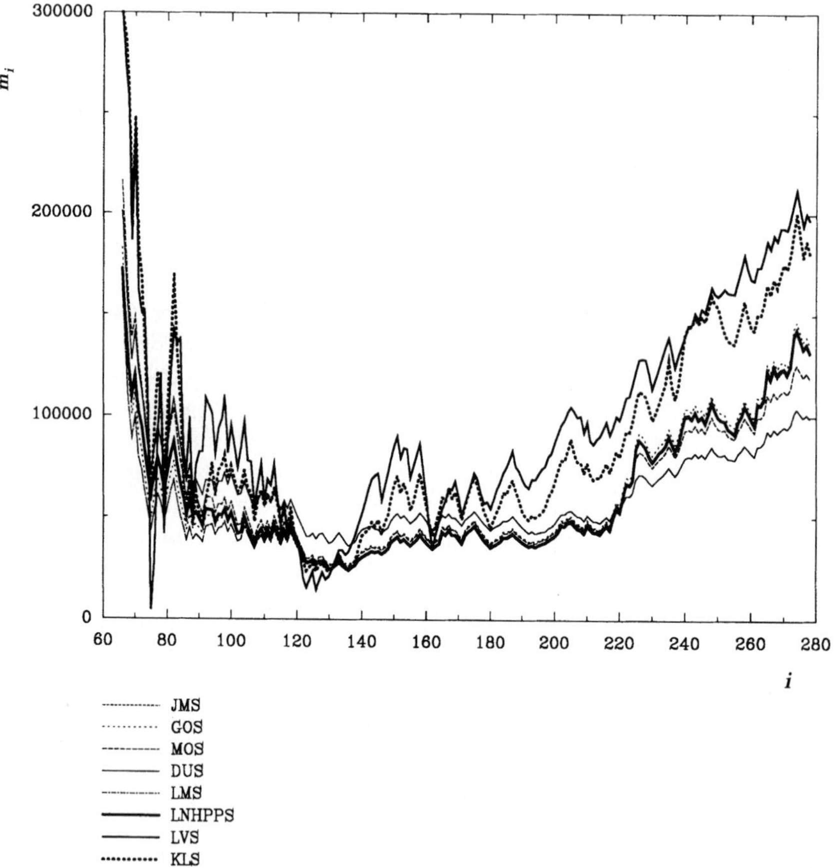

Figure 4.15 Successive median predictions from eight recalibrated models, of the time to next failure, T_i, $i = 66, \ldots, 278$, for data set SS3. Notice how much closer in agreement these recalibrated predictions are when compared with the corresponding raw predictions in Fig. 4.3.

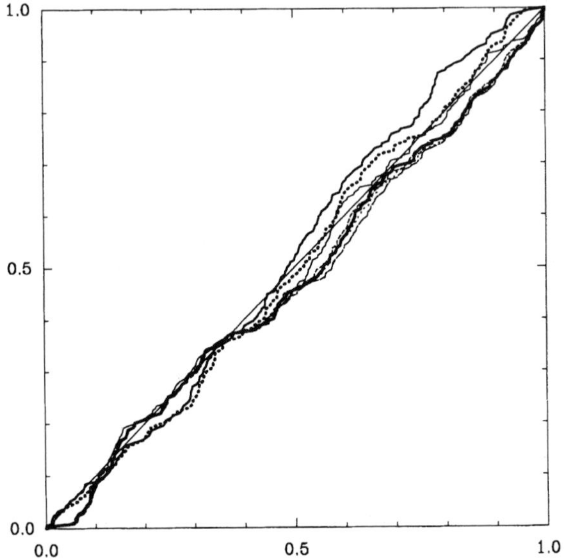

JMS 0.084 (5%–10%)
GOS 0.073 (10%–20%)
MOS 0.063 (insignificant at 20% level)
DUS 0.056 (insignificant at 20% level)
LMS 0.085 (5%–10%)
LNHPPS 0.068 (insignificant at 20% level)
LVS 0.087 (5%–10%)
KLS 0.064 (insignificant at 20% level)

Figure 4.16 u-plots and KS distances and significance levels for predictions of T_i, $i = 66, \ldots, 278$, from eight recalibrated models for data set SS3. These plots are now much closer to the line of unit slope than where the u-plots for the corresponding raw predictions (see Fig. 4.10), and the departure is now statistically insignificant, indicating that recalibration has removed bias in the raw predictions.

sequence of predictions, it is not really necessary to know beforehand whether suitable conditions for recalibration exist—we can merely check after the event to see whether there has been an overall improvement.

Recalibration looks like a powerful general technique for improving on the predictive accuracy of any* software reliability growth model. Indeed, it may have applications in other areas of forecasting.

* In this chapter, recalibration is applied only to continuous-time models, but it should be noted that it is also possible to apply recalibration to discrete-time models [Wrig88; Wrig93], where the observations and predictions to be made relate to the number of failures observed in the next period of time.

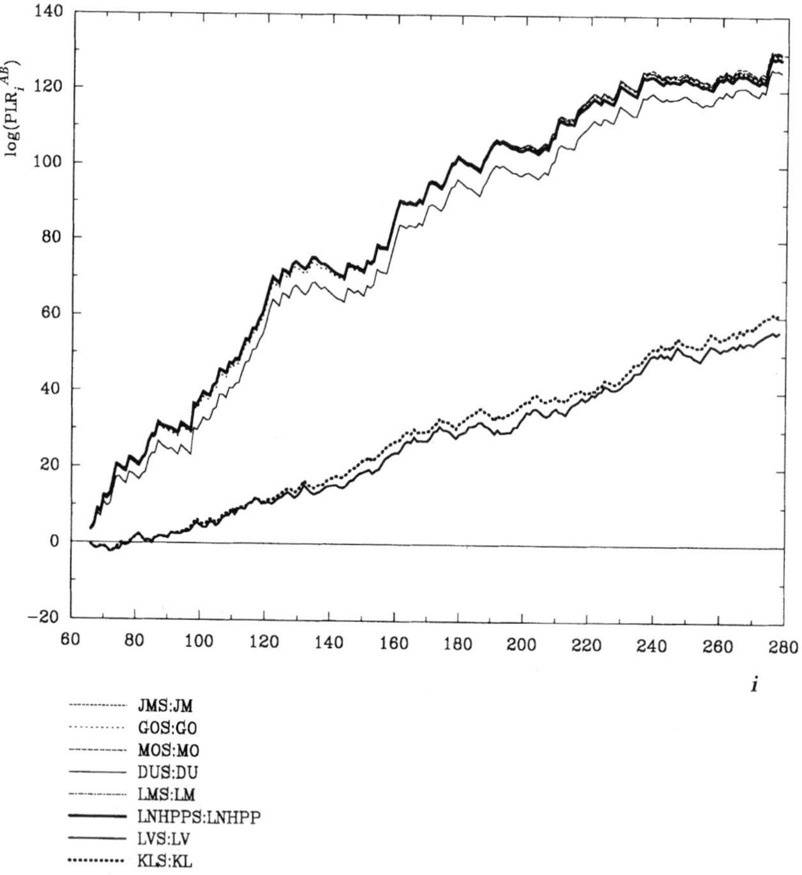

Figure 4.17 Log(PLR) plots for the recalibrated predictions versus the corresponding raw predictions of T_i, $i = 66, \ldots, 278$, for data set SS3. These plots indicate that the recalibrated predictions are much more accurate than the raw predictions; the least improvement is shown for LV and KL, but from Fig. 4.7 it can be seen that these models were initially better than the others and so there was less room for improvement.

4.5 A Worked Example

We have seen in previous sections of this chapter how the different techniques for analyzing predictive accuracy and for recalibrating predictions work on some data sets, SYS1 and SS3. We now present another worked example in which the techniques are used in the way in which we recommend they be used in practice.

Our new data set, CSR1, was collected from a single-user workstation at the Centre for Software Reliability (CSR), and represents some 397 user-perceived events: genuine software failures, together with events arising, for example, from usability problems and inadequate documentation. Figure 4.18 shows the data, and Fig. 4.19 shows a succession of median predictions from the same eight models used previously. There are two striking things to note here: first, there is little evidence of reliability growth until about halfway through the data set; and second, there is again quite marked disagreement between the different models when this growth does start. The u-plot of Fig. 4.20 shows that all models are performing very badly, since all the KS distances are highly significant. More to the point, there are great differences in the *nature* of the prediction errors being made. Thus JM, GO, LM, and LNHPP are too optimistic (the plot is almost everywhere above the line of unit slope) while LV and KL are pessimistic (the plot is below the line of unit slope). MO and DU, on the other hand, have a pronounced S-shaped u-plot, intersecting the line of unit slope at about (0.5,0.5). This indicates that their *medians* are quite accurate, but that estimates of other points on the distribution of time to next failure will be inaccurate: estimates of probabilities of *small* times to failure will be too optimistic, those of *large* times will be too pessimistic.

The PLR analysis in Fig. 4.21 shows that KL is performing best overall, with LV second. The relatively poor performance of the other mod-

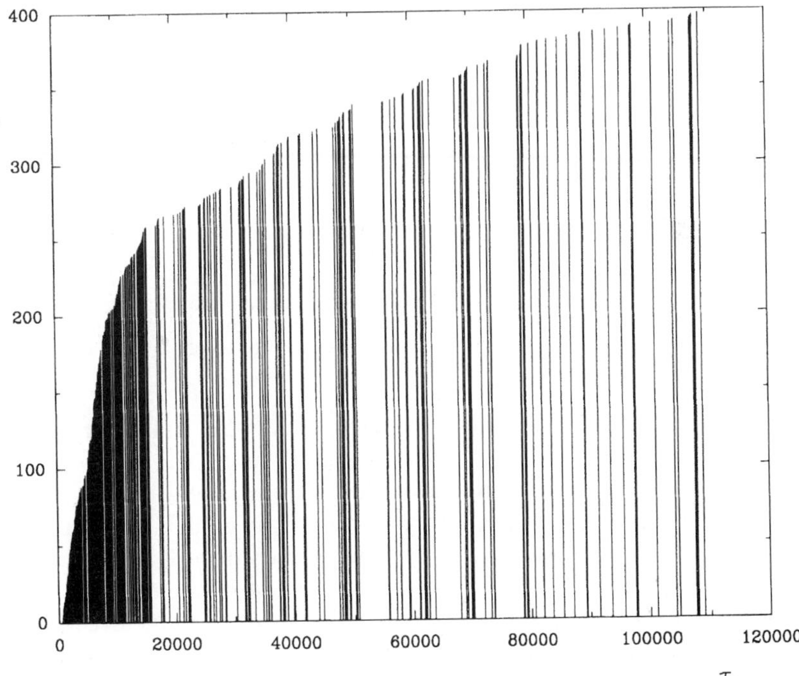

Figure 4.18 Data set CSR1 shown as the cumulative number of failures, i, versus the total elapsed hands-on time measured in minutes, $\tau_i = \sum_{j=1}^{j=i} t_j$, $i = 1, \ldots, 397$. This data, collected from a single-user workstation at CSR, represents some 397 user-perceived failure events.

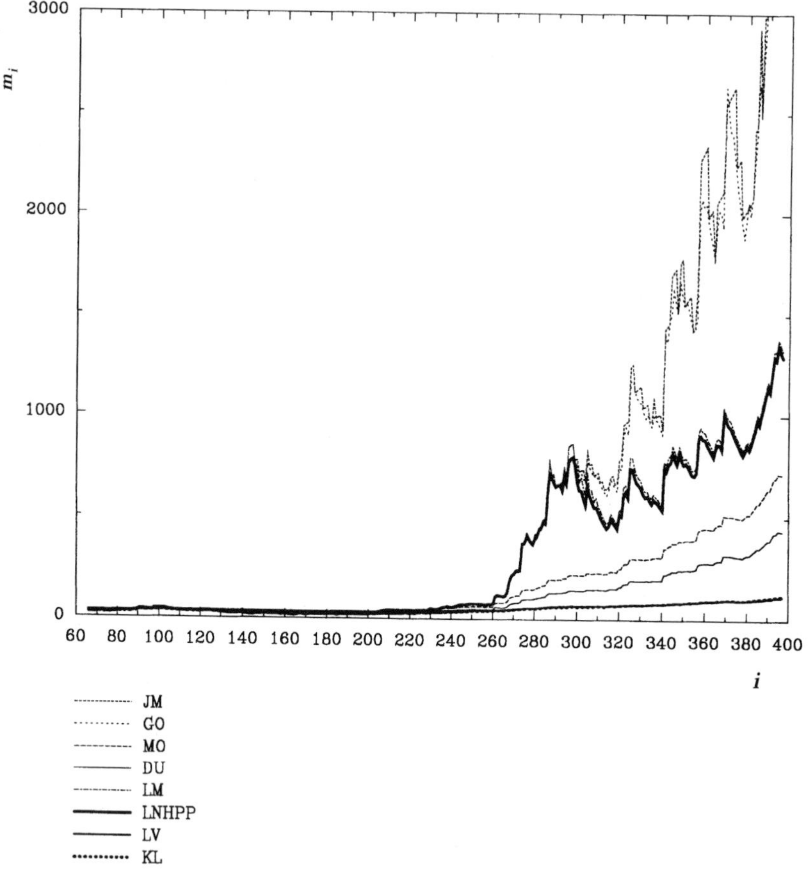

Figure 4.19 Successive median predictions from eight raw models, of T_i, plotted against i for $i = 66, \ldots, 397$ for data set CSR1. Notice how these median predictions are in close agreement in the first half of the data set where there is little evidence of reliability growth, but that they diverge, and increase, in the second half.

els is partly due to bias, as shown by the u-plots, and in some cases by their being too noisy (see the great fluctuations in the medians, for example, in Fig. 4.19). Once again, none of the raw predictions can be trusted according to the u-plot analysis, and these models are thus candidates for recalibration. Figure 4.22 shows the effect of this upon the median predictions: there has been some change in the medians from those obtained from the raw models, and it is in the right direction in view of the original u-plot indications of pessimism or optimism. The u-plot of the recalibrated predictions (Fig. 4.23) confirms that there has indeed been an improvement in comparison with Fig. 4.20. However, only KLS has a plot that does not significantly differ from the line of unit slope (although MOS, DUS, LNHPPS, and LVS are only just sig-

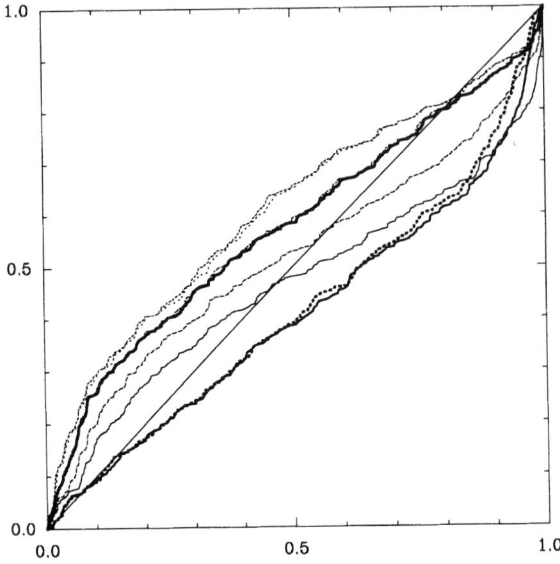

....	JM	0.206 (significant at 1% level)
....	GO	0.200 (significant at 1% level)
------------	MO	0.129 (significant at 1% level)
———	DU	0.197 (significant at 1% level)
-·-·-·-·-	LM	0.174 (significant at 1% level)
———	LNHPP	0.172 (significant at 1% level)
———	LV	0.213 (significant at 1% level)
....	KL	0.196 (significant at 1% level)

Figure 4.20 u-plots and KS distances and significance levels for predictions of T_i, $i = 66, \ldots, 397$ from eight raw models for data set CSR1. These plots indicate that all these predictions are significantly inaccurate for this data set, with some (e.g., JM and GO) being grossly optimistic and some (e.g., LV and KL) being grossly pessimistic, while others (e.g., MO) have more complicated departures of prediction from the truth than simple optimism or pessimism.

nificant at the 5 percent level). Notice that, in the case of MOS and DUS, while the u-plots have improved a great deal, there is little change in the medians (Fig. 4.19 and 4.22). This is expected, since the raw medians are quite accurate; however, other points on the raw predictive distributions are not accurate, and these will have been improved by the recalibration. Figure 4.24 shows a steady increase in all PLR plots and confirms that, in all cases, the recalibrated predictions are superior to the raw ones. The greatest improvement arising from recalibration is in DU, but this is largely because this model was so bad originally (see Fig. 4.21).

Figure 4.25 shows that after recalibration the best predictions are coming from DUS, with KLS and LVS next best. Thus in this case a user who wished to make further predictions on this data set would be advised to use the recalibrated DU model, bearing in mind, though, that this predictive analysis should be repeated at future stages in case there should be a reversal in fortunes between the various raw and recalibrated predictions from the different models. It is notable that here the recalibration has turned the *worst-performing* model, DU, into the *best,* DUS.

In the analysis of this data set we have deliberately taken no account of the fact that there seems to be little evidence of reliability

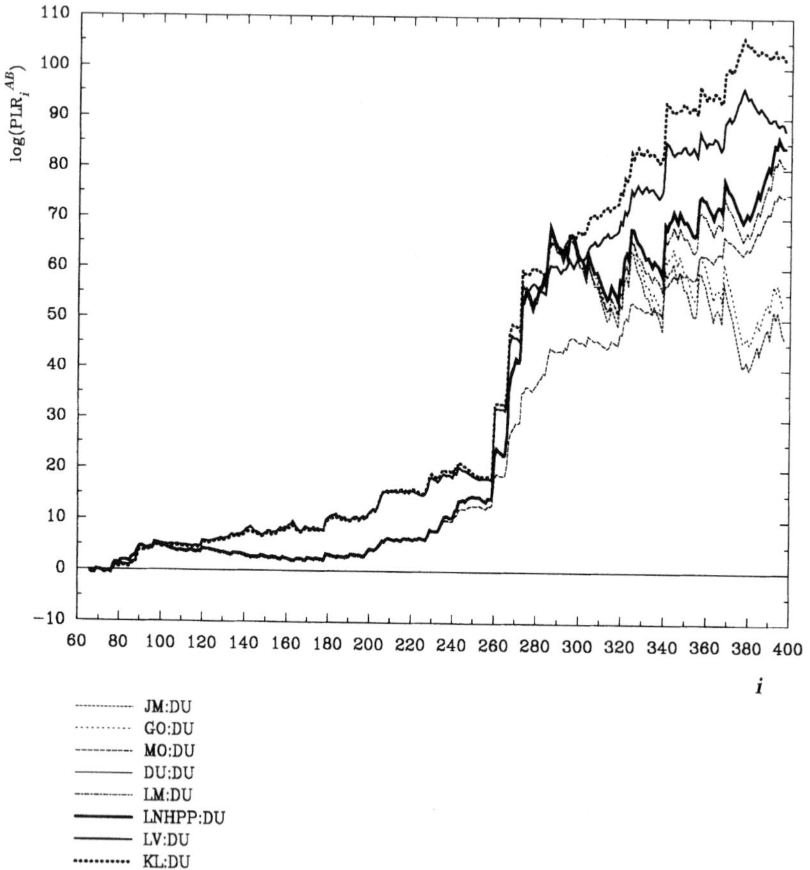

Figure 4.21 Log(PLR) plots for predictions of T_i, $i = 66, \ldots, 397$, from eight raw models comparing against DU for data set CSR1. This suggests that there are big differences in accuracy between these eight models and that LV and KL are generally giving the best predictions, and DU is generally giving the worst.

growth until quite late—rather, we have blindly applied the models and the recalibration procedure as would a naive user. Clearly, it would be a trivial matter to carry out some simple preprocessing of the data to detect the early stationarity (for example, applying simple tests for trend). In the event that there is no growth indicated in the early part on the data, it would be sensible to exclude this data and apply the growth models only to the *later* stages where growth *is* present.

For a similar analysis considering only failures that are *known* to be due to software faults in CSR1 data set, see Prob. 4.7.

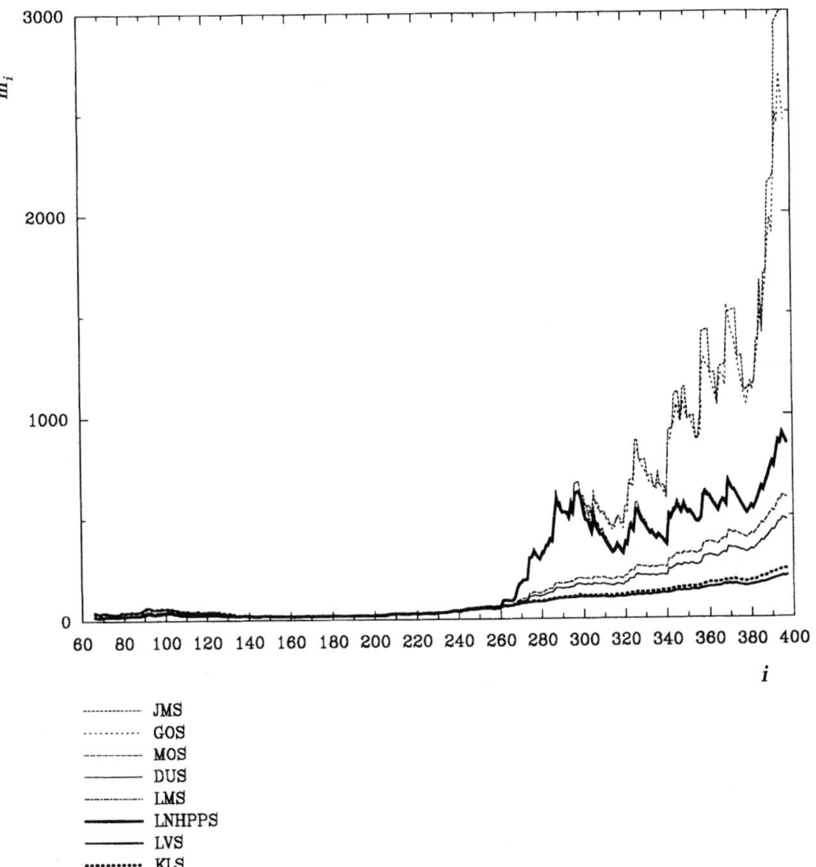

Figure 4.22 Successive median predictions from eight recalibrated models of T_i, plotted against i for $i = 66, \ldots, 397$ for data set CSR1. Comparing with the raw medians in Fig. 4.19, it can be seen that these are in closer agreement than before, but that they still diverge in the second half of the data set.

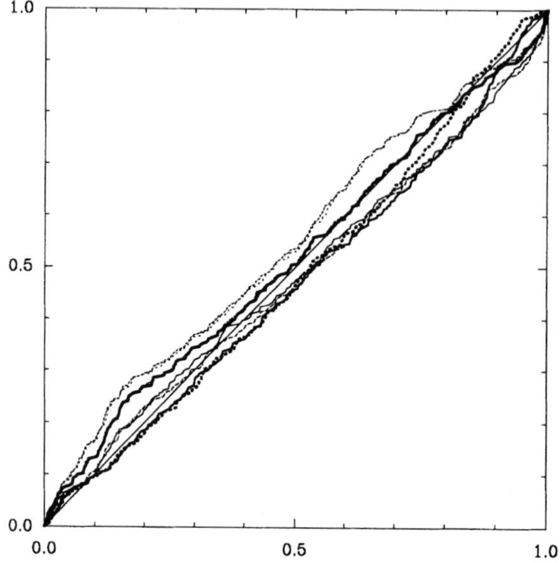

JMS	0.110 (significant at 1% level)
GOS	0.107 (significant at 1% level)
MOS	0.078 (2%–5%)
DUS	0.075 (2%–5%)
LMS	0.083 (1%–2%)
LNHPPS	0.081 (2%–5%)
LVS	0.080 (2%–5%)
KLS	0.055 (insignificant at 20% level)

Figure 4.23 u-plots and KS distances and significance levels for predictions of T_i, $i = 66, \ldots, 397$ from eight recalibrated models for data set CSR1. Notice how these have improved when compared with the raw u-plots in Fig. 4.20, indicating that the bias in the raw predictions has been reduced by recalibration.

4.6 Discussion

4.6.1 Summary of the *good* news: where we are now

In this chapter we hope we have convinced you of two things.

First, there are serious problems that need to be addressed concerning the accuracy of reliability growth models. There is no universally acceptable model that can be trusted to give accurate results in all circumstances; users should not trust claims to the contrary. Worse, we cannot identify a priori for a particular data source the model or models, if any, that will give accurate results; we simply do not understand which factors influence model accuracy.

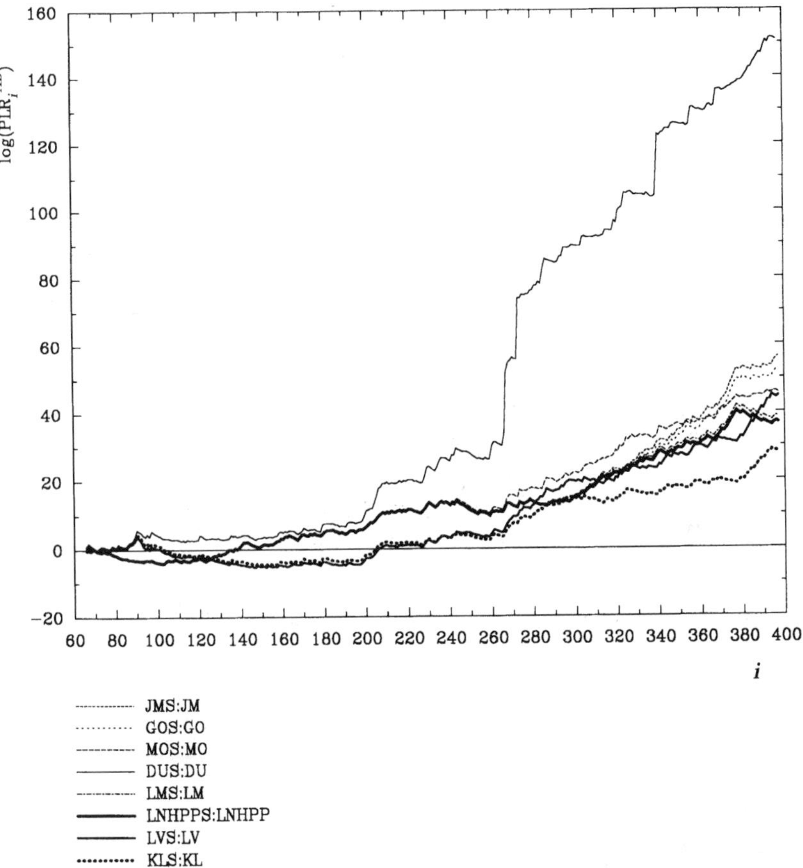

Figure 4.24 Log(PLR) plots for the recalibrated predictions versus the corresponding raw predictions of T_i, $i = 66, \ldots, 397$ for data set CSR1. These plots indicate that the recalibrated predictions are more accurate than the raw; the most dramatic improvement is shown for DU, but from Fig. 4.21 it can be seen that this model was most in need of improvement in the first place.

Second, and more hopefully, there are techniques which can rescue us from this apparent impasse; they allow the accuracy of the actual predictions being obtained on a particular data source to be analyzed. One of these techniques for analyzing the accuracy of predictions also brings with it a bonus: it is possible to use it to assess the errors in past predictions made by any raw model and hence to recalibrate future raw predictions in order to eliminate such errors. With this new approach to software reliability prediction, we believe that users will normally be able to obtain reliability measures and predictions in which they can have confidence, and that this confidence will be justified. In those situations where it is not possible to obtain accurate results from any of the models, even with recalibration, users will get a warning that this is the case.

It must be admitted that the ways of examining the accuracy of predictions that we have described are nontrivial, and users may find them at first quite unfamiliar. This is not surprising, since traditional statistical methods have tended to neglect the problem of prediction in favor of estimation. It is only recently that techniques such as PLR analysis have become available. However, the *use* of the techniques is really quite straightforward, normally involving nothing more than the simple graphical analysis we have seen in the examples. Further, these new measures are implemented in some of the current software reliability tools (SRMP, SMERFS, and CASRE) which are discussed in App. A.

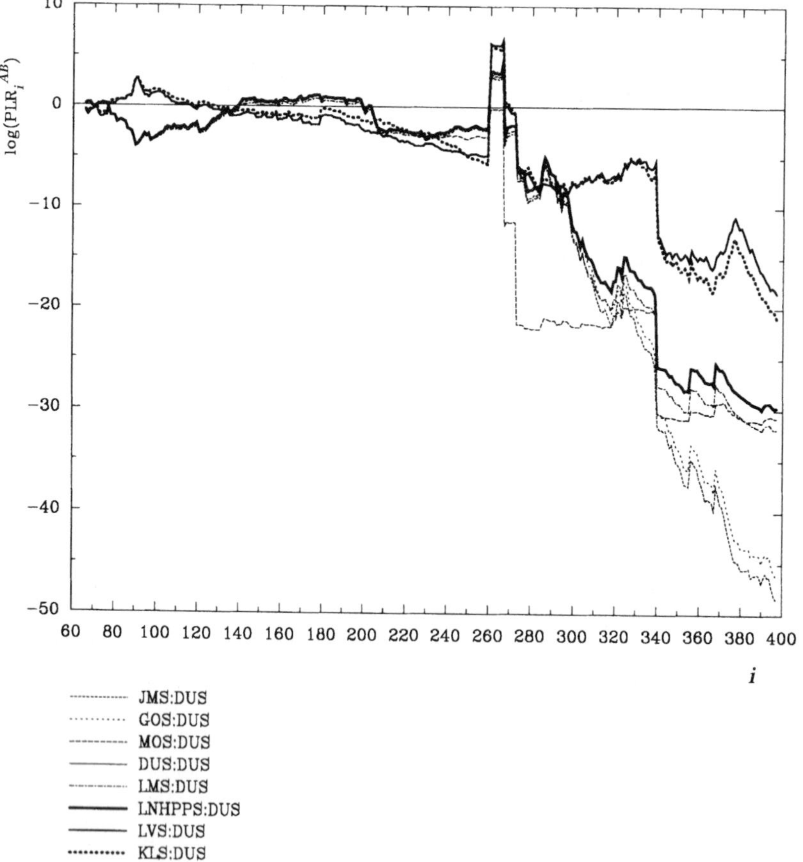

Figure 4.25 Log(PLR) plots for predictions of T_i, $i = 66, \ldots, 397$ from eight recalibrated models comparing against DUS for data set CSR1. This suggests that the best recalibrated predictions are coming from DUS, which we know from Fig. 4.21 was the worst before recalibration, with KLS and LVS next best.

4.6.2 Limitations of present techniques

One major limitation of the techniques for prediction evaluation and recalibration described in this chapter relates to the earlier discussion in Sec. 4.2.2 on long-term predictions. It was noted that prediction errors are likely to be different depending on the nature of the predictions being made and, in particular, that the nature of the error in one-step-ahead predictions is likely to be different than for longer-term predictions, for example, as we have seen, 20 steps ahead. For simplicity, the techniques described here have concentrated upon one-step-ahead predictions only. There are clearly practical restrictions when we try to extend these techniques to predictions further than one step ahead. Theoretically, an extension to n-steps-ahead predictions is fairly obvious; we could make many such predictions, and then evaluate their accuracy by comparison with the corresponding observations when they are finally later observed. The practical limitation of course lies with the value of n. The larger the value of n, the less likely it is that we will ever have enough data to make many such observations and thus to conduct such an analysis of accuracy, or to recalibrate such predictions. This problem becomes even worse when we consider predictions such as estimating how long it will take to achieve a target reliability.

Although these problems due to sparseness of data apply to a greater extent to the topics of evaluation and recalibration discussed in this chapter, they also apply to software reliability modeling in general. A major limitation of the whole software reliability growth approach is that it is really only practicable for those situations in which rather modest reliability levels are involved. If we require ultrahigh reliability, and need to evaluate a particular system in order to have confidence that such a target reliability has in fact been achieved, these techniques will not be sufficient. The problem, of course, lies not in a deficiency in the reliability growth approach itself, but in the fact that the amounts of data needed are prohibitively large. It has been shown in [Litt93] that the length of time needed for a reliability growth model to acquire the evidence that a particular target mean time to failure has been achieved will be *many times* that target. Worse, this multiplier tends to become larger for a higher target reliability—there is a law of diminishing returns operating in software reliability growth. This kind of result seems to occur whatever model we use and whatever the nature of the reliability measure adopted, and effectively precludes these kinds of techniques from providing evidence that a system has achieved ultrahigh reliability.

Another serious restriction to the usefulness of all these techniques lies in their need for the inputs to be selected in the same way during the collection of data as it will be in the period to which the predictions relate. Thus, if we wish to predict the reliability of a program in its operational environment, we need to base our predictions upon failure data collected when the software was operating in such an environment (or good simulated approximation of it). In this sense, the models (and recalibration) work by a sophisticated form of extrapolation, and we can expect the results to be accurate only if past and future are similar. For some applications, constructing a test environment that is a realistic replica of an operational one is not too difficult, but it must be admitted that sometimes this is a difficult task. On the other hand it could be said that some reasonable approximation to the intended operational profile should be considered to be part of the specified requirements for a system, rather than this just being limited to the functional requirements. There is a sense in which it could be said that not knowing the expected operational profile is like not having completely specified the requirements of the real-world problem to which the software is intended to be the solution.

Furthermore, the notion of a *single* operational environment can be too restrictive. Some programs go out into the world and are used in different ways by many users. These users will then often experience different reliabilities for the same program. Of course, we could construct many different test environments to try to reproduce the different types of operational use, but this would be expensive. Ideally, we would like to be able to take the failure data from a (nonrepresentative) test environment and use this together with information about the operational environment to predict operational reliability. Chapter 5 discusses operational profile techniques in detail.

4.6.3 Possible avenues for improvement of methods

It has been our experience from using the techniques for evaluating predictive accuracy and recalibration that with the many current models it is usually possible to obtain trustworthy results from one of them—either before or after recalibration. It has also been our experience that having more sophisticated models does not necessarily lead to predictions (either before or after recalibration) which are more robust or applicable over a wider range of data sets than those with simpler assumptions. Unless there are pressing reasons to the contrary, we believe that research would be better conducted in areas other than model building.

Having said that, some of the present models and the analysis techniques could benefit from further work. For example, it is hard to predict far into the future with some models, and exact results are not available. Similarly, as discussed in the previous section, there has not been much work on the analysis of the accuracy of such predictions. Depending upon their precise nature, such predictions may require us to develop more advanced versions of the analysis techniques described here.

In addition to this there are other possible ways in which these methods for improving raw predictions can themselves be improved. For example, as we observed earlier with the CSR1 data in Sec. 4.5, there are some data sets for which, even though recalibration gives dramatic improvement over the raw predictions, there is still room for further improvement. In these cases it is apparent that the recalibrated predictions are still biased because there is nonstationarity in the raw prediction errors. There are several possible methods which could be investigated in such cases. We could apply the recalibration method again to those recalibrated prediction sequences which are still biased. Alternatively, in the presence of nonstationary raw prediction errors it is reasonable to assume that the most recent prediction errors reflect more accurately the current prediction error than those further into the past; it would thus seem sensible to use only these most recent predictions in recalibrating the current prediction. This, in turn, naturally leads us to the possibility of investigating methods which formally test for changes in the prediction errors so that we can decide which of the past raw predictions to use in recalibrating the current prediction. Investigations so far indicate that applying recalibration using only very recent predictions tends to eliminate bias successfully (i.e., good u-plots result) but sometimes this decrease in bias is outweighed by an increase in noise in the resulting recalibrated predictions, and so there is a trade-off to be made here. An alternative to the search for an optimum window of predictions in such cases (i.e., a window which results in bias reduction that is not outweighed by increased noise) might be to investigate the possibility of direct methods for the elimination of noise—i.e., smoothing techniques.

A related subject is the investigation of other techniques for improving raw reliability predictions, such as the combining techniques which are considered in Chap. 7. Here any group of predictors (raw or recalibrated) may be combined to form a new predictor. Like recalibration, the new predictors generated from these combination techniques are genuinely predictive (being based only on past data) and so the analysis techniques discussed in this chapter can be used to assess the benefit gained from combination. Various combination techniques have been investigated and the most promising seem to be those where the combination depends on past predictive performance of the initial predictors; for example, where the combined predictor is a combination with more weight given to those initial predictors which have performed the best in the (recent) past. Investigation so far indicates that the main benefit of these combination techniques is that they result in a new predictor comparable with the best of the initial predictors. The main advantage of these techniques is that the result is *automatic* selection of a best predictor for a particular data set. This is important, since one major criticism of reliability modeling is that the user of such techniques needs to be reasonably expert. There is much further work to be done in this area: for example, trying more sophisticated combination methods, testing for appropriate past intervals of predictions on which to base combination at each prediction stage, and so on.

The problem outlined in the previous section of predicting the reliability of a program in a different operational environment from the one in which the failure data has been collected is an important one that might benefit from research. There has been some work on this problem [Cheu80, Litt79b], based on a structural decomposition of the software, where the operational profile of a program is characterized by the Markovian exchanges of control between its modules. The idea here is that the reliability estimation for the modules could be performed once and for all in a testing environment, using the reliability growth models, and then the reliability of the overall program could be predicted for any new operational environment merely by estimating the parameters of the Markov process for the new environment. This latter task should be much easier than the reliability estimation. There seems to be no experience of using these ideas, however, and it might be questioned whether some of the modeling assumptions are realistic.

A criticism that is often made of the reliability growth models is that they give their answers far too late—what is needed, it is stated, is a means of estimating and predicting the reliability of a system at a much earlier stage in its development so that corrective action can be made if necessary. We are skeptical about being able to make genuine predictions of final system reliability at an early stage, but it may be possible to identify attributes of the early development process that will indicate potential future problems.

A more promising approach might be to try to identify some attributes of process and product that can be used *with* the later failure data in order to obtain more accurate models. There has been considerable interest in the statistical literature over recent years in stochastic models with such explanatory variables; the problem in this case seems to be that of identifying variables with genuine explanatory power.

4.6.4 Best advice to potential users

The first and most important advice we would give if you are setting out to measure and predict software reliability is: be skeptical. There is no model that can be relied upon to be accurate under all circumstances (although there do seem to be some models that are inaccurate on most data sources). Nor can we identify a priori those circumstances where a particular model *is* appropriate and *will* give accurate results.

In the face of these difficulties, we believe that there is no alternative but to adopt the eclectic approach that we have described here. Many models should be used simultaneously, and their output compared with the actual failure times using the techniques we have described. The result in most cases will be that reliability predictions will be identified that are trustworthy with respect to certain important types of possible error, and this trustworthiness will be *demonstrated.* The latter point is particularly important—with our approach there is no need to appeal to dubious arguments such as model plausibility, or past good performance on other data sets.

Finally, we have a bonus in our recalibration technique, which seems to work in a high proportion of cases, giving results that are better than those of the corresponding raw models. Experience of applying this recalibration technique has shown that it often gives dramatic improvement over the raw predictions, and only in rare circumstances will marginally worse predictions result.* Once again, as a user you do not need to, and should not, *trust* our claims for the efficacy of this technique—rather you should treat it as another source of competing predictions that need to be analyzed for accuracy on your data, using the methods we have described, just as with any other predictions.

Although the techniques we have described depend upon rather novel and subtle statistical methods, we think that their actual use and interpretation from the graphical presentations are comparatively straightforward. This is aided by the use of some of the software reliability tools which are discussed in App. A. Our advice if you are contemplating measuring and predicting software reliability is to go ahead and try our approach. Most times you will get results you can trust. In those rare cases where none of the raw or recalibrated models work, our techniques will give you a warning.

4.7 Summary

The techniques we have described here are important because they largely resolve a basic dilemma of software reliability modeling: a user is now faced with a plethora of models, but no one of them can be rec-

* This sometimes occurs when the raw model predictions are already unbiased and so there is no room for further improvement. In such circumstances the recalibrated and raw predictions are approximately the same, although recalibration may add some noise to the predictions.

ommended for universal use. Indeed it is our belief that the relatively poor take-up of software reliability modeling techniques has been a result of certain models being sold as universal panaceas. Users rightly adopt an attitude of "once bitten, twice shy" when they see these models occasionally giving ludicrous results.

We think that the techniques we have developed provide a means to overcome these difficulties and that it is now possible to measure and predict software reliability for the relatively modest levels that are needed in the vast majority of applications. Most important, the techniques provide a means whereby the user can be *confident* that the results are sufficiently accurate for the particular program under examination. There is thus no need to subscribe to dubious claims about the inherent plausibility of a particular model in order to have some assurance that the reliability figures can be trusted.

One of the analysis techniques described in this chapter also brings with it a bonus: it allows us to assess the nature of the inaccuracy of past predictions and to recalibrate future predictions in order to improve predictive accuracy. The examples we chose for this chapter are ones in which the raw models perform rather badly. We did this deliberately to show the power of the recalibration technique, but it is often the case that some individual raw models will perform reasonably well even before recalibration. From a user's point of view, however, this is immaterial. The recalibration procedure is easy to use and is genuinely predictive, so it should be applied as a matter of course; then it is easy to use the analytical methods to find which of the many different (raw and recalibrated) versions is performing best for the data of interest.

Problems

4.1 *a.* Give two reasons why techniques for analyzing the results of applying software reliability models are needed for use with each new data set to which they are applied.

b. State the main objective of practical interest of these techniques.

c. Briefly describe the general approach to predicting reliability that we are advocating in this chapter.

4.2 Explain what is meant when we say that a sequence of reliability predictions is

a. Optimistic

b. Pessimistic

c. Consistently biased

d. Noisy (compared with the truth)

4.3 Discuss all the relative advantages and disadvantages of the following techniques for analyzing predictive accuracy:

a. The variability as defined in Sec. 4.3.1.
b. Techniques which compare sequences of point predictions of the time between failures T_j with the (later observed) time between failures t_j.
c. Prequential likelihood ratio
d. The u-plot
e. The y-plot

4.4 Consider the following two prediction systems. Assume that the time to next failure, T_j, is exponentially distributed with failure rate

$$\hat{\lambda}_j = \frac{n}{\sum_{r=j-n}^{j-1} t_r}$$

and that for prediction sequence A, $n = 1$, and prediction sequence B, $n = 20$.

In the presence of data for which each time between failures is exponentially distributed and which exhibits reliability growth, discuss what you think the nature of the errors would be in the two prediction sequences suggested here. Describe how these errors are likely to be shown in the u- and y-plots and the prequential likelihood ratio.

4.5 Briefly describe the recalibration technique. Under what circumstances would you expect this technique to *eliminate* inaccuracies in a sequence of raw model predictions?

4.6 Briefly discuss some limitations of the techniques for analyzing accuracy and the recalibration technique, as described in this chapter.

4.7 Data set CSR2 is a subset of CSR1 where only failures that are known to be due to software faults are considered. Perform an analysis on CSR2 similar to the one applied to CSR1 in Sec. 4.5.

4.8 Data set CSR3 is another subset of the data previously analyzed in this chapter (CSR1), but this time failures related only to Pascal programming are included. Tables 4.5, 4.6, and 4.7 (in the Data Disk) show raw and recalibrated one-step-ahead predictions of T_i, $i = 66, \ldots, 104$ that result from applying three models, JM, DU, and KL.

a. Draw plots of the *raw* median predictions against the prediction stage i for these three models. Discuss these plots.
b. Draw the u-plots, and calculate the *KS* distances, for the three *raw* prediction sequences. From Table 4.8, in the Data Disk, say which of these plots is significantly far from the line of unit slope according to these *KS* distances. Based on these u-plots *only,* state which model is giving the most accurate *raw* predictions and which is giving the least accurate predictions. Comment on what the shape of the u-plots for the models which are giving inaccurate predictions tells us about the *nature* of the *raw* prediction errors in each case.

c. Choosing the raw DU model as the reference against which to compare, draw the log(PLR) plot, as shown in the previous examples for these raw prediction sequences (i.e., JM versus DU and KL versus DU). According to this PLR analysis, which raw model is the most accurate, and which is the least accurate? Does this analysis confirm the previous u-plot analysis?

4.9 For the data set CSR3 and the predictions in Tables 4.5, 4.6 and 4.7:

a. Draw the median plot (again against i) for the three sequences of *recalibrated* predictions. Comment on these plots in comparison with the equivalent raw median plots.

b. Draw the u-plots, and calculate the *KS* distances, for the three *recalibrated* prediction sequences. As before, from Table 4.8, say which of these plots is significantly far from the line of unit slope according to these *KS* distances. Comment on these plots in comparison with the equivalent raw u-plots. Discuss whether recalibration has effectively eliminated bias initially present in the raw prediction sequences.

c. Choosing the DUS model as the reference against which to compare, draw the log(PLR) plot as shown in the previous examples for these recalibrated prediction sequences (i.e., JMS versus DUS and KLS versus DUS). According to this PLR analysis, which recalibrated prediction sequence is the most accurate, and which is the least accurate? What does a comparison of this PLR analysis with the equivalent PLR analysis for the raw models suggest?

d. Draw log(PLR) plots for the recalibrated versus the raw prediction sequences (i.e., JMS versus JM, DUS versus DU, and KLS versus KL). Discuss whether these plots show that recalibration has made the predictions more accurate. According to these plots, which model shows the most improvement via recalibration, and which shows the least?

4.10 According to the analyses and plots in Probs. 8 and 9, which of the six predictions shown in Tables 4.5, 4.6, and 4.7 would you choose to use for the next one-step-ahead prediction (i.e., of T_{105} for the data set in CSR3)? Discuss why.

Chapter

5

The Operational Profile

John Musa, Gene Fuoco, Nancy Irving, Diane Kropfl
AT&T Bell Laboratories

Bruce Juhlin
U.S. West

5.1 Introduction

A software-based product's reliability depends on just how a customer will use it [Musa87]. Making a good reliability estimate depends on testing the product as if it were in the field. The operational profile, which is a quantitative characterization of how a system will be used, is thus essential in software reliability engineering (SRE). Operational profile theory can be applied to hardware as well as software, and even to human components. Thus it is applicable to complete systems. The operational profile shows you how to increase productivity and reliability and speed development by allocating development and test resources to functions on the basis of use. It helps you plan test activities, generate test cases, and select test runs.

Using an operational profile to guide system testing ensures that if testing is terminated and the software is shipped because of imperative schedule constraints, the most-used operations will have received the most testing, and the reliability level will be the maximum that is practically achievable for the given test time. In guiding regression testing, it tends to find, among the faults introduced by changes, the ones that have the most effect on reliability.

An example of the benefits from developing and applying the operational profile is shown by AT&T's International Definity® project (a PBX switching system). This project combined the operational profile with other quality-improvement techniques to reduce customer-reported problems and maintenance costs by a factor of 10, system-test interval by a factor of 2, and product-introduction interval by 30 percent [Abra92]. The system experienced no serious service outages in the first two years of deployment; customer satisfaction improved significantly. The marked quality improvement and a strong sales effort resulted in an increase in sales by a factor of 10.

In a similar quality-improvement program, Hewlett-Packard applied software reliability engineering and the operational profile to reorganize their system-test process for a multiprocessor operating system. With automated test and failure recording and using the operational profile to guide testing, they reduced system-test time and cost by at least 50 percent.

The cost of developing an operational profile varies. Our experience indicates that the effort to construct the operational profile for an average project—about 10 developers, 100,000 source lines, and a development interval of 18 months—is about one staff month. Large projects can cost more, but the increase is clearly less than linear with project size. International Definity invested two to three staff years in extensive customer study that led to an operational profile. Of course, every project requires good knowledge of the customer base, so only a portion of this effort can reasonably be charged to the operational profile. Also, the work can be written off over several releases, with only minor updating needed between them.

Experience to date indicates that operational profiles are beneficial even when very simple and approximate. For example, one project used an operational profile defined on only five operations. However, defining operational profiles in the range of 50 to 200 operations has usually been definitely worth the extra effort.

5.2 Concepts

A *profile* is simply a set of disjoint (only one can occur at a time) alternatives called *elements,* each with the probability that it will occur. If *A* occurs 60 percent of the time and *B* 40 percent, for example, the profile is *A,* 0.6 and *B,* 0.4.

In order to select and define the terms we will use in analyzing a work process and developing the operational profile for the system that will implement the activities of the work process, we must recognize two practical needs.

The first is the need to distinguish between the view of the system taken in specifying its requirements and the view of the system as it is built. We will use terms containing the word *function* at the requirements stage and terms containing the word *operation* when dealing with the system as it is being built.

The second need arises from the situation that is common to most work processes. There is a need to talk about tasks that represent the smallest divisions of work that can be initiated by external intervention, either human or by a system external to the one being analyzed. Although work can always be divided into smaller packages, there is no useful purpose and only greater cost and reliability risk involved in allowing initiation access to these packages if the same sequence of work packages will always be followed. We will call these smallest initiable divisions *runs*. In a switching system, a run might be a telephone call. In interactive systems, it might be a command input by a user. In transaction-based systems, it might be a transaction. In an aircraft-control system it might be a maneuver.

Runs are associated with input states. The *input state* is the complete set of input variables of the system, an *input variable* being any data elements that exist external to the system and influence it. For example, externally initiated interrupts, such as interrupts generated by the system clock, by operator actions, and by other components of the system outside the program, are input variables. Intermediate data computed by the program during a run and not existing external to the program are not input variables. Hence, interrupts generated directly by a run or interrupts that are determined from other input variables (for example, overflow and underflow) are not input variables.

Input variables don't just include the parameters that are explicitly transmitted. For example, data elements that affect a system may be unknown to the designers; nevertheless, they are input variables. The concept of an input variable is logical, not physical. For example, a physical memory location can be time-shared by different input variables.

Runs that have identical input states are said to belong to the same *run type*. Airline-reservation transactions that are exact duplicates have the same run type. However, reservations made for different people, even on the same flight, are different run types. If you test all run types, you have exhaustively tested the system. You do not need to execute repeated runs or instances of the same run type.

A *function* is a set or grouping of run types, as conceived at the requirements stage. An *operation* is a set or grouping of run types for the system as built. One might ask why we should group run types. The main reason is that practical systems usually have astronomical numbers of run types. It is totally impractical to collect usage on run types, unless you do it only for a very small and important subset. We need a much smaller number of elements (generally not more than hundreds) on which we will collect usage data. Functions and operations are defined and used for that purpose. The *functional profile* is a profile of functions; *operational profile,* of operations. A run (and hence function or operation) is a logical rather than physical concept. It can extend over multiple machines (for example, in distributed systems). It can execute in segments of time rather than continuously.

It may be helpful at this point to view some of these concepts graphically. The set of all possible input states for a system is called the *input space,* as shown in Fig. 5.1. Each input state and hence run type is represented by a point in this space. An operation is represented by a domain in the input space. A run type can belong to only one operation. The domains of different operations do not overlap. A function can't be directly represented in the input space because inputs are not defined until design is complete. However, you could look at a function as implying a domain in the input space. Such a domain would not be identical to the domain of an operation unless the function maps directly one-to-one to the operation.

Execution of runs is represented by selection of points from the input space. If you repeat the same run type, you are selecting the same point again.

5.3 Development Procedure

The operational profile is usually developed by some combination of systems engineers, high-level designers, and test planners, with strong participation from product planning, marketing professionals, and customers.

To determine an operational profile, you look at use from a progressively narrowing perspective—from customer down to operation—and, at each step, you generate an intermediate profile by specifying

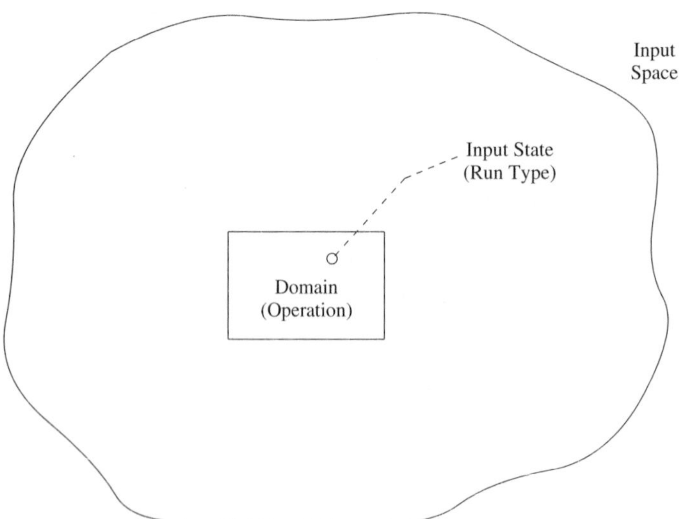

Figure 5.1 Some operational profile concepts.

the probability that each of the elements in that step will be used. This procedure represents the best current approach, based on experience with a variety of projects. We illustrate the procedure by developing, step by step, a simple operational profile for a private branch exchange (PBX). However, the procedure is generally applicable to all kinds of applications, with just minor tuning.

In many cases, usage information is available or can be estimated, most easily in terms of rates like transactions per hour. But these data are not true profiles until you convert them to probabilities by dividing by the total transactions per hour. Converting to probabilities is helpful because you can make a quick completeness check by seeing if the probabilities add to 1. On the other hand, the raw data are useful to recreate actual traffic levels in test.

You will need to establish the granularity (number of elements for which you collect occurrence probabilities) and accuracy (error in estimated occurrence probabilities with respect to those actually experienced in the field) needed for the operational profile. You should base these decisions on the net economic gain resulting from the better decisions that result from more fine-grained and accurate data, minus the extra cost of gathering and analyzing these data being considered. In many cases, however, you will use informed engineering judgment rather than a formal economic analysis. The engineering judgment will be based on such factors as product complexity, product maturity, product cost, and schedules. In practice, you must limit profiles to several hundred (several thousand, at most) elements, because the cost of developing them increases approximately in proportion to the number of elements. Reliability measurements are generally robust with respect to inaccuracies in determining the operational profile [Musa94].

Is use the only factor you should consider in developing operational profiles? What about infrequently executed functions whose failure might lead to disastrous results, such as the function that shuts down an overheating nuclear reactor? This concern can be handled by considering criticality, which we cover in Sec. 5.3.3.

Developing an operational profile to guide testing involves as many as five steps:

- Developing a customer type list
- Developing a user type list
- Listing system modes
- Developing a functional profile
- Converting the functional profile to an operational profile

In the first four steps, you progressively break down system use into more detail. Customer types (large retail stores) break down into user types (sales clerks and information-system specialists). A single user type may invoke several system modes (information-system specialists perform both database cleanup and generate reports). In turn, each system mode has several functions (the generate-reports mode has several types of reports). In the fifth step, functions evolve into operations as the system is implemented.

Some steps may not be necessary in a particular application. A customer list is unnecessary if you have only one customer or if all customers use the system the same way. Sometimes you can skip the functional profile, especially when the requirements are so detailed they specify how users will execute the system to accomplish their tasks. At some other times the information you need to develop the operational profile is not available until the design or even a substantial part of the implementation is complete, so you must develop the functional profile if you want to have guidance in allocating development resources and determining priorities during the design and implementation phases.

Even if you have all the information you need to develop the operational profile before design commences, you may prefer to generate the functional profile first. Because it generally has fewer elements, it is easier to develop and use for guiding pretest development than an operational profile. Should you decide to develop the operational profile directly, you should consider the tasks outlined in the functional-profile step in combination with those in the operational-profile step.

The procedure can conceivably be iterative. If you have an existing system, you may determine the current operational profile, then analyze your current and prospective future customer groups, and then proceed through the steps to obtain a modified operational profile.

At each step, you must determine the level of detail you need. Whether you distinguish and treat an item differently at a given step will depend on the net economic gain for doing so. For example, in developing a customer list broken down by industry, it may be cost-effective to distinguish certain important customers with the intention of performing special testing on the product supplied to them. The degree of detail does not have to be uniform across the system. For example, some important system modes may require greater levels of detail.

When attaining an average reliability over all of a system's applications is acceptable, there may be no need for more than one operational profile. You must still separately identify different customers, users, and system modes so that you can weight the contribution each makes to the operational profile. If it is important to assure a particular reliability for a particular use (even if all reliability objectives are the same), then you must determine multiple operational profiles. You may also need multiple operational profiles if the system will operate with different hardware configurations. Finally, lab and test resource limits may force you to divide testing, using different operational profiles.

Sometimes a software product is part of a network of systems. In that case, it may be useful to develop an operational profile for the entire network before developing the operational profile for the product. This supersystem profile can be very useful to determine which systems in the network are most important and should receive the most attention. It is also possible to decompose a system into subsystems and to develop an operational profile for each.

All profiles that are developed should be baselined and placed under change control, with appropriate traceability requirements.

As far as we now know, the operational profile is independent of design methodology—its determination will not be affected by an object-oriented approach, for example. The one exception might be a case in which functions designed with one methodology map to a considerably different set of operations when designed with another.

5.3.1 Customer type list

A customer is the person, group, or institution that is acquiring the system. A customer type, the key concept here, is a set of customers who will use the system in the same way. Large pharmacies use a switching system very much like other large retailers and thus could be grouped with them, even if they are not in the same market segment. The customer type list is the complete set of customer types.

You obtain information on potential customers from marketing data for related systems, modified by marketing estimates that take into account the new system's appeal. The business case developed for a proposed product usually includes the expected customer base. It is a valuable source for developing operational profiles, analyzing performance, and reviewing requirements.

Example 5.1 As an example, consider a hypothetical PBX that is sold to institutions for internal use and, of course, external connections. Assume there are two customer types, large retail stores and hospitals.

5.3.2 User type list

A system's users are not necessarily identical to its customers. A user is a person, group, or institution that employs, not acquires, the system. A user type is a set of users who will employ the system in the same way. By identifying different user types, you can divide the task of developing the operational profile among different analysts, each an expert on their user type. The user type list is the set of user types. Sometimes the users are customers of your customers; sometimes they are internal to your customer's institution. In any case, different users may employ the system differently. The differences may be the result of job roles—an entry clerk will view an insurance company's claim-processing system differently than an actuary.

You derive the user type list from the customer type list by refinement: looking at each customer type and determining which user types exist. If you find similar user types among different customer types, you should combine them.

Example 5.1 (cont.) In our example, user types in each customer type include telecommunications users (people making calls and sending data), attendants (internal operators who answer the main number), a system administrator (who manages the system and adds, deletes, and relocates users), and maintenance personnel (who test the system periodically and diagnose and correct problems).

Each of these user types employs the system differently.

5.3.3 System mode list

A system mode is a set of functions or operations that you group for convenience in analyzing execution behavior. A system can switch among modes so that only one is in effect at a time, or it can allow several modes to exist simultaneously, sharing the same resources.

For each system mode, you must determine an operational (and perhaps functional) profile. Thus multiple system modes means multiple operational and perhaps functional profiles. The same function or operation can occur in different system modes.

There are no technical limits on how many system modes you can establish. You must simply balance the effort and cost to determine and test their associated operational profiles against the value of more specialized information and organizational convenience they provide.

Some bases for characterizing system modes, with examples, are

- *Relatedness of functions/operations to larger task.* System administration, data entry, customer representative queries, transaction processing, report generation.
- *Significant environmental conditions.* Overload versus normal traffic; initialization (start-up or reboot for failure recovery) versus continuous operation (includes warm start after an interruption); system location; time.
- *Operational architectural structure.* Online retail sales mode versus after-hours billing mode.

- *Criticality.* Shutdown mode for nuclear power plant in trouble.
- *Customer or user.* Customer group or user group requiring special functions/operations.
- *User experience.* Novice versus expert mode.

When a system has different priorities for its tasks, it is particularly important that system modes be defined for both normal traffic and heavy traffic conditions, because their operational profiles will differ. For example, when you have a normal load of feature-oriented tasks, more low-priority tasks such as audits and housekeeping operations will execute. Occurrence probabilities of such low-priority operations may be zero under heavy traffic conditions.

Defining different system modes is a convenient way of accommodating changes in the operational profile as users become more experienced. In practice, you can capture the variations in experience with two extremes, novice and expert, mixed in different proportions.

Some systems control the operations they will accept on the basis of environmental variables, such as traffic level and system-capability status, in order to reject noncritical, nonfunctioning operations and dedicate capacity to more critical ones. If a system must function in these conditions, each of these situations should be established as a system mode and tested with the guidance of separate operational profiles.

It is most convenient to group critical operations into one or more system modes, where each system mode incorporates operations of the same criticality. Critical system modes will then receive accelerated or increased testing. The factor of acceleration or increase is usually selected to yield enough execution time for the critical functions to assure achieving a desired level of failure intensity with acceptable confidence. Failure intensities measured in accelerated testing can be transformed to the values they would have had without the acceleration. The case study in Sec. 5.8 deals with critical but infrequent operations.

To measure criticality, consider value added (increased revenue or reduced cost) by an operation or the severity of the effect when it fails. Effects include risk to human life, cost, or reduction in capability. Cost consists of direct and indirect (damage to reputation) revenue loss and the cost of failure workaround, resolution, and recovery. In some cases, an operation can fail in different ways, with different severities. We use the average of the severities, weighted by relative probability, as the operation's criticality.

In considering financial effect, old operations can be more critical than new operations because their failure disrupts existing capabilities that users rely on. At least part of this effect may be captured by higher occurrence probabilities for these operations. On the other hand, new operations may be critical to the success of a new product, yet may not have a very high estimated occurrence probability. You may have to assign them a high criticality to reflect their importance.

It is common to use four criticality categories, each separated from the next most critical by one order of magnitude of effect. You must define a failure intensity objective for each criticality category and all must be met to ensure satisfactory operation.

The margin for error in reliability estimates is almost always smaller for the most critical category. So the effects of environmental input variables, such as traffic fluctuations and entry errors, will often be material for the critical category; testing for operations in that category must cover them.

Example 5.1 (cont.) The sample PBX has five system modes:

- Telecommunications business use
- Telecommunications personal use
- Attendant use
- Administration
- Maintenance

The last three system modes represent user types. They are disjoint in that they do not share functions or operations. The first two modes share most functions or operations and could be combined. However, both the functional and operational profiles for the two modes are expected to be very different. Hence we will separate these modes so that all modes may be viewed as disjoint. Note that we are separating the modes only to ease the job of analyzing them. It does not imply that different modes can't execute simultaneously.

5.3.4 Functional profile

The next step is to break each system mode down into the functions it needs—creating a function list—and determine each function's occurrence probability.

Functions, as noted, are defined from the user's perspective; they do not necessarily consider architectural or design factors. They are established during the requirements phase and are closely related with requirements. In general, developing a functional profile is considered part of the job of developing the requirements. The functional profile is used in the management of the architecture and design phases and in the design of the architecture itself. The functional profile is baselined and placed under change control, with appropriate traceability requirements, just as the requirements are.

Because you determine the functional profile before design begins, it can help guide the allocation of resources during design, coding, unit test, and possibly subsystem test. Of course, to allocate resources and set priorities, you must consider other factors as well, such as risk and developer expertise.

5.3.4.1 Number of functions. A functional profile does not have a set number of functions, but it typically involves between 20 and several hundred. The number generally increases with project size, the number of system modes, the number of major environmental conditions, and function breadth—the extent to which a function accommodates task variations.

Functions should be defined such that each represents a substantially different task, in the sense that we are likely to assign a different priority and allocate different resources to the development of, or design a different architecture for, that part of the system that supports that task. The task can be substantially different either as a result of work accomplished (most common) or the environment encountered. Examples of different environments might be different equipment or different traffic levels (normal and overload). You are likely to need to define different functions if tasks differ considerably in criticality; the run types you group in a function should have approximately the same criticality, because they will be treated as if they did.

5.3.4.2 Explicit versus implicit. Functional, operational, functional scenario, and operational scenario profiles can all be expressed in two forms, explicit and implicit, although it is usually easiest to express the latter two profiles in implicit form. *Explicit* and *implicit* refer to different ways of specifying functions and operations and hence selecting them for execution. At this point you must choose between an explicit or implicit operational profile or some combination of the two because that determines if you should develop an explicit or implicit functional profile.

In order to distinguish the two forms, we first need to define what we mean by "key input variable." We will, for brevity, give the definition in terms of operations, but it is equally applicable to functions. A *key input variable* is an input variable that is common to the input states of two or more operations, and whose value is needed to differentiate among some of these operations. In many cases, the values of a key input variable that differentiate operations are actually ranges, which are called *levels.* The name of the operation is a key input variable. A parameter may be a key input variable if two or more operations have the same name and the value of the parameter is the only way of distinguishing between them.

A profile is *explicit* if each element is designated by simultaneously specifying the values of all the key input variables necessary to identify it. A profile is *implicit* if it is expressed in terms of sequences of subprofiles, each subprofile representing the possible values of one key input variable and their conditional probabilities of occurrence, given the values specified for the previous key input variables in the sequence.

Suppose you have two key input variables, *C* and *D*, each with three values. For simplicity, assume that the variables are independent (if not, the subprofiles become more complex since all the preconditions must be stated). We can define nine operations based on the values of these key input variables. Example implicit and explicit operational profiles for these operations are given in Table 5.1.

An implicit profile is most conveniently expressed as a directed graph or a tree with the nodes representing key input variables and the branches, their values, and the associated conditional probabilities. For example, Fig. 5.2 shows sample "call trees" used by International Definity. It represents an implicit operational profile. Instead of selecting test cases from a complete list of all possible paths with associated probabilities (explicit profile), you select from each set of branch alternates with their associated branch probabilities. An explicit profile can always be determined from an implicit profile by tracing all paths through the directed graph or tree, multiplying the conditional probabilities of the branches together. Note how a test call is generated by pairing the call trees for a calling and a receiving party.

The chief advantage of the implicit profile is that it usually requires you to specify fewer elements—as few as the *sum* of the number of levels of the key input variables, depending on the amount of indepen-

TABLE 5.1 Sample Implicit Operational Profile

Subprofile C		Subprofile D	
Key input variable value	Occurrence probability	Key input variable value	Occurrence probability
C1	0.6	*D1*	0.7
C2	0.3	*D2*	0.2
C3	0.1	*D3*	0.1

Sample Explicit Functional Profile

Key input variable values	Occurrence probability
C1D1	0.42
C2D1	0.21
C1D2	0.12
C3D1	0.07
C1D3	0.06
C2D2	0.06
C2D3	0.03
C3D2	0.02
C3D3	0.01

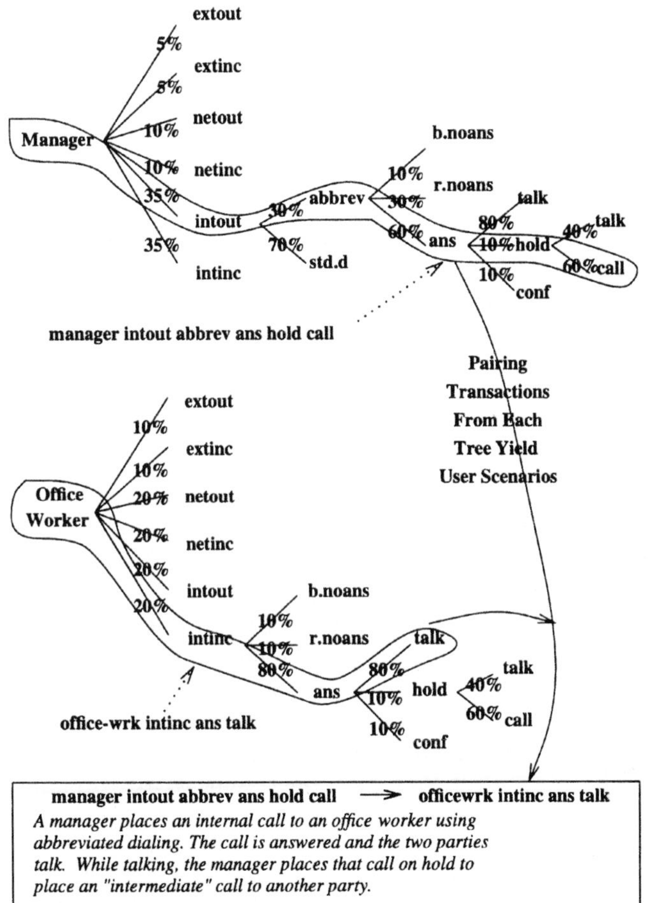

Figure 5.2 Sample call trees.

dence among these variables. Using an explicit profile, the number of elements you must specify can be as high as the *product* of the number of levels of the key input variables. The implicit profile can then be used in cases where the number of elements of an explicit profile would be too large. Alternatively, use of the implicit profile may give you finer granularity in measuring usage for the same effort you would use for an explicit profile.

The implicit approach is suited to transaction-based systems, in which processing depends primarily on transaction attributes that have known occurrence probabilities. A system to generate personalized direct mail, for example, depends on customer attributes such as location, income, and home ownership.

An implicit profile is particularly easy to construct when the key input variables that characterize a function or operation tend to present themselves sequentially in the description of the task that is being accomplished, such as in the call trees of Fig. 5.2.

5.3.4.3 Initial function list. The initial function list focuses on features, which are functional capabilities of interest and value to users. It consists of one list if you are developing an explicit profile, and one list for each key input variable if you are developing an implicit profile. System requirements are usually the best source of information on features. If you have trouble identifying the function, it is often because the requirements are incomplete or fuzzy. User input is vital in creating the initial function list. Only those who have practical experience with the existing work process can uncover problems with a proposed process. For military projects, part of the request for proposal may contain a "Design Reference Mission Profile" which, in turn, may contain descriptions of system modes, functions, and tasks performed and environmental factors. The mission profile serves as a good basis for developing a functional profile.

You can use a prototype as a second verifying source, but you must use it with care, because often a prototype implements only some functions. The most recent version of the product can also serve as a valuable check, but of course it lacks the new functions planned for the next version. Sometimes there is a draft user manual, written to enhance communication with users, that you can check, but it will probably emphasize functions activated by commands, not functions activated by events or data.

Example 5.1 (cont.) In the PBX example, we will generate an explicit profile for the administration system mode functions. The initial function list has four elements because the system-administration mode has four principal functions: adding a new telephone to the exchange, removing a telephone, relocating a telephone or changing the service grade provided, and updating the online directory.

5.3.4.4 Environmental variables. Now you should identify the environmental input variables and their values or value ranges that will require separate development efforts, such as substantial new modules. Environmental variables describe the conditions that affect the way the program runs (the control paths it takes and the data it accesses), but do not relate directly to features. Hardware configuration and traffic load are examples of environmental variables. Probably the best approach is to have several experienced designers brainstorm a list of environmental variables that might cause the program to respond in different ways, and then decide which of these would likely have a major effect on the program.

Example 5.1 (cont.) In the PBX example, telephone type is an environmental variable that has a major effect on processing. Although telephone type can have several values, here only analog (*A*) and digital (*D*) telephones have substantially different effects on processing. So there are two levels for the environmental input variable, *A* and *D*.

When environmental variables and their values are associated with their occurrence probabilities, you have an *environmental profile*. The configuration profile used by DEFINITY (Sec. 5.7.3) is an example of an environmental profile.

5.3.4.5 Final function list. Before you create the final function list, you should examine dependencies among the key environmental and feature variables. If one variable is totally or almost totally dependent on another, you can eliminate it from the final function list. If one variable is partially dependent on another, you must list all the possible combinations of the levels of both variables, along with all the independent variables. You will have one final function list for an explicit profile. For an implicit profile, the number of function lists will equal the number of feature and environmental key input variables.

The number of functions in the final function list is the product of the number of functions in the initial list and the number of environmental variable values, minus the combinations of initial functions and environmental variable values that do not occur.

Example 5.1 (cont.) The final function list for the PBX, shown in Table 5.2, is developed from the initial function list enumerated above and the telephone type environmental variable. It has seven elements: the three initial functions with two environmental variable values, plus the initial function "online-directory updating," which is not affected by telephone type.

5.3.4.6 Occurrence probabilities. The best source of data to determine occurrence probabilities is usage measurements taken on the latest release, a similar system, or the manual function that is being automated. Usage measurements are often available in system logs, which

TABLE 5.2 Final Function List

Function	Environmental variable
Relocation/change	*A*
	D
Addition	*A*
	D
Removal	*A*
	D
Online-directory updating	

are usually machine-readable. Note that these measurements are of operations, not functions, so they must be combined (usually by simple addition) when a function maps to more than one operation.

Occurrence probabilities computed with these data must be adjusted to account for new functions and environments and expected changes due to other factors. Most systems are a mixture of previously released functions, for which you may have measurements, plus new functions, for which you must estimate use. Although estimates are less accurate than measures, the total proportion of new functions is usually small, perhaps 5 to 20 percent, so the functional profile's overall accuracy should be good.

In the rare event that a system is completely new and the functions have never been executed before, even by a similar system or manually, the functional profile could be very inaccurate. However, it is still the best picture of customer use you have and so is valuable.

The process of predicting use alone, perhaps as part of a market study, is extremely important because the interaction with the customer that it requires highlights the functions' relative value. It may be that some functions should be dropped and others emphasized, resulting in a more competitive product. Reducing the number of little-used functions increases reliability, speeds delivery, and lowers cost.

Example 5.1 (cont.) In the sample PBX, there are 80 telephone additions, 70 removals, and 800 relocations or changes per month. Online-directory updating represents 5 percent of the total use in the system-administration mode.

We will assume that the occurrence probability for the system-administration mode is 0.02. Thus the overall occurrence probability for each of these functions, without consideration of environmental factors, is the product of their occurrence probability and the system-administration mode's occurrence probability in the overall system. Table 5.3 shows the resulting segment or part of the initial functional profile.

To take into account environmental factors, assume that 80 percent of the telephones are analog and 20 percent are digital. The environmental profile is shown in Table 5.4.

Also assume that the occurrence probabilities of the first three functions and telephone type are independent. To determine the final functional profile, you

TABLE 5.3 Sample Initial Functional Profile Segment

Function	System-administration-mode occurrence probability	Overall occurrence probability
Relocation/change	0.80	0.0160
Addition	0.08	0.0016
Removal	0.07	0.0014
Online-directory updating	0.05	0.0010

TABLE 5.4 Sample Environmental Profile

Telephone type	Occurrence probability
Analog (*A*)	0.8
Digital (*D*)	0.2

multiply the values of the environmental profile by the values of the initial functional profile to obtain the final functional profile segment for the system-administration mode in Table 5.5.

5.3.4.7 Functional and operational profiles with correlated elements. It is desirable to define functions and operations such that their probabilities of selection are independent of previous functions/operations selected. Then you only need to determine occurrence probabilities for the functions/operations in your list. The foregoing implies that if you have a sequence of functions/operations that are highly correlated, you should try to bunch them into one function/operation.

You can assume that functions/operations with little correlation are independent, but you must recognize the fact of your approximation. The risk here is that independent random selection will distort the true occurrence probabilities to some extent. Positively correlated sequences will occur less frequently than they do in reality, increasing the risk that failures occurring in them may be missed. Negatively correlated sequences will occur more frequently than they do in reality, wasting test and debugging resources by overemphasizing failures associated with them.

5.3.5 Operational profile

The functional profile is a user-oriented profile of functions, not the operations that actually implement them. But it is operations, not functions, that you test. An operation represents a task being accomplished

TABLE 5.5 Sample Final Functional Profile Segment

Function	Environment (telephone type)	Overall occurrence probability
Relocation/change	*A*	0.0128
	D	0.0032
Addition	*A*	0.00128
	D	0.00032
Removal	*A*	0.00112
	D	0.00028
Online-directory updating		0.00100

by the system, sometimes in a particular environment, as viewed by the people who will run the system (also as viewed by testers, who try to put themselves in this position). To allocate testing effort, select tests, and determine the order in which tests should be run, the operational profile must be available when you start test planning.

Functions evolve into operations as the operational architecture of the system is developed. The *operational architecture* is the way the user will employ operations to accomplish functions. There is often some, but rarely complete, correlation between the operational architecture and the system architecture, which determines how modules and subsystems combine into the system.

A function may evolve into one or more operations, or a set of functions may be restructured into a different set (and different number) of operations. Thus the mapping from functions to operations is not necessarily straightforward. For example, an administrative function in a switching system might be to relocate a telephone. This single function may be implemented by two operations, removal and installation, because these tasks may be assigned to different work groups. Generally, there are more operations than functions, and operations tend to be more refined. An operation is usually more differentiated than a function.

The principal steps in determining the operational profile are to list the operations and determine the occurrence probabilities.

5.3.5.1 Listing operations. You use the functional profile to develop the list of operations, mapping functions to operations by following the operational architecture of the system (the way the operations combine to accomplish the functions). Since functions differ from one another by virtue of implementing substantially different tasks, operations will generally be distinguished from one another by substantially different processing. Different operations will usually execute substantially different code paths. Thus the definition of *operation* can be affected by program structure. You will usually want to select at least one test case for each operation, as each has a substantial risk of experiencing a failure that is not experienced by other operations. As with functions, operations may differ as the result of work accomplished or environment encountered.

If possible, it is desirable to define functions such that functions and operations will map one-to-one. This will greatly simplify deriving the operational profile from the functional profile. It requires, concurrent with requirements development, consideration of architectural factors, design factors, and practical constraints on the execution time of operations. If you are developing an operational profile for an existing system, there will be a natural tendency for functions and operations to be similar.

Creating and examining a list of those events that initiate program execution (such as commands or transactions) may help you create the operations list. If the events have parameters, consider the effects of different parameter values. If a value of a parameter causes significantly different processing to occur, you may want to define a new operation. If there are N significantly different kinds of processing associated with an event as a result of different parameter values, then the original function associated with the event should be replaced by N operations. In creating the list, you must also consider environmental variables.

The definition of a run should imply an execution time that is short enough so that sufficient executions exist during:

1. Field operation to permit satisfactory accuracy in characterizing usage
2. Test to permit satisfactory accuracy in reproducing usage

Also, the run should be short enough so that the input state needed to characterize its interaction with the environment is not excessively long. For example, a complete flight of a space vehicle or aircraft might be defined as a run, but the execution time would be too long to meet the constraints just noted. You might then define the runs such that their time durations correspond to the time of a flight maneuver for the vehicle. Examples of grouping of such runs into operations might be "turn," "climb" (including dive), and "steady flight." These operations are probably not correlated with each other. However, the input states and hence runs *are* because the vehicle's position and velocity can change only a limited amount during the time of a maneuver. This must be handled in test by selecting a sequence of runs (input states) within the sequence of operations chosen that recognizes the limitations.

Avoid excessive interaction between operations. When sequences of tasks occur such that substantial amounts of data must be passed between them, consider defining the entire sequence as a run. If the system is reinitialized from time to time, it is a good idea to define runs so that they do not cross reinitialization boundaries.

Now you need to verify that the list of operations is as complete as you can reasonably make it. First, you develop a list of input variables and their ranges of values that is practically complete. A "practically complete" list identifies all input variables except those that take on one value with very high probability. You are ignoring and thus won't be testing the alternate values. This is acceptable because they occur so rarely that they have little effect on reliability even if they fail. The degree to which you can do this decreases for systems requiring higher reliability.

You then create a representation of the input states, also making it practically complete. Because the identification process will never be perfect, you should employ other strategies, such as reducing the number of input states and using indirect input variables, described later, to ensure that you handle hidden input variables properly. The amount of effort you put into this should be based on reliability requirements, the cost of the extra effort, and any information you have on the probability that these interactions will occur.

5.3.5.2 Reducing number of operations. If developing the operational profile is burdensome because the operations list is too long, you essentially have three options in redefining it (we are not discussing test selection here, which will be covered in Sec. 5.4):

- Reduce the number of run types.
- Increase the number of run types grouped per operation.
- Ignore the remaining set of run types expected to have total occurrence probability appreciably less than the failure intensity objective of the system.

Reducing the number of run types has the added benefits of reducing the testing effort and perhaps design and implementation costs. Practically speaking, you can reduce the number of run types either by reducing the number of input variables or the number of values for each input variable. In general, the number of input variables is more likely to influence program control flow and failure behavior than the number of values, so you should give this more attention. Some ways to reduce the number of input variables are:

- Reduce functionality.
- Reduce the number of possible hardware configurations.
- Restrict the environment the program must operate in.
- Reduce the number of types of faults (hardware, human, software) the system must tolerate.
- Reduce unnecessary interaction between successive runs.

All these approaches have costs, in addition to the costs of analysis and redesign. The first four, which change the system's features, may involve customer objections, less flexibility, less robustness, or reduced reliability, respectively. The disadvantage associated with reducing operations may be more apparent than real. It may be possible to build systems with the same functionality but fewer operations by applying the *reduced-operation software* concept [Musa91a], analogous to reduced-instruction-set computing. With this approach, you do not implement operations that occur rarely. Instead, they are accomplished by executing sequences of other operations or combining other operations with manual intervention. To decide which operations should not be implemented, look at the economic trade-off between reduced development cost and potentially higher operating costs.

The fifth option, reducing unnecessary (not required for functional reasons) interaction between successive runs, is highly desirable. It requires only changes in design or operational procedures, not negotiation with customers. Reducing interaction not only simplifies test planning, but substantially reduces the risk of failure from unforeseen causes. You must recognize, however, that the extent to which you can do this may be limited. And there is usually some cost in greater execution time.

Some ways to reduce unnecessary interaction are as follows:

- Design the control program to limit the input variables that application programs can access at any one time (information hiding).
- Reinitialize variables between runs. Because it may be difficult to determine with high confidence which input variables are influencing runs, it may be simplest to reinitialize all of them between runs. If the resulting overhead is excessive, reinitialize periodically, which reduces overhead but allows more interaction.
- Use synchronous (time-triggered) instead of asynchronous (event-triggered) design. Synchronous design lets you better control the input variables that are in play at any time. However, it may add overhead; it requires extra measurement and planning to prevent functions from being aborted when deadlines are missed; and it may be a less natural fit with the problem being solved, resulting in a less compact design.

Reducing interactions has a higher risk than the other approaches to reducing input space. It is more complex and hence more error-prone, so "sneak" interactions may remain. Also, we know less about how to best exploit reduced interactions to reduce testing.

The second option to reducing the number of operations, increasing the number of run types grouped per operation, involves increasing the difference in occurrence probabilities among run types required to establish separate operations. Operations that do not meet the higher differentiation standard are merged, provided they share the same input variables. If the number of randomly selected tests in the merged operation equals the sum of the number of tests for its components, the risk of missing a failure is not substantially changed, providing the failure probability of a run type in each of the components is approximately the same [Haml90]. Greater grouping does not reduce the amount of testing required; it just decreases the amount of effort required to develop the operational profile. There is an extra cost for analysis, however.

The run types you group should have approximately the same criticality and probability of occurrence, because you will give them the same priority in test and test them to the same degree of intensity. If they also share the same input variables and execute the same code path, the job of test selection (see Sec. 5.4) will be simplified, but this condition is not essential. Consider an airline reservation system. We will group all the single-leg flight reservations, since their run types share the input variables of passenger name, flight number, originating city, terminating city, and so on. A two-leg reservation, on the other hand, is a different operation with a different set of key input variables, which include the second flight number and the connecting city.

If you have different operations with the same input variable sets, you should consider merging them unless they have substantially different criticalities or occurrence probabilities. In the latter case, maintaining them separately provides the basis for nonuniform testing, that is, testing the more frequently occurring operation more intensely.

The reduction in operations may even be on a temporary basis. You may develop an operational profile with a moderate number of elements for the first version of a software product, refining it for later versions only if you discover in the field that the reliability predictions from test are in error.

The third option, excluding the remaining set of run types expected to have total occurrence probability appreciably less than the failure intensity objective of the system, can happen automatically if the number of test cases is limited and they are selected in accordance with the occurrence probability of the operations. Let the sum of the occurrence probabilities of the excluded run types equal p_E. Assume the failure intensity at the start of test is λ_0; at the end, λ_F. Assuming that faults initially are distributed uniformly with respect to operations, then operations contribute to the failure intensity in proportion to their occurrence probability. The excluded operations will contribute $p_E\lambda_0$ to the failure intensity at the start of test. This number will be the same or less at the end, assuming that no faults are spawned that could cause any excluded operation to fail. Because this contribution will not be measured, λ_F will be low by, at most, this amount. Let ε be the maximum acceptable error in measuring failure intensity. Then, setting ε equal to $p_E\lambda_0$, you obtain the allowable value of

$$p_E = \frac{\varepsilon}{\lambda_0}$$

Suppose the failure intensity objective is 10 failures per 1000 CPU hours. It might be reasonable to set ε equal to one failure per 1000 CPU hours. If $\lambda_0 = 10^5$ failures per 1000 CPU hours, then $p_E = 10^{-5}$. This means that once the total occurrence probabilities of the operations you are testing reaches $1 - 10^{-5}$, you can ignore the rest. The higher the failure intensity objective (the lower the reliability), the more operations you can exclude. Obviously, as criticality increases, the degree to which functions can be excluded diminishes.

The set of operations should include all operations of high criticality, even if they have low use. The effect of not including operations of low criticality and low use will be negligible unless reliability requirements are very high. To increase the likelihood that all high-criticality operations are included, you should focus on tasks whose unsatisfactory completion would have a severe effect and carefully consider all the environmental conditions in which they may be executed. Postmortems of serious failures in previous or related systems often suggest some of these situations.

5.3.5.3 Occurrence probabilities. Since different system modes have different operational profiles but may share common operations, you may have to determine multiple occurrence probabilities for the same operation.

In some cases, there may be field data already existing on the frequency of events the system must respond to. You should expend some effort searching for such data, because it may provide the most cost-effective approach to determining occurrence probabilities. This is especially true if the alternative is building special measurement and recording tools.

There are two general ways to determine occurrence probabilities for operations:

- Count the occurrence of operations in the field.
- Rely on estimates derived by refining the functional profile.

The first is more accurate, but obviously can be done only if a previous release exists. When adding new operations to an existing system, you must supplement use records with estimates. You can also view a system modification as adding a new operational profile to an old one. The operational profile for the old system can be measured; for the new operations, estimated. The two parts are joined by weighting each one's occurrence probabilities by the proportion of total system usage that part represents.

It may take some effort to develop recording software, but you may be able to develop a generic recording routine that requires only an interface to each application. The recording software must instrument the system so that it extracts sufficient data about input variables to identify the operations being executed. If operations are independent and do not depend on the history of preceding operations, you need only to count the execution of each operation. If they are not independent, you must record the sequence of operations. You can later process the sequence to determine conditional probabilities. An operational profile can be recorded in either explicit or implicit form.

The recording process usually adds some overhead to the application. As long as this overhead is not excessive, it may be feasible to collect data from the entire user community. However, if the overhead is large, you will probably have to employ a user survey instead of recording. In sampling users, the same guidelines and statistical theory used for polling and market surveys apply; a sample of 30 or even fewer users may suffice to generate an operational profile with acceptable accuracy.

If the costs of obtaining occurrence probabilities are an issue, you may make measurements of moderate granularity and accuracy for the first version of a software product, refining them for later versions only if you discover in the field that the reliability predictions from test are in error.

If you will be using usage data for testing only, it is acceptable to directly drive testing by recording complete input states in the field. You need not determine the operational profile or create test cases. This saves time and effort, but these savings will be reduced by the extent to which you add new operations. For the new operations, you must estimate occurrence probabilities and develop test cases.

In order to estimate by refining the functional profile, determine the function to operation mapping. Then allocate the function occurrence probabilities to operations. In doing this, you may need to obtain occurrence probabilities of environmental variables whose values distinguish different operations. Sometimes the occurrence probabilities of certain key input variables can be found by simulating the operation of associated systems that determine them. For example, the operational profile of a surveillance system will depend on the frequencies of certain conditions arising in the systems being monitored.

The estimation effort is usually best done by an experienced systems engineer who has a thorough understanding of the businesses and the needs of the expected users, and how they will likely take advantage of the new functions. It is vital that experienced users review these estimates. Often, new functions implement procedures that had been performed manually or by other systems, so there may be some data available to improve the accuracy of the estimates.

It often helps to create an interaction matrix of key input variables plotted against other key input variables. This matrix reveals combinations of key input variables that do not occur or that interact. The remaining areas of the matrix represent regions where you can assume key input variables are independent and estimate the occurrence probability as the product of individual key input variable probabilities.

Let's examine two common types of systems, command-driven and data-driven (also called *transaction-based*).

Example 5.2 Command-driven system The PBX is a *command-driven* system. In implementing the features of the system-administration mode, assume that this command set was developed:

```
relocate <old location> <new location>
add      -s <service grade> <location>
remove   <location>
update
```

The designers decided to handle the function "change of service grade" by removing the old service and adding a new one. As you consider the parameters, you note that location does not affect the nature of the processing. However, the service grade does because the features provided are substantially different for staff, secretaries, and managers. So you refine the add command into three operations and obtain the operations list:

```
relocate <old location> <new location>
add      -s staff <location>
add      -s secretary <location>
add      -s manager <location>
remove   <location>
update
```

All these commands, except update, account for 0.019 of the occurrence probability; update accounts for 0.001. Suppose that the expected 80 additions of service per month break down into 70 staff, 5 secretaries, 5 managers. There will be 780 relocations and 20 changes of service grade each month, the latter representing promotions to manager. There will be 70 removals proper and 20 removals created as the result of change of service grade, yielding a total of 90 removals. The part of the operational profile for the system-administration mode is shown in Table 5.6.

TABLE 5.6 Operational-Profile Segment Based on Features

Command	Transactions per month	Occurrence probability
relocate	780	0.0153
remove	90	0.0017
add -s staff	70	0.0014
update		0.0010
add -s manager	25	0.0005
add -s secretary	5	0.0001

You proceed in this fashion until you have accounted for all the ways the system can be employed. Now you must consider the possible expansion of the operation list to account for environmental variables that could change the processing (and thus result in different failure behavior). There will usually be environmental variables that affect the processing sufficiently to require testing based on some of their values that you must now consider, even though they were not sufficiently major to be considered in the development of the functional profile. For simplicity, assume that the environmental variables may interact with feature variables in determining occurrence probabilities. For example, certain features may be executed at constant occurrence *rates* but as traffic increases, their occurrence *probabilities* decrease.

Example 5.2 (cont.) In our sample system, the environmental variable is telephone type: the system must handle both analog and digital telephones. The operational profile in Table 5.6 will thus expand under this environmental variable into 11 operations (online-directory update is not affected by telephone type). Let's exclude directory update and consider the part for analog telephones *A*, which will have occurrence probabilities that are 80 percent of those for all configurations.

Assume that system load is such an environmental variable. If system-administration functions are performed when the system is in an overload condition because of heavy communication traffic, processing may be affected (administrative requests might be queued, for example). Assume that this occurs 0.1 percent of the time.

To generate the segment of the operational profile we are considering, first multiply all values in Table 5.6 by 0.8 to give the occurrence probabilities for analog telephones. Then multiply by 0.999 to obtain the occurrence probabilities for normal load, or by 0.001 to obtain the occurrence probabilities for overload. Table 5.7 is the new operational profile segment.

TABLE 5.7 Operational Profile Segment Based on Features and Environment

Command	Environment	Occurrence probability ($\times 10^{-6}$)
relocate	Normal load	12,228.00
remove	Normal load	1,359.00
add -s staff	Normal load	1,119.00
add -s manager	Normal load	400.00
add -s secretary	Normal load	79.90
relocate	Overload	12.24
remove	Overload	1.36
add -s staff	Overload	1.12
add -s manager	Overload	0.40
add -s secretary	Overload	0.08

Some operations in Table 5.7 occur very infrequently. You should seriously question if it is really necessary to test all of them. Consider eliminating the "add -s secretary under overload conditions."

Example 5.3 Data-driven system Financial and billing systems are commonly *data-driven*. Suppose a telephone billing system was designed as two subsystems. The sort subsystem receives call transactions and sorts them by billing period and account number, grouping all the items for one account for the current billing period. The account-processing subsystem processes the charge entries for each account for the current billing period and generates bills.

The reliability you want to evaluate is the probability of generating a correct bill. This involves determining the reliability of each subsystem over the time required to process the bill or the entries associated with the bill, and then multiplying the reliabilities. You must determine an operational profile for each subsystem.

Because this design was not anticipated when the functional profile was developed, the relationship between the functional profile and the two operational profiles is complex. For example, typical functions may have been bill processing, bill correction, and the identification of delinquent customers. The bill-processing function relates to operations in both subsystems, but the other two functions relate only to the account-processing subsystem.

The first subsystem, the sort subsystem, will have relatively few operations and a simple operational profile. The operation for processing correct charge items has an occurrence probability greater than 0.99; other operations handle missing data, data with recognizable errors, and so on. You should be able to estimate occurrence probabilities from past data on the frequency and type of errors.

The second subsystem, the account-processing subsystem, has an operational profile that relates to account attributes. Its operations are classified by service (residential or business), use of a discount calling plan (non, national, or international), and payment status (paid or delinquent), resulting in 12 operations.

Assume that the service classification is 80 percent residential and 20 percent business. A national discount calling plan is used by 20 percent of subscribers; international, 5 percent. Only 1 percent of accounts are delinquent. Table 5.8 shows the set of operations and their associated probabilities.

TABLE 5.8 Operational Profile Account-Processing Subsystem of Billing System

Operation	Occurrence probability
Residential, no calling plan, paid	0.5940
Residential, national calling plan, paid	0.1584
Business, no calling plan, paid	0.1485
Business, national calling plan, paid	0.0396
Residential, international calling plan, paid	0.0396
Business, international calling plan, paid	0.0099
Residential, no calling plan, delinquent	0.0060
Residential, national calling plan, delinquent	0.0016
Business, no calling plan, delinquent	0.0015
Business, national calling plan, delinquent	0.0004
Residential, international calling plan, delinquent	0.0004
Business, international calling plan, delinquent	0.0001

If transaction use is described in terms of transaction rates, you obtain the occurrence probabilities by dividing the individual transaction rates by the total transaction rate and multiplying this by the probability of transaction occurrence (with respect to other operations). If all the operations are transactions, the last step is not necessary.

5.4 Test Selection

The operational profile is used to select operations to execute in test in accordance with their occurrence probabilities. Testing driven by an operational profile is very efficient because it identifies failures (and hence the faults causing them), on average, in the order of how often they occur. This approach rapidly increases reliability—reduces failure intensity—per unit of execution time because the failures that occur most frequently are caused by the faulty operations used most frequently. Users will also detect failures in the order of their frequency if they have not already been found in test.

Since an operation represents a group of run types, the *coarse grain* selection of the operation must be followed by the *fine grain* selection of a run type. Although selection of the operation can be based on usage (and criticality), the fine grain selection must be very simple and easy to implement because of the large number of elements in the population from which you are selecting. Of course, you also want it to be efficient in the sense of requiring the smallest possible number of tests to assure a specified reliability at the required confidence level.

Random selection of run types within an operation is a common strategy; it is probably best when you have little information that might affect the distribution of failing run types within an operation. An example of pertinent information would be a processing difference between groups of run types, where it is known that the code associated with one processing alternative is considerably more complex.

However, when some information is available, it is useful to profit from it by dividing the operation into run categories. A *run category* is a group of run types that represent part of an operation. The information that might affect the distribution of failing run types is used to attempt to select run categories or sets of run types that are *homogeneous*. Run categories are homogeneous if any one run type represents the entire set in the sense that all have the same failure behavior. Thus if a test of one of them fails, all will fail. Similarly, a successful execution of one run type means the entire homogeneous set will execute successfully. Clearly, identification of homogeneous sets of run types will reduce the amount of testing required for a specified level of reliability. In practice, it is very difficult to identify homogeneous sets with certainty; hence we define a run category as being *near homogeneous*.

You should establish run categories such that they have approximately equal occurrence probabilities. This is because selection of run categories from operations is done on a uniform basis, usage information not being available at this level.

To define run categories that approach homogeneity, look for run types that at least share the same input variables and execute the same code path. Try to find ranges of values for each input variable over which essentially the same processing occurs.

Although you could in theory select only one run type from a run category, it is probably better to pick two or more and do it randomly to counter the risk that homogeneity is often not achieved. Thus, the sequence of selections that occurs when using run categories is operation, run category, run type.

Selection should be with replacement for operations, run categories and run types. *Replacement* means that, after selection, an item (for example, operation or run type) is returned to the list from which it was chosen so that it is not excluded from reselection. One might argue that replacement for run types wastes test resources because of the possibility of duplication. However, the number of run types is so large that the probability of this happening is infinitesimal.

Selection could be performed without replacement, in which an element can be chosen only once. This is unwise for operations because they can be associated with multiple faults. There is a high risk that different run types within an operation may show different behavior.

5.4.1 Selecting operations

With an explicit operational profile, you select operations directly in accordance with their occurrence probabilities. With an implicit operational profile, you select operations by choosing the level of each key input variable in accordance with its occurrence probability, which implicitly selects the operation at the conjunction of these values.

If different profiles (system modes) occur at different times in the field, you should conduct separate tests. However, if they occur simultaneously, testing should be concurrent, because system modes running simultaneously can interact. The execution time allocated to each system mode should be proportional to its occurrence probability. Concurrent testing in effect combines multiple operational profiles into a single one.

If different versions of the software product are supplied to different customers, they may differ primarily in system-mode profiles. If interaction among system modes is nonexistent or small, you can test each system mode independently. Failure intensities for the different customers can be obtained by weighting the system-mode failure intensities by the occurrence probabilities. The result is substantial savings in test time. You may also want to test several operational profiles that represent the variation in use that can occur among different system installations to determine the resulting variation in reliability.

If possible, you should select operations randomly to prevent some unrealized bias from entering into the testing process. Data corruption often causes such a bias. Data corruption increases with execution time since the last reinitialization, so if one operation is always executed early and another always late, your tests may miss significant failure behavior.

It is wise to randomly select as many key input variables as possible. Random selection is feasible for operations with key input variables that are not difficult to change. However, some key input variables can be very difficult and expensive to change, such as one that represents a hardware configuration. In this case, you must select some key input variables deterministically, because changing these variables during system test must be scheduled. Carefully consider the bias that might result from those you select deterministically and try to counter it. For example, reinitialize the system at random times to avoid data-corruption bias.

5.4.2 Regression test

Regression testing can be a substantial portion of the overall test effort. Regression tests are run after changes have been made to uncover spawned faults. Spawned faults are faults introduced while removing other faults. Because changes are frequently grouped and introduced periodically, regression testing is also usually periodic. A week is a common interval, although intervals can be as short as a day or as long as a month.

Some testers say regression testing should focus on operations that contain the changed code. This view makes sense only if you are sure the possible effects of the changes are isolated to those operations or if system reliability requirements are low so that cross-effects to other operations do not matter. However, in most cases you cannot rely on isolation, and potential cross-effects can cause unacceptable deterioration in system reliability. So all operations should be considered when planning a regression test. However, a change generally results in a smaller probability of failure than a new program, so it isn't really necessary to retest every operation after every change.

It is inefficient to cover operations of unequal occurrence frequency with equal regression testing; hence, operations should be selected in accordance with the operational profile. Now the possibility exists of integrating regression testing with regular system testing. You can achieve substantial savings in test resources and time by making your tests do double duty.

5.5 Special Issues

As we used the operational profile on several projects, we encountered some special situations for which solutions had to be researched. We address the most important of these cases here.

5.5.1 Indirect input variables

Sometimes the relationship among observable task and environmental variables and input states is not clearly discernible, at least not without an expensive effort. In this case, you can establish and employ indirect input variables to control test selection. An indirect input variable is believed to affect processing, but is not used by the program directly. In many cases, you will be interested in establishing indirect *key* input variables.

Consider traffic load. It is neither practical nor enlightening to determine which input-variable values are caused by heavy traffic and directly affect processing. It is better to actually generate a heavy traffic load and observe the results. The program accesses no traffic-level variable, but you can consider the traffic level generated as an indirect input variable. You can select levels of these indirect input variables randomly, in accordance with estimated occurrence probabilities.

Indirect input variables are particularly useful for handling the effects of data corruption. Data corruption is the accumulated degradation in data with execution time that results from anomalies in intermediate variables that do not represent failures. Some of these data are in reality input variables for other operations, but the interaction is often not known. In this case, you can define an indirect input variable called *soak time* in terms of hours of execution and plan to test several different values of this variable. You may implicitly select the values by performing a *soak test,* in which you continuously increase soak time up to a limit, with operations randomly chosen in accordance with the operational profile in this interval. In either case, you should include a soak time slightly less than the reinitialization interval you expect to use in the field.

5.5.2 Updating the operational profile

An operational profile can change during the life of a product, especially when new features are regularly made available through new releases. Each new release will necessitate modifying the operational profile. Because it is best to base the modified operational profile on measured data, a regular operational-profile measurement program is recommended.

In the long run, the simplest way to do this is to build the measurement capability into the system. This involves counting and recording the number of runs of each run type. You can combine this measurement system with a failure-detection and -recording function or other performance-measurement system. The most economic and reliable way to collect data is through periodic reporting over telecommunication channels to a central location. If this is not feasible, you can collect data on a removable medium that is mailed periodically to a processing center.

Some designers may be concerned about performance degradation caused by the recording function. For the amount of data needed and the length of the runs involved, performance degradation is unlikely, but recording excessive amounts of data could cause a problem. If performance does become a problem, you can sample a set of sites or a set of time periods, as long as you are careful to sample randomly. Built-in recording may not happen until suppliers and customers learn through experience to appreciate its value. In this case, the best approach is to take measurements at a randomly selected sample of sites. Root-cause failure analysis may also provide data, because it sometimes leads to uncovering system uses that were not known and hence not tested.

Generally, operational profiles should be updated when there are major releases that represent substantial changes in capabilities and expected use. As a system passes through different versions or releases, the functional profile usually needs updating less frequently than the operational profile, because it is used mainly to prioritize tasks and allocate resources and thus can be less refined.

If new functions are added, their occurrence probabilities must be estimated. Suppose that the new functions' usage totals p_N. If the new functions do not affect the occurrence probabilities of the old functions except by adding to the overall set of functions, the old functions' probabilities are adjusted by multiplying by $(1 - p_N)$. However, if some old functions are replaced or otherwise affected, the probabilities are adjusted individually.

5.5.3 Distributed systems

You can apply operational-profile techniques to distributed or networked systems if they are engineered, tested, and managed as a whole. This implies that "operation" refers to a task that involves part or all of the total system, not just one component. There is nothing that restricts the concept of an operation to a program that executes on a single machine.

All the concepts relating to input space—run, run type, run category, operation, and function—and failures are logical, in the sense that they can span a set of software, hardware, and human components. For example, a run can consist of a series of segments, each executed as a process by a server, with the servers being implemented on the same or different machines.

The functional profile can be used to guide resource allocation and set priorities in development with respect to the entire system. The operational profile can guide testing of the entire system as a unit.

Delineating run types, run categories, and operations for distributed and networked systems can be more complex because the set of environmental variables can be appreciably larger. Although going from a centralized to a distributed system does not increase the number of task variables, it often increases the effective number of environmental variables, such as traffic load and soak time, because you may have to specify and measure them with respect to individual machines.

You can counter the foregoing proliferation of environmental variables by carefully designing both the system and its operating procedures. For example, you can design a system so that all machines have similar traffic loads (as a percentage of capacity). And you can equalize soak time by synchronizing reinitializations.

You can, of course, also apply the operational profile to any subsystem as long as that subsystem has operations that relate directly to users.

5.6 Other Uses

Although it was developed to guide testing, the operational profile can also guide managerial and engineering decisions throughout the life cycle, including requirements specification, design, implementation, and testing. Because it ranks features by how often they will be used, it suggests development priorities.

A prioritized *operational development* approach is potentially a very competitive, customer-oriented way to sequence new-product introduction: make the most-used features (operations) available very quickly and provide less-used features in subsequent releases. Development of a specified release proceeds incrementally by operations. This approach is different from traditional incremental development approaches, which proceed incrementally by modules. Since operational development is relatively new, experience will be required to identify and resolve development issues that may arise.

The functional profile improves communication between developer and customer and within the customer organization by making expression of needs more precise. It may highlight types of use not anticipated by the developers. It may cause users to think about their needs in greater detail. For example, when a developer asks which functions are needed to support maintenance and how often they will be used, it stimulates users to think about, discuss, and study what the maintenance procedures should be.

The operational profile can also be used in performance analysis. If you multiply each operation's occurrence probability by the system's overall run or transaction-execution rate, you obtain the run or transaction rates for each operation. This information is used for performance analysis and performance testing. Among other uses, it can help determine the number of servers a client-server system requires.

Finally, the operational profile is an educational aid. It organizes work in a manner that is closely related to user work processes. It can direct the customer's training efforts toward the most-used operations. For user manuals, the operational profile suggests the order in which material should be presented (most-used first) and the space, time, and care that should be devoted to preparing and presenting it.

By employing an operational profile for multiple purposes, we lower its cost per use.

5.7 Application to DEFINITY®

5.7.1 Project description

The Global Business Communications System (GBCS) division of AT&T provides private branch exchanges (PBXs) to businesses. A PBX is a telecommunication system for businesses that provides phone services within buildings and out into the public telephone network. The DEFINITY G3 line of PBXs comes in a variety of models that serve the needs of customers from all areas of industry and in sizes from around 80 lines to tens of thousands.

DEFINITY has a central processor running a program of about one and a half million lines of source code. In addition, there are as many as several hundred distributed processors (line, trunk, and other interfaces) each running programs ranging from 2000 to 250,000 lines of source code.

5.7.2 Development process description

In 1989, DEFINITY development processes were reengineered to focus more on customer satisfaction. During this reengineering process, research indicated that SRE principles could form the base of a complete product development process that was oriented toward satisfying customers. The resulting development process is called Customer Satisfaction Based Product Development. Its components include rigorous software development techniques (including design teams, code inspections, and developer testing), an incremental development life-cycle model, and quality factor assessment (the assessment of customer-oriented product quality metrics during the development cycle). These processes are now applied to all DEFINITY releases and other products besides PBXs.

SRE is woven into this development process in the following way:

- Customer satisfiers are determined (reliability is a key quality requirement).
- Metrics to measure those quality requirements during product development are defined (various failure-rate metrics are used for reliability measures).
- Customer usage of the DEFINITY product is documented in detail (operational profiles are defined).
- Methods for assessing quality (reliability) during development are devised.

5.7.3 Describing operational profiles

Multiple separate operational profiles are created for the DEFINITY product, rather than one all encompassing profile. This is because a single test environment that represents all DEFINITY customers cannot be effectively, efficiently, or realistically created. Instead, an operational profile is created for each customer type in the customer profile.

Operational profile definitions start with customer models derived from marketing, sales, manufacturing, user groups, and other data sources. These models define typical or generic customers from each of about 12 key business/industry areas (e.g., banking, universities, factories). This forms a customer profile. For each customer type, the set of users in that profile is described. Table 5.9 is part of the user profile for a bank.

The user percentage and call rate are determined for each user in the profile. Together, these allow a usage distribution for those users to be computed. As work was done to define the users for each customer in the profile, the DEFINITY project recognized that users with similar usage behaviors could be grouped into a common usage description. These user descriptions are called *generic users.*

Each operational profile created has essentially one system mode called a *busy hour.* This represents a customer's busiest hour of usage across a typical week. More stressful usage modes are studied independently via stress tests designed by system test engineers.

Initially, the functional profile was defined to be simple and focus on only a single basic PBX function—making and/or receiving a phone call (though with more than 150 features on a DEFINITY PBX, there's no such thing as a simple phone call). This decision was based on the fact that the vast majority of a PBX's users were telephone users and that the main PBX function they employed was making/placing calls. Thus, the major component of system usage (as measured by transactions, system hours, or CPU hours), and therefore software usage, was accounted for by modeling phone calls. Since that time, the project has subsequently defined other users (e.g., system administrators and maintenance technicians) and their corresponding functional profiles.

An environmental profile, called a *configuration profile,* is also defined. It is a set of configuration descriptions representing those used by the customers in the customer profile. The descriptions specify the parameters needed to describe the hardware and software environment in which the functional profile takes place. The parameters include such things as number of PBXs, types of processors used, types of trunks between PBXs, and number of analog stations.

To describe the operational profiles, a tree-based approach is used. For each user, a *call tree* is defined that describes their telephone usage. The tree-based approach allows for expression of context-dependent occurrence probabilities (i.e., conditional probabilities). This means that the probability of a feature's usage can change depending on when in a call the feature is used. A set of tools is used to automatically create complete telephone calls (run types) from the call trees. Figure 5.2 shows an example of two simplified call trees yielding a simple run type. The tools, using the frequencies defined in the call trees, generate samples that are proportioned according to customer usage.

This method substantially automates the generation of customer-oriented test cases and, of course, provides the customer-like testing (operational-profile-based testing) needed to estimate a system's relia-

TABLE 5.9 A User Profile

Customer Type = Bank				
User name	Generic user type	User percentage	Call rate (c/hr)	User prob.
Secretary	Secretary	20	10	0.379
Attendant	Attendant	1	24	0.046
Night-service	Attendant	1	8	0.015
Agent	Call-center agent	1	15	0.028
Supervisor	Call-center supervisor	1	3	0.006
Executive	Manager	3	3	0.017
Tellers	Worker	15	2	0.057
Office workers	Worker	52	4	0.395
Investment counselors	Administrators	6	5	0.057

bility. An added benefit is greatly enhanced tester productivity since the vast majority of run types and test cases are automatically produced by this method.

Call trees are implicit operational profiles—selections are made directly from the frequency/probability distributions of customers, users, functions, and operations rather than from a listing of all possible operations (an explicit approach). Since each customer may have as many as 20 different users, and each user tree may have hundreds of branches (complete paths through the trees), the possible number of run types is extremely large (estimated to be in the 10^8 range). Consequently, enumerating all run types to create an explicit profile is not feasible.

5.7.4 Implementing operational profiles

A key to this operational profile implementation is the selection methods used across the various profiles. To select customers and configurations, this technique selects ones that are both of high probability and (more) likely to fail. These configuration and customer choices are made independently since experience has indicated that (nearly) all combinations exist in the DEFINITY customer base (or are at least possible).

The customers/configurations selection strategy begins by deterministically (not randomly) selecting those with the highest usage probabilities. The selections are then modified by adding or removing configuration components based on knowledge of the likelihood of failure of the components. (Though perhaps difficult to quantify, knowledge of product failure behavior is available during the development process. It includes such things as which code has changed, which circuit packs are new, which functional interactions exist, what the "traditional" trouble areas are, and so on.)

This is a good strategy from the test resource perspective: by following this strategy, the largest proportion of customers are covered with the fewest selections. It is also good from the quality-improvement perspective since it uses failure- and usage-likelihood information in combination. This will most rapidly improve customer-perceived quality.

Once the customer and configuration are selected (deterministically), the run types to execute are selected randomly (as explained earlier) from that customer's user call trees according to usage probabilities.

The system test organization implements this operational profile approach by first documenting customer, user, and configuration selections in the system test environment and strategy planning documents. These documents guide the creation of individual test plans, one for each quality (reliability) assessment done during the development interval. The test plans consist of configuration information (environment), usage information (traffic loads and user run types), and other system-level test cases. Using the information in the test plan, the basic execution process is to set up the test lab into a customer-like configuration and operate it as a customer would by running traffic and executing user run types. Failure data observed from this process are fed into reliability analysis tools that plot reliability and other quality metric graphs.

5.7.5 Conclusion

As described earlier in this chapter (see Sec. 5.1), initial experience with SRE-based product development for DEFINITY was quite successful (other factors also influenced these results—see [Abra92]). Subsequent applications of these techniques continue to yield extremely beneficial results both in terms of product quality as well as development time and cost. You can find out more about these operational profile techniques in [Juhl92a] and the overall SRE approach in [Juhl92b] and [Juhl93].

5.8 Application to FASTAR^{SM} (FAST Automated Restoration)

5.8.1 System description

AT&T's long distance network provides ultrareliable telecommunications services. The network is composed of fiber light-guide systems connected by Digital Cross Connect Systems. With the advent of fiber-optic technology, the capacity of the network has increased along with the consequences of events such as cable cuts caused by backhoes, train derailments, and ice storms. Fiber systems are vulnerable to damage due to cable cuts, and a large cut could easily affect over 100,000 telephone circuits. FASTAR, AT&T's Fast Automated Restoration Platform, alleviates the impact of fiber cable cuts by reducing the time it takes to restore service from hours to minutes.

In November 1988, prior to FASTAR, a fiber cable cut in the Newark, New Jersey, area caused the loss of over 270 DS3 paths. A DS3 path consists of 672 telephone circuits and is the unit of transmission and restorability in the AT&T long-distance network. Thus more than 180,000 telephone circuits we affected. It took more than 15 hours to repair the cable and reestablish service. After FASTAR was deployed, a cable cut between Kansas City and St. Louis severed over 250 DS3 paths. It took considerably less than the 5-minute restoration objective to restore service using FASTAR technology.

Two key systems manage FASTAR restoration capabilities. These are the Restoration Node Controller and the Central Restoration System. The Restoration Node Controller is a UNIX®-based system with instances in more than 200 AT&T digital central offices. It monitors the Lightguide Terminating Equipment and Digital Cross Connect Systems for alarm conditions indicating a fiber cut or component equipment failure. The Central Restoration System, also a UNIX®-based system, controls the overall restoration process. This system utilizes unused capacity in the AT&T network to dynamically reroute traffic around failures. Users interact with the Central Restoration System to monitor restoration progress and handle exception conditions.

Figure 5.3 provides a diagram of the FASTAR architecture. If a cable between office A and office C is cut, the Restoration Node Controller in each of these offices detects and reports the failure to the Central Restoration System. Next, the Central Restoration System computes optimal DS3 restoration paths between offices A, B, and C and implements these paths by sending appropriate commands to the Digital Cross Connect System in each office.

Software validation of the UNIX®-based systems that control the restoration process was critical to the success of FASTAR. Since the Restoration Node Controller and Central Restoration System have the power to rearrange the AT&T network, software defects in these

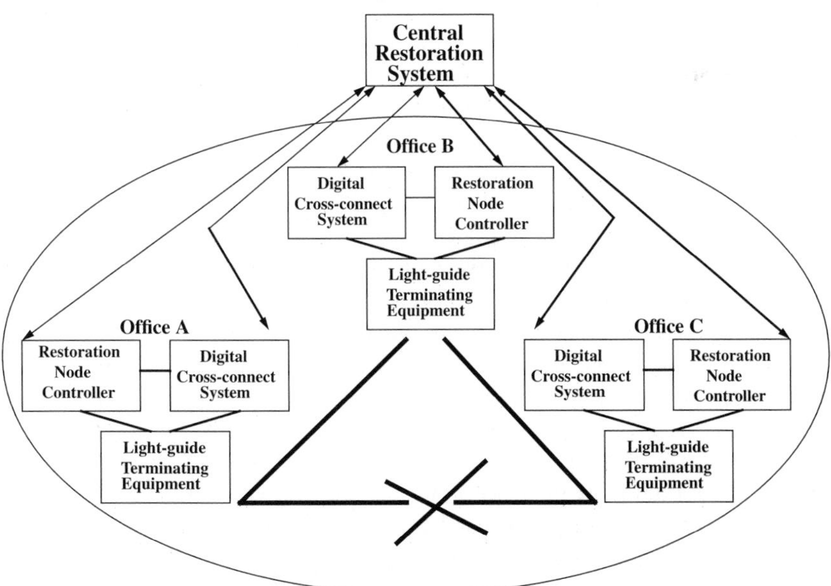

Figure 5.3 FASTAR℠ architecture.

systems could cause severe network service interruptions. As the development team for FASTAR, we selected software reliability engineering (SRE) to verify that stringent reliability objectives had been met. (Throughout the remainder of this section, *we* refers to the FASTAR development team.)

The success of the FASTAR SRE program was based on our focus in four key areas: understanding customer expectations, deriving the operational profile, developing the test environment, and executing the load/stress/stability test program.

5.8.2 FASTAR: SRE implementation

5.8.2.1 Understand customer expectations. The customers for FASTAR are the AT&T business units that provide business and consumer long Distance and 800 services and the Network Operations group that maintains the AT&T network. The job of these AT&T organizations is to provide a reliable network for the millions of business and residential consumers who use AT&T telecommunications services every day. FASTAR helps them meet the demands of these consumers.

These customers demand high levels of quality, reliability, availability, and performance. They expect the systems that compose FASTAR to not only meet performance objectives but also operate continuously and flawlessly. They want to be absolutely certain that the system has no defects that could negatively impact long-distance service.

Our goal as the development managers for the Central Restoration System and the Restoration Node Controller is to ensure that our organization delivers on our customers' high demands. Our SRE program allows us to do just that. With SRE, we are able to verify FASTAR operational reliability and assess performance under projected field operation. To do this, we developed an operational profile.

5.8.2.2 Derive operational profile. As previously noted, an operational profile characterizes the operating conditions for the system—that is, how the software will be used in the field. We derived the initial version of the FASTAR operational profile using a computer simulation model of FASTAR. This first profile focused solely on cable-cut scenarios. We defined the typical and worst-case cable-cut incidents from simulation results, and derived the frequency of various cable-cut scenarios from historical data. Figure 5.4 displays the FASTAR operational profile for cable-cut scenarios. It describes the probability of small, medium, and large cable cuts occurring. We estimate that 10 large cable cuts occur in the AT&T fiber network each year.

As development proceeded, we recognized the need to define a richer operational profile that described all the system inputs and outputs in

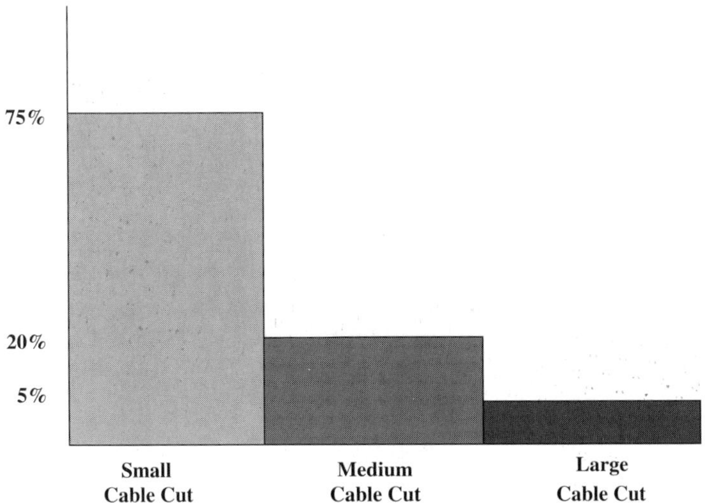

Figure 5.4 FASTAR^{SM} operational profile. Probability of small, medium, and large cable cuts.

order to adequately test the system. We added background events to the profile. We defined *background events* as all non-cable-cut activities that could occur on the system. These included activities such as database provisioning, maintenance operations, network management operations, and single DS3 path failures caused by component equipment failures. While major cable cuts occur approximately 10 times during a year, background events occur continuously.

After close examination of the FASTAR operational profile, we determined that the operating conditions for the Central Restoration System were quite different than that of the Restoration Node Controller. We viewed the operating scope of the Central Restoration System as the entire AT&T network. For the Restoration Node Controller, we viewed the operating scope as a single digital central office. In order to take these important differences into account in our test program, we decided to define distinct operational profiles for each of the two systems.

In the operational profile for the Central Restoration System, we were concerned about the overall FASTAR profile and the impact of receiving data from over 200 Restoration Node Controllers, maintaining communications to over 200 Digital Cross Connect Systems and processing commands from 50 simultaneous users. Special attention was paid to collecting data that described how users actually interacted with the system. For the Restoration Node Controller, we developed one operational profile that represented all the offices and focused on the worst-case load in the largest AT&T digital central offices.

We derived the operational profile for each of the systems from discussions with customers and from log data collected from Beta Test versions of the system. The frequency of event occurrences in the Central Restoration System dwarfed that of the Restoration Node Controller. For the Central Restoration System, 10 major cable-cut events are expected in a year. For the Restoration Node Controller, any single system can expect to participate in less than one cable-cut event each year. The difference in background events is even more dramatic. Forty thousand background events are executed on the Central Restoration System every day due to the many users who interact with the system. For the Restoration Node Controller, 500 background events are performed each day. After fully understanding the operating conditions for the software, our next challenge was to build a test environment to take advantage of the operational profile.

5.8.2.3 Develop test environment. We began FASTAR testing by using real network facilities and central office equipment in a laboratory. However, this did not allow us to test the field operational profile. It was not possible or feasible to test the system's maximum configuration. We augmented the test lab with a simulated test environment that could handle all the inputs and outputs identified in the operational profile.

For the Central Restoration System, we developed a Network and User Simulator (see Fig. 5.5). It can simulate the actions of more than 200 Restoration Node Controllers and Digital Cross Connect Systems and over 50 simultaneous users. It provides an environment to test the Central Restoration System with the worst-case cable-cut scenarios that can occur in the AT&T network in the safety of our lab environment.

For the Restoration Node Controller, we developed an Office Simulator (see Fig. 5.3). It simulates the maximum office configuration. The Office Simulator supports the simulation of direct connections to Lightguide Terminating Equipment and Digital Cross Connect Systems. It provides an environment to test the Restoration Node Controller with worst-case cable-cut events in AT&T's largest offices in the safety of our lab.

Both simulation environments were designed with a programmable interface. This allowed us to develop automated test scripts to drive the test runs. We wrote automated test scripts in the Network and User Simulator environment to simulate the operational profile of the Central Restoration System. For example, user scripts mirror the operations of the various users, and alarm scripts simulate the cable-cut alarms from the Restoration Node Controller. We wrote automated test scripts in the Office Simulator environment to simulate the operational profile of the Restoration Node Controller. For instance, alarm scripts simulate cable-cut alarms from Lightguide Terminating Equipment.

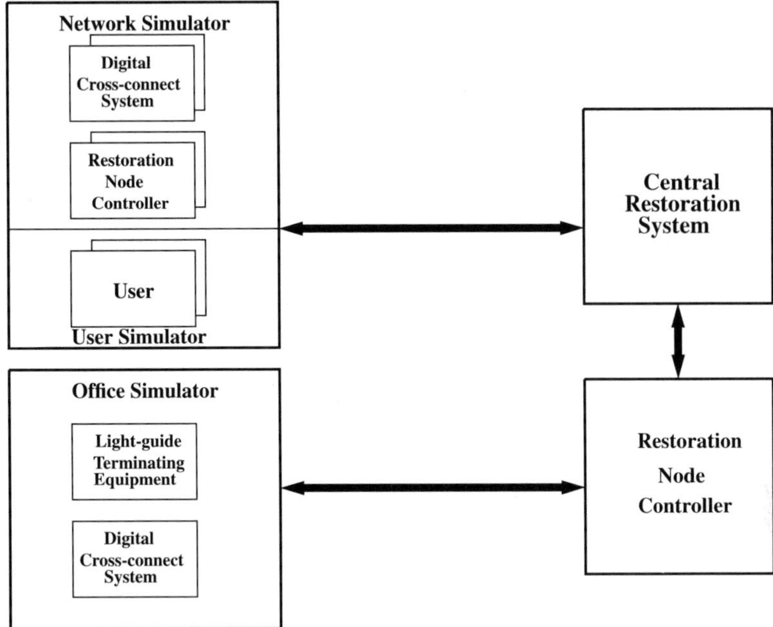

Figure 5.5 Simulator test environment.

Once the test environment was developed, we had the tools in place to execute our load/stress/stability test program.

5.8.2.4 Execute load/stress/stability test program. The purpose of our load/stress/stability test program was to ensure that the Central Restoration System and Restoration Node Controller met our customer's stringent reliability objectives for FASTAR. We wanted to be certain that FASTAR did what it was supposed to do and, more important, did not do anything that it was not supposed to do. We orchestrated load/stress/stability tests by executing each system's operational profile in its respective test environment. We found and fixed defects and reran the tests. Using this process, failures occurred less frequently and the reliability of FASTAR improved over time.

During our load/stress/stability test program, we tested the Central Restoration System and Restoration Node Controller under the same conditions that would be encountered in the field. These tests were performed after the individual commands and operations had been functionally verified. Load tests mirrored the operational profile of the two systems. Stress tests executed worst-case cable-cut scenarios on each of the systems. Stability tests verified each system with its operational profile for a minimum of 100 hours of continuous operations. Often, stability tests ran for over one month.

The FASTAR operational profile showed that cable cuts happen very infrequently. Restoration of cable cuts was certainly the most critical operation of the system. Since it was not feasible to execute the test program for a year to simulate the expected 10 cable cuts, we designed accelerated test runs. In the case of the Restoration Node Controller, load was accelerated by a factor of 24 during stability tests. This allowed us to execute an entire day's activities in one hour. Hence, we could execute a year's operational profile in the test environment within a matter of weeks. For the Central Restoration System, load was accelerated by a factor of 1.25 during stability tests and by a factor of 50 during stress tests.

We measured test results for each load/stress/stability test run and tracked the growth of reliability over time. The metrics we used for tracking results were DS3 paths correctly reported by the Restoration Node Controller and DS3 paths correctly rerouted by the Central Restoration System. When we started obtaining load/stress/stability test results, 90 percent of DS3 paths were correctly reported and rerouted. We continued to improve the system, run tests, measure results, and fix defects. When we were ready to release FASTAR, reliability had grown above the 99 percent mark. Still we continued to improve the system until our results reached nearly 100 percent.

5.8.3 FASTAR: SRE benefits

SRE was instrumental to the success of FASTAR by ensuring that reliability objectives had been satisfied prior to introducing the system into the AT&T network. SRE results guided us in making the critical decision on when to release FASTAR.

The major benefit from SRE was that it gave us the confidence to deploy the system. In fact, we believe that without SRE we would have not been able to release FASTAR, because we had no other way to be certain that the system would not have a defect that could seriously impair the operation of the AT&T network. With the results we obtained from SRE, we were able to decide when the system was ready to be released, and we were confident that FASTAR would dramatically improve network operations. Our SRE prediction has proven to be accurate. FASTAR handles single DS3 restorations on a daily basis and major cable cuts throughout the year.

5.9 Application to the Power Quality Resource System (PQRS)

5.9.1 Project description

In recent years, AT&T has placed increased emphasis on the role of AC and DC power systems and other network infrastructure elements with respect to network reliability. While normally maintaining a low profile among the more exciting, high-visibility technologies in use today, power and infrastructure systems must be in place, engineered correctly, and maintained appropriately to ensure reliable operations of the network elements they support.

In mid-1992, AT&T's Network Services Division, which operates the core network, deployed a new internal application to support network operations and engineering of power and infrastructure systems. The Power Quality Resource System (PQRS) maintains an inventory of the major units of AC and DC power systems and infrastructure elements, including building environmentals such as chillers. In addition, PQRS contains algorithms to calculate fuel and battery reserve time. PQRS provides the capability to calculate the number of hours the office can run on auxiliary power generated by its standby engines and by battery backup.

A typical use of PQRS involves support of the demand (or reactive) maintenance process. In the event of a power failure alarm, for example, AT&T's surveillance and alarm center personnel will determine the appropriate response, given a number of factors including battery reserve time, fuel reserve, or availability of a portable engine, and so on—information extracted from PQRS upon demand.

The project team applied state-of-the-art methods and tools in the development of PQRS. In the preliminary planning stages for the project, a decision was made to apply SRE—in particular, operational profile testing.

5.9.2 Developing the operational profile

5.9.2.1 Initial functional profile derived from DFDs. The PQRS requirements team used dataflow diagrams (DFDs) and entity relationship diagrams (ERDs) to model the application's functions and stored data. The level 0 DFD is used to identify the major processes and functions of the system. The level 0 diagram is the DFD directly beneath the context diagram in a leveled set of DFDs, and it represents the highest-level view of the major functions within the system and the major interfaces between those functions [Your89]. The initial functional profile was derived from PQRS's level 0 DFD.

At this early point in the development cycle, the team estimated transaction volume in terms of broad ranges and used the information as input to the formulation of the hardware and software architecture of the system.

5.9.2.2 Final functional profile. The project team used a process known as *architecture discovery* to understand the user's expectations, to identify the problem to be solved, and to determine if a solution (partial/whole) already exists. As the software architecture solution began to be defined, logical groupings of transactions emerged. The transaction classes were groups of transactions which were roughly equivalent in terms of CPU utilization, software architecture elements applied, user think time, and performance/response time.

The architecture team turned over a list of 21 transaction classes to the requirements team to develop estimates of daily system-usage volumes (best and worst case) by user group for the first and fourth years of operation. The requirements team pulled in a subject matter expert from the user community to help produce the estimates.

The architecture team used the functional profile to finalize the resource budgets and system configuration. The team also established a plan to instrument the system so that field data could be collected to assess the system's performance, to identify usage trends, and to validate/update the estimates that were used for the performance model and for the operational profile.

5.9.2.3 Operational profile. Over time, PQRS's project-specific definition of *operational profile* has evolved to the following: listing of each transaction, mapping of each transaction to an operation, execution frequency of each operation, and usage characteristics (time of day, number of users). The definition does not include environmental and customer-type variables, as they are not factors for this internal product.

About 3 months prior to system test, members of the project team met to finalize the operational profile. By that point, the application itself was well understood. With much discussion and lively interchange, 56 individual transactions were identified and mapped to 12 operations. The rationale for aggregating the transactions followed the logic of the architecture phase: that roughly equivalent transactions could be grouped based on CPU utilization and software architecture elements involved. Further, due to the difficulty (and inherent inaccuracy) in estimating transaction volumes at the lowest level (add battery record, view battery record, modify battery record, etc.), the team agreed that the aggregate approach was appropriate for this data-intensive application.

PQRS's heaviest users (in terms of numbers of transactions they were expected to generate) work regular office hours, and most are in the eastern time zone. The project team settled on three system modes for the initial operational profile: off hours, prime-time peak, and prime-time nonpeak. Experience with the production system has validated these assumptions.

With a total number of transactions expected during an average business day and considering the predominant daytime usage, it was easy to estimate the off-hours volume by class. To segregate the remainder between peak and nonpeak hours, the team approximated prime-time peak as 50 percent higher than prime-time nonpeak.

5.9.2.4 Updating the operational profile. With the instrumentation provided in PQRS's software to log transaction volumes at the lowest level, including their performance, it has been simple for the project team to update the operational profile for each new release. Following the initial operational profile testing of release 1.0, the team has further condensed the number of operations. Every transaction is mapped to one of seven basic operations. For each new release, the seven basic operations are updated to include functionality delivered in the previous release, and the new functionality is isolated in three separate, additional operations to ensure thorough test coverage of the new capabilities, but in proportion to their expected usage.

PQRS's logs are shipped regularly from the production site to the development machine. Numbers of login sessions and transactions are tracked by class, by user, and by hour of the day. The data are also analyzed for transaction mix and volumes during network emergencies such as Hurricane Andrew.

5.9.3 Testing

The primary objective of the project team in testing in accordance with the operational profile was to certify PQRS's software quality from the users' viewpoint. The team expected to identify software failures occurring as a result of combinations of transactions or due to hours of continuous operation, failures not observable through traditional functional testing.

5.9.3.1 Tools. A high degree of automation has always been an assumption with respect to operational profile testing for both test generation and test execution. The test team developed a test executive that controls generation of test scripts and executes them based on the operational profile. Every hour, a scheduled job begins executing, and it performs the following:

1. Determine system mode for the next hour and number of users who will log in.
2. Determine number of transactions by class that will be executed; randomly select individual transactions within the class to be executed; generate test cases in real time based on a set of fixed, valid data.
3. Randomly map test cases to users and determine a random minute within the hour for the start of each user session.
4. Create an execution script for each user.

During each hour, the test executive provides overall control for execution of the scripts and monitoring mechanisms.

5.9.3.2 Varying occurrence probabilities. Due to the simplicity of the design of the test executive, the test team has been able to vary the occurrence probabilities and transaction volumes by class. Since the operational profile is only an estimate at best, the team has found it useful to vary it a bit to reflect the production environment, i.e., every day in the field will not be an average day. This has resulted in the detection of at least one failure that may not have been detected in other phases of testing. This follows from the expectation that reliability will change when the environment changes [Musa87].

With such a data-intensive product, and each new release delivering additional inventory capability (i.e., new screens and tables), the team has at times intentionally increased the rate of inventory transactions significantly above the norm to evaluate the results. And due to heavy usage of PQRS's reporting capabilities during network emergencies, the test team has also varied the mix of transactions to simulate non-average field conditions.

5.9.3.3 Extension to performance and stress testing. Because PQRS was instrumented to track transactions and performance, performance testing is not a separate testing discipline for the project. During the intervals when the operational profile is being executed, the system logs are monitored closely for anomalies in performance.

The simplicity of the design of the operational profile test executive has also made it extensible to stress testing. Transaction volumes, transaction mix, and numbers of users are systematically intensified and the logs examined for evidence of failures and to evaluate performance.

5.9.4 Conclusion

Development of the operational profile was an extension of work already performed for understanding the customers' requirements. With the inclusion of application measurements and logging, it has been a relatively simple matter to keep the profile updated for each release.

The benefits realized from testing in accordance with the operational profile include detection of several software faults not observed (and likely not observable) during traditional functional testing. It has certified the quality of the delivered product.

The investment made in automation continues to pay back, in its ability to run load testing continuously for two weeks without intervention and in its extensibility to stress testing and application for regression testing.

5.10 Summary

At AT&T, software reliability engineering, which includes the operational profile, was approved as a "best current practice" (see Chap. 6) in 1991. To qualify as a best current practice, a technique must have substantial project application with a documented, favorable benefit-to-cost ratio, support by world-class technology, and mechanisms for technology transfer (courses, reference material, jump starts and consulting, tools) in place. It must pass probing reviews by two committees of senior software managers [Ever93].

AT&T has used SRE and the operational profile to ensure the success of many projects, including such critical ones as DEFINITY, FASTAR, and PQRS. In one large software-development organization, it is being fully integrated into the development process. AT&T and other companies (for example, Hewlett-Packard) have found that application of the operational profile yields substantial savings in test costs and hence total project cost. You can expect to save even more if you use the operational profile to guide other development phases as well.

Problems

5.1 What simplifications should be made in the procedures for developing an operational profile for a software-based product for internal use in a company?

5.2 When can you go directly to an operational profile without creating a functional profile?

5.3 Can different customer groups have the same user groups?

5.4 Systems in heavy traffic conditions often will not allow the execution of low-priority operations such as maintenance and backup. How do you handle the effect on the operational profile?

5.5 Is it acceptable to merge a number of noncritical, rarely occurring operations into one operation?

5.6 What is a common failing in creating the function list?

5.7 Can an operational profile be developed for operations that span multiple machines?

5.8 What is *reduced-operation software?*

5.9 Assume you are the development manager on a software project for an airplane flight control system. How would you implement an SRE program for this software development effort? Include the major steps you would undertake to ensure the success of this program.

5.10 Discuss the advantages and disadvantages of aggregating individual transactions in the formulation of the operational profile.

5.11 Discuss the benefits of instrumenting your application to record field data.

Part

2

Practices and Experiences

Chapter

6

Best Current Practice of SRE

Mary Donnelly, Bill Everett, John Musa, and Geoff Wilson
AT&T Bell Laboratories

6.1 Introduction

This chapter describes the best current practice (BCP) for doing software reliability engineering (SRE) as adopted by AT&T. It represents an integrated consensus of some 70 software project managers and engineers based on practices employed by a large number of projects within AT&T. Consequently, to maintain its integrity, we have not incorporated material from other sources.

The practice of SRE provides the software engineer or manager the means to predict, estimate, and measure the rate of failure occurrences in software (including firmware). Such measures are understandable to your customer. Using SRE in the context of software engineering, you can:

- Analyze, manage, and improve the reliability of your software products.
- Balance customer needs for competitive price, timely delivery, and a reliable product.
- Determine when the software is good enough to release to your customer, minimizing the risks of releasing software with serious problems.
- Avoid excessive time to market due to overtesting.

Although portions of SRE are based on sophisticated statistical concepts, available software tools as discussed in App. A allow the average software developer or engineer to apply SRE easily, without the need for statistical background.

The practice of SRE may be summarized in six steps:

1. Quantify product usage by specifying how frequently customers will use various features and how frequently various environmental conditions that influence processing will occur.

2. Define *quality* quantitatively with your customers by defining failures and failure severities and by specifying the balance among the key quality objectives of reliability, delivery date, and cost to maximize customer satisfaction.

3. Employ product usage data and quality objectives to guide design and implementation of your product and to manage resources to maximize productivity (i.e., customer satisfaction per unit cost).

4. Measure reliability of reused software and acquired software components delivered to you by suppliers, as an acceptance requirement.

5. Track reliability during test and use this information to guide product release.

6. Monitor reliability in field operation and use results to guide new feature introduction, as well as product and process improvement.

This chapter will help assess the benefits and costs of doing SRE in your organization or project. It will also aid you in visualizing how to practice SRE and how to get started. It provides information on resources and examples of successful applications.

6.2 Benefits and Approaches to SRE

SRE predicts, models, estimates, measures, and manages the reliability of software-based products. It extends from product conception through delivery and use by the customer. Again, *reliability* is the probability that a hardware or software system or component does its required functions without failure for a specified period of time under specified operating conditions.

Software reliability varies with how and in what environment the software is used. Characterizing customer operating conditions as precisely as possible is an important part of SRE. This is done with a *profile* or set of alternative uses and their occurrence probabilities under different environmental conditions, as discussed in Chap. 5. Early in the software development life cycle, you deal with *functions* or tasks needed by the user in different environments and determine a *functional profile.* Later, when you know how tasks will be implemented by the system as *operations,* you translate the functional profile to an *operational profile.*

6.2.1 Importance and benefits

Most surveys of users of software-based systems show that reliability ranks first on the list of customer satisfiers. Eighty percent of AT&T's largest customers considered reliability to be *the most important quality attribute* to them. With greater use of software in products, the proportion of total failures that are software related is increasing. Some projects report that the number of customer-reported software failures of their products exceeds the number of hardware failures. To be successful in the marketplace a product must meet the quality expectations of its customers. To meet this end, you must be able to measure quality from your *customer's* perspective.

Fault-based measures commonly used in the software development industry have served well as developer-oriented measures of quality. They have helped to improve the quality of development processes in the past and will continue to play an important role. However, users of software products experience failures, not faults. Your customers are not concerned as much with how many faults there are in your software product as they are with how often the product will fail and the impact such failures will have on the job they must do. Evaluating reliability of software from the customer's perspective requires *failure-based measures.*

SRE will help your project

- *Satisfy customer needs more precisely.* Having precise reliability requirements focuses development on meeting your customers' reliability needs. Reliability requirements enable system testers to concretely verify that the finished product meets customers' needs before it is released.
- *Deliver earlier.* Delivering the exact reliability needed by the customer avoids wasting time for unneeded extra testing.
- *Increase productivity.* By using the functional and operational profiles to focus resources on the *high-usage* functions or operations and by developing and testing for *exactly* the reliability needed, productivity is improved.
- *Plan project resources better.* Before testing begins, SRE supports prediction of the amount of system test resources needed, avoiding unnecessary waste and disruption due to unpleasant surprises.

6.2.2 An SRE success story

AT&T's International DEFINITY® PBX started a new quality program that included doing SRE along with other proven quality methodologies [Abra92]. The SRE part of the program included

- Defining an *operational profile* based on customer modeling
- Generating test cases automatically based on frequency of use reflected in the *operational profile*
- Delivering software in increments to system test with quality factor assessments (*reliability* being one factor)
- Employing clean-room development techniques together with feature testing based on the *operational profile*
- Testing to reliability objectives

The quality improvement from the previous major release was dramatic:

- A *factor-of-10 reduction* in customer-reported problems
- A *factor-of-10 reduction* in program maintenance costs
- A *factor-of-2 reduction* in the system test interval
- A *30 percent reduction* in new product introduction interval

In addition, no serious service-affecting outages were reported in the first two years of operation. There was significant improvement in customer satisfaction. The reliability improvement and an aggressive sales plan have pushed sales to 10 times those for the previous version. Items contributing to these successes were as follows:

- Using *reliability* as a release criterion prevented excessive customer-reported problems and associated maintenance activity.
- Using *operational-profile-driven testing* increased test efficiency: 20 percent of the operations represented 95 percent of the use; 20 percent of the faults caused 95 percent of the failures; testing the 20 percent high-usage operations first speeded reliability improvement.

6.2.3 SRE costs

The principal cost in applying SRE is determining the operational profile. The effort depends on the number of operations defined and the precision of their occurrence probabilities. You must use engineering judgment to control the amount of work. In our experience, effort has ranged from one staff week to one staff year, depending on the size and the complexity of the project. The average effort (for a project with 10 developers, approximately 100,000 source lines and a development interval of about 18 months) is about 2 staff months. Once you develop the operational profile for a product, you need only update it for subsequent releases, a much smaller task. Another cost is associated with processing and analyzing failure data during reliability growth testing, which requires about 4 hours per week. The total SRE effort during a test is thus usually less than 0.3 staff month. There is a training cost in starting to apply SRE. At least one project representative needs a course in SRE. Also, engaging an SRE consultant to transfer SRE knowledge to the project during initial implementation (jump-start consulting) is cost-effective. The cost (about one staff month of consultant's time) is offset by preventing costly mistakes in applying SRE.

Most SRE activities involve using SRE measures to better perform tasks that projects normally do anyway. SRE does not contribute more cost to these tasks. As most projects have multiple releases, and SRE cost drops sharply after initial application, the per-release cost of SRE is about one staff month. The very largest projects (over 1000 software developers and multiple large operational profiles) do not exceed an effort of one person full time. Thus, for most projects, SRE costs considerably less than 1 percent of total project cost.

6.2.4 SRE activities

Figure 6.1 illustrates SRE activities across the phases of the software product life cycle. The phases, of course, need not follow a neat sequence, and neither do the SRE activities. There is considerable overlap and iteration. Each SRE activity is therefore simply placed in the phase in which most of the effort occurs. Sections 6.3 to 6.6 each discuss the activities of one phase in detail.

6.2.5 Implementing SRE incrementally

Most projects start by implementing just some of the SRE activities. As they learn to apply and profit from these activities, they add additional ones. A typical implementation sequence is shown in Table 6.1, with the benefits from each step noted. The sequence applies to both new and existing projects. This incremental approach keeps the rate of change in your development process to a manageable level.

The order of implementing the sets of activities in Table 6.1 is the recommended one. However, there is considerable *flexibility* in choosing the sets of activities to implement, and in modifying the sequence to meet your project's needs. If there are external factors that hamper the implementation of a particular set, implement another set of activities in the sequence and return to the first one when the difficulties are resolved. For example, although monitoring field reliability is important and should be implemented early, the difficulties associated with obtaining field data may require it to be implemented later. It's a good practice to have an expert check the SRE implementation plan to make sure you haven't inadvertently left out a prerequisite activity. The section references in the "Details" column of Table 6.1 indicate where to read more about the activities.

6.2.6 Implementing SRE on existing projects

There is no essential difference between new and existing projects in applying SRE for the first time. After it has been applied to one release, however, you will need much less effort for succeeding releases. Most of the activities noted in Fig. 6.1 will require only small updates after they have been completed one time.

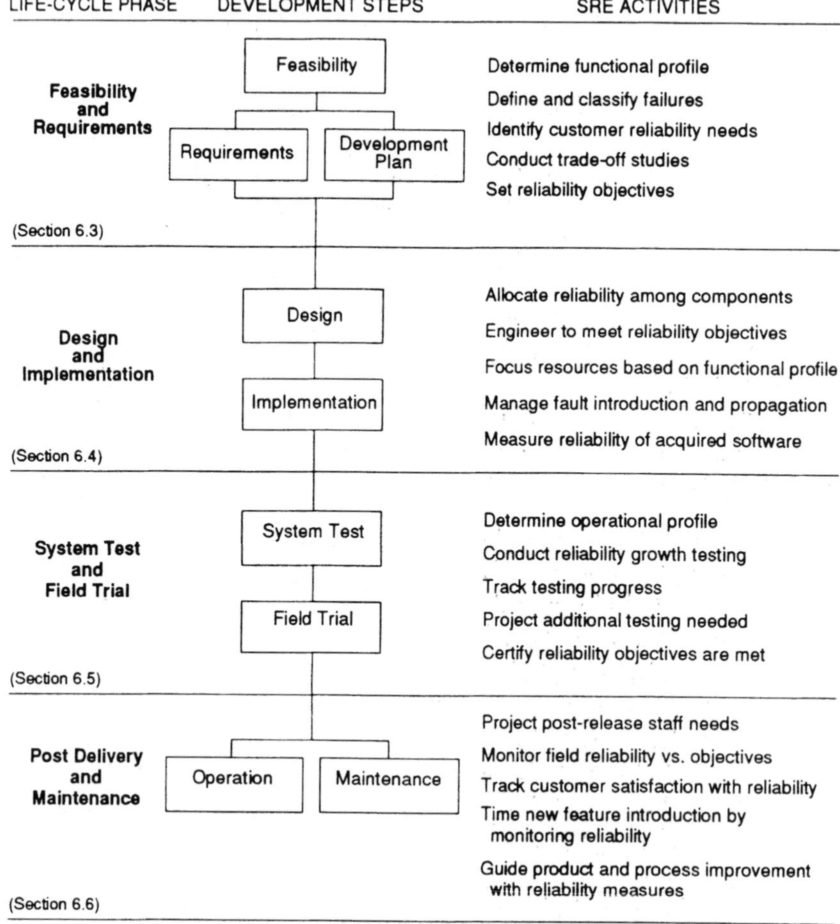

Figure 6.1 SRE activities in the software product life cycle.

TABLE 6.1 Typical Incremental Introduction of SRE

Set of activities	Benefits	Details
1. Conduct reliability growth testing, track testing progress	Know exactly what reliability your customer would experience at different points in time if you released the software at those points	6.5
2. Determine functional and operational profiles	Speed up time to market by saving test time, reduce test cost	6.3, 6.5
3. Define and classify failures, identify customer reliability needs, set reliability objectives, certify reliability objectives are met, project additional testing needed	Release software at a time that meets customer reliability needs but is as early and inexpensive as possible	6.3, 6.5
4. Monitor field reliability versus objectives, track customer satisfaction with reliability	Maximize likelihood of pleasing customer with reliability	6.6
5. Time new feature introduction by monitoring reliability	Ensure that software *continues* to meet customer reliability needs in the field	6.6
6. Focus resources based on functional profile	Speed up time to market by guiding development priorities, reduce development cost	6.4
7. Allocate reliability among components	Reduce development time and cost by striking better balance among components	6.4
8. Measure reliability of acquired software	Reduce risks to reliability, schedule, cost from unknown software	6.4
9. Engineer to meet reliability objectives	Reduce development time and cost with better design	6.4
10. Guide product and process improvement with reliability measures	Maximize cost-effectiveness of product and process improvements selected	6.6
11. Manage fault introduction and propagation	Maximize cost-effectiveness of reliability improvement	6.4
12. Project postrelease staff needs	Reduce postrelease costs with better planning	6.6
13. Conduct trade-off studies	Increase market share by providing better match to customer needs	6.3

6.2.7 Implementing SRE on short-cycle projects

Small projects or releases or those with short development cycles may require a modified set of SRE activities to keep costs low or activity durations short. A reasonable approach is to select a reduced group of sets of activities from Table 6.1, following approximately the order listed. Leave out sets of activities whose benefits for your project do not justify their costs or time durations.

Determining the functional and/or operational profiles is often the SRE activity that takes the most cost and time. Reduction in cost and time can be obtained by limiting the number of elements in the profile [Musa93] and by accepting less precision.

One difficulty with small projects is the likelihood of only a small sample of failures occurring during reliability growth testing. You can still track testing progress, but not as precisely as you might wish.

6.3 SRE During the Feasibility and Requirements Phase

Although the makeup of this phase may vary across projects, this section describes the SRE activities, outlined in Fig. 6.1, that are conducted during the feasibility and requirements stages. The feasibility stage involves product concept development. The requirements stage involves the development of detailed product requirements and a plan to develop the product.

6.3.1 Feasibility stage

The output of the feasibility stage is either a feasibility report, product prospectus, or a business plan. This defines a certain market and explores the potential of the product to meet that market. It also assesses the capability of the organization to produce the product for the market in the time frame needed, at a price and level of reliability desired by the customer relative to their competitors. For government contract work the output consists of a response to a request for proposal (RFP), which contains many of the items described above.

6.3.1.1 Determine functional profile. To determine the *functional profile,* you must first establish the set of functions for the product. Functions are characterized in terms of *both* the tasks performed and the environmental factors that influence processing. For example, functions of a telephone PBX system would include the types of telephone calls placed and received by subclasses of users (e.g., managers, secretaries, and engineers). In addition, they would also contain information on the environment, such as the types of telephone sets configured on the system and call features (for example, call forwarding) configured on the sets by each class of user.

In the case of both functional and operational profiles, you can account for *criticality* of functions or operations by weighting them.

Requirements are sometimes developed in great detail, so that in effect they incorporate some of the system architecture and actually specify the operations performed by the system. In that case, you can determine an operational profile directly in this stage, rather than after design and implementation.

Quality function deployment (QFD) is a useful method of working with your customers to identify functions that satisfy their needs. Having them ask, "How often do I visualize that need occurring?" and "How costly is it to me when that need is not satisfied?" helps in defining a functional profile and in defining classes of failures. Having a customer answer these questions also helps them rank their needs in completing the QFD process. For more detailed information on the functional profile see Chap. 5.

6.3.1.2 Define and classify failures. You should define *failure* from your customer's perspective. Start with similar products with the same customer base as your new product and determine the customer's failure experiences with them. Distinguish software failures from hardware and procedural failures.

A good practice is to group identified software failures into a few severity classes (say, three or four). This grouping should be done from the viewpoint of the effect of failures on the customer's ability to conduct business. The effect can be measured in terms of cost, service degradation, or safety. Table 6.2 gives an example based on service degradation for a telephone switching system.

There is a trade-off here. More classes require more effort later in the life cycle in collecting and analyzing data for each class, whereas fewer classes give a coarser resolution of the effect on the customer.

6.3.1.3 Identify customer reliability needs. You identify customer reliability needs at a high level in this stage. A small team conducts the assessment while defining other aspects of the product (e.g., feature set content, capacity, and performance capabilities). A recommended team consists of a system engineer, a system architect, a marketing (product planning) person, a customer representative (marketing may serve as a customer surrogate), a reliability analyst, and a system tester. The marketing person is a likely candidate to lead this team.

Establish who (other suppliers) and what (alternative products) your competitors are and assess their reliability capabilities. A good way of defining the level of reliability required is to relate the product to an existing product or set of products having the same customer base. For

TABLE 6.2 Severity Classification Based on Service Degradation

Severity classification	Definition	Example
Catastrophic	Entire system failed, no functionality left	No one can get dial tone
Severe	A high-priority customer feature is not working	You can make local but not long-distance calls
Significant	Customers must change how they use the system	You can't use your calling card in a pay phone but must read number to operator
Minor	Problem is not noticeable by customers	Some maintenance functions are not currently performed

example, relating a new product to an existing switching system product, a reliability assessment might state "product X should have a reliability comparable to switching system Y used in the customer central office."

As a minimum, determine an approximate acceptable failure intensity for each severity class. Typical acceptable values of failure intensity can range from one failure per 100 hours (low-severity failures for routine business applications) through one failure per billion hours (air traffic control or nuclear power plant shutdown). This approach was used within AT&T to establish the reliability of a large network system which included 337 thousand new-end changed source lines (KNCSL) of new software reused from previous products and of a PBX system with over 1100 thousand lines of code (KLOC).

6.3.2 Requirements stage

The requirements stage involves preparing a detailed requirements specification for the product and laying out a development plan. The *requirements specification* expands the needs and high-level features defined during the feasibility stage. It includes attributes such as product reliability, availability, performance, and capacity. A requirements specification must have a section defining the reliability requirements of the product. The *development plan* outlines the resources, costs, and schedules needed to develop the product. You determine resources, costs, and schedules from the product requirements specification, *including* the reliability specifications. The development plan should include adequate resources and schedule for reliability-related activities. These activities include reliability training of staff (Sec. 6.7.1) and particular reliability activities conducted during each phase of the product life cycle (Secs. 6.3 through 6.6).

The reliability assessment started in the feasibility stage is refined in this stage in forming your reliability requirements. You establish specific quantified reliability objectives. These are based on the functional profile and failure definitions you have determined and that you continue to refine. For example, for a PBX product used in a telemarketing application, you might specify that a software failure that could cause a system outage should occur no more than once every three months. When such an outage occurs, it should be recoverable in less than 30 minutes.

In this stage, the system engineer would generally serve as team leader of the reliability assessment team formed in the feasibility stage. You should also seriously consider adding a field support person to the team.

6.3.2.1 Conduct trade-off studies. A major cost in developing your product is associated with testing in general and with reliability growth testing in particular. For some product developments, testing accounts for over half of the development cost. Trade-off studies help you in setting objectives for reliability, cost, and delivery date. Investigate the balance among these attributes and functionality with respect to reliability growth testing and current software engineering technology.

Reliability and functionality. The number of functions is correlated with the number of lines of code developed, total faults introduced, and hence failure intensity. Thus, increasing functionality generally decreases reliability. Increased levels of reliability generally equate to increased levels of testing, which means increased time and cost.

Reliability, cost, and delivery date. Increasing the failure intensity objective (and hence reducing reliability) reduces reliability growth testing time and cost but increases the cost associated with field failures. Cost associated with field failures includes cost to the *supplier* in terms of repair, field support service, and potential lost future business. In addition, there is cost to the *customer*. For simplicity, we assume that the field failure cost increases linearly with the number of failures, although this assumption is probably conservative.

You can plot the total life-cycle cost (defined here to be the sum of the cost of doing reliability testing and field failure cost) versus the failure intensity objective (left-hand plot of Fig. 6.2). There is an optimum value of failure intensity objective for which the life-cycle cost is minimum. As field failure cost will vary with the failure severity class, individual trade-off studies can be done for each. Likewise, you can plot the time to do reliability growth testing versus the failure intensity objective (right-hand plot of Fig. 6.2) to determine which delivery date would correspond to a specified objective. The SRE tools discussed in App. A will produce plots like these.

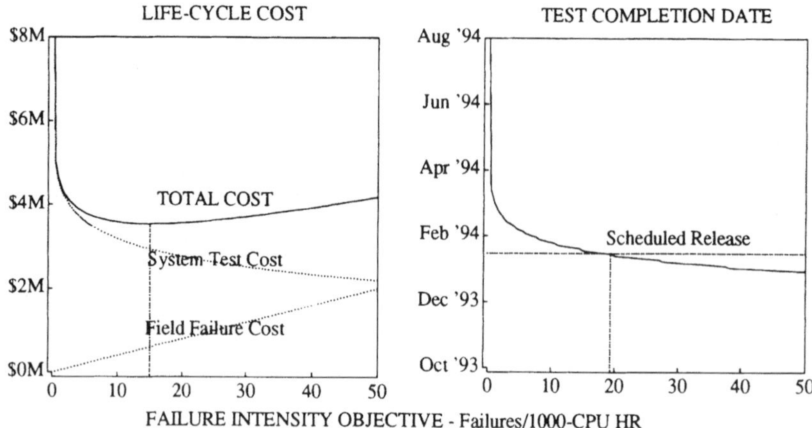

Figure 6.2 Cost and release date trade-offs.

Modeling to support trade-off studies. Currently, parameters of some reliability growth models can be predicted from product and development process characteristics. Product characteristics include such items as newly developed lines of code and lines of reused code. Process characteristics depend on the development environment and development organization. Determine them for the same or a similar situation. They include such quantities as requirements volatility, thoroughness of design documentation, and programmer experience level. Most process characteristics are incorporated in models through their effect on fault density.

Chapter 7 of [Musa87] provides details on conducting trade-off studies using one such model. Examples of their application and details on the model employed in such studies are also provided. Since these studies are performed early in the product life cycle, be aware that there can be substantial errors in absolute results, although relative results are usually valid.

6.3.2.2 Set reliability objectives. Separate reliability objectives are established for each failure category. Usually, system reliability objectives are set first (chap. 4 in [Ever90] and secs. 3.7.1 and 4.7.1 in [SAE90]) and then allocated between hardware and software. Factors that influence setting software reliability objectives include:

- Explicitly stated reliability requirements from a request for proposal or standards document
- Reliability performance of and customer satisfaction with previous releases or similar products

- Capabilities of competition (including both direct competitors and indirect ones such as the manual methods the product is intended to displace)
- Trade-offs with other characteristics such as performance, delivery date, and cost
- Warranty considerations
- Potential of reusing highly reliable components from other software systems
- Technology capabilities and constraints (e.g., use of fault-tolerant techniques)

For example, one project set reliability objectives on a particular category of failures based on customer experiences with existing similar products. Another project set reliability objectives for its new products by relating customer acceptance of previous products and failure rates observed during their system test.

As another example, a large-scale switching system has established objectives on software asserts, audits, peripheral processor interrupts, and system interrupts, based on the number of telephone calls originated. The project combines these measures to compute a stability index that also has a particular objective associated with it. The stability index objective is based on measures from previous releases of the switching system software and from customer satisfaction with these releases. See, for example, [Berg89] and [DiMa91].

Effect on architecture. Reliability requirements may strongly influence the architecture adopted for a product. In turn, changes to architecture may dramatically affect reliability. During this phase of the life cycle and continuing into the design and implementation phase, the architecture evolves through successive iterations. There may be successive reviews in this iterative process referred to as *discovery* reviews. The reliability assessment conducted during each of the stages in this phase provides valuable information for these reviews. The reliability analyst should participate in each of these reviews.

Availability. Availability is an important consideration in setting reliability objectives. It depends on how much time elapses after a failure before service can be restored. For example, for one product, the category of failures for which reliability objectives were set was those failures that required a reboot of the system to restore service. The particular reliability objectives were satisfactory only if the reboot time was under 15 minutes. Consequently, the project included an objective on the reboot time as part of the reliability objective.

6.4 SRE During Design and Implementation Phase

Although the structure of this phase may vary across projects, this section describes the SRE activities, outlined in Fig. 6.1, that are conducted during the design and implementation stages.

6.4.1 Design stage

The design stage involves translating a requirements specification into a design of the software product. During the implementation stage, the design is used to implement the code for the software programs.

The *system architecture,* expressing the system concept in terms of hardware and software components and the interfaces among them and with the external environment, is completed during this stage. As described in Sec. 6.3, the architecture evolves through successive iterations. A reliability analysis can assess whether the successive iterations of the architecture will satisfy reliability and availability requirements, as will be discussed in subsequent sections.

6.4.1.1 Allocate reliability among components. While defining the architecture, consider alternative ways of dividing the system into components while achieving the overall reliability objective. Various factors should be considered when you divide the system into components (see [Musa87], pp. 85–88). These factors include the physical nature of the system, the nature of previously collected data (for example, what sets of similar elements of known reliabilities exist), the need to track a particular component for project management purposes, and the amount of effort required for data collection. [Fran93] and [Pant91] describe component analysis experiences.

To determine the reliabilities required for the components, first make a trial allocation of the reliabilities. Next, calculate the system reliability using the trial allocation. Adjust the allocation so that the system reliability requirement is met, along with approximate equality of development time, difficulty, and risk for the components and minimum total system cost.

6.4.1.2 Engineer to meet reliability objectives. There are several methods for engineering the product to meet reliability objectives.

Plan recovery strategies. Many software failures result from transient environmental conditions such that if execution of the software is simply retried, the failure will not repeat. However, before execution is retried, some attempt should be made to repair possibly damaged data. Also, execution needs to be restarted from some known (possibly previously "checkpointed") place of execution. Finally, mechanisms should be in place to determine when a failure has occurred and to prevent further execution so as to contain damage to program data. [Lee90] discusses techniques of failure detection, damage confinement, and failure recovery.

Use redundant software elements. Redundant software elements can increase reliability only if they are not exactly the same copies. One approach is to have different groups develop them independently [Aviz85]. However, you probably can't achieve completely independent development in practice. Hence, the possible improvement is limited. Therefore, developers have used redundant software only in ultrareliable systems (typically, systems with failure intensity objectives less than 10^{-6} failure/CPU hr). Chapter 14 will discuss fault-tolerant software reliability engineering techniques in detail.

Identify high-risk areas. Two techniques used in safety-critical and ultrareliable systems design that are beginning to find their way into software design are FMEA and fault tree analysis. FMEA (failure modes and effects analysis) is a bottom-up technique that starts by defining failure modes of the components and then assesses how they can cause systemwide failures. Fault tree analysis (see Chap. 15 for details) is a top-down technique that starts with failures at the system level and successively decomposes and relates these failures to failures at the subsystem and component levels. Although FMEA and fault tree analysis are not extensively used for software in general, these techniques are finding applications in safety-critical software (e.g., see [Leve86]).

6.4.1.3 Focus resources based on functional profile. The functional profile can help you, as a developer, focus on what is really important from the customer's standpoint. The information it provides on the frequency of use and criticality of different functions can help weigh design alternatives. For example, a designer might opt for a simpler manual recovery design for a condition that occurs infrequently rather than for a more complex automated recovery design.

6.4.2 Implementation stage

6.4.2.1 Focus resources based on functional profile. The functional profile can also help allocate effort during the implementation stage, based on the relative usage and criticality of different functions. For example, you might expend more inspection effort or do more thorough testing for high-usage than low-usage functions. Similarly, the functional profile can provide helpful guidance for ordering the time periods scheduled for developing the functions (highest use and criticality first).

6.4.2.2 Manage fault introduction and propagation. Since faults are the underlying cause of failures in software, controlling the number of faults introduced in each development step and the number of faults that propagate undetected to the next development step is important in managing product reliability. Although we discuss the topic in this phase, you must manage faults across *all phases* of the life cycle. Many development practices affect fault management. A few of the more important ones are as follows:

- *Practicing a development methodology.* Using a common approach in translating high-level design into code, and in documenting it, is particularly important for larger projects. It facilitates good communication between project team members, helping reduce introduction of faults into the software.
- *Constructing modular systems.* A modular system consists of well-defined, simple, and independent parts interacting through well-defined interfaces. Small, simple modules are easier for designers and programmers to build and hence less prone to faults being introduced through human error. Also, modular designs are more maintainable and hence decrease the chances that detected faults are incorrectly repaired. [Ever90] provides a list of criteria for decomposing systems into manageable sets of modules.
- *Employing reuse.* Reuse of software components that have been well tested for an operational profile that is close to that expected for your system reduces fault introduction. The alternative is to develop new components. They will almost certainly have more faults than the properly reused ones.
- *Doing unit and integration testing.* Testing plays a major role in preventing faults from propagating to a next development step. Unit tests verify modules' functions as specified in their low-level (or module) designs. Integration tests verify that modules interact as specified in the high-level design (or architecture). [ISO87] requires design verification through tests, design reviews, and other measures. [ANSI86] requires that software projects maintain test plans and recommends the contents of these plans.
- *Conducting inspections and reviews.* You can review or inspect requirements, design documents, software code, user manuals, user training materials, and test documents. Both reviews and inspections use a small team of people to compare the output of a development step with what was specified on input to that step.
- *Controlling change.* Many failures result from change in the intermediate items produced as part of the completed product. Such inter-

mediate items include the code of software components, design and requirement specifications, test plans, and user documentation. To reduce the occurrence of such failures, you need to manage the various versions of such items and how they go together to produce the completed product. This is called *version control.* You must also maintain an orderly procedure for submitting, tracking, and completing requested changes to items (referred to as *change control*). Reducing the rate of change of requirements generally increases reliability. Projects often refer to requested changes as *modification requests* or MRs. Version and change control are together referred to as *configuration management.*

6.4.2.3 Measure reliability of acquired software. If you use acquired software in your product (i.e., software that was not developed or tested in previous releases of your product), you will have to decide if the reliability of the software should be certified for your application. Acquired software may be a commercial off-the-shelf program, reused modules (increasingly common for productivity reasons), or software delivered by a contractor.

A concern is that acquired software may have been tested and used under a different set of conditions than is expected for your application. Therefore its reliability may be different in your application than in other applications. In such a case, the reliability should be certified using the operational profile for your application. Certify acquired software as early as possible. This allows you time to take action if the software displays a level of reliability that is less than what you require.

Reliability demonstration testing. Certifying the reliability of existing software can be done by using reliability demonstration testing. Select test cases at random according to the operational profile. Do not fix the underlying faults that cause failures. The test tells you after each failure whether the software should be accepted or rejected or whether you should continue testing.

A tool can be useful to construct the chart shown in Fig. 6.3 and to plot failure times on it (see App. A). The action you take depends on the region in which the failure point is located. Note that you continue testing after the first three failures in the example, but stop testing and accept the software after the fourth. The test is based on sequential sampling theory.

6.5 SRE During the System Test and Field Trial Phase

System test and field trial activities certify that the software requirements of the product are met and that the product is ready for general use by the customer. The system test stage is critical, since it is the last stage in the development process where corrective action can be taken to improve the reliability of the product before release to the first customer.

The field trial stage validates the specifications and system test reliability in a customer's environment. It is the first use of the product at a customer site. The end of this stage marks the general availability of the product to all customers.

This section describes the SRE activities outlined in Fig. 6.1 that are conducted during this phase.

6.5.1 Determine operational profile

Determining the operational profile is an important part of test planning, which generally occurs substantially ahead of the system test stage proper. The operational profile is a set of operations and their associated probability of occurrence. Operations are characterized by considering both tasks performed *and* environmental factors that influence processing. An operation may represent a command, or a command with its parameters or input variables set within certain ranges, executing in a particular environment. For example, separate operations might represent the same command executing in normal and overload traffic environments. Test cases must be based on the operations as they are implemented in the system, rather than on the functions conceived during system definition.

Test planners usually determine the operational profile, with extensive collaboration from system engineers and designers. It is desirable to involve test planners in the feasibility and requirements phase. The

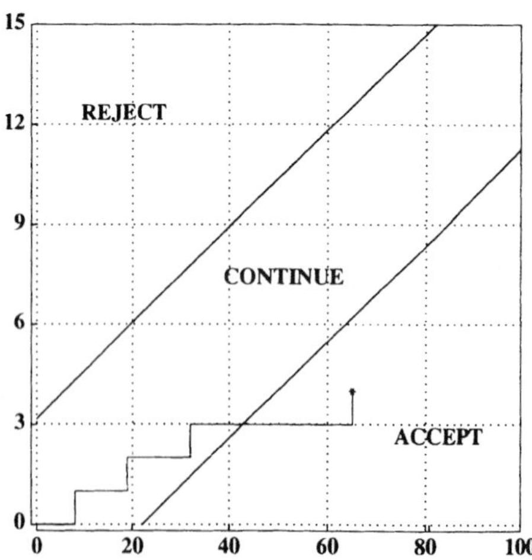

Figure 6.3 Reliability demonstration chart: failures versus execution time.

members of the team work together to specify the operational profile and to create test cases in conformance with the profile.

There are two main ways of deriving the operational profile used during testing. One is recording actual operation of a previous release or existing similar system. The other is estimating the operational profile, starting from the functional profile developed during the feasibility and requirements phase (Sec. 6.3). You often use some combination of both approaches.

Multiple operational profiles. It may be necessary to develop different operational profiles for different market segments with different applications. As an example, a point-of-sale system in a supermarket located in an urban area is likely to have a different usage profile than one in a suburban area. Also, you might fine-tune a special version of the system to meet a customer's high-reliability requirement for a particular set of functions. There are no technical limitations to the number of operational profiles you can define, but you are practically limited by the costs of developing and using them.

Ultrareliable operations. Catastrophic failures demand extra preventive effort. The frequency at which such failures occur is usually low (almost zero). The entire system need not be highly reliable; only the critical operations demand high reliability. For example, in a nuclear reactor power system, the alarm and shutdown operations must not fail. These operations (and only these operations) should have ultra-reliable objectives. You may wish to establish a separate operational profile for them and test them separately.

For more detail on the determination of the operational profile, see Chap. 5.

6.5.2 System test stage

6.5.2.1 Conduct reliability growth testing. In reliability growth testing, system testers execute test cases in proportion to how often their corresponding operations occur in the field, as characterized by the operational profile. By mirroring customer use, reliability growth testing is likely to find the failures that cause the greatest customer dissatisfaction and will reflect the reliability the customer will experience.

You can select more than one test case per operation. First, select the operation randomly, in accord with its probability of occurrence. Note that frequently used operations tend to be selected first. Then select the test case randomly from those that belong to the operation, avoiding repetition. When failures occur, identify and remove the faults that are causing them. Repeated failures that occur during the period while failures are being resolved are not counted. When only the first occurrence of failures is counted, the failure intensity is based on the unknown faults remaining in the software. Failure intensity decreases with execution time (reliability growth).

The goal of reliability growth testing is to attain a level of confidence that the software product is being released with reliability that meets customers' needs. An example of many projects that have used SRE for this purpose is the case study described in [Ehrl90]. Reliability growth testing is usually the last step in system test. However, you need to allow enough execution time to demonstrate that the reliability objective is met.

Test automation. Investing some effort in automating the reliability growth testing process will often pay off. You can usually automate test selection and failure identification and recording. There are some failures you must identify manually, because you cannot specify their symptoms in advance. If automatically identified failures represent a constant proportion of all failures, you can rely on automatic identification and apply a correction factor.

Related types of testing. Certain special types of testing often meet the criteria for reliability growth testing. You may be able to combine failure data from these tests with reliability growth testing data to yield better reliability estimates.

- *Regression testing* ensures that old functions continue to work in the face of changes such as repair of problems and incorporation of new functions. Using the operational profile to drive regression testing is a particularly efficient way to accomplish this function.
- *Feature testing* verifies that the features/functions of a system are present and work as specified. It usually proceeds sequentially by functions, concentrating on one function and then another. Testers at present ordinarily don't use the operational profile to select or execute feature test cases. Thus, the rate at which failures occur does not reflect the rate at which the customer would see failures. Combining such data with reliability growth testing data is not advisable.

  However, with some effort, you can select test cases randomly in proportion to the frequencies specified by the operational profile, as noted at the start of this section. You can then use failure execution time data with existing software reliability models to estimate reliability. For more information see Chap. 5. Feature testing based on an operational profile is often more effective, because features are tested with user operations. This has been done in International DEFINITY [Abra92].

- *Performance and load testing* not only locates load/stress points at which the system fails to meet objectives, but also certifies that the software satisfies certain objectives regarding response time, throughput rates, start-up time, and capacity. Use the operational profile to drive performance and load testing so that it reflects customer usage. Since there is often a tendency to focus on peak-period usage, and systems behave differently under different load conditions, care must be taken to test at different levels if you wish to include the failure data in your reliability estimates.

Data collection. You will need to collect during system test the data shown in Table 6.3. The data are classified by the SRE activities you expect to perform. Include answers to the following questions in your planning:

1. Who will gather the data?
2. How will the data be collected?
3. What tools will be needed to support the data collection?
4. Who will analyze and interpret the data?

Measuring execution time. The use of SRE models during system test assumes that you can measure the execution time when failures occur. CPU time is a direct measure of execution time.

TABLE 6.3 Data to Collect in System Test

Type of data to be collected	SRE activity
1. Execution time of failures or another measure that can relate to execution time	Track testing progress, project additional testing needed, certify reliability objectives are met
2. Severity classification of failures	
3. Resource usage data • Tester time for failure identification • Developer time for failure resolution • Computer time for failure identification and resolution	Project additional calendar time needed for test
4. Number of faults found 5. Developed (new and modified) code in source instructions 6. Number of new faults spawned during failure resolution 7. Average instruction execution rate of processor 8. Total code in object instructions	Conduct trade-off studies (cost and schedule with reliability) for next generic or a new product with similar software and development characteristics

Several tools exist to measure the CPU time to a failure for a UNIX® application. UNIX® produces an entry in a process accounting file whenever a process is terminated, which can be extracted using the UNIX® "acctcom" administrative command. You can write a simple program to process the accounting file and record the execution time and calendar time when a failure occurred in the correct format for the software reliability tool.

Approximating execution time. CPU time is the preferred way of measuring execution time, but sometimes you cannot easily obtain it. In that case, you can estimate execution time by a variety of other means. You can use any measurement that is correlated with execution time. Examples are clock time, weighted clock time, number of commands executed [Ehrl90], telephone calls processed [Harr89], and interrupts processed. If the software fully utilizes its processor and is operating continuously through the time period, then execution time is equivalent to clock time. For weighted clock time, you can approximate execution time by the product of clock time and the system utilization.

6.5.2.2 Track testing progress and certify that reliability objectives are met. During reliability growth testing, failure data is collected and a software reliability tool (App. A) is used to track testing progress and project additional testing needed. Based on progress, management can make any necessary adjustments in resources and schedule as system testing continues. If you estimate reliability on a per-component basis, you can identify components with reliability problems for particular attention. When the current failure intensity reaches the failure intensity objective, you can certify that the reliability objective is met. You may need to do this for each severity class.

Adjusting for incremental delivery to system test. Software reliability models assume a stable program executing in a constant environment. However, software may change because of requirements changes or integration of parts during development. There are three approaches to handling software evolution during system test to get good reliability estimates:

1. Ignore change, and let the model adapt for itself. This is the best solution when the software is changing slowly in a continuous fashion and there is a final period of stability.
2. View the software change in terms of the addition or removal of independent components. This is best when you have a small number of changes, each an independent component.
3. View changes as occurring throughout the program. Here you adjust the failure times to what they would have been if the complete software had been present at the start of test. This is the best approach

when you have many changes of medium size, and it can be handled automatically by SRE Toolkit (see App. A and the Data and Tool Disk).

A detailed description of the three approaches to adjusting for incremental delivery of software during system test is given in [Musa87].

6.5.3 Field trial stage

When system testing is complete, software moves to the next stage, field trial. Field trial is sometimes referred to as *beta test* or *first office application* (FOA). It is advantageous if the field trial location has an operational profile that is close to the main-line usage of the product. You should have a field trial plan that includes failure recording procedures.

6.5.3.1 Certify that reliability objectives are met. During field trial, you collect failure data from the field site. You use field failure data and a software reliability tool to measure the reliability of the product in the field. Then you compare this with the reliability of the product measured at the end of system test.

Several factors can cause the field trial reliability to differ from the system test reliability:

- The definition of what the customer perceives as a failure is different from the definition used in testing the product.
- Inaccurate data collection during system test and/or field trial.
- The field and test operational profiles differ, the test environment not accurately reflecting field conditions.

Use of reliability growth modeling. If you resolve failures during the field trial and count only the first occurrence of each failure, you can apply a reliability growth model. The combined failure data from system test and from field trials can be concatenated, provided that failure definitions and the operational profile remain the same.

Example 6.1 Figure 6.4 is an example of the shape of the reliability growth model fitted to combined stability test (reliability growth test) and beta test failure data. The results in this example show that more failures were experienced during beta test than were expected at the end of system test [Ehrl90]. A discontinuity in the slope of the measured failure behavior is apparent. Based on stability test data, one additional failure had been expected during beta test. However, 16 additional failures occurred. Analysis indicated that the additional failures occurred because the operational profile used during stability test differed significantly from the beta test operational profile. The profile used in stability test did not include start-up operations such as database provisioning. Thus, behavior like that experienced can be a valuable warning sign that your testing is not realistic and needs to be modified.

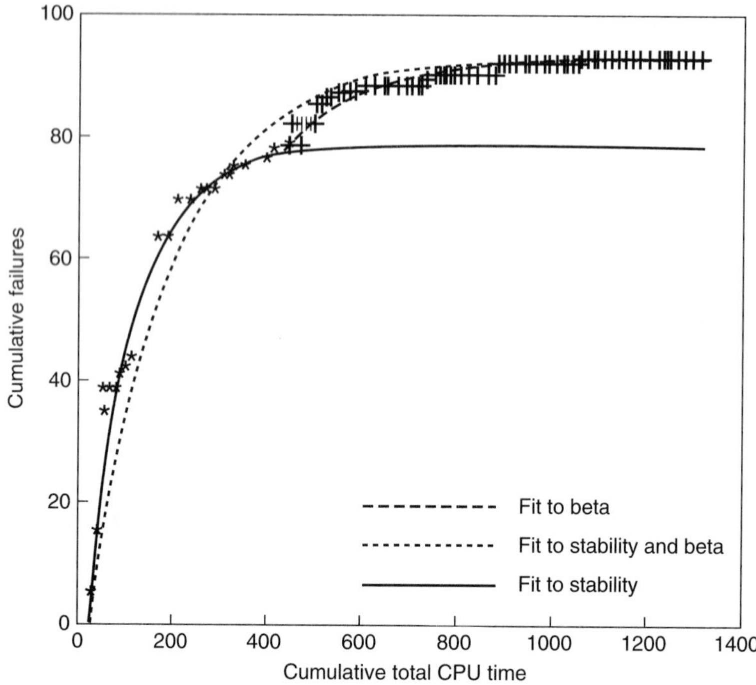

Figure 6.4 Measurements. System T stability (08/02/88–11/27/88) and beta test (12/01/88–03/21/89).

6.6 SRE During the Postdelivery and Maintenance Phase

During the postdelivery and maintenance phase, you deploy the product to your customers. Maintenance consists of removing the faults associated with failures reported by customers. This section describes the SRE activities that are conducted during this phase.

6.6.1 Project postrelease staff needs

You can use reliability models to project staff needs following the release of a software product. This includes:

1. The customer's operations staff to support service recovery following failures
2. The supplier's staff to handle customer-reported failures
3. The supplier's software development staff to locate and remove faults associated with customer-reported failures

When failures are not resolved during operations, constant reliability models (models with constant failure intensity) are used to project items 1 and 2 for a given release. This is the situation between maintenance releases of delivered software products when no fixes or patches are introduced in the software. Less severe faults are generally not corrected between maintenance releases. When severe failures are resolved, use reliability growth models to project item 3.

6.6.2 Monitor field reliability versus objectives

If your organization has operations responsibility, you will find software reliability measurements useful for monitoring the reliability of the operating software. If not, you should attempt to get these data from your customer as an index of customer satisfaction. Failure intensity is approximately constant for a given release. However, there may be a period of reliability growth just after installation of a new release due to field fixes [Chri88].

Several projects at AT&T and elsewhere have reported on their experiences in analyzing failure data collected from field sites. The 5ESS U.S. telephone switch release 5E6 used software reliability to track product reliability after release to the field sites. An analysis of the data collected in the first month of operations showed that 5E6 met its projected reliability goals. Further analysis showed that 5E6 was better than the previous release after one year of operation. Field analysis identified one particularly troublesome failure, which received special attention during the development of the next release.

5ESS International collected failure intensity data from customer locations after release for four different time periods [DiMa91, Pant91]. They used this data to validate that the estimated failure intensity at the end of verification testing matched what was being observed at customer sites. The present failure intensity in the field varied about 25 percent around the corresponding failure intensity measured at the end of verification. However, the average failure intensity (total failures divided by the total execution hours) for each of the four time periods was 15 percent lower than the average failure intensity for the last three verification loads. Discrepancies were attributed to differences in the operational profiles used during verification testing and the customer's environment. The project used failure intensity and other metrics to assess the quality of the product and the development process [DiMa91].

If you observe differences in reliability in the customer's environment from what was predicted by system test, you should consider the same possible causes as were listed for the field trial stage in Sec. 6.5.3.1.

If reliability differs because the field and test operational profiles do not match, you need to find the source of the mismatch and take appropriate corrective action. The mismatch may be either in tasks or environmental factors. As an example of the latter, simulators used in test to replace hardware components may not have faithfully reflected the operation of the replaced components. If the difference is substantial, you may wish to use an updated profile for the next release. Example 6.1 shows how differences in the operational profile between system test and beta test can affect measured reliability [Ehrl90].

Collecting failure data. To do software reliability estimation during operation, collect failure data that is tied to the execution time of the software, just as you did during reliability growth testing. Thus you need to determine total execution time across many customer sites. In field operations, more people will be involved, and you will need to carefully plan your data collection. For more information, see Chap. 11.

Some users may not report a given failure if they are not certain that a failure occurred or if they have focused on quick recovery rather than reporting. Thus, there is a need to motivate users to report failures and provide feedback so they will continue to do so.

For a true measure of field failure intensity, you need information about *all* failures. For other purposes, information about just the first occurrence of each failure (as provided by modification requests or MRs) will suffice. For example, MRs can be used to size the programming staff needed to remove faults. Collecting MRs is less expensive than manually collecting all failure occurrences. You may choose from several potential sources for obtaining failure data, but understand that each source has its advantages and limitations.

Using data from trouble tracking systems. To collect data on failures, many projects use a trouble-tracking system. In a typical operation, when the customer at a field site encounters a failure, they call in a trouble report. A "TR" (trouble report) number is assigned and information about the failure is entered into the system. The field support person assigned to the failure categorizes it (e.g., hardware, operator, software) and assigns a severity class.

The severity assigned depends on

- The extent to which the problem degrades system operation
- The lack of a work-around
- The customer's perception of the failure

If the failure is judged to be a new one, the field support person opens a modification request (MR). Although the same failure is likely to be reported from more than one site, resulting in multiple TRs, only one MR is (should be) opened. Thus, the number of MRs shows the *first occurrences* of failures, while TR numbers include repetitions of the same failures at different or even the same sites. An estimate of failure intensity based on first occurrences of failures will yield an estimate of the failure intensity that will exist when the faults causing the reported failures have been removed.

One cannot assume there will be a TR for *every* occurrence of a failure in the field because some may not be reported. In practice, then, the number of TRs will fall *between* the number of first-occurrence failures and the total number of failures occurring in the field.

Talking directly to users. The operations staff at the field sites may maintain failure logs. Talking with the users and examining these logs can provide a true picture of the failures occurring. The discussion may clear up misunderstandings, for example, when the number of TRs is low, yet the customer voices dissatisfaction. This might occur if a project organization has been unresponsive to field problems in the past. To reduce the expense of this approach, sample just a few sites and adjust the results to estimate the total number of failures that occurred.

Automated failure data collection. The problem with TR and MR systems is that they were not designed to collect failure data. Some recent practitioners have reported that the practical extension of SRE to software systems' field usage requires instrumenting data collection so that the burden of data collection does not degrade the data. Under such an arrangement, field systems monitor their own health and then report data back to the development machine for analysis and interpretation.

6.6.3 Track customer satisfaction

Tracking field reliability in relation to objectives is necessary but not sufficient by itself. Select a sample of customer sites and survey their level of satisfaction with product reliability. You may be meeting your objectives but your customer may not be satisfied. Dissatisfaction may be due to inappropriate objectives being set or to other factors appearing in their use of the product. If there is dissatisfaction, you will want to follow up by modifying the objectives or by making any necessary field support service and product changes.

6.6.4 Time new feature introduction by monitoring reliability

Changes to add new functionality to a system will also likely add new defects, causing the failure intensity to rise. If the addition of new features is or can be separated from the removal of previous faults, a field operations manager may wish to use discretion in deciding when the new features are installed. The failure intensity of the system will exhibit a general stability about some value over the long term, but with swings around this value when newly developed features are periodically incorporated. Failure intensity will increase just after you add new features. Periods in which fixes are installed to remove faults will exhibit decreasing failure intensity.

A field operations manager is often faced with conflicting demands. Some users want certain new features to be introduced as soon as possible. Other users, employing existing features, will insist that reliability be as high as possible. If these conflicts can be negotiated and a failure intensity objective established, the manager's job is then simplified. New features are introduced only when the failure intensity is below the objective.

The manager may use the amount of margin below the service objective as a guide to the size of the change to be permitted (see "Impact of Design Change," pp. 204–205, in [Musa87] for instruction on estimating this size). [Hami78] discusses an SRE application much like the one just described.

6.6.5 Guide product and process improvement with reliability measures

First, categorize field failures for analysis by their severities and frequencies experienced (if available). One might, for instance, analyze failures of severities 1 and 2 that exceed a certain frequency. Note that the frequency of a failure can vary from site to site. Once the selection of failures has been made, a root-cause analysis can begin on each underlying fault causing the failure to determine:

- Where and why the fault was introduced
- Why it escaped detection earlier in the development cycle
- What process change(s) are needed to reduce the probability that similar faults will be introduced in the future or at least increase the probability that such faults will be detected in the stage(s) where they are introduced

6.7 Getting Started with SRE

In the previous sections, you learned how and when to do SRE in your project. This section will help you:

1. Prepare your organization to do SRE.
2. Find information and support for doing SRE.
3. Do an SRE self-assessment.

6.7.1 Prepare your organization for SRE

6.7.1.1 SRE as a process. A key factor for a successful implementation of SRE is integrating SRE activities into an organization's software development process. First, you need to understand how SRE activities interrelate with development activities. These interrelationships are summarized in Fig. 6.1 and described in Secs. 6.3 through 6.6. Second, you need to understand *who* is to do *what* task or activity and *when* they are to do it. Table 6.4 summarizes the people who are involved in doing SRE and the life-cycle phase in which they are most likely involved. Large organizations may benefit in tailoring an SRE process for their organization.

6.7.1.2 Seven-step program. Two important ingredients for successfully introducing SRE into your organization are commitment by management and motivation of staff.

Table 6.5 is a sample seven-step implementation program that was followed with one organization.

The program first focuses on getting up-front management commitment by developing awareness of SRE and the benefits of doing it through a personal briefing. The level of commitment can be measured by the willingness of your management to expend resources and to review progress periodically in completing the steps in this program.

The program motivates your staff by providing adequate training and consulting support so that people understand and can do the jobs that are expected of them. Jump-start consulting ensures team members responsible for implementing SRE are properly supported in their efforts. It provides guidance, constructive critique, tutoring, and problem solving as required by project needs. Implementation might consist of one (or more) 4- to 6-month efforts with your team of one or more members who work part-time on the effort. It is important to designate one member of the team as a decision-making representative for your project.

Most efforts focus on first implementing SRE within system test to monitor and track reliability growth. On successfully completing this initial effort, you can add setting reliability objectives and defining an operational profile that better reflects customer usage of the product.

The program in Table 6.5 would be appropriate for organizations ranging from 50 to several thousand people. If your organization is smaller, parts of this program can be used to tailor a more appropriate program for you.

It is certainly possible to use outside experts instead of training your own personnel on a project if necessary. However, this is generally

TABLE 6.4 People Involved in Doing SRE

Job function	Software life-cycle phases			
	Feasibility and requirements	Design and implementation	System test and field trial	Postdelivery and maintenance
Product manager	X		X	
Project manager	X	X	X	
Development manager		X	X	
Reliability engineer	X	X	X	X
Systems analyst				
System engineer	X	X		
Software architect	X	X		
Software designer		X		
Programmer		X		
Test manager	X		X	
Quality assurance engineer		X	X	X
Test designer		X	X	
System tester	X		X	
Installation and operations manager	X			X
Users	X			X

TABLE 6.5 SRE Start-Up Program for Organizations

Step	Program element	Target audience	Purpose	When
1	SRE briefing	Executive management	SRE awareness; considerations for initial application.	0
2	Project manager overview course	Managers with project system engineering, development, or system test responsibility	SRE awareness for managers who will select potential projects for SRE implementation.	0 + 3 weeks
3	Two-hour follow-up meeting	Managers involved in step 2	Respond to questions and concerns, give advice. Identify one or more initial implementation efforts.	0 + 5 weeks
4	Project staff overview course	Staff of project using SRE	Prepare team members not needing in-depth SRE knowledge and skills.	0 + 8 weeks
5	SRE practitioner course	Staff directly involved in SRE implementation effort	Prepare team members needing in-depth SRE knowledge and skills.	0 + 8 weeks
6	SRE project planning course	Individual SRE implementation teams	Develop an action plan for initial implementation.	0 + 10 weeks
7	Jump-start consulting	Individual SRE implementation teams	Provide direct consulting to support SRE implementation effort.	After week 10

TABLE 6.6 Contacts for Support Resources

Items	Contact
AT&T SRE courses	AT&T Technical Education Center 1-800-TRAINER
AT&T SRE Toolkit	See enclosed Data and Tool Disk
IEEE SRE video (3 hrs)	IEEE Computer Society Press 800-272-6657, order number 1994AV
Software Reliability: Measurement, Prediction, Application by Musa, Okumoto, Iannino	McGraw-Hill 800-338-3987

undesirable because these experts will lack specific project knowledge; it will be much more difficult to integrate SRE with your development process; and you will not be preparing your people for the future.

Experience indicates that the development of the functional and operational profiles are the activities where you are most likely to need expert consultation.

6.7.2 Find more information or support

Table 6.6 lists several contacts for finding more information or support. The particular contacts shown may become out of date between updates to this text, but a reasonable amount of diligence should lead the reader to the desired information.

6.7.3 Do an SRE self-assessment

Use the statements in the following subsections to assess the conformance of your project or process with the best current practice of SRE. For each statement below that is completely true, score the number of points indicated at the beginning of the statement. The activities in each phase correspond to those listed in Fig. 6.1 and discussed in Secs. 6.3 through 6.6. Note that the activities can overlap into other phases as well. For any statement that is partially true, score 1 point. If you can justify why a particular statement is not applicable or not cost-effective for your project, you may take full credit for that statement and attach a written explanation of your justification.

Conformance level is based on the total points received as follows:

Total score	Conformance level
60 to 64	Fully conforms
45 to 59	Mostly conforms
25 to 44	Partially conforms
0 to 24	Does not conform

6.7.3.1 Feasibility and requirements phase ______ points

In writing your requirements specification, you:

(3) Determine functional profile (alternatively, may determine operational profile directly)

(3) Define and classify failures

(3) Identify customer reliability needs

(2) Conduct trade-off studies to help set objectives for reliability, delivery date, functionality, and cost

(3) Set reliability objectives

6.7.3.2 Design and implementation phase ______ points

As you define the architecture and design, you:

(2) Allocate system reliability to components so that the overall reliability objective is met

(2) Engineer to meet reliability objectives

During implementation, you:

(2) Focus resources based on functional profile

(2) Manage fault introduction and propagation

(2) Measure reliability of acquired software

6.7.3.3 System test and field trial phase ______ points

During product validation, you:

(3) Determine operational profile

(3) Conduct reliability testing, consistent with the operational profile

(3) Track testing progress, acting on differences between expected and achieved reliability

(2) Project additional testing needed

(5) Certify that reliability objectives are met before release

6.7.3.4 Postdelivery and maintenance phase ______ points

Before product release, you:

(2) Project postrelease staff needs

After product release, you:

(3) Monitor field reliability versus objectives, acting on differences

(2) Track customer satisfaction with reliability

(2) Guide new feature introduction by monitoring reliability

(3) Guide product and process improvement with reliability measures

6.7.3.5 Organizational and project preparation ______ points

Your organization and project demonstrate adequate preparation for SRE through:

(2) Visible management commitment

(2) Training of at least one local expert in SRE application

(2) An agreed-upon set of reliability metrics

(2) A supported set of SRE tools

(2) An agreed-upon and monitored set of expected SRE benefits

(2) Planning reliability-related activities, and providing adequate resources and schedule time for them

TOTAL: ______ points

6.8 Summary

SRE presents a life-cycle approach to managing software reliability. It provides a software engineer or manager the means to estimate and measure the rate of failure occurrence in software. The main focus of SRE is on how the customer will use the product in their environment. Software product usage is part of the reliability definition.

During the *product feasibility and requirements* phase, the functions the product will perform for each user, the frequencies of use of these functions, and criticality are defined. These functions establish the functional profile. Failures are defined and categorized from the product-user perspective. The reliability objectives for different uses of the product are established based on trade-off studies between functionality, reliability, cost, and schedule. Tools are used to determine these trade-offs.

During the *design and implementation* phase, the developer allocates reliability objectives between the hardware and software components. The functional profile helps focus development resources according to frequency of customer usage and criticality. Operations are characterized by considering both the tasks to be performed and the environmental factors that influence processing. Since most software applications are built from acquired software (software not developed or tested in previous releases of the product), the reliability of this software has to be certified. This certification can be done using a reliability demonstration testing tool.

During the *system test and field trial* phase, the focus is on ensuring that the completed software meets the reliability objectives as specified in the requirements. The functional profile is refined into an operational profile that is used to select operations during system test in accordance with the occurrence probability. The philosophy of operational profile testing is to test the operations the customer will most likely use, and time is not spent on testing little-used and noncritical operations. Failures are reported and faults removed. Tools use the failure data to determine the current failure intensity and estimate release date. The system is released when the failure intensity objective (software reliability objective) has been achieved. This avoids excessive time due to overtesting. The reliability objective for the product can be determined by combining the hardware reliability objective and the software reliability objective.

The practice of SRE continues during *postdelivery and maintenance.* Field reliability is monitored against established product objectives and customer satisfaction. This information can be used to improve the reliability of future product releases and to improve the quality of the development process.

Problems

6.1 Studies to date show that up-front SRE investment during the development cycle results in earlier delivery, increased productivity, lower maintenance cost, and satisfied customers.

a. What SRE activities are important to achieve this payback?
b. What benefits are achieved?
c. In what phase of the life cycle do these activities occur?

6.2 A software reliability program requires that the development cycle of the product be definable and measurable. Reliability cannot be assumed if it cannot be defined and measured. A successful metrics program critically depends upon the quality of the data that is needed as input.

a. What type of data is needed to establish the functionality of the product?
b. What type of data is needed to establish a reliability objective?
c. What type of data is needed during reliability growth test to certify that the reliability objectives of the system are met?
d. What type of data should be collected during reliability growth test to provide historical data needed to establish a reliability objective for the next release or for a new product similar to this product?

6.3 The current airline reservation system has been in existence for 3 years. During this time three major problems have occurred:

- *System performance.* Transaction processing during the busy period has not been acceptable. The response time is adequate when the system is lightly loaded. It becomes a problem around 10 A.M. and remains a problem to around 3 P.M. Response time is particularly bad from 11:30 to 1:30.

- *System availability.* The system is unavailable because the data base fails and must be restarted.
- *Cost of new functions.* The reservation system is a dynamic one and is frequently updated to include new services. Travel reservation personnel are saying that the costs of implementing new features are excessive.

  a. A new release for the software is now needed. Your job as a system engineer/analyst is to establish a functional profile and to negotiate with the customer on:

  - Performance requirements
  - Reliability requirements
  - Cost

  (1) What is your first step?
  (2) What information is needed to determine the functional profile?
  (3) Establish the definition of failures for this system.
  (4) Categorize these failures into severity classifications.
  (5) How would you establish the functionality and failure intensity objective for the new software?
  (6) How does decreasing the number of features increase reliability of the product?
  (7) Where in the life cycle of the new release should inspections be scheduled?

  b. The software is now in the design stage. Your job as reliability engineer is to ensure that the reliability requirements for the software are met.

  (1) How can the total reliability (hardware and software) of the airline reservation system be determined?
  (2) To update the transaction database, a large amount of acquired software will be used. How can you determine if the reliability of the acquired software meets the reliability requirements for the system?

  c. The software has completed the implementation stage and is entering the system test stage. Your job as lead system tester is to ensure that the reliability objectives of the software will be met on release.

  (1) What information is needed to determine the operational profile?
  (2) Failure execution time may be hard to measure. What other measure could you use? What will be the unit of the failure intensity objective?
  (3) What type of information is important to the test manager?
  (4) How will you track the progress of system test and determine when the software reliability objective is met?
  (5) Often the entire software is not available for system test. Can you use SRE tools with incremental development?

  d. The software is now in operation in the field. Your job as reliability engineer is to determine if the field reliability of the software differs from the reliability that was measured at the end of system test. If the reliability is different, what are the main factors that could have contributed to the difference?

Chapter 7

Software Reliability Measurement Experience

Allen P. Nikora
Jet Propulsion Laboratory

Michael R. Lyu
AT&T Bell Laboratories

7.1 Introduction

The key components in the SRE process, as described in Chap. 6, include reliability objective specification, operational profile determination, reliability modeling and measurement, and reliability validation. These techniques were applied to several internal projects developed within Jet Propulsion Laboratory (JPL) and Bell Communications Research (Bellcore). The project background, reliability engineering procedures, data collection efforts, modeling results, data analyses, and reliability measurements for these projects are presented in this chapter. Model comparisons for the software reliability applications, lessons learned with regard to the engineering effort, and directions for current and future software reliability investigations are also provided.

One major thing we observed is that for the failure data we analyzed, no one model was consistently the best. It was frequently the case that a model that had performed well for one set of failure data would perform badly for a different set. We therefore recommend that for any development effort, several models, each making different assumptions about the testing and debugging process, be simultaneously applied to the failure data. We also recommend that each model's applicability to the failure data be continuously monitored. Traditional goodness-of-fit tests, such as the chi-square or Kolmogorov-Smirnov tests, can be used. In addition, the model evaluation criteria described in Chap. 4 are also strongly recommended.

Another discovery is that, of the software development efforts we studied, few had quantitative reliability requirements that were measurable. Strictly speaking, it is not necessary to have a reliability requirement for a system in order to apply software reliability measurement techniques. It is quite possible to measure a software system's reliability during test and make predictions of future behavior. However, the existence of a requirement is very helpful in that:

1. Specifying a reliability requirement helps the users and developers focus on the components of the system that will have the most effect on the system's overall reliability. Potentially unreliable components can be respecified or redesigned to increase their reliability.
2. A reliability requirement will serve as a goal to be achieved during the development effort. During the testing phases, software developers and managers can estimate software reliability and determine how close it is to the required value. The difference between current and required reliability can be converted into estimates of the time and resources that will be required to achieve the goal.

We also discovered that one of the most important aspects in an SRE program is identifying the data to be collected and setting up mechanisms to ensure that the data collected are complete and accurate. We found that development organizations generally have the capability to collect the type of data that is required to use software SRE techniques. Every software development effort that we studied has a mechanism for recording and tracking failures that are observed during the testing phases and during operations. Most projects also have requirements for the test staff to keep an activity log during the testing phases. Properly used, these data collection mechanisms would provide accurate failure data in a form that could easily be used by many currently available software reliability models. However, since many software managers and developers are not aware of the types of analysis that can be done with these data, they do not devote the effort required to ensure that the collected data are complete and accurate.

Finally, we discovered that a properly defined linear combination of model results produced more accurate predictions over the set of failure data that we analyzed than any one individual model [Lyu92c]. This linear combination modeling scheme is discussed in detail.

7.2 Measurement Framework

To enhance a company's ability to deliver timely, high-quality products through an application of SRE practices, as well as to help ensure that software vendors deliver high-quality component products, several elements are included in our investigation. Figure 7.1 shows an SRE framework in our current practice. You can see that this framework is similar to that displayed in Fig. 6.1; however, it is more focused on the product life-cycle phases during system test and postdelivery.

First, customer usage is quantified by developing an operational profile. Second, quality is defined quantitatively from the customer's viewpoint by defining failures and failure severities, by determining a reliability objective, and by specifying balance among key quality objectives (e.g., reliability, delivery date, and cost) to maximize customer satisfaction. We then advocate the employment of operational profile and quality objectives to manage resources and to guide design, implementation, and testing of software. Moreover, we track reliability during testing to determine product release. This activity may be repeated until a certain reliability level has been achieved. We also analyze reliability in the field to validate the reliability engineering effort and to introduce product and process improvements.

From Fig. 7.1 we can identify four major components in the SRE process, namely, (1) *reliability objective,* (2) *operational profile,* (3) *reliability modeling and measurement,* and (4) *reliability validation.* A reliability objective is the specification of the reliability goal of a prod-

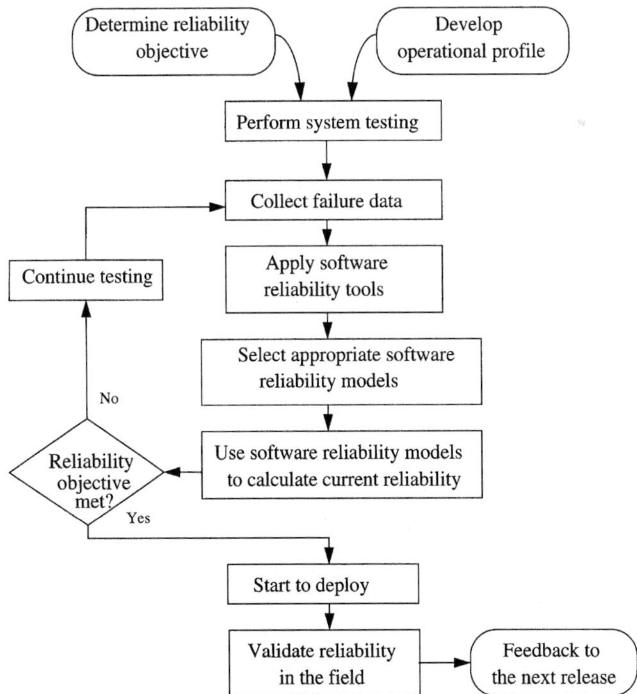

Figure 7.1 Software reliability engineering process overview.

uct from the viewpoint of the customer. If a reliability objective has been specified by the customer, that reliability objective should be used. Otherwise, you can select a reliability measure which is most intuitive and easily understood, and then determine the customer's tolerance threshold for system failures in terms of this reliability measure. For example, customer A might be mostly concerned with the total number of field failures product X may produce. Therefore, the reliability objective could be specified as, say, "product X should not produce more than 10 failures in its first 50 months of operation by customer A."

Operational profile concepts and techniques are described in Chap. 5. It is a set of disjoint alternatives of system operation and their associated probabilities of occurrence. The construction of an operational profile encourages testers to select test cases according to the system's operational usage, which contributes to more accurate estimation of software reliability in the field.

Reliability modeling is an essential element of the reliability estimation process. It determines if a product meets its reliability objective and is ready for release. You are required to use a reliability model to calculate, from failure data collected during system testing (such as failure report data and test time), various estimates of a product's reliability as a function of test time. Several interdependent estimates make equivalent statements about a product's reliability. They typically include the product's failure intensity as a function of test time t, the number of failures expected up to test time t, and the mean time to failure (MTTF) at test time t. These reliability estimates can provide the following information useful for product quality management:

1. The reliability of the product at the end of system testing.
2. The amount of (additional) test time required to reach the product's reliability objective.
3. The reliability growth as a result of testing (e.g., *failure intensity improvement factor*, defined as the ratio of the value of the failure intensity at the start of testing to the value at the end of testing).
4. The predicted reliability beyond the system testing already performed. This can be, for example, the product's reliability in the field, if the system testing has already been completed, or the predicted reliability at the end of testing, if the system testing has not yet been completed.

Chapter 3 gives a comprehensive survey on existing reliability models. Despite the existence of more than 40 models, the problem of model selection and application is manageable. Guidelines and statistical methods for selecting an appropriate model for each application are developed in Chap. 4. Furthermore, experience has shown that it is sufficient to consider only a dozen models from among the 40 models, particularly when they are already implemented in software tools (see App. A).

Using these statistical methods, best estimates of reliability are obtained during testing. These estimates are then used to project the reliability during field operation in order to determine if the reliability objective has been met. This procedure is an iterative process since more testing will be needed if the objective is not met. When the operational profile is not fully developed, application of a test compression factor can assist in estimating field reliability. A *test compression factor* is defined as the ratio of execution time required in the operational phase to execution time required in the test phase to cover the input space of the program. Since testers during testing are trying to "break" the software by searching through the input space for difficult execution conditions, while users during operation execute the software at only a normal pace, this factor represents the reduction of failure rate (or increase in reliability) during operation with respect to that observed during testing.

Finally, the projected field reliability has to be validated by comparing it with the observed field reliability. This validation not only establishes benchmarks and confidence levels of the reliability estimates, but also provides feedback to the SRE process for process improvement and better parameter tuning. For example, the model validity could be established, the growth of reliability could be determined, and the test compression factor could be refined.

Various components in this SRE framework are discussed in detail below.

7.2.1 Establishing software reliability requirements

Software reliability requirements are specified during earlier development phases, and SRE techniques are used to estimate the resources that will be required to achieve those requirements during test and operations. The resource requirements are translated into testing schedules and budgets. Resource estimates are compared to the resources actually available to make quantitative, rather than qualitative, statements concerning achievement of the reliability requirements.

7.2.1.1 Expressing software reliability. Reliability and reliability-related requirements can be expressed in one of the three following ways:

1. Probability of failure-free operation over a specified time interval
2. MTTF
3. Expected number of failures per unit time interval (failure intensity)

The first form, the basic definition of software reliability, is a probabilistic statement concerning the software's failure behavior. The other two forms can be considered relating to reliability. Reliability and reliability-related requirements must be stated in quantitative terms. Otherwise, it will not be possible to determine whether the requirements have been met. To help in understanding how to develop these requirements, examples of testable and untestable reliability requirements are given in the following paragraphs.

The following statements, paraphrased from a JPL software development effort, represent a requirement for which SRE can be used to determine the degree to which that requirement has been met.

> Reliability quantifies the ability of the system to perform a required function under the stated conditions for a period of time. Reliability is measured by the MTTF of a critical component. Under the expected operational conditions, documented elsewhere in this requirements document, the probability of the MTTF for the software being greater than or equal to 720 hours shall be 90 percent.

The above requirement is stated in a testable manner. If the expected operational conditions are stated in terms of the operational hardware configuration and the fraction of time each major functional area is expected to be used (the operational profile), the test staff can then design tests to simulate expected usage patterns and use reliability estimates made during these tests to predict operational reliability.

Confidence bounds should be associated with reliability or reliability-related requirements. If the above MTTF requirement had been stated as being simply 720 hours, it would have been possible to meet that requirement with a very wide confidence interval (for example, 90 percent probability of the MTTF lying between 200 and 1240 hours). This could have resulted in the delivery of operational software whose MTTF was considerably less than the intended 720 hours. Yet the end users of the delivered software would be told that the reliability requirement had been met. Not until the software was actually operated would the users realize the discrepancy. To avoid this problem, express the reliability requirement as the minimum value of the confidence interval. This will allow the end users to know the probability of the software meeting its reliability requirement, and permit them to plan accordingly. It is often needed to specify a tighter confidence interval. The price to pay for this improvement, though, is the need for extra validation effort to establish the tighter confidence interval.

An example of an untestable reliability-related requirement is now given. Again, the text is paraphrased from that found in a JPL development effort's system requirements document.

> The system is designed to degrade gracefully in case of failures. As a first priority, system fault protection shall ensure that no system failures or component failures will compromise system integrity. As a second priority, minimum mission science objectives previously described in this document shall not be compromised. Accordingly, each instrument shall be designed so that if one fails (either through hardware or software failures), it will not jeopardize the safety of the system or damage adjacent instruments. This includes provision for isolation from the system via the instrument power supply. If a system fault occurs, the system will automatically stop any science data gathering and go to a safe state. After a safe state is achieved and subsystems are reinitialized, science can be resumed.

The foregoing type of requirement, frequently seen in industry for critical applications, does not provide a basis for measuring the reliability of the system under development, as it contains no quantitative statements concerning the system's failure behavior. Rather, it is a statement of design constraints that are intended to localize damage resulting from a component failure to the immediate area (e.g., assembly, subsystem) in which the failure occurred. During subsequent phases of system development, it may indeed be possible to determine whether such constraints have been reflected in the system design and implementation. However, this information alone is not sufficient to make quantitative statements concerning the system's reliability. Although specifying constraints such as these is an important aspect of system specification, specific reliability requirements, similar in form to the first reliability requirement discussed in this section, would have to be provided if it were intended to use SRE techniques to determine compliance to a reliability requirement.

7.2.1.2 Specifying reliability requirements. To specify reliability requirements, use one or more of the three methods described below. The methods are [Musa87]:

1. System balance
2. Release date
3. Life-cycle cost optimization

It is possible to use one of these methods for developing the requirements for one component of the system, and another for a separate component.

The *system balance* method is primarily used to allocate reliabilities among components of a system based on the overall reliability requirement for that system. The basic principle of this method is to balance the difficulty of development work on different components of the system. The components having the most severe functional requirements or being the most technologically advanced are assigned less stringent reliability requirements. In this way, the overall reliability requirement for the system is met while minimizing the effort required to implement the most complex components. For software, this might translate to assigning less stringent reliability requirements to functions never before implemented or functions based on untried algorithms. This approach generally leads to the least costly development effort in the minimum time. The system balance method is frequently used in developing military systems.

The second approach is used when the release date is particularly critical. This is appropriate for flight systems facing a fixed launch time, or commercial systems aiming at delivery within a profit window. The release date is kept fixed in this approach. The reliability requirement is either established by available resources and funds, or is traded off against these items. With this approach, it is desirable to know how failure intensity trades off with release date. First, the way in which the failure intensity trades off with software execution time is determined. This execution time is then converted to calendar time. The following example uses the Goel-Okumoto exponential Poisson model (GO) model and Musa-Okumoto logarithmic Poisson (MO) model for illustrations.

Example 7.1 For the GO model, the relationship between the ratio of failure intensity change during test and the execution time is given by (see Sec. 3.3.2)

$$t = \frac{1}{b} \ln \frac{\lambda_0}{\lambda_F} \tag{7.1}$$

where t = elapsed execution time
λ_0 = initial failure intensity
λ_F = required failure intensity
b = failure detection rate per failure

This model also has a parameter N, which specifies the number of failures that would be observed if testing were to continue for an infinite amount of time. For the MO model, the relationship between the ratio of failure intensity change during test and the execution time is given by (see Sec. 3.5.3)

$$t = \frac{1}{\theta\lambda_0}\left(\frac{\lambda_0}{\lambda_F} - 1\right) \tag{7.2}$$

where t, λ_0, and λ_F as above
θ = failure intensity decay parameter

For this example, the failure history data from one of the testing phases of a JPL flight program (see J3 in the Data Disk) are used. Applying the GO and MO models to this data set, the following model parameter and failure intensity estimates are obtained:

Goel-Okumoto	Musa-Okumoto
λ_0 = 0.3383 failures/CPU hour	λ_0 = 0.3249 failures/CPU hour
N = 414.76 failures	θ = 0.001256/failure
b = 0.0008156 per failure	

The above equations can be used to determine the amount of test time that will be needed for various failure intensity improvement factors:

Failure intensity improvement factor	Execution time (CPU hours)	
λ_0/λ_F	GO model	MO model
10	2,823	22,052
100	5,647	242,573
1,000	8,670	2,442,782
10,000	11,293	24,499,873

Note the differences between the predictions made by the two models. In the MO model, the relationship between additional execution time needed and the improvement factor is linear, while in the GO model it is logarithmic. At this point, a choice between the two models must be made. Since it is not possible to know a priori which model is best suited to the data, the applicability of models to a set of failure data must be evaluated while the models are being applied. Once the model most applicable to the failure data has been identified, that model's relationship between failure intensity improvement factor and execution time can be used in conjunction with the relationship between execution and calendar time to determine the failure intensity requirement.

The basis of the third approach, *life-cycle cost optimization,* is the assumption that reliability improvement is obtained by more extensive testing. Costs and schedules for nontesting phases are assumed to be constant. The part of development cost due to testing decreases with higher failure intensity requirements (i.e., more failures are allowed), while the operational cost increases. The total cost therefore has a minimum. This is shown below in Fig. 7.2.

To find this minimum, testing cost as a function of failure intensity must be computed. If testing cost can be related to calendar time, and if the relationship between calendar and execution time is known [Musa87], this calculation can be done for a specific model. Similarly,

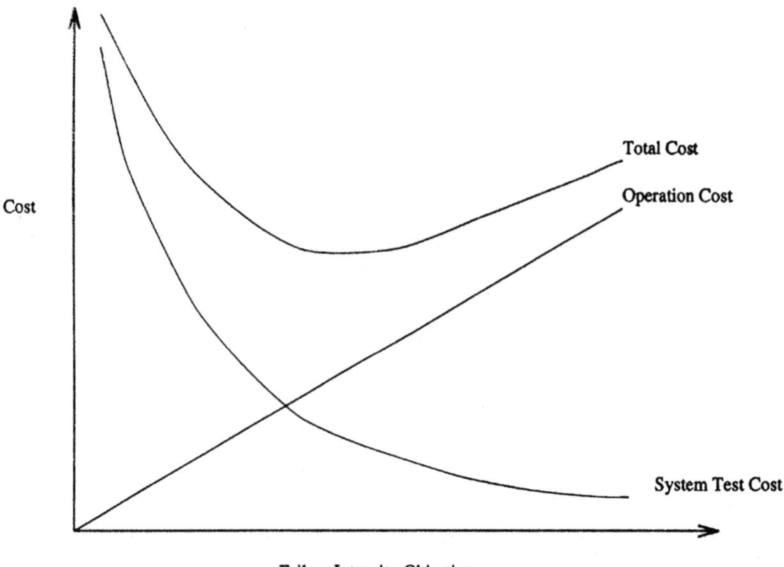

Figure 7.2 Reliability objective by life-cycle cost optimization.

the operational cost as a function of failure intensity could be computed [Ehrl93]. The following costs could be considered:

1. Terminating an improperly functioning program in an orderly manner
2. Reconstructing affected databases
3. Restarting the program
4. Determining the cause(s) of the failure
5. Developing procedures to prevent further failures of that type
6. Repairing the fault(s) causing the failure if the severity and criticality of the failure warrants corrective action
7. Testing the software to validate any repairs
8. Effect of similar failures in the future on mission or program success
9. Loss of customers' goodwill
10. Other costs, such as settling lawsuits in the event of failures in life-critical systems (e.g., commercial avionics, medical systems)

As a result, the cost of operational failures depends on many complicated factors and is hard to determine accurately. In particular, the last two types of costs may be nonlinear with increasing failure intensity.

However, we may start by assuming that failures are equally costly in each severity class. Another simple alternative is to assume all operational failures cost the same, in which case an average cost figure, normally available in each corporation, could be used. This number typically ranges from \$10,000 to \$100,000, depending on the size and the criticality of each project.

Note that the cost of testing could be expressed as an increasing function of time or number of test cases. Three conditions are normally considered: (1) the cost of testing is linear, i.e., it is constant per unit time; (2) it is linear up to time t_{max}, and infinite beyond that, i.e., that project has to be finished by the time t_{max}; and (3) initially it is linear, while later it increases exponentially due to the loss of credibility, lost market window, penalties, etc.

Determination of the failure intensity requirement then becomes a constrained-minimum problem that can be solved analytically or numerically. A typical economic model [Dala88, Dala90] is illustrated in Example 7.2.

Example 7.2 This model includes costs and benefits derived from trade-off between testing and operation cost due to failure. For simplicity, it is assumed that fault and failure have a one-to-one relationship, and could thus be referred simultaneously. Let

N = expected total number of faults in the program
$K(t)$ = number of faults observed up to time t
x = cost of fixing a fault when found during testing
y = cost of fixing a fault when found in the field
$c = (y - x)$ = net cost of fixing a fault after rather than before release

Further, we assume that there is a known nonnegative monotone increasing function $g(t)$ that gives the sum of the cost of testing up to time t plus the opportunity cost of not releasing the software up to time t. Here we also assume that all the failures are equally costly.

Now the following total cost of testing up to time t could be formulated as follows:

$$\begin{aligned} L(t, K(t), N) &= g(t) + xK(t) + y(N - K(t)) \\ &= g(t) - cK(t) + yN \end{aligned} \tag{7.3}$$

It can be shown that if the amount of time it takes to find a fault X during testing is distributed with a known distribution function $F_X(t)$, and the failure times are independent, then the stop-testing rule turns out to be

$$\frac{g'(t)F_X(t)}{cf_X(t)} \geq K(t) \tag{7.4}$$

where $f_X(t)$ is the density function of $F_X(t)$.

Now if we take $g(t)$ to be linear, i.e., $g(t) = g \cdot t$, and if we apply the GO model (see Sec. 3.3.2) for $F_X(t)$, namely, $F_X(t)$ is $1 - e^{-bt}$ and $f_X(t)$ is be^{-bt}, then the stopping rule in Eq. (7.4) reduces to

$$(g / bc)\,(e^{bt} - 1) \geq K(t) \tag{7.5}$$

Note that this stopping rule depends on $g(t)$ and c only through the ratio g/c. Also note that $K(t)$ can be estimated and predicted by

$$K(t) = N(1 - e^{-bt}) \tag{7.6}$$

7.2.2 Setting up a data collection process

When you set up an SRE program, you should avoid the ambition to keep every bit of information about the project and its evolvement over the life cycle. Often, people do not have a clearly defined objective for the data collection process. As a result, much effort is expended with little gain. There have been many instances in which large data collection efforts have been implemented without any capability to analyze the data. Clearly defined objectives are necessary to help define the SRE requirements. In addition, when a large amount of data are required, the development staff is usually affected. Cost and schedule suffer because of the additional effort of collecting the data. Project management complains about the large amount of overhead involved in the data collection without any constructive feedback that could help the development process.

Therefore, we recommend you use the following sequence of steps to set up a data collection process:

1. Establish the objectives. Establishing the objectives is often the distinguishing point between successful and unsuccessful data collection efforts.

2. Develop a plan for the data collection process. Involve all of the concerned parties in the data collection and analysis. This includes designers, coders, testers, quality assurance staff, and line and project software managers. This ensures that all parties understand what is being done and the impact it will have on their respective organizations. The planning should include the objectives for the data collection and a data collection plan. Address the following questions:
   a. How often will the data be gathered?
   b. By whom will the data be gathered?
   c. In what form will the data be gathered?
   d. How will the data be processed, and how will they be stored?
   e. How will the data collection process be monitored to ensure the integrity of the data and that the objectives are being met?
   f. Can existing mechanisms be used to collect the data and meet the objectives?
   g. How much effort will be required to collect the data over the life of the project?

3. If any tools have been identified in the collection process, their availability, maturity, and usability must be assessed. Commercially available tools must not be assumed to be superior to internally developed tools. Reliability, ease of use, robustness, and support are factors to be evaluated together with the application requirements. If tools are to be developed internally, plan adequate resources—cost and schedule—for the development and acceptance testing of the tool.
4. Train all parties in use of the tools. The data collectors must understand the purpose of the measurements and know explicitly what data are to be collected. Data analysts must understand a tool's analysis capabilities and limitations.
5. Perform a trial run of the data plan to iron out any problems and misconceptions. This can save a significant amount of time and effort during software development. If prototyping is being done to help specify requirements or to try out a new development method, the trial-run data collection could be done during the prototyping effort.
6. Implement the plan. Make certain that sufficient resources have been allocated to cover the required staffing and tool needs, and that the required personnel are available.
7. Monitor the process on a regular basis to provide assurance that objectives are met and that the software is meeting the established reliability goals.
8. Evaluate the data on a regular basis. Don't make the reliability assessment after software delivery. Waiting until after delivery defeats the usefulness of software reliability modeling because you have not used the information for managing the development process. Based on the experiences reported in [Lyu91a], weekly evaluation seems appropriate for many development efforts.
9. Provide feedback to all parties. This should be done as early as possible during data collection and analysis. It is especially important to do so at the end of the development effort. It is very important to provide feedback to those involved in data collection and analysis so they will be aware of the impacts of their efforts. Parties who are given feedback will be more inclined to support future efforts, as they will have a sense of efficacy and personal pride in their accomplishments.

7.2.3 Defining data to be collected

Many projects already have in place some data collection mechanisms for failure data. For example, JPL has Problem/Failure Report (P/FR),

AT&T Bell Laboratories, Bellcore has Modification Request (MR) database, and IBM has Authorized Program Analysis Report (APAR). These mechanisms track the date and time at which the failure was observed, a description of the failure, and some information about the system configuration at the time the failure was observed. Specific information that needs to be collected is listed in the following subsections.

7.2.3.1 Time between successive failures. Collect the execution time between successive failures first. If execution time is unavailable, testing time between successive failures, measured by calendar time, can be used as a basis of approximation. Collect the start and completion time of each test session. If time-between-failures data cannot be collected, then collect test interval lengths and the number of failures encountered during each test interval. In many cases, this failure-count (or failure frequency) information is more easily collected than the time-between-failure information. Test interval lengths should also be accurately recorded. If possible, collect the CPU utilization during the test periods to determine the relationship between CPU and calendar time.

For many development efforts, failure-count information is the only available type. However, some software reliability tools can use only time between failures as input. In this instance, the failure-count data can be transformed to time-between-failures data in one of two ways described in Sec. 1.4. Since the uncertainty in reported failure times affects the accuracy of modeling results, problem-reporting mechanisms should be structured such that the mechanism's resolution is greater than the average interfailure time throughout the test cycle.

7.2.3.2 Functional area tested. This can be done with reference to a software requirements document or a software build plan. Reliability predictions may be dramatically different when this information is or is not available. The importance of tracking this information is illustrated in the following example.

Example 7.3 Failure data set J3 in the Data Disk is used for this example. The software reliability estimates are made using software reliability modeling tool SMERFS and CASRE (see App. A for descriptions). The Goel-Okumoto NHPP model was applied to the data. The software is assumed to be composed of two largely independent functional areas, and each functional area would be executed 50 percent of the time during operations. In producing the estimates seen in Fig. 7.3, the model was first applied to the entire set of failure data. This yields an estimated failure rate of three failures per week at week 41 of the testing phase.

The actual failure rate curve, however, is bimodal. There is clearly a change in the test procedure after week 14 of the testing phase. If the two functional areas are tested such that the first functional area is tested during the first 14 weeks,

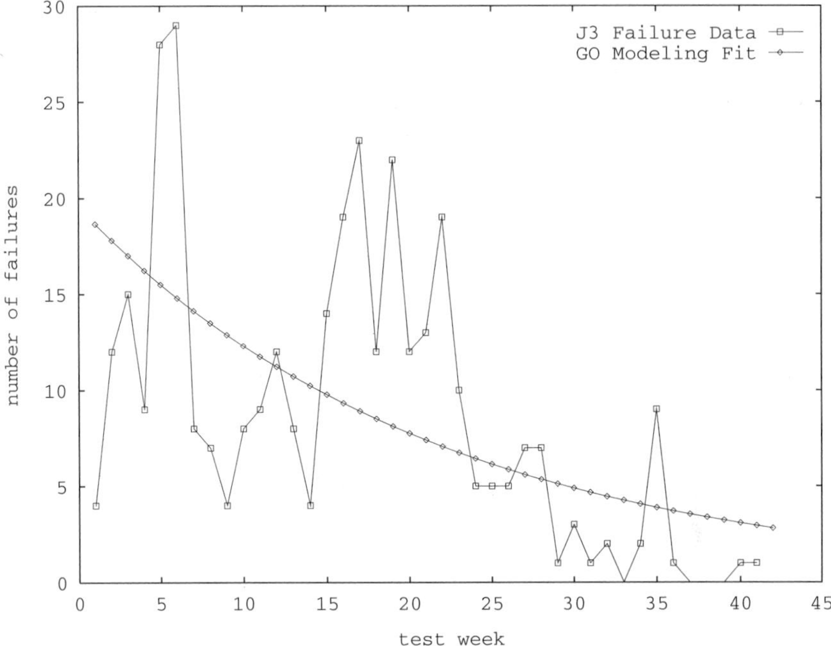

Figure 7.3 Application of GO model to entire data set.

while the second functional area is tested after week 14, then the reliabilities of the two functional areas can be separately modeled to yield a more accurate reliability estimate.

Figure 7.4 shows the reliability estimates for the two individual functional areas. By the end of week 14, the expected number of failures per week is 8 for the first functional area. During the interval between weeks 15 and 41, only the second functional area is tested. By the end of week 41, the expected number of failures per week is 1. If the software is delivered to operations at the end of week 41, it is seen that during operations, 4 failures per week can be expected while executing the first functional area, and 0.5 failures per week can be attributed to the second functional area. The resulting estimate of 4.5 failures per week is significantly different from the 3 failures per week that were estimated without taking the change in test focus into account.

As a numerical comparison, the mean square error for the predictions in Fig. 7.3 is 42.9, while that for the predictions in Fig. 7.4 is 28.3, a significant improvement. Note that the mean square error for the predictions in weeks 15–41 in Fig. 7.4 further drops to 14.2. The close fit in this period can been seen in the figure.

This analysis also shows that the first functional area needs more testing if it occurs frequently in the operational profile.

7.2.3.3 Changes during testing. Significant events that may affect the failure behavior during test include:

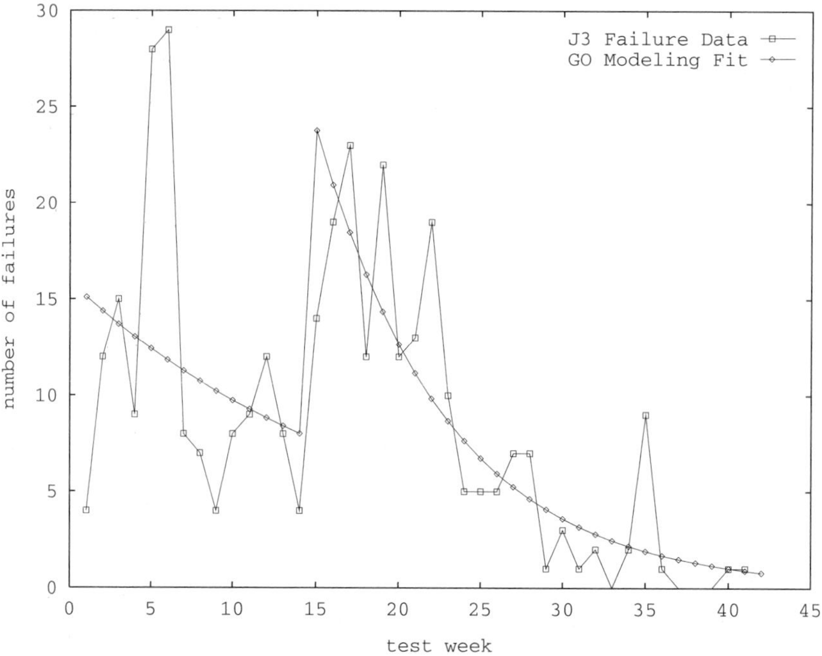

Figure 7.4 Separate GO model application of distinct functional areas.

1. *Addition of functionality to the software under test or significant modification of existing functionality.* If the software under test is still evolving, the failure intensity may be underestimated during the early stages of the program's development, yielding overly optimistic estimates of its reliability.

2. *Increases or decreases in the number of testers.* This will, for example, increase or reduce the failure-count data (expressed in calendar time) as testers are added to or taken away from the development effort. The time spent by each tester in exercising the software must be recorded so that the failure-count or time-between-failures inputs to the models are accurate.

3. *Changes in the test environment.* Examples are addition/removal of test equipment and modification of test equipment. If the test equipment is modified during a test phase to provide greater throughput, the time-between-failures and failure-count data recorded subsequently to the modification will have to be adjusted. For instance, if the clock speed in the test computer is increased by a factor of 2, the test intervals subsequent to the clock speed increase will need to be half as long as they were prior to the speedup if failure-count information is being recorded. If time-between-failures information is being recorded, the interfailure

times recorded subsequent to the speedup will have to be multiplied by 2 to be consistent with the times between failures recorded before the speedup occurred.

4. *Changes in the test method.* Examples are switching from white-box to black-box testing and changing the stress of software during test. If the test method changes during a testing effort, or if the software is exercised in a different manner, new estimates of the software's reliability will have to be made, starting at the time when the testing method or testing stress changed.

7.2.3.4 Other considerations. Interfailure times expressed in terms of CPU time are the preferred data. However, failure-count data are also recommended since existing problem-reporting mechanisms can often be used. The relative ease of collecting this information will encourage the use of SRE techniques. Currently, most problem-reporting systems collect the number of failures per unit test time interval. If your projects have existing mechanisms for collecting software failure data during developmental testing, use these data to obtain time-between-failures or failure-count data.

If failure-count data are used, a useful length for the test interval must be determined. This is influenced by such considerations as the number of testers, the number of available test sites, and the relative throughputs of test sites. Many testing teams summarize their findings on a weekly basis. Typically, a week during subsystem or system-level testing is a short enough period of time that the testing method will not change appreciably. Enough failures can be found in a week's time during the early stages of test to warrant recomputing the reliability on a weekly basis.

Many development projects require that test logs be kept during developmental and system-level testing, although the information recorded in these logs is generally not as accurate as that tracked by the problem-reporting system. Used as intended, these logs can be utilized to increase the accuracy of the failure-count or time-between-failures data available through the problem-tracking system. Without much effort beyond what is required to record failures, the following items can be collected:

1. *Functionality being tested.* The functionality can be related to items in a software build plan or requirements in a software requirements document. The reliability for each functional area should be modeled separately.
2. *Test session start date and time.*
3. *Test session stop date and time.*

In addition, it may be possible to gather CPU utilization data from the test bench's accounting facilities for each test period recorded.

If only one functional area is to be tested during a session, record only one start and stop time. If more than one functional area is to be tested, however, start and stop times should be recorded for each functional area. If testing is being done at more than one test site, keep a log at each test site. To determine test interval lengths, use the test logs from all test sites to determine the amount of testing time spent in a fixed amount of calendar time. Count the number of unique failure reports from all test sites written against that functional area in the chosen calendar interval to determine the failure-count data. These failure counts and test interval lengths can then be used as inputs to software reliability models. Note that the reliability of each functional area is separately determined.

7.2.4 Choosing a preliminary set of software reliability models

After specifying the software reliability requirements, you need to make a preliminary selection of software reliability models. Examine the assumptions that the models make about the development method and environment to determine how well they apply to your project. For instance, many models assume that the number of faults in the software has an upper bound. If software testing does not occur until the software is relatively mature and there is a low probability of making changes to the software actually being tested, models making this assumption can be included in the preliminary selection (e.g., Goel-Okumoto model, Musa basic model). If, on the other hand, significant changes are being made to the software at the same time it is being tested, it would be more appropriate to choose from those models that do not assume an upper bound to the number of faults (e.g., Musa-Okumoto and Littlewood-Verrall models). Many models also assume perfect debugging. If previous experience on similar projects indicates that most repairs do not result in new faults being inserted into the software, choose from those models making this assumption (e.g., Goel-Okumoto model, Musa-Okumoto model). However, if a significant number of repairs result in new faults being inserted into the software, it is more appropriate to choose from those models that do not assume perfect debugging (e.g., Littlewood-Verrall model).

It is important to note that there is currently no known method of evaluating these assumptions to determine a priori which model will prove optimal for a particular development effort [Abde86]. You are advised that this preliminary selection of models will be a qualitative, subjective evaluation. After a model has been selected, its performance during use can be quantitatively assessed (see Chap. 4). However, these assessment techniques cannot be applied to the preliminary selection.

If a model has been shown valid for a similar project or the early release of the same project, use that model continuously and consistently. If you have no practical experience with software reliability models, you are advised to use the following models, as recommended by AIAA [AIAA93]. The order of this list is arbitrary:

1. Generalized exponential model (see Sec. 3.7.1), which includes Jelinski-Moranda model (JM) [Jeli72] and Shooman model [Shoo73] (also in Sec. 3.3.1), Musa basic model (MB) [Musa79a] (also in Sec. 3.3.4), and Goel-Okumoto model (GO) [Goel79] (also in Sec. 3.3.2)
2. Schneidewind model (SM) [Schn75] (also in Sec. 3.3.3)
3. Musa-Okumoto logarithmic Poisson model (MO) [Musa84] (also in Sec. 3.5.3)
4. Littlewood-Verrall model (LV) [Litt73] (also in Sec. 3.6.1)

7.2.5 Choosing reliability modeling tools

Many software reliability tools are available to model and measure software reliability automatically. See App. A for a comprehensive survey.

In our study we use two tools: SRMP [Litt86] and CASRE [Lyu92d]. The CASRE tool calculates a product's reliability (the present reliability as well as future predictions of reliability) as a function of test time, and represents it in terms of several interrelated reliability measures, such as cumulative number of failures, failures per time interval, and the product's reliability function. This enables us to analyze a product's reliability from several points of view. CASRE is capable of providing product reliability estimates not only during system testing but during the product's field operation as well. In the latter case, product reliability is expressed as a function of field operation time. CASRE allows users to select and apply existing software reliability models to the data displayed in the work space. These models come from the model library of the SMERFS tool [Farr88], and consist of two categories based on their input data: time-between-failures models take the sequence of times between failures as the input, while failure-count models take number of failures per interval as the input.

7.2.6 Model application and application issues

After setting up a data collection mechanism and selecting the model(s) and tool(s), measurement of software reliability can be started. Do not attempt to measure software reliability during unit test. Although failures may be recorded during this testing phase, the individual units of code are too small to make valid software reliability estimates. Our experience indicates that the earliest point in the life cycle at which meaningful software reliability measurements can be made is at the subsystem software integration and test level. Experience gained in our study, as well as empirical evidence reported in [Musa87], suggests that software reliability measurement should not be attempted for a software system containing fewer than 2000 lines of uncommented source code. Instead, other measures (e.g., statement coverage, data and control flow coverage, data definitions and uses) could be investigated. Chapter 12 provides some emerging techniques in this area.

We now turn to the assumptions made by some of the more widely used software reliability models. Chapter 3 discusses the model assumptions in detail. These assumptions are made to cast the models into a mathematically tractable form. However, there may be situations in which the assumptions for a particular model or set of models do not apply to a development effort. In the following paragraphs, specific model assumptions are listed and the effects they may have on the accuracy of reliability estimates are described.

1. *During testing, the software is operated in a manner similar to the anticipated operational usage.* This assumption is often made to establish a relationship between the reliability behavior during testing and the operational reliability of the software. In practice, the usage pattern during testing can vary significantly from the operational usage. For instance, functionality that is not expected to be frequently used during operations (e.g., system fault protection) will be extensively tested to ensure that it functions as required when it is invoked.

When the operational usage distribution is not obtainable, one way of dealing with this issue is to model the reliability of each functional area separately, and then use the reliability of the least reliable functional area to represent the reliability of the software system as a whole. Predictions of operational reliability that are made this way will tend to be more pessimistic than the reliability that is actually observed during operations, provided that the same inputs are used during test as are used during operations. If the inputs to the software during test are different from those during operations, there will be no easily identifiable relationship between the reliability observed during test and operational reliability.

2. *There are a fixed number of faults contained in the software.* Because the mechanisms by which faults are introduced into a program during its development are poorly understood at present, this assumption is often made to make the reliability calculations more tractable. Models making this assumption should not be applied to

development efforts during which the software version being tested is simultaneously undergoing significant changes (e.g., 20 percent or more of the existing code is being changed, or the amount of code is increasing by 20 percent or more). Among the models making this assumption are the Jelinski-Moranda, the Goel-Okumoto, and the Musa Basic models. However, if the major source of change to the software during test is the correction process, and if the corrections made do not significantly change the software, it is generally safe to make this assumption. In practice, this would tend to limit application of models making this assumption to subsystem-level integration or later testing phases.

3. *No new faults are introduced into the code during the correction process.* Although introducing new faults during debugging is always possible, many models make this assumption to simplify the reliability calculations. In many development efforts, the introduction of new faults during the correction process tends to be a minor effect. If the volume of software (measured in source lines of code) being changed during correction is not a significant fraction of the volume of the entire program, and if the effects of repairs tend to be limited to the areas in which the corrections are made, this assumption is deemed acceptable. In the event that code is changing quickly or new faults are introduced when trying to fix old faults [Leve90], reliability models are still adaptable by examining the code "churns" [Dala94].

4. *Detections of failures are independent of one another.* This assumption is not necessarily valid. Indeed, evidence shows that detections of failures occur in groups, and there are some dependencies in detecting failures. However, this assumption enormously simplifies the estimation of model parameters. Determining the maximum likelihood estimator of a model parameter, for instance, requires the computation of a joint probability density function (pdf) involving all of the observed events. The assumption of independence allows this joint pdf to be computed as the product of the individual pdf's for each observation, keeping the computational requirements for parameter estimation within practical limits.

Practitioners using any currently available models have no choice but to make this assumption. Almost all the models analyzed in Chap. 3 make this assumption. Nevertheless, studies from AT&T, Hewlett Packard, and Cray Research report that the models produce fairly accurate estimates of current reliability in many situations [Ehrl90, Rapp90, Zinn90]. If the input data to the software are independent of each other, failure detection dependencies may be reduced.

When the above assumptions are deemed necessary for analytical approaches to reliability modeling, other techniques have been developed to relieve some of these assumptions. Simulation approaches (see Chap. 16) and neural networks (see Chap. 17) are two of the promising attempts.

7.2.7 Dealing with evolving software

Most models described in Chap. 3 assume that the software being tested will not be undergoing significant changes during the testing cycle. This is not always the case. A software system undergoing test may be simultaneously undergoing development, with changes being made to the existing software or new functionality being added periodically. To accurately model software reliability in this situation, changes made to the software have to be taken into account. Three approaches in handling changes to a program under test are available (see also Sec. 6.5.2.2):

1. Ignore the change.
2. Apply the component configuration change method.
3. Apply the failure time adjustment technique.

Ignoring changes is the simplest method, and is appropriate when the total volume of changes is small compared to the overall size of the program. In this case, the continual reestimation of parameters will reflect the fact that some change is in fact occurring.

The *component configuration change* approach is appropriate for the situation in which a small number of large changes are made to the software, each change resulting from the addition of independent components (e.g., addition of the telemetry gathering and downlinking capability to a spacecraft command and data subsystem). The reliability of each software component is modeled separately. The resulting estimates are then combined into a reliability figure for the overall system.

The *failure time adjustment* approach is most appropriately used when a program cannot be conveniently divided into separate independent subsystems and the program is changing rapidly enough to produce unacceptable failures in estimating the software's reliability. The three principal assumptions that are made in failure time adjustment are:

1. The program evolves sequentially. At any one time, there is only one path of evolution of the program for which reliability estimates are being made.
2. Changes in the program are due solely to growth. Differences between version k and version k+1 are due entirely to new code being added to

version k. In practice, there may be reductions in one area of the code between versions k and k+1, while growth in other areas occurs. If the reductions are small in comparison to the growth, as often occurs in repairing faults, they can usually be ignored.

3. The number of faults introduced by changes to the program are proportional to the volume of new code.

7.2.8 Practical limits in modeling ultrareliability

It is important to note a limitation of applying software reliability modeling techniques to verify systems for ultrahigh reliability (e.g., one failure per 10^7 hours of operation). It could be shown [Butl91] that quantification of software reliability in the ultrareliable regime is infeasible, since the required amount of testing time exceeds practical limits. For example, a system having a required probability of failure of 10^{-7} for a 10-hour mission implies that MTTF of the system (assuming exponentially distributed) T_F is approximately 10^8 hours. There are two basic approaches: testing with replacement, and testing without replacement. In either case, testing continues until r failures have been observed. In the first case, when a system fails, a replicated system is put on test in its place. In the second case, the failed system is not replaced. For the first case, the expected time on test, D_t, is given by

$$D_t = T_F \frac{r}{n} \tag{7.7}$$

where n is the number of items placed on test. For the second case, the expected time on test is

$$D_t = T_F \sum_{j=1}^{r} \frac{1}{n-j+1} \tag{7.8}$$

If r is set to 1, this gives the shortest test time possible. Table 7.1 shows the expected test duration as a function of the number of test replicates, n. The expected test time with or without replacement is the same in this case.

TABLE 7.1 The Expected Test Duration as a Function of *n*

No. of replicates (n)	Expected test duration D_t
1	10^8 hours = 11415 years
10	10^7 hours = 1141 years
100	10^6 hours = 114 years
1,000	10^5 hours = 11.4 years
10,000	10^4 hours = 1.14 years

To get satisfactory statistical significance, larger values of r are required, which translates to even more testing. Given that economic considerations rarely allow the number of test replicates to be greater than 10, life testing of ultrareliable systems looks quite hopeless.

We should note, however, that the critical software function which requires such an ultrareliability seldom executes the complete period of the 10-hour mission. In fact, it could only require a small portion of the CPU time (e.g., the final landing approach of a long airplane flight). If we assume that only 0.1 CPU hour of the 10-hour mission requires this 10^{-7} failure probability, then T_F becomes approximately 10^6 CPU hours for the critical function. Consequently, the numbers in Table 7.1 become those in Table 7.2.

It is noted that the critical function could be tested in a more powerful CPU, which is equivalent to an increase of the number of replicates. For example, if we use 10 replicates, each running a CUP that is 100 times faster than the original one, then the goal could be practically achieved in 42 CPU days. There are, of course, obstacles to overcome before this kind of testing and validation can happen. But its achievement would not be completely infeasible.

7.3 Project Investigation at JPL

For project applications in SRE practice, we have conducted a study on SRE techniques using JPL projects. The objectives of this study include:

1. Examine the applicability of software reliability models to real-world projects.
2. Apply model selection criteria and compare models.
3. Determine if there is a best model suitable for all applications.
4. Evaluate the cost-effectiveness of SRE techniques.

7.3.1 Project selection and characterization

Data set J1. Project J1 was one of the first spacecraft in which a significant fraction of the functionality was provided by software. This software system, totaling approximately 14,000 lines of uncommented

TABLE 7.2 The Expected CPU Test Duration as a Function of n

No. of replicates (n)	Expected CPU test duration D_t
1	10^6 hours = 114 years
10	10^5 hours = 11.4 years
100	10^4 hours = 1.14 years
1,000	10^3 hours = 42 days
10,000	10^2 hours = 4.2 days

assembly language, was divided among three real-time embedded subsystems: the Attitude and Articulation Control Subsystem (AACS), the Command and Control Subsystem (CCS), and the Flight Data Subsystem (FDS). The failure data we analyzed come from spacecraft system testing, at which point the AACS, CCS, and FDS had been integrated into the spacecraft. Among the items recorded on the P/FR during system test are (1) time of failure, (2) failure type, and (3) subsystem in which the failure occurred. During J1 system test, approximately 9.5 faults per thousand lines of code (KLOC) were discovered.

Data set J2. Launched in 1989, project J2 was developed as a planetary orbiter carrying an atmospheric probe. As with the project J1, a large fraction of project J2's functionality was provided by software. Approximately 7000 uncommented source lines of HAL/S were implemented for the AACS, while about 15,000 source lines of assembly language were developed for the Command and Data Subsystem (CDS). Project J2 failure data come from spacecraft system testing. During J2 system test, approximately 10.2 faults per KLOC were discovered.

Data set J3. Failure data for the project J2 CDS during one phase of subsystem-level integration testing were available for analysis. We were able to reconstruct some elements of the testing profile. For example, it was known to us that the number of hours per week during which testing occurred was nearly constant throughout this phase, which was composed of two testing stages. In addition, the main functional areas of the software received roughly the same amount of testing every calendar week. This information resulted in the failure data being more accurate than that for other projects. During J3 subsystem test, approximately 10.1 faults per KLOC were discovered.

Data set J4. Like project J2, project J4 has an AACS and a CDS, and the number of uncommented source lines of code for each is roughly the same as that for project J2. As with projects J1 and J2, the failure data come from the spacecraft system test period. During J4 system test, approximately 8.0 faults per KLOC were discovered.

Data set J5. Project J5 is a facility for tracking and acquiring data from earth resources satellites in high-inclination orbits. Totaling about 103,000 uncommented source lines of code, the software is written in a mixture of C, Fortran, EQUEL, and OSL. About 14,000 lines were reused from previous efforts. The failure data reported here were obtained from the development organization's anomaly reporting system during software integration and test. During J5 system test, approximately 3.6 faults per KLOC were discovered.

This variety of project data would give us a chance to see whether the reliability measurement techniques developed for one type of development effort would work well for another.

7.3.2 Characterization of available data

For all of the JPL efforts, the following data were available:

1. Date on which a failure occurred
2. Failure description
3. Recommended corrective action
4. Corrective action taken
5. Date on which failure report was closed.

For each of the flight projects, the severity of each failure was also available.

Note that the following items were not systematically recorded, and were generally unavailable for use in the modeling effort:

1. *Execution times between successive failures,* or comparable information (e.g., total time spent testing during a calendar interval).
2. *Test interval lengths;* it was therefore necessary to assume that they were constant.
3. *Operational profile information* (e.g., functional area being tested, referenced to requirements or design documentation; subsystem being tested; points at which the testing method may have changed.)

The data collected from these development environments tend to be very noisy, and the assumptions of most software reliability models do not necessarily hold under the described circumstances. Nevertheless, failure data collected based on calendar time are typically under similar circumstances in many other projects.

7.3.3 Experimental results

In the reliability analysis of the JPL project data J1 through J5, we have to assume that the test time per unit interval of calendar time was relatively constant and that the testing method remained constant, since this information was not systematically recorded. Largely because of this lack of information, we decided to model the reliability of the facility as a whole, rather than attempt to model the component reliabilities. Subsequently, we applied the SRMP reliability tool to the five JPL projects and obtained the following model comparison results. Note that all the JPL project data were collected in failure-count format, and we had to convert the data into time-between-failures format for proper execution by SRMP. Random distribution of the grouped failure data was assumed for the conversion.

We evaluated a number of models surveyed in Chap. 3 and selected six models—JM, GO, MO, Duane model (DU) [Duan64] (also in Sec.

3.5.1), Littlewood model (LM) [Litt81], and LV—for project applications [Lyu91b]. Tables 7.3 to 7.7 summarize the analysis of model applicability for the JPL efforts. For each development effort, the models applied were evaluated with respect to evaluation criteria (Sec. 4.3), including model accuracy (prequential likelihood value), model bias (u-plot), bias trend (y-plot), and variability. The value for each criterion is given in the tables, while the corresponding ranking is given in parenthesis. Each of these criteria was given equal weighting in the overall ranking.

From Tables 7.3 to 7.7 we found that there was no one best model for the development efforts that were studied. This is consistent with the findings reported in Chap. 4. It is easy to see that a model that performs well for one development effort may do poorly in another. For instance, the Littlewood-Verrall model performs very well for the first three data sets—in fact, it outperforms all of the other models. However, it comes in last for the remaining two projects. This inconsistency is repeated for the other five models as well. There were no clear differences between the development processes for the five JPL applications, certainly none that would favor the selection of one model over another prior to the start of test. These findings suggest that multiple models be applied to the failure data during the test phases of a development effort, preferably models making different assumptions about the failure detection and fault removal processes. In addition, the models should be continually evaluated for applicability to the failure data. The model(s) ranking highest with respect to the evaluation criteria should then be chosen for use in predicting future reliability.

7.4 Investigation at Bellcore

After the study of JPL historical project data, we learned the lesson that data collection plays a crucial role in SRE applications. We also learned that multiple models should be applied to project data and the selection of best model(s) should be done continuously. Another study was performed to investigate Bellcore projects for SRE applications [Carm95]. The objectives of this study were:

1. Apply a better data collection effort and observe the effect.
2. Search better model(s) for particular projects as a posteriori.
3. Observe and quantify the growth of reliability during testing.
4. Classify the characteristics of reliability models.

7.4.1 Project characteristics

Project B1 is a key telecommunications software system for daily telephony operations. This system has been in existence for over 10

TABLE 7.3 Model Rankings for J1 Data

Measure	JM	GO	MO	DU	LM	LV
Accuracy	894.7 (6)	573.7 (3)	571.5 (2)	586.6 (4)	829.9 (5)	549.1 (1)
Bias	0.2994 (5)	0.2849 (3)	0.2849 (3)	0.2703 (2)	0.2994 (5)	0.0793 (1)
Trend	0.0995 (5)	0.0965 (3)	0.0957 (2)	0.2551 (6)	0.0994 (4)	0.0876 (1)
Variability	∞ (5)	13.81 (3)	9.225 (2)	8.402 (1)	∞ (5)	24.51 (4)
Overall rank	(6)	(3)	(2)	(4)	(5)	(1)

TABLE 7.4 Model Rankings for J2 Data

Measure	JM	GO	MO	DU	LM	LV
Accuracy	1074 (2)	1075 (4)	1078 (5)	1098 (6)	1074 (2)	1051 (1)
Bias	0.3378 (3)	0.3378 (3)	0.3379 (5)	0.1944 (1)	0.3382 (6)	0.2592 (2)
Trend	0.4952 (3)	0.4954 (4)	0.5041 (6)	0.4618 (2)	0.4954 (4)	0.1082 (1)
Variability	2.607 (3)	2.593 (2)	2.395 (1)	4.541 (5)	2.624 (4)	23.33 (6)
Overall rank	(2)	(3)	(5)	(4)	(6)	(1)

TABLE 7.5 Model Rankings for J3 Data

Measure	JM	GO	MO	DU	LM	LV
Accuracy	643.0 (3)	639.3 (2)	681.1 (5)	728.5 (6)	643.0 (3)	612.3 (1)
Bias	0.1783 (3)	0.1783 (3)	0.1700 (1)	0.1748 (2)	0.1784 (5)	−0.2581 (6)
Trend	0.3450 (3)	0.3408 (2)	0.4262 (5)	0.4282 (6)	0.3450 (3)	0.2426 (1)
Variability	4.042 (5)	3.908 (4)	2.673 (3)	2.287 (1)	4.042 (5)	2.564 (2)
Overall rank	(3)	(2)	(3)	(5)	(6)	(1)

TABLE 7.6 Model Rankings for J4 Data

Measure	JM	GO	MO	DU	LM	LV
Accuracy	627.1 (3)	627.1 (3)	627.1 (3)	616.0 (1)	627.1 (3)	622.9 (2)
Bias	0.2968 (4)	0.2968 (4)	0.2969 (2)	0.1858 (1)	0.2969 (2)	–0.3483 (6)
Trend	0.2399 (3)	0.2399 (3)	0.2399 (3)	0.2180 (2)	0.2399 (3)	0.1429 (1)
Variability	1.007 (1)	1.007 (1)	1.007 (1)	2.003 (5)	1.009 (4)	5.563 (6)
Overall rank	(3)	(3)	(1)	(1)	(5)	(6)

TABLE 7.7 Model Rankings for J5 Data

Measure	JM	GO	MO	DU	LM	LV
Accuracy	915.7 (1)	915.8 (4)	915.7 (1)	925.5 (6)	915.7 (1)	920.5 (5)
Bias	0.3023 (1)	0.3023 (1)	0.3023 (1)	0.4249 (6)	0.3023 (1)	–0.3672 (5)
Trend	0.0606 (1)	0.0615 (3)	0.0620 (4)	0.0918 (5)	0.0606 (1)	0.1009 (6)
Variability	1.587 (3)	1.540 (2)	1.395 (1)	1.650 (5)	1.589 (4)	3.189 (5)
Overall rank	(1)	(4)	(2)	(5)	(2)	(5)

years and it is deployed by all the regional Bell operating companies. The whole system includes around 1 million lines of C source code, with the main application being composed of 700K lines of code. During testing of various project B1 releases, complex interactions with other large telecommunications systems are involved. Since test metrics were collected in an automatic testing environment, some approximations to software execution time are available, which include the number and size of messages received per day, as well as total and unique test cases executed per day. The failure reports represent testing activities conducted by a group of 15 staff members that were involved with testing the current release, which includes about 250K lines of new and changed lines of code.

7.4.2 Data collection

Failure data for project B1 are collected from Bellcore internal problem tracking systems. This database stores information about all the failures (i.e., Modification Requests, or MRs) found during testing and operation. The discovery date, description, originator, severity, and other tracking information are associated with each failure. A query is available to return the number of failures found on each testing day. Staff time related information is collected manually for the project. The data collection form for this process is shown in Fig. 7.5. In addition, project B1 is able to automatically extract some time-related records to represent the intensity of testing.

From several months' effort of software failure data collection during system testing, the following scenarios were made available for the project (B1):

1. B1.calendar: This data set collects software failure data reported during B1 system testing, based on calendar time.
2. B1.staff: This data set records B1 system testing failures based on staff time reported by each tester during testing.
3. B1.all_test: This data set records B1 failures based on the total test cases executed per testing day. The test case information is automatically collected.
4. B1.uniq_test: This data set records B1 failures based on the number of unique test cases executed each day. Repeated test cases run on the same day are not counted. This information is automatically collected.
5. B1.message: This data set records B1 failures based on the messages the system sends out. The number of messages is considered an indication of the intensity of software execution. This information is automatically collected.

7.4.3 Application results

We used the CASRE tool to apply software reliability models to the Bellcore data sets. There are two types of models in CASRE: time-between-failures (TBF) models and failure-count (FC) models. Table 7.8 presents a comparison of TBF models, including LV, geometric model (GEO) [Farr83] (also in Sec. 3.5.2), MB, JM, and MO, for the project B1 data using messages as a time measure (B1.message). Table 7.9 shows comparable results for FC models, which include generalized Poisson model (GP) [Farr83], Brooks and Motley Poisson model (BMP) and binomial model (BMB) [Farr83], NHPP (same as GO) model, and Yamada delayed S-shaped model (YSS) [Yama83] (also in Sec. 3.4.2).

The first row lists the models being compared. These are followed by the rows that record results from several model evaluation criteria, discussed in Sec. 7.3.3, and goodness-of-fit measure (Kolmogorov-Smirnov test for TBF data, chi-square test for FC data). Rank ordering

Test Data Collection Sheet

<Project Name>

Testing phase: ____________ Week no.:____________ Tester ID: ____________

Monday's date: ____________

	Mon.	Tues.	Wed.	Thurs.	Fri.	Sat.	Sun.
Calendar working time (hours)*							
Staff testing time (hours)**							
No. of total test cases run							
No. of unrepeated test cases run							
No. of severity 1 failures							
No. of severity 2 failures							
No. of severity 3 failures							
No. of severity 4 failures							

* Record the official working hours at the company (usually 7.5 hours).

** Record the tester's time (hours) spent on system testing. Include: (1) functional test, (2) regression testing (3) test case preparation.

NOTE: Do not count tester time spent meeting with developers regarding MR fixes.

Figure 7.5 Sample data collection form.

TABLE 7.8 TBF Model Comparisons for B1.message Data

Measure	LV	GEO	MB	JM	MO
Accuracy	526.8 (1)	529.5 (2)	529.8 (4)	529.5 (3)	529.9 (5)
Bias	0.127 (5)	0.113 (3)	0.080 (2)	0.067 (1)	0.120 (4)
Trend	0.0940 (1)	0.1490 (2)	0.1644 (5)	0.1643 (4)	0.1511 (3)
Variability	1.85 (2)	1.78 (1)	2.76 (4)	2.80 (5)	1.87 (3)
Goodness-of-fit	0.045 (1)	0.107 (4)	0.104 (2)	0.111 (5)	0.105 (3)
Overall rank	1	2	3	4	5

TABLE 7.9 FC Model Comparisons for B1.message Data

Measure	GP	BMP	NHPP	BMB	YSS
Accuracy	99.87 (1)	104.12 (3)	103.63 (2)	104.80 (4)	118.03 (5)
Goodness-of-fit	42.91 (1)	50.09 (2)	55.42 (4)	50.29 (3)	60.38 (5)
Degree of freedom	16	19	19	19	12
Overall rank	1	2	3	4	5

of the measure for each criterion is listed in parentheses. Overall ranks are provided in the last row. We can see for B1.message data, LV performs the best among the TBF models, while among the FC models, the GP model performs the best.

Tables 7.10 and 7.11 list, for B1.message data, the estimated times between failure, failure rates, and the factor of reliability growth for the TBF and FC models, respectively. To capture the growth of reliability from each model's viewpoint, we define a reliability growth factor (RGF) to be

$$\text{RGF} = \frac{\text{final time between failures}}{\text{initial time between failures}} \quad \text{(for TBF models)} \tag{7.10a}$$

$$= \frac{\text{initial failure rate}}{\text{final failure rate}} \quad \text{(for FC models except the YSS model)} \tag{7.10b}$$

TABLE 7.10 Time (Messages) Between Failures and Reliability Growth Estimated by TBF Models

Measure	GEO	JM	LV	MB	MO	Average
Initial TBF	798	896	817	909	823	849
Final TBF	3277	4213	3790	4047	3269	3719
RGF	4.11	4.70	4.64	4.45	3.97	4.37

TABLE 7.11 Failure Rates (Per Day) and Reliability Growth Estimated by FC Models

Measure	BMB	BMP	GP	NHPP	Average
Initial failure rate	3.34	3.38	2.92	3.30	3.24
Final failure rate	0.65	0.64	0.46	0.66	0.60
RGF	5.16	5.31	6.29	5.02	5.45

In other words, RGF is the same as the failure intensity improvement factor discussed in Example 7.1. Note that RGF is not defined for the YSS model.

The overall comparison of the five Bellcore data sets is summarized in Table 7.12 for the TBF models, and in Table 7.13 for the FC models. From these two tables we can see that for the Bellcore project data, LV is the best TBF model. For the FC type models, the GP model is the best one.

Table 7.14 summarizes the overall indication of level of data convergence and reliability growth for each data set, across all TBF models. Table 7.15 presents an analogous summary for the FC models. The second column in these tables, first convergence point, represents the number of data points upon which at least one model converges, divided by the total number of data points. Its percentage ratio is given in parentheses. The third column, common convergence point, is given

TABLE 7.12 Overall Model Comparisons of TBF Models

Model	GEO	JM	LV	MB	MO
B1.calendar	(5)	(3)	(1)	(2)	(4)
B1.staff	(5)	(3)	(1)	(2)	(4)
B1.all_test	(5)	(1)	(1)	(3)	(4)
B1.uniq_test	(5)	(1)	(2)	(3)	(4)
B1.message	(2)	(3)	(1)	(3)	(5)
Sum of rank	44	33	25	36	47
Total rank	(4)	(2)	(1)	(3)	(5)

TABLE 7.13 Overall Model Comparisons of FC Models

Model	BMB	BMP	GP	NHPP	YSS
B1.calendar	(4)	(2)	(3)	(1)	(4)
B1.staff	(3)	(3)	(1)	(5)	(1)
B1.all_test	(4)	(3)	(1)	(5)	(1)
B1.uniq_test	(4)	(3)	(1)	(5)	(2)
B1.message	(4)	(2)	(1)	(3)	(5)
Sum of rank	19	13	7	19	13
Total rank	(4)	(2)	(1)	(4)	(2)

by the number of points at which all models converge divided by the total number of points. The percentage ratio is also in parentheses. A high ratio indicates the parameter estimation did not converge until very late. This would happen when the data set is very noisy.

From Tables 7.14 and 7.15, we can make following observations:

1. When a reliability model is applied to a data set, it usually requires some failure observations in the estimation process for the model to get convergence. On the average, TBF models take at least 27 percent of the data to get initial convergence, while FC models require only 6 percent of the data. However, even if a model can converge very early, we still recommend that you use at least 30 observations (failures for TBF models or intervals for FC models) or 30 percent of the total data points for parameter estimation in the model application.
2. It usually takes quite a few data points before all the models converge, particularly for TBF models. In some cases a TBF model would not converge until a large amount (say, 86 percent) of the failure data are observed.
3. Not only do FC models converge earlier than TBF models, but they normally have a higher RGF than TBF models. In general, the data sets with an earlier converging point would have a larger RGF.
4. The B1 project tracks reliability growth well during testing, using either calendar time, staff time, or test-related time (test cases exe-

TABLE 7.14 Overall RGF of TBF Models for Each Data Set

Project data	First convergence point	Common convergence point	RGF
B1.calendar	31/150 (20.6%)	102/150 (68.0%)	5.10
B1.staff	34/150 (22.7%)	130/150 (86.7%)	3.57
B1.all_test	34/150 (22.7%)	130/150 (86.7%)	3.46
B1.uniq_test	77/150 (51.3%)	130/150 (86.7%)	4.20
B1.message	32/150 (21.3%)	90/150 (60.0%)	4.37
Average	(27.7%)	(77.6%)	4.14

TABLE 7.15 Overall RGF of FC Models for Each Data Set

Project data	First convergence point	Common convergence point	RGF
B1.calendar	5/85 (5.9%)	33/85 (38.8%)	6.52
B1.staff	5/85 (5.9%)	55/85 (64.7%)	4.67
B1.all_test	4/68 (5.9%)	44/68 (64.7%)	4.35
B1.uniq_test	4/68 (5.9%)	44/68 (64.7%)	5.81
B1.message	5/71 (7.0%)	14/71 (19.7%)	5.45
Average	(6.1%)	(50.5%)	5.36

cuted, messages sent by the system). This consistency indicates that this particular release has a well-controlled testing procedure and a smoothly conducted testing activity, which is confirmed when evaluating the software engineering process of the project.

7.5 Linear Combination of Model Results

Our other finding is that linear combinations of model results, even in their simplest format, appear to provide more accurate predictions than the individual models themselves [Lyu91c]. Basically, we adopt the following strategy in forming combination models:

1. Identify a basic set of models (the component models). If you can characterize the testing environment for the development effort, select models whose assumptions are closest to the actual testing practices.
2. Select models whose predictive biases tend to cancel each other. As previously described, models can have optimistic or pessimistic biases.
3. Separately apply each component model to the data.
4. Apply certain criteria to weight the selected component models (e.g., changes in the prequential likelihood) and form a combination model for the final predictions. Weights can be either static or dynamically determined.

In general, this approach is expressed as a mixed distribution,

$$\hat{f}_i(t) = \sum_{j=1}^{n} \omega_j(t)\, \hat{f}_i^j(t) \tag{7.11}$$

where n represents the number of models, $\hat{f}_i^j(t)$ is the predictive probability density function of the jth component model, given that $i - 1$ observations of failure data have been made. Note that

$$\sum_j \omega_j(t) = 1 \qquad \text{for all } t\text{'s}$$

The linear combination model tends to preserve the features inherited from its component models. Also, because each component model performs reliability calculations independently, the combination model remains fairly simple. The component models are plugged into the combination model only at the last stage for final predictions.

Selecting appropriate component models is, of course, important to the success of the combination model. The parameter-estimation method you select to implement the component models may, to a certain extent, affect the combination model's prediction validity. We feel that the Goel-Okumoto (GO), Musa-Okumoto (MO), and Littlewood-Verrall (LV) models are the best candidates for our linear combination models. We selected them because in our investigations, we found that their predictions were valid [Lyu92c]. Other practitioners have also found that they perform well, and they are widely used [AIAA93]. Another reason is that they represent different model categories. GO represents the exponential-shaped NHPP model; MO represents the logarithmic-shaped NHPP model; and LV represents the inverse-polynomial-shaped Bayesian model. Finally, at least with the data set we analyzed, the biases of these models tend to cancel out. GO tends to be optimistic, LV tends to be pessimistic, and MO might go either way.

We experiment with three types of combinations. The goal of each is to reduce the risk of relying on a specific model, which may produce grossly inaccurate predictions, while retaining much of the simplicity of using the component models. These combinations are:

1. Statically weighted combinations
2. Dynamically weighted combinations in which weights are determined by comparing and ranking model results
3. Dynamically weighted combinations in which weights are determined by changes in model references.

7.5.1 Statically weighted linear combinations

This type of model is the simplest combination to form. Each component model has a constant weighting which remains the same throughout the modeling process. The main statically weighted combination is the equally weighted linear combination (ELC) model, which is formed by the arithmetic average of all the component models' predictions, namely,

$$\mathrm{ELC} = \frac{1}{3}\mathrm{GO} + \frac{1}{3}\mathrm{MO} + \frac{1}{3}\mathrm{LV}$$

This model follows a strategy similar to that of a Delphi survey, in which authorities working independently are asked for an opinion on a subject, and an average of the results is taken.

7.5.2 Weight determination based on ranking model results

Combination models may produce more accurate results if the weights are dynamically assigned rather than remaining static throughout the modeling process. One way of dynamically assigning weights is based on simply ranking component model results. If a combination model contains n components, choose a set of n values that can be assigned to the components based on a ranking of model results. One of the combinations is the median-weighted linear combination (MLC) model, formed by the following: for each failure, the component models would be run, and the results of the models would then be compared. The models predicting the highest and lowest times to the next failure would then be given weights of 0 in the combination, while the prediction in the middle would be given a weight of 1.

The other combination of this type is the unequally weighted linear combination (ULC) model. This model is similar to MLC except that optimistic and pessimistic predictions contribute to the final prediction. The prediction is not determined solely by the median value. Here we use weightings similar to those in the *Program Evaluation and Review Technique:*

$$\frac{1}{6}O + \frac{4}{6}M + \frac{1}{6}P$$

where O represents an optimistic prediction, P a pessimistic prediction, and M the median prediction.

7.5.3 Weight determination based on changes in prequential likelihood

The dynamically weighted linear combination (DLC) model is the one in which weights are both dynamically determined and assigned. The basis for determining and assigning weights is the changes in model preferences over a small number of observations.

In the DLC model, we assume that the applicability of any individual model to the project data may change as testing progresses. Therefore, the component models' weights will change according to changes in a model's applicability. Here, we use changes in prequential likelihood—a measure that denotes a model's accumulated accuracy—to assign weights to the component models, which could be taken over a few or many time frames. As a baseline, we formed the simplest DLC model by choosing an observation window of one time frame before each prediction as the reference in assigning weights.

7.5.4 Modeling results

In order to determine the validity of the linear combination modeling scheme, we use six models selected in Sec. 7.3.3 as a reference group to compare with the experimental group of linear combination models.

Modeling results for this comparison came from three sets of published data in [Musa79]. These data sets are also listed as SYS1, SYS2, and SYS3 in the Data Disk. Table 7.16 shows the result of SYS3 data application.

In Table 7.16, numbers in each row represent the computed measure under each criterion, with ranks in parentheses corresponding to the models in columns. The last row, "Overall rank," was determined by equally treating all the four criteria. Note that the "starting data" indicates when the model predictions began; previous data points were used for parameter estimations. This starting point was chosen such that a small but reasonable set of data points could be used for the parameter estimations.

It is observed from this table that the proposed linear combination models performed relatively well compared with the other six models. Model application to other data sets in [Musa79] also showed similar results.

7.5.5 Overall project results

Tables 7.17 and 7.18 list the performance comparisons for the three data sets from [Musa79] and the five data sets from JPL (J1 through J5). The overall comparison is done by using all four measures in Table 7.17, or by using the prequential likelihood measure (the accuracy criterion) alone in Table 7.18, since it is judged to be the most important one. In general, we consider a model as being satisfactory if and only if it is ranked 4 or better out of the 10 models for a particular project. To extend this idea, we define a *handicap* value, which is calculated by subtracting 4 (the *par* value) from the rank of a model for each data set before its ranks are summed up in the overall evaluation (or subtract 32 from the "Sum of rank" row in Tables 7.17 and 7.18). A negative handicap value represents satisfactory overall performance for the eight data sets.

We can observe several important points from these summary tables:

1. There are two sets of models under investigation here: the set of single models, and the set of combination models. In general, the set of combination models perform better than the set of single models. The acceptable models (those with a negative handicap), when considering all four measuring criteria (Table 7.17), are exactly the four linear combination models. When considering the accuracy criterion alone (Table 7.18), the three acceptable models, DLC, ELC, ULC, also belong to the combination model set. By evaluating the handicap value, we also note that the combination models usually beat the other single models with a significant margin.

TABLE 7.16 Model Comparisons for Data Set SYS3

Recommended Models: (1) DLC, (2) MLC, (3) ULC, (4) ELC, (4) MO

Data Set 3 (207 data points; starting data—60)										
Measure	JM	GO	MO	DU	LM	LV	ELC	ULC	MLC	DLC
Accuracy	−811.1	−811.2	−811.1	−814.3	−811.3	−812.7	−810.8	−810.8	−811.1	−809.1
	(4)	(7)	(4)	(10)	(8)	(9)	(2)	(2)	(4)	(1)
Bias	0.0835	0.0761	0.0586	0.0994	0.0829	0.0845	0.0640	0.0594	0.0586	0.0649
	(8)	(6)	(1)	(10)	(7)	(9)	(4)	(3)	(1)	(5)
Trend	0.0623	0.0663	0.0487	0.0740	0.0602	0.0630	0.0467	0.0474	0.0480	0.0462
	(7)	(9)	(5)	(10)	(6)	(8)	(2)	(3)	(4)	(1)
Variability	5.384	5.209	4.088	2.426	6.002	3.714	4.224	4.196	4.073	3.901
	(9)	(8)	(5)	(1)	(10)	(2)	(7)	(6)	(4)	(3)
Overall rank	(6)	(8)	(4)	(9)	(9)	(6)	(4)	(3)	(2)	(1)

TABLE 7.17 Overall Model Comparisons Using All Four Criteria

	Summary of Model Ranking for Each Data by All Four Criteria									
Model	JM	GO	MO	DU	LM	LV	ELC	ULC	MLC	DLC
SYS1	(10)	(9)	(1)	(6)	(8)	(6)	(4)	(2)	(3)	(5)
SYS2	(9)	(10)	(6)	(7)	(8)	(1)	(4)	(5)	(2)	(2)
SYS3	(6)	(8)	(4)	(9)	(9)	(6)	(4)	(3)	(2)	(1)
J1	(10)	(7)	(6)	(7)	(9)	(2)	(2)	(4)	(5)	(1)
J2	(5)	(7)	(10)	(6)	(9)	(4)	(1)	(3)	(8)	(2)
J3	(8)	(6)	(6)	(8)	(10)	(1)	(1)	(1)	(4)	(5)
J4	(5)	(5)	(8)	(1)	(9)	(10)	(1)	(5)	(4)	(3)
J5	(1)	(5)	(1)	(9)	(3)	(10)	(8)	(7)	(3)	(6)
Sum of rank	54	57	42	53	65	40	25	30	31	25
Handicap	+22	+25	+10	+21	+33	+8	−7	−2	−1	−7
Total rank	(8)	(9)	(6)	(7)	(10)	(5)	(1)	(3)	(4)	(1)

TABLE 7.18 Overall Model Comparisons by the Accuracy Measure

	Summary of Model Ranking for Each Data Using the Accuracy Measure									
Model	JM	GO	MO	DU	LM	LV	ELC	ULC	MLC	DLC
SYS1	(10)	(9)	(2)	(8)	(6)	(7)	(5)	(4)	(3)	(1)
SYS2	(7)	(9)	(4)	(10)	(7)	(1)	(4)	(4)	(3)	(2)
SYS3	(4)	(7)	(4)	(10)	(8)	(9)	(2)	(2)	(4)	(1)
J1	(10)	(7)	(6)	(8)	(9)	(2)	(3)	(4)	(5)	(1)
J2	(5)	(7)	(9)	(10)	(5)	(4)	(2)	(3)	(8)	(1)
J3	(6)	(5)	(8)	(10)	(6)	(2)	(3)	(4)	(8)	(1)
J4	(6)	(6)	(6)	(2)	(6)	(5)	(3)	(4)	(6)	(1)
J5	(2)	(6)	(2)	(10)	(2)	(9)	(8)	(7)	(2)	(1)
Sum of rank	50	56	41	68	49	39	30	32	39	9
Handicap	+18	+24	+9	+36	+17	+7	−2	0	+7	−23
Total rank	(8)	(9)	(6)	(10)	(7)	(4)	(2)	(3)	(4)	(1)

2. By weighting or averaging the predictions from the three well-known component models, GO, MO, and LV, the combinational models appear to be less sensitive to potential data noise than their component models and other single models. This is reflected in the investigated data sets which include both execution-time-based data and calendar-time-based data. Moreover, when we examine all project data for the evaluation criteria, we can see that the combination models could *sometimes* outperform all their component models, but they *never* perform worse than the worst component model.

3. The DLC and ELC models perform rather consistently. Most other models seem to perform well for a few data sets but poorly for other data sets, and the fluctuation in performance is significant. By preserving good properties from the three well-known models with equal weightings, the ELC model achieves a good overall performance, as expected. On the other hand, since the DLC model is allowed to dynamically change its weightings according to the outcome of the accuracy measure, it is not surprising to see it consistently produce the best accuracy measure for almost every data set. This consistency suggests that, if you use whatever accuracy measures you deem the most important as the weighting criterion in forming the DLC model, you will get the best results.

7.5.6 Extensions and alternatives

You can extend or alter our basic approach in the following ways:

1. Extend the DLC model by increasing the size of the observation window from one time frame to N time frames. The DLC model consistently produces the best accuracy measure, but with only one observation window, it might fail to note a global measurement trend. Thus, a natural extension is to enlarge the window.
2. Try to apply models other than GO, MO, and LV as component models. If some models perform well in a particular data set, they should be the candidate component models to form a combination model.
3. Use more than three models as component models. We believe that the more component models you apply, the better the prediction. However, more computations are required, and the returns may diminish as more models are added.
4. Apply alternative weighting schemes that are based on project criteria and engineering judgments. Our approach is flexible enough that you can decide how you want to form a combination model.
5. Use the combination models themselves as component models to form another combination model.

6. As the original assumptions behind each model become lost through the layers of linear combinations, a distribution-free (nonparametric) modeling technique may emerge.

In our investigation, the most promising approach was to extend the DLC model. We considered a DLC model with a fixed *N* window, DLC/F, and a DLC model with a sliding *N* window, DLC/S. Figure 7.6 shows how the two models differ.

In the DLC/F model, the weight assignments for each model are based on changes in the accuracy measure over the last *N* observations. The weight assignment for each model remains fixed for the next *N* predictions. At the end of that time, the weights are recomputed according to the changes in accuracy over the last *N* observations. To compute the weight of a component model, you first determine the amount of change in component model A's accuracy measure over the last *N* observations. You then identify component model B, the component model whose accuracy measure changed the most. The unnormalized weight for A is simply the ratio of the change in its accuracy measure to the change in B's accuracy measure.

In the DLC/S model, you recompute the weight assignments for each model at each data point, using changes in the accuracy measure over the last *N* observations as the basis for determining each model's weight. To compute weights for component models, the procedure is the same as that in the DLC/F model.

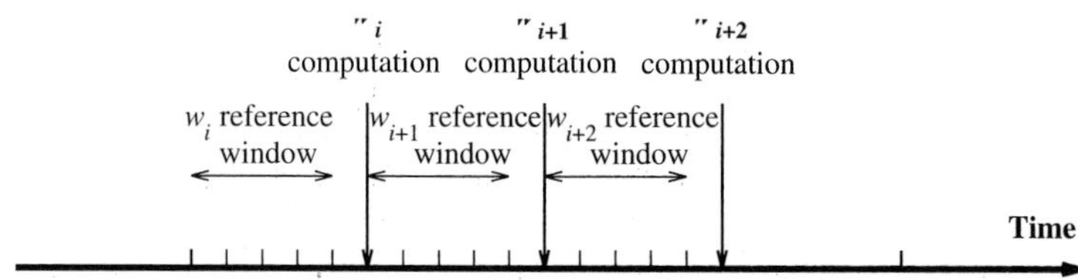

Figure 7.6*a* The DLC model with a fixed observation window.

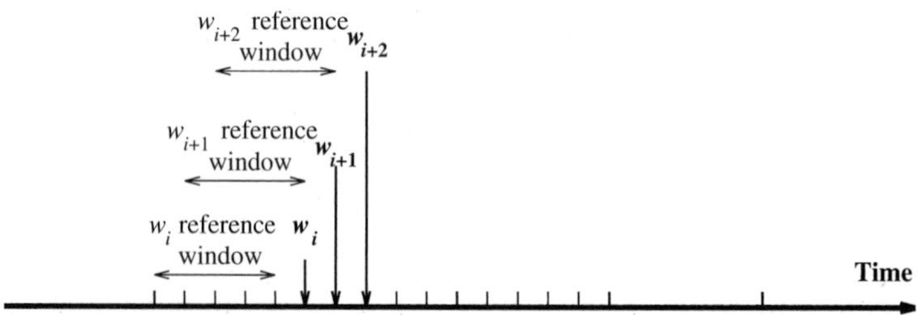

Figure 7.6*b* The DLC model with a sliding observation window.

Figure 7.7 summarizes the accuracy measure of the DLC/F and DLC/S models, normalized with respect to the number of measured points in each data set before being summed up for the eight data sets.

As Fig. 7.7 shows, the DLC/S model is generally superior to the DLC/F model. This result is not surprising, since DLC/S allows the observing window to advance dynamically as step-by-step prediction moves ahead. In general, the accuracy of the DLC/F model deteriorates when the window becomes larger. The DLC/S model's performance, on the other hand, improves when the window becomes larger, but only slightly larger. We found that a window size of three to four time frames is optimal.

Of course, the best window size depends on your development environment, testing scheme, and operational profile, but, in general, the window size should be fewer than five time frames, since the model is then able to catch fast shifts in model applicability among the component models.

The accuracy measure in Fig. 7.7 is the prequential likelihood, but other accuracy measures, such as the Akaike information criterion—another criterion to denote how close a prediction is to the actual data [Khos89]—or mean square error, are also feasible. The main strength of the DLC models is that they combine component models in a way that lets the output be fed back for model adjustment.

The fundamental approach of the linear combination models is simple. However, by applying more complicated procedures, we risk losing the individual model's assumptions about the physical process. It then

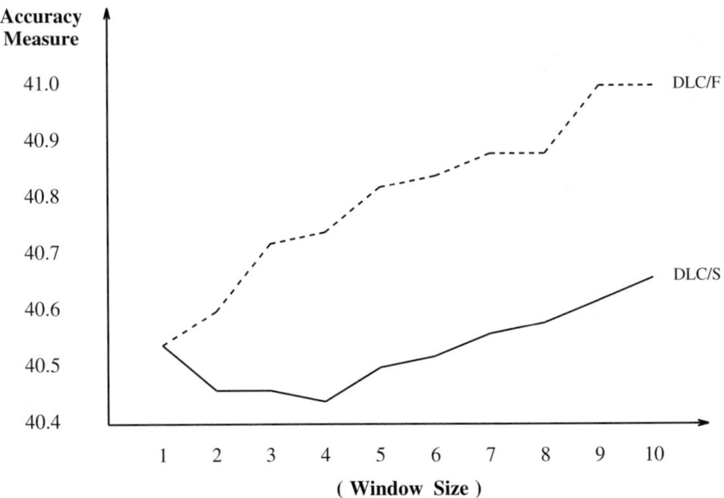

Figure 7.7 Summary of the DLC/F and DLC/S models for windows up to 10 time frames.

becomes harder to get insight into the process of reliability engineering. Most reliability models view software as a black box from which to observe failure data and make predictions. In that context, our combination models do not degrade any properties assumed in current reliability-modeling practices.

7.5.7 Long-term prediction capability

Our results have shown that the combination models perform well in making step-by-step predictions—in which you can adjust the model's parameters for each prediction—but we also want to determine how they perform in making long-term predictions, say, 20 failures ahead. For this evaluation, we select the ELC and DLC models and compare them with the GO, MO, and LV component models. Figure 7.8 shows the prediction curve for each model for the data set J3.

We use the first 152 data points J3, or up to 777 cumulative test hours as indicated by the dashed line, to estimate each model's parameters. Immediately following this estimation stage is the prediction stage. For the project J3, these two stages follow the project's natural breakdown into two testing stages.

For the DLC model, we compute model preferences and weights in the estimation phase, and fix the weight assignments in the prediction phase. From Fig. 7.8 we can observe that LV's prediction curve is too

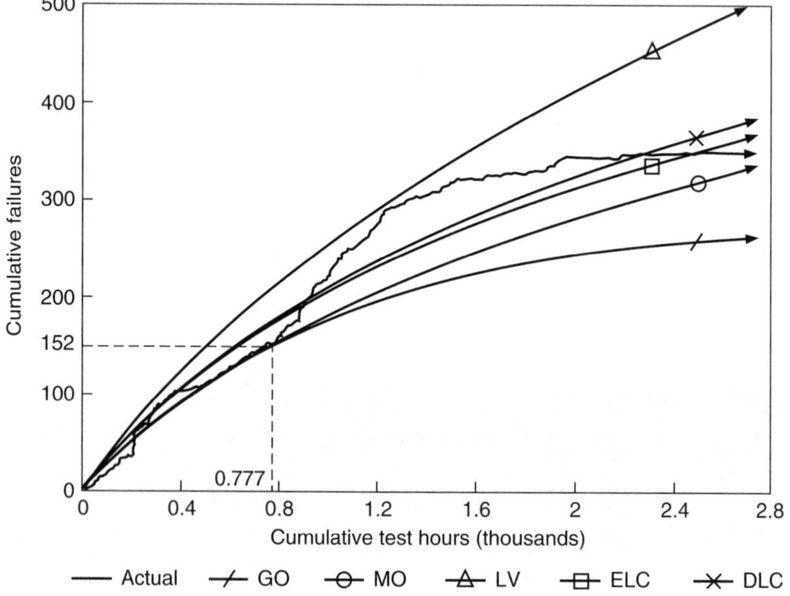

Figure 7.8 Long-term predictions for data set J3 from several models.

pessimistic, and GO's and MO's are too optimistic. In fact, all three curves for the component models are out of the actual project data curve. ELC and DLC, on the other hand, compensate these extremes and make rather reasonable long-term predictions.

To show quantitative comparisons of long-term predictions, we use mean square error instead of prequential likelihood. Prequential likelihood is more appropriate for comparing step-by-step predictions, while the mean square error provides a more widely understood measure of the distance between actual and predicted values.

Table 7.19 shows the summary of long-term predictions. The value in each project raw represents the mean square errors for a model applied to the project data in that raw, and the model ranking is shown in parentheses. The values under "Sum of mean square errors" and "Sum of ranks" indicate that the ELC and DLC models generally perform better than the component models. Even though the component models make a better prediction than the ELC and DLC models on several occasions, they also perform significantly worse on others. The ELC and DLC models, on the other hand, never make the worst long-term predictions.

7.6 Summary

We have initiated SRE programs in real-world environments for better specification and tracking of software reliability for different projects. We lay out the framework of this SRE process, which includes the most current state of practice in industry. In applying the reliability-objective-setting method and the software reliability modeling and measurement techniques, we obtain some modeling results that look promising.

TABLE 7.19 Summary of Long-Term Predictions.

Summary of Model Ranking for Long-Term Predictions Using Mean Square Errors					
Data Model	GO	MO	LV	ELC	DLC
SYS1	2117 (5)	687.4 (4)	567.7 (3)	266.7 (2)	169.7 (1)
SYS2	1455 (5)	1421 (4)	246.1 (1)	930.5 (2)	955.7 (3)
SYS3	480.0 (2)	253.2 (1)	2067 (5)	745.5 (3)	779.8 (4)
J1	1089 (4)	782.9 (2)	5283 (5)	130.1 (1)	876.7 (3)
J2	4368 (4)	4370 (5)	539.3 (1)	2171 (3)	1791 (2)
J3	4712 (5)	3073 (3)	4318 (4)	1322 (2)	1141 (1)
J4	3247 (4)	3248 (5)	219.5 (1)	1684 (3)	1354 (2)
J5	60.22 (3)	60.12 (1)	104.45 (5)	68.44 (4)	60.15 (2)
Sum of mean square errors	17528.5	13896.6	13345.0	7317.3	7128.3
Sum of ranks	(32)	(25)	(25)	(20)	(18)
Overall rank	(5)	(4)	(3)	(2)	(1)

These results indicate that model performances are dramatically different depending on the context of different projects, and the use of multiple models is deemed necessary. Moreover, the reliability growth phenomenon is better demonstrated when the SRE mechanism is put in place. It is noted that the data collection process is the key to successful measurement of software reliability. In particular, failure data should be scrutinized for better classification of real software failures against the current release, and more data should be collected automatically for accuracy and reasons of economy. The application of software reliability tools also greatly simplifies the tedious job of reliability measurement and model comparison. Finally, the linear combination modeling scheme is introduced as a simple technique to increase accuracy in software reliability measurement.

In summary, we believe that when the SRE application receives more attention and wider implementation in industry, more insights leading to improvement in product quality and software development process will gradually emerge.

Problems

7.1 Analyze the failure reporting and tracking mechanisms used by a software development organization with which you're familiar. Compare the data collected by these mechanisms with the minimum set of failure data described in this chapter. Report on the suitability of your failure reporting and tracking mechanisms for software reliability estimation, and describe any changes that would result in a more suitable mechanism.

7.2 How has your development organization, or an organization you know, set reliability requirements? How do the requirements compare to the two examples given in this chapter (Sec. 7.2.1.1)? Which of the three methods of setting requirements (Sec. 7.2.1.2) has the organization used, or was another method used? Why was the method chosen?

7.3 How does your development organization, or the organization you know, estimate and forecast software reliability? How does the organization choose the model(s) used? How does the method of selection compare to that presented in this chapter?

7.4 Using the guidelines given in this chapter, write a plan that your organization could use to guide them in collecting data for software reliability measurement.

7.5 Show Eq. (7.4) is the stop-testing rule based on the assumptions in Example 7.2.

7.6 For the data set J3, suppose we have a system that is integrated in two stages. Only a portion of the system is tested during the first stage, which lasts

14 weeks. After the first stage, the remainder of the code is added to the system, at which point it is tested for 26 more weeks. At this point, the curve representing the expected number of failures will switch to the one that would have occurred for a system in its final configuration. The curve, however, is temporally translated, the amount of translation depending on the number of failures that were experienced during the first test stage.

The parameters for the first and second stages, using the Goel-Okumoto model, are as follows:

	a	b
First stage (weeks 1–14)	317	0.0487787
Second stage (weeks 15–40)	413	0.0461496

a. Plot the mean value function for each stage of integration, using the model parameters in the table above.
b. Determine the amount of time by which the mean value function during the second stage of integration is translated from the mean value function that would have been observed had the entire system been in place at the start of testing.

7.7 Given a project data set, the estimate of b is 1/57.6 in Eq. (7.5) for the applied GO model. The loaded salary for a single tester is $1000 per day, and there are six full-time testers in the project. Further suppose that the cost of fixing a fault during testing is $200, and that for fixing a fault in the field is $2200. It is estimated that a total of 1300 faults exist in the software.
a. Draw the curves similar to Fig. 7.2. Write down the equations for each curve.
b. Draw the two curves representing the two sides of Eq. (7.5).
c. When should the testing be stopped?
d. Repeat items *b* and *c* for 10 testers and 2 testers, respectively.

7.8 Why isn't RGF defined for the YSS model?

7.9 Comparing with prequential likelihood, what are the advantages and disadvantages of using reliability growth factor (RGF) to determine the model validity during testing?

7.10 Why do combination models provide better results, on average, than individual models? Can you think of other methods to increase the prediction accuracy of models? What limitations do combination models have? Under what circumstances are these limitations important?

7.11 The linear combination models are applied mainly to one type of data in this chapter. Is it TBF data type or FC data type? For each data type, discuss which linear combination models could be formed easily, and which could not.

Chapter

8

Measurement-Based Analysis of Software Reliability

Ravishankar K. Iyer
University of Illinois

Inhwan Lee
Tandem Computers Inc.

8.1 Introduction

Software reliability and quality must be built in, starting in the early design phase, and maintained throughout the software life cycle. Essential to this process is a sound understanding of software reliability in production environments. There is no better way to acquire this understanding than through the direct measurement and analysis of real systems. Direct measurement means monitoring and recording naturally occurring errors and failures in a running system under user workloads. Analysis of such measurements can provide valuable information on actual error/failure behavior, identify system bottlenecks, quantify reliability measures, and verify assumptions made in analytical models.

Typically, a software engineer must decide what data to gather and analyze, sometimes without the benefit of guidance, experience, or easily available intuition. How to obtain general models from experiments or measurements made in a particular environment is by no means clear. This chapter discusses the current issues in this area. The discussion centers around techniques, our experiences, and major developments. The chapter discusses measurement techniques, analysis of data, model identification, analysis of models, and the effects of workload on software reliability. For each field, the key issues are discussed and then detailed techniques and representative work are presented. Analytical modeling techniques and statistical techniques relevant to the discussions are reviewed in App. B.

8.2 Framework

This section discusses the framework of measurement-based analysis and reviews past work in the area of software reliability in the operational phase.

8.2.1 Overview

Once general directions are set, a measurement-based study consists of two phases: measurement and analysis (Fig. 8.1). In the measurement phase, you develop instrumentation techniques and make measurements. You can conduct a measurement-based study of operational software using two types of data: human-generated software error reports and machine-generated event logs. The former provide detailed information about the underlying software faults (or defects) and the associated failure symptoms, while the latter provide accurate information on the timing of software failures and recovery. Measurement techniques are discussed in Sec. 8.3.

Given field error data collected from a real system, the analysis consists of five steps, as shown in Fig. 8.1*b:* (1) preprocessing of data, (2) analysis of data, (3) model structure identification and parameter estimation, (4) model solution, if necessary, and (5) analysis of models.

In step 1, you extract necessary information from the field data. The processing in this step requires detailed understanding of the target software. It can also require detailed knowledge of the operating system and system operation. The actual processing depends on the types of data. The information in human-generated reports is

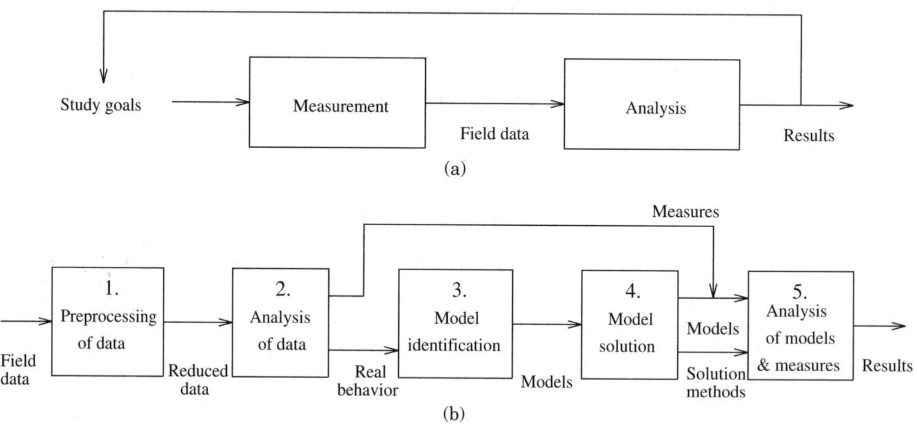

Figure 8.1 Measurement-based analysis: (*a*) overall framework; (*b*) analysis phase.

usually not completely formatted. Therefore, this step involves understanding the situations described in the reports and organizing the relevant information into a problem database. In contrast, the information in automatically generated event logs is already formatted. Data processing of event logs consists of extracting error events and coalescing related error events. Section 8.4.1 discusses the preprocessing of data.

In step 2, you interpret the data. Typically, you begin this step with a list of measures to evaluate. However, you can identify new issues that have a major impact on software reliability during this step. Results from step 2 are reliability characteristics of operational software in actual environments and issues that must be addressed to improve software reliability. Sections 8.4 and 8.5, which cover this step, discuss fault and error classification, error propagation, error and failure distribution, software failure dependency, hardware-related software errors, evaluation of software fault tolerance, error recurrence, and diagnosis of recurrences.

In step 3, you identify appropriate models (such as Markov models) based on the findings in step 2. You identify model structures and realistic ranges of parameters. Identified models are abstractions of the software reliability behavior in real environments. Proposed software reliability models include: performability models [Hsue88, Lee93a], an error and recovery model [Hsue87], a software reliability model that captures the effects of faults on the overall system [Lee94b], and workload-dependent software reliability models [Cast81, Iyer82a]. Statistical analysis packages such as SAS [SAS85] or measurement-based reliability analysis tools such as MEASURE+ [Tang93b] are useful at this stage. Step 3 is covered in Secs. 8.6 and 8.7.

Step 4 involves either developing or using known techniques to solve the model. Model solution allows you to obtain measures, such as reliability, availability, and performability. The results obtained from the model must be validated against real data. You can use reliability and performance modeling and evaluation tools such as SHARPE [Sahn87] in this step. In step 5, you answer what-if questions, using the identified models. You vary factors in the models and evaluate the resulting effects on software reliability. You determine reliability bottlenecks and predict the impact of design changes on software reliability. Section 8.6, which covers this step, discusses software reliability modeling in the operational phase and the modeling of the impact of software failures on performance, detailed error and recovery processes, and software error bursts. You use knowledge and experience gained through analysis to plan additional studies and to develop the measurement techniques as shown in Fig. 8.1*a*.

8.2.2 Operational versus development phase evaluation

Figure 8.2 shows a simplified software life cycle. To construct new software or to add a new feature, you begin with requirements and then design, implement, and verify the software. After verification, the software is released to the field. Problems found in the field are diagnosed, fixes are made, and interim versions of the software are released to the field. As a result, many versions of the same software exist in the field at the same time. The process in Fig. 8.2 is repeated until the software becomes obsolete.

You can perform an experimental evaluation of software reliability at different phases of the software's life. In the development phase, data are generated as a result of code inspection and software testing. Many studies have addressed the evaluation of data collected during the development stage. However, the reliability of operational software can be quite different from that of the software in its development stage. In the operational phase, the software update rate is relatively low. Due to the differences among the fault severities (i.e., their impact on system functionality) and due to software fault tolerance features in a system, not every software fault has the same impact on software reliability. Workloads, interaction between software and hardware platforms, and operational environment are also factors that affect reliability. Thus, you cannot accurately estimate software reliability in the operational phase using only the data collected during the development phase. Understanding the reliability of software requires direct measurement during the operational phase.

8.2.3 Past work

Measurement-based reliability analysis of operational software has evolved significantly over the past 15 years. Many studies have been published. Table 8.1 lists some of the studies that are closely related to

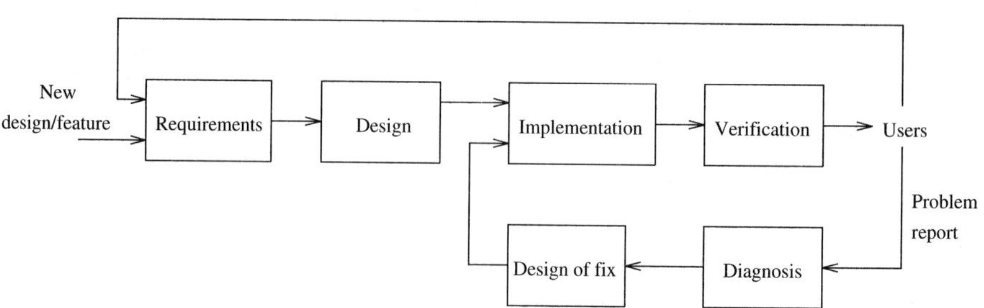

Figure 8.2 Software life cycle.

the theme of this chapter. These studies addressed the issues of fault categorization, error/failure and recovery distributions, error propagation, failure dependency, the impact of software faults on system performance and reliability, evaluation of software fault tolerance, recurrent software failures, and failure diagnosis.

8.3 Measurement Techniques

Measurement is plagued by numerous theoretical and practical difficulties. The question of what and how to measure is a difficult one. Most studies use a combination of installed and custom instrumentation. From a statistical point of view, you should collect a considerable amount of data for sound evaluations, because the accuracy of estimation is directly related to the number of samples. But the management of collected data is a nontrivial task. In an operational system, you can measure only detected errors. In modern computer systems, especially in fault-tolerant systems, failures are infrequent and, to obtain meaningful data, you should make measurements over a long period of time. Also, you should expose the measured system to a wide range of usage conditions for the results to be representative. Further, you should work with users as well as development and service organizations to collect data in the operational phase.

TABLE 8.1 Measurement-Based Studies of Software Reliability

Category	Issues	Studies
Data coalescing	Analysis of time-based tuples Clustering based on type and time	[Tsao83, Hans92] [Iyer86, Lee91, Tang93a]
Software fault classification	Fault and error profile	[Lee93b, Tang92c, Hsue87] [Chil92, Thay78, Endr75]
Reliability census	Contribution of software to system reliability	[Gray90, Leve90]
Basic reliability characteristics	Error/failure bursts TTE/TTF/TTR distributions	[Iyer86, Hsue87, Tang93a] [McCo79, Iyer85b, Lee93a]
Failure dependency	Hardware-related & correlated software errors Two-way and multiway failure dependency	[Iyer85a, Tang92b, Lee93a] [Duga91, Lee91, Tang91]
Error propagation	First error, propagation mode, error detection	[Lee93b]
Software fault tolerance	Recovery routines Process pairs	[Vela84, Hsue87] [Gray85, Gray90, Lee92, Lee93b]
Recurrences and failure diagnosis	Preventive software service Symptom-based diagnosis of recurrences	[Adam84] [Lee94a]
Software reliability modeling	Performability models for error detection/recovery Two-level models for operating systems Modeling of multiple errors Reliability modeling in the operational phase	[Hsue87, Hsue88] [Lee93a, Tang93a, Lee92] [Hsue87] [Lee94b]
Workload dependency	Workload-dependent software failure models	[Cast81, Cast82, Iyer82a] [Iyer85b, Mour87]

Establishing a sound data collection process requires ongoing cooperation between data collectors and data consumers (e.g., a practitioner). You can make two types of measurements: *on-line machine logging* and *manual reporting*. On-line logging of errors during machine operation is usually performed automatically by the operating system. Manual reports are generated by three types of data collectors: users, problem analysts, and software developers. Both types of data collection are essential for believable reliability analysis. Ideally, you should be able to cross-reference the two types of data for most incidents. Definitions and forms for data collection change as the data collection process, the software, and the hardware evolve. A sound data collection process is slow building, but it can break down easily.

The following subsections discuss issues in instrumentation and in evaluating collected data, for automatic machine logging and manual reporting.

8.3.1 On-line machine logging

Most large computer systems provide error-logging software in the operating system. This software records information on errors occurring in the operating system and its various subsystems, such as the memory, disk, and network subsystems, applications, as well as information on system events, such as reboots and shutdowns. The reports usually include information on the location, time, and type of the error, the system state at the time of the error, and error recovery (e.g., retry). The reports are stored chronologically in a permanent system file.

Figure 8.3 shows a simplified picture of on-line event logging. The collector is a system process which is in charge of event logging and event log management. Application processes can generate events when they detect abnormal conditions by means of their internal consistency checks. System processes usually generate three types of events: problems in the software components that run as system processes, problems in applications that are detected by system processes, and abnormal hardware conditions. When necessary, the human operator can intervene and collect additional data, such as the dump of a process state or the dump of a processor memory. These dumps are not usually stored in event logs because of their size, so they constitute a part of human-generated error reports discussed in the next subsection. However, they can be treated as a part of on-line machine logs in an advanced environment in which many operator tasks are programmed into the data collection module of the operating system.

Figure 8.4 shows a sample error entry extracted from a machine log from a Tandem system [TAND89]. The information in the event was decoded to make it readable. An error record consists of a header and a

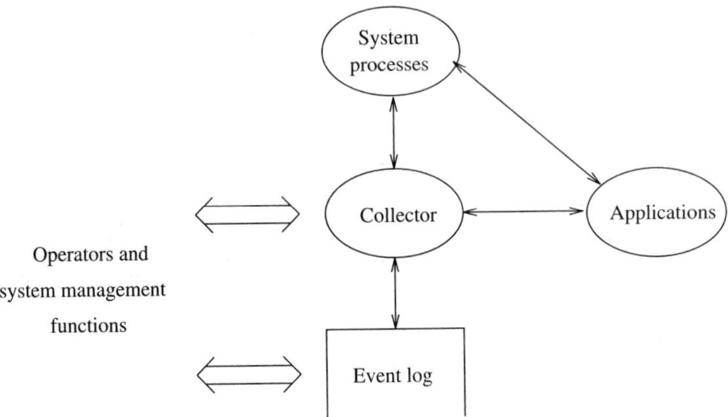

Figure 8.3 On-line event logging.

body. The header contains general information, such as the time of occurrence, the subsystem and device affected, and the type of the event. Typically, all errors have the same header format. In this example, the event reports a processor halt seemingly caused by a software fault. The body contains detailed information about the event. The format of the body differs from event to event. In Fig. 8.4, the body contains the apparent cause of the halt from an operating system perspective (halt error code) and a summary of the processor state at the time of halt.

An event in an on-line log is structured and coded in a predefined format. Issues in creating the instrumentation for automatic logging include the definition of the set of events to be reported, the signature

Time	Subsystem	Device	Event
06SEP91 09:57:00	CPU	CPU-2 SECT-1 CAB-1	CPU-Software-Halt
	CPU-Type:	3	
	Halt-error-code:	%4040	
	OS-Type:	0	
	P-register:	%60544	
	E-register:	%3407	
	L-register:	%7250	
	Current-space-id:	%147	
	Coldload-address:	%351	
	Current-PCB-address:	%107200	
	PCB-base-address:	%100100	
	DDT-status:	%10,%0,%0,%343,%120	
	DDT-error-bits:	%0,%0,%0,%0,%2,% 0,%0,%0,%0,%0,%0,%210	
	Register-file:	%%4040,%0,%4317,%1 ,%0,%57,%1360,%12742,%0,%170000 %100,%0,%177440,%53,%20,%1	

Figure 8.4 Sample error entry in error log.

format of each event, and the meaning of each field in an event. These issues are usually addressed at the system design stage, and the resulting on-line error logging is an operating system function. Related issues are the reporting mechanism between the operating system and other subsystems and the event management within the operating system. Such instrumentation should consider the possibility of introducing new events as subsystems and situations are added. Clearly, the meaning of each event is valid only within a system. You should consider the differences in hardware/software error detection and logging mechanisms when evaluating the logs from different types of systems.

The main advantage of on-line automatic logging is its ability to record a large amount of information about transient errors and on-line error recovery, which cannot be done manually. It records nearly 100 percent of key events and provides accurate timing information. However, there are several challenges in evaluating on-line logs.

First, on-line error logs do not usually provide information on underlying faults and off-line diagnosis. Also, under some crash scenarios, the system may fail too quickly for any error messages to be recorded. Therefore you should supplement machine logs with manual (human-generated) reports. Second, modern computer systems are reliable, and you should make a long period of measurement (often on a number of systems) to conduct a meaningful analysis. The size of the data can be huge. You should develop software tools to manage the data and to automate basic analysis steps. Third, the meaning of a record and the format of an event in a log can differ between versions of the operating system and between machine models. This is natural because the software and hardware of a system evolve. Thus, you should update software tools to ensure against such discrepancies.

8.3.2 Manual reporting

Manual reporting is initiated by problems found in the field (Fig. 8.2). A problem could be simple in nature, such as a misunderstanding of software features or a minor cosmetic error, or it could be as severe as a system crash or loss of data. Initially, a report contains information provided by the user, such as the time of occurrence, severity, system identification, and a description of the problem. In the case of a system crash or loss of data, additional information (e.g., a processor memory dump) is also provided. As the reported problem is diagnosed and fixed by analysts and developers, the log of all diagnostic actions, analysis history, and information on the underlying faults, failure symptoms, and fixes are appended to the report. Such information is difficult to describe using a fixed format. As a result, a manual report of a software problem is mainly a collection of textual descriptions. Only the header has a fixed format common in all reports. Another type of report, called an *operator log,* is generated by the system operator. An operator log contains information on system crashes, failure diagnosis, and hardware and software updates.

Figure 8.5 shows a sample manual report extracted from the Tandem Product Report (TPR) database [TAND85]. A TPR is used to report all problems, questions, and requests for enhancements by customers or Tandem employees concerning any Tandem product. The figure shows mainly the header, which provides fixed fields for the information such as the date, problem type, urgency, customer and system identifications, and brief problem description. The body of a TPR is a textual description of all actions taken by Tandem analysts in diagnosing and fixing the problem. If a TPR reports a software failure, the body of the TPR also includes the log of memory dump analyses performed by analysts.

Software error reports contain detailed information about the underlying faults, symptoms, and fixes. As a result, you can use such reports to address many software reliability issues. There are two major challenges in evaluating manual reports. First, underreporting can be significant. It is estimated that the majority of processor software failures in Tandem systems are not reported [Lee93b, Gray90]. Ideally, a cross-referencing between on-line logs, manual reports, and operator logs should be possible. Second, since they are textual reports generated by humans, you cannot analyze them by automatic tools. Usually, you should reorganize the raw data into a structured database. This involves data categorization, that is, generating categories and counting instances for each category. This in turn requires understanding the details of problems long after their cases are closed, when important information may no longer be available. Such reorganization can

Tandem Product Report

TPR number: 91-01-03 17:50 | Severity: 2

Product Name: GUARDIAN Kernel | Origination: ABC Financial Inc.
Classification: software problem | 777 Lawrence Street
| Chicago, IL 60661

Date Received: 91-01-03 14:54
Date Returned: 91-01-10 10:49 | System Number: 0056983

Accompanying Information: dump file location \ABC.prs.jan031750.*

Problem Description: Halts on CPUs 4 and 5.
Process $ABC runs in CPU 4 backed up in CPU 5

- -

Response:
All actions including dump analyses taken by Tandem analysts to diagnose the problem.

Figure 8.5 Human-generated software error report.

be a serious hurdle, consuming most of the evaluation effort. You can resolve this problem by generating categories before collecting data. You can provide additional space for some free text to collect information that is specific to a failure.

Table 8.2 shows an example of data categorization to collect and analyze reasons for code changes [Basi84a]. With the categories, data collectors (developers, in this case) can just mark an appropriate category on a code update. This is the most efficient and accurate way of collecting data, and it allows you to analyze the data automatically (i.e., using programs) later. In the example, the reason for collecting the information would be to take action to minimize the number of code changes in the future. Unfortunately, category generation is an imprecise science. It is usually difficult to keep categories orthogonal. That is, categories tend to overlap. Also, different people can interpret a category differently. In practice, you can overcome these problems by using a small number of well-defined categories (see Chap. 9). You should generate categories for each question to answer. Studies have shown that, with a well-defined form, it takes a minimal amount of time for human collectors to fill out the form when a case is closed.

8.4 Preliminary Analysis of Data

This section discusses preprocessing of data, fault and error classification, error propagation, and distribution identification. Such analyses investigate basic software reliability characteristics.

8.4.1 Data processing

Usually, field failure data contain a large amount of redundant and irrelevant information in various formats. Thus, you should preprocess data to extract necessary information and to put it into a database for subsequent analyses. Preprocessing varies with the types of data.

TABLE 8.2 Sample Category Generation

Issue	Category
Type of change	Error correction
	Planned enhancement
	Implementation of requirements change
	Improvement of clarity, maintainability, or documentation
	Improvement of user services
	Insertion/deletion of debug code
	Optimization of time/space/accuracy
	Adaptation to environment change
	Other

8.4.1.1 Preprocessing of automatically generated error logs. Information in error logs is usually coded and structured because it is generated automatically by the operating system. Details of preprocessing are machine-dependent because of the differences in error detection and logging mechanisms and semantics among the systems. You usually perform two major types of processing other than reformatting: *data extraction* and *data coalescing.* Data extraction means that you select the events and fields that are necessary for the analysis. Data coalescing is necessary, because a single fault in the system can result in many repeated error reports in a short period of time. To ensure that the subsequent analyses will not be distorted by these repeated reports, you should coalesce entries that correspond to the same problem into a single event.

A commonly used data-coalescing algorithm [Iyer82a] is merging all error entries of the same error type that occur within a ΔT interval of each other into a tuple. The algorithm is as follows:

```
IF <error type> = <type of previous error>
    AND <time away from previous error> ≤ ΔT
THEN <put error into the tuple being built>
ELSE <start a new tuple>
```

A tuple reflects the occurrence of one or more errors of the same type that occur in rapid succession. It can be represented by a record containing information such as the number of entries in the tuple and the time duration of the tuple.

You can make two kinds of mistakes in data coalescing: *collision* and *truncation* [Hans92]. A collision occurs when the detection of errors caused by two faults are close enough in time (within ΔT) such that they are combined into a tuple. A truncation occurs when the time between two errors caused by a single fault is greater than ΔT. In this case, the two reports are split into different tuples. If ΔT is large, collisions are likely to occur. If ΔT is small, truncations are likely to occur. You can determine the value of time-interval threshold based on data. Collision is not a big problem if you use the error type and device information in data coalescing as shown in the above coalescing algorithm. Truncation is not considered to be a problem [Hans92] because there are techniques available to deal with truncations [Iyer90, Lin90]. These techniques have been used for fault diagnosis and failure prediction.

8.4.1.2 Preprocessing of human-generated problem reports. Some information in manual reports, such as a header that includes the date, severity, and product and system identifications, is structured. The format of the rest of the report depends on the data collection process. As explained in Sec. 8.3, you usually perform the preprocessing in three steps: (1) understanding the situations described in the reports, (2) generating categories, and (3) counting the instances of each category and constructing a database. If data categorization is done in advance and the data is collected accordingly, you may be able to skip the first and second steps.

8.4.2 Fault and error classification

Faults and errors identified from a software system can provide clues of how to fine-tune the software development environment and how to improve error detection and recovery. Fault and error categorization is frequently used in addressing such issues. Most studies have addressed the issues by using faults found during the development phase [Thay78, Endr75, Basi84a]. However, fault and error profiles of operational software are just as informative and can be quite different from those of the software in its development phase because of the differences in the operational environment and the maturity of software. Therefore, to improve software quality, it is important to investigate software fault and error profiles in the field. Here we introduce fault and error profiles obtained using field data collected from Tandem GUARDIAN, IBM MVS, and VAX VMS operating systems [Lee93b, Hsue87, Tang92c].

8.4.2.1 GUARDIAN. Table 8.3 shows the results of a fault classification using 153 Tandem Product Reports (TPRs) that contain logs of processor dump analyses of software failures performed by analysts. The table shows both the number of TPRs and the number of unique faults. The differences between the two represent multiple failures caused by the same fault. From Table 8.3, you can see what kinds of faults the developers introduced. "Incorrect computation" refers to an arithmetic overflow or the use of an incorrect arithmetic function (e.g., use of a signed arithmetic function instead of an unsigned one). "Data fault" refers to the use of an incorrect constant or variable. "Data definition fault" refers to a fault in declaring data or in defining a data structure. "Missing operation" refers to an omission of a few lines of source code. "Side effect of code update" occurs when not all dependencies between software modules are considered when updating software. "Unexpected situation" refers to cases in which the software designers did not anticipate a legitimate operational scenario, and consequently the software did not handle the situation correctly. You can see from the table that "Missing operation" and "Unexpected situation" are the most common types of software faults in Tandem systems. Additional code inspection and testing efforts can be directed for identifying such faults.

TABLE 8.3 **Software Fault Categorization for GUARDIAN**

Fault Category	No. faults		No. TPRs	
Incorrect computation		3		3
Data fault		12		21
Data definition fault		3		7
Missing operation:		20		27
—Uninitialized pointers	(6)		(7)	
—Uninitialized nonpointer variables	(4)		(6)	
—Not updating data structure on the occurrence of certain events	(6)		(9)	
—Not telling other processes about the occurrence of certain events	(4)		(5)	
Side effect of code update		4		5
Unexpected situation:		29		46
—Race/timing problem	(14)		(18)	
—Errors with no defined error-handling procedures	(4)		(8)	
—Incorrect parameters or invalid calls from user processes	(3)		(7)	
—Not providing routines to handle legitimate but rare operational scenarios	(8)		(13)	
Microcode defect		4		8
Others (cause does not fit any of the above class)		10		12
Unable to classify due to insufficient information		15		24
All		100		153

A software failure caused by a newly found fault is referred to as a *first occurrence;* a software failure caused by a previously reported fault is referred to as a *recurrence.* The 153 TPRs whose software causes were identified occurred due to 100 unique faults (Table 8.3). Out of the 100 software faults observed during the measured time window, 57 faults were diagnosed before the time window (i.e., were recurrences) and 43 were newly identified during the time window (i.e., were first occurrences). That is, about 72 percent (110 out of 153) of the TPRs reported recurrences of previously reported software faults. The issue of recurrence is discussed further in Sec. 8.5.4.

8.4.2.2 MVS. In MVS, software error data on the type of detection (hardware and software) and recovery are logged by the system onto a data set called SYS1.LOGREC. Each error record in the LOGREC data contains bits describing the type of error, its severity, and the results of hardware and software attempts to recover from the problem. The general software error status indicators are TYPE (of detection), EVENT (causing the detection), and ERRCODE (code of symptom of the error). Based on the ERRCODE information provided by the system, eight classes of errors, which reflect commonly encountered problems, were defined [Hsue87]:

1. *Control* (CTRL) indicates the invalid use of control statements or invalid supervisor calls.
2. *Deadlock* (DLCK) indicates endless loops, wait states, or violation of system- or user-defined time limits.

TABLE 8.4 Software Error Classification for MVS

(Measurement period: 12 months)

Error type	Frequency	Percent
Control	213	7.72
Deadlock	23	0.84
I/O & data management	1448	52.50
Program exception	65	2.43
Storage exception	149	5.40
Storage management	313	11.35
Others	66	2.32
Multiple error	481	17.44
All	2758	100.00

3. *I/O and data management* (I/O) indicates a problem occurred during I/O management or during the creation and processing of data sets.
4. *Storage management* (SM) indicates an error in the storage allocation/deallocation process or in virtual memory mapping.
5. *Storage exception* (SE) indicates addressing of nonexistent or inaccessible memory locations.
6. *Programming exception* (PE) indicates a program error other than a storage exception.
7. *Others* (OTHR) indicates errors which do not fit any of the above categories.
8. *Multiple errors or error bursts* (MULT) indicates error bursts consisting of different types (listed above) of errors.

Table 8.4 lists the frequencies of different types of software errors defined above. You can see that more than one half (52.5 percent) of software errors are I/O and data management errors and another 11.4 percent of the errors are storage management errors. This result is probably related to the fact that a major feature of MVS is multiple virtual storage organization. Also, I/O and data management is a high-volume activity critical to the proper operation of the system. It is therefore expected that their contributions are significant. You can also see that a significant percentage of errors are multiple errors, indicating that error detection and recovery need to take multiple errors into account (to be discussed further in Sec. 8.6.4).

8.4.2.3 VMS. Software errors in a VAXcluster system are identified from *bugcheck* reports in the error log files. All software-detected errors were extracted from bugcheck reports and divided into four types in [Tang92c]:

TABLE 8.5 Software Error Classification for VMS

(Measurement period: 10 months for VAX1 and 27 months for VAX2)

Error type	Frequency (VAX1)	Frequency (VAX2)	Fraction (%), combined
Control	71	26	50.0
Memory	8	4	6.2
I/O	16	44	30.9
Others	1	24	12.9
All	96	98	100

1. *Control.* Problems involving program flow control or synchronization. For example, "Unexpected system service exception," "Exception while above ASTDEL (Asynchronous System Traps DELivery) or on interrupt stack," and "Spinlock(s) of higher rank already owned by CPU."
2. *Memory.* Problems referring to memory management or usage. For example, "Bad memory deallocation request size or address," "Double deallocation of memory block," "Pagefault with IPL (Interrupt Priority Level) too high," and "Kernel stack not valid."
3. *I/O.* Inconsistent conditions detected by I/O management routines. For example, "Inconsistent I/O data base," "RMS (Record Management Service) has detected an invalid condition," "Fatal error detected by VAX port driver," and "Invalid lock identification."
4. *Others.* Other software-detected problems. For example, "Machine check while in kernel mode," "Asynchronous write memory failure," and "Software state not saved during powerfail." These are actually not software-related errors although their statistics are included.

Table 8.5 shows the frequency for each type of software-detected error for the two measured VAXcluster systems. You can see that nearly 13 percent of software-detected errors are type "Others," and almost all of them belong to VAX2. The VAX2 data show that most of these errors are "machine check" (i.e., CPU error). The VAX1 error logs do not include CPU errors in the bugcheck category. A careful study of the VAX error logs and discussions with field engineers indicate that different VAX machine models may report the same type of error (in this case, CPU error) to different classes. Thus, it is necessary to distinguish these errors in the error classification. Most "Others" errors are judged to be nonsoftware problems.

8.4.3 Error propagation

Given that a complete elimination of software faults in a large, continually evolving software system is difficult, it is important that the software handles the effects of software faults efficiently. Such a design requires understanding the effects of software faults and establishing efficient software fault models. While efficient models for hardware faults exist, the issue of software fault models is open.

You can build software fault models from two perspectives: software engineering and software fault tolerance. Examples of software fault models built from the software engineering perspective are those resulting from software fault categorization. You can use such models for fine-tuning the software development environment and for avoiding or eliminating software faults. Software fault models built from the software fault tolerance perspective are those based on a knowledge of faults, the effects of software faults (i.e., errors), error propagation, or a combination of these. You can use such models for designing efficient error detection, diagnosis, and recovery strategies. This subsection discusses a re-creation of error propagation using the 153 TPRs used to create Table 8.3 in Sec. 8.4.2, to build a model from the software fault tolerance perspective.

The term *first error* is defined as the immediate effect of a software fault on the processor state when the fault is exercised. In other words, the first error of a software fault refers to the first program variable that acquires an incorrect value because of the fault. The first errors identified from the 153 TPRs were classified into the five categories [Lee93b]:

1. *Single address error.* An incorrect address word is developed.
2. *Single nonaddress error.* An incorrect nonaddress value is developed. Instances in this category are further divided into four subclasses: incorrect field size, incorrect index, incorrect flag, and the rest.
3. *Multiple errors.* Multiple errors are generated at once. Instances in this category are further divided into two subclasses: (1) random corruption in a memory area without regard to the data structure (e.g., a corruption caused by a stack area overlap or a missing initialization of a memory area) and (2) multiple regular errors in data structure (e.g., memory management tables become inconsistent due to a partial update, or a request buffer is overwritten by another request).
4. *Others.* The first error does not fit any of the above categories (e.g., an invalid request caused by a race condition).
5. *Unable to classify.* The first error cannot be identified due to insufficient information in the TPRs.

The propagation characteristics of first errors were classified into three groups: *no propagation, further corruption,* and *quick detection.*

No propagation refers to cases in which there is no possibility of error propagation, i.e., the first error is certain to be detected on the first access. Further corruption refers to error propagation across processes and the generation of more errors. Quick detection lies between the above two propagation modes. In this situation, there is no guarantee that there will be no propagation. The problem is detected quickly, after the first error is accessed for the first time, while the task that made the first access is executed.

Figure 8.6 shows an overall picture of error propagation, from underlying software faults to problem detection. A circle or a rectangle represents a category, and the numbers inside it represent the number of TPRs in that category and its percentage of the 153 TPRs. An arrow represents a transition, and the associated number represents a branching probability from the source state. For example, you can see that data faults account for 14 percent of the faults, and if a fault in this category is exercised, there is a 24 percent chance that an incorrect address will be generated. Figure 8.6 captures all major error propagation paths that must be eliminated. You can observe from the figure that address errors are difficult to handle with consistency checks. The data show no instances in which "Single address" error is guaranteed to be detected on the first access.

In Figure 8.6, "No propagation" is a desired state, because it does not threaten the integrity of the data in the system. It is a significant state

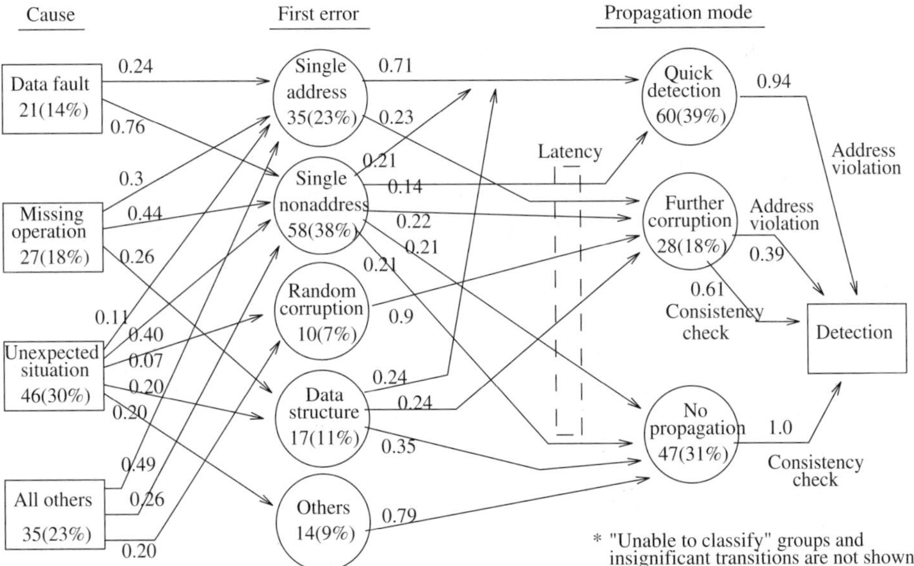

Figure 8.6 Error propagation model.

in the measured system because of the use of redundant data structures and consistency checks. You can see that all instances of "No propagation" are detected by consistency checks. In 94 percent of the instances of "Quick detection," problems are detected due to address violations; the rest are detected by consistency checks.

"Further corruption" is a dangerous state, in that error propagation can occur recursively and multiple errors are generated until the problem is detected. Note that some of the errors may break the fault-containment boundary assumed for on-line recovery and thus cause another problem later. Any process that accesses corrupted data can potentially assert a halt, and thus a single fault can cause a variety of failure symptoms, which may complicate the diagnosis.

8.4.4 Error and recovery distributions

Probably the most basic software reliability characteristics are time to failure/error (TTF/TTE) and time to repair (TTR) distributions. This subsection discusses error/failure frequency and empirical distributions built from data.

8.4.4.1 Error/failure frequency. It is often convenient to count the numbers of different types of errors and failures during the measurement period. You can make an easy comparison of error types and can also identify reliability bottlenecks using these counts. Table 8.6 shows the error/failure statistics for a VAXcluster system [Tang93a]. In the table, I/O errors include disk, tape, and network errors. Machine errors include CPU and memory errors. Software errors are software-related errors. Recovery probability is the probability that an error does not cause a machine crash.

You can identify two bottlenecks from the table. First, although software errors constitute only a small portion of all errors (0.3 percent), they result in significant failures (25 percent). This is because software errors have a very low recovery probability (0.1). Second, the major error category is I/O errors (93 percent), i.e., errors from shared

TABLE 8.6 Error/Failure Statistics for the VAXcluster

	Error		Failure		
Category	Frequency	Fraction (%)	Frequency	Fraction (%)	Recovery probability
I/O	25807	92.9	105	42.9	0.996
Machine	1721	6.2	5	2.0	0.970
Software	69	0.3	62	25.3	0.101
Unknown	191	0.7	73	29.8	0.618
All	27788	100.0	245	100.0	0.99

resources. This category of error has a very high recovery probability (0.996). However, these errors still result in nearly 43 percent of all failures. This result indicates that, although the system is generally robust with respect to I/O errors, the shared resources still constitute a major reliability bottleneck due to the sheer number of errors. Improving such a system may require using an ultrareliable network and disk system to reduce the raw error rate, not just providing high recoverability.

8.4.4.2 Error distributions. A realistic, analytical form of TTE distribution is essential in modeling and evaluating software reliability. You can obtain such distributions using the procedure described in App. B. You can sometimes satisfactorily represent a raw distribution by multiple distributions, which are chosen based on data, prior knowledge, and intuition. You can gain insights into different aspects of the data from each of these fits. Often, for simplicity or due to lack of information, the TTE is assumed to be exponentially distributed [Arla90, Lapr84].

Figure 8.7 shows the empirical TTE or TTF distributions fitted to analytic functions for Tandem GUARDIAN, DEC VAX VMS, and IBM MVS operating systems [Lee93a]. Here, a failure means a processor or machine failure, not a system failure. None of these distributions fit simple exponential functions. The fitting was tested using the Kolmogorov-Smirnov or chi-square test at a 0.05 significance level. This

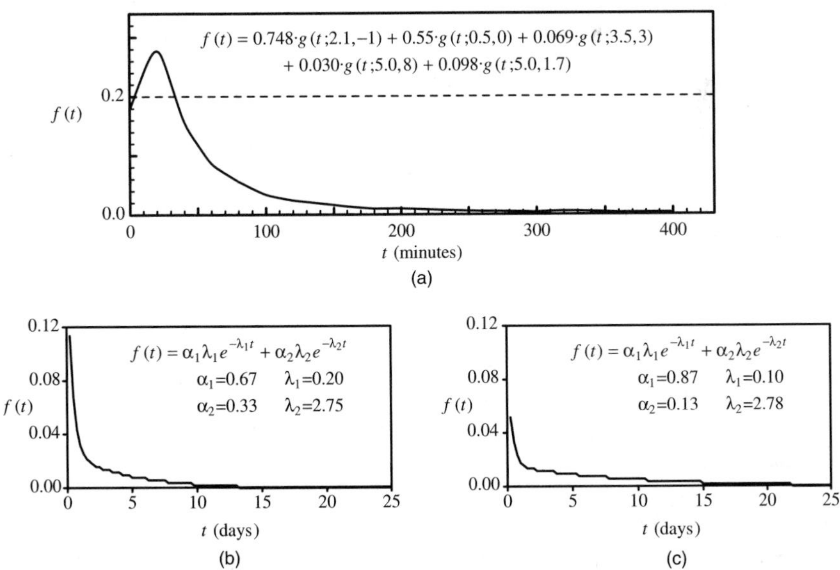

Figure 8.7 Empirical software TTE/TTF distributions. (*a*) IBM MVS software TTE distribution; (*b*) VAXcluster software TTE distribution; (*c*) Tandem software TTF distribution.

result conforms to the previous measurements on IBM [Iyer85a] and DEC machines [Cast81, McCo79]. Several reasons for this nonexponential behavior, including the impact of workload, were documented in [Cast81].

The two-phase hyperexponential distribution provided satisfactory fits for the VAXcluster software TTE and Tandem software TTF distributions. An attempt to fit the MVS TTE distribution to a phase-type exponential distribution led to a large number of stages. As a result, the multistage gamma distribution was used. It was found that a five-stage gamma distribution provided a satisfactory fit.

Figure 8.7*b* and *c* shows that the measured software TTE and TTF distributions can be modeled as a probabilistic combination of two exponential random variables, indicating that there are two dominant error modes. The higher error rate, λ_2, with weight α_2, captures both the error bursts on a single instance of an operating system and concurrent errors on multiple instances of an operating system (Sec. 8.5.1). The lower error rate, λ_1, with weight α_1, captures regular errors and provides an interburst error rate.

These error bursts may be repeated occurrences of the same software problem or multiple effects of an intermittent hardware fault on the software. Actually, software error bursts have been observed in laboratory experiments reported in [Bish88]. The study showed that, if the input sequences of the software under investigation are correlated (rather than being independent), one can expect more bunching of failures than those predicted using a constant failure rate assumption. In an operating system, input sequences (user requests) are highly likely to be correlated. Hence, a defect area can be triggered repeatedly.

8.4.4.3 Recovery distributions. Figure 8.8*a* plots the spline-fit for the TTR distribution of multiple software errors in the MVS system [Lee93a]. A multiple software error is an error burst consisting of different types of software errors. The TTR distribution for multiple software errors is presented because these errors have longer recovery times than other software errors and are more typical in terms of recovery process (Table 8.14 in Sec. 8.6.3). A three-phase hyperexponential function could be used to approximate the distribution, suggesting a multiple mode recovery process. Because most MVS software errors do not lead to system failures, the TTR for multiple errors is short, although these errors take the longest time to recover of all software errors.

Figure 8.8*b* and *c* plots the empirical software TTR distributions for the VAXcluster and Tandem systems. Because of their peculiar shapes, the raw distributions are provided. Since each system has different error semantics, recovery procedures, and maintenance environments, you cannot compare the measured systems in terms of TTR distribution. In the VAXcluster (Fig. 8.8*b*), you can see that most of the TTR

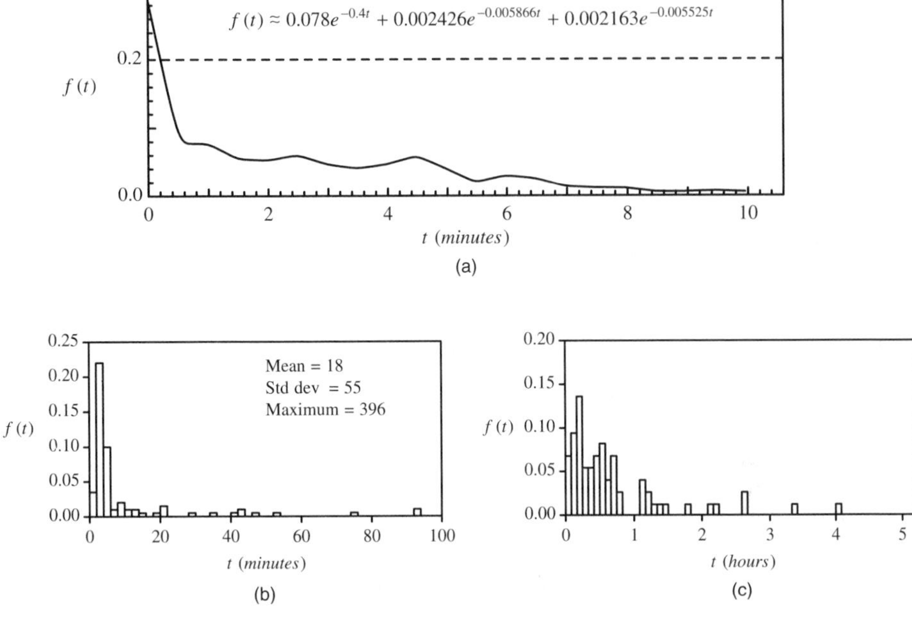

Figure 8.8 Empirical software TTR distributions. (*a*) MVS multiple software error TTR distribution; (*b*) VAXcluster software TTR distribution; (*c*) Tandem software TTR distribution.

instances (85 percent) are less than 15 minutes. This is attributed to those errors recovered by on-line recovery or automatic reboot without shutdown repair. However, some TTR instances last as long as several hours (the maximum is about 6.6 hours). These failures are, in our experience, probably due to a combination of software and hardware problems. Since the Tandem system does not allow an automatic recovery from a halt and all events considered are processor halts due to software, its TTR distribution (Fig. 8.8*c*) reflects the time to collect failure data and to reload and restart by the operator.

Typically, analytical models assume exponential or constant recovery times. You can see from Fig. 8.8 that this does not apply universally. None of the three TTR distributions is a simple exponential. For the MVS system, since the recovery is usually quick, a constant recovery time assumption may be suitable. For the VAXcluster and Tandem systems, neither exponential nor constant recovery time can be assumed. You should use more complex multimode functions to model these TTR distributions.

8.5 Detailed Analysis of Data

After preliminary analysis of data, you can perform a series of analyses that evaluate features specific to the measured software system and data. You can gain insights into the types of analysis to be performed additionally from the results of preliminary analysis. You can also perform a detailed analysis based on specific analysis goals set in advance. This section discusses the analysis of failure dependency, hardware-related software failures, evaluation of software fault tolerance due to the use of process pairs and recovery routines, and the issue of recurrence.

8.5.1 Dependency analysis

Many underlying dependencies can exist among measured parameters and components. Examples are the dependency between workload and failure rate and the dependency or correlation among failures on different system components. Failure dependency is a special concern in fault-tolerant systems and highly parallel systems. Nonetheless, few measurement-based studies have addressed this issue. While you can use analytic methods, such as Markov modeling, to represent the failure dependencies identified, you can identify the types of dependencies that exist in actual systems and the range of realistic dependency parameters based only on field data. Understanding and quantifying such dependencies is important for developing realistic models and hence better designs. This subsection introduces a real example of correlated software errors and two studies of failure dependency based on real data: (1) an analysis of the two-way dependency between errors on two different machines in a VAXcluster system [Tang93a] and (2) an analysis of multiway dependency among failures on multiple processors in a Tandem fault-tolerant system [Lee91].

8.5.1.1 Correlated software errors. When multiple instances of a software system interact with each other in a multicomputer environment, you should consider the issue of correlated failures. Several studies ([Tang90, Wein90, Lee91]) found that significant correlated processor failures exist in multicomputer systems. To understand how correlated software failures occur, we will examine a real case in detail.

Figure 8.9 shows a scenario of correlated software failures observed in a seven-machine VAXcluster [Lee93a]. In the figure, Europa, Jupiter, and Mercury are machine names in the VAXcluster. A dashed line represents that the corresponding machine is in a failure state. Initially, a network error (net1) was reported from the CI (computer interconnect) port on Europa. This resulted in a software failure (soft1) 13 seconds later. Twenty-four seconds after the first network error (net1), additional network errors (net2,net3) were reported on the second machine (Jupiter), which were followed by a software failure (soft2). The error sequence on Jupiter was repeated (net4,net5,soft3) on the third machine (Mercury). The three machines experienced software failures concurrently for 45.5 minutes. All three software failures occurred shortly after network errors occurred, so they were probably network-error-related.

Note that the above scenario is a multiple-component-failure situation. A substantial amount of effort has been directed at developing general system design principles against correlated failures. Still, correlated failures exist due to design holes and unmodeled faults. Generally, correlated failures can stress recovery and break the protection provided by the fault tolerance.

8.5.1.2 Two-way dependency. The first step in a dependency analysis is to build a data matrix based on the measured data. Assume that there are n components in the measured system and that the measured period is divided into m equal intervals of Δt (e.g., 30 minutes). Then you can construct an $m \times n$ data matrix such that the element (i, j) of this matrix has a value of 1 if component j experiences an error or a failure during the ith time interval; otherwise, it has a value of 0. Alternatively, you can define the value of the element (i, j) of the matrix as the number of errors or failures occurred in component j during the ith interval. Note that the jth column of the matrix represents the sample error or failure history of component j, while the ith row of the matrix represents the state of the components in the ith time interval.

You can calculate correlation coefficients based on the data matrix. Each time, you pick up two columns (X_i and X_j) to calculate cor(X_i,X_j). Table 8.7 lists the average correlation coefficients of the 21 pairs of machines in a seven-machine VAXcluster for different types of errors and failure [Tang93a]. The table also lists the recovery probability for each error type. You can see that disk errors have the strongest corre-

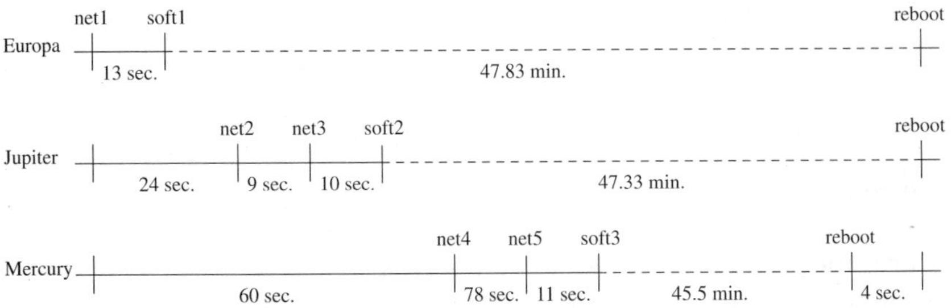

Note: soft1, soft2, soft3 — Exception while above asynchronous system traps delivery or on interrupt stack.
net1, net3, net5 — Port will be restarted. net2, net4 — Virtual circuit timeout.

Figure 8.9 A scenario of correlated software failures.

lation. This is because errors in the disk subsystem often affect multiple machines because of the sharing of disks. For similar reasons, network errors are strongly correlated across machines. While software error correlation across the machines is low, software failure correlation across them is significant because of the low recovery probability from a software error. This result is significant because even a small failure correlation can have a significant impact on system availability.

8.5.1.3 Multiway dependency. The limitation of correlation analysis is that the correlation coefficient can quantify a dependency between two variables only. However, dependencies may exist within a group of more than two variables or even among all variables. For example, in a distributed system, a disk crash can cause failures on those machines whose operations depend on a set of critical data on the disk, resulting in multiway failure dependency in these machines.

Multivariate analysis techniques allow you to analyze multiway failure dependency. Principal component analysis, factor analysis, and cluster analysis were used to identify the multiway failure dependency (see App. B) in [Lee91]. Table 8.8 shows the results of factor analysis using processor halt data collected from an eight-processor Tandem system.

According to [Dill84], factor loadings greater than 0.5 are usually considered significant. However, in reliability analysis, factor loadings

TABLE 8.7 Average Correlation Coefficients for VAXcluster Errors

	Error						Failure
	All	CPU	Memory	Disk	Network	Software	All
Correlation coefficient	0.62	0.03	0.01	0.78	0.70	0.02	0.06
Recovery probability	0.99	0.97	1.00	0.99	0.99	0.08	—

TABLE 8.8 Factor Pattern of Processor Halts in a Tandem System

Processor	Common factor 1	Common factor 2	Common factor 3	Common factor 4	Communality
1	0.997	−0.004	−0.069	0.023	1.00
2	0.000	0.000	0.000	0.000	0.00
3	0.061	0.012	0.853	−0.133	0.75
4	0.001	0.999	−0.011	0.021	1.00
5	0.982	−0.000	0.188	−0.018	1.00
6	−0.001	0.447	−0.005	0.009	0.20
7	0.047	−0.002	0.862	0.506	1.00
8	−0.007	0.762	0.090	0.641	1.00
Var.	1.965	1.781	1.519	0.685	
Var. %	24.6	22.3	19.0	8.6	

lower than 0.5 can be significant because even a small correlation can have a significant impact on system reliability. The results of factor analysis (Table 8.8) show that there are four common factors. You can see that, for example, common factor 1 captures the dependency between processors 1 and 5 and accounts for 24.6 percent of the total variance. Common factor 2 captures the multiway dependency among processors 4, 6, and 8, although the contribution of processor 6 is smaller (0.447^2, that is, 20 percent of its variance is explained by this factor). Common factor 2 explains 22.3 percent of the total variance. You can identify hidden failure dependencies and model the impact of design improvements on system reliability from such an analysis. The development of techniques to model such multiway dependencies efficiently is an area of future work.

8.5.2 Hardware-related software errors

When software is running on hardware platforms, interactions between hardware and software occur. Such interactions and their effects on system reliability are particularly difficult to comprehend. This is further compounded by the lack of real data. Results based on actual measurements and experiments are essential for developing a clear understanding of the problem.

The operating system's handling of software errors related to hardware was first studied using on-line event logs in [Iyer85a]. Such errors are described as *hardware-related software errors* (or HW/SW errors). More precisely, if a software error (failure) occurs in close proximity (within a minute) to a hardware error, it is called a hardware-related software (HW/SW) error (failure). You can explain hardware-related software errors in several ways. For instance, a hardware error, such as a flipped memory bit, may change the software conditions, resulting in a software error. Therefore, even though the error is reported as a software error, it is actually caused by faulty hardware. Another possibility is that software may fail to handle an unexpected hardware status, such as an unusual but legitimate condition in the network communication. This is a software design flaw. Sometimes, both the hardware error and the software error are symptoms of another, unidentified problem.

Table 8.9 shows the frequency and percentage of HW/SW errors/failures (among all software errors/failures) measured from an IBM 3081 system running MVS [Iyer85b] and two VAXclusters [Tang92b]. In the IBM system, approximately 33 percent of all observed software failures are hardware-related. HW/SW errors are found to have large error-handling times (high recovery overhead). The MVS data show that the system failure probability for HW/SW errors is close to three times that for software errors in general and that the operating system is seldom able to diagnose that a software error is hardware-related. The VAXcluster data show that most hardware errors involved in HW/SW errors are network errors (75 percent). This is probably because processes rely heavily on communications through the network in the multicomputer system.

8.5.3 Evaluation of software fault tolerance

Two major approaches proposed for software fault tolerance are recovery blocks and N-version programming [Aviz84, Rand75] (see Chap. 14). Both of these approaches require multiple, independently generated versions of software. As a result, they are not easily applicable to large, continually evolving software systems due to cost constraints, although critical code sections can be protected by these techniques.

It has been observed that some techniques originally intended for hardware fault tolerance can cope with software faults [Gray85, Gray90]. Detailed evaluation of software fault tolerance achieved by the use of process pairs in the Tandem GUARDIAN operating system and recovery routines in the IBM MVS operating system has been performed [Lee95, Vela84]. Process pairs are an implementation of the checkpointing and restart technique, which is a general approach. Recovery routines are a systematic implementation of exception handling. [Lee95] showed that the use of process pairs in Tandem systems, which was originally intended for tolerating hardware faults, allows the system to tolerate about 75 percent of reported field faults in the system software that cause processor failures. The loose coupling between processors, which results in the backup execution (the processor state and the sequence of events occurring) being different from the original execution, is a major reason for the measured software fault tolerance. This result shows that there is another dimension in achieving software fault tolerance. (Refer to the cited works for further details.) Clearly, software reliability can be improved by designs exploiting such knowledge in similar environments. Recently, attempts have been made to exploit the subtle nature of some software faults to tolerate such faults in user applications using checkpointing and restart [Huan93, Wang93].

TABLE 8.9 Hardware-Related Software Errors/Failures

Category	HW/SW errors		HW/SW failures	
Measures	Frequency	Percent	Frequency	Percent
IBM/MVS	177	11.4	94	32.8
VAX/VMS	32	18.9	28	21.4

8.5.4 Recurrences

[Lee93b] showed that about 72 percent of reported field software failures in Tandem systems are recurrences (Sec. 8.4.2). Recurrences are not unique in Tandem systems. A similar situation exists in IBM systems [Adam84] and AT&T systems [Leve95]. This shows that the number of faults identified in software is not the only important factor. Recurrences can seriously degrade software reliability in the field.

Recurrences exist for several reasons. First, designing and testing a fix of a problem can take a significant amount of time. In the meantime, recurrences can occur at the same site or at other sites. Second, the installation of a fix sometimes requires a planned outage, which may force users to postpone the installation and thus cause recurrences. Third, a purported fix can fail. Finally, and probably most importantly, users who did not experience problems due to a certain fault often hesitate to install an available fix for fear that doing so will cause new problems.

This subsection discusses two issues to reduce the impact of recurrences: software service policy to minimize the number of recurrences taking the cost of service into consideration [Adam84] and automatic diagnosis of recurrences based on their symptoms [Lee94a].

8.5.4.1 Preventive software service. *Corrective service* is the process of eliminating a software fault from a user's code after the fault caused a problem to the user. *Preventive service* is the process of eliminating a software fault from a user's code when the fault has not yet caused a problem to the user. Preventive service can potentially reduce the number of recurrences, but it requires resources to prepare, distribute, and install fixes. More important, it can cause additional problems because of faults in the fixes. Then question is: what is the optimal preventive service policy?

Based on the failure and shipment data of IBM products, [Adam84] proposed a procedure to predict the number of recurrences. Table 8.10 shows a sample rediscovery matrix constructed using the procedure. Here the terms *recurrence* and *rediscovery* are used interchangeably. The rows and columns of the matrix are labeled by months counted from the time of first customer shipment. The entry (i, j) of the matrix is the number of projected rediscoveries in the user base during month i caused by faults first discovered in month j. The total of the numbers in the ith row is the total number of rediscoveries expected in month i. The numbers are projected for a hypothetical product that has steady month-to-month growth of usership, assuming that all users use the initial version of the product.

You can see from the rediscovery matrix that the number grows steadily down a column and diminishes strongly to the right across the

TABLE 8.10 Rediscovery Matrix

		Discovery month																	
		1	2	3	4	5	6	7	8	9	10	11	12	13	14	15	16	17	18
	1	7	0	0	0	0	0	0	0	0	0	0	0	0	0	0	0	0	0
	2	29	9	0	0	0	0	0	0	0	0	0	0	0	0	0	0	0	0
	3	44	26	7	0	0	0	0	0	0	0	0	0	0	0	0	0	0	0
	4	59	35	19	6	0	0	0	0	0	0	0	0	0	0	0	0	0	0
	5	73	43	24	15	5	0	0	0	0	0	0	0	0	0	0	0	0	0
	6	88	52	28	17	12	4	0	0	0	0	0	0	0	0	0	0	0	0
	7	103	61	33	20	14	10	4	0	0	0	0	0	0	0	0	0	0	0
	8	117	69	38	23	16	11	8	3	0	0	0	0	0	0	0	0	0	0
Rediscovery	9	132	78	42	26	18	13	9	7	3	0	0	0	0	0	0	0	0	0
month	10	147	87	47	29	20	14	10	8	6	2	0	0	0	0	0	0	0	0
	11	162	95	52	32	22	15	11	9	7	5	2	0	0	0	0	0	0	0
	12	176	104	57	35	24	17	12	9	7	6	5	2	0	0	0	0	0	0
	13	191	113	61	38	25	18	13	10	8	6	5	4	2	0	0	0	0	0
	14	206	121	66	41	27	19	14	11	8	7	5	4	3	1	0	0	0	0
	15	220	130	71	44	29	21	15	12	9	7	6	5	4	3	1	0	0	0
	16	235	139	76	47	31	22	16	12	10	8	6	5	4	3	3	1	0	0
	17	250	147	80	50	33	24	17	13	10	8	6	5	4	4	3	3	1	0
	18	264	156	85	52	35	25	18	14	11	9	7	6	4	4	3	3	2	1

row. The variation down the column reflects the continual entry of new users who can have problems; the decrease to the right reflects the diminishing virulence of faults found in later months. Table 8.10 shows that the large numbers all occur in the columns to the left. This indicates that you might be better off by limiting preventive software service only to a relatively small number of highly visible faults that cause problems in leftmost columns.

8.5.4.2 Automatic diagnosis of recurrences. The above mentioned study ([Adam84]) and the reasons for recurrence indicate that recurrences will continue to be a significant part of field software failures. Then the question is: how can you handle recurrences efficiently? An approach to automatically identify recurrences based on their symptoms has been proposed in [Lee94a]. The approach is based on an observation that failures caused by the same fault often share common symptoms [Lee93b]. Specifically, the study proposed the comparison of failure symptoms, such as the stack trace and code location where problems were detected, as a strategy for identifying (i.e., diagnosing) recurrences. A stack trace is the history of procedure calls made by the active process at the time of failure. It represents the software function that detected a problem.

Figure 8.10 illustrates the type of automatic diagnosis environment envisioned. The diagnosis tool is connected with many user systems by an on-line alarm system. All previously reported failure symptoms and associated information, such as underlying faults and fixes, are stored in a database. On a failure alarm, the tool accesses the system that sent the alarm, extracts the values of the common symptoms (e.g., a stack trace and a detection location), and compares them with those of previously reported faults in the database. If a match is found in the

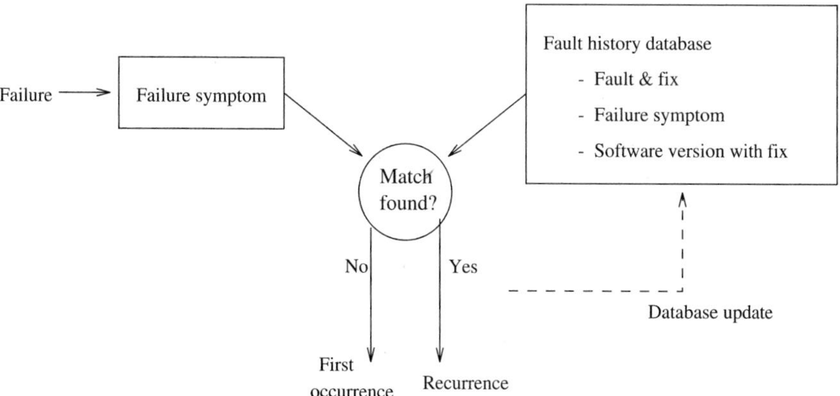

Figure 8.10 Diagnosis environment.

database, the new failure is declared a recurrence of the corresponding fault; otherwise, it is declared a first occurrence. In the case of recurrence, the tool also identifies an available fix. After the diagnosis, the database is updated with new failure data.

To apply symptom-based diagnosis of software failures, you should consider the following two extremes: a software fault can cause failures with different symptoms, and two software faults can cause failures with identical symptoms. Figure 8.11 illustrates the first extreme: two failures caused by the same software fault have different stack traces. In the figure, a circle represents a procedure call, and an arrow represents the execution within a procedure. Figure 8.11 shows a failure in which the base procedure MAINLOOP called the procedure NEXTREQ, which in turn called the procedure MONITORPRIMARY. MONITORPRIMARY called the procedure TK_PROCESS_TK_CKPT, in which a fault was exercised and a processor halt was asserted. In another failure, the same sequence was repeated, except that MAINLOOP reached MONITORPRIMARY through the procedure INITIALIZE. This calling path is also shown in the figure. Each chain of procedure calls forms a stack trace and is represented by a set of connected solid arrows in the figure. Because the software structure is modular, there can be different program paths that reach the faulty code section. Figure 8.11 shows two such paths. Each of the paths gives a distinct stack trace.

Another example of the first extreme is the case of a wide range of corruption in shared data. In this case, any software function can detect some of the errors and assert a processor halt. This would lead to widely different stack traces, problem detection locations, and error patterns.

The second extreme to consider is that different faults can cause failures with identical symptoms. A procedure typically contains multiple

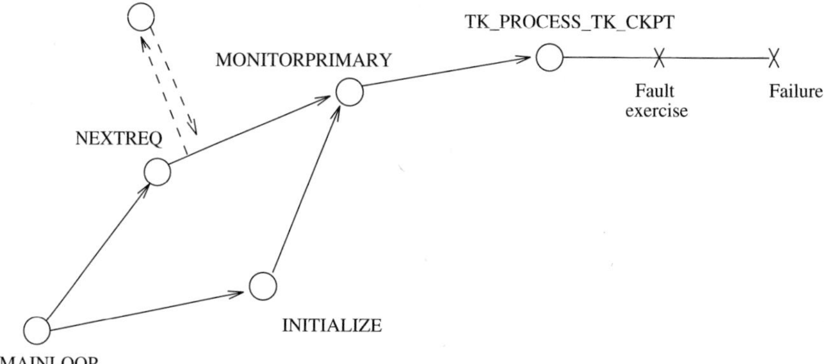

Figure 8.11 A single fault causing failures with different symptoms.

checks, and these checks test different conditions. As a result, errors caused by different faults can be detected within the same procedure, thus resulting in failures with identical stack traces.

You can clearly see that the effectiveness of a diagnosis strategy under the two extremes must be evaluated using the actual data. The proposed strategy was applied using the failure data from two Tandem system software products [Lee94a]. Then the results obtained were compared with the actual diagnosis and repair logs by analysts. Results of the comparison showed that between 75 and 95 percent of recurrences can be identified successfully by matching stack traces and problem detection locations. Less than 10 percent of faults are misdiagnosed.

The results show that the proposed automatic diagnosis of recurrences allows analysts to diagnose only one out of several software failures (i.e., primarily the failures caused by new faults). In the case of a recurrence for which the underlying cause was identified, the diagnostic tool can rapidly identify a solution. In the case of a recurrence for which the underlying cause is being investigated, the diagnostic tool can prevent a repeated diagnosis by identifying previous failures caused by the same fault. These benefits are not free. Misdiagnosis is harmful, because a single misdiagnosis can result in multiple additional failures. (Such a danger exists in diagnoses by analysts, also.) You should implement the proposed approach in a pilot. You should make measurements to determine how well the approach works in real environments and to make design trade-offs.

8.6 Model Identification and Analysis of Models

The data analyses discussed in the previous sections reveal the software reliability behavior in real environments. Specifically, they identify the model structure and the range of parameter values. You can use this information to tune existing analytic or simulation models and to build new models. Then you can use the new models to predict various reliability characteristics in a new design by evaluating the model characteristics with a different set of parameters. This section discusses the modeling of the impact of software failures on performance, software reliability modeling in the operational phase, modeling of error detection and recovery, and modeling of software error bursts.

8.6.1 Impact of failures on performance

One of the key measures in evaluating gracefully degraded systems is the impact of failures on system performance or service capacity. In fault-tolerant systems, it is also important to evaluate the effectiveness of various fault-tolerance techniques implemented to enhance software reliability. This subsection discusses the modeling of the impact of software failures on performance. It also evaluates the operating system fault tolerance achieved due to the built-in, single-failure tolerance in the Tandem system by conducting Markov reward analysis (App. B). Figure 8.12 shows a Markov model built using processor halt logs collected from a 16-processor Tandem system [Lee92]. In the figure, S_i represents the system state in which there are i failed processors because of software faults and $r_{i,j}$ represents the transition rate from S_i to S_j.

Two reward functions are defined in the analysis (Eqs. (8.1) and (8.2)). In these equations, r_i represents the reward rate for S_i. The first function (SFT) reflects the fault tolerance of the Tandem system. In this function, the first processor halt does not cause any degradation. For additional processor halts, the loss of service is proportional to the number of processors halted. The second function (NSFT) assumes no fault tolerance. The difference between the two functions allows evaluation of the improvement in service due to the built-in fault tolerance mechanisms.

SFT (single-failure tolerance):

$$r_i = \begin{cases} 1 & \text{if } i = 0 \\ 1 - \dfrac{i-1}{16} & \text{if } 0 < i < 16 \\ 0 & \text{if } i = 16 \end{cases} \tag{8.1}$$

NSFT (no single-failure tolerance):

$$r_i = 1 - \frac{i}{16} \qquad \text{if } 0 \leq i \leq 16 \tag{8.2}$$

Based on the above reward functions, the expected steady-state reward rate is evaluated for software, nonsoftware, and all halts. The

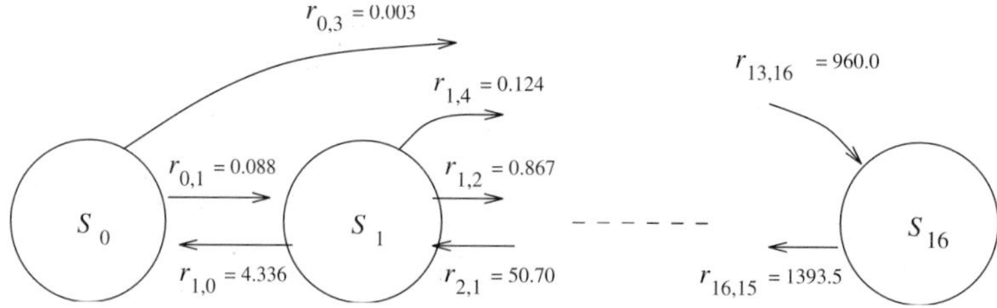

Figure 8.12 Measurement-based Markov model.

steady-state reward rate represents the relative amount of useful service the system can provide per unit of time in the long run; it is a measure of service-capacity-oriented software availability. The steady-state reward-loss rate (or simply, reward loss) represents the relative amount of useful service lost per unit of time due to processor halts.

The results of analysis are given in Table 8.11. Rows with "SFT" and "NSFT" show the estimated steady-state reward-loss with SFT and NSFT, respectively. The bottom row shows the improvement in service (i.e., reduction in reward loss) due to the fault tolerance. You can see that the single-failure tolerance in the measured system reduces the service loss due to software halts by 89 percent and the service loss due to nonsoftware halts by 92 percent. This clearly demonstrates the effectiveness of the implemented fault-tolerance mechanisms against software failures as well as nonsoftware failures. You can also see that software problems account for 30 percent of the service loss in the measured system (with SFT).

8.6.2 Reliability modeling in the operational phase

Software reliability models typically attempt to relate the history of fault identification during the development phase, verification efforts, and operational profile [Musa87, Rama82]. Usually, it is assumed that software is an independent entity and each identified fault has the same impact. However, our results indicate that there are other factors that significantly affect software reliability in real environments. First, a single, highly visible software fault can cause many failures, and recurrences can seriously degrade software reliability in the field. Second, for a class of software, the fault tolerance of the overall system can significantly improve software reliability by making the effects of software faults invisible to users. Clearly, reliability issues for operational software in general can be quite different from those for the software in the development phase.

TABLE 8.11 Loss of Service Caused by Processor Halts in the Tandem System

Measure		Software	Nonsoftware	All
NSFT	Reward	0.00062	0.00205	0.00267
	Loss	23.2	76.8	100
SFT	Reward	0.00007	0.00016	0.00023
	Loss	30.4	69.6	100
Improvement		89%	92%	91%

This subsection discusses the factors that determine software reliability in the operational phase, using a case study of the Tandem GUARDIAN operating system [Lee94b].

8.6.2.1 Model construction. A hypothetical eight-processor Tandem system whose software reliability characteristics are described by the parameters in Table 8.12 was considered. Here the term *software reliability* means the reliability of an overall system when only the faults in the system software are considered. A system failure was defined to occur when more than half of the processors in the system failed. All parameters in the table except λ and μ were estimated based on the measured data (Secs. 8.4.2 and 8.5.3). The values of λ and μ were determined to mimic the 30 years of software mean-time-between-failures (MTBF) and the mean-time-to-repair (MTTR) characteristics reported in [Gray90]. Thus, the objectives of the analysis are to model and evaluate reliability sensitivity to various factors, not to estimate the absolute software reliability.

With the use of process pairs, a fault in the Tandem system software can cause a single or double processor halt. Also, a double processor halt can cause additional processor halts if the two halted processors control key system resources that are needed by other processors. (Refer to [Lee95] for further details.) In Table 8.12, "P(double CPU halt | software failure)" is the probability that a double processor halt (i.e., the failure of a process pair) occurs given that a software failure occurs. A software failure refers to a processor halt due to software. Similarly, "P(system failure | double CPU halt)" is the probability that a system failure occurs given that a double processor halt occurs. These two parameters are used to describe the major failure mode of the system because of software. The parameter "P(system failure | single CPU halt)" represents the secondary failure mode, which captures single processor halts severe enough to cause system coldloads. The table shows these probabilities for first occurrences, recurrences, and unidentified failures. Unidentified failures refer to the cases in which

TABLE 8.12 Estimated Software Reliability Parameters

Failures	First occurrence	Recurrence	Unidentified
Failure rate	$\lambda_f = 0.24\lambda$	$\lambda_r = 0.61\lambda$	$\lambda_u = 0.15\lambda$
P(double CPU halt | software failure)	$C_{df} = 0.23$	$C_{dr} = 0.18$	$C_{du} = 0.0$
P(system failure | double CPU halt)	$C_{sdf} = 0.44$	$C_{sdr} = 0.63$	$C_{sdu} = 0.0$
P(system failure | single CPU halt)	$C_{ssf} = 0.05$	$C_{ssr} = 0.0$	$C_{ssu} = 0.0$

Failures:
Software failure rate = λ = 0.32/year

Recovery:
Recovery rate = μ = 1/hour

analysts believed that the underlying problems are software faults but had not yet located the faults.

Figure 8.13 shows the Markov model. In the model $S_i, i = 0,\ldots, 4$ represents that i processors are halted because of software faults. A system failure is represented by the S_{down} state. To evaluate software reliability, no recovery from a system failure is assumed. That is, the system failure state is an absorption state. The R_i state represents an intermediate state in which the system tries to recover from an additional software failure (ith processor halt) using process pairs.

If a software failure occurs during the normal system operation (i.e., when the system is in the S_0 state), the system enters the R_1 state. If the failure is severe enough to cause a system coldload, a system failure occurs; otherwise, the system attempts to recover from the failure by using backup processes located in other processors. If recovery is successful, the system enters the S_1 state; otherwise, a double processor halt occurs. If the two halted processors control key system resources (such as a set of disks) that are essential for system operation, the rest of the processors in the system also halt and a system failure occurs; otherwise, the system enters the S_2 state and continues to operate. The value of r, the transition rate out of an R_i, is small and has virtually no impact on software reliability; a value of one transition per minute is used in the analysis.

In Fig. 8.13, the three coverage parameters C_d, C_{sd}, and C_{ss} are calculated from Table 8.12:

$$C_d = \text{P(double CPU halt} \mid \text{software failure)} = \frac{\lambda_f C_{df} + \lambda_r C_{dr} + \lambda_u C_{du}}{\lambda_f + \lambda_r + \lambda_u} \tag{8.3}$$

$$C_{sd} = \text{P(system failure} \mid \text{double CPU halt)} = \frac{\lambda_f C_{df} C_{sdf} + \lambda_r C_{dr} C_{sdr} + \lambda_u C_{du} C_{sdu}}{\lambda_f C_{df} + \lambda_r C_{dr} + \lambda_u C_{du}} \tag{8.4}$$

and

$$C_{ss} = \text{P(system failure} \mid \text{single CPU halt)} = \frac{\lambda_f C_{ssf} + \lambda_r C_{ssr} + \lambda_u C_{ssu}}{\lambda_f + \lambda_r + \lambda_u} \tag{8.5}$$

From the model in Fig. 8.13, you can evaluate software reliability (i.e., the distribution of the time for the system to be absorbed to the system failure state, starting from the normal state). You can use tools such as SHARPE [Sahn87, Sahn95] to evaluate the distribution.

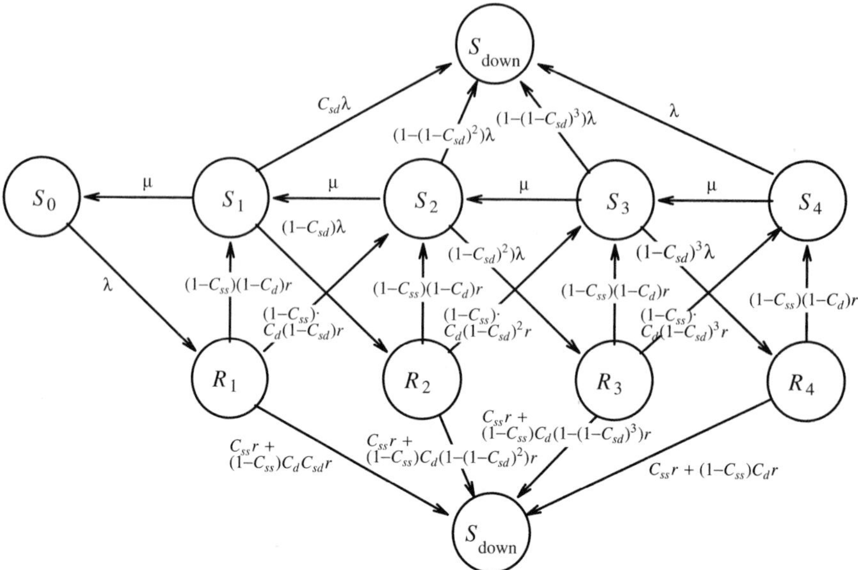

Figure 8.13 System-level software reliability model.

8.6.2.2 Sensitivity analysis. Table 8.13 shows the six factors considered. The second column of the table shows activities related to these factors, and the third column shows the model parameters affected by the factors. The coverage parameters C_d and C_{sd} are determined primarily by the robustness of process pairs and the system configuration, respectively. For example, C_d can be reduced by conducting extra testing of the routines related to job takeover. The parameter C_{sd} is primarily determined by the location of failed process pairs and the disk subsystem configuration. The recovery rate μ can be improved by automating the data collection and reintegration process.

Figure 8.14 shows the software MTBF evaluated using the model in Fig. 8.13 while varying the six factors in Table 8.13, one at a time. You can see that C_d and C_{sd} are almost as important as λ in determining the

TABLE 8.13 Factors of Software Reliability

Factor	Activity	Related parameters	
		Detailed	Overall
Software failure rate	Software development	λ_f, λ_r, λ_u	λ
Recurrence rate	Software service	λ_r	λ, C_d, C_{sd}, C_{ss}
Coverage parameter C_d	Robustness of process pairs	C_{df}, C_{dr}, C_{du}	C_d
Coverage parameter C_{sd}	System configuration	C_{sdf}, C_{sdr}, C_{sdu}	C_{sd}
Coverage parameter C_{ss}	—	C_{ssf}, C_{ssr}, C_{ssu}	C_{ss}
Recovery time	Diagnosability/maintainability	μ	μ

software MTBF. For example, a 20 percent reduction in C_d or C_{sd} has as much impact on software MTBF as an 18 percent reduction in λ. (The figure shows that the impact is approximately a 20 percent increase in software MTBF.) This result is understandable because the system fails primarily because of a double processor halt causing a set of disks to become inaccessible, not because of multiple independent software failures. You can also see that the recurrence rate has a significant impact on software reliability. A complete elimination of recurrences ($\lambda_r = 0$ in Table 8.12) would increase the software MTBF by a factor of 3.

Typically, it is assumed that the number of faults in software is the only major factor determining software reliability. Figure 8.14 clearly shows that in the Tandem system there are four degrees of freedom in improving software reliability: the number of faults in software, the recurrence rate, the robustness of the process pairs, and the system configuration strategy. The first two are general factors, and the last two are system-specific factors. Efforts to improve software reliability can be optimized by estimating the cost of improving each of the four factors.

8.6.3 Error/failure/recovery model

This subsection discusses the modeling of the detailed error detection and recovery processes in an operating system, using the data from the IBM MVS system running on an IBM 3081 mainframe [Hsue87]. The MVS system attempts to correct software errors using recovery routines. The philosophy in MVS is that for major system functions the designer envisions possible failure scenarios and writes a recovery routine for each. It is, however, the responsibility of the installation (or the user) to write recovery routines for applications.

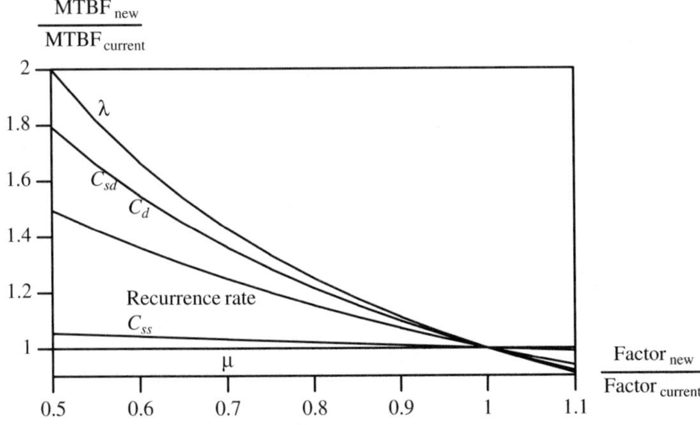

Figure 8.14 Software MTBF sensitivity.

More than one recovery routine can be specified for the same program. If the current recovery routine is unable to restore a valid state, the recovery manager can give control to another recovery routine, if available. This process is called *percolation*. The percolation process ends if a routine issues a valid retry request or if no more recovery routines are available. An error recovery can result in any of the following four situations:

1. Resume op (resume operation). The system successfully recovers from the error and returns control to the interrupted program.
2. Task term (task termination). The program and its related subtasks are terminated, but the system does not fail.
3. Job term (job termination). The job in control at the time of the error is aborted.
4. System failure. The job or task, which was terminated, is critical for system operation. As a result of the termination, a system failure occurs.

8.6.3.1 Model construction. The model consists of eight types of error states (Table 8.14) and three states resulting from error recoveries. Figure 8.15 shows the model, where a circle represents a state and an arrow represents a transition with an associated transition probability. The normal state represents the operating system running error-free. Note that the system failure state is not shown in the figure. This is because the occurrence of system failure was rare, and the number of observed system failures was statistically insignificant. Given that the system is in state i, the probability that it will go to state j, p_{ij}, can be estimated from the data as follows:

$$p_{ij} = \frac{\text{observed number of transitions from } E_i \text{ to } E_j}{\text{observed number of transitions out of } E_i} \tag{8.6}$$

TABLE 8.14 Mean Waiting Time

State	No. observations	Mean waiting time (sec.)	Standard deviation
Normal (error-free)	2757	10461.33	32735.04
CTRL (control error)	213	21.92	84.21
DLCK (deadlock)	23	4.72	22.61
I/O (I/O & data management error)	1448	25.05	77.62
PE (program exception)	65	42.23	92.98
SE (storage or address exception)	149	36.82	79.59
SM (storage management error)	313	33.40	95.01
OTHR (other type)	66	1.86	12.98
MULT (multiple software error)	481	175.59	252.79

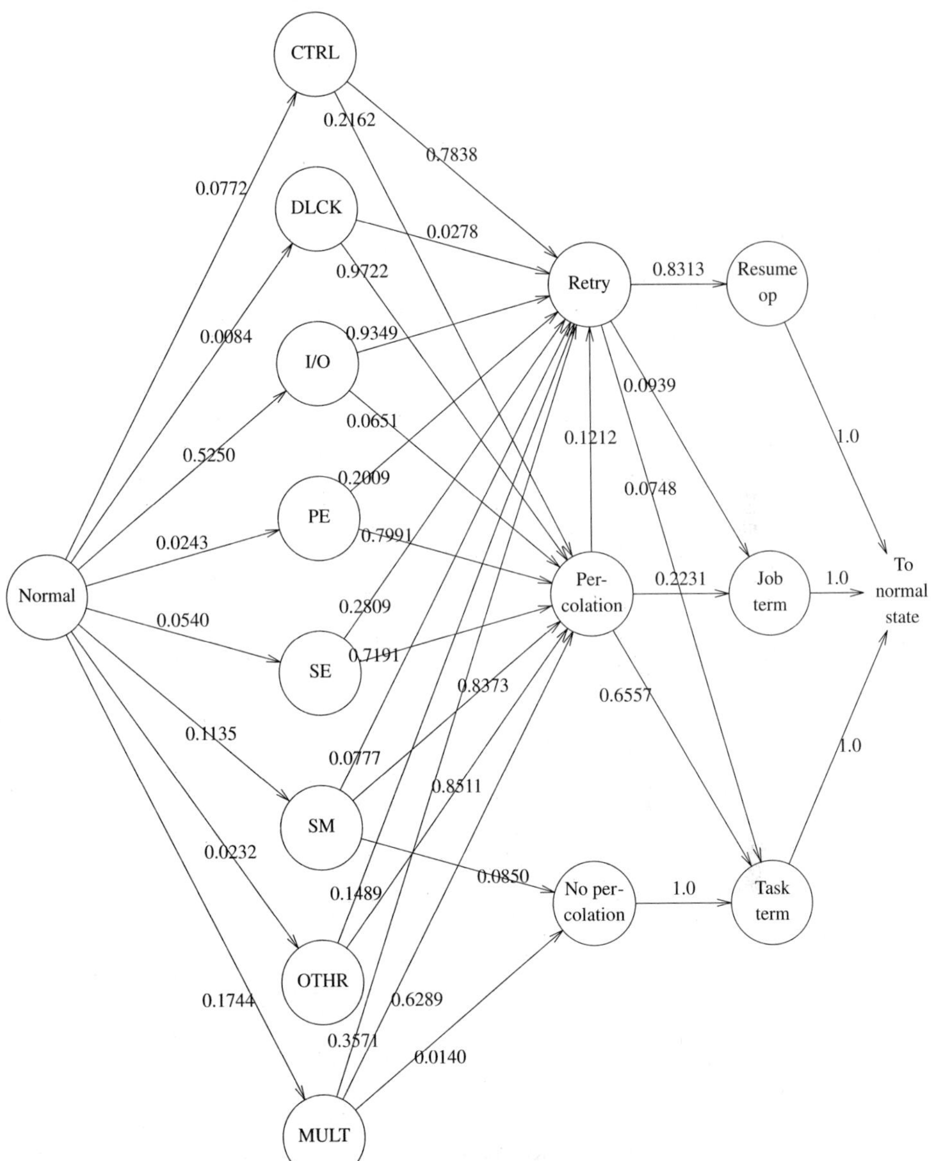

Figure 8.15 MVS software error/recovery model.

An error recovery can be as simple as a retry or as complex as requiring several percolations before a successful retry. The problem can also be such that no retry or percolation is possible. You can see from Fig. 8.15 that about 83.1 percent of all retries are successful. You can also see that 93.5 percent of I/O and data management errors and 78.4 percent of control-related errors resulted in a direct retry. These observations indicate that most I/O- and control-related errors are relatively easy to recover from compared to the other types of errors, such as deadlock or storage errors.

Table 8.14 shows the mean-waiting-time characteristics of the normal and error states in the model. (See Sec. 8.4.2 for the definitions of error types.) You can see that the average duration of a multiple error is at least four times longer than that of any type of single error, which is typically in the range of 20 to 40 seconds, except for DLCK (deadlock) and OTHR (others). The average recovery time from a program exception is twice as long as that from a control error (21 seconds versus 42 seconds). This is probably due to the extensive software involvement in recovering from program exceptions.

8.6.3.2 Model evaluation. Table 8.15 shows the following steady-state measures evaluated from the model. The detailed definitions of these measures are given in [Howa71].

Transition probability (π_j)	Probability that the transition is to state j, given a transition to occur
Occupancy probability (Φ_j)	Probability that the system occupies state j at any time point
Mean recurrence time ($\overline{\Theta}_j$)	Mean recurrence time of state j

The occupancy probability of the normal state can be viewed as the operating system availability without degradation. The state transition probability, on the other hand, characterizes error-detection and recovery processes in the operating system. Table 8.15*a* lists the state transition probabilities and occupancy probabilities for the normal and error states. Table 8.15*b* lists the state transition probabilities and the mean recurrent times of the recovery and result states. A dash (—) in the table indicates a negligible value (less than 0.00001). You can see that the occupancy probability of the normal state in the model is 0.995. This indicates that 99.5 percent of the time the operating system is running error-free. In the other 0.5 percent of the time, the operating system is in an error or recovery state. In more than half of the error and recovery time (that is, 0.29 percent out of 0.5 percent) the operating system is in the multiple-error state.

By solving the model, you can find that the operating system makes a transition every 43.37 minutes. Table 8.15*a* shows that 24.74 percent of all transitions made in the model are to the normal state, 24.73 percent to error states (obtained by summing the π's for all error states), 25.79 percent to recovery states, and 24.74 percent to result states. Since a transition occurs every 43 minutes, you can estimate that, on

TABLE 8.15 Error/Recovery Model Characteristics

Measure	Normal state	Error state							
		CTRL	DLCK	I/O	PE	SE	SM	OTHR	MULT
π	0.2474	0.0191	0.0020	0.1299	0.0060	0.0134	0.0281	0.0057	0.0431
Φ	0.9950	0.00016	—	0.00125	0.000098	0.000189	0.00036	—	0.002913

(a)

Measure	Recovery state			Result state		
	Retry	Percolation	No-percolation	Resume op	Task term	Job term
π	0.1704	0.0845	0.0030	0.1414	0.0712	0.0348
$\overline{\Theta}$(hr.)	4.25	8.55	241.43	5.11	10.16	20.74

(b)

the average, a software error is detected every 3 hours and a successful recovery (i.e., reaching the "resume op" state) occurs every 5 hours. Table 8.15*b* also shows that more than 40 percent of software errors lead to job or task terminations, thus causing the loss of service to users. However, only a few of these terminations lead to system failures. This result indicates that recovery routines in MVS are effective in avoiding system failures, but are not so effective in avoiding user job terminations.

8.6.4 Multiple-error model

The error/failure/recovery model and analysis using the model in Sec. 8.6.3 showed that multiple errors are a significant source of system degradation in the MVS system. Figure 8.16 shows a semi-Markov model for a multiple error developed from the data from an IBM MVS system [Hsue87] (Secs. 8.4.2 and 8.4.4). The model was constructed assuming zero waiting time in the normal state (i.e., assuming the occurrence of a multiple error). The figure not only illustrates the interactions among different software errors, but also provides detailed information on the occurrence of transitions. For example, if a program exception error (PE) occurs, there is about a 63 percent chance that a storage exception error (SE) will follow. Further, there is about a 50 percent chance that a storage error (SE or SM) will be followed by another error of the same type.

Table 8.16 lists the characteristics for a multiple error obtained by solving the semi-Markov model described in Fig. 8.16 with a zero holding time in the normal state (i.e., given that a multiple error occurs). In the table, e_j (entry probability) represents the probability that the system enters state j, given an entrance to occur [Howa71]. You can see (from π, transition probability) that nearly 30 percent of the transitions are made to the storage exception state when the system enters a multiple error mode. Once in a multiple error mode, a storage exception error occurs every 1 minute and 45 seconds ($\overline{\Theta} = 0.0292$ hours in Table 8.16), while the average duration of multiple errors is about 2 minutes and 56 seconds ($\overline{\Theta} = 0.0489$ hours, the recurrence time of the normal state). Note that the average duration of a multiple error predicted here from the model is very close to the mean duration of a multiple error, 175.5 seconds obtained from the real data, listed in Table 8.14. This provides evidence that the semi-Markov process is a good model for the measured system. As soon as an entry into a multiple error is made, consecutive errors are detected almost every 31 seconds (by taking the reciprocal of the sum of all entry probabilities e in Table 8.16). This indicates that about five to six errors will be detected, on average, once a multiple error occurs.

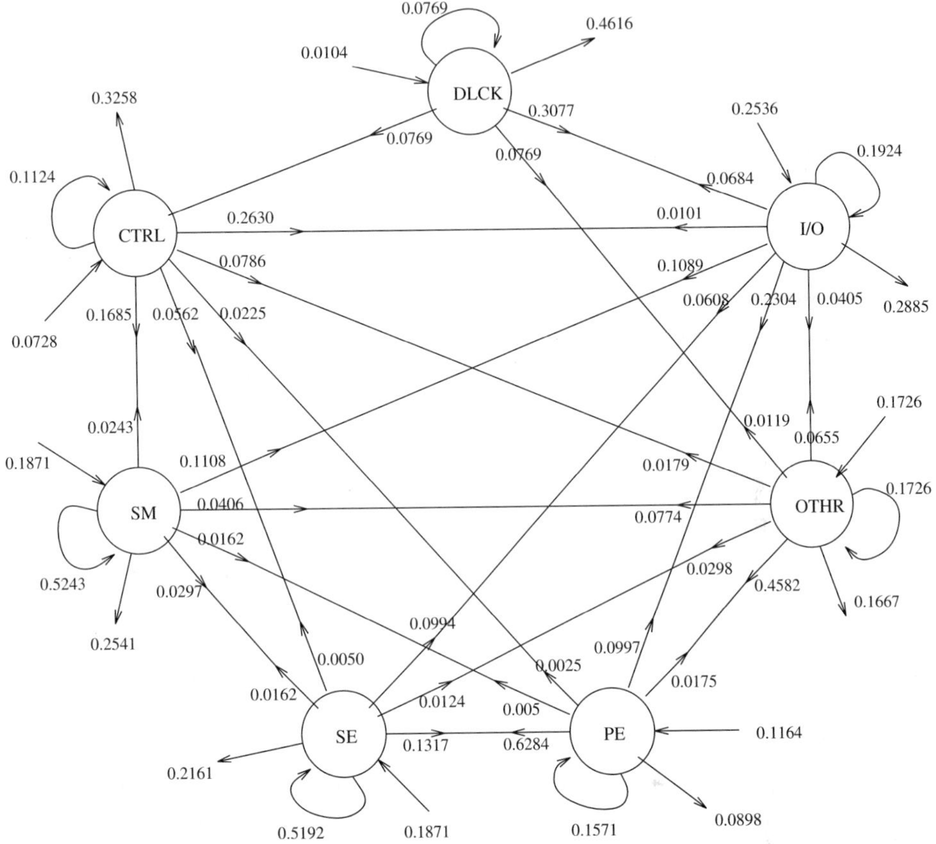

Figure 8.16 State transition diagram of multiple error (MULT).

8.7 Impact of System Activity

This section discusses the relationships between software failures and various workload parameters. Several studies have shown that you cannot consider software reliability in real environments without taking the system workload into account. [Cast81, Cast82,] and [Iyer82a] proposed analytic or regression models of such relationships. Markov models of such relationships have been proposed in [Hsue88].

8.7.1 Statistical models from measurements

8.7.1.1 Workload-dependent cyclostationary model. An early study [Cast81] introduced a workload-dependent cyclostationary model to characterize system failure processes. The model is based on the observation of the periodic nature of daily workload profile and failures. The

TABLE 8.16 Characteristics of Multiple Errors

Measure	Normal state	Error state						
		CTRL	DLCK	I/O	PE	SE	SM	OTHR
π	0.1767	0.0327	0.0048	0.1451	0.1473	0.2957	0.1360	0.0617
Φ	0	0.0648	0.0130	0.3004	0.0837	0.2202	0.2717	0.0462
$\bar{e}$	0.00568	0.00105	0.00015	0.00466	0.00473	0.00950	0.00437	0.00198
Θ (hr)	0.0489	0.2647	1.8126	0.0596	0.0587	0.0292	0.0636	0.1401

underlying idea is that a higher workload implies that the kernel of the operating system is exercised more per unit of time, increasing the probability of system failure. It is assumed that the instantaneous failure rate of a system resource can be approximated by a function of the usage of the resource considered. Specifically, the failure rate of a particular resource, $\lambda(t)$, is assumed to be

$$\lambda(t) = au(t) + b \tag{8.7}$$

where $u(t)$ is a usage function of the resource that, in turn, consists of a deterministic, periodic function of time, $m(t)$ and a modified, stationary gaussian process, $z(t)$:

$$u(t) = m(t) + z(t) \tag{8.8}$$

The failure arrivals are assumed to follow a Poisson process. Thus, the failure process involves two stochastic processes: a Poisson process and a gaussian process. Such a process is defined as a *doubly stochastic process.* The following workload-dependent cyclostationary reliability function due to software is derived:

$$R(t) = 1 - \phi(t)e^{-k_1 t - k_2(1 - e^{-k_3 t}) - k_4(1 - e^{-k_5 t})} \tag{8.9}$$

where $\phi(t)$ is a periodic function of time, depending on the periodic component of $\lambda(t)$ and k_1, k_2, k_3, k_4, and k_5 are constants determined from the failure and usage process characteristics (Eqs. (8.7) and (8.8)).

8.7.1.2 Load hazard model. In [Iyer82a], a load hazard model was introduced to measure the risk of a failure as the system activity increases. The proposed model is similar to the hazard rate defined in reliability theory. Given a workload variable X, the load hazard is defined as

$$z(x) = \frac{P[\text{failure in load interval } (x, x + \Delta x)]}{P[\text{no failure in load interval } (0, x)]\ \Delta x} = \frac{g(x)}{1 - G(x)} \tag{8.10}$$

where $g(x)$ is the probability density function (pdf) of the variable "a failure occurs at a given workload value x" and $G(x)$ is the corresponding cumulative distribution function (cdf). That is,

$$g(x) = P(\text{failure occurs} \mid X = x) = \frac{f(x)}{l(x)} \tag{8.11}$$

where $l(x)$ is simply the pdf of the workload in consideration:

$$l(x) = P(X = x) \tag{8.12}$$

and $f(x)$ is the joint pdf of the system failure and the workload:

$$f(x) = P(\text{failure occurs and } X = x) \tag{8.13}$$

The load hazard $z(x)$ (in close analogy with the classical hazard rate in reliability theory) measures the incremental risk involved in increasing the workload from x to $x + \Delta x$. A constant hazard rate implies that failures are occurring randomly with respect to the workload. An increasing hazard rate on the increase of X implies that there is an increasing failure rate with increasing workload.

The load hazard model was applied to the software failure and workload data collected from an IBM 3081 system running the VM operating system [Iyer85b]. Based on the collected data, $l(x)$, $f(x)$, $g(x)$, and $z(x)$ were computed for each workload variable. Figure 8.17 shows the $z(x)$ plots for three selected workload variables:

OVERHEAD	The fraction of CPU time spent on the operating system
PAGEIN	The number of page reads per second by all users
SIO (start I/O)	The number of input/output operations per second

The regression coefficient, R^2, which is an effective measure of the goodness of fit, is also shown in the figure.

You can see from the hazard plots shown that the workload parameters appear to be acting as stress factors, i.e., the failure rate increases as the workload increases. The effect is particularly strong in the case

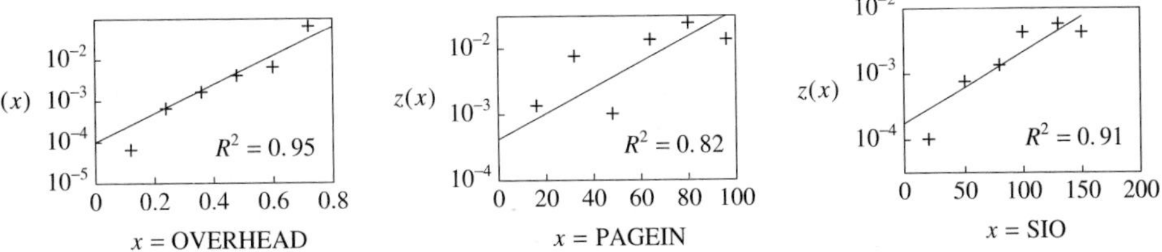

Figure 8.17 Workload hazard plots for an IBM 3081 system.

of the interactive workload measures OVERHEAD and SIO. The correlation coefficients of 0.95 and 0.91 show that the failure process closely fits an increasing load hazard model. The risk of a failure also increases with increased PAGEIN, although at a somewhat lower correlation (0.82). Note that the vertical scale on these plots is logarithmic, indicating that the relationship between the load hazard $z(x)$ and the workload variable is exponential, i.e., the risk of a software failure increases exponentially with increasing workload.

It was hypothesized that, in addition to the reasons reported in [Cast81], there are other load-induced effects [Iyer82b]. The first is the latent discovery effect. Problems must be detected in order to cause failures. Even if failures may not be caused by increased workload, they are revealed by this factor. The second effect is the load-induced software failures. Many typical software faults exist in the operating system. These faults can be divided in two groups, those triggered under high load and those that are load-independent but appear to be load-induced because of an increased execution time effect.

8.7.2 Overall system behavior model

This subsection introduces a measurement-based performability model based on error and resource-usage data collected on a production IBM 3081 system running under the MVS operating system [Hsue88].

8.7.2.1 Workload model. The workload data were collected by sampling, at predetermined intervals, four resource usage meters:

CPU	The fraction of the measured interval for which the CPU is executing instructions
CHB	The fraction of the measured interval for which the channel is busy and the CPU is in the wait state (commonly used to measure the degree of contention in a system)
SIO	The number of successful start I/O and resume I/O instructions issued to the channel
DASD	The number of requests serviced on the direct-access storage device

At any interval of time, the measured workload is represented by a point in a four-dimensional space (CPU, CHB, SIO, DASD). Statistical cluster analysis (App. B) is used to divide the workload into similar classes according to a predefined criterion. This allows you to concisely describe the dynamics of system behavior and extract a structure that already exists in the workload data. Each cluster (defined by its centroid) is then used to depict a system state, and a state-transition diagram (consisting of intercluster transition probabilities and cluster sojourn times) is developed. A k-means algorithm [Spat80] is used for clustering.

Figure 8.18 shows the workload model built by the above procedures using the CPU and CHB data. This combination was found to best describe the CPU-bound load, while models based on SIO and DASD were found to best describe the I/O workload. Note that the null state W_0 has been incorporated to represent the state of the system during the nonmeasured period. (The measurements were not made continuously during the entire measurement period.) The time spent in the null state is assumed to be zero. Table 8.17 shows the results of the clustering operation. You can see that for about 36 percent of the time the CPU was heavily loaded (0.96), and for 76 percent of the time the CPU load was above 0.5.

8.7.2.2 Resource-usage/error/failure model. Error data during the measurement period were passed through a coalescing algorithm and then through an additional reduction technique based on the probabilistic relationships between errors [Iyer90]. The resulting errors were then classified into five classes:

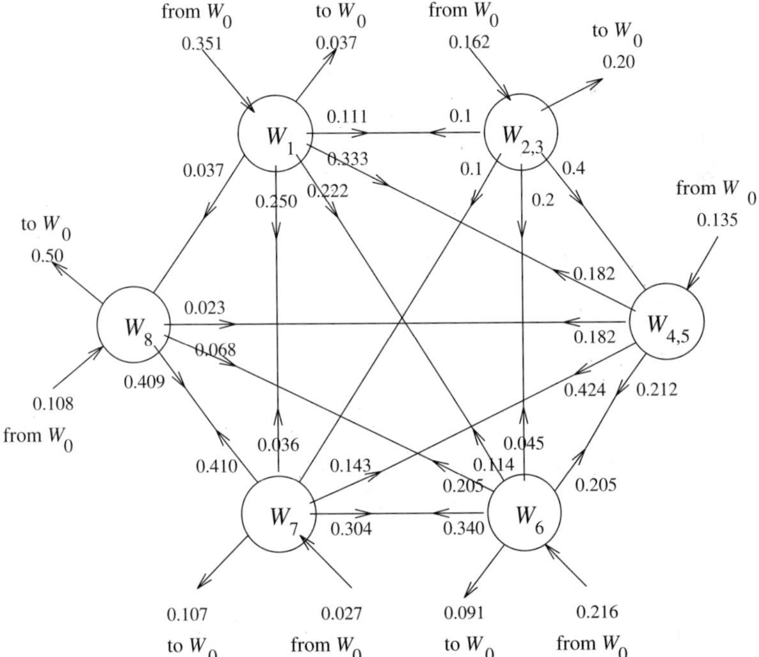

Figure 8.18 State transition diagram of CPU-bound load.

TABLE 8.17 Characteristics of CPU-Bound Workload Clusters

Cluster id	% of obs	Mean of CPU	Mean of CHB	Std. dev. of CPU	Std. dev. of CHB
W_1	7.44	0.0981	0.1072	0.0462	0.0436
W_2	0.50	0.1126	0.5525	0.0433	0.0669
W_3	2.73	0.1547	0.2801	0.0647	0.0755
W_4	12.41	0.3105	0.1637	0.0550	0.0459
W_5	0.74	0.3639	0.3819	0.0365	0.1923
W_6	17.12	0.5416	0.1287	0.0560	0.0511
W_7	22.58	0.7207	0.0848	0.0576	0.0301
W_8	36.48	0.9612	0.0168	0.0362	0.0143

R^2 of CPU = 0.9724
R^2 of CHB = 0.8095
overall R^2 = 0.9604
(R^2: the square of correlation coefficient)

1. CPU — Errors that affect the normal operation of the CPU; may originate in the CPU, in the main memory, or in a channel
2. CHAN — Channel errors (the great majority are recovered)
3. DASD — Disk errors, recoverable (by data correction or instruction retry) and nonrecoverable
4. SWE — Software incidents due to invalid supervisor calls, program checks, and other exceptions
5. MULT — Multiple errors that affect more than one type of component (i.e., involving more than one of the above)

The recovery procedures were divided into four categories based on recovery cost, which was measured in terms of the system overhead needed to handle an error. The lowest level (hardware recovery or HWR) involves the use of an error correction code (ECC) or hardware instruction retry; it has minimal overhead. If hardware recovery is not possible or unsuccessful, software-controlled recovery (SWR) is invoked. This could be simple (e.g., terminating the current program or task in control) or complex (e.g., invoking a specially designed recovery routine(s) to handle the problem). The third level, alternative (ALT), involves transferring the tasks to functioning processor(s) when one of the processors experiences an unrecoverable error. If no on-line recovery is possible, the system is brought down for off-line (OFFL) repair.

The separate workload, error, and recovery models developed were combined into a single model, shown in Fig. 8.19. Due to the complexity of the entire model, the figure shows only a part of the model. The null state W_0 is not shown in the diagram. The model in Fig. 8.19 captures the workload-dependent error and recovery process in the system. The model has three classes of state: normal operation states (S_N), error states (S_E), and recovery states (S_R). Under normal conditions, the system makes transitions from one workload state to another. The occurrence of an error results in a transition to one of the error states. The system then goes into one or more recovery states after which, with a high probability, it returns to one of the workload states. You can see from the state transition diagram that nearly 98.3 percent of hardware recovery requests and 99.7 percent of software recovery requests are successful.

8.7.2.3 Performability analysis. The resource-usage/error/recovery model was used to evaluate the performability of the system. Reward functions were used to depict the performance degradation due to errors and due to different types of recovery procedure (App. B). Since the recovery overhead for each error event in the modeled system is approximately constant, the total recovery overhead, and thus the reward, depends on the error rate during the event. On this basis, the reward rate r_i (per unit time) for each state of the model is defined as

$$r_i = \begin{cases} \dfrac{s_i}{s_i + e_i} & \text{if } i \in S_N \cup S_E \\ 0 & \text{if } i \in S_R \end{cases} \tag{8.14}$$

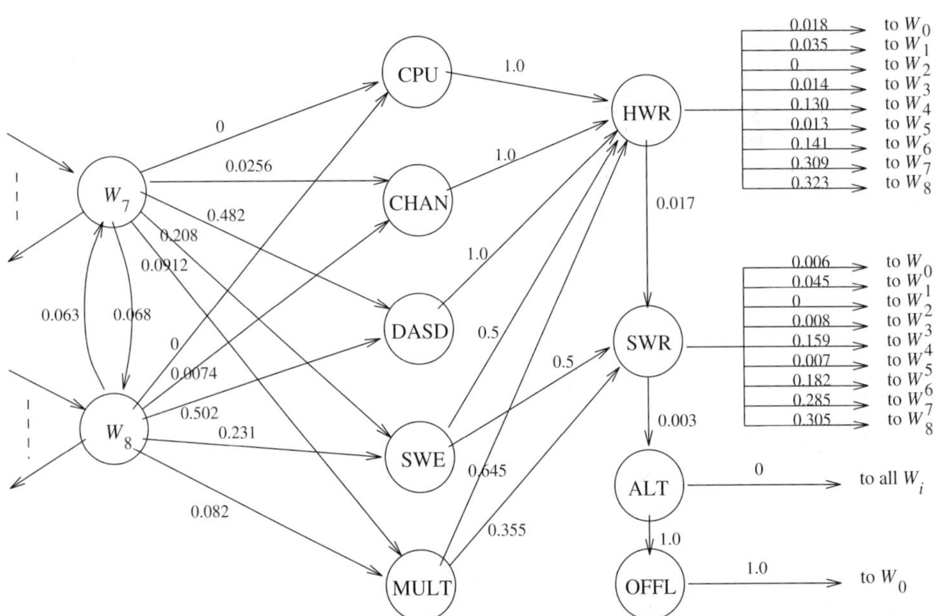

Figure 8.19 State transition diagram of resource-usage/error/recovery model.

where s_i and e_i are the service rate and the error rate in state i, respectively. Thus one unit of reward is given for each unit of time when the system stays in the normal states S_N. The reward rate decreases with increasing number of errors generated in an error state. Zero reward is assigned to recovery states.

The reward rate of the modeled system at time t is a random variable $X(t)$. Therefore, the expected reward rate $E[X(t)]$ can be evaluated from $E[X(t)] = \Sigma_i p_i(t) r_i$ where $p_i(t)$ is the probability of being in state i at time t. The cumulative reward by time t is $Y(t) = \int_0^t X(\sigma) d\sigma$, and the expected cumulative reward is given by

$$E[Y(t)] = E\left(\int_0^t X(\sigma) d\sigma\right) = \sum_i r_i \int_0^t p_i(\sigma) d\sigma \tag{8.15}$$

The impact of different types of errors were evaluated by calculating the expected reward rate with different definitions of absorption state. In Fig. 8.20, "OFFL" represents the expected reward rate when only off-line repairs are considered as an absorption state. This curve actually represents the system reliability. "MULT" represents the expected reward rate when off-line repairs and multiple errors are considered as an absorption state. The difference between the two curves captures the impact of multiple errors on performability.

8.8 Summary

In this chapter, we discussed the current issues in the area of measurement-based analysis of software reliability in the operational phase. The discussion centered around techniques, our experiences, and major developments in this area. This chapter addressed measurement techniques, analysis of data, model identification, analysis of models, and the effects of workload on software reliability. For each field, we discussed the key issues and then presented detailed techniques and representative work.

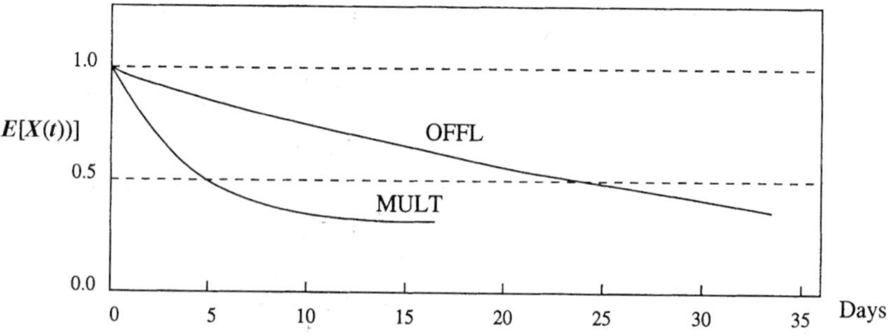

Figure 8.20 Expected reward rate.

Significant progress has been made in all these fields over the past 15 years. Increasing attention is being paid to: (1) combining analytical modeling and experimental analysis and (2) combining software design and evaluation. In the first aspect, state-of-the-art analytical modeling techniques are being applied to real operational software to evaluate various reliability and performance characteristics. Results from experimental analysis are being used to validate analytical models and to reveal practical issues that analytical modeling must address to develop more representative models. In the second aspect, software failure data from the operational phase are being used to identify and address software design issues for improving software reliability. Efficient on-line recovery and off-line diagnosis techniques are being developed based on data collected from the operational phase. Further interesting studies and advances in this area can be expected in the near future.

Problems

8.1 Discuss the power and limitations of measurement-based approach, as compared with analytic or simulation-based approach.

8.2 Reliability characteristics of operational software can be quite different from those of the software in its development phase. List the factors that contribute to such differences.

8.3 Describe general steps to build a software reliability model from measurements. What is the use of a measurement-based model?

8.4 It has been shown that software errors tend to occur in bursts. Discuss the reasons for error bursts. What are the effects of error bursts on software reliability?

8.5 Software and hardware components of a computer system may not fail independently of each other. Discuss the reasons for such correlated failures. Discuss the techniques for analyzing two-way and multiway failure dependencies.

8.6 Checkpointing and restart implemented in distributed transaction processing environments can allow a system to tolerate certain software faults. What are the reasons for the software fault tolerance? What are the factors that determine the level of software fault tolerance achieved with the technique in such environments? What are the advantages and disadvantages of using the above technique as compared with using the techniques such as N-version programming and recovery blocks?

8.7 It has been shown that, in environments where many users run the same software, the majority of field software failures are recurrences. What are the reasons for recurrences? What are the effects of recurrences on software reliability? How can we reduce such effects?

8.8 What are the effects of increased system activity on software reliability in an operational system? Discuss the reasons for such relationships.

8.9 Table 8.18 shows software time-to-failure (TTF) data measured on a multicomputer system. Table 8.19 shows the completion time (CT) of a benchmark running on a multicomputer system under different workload conditions. The time in Tables 8.18 and 8.19 represents the time at the end of the corresponding time interval. For example, the first column of Table 8.18 indicates that there are 29 TTF instances whose values are smaller than 1 day. Do the following work using the data:

a. Construct an empirical distribution for each set of data.
b. Fit both empirical distributions to an exponential function, the TTF distribution to a two-phase hyperexponential function, and the CT distribution to a two-phase hypoexponential function, respectively.
c. Test the goodness of fits using the chi-square test.

8.10 Table 8.20 (shown below and in the Data Disk) gives processor failure data collected from a distributed system consisting of five processors connected by a local network. Each record in the table has the following format:

Processor id	Failure time	Recovery time	Error type

The time unit is second and time 0 is 12 A.M., 10/1/1987. The measurement started from 12 A.M., 12/9/1987 (29,548,800), and ended at 12 A.M., 8/15/1988 (51,148,800), covering 250 days. The error type means the type of error that causes a processor failure. Possible error types are CPU, I/O (network or disk problems), software, and unknown. Do the following work using the data:

a. Obtain failure rate and recovery rate for each processor.

TABLE 8.18 Software TTF Data from a Multicomputer

TTF (days)	1	2	3	4	5	6	7	8	9	10	11	12	13
Frequency	29	8	6	5	3	3	1	3	1	1	1	2	1
TTF (days)	14	15	15	17	18	19	20	21	22	23	24	25	26
Frequency	0	2	0	1	0	0	0	0	0	0	0	0	1

TABLE 8.19 Completion Time of a Benchmark

Time (min.)	2	4	6	8	10	12	14	16	18	20	22	24
Frequency	2	10	12	18	16	13	15	7	6	4	2	6
Time (min.)	26	28	30	32	34	36	38	40	42	44	46	48
Frequency	4	1	0	1	4	0	0	1	1	0	0	0

TABLE 8.20 Processor Failure Data from a Five-Processor Multicomputer System

Processor id	Start time	End time	Error type
1	29604556	29605120	Software
1	29704893	29706486	I/O
1	29770774	29772334	Software
1	29779466	29779946	I/O
1	29918361	29919001	I/O
1	29938155	29938995	Unknown
1	29968514	29969314	I/O
1	30204850	30206947	I/O
1	30300136	30300482	I/O
1	30315829	30316496	I/O
1	30552159	30555408	Unknown
1	30571134	30571529	I/O
1	31762359	31762897	I/O
1	31830453	31831347	I/O
1	31837833	31838304	I/O
1	31839160	31839628	I/O
1	31951476	31952241	I/O
1	32123531	32124925	I/O
1	32126834	32127160	I/O
1	32177392	32178646	I/O
1	32963455	32964054	Software
1	33014870	33015438	I/O
1	33152933	33153737	Software
1	34616577	34617326	Software
1	34770846	34771459	I/O
1	37813703	37814561	Unknown
1	38007128	38049817	I/O
1	38955976	38956597	Unknown
1	38961843	38962658	Unknown
1	39465650	39467247	I/O
1	39809295	39810575	Unknown
1	40069978	40071607	I/O
1	41000249	41001273	Software
1	41366807	41387784	Software
1	41391480	41392113	Software
1	42272616	42273174	Software
1	42831896	42833058	Software
1	43309767	43313204	Software
1	43348292	43350322	Software
1	43952410	43953022	Software
1	44877091	44877998	Software
1	45841909	45842888	Software
1	46961851	46962724	Software
1	48878979	48880349	Unknown
1	48888392	48890586	Software
2	29570604	29570904	I/O
2	29577262	29577562	I/O
2	29767256	29767556	I/O
2	29782058	29782358	I/O
2	29788920	29789718	I/O
2	29886930	29887230	I/O

TABLE 8.20 ***(Continued)*** **Processor Failure Data from a Five-Processor Multicomputer System**

Processor id	Start time	End time	Error type
2	29909506	29909806	I/O
2	29910884	29911926	I/O
2	29913095	29913465	I/O
2	29914121	29915273	I/O
2	29916032	29916705	I/O
2	29917194	29917844	I/O
2	29918236	29919428	I/O
2	29939825	29940125	Unknown
2	29946828	29947128	Unknown
2	29949602	29950199	I/O
2	29953804	29954104	I/O
2	29957176	29957476	I/O
2	29963079	29963379	I/O
2	29964579	29966271	I/O
2	29967435	29968115	I/O
2	30550260	30550560	Unknown
2	30550946	30553816	Software
2	30660369	30660669	Unknown
2	31774557	31774857	I/O
2	31775859	31776450	I/O
2	31781002	31781783	I/O
2	31832367	31832781	I/O
2	31839101	31841182	I/O
2	32122929	32129036	I/O
2	32176731	32177250	Software
2	32178134	32180594	I/O
2	32183767	32184321	I/O
2	32449592	32450399	Unknown
2	32962291	32962591	Unknown
2	32975370	32975670	I/O
2	32976674	32976974	I/O
2	32983427	32983727	I/O
2	33049654	33050104	I/O
2	33052795	33053095	I/O
2	33057253	33057553	I/O
2	33059795	33060095	I/O
2	33087233	33087533	I/O
2	33089396	33089696	I/O
2	33120965	33121265	Unknown
2	33148035	33148430	I/O
2	34011900	34012200	Unknown
2	34770845	34771810	I/O
2	34774453	34774753	Unknown
2	34775145	34776270	I/O
2	34777013	34777313	I/O
2	34777969	34778269	I/O
2	34780806	34781106	I/O
2	35659389	35662510	Unknown
2	35668585	35668885	I/O
2	35725413	35725713	I/O
2	35726840	35727669	I/O

TABLE 8.20 ***(Continued)*** **Processor Failure Data from a Five-Processor Multicomputer System**

Processor id	Start time	End time	Error type
2	35730910	35731210	I/O
2	35744817	35745117	I/O
2	35753244	35753544	I/O
2	36785044	36785772	Unknown
2	36789532	36789988	Software
2	36796257	36847121	I/O
2	38249305	38249785	Software
2	38251655	38252099	Unknown
2	38744311	38744777	Software
2	38745674	38746341	CPU
2	38955454	38956597	Unknown
2	39805355	39808038	I/O
2	43064089	43065444	Unknown
2	44732995	44733453	Software
2	45221452	45221917	I/O
2	46375146	46375583	Unknown
2	49391794	49392273	Software
2	50068269	50069049	I/O
3	30550976	30554633	Software
3	31760114	31760624	Software
3	32806356	32806844	Software
3	33152933	33153558	Software
3	34370843	34385770	I/O
3	34779280	34779754	Unknown
3	36783938	36786522	I/O
3	36787771	36788262	Software
3	37800626	37811789	I/O
3	37812929	37813548	Software
3	43175442	43175990	Software
3	43326842	43327797	Unknown
3	43330318	43330785	CPU
3	43331708	43332312	CPU
3	43334898	43338477	CPU
3	43338720	43340663	I/O
3	43342983	43345110	CPU
3	43691509	43692018	Software
3	43693033	43693689	Unknown
3	43693580	43694622	I/O
3	43695584	43696455	Unknown
3	43697283	43698493	I/O
3	47651456	47651969	Software
3	49057997	49058626	Software
3	49568366	49568810	Unknown
3	50043031	50043500	Software
3	50697666	50698119	Unknown
3	50930312	50930764	Unknown
4	29939050	29940425	I/O
4	29943202	29948396	I/O
4	30550948	30554287	I/O
4	30762674	30762976	I/O
4	34777878	34778529	I/O

TABLE 8.20 ***(Continued)*** **Processor Failure Data from a Five-Processor Multicomputer System**

Processor id	Start time	End time	Error type
4	37563700	37567137	I/O
4	37811277	37811786	I/O
4	38956002	38963057	I/O
4	39204773	39205074	I/O
4	43175015	43175315	Unknown
4	47239532	47243366	I/O
4	47641698	47642345	I/O
4	48939418	48940072	Unknown
4	49144906	49145430	I/O
4	50662627	50663276	Unknown
4	50668168	50672456	I/O
4	50758111	50758751	I/O
4	50941271	50943381	I/O
5	30545108	30545606	Software
5	30551262	30553813	Unknown
5	31769662	31770215	Software
5	31953896	31954395	Unknown
5	33152335	33153779	Unknown
5	33153616	33156417	Software
5	34774852	34780711	I/O
5	37813181	37813664	Unknown
5	38955806	38962854	Unknown
5	40928410	40934268	Software
5	40936013	40936767	Unknown
5	43189066	43193507	Software
5	43252583	43254201	Unknown
5	43256847	43257890	Unknown
5	43328379	43333113	Software
5	44903066	44903945	Unknown
5	47064423	47069097	I/O
5	49125607	49126676	Software
5	49478273	49478888	Unknown
5	50618397	50623146	Software

b. Assuming failures on different processors are independent, build a Markov model based on the failure and recovery rates obtained in item *a.*

c. Assuming the modeled system is a three-out-of-five system, solve the model (using SHARPE [Sahn87, Sahn95] or similar tools) to obtain the reliability of the system. (Note: To obtain SHARPE, contact Professor Kishor Trivedi at Duke University. Phone: (919) 660-5269, e-mail: kst@ee.egr.duke.edu.)

d. Build a measurement-based Markov model using the data without assuming failures on different processors are independent.

e. Solve the measurement-based model (using SHARPE or similar tools) to obtain the reliability of the three-out-of-five system, and compare the result with that obtained in item *c.*

f. Construct a failure data matrix and then use the matrix to calculate correlation coefficient for each pair.

Chapter

9

Orthogonal Defect Classification

Ram Chillarege
IBM Watson Research

9.1 Introduction

One of the perpetual challenges for measurement in the software development process is to provide fast and effective feedback to developers. Traditional techniques, although they provide good report cards, seldom have the fine insight into the process or product to truly guide decision making. Thus it is not uncommon to witness decisions guided more by intuition than by true measurement, analysis, and engineering.

Orthogonal defect classification (ODC) makes a fundamental improvement in the level of technology available to assist software engineering decisions via measurement and analysis. This is achieved by exploiting software defects that occur all the way through development and field use, capturing a significant amount of information. ODC extracts the information from defects cleverly, converting what is semantically very rich into a few vital measurements on the product and the process. These measurements provide a firm footing upon which sophisticated analysis and methodologies are developed. Thus it is possible to emulate some of the detail and expansiveness of qualitative analysis with the low cost and mathematical tractability of quantitative methods.

At IBM Watson Research we began a program to place ODC in the real world of software development. Over the past few years, it has been deployed at a dozen IBM locations, worldwide, in over 50 projects. It has also been extended to apply at different parts of the development cycle and different layers of decision making. Over time there have been analytical methods, tools, methodologies, feedback techniques, diagnosis procedures, and support processes developed to fit different needs. When applied to reduce the cost of classical root-cause analysis, it achieves cost reductions by a factor of 10. An organization that fully employed ODC, coupled with the Butterfly model [Bass93], has seen a cycle-time reduction by a factor of 3, and achieved a defect reduction by a factor of 80 in 5 years.

This chapter is designed to provide an overview of ODC, complete with examples illustrating its real-world application. It begins with an overview of the domain of defects in software development, followed by examples which motivate the ODC concept. Since the concepts are fairly new, we have chosen to describe two attributes—the defect type and trigger—in detail, which provide measurement instruments on the development process and the verification process. The latter part of the trigger section illustrates how the two together provide measures of effectiveness. These sections are complete with definitions so that it is possible to start some sample prototypes. ODC is primarily a multidimensional measurement system, which allows for very creative analysis. The end of this chapter hints at this and briefly sketches the current implementation at IBM, which includes two additional attributes: source and impact. We have, of course, assumed that classical measures such as severity and process-phase identifiers exist, since most defect-tracking systems provide them. The key in all such endeavors is to set up a measurement system (not merely a classification taxonomy) that is clean, expandable, and broadly applicable. We believe ODC makes a significant stride in accomplishing that.

9.2 Measurement and Software

Software, as most of us know, is a very difficult area in which to develop crisp in-process measurements and analysis techniques. Nevertheless, the need to get a grasp on the software development processes is vital to manage it as a business. This need becomes ever more critical as the software industry grows, reaching almost $100 billion in 1995,* and becomes more competitive. The task has enchanted software engineering for decades, but the solutions available were much too primitive to significantly impact the level of technology in practice. The best practices in the software industry have therefore remained largely human-intensive processes, which are qualitative, suffer poor repeatability, and have difficult introduction barriers.

The software development process is amorphous by nature—be it waterfall, iterative development, or an undefined chaotic process. The definitions of activities within a process and transitions between them are dependent largely on human behavior as opposed to being enforced by physical restrictions or conceptual roadblocks. The few crisp separa-

* *Business Week* summary of the computer industry, 1995.

tions between activities are primarily due to the rigidity of tools and their limitations. Thus, measurement in the software development environment is a tough challenge until tools exist to automatically extract them. As technology evolves and new tools are invented, they directly compete with some of the activities defined within a process. A technology might render an existing process-based activity ineffective or even unnecessary. Thus, processes have to be flexible and sensitive to accommodate such advances. At the same time, the measurement system needs to make the corresponding compensations. For instance, code inspection used to include a large number of checks to guard against errors due to the operational semantics of languages. As syntactic checkers and tools such as Lint became more powerful, they rendered some of these checks unnecessary. However, when the code inspection process and related measurements did not quickly adapt to these advances, some development communities reacted by doing away with code inspections altogether. In this particular case, the resultant loss was significant, since inspections addressed a much broader set of issues.

Measures related to software defects have survived the evolution of software development processes and are still widely used despite large variability in processes. The popular belief is that this is because defect counts provide a measure of product quality and, indirectly, productivity. However, the real reason, we believe, is far more subtle. A software defect signifies stoppage in the product development process. By the time the defect is resolved several activities and pieces of work occur. Thus, the defect has the potential to capture a variety of information on the product and the process—thereby providing an excellent measurement opportunity. Thus, defect-related information is actively used for a variety of purposes ranging from work completion to resource management to schedule estimation to risk analysis, and even continuous improvement.

This chapter is an exposition on the use of defects to measure, manage, and understand the software development process. Although the use of defect data has existed for years, its exploitation has been limited due to the lack of some fundamental insights. Orthogonal defect classification provides this insight and a framework to achieve the next order of technology.

9.2.1 Software defects

The word *defect* tends to include in its meaning more than a mathematician would like to attribute to it. From the perspective of strict definition it often captures the fault, sometimes the error, and often the failure. Given the wide range of meanings that could be attributed to a defect we need to clarify how defect data are used, what aspect is being used, and for what purpose. Before we delve further we must first understand the kind of defects that appear in software development, and arrive at a reasonably unambiguous definition for the word *defect.*

Software defects occur all the way through the life cycle of software development—from conception of product to end of life. The vernacular of development organizations tends to name and treat defects as different objects depending on when or where they are found. Some of the more common names are *bug, error, comment, program trouble memoranda, problem,* and *authorized program analysis report* (APAR). For starters, let us describe a couple situations where defects are identified, and then develop a more unifying definition.

When design documents and requirements are written, they are usually captured in plain text. Although there is increasing emphasis on documenting them in design tools, that is yet an evolving technology. When these documents are reviewed among peers, they can result in comments that question or critique the design. These comments may eventually result in changes. The concept of *failure* here is broader than its strict definition. A potential failure is identified by the human recognizing a departure, exception, or a gaping hole in the design. The corrective action results in changes that fix a likely fault. The comments and the resultant changes are essentially defects. Unfortunately, from a measurement perspective, quite often these defects are not formally captured by an organization and can be lost in desk drawers.

When a customer calls with a *problem* experienced with a product, it might be due to a software failure caused by a fault. On the other hand, not all problems experienced are due to the classical software programming bug causing a failure. More often than not (sometimes 80 to 90 percent), a customer calls experiencing difficulties due to poor procedures, unclear documentation, poor user interfaces, etc. The product may actually be working as designed, but poorly and much to the dissatisfaction of the customer. In some of these cases, the vendor may admit to the poor workings of the product and open a defect against it. This could eventually result in a fix being developed and distributed.

One of the primary difficulties with the notion of failure in software is that it is more amorphous than in hardware. The scientific definition accepted for *failure* is "deviation of the delivered service from compliance with the specification" [Lapr92a]. However, there is rarely a well-documented specification for most software in the industry. It is common practice to recognize a failure when a piece of software does not meet customer expectations. The corresponding fault can be equally obscure to identify, particularly in areas such as usability. The terms *fault, error,* and *failure* provide a good conceptualization model that we can draw from. However, for the practicality of implementation, ease of understanding, and a tangible connection to the real world, we develop the concept of a *defect:* simply put, it is a necessary change to the software.

There is a subtlety in saying that the *necessary* change is the defect. This is because it could be the case that a change was necessary but was not executed. It may have been forgotten, or remembered but without the resources to fix it. It is still a defect, since it was deemed a necessary change. Treating the necessary change as a defect ties the metaphysical concept of a fault, error, and sometimes failure to a physical action on the product that is more traceable. No matter what the development environment, the activity is specific and can become the anchor point from which other measurements can follow.

A software product usually begins with some set of requirements, either explicitly stated by a customer or identified through a vision of the market. Between the requirements and the availability of the product, there is design, code development, and test. The words *design, code,* and *test* do not automatically imply a pure waterfall process. On the other hand, it is hard to imagine a successful product developed without requirements, or code written without a design, or tests conducted without code. A pure waterfall process tends to have these phases well identified and separated with documents that capture the essence of these phases, providing well-defined handoffs between them. In more recent times, the small team with iterative development is popular, where the reliance on documentation and distinct handoffs are less emphasized. However, having some record of completion and milestones within a process is not only useful for project management but necessary for internal communication.

No matter what the implementation of a software development process, there are artifacts that are developed and storage mediums where the artifacts are recorded. Depending on the tools and methods, these artifacts may be on paper, images on tape, code in libraries, meeting minutes, discussions yielding decisions, etc. Furthermore, there is a time after which a work item is considered committed. It may not yet be completed, but being committed implies a clear record of intent. Any further necessary changes to the work item that becomes a product is considered a defect. Depending on the tools used in a development process, the identification and tracking of defects may be easy or difficult.

A process usually has several checks interspersed to ensure that the product being developed meets the record of intent. These checks could be reviews, inspections, informal tests, formal functional tests, stress tests, etc. Each of these verification efforts can identify deviations to the intent, which warrant change. Anything that requires change is a defect. Thus, there are defects that arise from requirements inspection, design inspection (usually, a high level and a low level), a code inspection (of which there might be one or two), a unit test, a functional verification test, and a system test. All these verification efforts can yield defects. Depending on what is included in a count, we find the number of defects per thousand lines of code varies, from as low as 10 to as high as 120.

9.2.2 The spectrum of defect analysis

Analysis of software defects has existed for a long time in the industry. One of the more common forms is bean counting for purposes such as estimating completion time and warranty cost. Another popular form of defect analysis is qualitative—to recognize the types of errors committed and guide defect prevention. Stepping back from the variety of methods of defect analysis, we can recognize a broad spectrum in its usage. The two extremes of this spectrum are distinctly defined, and Fig. 9.1 captures some of its elements. The left-hand extreme signifies purely quantitative methods such as mathematical and statistical methods. The right-hand extreme signifies purely qualitative analyses such as those employed in quality circles and defect prevention programs. There is a large white space between these extremes, which is the subject of this chapter. Before we delve into this white space, let us examine the extremes first.

An example of the left-hand extreme is statistical models of defect discovery. One of the well-known examples is the Raleigh model. This is an abstraction that is simple and intuitive, and has found extensive use. Another example is the software reliability models, several of which are discussed in this handbook (see Chaps. 3, 4, 6, and 7). As useful as these are, one has to recognize that they are the mathematicians' approximation of the defect process. Defect counts measure just one of the many effects of the complex human process of software development. In and of itself it represents a small part of the information from

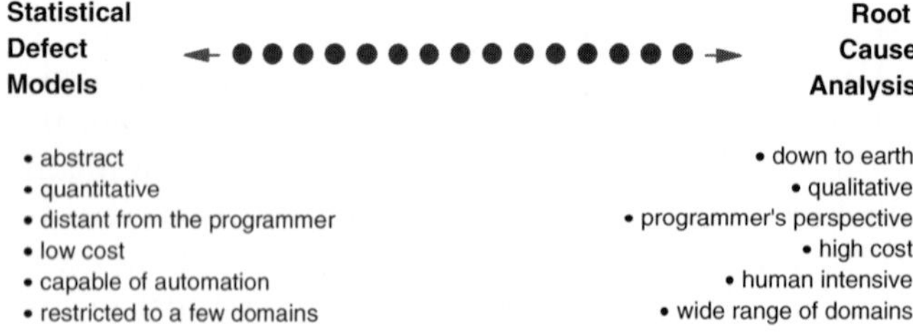

Figure 9.1 The spectrum of process measurement and analysis.

the software development process. We do not understate its implication or use, but recognize up front the overall scope and opportunity that is exploited or left unexploited.

A good example of the right-hand extreme is the classical approach toward defect prevention using causal analysis of defects. The origins are traceable to Demming and Juran and a more recent implementation of the process described in [Mays90, Hump89]. The methods employed are detailed qualitative analysis of defects, often conducted by a small team of people. The goal is to identify practices or oversights that could be prevented by implementing corrective or educational actions in the development organization. This is not a quick process, either for the analysis or the implementation of the program. For example, a team of four people discussing defects could reasonably work through three or four in an hour, yielding a cost of one person-hour per defect for the analysis phase. This is usually followed by action teams that execute the plans and directions developed from such analysis. It is not uncommon to see organizations that have developed ambitious action lists without the resources or commitment to execute them. The challenge is mostly one of prioritization and knowing the cost/benefit of such actions. This fact does not detract from the success of defect prevention. There have been significant improvements in quality and productivity reported. The challenge is how to do it cleverly. The traditional methods of laborious qualitative analysis followed by poor prioritization do not make it attractive in a world of short cycle time and reduced budgets.

Between the two extremes of the spectrum (quantitative statistical defect models and qualitative causal analysis) is a wide gap. This gap is characterized by a lack of good measurement methods that are meaningful to the developer and that exploit good engineering methods. At one extreme, the traditional mathematical modeling efforts tend to step back from the details of the process and to approximate defect detection by a statistical process [Litt73, Ohba84]. When calibrated, some of these methods are shown to be quite repeatable. However, they do not provide timely feedback to the developer in terms of available process controls. At the other extreme, the causal analysis mechanism is qualitative and labor-intensive; it can provide feedback on each individual defect. However, in a large development effort it is akin to studying the ocean floor with a microscope. It does not naturally evolve into abstractions and aggregations that can feed into engineering mechanisms to be used for overall process control.

It is not as though there has been no work done between these extremes. There is a myriad of reported research and industry attempts to quantify the parameters of the software development process with "metrics" [IEEE90a, IEEE90b]. Some efforts have been more successful than others. For example, the relationship between the defects that occur during software development and the complexity of a software product has been discussed in [Basi84a]. Such information, when compiled over the history of an organization [Basi88], will be useful for planners and designers. On the other hand, the focus of empirical studies has largely been to validate hypotheses that could be turned into a set of general guidelines. Unfortunately, the variability in productivity, skill, and process makes such findings difficult to establish. Each develolpment effort appears unique, making the task of treating them as repeatable experiments hard. Over the years, this has led to disillusionment of software measurement and in some extremes a distaste for the effort, particularly when developers are both skeptical about process change and resistant to the extra burden. Yet, it remains one of the most important technological areas in which to make progress, given where the software industry is headed.

As we shall see, this cause is not without hope. Only recently have there been studies to examine the feasibility of serious analytical software engineering. The work explored the capability of taking the semantically rich information from the defect stream and turning it into measurements. At the same time it tried to establish the existence of information that could predict the behavior of a software development effort via such measurements. The successes illustrated that a new class of methods can be developed that rely on semantic extraction of information linking the qualitative aspects from the right extreme of the spectrum to measurable computable aspects from the left extreme. The semantic extraction is done via classification. The link with the right extreme occurs when the classification has properties that make it a measurement. It should not be confused with a mere taxonomy of defects such as [IEEE87b], which serves a descriptive purpose. ODC makes the classification into a measurement that helps bridge the gap.

In summary, although measurements had been extensively used in software engineering, it still remained a challenge to turn software development into a measurable and controllable process. Why is this so? Primarily because no process can be modeled as an observable and controllable system unless explicit input-output or cause-and-effect relationships are established. Furthermore, such causes and effects should be easily measurable. It is inadequate to propose that a collection of measures be used to track a process, with the hope that some subset of these measures will actually explain the process. There should at least be a small subset that is carefully designed based on a good understanding of the mechanisms within the process.

Looking at the history of software modeling, it is evident that little heed has been paid to the actual cause-effect mechanism, let alone investigations to establish them. At the other extreme, when cause and effect was recognized, though qualitatively, it was not abstracted to a level from which it could graduate to engineering models. To the best of our knowledge, in the world of in-process measurements, until recently there has been no systematic study to establish the existence of measurable cause-and-effect relationships in a software development process. Without that insight and a rational basis, it is difficult to argue that any one measurement scheme or model is better than another.

9.3 Principles of ODC

Orthogonal defect classification (ODC) is a technique that can bridge the gap between quantitative methods and qualitative analysis. It does so by bringing in scientific methods by defining a measurement system in an area that has been historically ad hoc. This naturally provides a firm footing upon which sophisticated and detailed analysis can be developed. Fundamentally, we extract semantic information in defects via classification. ODC properties ensure that the classified data become measurements. As these measurements are related to the process and environment they provide the instrumentation for very detailed and precise feedback. Thus defects which are rich in information can be scientifically exploited to assist the decision-making process in software engineering.

9.3.1 The intuition

ODC is best described with an example that captures some of the motivations and provides an intuitive understanding of the concept. The detailed technical description can then be built on this base. We do so by illustrating, in Example 9.1, a situation from the real world. The objective is to contrast the classical methods of growth modeling with what can be achieved via semantics extraction from defects.

Example 9.1 The example is from the development of a component of 80,000 to 100,000 lines of code in an operating systems product. During the last few drivers (and months) of system test it became evident that there was a crisis in stability and completion. The top part of Fig. 9.2 shows the cumulative number of defects over time. Ideally, it should plateau, signifying a decreasing number of defects being detected and promising fewer defects in the field. Although the figure shows a slight plateau, it is artificial since these data did not include defects found in the field. It is the steep increase in the defect rate during period 3 leading to the near doubling of development defects, which identifies the criticality of the situation. Classical growth curve modeling techniques would recognize this trend and identify the problem. The issue is that by the time growth modeling can identify the problem, it is too late to take all but some desperate reactive measures.

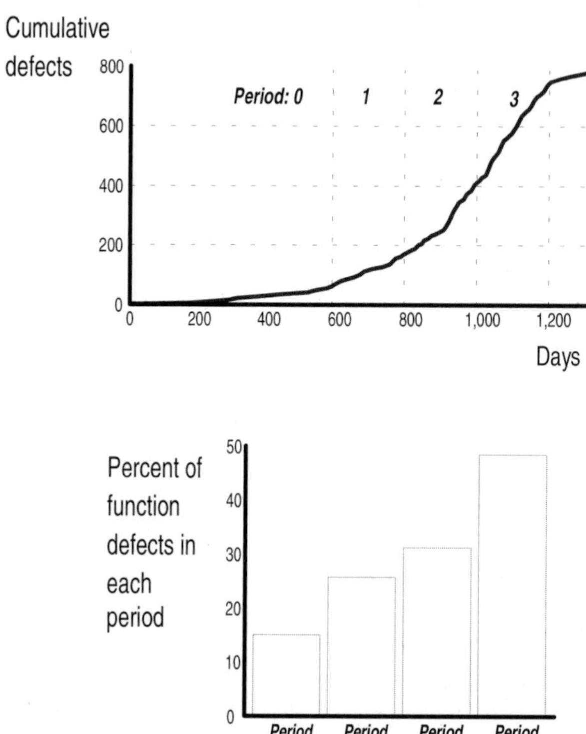

Figure 9.2 Total defects and proportion of function-type defects.

We attempt to do better than raw counts of defects by using the semantic information in them. To do so, we categorized defects into these classes: *assignment, checking, function, interface,* and *timing.* In the paradigm of programming, there are only certain ways to fix a programming problem. These categories capture the essence of what was fixed, thereby identifying the nature of work necessary to fix the defect. This we call the *defect type.* Samples of defects from the three periods are categorized into this defect type attribute. We then examine how the distribution contributed by defects changes as a function of time. For the purposes of illustration, the lower part of Fig. 9.2 shows just the proportion of defects that have the type function during each period.

The early periods of development are characterized by larger amounts of design, whereas the latter parts are characterized by greater amounts of system test and less of function test. Thus, the expectation would be that the proportion of defects of type function would be larger initially and smaller later. However, the data show exactly the opposite trend. Period 3, which was largely system test, shows close to 50 percent of the defects being of type function. The fact that the proportion of functional defects kept rising is discernible even in period 2. This identifies the crises that occurred by using semantic information almost six months earlier than by using raw defect counts. Furthermore, it also points to the potential cause of the problem and motivates corrective measures. In this case, it will require the appropriate skills (possibly design) to start examining the code and design. Reactive measures such as redoubling the test effort are unlikely to be as effective.

Example 9.1 illustrates the use of qualitative information in defects converted to a quantitative measure to make earlier predictions than more traditional quantitative methods. In addition, it provides clues to the reasons, which are translatable to recommendations for action. In Example 9.1, a causal analysis team could be directed to focus on a few of the function defects to provide further guidance to the development team. This approach avoids "boiling the ocean" to determine causality, since the problem and scope are better understood.

We need to extend this idea further toward a general case. Figure 9.3 shows a hypothetical distribution of defect types across the phases of design, unit test, integration, and system test. For the purposes of illustration we show just four defect types: function, assignment, interface, and timing. The fact that the process phases are shown in sequence does not imply a strict waterfall development process. As long as these activities exist (in any order or repeatedly), defects from these activities are used to construct the four defect-type distributions. The concept is that we examine the normalized distribution of all defects found during a phase against what the process should achieve. The bar representing function defects is steadily decreasing from design all the way to system test. This would make sense given that the intent of a design phase is to deal with functional issues and the expectation is that fewer of them have to be dealt with at system test. It is reasonable to anticipate that the proportion of timing defects would increase quite the opposite way to functional defects. System test occurs when the product is on the real hardware and is more likely to be stressed by timing conditions. The assignment and checking kinds of defects are likely to peak during unit test and fall either before or after that phase, whereas interfaces defects would possibly peak during the integration test and fall off on either side of those process stages. By defining a distribution that changes with the process activity we have created a very powerful instrument. *This instrument will allow us to measure the progress of a product through the process.* Changes in the distribution are easy to measure and are invariant to the total number of defects injected by a development community. A departure from the expected distribution or a change from the expected trend identifies problems and recommends possible corrective action. For instance, had the defect-type distribution at system test looked like that of unit test, we could argue that although the product met physical schedule dates it probably hadn't progressed logically. The offending defect type would be in a large number of function

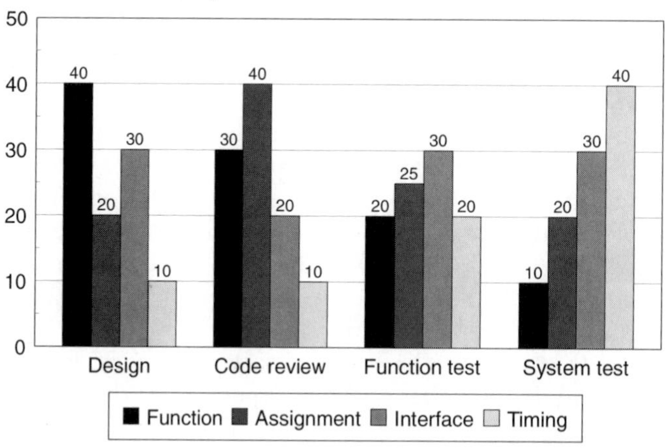

Figure 9.3 Change in the defect-type distribution with phase.

and assignment defects relative to the expected numbers, requiring that the corrective actions address those departures.

9.3.2 The design of orthogonal defect classification

The preceding was a hypothetical discussion of defect-type categories and what that could mean in the process space. In actuality, we use more than four defect types, which we illustrate with some real-life examples. It is useful at this point to conceptualize what it is that we are doing differently and why it works for us. Notice that we carefully extract semantics of defects using a classification scheme. The classification scheme is able to extract information that tells us how well the product is progressing on a scale that is defined within the process. The categories themselves have been carefully chosen. Otherwise, we would not have the kind of effects that we would desire from such measurement. So, clearly, there is an issue of defining the value set into which an attribute is categorized. The value set should provide an adequate range to provide the differentiation and resolution desired within the process space. These requirements boil down to a set of necessary and sufficient conditions that make it orthogonal defect classification. The orthogonality here is in the value set associated with the particular attributes such as defect type. When these values are independent of each other (at least reasonably, since it is a semantic translation) it provides for easy categorization.

ODC essentially means that we categorize a defect into classes that collectively point to the part of the process that needs attention, much like characterizing a point in a cartesian system of orthogonal axes by its x, y, and z coordinates. In the software development process, although activities are broadly divided into design, code, test, and service, each organization can have its variations. These process stages often overlap, with consecutive releases being developed in parallel. With a large product these process stages can be carried out by different organizations, while for small products people may be shared across products. Therefore, for ODC to become a measurement system that allows for the analysis of such complexity, it should be invariant to these boundaries. The classification should be consistent across process stages; otherwise it is almost impossible to study trends across them. Ideally, the classification should also be quite independent of the specifics of a product or organization. If the classification is both consistent across phases and independent of the product, it tends to be fairly process-invariant and can eventually yield relationships and models that are very useful. Thus, a good measurement system that allows learning from experience and provides a means of communicating experiences between projects has at least three requirements:

- Orthogonality
- Consistency across phases
- Uniformity across products

One of the pitfalls in classifying defects is that it is a human process and subject to the usual problems of human error, confusion, and a general distaste if the use of the data is not well understood. However, each of these concerns is resolved if the classification process is simple, with little room for confusion or possibility of mistakes, and if the data can be easily interpreted. If the number of classes is small, there is a greater chance that the human mind can accurately resolve them [Mill90]. Having a small set to choose from makes classification easier and less error-prone. When orthogonal, the choices should also be uniquely identified and easily classified.

9.3.3 Necessary condition

There exists a semantic classification of defects such that its distribution, as a function of process activities, changes as the product advances through the process.

The earlier examples help explain this necessary condition, since they discussed not only what it means, but how it could be used. There are, however, a few subtleties and details that merit discussion. It also helps to compare ODC with more traditional approaches to clarify this scheme and illustrate the differentiation.

Fundamental to the use of the change in distribution of defects to meter the advancement of a product in a process is the existence of such changes. All these years, while there has been significant research in closely related areas such as metrics, software reliability, taxonomy for defect classification, and root-cause analysis, etc., there were almost no studies that tried to quantify the existence of properties that allowed us to extract semantics and turn them into measurements. Thus, while studies reported statistics on causes of defects and the proportion of escapes from various stages of development, they stopped short of developing a comprehensive measurement methodology. This was not a simple oversight. It is a difficult problem, which requires the demonstration of properties that make a connection between semantics and measurement possible. A breakthrough study that attempted to uncover the existence of such properties relating the semantics in defect content to the overall response from a development effort is discussed in [Chil91]. This became the stepping-stone to help formulate the concepts in ODC.

However, it is easy to confuse semantic classification of defects with direct process-based measurement. This difference is subtle but important. Take, for example, the defect type attribute. It is primarily defined on the paradigm of programming as opposed to the process of how to do it. So the value set is about the meaning of what is done as opposed to how it is done. This has the advantage that even though the underlying process may change or be undefinable, the measurements are possible. Thus, they allow the process to be changed when measurements from the very process are used for the analysis that motivates the change. This would not be possible if the measurements are directly tied to the process, since then the very first adjustment to the process destroys the measurement system.

This point is best illustrated with an example that is commonplace in the industry. A popular classification of defects is the value set of where it is believed to have been inserted. So, for instance, the values would comprise the process activities such as design, coding, unit test, function test, and system test. This can be used to estimate escapes from the various stages of development, yielding a causality measure that can be quite useful. The distribution of this value set may also change as a function of activity (especially since the value sets themselves are the activities). Unfortunately, as simple and straightforward as this may seem, it is plagued with several problems. First, practitioners are quick to point out that the answer to the above question tends to be error-prone. Programmers, while fixing a defect, are too closely focused on the product to step back and reflect on the process. Thus the most common answers to "where the defect is injected" are "the earlier stage" or "requirements," which do not help much. Second, a causality mapped directly on the existing process has limited longevity. If the process is changed or altered (which is sometimes the goal of the exercise), then the measurements so far are subsequently invalid. Third, use of these data, inferences, and learning are limited to this project or to processes that are identical to this one. Finally, it cannot work where the process is not well defined or the process is being changed dynamically to suit the pressures of changing requirements. Such direct classification schemes, by the nature of their assumptions, qualify as good opinion surveys but do not constitute a measurement on the process.

Semantic classification that is based on the meaning of what is done is more likely to be accurate, since it is tied to the work just completed. It is akin to measurements of events in the process, as opposed to opinions of the process. There is an important advantage in the semantic classification of a defect, such as *defect type,* over an opinion-based classification, such as *where injected.* This semantic classification is invariant to process and product, but requires a mapping to process stages. This mapping, such as associating function and algorithm defects to a process activity (e.g., design or low-level design), provides the flexibility to keep the measurement system stable. Furthermore, this neutrality with products, processes, and even implementation methodologies offers the opportunity that these measurements could be benchmarked across the industry.

9.3.4 Sufficient conditions

The set of all values of defect attributes must form a spanning set over the process subspace.

The sufficient conditions are based on the set of elements that make up an attribute, such as *defect type.* Based on the necessary conditions, the elements need to be orthogonal and associated with the process on which measurements are inferred. The sufficient conditions ensure that the number of classes is adequate to make the necessary inference. Ideally, the classes should span the space of all possibilities that they describe. The classes would then form a spanning set, with the capability that everything in that space can be described by these classes. If they do not form a spanning set then there is some part of the space on which we want to make inferences that cannot be described with the existing data. Making sure that we have the sufficiency condition satisfied implies that we know and can accurately describe the space into which we want to project the data.

Given the experimental nature of the work, it is hard to a priori guarantee that sufficiency is met with any one classification. Given that we are trying to observe the world of the development process and make inferences about it from the defects coming out, there are the tasks of (1) coming up with the right measurement, (2) validating the inferences from the measurements with reference to the experiences shared, and (3) improving the measurement system as we learn more from the pilot experiences. However, this is the nature of the experimental method [Chil90]. For example, in the first pilot [Chil91], the following defect types evolved after few classification attempts: function, initialization, checking, assignment, and documentation. This set, as indicated earlier in this section, provided adequate resolution to explain why the development process had trouble and what could be done about it. However, in subsequent discussions [IBM90] and pilots it was refined to the current eight. Given the orthogonality, in spite of these changes several classes such as *function* and *assignment* and the dimension they spanned (associations) remained unchanged.

9.4 The Defect-Type Attribute

A programmer making the changes for a defect is best suited to pick the defect type. The selection of defect type captures the nature of the change. These types are simple in that they should be obvious to a programmer without much room for confusion. In each case a distinction is made between something *missing* or something *incorrect.*

Function. A function defect is one that affects significant capability, end-user features, product application programming interface (API), interface with hardware architecture, or global structure(s). It would require a formal design change.

Assignment. Conversely, an assignment defect indicates a few lines of code, such as the initialization of control blocks or data structure.

Interface. Corresponds to errors in interacting with other components, modules, device drivers via macros, call statements, control blocks, or parameter lists.

Checking. Addresses program logic that has failed to properly validate data and values before they are used, loop conditions, etc.

Timing/serialization. Timing/serialization errors are those that are corrected by improved management of shared and real-time resources.

Build/package/merge. These terms describe errors that occur due to mistakes in library systems, management of changes, or version control.

Documentation. Errors can affect both publications and maintenance notes.

Algorithm. Errors include efficiency or correctness problems that affect the task and can be fixed by (re)implementing an algorithm or local data structure without the need for requesting a design change.

The defect types are chosen so as to be general enough to apply to any software development, independent of a specific product. Their granularity is such that the classifications apply to a defect found in any phase of the development process, yet can be associated with a few specific activities in a particular process. The defect types should also span the space of these phases to satisfy the sufficient condition. For instance, a typical association that occurs is to tie the functional defect to the design aspects of the process. Thus, no matter where the defect is found, if the distribution peaks with function dominating the distribution, it is indicative of activity that escaped the design phases. It is not as though function defects may only be found at a design review; they probably will be found throughout the development process. The issue is how many, and whether they dominate the overall mix of work that needs to take place during an activity. Similarly, an assignment and checking defect may be primarily associated with the coding phase and expected to be weeded out with code review and unit-test-type activity. These could peak repeatedly in the case of iterative development in those phases. However, when the function tests tend to be dominated by those types of defects, it is reflective of escapes from earlier verification phases, and impacts the overall productivity of the function test activity. The choice of the defect types are different enough so that they span the development process through all its activities. This allows us to use the distributions to provide feedback on the process, especially in the language that programmers can relate to.

Example 9.2 Figure 9.4 shows you the defect-type distribution of a product moving through the stages of high-level design, low-level design, code, and unit test. These data reflect a real product version of the hypothetical picture that we described earlier. We have chosen to show the total number of defects within each of these activities, as opposed to the normalized distribution, to also reflect a sense of volume that occurs in these phases. Notice that the bar corresponding to function defects has been steadily decreasing from high-level design all the way to unit test and is also decreasing in the rank order among the bars within each of these activities. At the same time notice that the assignment and checking types of defects are increasing both in volume and rank order among the other defect types as the product moves from high-level design into code review. Similarly, the algorithm types of defects tend to be peaking at low-level design and then trailing off into code review. This change in defect-type distribution is reflective of all the various discussions that we have had so far regarding the semantic extraction and explanation of how ODC works.

Example 9.3 There is another presentation of a defect-type distribution in Fig. 9.5. These curves provide a graphical display for a categorical data series so that an ordinate through the curves has intercepts that add up to 100 percent. Thus,

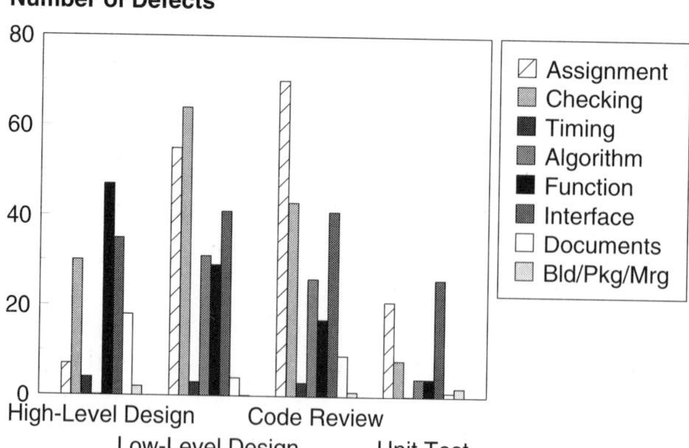

Figure 9.4 The defect type and process associations.

these curves show an instantaneous change in the distribution of defect data as a continuous curve created by smoothing the distribution over a moving window. The curve is a combination of a simple moving average and a cosine arch moving average applied to the binary representation of each category [Biya95]. The figure shows four groups of defect types: (1) assignment and checking, (2) function and algorithm, (3) timing and interface, and (4) the rest of them. The idea being that we would like to examine how the distribution of these groups of defect types changes as the product advances through development. These curves represent the instantaneous change in its distribution. Note that the early part of development has a higher fraction of functional defects, which decreases through time, while the timing component, which was originally low, is increasing. The assignment and checking type of defects change as the process phases change. This representation is intuitive, providing a concise representation of the overall data.

9.5 Relative Risk Assessment Using Defect Types

ODC data provide a foundation of good measurements that can be exploited for a variety of new analysis methods. One of the natural extensions is illustrated by using the defect-type data to significantly enhance the methodology of growth models. This section illustrates the development of such an extension to yield relative risk assessments, which are useful during the shutdown of a product release.

Chapter 3 provided a detailed discussion on growth models. Our experience in the practical use of these methods is that they are usually more successful with data from late system test or early field test. Their application to function/component test is limited in their current form. This criticism is what troubles the development manager who finds that current growth-curve-based analysis works only too late in the development cycle to make a difference.

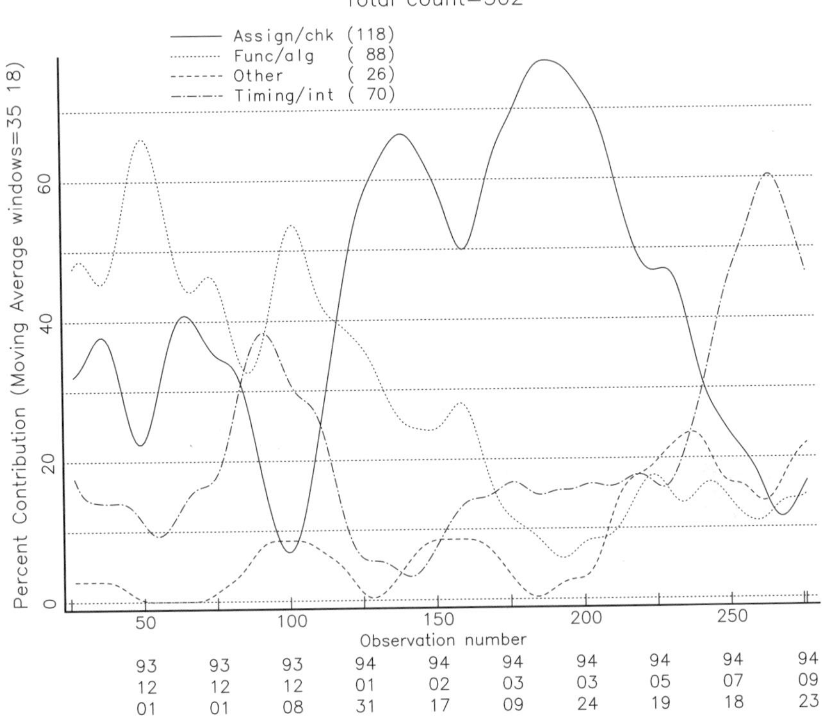

Figure 9.5 A doubly smoothed presentation of defect-type distribution.

We combine ODC with growth modeling to provide far greater insight than is commonly available with the typical growth models. There are two elements to this insight: one contributed directly from ODC and the other from assessing the relative growth of different groups of defects. Examining them against a common abscissa is what provides the additional insight to help make key qualitative inferences that drive decisions. To illustrate these ideas, we first need to step back and reflect on the qualitative aspects of a typical growth curve. Next we factor in ODC.

9.5.1 Subjective aspects of growth curves

Figure 9.6 shows a typical reliability growth curve with the cumulative number of defects on the ordinate and calendar time on the abscissa. This is one of the fairly standard representations that we use for this discussion. There are, however, several variations of these. The ordinate may represent failure rate or failure density. The abscissa may represent calendar time, execution time, test cases run, percent of test cases, etc. For this illustration, we restrict our attention to growth

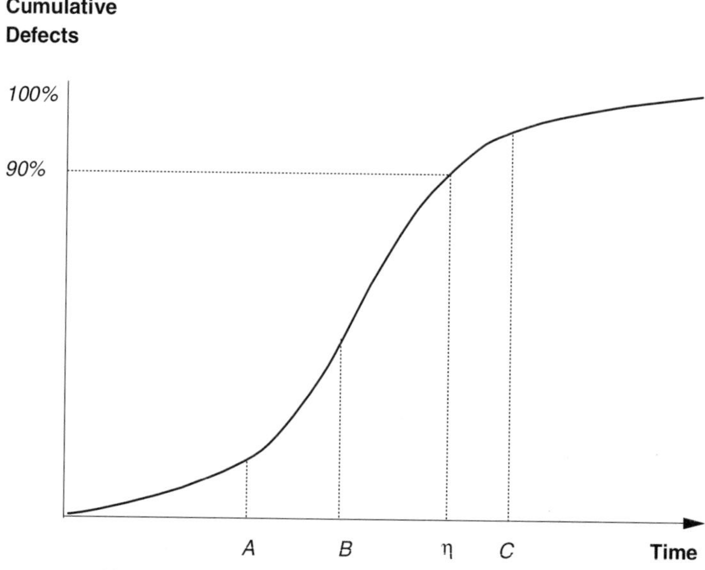

Figure 9.6 Typical growth curve.

curves with the cumulative number of defects on the ordinate and calendar time on the abscissa. The ideas that are proposed may map into other representations as well.

The growth curve in Fig. 9.6 is meant to show the span of development periods beginning with function/component test, continued into system test and possibly the early part of field life. For this discussion, we identify a few key points on the growth curve that are projected down on the time line. These are annotated as A, B, C, and η. Point A is when the test effort is ramped up, which is often visible when test takes awhile to be ramped up. Point B is computable when there is an inflection in the growth curve. In our experience, its existence is a good indicator to the modeler that the subsequent predictions become more stable. Between points A and B the curve can be accelerated depending on which fraction of function test is executable. Often there is parallel development of code and execution of test until a large part of the product can be integrated. Point C, commonly called the *knee* of the curve, is a classic indication of the begining of the end of the test effort. An ideal time to release a product is after the knee in the curve is observed, which reduces the exposure of defects found in the field. In practice, several variances occur: products are not shipped after the knee, or the knee can occur in the field. There are cases where two knees occur: one before shipping and another a few months out into the field.

It is not necessary that these three points be identifiable on each growth curve—for instance, some of them do not have an inflection point at all. When they are identifiable, they provide important points on the time line to identify progress of the development effort. Another important point that we find useful, from practice, is to identify the point at which 90 percent of the predicted total number of defects are found. In Fig. 9.6 this is projected to the time line and annotated as η. It will be referred to as the η point. These points are sometimes visible and identifiable in a growth curve and sometimes not. This is dependent on the data and the nature of the growth curve. The η point provides a milestone in the development cycle from which to make comparative assessments.

9.5.2 Combining ODC and growth modeling

Separate growth curves can be generated for each of the defect-type categories, demonstrating their relative growth. Since several of these categories could be sparse (such as build/package/merge) it is more meaningful to collapse categories to reflect broader aspects of the development process. Function and algorithm defects capture the high-level-design and low-level-design aspects of the product. Similarly, assignment and checking tend to be related to coding quality. Thus a reasonable collapsing of the categories provides useful subdivisions of the data, making the relative comparison far more comprehensible.

To illustrate the ideas, Fig. 9.7 shows an exaggerated version of possible growth curves with collapsed categories. The curve on top shows the overall growth curve, and at time *T* it is hard to predict the end of development. However, when split by three groups of defect types (shown in the lower graph), there is greater insight on the dynamics of the development. It is obvious that function and algorithm defects have stabilized, given that the growth curve has reached its knee, implying that the design aspects of the product are possibly stable. On the other hand, the code quality represented by assignment and checking defects has not stabilized anywhere close to the degree that function defects did. Yet, the growth curve has well passed the inflection point, and the knee of the curve is predictable within reason. Between the growth curves of function+algorithm and assignment+checking it appears that the code parts of the product will stabilize shortly after *T*. Thus if the testing efforts are continued at the current rate and pace, the product should stabilize as far as these elements. On the other hand, this is not the case with the third growth curve, which represents user interface and messages defects. This curve is clearly rising very rapidly and the prediction of when it will stabilize is much further out. Since these defects are driving the volume, a separate decision has to be made regarding the risk due to these defects.

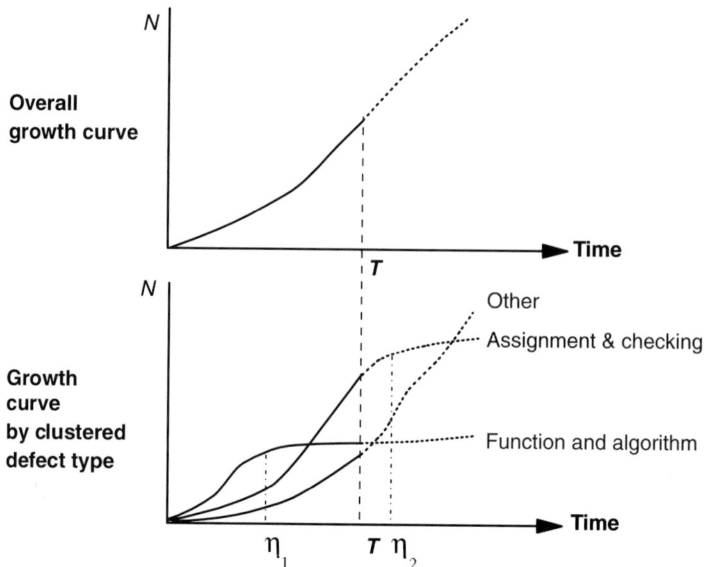

Figure 9.7 ODC for risk assessment (illustrating relative growth using ODC).

Looking at the relative growth curves, a development manager could respond to what is occurring in the product by carefully choosing the right skill mix and staffing levels during the later parts of testing. It is evident that the lead developers with the design skills are not critical at time T and could be working on the next release. Defects of type assignment+checking, representing coding issues, will continue being opened at current rates, which will need the appropriate staffing to handle the volume. However, the volume is dominated by defects of type miscellaneous that contain messages, panels, and interfaces. There is a major exposure here, since the end is not in sight, and the management has to deal with stabilizing this aspect of the product. Since the type of problems are known, management has the opportunity to respond to it by process changes and by bringing the right type of skills and experience to bear. Also, the severity of the defects can be examined to understand the risk of shipment without complete closure of the open problems.

Example 9.4 Data for this example are taken from a large project with several tens of thousands of lines of code (see ODC1.DAT on the Data Disk). The time frame includes function test and systems test, and the current date of the analysis is around two months from the desired ship date. Figure 9.8 shows the trend of the cumulative number of defects, which appears to be steadily growing, and stabilization of the product is not in sight. The developers' perception was that the product is not yet stable, and the growth model reaffirms that belief. The defect discovery rate is high, and the volume is not likely to be handled despite

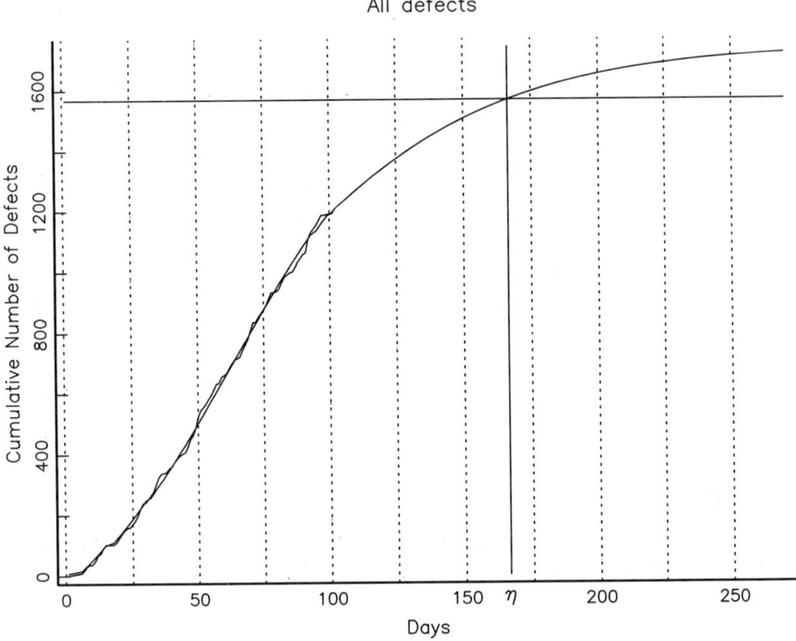

Figure 9.8 Overall cumulative defects.

increased staffing. The question of why and what to do to meet schedule while reducing the risk in the field is not evident from this level of analysis.

To gain more insight into the data, we use the ODC defect type to split the defects into three categories: *function* defects, *assignment+checking,* and all others termed *miscellaneous.* The last category predominantly consists of *documentation* and *panel+message* defects. Figure 9.9 shows the separate growth curves for the three categories superimposed on each other. Observe that the defect growth for *function* and *assignment+checking* defects is slowing down, and both of these categories are expected to stabilize soon. The growth of defects in the *miscellaneous* category, however, shows no signs of stabilization.

We decided to predict the future course of the growth curve using the inflection S-shaped model (Sec. 3.3.6),

$$N(t) = n\frac{1 - e^{-\phi t}}{1 + \psi e^{-\phi t}}$$

where $N(t)$ is the cumulative number of defects found by time t, n is the total number of defects originally present, and ϕ and ψ are model parameters related to the defect detection rate and the ratio of masked/detectable defects. We were able to fit the inflection S-curve to each of the first two categories (function and assignment/checking). The growth curve for the miscellaneous category, however, had not yet reached its knee, and it was not far enough advanced to fit an S-curve to it in the normal manner. We were, however, able to fit an S-curve by assigning a fixed value for one of the parameters ψ, using a guess, based on fitting the model to the entire data. Figures 9.10, 9.11, and 9.12 show the growth curves for

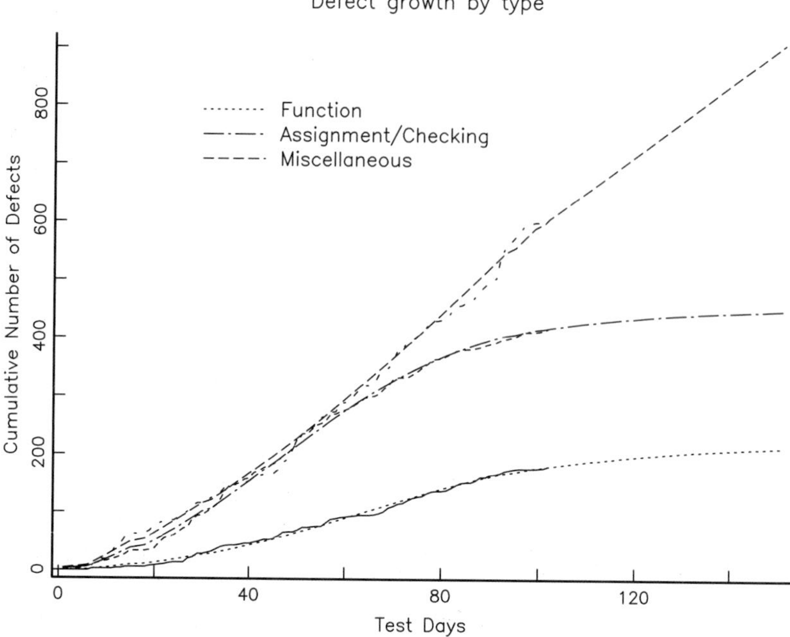

Figure 9.9 Cumulative defects by defect type.

the function defects, the assignment and checking defects, and the miscellaneous defects, respectively. In each of these curves, there is a horizontal line corresponding to 90 percent of the estimated number of defects in this category and the projection to the abscissa showing the η point. Note that the η point for function defects is around day 125, whereas that for the assignment and checking is at day 100, and the η point for the miscellaneous defects doesn't intercept the projection until all the way past day 250.

We are near day 100, and need to make decisions regarding the actions to follow in the next 60 days to meet the desired release date. From the curves it is evident that the code quality, represented by assignment+checking defects, is likely to stabilize, since we are already at the η point. On the other hand, the function defects would stabilize in the next month or so given that the η point is predicted to occur in 25 days. On the other hand, the miscellaneous defects are unlikely to stabilize given the current testing and development activity. As a result of the relative growth comparison we could say that a slight exposure exists regarding design, and the critical issue may be the miscellaneous defects. Therefore, maintaining the current test and development team will probably address the code quality aspects, but would need additional skills and resources on the other two issues. As we found out, in this project some key design skills were removed from the development team to work on the next release several weeks ago. Given this analysis and inference these skills were redirected back into this release, whereas the miscellaneous defects were a larger problem given their volume. A further analysis of those defects showed a large number of severity 3 and 4 (as opposed to 1 and 2, the higher-severity defects). Thus, releasing with several of them open was not deemed a major exposure. As it worked out, this product had

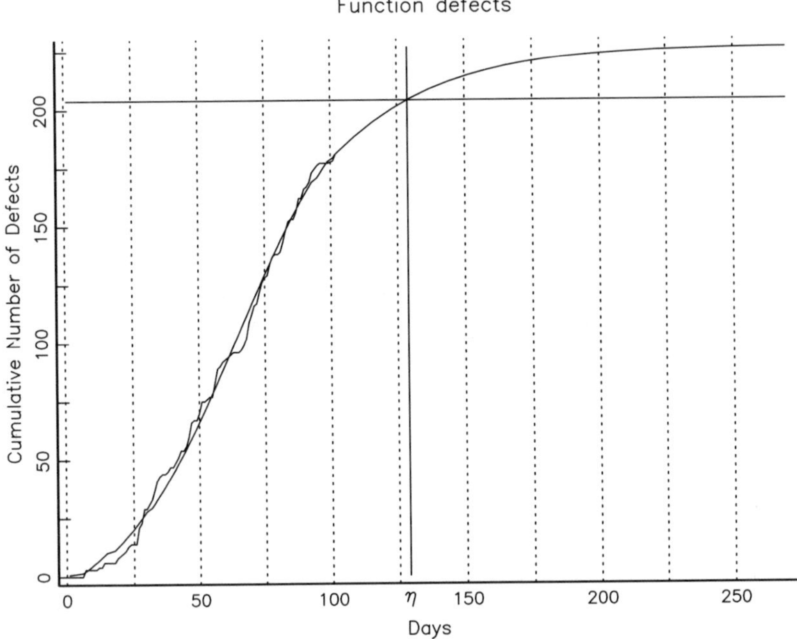

Figure 9.10 Cumulative defects: function.

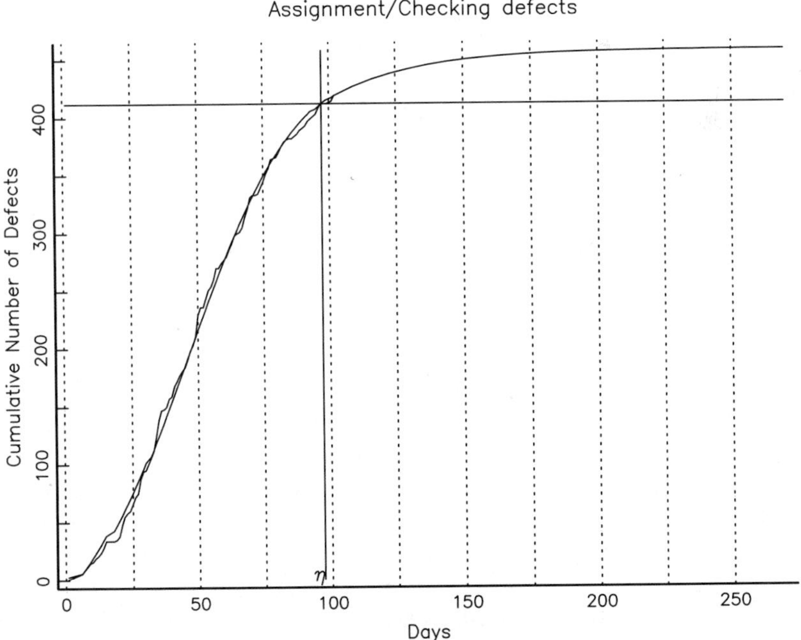

Figure 9.11 Cumulative defects: assignment/checking.

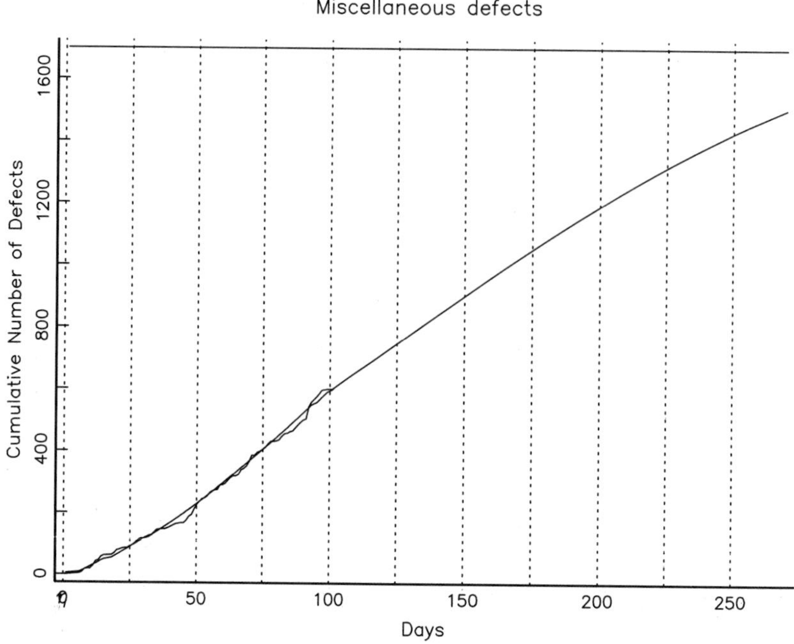

Figure 9.12 Cumulative defects: miscellaneous.

one of the higher quality ratings in the field and these decisions made during the shutdown helped not only to reduce risk but also to meet schedule and assure good field reliability.

9.6 The *Defect Trigger* Attribute

The concept of the software trigger is relatively new to the area of defect classification as opposed to defect type, which has parallels in earlier literature (although they may not have provided the measurement capability defined by ODC). The defect trigger is a new idea and therefore needs to be carefully understood.

9.6.1 The Trigger Concept

The trigger, as the name suggests, is what facilitated the fault to surface and result in a failure. It is therefore used to provide a measurement on the verification aspects of the development process. Just as the defect type provides an instrument on the progress of development, the trigger will provide a corresponding instrument on verification of testing.

We need to tear apart this activation process of faults in greater detail to appreciate the nuances of the triggering process. Before we do that, let us reflect on the nature of software faults for a moment. Software faults are dormant by nature. They can lie undetected for a long period of time—commonly, the entire development cycle—and then be detected when a product is introduced in the field. The various verification and testing activities provide mechanisms to detect these faults. Often they verify what should work. Sometimes they are designed to create conditions that would emulate customer usage and thereby identify the faults that escaped the earlier test stages. The question to ask is: what activates the otherwise dormant faults, resulting in failures? This catalyst is what we call the *trigger.*

There are really three different classes of software triggers. These come about by the three substantially different activities of verification that are commonly employed in software—review, unit/function test, and system test. The distinction arises from how they attempt to detect faults. Review is a passive process, since there is nothing to execute. The unit/function test actively checks the implementation by execution of the code, driven by triggers that are structural and compositional. System test emulates usage under customer environmental conditions.

The review process (which includes inspection) is geared to identify pitfalls in a product using the design documents and code. The triggering mechanisms appear when someone thinks about the product, examines a design, discusses an implementation, etc. These are human triggers that result in the identification of faults by thinking about factors such as design conformance, compatibility with other releases, rare situations, and operational semantics. When a product is being tested, either unit test or function test faults are identified because a test failed or did not complete. The trigger really underlies the test case. That is the reason why a test case was written in the first place—to check for coverage, functional completeness, etc. In another sense, it is the thought behind the design of a test that is the trigger. In the case of systems test, the product is usually stressed and taken through the scenarios to which most customers would subject it. The mechanisms that identify faults are those that would also identify faults in the field, such as stress, workload, and software configurations. Contrasted with the unit/function test triggers, these are the set of things that happen to the product as opposed to what is done to it.

To put triggers in perspective, let us for a moment digress and discuss the more commonly known attributes of failures. This will help differentiate what triggers are and clarify any potential confusion. Some of the more commonly discussed attributes of failures are their *failure modes* and characteristics such as *symptom, impact,* and *severity.* The *symptom,* a visible attribute, is the characteristic displayed as a result of the failure and the net effect on the customer. For instance, the symptom attributes reported in the IBM service process have a value set such as hang, wait, loop, incorrect output, message, and abnormal termination (abend). Fault injection experiments also use a similar attribute (often called *failure* or *failure mode*) with a value set such as no error, checksum, program exit, timeout, crash, reboot, and hang [Kana95, Kao93, Huda93]. The *impact* is an attribute that characterizes the magnitude of outage caused (severity) such as timing, crash, omission, abort fail, lucky, and pass [Siew93]. At first glance, it is not uncommon to confuse the symptom with the trigger. However, they are very different and orthogonal to each other. In simple terms, the trigger is a condition that activated a fault to precipitate a reaction, or series of reactions, resulting in a failure. The symptom is a sign or indication that something has occurred. In other words, the trigger refers to the environment or condition that helps force a fault to surface as a failure. A symptom describes the indicators that show a failure has occurred, such as a message, an abend, or a "softwait." Thus, a single trigger could precipitate a failure with any of the above symptoms or severities, and, conversely, a symptom or severity could be associated with a variety of trigger mechanisms.

The intent of capturing the triggers is to provide a measurement of the verification aspects of software development. Essentially, triggers need to conform to the same rules of ODC as did the defect types. Then they would provide a measurement on the verification process. To briefly summarize, it requires that the distribution of an attribute (such as trigger) changes as a function of the activity (process phase or time) to characterize the process. In addition, the set of triggers should form a spanning set over the process space for completeness. Changes in the distribution as a function of activity then become the instrument, yielding signatures, which characterizes the product through the process. This is the point at which the trigger value set is elevated from a mere classification system to a measurement of the process and qualifies as an ODC. The value set has to be experimentally verified to satisfy the stated necessary and sufficient conditions. Unfortunately, there is no shortcut to determine the right value set. It takes several years of systematic data collection, experimentation, and experience with test pilots to establish them. However, once established and calibrated, they are easy to roll out and "productionize." We have the benefit of having executed ODC in around 50 projects across IBM, providing the base to understand and establish these patterns. We would have liked to have one set of triggers that apply across the entire life cycle of development. Realistically, given the nature of the verification technology today, there are at least three distinctly different activities that need to be captured. Thus the triggers are in three sets, each of which span the process on which they are defined. In the following subsections we will define the triggers and illustrate their use with data from real examples.

9.6.2 System test triggers

System test usually implies the testing that is done when all the code in a release is mostly available, and workload similar to what a user might generate is used to test the product. These triggers characterize that which regular use of the product in the field would generate. They therefore apply to system test in the field.

Recovery/exception handling. Exception handling or recovery of the code is initiated due to conditions in the workload. The defect would not have surfaced had the exception handling process or the recovery process not been called.

System start-up and restart. This has to do with a product being initialized or being shut down from regular operation. These procedures can become significantly involved in applications such as database. Although this would be considered normal use of the product, it reflects the operations that are more akin to maintenance rather than regular operations.

Workload volume/stress. This indicates that the product has been stressed by reaching some of the resource limits or capability limits. The types of stresses will change depending on the product, but this is meant to capture the actions of pushing the product beyond its natural limits.

Hardware configuration and software configuration. These triggers are those that are caused by changes in the environment of either hardware or software. It also includes the kinds of problems that occur due to various interactions between different levels of software precipitating problems that otherwise would not be found.

Normal mode. This category is meant to capture those triggers where nothing unusual has necessarily occurred. The product fails when it was supposed to work normally. This implies that it is well within resource limits or standard environmental conditions. It is worthwhile noting that whenever normal mode triggers occur in the field it is very likely that there is an additional trigger attributable to either review or function test that became active. This additional level of classification by a function test or review trigger is recommended for field defects.

9.6.3 Review and inspection triggers

When a design document or code is being reviewed, the triggers that help find defects are mostly human triggers. These triggers are easily mapped to the skills that an individual has, providing an additional level of insight.

Backward compatibility. This has to do with understanding how the current version of the product would work with earlier versions or maintain n to $n + 1$ (subsequent release) compatability. This usually requires skill beyond just the existing release of the product.

Lateral compatability. As the name suggests, this trigger has to do with how this product would work with the other products within the same software configuration. The experience required by the individual should span the subsystems of the product and also the application program interface of the product with which it interacts.

Design conformance. These faults are largely related to the completeness of the product being designed with respect to the requirements and overall goals set forth for the product. The skills required for finding these kinds of triggers has more to do with an understanding of the overall design than with the kinds of skills required to ensure compatibility with other products.

Concurrency. This has to do with understanding the serialization and timing issues related to the implementation of the product. Specific examples are locking mechanisms, shared regions, and critical sections.

Operational semantics. This has to do largely with understanding the logic flow within the implementation of a design. It is a trigger that can be found by people who are reasonably new but well trained in software development and the language being used.

Document consistency/completeness. This has to do with the overall completeness of a design and ensures that there is consistency between the different parts of the proposed design or implementation. The skill is clearly one that requires good training and implementation skills, but may not require significant in-depth understanding of the products, dependencies, etc.

Rare situation. These triggers require extensive experience of product knowledge on the part of the inspector or reviewer. This category also recognizes the fact that there are conditions peculiar to a product that the casual observer would not immediately recognize. These may have to do with unusual implementations, idiosyncrasies, or domain specific information that is not commonplace.

9.6.4 Function test triggers

One of the primary differences between function test and the other set of triggers is that the meaning of the trigger needs to be more complex. Since the defining question for the trigger "why did the fault surface?" would result in the answer "test case," the definition of trigger involves a finer refinement.

The question becomes "why did you write the test case?" Thus the triggers that are identified reflect the different motivations that drive the test case generation. Therefore, it is feasible to actually identify the triggers for each test case as it is written. It is not necessary that the triggers be classified only after a fault is found. Each test case would then have a trigger associated with it. The trigger distribution is then reflective of the different methods and coverages intended through the test plan. These test cases should also be mapped into the white box and black box of testing.

Test coverage. This refers to exercising a function through the various inputs to maximize the coverage that is possible of the parameter space. This would be classified as a black-box test trigger.

Test sequencing. These are test cases that attempt to sequence multiple bodies of code with different sequences. It is a fairly common method of examining dependencies which exist that should not exist. This is also a black-box test.

Test interaction. These are tests that explore more complicated interactions between multiple bodies of code usually not covered by simple sequences.

Test variation. This is a straightforward attempt to exercise a single function using multiple inputs.

Simple path coverage. A white-box test that attempts to execute the different code paths, increasing statement coverage.

Combination path coverage. Another white-box test that pursues a more complete signal of code paths, exercising branches and different sequences.

9.6.5 The Use of Triggers

Once we understand what the trigger data capture we can begin to appreciate the different potential uses of the trigger concept. Triggers can be used on their own to measure the effectiveness of the verification phase, and they can also be used in conjunction with the other categories in ODC to provide further insight into the cause of a process situation. In the following we will illustrate the use of triggers by showing examples from pilot studies conducted at IBM. Some of these examples will use the trigger category in conjunction with the defect type to illustrate the dynamics occurring in a particular process phase. The type of trigger that is used will change depending on which process phase we are looking at. Triggers can also be used with field data to recognize the different environmental stresses that are placed on a product.

The concept of the trigger provides insight not on the development process directly, but on the verification process. Discussing a few examples that use triggers gives us a much better understanding of how this works. We will do so by examining a few specific situations and illustrating the kind of inferences that can be drawn from the trigger data. We begin by first examining a project in the high-level-design phase in Example 9.5 and then follow it up with triggers in the field in Example 9.6.

Example 9.5 This example is from the high-level design inspection of a middleware software component (see ODC2.DAT on the Data Disk). The component's API was intended for use with several other products and vendor applications. The example uses the idea of triggers combined with the defect type to illustrate measuring the effectiveness of the inspection. Figures 9.13 and 9.14 show the distribution of defect types and triggers subgrouped by defect types. Let us factor into these distributions our expectations and critique the situation. Studying the defect-type distribution, we notice that it is typical of what a high-level inspection should produce: the number of function defects is fairly large—the mode being documents, which is understandable given that it was a document review. The trigger distribution shows that the largest number of defects were found by the operational semantics trigger. This again is explainable given that completeness and correctness are major issues considered in a high-level-design inspection. Given that this is a middleware component that will be used by several other products, interfaces are key. Furthermore, lateral compatibility is important since it is middleware. What is surprising is that there are a small number of interface defects found using the lateral compatibility trigger. Defects found using the lateral compatibility trigger are mostly function defects. Given the nature of this component, this raises serious questions regarding the skills of the inspection team, particularly from a cross-product perspective. A check of the team's membership found few people with that particular skill.

In this case, an additional review was requested to fill the gaps, and two experts (including an IBM fellow) found the defects shown in Figs. 9.15 and 9.16. It was

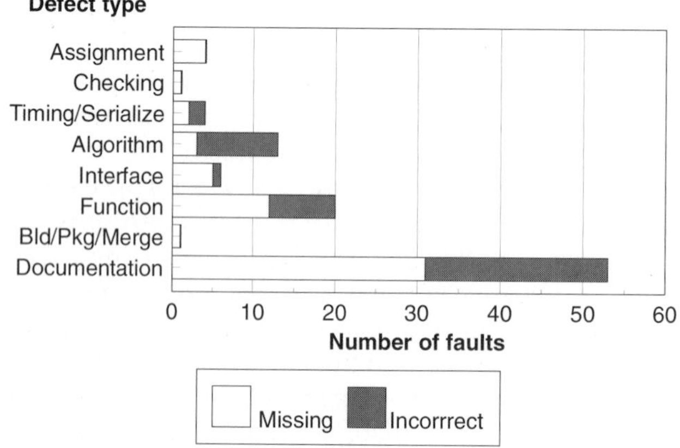

Figure 9.13 Defect-type distributions at first high-level design.

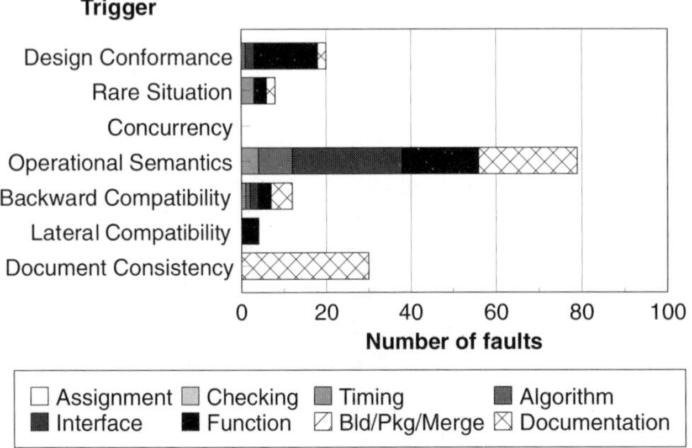

Figure 9.14 Defect-trigger distributions at first high-level design.

possible to advise these experts to focus their efforts along the dimension that we suspected was weak rather than redo the entire inspection. The second defect-type distribution, like the former, is characteristic of a high-level design inspection—namely, large numbers of document and function defects. From the trigger distribution in Fig. 9.16, it is clear that a substantial number of lateral compatibility triggers were being used to identify defects. In addition, the lateral compatibility trigger found many different defect types, indicating a more detailed review. In this case, 102 defects were found due to the additional review—in precisely the areas where deficiencies were suspected. The savings due to this early detection exceeds more than $1 million in development and service costs.

Note that this is identified using the cross product of the defect type and the trigger. The feedback was available right after the inspection—extremely fast and

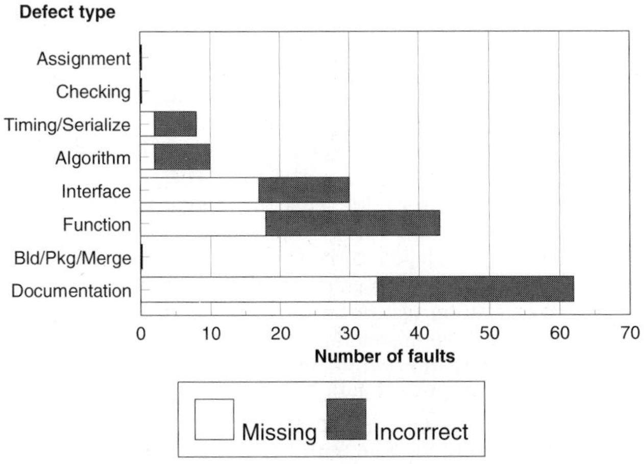

Figure 9.15 Defect-type distributions at second high-level design.

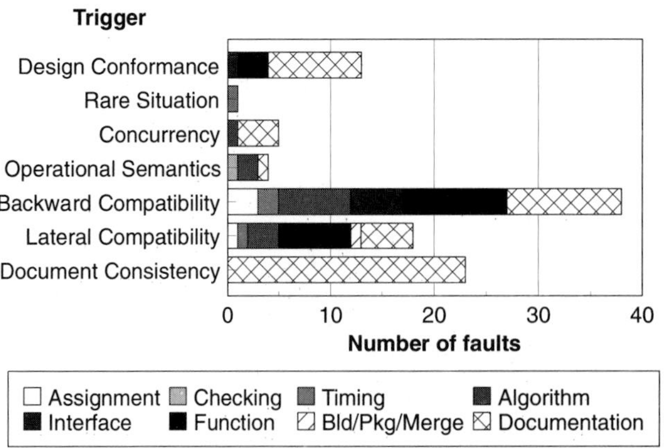

Figure 9.16 Defect-trigger distributions at second high-level design.

actionable feedback quite unusual for the software industry. Traditional methods rely on the volume of defects being found compared with earlier statistics, which only make broad inferences. Given the wide variances of defect injection rates, the credibility of such inferences is often questioned. Classical root-cause analysis, after considerable expense, would reveal the nature of defects found, but could not react to the omissions. Furthermore, two-dimensional cross products are hard to correlate mentally in qualitative analysis.

Example 9.6 This example shows trigger distribution of defects found in the field. The data are from a two-year period of a product in the field. Two years is a reasonable length of time, since the bulk of the defects are usually found during this period. There are several inferences to be drawn from Fig. 9.17. First, the trigger distribution changes as a function of time for the different triggers. Recall the ODC necessary and sufficient conditions, which need to be empirically established. The change in distribution as a function of time signifies meeting the necessary condition. Second, the trigger distribution indicates to us when a particular product is likely to have the maximum defects from a particular trigger. This information is vital to develop testing and service strategies. For instance, the fact that hardware configuration and stress-based triggers tend to peak in later years would allow for a testing strategy that focuses on weeding out the triggers that peak earlier. This could be exploited if there is an opportunity to refresh the release in the field with a better-tested upgrade within the next year or so. Third, knowing the trigger profiles allows us to project the number of defects that appear in the field better. There are several techniques that could be developed in the future. However, for a simple intuitive understanding, consider comparing trigger distributions of the past release's field to this release's system test. A better coverage in system test of areas that the customer hits hard would result in a smaller field fallout. This assessment, combined with the detection profile in the field, allows us to make more accurate projections of the number of defects to be found in the first, second, and third quarters following a release. Having a better projection based on triggers allows us to do service planning and staff the functions better by skill group.

System Test Triggers

Number of faults by quarter

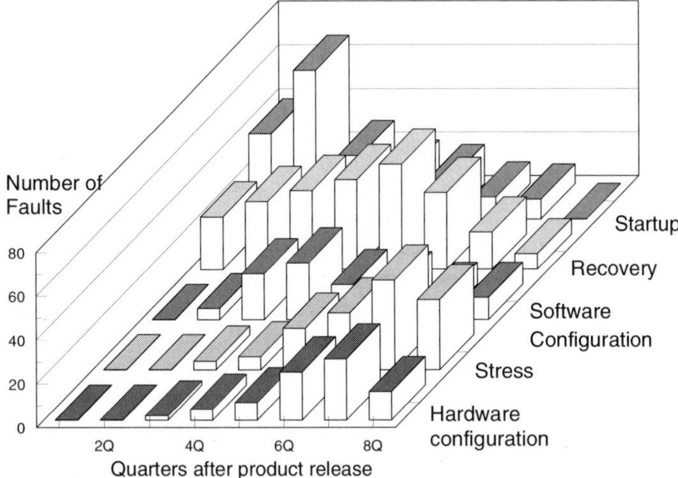

Figure 9.17 Triggers of defects found in the field. Subsets of system test triggers showing number of faults by quarter.

Although this section does not show data on trigger distribution through function tests, the discussion on the review triggers and the system test triggers should provide good initial understanding of how triggers work. For a further discussion of triggers there are several articles that are recommended. The ODC paper provides an overview of the concept of the trigger and illustrates some data on both the review and test process [Chil92]. A more detailed discussion on the test process exists in [Chaa93], where the trigger concept is expounded and examples from several pilots are included. For an understanding of how the trigger concept can be levered to guide fault injection and characterize the field performance of the system, [Chil95] provides a lot of information.

9.7 Multidimensional Analysis

This chapter has so far primarily focused on two attributes: namely, the defect type and the trigger. Each of these attributes has a specific purpose from a measurement perspective. The defect type is a measure related to the development process, and the trigger to the verification process. Both attributes are of a causal nature: the defect type is "what is the meaning of the fix," and the trigger is "what was the catalyst to find the defect." The fact that the value set conformed to the properties of ODC is what made these classifications into measurements.

ODC does not imply only these two classification attributes. In fact, any classification can be considered ODC if the attribute-value set conformed to the necessary and sufficient conditions. However, to build a measurement system with a firm footing, a substantial amount of piloting and experimentation needs to be conducted to verify the properties. In theory, there could be any number of attribute-value sets, each of which meets ODC requirements—providing a large space of measurements. The attribute-value sets could address different issues about the product or the process. Each attribute does not have to be independent of the other, but the values within an attribute need to be. However, having attributes that are highly dependent on each other, with highly correlated value mappings, does not make for useful measurement.

Having multiple attribute-value sets that conform to ODC properties provides a rich measurement opportunity. It allows for the analysis using multiple attributes to be easily interpreted, be they correlations, subsets, functional relationships, etc. In fact, the multidimensional nature of this measurement provides fertile ground for data mining. Having a large body of such data from several products or releases makes it particularly amenable for developing models and examining properties, trends, and characteristics. This is useful to develop an understanding of a development experience, as well as to characterize teams, environments, practices, etc.

At first glance it seems relatively easy to come up with attributes that potentially could be useful. However, it takes considerable experience to find the truly useful attribute-value sets. Thus, it is not uncommon to see teams coming up with recommendations to improve the classification or add new attributes. The danger in arbitrarily adding to or changing the measurement system is that before one is verified to be ODC, widely deploying it could be an unproductive exercise. Furthermore, it is important not to thrust too many attributes on a development team and scare them away. We have chosen to introduce just four new attributes over and above what is traditionally in place.

Figure 9.18 shows six attributes and their purposes. The italicized attributes are recommended as starters for ODC. Defect type, trigger, source, and impact are four attributes that are introduced as new additions on top of the standard measurements that most defect-tracking mechanisms provide. To help put this in perspective, two commonly used attributes—phase found and severity—are also shown. Most defect-tracking tools commonly have between five and fifteen such attributes to categorize defects. Many of them never get used, or when used, it is not uncommon for organizations to never use the data! In sharp contrast, the ODC approach uses few attributes, but very carefully designs them.

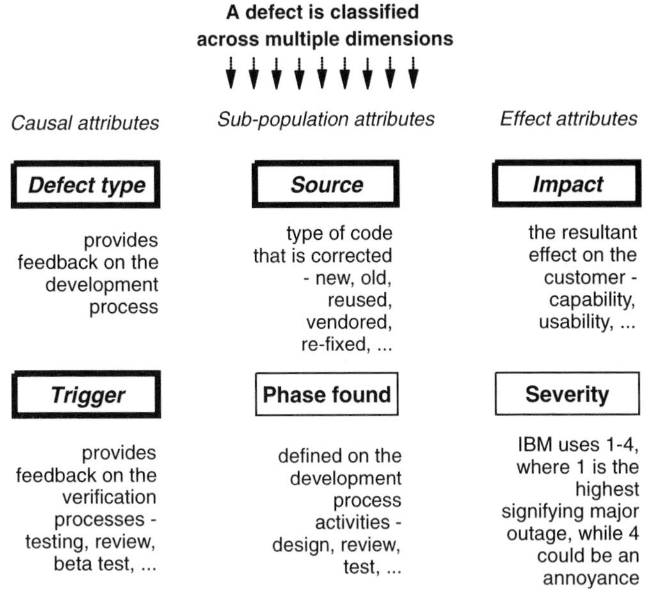

Figure 9.18 Dicing a defect, generating multidimension data.

These six attributes are further grouped under the broad areas of cause, effect, and subpopulation identifiers. This helps us visualize a framework on which these attributes could be used. Since every defect will have each of these classifications, analyzing a collection of defects allows us to statistically develop models that relate cause with effect. Furthermore, the subpopulation identifiers allow us to slice and dice the data and provide greater visibility of the underlying issues within a software development process.

One of the key advantages of having the data along the dimensions shown in the figure is that this provides a good minimal set for a variety of purposes. For example, root-cause analysis usually requires a few cause-and-effect attributes, particularly if we want to diagnose an issue from a customer's perspective. Thus, if we want to understand how to best improve the serviceability of a product, the ODC data sets provide a clear and efficient diagnosis search path. The impact attribute would be used to create a subset including reliability, maintainability, and serviceability defects. The subset is then examined using the defect type and trigger to understand the reason such defects escape into the field and the kind of faults that are being committed to cause the impact. This understanding is then translated into recommendations for actions. To further reduce the search space to apply such actions, the source category can be used to explore whether certain kinds of code—new code, old code, vendored code, etc.—dominate the volume of such problems.

The data requirements document [IBM95] provides the details of the attributes and values of the latest version of ODC. This includes values and definitions for the attributes that are currently tested to meet the ODC requirements. The document also includes any enhancements made in ODC, applied across different types of development—software, hardware, information, etc. It also includes new attributes as they are invented and the uses developed for them.

Having multidimensional ODC-based measurements, not just classification, opens up a new world for analysis. Fairly systematic methods for diagnosis can be established for the commonly arising problems. At the same time it keeps open opportunities to explore via data mining methods.

9.8 Deploying ODC

The deployment of a technology such as ODC requires careful thought and considerable insight into the means of process insertion. Most practitioners would recognize that technology transfer is a difficult business. Process transfer is yet another order of magnitude harder and especially so in software. This is because, unlike a technology that can be captured in a tool or a design which impacts a product group, process transfer in software requires that every programmer change a little. Although the change may be minor in terms of the actual work a programmer does, getting acceptance of the concepts and buy in through the organization is a major undertaking.

Unless programmers quickly see the value of ODC, it is hard to sustain their interest and commitment to provide good data. This quickly becomes an exercise in managing all the processes to execute ODC. Knowing the processes and having the necessary skills are the minimum requirements. Being able to quickly recognize when they are not working and reacting to them effectively is the difference between success and failure. At Watson Research, we started as technologists and teamed with our divisional partners to do deployment. It quickly became evident that the split was artificial. Both teams needed to understand the technology and the nuisances of the real world to be effective. We learned to create processes that were necessary and developed schemes to maintain and troubleshoot them.

Figure 9.19 identifies some of the key processes. It also divides the range and scope of deployment into *pilot, staged production,* and *production,* indicating the growth of deployment in an IBM lab. The idea is that initially an organization would usually start off with a pilot project, almost as a trial. These usually last between three months and one year, and become the proving ground for ODC at the pilot stage. Most of the processes were owned by Watson Research, and the responsibilities of the participating lab were limited. As we made progress, we would develop the skills in the organization to own more of the processes, reducing the responsibility and involvement of the research team. In the best cases, we were able to obtain ownership of more than 70 percent of the processes in around 18 months. Results from the use of ODC in projects across the company are described in [Bhan94]. At the end of 1995, we had close to 50 projects in about a dozen labs. Two labs could be considered to be well into staged-production.

The cost of ODC is quite low. There is an up-front cost in terms of modifying the tool set and providing education. The execution cost is dramatically lower if a developer is already using a change control system. This is because most change control systems require that the programmers update a panel, and ODC requires only four additional fields (in most cases), which is a small delta cost. The subsequent costs are incurred in analyzing the data, which is mostly tool cost and either management or technical review which runs approximately two hours a month (on average). This can be rolled into existing quality programs or quality circle efforts, thereby not requiring additional effort.

When ODC is used to enhance the quality circle of the defect prevention process (DPP) [Mays90] significant savings can be accrued in analysis costs. Typically, DPP-related efforts cost in the range of one person hour per defect. Imagine four people in a room analyzing defects. They usually do a detailed root-cause analysis of around four or five defects in an hour. This one hour usually includes not only qualitative analysis but also identifying a potential solution and writing it down as an action item for the organization to execute. Given such high costs, it is again not common for organizations to be able to do

Pilot Projects	Staged Production	Regular Production
Lab Ownership	**Lab Ownership**	**Lab Ownership**
Classification	Classification	Classification
Decisions	Decisions	Decisions
Actions	Actions	Actions
Watson Ownership	ODC Education	ODC Education
ODC Education	Advocacy	Advocacy
Advocacy	Data collection tools	Data collection tools
Data collection tools	Process definition	Process definition
Process definition	**Watson Ownership**	Analysis
Analysis	Analysis	Feedback
Feedback	Feedback	Databases
Databases	Databases	**Watson Ownership**
Consultation	Consultation	Consultation

Figure 9.19 Deployment of ODC.

DPP on every defect, since they usually run into thousands. The ODC classification, which extracts cause and effect, usually takes only two minutes when done retrospectively. Granted that the granularity of the measurement is very coarse, its low cost allows full coverage over the defect population. The analysis of these data provide a statistical means to do causal analysis by associating cause and effect. This now occurs not on each defect, but on a collection of them, and is appropriately timed at the exit of a development phase. Since the analysis of the data (which may even be qualitative) is amortized over several of them, the overall cost is reduced by about an order of magnitude (according to our estimates) when including all the time costs involved.

9.9 Summary

Orthogonal defect classification fundamentally improves the technology for in-process measurement for the software development process. This opens up new opportunities for developing models and techniques for fast feedback to the developer, thus addressing a key challenge that has been nagging the community for years. At one end of the spectrum, research in defect modeling focused on reliability prediction, treating all defects as homogeneous. At the other end of the spectrum, causal analysis provided qualitative feedback on the process. The middle ground did not develop, primarily because the basic discoveries establishing the feasibility were not yet there. This work is built on some fundamental breakthroughs, which show that certain cause-effect relationships are measurable. Furthermore, the measurement system is definable on the semantic information contained in the defect stream. ODC provides the basic capability to extract signatures from defects and infer the health of the development process.

Our experience with ODC indicates that it can provide fast feedback to developers. Developers find this a useful method to gain insight they did not have before. It also provides a reasonable level of quantification to help make better management decisions to significantly impact cost and opportunity. There are several levels of analysis and feedback that can be built on ODC. The published literature discusses trend analysis, relative risk reduction, data mining, prediction methods, and assisting root-cause analysis. When used to assist root-cause analysis, it can cut the cost by a factor of 10 compared to traditional methods. It can be used as a general diagnostic tool retroactively to assess problem situations in development organizations. ODC has since been extended into information development and non-defect-oriented issues, and has been applied to hardware (microcode) development.

Problems

9.1 Define a process with three stages. Take the eight defect types from Sec. 9.4 and draw the expected defect type distribution to signify the ideal signature. Explain why the mode occurs in each of the phases and its relative size compared to the category that is second to the mode.

9.2 For the process described in Prob. 9.1, increase the process to five stages. Now modify the distributions to accommodate the addition of process stages. Redraw the distributions with the abscissa to represent number of defects, instead of percent of defects.

9.3 Consider release 2 of a product made up of 80 percent of old code (from release 1) and 20 percent of new code developed in release 2. Defects are found during testing from the old code and the new code. Write down an expectation of the defect-type distribution of the new code and the old code. Defend your position. If we had information on the defects found in the field use of release 1, how would that influence your expectations? Develop a hypothetical example.

9.4 Take data from `ODC3.DAT` on the Data Disk. Develop defect-type distributions for the design phase and the code/unit-test phase. Compare the distributions and assess the trends in the changes. Next compute the proportion of missing to incorrect defects from the two phases and explain the difference between the two phases. Develop feedback to the development team based on your analysis.

9.5 Suppose we have triggers of defects found during the system test and the first six months' usage in the field after product release. Argue what the differences or similarities should be between the trigger distribution of the system-test defects and the field defects. Would they be (*a*) identical, (*b*) complementary, (*c*) unrelated? Explain why.

9.6 Study the trigger distributions of defects reported in reference [Chil95]. What would you recommend to the development team that is developing the next release of this product?

9.7 How would your recommendations change if you know that the triggers from the defects in Prob. 9.6 come from three different releases? For simplicity let us assume that all the system-test-triggered defects are from release 1, the function-test-triggered defects from release 2, and the others from release 3. Now, if we were to make a recommendation for the development of release 4, how would it be different from those of Prob. 9.6?

9.8 Develop defect types for the art of writing a paper. To do so, use the experience of writing a technical paper to identify defects.

a. Define what a defect means in this activity.
b. Define the parallel to the defect type and trigger for these defects.
c. Collect defects from a paper-writing project and classify them by defect types and triggers.

d. Develop the distributions as a function of the phases of writing a paper. If the phases cannot be clearly identified, then develop them as a function of time.

9.9 Take the data sets of `ODC3.DAT` to `ODC6.DAT` from the Data Disk and analyze the defect-type distribution by doing simple trend analysis to raise issues that should be of concern. To do so, develop distributions (such as in Figs. 9.13 to 9.16) to obtain insight. Specifically, generate defect-type distribution as a function of phase, and the trigger versus type distributions. Additional insight can be gained by looking at additional attributes in the data sets. More sample data sets are available from the Web site: `http://research.ibm.com/softeng`.

9.10 Take the data for Example 9.4 and try to do a similar analysis on relative risk using a different grouping of defect types. What are your conclusions? Are they different from the stated example?

9.11 What is the parallel to the risk assessment (Sec. 9.5) using triggers instead of using defect types? Discuss applications for this new approach.

Chapter

10

Trend Analysis

Karama Kanoun and Jean-Claude Laprie
LAAS-CNRS, Toulouse, France

10.1 Introduction

Generally, software reliability studies are based on the application of reliability growth models to evaluate reliability measures. When performed on a large base of deployed software systems, the results are usually of high relevance (see [Adam84, Kano87] for examples of such studies). However, the utilization of reliability growth models during the early stages of development and validation is much less convincing; when the observed times to failure are in the order of minutes or hours, the predictions based on such data can hardly predict mean times to failure different from minutes or hours, which are far below any acceptable level of reliability! In addition, when a program under validation becomes reliable enough, the times to failure may simply be so large that applying reliability growth models to data collected during the end of validation is impractical due to the (hoped for) scarcity of failure data. On the other hand, in order to become a true engineering exercise, software validation should be guided by quantified considerations relating to its reliability. Statistical tests for trend analysis provide such guides.

This chapter addresses the problem of reliability growth analysis; it shows how reliability trend analyses can help the project manager control the progress of the development activities and appreciate the efficiency of the test programs. Reliability trend changes occur for various reasons. They may be desirable and expected (such as reliability growth due to fault removal) or undesirable (slowing down of testing effectiveness, for example). Timely identification of the latter allows the project manager to make the appropriate decisions in order to avoid problems that may surface later.

We introduce the notions of reliability growth over a given interval and local reliability trend change, allowing a better definition and understanding of the reliability growth phenomena. The already existing trend tests are then revisited using these concepts. We put the emphasis on the way trend tests can be used to help the management of the testing and validation process and on practical results that can be derived from their use. It is shown that, for several circumstances, trend analyses give information of prime importance to the developer. We also discuss their extension to software static analysis (e.g., specification and code inspection or review).

It is worth noting that, generally, most companies are accustomed to trend analysis during software testing (see e.g., [Grad87, Ross87, Vale88]). However, trend analyses are usually applied intuitively and empirically rather than in a quantified and well-defined manner. Moreover, such analyses are commonly restricted to failures reported during software execution. It is undoubtedly important to manage software testing, but equally important to manage the earliest phases of the verification and validation activities (for instance, static analysis through inspections, walk-through or code review) since efficient early static analyses significantly reduce subsequent development cost. We will thus discuss the extension of the trend analyses to data derived from static analysis before software execution (testing).

This chapter focuses on trend analysis. First, emphasis is placed on the characterization of reliability growth via the subadditive property and its graphical interpretation. Then we briefly present the Laplace test, which is a conventional trend test, and outline its relationship with the subadditive property. We then show how trend tests can be used to help manage the validation process before illustration on several data sets from real-life systems. Finally, the last section extends the application of trend tests to trouble reports recorded during static analysis of the software.

10.2 Reliability Growth Characterization

Lack of software reliability stems from the presence of faults. It is manifested by failures which are due to fault sensitization (see Chap. 2). Removing faults should result in reliability growth. However, this is not always the case, due to the complexity of the relationship between faults and failures, and therefore between faults and reliability, which was noticed long ago (see e.g., [Litt79a]). Basically, complexity arises from a double uncertainty: the presence of faults and the fault sensitization via the trajectory in the input space of a program.* As a conse-

* By way of example, the data published in [Adam84] concerning nine large software products show that for a program with a mean lifetime of 15 years, only 5 percent of the faults were activated during this period.

quence, reliability trend changes can occur, which may be due to a wide range of phenomena, such as

- *Variation in the utilization environment.* Variation in the testing effort during debugging, change in test sets, addition of new users during the operational life, etc.
- *Dependence between faults.* Some faults can be masked by others, they cannot be activated as long as the latter are not removed [Ohba84].

Reliability decrease may not, and usually does not, mean that the software has more and more faults. It is just an indication that the software exercises more and more failures per unit of time under the corresponding conditions of use. Corrections may reduce the failure input domain, but more faults are activated or faults are more frequently activated due to operational profile changes. However, during fault correction, new faults may also be introduced—regression faults—that are likely to affect the ability of the software to deliver a proper service, depending on the conditions of use. Last but not least, reliability decrease may be due to specification changes, as exemplified by the experimental data reported in [Kenn92].

10.2.1 Definitions of reliability growth

A common definition of reliability growth is that the successive interfailure times tend to become larger, i.e., denoting $T_1, T_2, \ldots,$ the sequence of random variables corresponding to interfailure times:

$$T_i \underset{st}{\leq} T_j \qquad \text{for all } i < j \tag{10.1}$$

where $\underset{st}{\leq}$ stands for *stochastically smaller than* (that is, $P\{T_i < v\} \geq P\{T_j < v\}$ for all $v > 0$). Under the stochastic independence assumption, Eq. (10.1) is equivalent to $F_{Ti}(x)$, denoting the cumulative distribution function of T_i:

$$F_{Ti}(x) \geq F_{Tj}(x) \qquad \text{for all } i < j \text{ and } x > 0 \tag{10.2}$$

An alternative to the (restrictive) assumption of stochastic independence is to consider that the successive failures are governed by a nonhomogeneous Poisson process (NHPP). Let $N(t)$ be the cumulative number of failures observed during time interval $[0, t]$, $H(t) = E[N(t)]$, its mean value, and $h(t) = dH(t)/dt$ its intensity, i.e., the failure intensity. A natural definition of reliability growth is then that the increase in the expected number of failures tends to become lower, i.e., that $H(t)$ is concave, or equivalently that $h(t)$ is nonincreasing. However, there are several situations where, even though the failure intensity fluctuates locally, reliability growth may take place on average on the considered time interval.* An alternative definition allowing for such local fluctuations is that the expected number of failures in any initial interval (i.e., of the form $[0, t]$) is no less than the expected number of failures in any interval of the same length occurring later (i.e., of the form $[x, x + t]$). The independent increment property of an NHPP enables us to write the latter definition as

$$H(t_1) + H(t_2) \geq H(t_1 + t_2) \qquad \text{for all } t_1, t_2 \geq 0 \text{ and } 0 \leq t_1 + t_2 \leq T \qquad (10.3)$$

where inequality is assumed strict for at least one couple (t_1, t_2). When Eq. (10.3) holds, the function is said to be *subadditive* (see e.g., [Holl74]). When Eq. (10.3) is reversed for all $t_1, t_2 \geq 0$ and $0 \leq t_1 + t_2 \leq T$, the function is said to be *superadditive,* indicating reliability decrease on average.

Equation (10.3) is very interesting, since it allows for local fluctuations: locally subintervals of reliability decrease may take place without affecting the nature of the trend over the whole time interval considered. When $h(t)$ is strictly decreasing over $[0, T]$, Eq. (10.3) is verified, but the converse is not true. This is detailed in the next subsection. The case where $h(t)$ is strictly decreasing (respectively, increasing) is usually referred to as *strict* or *monotone* reliability growth (respectively, decrease).

10.2.2 Graphical interpretation of the subadditive property

Let C_t denote the portion of the curve representing the mean value function over $[0, t]$ as shown in Fig. 10.1, and L_t be the line joining the two ending points of C_t (i.e., the chord from the origin to point $(t, H(t))$ of C_t). Let $\mathcal{A}_H(t)$ denote the difference between (1) the area delimited by C_t and the coordinate axis and (2) the area delimited by L_t and the coordinate axis. With these notations, if $H(t)$ is subadditive over $[0, T]$, then

$$\mathcal{A}_H(t) \geq 0 \qquad \text{for all } t \in [0, T] \qquad (10.4)$$

This property can be shown as follows. Let us divide the interval $[0, t]$ in K small time intervals of length dt, that is, $t = Kdt$. K may be

* The NHPP assumption (more precisely, the property of independent increments) is essential since a stationary process which is a non-Poisson process may undergo transient oscillations that cannot be distinguished from a trend in a nonstationary Poisson process (see, for instance, [Asch84, Gned69] for renewal processes).

even or odd. Let us consider the even case. In Eq. (10.3), let t_1 successively take the values $\{0, dt, 2dt, 3dt, \ldots, (K/2)dt\}$ and $t_2 = t - t_1$. Equation (10.3) successively becomes

$$H(0) + H(Kdt) \geq H(t)$$

$$H(dt) + H((K-1)dt) \geq H(t)$$

$$H(2dt) + H((K-2)dt) \geq H(t)$$

$$\ldots$$

$$H\left(\frac{K}{2}dt\right) + H\left(\frac{K}{2}dt\right) \geq H(t)$$

Summing over the $(K/2) + 1$ inequalities gives

$$\sum_{j=0}^{K} H(jdt) + H\left(\frac{K}{2}dt\right) \geq \left(\frac{K}{2} + 1\right) H(t)$$

Replacing K by t/dt and taking the limit when dt approaches zero lead to

$$\int_0^t H(x)\,dx \geq \frac{t}{2} H(t)$$

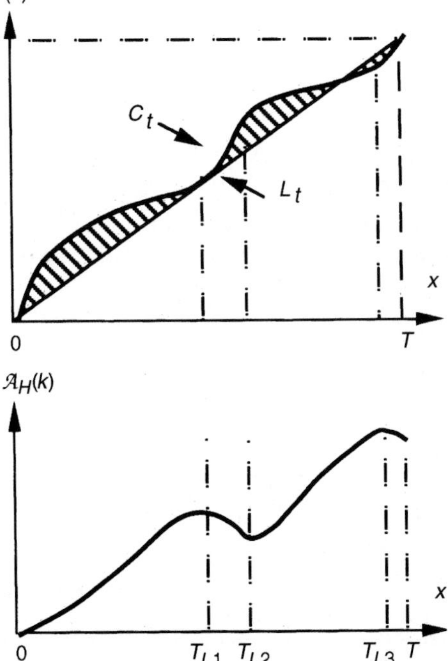

Figure 10.1 Graphical interpretation of the subadditive property.

The left term corresponds to the area delimited by C_t and the coordinate axis; the right term corresponds to the area between L_t and the coordinate axis.

Equation (10.3) implies Eq. (10.5):

$$\int_0^t H(x)\,dx - \frac{t}{2}H(t) \geq 0 \qquad \text{for all } t \in [0, T] \tag{10.5}$$

That is, $\mathcal{A}_H(t) \geq 0$.

It can also be shown that Eq. (10.5) implies Eq. (10.3), which means that Eqs. (10.3) and (10.5) are equivalent. When K is odd, derivation can be handled in a similar manner.

Throughout this chapter, $\mathcal{A}_H(t)$ is called the *subadditivity factor*.

With this graphical representation, the subadditive property is easily identified. For example, the function considered in Fig. 10.1 is subadditive over $[0, T]$; there is thus reliability growth over the whole time interval.

10.2.3 Subadditive property analysis

It is worth noting that, for a subadditive function over $[0, T]$ when t varies from 0 to T, the difference between the two areas, $\mathcal{A}_H(t)$, may increase, decrease, or become zero without being negative. The variations of $\mathcal{A}_H(t)$ indicate *local* trend changes.

Let us consider a subadditive function; $\mathcal{A}_H(t)$ is thus positive and increasing at the beginning, and

- Without local trend change, the mean value function is concave, leading to $\mathcal{A}_H(t)$ positive and increasing over the considered interval. Such a situation is illustrated by case A in Fig. 10.2,
- In case of local trend change, the mean value function is no longer concave and the difference between the two areas is not increasing

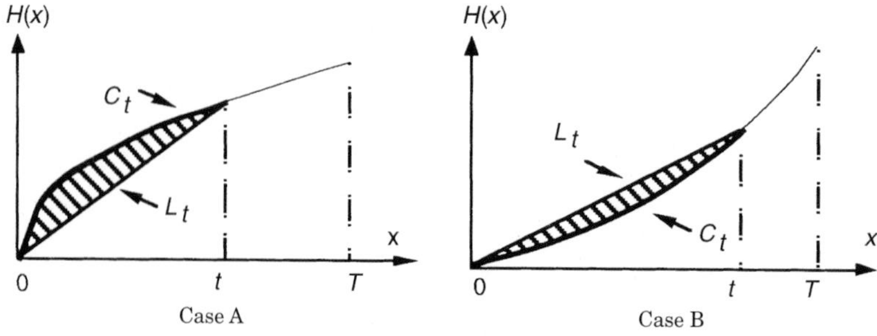

Figure 10.2 Subadditivity (left) and superadditivity (right) without local trend variation.

over the considered interval. Figure 10.1 gives an example of such a situation. $\mathcal{A}_H(t)$ takes its maxima (minima) when its derivative is null. Let T_{L1} denote the time at which the first maximum takes place. From T_{L1}, $\mathcal{A}_H(t)$ is decreasing (denoting local reliability decrease) up to the next point where the derivative is null again (point T_{L2} of Fig. 10.1). From T_{L2}, $\mathcal{A}_H(t)$ is increasing again (denoting local reliability growth) and so forth.

In fact, Fig. 10.1 shows a situation with two subintervals of local reliability decrease (namely, intervals $[T_{L1}, T_{L2}]$, and $[T_{L3}, T]$) despite reliability growth on the whole interval $[0, T]$, since the function is subadditive over $[0, T]$.

Let $\mathcal{A}_h(t)$ denote the derivative of $\mathcal{A}_H(t)$ given by

$$\mathcal{A}_h(t) = \frac{d}{dt}\mathcal{A}_{\mathrm{H}}(t) = \frac{d}{dt}\left[\int_0^t H(x)\,dx - \frac{t}{2}H(t)\right] = \frac{1}{2}[H(t) - t \cdot h(t)] \qquad (10.6)$$

As for $\mathcal{A}_H(t)$, a simple graphical interpretation of $\mathcal{A}_h(t)$ leads to the following results: $\mathcal{A}_h(t)$ corresponds to half the difference between (1) the area delimited by $h(t)$, the failure intensity, and the coordinate axis and (2) the area of the rectangle $(t, h(t))$. Local trend change takes place at points T_L, which are such that $\mathcal{A}_h(T_L) = 0$ (where both areas are equal).

For a subadditive function, taking the first point of local trend change as the time origin would lead to a superadditive function from this new time origin to the following point of local trend change (since the curve giving the cumulative number of failures is concave over this time interval).

The preceding remarks also hold for a superadditive function. At the beginning, the difference between the two areas is negative and decreasing, and

- Without local reliability fluctuation, the mean value function is convex, leading to a negatively decreasing $\mathcal{A}_H(t)$ (Fig. 10.2, case B).
- In case of local reliability fluctuation, $\mathcal{A}_H(t)$ takes its first minimum at T_L (such as $\mathcal{A}_h(T_L) = 0$). From T_L, $\mathcal{A}_H(t)$ is then increasing (indicating local reliability growth) up to the next point of local trend change, and so on.

10.2.4 Subadditive property and trend change

There exist more complex cases, however, where the cumulative number of failures is neither subadditive nor superadditive over the considered interval. Since the notion of subadditivity/superadditivity is related to a given interval, a change in the time origin leads to subadditive or superadditive functions over the subintervals of the new considered interval. Two such cases are depicted in Fig. 10.3.

For case C, the function is superadditive before T_G, denoting reliability decrease over $[0, T_G]$. T_G corresponds to the point where $\mathcal{A}_H(t)$ changes signs ($\mathcal{A}_H(T_G) = 0$): the function is no longer superadditive. T_L denotes the point where $\mathcal{A}_H(t)$ is no longer decreasing ($\mathcal{A}_h(T_L) = 0$), denoting local trend change. However, the function continues to be superadditive up to point T_G. On the subinterval of time between T_L and T, the curve is concave, indicating reliability growth over $[T_L, T]$.

Situation D is the converse of that of C. Up to point T_G, the cumulative number of failures is subadditive, denoting reliability growth over $[0, T_G]$; from T_G, it is no longer subadditive. On $[T_L, T]$ the function is superadditive, corresponding to reliability decrease over this time interval. Combining C and D leads to situations where the trend may change more than once.

10.2.5 Some particular situations

What precedes shows that the notion of reliability growth is related to the interval of time considered and, thus, strongly associated with the origin of the time interval. Two types of particular situations can therefore be found in practice: (1) when the subadditivity factor is constant (or null) over a given interval and (2) when $\mathcal{A}_h(t)$ varies but remains positive over a given interval while the concavity of $H(t)$ may change. These two specific cases will be reviewed.

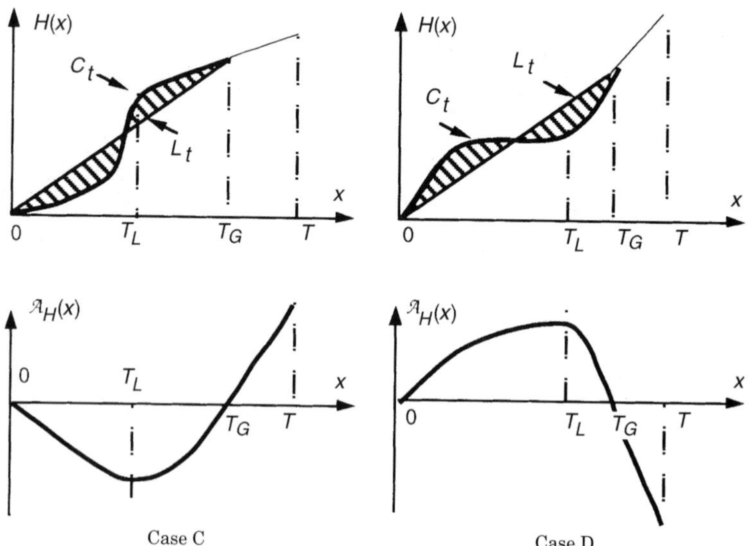

Figure 10.3 Subadditivity/superadditivity and local trend variation.

The first case (where $\mathcal{A}_H(t)$ is constant or null over a given interval, say, $[t_1, t_2]$) is characterized by the fact that the derivative of $\mathcal{A}_H(t)$, $\mathcal{A}_h(t)$, is null over $[t_1, t_2]$. Integration of $H(t) - th(t) = 0$ leads to a linear cumulative number of failures function, i.e., a constant failure intensity over $[t_1, t_2]$. The constancy of $\mathcal{A}_H(t)$ thus indicates *stable reliability* over this time interval.

Finally, the case of $\mathcal{A}_h(t)$ being positive over a given interval while the concavity of $H(t)$ may change leads to the notion of transient or temporary behavior. Positive $\mathcal{A}_h(t)$ means that $\mathcal{A}_H(t)$ is not decreasing over the considered interval. This is shown in the example in Fig. 10.4. $H(t)$ is subadditive; $h(t)$ is fluctuating, leading to $H(t)$ concavity change; whereas $\mathcal{A}_H(t)$ is not decreasing ($\mathcal{A}_H(t)$ is not shown). The transient variations of $h(t)$ cannot be detected by the sign of $\mathcal{A}_H(t)$ and do not correspond to a trend variation as defined by the subadditive property. They are due to the random nature of the process and are identified as a *transient* or *temporary* behavior of the software.

Defining reliability growth through the subadditive property is thus very attractive since it is not sensitive to the transient and temporary behavior. The subadditive property constitutes a form of smoothing of the software behavior, as shown in Fig. 10.4.

10.2.6 Summary

Reliability growth/decrease is entirely characterized by the subadditivity factor $\mathcal{A}_H(t)$ and its derivative $\mathcal{A}_h(t)$. $\mathcal{A}_H(t)$ gives information about the trend on average over a given interval, whereas $\mathcal{A}_h(t)$ informs about local trend variation as follows:

- $\mathcal{A}_H(t) \geq 0$ over $[0, T]$ implies reliability growth on average over $[0, T]$.
- $\mathcal{A}_H(t) \leq 0$ over $[0, T]$ implies reliability decrease on average over $[0, T]$.
- $\mathcal{A}_H(t)$ constant over $[0, T]$ implies stable reliability on average over $[0, T]$.
- Changes in the sign of $\mathcal{A}_H(t)$ indicate reliability trend changes.

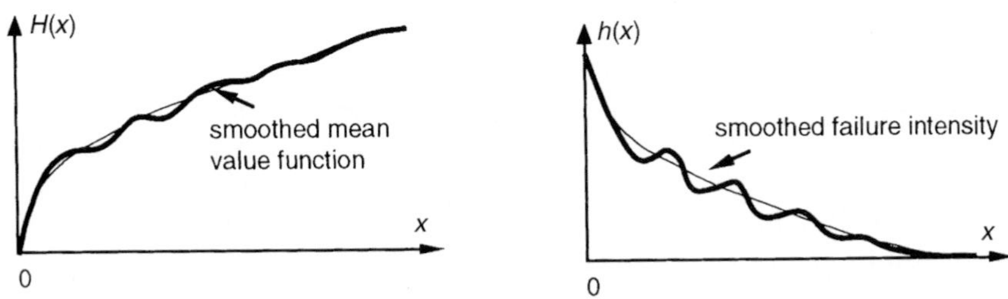

Figure 10.4 Subadditivity and transient/temporary behavior.

- $\mathcal{A}_h(t) \geq 0$ over a subinterval $[t_1, t_2]$ implies local reliability growth over $[t_1, t_2]$.
- $\mathcal{A}_h(t) \leq 0$ over a subinterval $[t_1, t_2]$ implies local reliability decrease over $[t_1, t_2]$.
- Changes in the sign of $\mathcal{A}_h(t)$ indicate local reliability trend changes.
- Transient variations of the failure intensity are not detected by the subadditivity property.

10.3 Trend Analysis

Reliability growth can be analyzed by trend tests. In this section we will present only the most often used and most significant trend tests and place the emphasis on the relationship between the Laplace test (the most common one) and the subadditive property. The presentation of the tests is followed by a discussion of how they can be used to follow up software reliability.

Failure data can be collected in one of two forms: *interfailure times* or *number of failures per unit of time*. These two forms are related. Knowing the interfailure times enables us to obtain the number of failures per unit of time (the second form needs less precise data collection).

The use of data in the form of number of failures per unit of time reduces the impact of transient variations on software reliability analysis and evaluation. The unit of time is a function of the type of system usage as well as the number of failures occurring during the considered units of time, and it may be different for different phases. For instance, since more failures are likely to occur during development, the selected unit of time may be smaller than the one selected for operational life.

10.3.1 Trend tests

There are a number of trend tests which can be used to help determine whether the system undergoes reliability growth or decrease. These tests can be grouped into graphical and analytical tests [Asch84]. Graphical tests consist of plotting some observed failure data such as the interfailure times or the number of failures per unit of time versus time in order to visually obtain the trend displayed by the data. As such they are informal. Analytical tests correspond to more rigorous tests since they are based on statistical considerations. The raw data are processed to derive trend factors. The principle of analytical tests is to test a null hypothesis H_0 versus an alternative H_1. Usually, H_0 corresponds to one of the following assumptions for the underlying process: it is assumed to be either (1) a homogeneous Poisson process

(HPP) or (2) a stationary renewal process. Very often, H_1 corresponds to "the process undergoes monotonic trend," i.e., increasing (decreasing) interfailure times or decreasing (increasing) failure intensity.

Theoretical definition and comparison of analytical trend tests have given rise to several publications [Cox66, Asch84, Gaud90]. In the latter reference, detailed presentation, analysis, and comparison of some analytical tests (e.g., Laplace, MIL-HDBK 189, Gnedenko, Spearman, and Kendall tests) are presented. In particular, it is shown that

- From a practical point of view, all these tests yield similar results for the detection of reliability trend variations.
- The Spearman and Kendall tests have the advantage of being based on less restrictive assumptions (that is, H_0: the underlying process is a renewal process).
- The Gnedenko test is interesting since it uses exact distributions.
- From the optimality point of view, the Laplace test is superior and recommended for use when the NHPP assumption is made (even though its significance level is not exact and its power cannot be estimated).

These results confirm our experience in the processing of real failure data. We have observed the agreement between the results of these various tests and the superior efficiency of the Laplace test.

All the aforementioned tests are performed relative to a monotonic trend. Linked with the subadditive property, a test for subadditivity (referred to subsequently as the Hollander test) was derived by Hollander and Proschan in [Holl74] and Hollander in [Holl78]. The Hollander test deals with H_0 and H_1 defined by:

H_0: the failure process is an HPP

H_1: the mean value function is superadditive

It is thus more general than the previous ones and also more in line with our definition of reliability growth/decrease. Further details on the Laplace and Hollander tests will be provided in the following subsections.

The trend can be analyzed using interfailure times data or failure intensity data, both of which we will now examine.

10.3.1.1 Interfailure times. Two trend tests are commonly carried: the arithmetical mean and the Laplace tests. The *arithmetical mean* of the interfailure times is a popular test. It consists of calculating the arithmetical mean $\tau(i)$ of the observed interfailure times θ_j, $j = 1, 2, \ldots, i$ (θ_j are realizations of T_j):

$$\tau(i) = \frac{1}{i} \sum_{j=1}^{i} \theta_j \tag{10.7}$$

An increasing series of $\tau(i)$ indicates reliability growth and, conversely, a decreasing series suggests reliability decrease. This straightforward test is directly related to the observed data. A variant of this test consists of evaluating the mean of interfailure times over periods of time of the same length in order to put emphasis on the local trend variation.

Let $N(T)$ denote the cumulative number of failures over the observation period $[0, T]$. The *Laplace test* [Cox66] consists of calculating Laplace factor, $u(T)$ which is derived as follows. The occurrence of events is assumed to follow an NHPP whose failure intensity is decreasing and given by

$$h(t) = e^{a+bt} \qquad b \leq 0 \tag{10.8}$$

If $b = 0$, the Poisson process becomes homogeneous and the occurrence rate is time-independent. Under this hypothesis ($b = 0$, that is, H_0: the failure process is an HPP), the test procedure is to compute:

$$u(T) = \frac{\dfrac{1}{N(T)} \displaystyle\sum_{n=1}^{N(T)} \sum_{j=1}^{n} \theta_j - \dfrac{T}{2}}{T \sqrt{\dfrac{1}{12N(T)}}} \tag{10.9}$$

This factor may be evaluated step by step, after each failure occurrence, for instance. In this case T is equal to the time of a failure occurrence, say, failure i, and failure at time T is to be excluded. Equation (10.9) thus becomes

$$u(i) = \frac{\dfrac{1}{i-1} \displaystyle\sum_{n=1}^{i-1} \sum_{j=1}^{n} \theta_j - \dfrac{\displaystyle\sum_{j=1}^{i} \theta_j}{2}}{\displaystyle\sum_{j=1}^{i} \theta_j \sqrt{\dfrac{1}{12\,(i-1)}}} \tag{10.10}$$

Practical use of Laplace test in the context of reliability growth can be summarized as follows:

- Negative values of the Laplace factor indicate a decreasing failure intensity ($b < 0$).
- Positive values suggest an increasing failure intensity ($b > 0$).
- Values varying between −2 and +2 indicate stable reliability.

These practical considerations are derived from the significance levels associated with the normal distribution; e.g., for a significance level of 5 percent,

- The null hypothesis "H_0 : HPP" versus "H_1 : the failure intensity is decreasing" is rejected for $u(T) < -1.645$.
- The null hypothesis "H_0 : HPP" versus "H_1 : the failure intensity is increasing" is rejected for $u(T) > 1.645$.
- The null hypothesis "H_0 : HPP" versus "H_1 : there is a trend" is rejected for $|u(T)| > 1.96$.

The Laplace test can be simply interpreted as follows:

- $T/2$ is the midpoint of the observation interval.
- $1/[N(T) \sum_{n=1}^{N(T)} \sum_{j=1}^{n} \theta_j]$ corresponds to the statistical center of the interfailure times.

Under the assumption of failure intensity decrease (increase), the interfailure times θ_j will tend to occur before (after) the midpoint of the observation interval; hence the statistical center tends to be smaller (larger) than the mid-interval.

10.3.1.2 Failure intensity and cumulative number of failures. Two very simple graphical tests can be used: the plots giving the evolution of the observed cumulative number of failures and the failure intensity (i.e., the number of failures per unit of time) versus time, respectively. The inevitable local fluctuations exhibited by experimental data make smoothing necessary before the reliability trend can be determined, and favor the cumulative number of failures rather than failure intensity. Reliability trend is then related to the subadditive property of the smoothed plot, as seen in Sec. 10.2.

The formulation of the *Laplace test* for failure intensity (or cumulative number of failures) is as follows. Let the time interval [0, T] be divided into k units of time of equal length, and let $n(i)$ be the number of failures observed during time unit i. Following the method outlined in [Cox66], the expression of the *Laplace factor* is given by (for a detailed derivation consult [Kano91a])

$$u(k) = \frac{\sum_{i=1}^{k} (i-1)n(i) - \frac{(k-1)}{2} \sum_{i=1}^{k} n(i)}{\sqrt{\frac{k^2-1}{12} \sum_{i=1}^{k} n(i)}} \qquad (10.11)$$

The same results as previously stated apply: negative values of $u(k)$ indicate a decreasing failure intensity (reliability growth) whereas positive values point out an increasing failure intensity (reliability decrease).

The *Hollander test* for subadditivity [Holl74] consists of evaluating the statistic Q_n based on the times of failures

$$s_i = \sum_{j=1}^{i} \theta_j$$

$$Q_n = 2K_n/n(n-1)(n-2)$$

$$K_n = \sum\nolimits^* \left[\phi(s_{\alpha 3} + s_{\alpha 2}, T) - \phi(s_{\alpha 3}, s_{\alpha 1} + s_{\alpha 2}) \cdot \phi(s_{\alpha 1} + s_{\alpha 2}, T)\right] \quad (10.12)$$

where $n = N(T)$, $\phi(a, b) = 1$ if $a \le b$, else $\phi(a, b) = 0$, and $\sum^*$ is over all $\frac{1}{6}n(n-1)(n-2)$ choices of subscripts such that $1 \le \alpha 1 < \alpha 2 < \alpha 3 \le n$. Critical values of the K_n statistic are given in the same reference for various levels of significance.

10.3.1.3 Relationship between the Laplace test and the subadditive property. The Laplace test may be used in the same way as any statistical test with significance levels as indicated above. However, we derive a relationship between the Laplace factor and the subadditivity factor allowing extension of the properties of the latter.

Let $n(i)$ denote the number of failures during the ith unit of time (i.e., $N(k) = \sum_{i=1}^{k} n(i)$). The numerator of Eq. (10.11) can be written as

$$\sum_{i=1}^{k} (i-1)[N(i) - N(i-1)] - \frac{(k-1)}{2} N(k)$$

which is equal to

$$\left[kN(k) - \sum_{i=1}^{k} N(i)\right] - \frac{(k-1)}{2} N(k) = \frac{k+1}{2} N(k) - \sum_{i=1}^{k} N(i)$$

Equation (10.11) thus becomes

$$u(k) = -\frac{\displaystyle\sum_{i=1}^{k} N(i) - \frac{k+1}{2} N(k)}{\sqrt{\dfrac{k^2-1}{12} N(k)}} \quad (10.13)$$

The $u(k)$ numerator is nothing other than the subadditivity factor, $\mathcal{A}_H(k)$. Therefore, testing the sign of $u(k)$ leads to testing the sign of the difference of areas between the curve plotting the cumulative number of failures and the chord joining the origin and the current cumulative number of failures. This shows that the Laplace factor (fortunately) integrates the unavoidable local fluctuations which are typical of experimental data, because the numerator of this factor is directly related to the subadditive property.

In the previous section certain features related to the subadditive property were introduced (i.e., reliability growth over a given interval and local trend change). We use a simple hypothetical example to illustrate the relationship between these features and the Laplace test. Figure 10.5 shows the failure intensity considered, the corresponding cumulative number of failures, $N(k)$, the derived subadditivity factor, and the evaluated Laplace factor.

Considering the whole data set (Figure 10.5*a*) leads to the following comments:

- $\mathcal{A}_H(k)$ is negative until point 9, thus indicating superadditivity and hence reliability decrease up to this point.
- The trend of $\mathcal{A}_H(k)$ changes around point 6, indicating local trend change. (This is also noticed when looking directly at the failure intensity, which is decreasing from point 6.)
- The sign and variations of the Laplace factor follow the sign and variations of $(-\mathcal{A}_H(k))$.

If we consider the data set from point 6 and plot the same measures (Fig. 10.5*b*), the results of this time origin change are as follows:

- $\mathcal{A}_H(k)$ is positive for each point showing reliability growth over [6, 21].
- The Laplace factor becomes negative.

To conclude, the denominator in the expression of the Laplace factor (Eq. (10.13)) usually does the following:

- Amplifies the Laplace factor variations when compared to those of $\mathcal{A}_H(k)$, at the beginning of the time interval considered
- Reduces the scale variation of the Laplace factor when compared to the variations of $\mathcal{A}_H(k)$ on the whole time interval, as it acts as a norming factor

It is also worth noting that changes in the time origin similarly impacts the subadditivity factor and the Laplace factor. However, the change in the time origin does not result in a simple translation in all situations.

The preceding statements are now illustrated by a more complex case corresponding to the experimental data of the TROPICO-R

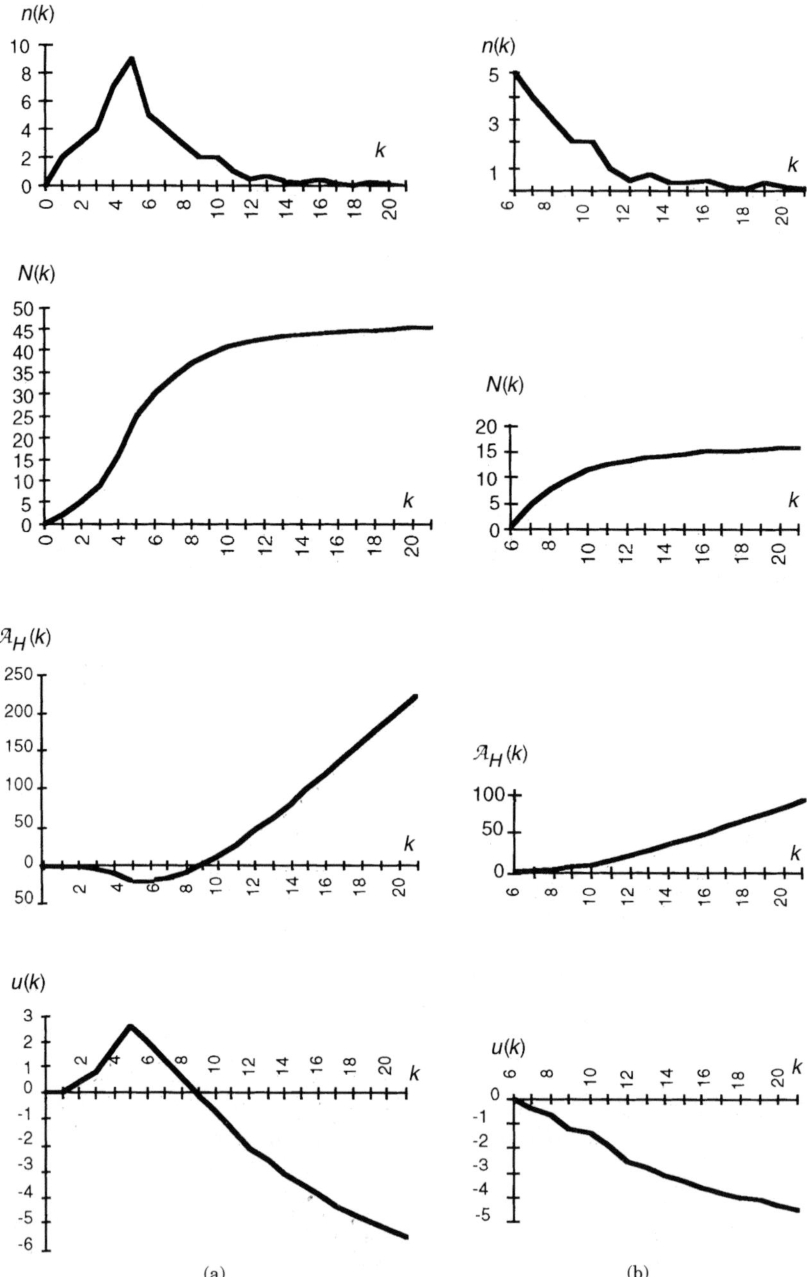

Figure 10.5 Example of relationship between failure intensity, cumulative number of failures, subadditivity factor, and Laplace factor.

switching system studied in [Kano91a]. Figure 10.6 gives the Laplace factor for the whole data set from validation to operation. At the beginning of validation, a reliability decrease took place, due to the occurrence of 28 failures during the third unit of time, whereas only 8 failures had occurred during the first two time units, and 24 failures occurred during the next two time units. This is a common situation at the start of validation: reliability decrease is due to the activation of a large number of faults. Applying the Laplace test without the data belonging to the two first units of time leads on average to reliability growth from unit time 3 despite local trend changes (Fig. 10.7). The evolution of the subadditivity factor $\mathcal{A}_H(k)$ is shown in Fig. 10.8, which also depicts the influence of the first two data items. Even though only two data items were removed, the comparison of Figs. 10.6 and 10.7 (and of the curves of Fig. 10.8) confirms the previous remarks, that is,

- The curve's shape is preserved when suppressing the first data items, which cause the reliability decrease at the beginning and preservation of the local trend change points.
- $\mathcal{A}_H(k)$ seems less sensitive to the local trend variations when compared to the Laplace factor. This difficulty may be overcome by considering, for instance, a reduced data set as indicated in Fig. 10.9, which depicts $\mathcal{A}_H(k)$ over the validation phase only.

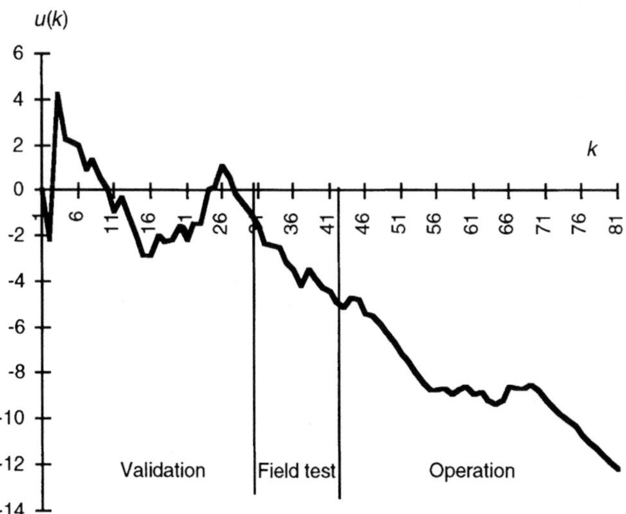

Figure 10.6 Laplace factor for the TROPICO-R considering the whole data set.

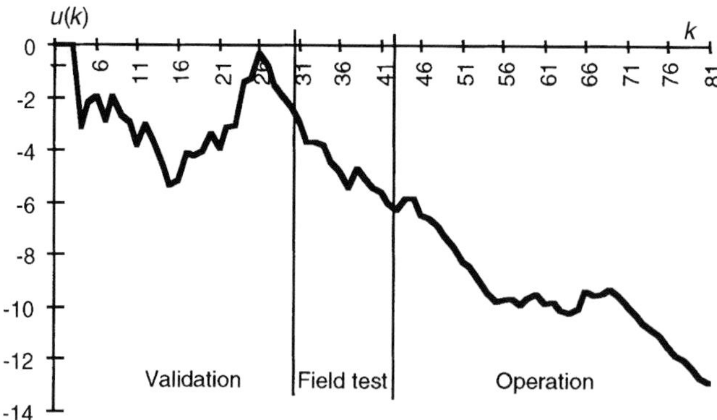

Figure 10.7 Laplace factor for TROPICO-R without considering the first two units of time.

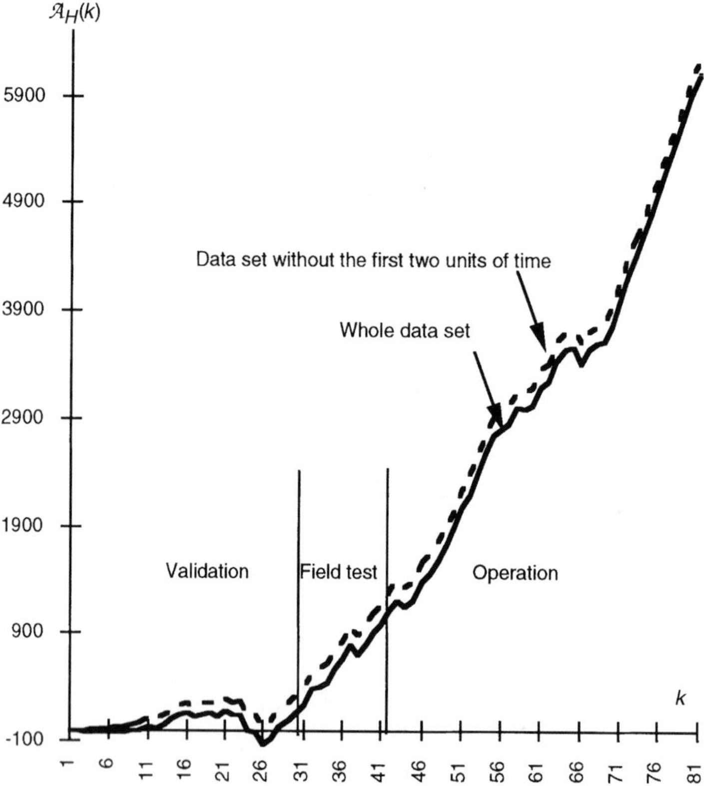

Figure 10.8 Subadditivity factor for TROPICO-R with and without considering the first two units of time.

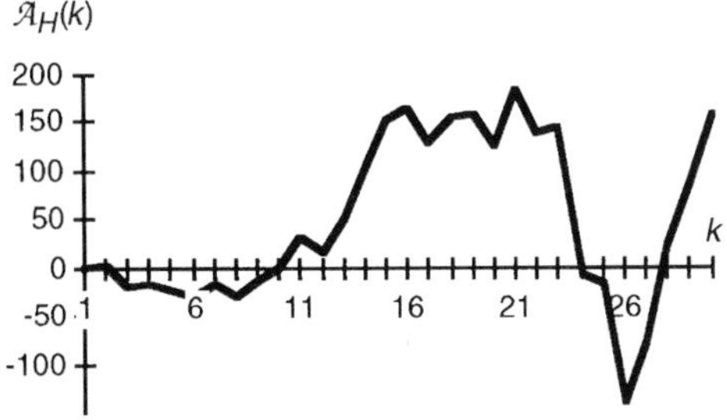

Figure 10.9 Subadditivity factor for TROPICO-R for the validation phase.

10.3.2 Example

By way of example, we illustrate the features of the Laplace factor introduced in the previous paragraph. The data are those collected on system 2 presented in [Musa79], denoted S2 in this chapter. Fifty-four failures occurred during the observation period covering system testing.

The left column of Table 10.1 gives the number of failures, i; the second column lists the execution time (in seconds) from system restart after failure $i - 1$ to failure i. We use Eq. (10.10) to evaluate the Laplace factor, $u(i)$, from $i = 2$ up to $i = 54$. Numerical values of $u(i)$ are given in the third column of Table 10.1. Certain values are worth commenting upon. Time to failure 2 is larger than time to failure 1. As a result $u(2)$ is negative, indicating reliability growth. The times to failures are still increasing up to failure 8, and the Laplace factor is also negative and decreasing, indicating reliability growth over [1, 8]. Time to failure 9 is smaller, thus evidencing local variation which leads to an increasing but still negative Laplace factor, indicating reliability growth over [1, 9], and so on. The Laplace factor is indeed negative over all the period considered. It is illustrated in Fig. 10.10*a*. This figure shows that from failures 31 to 41, $u(i)$ is increasing, indicating a local reliability decrease over this time interval despite a global reliability growth. If we consider data items from failure 31 only and evaluate again $u(i)$ for $i = 32$ to 54, the Laplace factor becomes positive up to $i = 42$, confirming reliability decrease over this period of time. The numerical results are given in the right column of Table 10.1, and the corresponding curve in Fig. 10.10*b*.

Consider the failure intensity for the same system. It is obtained by computing the number of failures over periods of time of equal length (called *units of time*). Cumulative execution time obtained by summing all the times to failures is 108,708 s. The unit of time considered is 5000 seconds of execution time, which leads to 22 units of time. This choice is a trade-off. Indeed, if a small unit of time (2000–3000 s) were considered it would lead to several units of times during which zero failure would be observed mainly during the last period of observation, and, on

TABLE 10.1 Times to Failures and Laplace Factor for System S2

(In seconds of execution time)

Failure no. (i)	Time to failure (seconds)	Laplace factor $u(i)$	Laplace factor (from 31)
1	191	0.00	
2	222	–0.13	
3	280	–0.31	
4	290	–0.36	
5	290	–0.36	
6	385	–0.55	
7	570	–0.93	
8	610	–1.15	
9	365	–0.97	
10	390	–0.86	
11	275	–0.64	
12	360	–0.57	
13	800	–0.99	
14	1,210	–1.59	
15	407	–1.4	
16	50	–0.95	
17	660	–1.07	
18	1,507	–1.73	
19	625	–1.67	
20	912	–1.78	
21	638	–1.72	
22	293	–1.47	
23	1,212	–1.75	
24	612	–1.67	
25	675	–1.64	
26	1,215	–1.86	
27	2,715	–2.6	
28	3,551	–3.35	
29	800	–3.19	
30	3,910	–3.79	
31	6,900	–4.68	0.00
32	3,300	–4.78	1.88
33	1,510	–4.62	2.07
34	195	–4.28	2.62
35	1,956	–4.22	2.41
36	135	–3.89	2.88
37	661	–3.65	3.07
38	50	–3.33	3.47
39	729	–3.14	3.53
40	900	–2.99	3.50
41	180	–2.71	3.79
42	4,225	–3.19	2.44
43	15,600	–4.97	–0.59
44	0	–4.65	–0.09
45	0	–4.34	0.38
46	300	–4.07	0.76
47	9,021	–4.77	–0.31
48	2,519	–4.72	–0.23
49	6,890	–5.06	–0.69
50	3,348	–5.06	–0.67
51	2,750	–5.00	–0.58
52	6,675	–5.25	–0.91
53	6,945	–5.48	–1.19
54	7,899	–5.73	–1.49

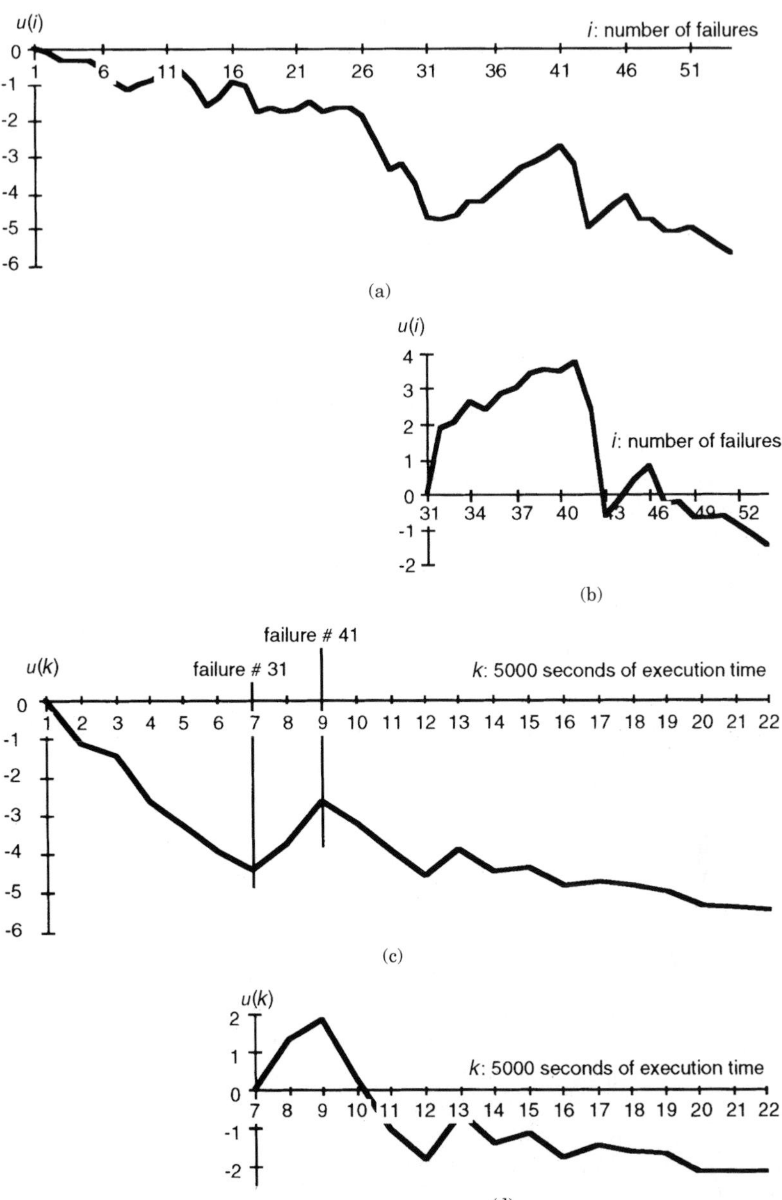

Figure 10.10 Laplace factor for system S2. (*a*) Laplace factor for the times to failure considering the whole data set. (*b*) Laplace factor for the times to failure from failure 31. (*c*) Laplace factor for the failure intensity considering the whole data set. (*d*) Laplace factor for the failure intensity from unit time 7.

the other hand, a larger unit of time would lead to a smaller number of units of time and hence to less detailed information.

The first three columns of Table 10.2 list, respectively, the number of time unit, the corresponding number of failures during this time unit, and the Laplace factor evaluated using Eq. (10.11) or Eq. (10.13), which are equivalent. The Laplace factor is also displayed in Fig. 10.10*c* and shows a reliability decrease between unit times 7 and 9. Failure 31 occurred during unit of time 7, and failure 42 during unit of time 9. The comparison of Fig. 10.10*a* and *c* shows that the Laplace factor gives similar results when considering failure intensity or times to failure. Application of the Laplace test to failure data from the 7th unit of time (last column of Table 10.2 and Fig. 10.10*d*) leads to results similar to those obtained when considering data items from failure 31.

10.3.3 Typical results that can be drawn from trend analyses

Trend analyses are a great help when it comes to appreciating the efficiency of test activities and controlling their progress. They are particularly helpful for following up the software development. Indeed, graphical tests are often used in the industry [Grad87, Ross87,

TABLE 10.2 Number of Failures Per Periods of 5000 s and Laplace Factor for System S2

Unit of time (k)	Failure intensity	Laplace factor $u(k)$	Laplace factor (from 7)
1	12	0.00	
2	7	−1.15	
3	6	−1.47	
4	2	−2.67	
5	2	−3.28	
6	1	−3.96	
7	1	−4.40	0.00
8	4	−3.73	1.34
9	6	−2.66	1.85
10	1	−3.22	0.26
11	0	−3.95	−1.02
12	0	−4.56	−1.86
13	4	−3.90	−0.62
14	0	−4.46	−1.42
15	2	−4.38	−1.19
16	0	−4.85	−1.81
17	2	−4.71	−1.48
18	1	−4.84	−1.61
19	1	−4.96	−1.71
20	0	−5.34	−2.17
21	1	−5.40	−2.17
22	1	−5.45	−2.17

Vale88]—even though they are referred to differently (e.g., descriptive statistics or control charts).

Also worth pointing out here is that the role of the trend analysis is only to *draw attention* to problems that might otherwise pass unnoticed until it is too late, thus providing an early warning likely to speed up the search for a solution. Trend analysis can be used to enrich the interpretation of someone who knows the software from which the data are derived, as well as the development process and the user environment.

In the following, three typical situations are outlined: reliability decrease, reliability growth, and stable reliability.

Reliability decrease at the beginning of a new activity is generally expected and considered normal. Examples of such activities are

- New life cycle phase
- Change in the test sets within the same phase
- Addition of new users
- Activation of the system in a different profile of use

Also, reliability decrease may result from regression faults. Trend analysis allows this kind of behavior to be noticed. If the duration of the decrease period seems long, there may be cause for alarm. In some situations, if it continues to decrease there may be some problems within the software. Analyzing the reasons for this decrease as well as the nature of the activated faults is of prime importance in these kinds of situations. Such analysis may result in the decision to reexamine the corresponding software part.

Reliability growth following reliability decrease is usually welcomed, since it indicates that, after removal of the first faults, the corresponding activity reveals fewer and fewer faults. When calendar time is used, mainly in operational life, sudden reliability growth may result from a period of time during which the system is less used or not used at all; it may also be due to some failures that are not recorded. When this is noticed, particular care must be taken and, more important, the reasons for this sudden increase have to be analyzed.

Stable reliability indicates that either (1) the software does not undergo corrective maintenance or (2) the corrective actions performed have no visible effect on reliability. When the software is under validation, stable reliability with almost no failures means that the corresponding activity has reached a saturation: the application of the corresponding test sets does not reveal new faults. One has to either stop testing, introduce new test sets, or proceed to the next phase. More generally, it is recommended that the application of a test set continue as long as it exhibits reliability growth and end when stable reliability with almost no failures is reached. Thus, in practice, if stable reliability has not been reached the validation team (and the manager) may decide to continue testing before software delivery (since it will be more efficient and cost-effective to do so) and to remove faults during validation rather than during operation.

Finally, trend analyses may greatly help reliability growth models to give better estimations, since they can be applied to data displaying trends in accordance with their assumptions rather than blindly. Applying reliability growth models blindly may lead to nonrealistic results when the trend displayed by the data differs from that assumed by the model. Failure data can be partitioned according to the trend:

- In case of reliability growth, most of the existing reliability growth models can be applied.
- In case of reliability decrease, only models allowing an increasing failure intensity can be applied.
- When the failure data exhibit reliability decrease followed by reliability growth, an S-shaped model [Ohba84] can be applied.
- When stable reliability is noticed, a constant failure intensity model can be applied (HPP model); reliability growth models are in fact not needed.

10.3.4 Summary

In this section, we have presented a few trend tests and tried to keep the presentation as simple as possible by skipping mathematical developments and giving graphical and practical interpretations. The Laplace and the Hollander tests can be used as conventional statistical tests with significance levels. However, the graphical interpretation of the subadditive property and the link between the Laplace factor and the subadditivity factor enable both local trend change and trend on average to be identified at a glance. In practice, we will mainly plot the Laplace factor and possibly the subadditivity factor in order to follow up the software reliability. Processing of the failure data from system S2 showed the benefit of using the Laplace factor to identify local trend changes as well.

10.4 Application to Real Systems

This section is intended to illustrate the type of results that may be expected from trend analysis during development and operational phases, as well as from the application of reliability growth models.

Since the previous section showed the link between the Laplace factor and the subadditivity factor, we will use both. The aim of this section is simply to illustrate some of the points introduced in the previous section, and not to make detailed analyses of the data sets considered. For further details about the systems considered, you may consult the publications referenced. We will analyze the trend of five data sets, some of them being in the form of times to failures and the others being in the form of failure intensity. In order to show the consistency of the results derived from the various trend tests, more than one test will be applied for some data sets.

The considered software systems are as follows:

1. System *SS4* of [Musa79]
2. The system also considered in [Musa79] referred to as *S27*
3. The system corresponding to the switching system of section 2 in [Kano91a], called *SS1*
4. The so-called *SS2* system, corresponding to the switching system observed during validation and part of operational life [Kano93b]
5. The system corresponding to an avionic application, referred to as *SAV*

For each one, we give the results of the trend analysis and comment on the type of reliability growth models that could be (or has been) used. The analyses are performed using SoRel, a tool for reliability analysis and evaluation presented in App. A.

10.4.1 Software of system SS4

Failure data gathered on SS4 correspond to operational life. Application of the arithmetical mean test in Fig. 10.11*a* shows that the mean time to failure is almost constant: about 230,000 units of time. The corresponding Laplace factor given in Fig. 10.11*b* oscillates between –2 and +2, also indicating stable reliability for a significance level of 5 percent.

As for system S2 considered in Sec. 10.3, we evaluate the failure intensity considering a unit of time of 10^6 seconds of execution time. The application of Laplace test to the failure intensity (displayed in Fig. 10.11*c*) also indicates stable reliability at the same significance level. For this system, a constant failure rate (i.e., HPP model) is well adapted to model the software behavior and is simpler to apply than a reliability growth model. This is not surprising since the software was in operational life without corrective maintenance. The behavior of the software is thus similar to that of the hardware:

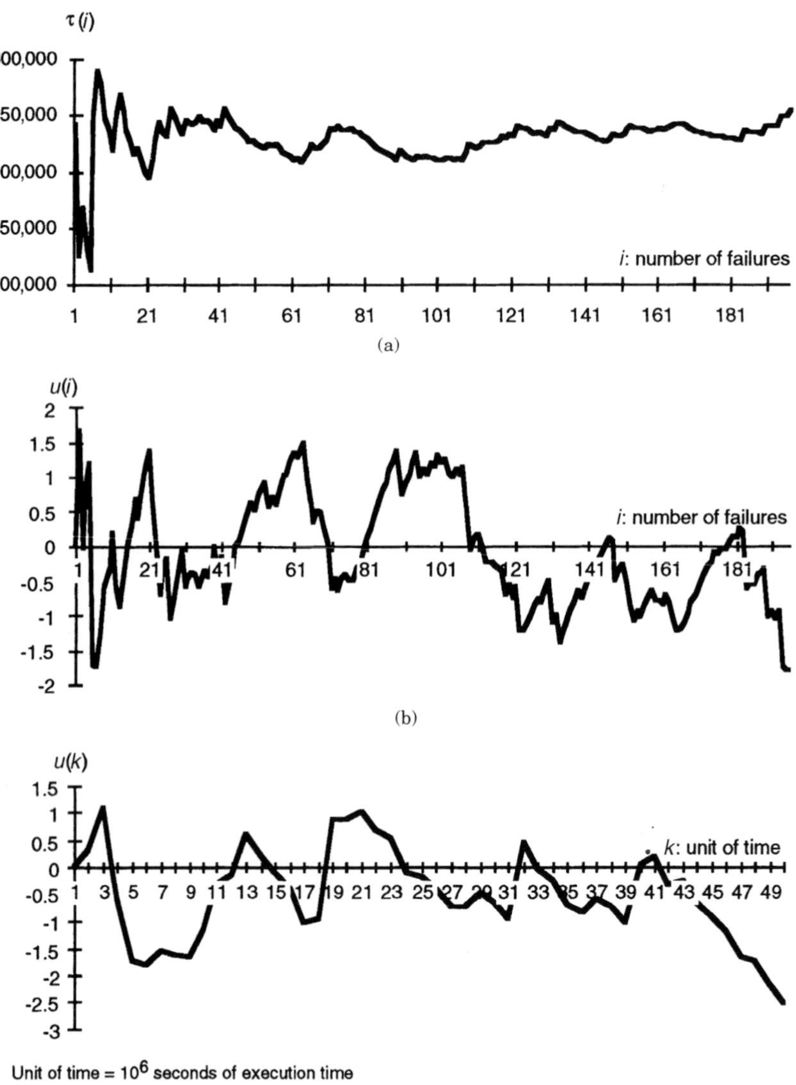

Figure 10.11 Trend tests for SS4. (*a*) Arithmetical mean of the times to failure. (*b*) Laplace factor of the times to failure. (*c*) Laplace factor of the failure intensity.

- For the hardware, the repair actions are intended to replace the failed part by another one which is identical.
- For nonmaintained software, the system is restarted with an input pattern different from the one having led to failure.

In both cases the system's ability to deliver a proper service is preserved (i.e., stochastic identity of the successive times to failure).

10.4.2 Software of system S27

S27 is an example of systems that exhibit two phases of stable reliability. The transition between them took place around the 24th failure, as indicated in Fig. 10.12. This system was under test and the reasons of this sudden change (which may be due to a singular behavior of the software) must be investigated. Unfortunately, the published data did not allow us to identify the reasons of this behavior. In this case, data may be partitioned into two subsets, each one being modeled by a constant failure rate: the failure rate of the second subset (from 24 to 42) being lower than the failure rate of the first. If we remove failure data up to failure 23 and again apply the Laplace test, the corresponding factor shown in Fig. 10.12*c* confirms the stable reliability over [24–41], except for two points.

Figure 10.12*a* and *b* illustrates the link between a graphical test (the mean of the interfailure times) and the results of the Laplace factor. Both of them point out the discontinuity in software behavior.

10.4.3 Software of system SS1

Trend tests accounting for the whole data set collected on this system are displayed in Figs. 10.6 and 10.7. Applying the Laplace test separately to each phase (ignoring data collected during the previous phases) is illustrated in Fig. 10.13.

The following comments apply to both Figs. 10.6 and 10.13:

- Reliability decrease from $k = 14$ to $k = 25$ was induced by the changes in the nature of the tests within the validation phase. This period corresponds to the application of *quality* and *performance* tests after *functional* tests in the previous period. This decrease is due to their dynamic nature (traffic simulation) which has activated new parts of the program.
- Transitions from validation to field test and from field test to operation did not give rise to a reliability discontinuity, which means that the tests applied during the end of validation are representative of operational conditions.
- Figure 10.6 indicates that from $k = 55$ up to $k = 70$ reliability tends to be stabilized: $u(k)$ is almost constant, suggesting stable reliability. However, when considering the trend results obtained for operational data only in Fig. 10.13 we notice in fact a reliability decrease over this time interval. The difference in perception of the reliability variation (from reliability growth to stable reliability or reliability decrease) is related to the interval of time considered. When considering the whole data set, a relative stable reliability is observed, and when considering only operational failure data, a relative reliability

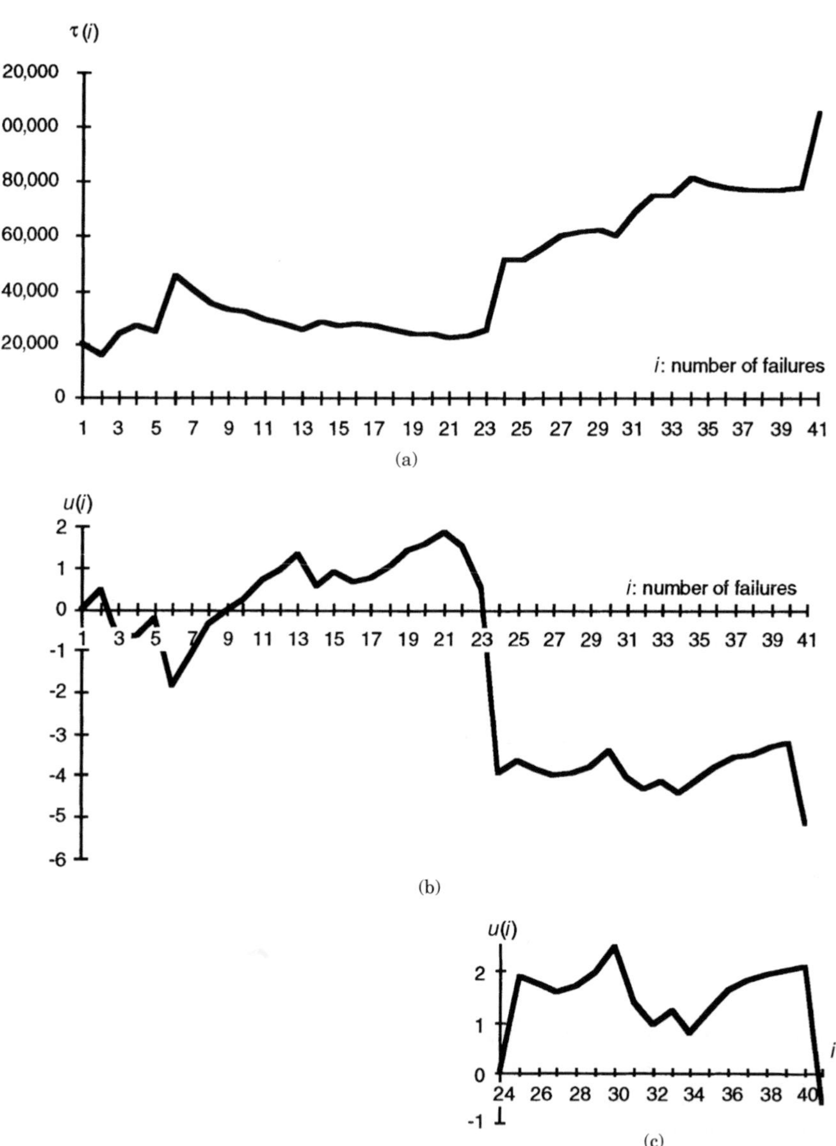

Figure 10.12 Trend tests for S27 considering the times to failure. (a) Arithmetical mean of the times to failure. (b) Laplace factor of the times to failure. (c) Laplace factor from the 24th failure.

decrease is observed. It can also be noted that the trend change points do not vary from Fig. 10.6 to Fig. 10.13.

- From $k = 70$, the trend is reversed. This failure behavior is directly related to the number of installed systems over the periods considered, during which about 12 systems were installed and the number

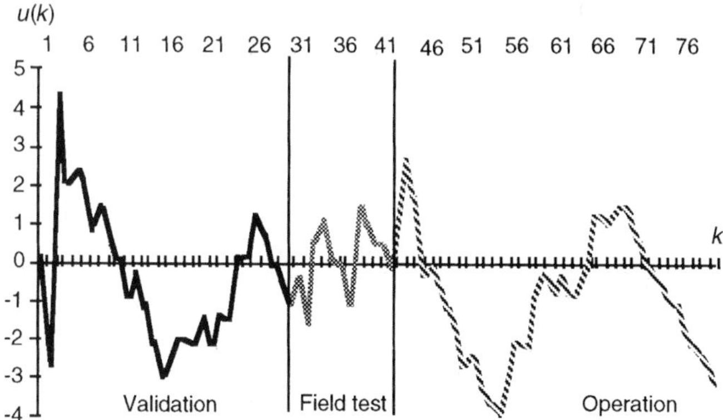

Figure 10.13 Laplace factor of SS1 for each phase.

of failures reported by the users increased. By time unit 70, a new generation of systems had been released and no additional former system had been installed, which corresponds to the period of reliability growth from time unit 70.

Applying the reliability growth models blindly to this data set would have produced no significant results. However, taking into account the increasing number of installed systems and using the trend analysis results led to trustworthy predictions from reliability growth models. These results [Kano91a] are in agreement with those observed later.

10.4.4 Software of system SS2

The subadditivity factor, $\mathcal{A}_H(k)$, for this system is given in Fig. 10.14. SS2 displayed a reliability decrease during validation; reliability growth took place during operational life only. This is confirmed by Fig. 10.15, where the subadditivity factor for operational life is applied to the data collected during operation only. It can also be seen that some reliability fluctuations took place starting from unit time 15; this fluctuation is due to the introduction of new users. Clearly, no reliability growth model can be applied during validation. Nonetheless, an S-shaped model can be applied to the whole data set. Also, any reliability growth model with a decreasing failure rate can be applied to the data collected during operation (from unit of time 9) [Kano93b].

10.4.5 SAV

We consider the data collected during 70 units of time including the end of validation and operational life. Only a few failures were discovered during operation (which started at unit time 28), and even these

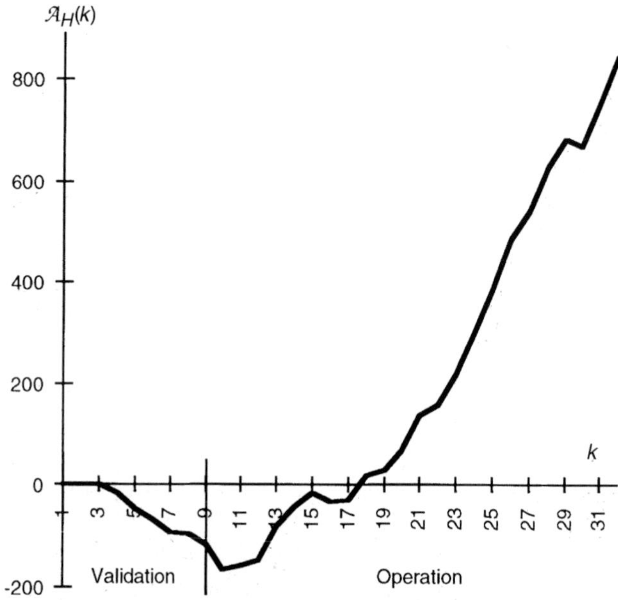

Figure 10.14 Subadditivity factor for SS2 considering the whole data set.

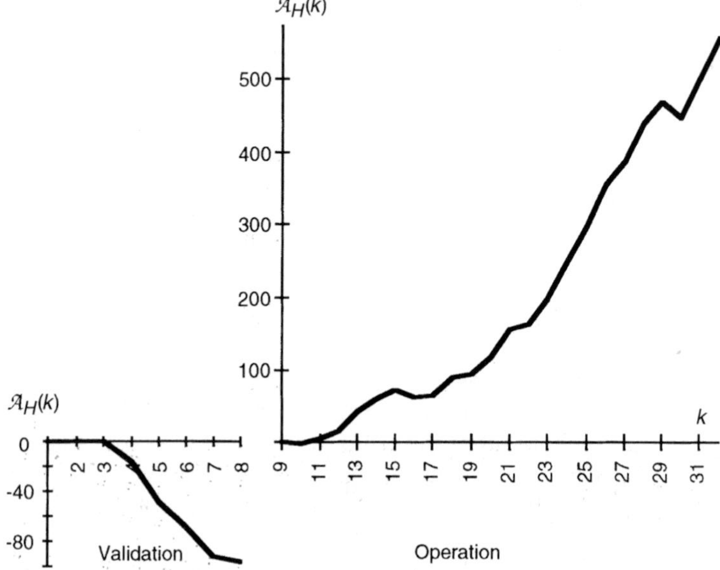

Figure 10.15 Subadditivity factor for SS2 considering each phase separately.

failures were detected by the software manufacturer during introduction of new functionalities (specification changes). The Laplace factor for this system is given in Fig. 10.16. The reliability decrease around the 24th unit of time is due mainly to the introduction of new versions corresponding to changes in the specifications. It can be seen that a significant reliability improvement took place during operation (when considering the whole data set).

10.5 Extension to Static Analysis

10.5.1 Static analysis conduct

It is well known that software fault-fixing in the earlier development phases is much less expensive than fault-fixing at a later stage of development and during operation [Boeh81]. It is also well known that static analysis (carried out either by means of walk-through or code review or inspections) substantially reduces the corrective maintenance. Thus it is important to provide the software developer with some statistical criteria to guide the decision to drop from one phase to the following phase of the inspection process or testing.

The figures published in [Faga76, Ross87, Bush90, and Saye90] show that, for systems undergoing thorough walk-throughs or inspections, the majority of faults are detected before software execution (75 to 95 percent of the faults being found before software testing). For these systems, the analysis of data collected during testing can be advantageously preceded by analysis performed on data related to the trouble reports recorded during walk-throughs or inspections.

Generally, walk-throughs and code review vary greatly in terms of regularity and thoroughness, whereas inspections have well-established

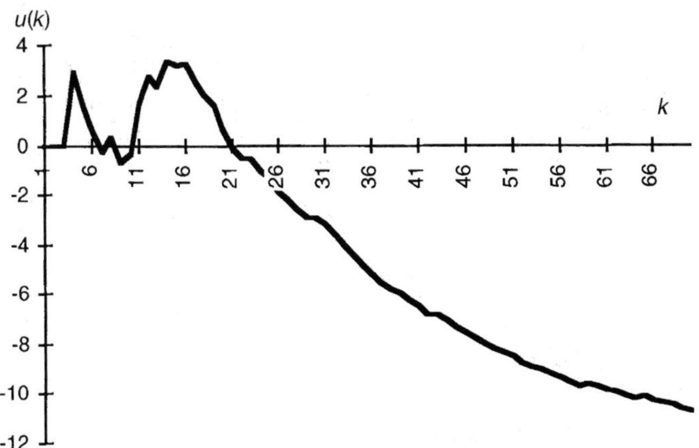

Figure 10.16 Laplace factor for the observed failures of SAV.

and rigorous procedures [Faga76]. During inspections, exit from one operation to the following one is based on criteria that are checkpoints in the development process through which every programming project must pass. The sets of exit criteria are defined for each project and should be as objective as possible so as to be repeatable [Faga86]. For walk-throughs, such criteria do not exist and exit from the different operations is left to responsible judgment.

Faults detected during static analysis of the code and during testing in the absence of static analysis are faults located in the code; using the same approach in both phases seems natural. For design-level inspections, even though the nature of the detected faults may differ from those detected later, data analysis may be conducted as the analysis of failure reports recorded during testing and operation. Inspection progress can thus be monitored using trend analysis results (in addition to the exit criteria already used for exit between operations)* as for testing. However, due to the differing nature of the faults detected during the various inspection levels (or phases), each level has to be monitored separately to handle data of the same nature (note that this is common practice when processing data from different test phases).

As far as we know, statistical processing of information that can be derived from troubles reported during inspection or walk-through phases is seldom used to guide the management of these phases; the work published in [Grad86] constitutes an exception. Generally, these data are either processed together with data from software testing by application of reliability growth models, as carried out in [Ross89], or processed by a tracking model based on the results related to previous similar projects as in [Kan91] in order to approximate the final quality index of the software and not to guide its management as proposed here.

Theoretical aspects and practical results presented in Secs. 10.2 and 10.3 can thus be adapted to faults detected by static analysis. Data in the form "number of faults detected per unit of time" is better suited to these phases, since the supplier is more interested in the process of removing faults than in evaluating intervals between two fault detections. The choice of unit of time duration is determined by the duration of the inspection phases and the number of faults detected. The unit of time may range from a few hours to one day when several faults are detected during such periods, or a few days when less faults are detected; and the unit of time can be changed from one phase to the

* It is worth noting that exit criteria for software inspection and monitoring criteria using trend tests are not contradictory. The first one has to be applied to internal operations within an inspection level, whereas the second constitutes a criterion based on the number of troubles detected by this activity and helps make the decision to exit the inspection level considered.

next. However, since the software is not executed during inspection, talking about reliability growth or decrease is meaningless. We are interested in the evolution of the number of troubles reported versus time and not in the evolution of the interfailure times or number of failures. Nevertheless we will abusively use "reliability growth" (respectively, decrease) to characterize situations where the number of trouble reports is decreasing in time (respectively, increasing).

10.5.2 Application

Consider again SAV, the software of the avionic application studied in the previous section. For this system, troubles detected during specification and code review have been recorded in trouble reports analogous to failure reports. Since the system specifications kept changing during the life cycle, trouble reports were drawn up even when the system was in operation (while adding new parts to the software). For this system, more than 50 percent of faults were detected by specification and code review.

The Laplace factor corresponding to the trouble reports is given in Fig. 10.17 which, as in the case of software execution, reveals an almost steady reliability growth from unit of time 16. Reliability fluctuation at the beginning is due to the review of new specifications and the corresponding software code. From unit of time 25, it is interesting to note that the very local fluctuations of the Laplace factor corresponding to trouble reports (indicated by the arrows in Fig. 10.18) are also followed by local fluctuations of the Laplace factor corresponding to software failures. The time lag corresponds to the time interval between the review of the new part of the software (either specification or code) and the execution (testing) of this part of the software.

10.6 Summary

In this chapter, we have characterized reliability growth using the notion of the subadditive property. Then a graphical interpretation of this property was derived and we have shown the equivalence between this property and the Laplace factor, thus allowing for the Laplace test to be extended to local trend-change identification.

We have shown (1) that trend analyses constitute a major tool during the software development process, from static analysis to system integration and (2) how the results can guide the project manager to control the progress of the development activities and even to make the decision to reexamine the software for specific situations. Extension of trend analyses to trouble reports from static analysis is all the more useful as the majority of faults are detected by design and code inspec-

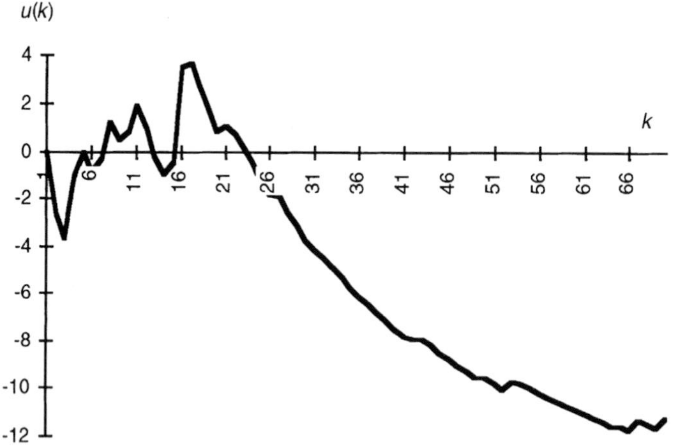

Figure 10.17 Laplace factor for the trouble reports related to SAV review.

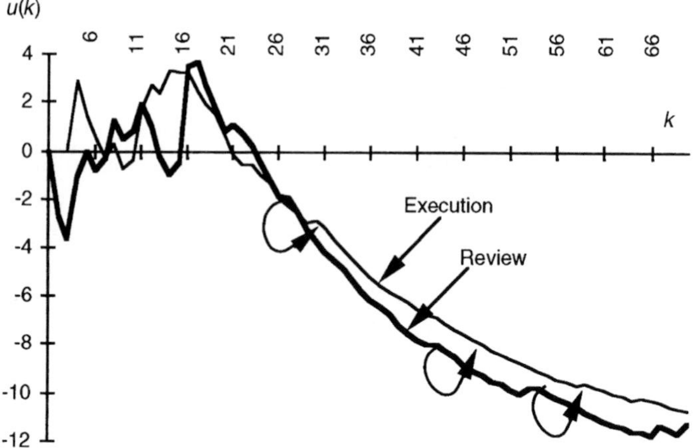

Figure 10.18 Laplace factor for the trouble reports and for the observed failures related to SAV.

tion; monitoring the inspection activities is thus of prime importance in these situations.

Trend analyses are also helpful when reliability evaluation is needed. They allow periods of reliability growth and reliability decrease to be identified in order to apply reliability growth models to data exhibiting trends in accordance with their modeling assumptions. Trend analysis and reliability growth models are part of a global method for software reliability analysis and evaluation which is presented in [Kano88, Kano93b] and which has been successfully applied to data collected on real systems [Kano87, Kano91a].

Problems

10.1 The table in Fig. 10.19 gives the successive interfailure times observed during the validation test of an application software (read from left to right). Which trend tests can you apply to this data set? Apply at least one of them. Does this curve or the results of the trend test application reveal a possible abnormal behavior?

10.2 Assuming that Fig. 10.19 represents the observed failure intensity (number of failures per week), answer the same questions as in Prob. 10.1.

10.3 The Laplace factor calculated from the failure intensity data collected during testing is plotted in Fig. 10.20. Identify the various periods of reliability growth/decrease. Can you think of some reasons for this reliability decrease? Comment on this and recommend one or more reliability growth models which could be applied according to the trend.

10.4 After three months of software testing without specification changes, the observed failure intensity is given in Fig. 10.21. Identify the period(s) of reliability decrease. What could be the reasons for this decrease? (Give some reasons that seem acceptable from a tester's point of view, and others that could help improve the validation procedures.)

10.5 Repeat Prob. 10.4 assuming two new versions of the software have been introduced due to specification changes. Locate approximately the times of the introduction of the new versions. Comment on this.

10.6 In the text (Sec. 10.2.2), we have shown how Eq. (10.3) implies Eq. (10.5) in the case where K is even. Show this implication when K is odd.

12	10	16	13	6	7	6	5	7	9	8	9	7	5	6
3	5	3	7	9	8	10	9	12	10	14	12	15	13	

Figure 10.19

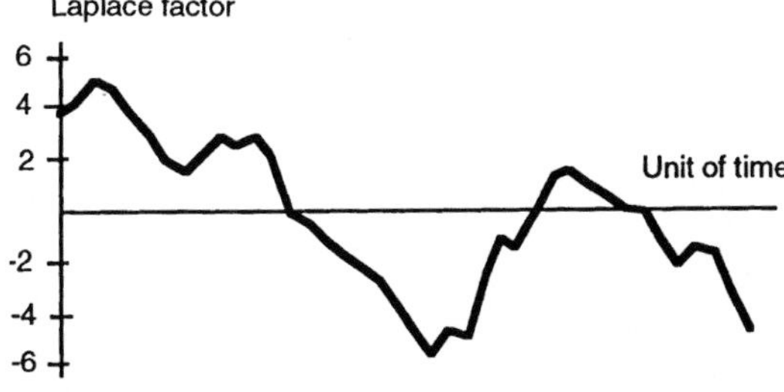

Figure 10.20

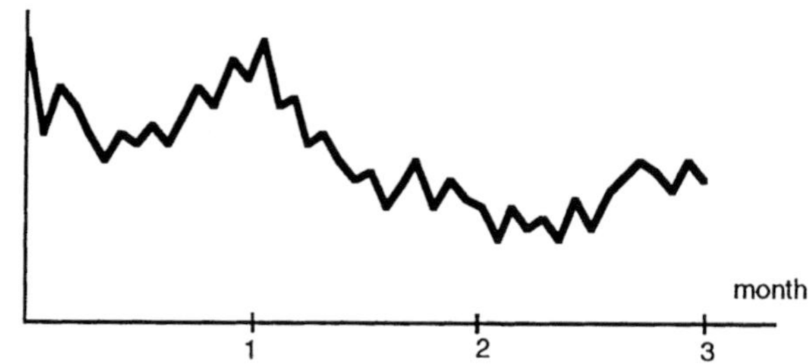

Figure 10.21

10.7 The observed failure intensity during the last six months of software testing is given in Fig. 10.22*a* (number of failures per week). It is assumed that there are no quantified reliability objectives. Our aim in this exercise is to use qualitative and informal criteria from trend test results and the observed failure intensity to guide the development process. The informal criteria for software delivery is the following: "the software has reached a stable reliability behavior with a few failures per week—more precisely, less than 10 failures per month."

a. Plot the failure intensity and the corresponding Laplace factor. Delivery of the software is planned for the end of the year. Does this aim seem reachable?

b. The failure intensity observed during the following three months (months 7 to 9) is given in Fig. 10.22*b* (number of failures per week). Comment about the trend. Do you think that it is still reasonable to plan delivery for the end of the year?

c. The failure intensity observed during the following three months (months 10 to 12) is given in Fig. 10.22*c* (number of failures per

30	31	25	30	28	27	32	25	30	28
29	25	27	28	26	25	23	24	19	20
17	15	16	12	15	17				

Figure 10.22(*a*)

12	15	13	12	9	12	10	11	9
10	14	15						

Figure 10.22(*b*)

17	16	14	17	15	10	8	9	6	7
5	3	4							

Figure 10.22(*c*)

week). At the end of the 10th month do you think that it is still reasonable to plan delivery for the end of the year? Plot the overall failure intensity and the Laplace factor. What could be the reasons for the failure intensity increase at the beginning of the last quarter?

10.8 The average failure intensity observed during four weeks of testing is (assuming seven working days):

- 5 failures per day the first week
- 3 failures per day the second week
- 2 failures per day the third week
- 0.2 failures per day the fourth week

Plot the failure intensity and the cumulative number of failures. Show that the latter is subadditive over the considered period. Plot the Laplace factor.

10.9 After 12 weeks of testing, the observed failure intensity can be approximated as follows:

- For $0 \leq t < 3$, $h(t) = 2 + 3t$
- For $3 \leq t < 7$, $h(t) = 17 - 2t$
- For $7 \leq t < 9$, $h(t) = 10 - t$
- For $9 \leq t \leq 12$, $h(t) = 1$

Plot the failure intensity and the cumulative number of failures. What about the subadditive property? Locate approximately the region of trend change. Plot the Laplace factor.

10.10 The failure intensity (i.e., the number of failures per week) observed during the validation of a software system is given in Fig. 10.23 (read from left to right). Plot the failure intensity and the Laplace factor. What conclusions can be drawn for the trend? Partition the data according to the trend and plot the Laplace factor for the subset displaying reliability growth.

15	17	16	19	20	17	20	19	21	19
25	28	26	24	26	25	23	24	19	20
17	15	16	12	15	17	12	15	13	12
9	12	10	11	9	13	10	9	10	8
7	9	5	6						

Figure 10.23

Chapter

11

Field Data Analysis

Wendell D. Jones
BNR Inc.

Mladen A. Vouk
North Carolina State University

11.1 Introduction

The role and functionality of software in modern computer-based systems is growing at a tremendous rate. At the same time, pressures are mounting on software developers to deliver and maintain software of better quality. Current experience indicates that, as organizations create more complex systems, software failures are an increasing proportion of system failures, while the information about these failures is frequently less than complete, uniform, or precise.

For example, field data on large telephone switching systems indicate that software is responsible for 20 to 50 percent of complete system outages. Figure 11.1 illustrates the percentage of reported causes of total system outages (due to hardware, software, and other causes) for two large telecommunications systems [Leve89, Leve90, Cram92]. The values indicated are averaged over several releases. Although both systems have similar overall functionality, there are some remarkable differences that underline an important, and often observed, property of software field reliability data—*variability*.

When examining individual releases for system A, about 30 to 60 percent of outages were attributed to hardware (some of which may have involved a combination of hardware and software problems), about 20 to 25 percent were attributed to software, while procedural and other errors accounted for the remainder of the outages [Leve90, Leve93]. In the case of system B, 3 to 7 percent of outages were attributed to hardware, and between 15 and 60 percent (depending on the maturity of the release) could be attributed to software. The figures

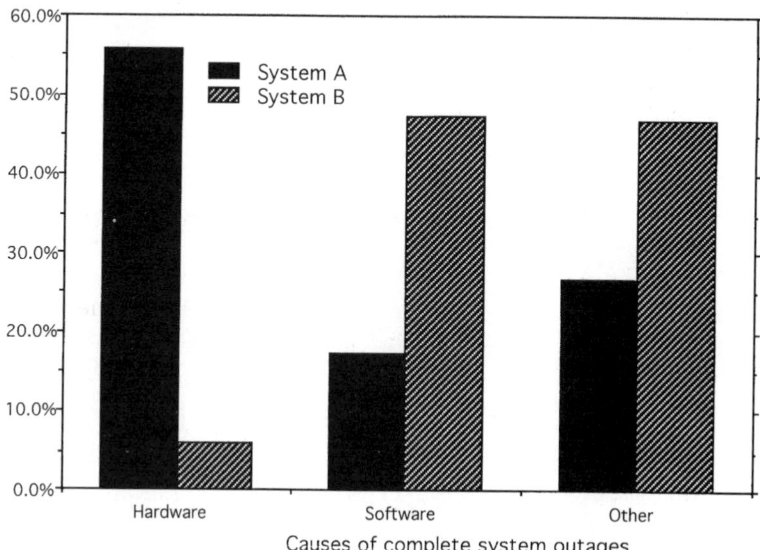

Figure 11.1 Causes of complete system outages averaged over several releases for two large telecommunication systems: System A [Leve90] and System B [Cram92].

reported for system A are closer to the distributions reported for operating systems [Iyer85a, Iyer85b]. The variance between systems A and B is due to, at least in part, the lack of a precise definition for software outage categories. It may also differ due to the functional implementation strategy of the two systems (for example, system A may implement more functionality in hardware). Whatever the reasons, it is not easy to compare the two systems and draw objective conclusions.

Examples like the one above can be found in all application areas. Therefore, it is not surprising that there are industrial, national, and international efforts to standardize software reliability data collection and analysis processes. For example, in the United States, Bellcore is an organization that acts as a software-quality watchdog from within the telecommunications community. Bellcore requires collection of outage data for all network switching elements, analysis of the data, and classification of the data by cause of failure [BELL89]. In fact, the U.S. Federal Communications Commission (FCC) mandates reporting of certain types of switch failures [FCC92].

A proper collection and analysis of *software* failure data lies at the heart of a practical evaluation of the quality of software-based systems. This is especially true when we consider analysis of software *field data* as opposed to test data. There is usually much less control over what is actually collected in the field; often analyses are based on the available historical data; and usage of the system usually cannot be stopped to await the analysis of the data. In addition, organizations are much more sensitive to disclosure of field data due to competitive pressures.

The *goal of this chapter* is to provide insight into the process of collection and analysis of software reliability field data through a discussion of the underlying principles and case study illustrations. A distinction is made between (1) the data collected from the actual operational sites where software is used by its intended users during field tests or in day-to-day production and (2) the data collected during *controlled* system tests and experiments with operational software. The latter categories were discussed in the earlier chapters, and therefore are not considered. In the next two sections we discuss data collection principles and the basics of practical data screening and analysis. This is followed by sections that provide definition and discussion of four important topics in reliability studies—*calendar-time* analysis, *usage-time* analysis, *special-event* analysis, and *availability* analysis. Field analysis of other dependability measures, such as safety and security, is not examined in this chapter.

11.2 Data Collection Principles

11.2.1 Introduction

Software reliability is often expressed in terms of probability of failure in a given time, or in terms of the failure intensity, which is the number of failures per unit time. Minimum data requirements for calculating one expression may be slightly different than the other. Furthermore, precision in the data collection mechanism may affect the variance in reliability parameter estimates or field predictions. For example, as discussed in Chap. 1, the basic information required to perform reliability analyses includes the amount of time a software system is in operation and the exact times that failures occur. A less precise, but usable, alternative would be condensed data that reports only the total number of failures observed over a period of time. Also, additional data may be required if we wish to do more than analyze the reliability of the product. For example, if we desire to determine the availability of the product, we need both failure repair and failure severity information.

For the purpose of our discussion, we will say that whenever there is a need to make an evaluation of, or draw a conclusion based on, software reliability or availability, we conduct a *study*. Software reliability studies must have clearly defined objectives, goals, and analysis methods so that efficient use may be made of the existing data and that the cost of collecting required supplemental data is minimized. The data needed for collection and its subsequent analysis should be related to the *goals* of the study. In reliability field data analysis, some important goals are (1) to *assess* the actual quality and reliability of a software product in its operational environment (which in turn assists in determining compliance with requirements or regulations and with the planning of maintenance resources); (2) to *relate* field failure behavior of software to its usage in the field and to its development and maintenance processes through *models;* and (3) to *predict* software behavior in the field and *control* its *field quality* by controlling its development, testing, and maintenance processes and methods.

In industry the first goal has preeminence at this time, and it is the logical first step when conducting field analysis. For example, [Hude92] provides an illustration of how field data analysis can be used to plan maintenance resources. This paper also illustrates how Nortel made progress in relation to goal 2. Goals 2 and 3 are difficult and require that field analysis be supplemented with process and product information, but achieving these goals is needed to impact the software development process and assist in its maturing. Although various organizations may have different goals, exact and detailed goals are needed to properly carry out a study [Basi84b] or any other software-related task [Boeh89, Boeh91].

11.2.2 Failures, Faults, and Related Data

Definitions for failures and faults are given in Chap. 1. More comprehensive definitions that include human errors are given in [IEEE88b, Lapr92a, Gert94]. Accurate field collection of this information and related data is essential. In addition to recording the failures and the times of corrective actions, other information is helpful for a full analysis (e.g., [IEEE88a, IEEE88b, BELL90a, Mell93]). Table 11.1 provides an example of the data that can help a designer take corrective action and also allow an analyst to properly segment and prepare data for system-level software reliability analysis. In the table, we distinguish between general classifiers, such as date and time of failure, and software-specific classifiers, such as software version information and causal analysis information.

We caution that Table 11.1 is not a form for data collection and therefore should not be used as such. The information in Table 11.1 is usually drawn from a variety of sources: customers, field support personnel, problem screeners, designers, system engineers, and maintenance personnel, including patch applicators. However, it would be very difficult for a reliability analyst to gather this information individually for all failures. Instead, what is needed is a toolset that allows integration of information (whether preexisting or current) from many sources and a variety of forms (e.g., reports, files, or databases) so that an analyst can create a table similar to Table 11.1.

TABLE 11.1 Examples of Fields Required for Reliability Analysis

Note	General classifiers	Example
Required	Date failure occurred	921214
	Time failure occurred	045600
	Date failure was reported	921214
	Tracking number or identifier (it often helps to make these identifiers as informative as possible)	ATCH-E2-1-00076
	Customer name or code	American Technology
Recommended	Site code or comparable entity	CHCGILAA34F
	Customer severity of failure (for example, critical, high, medium, low)	High
	Degradation	
	Level of degradation to system (percent)	5
	Duration of degradation (minutes)	23
	Apparent cause—top-level classification (determined at time of screening, e.g., hardware, software)	ISDN call processing
	Root cause (to be determined later by vendor)	Table control and configuration
	System or subsystem level of failure	ISDN
	Status in investigation (not under inv., under inv., closed, resolved)	Resolved
	Problem resolution process	
	Problem owner	J. Doe
	Status of problem (open, fixed, rejected, resolved)	Resolved
	Is the fix available? (Y or N)	Y
	Is this problem a duplicate of previous one? (Y or N) or the ID no. of the duplicate	N
	Resolution date	921220
	Software-specific classifiers	
Required	Software version	8.1
Recommended	Version of software in underlying operating system	4.0
	Problem at install? (Y or N)	N
	Failure type (executable or data)	Executable
	High-level cause	Design logic
	Design or correction fault if executable	
	Design or procedural fault if data	
	Text describing the failure or the input state that reproduces the failure	ISDN PRI trunks do not come up on warm restart when . . .
	Patch created (Y or N)	Y
	Patch process	
	Patch identifier	P-0192-064
	Status of patch (D—documented, C—coded, T—tested, A—available, GA—generally available)	GA
	Date patch is created	921221
	Version patch is written for	8.0+

A number of larger organizations have developed their own (proprietary) systems for collection and analysis of reliability data (e.g., ALCATEL, AT&T, BNR, IBM, StorageTek). There are also some commercial (e.g., [Soft93]), research (e.g., [Mos194]), and public domain [GNU95] computer-based systems for collection and analysis of software quality data (see also App. A). These systems require organization-specific customization and augmentation of their functionalities. The decisions on which data to collect, how to collect the data (for example, automated versus manual), and how to *verify correctness* of the collected information are some of the most crucial decisions an organization makes in its software reliability engineering program. Therefore they should be given appropriate attention and visibility.

Partnering with customers is essential. Without the customer's assistance it is very difficult to collect adequate field data for system analysis. The customers should know why the data are needed, how the data will be used, and how they will benefit from the analysis. Providing feedback to the customer regarding the information that is gleaned from customer field data is of great importance. It will enhance the quality of the data collected and provide customer focus that leads to quality improvement.

11.2.3 Time

In general, the more often that a (faulty) product is used, the more likely that a failure will be experienced. A full implementation of software reliability engineering requires consideration of software usage through determination of *operational profile*(s) and analysis of observed problems in that context (see Chap. 5). For example, if a software subsystem (or module) is found to exhibit an excessive number of field problems, it should be established whether this is due to very frequent usage of a component that has an average residual fault density (perhaps expressed as number of faults per line of code) or due to an excessive residual fault density in a component that is being used at the rate typical for most other product components. Reengineering of both subsystems may be required. However, the evaluation of the process that created each subsystem would be very different. For the first case, understanding the demanding requirements that are associated with the highly utilized components is of primary importance. In the second case, implementation quality is paramount. The first-case subsystem may also need extensive verification. Central to these issues is the product usage time.

Time is the execution exposure that the software receives through usage. As stated in Chap. 1, experience indicates that the best measure of time is the actual central processing unit (CPU) execution time (see also [Musa87]). However, CPU time may not be available, and it is often possible to reformulate the measurements and *reliability models* in terms of other exposure metrics: calendar time, clock time, in-service time (usually a sum of clock times due to many software applications running simultaneously on various single- or multiple-CPU systems), logical time (such as number of executed test cases or fraction of planned test cases executed), or structural coverage (such as branch achieved statement or branch coverage) [Musa87, Tian93a, Tian93b]. In-service time usually implies that each system is treated as one unit whether it has one or several CPUs. Also, 100 months of in-service time may be associated with 50 months (clock time) of two systems or 1 month (clock time) of 100 systems. In many cases, in-service time like clock time will be proportional to system execution (CPU) time. For this chapter, the term *usage time* will refer to any of CPU, execution, clock, or in-service time.

In considering which time to use, it is necessary to weight factors such as appropriateness of the metric, availability of the data, error-sensitivity of the metric, and its relationship to a particular model. An argument in favor of using usage or calendar time instead of, for example, structural software coverage, is that engineers often are more comfortable with time than any other exposure metric. Moreover, in order to combine hardware and software reliability into one overall reliability metric, the time (whether calendar or usage) approach may be essential (see Chap. 2).

11.2.4 Usage

Ideally, one should have a record of everywhere the system is used, and some information on how it is used. An example of the needed data related to the usage information is given in Table 11.2. Also given in the table is a sample of some additional information that aids various analyses. This type of information allows calculation of metrics such as the total number of systems in operation on a given date and total operation time accumulated over all licensed systems running a particular version of the software.

Some operating systems support collection of usage data better than others. For example, processes can be created in UNIX that allow tracking of when the software is accessed, who accesses it, how frequently it is accessed, and how long the user accesses it. This allows collection of usage data at the CPU level. However, to do this in a thorough manner, more exact knowledge of the users (through licenses and other means) is often necessary, as is access to the user's system.

Although license information is often available, usage information may be less accessible. Thus, it may be necessary to statistically sample the user population to determine certain types of usage informa-

TABLE 11.2 Example of Usage Fields

Note	Field description	Example
Required	Site code or comparable entity	CHCGILFH34F
	It must match the information in the failure classification, such as the one shown in Table 11.1	
	Version of software being used	8.1
	Date software was cut over to the above version	921201
	Version of software with which the product is being used (if applicable, e.g., HP-UX 9.0)	NA
	System configuration data (e.g., hardware processor, other software loaded with the product)	MC68050
Recommended	Date/time when software installation began	921201-033001
	Date/time when software installation ended	921201-055500
	Were there any aborts? (Y or N)	N
	Is the usage under special circumstances (trials, tests, official beta testers, etc.)?	N
	Number of licenses or users at the site	1
	Last date any field in this section changed	921202

tion. In many cases, measuring the clock time associated with usage will be a sufficiently accurate measure of exposure.

For unlicensed software, or software sold through third-party vendors, the methods can be more troublesome. Crude estimates of units sold are only part of the equation, since you need to know when they were sold (and when the product is first used, or replaced with a later version or another product). You can estimate the relative usage of a product through statistical sampling methods. In any case, some combination of statistical sampling with estimates of units sold is much better than using calendar time because of the so-called loading, or ramping, effect discussed in Sec. 11.4. If this effect is not accounted for, then we are assuming constant usage over time for most models. As a consequence, field reliability may initially appear to be better than forecasts based on system testing since the system will have little usage in its early life. Later, when customers buy the new release in larger quantities and the majority of the failures occur, the reliability will be below the forecasts.

11.2.5 Data granularity

In collecting usage and other data, remember that the useful precision of the estimate/prediction of reliability is always less than the precision of the data. For example, predictions for how many failures will occur during a particular week will be of little use if the data are only collected monthly. Therefore, choosing the right granularity is very important. For example, time intervals for data sampling or aggregation may be one second, one hour, one day, one week, one month, 10 test cases, one structural branch, or some other value. The time granularity of the raw data determines the lower limits of meaningful micromodeling and analyses that can be performed.

For a different illustration, consider prediction of the time to next failure, a standard metric in reliability analysis. With field data, predicting the time to next failure or even the next five failures is usually impractical. In many cases when field data are assimilated for analysis, groups of failures (say, 5 to 10 in size) are commonly associated with the same time frame (say, one calendar week). Predicting that the next failure will occur within the next 10 usage weeks with a probability of 0.95 will not help the customer, since 10 usage weeks may correspond to three calendar days. Thus, by the time all the data have been collected and analyzed, the next failure has *already* occurred. Field usage is very different from the laboratory test environment, where one can interrupt the testing and assess the reliability of the system before continuing with another round of tests. Field usage is continuous; therefore, analysis should be commensurate with practical data collection delays and should focus on longer-range forecasting and estimation since this can be adequately done even when the failure and/or usage data are lumped together.

11.2.6 Data maintenance and validation

In practice, a large amount of failure data may be entered manually by field support personnel from customer reports or interviews. Some software systems have internal or independent mechanisms that detect failures of various types and record that data automatically for later retrieval and processing. Even if such an automated system is in place, some data may still need to be entered manually simply because the data entry program either cannot function during a failure state or cannot recognize all failure states. Furthermore, some automated systems often cannot distinguish between hardware and software failures, and thus manual identification is required. Nevertheless, for any system, information surrounding a failure needs to be recorded as accurately as possible and data entry and database systems should be designed in such a way that all of the pertinent information is available to a reliability analyst.

Automation of date and time entries, implementation of intra- and interdata-record error and consistency checking, and standardization of entries will ensure that the analyst will have the best data possible from which to draw information. The database that holds the field data must be updated and cross-checked as new data become available or as existing data are found to be inaccurate. The importance of consistency checking cannot be overstressed. Unfortunately, it is an area that most data collection systems overlook. The effects of data discrepancies can be very pronounced, especially in the early deployment life when the usage data are sparse. For example, even a relatively small mistake in accounting for the sites involved, or in associating failures with the appropriate software releases, can have considerable impact on the failure count and the computation of the failure intensity.

Validation and maintenance of the collected data is an absolute necessity. It is our experience that it may also be a very time-consuming and tedious activity unless appropriate tools and methods are used. If you suspect that collection errors exist, then you may need to perform an initial investigation into the amount and nature of possible data collection errors. This can be done through computations as well as visually. All information, including out-of-date records, should be kept for historical analysis purposes. The analyst's worst nightmare is coming across a database that contains all the fields required to do analysis and yet the old data is thrown away because it is no longer current and thus perceived to be of little value. For example, if there is only one record in a company's data repository for each site concerning software load information, then usually only the *current* software load information is stored and the historical usage information on past loads is not retrievable. If this occurs, then create a new database that archives records of the old usage information. It will be worth the effort after only a few months, since this information is critical for computing and comparing the field reliability of different software loads.

Distinguishing different sites or installed software systems with code identifiers is important. Codes allow for segmentation of customers and provide quicker access to the relevant information. Also, codes allow the usage to be linked with the problems experienced by customers. It is very important that the identifiers used by a customer service organization to track problems are the same as the identifiers used by the marketing/engineering personnel to track software installations, especially early in the deployment of new software. The customer information recorded by installation and shipping personnel, help-line personnel, and license agreement personnel, etc., should be consistent and available to analysts.

11.2.7 Analysis environment

For proper analysis, many pieces are required that must work well together. First, there must be processes and tools in place to collect the raw data. There must also be an appropriate storage mechanism for the data, which is usually a database. If the database does not allow for easy data scanning, manipulation, and processing, then some other system should be in place to allow cursory examination and filtering of inappropriate or corrupt data. Of course, corrupt data should be corrected if possible, or at least marked as such. After filtering, an environment for merging data from different sources should be in place, since the data needed for failure analysis often reside in different systems. Also, some data may need to be transformed. Finally, for modeling and estimation, an environment that supports statistical methods should be available, as well as a good data-graphing tool. Depending on how the data will be used in a given environment, various information feedback mechanisms may be needed for different job roles that utilize that information.

An adequate environment may contain the following: (1) high-end networked color-graphic workstation, PC, or mainframe computing platform with a graphics terminal; (2) a data collection system linked to a multidimensional database management system; (3) manipulation, filtering, and data merging system such as SAS/BASE or SPSS; (4) software reliability modeling tools such as SMERFS, CASRE, or SoRel (see App. A); and (5) commercially available statistical analysis and visualization systems such as SAS/STAT and SAS/INSIGHT, SPSS, Systat, DataDesk, S or S+, Data Explorer, or AVS.

A general statistical analysis package is often a must, even if a reliability estimation tool is available. Most reliability packages are focused on parameter estimation and model-aptness of well-known models. However, many do not easily take into account covariates (i.e., variables that may be related to the quantity of interest, such as failure intensity, in some well-defined way), or support other standard statistical methods. Covariates are used infrequently at present but may be used more and more with the core models as analysts become more aware of their potential. Examples of covariates include a patch metric that indicates what percentage of patches are successful, and a usage-related metric that indicates how many (or what percentage of) sites have the latest software release. Both of these metrics vary with calendar or usage time and thus would be suitable covariate candidates. The patch metric may indicate local trends in the reliability growth (or degradation) if, for example, a group of patches were applied that did not fix the faults intended and instead caused additional failures. These additional failures may cause a deviation from the natural trend in reliability growth that would be explained by a patch metric covariate.

11.3 Data Analysis Principles

In statistics, analysis of data is usually considered exploratory or confirmatory. *Exploratory* analysis includes techniques in which conjecture associations are only beginning, and the objective is simply to explore the potential nature of the data. *Confirmatory* techniques are typically used after some body of evidence has emerged to confirm or challenge the prevailing wisdom or current thought. The *hypothesis test* is a tool very frequently used in confirmatory analysis.

Several exploratory data analysis techniques are particularly relevant in the analysis of software failure and fault data. They are *plots and graphs, data modeling* and associated diagnostics, *data transformation,* and *data resistance.* Each technique has its own special utility, but they can often be used in combination with each other. Confirmatory analysis techniques are rarer in software reliability since the nature of software failures is still very complicated. For example, confirmatory tests in the form of *trend analysis* are described in the preceding chapter. However, there is limited agreement among researchers as to the most appropriate underlying process that is descriptive and robust enough to characterize and predict the nature of software failures. Thus exploratory techniques predominate software reliability analysis in practice.

It is often assumed that in the field software exhibits (real or apparent) reliability growth. But, this assumption needs to be validated in each study. There are two primary reasons for the assumption of reliability growth. First, most software systems can be patched relatively easily. In fact, patching is one of the great advantages of software over hardware. Faults are corrected while the system is in operation, and the system subsequently experiences reliability growth. Second, users of the system may become familiar with the imminent-failure states through firsthand experience, or information from other users or the vendor. This information tends to allow the user to avoid failure modes until a correction occurs.

In the following subsections we will examine various elementary data analysis principles. For a more complete treatment of exploratory data analysis see [Tuke77]. Visual data exploration is discussed in [Clev93, Eick92, Eick94]. We present the ideas using field data from a large release of software from a major digital telecommunications company. The data set, called DataSet 1, is on the Data Disk. In most cases, we will be concerned with reliability growth models, although most of the techniques we discuss will apply to a variety of other models and analyses.

11.3.1 Plots and graphs

Plots and graphs are very powerful tools in exploratory analysis, particularly when coupled with color graphics [Clev93]. It is often the case that an analyst can determine very quickly the initial relationships and associations in a data set using scatterplots, line plots, stem-and-leaf plots, dot plots, and schematic or box plots. In software reliability, you often see plots of the main variables of interest. For example, for DataSet 1 the line plot in Fig. 11.2 illustrates the relationship between the total number of sites using the software release related to DataSet 1 (version N) and *calendar time*. We see that the number of offices is initially low, but quickly *ramps* up to the point of saturation. After the next release becomes available, the number of offices having version N steadily declines as customers migrate to the new release $N + 1$. This graph illustrates that the usage of version N is far from constant in calendar time, an important factor to consider when examining the reliability of this software, since usage often will not be proportional to calendar time.

Another frequently used graph in software reliability illustrates the relationship between cumulative software failures and usage time. For example, this graph is stipulated by Bellcore as a mandatory graph that U.S. telecommunications suppliers must provide in their reliability and quality reports [BELL90b]. Figure 11.3 is an example of this graph for system DataSet 1. Note that the data have been normalized to protect proprietary information. The main effect of normalization on the analysis is one of scaling. Therefore, in essence, the analysis of the nonnormalized data would be the same.

Based on Fig. 11.3, we may conjecture that some simple functional relationship may exist between cumulative failures and time. In fact, two potential functional relationships are shown in the figure using models that were defined in Chap. 3. If you think that both models

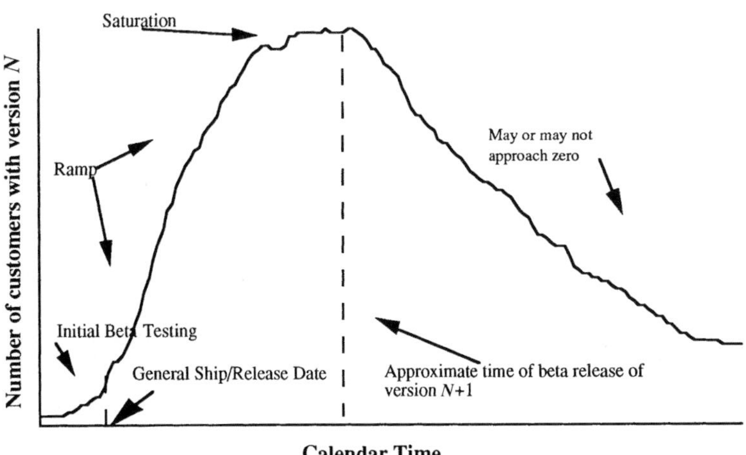

Figure 11.2 The *loading* or installation *ramping* effect (DataSet 1).

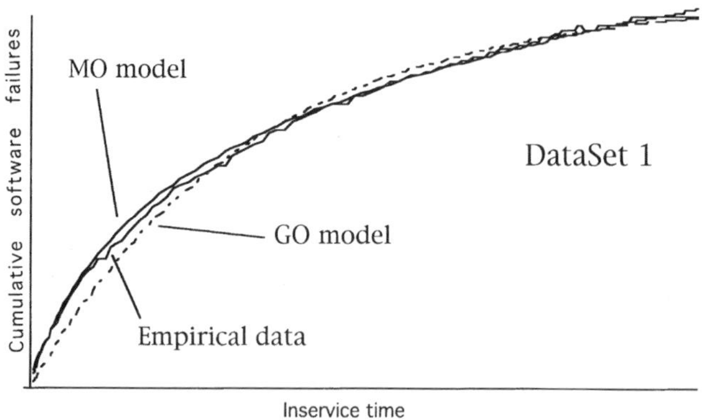

Figure 11.3 Two potential functional relationships: Musa-Okumoto (MO) model and Goel-Okumoto (GO) model for DataSet 1.

appear to fit or describe the data equally well then you have encountered the unfortunate limitations of perception with curved graphs. It is very difficult to distinguish one type of curve from another. The fitted curves are actually very different functions; one is a logarithmic function and the other is an exponential function. Therefore, the moral is *do not use* cumulative failure plots to determine functional relationships or compare different functional relationships. Although either model may be useful for interpolation, it is the extrapolation (or predictions) of the behavior that is of primary interest to a reliability engineer. These two functions have vastly different extrapolations. Thus, graphs of the cumulative failures should in practice be limited to depicting the failures for a given release against a predicted curve, or in simultaneously comparing several releases in an overlay plot.

Failure intensity is the rate of change in the expected cumulative failures. It can be quantified by the number of failures per unit time. Since the failure intensity changes over time, we are interested in the instantaneous failure intensity and how it changes with respect to time, or how it changes with accumulation of failures. Figure 11.4 is a scatterplot of the failure intensity of release DataSet 1 with a group size of 5 (percent)* against the cumulative failure count (in this case normalized to the total number of recorded failures).

Failure intensity *should* play an important role in any reliability analysis. Many of the graphs illustrated in this text (including Fig. 11.4) and many graphical diagnostics require calculation of the approximate failure intensity from empirical data. This calculation has many bene-

* Note that grouping of (unique) failures by percentage does not diminish the general analysis, even though specific values are hidden. In fact, this provides an excellent vehicle for definition of a canonical model that may carry over to the next release.

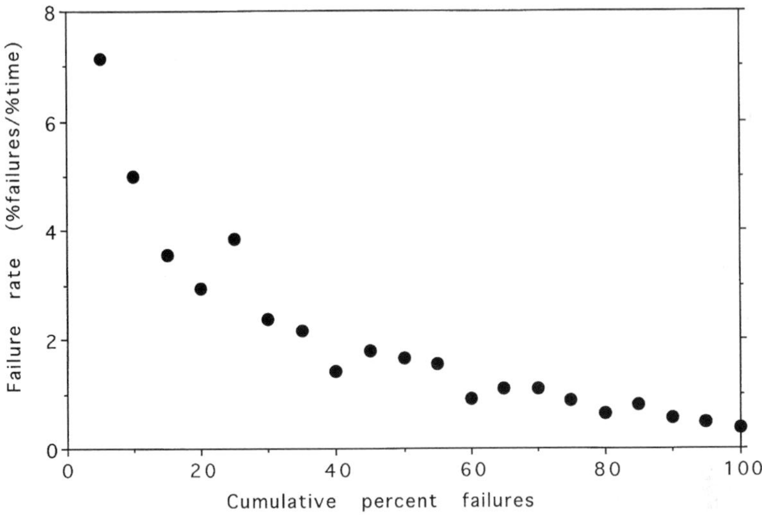

Figure 11.4 Scatterplot of the failure intensity of DataSet 1. Time is measured in in-service units.

fits: the empirical failure intensity can be measured and quantified, graphs of the failure intensity may indicate appropriate functions, and parameters for certain models may be successfully estimated from the empirical failure intensity using ordinary least squares (in addition to more complex estimation methods such as maximum likelihood). Inspection of Fig. 11.4 reveals that the failure intensity appears to decrease (indicating reliability growth) in a nonlinear fashion, and that the variance in the failure intensity becomes smaller as it approaches zero.

The obvious and uniform decreasing trend exhibited in Fig. 11.4 may not be as obvious in other situations. For example, immediately after initial deployment of a release (during the so-called transient period where the usage load is low and small errors in the data can drastically affect all metrics, including failure intensity), or where the data have large variance, we would like to confirm that reliability growth actually occurs before we commit to a particular (global) reliability growth model. The primary means for determining if reliability growth exists is the use of trend tests, which are discussed in Chap. 10. You are invited to perform the trend tests for DataSet 1 and DataSet 2 (described further in Sec. 11.5.1 and on the Data Disk) where usage is expressed in calendar-time units.

For example, when plotted, DataSet 2 exhibits unimodal failure intensity, its mean value function is S-shaped, and the reliability growth (on the calendar-time scale) does not occur prior to 8 to 10 months into the field usage.* Graphs of these quantities are given in Sec. 11.5.1. Analysis shows that one cannot be statistically certain of a confirmed global downward trend before approximately 19 months after release. This is often too long to wait for any modeling to be useful from a practical perspective. Many systems that have a unimodal field failure intensity with respect to calendar time often have a dramatically different behavior with respect to usage time (see example in Sec. 11.4). A recalibration of the data with respect to usage may greatly enhance the timeliness of the reliability modeling when usage can be estimated. In general, S-shaped models do not lend themselves to quick estimation even though the functional form may be accurate for the functional characterization considered (in this instance, failure rate versus calendar time).

An alternative may be to reduce the influence of, or even remove, the initial data where the failure intensity is increasing and fit a model on the remainder data. Examples of this approach include various forms of *data aging* such as smoothing based on a moving average (e.g., [BELL89]; also see Sec. 11.8.2) and exclusion of transient behavior data (e.g., [Mart91], see Sec. 11.5.3). The idea behind data aging is that we assign more weight to more recent failure data if we believe that the failure process changes rapidly enough that old data are not representative of the current failure process. On the other hand, if the failure process remains essentially the same throughout our observation period, then we should model using as many of the observations as possible. A discussion of this topic is given in Sec. 3.3.3; also see Sec. 11.7.2. It must be noted that weighting or elimination of early data, or weighting and elimination of outliers in general, needs to be done with great caution and with considerable expert help from a trained statistician and/or reliability engineer. It is very easy to incorrectly reduce the influence of parts of data and fit a reliability model which has no predictive validity. For example, in the case of DataSet 2, it is better to use a model which has a unimodal failure intensity function, since that behavior is characteristic of that system, than to eliminate early data.

11.3.2 Data modeling and diagnostics

Models are very important to engineers. Most useful models are predictive, and some models may be used to direct development and maintenance process management. We will assume, for convenience, that software failures occur in accordance within the general framework of the nonhomogeneous Poisson process (NHPP). In principle, this

* In fact, there appears to be an initial increase in failure intensity that may be due to the ramping effect of the user base.

assumption, which underlies many of the models, should be confirmed before we attempt to fit these models to data. A test for Poisson process assumption is described in [Cox78]. The test requires information on true interfailure times, something that may be difficult to obtain for the field data. The NHPP framework is very flexible and is not limited by specific assumptions that were common with initial models (for example, the assumption of instantaneous perfect repair of faults or the total number of failures is constant but unknown). It also allows for the use of covariates in the mean-value function that may or may not be directly tied with usage time.

11.3.3 Diagnostics for model determination

Model determination is perhaps the most underrated aspect to modeling failure data. Many naive practitioners often will examine only one model, especially when the model agrees with their assumptions or beliefs about the failure process. Also, practitioners may have viewed a graphical representation of some of the more common models, such as the GO model, and thought, *Yes, my data looks like that!* This leads to *the* question. What does failure data look like? Also, can we use the "looks" to choose the most appropriate model? The answer is a strong *yes*. There is one caveat: it depends on exactly how the data is presented.

11.3.3.1 Graphical diagnostics for model determination. Used correctly, graphical methods can be a very powerful tool to quickly determine which models may be appropriate or, especially, inappropriate. Graphical diagnostics have a long history of use in many applications, but especially in statistics. For example, there are standard plots that statisticians use to examine assumptions concerning normality of errors, or whether data from a sample is from a particular distribution. Many of these plots take advantage of the innate ability humans have in detecting straight lines; we are much less adept at distinguishing different types of curves. Many diagnostic plots graph one variable with respect to another, the object being to ascertain linearity or nonlinearity. If a linear relationship exists, then based on how the data are (or are not) transformed from the original variables, a functional relationship can be established between the two variables of interest. In our case, we are primarily interested in establishing the relationship between failures and time.

We have already seen from Fig. 11.4 that the failure intensity of release DataSet 1 is not linear with respect to the cumulative failures. Figure 11.5 shows a linear fit overlaid on the failure intensity curve. Obviously there are persistent deviations from the linear fit which would be confirmed by examining the graph of the *residuals* of the fit.

Examination of residuals *should* be a part of any serious modeling study. In our case, the residuals are serially correlated (a common symptom of a poor predictive model), indicating that the failure rate is significantly nonlinear with respect to the cumulative number of failures.

[Musa87] and [Jone91] examined the long-term relative predictive error of several models over time for many releases of field reliability data. This method is a historical validation technique and thus requires historical data if it is to be used. That is, one calculates total failure forecasts at several points earlier in the release cycle given the data that would have been available at that time. The long-term forecasts are then compared against the actual values and a relative error (in this case, a relative *predictive* error) is computed and plotted.

Consider the relative error plot for the MO model in Fig. 11.6 using the reliability data from three software releases of the same software system. A good model tends to have values of relative error close to zero, and tending toward zero over time. The variance in the relative predictive error is usually greatest at first, and then narrows as the model has both more data for model stability and as forecasts are not as far into the future. A lack of symmetry in the relative error indicates a possible bias in the candidate model and usually implies that the candidate model is either not appropriate for prediction or may need recalibration. In Fig. 11.6 we see that the MO model has little bias except at the very end where the relative error is small.

As introduced in Chap. 4, u-plots and plots based upon the prequential likelihood [Abde86, Broc92, DeGr86] are another source of candidates for graphical diagnostics. However, the mathematics are very

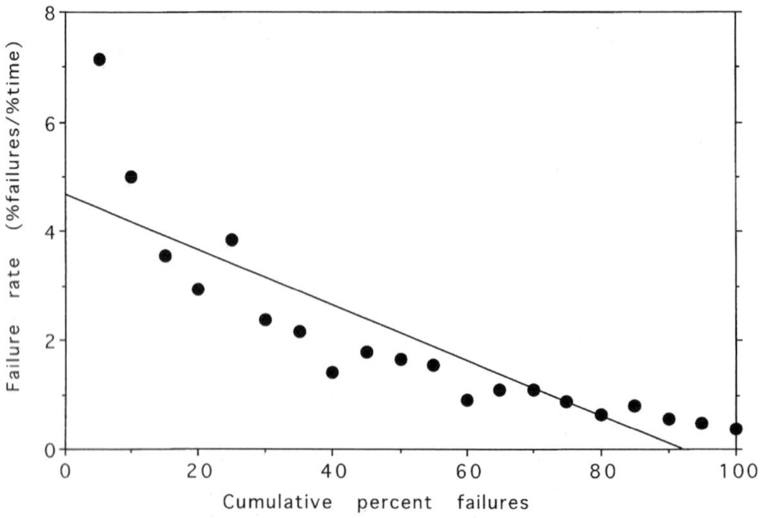

Figure 11.5 Linear fit through the failure intensity of DataSet 1.

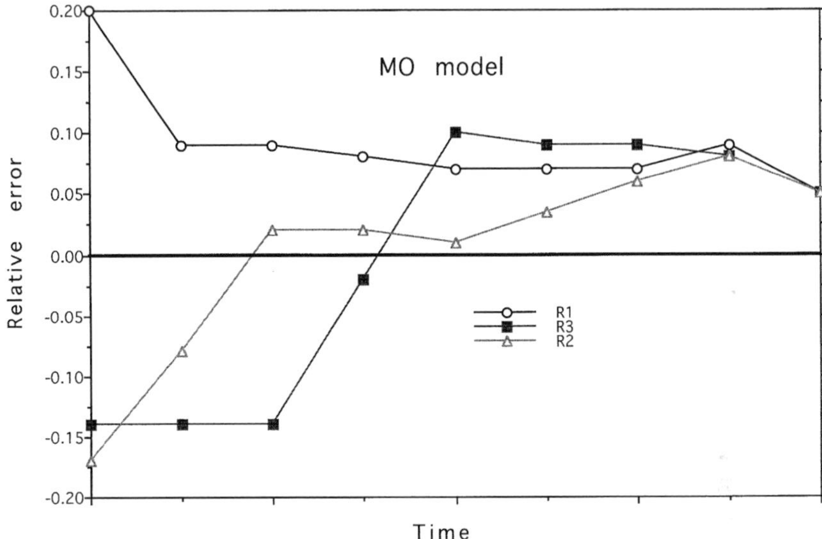

Figure 11.6 Relative error of long-term forecasts for three software releases (MO model).

complex for creating *u*-plots and PLR (prequential likelihood ratio) plots for more than just the next failure. Thus, they are primarily used when the prediction of the time to the *next* failure is important. As we mentioned earlier, the nature of failure event recording by the customer and vendor coupled with the data assimilation process usually leads to the retrieval of field failures in groups. Often the exact time of failure is not recorded—only the time when it was entered into a database. In any case, in considering the field data, we are not usually interested in when the very *next* failure event will occur, but rather how many will occur over time, and whether we can find subsequent interpretations for the parameters.

11.3.3.2 Computational diagnostics for model determination. Useful computational diagnostics typically fall into one of two categories: prediction error and overall fit. In previous discussions, we stated that accurate long-term predictions are an appropriate and important aspect of modeling field data. It is preferable to determine the accuracy of long-term predictions, or overall model behavior, especially when you wish to direct development processes based on the values of the model parameters. Therefore, certain short-term prediction diagnostics, such as prequential likelihood, are not examined in this section but are addressed in Sec. 4.3.

Computation of relative predictive error for reliability analysis was more formally stated in [Chan92]. Chan applied the idea of relative predictive error to both short-term and long-term predictions. Let ξ_i be the relative error of the predictive model at time t_i. Then, for both long- and short-term predictions, we define the relative predictive error to be

$$\xi_i(\Delta) = \frac{\hat{\mu}_i(t_{i+\Delta}) - (i + \Delta)}{(i + \Delta)} \tag{11.1}$$

where $\hat{\mu}_i(t)$ is the forecast of the total number of failures by time t calculated at the ith failure time. For short-term predictions, typical values for Δ would be 5, 10, or 20, depending on what is meaningful to the organization and the reliability system. However, we must again remember that for field data, very short-term predictions are usually useless due to the nature of reporting and collecting data. Therefore, for long-term predictions, we are most often interested in the relative error of the predictions at some standardized time value t, where t is large so that comparisons can be made between releases. We may also be interested in relative errors for t_m where m is the total number of failures of the system (that is, $\Delta = m - i$).

In addition to relative predictive error, [Khos91] used the Akaike Information Criterion (AIC) [Akai74] as a model comparison method based on maximum likelihood. Although it is a means of indicating which model is better overall when compared relatively to another model, the values from the AIC metric are not as useful in determining how well suited any of the models are in absolute terms. That is, the AIC indicates closeness of the data to a relative distribution but does not, for example, convey how accurate any forecasts may be in the very comprehensible way that relative predictive error does.

Some traditional statistical modeling computational diagnostics should be avoided with software reliability models. One of these is the r-squared statistic, a value related to the lack of fit (sum of the squared errors). The r-squared statistic can be deceiving in this context since the r square is usually computed from a model based on a regression analysis using the failure intensity (which is, in turn, based on an approximation using grouped failures). In general, the larger the group size chosen (which is somewhat arbitrary), the larger the r square will be for the same data since the larger group size tends to smooth the data, thus eliminating variance in a trend. Comparisons of r-squared values from data set to data set are almost always suspect.

11.3.4 Data transformations

Transformations are a powerful mechanism for understanding data. Determining appropriate metrics and how the metrics are related is the key to understanding random phenomena.

We have seen that a linear relationship does not exist between the failure rate and the cumulative failures for DataSet 1. Can some transform be used to examine other potential relationships? Table 11.3 illustrates several transforms that can be used to diagnose appropriate or inappropriate models. For example, the MO model exhibits a linear relationship between the log of the failure intensity and the cumulative failures, while the Duane model is linear in the log of the intensity versus the log of the cumulative failures. All the models in Table 11.3 use transforms of μ, λ, or τ. Also, all of the transforms can be easily calculated on most spreadsheets or statistical packages for quick analysis. Both SMERFS and CASRE support these types of data transformations. Some of these relationships, and the associated computational and graphical techniques required to perform this graphical diagnostic, are found in [Musa87, Jone91, Xie91a, Xie91b, Jone93]. The key relationship is the one between the failure intensity and the cumulative failures. Data transformations are especially effective when used in combination with graphs and plots.

We illustrate the transform approach using DataSet 1. The scatterplot with a regression line fit in Fig. 11.7 is the DataSet 1 failure intensity (λ) versus cumulative failures (μ) after taking a log transformation of the failure intensity. In this case, the log transformation creates an almost textbook linear fit. From Table 11.3 we see that the linearized MO model conforms with this transformation and may be the appropriate one to use. You should review Chap. 3 regarding the actual estimation of model parameters and derived variables. For a more complete discussion on curve fitting, regression analysis, and related diagnostics, see [Drap86].

11.4 Important Topics in Analysis of Field Data

In the case of a multirelease system, at different calendar times different software releases are installed at a different number of sites. This means that the usage intensity of a particular software load varies over calendar time and accumulates usage according to the amount of time the sites using the release have been in service. Therefore, from

TABLE 11.3 Linear Relationships in Reliability Growth Models

Model	Primary linear relationship	Other linear relationships (if any)	Parameters
GO model	$\lambda = \alpha\beta - \alpha\mu$	$\ln(\lambda) = \ln(\alpha\beta) - \alpha\tau$	α β
MO model	$\ln(\lambda) = \ln(\lambda_0) - \theta\mu$		λ_0 θ
LV model	$1/\lambda = \beta_0 + \beta_1 \mu$		β_0 β_1
Duane (Crow) model	$\ln(\lambda) = f(\alpha\beta) - \dfrac{\alpha - 1}{\alpha} \ln(\mu)$	$\ln(\mu) = \ln(\beta) + \alpha \ln(\tau)$	α β

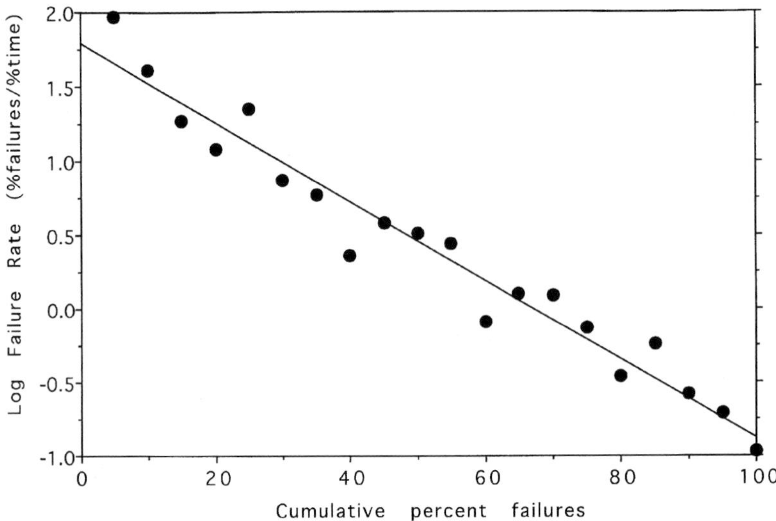

Figure 11.7 Log transform of DataSet 1 failure intensity.

both hardware and software viewpoints, in-service time is a more representative and relevant measure of usage than calendar time. However, in many cases, calendar time is a measure that better reflects the perception of users (such as the telecommunications companies) since calendar-time availability and degradation of services are very important from the customers' point of view. Simply stated, the context may dictate whether one or both viewpoints (calendar time and in-service time) are appropriate for analysis.

When discussing the quality of software in operational use, it is instructive to employ a classification based on the usage characteristics of the product and the nature and availability of the field data. As seen in previous chapters, it is well known that the software usage profile is a dominant factor that influences the reliability [Musa93], and that the software execution time is a better time domain than calendar time since it automatically incorporates the workload to which the software is subjected [Musa87]. The influence of measuring usage on reliability modeling as an alternative to calendar time is demonstrated by the example in this section. However, in practice, we may have to make a statement about the quality of the software without having direct information about its usage, and without having available a large number of failure events. Therefore, in the following sections, we will discuss three classes of field reliability data analysis: calendar-time, usage-time, and special-event analyses. In Sec. 11.8, we will discuss the related concept of availability.

11.4.1 Calendar time

Calendar-time analysis arises in situations where failures are reported only in the calendar-time domain and precise information about the usage of the software may not be available. We see this type of constraint in wide-distribution software—software that is developed for the purpose of selling on the open market to many customers, or for nonprofit distribution to anyone who wishes to install it. Its usage often builds to thousands, or even hundreds of thousands, of independent systems. However, direct monitoring of the usage rate of such software is not always feasible, or is not practiced. This is especially true of commercial wide-distribution software [Boeh89], shrink-wrapped or off-the-shelf software, and freeware. Examples of wide-distribution commercial software are Microsoft Windows, WordPerfect, DEC's Ultrix, commercial PC and workstation compilers, and freeware such as the GNU family of software products. We discuss calendar-time analysis in detail in Sec. 11.5.

11.4.2 Usage time

It should not be surprising that the many organizations that are prominent in the practice of software reliability engineering (SRE) deal with telecommunications and safety-critical applications.* Other application areas include reservation systems, banking transaction systems, database engines, operating systems, medical instruments, etc. For many of these systems, reliability is one of the most important, if not *the* most important, attribute of the system. This implies the need for accurate and detailed information about the system usage. Usage-time analysis can be performed when more precise information about software usage is available. This is often true for software that is developed for the purpose of selling to a specialized market such as the examples given above. Its usage may build up to hundreds or thousands of independent systems, yet the users of the software are known and well documented, and direct monitoring of the usage rate of the software is feasible and is practiced. We discuss usage-time analysis in detail in Sec. 11.6.

---

* For example, *telecommunication systems, networks:* ALCATEL, Bell Laboratories/AT&T, Bellcore, BNR/Nortel, Ericsson/GE, Fujitsu, IBM, Motorola TELEBRAS; *advanced avionics and space systems:* Boeing, CNES, Hughes Aircraft, LORAL (ex IBM Federal Systems), JPL, NASA, USAF; *other systems:* Cray, Digital, Hewlett-Packard, Hitachi, Intel, Sun Microsystems, StorageTek.

11.4.3 An example

The following example helps underscore the issues driving the above classification. Figure 11.8 shows the actual field data for a large-scale limited-distribution telecommunications product. We plot the concurrent changes in the number of installed systems of a particular software release (DataSet 1 on the Data Disk) over calendar time, the corresponding failure rate in terms of calendar time (failures per week), and failure rate per system in-service week. Note the dramatic difference between the failures per calendar week and the failures per system in-service week.

From Fig. 11.8, we see that the calendar-time failure rate is initially low (indicating apparent high reliability), then begins to climb (apparent reliability degradation), and finally reaches a peak just before the deployment reaches its peak. A naive analyst might mistakenly conclude that a disaster is in the making. In fact, the system is behaving as it should—the problem is an inherent deficiency in the failure rate metric. As the rate of deployment peaks, the reliability appears to improve dramatically, and the failure rate drops steadily thereafter.

However, we see a different picture when we examine the failure rate in terms of failures per system in-service week (that is, normalized with respect to the deployment function) or per usage load on the system. The normalized failure rate is initially high, but then decreases dramatically in the first few weeks after the system has been deployed. As the deployment curve peaks, the reliability growth may slow but reliability continues to improve.

Obviously, the model that describes the failure behavior of this system will depend very strongly on whether we have the actual system

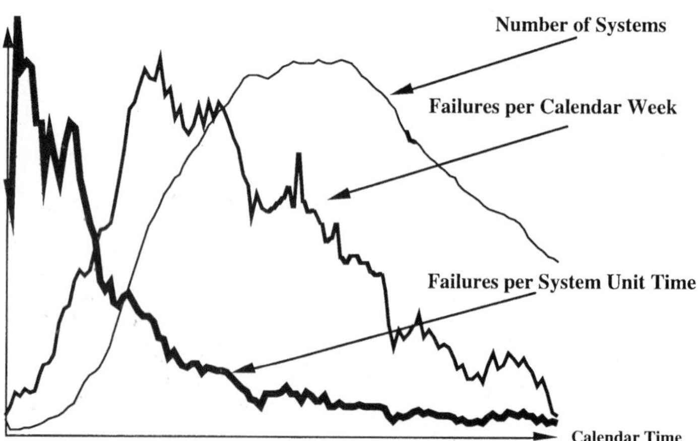

Figure 11.8 Influence of usage on computed failure intensity.

usage information or not. The number of failures per calendar week is a direct function of the true reliability of the system *and* the deployment function of the system. Reliability growth may be difficult, if not impossible, to discern from the calendar-based view. While failures per calendar week may be a natural, and important, metric to a customer service organization, it is usually far from suitable for making inferences about the reliability of the system [Musa87].

11.5 Calendar-Time Reliability Analysis

The principal characteristic of wide-distribution software is that it is used by many users at many customer sites. This software lives in the world of multiple releases, and for this type of software, by definition, we often do not know who the users are or how they use it. Although we may know how many licenses there are, we may not know how intensively each copy is used. When dealing with wide-distribution commercial software we often have a large user base with each user experiencing his or her own level of reliability. Some users may run for months without a disruption, while others may run for only a few hours before running into a problem. It all depends on the user's software usage profile. Yet, despite the fact that reliability of a software system is important to customers of commercial software products, they generally do not keep good records on execution time, and they seldom report on their reliability experience. What they do report to software development organizations is the occurrence of specific failures, with the expectation of getting the underlying defect(s) fixed so that the failures do not reoccur. This is possibly why many commercial software development organizations focus on the number of remaining defects rather than reliability, or mean time to failure, as the measure of software quality.

[Musa87] discusses the advantages and disadvantages of the calendar-based analysis in great detail, and shows that although a general Weibull-type failure intensity model can describe calendar-time system behavior, the fit is often inferior to the one obtained using execution-time-based intensity. But it is also pointed out that in practice managers and users may be more attached to the calendar-time domain since it is closer to the world in which they make decisions.

The following case studies illustrate practical analyses of calendar-time data. We consider unimodal models, and the use of calendar-time-based failure intensity to focus on the user perception of the software quality. In the first case study, analysis is biased toward the view software developers may take when dealing with field defects, while the second study is strongly biased toward the user view. We leave it as an exercise for you to research and discuss the bias, if any, in the remaining examples.

11.5.1 Case study (IBM Corporation)

One approach to analyzing field data for wide-distribution commercial software is described in detail in [Kenn92, Kenn93a, Kenn93b]. The idea is to decouple the concept of individual system reliability from the notion of how many defects are left in the code as a whole, and to use the latter to quantify the quality of the software through a Weibull-type field-defect model. The approach is based on the assumption that for the software developers the failure count is of special interest because it implies a certain software maintenance workload, and that by estimating the number of defects remaining in the code it is possible to distill the experience of thousands of users down to one number that characterizes the quality of the software product as a whole.

[Kenn93a] developed a calendar-time model for a multirelease product using Trachtenberg's general theory of software reliability [Trac90]. Since direct usage information was not available, it was assumed that, within the period most interesting for the study, the workload on the system as a whole increased as a power function of calendar time. The general form of the failure intensity for the resulting Weibull field-defect model is

$$\lambda = N\left(\frac{\alpha}{\beta}\right)\left(\frac{t}{\beta}\right)^{\alpha-1} \exp\left(-\frac{t}{\beta}\right)^{\alpha} \tag{11.2}$$

where N is the initial number of defects in the software, t is the calendar time and α and β are the Weibull parameters. Under the assumptions made in the study, λ is both the average defect discovery rate and the average defect removal rate. Parameter estimation for α and β was done by maximizing their conditional likelihood. The estimate of N was obtained through substitution of the estimated parameters α and β and of the number of observed failures at the point of censoring in to the cumulative distribution function. Of course, other approaches to estimation can be used.

In [Kenn93a] two data sets from releases of established IBM software products were used to demonstrate the model. One data set contains 36 months of defect-discovery times for a release of *controller software* consisting of about 500,000 lines of code installed on over 100,000 controllers. The other contains 24 months of defect-discovery times for a release of a commercial *software product* consisting of about 1 million lines of code installed on 10,000 systems. The defects are those that were present in the code of the particular release of the software and were discovered as a result of failures reported by users of that release, or possibly of the follow-on release of the product.

The first of the above data sets is on the Data Disk as DataSet 2. We illustrate the results in Fig. 11.9. The figure shows the number of unique defects reported per month against the month after the first customer shipment and the associated Weibull model, which has an S-shaped cumulative distribution function. The downside of using an S-shaped model, such as the Weibull field-defect model, is that, in this case, a reasonable and stable estimate of N could not be obtained before about 16 months of data were available for the *controller software,* and about 18 months of data were available for the *software product* set, although preliminary (and less accurate) estimates could be obtained as early as 10 to 12 months after release of the software to the customers.

It is a common experience that when a new software release is made available for customer use, the reporting of field problems initially rises to a peak and then tails off as the release ages [Uemu90, Ohte90, Yama91, Mart90, Leve90]. When the next release is shipped to customers, we again see the field problem reports rise. It turns out that this increase is not totally due to defects inserted into the new release. In addition to discovering the defects added through the new release, the new release often stimulates discovery of the latent defects, that is, the defects that were inserted into the prior code releases but never discovered. This phenomenon aggravates the stability of a new release in its early days, and makes predictive modeling difficult. We call the phenomenon the *next-release effect* [Kenn92, Kenn93a, Kenn93b].

The next-release effect can be seen in Fig. 11.10. The figure shows an overlay plot of the frequency of reported problems for several releases of the *controller software.* The data are smoothed using a three-point symmetric moving average. All releases use common timescale, months after

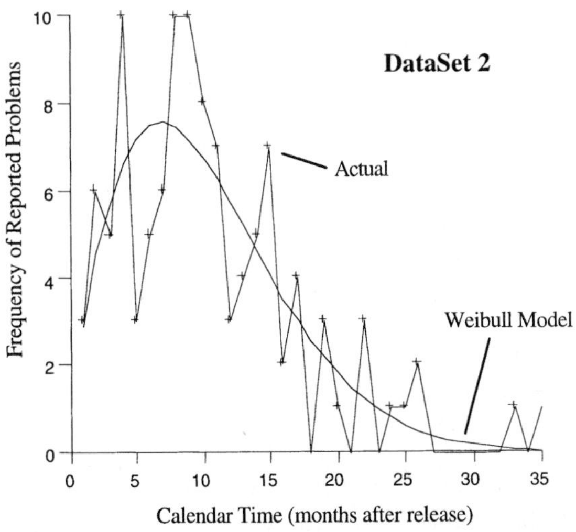

Figure 11.9 Frequency distribution and its Weibull model (DataSet 2).

release X was shipped. The time span covers six releases, but for simplicity we show only three of them: X, $X + 1$, and $X + 2$. We see the effect subsequent releases have on release X as multiple peaks in the release-X-associated problems around months 9, 12 to 13, and to a lesser extent at months 16 to 19, 25, and 34. These peaks were correlated with the switchover of the customers to the next release, and the onset of reports from the next release of the product [Kenn92]. The release of new code stimulates discovery of defects in the prior releases of the code. For example, the defects present in the code developed for release X were reported as problems during field use of release $X + 1$ and traced back to release X code. The next-release effect is further discussed in the context of the space shuttle flight software failures (see Sec. 11.7.2).

It is interesting to note that the above analysis, from the data collection perspective, requires that the detected defects be counted against the release into which they were inserted, which is not necessarily the release on which the first failure occurred. This means that a mapping would have to be established between the field failures and the version from which the corresponding faults originate, information that may not be readily available in many organizations.

11.5.2 Case study (Hitachi Software Engineering Company)

The Japanese software industry has a long and distinguished record of considering the quality of software they ship to their customers as a

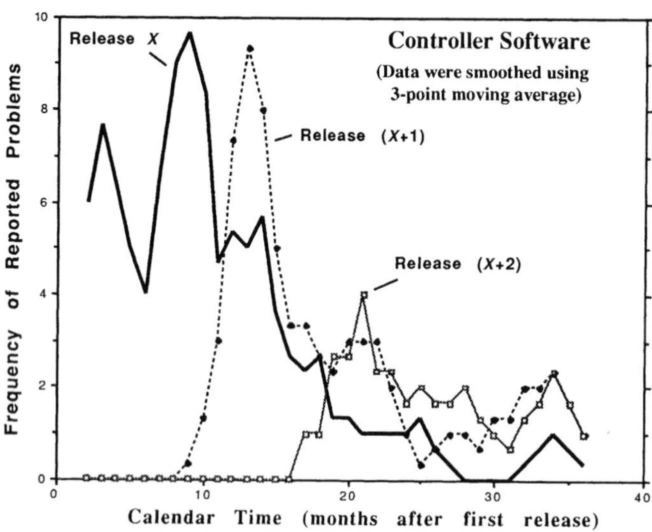

Figure 11.10 Smoothed frequency distribution for releases X, $X + 1$, and $X + 2$.

very serious issue [Naka92, Ishi91]. Good examples of such companies are Fujitsu and Hitachi.

For instance, Hitachi Software Engineering Company Limited, a part of Hitachi Limited, is one of the largest software houses in Japan. About 20 percent of the systems developed at Hitachi Software have 5 million lines of code, while the average size of a system is about 200,000 lines of code. Hitachi Software uses statistical control to improve both the quality of the software they ship and the quality of the process they use to develop it. During the development, Hitachi Software engineers predict the defect content of their product and derive the test-stopping criteria using a Gompertz curve fault model. After the product is released, software field data is routinely collected, and the information is fed back into the software development process to effect further improvements [Onom93, Onom95]. The overall goal is customer satisfaction and the key value is the number of failures that a customer may experience per calendar month.

Hitachi Software tracks the number of system failures detected at customer sites. This information is transformed into the *field failure ratio,* the number of system failures per month per thousand systems [Onom93]. Figure 11.11 shows the percentage change in that ratio over a 13-year period (DataSet 5 on the Data Disk). The ultimate target is zero field defects, and more immediate targets are set with the aim of having as small a number of problems as possible emerge at customer

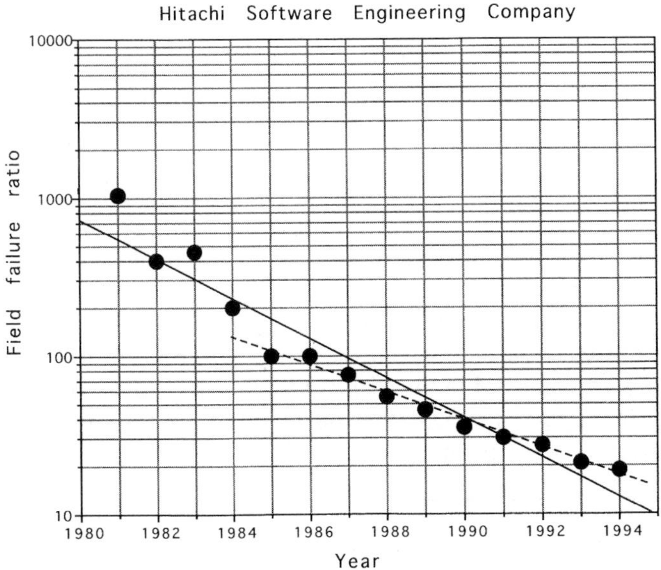

Figure 11.11 Field failure ratio.

sites. To emphasize this, Hitachi Software measures the productivity of its engineers not in terms of the number of lines of code produced per hour, but in terms of the number of debugged lines of code per hour. For example, in 1990 only about 0.02 percent of the faults detected during a project life cycle ended up as field failures [Onom93, Onom95].

11.5.3 Further examples

AT&T. An interesting calendar-time birth–death model was developed by Levendel [Leve87, Leve89, Leve90, Leve93]. Levendel defines and models a set of laws that govern the software defect detection and removal process. He uses these models to describe and predict the behavior of software field failures. The model includes analyses for incremental defect detection, removal, and reintroduction rates. The underlying assumption is that the defect introduction and removal is governed by Poisson distributions. For example, his simulation shows that for every three defects repaired as much as one defect may be reintroduced. The defect rate (intensity) model envelope is a *unimodal Poisson-type shape.* Levendel also discusses quality estimators such as the number of defects to repair, current number of defects, testing coverage and repair intensity, and testing process quality and effectiveness. The laws and models were applied to a large telecommunications switching product (5ESS), and were found to be good descriptors and reasonable predictors of the system behavior.

TELEBRAS and ALCATEL. Several interesting approaches to analysis of failure data and calendar-time usage information can be found in the extensive studies of field reliability and availability of the TELEBRAS TROPICO R digital switching systems (e.g., Chap. 10, [Mart90, Mart91, Kano91a, Lapr91]) and of the ALCATEL E-10 system ([Kano87]). For example, [Mart91] applied trend tests, and fitted the exponential and gamma [Yama85] models to the TROPICO-R 4096 system test and operational data (on the Data Disk, DataSet 4). [Mart91] experimented with the removal of some initial data to avoid spurious results due to transient behavior usually found in the initial recorded usage period. You are encouraged to calculate and plot DataSet 4 intensity, the corresponding Laplace trend graph, and then to attempt to fit MO, GO, and hyperexponential models and discuss the results (first to all data, and then to the data after time unit 10). Kanoun et al. reported on a similar study performed on the TROPICO-R 1500 system (DataSet 3) [Kano91].

The validity of the hyperexponential reliability model was explored using the data from the ALCATEL E-10 switch [Kano87] and from the TROPICO-R system [Lapr91]. [Lapr91] also illustrated how trend tests help to partition the observed failure data according to the assumptions of the reliability growth models. It is worth noting that TROPICO-R data (DataSet 3) appear to show the influence of the usage ramping, but a direct hyperexponential fit treats that as an initial instability and essentially overrides it. On the other hand, the approach taken by [Mart91], where the initial data were discarded, simply removes the transient behavior. We want to stress that, although in some situations this is a valid approach,* in general, any elimination of early data (or other outliers) has to be done with great caution and with considerable expert help because it can lead to models that have no predictive validity. Some related results are given in Chap. 10.

11.6 Usage-Based Reliability Analysis

As vendors and customers form closer alliances due to stringent reliability expectations, usage data will be more accessible. Currently, Bellcore [Bell90b] requires that telecommunication vendors in the United States systematically record software usage and a variety of metrics that quantify the quality of software releases. In fact, it is likely that in the near future, industries such as medical software [Frie91] will be subject to similar requirements from some outside agency. In this section, we show how software reliability analysis can be conducted when sufficient usage information is available.

11.6.1 Case study (Nortel Telecommunication Systems)

The reliability behavior of Nortel's DMS (Digital Multiplexing System) software was initially studied by Jones [Jone91, Jone92]. The focus was the comparison of the predictive accuracy and goodness-of-fit of various models along with a comparison of parameter estimation methods. The ultimate goal was to determine appropriate modeling methods for Nortel's DMS software. A comparison was made of the ability of various models to forecast the total number of field failures and corresponding faults. In addition, the reliability model aptness or goodness-of-fit during alpha and beta test was examined. Finally, given a model, a comparison was made of the two popular methods for estimating parameters (maximum likelihood and least squares).

---

* In situations where the failure observations cover a long time period of time, old data may not be as representative of the current and future failure process as recent data. In such cases, justified data aging may be an appropriate approach (see Secs. 11.7.3 and 11.8).

By examining several releases over a period of time, [Jone92] used a variety of numerical and graphical diagnostics to conclude that the MO model was the most appropriate model for the DMS software releases both in the field and during alpha and beta field testing. An example using release R8 (a large software release of a telecommunications product) is shown in Fig. 11.12. In Fig. 11.12*a*, we see that the failure intensity does not appear to be linear with respect to failures. However, the log transformation of the failure intensity shown in Fig. 11.12*b* does appear to greatly linearize the data, as well as homogenize the variance of the failure intensity. From this and other analyses, it was concluded that the MO model was most appropriate for this software system.

In a follow-up study, parameters of the field MO model were related to metrics of the development cycle and to the deployment characteristics of the software [Hude92]. It was found that for DMS systems, the decay parameter θ of the MO model was directly related to the number of systems deployed. If a release had wide deployment, the decay rate of the failure intensity was less than when a release had limited deployment. Also, the initial failure intensity (parameter λ_0 of the MO model) in the field was found to be directly related to the failure intensity measured during alpha and beta test.

11.6.2 Further examples

AT&T telecommunication systems. [Ehrl90, Ehrl93] examined system test and field data from the beta test of the AT&T System T software.

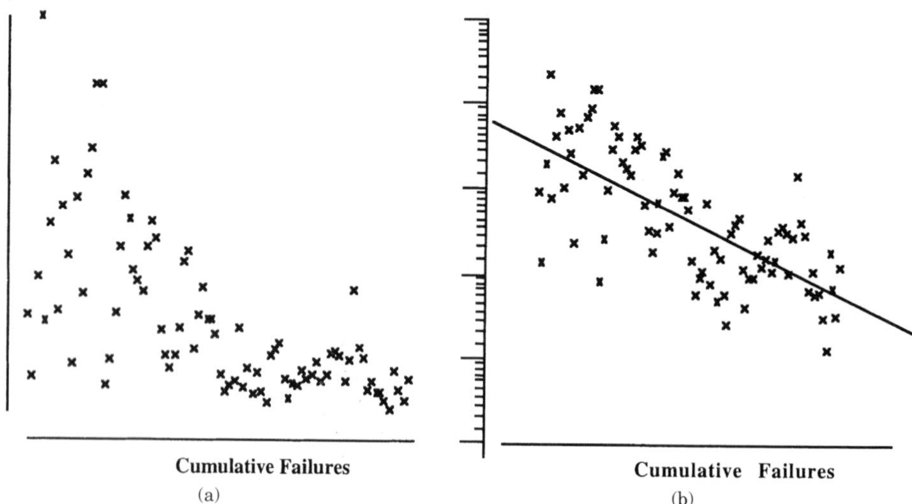

Figure 11.12 (*a*) Reliability modeling of the Nortel DMS software. Graph of failure intensity for R8 during alpha- and beta-test phase. (*b*) Reliability modeling of the Nortel DMS software. Graph of log failure intensity for R8 during alpha- and beta-test phase.

The more recent work [Ehrl93] is particularly interesting since the authors demonstrated a procedure for testing Poisson process assumptions. Poisson processes are often used when modeling reliability growth. Their candidates for modeling their failure data were the GO, MO, and Duane models. The GO model was chosen for System T since it had the smallest fitted mean square error.

VAX/VMS operating system. [Tang92] examined the software reliability of the VAX/VMS operating system on two VAX clusters. Analysis considerations included examining distributions of the time to failure, time to repair, and time between failures. Also of interest were software failures that were hardware-related and estimates of unavailability due to software. For the systems under study, the unavailability due to software was on the order of 10^{-4}. As a contrast, telecommunications systems are usually required to have an unavailability due to all causes of less than 10^{-5}. The authors of [Tang92] used a modified GO model in which they assumed that an asymptotic steady-state constant term existed for the failure intensity. It is interesting to note that this model is similar to the hyperexponential model [Kano91].

CNES space and avionics system. [Vale92] examined two data sets related to space systems that had operational or field failure data. The goal for this study was to determine which reliability growth model would be the most appropriate for the authors' software systems. They initially selected five models: Musa model (basic execution time), Littlewood-Verrall, GO model, Weibull (Duane) model, and the MO model. They were also interested in determining if there were relationships between the development environment or development metrics and the appropriate software reliability growth model. The diagnostics used in the model determination included Kolmogorov-Smirnov test on a u-plot and evolving u-plot along with the relative predictive error. Their data suggested that field failures from one project in one category were best modeled by the MO model, while field failures from another project in a different category were best modeled by the Duane model.

Bellcore software quality measurements. A very interesting issue is how reliability models relate to the overall software process [Naka92, Paul93] and how classical quality control techniques, such as quality trend charts [Hoad81, Hoad86], can be applied to evaluate the quality of a series of software product releases. [Weer94] examined two sets of data belonging to two telecommunications products in the light of the Hoadley's Quality of Measurement Plan (QMP). Both sets contained data on three releases of the product. In their paper the authors describe how failure data from software processes can be displayed using QMP trend charts, and how the approach can be used to compare a number of software releases to see if there is an increase or decrease in the software quality over the releases, where the quality is measured through the number of unique field failures (faults) and the fault density (faults per 10,000 lines of code). To make fault estimates, the authors experiment with exponential, Pareto, and Weibull distributions for fault detection times (the time scale is "system months of field operation"), and they use a Bayesian methodology to combine the data from all releases to produce quality index estimates. This type of analysis will gain in importance as software process maturity of organizations increases, and as the organizations start using their test and field deployment failure data to control software field maintenance processes and provide immediate and active feedback to the process of developing the next release of their software product [Vouk93b].

11.7 Special Events

Some classes of failures may be of special interest, and may be considered more important than others. These could be failures that are categorized as having life-threatening or extremely damaging consequences, or failures that can be very embarrassing or costly. The need to recognize early the potential of a software-based system for special-event problems is obvious. How to achieve this is less clear. In general, it is necessary to link the symptoms observed during, say, software testing phases or early deployment phases with the effects observed in the later operational phases.

In that context, the key is identification of these failure modes, and of the events that lead to these failures. Failures modes that are absolutely unacceptable should *not* be analyzed using only probabilistic methods since these methods are inherently incapable of assuring the level of reliability that is required for such systems. Some other techniques, such as formal methods, should be used to complement the analyses [Schn92b]. Ultrahigh reliability systems pose special problems and require dependability assessment techniques. A discussion of these issues can be found in [Butl93] and [Litt93].

However, special-event failures to which one is willing to attach a probability of occurrence (say, above 10^{-7}) may be analyzable through the concept of risk. This concept forms a bridge between the probabilistic reliability aspects and the critical and economic considerations of any system [Ehre85, Fran88, Boeh89]. A risk model identifies a set of software reliability engineering indicators or symptoms, and relates them to the expected behavior of the software in the field. Once risks have been identified, analyzed, and prioritized (risk assessment), a risk control strategy has to be defined and implemented. In practice, risk assessment and control requires a very thorough understanding of the problem area, solution alternatives, and corresponding impacts. Furthermore, the process is invariably complicated by the fact that the probability and/or loss estimates are subjective, at least to some extent, and that our information about the system states and associated impact likelihoods is never perfect. For example, we have to take into account the probability that our risk control decisions, based on the computed risks, will fail to avert the risk, or will be wasted since the risk would not have materialized in any case. Before applying software risk assessment and control techniques, you are urged to consult the excellent works of [Boeh91, Boeh89, Char89, Fran88, Ehre85] on software risk analysis, the papers and references in [IEEE94] on software safety, and the *Human Reliability and Safety Analysis Data Handbook* [Gert94].

An example of a special event that could be regarded through the probabilistic prism is an FCC-reportable failure. In part owing to a series of operational problems that have embarrassed the switching industry in the past several years,* FCC has issued a notification to common carriers regarding service disruptions that exceed 30 minutes and affect more than 50,000 lines. Since March 1992, any outage of this type needs to be reported to FCC within 30 minutes of its occurrence [FCC92]. These FCC-reportable events are relatively rare, but such outages may have serious safety implications.† Since the information itself can command considerable public visibility and attention, such failures may have serious business implications as well. An example is an advertisement that appeared in the *USA Today* on April 15, 1993 [USAT93]. This AT&T advertisement woos 800-service customers by comparing the AT&T and MCI reliability performance over the previous year in terms of, among other things, lost and abandoned calls and the number of FCC-reported outages.

11.7.1 Rare-event models

The key issue is the probability of occurrence of rare events. Computation of the probability of rare software events is not a solved problem, and perhaps not even a fully solvable problem. However, whatever results are available must be presented not as a point estimate but as a range or interval: for example [lowerbound, upperbound]. Often, 95 percent confidence interval is used. We present some very simple models which serve to highlight the issues involved, and indicate the difficulty of the problem.

* For example, the January 1990 AT&T outage [Lee92a] and the DSC signal transfer point fiasco [Wats91].

† For example, through impact on emergency services such as 911 calls.

11.7.1.1 No-failure model. It can be shown (e.g., [Dura84, Ehre85, Howd87]) that if N representative (operational profile) random test cases are executed and no failures are found, then an upper bound, p_u, on the failure probability of the system, at α confidence level, is given by the following expression:

$$p_u = 1 - (1 - a)^{1/n+1} \tag{11.3}$$

This is the distribution function of the *modified* geometric probability mass function which is used when one counts the number of trials before (but *not* including) the first "failure" [Triv82]. Typically, $a = 0.95$ (95 percent confidence bound). For example, given that we have run for 10,000 in-service hours without experiencing a single FCC reportable failure, an upper 95 percent confidence bound on the probability of failure per in-service hour is

$$p_u = 1 - (1 - 0.95)^{1/10001} = 1 - 0.9997 = 0.0003 \tag{11.4}$$

So the model, given continuation of execution in the same environment, is [0.0,0.0003] failures per in-service hour (to one significant digit). A more sophisticated analysis, based on Bayesian estimation, is offered by [Mill92]. Equation 11.4 is then a special case where prior knowledge about the quality of the system is not incorporated into the calculation.

11.7.1.2 Constant-failure-rate model. If some failure information is available, and it can be assumed that the failure rate, or failure intensity, is constant,* then we deal with two cases: (1) a gamma (exponential) distribution, if the number of failures is fixed but the total exposure time is a random variable; or (2) the Poisson distribution, if the number of failures is a random variable but the total exposure time is fixed. In both cases, standard statistical confidence bounds for these distributions can be used to evaluate the information.

The simplest model is the one where we estimate the probability of the undesirable events based on the counts of these events:

$$P(S_f) \simeq \frac{n_f}{n} \tag{11.5}$$

where n_f is the number of failure events, and n is the usage exposure expressed as the number of intervals in which we wish to estimate.

For example, given that a telecommunications organization experiences three FCC-reportable failures in one year [USAT93], and if we

* Or, at least, a relatively slowly varying function of time.

assume that the failures are mutually independent and the rate is relatively constant,* then (using 95 percent Poisson bounds [Triv82]) in the following year we may expect between one and seven FCC-reportable failures. Similarly, if the constant annual failure rate is 13, then the 95 percent confidence-bound model is [7, 19] FCC-reportable failures per year.

11.7.1.3 Reliability growth. If the usage rate of the product is growing, but its quality remains approximately the same or grows at a lower rate than the product usage, then although per-site or per-system failure rate may be roughly constant (or may even be improving), the overall number of reported problems will grow. In that case, it is necessary to model the per-site failure rate. For example, let function $S(t)$ describe the number of sites that use a particular release of a product at some calendar time t (see Fig. 11.2). This shape can often be described using a Poisson [Leve90], or perhaps Weibull-type, envelope, such as

$$S(t) = K \frac{\alpha}{\beta} t^{\alpha - 1} e^{-(t/\beta)^{\alpha}} \tag{11.6}$$

Combined with historical information about the usual position of the envelope mode, and other model parameters, and the marketing information about a release (e.g., the total number of sites expected to run this release), it may be possible to predict $S(t)$ relatively early in the life cycle of a release. This yields an estimate of the overall load on the software release. If this function is then combined with the one describing the quality of the release, it may be possible to make early and accurate predictions of the outage rates.

An example of the quality function, $q(t)$, may be the annual variation of per-office failure rate, perhaps along the lines seen in Fig. 11.11 for Hitachi Software. Note that the problem is somewhat different from traditional time-dependent reliability modeling. The assumptions are that the exposure time is the calendar time, that $q(t)$ is a slowly varying function of time compared to $S(t)$, and that $S(t)$ is relatively independent of $q(t)$. In many practical situations this may be true, and $q(t)$ of a release may be fairly constant over the life cycle of a release (except, perhaps, in the very early field release stages [Cram92]). Hence, although the solution presented by Eq. (11.7) is exceedingly simple, it may be adequate; that is

$$f(t) = S(t) * q(t) \tag{11.7}$$

* Or that it is at least a function that changes very slowly over a two- to three-year period.

may estimate the average number of field outages per unit time.* Whether $f(t)$ estimates the number of outages for a release or for all active sites will depend on whether $S(t)$ represents a single release or is a combined function. The confidence bounds would have to be computed based on the standard error of the site estimates and the $q(t)$ error.

Different models can be used to described the growth of quality. It may also be possible to use all available failure data, not just the special-event data, to estimate reliability growth, and then make assumptions about the proportional growth in the reliability with respect to the special events. A more detailed discussion of this approach can be found in [Schn92b].

11.7.2 Case study (space shuttle flight software)

Space shuttle onboard flight (SSOF) software is an example where a team of experienced software reliability engineers evaluated a number of reliability models and selected the models that best matched the rare-event failure history of that software [Schn92b, Schn93c].

The team carefully evaluated all assumptions on which the models were based and made sure that all restrictions they imposed were accounted for in the analysis of the real software. The execution time of the software under investigation was estimated using test records of digital flight simulators and records of the actual shuttle flights. The failure data collected over a 12-year period were used to validate the models. All detected faults were considered in any operational-like execution, whether the user was aware of the fault or not [Schn92b]. The events were quite rare—at most several per usage-year of a module, and decreasing in frequency. The researchers fitted different models, made predictions, and compared the results to the actual data. They defined and applied different data aging criteria† to account for the fact that old data may not be as representative of the current and future failure process as recent data. In fact, they found that if they gave lower weight to, or even excluded, earlier data they could get more accurate predictions of future failures [Schn93c]. The Schneidewind model provided the most accurate fit over the investigated period.

The data used in the preceding modeling is on the Data Disk (DataSet 6). The data was provided by NASA [Prue95] and reflects the flight software failure history from January 1, 1986, through December

---

* The rarer the event, the longer the time period.

† Examples of data aging include moving average and exponential smoothing. See Sec. 11.8 for application of data aging in availability studies.

1, 1994. The data sets include information about the severity of the failures, information about the circumstances in which a failure was observed (TESTING, TRAINING, FLIGHT), and the information about the software version in which the failure was observed and in which it was originally introduced. Figure 11.13 shows the cumulative failure count over that period, and Fig. 11.14 shows the total yearly failure rate by severity. The exposure time is calendar time. These data show that only one failure was recorded on a flight and it was of low-severity level 3. The remaining 99 failures were found during planned verification testing and training use of the software. The NASA standard, and experience for the past five years, has been that SSOF software fault rates are in the range 0.1 to 0.2 faults of any severity per 1000 lines of changed code [Prue95]. Furthermore, all but one failure were detected prior to flight, and no potential severity 1 or 2 failures have *ever* occurred in flight. The severity 3 flight failure involved a benign annunciation issue analyzed postflight. This success is less surprising when one realizes that the software organization that develops SSOF is one of the very few software organizations in the world that has been classified as a level 5 on the SEI software process scale [Paul93, Kits91].

Severity classification used for SSOF failures is rather unique to avoid confusion with many other severity definitions used on other software projects [Prue95]. Full definitions are given on the Data Disk in the DataSet 6 file. When discussing the loss of or injury to the crew or vehicle, even a single severity 1 problem may be considered as a seri-

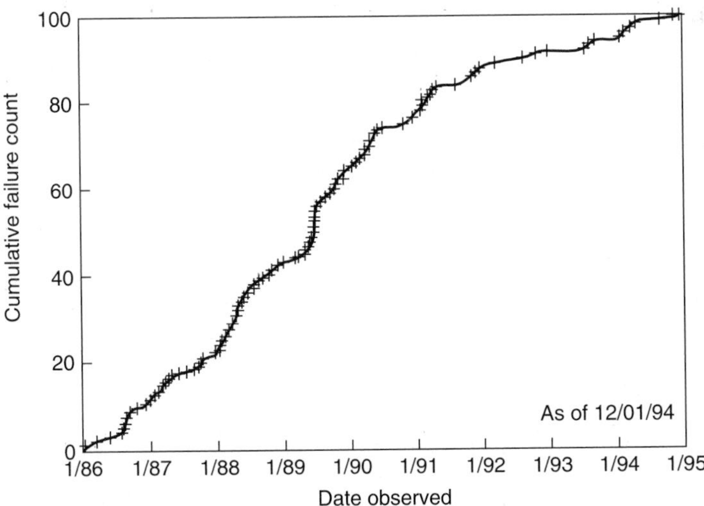

Figure 11.13 Cumulative failure count for SSOF software over a nine-year period [Prue95].

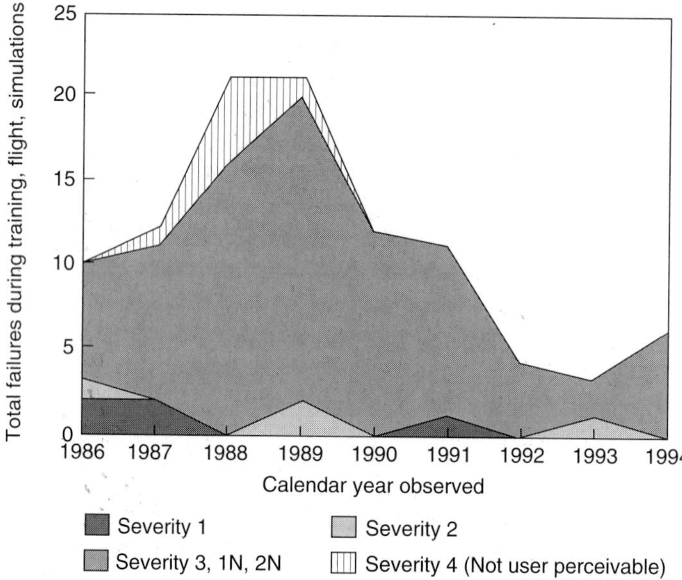

Figure 11.14 SSOF software yearly failure rate over the past nine years, and the severity of the observed failures [Prue95]. Since 1985 only one failure has been experienced in flight due to a coding error. That failure (in 1989) involved a benign annunciation issue analyzed postflight (severity 3).

ous oversight and cause for concern. Hence, SSOF severity definitions are very conservative. NASA defines as severity 1 any problem that has even the remotest probability of ever occurring in normal operational use of the shuttle. The experience is that severity 1 and 2 problems almost always require highly off-nominal shuttle operations or multiple hardware failures within millisecond windows to result in an actual failure. Although these situations have very low probability of occurring, NASA takes severity 1 and 2 failures very seriously and requires detailed analysis and corrective action on each.*

Figure 11.15 illustrates the next-release effect as observed in the SSOF software. The filled circles represent the failures, attributed to the first system release (REL A) of the code, that were precipitated through the execution of a later release. The release execution parallelism derives from concurrent testing and use of several releases under different conditions.

It is important to note that the Schneidewind model was not used as the principal indicator of software reliability, but only to add confi-

* This is also done for shuttle hardware failures.

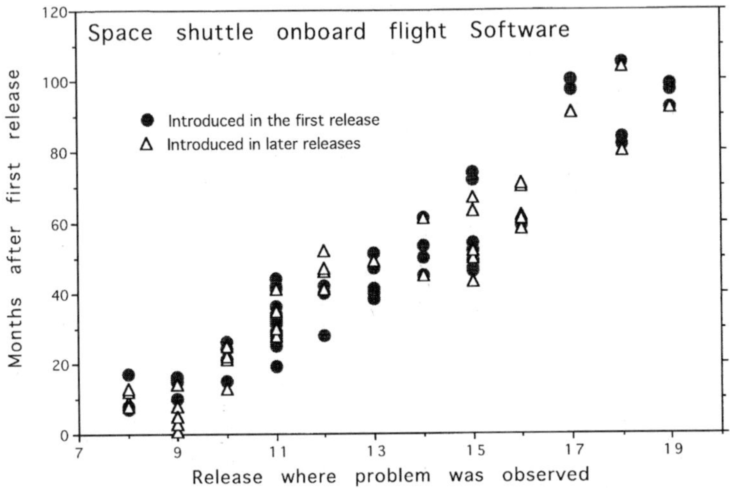

Figure 11.15 This dot plot illustrates the parallelism in the usage of different SSOF software releases. Filled circles represent failures, originating in release 1 (or release A) of the software, that were triggered through the next-release effect when the system release shown on the x axis was used.

dence to failure probabilities obtained from formal certification processes. It was concluded that a credible use of software reliability models for prediction of rare events is possible, but that this has to be accompanied by a careful evaluation of the model assumptions and constraints, a validation of the predictive capabilities of the model, and an understanding of what the predictions really mean. [Prue95] noted that while complex software may never be proven to be perfect, the shuttle software has a NASA commitment to be as close as possible.

11.8 Availability

11.8.1 Introduction

An important concept that is closely related to reliability is software availability. The importance stems from prevalent industry specifications related to reliability and availability. For example, one of Bellcore's primary requirements is for the availability of telecommunications network elements. Their target is about 3 minutes of downtime per year. Availability is simply the probability that the system will be available when demanded, and it depends on both the reliability and the reparability of the system. We briefly explore the practical evaluation of system availability by using the following example.

[Cram92] reports on the availability of a large multirelease telecommunications switching system. The system in this study has two principal switching products running similar software, but distinguished by their hardware compositions. We will refer to these separate systems (or products) as P1 and P2. Since the software running on these systems generally changes more frequently than the hardware, a new software release will represent the upgrade to a new system. A software release is normally installed at hundreds of sites. To distinguish among the releases, we use release numbers (R7, R8, etc.). Software libraries for this system exceed 10 million lines of high-level code. A typical executable software load consists of approximately 7 million lines of high-level code, of which about 10 percent is new or modified code. The data used in this example come from the operational phase of the software. The data are collected on a regular basis as part of software process and product quality assurance activities at the organization that developed the system.

11.8.2 Measuring availability

11.8.2.1 Instantaneous availability. Instantaneous availability is the probability that the system will be available at any random time t during its life [Sand63, Triv82]. We estimate instantaneous availability in a period i as follows:

$$\hat{A}(i) = \frac{\text{uptime in period } i}{\text{total in-service time for period } i} \tag{11.8}$$

where the in-service time is the total time in the period i during which all hosts of a particular type (e.g., processor A, processor B), at all sites, operated a particular software release (whether fully operational, partly degraded, or under repair), while uptime is the total time during period i at which the systems *were not* in the "100 percent down" state (or total system outage state).* Correspondingly, the instantaneous unavailability estimate is $(1 - \hat{A}(i))$. Associated with this measure are instantaneous system failure, $\lambda(i)$, and recovery rates, $\rho(i)$, which are estimated as follows:

$$\hat{\lambda}(i) = \frac{\text{number of outages in period } i}{\text{total uptime for period } i} \tag{11.9}$$

$$\hat{\rho}(i) = \frac{\text{number of outages in period } i}{\text{total downtime for period } i} \tag{11.10}$$

---

* The equation can be customized with other definitions of uptime that suit the need. For example, we could define *uptime* as only the states where the system was 80 to 100 percent operational.

where in-service time for period i is the sum of the downtime and uptime in that period.

11.8.2.2 Average availability. Since the raw data are often noisy, the data are usually presented after some form of smoothing, or data aging, has been applied. This gives rise to a family of smoothed availability metrics (note there is an analogous family of smoothed reliability metrics). Examples are one-sided moving average and symmetrical moving average, such as 11-point symmetrical moving average. An extreme form of smoothing is provided by the *average,* or *uptime,* availability. Uptime availability is the proportion of time in a specified interval $[0,T]$ that the system is available for use [Sand63, Shoo83]. We estimate uptime availability up to and including period i as follows:

$$A_c(i) = \frac{\sum_{x=1}^{i} \text{uptime in period } x}{\sum_{x=1}^{i} \text{total in-service time for period } x} \tag{11.11}$$

Total uptime and total in-service time are cumulative sums starting with the first observation related to a particular release. Uptime includes degraded service. Associated with uptime availability are average system failure, $\hat{\lambda}_c(i)$, and recovery rates, $\hat{\rho}_c(i)$, which are Eq. (11.11) analogues of Eqs. (11.9) and (11.10).

11.8.3 Empirical unavailability

Figure 11.16 illustrates a typical unavailability observed for the system described in [Cram92]. In addition to the instantaneous data, we show the influence of different smoothing approaches. For example, [Cram92] found that the 11-point symmetrical moving-average smoothing was useful for examining trends in the instantaneous unavailability. Each raw data point on the graph corresponds to the data collected during one calendar period.* Abrupt changes in instantaneous unavailability are smoothed by uptime averaging. Under the assumption that product unavailability becomes smaller with time, we would expect uptime unavailability estimates to be generally conservative. Unavailability curves similar to that in Fig. 11.16 were observed for the TROPICO 4096 system described in [Lapr91] (DataSet 4 on the Data Disk; also see Sec. 2.4.4).

---

* For example, one week or one month. *Note:* In order to draw the raw data on the logarithmic scale, the data points (periods) where no failures were observed (i.e., zero failure rate) were censored and only the adjacent nonzero failure rate points are shown.

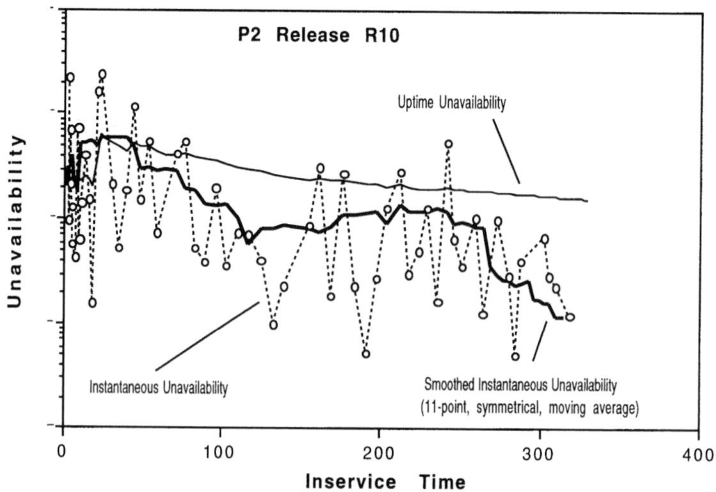

Figure 11.16 Illustration of empirical unavailability data and of the effect of some smoothing options applied to release R10 of P2.

There is often a period, immediately after the product is made available to customers, in which considerable oscillation is observed in unavailability. We refer to the time period from the point where the product is made available to the customers (i.e., time zero) to the point where the instabilities abate as the *transient region.* It corresponds to the transient part of the availability function. It is interesting to note the maximum in the initial part of the smoothed P2 unavailability function is a characteristic of reliability growth [Lapr90b]. In Fig. 11.16 the duration of this region of instability is about 20 to 50 in-service time units, but in general, it depends on the product type and release. Once the instability had decayed, all releases exhibited fairly smooth unavailability decay curves, which in this case could be approximated by almost straight lines [Cram92].

11.8.3.1 Failure and recovery rates. Two measures which directly influence the availability of a system are its failure rate and its field repair rate (or software recovery rate). In a system which improves with field usage we would expect a decreasing function for failure rate with in-service time (implying fault or problem reduction and reliability growth). Failure rate is connected to both the operational usage profile and the process of problem resolution and correction. Measured recovery rate depends on the operational usage profile, the type of problem encountered, and the field response to that problem (i.e., the duration of outages in this case). If the failures encountered during the operational phase of the release do not exhibit durations that would be preferentially longer or shorter at a point (or period) in the life cycle, then we would expect the instantaneous recovery rate to be a level function with in-service time (with, perhaps, some oscillations in the early stages). This behavior was generally observed in both the [Cram92] and the [Lapr91] investigations. It is interesting to note that [Cram92] observed recovery rates at least 3 to 4 orders of magnitude larger than the failure rate. It was also found that the recovery rate was approximately constant, so the availability was governed primarily by the stochastic changes in the failure rate.

11.8.4 Models

The time-varying nature of both the failure rate and, to a lesser extent, the repair rate indicates that a full availability model should be nonhomogeneous. In addition, the distribution of outage causes, as well as the possibility of operation in degraded states, suggest that a detailed model should be a many-state model. Nonetheless, a very simple two-state model may provide a reasonable description of the system availability beyond the transient region. It can be shown that system availability $A(t)$ and unavailability $\bar{A}(t) = 1 - A(t)$, given some simplifying assumptions, is (e.g., [Triv82, Shoo83]):

$$A(t) = \frac{\rho}{\lambda + \rho} + \frac{\lambda}{\lambda + \rho} e^{-(\lambda + \rho)t} \tag{11.12}$$

It can also be shown that uptime availability can be formulated as

$$A_c(T) = \frac{\rho}{\lambda + \rho} + \frac{\lambda}{(\lambda + \rho)^2 T} - \frac{\lambda}{(\lambda + \rho)^2 T} e^{-(\lambda + \rho)T} \tag{11.13}$$

The system becomes independent of its starting state after operating for enough time for the transient part of the preceding equations to decay away. This steady-state availability of the system is $A(\infty) = \text{limit}\ \{A(t = T \rightarrow \infty)\}$, i.e.,

$$A(\infty) = \frac{\rho}{\lambda + \rho} \tag{11.14}$$

The preceding model represents a two-state system which can be either fully operational or completely off-line and under repair. However, realistic systems, like the ones discussed in our case studies, not only have failure rates and repair rates which vary with time and can have different down states (e.g., FCC-reportable or not [FCC92]), but they can also function in more than one up state (i.e., the system may remain operational but with less than 100 percent functionality for some failures). Thus, a many-state nonhomogeneous Markov model may be more appropriate for describing the details of such systems (e.g., [Triv75, Lapr92b, Ibe92]). Nevertheless, a classical two-state model for availability of recoverable systems can be used to approximate behavior of more complex nonhomogeneous systems.

11.8.4.1 Practical approximations. An approximation that may work quite well is what we will call the *steady-state approximation.* It is based on the observations made by [Triv75, Shoo83]. We note that once the system has been operational for some time, the steady-state Eq. (11.14) may be used to approximate the instantaneous availability by assuming a piecewise-constant variation of λ and ρ in time. Letting $\hat{\lambda}(t)$ and $\hat{\rho}(t)$ be estimates at time t for λ and failure rate, ρ, respectively, we can estimate instantaneous availability as

$$\hat{A}(t) = \frac{\hat{\rho}(t)}{\hat{\lambda}(t) + \hat{\rho}(t)} \tag{11.15}$$

The $\hat{\lambda}(t)$ and $\hat{\rho}(t)$ approximations can be obtained from the empirical data: the former through application of a reliability model and the latter is often assumed to be a constant (e.g., [Lapr91]).

The following example provides a simple illustration of the application of the preceding approximation. We consider the release R11 for product P2. From other work [Cram92] we know that the uptime recovery rate for this release is approximately constant once sufficient in-service time has passed. We make the simplifying assumption that the recovery rate is constant and choose it to be the average of the period being considered (i.e., it is the uptime recovery rate of the sample point with the largest in-service time). Furthermore, the MO model provides a good descriptive, as well as predictive, model for the failure rate of the P1 and P2 systems [Jone91, Jone92].

The MO failure rate equation with the parameters obtained from a fit and constant repair rate were used to compute the steady-state approximations for instantaneous unavailability. The results are shown Fig. 11.17. The figure also shows the result of another, more accurate, computational approximation we call *n-step approximation.* The n-step transition approximation [Cram92] is based on numerical solution of Chapman-Kolmogorov equations that describe the system states.

It is interesting to note that the n-step approximation reflects the transient region maximum expected in the unavailability function of a system that experiences reliability growth [Lapr92b], while the steady-state approximation does not exhibit this mode. However, the results from the n-step and steady-state approximations practically coincide

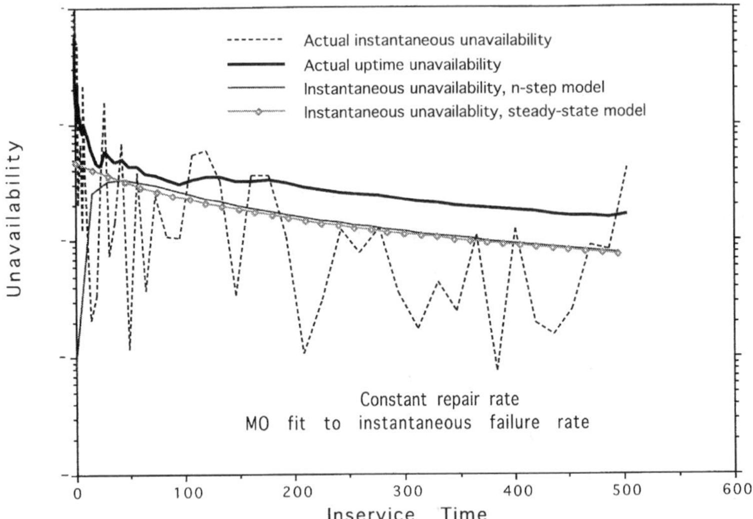

Figure 11.17 Unavailability modeling using the MO failure intensity model and constant repair rate. Both the MO parameters and the average repair rate were estimated on the basis of *all* data. The data are for system P2, release R11.

once past the transient period, and for all practical purposes, the computationally simpler steady-state approximation may be all that is needed to model availability of a system. Of course, both approximations lie below uptime unavailability (shown in the figure as a thick solid line) because the instantaneous unavailability is less conservative than the uptime unavailability.

11.8.4.2 Prediction. In practice, a model would be used to predict future unavailability of a system. Of course, only the data up to the point from which the prediction is being made would be available. In this example, we refer to the point at which the prediction is made as the data *cut-off point.* The prediction of future unavailability will differ from the true value depending on how well the model describes the system.

In Fig. 11.18, we show instantaneous and uptime unavailability using the steady-state approximation, average recovery rate at the cut-off point, and the MO failure fit to points from the beginning of the operational phase of the release up to the cut-off point. We see that the approximation for uptime unavailability appears to follow the empirical uptime unavailability quite well. Similar results have been obtained for other releases of the same product. Of course, in practice, predictive characteristics of a model should be checked more formally using tests such as u-plots or relative error calculations (see Sec. 11.3.3.2). However, the lesson is that, from a practical perspective, a

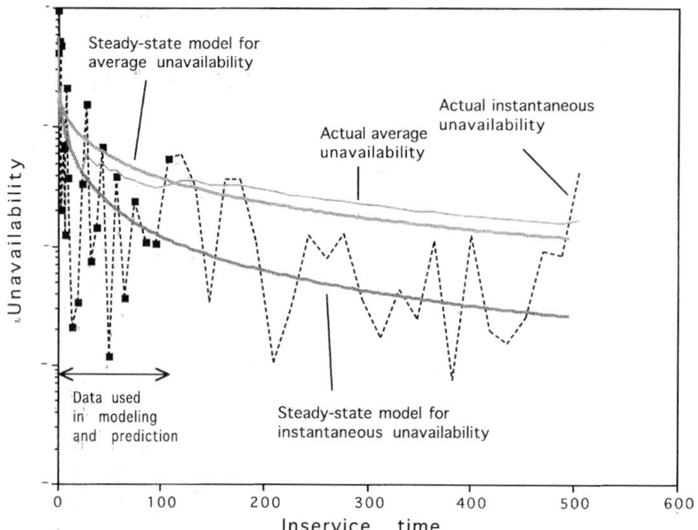

Figure 11.18 Unavailability was modeled using the steady-state model. Failure intensity was modeled using MO model and average repair rate. Both the MO parameters and the average repair rate were estimated on the basis of the first 100 in-service time units. The data are for system P2 release R11.

relatively simple availability model can have quite reasonable predictive properties for a system that is being released and maintained in a stable environment.

Availability models can be constructed using other assumptions, including time-varying repair rate, and different (appropriate) software reliability models. An example is the availability model constructed in [Lapr91] using the constant-repair-rate assumption, and the hyperexponential reliability model to fit the empirical failure data for the TROPICO-R 4096 switch software. The model is based on calendar-time usage, rather than on in-service-time usage, and it has good predictive characteristics (see Sec. 2.4.4).

11.9 Summary

Analysis of field data is an extremely important software reliability engineering activity. It enables quantitative and qualitative assessment of the product quality during its actual usage; it provides the link between software quality in the field and software life-cycle processes; and it provides the basis for active control of software field quality. It is essential that you perform the reliability analysis on properly collected data, using adequate tools and appropriate software reliability models. The key data collection issues are (1) consistent definition of failures and faults, (2) measurement of the product usage, and (3) the data granularity. Analysis tools and methods include graphs and plots. In that context, it is interesting to note that an approach that can be very useful, but is often overlooked in practice, is reliability model selection based on graphical diagnostics. The customer's usage of the product is very important to understanding of the current or future reliability of a system. If CPU-time-usage data are difficult to obtain (as is often the case), field failure rates based on calendar time can be employed. Experience shows that both calendar-time- and usage-time-based models can be used effectively to predict system behavior. In the case of critical systems, and in situations where we are dealing with rare failure events, common software reliability models may not be adequate and special methods need to be used. A concept that is closely related to reliability, and has many practical implications, is system availability. In addition to failure data, availability analysis requires collection of information about corresponding system recovery rates.

Problems

11.1 Outline a study document for investigation of the field reliability of your favorite software system. Include explicit study goals, a template for data collection and an outline of the processes and methodology you intend to use to validate your data, and analyze and present the results.

11.2 *a.* List at least five important failure data collection issues.
b. Explain the statement: "Ten usage weeks may correspond to three calendar days."

11.3 What is the difference between exploratory and confirmatory data analyses and techniques?

11.4 What are the advantages and disadvantages of using plots, graphs, and graphical model selection and diagnostic tools? Explain and give examples.

11.5 Using DataSet 1 (large telecommunications system):
a. Analyze the usage and office data and comment on any anomalies. Are they explainable?
b. Calculate the failure intensity using failure grouping of 10 percent and plot the results.
c. Compare the plot with Figs. 11.4 and 11.7 and comment on the difference, if any.

11.6 Perform Laplace trend analysis of the DataSet 1 using one of the automated tools (e.g., SoRel, described in Sec. A.7).

11.7 Using DataSet 1 (large telecommunications system):

a. Calculate the maximum likelihood estimates for the parameters of the MO model based on all available data.
b. Calculate the maximum likelihood estimates for the parameters of the MO model at 10 percent time intervals and forecast the end time. Compute the relative error of the prediction at each time point and create a relative error plot using the maximum likelihood estimates (MLE).
c. Choose a model other than the log Poisson and repeat item *b.* Is the new model better or worse? Explain and justify using a metric such as u-plot.

11.8 *a.* Use DataSet 1 from the Data Disk and replot Fig. 11.8.
b. Can we analyze field data using usage-time-based reliability models in the calendar-time domain? Explain, giving examples.

11.9 What is the relationship between the field usage of the software and the number of sites at which the product is installed? Using information in DataSet 1 and Fig. 11.8, develop an analytic form for this relationship.

11.10 What is the difference between failures or outages per in-service time, and failures and outages per system per calendar year? If the product is a telephone switching software, which one would you use to examine quality of service offered to a typical telephone user? Explain.

11.11 What are the advantages and disadvantages of using S-shaped reliability models for modeling field data? Explain and give examples.

11.12 Perform an exploratory analysis of the DataSet 2 (IBM Corporation *controller software*).
a. Group the data into categories one month long and compute the corresponding failure frequencies; plot the frequency against the calendar time.
b. Apply symmetrical 3-month and 5-month moving-average smoothing to the frequency data and overlay the results on the frequency plot from item *a.* How do results change if the moving average is asymmetrical (only the older data are used to adjust the current value)?
c. For each failure, calculate its corresponding time to failure. Tabulate the results.
d. Compute calendar-time failure intensity using failure groups of size 5; plot the failure intensity against the calendar time.
e. Compute and plot Laplace trend for the data set.
f. Try to linearize the data.
g. Plot cumulative failure distribution against calendar time.
h. Discuss your results.

11.13 *a.* Based on Prob. 11.12 results, recommend a model.
b. Fit the model to the data, record the parameters, and overlay the plot of the modeled and empirical failure intensity, and modeled and empirical cumulative failure distributions.

c. Discuss the validity and predictive capabilities of the model by showing how well it predicts the total cumulative failure count in month 36, given data up to month 12, month 18, month 24, and month 30.
d. Use a computational diagnostic to evaluate the predictions (justify the use of this particular diagnostic).

11.14 What is the next-release effect? Explain and give examples.

11.15 Perform full reliability analysis of DataSet 3.

11.16 Fit and justify a model for DataSet 5. What can we expect the field failure ratio to be in 1996? Provide upper and lower bounds for this estimate.

11.17 Look up u-plots and prequential likelihood tests. Apply these methods to one of the analyses requested in the previous problems. Explain and justify your approach and the results.

11.18 A software system has a failure intensity objective of 0.005 failures per CPU hour. During beta test the system runs for 700 CPU hours without a failure.

a. What is the upper 95 percent confidence bound on the program failure intensity?
b. If the upper 99 percent confidence bound on the failure intensity must be below 0.005, how many *more* CPU hours would you have to beta-test the system without experiencing a failure.

11.19 *a.* Why is it that time to next failure may be totally inapplicable to field data?
b. Perform an exploratory analysis of DataSet 6, including next-release effect and parallelism analyses. Use dot plots. Write an exploratory analysis report on SSOF.
c. Is the Weibull defect model a viable model for SSOF? Discuss, using examples and analyses based on DataSet 6.

11.20 Describe a simple two-state Markov chain model for availability and derive the basic relationships for instantaneous and long-term (steady-state) availability.

11.21 *a.* Use Shooman's steady-state approximation model to analyze availability for TROPICO R-4096 switching software given in DataSet 4.
b. Compare the results with the hyperexponential model.

Part

3

Emerging Techniques

Chapter

12

Software Metrics for Reliability Assessment

John C. Munson
University of Idaho

Taghi M. Khoshgoftaar
Florida Atlantic University

12.1 Introduction

Software development is a complicated process in which software faults are inserted in code by mistakes on the part of program developers. For the purpose of software reliability engineering, it is important to understand this fault insertion phenomenon. The pattern of the faults has been shown to be related to measurable attributes of the software. Consider the case of a large software system. Typically, this system will contain many subunits or modules. Each of the modules may be characterized in terms of a set of attribute measures. It would be quite useful to be able to construct predictive models for software faults based on these attribute values.

Among various software attributes, we focus on complexity metrics. This is based on the observation that software complexity has a direct impact on its quality. Some programs are easy to understand, easy to modify, and account for little of the expense in the development of the software systems of which they are components. Other programs seem almost beyond comprehension, even to their authors. These programs are nearly impossible to modify without inserting multiple faults, and they account for much of the expense in the development of the software systems of which they are components. Between these extremes lies a range of programs of intermediate complexity. Many program attributes, considered together, account for this observed variability. A large set of interrelated software complexity metrics quantify these static program complexity attributes. The size of this set, and the interrelationships among its elements, cause difficulties in understanding software complexity.

We also note that the initial reliability of a software system is largely determined during program design. One distinct aspect of the software design process that lends itself to measurement is the decomposition of the functionality of a system into modules and the subsequent interaction of the modules under a given set of inputs to the software. The reliability of a software system may be characterized in terms of the individual software modules that make up the system, as well as their executions. The likelihood that a component will fail is directly related to the complexity of that module. If it is very complex the fault probability is also high. Furthermore, a typical large software system might consist of many hundreds of distinct software modules. When the software is executing any one of many possible functionalities, only a small subset of the code is actually executing. The reliability of a software system, then, is a function of software modules that are actually executing and the fault density of these modules. In order to model the reliability of a software system, we must be able to characterize the dynamic characteristics of the software.

For each possible design outcome in a software design effort there will be a set of expected execution profiles, one for each of the anticipated program functionalities. The reliability of the system can be thought of in terms of the exposure of the program to complex modules while the program is running. This complexity will vary in relation to the execution profiles induced by the operating environment of the program. At the design stage, quantitative measures correlated to fault-proneness and product failure provide a means to begin to exert statistical process control techniques on the design itself as an ongoing quality-control activity. Rather than merely documenting the increasing operational complexity of a software product and therefore its decreasing reliability, you can also monitor the operational complexity of successive design adaptations during the maintenance phase. This effort can ensure that subsequent design revisions do not increase operational complexity and, especially, do not increase the variance among individual module's functional complexity.

In this chapter we describe the software metrics that can be obtained early in the life cycle for software reliability assessment. In particular, we introduce the measure of complexity attributes to predict the quality of software. We first present the techniques that reduce a large set of interrelated complexity metrics, respectively, to a smaller set of orthogonal metrics, and to a single metric. We then describe a method for quantifying execution profiles. Furthermore, we combine the concepts of static complexity and execution profile to produce dynamic complexity metrics, that is, metrics that quantify the complexity of software systems as they operate in a given environment. Finally, the usage of software complexity metrics in software reliability models is presented.

12.2 Static Program Complexity

Our ultimate objective in the software measurement process is to be able to characterize the quality of a software system in terms of some measurable software attributes. These software quality attributes might include such domains as the number of embedded faults in the software or the number of changes made to the software over its useful life. The problem with software quality attributes is that these attributes are known only at the end of the useful life of the software. It is a moot point whether or not a system has a low or a high fault density after the software has been taken out of service at the end of its career. In order to understand the quality of software, we need to examine different complexity metrics.

12.2.1 Software metrics

We have, over a period of time, observed a relationship between measures of software complexity and measures of software quality [Khos90]. An example of this would be the direct relationship and high correlation between the lines of code (LOC) metric and software faults [Khos92a]. There are many software complexity metrics. A number of these metrics are highly correlated with measures of quality such as fault count or change count. Measures of software complexity can be used as good predictors of software quality: for example, complex software modules are those likely to have a high fault count. Further, if a complex module is executed, it has a much higher likelihood of failing than a module that is not so complex. The important fact here is that measures of software complexity can be obtained very early in the software life cycle. Some may be obtained by measuring the source code, such as LOC. Some may be obtained from the high-level design, such as measures relating to the flow of program control. Some measures may even be taken on the software specifications themselves. Thus we can use software complexity measures as leading indicators of measures of software quality.

Since most of the existing metrics have common elements and are linear combinations of these common elements, it seems reasonable to investigate the structure of the underlying common factors or components that make up the raw metrics. The technique we have chosen to use to explore this structure is a procedure called *principal components analysis.* Principal components analysis is a decomposition technique that may be used to detect and analyze the relationships among the software metrics. When confronted with a large number of metrics measuring a single construct, it may be desirable to represent the set by some smaller number of variables that convey all, or most, of the information in the original set. Principal components are linear transformations of a set of random variables that summarize the information contained in the variables. The transformations are chosen so that the first component accounts for the maximal amount of variation of the measures of any possible linear transform; the second component accounts for the maximal amount of residual variation; and so on. The principal components are constructed so that they represent transformed scores on dimensions that are orthogonal [Muns89].

12.2.2 A domain model of software attributes

Through the use of principal components analysis, it is possible to have a set of highly related software attributes mapped into a small number of uncorrelated attribute domains. This solves the problem of multicollinearity in subsequent regression analysis [Khos90]. There are many software metrics in the literature, but principal components analysis reveals that there are few distinct sources of variation, i.e., dimensions, in this set of metrics. It would appear perfectly reasonable to characterize the measurable attributes of a program with a simple function of a small number of orthogonal metrics, each of which represents a distinct software attribute domain. Still, some metrics measure distinct program attributes. For example, Halstead developed a number of metrics now known as the software science metrics [Hals77]. Four of these metrics cannot be decomposed into other metrics:

- N_1, the total number of operators in a program
- N_2, the total number of operands in a program
- η_1, the number of unique operators in a program
- η_2, the number of unique operands in a program

From these primitive metrics, Halstead composed nonprimitive metrics, including

- $N = N_1 + N_2$, program length
- $V = N \log_2 (\eta_1 + \eta_2)$, program volume
- $\hat{E} = V\,[\eta_1 N_2 / 2\eta_2]$, estimated effort

While these metrics are sensitive to program size, they are not sensitive to program control flow; that is, programs with vastly different control flow structure can have identical Halstead metric values. Thus, Halstead's metrics do not measure complexity due to control flow.

On the other hand, McCabe developed a nonprimitive metric, the cyclomatic number, which does measure some aspects of control flow complexity [McCa76]. Given a strongly connected graph G, the cyclomatic number of G is the number of independent paths in G. This is given by $V(G) = e - n + p$, where e is the number of edges, n is the number of nodes, and p is the number of connected components. McCabe applied this graph theory by constructing a program control flow graph. In this directed graph, nodes represent entry points, exit points, segments of sequential code, or decisions in the program. Edges represent control flow in the program. Strong connectivity is satisfied with the addition of an edge from the exit node to the entry node. McCabe observed that, for a structured program with single entry and exit constructs, $V(G)$ is equal to the number of predicates in the program plus one.

While $V(G)$ is sensitive to program control flow complexity, it is not necessarily related to program size, that is, programs with vastly different counts for operators and operands can have identical cyclomatic numbers. Thus, Halstead's metrics and McCabe's metric measure two distinct program attributes. Each of these program attributes represents a source of variation underlying the measured complexity metrics.

12.2.3 Principal components analysis

A statistical technique like principal components analysis may be used quite effectively to isolate the distinct sources of variation underlying the set of software complexity metrics describing a software system. A multivariate data set might, for example, consist of values for each of m software attribute measures for a set of each of n program modules. These data can be represented by an n by m matrix. When applying principal components analysis, you typically seek to account for most of the variability in the m attributes of this matrix with $p < m$ linear combinations of these attributes. Each linear combination represents an orthogonal source of variation underlying the data set. Let $\mathbf{\Sigma}$ be the covariance matrix for the metric data set. Then $\mathbf{\Sigma}$ is a real symmetric matrix and, assuming that it has distinct roots, can be decomposed as

$$\mathbf{\Sigma} = \mathbf{T}\,\mathbf{\Lambda}\,\mathbf{T}'$$

where $\mathbf{\Lambda}$ is a diagonal matrix with the eigenvalues, $\lambda_1, \lambda_2, \ldots, \lambda_m$ on its diagonal

$\mathbf{\Sigma}_{j=1}^{m} \lambda_j = \text{trace}(\Sigma)$

$\mathbf{T}$ is an orthogonal matrix where column j is the eigenvector associated with λ_j

$\mathbf{T}'$ is the transpose of $\mathbf{T}$

The m eigenvectors in **T** give the coefficients that define m uncorrelated linear combinations of the original complexity metrics. These orthogonal linear combinations are the principal components of $\boldsymbol{\Sigma}$. The ratio $\lambda_j/\text{trace}(\boldsymbol{\Sigma})$ gives the proportion of complexity metric variance that is explained by the jth principal component. The first few principal components typically explain a large proportion of the total variance. Thus, restricting attention to the first few principal components can achieve a reduction in dimensionality with an insignificant loss of explained variance. A stopping rule selects $p < m$ principal components such that each one contributes significantly to the total explained variance, and the p selected components collectively account for a large proportion of this variance. A typical stopping rule selects principal components with associated eigenvalues greater than one.

The standardized transformation matrix, $\mathbf{T}*$, is constructed from **T** to produce p domain metrics for each of the n programs comprising the software system. An element t_{ij} of $\mathbf{T}*$ gives the coefficient, or weight of the ith complexity metric, $i = 1,2, \ldots ,m,$ for the jth domain metric, $j = 1,2, \ldots ,p$. Thus, given $\mathbf{z}_k$, the vector of standardized metrics for program module $k = 1,2, \ldots ,n$, $\mathbf{D}_k = \mathbf{z}_k\mathbf{T}*$ is a new vector of orthogonal domain metrics for the kth program module. The p domain metric values for this program module, $D_{k1}, D_{k2}, \ldots ,D_{kp}$, represent variation due to the p orthogonal complexity domains underlying the complexity data. The n values for the jth domain metric $D_{1j}, D_{2j}, \ldots ,D_{nj}$ are distributed with a mean of 0 and variance of 1. Since domain metrics are not directly observable, they are best interpreted in terms of domain loadings, that is, in terms of their correlations with the complexity metrics.

Example 12.1 Consider a sample metric data set consisting of metric values for N, V, $\hat{E}$, and $V(G)$ for the programs comprising a software system. Assume that principal components analysis of this data set reveals two principal components having eigenvalues greater than 1. Thus, two complexity domains represent significant sources of variation underlying the complexity metrics. Table 12.1 gives the pattern of domain loadings for these domains along with their associated

TABLE 12.1 Domain Pattern

Metric	Domain 1	Domain 2
N	**0.98**	0.11
V	**0.97**	0.09
$\hat{E}$	**0.91**	0.13
$V(G)$	0.12	**0.99**
Eigenvalue	2.75	1.02
% variance	68.83	25.61
Cumulative % variance	68.83	94.44

eigenvalues. The three Halstead metrics correlate strongly with the first domain, while $V(G)$ correlates strongly with the second domain. This observation leads to the interpretation that the first domain is related to size complexity, while the second domain is related to control flow complexity. These two domains account for, respectively, about 68.8 and 25.6 percent of the variance observed in the metric data. Table 12.2 gives the standardized transformation matrix, $\mathbf{T}_*$.

Consider program module k that has a vector of standardized metrics

$$\mathbf{z}_k = [1.284 \; 1.408 \; 0.777 \; -0.415]$$

The domain metric values for this program module may be obtained by postmultiplying the standardized metric values by the transformation matrix in Table 12.2 as follows:

$$\mathbf{d}_k = [1.284 \; 1.408 \; 0.777 \; -0.415] \begin{bmatrix} 0.364 & -0.046 \\ 0.361 & -0.061 \\ 0.334 & -0.015 \\ -0.119 & 1.020 \end{bmatrix}$$

$$= [1.286 \; -0.581]$$

In most linear modeling applications with software metrics, such as regression analysis and discriminant analysis, the independent variables, or metrics, are assumed to represent some distinct aspect of variability not clearly present in other measures. In software development applications, the independent variables (in this case, the complexity metrics) are strongly interrelated or demonstrate a high degree of multicollinearity. In cases like this, it will be almost impossible to establish the unique contribution of each metric to the model. One distinct result of multicollinearity in the independent measures is that the regression models developed using independent variables with a high degree of multicollinearity have highly unstable regression coefficients. Such models may be subject to dramatic changes due to additions or deletions of variables or even discrete changes in metric values.

12.2.4 The usage of metrics

Our objective is to build and extend a model for software attributes. This model will contain a set of orthogonal attribute domains. Once we

TABLE 12.2 Standardized Transformation Matrix, $\mathbf{T}_*$

Metric	Domain 1	Domain 2
N	0.364	–0.046
V	0.361	–0.061
$\hat{E}$	0.334	–0.015
$V(G)$	–0.119	1.020

have such a model in place we would then like to identify and select from the attribute domain model those attributes that are correlated with a software quality measure, such as number of faults. Each of the orthogonal attributes will have an associated metric value that is uncorrelated with any other attribute metrics. Each of these attributes may potentially serve to describe some aspect of variability in the behavior of the software faults in a program module. This further suggests that constructing a composite metric consisting of Halstead's metrics and McCabe's metric can lead to a better fault prediction capability [Lyu94a].

Some ill-considered attempts have been made to design software systems reflecting the complexity of the object being designed. The most notable of these attempts relates to the use of McCabe's measure of cyclomatic complexity $V(G)$. Magic values of cyclomatic complexity are being incorporated into the requirements specifications of some software systems. For example, we might choose to specify that no program module in the software system should have a cyclomatic complexity greater than an arbitrary value of, say, 15, which is used as a guideline in the design process.

Potentially catastrophic consequences may be associated with this univariate design criterion. First, there is little or no empirical evidence to suggest that a module whose cyclomatic complexity is greater than 15 is materially worse than one whose cyclomatic complexity is 14. Second, and most important, is the fact that if, in the process of designing a software module, we find that the module has a cyclomatic complexity greater than 15, the most obvious and common solution to the problem is to divide the software module into two distinct modules. Now we will certainly have two modules whose cyclomatic complexity is less than 15. The difficulty here is that instead of one program module we have created two, or possibly three, in its place. This will increase the macro complexity of measures related to complexity. In other words, we have decreased *cyclomatic complexity,* but we have increased *coupling complexity.* The result of this shortsighted decision may well be that the total *system complexity* will increase. This in turn will likely lead to a concomitant increase in total faults.

12.2.5 Relative program complexity

In order to simplify the structure of software complexity even further it would be useful if each of the program modules in a software system could be characterized by a single value representing some cumulative measure of complexity. The objective in the selection of such a function, g, is that it be related in some linear manner to software faults such that $g(x) = ax + b$, where x is some unitary measure of program complexity. The more closely related x is to software faults, the more valuable the function g will be in the anticipation of software faults. Previous research has established that the relative complexity metric ρ has properties that would be useful in this regard. The relative complexity metric, ρ, is a weighted sum of a set of uncorrelated attribute domain metrics [Muns90a, Muns90c]. This relative complexity metric represents each raw metric in proportion to the amount of unique variation contributed by that metric.

For an analysis concerned with the relative contributions of each program complexity domain to the complexity of each program, reduction to domain metrics is sufficient. For these applications, it is possible to compute the relative complexity metric for each program module k by forming the weighted sum of the domain metrics as follows: $\rho_k = \mathbf{d}_k\Lambda'_*$ where Λ_* is the vector of eigenvalues associated with the selected domains, Λ'_* is the transpose of this vector, and $\mathbf{d}_k$ is the vector of domain metrics for program module k [Muns90b]. The n values of ρ are distributed with a mean of 0 and a variance of

$$V(\rho) = \sum_{j=1}^{p} \lambda_j^2$$

where p is the number of selected domains, and λ_j is the eigenvalue associated with the jth domain. Thus ρ will take both positive and negative values. A scaled version of this metric

$$\rho'_k = \frac{10\rho_k}{\sqrt{V(\rho)}} + 50$$

is more easily interpreted. The scaled metric is distributed with a mean of 50 and a standard deviation of 10.

Example 12.2 Consider a program module k having the vector of domain metric values $\mathbf{d}_k = [1.286\ -0.581]$. The relative complexity for program module k may be computed by the multiplication of the transpose of a vector containing the eigenvalues from Table 12.1 as follows:

$$\rho_k = [1.286\ -0.581]\begin{bmatrix} 2.753 \\ 1.024 \end{bmatrix} = 2.946$$

The scaled relative complexity is simply,

$$\rho'_k = \frac{(10)(2.946)}{\sqrt{2.753^2 + 1.024^2}} + 50 = 60.03$$

From this scaled value it is easy to see that the scaled relative complexity of module k is roughly one standard deviation (10.03) above the mean relative complexity, 50, for all modules in the total software system.

12.2.6 Software evolution

From the standpoint of early reliability prediction, we would like to be able to use the measurements from past software development efforts to perform a preliminary assessment of fault density or reliability of current or active software development projects. In other words, we would like to have the ability to use a past system to serve as a baseline for a current development project. In essence, the objective is to use an existing database as a baseline for subsequent measures in a software system currently in development. We might choose, for example, to take the first build of a real-time control software system that was developed in the past and use this for a real-time control software system currently being developed. In this sense, all subsequent software measures on new systems will be transformed relative to the baseline system.

The ability to use information from past development projects in current design work is most important. This is due to the fact that many of the software quality and reliability attributes of a system can be measured only after the system has been in service for some time. If a software system under current development is directly comparable to one that has demonstrated quality and/or reliability problems in the past, there is evidence to suggest that the design had better be modified.

The attribute measures presented so far are *static* measures of the program. They measure such features of the program as its size and the complexity of its control structure. If the functionality of a program was extremely restricted, these static measures might well be sufficient to describe the program entirely. Most modern software systems, however, have a broad range of functionality. Consider, for example, the software system for a typical spreadsheet program. The number of distinct functions in such a system and the number of ways that these functions might be exercised are both very large numbers. In addition to static measures of program attributes, we must also be concerned with dynamic measures of programs as well.

In order to describe the complexity of an evolving system at any point in time, it will be necessary to know which version of each of the modules was a constituent in the program that failed. Consider a software system composed of n modules as follows:

$$m_1, m_2, m_3, \ldots, m_n$$

Now, let m_j^i represent the ith version of the jth module. With this nomenclature, the first build of the system would be described by the set of modules:

$$<m_1^1, m_2^1, m_3^1, \ldots, m_n^1>$$

We can represent this configuration more succinctly simply by recording the superscripts as vectors. Thus a system under development might look like the following sequence of module version sets:

$$\mathbf{v}^1 = < 1, 1, 1, 1, \ldots, 1 >$$

$$\mathbf{v}^2 = < 1, 2, 2, 1, \ldots, 1 >$$

$$\mathbf{v}^3 = < 2, 2, 3, 1, \ldots, 1 >$$

$$\mathbf{v}^4 = < 2, 3, 3, 2, \ldots, 2 >$$

$$\vdots$$

Thus, the ith entry in the vector $\mathbf{v}^n$ would represent the version number of the ith module in the nth build of the system.

A natural way to capture the intermediate versions of the software is to have the system development occur under a configuration management system. For a system running under configuration management, all versions of all modules can be reconstructed from the time the program was placed in the system. That is, the precise nature of $\mathbf{v}^n$ can be determined from the configuration management system.

The computation of the relative complexity of various releases or versions of a software system will occur as follows: for an initial build of a software system described by $\mathbf{v}^1$, transformation matrix will map the raw complexity metrics onto a set of reduced orthogonal domain metrics. From these, relative complexity values may be computed for the modules represented by the vector $\mathbf{v}^1$. The transformation coefficient matrix derived from the first build will not change subsequently, but will serve as a baseline for measuring changes in program complexity.

Associated with the ith program module, m_i^1, at the first build of a program, there is a corresponding relative complexity value of ρ_i^1. By definition, the adjusted relative complexity, ρ, of the program system at this first build will be

$$\rho^1 = \sum_i \rho_i^{v_i^1} = 50$$

As the system progresses through a series of builds, system complexity will tend to rise [Muns90b]. Thus, the system relative complexity of the

nth version of a system may be represented by a nondecreasing function of module relative complexity as follows:

$$\rho^n = \sum_i \rho_i^{v_i^n} \geq 50$$

where v_i^n represents an element from the configuration vector $\mathbf{v}^n$ described earlier.

This change in the overall relative complexity of an example system over time is presented pictorially in Fig. 12.1. It can be seen from this figure that the relative complexity of a system will rise fairly rapidly shortly after the first build of the system. It would further appear that the relative complexity becomes asymptotic to a value of, say, 55. This is not the case. The system complexity continues to rise, albeit more slowly, throughout the life of the software system.

12.3 Dynamic Program Complexity

The relative complexity measure, ρ, of a program is a measure of the program at rest. When a program is executing, the level of exposure of its modules depends on the execution environment. Consequently, both the static complexity of a software system and the system's operational environment influence its reliability [Khos93a]. The complex programs comprising a software system often contain a disproportionate number of faults. However, if in a given environment the complex modules are rarely exercised, then few of these faults are likely to become expressed as failures. Different environments will exercise a system's programs differently. The dynamic complexity is a measure of the complexity of the subset of code that is actually executed as a system is performing a

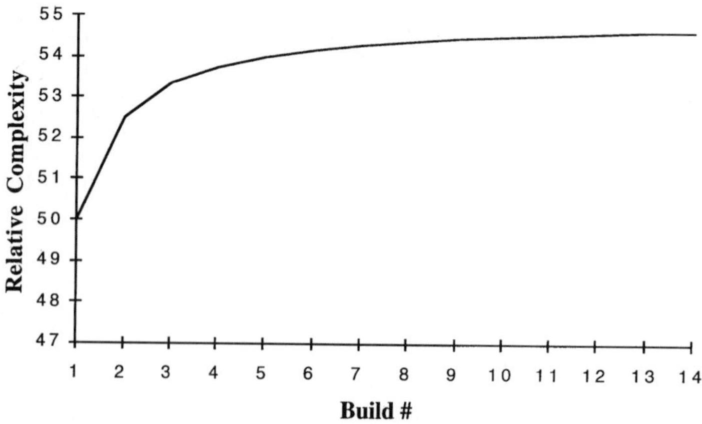

Figure 12.1 Change to relative complexity over time.

given function. A system's dynamic complexity is high in an environment that exercises the system's complex programs with high probability. It is likely that one or more potential scenarios induce inordinately large dynamic complexity. Identifying these scenarios is the first step in assuring that they receive the testing time that they warrant. This is evident in the concept of execution profile.

12.3.1 Execution profile

A software system is written to fulfill a set of functional requirements. It is designed in such a manner that each of these functionalities is expressed in some code component. In some cases a direct correspondence exists between a particular program module and a particular functionality. That is, if the program is expressing that functionality, it will execute exclusively in the module in question. In most cases, however, there will not be this distinct traceability of functionality to modules. The functionality will be expressed in many different code modules.

As a program is exercising any one of its many functionalities, it will apportion its time across one to many program modules. This temporal distribution of processing time is represented by the concept of the execution profile. In other words, if we have a program structured into n distinct modules, the execution profile for a given functionality will be the proportion of time spent in each program module during the time that the function was being expressed.

Another way to look at the execution profile is that it represents the probability p_i of execution occurring in module m_i at any point in time. When a software system is running a fixed function there is an execution profile for the system represented by the probabilities p_1, p_2, $p_3, \ldots, p_n$. For our purposes, p_i represents the probability that the ith module in a set of n modules is in execution at any arbitrary time.

Each functionality will have its own, possibly unique, execution profile. For a set of 10 hypothetical program modules, the execution profiles of two functionalities are shown in Fig. 12.2. From this example, we can see that for program module 6, there is a low probability of finding this module in execution at any time in the duration of the execution of function 1. For function 2, on the other hand, this same module shows a relatively high rate of use.

12.3.2 Functional complexity

The functional complexity ϕ of the system running an application with an execution profile is defined as

$$\phi = \sum_{j=1}^{n} p_j \rho_j$$

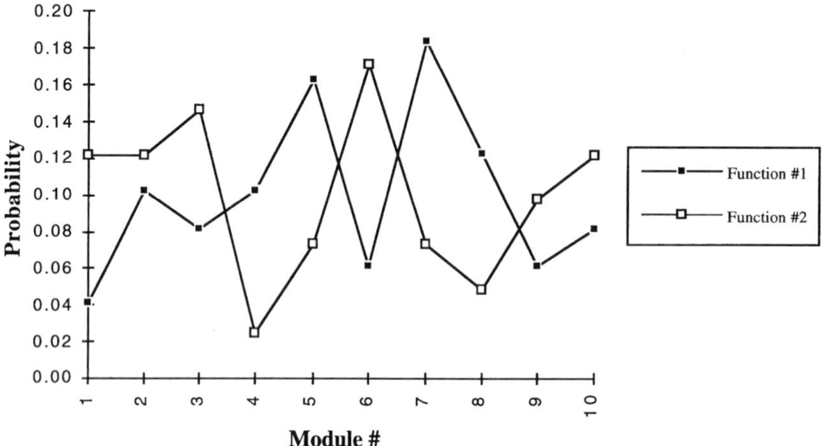

Figure 12.2 Two different execution profiles.

where ρ_j is the relative complexity of the jth program module and p_j is the execution probability of this module. This is simply the expected value of relative complexity under a particular execution profile. The execution profile for a program can be expected to change across the set of program functionalities. In other words, for each functionality, f_i, there is an execution profile represented by the probabilities p_1^i, $p_2^i, \ldots, p_n^i$. As a consequence, we can observe a functional complexity ϕ_i for each function, f_i execution, where

$$\phi_i = \sum_{j=1}^{n} p_j^i \rho_j$$

This is distinctly the case during the test phase when the program is subjected to numerous test suites to exercise differing aspects of its functionality. The functional complexity of a system will vary greatly as a result of these different test suites. A bar chart demonstrating the relationship of execution profile and relative complexity of a program running a scenario of low functional complexity is shown in Fig. 12.3. In Fig. 12.4 a high functional complexity test scenario is presented.

Given the relationship between complexity and embedded faults, we would expect the failure intensity to rise as the functional complexity increases. If an application is chosen in such a manner that high execution probabilities are associated with the complex modules, then the functional complexity will be large and the likelihood of a failure event during this interval would be relatively high. In Fig. 12.5, the operation of a hypothetical software system executing various functionalities across time is presented. From this figure, we would expect the software failures to be directly related to those periods when the functional complexity is high.

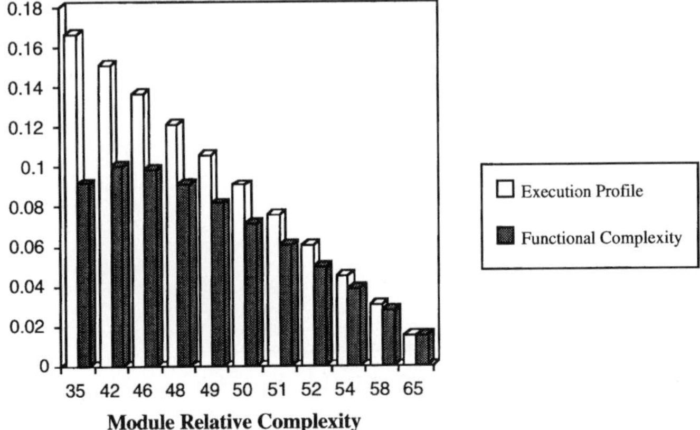

Figure 12.3 Low functional complexity.

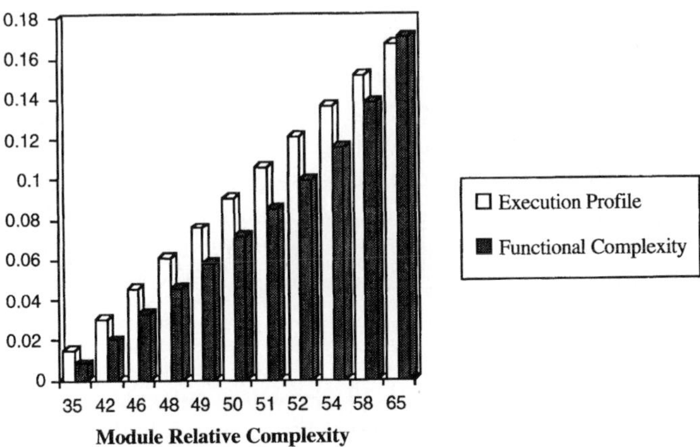

Figure 12.4 High functional complexity.

12.3.3 Dynamic aspects of functional complexity

System functional complexity can be determined in two dimensions. First, the functional complexity will vary in accordance with the function being executed. It will also vary as a function of the reconstitution of the software over builds. Thus, the functional complexity for function f_i at the jth build represented by $\mathbf{v}^j$ will be

$$\phi_{ij} = \sum_{j=1}^{n} p_k^i \rho_k^{v_k^j}$$

It is possible to determine the functional complexity for various execution profiles at varying stages of software maturity and thus to indi-

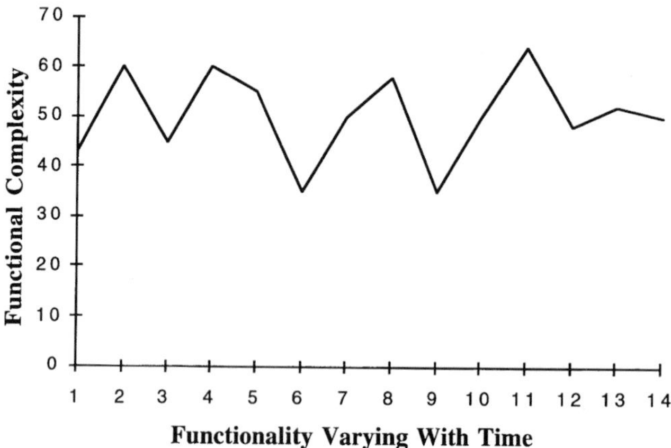

Figure 12.5 Varying functional complexity.

cate their likely failure intensity. In order to model correctly the reliability of a software system we have to determine the functionality of the program and how these functions will interact as the program executes. The latter information not only directs the formation of test suites but also provides the information necessary to formulate execution profiles. The functionalities that imply execution profiles which cause the functional complexity to increase merit our attention since these are the conditions that will increase failure rates for a given design.

Example 12.3 Programs may be seen to differ in terms of the variability of the system functional complexity. Some software systems will be fairly homogeneous in terms of their functionalities. There will be very little diversity in the range of things that the software will do. As a consequence, little variability will be observed in functional complexity from one application to another. This scenario is represented graphically in Fig. 12.6 for a sample set of 14 program modules under four distinct tests of the program. The execution profiles induced by each of these tests are similar. Thus little variation can be seen in the functional complexity from one test to another. It will be very easy to characterize the functional complexity of this system from a statistical perspective.

Figure 12.7 shows a very different software system where there is a substantial difference in functional complexity from one test case to another. It will not be nearly so easy to characterize the behavior of this program in terms of its functional complexity over varying test scenarios. Great diversity can be identified from the execution profiles. Some tests will result in high functional complexity while others will result in low functional complexity. Given the relationship between software complexity and software faults, some tests will lead to consistent failures while others will not. The most important message here is that a software system will fail in direct relationship to its functionality. This is a very predictable and understandable relationship.

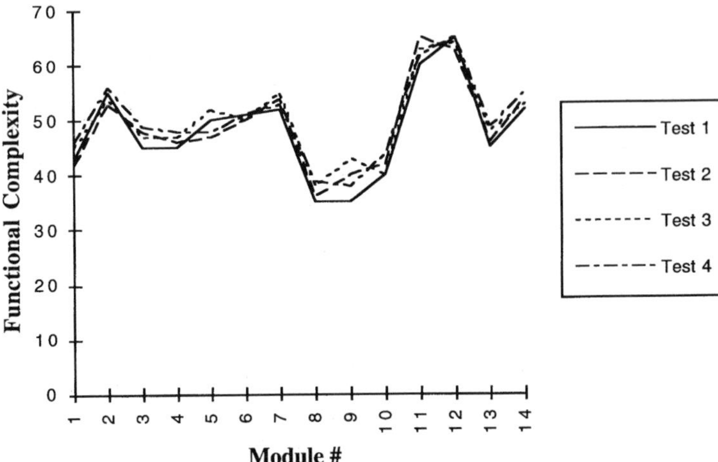

Figure 12.6 Low variability in functional complexity.

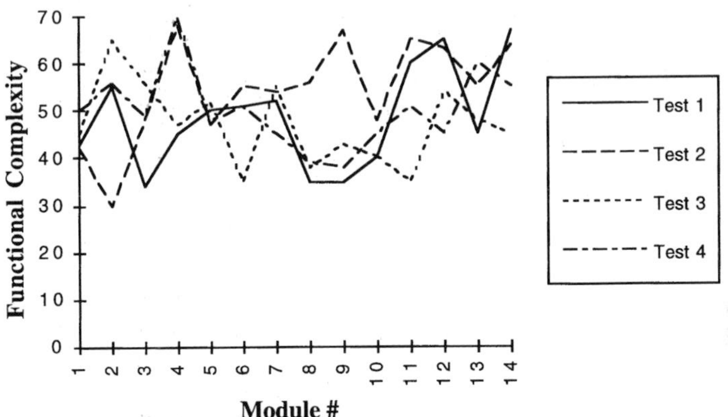

Figure 12.7 High variability in functional complexity.

12.3.4 Operational complexity

We must now come to terms with the fact that whenever a program executes, the changing functionalities will cause it to select only a subset of possible paths from the set of all possible paths through the control flow graph representation of the program. As each distinct functionality f_i of a program is expressed, a subset or *subgraph* of the program and each of its modules m_i will execute. The source code subset of the original program represented by the subgraph m_i will have a relative subgraph complexity ξ_i, where $\xi_i \leq \rho_i$. This relative subgraph complexity value will represent the complexity of just the code that was executed, which clearly cannot be more complex than the original program.

The *operational complexity* ω of a system running an application that generates an execution profile P is

$$\omega = \sum_i p_i \xi_i$$

The execution profile for a program will change over time as a function of system inputs. The relative subgraph complexity of a program will also change over time as a function of the same inputs. For each functionality f_i, there is an operational profile represented by the probabilities

$$\mathbf{P}^i = < p_1^i, p_2^i, \ldots, p_n^i >$$

For each functionality, f_i, there is also a complexity of module m_k on the jth build represented by ξ_k^j. For this functionality, the operational complexity of a system may be represented as

$$\omega_{ij} = \sum_k p_k^i \xi_k^{\nu}{}_k^j$$

The complexity, then, of a program will vary in direct relationship to the particular subgraph selected by each element in the set of program functionalities. Each subgraph has its own distinct complexity attributes.

12.4 Software Complexity and Software Quality

12.4.1 Overview

A distinct relationship exists between software faults and measurable program attributes. This information can yield specific guidelines for the design of reliable software. In particular, software complexity measures are distinct program attributes that have this property [Khos90]. Generally, if a program module is measured and found to be complex, then it will have a large number of faults. These faults may be detected by analytical methods, e.g., code inspections. The faults may also be identified based on the failures that they induce when the program is executing. A program may preserve a number of latent faults over its lifetime in that the particular manner that it is used may never cause the complex code sequences to execute and thus never expose the faults. Alternatively, a program may be forced to execute its complex code segments early in its life cycle and thus fail frequently early on, followed by reliable service after repair.

Code faults are not inserted by some random process. Faults occur in direct relationship to the complexity of the programming task. A programmer is faced with the task of converting a complex requirement into a complex algorithm in a rich programming language. It is quite reasonable to expect that the programmer will make mistakes. These mistakes will express themselves as faults in the program. From a maintenance perspective, it will be very expensive and time-consuming to find and to fix these faults. The real problem is to identify design rules that will restrict code faults from being introduced in the first place.

Typically, a small fraction of the modules comprising a software system tend to be complex. For example, [LeGa90] observed several software systems and found that only 4 to 6 percent of the modules were complex, 32 to 36 percent were simple, and the remaining modules fell between these extremes. The complex modules will cause great problems during software development and test. To take early actions that increase software reliability, software engineers must understand the relationships between software attributes that are measurable early in the product life cycle and the software quality characteristics that are not measurable until late in this cycle. Multivariate analytic techniques are necessary when approaching these relationships statistically, since both software complexity and software quality are multidimensional concepts. Software quality models exploit the relationship between static software complexity and software quality metrics. Software engineers fit software quality models to data collected from past projects. With a fitted model, engineers predict the number of faults that testing and operation will reveal in the modules of a similar ongoing project, or identify fault-prone programs of this project [Bria92, Henr91, Khos92b, Khos93c, Khos94a, Lyu95b].

In this section, we consider two multivariate techniques that are useful in developing software quality models: multiple discriminant analysis and multiple regression analysis. *Multiple discriminant analysis* is an analytic technique used to classify objects into two or more mutually exclusive and exhaustive groups based upon a set of independent variables. The independent variables are p measures of object attributes. For software quality models, the objects are program modules and the independent variables are software complexity measures. The classes are defined a priori based upon some criterion. For example, a program module could be classified as high- or low-risk, based upon the number of changes required to remove faults from the module. In this case, some value of change count, say, five, is the criterion. Thus if the module requires more than five changes to remove faults, then it is high-risk, otherwise it is low-risk. Discriminant analysis derives a linear combination of the independent variables that discriminates between the a priori groups such that misclassification error rates are minimized. Section 12.4.3 applies discriminant analysis to software quality control.

Multiple regression analysis is an analytic technique used to assess the relationship between a dependent variable and a set of independent variables. Again, the independent variables are p measures of object attributes, software complexity measures for software quality models. The dependent variable is a measure of some interesting quality attribute that is believed to vary with some linear combination of the measurable software attribute. For example, one might suspect that the number of changes required to remove faults from a module will vary with the static complexity of this module. Regression analysis is concerned with predicting the mean value of the dependent variable using known values of the independent variables. Section 12.4.4 applies multiple-regression modeling to software quality control.

[Schn92a] noted that metric-based models can give inconsistent results across development projects due to variations in product domains and other product characteristics, as well as variations in process maturity levels, development environments, and the skill and experience of people. To minimize the risk in applying quality models, validated criterion values of metrics obtained from one project are applied to another project. This procedure is performed at the completion of one effort and the inception of the other to determine the aptness of a quality model fitted to data from the completed effort for predicting results of the new effort.

12.4.2 The application and its metrics

Data collected during the development and maintenance of a Medical Imaging System (MIS) provide for examples in Secs. 12.4.3 and 12.4.4. MIS is a commercial software system consisting of approximately 4500 routines written in about 400,000 lines of Pascal, FORTRAN, and PL/M assembly code. MIS development took five years, and the system has been in commercial use at several hundred sites for three years. [Lind89] collected the number of changes made to each module due to faults discovered during system testing and maintenance, as well as 11 software complexity metrics for each of the modules that comprise MIS. The following list describes the software complexity metrics:

- *LOC* is the number of lines of code, including comments.
- *CL* is the number of lines of code, excluding comments.
- *TChar* is the number of characters.
- *TComm* is the number of comments.
- *MChar* is the number of comment characters.
- *DChar* is the number of code characters.

- $N = N_1 + N_2$ is program length, where N_1 is the total number of operators and N_2 is the total number of operands [Hals77].
- $\hat{N} = \eta_1 \log_2 \eta_1 + \eta_2 \log_2 \eta_2$ is an estimated program length, where η_1 is the number of unique operators and η_2 is the number of unique operands.
- $N_F = (\log_2 \eta_1)! + (\log_2 \eta_2)!$ is Jensen's estimator of program length [Lind89].
- $V(G)$, McCabe's cyclomatic number, is one more than the number of decision nodes in the control flow graph [McCa76].
- BW is Belady's bandwidth metric [Lind89], where $BW = 1/n \sum_i i\, L_i$ and L_i represents the number of nodes at level i in a nested control flow graph of n nodes. This metric is indicative of the average level of nesting or width of the control flow graph representation of the program.

The techniques we employ to analyze these data are not limited to this particular selection of metrics. The process would certainly benefit from a richer set than was available. Our goal is to demonstrate the modeling technique, not to justify the use of any particular selection of metrics. Before applying any modeling technique, software engineers must select a set of metrics that is suitable in their unique environment. The process of selecting and validating of metrics has been well studied in the software metrics literature [Muns89, Schn92a, Zuse91, Fent91].

We consider an MIS subset of 390 modules written in Pascal and FORTRAN for modeling (see `MIS.DAT` on the Data Disk). These modules consist of approximately 40,000 lines of code. When applying any modeling technique, an assessment of predictive quality is important. *Data-splitting* is a modeling technique that is often applied to test predictive quality. Applying this technique, one randomly partitions the data set to produce two data sets. The first data set is used for fitting the models. The remaining data set, the validating data set, provides for quantifying the predictive quality of the fitted models. Data-splitting randomly partitioned the 390 observations of MIS data into two sets, two-thirds of the observations comprising the fitting data set, and the remaining one-third comprising the validating data set.

Both multiple-regression modeling and discriminant analysis carry the assumption that no multicollinearity exists among independent variables. Violations of this assumption result in unstable models. For models based upon complexity data, domain metrics typically outperform correlated complexity metrics producing models with greater stability and predictive quality. The principal components analysis technique discussed in Sec. 12.2.3 will be used to create orthogonal domain metrics to eliminate potential problems of multicollinearity among the selected metrics.

The principal components analysis of the MIS-fitting data set produced two complexity domains. Table 12.3 gives the domain patterns of these two domains. This table shows the degree of relationship between each of the complexity metrics and the two domains. Domain 1 is strongly correlated with all of the metrics except *BW*. Each of these metrics are related to program size. Domain 2 is correlated with *BW*, a metric related to program control flow. Together, these two domains account for about 90 percent of the variability seen in the complexity metrics.

Table 12.4 gives the standardized transformation matrix, $\mathbf{T}*$, for the domains. This matrix and the vectors of standardized complexity measures from the fitting and validating data sets yield two domain metric values for each of the program modules in these data sets. This transformation matrix was produced during the principal components analysis of the fitting data set and then used as a baseline transformation for the validation data set. These domain metric values and the *changes* associated with each module provide data for illustrating the techniques presented in the following sections.

12.4.3 Multivariate analysis in software quality control

In the application of multiple discriminant analysis to program risk classification, the independent variables are p complexity domain metrics, and the criterion for class membership is a given value of a software quality measure related to program faults [Khos94a, Muns92]. A model is derived to optimally classify a collection of modules with known domain metric values and known class memberships. It is

TABLE 12.3 Principal Components Domain Patterns

Metric	Domain 1 Size	Domain 2 Control
TChar	**0.965**	0.192
LOC	**0.964**	0.213
CL	**0.941**	0.265
DChar	**0.932**	0.285
N_F	**0.917**	0.269
$\hat{N}$	**0.916**	0.273
N	**0.909**	0.306
TComm	**0.899**	0.107
MChar	**0.833**	−0.010
V(G)	**0.799**	0.481
BW	0.145	**0.964**
Eigenvalues	8.291	1.650
% variance	75.373	15.000
Cumulative % variance	75.373	90.037

TABLE 12.4 Standardized Transformation Matrix

	Domain 1	Domain 2
Metric	Size	Control
TChar	0.136	–0.074
LOC	0.131	–0.053
CL	0.112	0.004
DChar	0.105	0.026
N_F	0.106	0.014
$\hat{N}$	0.105	0.019
N	0.095	0.053
TComm	0.147	–0.140
MChar	0.166	–0.238
$V(G)$	0.025	0.256
BW	–0.235	0.912

expected that this model will achieve a low misclassification rate in a similar software development environment for untested program modules with known complexity metric values.

A two-class model classifies modules as either high-risk or low-risk based upon known domain metric values. A module is known to be high-risk or low-risk after a suitable period of testing and field experience reveals the number of changes required to remove faults discovered in it, that is, the criterion variable is *changes*. The criterion divides the set of modules into two classes, that is, modules having values of *changes* greater than some selected number are high-risk, while those having no more than this number are low-risk. Software engineers select this criterion variable value based upon the history of similar projects. An analysis of historical data will reveal the criterion value that isolates the set of modules that were considered troublesome in past development experience. The size of this set, and thus the appropriate value of the criterion variable, will vary with aspects of the product under development and the software development process.

One of several discriminant techniques may be appropriate for a given analysis. The choice lies with the types of the independent variables used in the analysis. The independent variables may be all quantitative, all qualitative, or a mixture of these two types. Applicable models in each of these cases use, respectively, linear, discrete, and logistic discrimination techniques [Dill84]. Since all of the software complexity metrics in this study are quantitative, we use a linear discriminant model and restrict our discussion to techniques of this type.

In the linear discriminant model that we develop, an observation, $\mathbf{x}$, is a vector of software complexity metrics. Let $\bar{\mathbf{x}}_j$ represent the mean of two classes, $j = 1, 2$. Then the generalized squared distance from an observation to the mean of each class is

$$D_j^2(\mathbf{x}) = (\mathbf{x} - \bar{\mathbf{x}}_j)^T \, \boldsymbol{\Sigma}^{-1} \, (\mathbf{x} - \bar{\mathbf{x}}_j)$$

where $\mathbf{\Sigma}$ is the pooled covariance matrix. Thus the posterior probability of membership of $\mathbf{x}$ in class j is

$$p_j(\mathbf{x}) = \frac{e^{-1/2D_j^2(\mathbf{x})}}{e^{-1/2D_1^2(\mathbf{x})} + e^{-1/2D_2^2(\mathbf{x})}}$$

The model assigns an observation $\mathbf{x}$ to the class j having greater posterior probability of membership, that is, the model selects j such that $p_j(\mathbf{x}) = \max(p_1(\mathbf{x}), p_2(\mathbf{x}))$.

We observe two aspects of quality in discriminant models. First, a model must be successful in classifying program modules having known complexity data, but unknown fault data. Second, a model must be able to perform this classification with little uncertainty. The misclassification rates of a model measure its success in classifying program modules. A model can commit two types of classification errors. A type 1 error occurs when a low-risk module is classified as high-risk. This could result in some wasted attention to low-risk modules. A type 2 error occurs when a high-risk module is classified as low-risk. This could result in an extension of the scheduled release date as more effort is required than planned for, or the release of a lower-quality product. The nature of the impacts of these error types suggests that the type 2 error rate is more important than the type 1 error rate in considering the quality of a classification model.

The model assigns a module to one of the two classes based upon some function of the module's complexity domain metric data. Modules with values of this function above some cutoff value fall in one class; the remaining modules fall in the other class. For some modules the function value will fall far from the cutoff value that determines class membership. These modules have a high probability of falling in the assigned class. For other modules the function value will fall close to the cutoff value. These modules have a relatively low probability of falling in the assigned class. For correct classifications, the model probability of membership in the opposite class is the uncertainty in the classification.

Example 12.4 We develop a discriminant model for classifying each MIS module as either high- or low-risk. The domain metric and change data values for the 260 modules in the MIS-fitting data set serve to fit this model. The value of the criterion variable, *changes,* is one. Modules requiring one or fewer changes to remove faults are low-risk, those requiring more than one change are high-risk. To magnify the difference between the high- and low-risk modules, we biased the training data set before training the models [Muns92]. We achieved this by removing all of the modules with values of *changes* between 2 and 9. This left 156 modules in the fitting data set: 126 low-risk modules and 30 high-risk modules.

Application of the fitted model to classify the 130 modules in the MIS testing data set serves to test the predictive quality of this model. The model classifies these modules based upon their domain metric values. Since the modules have known values of *changes,* the model's misclassification rates are known for this data set. Tables 12.5 and 12.6 give the results of the discriminant model for modules in the upper and lower extremes with regard to those with one or fewer fault-correcting changes and those with 10 or more fault-correcting changes. The modules appearing in Table 12.5 belong to the low-risk class. Those appearing in Table 12.6 belong to the high-risk class. These two tables give the domain metric values, the relative complexity metric value, the number of changes, and the model classification for the modules in the testing data set. Tables 12.5 and 12.6 also include the model uncertainty in correct classifications. Table 12.5 shows

TABLE 12.5 Classification Data for Modules with One or Fewer Changes

Program number	D_1	D_2	ρ'	Changes	Pred. group	Uncertainty
1	–0.63	–0.59	42.6	0	1	0.04
2	0.48	–1.02	52.7	0	2	—
3	–0.67	–0.26	42.8	0	1	0.04
4	–0.95	1.27	43.1	0	1	0.33
5	–0.33	0.98	48.6	0	1	0.35
6	–0.37	1.04	48.3	0	1	0.31
7	–0.80	0.52	43.1	0	1	0.07
8	–0.39	–0.08	45.9	0	1	0.06
9	0.05	–0.68	49.2	0	2	—
10	–0.38	–0.88	44.5	0	1	0.06
11	–0.85	–0.13	41.3	0	1	0.07
12	–0.76	–0.63	41.2	0	1	0.06
13	–1.43	2.75	41.3	0	2	—
14	–0.58	–0.85	42.5	0	1	0.04
15	–0.48	–0.73	43.7	0	1	0.04
16	–0.18	0.30	48.7	0	1	0.33
17	–0.70	–0.57	41.9	0	1	0.04
18	–0.42	–0.94	43.9	1	1	0.05
19	–0.66	–0.73	42.0	1	1	0.04
20	–0.48	–0.04	45.1	1	1	0.04
21	–0.55	0.17	44.8	1	1	0.04
22	–0.73	1.18	45.0	1	1	0.16
23	0.45	–0.47	53.5	1	2	—
24	–0.28	–0.22	46.7	1	1	0.09
25	–0.39	–0.80	44.5	1	1	0.05
26	–0.59	0.61	45.3	1	1	0.06
27	–0.23	–0.76	46.2	1	1	0.12
28	–0.59	–0.85	42.5	1	1	0.04
29	–0.75	–0.86	40.9	1	1	0.07
30	–0.85	–0.46	40.7	1	1	0.08
31	–0.41	–0.79	44.3	1	1	0.05
32	–0.23	–0.74	46.2	1	1	0.12
33	–0.67	–0.02	43.3	1	1	0.04
34	–0.23	0.65	48.9	1	1	0.38
35	–0.37	–1.12	44.1	1	1	0.07
36	–0.56	–0.75	42.9	1	1	0.04
37	–0.88	–0.29	40.7	1	1	0.09
38	–0.15	–0.15	48.1	1	1	0.26

that the model misclassified 4 of the 38 low-risk modules, yielding a type 1 error rate of about 10 percent. Table 12.6 shows that the model misclassified 4 of the 30 high-risk modules, giving a type 2 error rate of about 13 percent. The average uncertainty for high- and low-risk classifications is about 11 and 3 percent, respectively. Overall, this model misclassified about 12 percent of the modules in this study. This demonstrates an average uncertainty of about 7 percent.

12.4.4 Fault prediction models

In the application of multiple regression modeling to fault prediction, the independent variables are p complexity domain metrics, and the dependent variable is a software quality measure related to program faults [Khos90, Khos93b]. The first step in multiple regression modeling is model selection. In this step, one selects a subset of the p attributes to include in the regression. Several techniques are available for selecting this subset. These include stepwise regression, forward selection, backward elimination, the R^2 criterion, and C_p criterion.

TABLE 12.6 Classification Data for Modules with 10 or More Changes

Program number	D_1	D_2	ρ'	Changes	Pred. group	Uncertainty
101	2.40	1.46	76.4	10	2	0.00
102	−0.27	0.25	47.7	10	1	—
103	1.12	0.50	61.9	11	2	0.00
104	−0.04	−0.12	49.2	11	2	0.42
105	−0.28	1.01	49.2	11	1	—
106	1.53	−0.85	63.3	11	2	0.00
107	1.36	1.98	67.2	12	2	0.00
108	−0.07	−0.23	48.8	12	1	—
109	1.37	1.78	66.9	12	2	0.00
110	0.38	0.81	55.4	13	2	0.00
111	0.60	2.15	60.1	14	2	0.00
112	−0.20	0.97	49.9	14	2	0.33
113	2.57	−1.32	72.6	15	2	0.00
114	0.34	0.66	54.6	15	2	0.00
115	−0.53	−0.36	44.0	16	1	—
116	1.52	2.13	69.1	16	2	0.00
117	1.58	2.53	70.4	17	2	0.00
118	2.23	3.28	78.3	19	2	0.00
119	1.06	−0.28	59.8	20	2	0.00
120	0.25	−1.00	50.5	22	2	0.00
121	0.59	−1.21	53.4	25	2	0.00
122	0.96	0.01	59.4	28	2	0.00
123	3.98	−0.77	87.6	30	2	0.00
124	1.66	1.83	69.9	30	2	0.00
125	1.78	0.18	67.8	34	2	0.00
126	1.34	−0.34	62.5	38	2	0.00
127	2.53	−0.97	72.9	40	2	0.00
128	4.90	2.03	102.1	42	2	0.00
129	1.09	−1.12	58.5	46	2	0.00
130	4.28	0.08	92.2	98	2	0.00

In the *stepwise regression* analysis procedure, an initial model is formed by selecting the independent variable with the highest simple correlation with the dependent variable. In subsequent iterations new variables are selected for inclusion based on their partial correlation with variables already in the regression equation. Variables in this model may be removed from the regression equation when they no longer contribute significantly to the explained variance. There must be an a priori level of significance chosen for the inclusion or deletion of variables from the model. The second stepwise procedure is *forward inclusion.* In the case of this procedure, a variable once entered in the regression equation may not be removed. The third technique, *backward elimination,* forms a regression equation with all variables and then systematically eliminates variables, one by one, which do not contribute significantly to the model. For further details concerning model selection, refer to [Myer90].

Stepwise procedures for the selection of variables in a regression problem should be used with caution. These are useful tools for variable selection only in the circumstances of noncollinearity. We recommend a different set of procedures in the presence of collinearity. Once collinearity has been identified, a set of new variables, principal components, can be formed by using principal components analysis (see Sec. 12.2.3). These new variables will not be collinear. Then, stepwise procedures are used to select the factors which are important for predicting the dependent variable, which in our case will be an enumeration of programming faults.

Traditionally, the R^2 statistic is used almost exclusively in empirical studies in software engineering. Some distinct problems are associated with the use of R^2, which is defined as follows:

$$R^2 = \frac{\text{regression sum of squares}}{\text{sum of squares about the mean}}$$

Alternatively,

$$R^2 = \frac{\Sigma(\hat{Y}_i - \bar{Y})^2}{\Sigma(Y_i - \bar{Y})^2}$$

In that $\Sigma(Y_i - \overline{Y})^2$ is constant for all regression models, R^2 can increase only as independent variables are added to a regression equation, whether or not they will account for a significant amount of variance in the dependent variable. It is important to note that the R^2 statistic does not assess the quality of future prediction. If a model is sufficiently tailored to fit the noise and other aberrations in the data, then it is quite possible to develop a model that fits the data well but is worthless for future prediction. While we are interested in the fact that the model fit the data, our primary focus should be on the ability of the chosen model to render worthwhile future predictions.

The case for the C_p statistic is very different. C_p may be defined in terms of R_p^2 as follows:

$$C_p = \frac{(1 - R_p^2)(n - T)}{1 - R_T^2} - (n - 2p)$$

where n represents the number of observations and T represents the total number of parameters in the complete model. The statistic C_p is a measure of the total squared error in a regression. Thus, a researcher should choose a model with the smallest value of C_p. This statistic is to be preferred to R^2 because a penalty is introduced for overfitting the model with excess independent variables, which bring with them an additional noise component.

After selecting a model, we must fit it to the observed data. Some notation becomes helpful here. For N observations, the dependent variable values y_i will have corresponding predicted value, $\hat{y}_i$, produced by the model and a residual value $\varepsilon_i = y_i - \hat{y}_i$ representing the difference between the value predicted by the model and the observed value. For a model with p independent variables, $x_1, x_2, \ldots, x_p$, the least-squares estimation technique yields estimated model parameters, $\beta_0, \beta_1, \ldots, \beta_p$, such that, for $1 \le i \le N$,

$$\hat{y}_i = \beta_0 + \beta_1 x_{i1} + \beta_2 x_{i2} + \cdots + \beta_p x_{ip} \qquad \text{and the sum of} \qquad \sum_{i=1}^{N} (\hat{y}_i - y_i)^2$$

is minimized.

Example 12.5 Applying these concepts to the MIS data, we select a model for predicting *changes* for each MIS module given the domain metric values for these modules. The domain metric and change data values for the 260 observations in the MIS fitting data set serve to fit this model. The best model revealed by all model selection methods discussed above includes both domain metrics. The fitted model is given by

$$\mathit{Changes} = 7.15 + 7.07D_1 + 1.36D_2$$

The domain metric and change data values for the 130 observations in the MIS testing data set serve to measure the predictive quality of the fitted model. The average absolute error of the model on these data is 5.32.

12.4.5 Enhancing predictive models with increased domain coverage

One aspect of program variability that is not currently represented by any code metrics in the domain model of program complexity is a measure of the complexity of data structures in a program. For example, consider the case of a program to find the average value of a set of real numbers. This program may be written using only scalar values to accumulate the developing sum and a count of the numbers processed so far. On the other hand, the numbers may be copied into an array as they are read. After all of the numbers have been read, the contents of the array may be tallied to compute the sum. Clearly, these two programs will differ as a result of the complexity of the data structures that they will contain. They will also employ completely different algorithms to compute the sum. Hence, measures of their algorithmic complexity will also be different.

[Muns93] offered a measure of data structure complexity that is based upon a specification of the complexity of each data structure in the implementation language. The data structure complexity of a module, *DS,* is evaluated as the sum of the complexities of the data structures used in a program module.

Central to the idea of validating a new measure is the notion that it is measuring an attribute of programs not already being measured by another metric. That is, the new metric must map into a new orthogonal domain not already in the domain model. There must be some aspect of variability between programs that is attributable to the new metric that is not present to a large extent in other measures taken on the program. The utility of the new metric will be assessed by its ability to contribute new, distinct, and meaningful information to our understanding of program complexity.

For the present study, our metric analyzer for Ada code was augmented to compute data structure values for Ada source programs. This analyzer computes 16 complexity metrics for Ada program modules at the package level. In addition to *DS,* this analyzer computes a subset of the metrics defined in Sec. 12.4.2, including N_1, N_2, η_1, η_2, $V(G)$, and *BW,* along with the metrics defined in the following list:

- *Stmts,* the number of Ada statements
- *Paths,* the number of unique paths in the control flow graph
- *Cycles,* the number of cycles in the control flow graph
- *Max–Path,* the longest path in the control flow graph
- $\overline{Path}$, the average length of a path in the control flow graph
- $V(G)$, McCabe's cyclomatic complexity
- *CO,* the number of calls out of a package
- *CI,* the number of calls into a package
- *Global,* the number of global data references [Nav187]
- $\overline{Span}$ the number of levels up the procedure tree that the analyzer had to go to find the definition of each data item being referenced divided by the number of references [Nav187]

A total of 240 separately compilable Ada units or packages were measured. First, we were interested in the structure of the underlying complexity domains without the data structure metric, *DS*, present. The domain structure for this analysis is shown in Table 12.7. For the set of 15 metrics shown, there were four distinct domains. The resulting domain structure had four domains in it with a stopping rule for the analysis that the associated eigenvalues for each new domain be greater than or equal to 1.

Domain 1 shows a high correlation with *Stmts*, N_1, N_2, and *Paths*. These metrics all relate to size or volume of a program. Hence, we will identify this domain as relating to a *size* domain in our domain model. Similarly, domain 2 could be called a *control flow* domain, domain 3 an *action / reusability* domain, and domain 4 a *modularity* domain.

For the second analysis, the data structures metric, *DS*, was added to the set of 15 primitive metrics and the data were reanalyzed. The domain structure for this second analysis is shown in Table 12.8. In this case the resulting domain structure had five domains in it, again, with a stopping rule of 1 for the eigenvalues. The essential domain structure has been preserved from the first analysis to the second. That is, with only one exception, the size domain contains the same set of metrics in both analyses. Similarly, the control flow, action/reusability, and modularity domains contain the same sets of metrics in both

TABLE 12.7 Domain Pattern Without Data Structure Metric

	Domain1	Domain2	Domain3	Domain4
Metric	Size	Control flow	Action/ reuseability	Modularity
N_1	**0.960**	0.202	0.086	0.007
N_2	**0.951**	0.142	0.153	0.026
Stmts	**0.893**	0.350	0.092	−0.008
Global	**0.887**	0.278	0.027	−0.050
CO	**0.877**	0.189	0.029	−0.024
η_2	**0.644**	−0.042	0.443	0.095
Paths	**0.600**	0.374	−0.286	−0.126
Max–Path	0.328	**0.906**	0.068	−0.007
$\overline{Path}$	0.349	**0.892**	0.069	−0.023
Cycles	0.164	**0.772**	0.026	−0.045
$\overline{Band}$	0.102	**0.765**	0.372	0.104
η_1	0.118	**0.746**	0.480	0.057
$\overline{Span}$	−0.012	0.199	**0.713**	−0.162
V(G)	0.319	0.431	**0.546**	0.077
CI	−0.028	0.035	−0.087	**0.968**
Eigenvalue	5.345	4.026	1.515	1.016
% variance	35.633	26.840	10.100	6.773
Cumulative % variance	35.633	62.473	72.573	79.347

analyses. A new domain, however, is present in the second analysis that was not present in the first. This is the new domain containing the *DS* metric.

With the set of primitive metrics employed in this study, *DS* has served to identify another complexity domain. In this regard, it is important to note the eigenvalues reported in Tables 12.7 and 12.8. These eigenvalues represent the relative proportion of variance accounted for by each of the domains. The larger the eigenvalue the more variance attributable to each domain. The sum of the eigenvalues for the domains in each of the tables represents the total variance accounted for by that domain structure. The four domains displayed in Table 12.7 account for about 79 percent of the variance explained by the underlying metrics, while the five domains displayed in Table 12.8 account for about 84 percent of the variance explained by the underlying metrics. Thus, the increase in domain coverage by the addition of the data structures domain has increased the ability of the domain model to describe differences among the programs being measured.

12.5 Software Reliability Modeling

Current software reliability modeling approaches are, in some cases, simply extensions of hardware reliability models. Our view of complex

TABLE 12.8 Domain Pattern with Data Structure Metric

	Domain1	Domain2	Domain3	Domain4	Domain5
Metric	Size	Control flow	Data structures	Action/ reuseability	Modularity
N_1	**0.922**	0.197	0.111	0.153	–0.003
N_2	**0.899**	0.284	0.195	0.165	0.023
Stmts	**0.897**	0.119	0.135	0.099	0.006
Global	**0.871**	0.181	0.425	0.044	0.002
CO	**0.818**	0.141	0.527	0.059	0.006
η_2	**0.706**	0.295	–0.104	–0.108	–0.067
Paths	0.350	**0.894**	0.095	0.095	–0.000
Max–Path	0.372	**0.878**	0.095	0.099	–0.015
$\overline{Path}$	0.131	**0.811**	0.180	–0.050	–0.075
Cycles	0.087	**0.741**	0.187	0.437	0.046
Band	0.144	**0.730**	–0.013	0.452	0.128
DS	0.117	0.267	**0.860**	–0.027	–0.034
η_1	0.353	0.042	**0.841**	0.144	0.011
$\overline{Span}$	0.011	0.116	0.005	**0.840**	–0.117
V(G)	0.270	0.409	0.146	**0.546**	0.102
CI	–0.026	0.013	–0.019	–0.054	**0.980**
Eigenvalues	4.912	3.841	2.095	1.524	1.017
% variance	30.700	24.006	13.094	9.525	6.356
Cumulative % variance	30.700	54.706	67.803	77.328	83.684

software systems is colored by our experience with complex mechanical or electronic systems. The dynamic complexity of the software system will depend on the inputs to the system. The net effect of differing inputs to the system is that the operational or functional complexity of the system will change in response to the varying inputs. Given the association between module complexity and faults, it follows that as applications change over time intervals, so too will the likelihood of faults change with respect to time.

12.5.1 Reliability modeling with software complexity metrics

For the purpose of demonstration, we will now explore how the notions of relative complexity and functional complexity may be incorporated into a Bayesian model for reliability measurement. There are good reasons for employing a Bayesian technique in this modeling process. In this model, successive execution times between failures are independent random variables $T_1, T_2, \ldots, T_i, \ldots$, where T_i is the execution time of the software system being modeled, from the time of the repair of the $(i-1)$st failure to the ith failure. By convention, t_i will represent an observation of the random variable T_i. The T_i's are assumed to have an exponential probability density function (pdf) with a parameter λ of

$$f(t_i,\lambda(i)) = \lambda(i)e^{\lambda(i)t_i} \qquad t > 0 \qquad \lambda > 0$$

The parameter λ is related to the failure rate of a program. As the program progresses through the testing process, traditional hardware reliability modeling theory would have the failure rate diminish as fixes are made to the system, i.e.,

$$\lambda(i-1) > \lambda(i)$$

In software development applications, we cannot always assume that the system failure rate will improve as a result of a fix. Sometimes a fix will introduce faults of its own.

In the Littlewood-Verrall (Bayesian) model (see Sec. 3.6.1), the parameter λ is assumed to have a pdf of its own. Let the pdf of $\lambda(i)$ be denoted by $g(l, i, \alpha)$, where α is a parameter or vector of parameters. From the standpoint of mathematical tractability, the pdf of $\lambda(i)$ is chosen to have a gamma distribution in two parameters, α and $\psi(i)$ as follows:

$$g(l, i, \alpha) = \frac{\psi(i)[\psi(i)l\,]^{\alpha-1}\, e^{-\psi(i)l}}{\Gamma(\alpha)} \qquad t > 0 \qquad \lambda > 0$$

The parameter, $\psi(i)$, is essentially a scaling factor and is a monotonically increasing function of i. This assumption will guarantee the ordering of the distribution functions in i. Further, $\psi(i)$ is not estimated but is completely determined as a measure of a debugger's *behavior* at time i. The main problem here is that we have left the well-defined realm of mathematics and entered the realm of psychology. We would like to derive more substantive reliability models than those based solely on the attitudes or competencies of programmers.

It would seem reasonable that some measure of system complexity may be used for the ill-defined parameter, ψ. If, on the one hand, it is important that $\psi(i)$ be a monotonically increasing function of i, then the system relative complexity measure, ρ_s^i, would meet the monotonically increasing property as a function of time. Hence,

$$g(l, i, \alpha) = \frac{\rho_s^i(\rho_s^i l)^{\alpha-1} e^{-\rho_s^i l}}{\Gamma(\alpha)} \qquad t > 0$$

The property that $\psi(i)$ be a monotonically increasing function of i is an unnecessary restriction. This property will certainly ensure that the failure rate is a decreasing function of time. Empirical observations, however, do not support this view of failure rate. In many cases, we do observe an increase in failure rate during some time intervals.

Many dynamics operate on a program during the period it is measured for reliability modeling. As the functional complexity induced by test scenario on a program increases, so too will its exposure to code likely to contain faults. The failure rate at any time, i, ought to reflect which functions the program is executing during this time. Hence, we feel that the functional complexity ϕ_i at time i is a much better parameter for this model, in which case,

$$g(l, i, \alpha) = \frac{\phi_i(\phi_i l)^{\alpha-1} e^{-\phi_i l}}{\Gamma(\alpha)} \qquad t > 0$$

Consequently, two distinct variants in the Bayesian case are observed: one with relative complexity and one with dynamic complexity. In these modeling approaches some rather intensive measurements must be made on the software. It is not sufficient to record the time that the system failed; it is also necessary to measure the incremental versions of the systems in terms of their complexity as well as the operational profiles generated by test scenarios over time.

To complete the discussion of the Bayesian models, we will use the case where $\psi(i) = \phi_i$. It can be shown (see Prob. 12.13) that the maximum likelihood estimate for α, $\hat{\alpha}$, is obtained as

$$\hat{\alpha} = \frac{n}{\sum_{i=1}^{n} \ln\left(1 + \frac{t_i}{\phi_i}\right)}$$

Subsequently, the estimate for the current reliability of the software at the present time, n, is given by

$$\hat{R}(t_n) = 1 - \hat{F}(t_n) = \left(\frac{\phi_n}{t_n + \phi_n} \right)^{\hat{\alpha}}$$

As we can see from this functional relationship, the reliability of the system is directly dependent on the functional complexity induced by the operational profile of the test scenario during this nth time interval. The greater the functional complexity of the test, the less reliable will the software appear to be.

12.5.2 The incremental build problem

In the previous section we have taken a look at how software complexity attributes can be introduced into software reliability models. None of these approaches reflect the fact that most modern software systems are developed incrementally. This is yet another aspect of software development that must be incorporated into our thinking about software reliability modeling.

Functionality will be added incrementally to a developing core system. At any point in time the system is composed of a fixed set of modules. The precise status of the system at any particular build i will be given by the vector $\mathbf{v}^i$ introduced in Sec. 12.2.6. If we examine the contents of this vector, we will see that some modules have received extensive revision. Other modules have not been modified in some time. Those modules that have received continual changes will be substantially more failure-prone than those modules that have a longer period of stability. With this consideration in mind, we can observe that the granularity of the reliability modeling should be at the software module level and not on the software system as a whole [Schn92b].

Each program module in a total system is more than likely at a different stage of maturity as a system is developed. Most modern software systems begin with a nucleus of legacy code. This is code that has been ported from an older application. It has probably been run for some time. It may also be fairly fault-free. On the other hand, new program modules will be added to the system representing enhanced functionality of the software. These new modules will be added to the system over a period of time. At any particular build, the total system will consist of program modules at varying levels of maturity and, consequently, reliability.

Let $T^{v^i_j}$ be the estimated time to failure of each module m_j at the ith build of the software. The estimated time to failure of the total system, T_{SYS} on the ith build may be represented by

$$T^i_{SYS} = \frac{1}{\dfrac{1}{T^{v^i_1}} + \dfrac{1}{T^{v^i_2}} + \dfrac{1}{T^{v^i_3}} + \cdots + \dfrac{1}{T^{v^i_n}}}$$

This means of computing the reliability of a modular software system has been successfully used in the development of reliability estimates for the space shuttle onboard flight software system [Schn92b] (see Sec. 11.7.2).

12.6 Summary

This chapter examines software complexity measurement and software quality as these issues relate to software reliability. We describe the measurement of software attributes for early prediction of software quality. These attributes are primarily software complexity measures, which include relative program complexity and dynamic program complexity. Various strategies have been examined to exploit the relationship between software quality and software complexity. We also demonstrate how software complexity metrics can be included in software reliability models for the enhancement in their reliability predictions, and how reliability estimates for incrementally built systems can be obtained.

Problems

12.1 Software systems are characteristically different from hardware systems. From the standpoint of reliability modeling, exactly how does software differ from hardware?

12.2 System functional complexity is a dynamic measure of complexity. What is the relationship between the static complexity of a system as measured by relative complexity and the dynamic complexity of a system as measured by functional complexity?

12.3 What is the difference between functional complexity and operational complexity?

12.4 How would measurements be taken on a system to compute operational complexity?

12.5 How might existing models of software reliability be enhanced to incorporate measures of dynamic complexity?

12.6 List all the software metrics that strongly correlate with the second domain in Table 12.9.

12.7 Given a program module with the following standardized measurements,

$$\begin{aligned} \text{N2} &= -0.38485 \\ \text{N1} &= -0.40943 \\ \text{LOC} &= -0.41983 \\ \text{ELOC} &= -0.45814 \\ \text{ETA2} &= -0.42401 \\ \text{ETA1} &= -0.13556 \end{aligned}$$

TABLE 12.9 Domain Pattern

Rotated factor pattern (varimax rotation method)		
	Factor1	Factor2
N2	0.90650	0.40314
N1	0.90241	0.42068
LOC	0.88923	0.39994
ELOC	0.87983	0.44468
ETA2	0.76635	0.58308
ETA1	0.40602	0.90972
Eigenvalues	3.953055	1.864772

TABLE 12.10 Standardized Transformation Matrix, T1

Standardized scoring coefficients		
	Factor1	Factor2
N2	0.37179	–0.24400
N1	0.34825	–0.20546
LOC	0.35964	–0.23069
ELOC	0.30054	–0.13353
ETA2	0.04072	0.26228
ETA1	–0.65691	1.30095

and the transformation matrix in Table 12.10, what are the domain metrics for this module?

12.8 Given the data in Table 12.11, what is the relative complexity metric, ρ_k, and the scaled relative complexity metric, ρ'_k, for each program module?

12.9 Why is multicollinearity an important issue in software quality modeling?

12.10 For a discriminant model that classifies high-risk and low-risk modules, what is a type 1 error and what is a type 2 error?

12.11 What is a measure of the quality of predictions of a multiple linear regression model?

TABLE 12.11 Domain Metrics

Factor scores			
Module	Factor1	Factor2	Factor3
1	–0.505	–0.508	–2.752
2	–0.493	0.874	0.445
3	6.754	–0.322	1.787
Eigenvalues	7.048	2.560	2.547

12.12 List the steps of model development related to the *data-splitting* technique. Why is this technique used?

12.13 Solve the Bayesian model in Sec. 12.5.1. Namely, (1) Express the pdf of t_i given α and ϕ_i; (2) solve $\hat{\alpha}$; (3) obtain the reliability estimate at the present time n.

Chapter

13

Software Testing and Reliability

Joseph R. Horgan
Bellcore

Aditya P. Mathur
Purdue University

13.1 Introduction

It is believed that there is an important relationship between the estimation of reliability of a program, its structure, and the amount of testing it has been subjected to. Though one can imagine several ways of quantifying the amount of testing, we consider one or more measures of code coverage as possible quantifiers. Statement coverage, decision coverage, and data flow coverage are some of the code coverage measures. These measures are based on the structure, often detailed, of the software. Several software reliability theorists observe that the structure of the software should be closely followed in the analysis of reliability. [Broc90] suggests: "At some future time it may be possible to match a reliability model to a program via the characteristics of that program, or even of the software development methodology used."

[Musa87] has suggested a similar possibility. The importance of distributing testing according to a user's operational environment is a central theme of reliability estimation. In this context, characterization in [Goel85] is particularly apt: "To illustrate this view of software reliability, suppose that a user executes a software product several times according to its usage profile and finds that the results are acceptable 95 percent of the time. Then the software is said to be 95 percent reliable for that user."

As per the above quote, a program is tested according to its usage profile and then one or more of several reliability models applied to the failure data to obtain reliability estimates. Such an approach to reliability estimation fails to account for the difficulties in assessing accurate usage profiles and in accounting for the structure of the software. In this chapter we point out some of these difficulties and suggest two approaches for reliability estimation. Our approaches make use of code coverage explicitly in the estimation process, whereas the existing time-domain approaches as outlined in [Musa87] do not.

The remainder of this chapter is organized as follows. In Sec. 13.2 we present some concepts related to software testing. The problems encountered in establishing an operational profile are addressed in Sec. 13.3. The effect of nonavailability of an accurate operational profile on reliability estimation is also discussed in this section. Our first approach that combines the existing time-domain approaches of reliability estimation with coverage information obtained during system test is presented in Sec. 13.4. Another approach to viewing software reliability is to consider the risk associated with a program. In Sec. 13.5.1 we outline a model to estimate the risk associated with a program. This model does not use the time-domain approach in any form. Instead it uses various measures of code coverage to estimate risk.

13.2 Overview of Software Testing

A key question we address in this chapter is: "How does the nature of testing affect reliability estimation?" Below we lay the groundwork for an answer to this question by examining white-box testing.

13.2.1 Kinds of software testing

There are many ways of testing software. The terms *functional, regression, integration, product, unit, coverage,* and *user-oriented* are only a few of the characterizations we encounter. These terms are derived from the method of software testing or the development phase during which the software is tested. The testing methods *functional, coverage,* and *user-oriented* indicate, respectively, that the functionality, the structure, and the user view of the software are to be tested. Any of these methods might be applied during the *unit, integration, product,* or *regression* phases of the software's development. In this context the unit phase is the coding of small software components, the integration phase puts units together into larger components, and the product phase integrates the software into its final form. Regression testing pertains to the re-release of a modified software product.

13.2.2 Concepts from white-box and black-box testing

White-box, or coverage, testing uses the structure of the software to measure the quality of testing. It is this structural coverage and its measurement that we believe is of value in reliability estimation. We describe two coverage testing methods: mutation testing and data and control flow testing. Subsequently, we discuss the use of these methods in reliability estimation.

1. *Statement coverage* testing directs the tester to construct test cases such that each statement or a basic block of code is executed at least once.

2. *Decision coverage* testing directs the tester to construct test cases such that each decision in the program is covered at least once. A decision refers to a simple condition. Thus, for example, the C language statement **if** $(a < b \,||\, p > q) \ldots$ consists of two simple conditions, $a < b$ and $p > q$, and one compound condition. We say that a decision is *covered* if during some execution it evaluates to true and in the same or another execution it evaluates to false. In the above example, the two simple conditions must evaluate to true and false during some execution for the decision coverage criterion to be satisfied.

3. *Data flow coverage* testing directs the tester to construct test cases such that all the def-use pairs are covered. Consider a statement $S_1 : x = f()$ in program P, where f is an arbitrary function. Let there be another statement $S_2 : p = g(x, *)$ in P, where g is an arbitrary function of x and any other program variables. We say that S_1 is a definition and S_2 a use of the variable x. The two occurrences of x constitute a def-use pair. If the use of a variable appears in a computational expression, then such a pair is termed as a c-use. If the use appears inside a predicate then the pair is termed as a p-use. A path from S_1 to S_2 is said to be *definition-free* if no statement along this path, other than S_1 and S_2, defines x. Such a path is considered feasible if there exists at least one $d \in$ the input domain D such that when P is executed on d the path is traversed.

All statements in P that can possibly be executed immediately after the execution of some statement S are known as *successors* of S. We say that a c-use or a p-use is *covered* if the execution of P on some set of test cases causes at least one definition-free path to be executed from the defining statement to the statement in which the use occurs and to each of its successors. Further details of data flow testing may be found in [Horg90].

4. *Mutation testing* helps a tester design test cases based on a notion very different from that of path-oriented testing strategies such as the ones described above. Given a program P, mutation testing generates several syntactically correct *mutants* of P. A mutant is generated by making a change in P in accordance with a predefined set of rules. For example, one mutant, say M, of P can be generated by removing a statement from P. We say that a test case d distinguishes M from P if $P(d) \neq M(d)$. M is considered equivalent to P if $\forall d \in D, P(d) = M(d)$. Mutation testing requires a tester to generate test data that distinguish all nonequivalent mutants of P. Further details of mutation testing may be found in [Chio89].

Note that each of the four testing methods provides an *adequacy criterion* against which a test set can be evaluated. We say that a test set T consisting of one or more test cases is adequate with respect to the decision coverage criterion if all the decisions in the program are covered when executed against elements of T. T is adequate with respect to to the p-use criterion if all p-uses have been covered by T.* T is considered adequate with respect to mutation criteria if it distinguishes all the nonequivalent mutants of the program. Each of the preceding adequacy criteria is precise and measurable. Note that functional testing does not provide any such precise and measurable criteria.

It can be shown formally that if a test set is p-use or c-use adequate, then it is also decision adequate [Clar89]. We therefore say that data flow coverage *subsumes* decision coverage. Similar relationships have been investigated empirically among functional, data flow, and mutation testing. Evidence available so far [Math91, Wong93] suggests that test data which are mutation adequate are likely to be data flow adequate whereas a data flow adequate test set is less likely to be mutation adequate. Empirical evidence presented in Sect. 13.4.6 also suggests that even after a significant effort has been spent in functional testing, the test data so developed are not data flow adequate, and hence not mutation adequate. On the contrary, it has been shown [Howd80] that for several types of errors, structural testing is not sufficient, but functional testing is. Further, functional testing appears to be a necessity in any testing activity as it is the first step to verifying that the specific functions that a program is supposed to perform are indeed performed correctly.

Thus, taking empirical evidence, theoretical hierarchy [Clar89], and the practice of software testing into account, we justify the assumption that testing is carried out using a commonsense method first, i.e., functional testing followed by structure-based methods in the order of their expected cost benefits. Despite the existence of various testing methods, it is of interest to note that according to the current industrial practice, only functional testing is carried out in most environments.

13.3 Operational Profiles

A widely accepted definition of software reliability (R) is that it is the probability of failure-free operation of a system. By *system* we refer to the program (P) whose reliability is to be estimated. A variety of models have been proposed for estimating software reliability. Most of these are based on probabilistic principles. The ones that are popular

---

* There are several other data flow criteria that we have not mentioned in this paper. Definitions of the well-known data flow criteria are provided in [Clar89].

among researchers and practitioners make use of software failure data to estimate R. In reliability growth modeling, the failure data are obtained by testing P on a stream of inputs also known as test cases. Each test case (d) is a point in the input domain of P. To generate a test case the input domain is sampled based on an *operational profile.* As defined in Chap. 5, an operational profile is a list of occurrence probabilities of each element in the input domain of P. When P fails during testing, the time of failure is recorded and the software repaired. This process continues until some form of convergence of reliability estimates is achieved.

For most software, the input domain is extremely large and may be considered infinite for practical purposes. Thus, determination of the operational profile becomes a task to reckon with. Nevertheless, the operational profile is key to reliability estimation for most existing models used in practice, e.g., the Musa-Okumoto model. Not surprisingly, a significant amount of work has gone into developing procedures for estimating an operational profile. Chapter 5 also provides a detailed methodology of how an operational profile can be built. This methodology is dependent on input from the customer. In fact the first step in this methodology is to identify a customer profile. This profile is refined in a sequence of steps to obtain the operational profile, which in turn is dependent on how the users are expected to use the software.

Once an operational profile has been determined, you need to sample test cases from the input domain as per the occurrence probabilities. The software is then exercised against these test cases to obtain failure data. These data are then input to one or more models to estimate reliability.

In the procedure outlined above, the software is treated as a black box. Test cases are generated to test for specific *features* of the software. It has been suggested in [Musa93] that the number of test cases should be limited to several hundred or several thousand. However, neither the test case development nor the reliability estimates have any explicit relationship with how the software is exercised during testing; indeed, an implicit relationship exists. It is this lack of an explicit relationship that forms the basis of our argument against a purely black-box approach to reliability estimation.

13.3.1 Difficulties in estimating the operational profile

As mentioned earlier, an operational profile is an estimate of the relative frequency of use of various inputs to the program. The frequency is user dependent and is necessarily derived by some sort of usage analysis. Below we identify situations under which deriving an accurate operational profile may not be possible and hence you may have to rely on educated guesses. From our personal experience in software development and discussions with various development groups, we have come to believe that each of the scenarios described below is encountered by one or more developers and is not fictional. We also point out problems that may arise when an operational profile is inaccurate. The problems cited below are often encountered and discussed informally by practitioners; we are not aware of documentation.

New software. When a new system is designed, as opposed to modifying an existing system, one may not have any customer base for this system. As an example, consider the development of a system that will control an instrument for experimentation aboard a spacecraft. The experiment is one of its kind and has never been performed before. Features in this system will correspond to the requirements derived from an analysis of the instrument and the nature of its expected use. It is therefore likely to have a list of features but no existing customer base. Thus, we have to necessarily rely on guesstimates of occurrence probabilities for various features. If the system is designed to be fault tolerant, then one needs to guess the probabilities of failure of the application modules in the system. These probabilities will in turn determine the probabilities of how certain features of the fault manager will be exercised. Such failure probabilities may depend on a variety of relatively well understood phenomena (such as hardware failure) and not so well understood phenomena (such as data corruption due to cosmic rays). This is likely to add an extra degree of uncertainty to the occurrence probability estimates of features of the fault manager.

New features. New versions of an existing system may be continually under development. A new feature is added to the system assuming that one or more users will use it. Even though there exists a user base for the existing version of the system, there is no user base for the new version yet to be released. Once again the developer has to rely on guesstimates of the occurrence probabilities of the new features. The problem is further complicated by new features that might significantly alter the usage pattern of the existing system. If the users like a new feature they may not use an existing feature, thereby altering the usage frequency of this existing feature. Such a change may be difficult to anticipate, and the guesstimates of occurrence probabilities of various features could be very inaccurate.

Feature definition. A feature is often not a well-defined entity. For example, suppose that a system provides two features f_1 and f_2. Then, is the use of these features in different sequences also a feature? Adding all possible sequences of features into the operational profile might result in a very large profile, which is difficult to build and manage. As another example, suppose that a sort module is embedded in a large system. The module is internal and the user cannot access it directly. However, it supports two features f_1 and f_2. The system provides a feature f that occasionally uses the sort module. Should the operational profile treat only f as a feature or the combinations f,f_1, and f,f_2 as two distinct composite features?

Feature granularity. Consider a program that has a total of N lines of executable code. If the operational profile consists of k features, then the program has an average of k / N lines per feature. In practice there may be more or less lines per feature than the average. For a system with, for example, 100K lines of code and 100 features in the operational profile, we are likely to find features that correspond to more than 1000 lines of code. In order to test the code well, it would be desirable to specify the features with finer granularity, resulting in lesser lines of code per feature. However, if features are based on what a user uses directly, it may not be possible to specify features with a fine granularity.

Multiple and unknown user groups. An operational profile is intended to model one or more users. It is assumed that these users belong to a relatively homogeneous class. A reliability estimate given under such an operational profile is at best valid for the class of users for which the profile has been developed. A developer, such as the one who develops an operating system, might prefer to provide reliability estimates for the system independent of the user. It is not clear how to estimate an operational profile to meet such a requirement.

The above discussion leads us to believe that estimation of operational profiles is a difficult and error-prone task. Reliability estimation using operational profiles is often projected as "customer or user-centered" testing of a system. Based on arguments given above, we believe that it is at best a "known user-centered" approach. If an unknown user uses the system in a way that does not match with the operational profile, then there is no guarantee that the projected reliability figures will hold.

13.3.2 Estimating reliability with inaccurate operational profiles

As mentioned above, existing and popular models of reliability estimation make use of black-box testing to generate failure data. Below we argue that this approach might yield failure data leading to optimistic reliability estimates. Experimental evidence in support of our arguments appears in [Chen94b].

Inadequate test set. When using black-box testing based on an operational profile, the input tests are based on the features in the profile. A feature simply may not appear in an erroneous profile or the probability of its occurrence may have been erroneously estimated to be too low. This could result in not testing a feature or testing it scantily. The problem with such testing is that there is no program-based notion of the adequacy of a test set. Thus, after a program has been tested and you obtain the failure data, you have no way of determining how "good" the set of test cases was. The notion of adequacy that is used in such testing rests upon the reliability of statistical sampling from the input domain using the operational profile. This notion does not account for the fact that an inaccurate profile might result in a poor test set.

Thus, for example, if a feature is not tested at all, or tested but not thoroughly, and if there are errors in the implementation of that feature, then the failure data may not contain failures resulting from these errors. Such failure data might lead to an overestimate of reliability.

Coarse features. A feature could correspond to several lines of code. While using black-box testing, we construct several test cases to exercise the feature thoroughly. However, there is no measure of how well the feature has been exercised. There might be parts of the code related to this feature that never get exercised even though the feature occurs with a high probability in the operational profile. This is likely to happen when test cases are being randomly sampled from the input domain or a tester is generating them manually without a knowledge of how well the code corresponding to this feature has been exercised so far. Empirical data obtained from two applications that had been tested extensively over several years have indicated that indeed tests generated manually using a knowledge of program features and the functions used to implement them is insufficient to obtain a high level of code coverage [Horg92].

Inadequate testing of a feature is likely to result in misleading failure data and inaccurate reliability estimates. Note that we are assuming an accurate operational profile in this case. We have pointed out that despite this accuracy there is a possibility of obtaining misleading failure data.

Interacting features. In large systems, features often interact in a variety of ways [Zave93]. A simple form of interaction occurs when, say, feature f_1 works correctly when exercised before exercising feature f_2, but not otherwise. In large systems we deal with several hundred features. It is not clear how such interaction can be checked systematically when performing black-box testing. Once again, failure to check for faulty interactions may generate misleading failure data, leading to inaccurate reliability estimates.

Above we have listed several reasons why reliability estimates may be inaccurate. Currently there is a lack of data suggesting the extent of this inaccuracy. We are aware of one study which provides evidence in favor of the conjecture that an inaccurate operational profile may have a serious effect on reliability estimates [Chen94b]. Below we describe an approach that incorporates knowledge gained during white-box testing into reliability estimation, with the aim of reducing the effect of operational profile errors on reliability estimates.

13.4 Time/Structure-Based Software Reliability Estimation

An estimate of the probability of software failure within a specified time of operation is an important and useful metric. Such a metric, referred to as *software reliability,* is useful to both the software developer and its user. The developer can use this metric to decide whether to release the software or not. The user can decide whether to begin using the software or not at a given time. The importance of software reliability was realized several years ago and has been a major subject of research in software engineering. A large number and variety of models have been proposed to estimate software reliability. Often, these models have also been applied to data obtained from working software [Musa87]. The accuracy of these models, as measured against the predicted versus actual software failure, has varied from one project to another.

In the remainder of this chapter we describe two methods for estimating software reliability and the underlying rationale. A key feature of our methods is that they account for the fine structure of the software under development. This feature distinguishes our methods from the existing methods that employ time-domain models; it is also the basis of our claim that structure-based reliability methods are likely to provide more accurate reliability estimates than the existing time-domain-based methods.

13.4.1 Definitions and terminology

Let P denote a program under test whose reliability is to be estimated. During testing, P is executed on a test case d selected from the input domain D. The output of P obtained by executing it on d is denoted by $P(d)$. Each execution of P requires a test case and some CPU time. We assume that *testing effort* is measured either in terms of the number of test cases on which P is executed or through the cumulative CPU time for which P has been executed. The CPU time spent in executing P during testing is used in time-domain reliability models based on execution time. Let T_k denote the time at which the kth failure occurs and N_k the number of test cases used by time T_k. We define E_k, the effort spent in testing, as follows:

$$E_k \triangleq \begin{cases} T_k - T_{k-1} & \text{for time-based model} \\ N_k - N_{k-1} & \text{for test-case-based model} \end{cases} \tag{13.1}$$

Let e_i denote the effort spent during the ith execution of P. Then E_k can be expressed as

$$E_k = \sum_{i=l_1}^{l_2} e_i \tag{13.2}$$

where e_{l1} and e_{l2}, respectively, denote the effort spent in the first and last executions of P during the kth failure interval.

The reliability R of P is defined as the probability of no failure over the entire input domain. More formally, we have

$$R = \mathrm{P}\{P(d) \text{ is correct for any } d \in D\} \tag{13.3}$$

This definition can be cast in terms of a time-based definition. Let the cumulative effort S_k be defined as

$$S_k = \sum_{i=1}^{k} E_i \tag{13.4}$$

In the literature [Goel85], *reliability* is defined as the probability that a software system will not fail during the next x time units during operation in a specified environment. Here x is known as the *exposure period.* A more precise definition is given in [Yama85] using E_k and S_k as follows:

$$R(x \mid t) \equiv \mathrm{P}\{E_k > x \mid S_{k-1} = t\} \tag{13.5}$$

where $R(x \mid t)$ denotes the reliability during the next failure interval of x units, given the failure history during t units. $R(x \mid t) \to R$ as $x \to \infty$ if the test inputs are operationally significant.

13.4.2 Basic assumptions

Most models rely on certain assumptions that are often not satisfied in practice. Chapter 3 has identified these assumptions for various models. Several researchers have examined the validity of these assumptions. Here we examine one fundamental assumption: namely, the assumption that testing is carried out in accordance with the operational profile. This implies that the testers know and make use of the operational profile of the inputs. A knowledge of the operational profile implies knowing the frequency distribution with which test inputs are expected to be encountered when the software operates in its intended environment (Chap. 5). This frequency may presumably be used to decide which test inputs must be used during testing and in what order. Obviously, test cases not encountered during the monitoring of the environment will correspond to a frequency of zero in the profile. In Sec. 13.3 we have examined situations where an accurate operational profile may not be available.

The reliability models proposed herein impose a testing methodology on the tester. Such a methodology ensures (1) improved data input to a reliability model and a better reliability estimate and (2) that the predictions are less sensitive to the possible differences between the true operational profile and its approximation derived during testing.

13.4.3 Testing methods and saturation effect

We begin by describing a *saturation effect* that is associated with all testing methods. An understanding of this saturation effect is a key to the realization of the shortcomings of the application of existing models. A saturation effect refers to the tendency of an individual testing method to attain a limit in its ability to reveal faults in a given program. Figure 13.1 illustrates the saturation effect. As explained below, it is this limit that may cause significant over- or underestimates of reliability using existing models. The method presented herein accounts for the saturation effect [Chen92b].

13.4.4 Testing effort

As testing progresses, data (including calendar time, CPU time spent in executing the software under test, and the number of test cases developed) become increasingly available. Here we refer to the *later* phases of testing (e.g., the system test phase). A reliability model often uses some of the failure data generated during this phase. Musa's basic execution time model (see Sec. 3.3.4), for example uses the total CPU time spent executing the program under test; other researchers have used the number of test cases [Cheu80]. In our discussion below, we consider the CPU time and the number of test cases as indicators of *testing effort*. Thus, as testing effort increases, faults are discovered and removed. This results in an increase in program reliability. We shall denote the testing effort by t_x, where x indicates the testing method that was in use when the effort was measured.

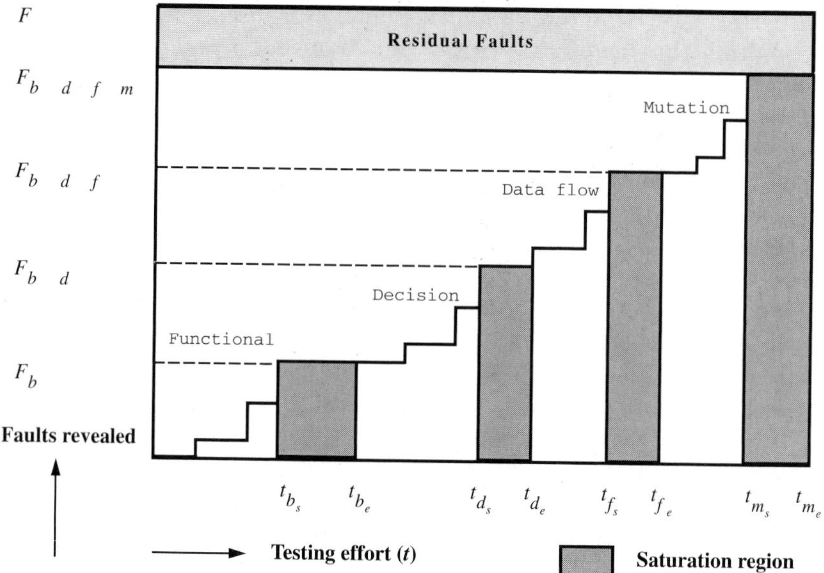

Figure 13.1 Saturation effect of testing methods assuming that the testing methods are applied in the following sequence: functional, decision, data flow, and mutation.

13.4.5 Limits of testing methods

At the start of testing, a program contains a certain number, say *F*, of faults. As testing proceeds the number of remaining faults decreases. However, when applied, each testing method has a limit on the number of faults that it can reveal for a given program. As shown in Fig. 13.1, we assume that for functional testing this limit is reached after t_{bs} units of testing effort has been expended. Also, functional testing has revealed F_b out of F faults when its limit is reached. In general, $F \geq F_b \geq 0$. Due to its imprecise nature, it is difficult, if not impossible, to determine when functional testing has been completed. In practice, a variety of criteria, both formal (e.g., a reliability estimate) and informal (e.g., market pressure), are applied to terminate functional testing. If no other form of testing is used, this also terminates testing of the product. Note that [Dala90] has formulated a method to decide when to stop testing.

It is reasonable to assume that as functional testing proceeds, the reliability of the software being tested grows when faults found are removed. However, once its limit has been reached, no additional faults are found. A tester, not knowing that the limit is reached, continues testing without discovering any more faults. If existing models for reliability estimation are used, e.g., the NHPP model of Goel and Okumoto [Goel79] then as functional testing proceeds beyond its limit the computed reliability estimate improves even though the reliability of the program remains fixed. The reliability estimate can be improved to any arbitrary limit by increasing the number of test cases executed in the saturation region.

In accordance with the scenario charted earlier, let us suppose that after t_{b_e} units of functional testing, we switch to decision-coverage-based testing. New test cases are developed to cover the yet uncovered decisions. Eventually, the limit of decision coverage is reached after a total of t_{d_s} units of testing. At this point $F_{b \cup d}$ faults have been revealed, with F_d being the number of faults revealed by decision coverage. Note that at this point 100 percent decision coverage may not have been achieved. However, the tester does not know that the limit has been reached and continues testing until t_{d_e}, by which time all decisions have been covered. Once again, empirical evidence suggests that $0 \leq F_b \leq F_{b \cup d} \leq F$.

We assume that the next switching occurs at time t_{d_e} to data flow testing and then at time t_{f_e} to mutation testing. As shown in Fig. 13.1, the limits of data flow and mutation are reached at times t_{f_s} and t_{m_s}, respectively, with a total of $F_{b \cup d \cup f}$ and $F_{b \cup d \cup f \cup m}$ faults revealed. We also assume that in general $0 \leq F_b \leq F_{b \cup d} \leq F_{b \cup d \cup f} \leq F_{b \cup d \cup f \cup m} \leq F$.

13.4.6 Empirical basis of the saturation effect

It is possible to construct examples of programs to show theoretically that every structure-based testing method will eventually reach its limit and thus fail to reveal at least one or more faults. This saturation effect has been illustrated for several structure-based methods by a few empirical studies in the past [Budd80, Girg86, Wals85]. Due to its imprecise nature, a proof that saturation effect holds for functional testing does not appear to be feasible, although Howden's work [Howd80] does provide some empirical justification. Below we present empirical justification based on another study with two relatively larger programs than the ones considered by Howden.

TEX [Knut86] is a widely used program in the public domain. It has been tested thoroughly for several years by Knuth [Knut89] and, as a result, a widely distributed test set [Knut84], named TRIPTEST, is available for testing TEX. Prior to installation, it is recommended that TRIPTEST be used to ensure that TEX indeed functions as intended by its author. TRIPTEST has been devised by Knuth primarily to test the functionality of TEX. As indicated in [Knut84], TRIPTEST exercises TEX in several ways that may be highly improbable in practice. Knuth has also documented [Knut89] all the errors discovered during the debugging and use of TEX. An examination [Demi91] of this list of over

850 errors of various kinds indicates that in spite of a fiendish amount of functional testing, errors have persisted in TEX. The above observation is indeed true for yet another UNIX® utility, namely, AWK, which has been tested for several years by Kernighan based on its functionality. However, errors continue to crop up, though with decreasing frequency, in AWK.

We used TEX and AWK to determine how much structural coverage is obtained using test data that has been derived from several years of functional testing. Using a data flow testing tool named ATAC [Horg94, Lyu94b], we decided to compute various coverage measures when TEX, Version 3.0, is executed on TRIPTEST. Table 13.1 lists these coverages. Notice that none of the four structural coverages is 100 percent. It is indeed possible that many of the blocks, decisions, p- and c-uses are indeed either infeasible or can be executed only under rare run-time conditions. Knuth does mention the fact that some parts of TEX that are related to such error conditions are not exercised by TRIPTEST [Knut84].

To ensure that not all of the uncovered structural elements of TEX correspond to error conditions, we examined the uncovered blocks and decisions and identified a few that are not related to processing error conditions arising at run time. Three such blocks, selected arbitrarily, were then removed from the original TEX code and TEX rebuilt. The rebuilt version was then executed against the TRIPTEST. The output generated by the rebuilt TEX was identical to that of the original TEX, thus showing that indeed TRIPTEST did not exercise the removed blocks.

An analysis similar to the one described above for TEX was also carried out for AWK. Several uncovered, though feasible, structural elements were discovered. These analyses strongly suggest that (1) intensive functional testing may fail to test a significant part of the code and, therefore, (2) may fail to reveal faults in the untested parts of the program. It is this empirical observation that justifies our claim that the saturation effect is exhibited by functional testing and that coverage data must be used during reliability estimation.

TABLE 13.1 Coverage Statistics of TEX and AWK

	Coverages (%)			
Program	Block	Decision	p-use	c-use
TEX	85	72	53	48
AWK	70	59	48	55

13.4.7 Reliability overestimation due to saturation

We now argue that the saturation effect can lead to overestimation of the reliability. Figure 13.2 shows the reliability R as faults are removed, and the estimate of R denoted by $\overline{R}$. The testing effort axis is labeled the same as in Fig. 13.1. Assuming that faults are independent, R increases as faults are removed from the program. $\overline{R}$ may, however, increase or decrease as faults are removed. This nonmonotonic behavior of $\overline{R}$ is due to the time dependence of the input data used by most models. Thus, for example, increasing interfailure times will usually lead to increasing $\overline{R}$ obtained from the Musa basic model.

We assume that the $\overline{R}$ generated by a model is a stochastically increasing estimate. This implies that even though $\overline{R}$ may fluctuate, it will eventually increase if the number of remaining faults decreases.

In Fig. 13.2, we indicate that as functional testing progresses, and faults are discovered and corrected, $\overline{R}$ increases. In general, however, it is not possible to detect when the saturation point, t_{b_s} in this case, has been reached. Thus, testing may continue well past the saturation point. As shown in the figure, testing in the saturation region does not increase R, though it does increase $\overline{R}$. The increase in $\overline{R}$ is explained by observing that the last value in the interfailure data, i.e., $(t - t_{b_s})$, is increasing without any new fault being detected. This increase in $\overline{R}$, while R remains constant, can lead to a significant overestimate of the

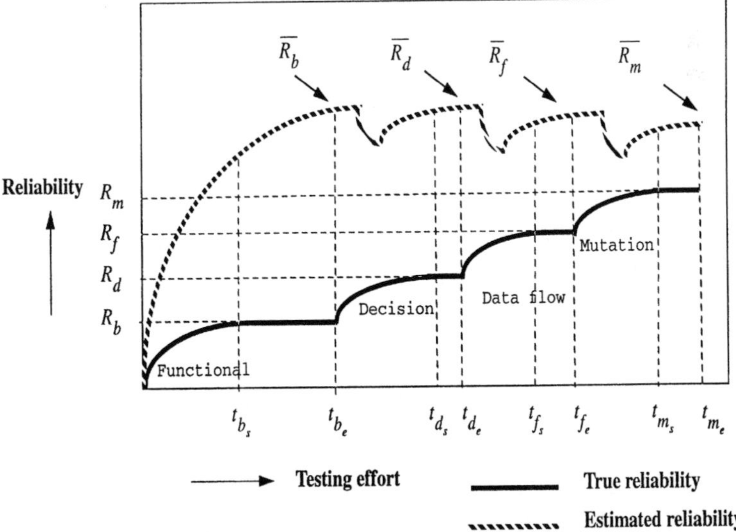

Figure 13.2 Overestimation of reliability due to saturation effect.

reliability. In Fig. 13.2, $\overline{R_b}$ is the estimate of the true reliability R_b at the end of functional testing.

The above reasoning applies to other phases of testing as well when white-box testing methods are being used. In each case, there exists a period of testing when $\overline{R}$ increases even though R remains fixed. Such an increase can lead to significant overestimates, as shown in Fig. 13.2.

Figure 13.2 indicates that R is a monotonically increasing function of testing effort in the growth region. This may not be always true. In general, the growth region will appear as in Fig. 13.3. Thus, for example, if t denotes CPU time spent in executing P, then R will grow during periods when faults are found; otherwise it will remain constant. This stepwise rise of R will cause $\overline{R}$ to fluctuate and increase stochastically, as dictated by the underlying model.

13.4.8 Incorporating coverage in reliability estimation

As mentioned earlier, during black-box testing we execute the system against test cases developed using the operational profile. Each test case has an effect on the *coverage* of various program elements. As a simple example, when program P is executed against test case $t_i, i \geq 1$, it may cause some statements to be executed for the first time, thus increasing the statement coverage. Below we outline an approach that

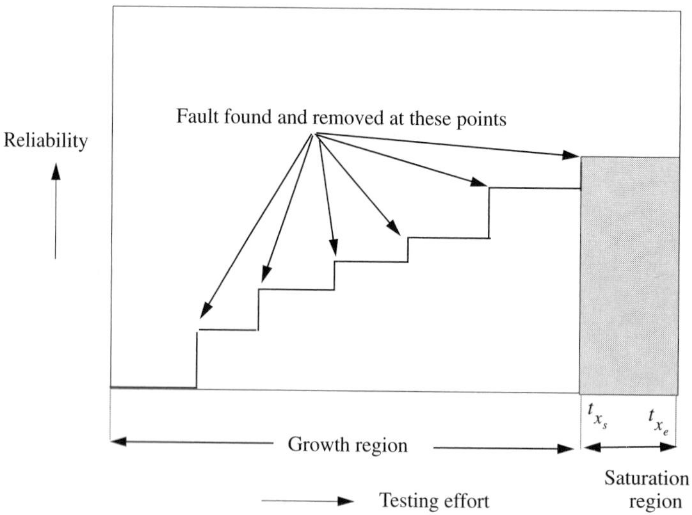

Figure 13.3 A realistic growth region.

makes use of coverage measures in estimating reliability. Our approach does not necessarily entail development of test cases using coverage measures; however, it calls for measurement of coverage during testing.

The time-structure-based approach outlined below is a simple extension of the the existing approach based on time-domain models. We emphasize that the use of time-structure-based approach does not require a change in the method used for the development of a test set; it does require the measurement of coverage such as block, decision, or data flow coverage. The pure structure-based models remove the notion of time in estimating the reliability and lead to another approach to reliability estimation. It is not yet clear which approach is the best to use in practice.

13.4.9 Filtering failure data using coverage information

We now describe an approach to incorporate coverage information in estimating software reliability. We begin by defining the notion of *useful* testing effort. A testing effort E_k is useful if and only if it increases some type of coverage. Note that the definition of usefulness does not specify which coverage should be increased for a test effort to be useful.

We might argue that in practice every test case, against which P has not been executed before, is useful. This argument is acceptable in accordance with our definition of usefulness if input domain coverage is considered to be one type of coverage. We know that there exist disjoint subsets D_i, $1 \leq i \leq n, n \geq 0$, of D, known as *partitions,* such that $\cup D_i = D$, that will cause P to behave identically. Thus, testing P on one element of D_i is equivalent to testing P on all elements of this partition. The problem, however, is that we cannot compute these partitions a priori. Instead, we rely on various testing methods to provide us with the relevant partitions. Therefore, we assume that input space coverage is *not* one of the coverage types to be considered in determining whether an effort is useful or not. Later we will explain how this assumption affects reliability estimates based on time/structure models.

We have already defined three types of coverages, namely, decision, data flow, and mutation. To illustrate the notion of usefulness, suppose that the first $k - 1$ test cases have resulted in a decision coverage of 35 percent. Now if the kth test case increases this coverage to, say, 40 percent, then we say that it is useful. In case the CPU time spent is the measure of testing effort, then an execution of P that causes an increase in decision coverage results in useful testing effort. Note that there are several ways of measuring structural coverage. It is not clear which is the best and should be used here. We return to this question later, in Sec. 13.4.10.

The effort E_k defined in Eq. (13.2) consists of one or more atomic efforts e_i. However, an e_i may be useless. To account for such useless efforts, which may bias the interfailure effort, we define

$$E_k^c = \sum_{i=l_1}^{l_2} \sigma e_i \tag{13.6}$$

where l_1 and l_2 are as in Eq. (13.2) and σ is the *compression ratio.* The quantity σ can be defined in several ways. Below we provide a simple definition. We consider alternate definitions in Sec. 13.4.10.

$$\sigma = \begin{cases} 1 & \text{if } e_i \text{ increases coverage} \\ 0 & \text{otherwise} \end{cases} \tag{13.7}$$

The use of compression ratio compresses the interfailure effort, E_k to E_k^c by ignoring the atomic effort that has been found useless. This process is illustrated in Fig. 13.4. Along the thick horizontal line, the testing effort is indicated. The leftmost upward-pointing arrow indicates the instant when testing began; subsequent upward arrows mark failure points. Two consecutive downward arrows bracket the atomic effort. The first atomic effort is bracketed by the leftmost upward arrow and the first downward arrow. The sequence of total effort spent between successive failures is indicated by the sequence of shaded boxes labeled "Observed." The sequence of shaded boxes, labeled "Useful" just below this line indicates the *filtered* effort data obtained by applying the compression ratio to the observed data.

The filtered effort data can now be used in any of the existing time-based models. Thus, for example, if the Musa model is being used to predict reliability, then the filtered data can serve as the modified sequence of interfailure times. If $\overline{R}_m$ and $\overline{R}_f$ are reliability estimates generated by the Musa basic model using, respectively, the original and filtered interfailure times, then $\overline{R}_f < \overline{R}_m$. The example below illustrates this relationship. Thus, filtering leads to a more realistic reliability estimate than the approach that uses unfiltered data. The filtered data can also be applied to any of the other models, such as the Goel-Okumoto model [Goel85].

Example 13.1 To show that filtered interfailure data result in more realistic reliability estimates, we generated hypothetical data corresponding to E_k. These data were filtered and reliability estimates computed using the Musa basic execution time model. The method for doing so is described below. Here we assume that the effort is measured in terms of CPU time.

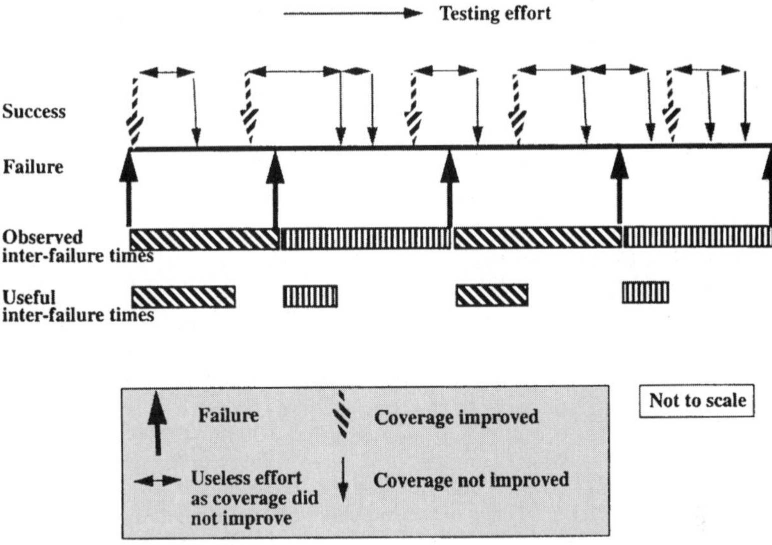

Figure 13.4 Filtering failure data using coverage information.

1. Assume that the per-fault hazard rate $\Phi = 0.05$ and the total number of expected failures $V = 100$.
2. The number of failures experienced by time t, denoted by $u(t)$ is computed as

$$u(t) = V\,(1 - e^{(-\Phi t)}) \tag{13.8}$$

3. The time to the ith failure, t_i, is computed from Eq. (13.8) as

$$t_i = \ln(V/(V - u))/\Phi \tag{13.9}$$

4. The failure interval between $(i - 1)$th and ith failure, Y_i, is $t_i - t_{i-1}$.
5. However, Y_i, as computed above, is monotonically increasing due to the use of Eq. (13.9). To obtain more realistic interfailure time data, we use Y_i as the mean of an NHPP process and generate the interfailure times. Let r be a uniform random number, $0 < r < 1$. We compute the interfailure times from Y_i as

$$E_i = Y_i \ln(1/(1 - r)) \tag{13.10}$$

6. Assume that P requires a constant time to execute on each test case. Let this time t_P, arbitrarily chosen, be 0.01 time unit. We then obtain the number of test cases n_i used in the ith failure interval as E_i/t_P.
7. Let r' be a uniform random variate, $0 < r' < 1$. The probability that a test case used at time t did not improve coverage is $1 - e^{(-0.01tr')}$. Using this information we identify which test cases are useless and hence contribute to useless effort. This information is used for compressing E_i to E_i^c.
8. Compute the new failure times $t_k = \Sigma_{i=1}^{k} E_k^c$, $1 \le k \le 100$.
9. Compute the new per-fault hazard rate Φ' for the uncompressed data and Φ'' from the compressed data. Maximum likelihood estimation is used in both cases.

10. Apply the Musa basic model to the uncompressed and compressed interfailure times to obtain the two reliability estimates, $\overline{R}(x/t)$ and $\overline{R}^c(x/t)$, respectively.

Using the uncompressed and compressed interfailure time data, we computed various reliability estimates. Figure 13.5 shows $\overline{R}(0.01 \mid t)$ and $\overline{R}^c(0.01 \mid t)$, i.e., the reliability for an exposure period of 0.01 time units at time t. Notice that both the estimates are almost equal but in all cases $\overline{R}^c(0.01 \mid t) \leq \overline{R}(0.01 \mid t)$. Over the entire time duration for 100 failures, we get $0.784 \leq \overline{R}(0.01 \mid t) \leq 0.999$ and $0.783 \leq \overline{R}^c(0.01 \mid t) \leq 0.998$.

The difference in the two estimates is significant in Fig. 13.6 where the exposure period is 10 time units. For this data set we obtained $0.0 \leq \overline{R}(10 \mid t) \leq 0.65$ and $0.0 \leq \overline{R}^c(10 \mid t) \leq 0.445$.

Reliability estimates were also obtained by fixing t and varying the exposure time. Figure 13.7 shows the estimates $\overline{R}(x \mid t)$ and $\overline{R}^c(x \mid t)$ where the values of the current time were set arbitrarily to the time at which the 84th failure occurred. The range of estimates obtained is $0.01 \leq \overline{R}(x \mid t) \leq 0.995$ and $0.003 \leq \overline{R}^c(x \mid t) \leq 0.993$. Figure 13.8 shows the estimates obtained by fixing t to the time when the 99th failure occured. The range of estimates obtained is $0.562 \leq \overline{R}(x \mid t) \leq 0.999$ and $0.343 \leq \overline{R}^c(x \mid t) \leq 0.998$. These data, and the data mentioned above, indicate

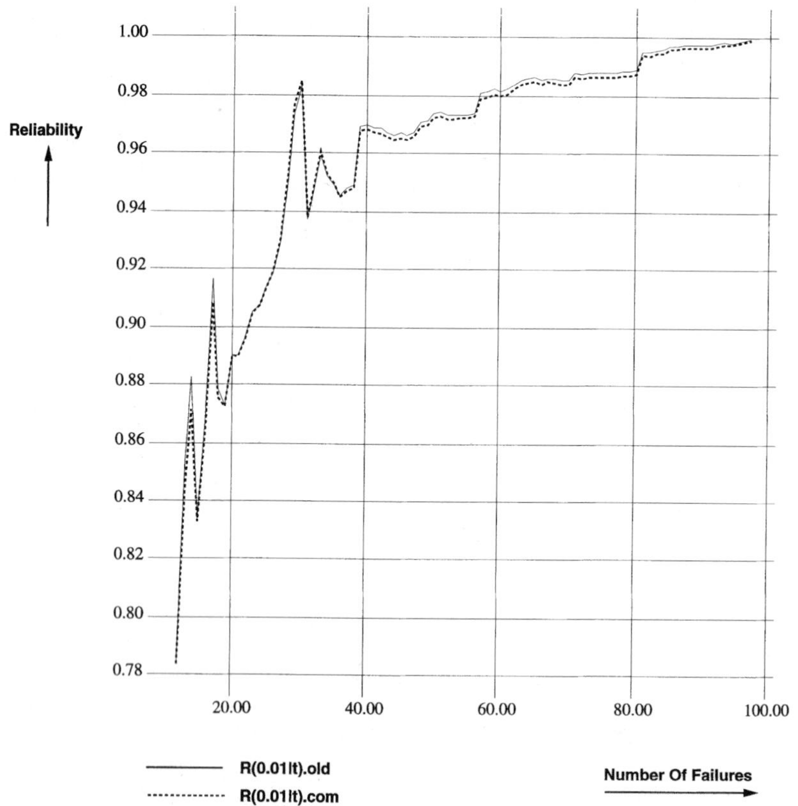

Figure 13.5 Variation in the reliability estimates with number of failures, $R(0.01 \mid t)$.

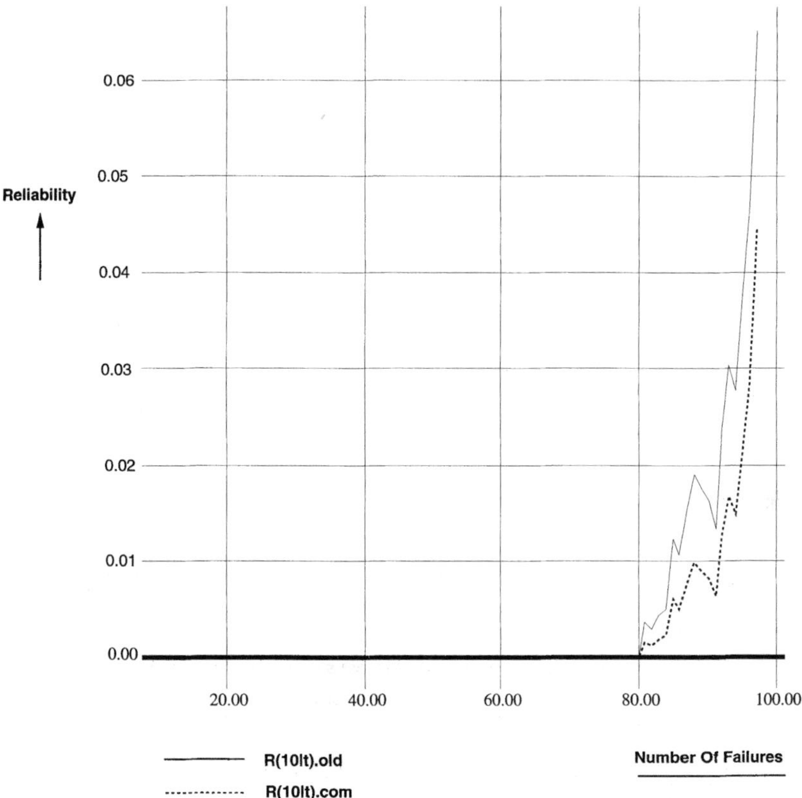

Figure 13.6 Variation in the reliability estimates with number of failures, $R(10\,|\,t)$.

that the estimates using the time structure model are conservative, as indicated by the ratio $\overline{R}(x\,|\,t)/\overline{R}^c(x\,|\,t)$, which ranged from 1 to 3.33.

13.4.10 Selecting the compression ratio

The notion of useless effort stems directly from the fact that the input domain of P can be partitioned into disjoint subdomains. Once such a partition is available, it is necessary to select just one test case from each subdomain. If two test cases are selected from one partition then one of them leads to useless effort. Even though domain partitioning is possible in theory, in practice it is difficult to determine such partitions for nontrivial programs. The white-box testing methods provide, at best, an approximation to such a partition. Thus, for example, if a test set covers a decision, we assume that any other test case that once again exercises the same decision is useless. It is easy to show by examples, and has also been shown empirically [Howd80], that such a test case may indeed reveal faults. This implies that what we consider as a

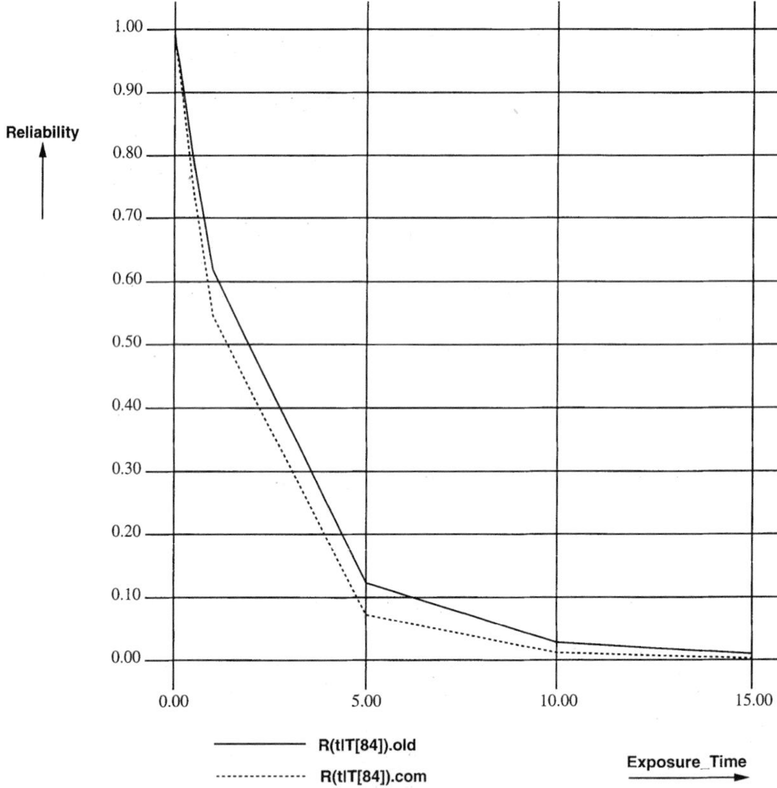

Figure 13.7 Variation in the reliability estimates with the exposure time, $R(x \mid 84)$.

test case amounting to useless effort may indeed be a useful test case that, when run successfully on P, has shown the nonexistence of a fault. Such a test case should therefore improve our reliability estimate. However, other than structural or mutation coverage, we do not have any other criterion to test the utility of a test case.

The above reasoning leads us to reconsider the definition of σ as given in Eq. (13.7). Toward this end, we make the following observations:

1. It is more likely for a test case to increase a coverage measure during the initial phases of testing than later. Thus, as coverage increases, it becomes increasingly difficult to construct a test case that will further increase coverage.

2. Once one or more coverage criteria have been satisfied, the likelihood of a test case, selected randomly, increasing coverage according to any remaining criteria, decreases.

As an example, suppose that T_d is a test set that covers all decisions but does not provide 100 percent data flow coverage. If a test case $d \notin$

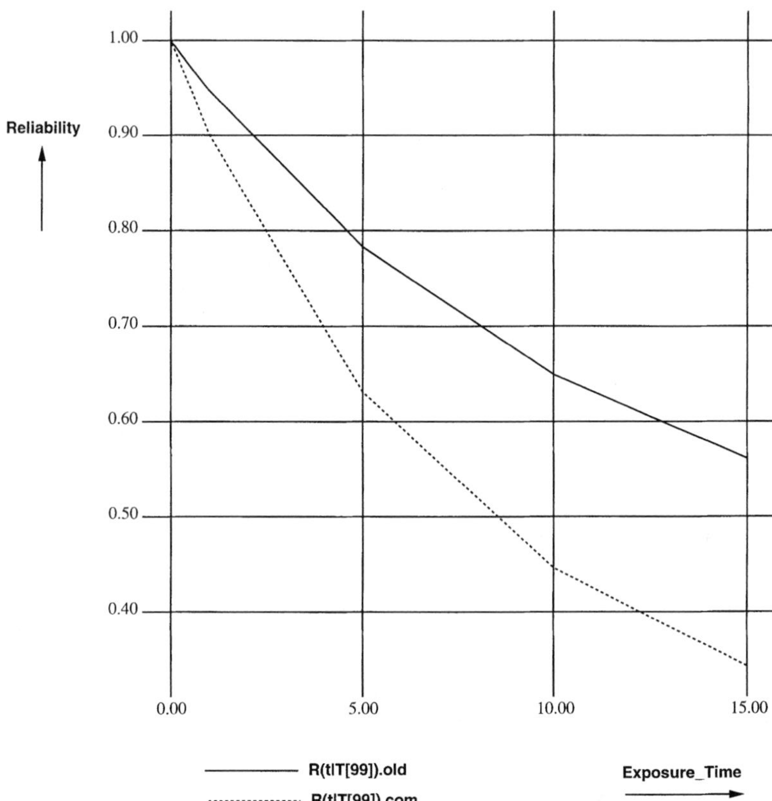

Figure 13.8 Variation in the reliability estimates with the exposure time, $R(x\,|\,99)$.

T_d is now selected randomly from the input domain, the likelihood of d increasing data flow coverage is less than its likelihood of increasing decision coverage when 100 percent decision coverage was not reached.

The above observations lead us to hypothesize that a test case d_1 may be more *important* than another test case d_2. We can modify Eq. (13.7) to account for this importance. The compression ratio can be made effort dependent. Thus, $\sigma \equiv \sigma(t)$ and $\sigma(t_1) < \sigma(t_2)$ if $t_1 < t_2$. Such a definition of σ will ensure that test cases that increase coverage during the later phases of testing get more importance than those that increase coverage during the early phases. Experiments carried out using another filtering method are described in [Chen94a].

13.4.11 Handling rare events

For a given test case $d \in D$, the failure of P on d, indicated by incorrect $P(d)$, is considered a rare event if Prob $\equiv P\{P(d)$ is incorrect$\} < \varepsilon$ for some arbitrarily small ε. If the operational profile is used during testing, then Prob is dependent on the profile itself. If the profile does not contain *d,* and hence *P* was most likely not exercised on *d,* then the failure might occur after a significant amount of effort has been spent during program operation. Such a failure is likely to be considered as a rare event arising due to the occurrence of a possibly rare input *d* during operation. If the profile is not used during testing, then Prob is the same as the probability of occurrence of *d* during operation.

In either of the two cases mentioned above, it seems impossible to determine such a test case during testing. This is specially true when only a negligible fraction of the input domain is accounted for during testing. Inclusion of coverage in reliability estimation helps decrease the likelihood of a failure-generating input arising in operation. Such a decrease takes place in two ways.

First, as mentioned above, coverage-based reliability estimates have been found to be more realistic compared to the ones that ignore coverage data. This is expected to lead to increased testing effort to raise the estimated reliability up to a cutoff level that may have been set by the management. Second, an examination of coverage helps the tester construct new test cases in addition to the ones constructed during functional testing. Such test cases are likely to reveal faults in code that remained uncovered during functional testing, based perhaps on the operational profile. Thus, failures that may have proved to be rare events during operation may in fact occur during testing.

13.5 A Microscopic Model of Software Risk

In this section we present a *risk model* for computing and/or interpreting the reliability numbers in conjunction with coverage data obtained during testing.

13.5.1 A testing-based model of risk decay

The computational basis for the risk model is the control and data flow measures. For purposes of discussion below we consider measures supported by ATAC, a data flow testing tool which reports various data flow coverages for a given test set. To fully capture the intuitive notion of the *risk of untested code,* other testing-based notions of risk that are intuitively independent of the data flow concept might also be considered. One such notion is provided by *mutation* testing [Choi89] and another by *domain* testing. By counting risk on three intuitively independent testing scales we might capture much of the notion of risk. For instance, during testing with ATAC we may be able to reduce the data flow risk of tested code to zero. The remaining mutation and domain risk would now provide a measure of residual testing risk, which could be taken into account in reliability and safety assessment.

Data flow testing measures the adequacy of a set of tests according to how well the tests exercise the statements, branches, and variable definition/use pairs in a program. For a given program P in the C language and a test set T for use with P, ATAC reports, among other data, a coverage score like

```
% blocks       % branches    % All-Uses
33(169/516)    21(86/414)    15(277/1852)
```

The above scores can be interpreted to mean that T exercised 33 percent of the 516 basic blocks, 21 percent of the branches, and 15 percent of the variable definition/use pairs in the program P. Having executed P on each element of T, one might view the above score as a multifaceted risk profile of P. A simple interpretation of these measures, assuming that all discovered faults have been repaired, is that by running the tests in T, we have reduced the risk associated with the untested blocks of P by 33 percent, that associated with untested branches by 21 percent, and of untested variable definition/use pairs by 15 percent. If another test set T_1 yields the coverage score

```
% blocks       % branches      % All-Uses
100(516/516)   100(414/414)    100(1852/1852)
```

we might say that P is risk-free when measured by block, branch, and all-uses testing. The conclusion of this sort of simple "risk" interpretation of coverage testing is that a set of tests that visit all blocks, branches, and def/uses in P eliminates all risk associated with P.

We now examine the notion of *risk* that originates from data flow coverage testing in the following examples. For simplicity, we restrict our examples to consideration of coverage of basic blocks; the model can be used to compute risk by including other data flow coverage statistics as well.

13.5.2 Risk assessment: an example

The program of Fig. 13.9 contains 12 basic blocks. These basic blocks are the indivisible units of control execution; every statment or expression in a basic block will be executed if any is executed. The simplest testing-based notion of risk is: *basic blocks (or statements) which remain untested are risky.* This dictum is simple, easily assessed, but seldom observed. Very few software organizations require every statement of code under test to actually be executed by some test. Occasionally, such an omission is justified. Some code is defensive code that cannot be executed, and some code can be executed only under conditions impossible to reproduce in a testing environment, but, often, statement coverage is simply not assessed.

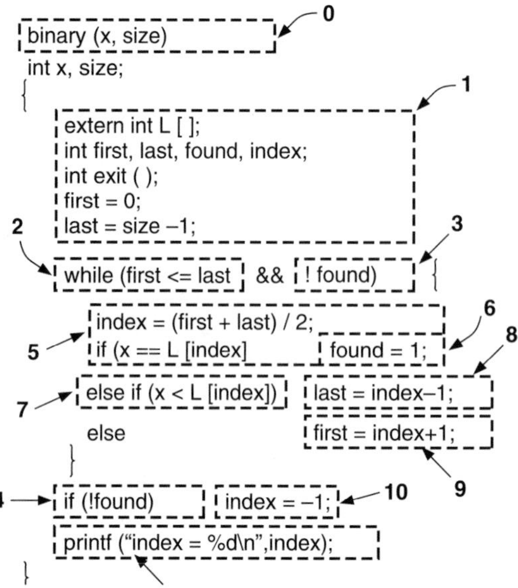

Figure 13.9 Basic blocks of a simple program.

Typically, we would run a set of tests like those displayed in Table 13.2.

Subsequent to running these tests we can calculate the coverage of the tests. Test t.1 yelds the following coverage:

```
> atac -s -n t.1 binary.atac
% blocks     % decisions % C-Uses     % P-Uses
----------- ----------- ----------- -----------
83(10/12)    70(7/10)     70(7/10)     61(17/28)   == total ==
```

Tests t1, t2, t3, and t4 together yield the following:

```
> atac -s -n t.[1-4] binary.atac
% blocks     % decisions % C-Uses     % P-Uses
----------- ----------- ----------- -------------
92(11/12)    90(9/10)     80(8/10)     71(20/28)   == total ==
```

The set of all 16 tests give the following coverage:

```
> atac -s -n t.* binary.atac
% blocks     % decisions % C-Uses     % P-Uses
----------- ----------- ----------- -------------
100(12)      100(10)      100(10)      93(26/28)   == total ==
```

TABLE 13.2 Sixteen Tests for binary.c

Variables	x	L[0]	L[1]	L[2]
Test t.1 values	0	0	1	2
Test t.2 values	0	0	1	3
Test t.3 values	0	0	2	3
Test t.4 values	0	1	2	3
Test t.5 values	1	0	1	2
Test t.6 values	1	0	1	3
Test t.7 values	1	0	2	3
Test t.8 values	1	1	2	3
Test t.9 values	2	0	1	2
Test t.10 values	2	0	1	3
Test t.11 values	2	0	2	3
Test t.12 values	2	1	2	3
Test t.13 values	3	0	1	2
Test t.14 values	3	0	1	3
Test t.15 values	3	0	2	3
Test t.16 values	3	1	2	3

Table 13.3 gives the number of visits to each block by each of the 16 tests as computed by ATAC.

Based on research in the fault-detection ability of coverage measures, we assume that statement coverage alone is not a good measure of risk reduction [Girg86]. Data flow testing measures the coverage of *branches* and various *definition/use* relationships [Horg91]. Covering these more complex aspects of code can be shown to reduce the exposure of code to faults, and thus risk. For instance, Fig. 13.10 displays

TABLE 13.3 Test Visit to Blocks

Blocks	0	1	2	3	4	5	6	7	8	9	10	11
t.1 visits	1	1	3	3	1	2	1	1	1	0	0	1
t.2 visits	1	1	3	3	1	2	1	1	1	0	0	1
t.3 visits	1	1	3	3	1	2	1	1	1	0	0	1
t.4 visits	1	1	3	2	1	2	0	2	2	0	1	1
t.5 visits	1	1	2	2	1	1	1	0	0	0	0	1
t.6 visits	1	1	2	2	1	1	1	0	0	0	0	1
t.7 visits	1	1	3	2	1	2	0	2	1	1	1	1
t.8 visits	1	1	3	3	1	2	1	1	1	0	0	1
t.9 visits	1	1	3	3	1	2	1	1	0	1	0	1
t.10 visits	1	1	3	2	1	2	0	2	1	1	1	1
t.11 visits	1	1	2	2	1	1	1	0	0	0	0	1
t.12 visits	1	1	2	2	1	1	1	0	0	0	0	1
t.13 visits	1	1	3	2	1	2	0	2	0	2	1	1
t.14 visits	1	1	3	3	1	2	1	1	0	1	0	1
t.15 visits	1	1	3	3	1	2	1	1	0	1	0	1
t.16 visits	1	1	3	3	1	2	1	1	0	1	0	1

data from an experiment in which our colleagues compared the statement coverage of unit tests for 28 modules of a single system to the number of system test faults found for each module. There is a clear relationship between high statement coverage in unit testing and low system test faults [Dala93].

13.5.3 A simple risk computation

Our model computes the risk of a code fragment by computing the risk of the constituent *testable attributes* of the code fragment. For the program `binary.c` these attributes are the 12 basic blocks, the 10 decisions, the 10 c-uses, and the 26 p-uses. We consider each of these attributes as carrying a unit of *static risk.* Each of these attributes is considered as a *receptor* of a potential defect. Of course, we do not know whether a given c-use, for example, is defective or not, but we do associate risk with it to account for the possibility of it being defective. Another way of looking at static risk in our model is to view it as a method of disproportionally distributing expected defects throughout the code. Using $\alpha_k(l_i), 1 \le k \le N$ to represent the static risk for all attributes of type k (e.g., c-uses) constituent in *locus* l_i (e.g., a line of code), we compute the static risk $\rho(l_i)$ for a given program for locus l_i as

$$\rho(l_i) = \sum_{k=1}^{N} \alpha_k(l_i) \tag{13.11}$$

Considering ζ_k defects per attribute as *prior information,* $\zeta\rho(l_i)$ is defined to be the *expected defects on prior information* for locus l_i:

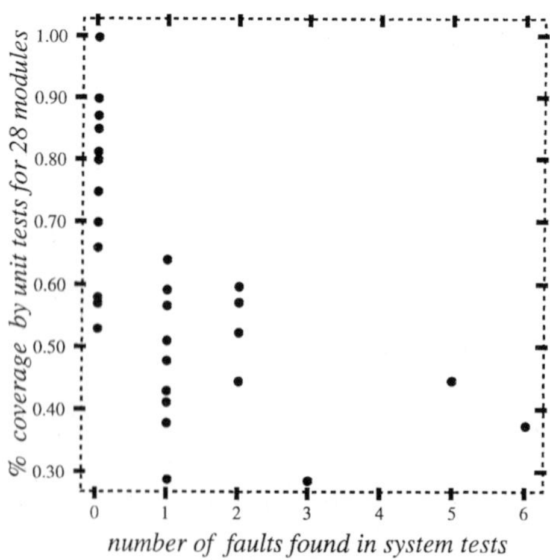

Figure 13.10 Relationship of unit coverage testing to system test faults for one system.

$$\zeta\rho(l_i) = \sum_{k=1}^{N} \alpha_k \zeta_k(l_i) \tag{13.12}$$

Using $\alpha_1(l_i)$ to represent blocks, $\alpha_2(l_i)$ decisions, $\alpha_3(l_i)$ c-uses, and $\alpha_4(l_i)$ p-uses, the static risk, $\rho(l_i)$, for locus l_i of `binary.c` is given by

$$\rho(l_i) = \alpha_1(l_i) + \alpha_2(l_i) + \alpha_3(l_i) + \alpha_4(l_i)$$

The expected defects on prior information is given by

$$\zeta\rho(l_i) = \alpha_1\zeta_1(l_i) + \alpha_2\zeta_2(l_i) + \alpha_3\zeta_3(l_i) + \alpha_4\zeta_4(l_i)$$

To be more concrete, suppose from prior project experience we believe that `binary.c` has 0.5 faults per 1000 noncommented source lines. Then, as `binary.c` has 17 noncommented source lines, it should have 8.5×10^{-3} faults. If we weigh all testable attributes equally (58 in this case), then there are approximately 1.47×10^{-4} faults per attribute. Relating that to a line of code is done through basic blocks. Line 13 of `binary.c`, "`else first = index + 1`", is involved in 1 basic block, 0 decisions, 1 c-use, and 5 p-uses. Therefore, we have

$$\alpha_1(\text{line } 13) = 1 \qquad \alpha_2(\text{line } 13) = 0,$$

$$\alpha_3(\text{line } 13) = \tfrac{1}{2} \qquad \alpha_4(\text{line } 13) = \tfrac{5}{3}$$

As each c-use participates in 2 basic blocks and each p-use participates in 3 basic blocks, we assign ½ of a c-use and ⅓ of a p-use for each occurrence in line 13. Then the static risk, ρ(line 13), for locus line 13 of `binary.c` is given by

$$\rho(\text{line } 13) = 1 + 0 + \tfrac{1}{2} + \tfrac{5}{3} = 3.17$$

As ζ_k is 1.47×10^{-4} per attribute in our example, the expected defects on prior information is given by

$$\zeta\rho(\text{line } 13) = 1.47 \times 10^{-4} \times 3.17 = 4.66 \times 10^{-4}$$

The expected defects on prior information for line 13 reflects our view that testable attributes are markers for defects. Therefore, when we calculate the static risk for line 13 as a portion of the static risk for the entire program, we distribute the expected defects of `binary.c` according to that risk. Thus, 5.5 percent (3.17/58) of the total static risk and the expected number of defects of `binary.c` are attributed by our model to line 13 of `binary.c`.

13.5.4 A risk browser

We have developed a tool named Risk Browser that allows a user to browse through the source code of a program displaying the risk associated with individual parts of the code. As an example, Fig. 13.11 shows the detailed display of static risk for the program `binary.c`. That is, the risk as measured by our model based upon the distribution of testable data flow attributes to the individual lines of `binary.c` before *any* tests are run. This fine-grained report of risk forms a baseline of the relative risk of the individual lines. Surprisingly, the 10th and 11th nonblank lines are considered most risky because they involve the highest number of data flow relations when compared with other lines in the code. In this respect, our static measure of risk is considerably different than control-flow-based measures such as cyclomatic complexity.

In a large software system the risk browser can present cumulative risk for various units of the system. In Fig. 13.11, the background window shows the relative cumulative static risk for the two files main.c (not presented here) and `binary.c`. As main.c is a simple driver pro-

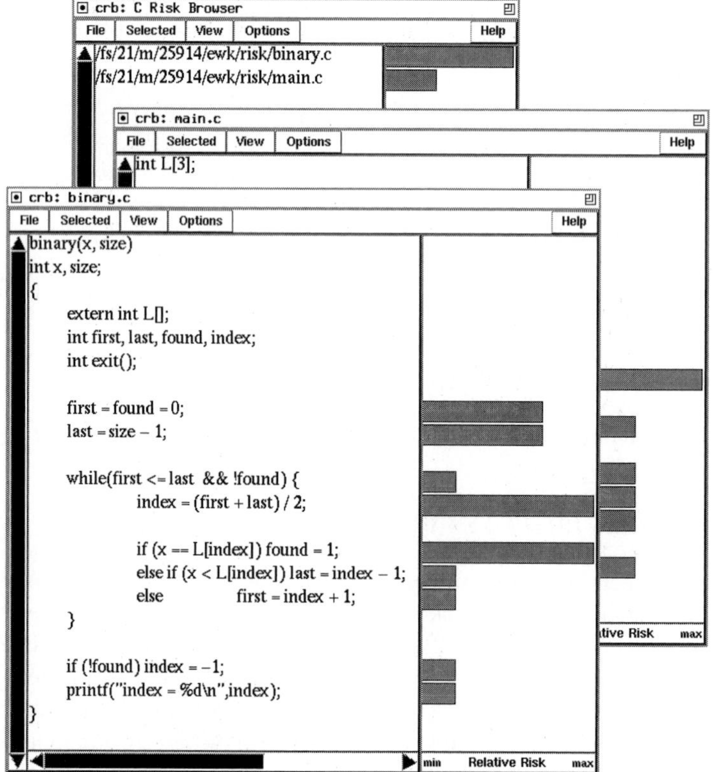

Figure 13.11 Static risk for `binary.c`.

gram, `binary.c` is shown to be considerably more risky. In all displays of risk we normalize against the most risky component of the display window. So lines 10 and 11 in the foreground window are shown with maximal risk, while `binary.c` in the background window is displayed with maximum risk.

Static risk is the start, and risk decays as testing progresses. Figure 13.12 shows the interaction of the risk browser and ATAC as the programmer attempts to reduce dynamic risk. The left foreground window shows the dynamic risk for `binary.c` after t.1 through t.8 have been run. The top right foreground window shows an ATAC display of uncovered blocks and the bottom foreground window shows an ATAC display of uncoverd decisions which remain in `binary.c` at this point in testing. The programmer crafts tests t.9 through t.16, which test these uncovered attributes, and the result is the final display of risk in Fig. 13.13. Here we see the original static risk (outlined) and the residual risk (darkened).

13.5.5 The risk model and software reliability

As ATAC collects visitation rates by test for each testable attribute, a more complex model of risk is possible. Rather than allowing the risk associated with an attribute to vanish once covered, we can allow the risk to asymptotically decay as visitation increases. We can construct

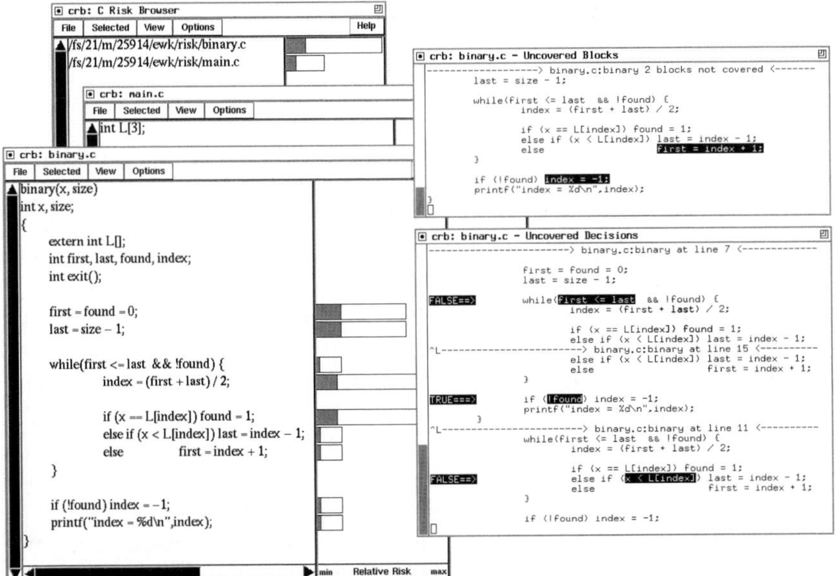

Figure 13.12 Dynamic risk for `binary.c` after execution on t.1 through t.8.

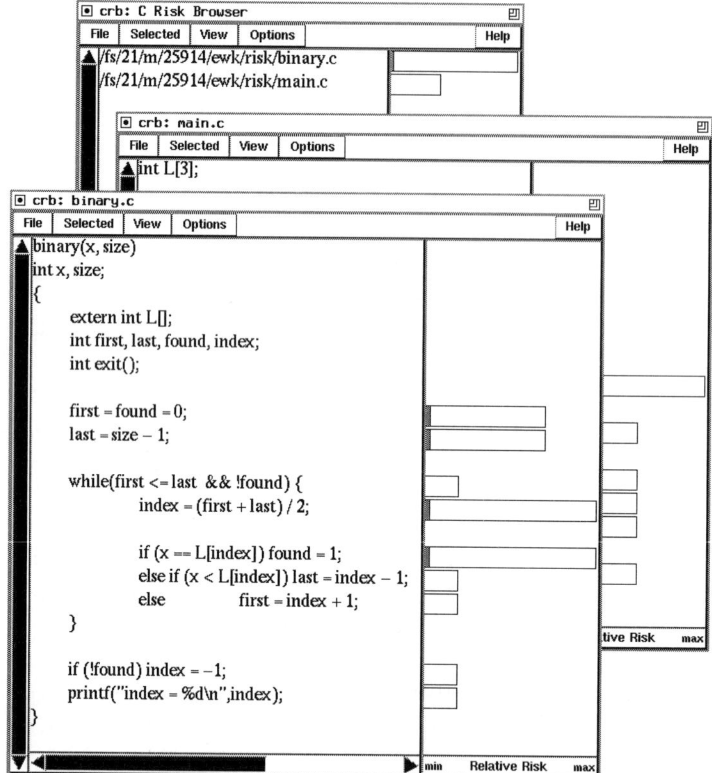

Figure 13.13 Dynamic risk for `binary.c` after t.1 through t.16.

confidence growth models similar to reliability growth models. Currently, the pragmatic value of such models is not known.

A more important relationship between coverage testing and reliability modeling involves the saturation effect explained earlier. Suppose that we calculate the reliability of `binary.c` based on the sequence of tests t.1 through t.16. This would be a trivial exercise, but we can ask "Should all the tests be counted as a measure of effort?" Surely, a sequence of 16 consecutive runs of t.1 would not count as 16 units of time or effort. An exact analysis using ATAC tells us that tests t.1, t.2, t.3, and t.8 define exactly the same computation paths in `binary.c`. The same is true of the sets {t.4}, {t.5, t.6, t.11, t.12}, {t.7, t.10}, {t.13}, and {t.9, t.14, t.15, t.16}. Thus, if our notion is that only testing which reveals something new about a program should be used in measuring reliability growth, we could restrict the reliability calculation to {t.1, t.4, t.5, t.7, t.9}. Moreover, if our notion is that only testing which reveals new coverage should be considered in reliability assessment, then only {t.4, t.13, t.16} need be considered. ATAC permits such measurements.

There is a problem of scale in these sorts of calculations. ATAC is used to monitor moderately large programs (up to 100,000 lines) during product testing. However, run-time overhead is sometimes several times the ordinary runtime. The data collection for exact analysis of path redundancy among tests is an additional burden. For large systems, the measurements required for our models may require off-line reprocessing of the tests so as not to interfere with the normal testing process.

13.6 Summary

In this chapter we have pointed to the problems encountered in reliability estimation in the presence of an inaccurate operational profile. To overcome these problems we have described two different methods of accounting for code coverage in software reliability estimation. The first method makes use of code coverage data to filter the failure data input to time-domain models. Any of the traditional time-domain models is then used to obtain reliability estimates. The coverage information can be obtained during the system test phase. Experiments conducted on small programs and on large simulated programs show that this method leads to more realistic estimates when compared with estimates obtained using the unfiltered data.

In the second method, code coverage measures and the program structure are used to assess the risk associated with a program. Highly reliable software is considered as software associated with low risk. Given visitations and coverage data for a program and a set of tests, a method of calculating risk has been described.

Problems

13.1 *a.* How does white-box testing differ from black-box testing?

b. What in your experience is the likelihood of obtaining 100 percent statement coverage from a test set derived using black-box testing?

c. Is it possible to test all functions from a test set that is derived to obtain 100 percent statement coverage?

d. For some program *P*, a test set *T* is adequate with respect to the statement coverage criterion. Give an example *P* for which *T* is not adequate with respect to the decision coverage criterion.

13.2 Consider the following program that inputs two integers *a* and *b* and computes *y*.

```
begin
    integer x,y,a,b;
    input(a,b);
    x=0; y=10;
```

```
    if a>0 then
                n=1
            else
                n=2
    endif;
    if b>0 then
                y=(n+1)*a
            else
                y=(n-1)*b
    endif;
    output (y);
end
```

a. Construct a test set T_s adequate with respect to the statement coverage criterion.

b. Construct T_d by adding test cases to T_s such that T_d is decision adequate.

c. Construct T_{pc} by adding test cases to T_s such that T_{pc} is *p*-use and *c*-use adequate.

d. A test set *T* is considered minimal with respect to some criterion *C* if removal of any test case from *T* will cause the remaining test set to be inadequate with respect to *C*. Which of the test sets constructed above are minimal?

13.3 *a.* Assume that program *P′* is constructed from *P* of Prob. 13.2 by replacing the statement $n = 2$ by $n = 3$. Consider *P′* to be an erroneous version of *P*. Which of the test sets constructed in Prob. 13.2 will cause *P′* to fail?

b. Let *T* be some test set that is adequate with respect to the statement coverage criterion for *P′*. Is *T* guaranteed to reveal the error in *P′* by causing *P′* to fail?

c. How does your answer to item *b* change if the statement coverage criterion is replaced by decision coverage? *p*-use coverage? *c*-use coverage?

d. Suppose that the input domain of *P* consists of all values of *a* and *b* such that $-5 \le a < 5$ and $-5 \le b < 5$. Let (a_1,b_1) be a randomly selected pair from the input domain. Let *P′* be executed on (a_1,b_1). What is the probability that *P′* will fail? How does this probability change as the range of *a* and *b* (i.e., the size of the input domain) increases?

13.4 For some user of program *P′* of Prob. 13.3, the operational profile has been specified as shown in Fig. 13.1. Suppose that *P′* is tested by randomly selecting a pair from the input domain using the operational profile given in Table 13.4.

a. With what probability will *P′* fail?

b. How does the probability in item *a* change as the probability of a test case, which satisfies $a < 0$ and $b < 0$, reduces?

c. Suppose that each time *P′* fails, the user incurs a cost *C*. What approximate cost will the user incur after 100 executions of *P′*?

TABLE 13.4 Sample Operational Profile for Prob. 13.4

	Input	Probability
1	$(a = 0, b > 0)$	0.1
2	$(a = 0, b = 0)$	0.005
3	$(a > 0, b > 0)$	0.7
4	$(a > 0, b = 0)$	0.1
5	$(a < 0, b < 0)$	0.05
6	All others	0.045

d. Suppose that P' was tested with respect to the operational profile given in Table 13.4 and that the error in P' was not revealed. P' is now delivered to a user whose operational profile is different from the one given in Table 13.4. The difference is in entries 3 and 6. These entries for our user are

$(a > 0, b > 0)$	0.4
All others	0.345

Recompute your answer to item *c* for the modified operational profile.

e. Now suppose that P' was tested to achieve 100 percent statement coverage. How will your answer to item *d* change? For decision coverage? For *p*-use and *c*-use coverage?

13.5 *a.* Why and how does the saturation effect affect the reliability estimate of a program?

b. Why is it that the use of code coverage in reliability estimation using random testing is likely to improve the estimates?

c. When using a "white-box" based approach to reliability estimation when is a test case considered useful?

d. Suppose that while testing for reliability measurement, we measure statement coverage. Now, suppose that a test case *t* does not increase the statement coverage. Will *t* be considered useful? Will it be considered useful if some other coverage were measured?

13.6 During the execution of a program *P*, we say that a rare event has occurred if *P* has been executed on an input that occurs with a very low probability. Which of the two testing methods—random or coverage-based testing—is more likely to cause this event to occur during testing? Provide a sample program to illustrate your answer.

13.7 Let *P* be a program with three features: f_1, f_2, and f_3. The program consists of 300 lines of executable source code. We test *P* by providing exactly three test cases, one to exercise each feature. Do you expect these test cases to provide 100 percent statement coverage? How does your answer change as the size of the program is increased and the number of features remains fixed? Explain your answer.

13.8 *a.* What is the basic difference between the approaches outlined in the chapter for reliability estimation using code coverage versus the risk decay model?

b. Why is it that statement coverage alone is not a good measure of risk reduction?

b. How is the static risk measure affected by increase in code coverage?

13.9 Obtain ATAC program from the following Internet ftp address.

ftp site: `flash.bellcore.com`, *login*: `anonymous`, *password*: `your address`, *directory*: `atac`

Get the `README` file and the archive file "`atac3.3.13.tar.Z`" or the latest version. Read the `README` file and get familiar with the `atac` package.

a. Type up the program `binary.c` shown in Fig. 13.9. Apply `atac` to count its blocks, decisions, c-uses, and p-uses. Verify that there are indeed 1 block, 1 c-use, and 5 p-uses in line 13. You need to write a simple `main.c` program to call the `binary` routine.

b. Apply `atac` to the program in Prob. 13.2 and measure the coverages obtained from your test sets.

c. Apply `atac` to the mutated program in Prob. 3.13 and determine which of your test cases detect the error.

Chapter

14

Fault-Tolerant Software Reliability Engineering

D. F. McAllister and M. A. Vouk
North Carolina State University

14.1 Introduction

Software development processes and methods have been studied for decades. Despite that, we still do not have reliable tools to guarantee that complicated software systems are fault-free. In fact, it may never happen that we will be able to guarantee error-free software. The reason is that the two basic ways of showing that software is correct, proof of program correctness and exhaustive testing, may never be practical for use with very complex software-based systems, although reuse of reliable software building blocks (objects) may go a long way toward achieving that goal. Techniques for proving software correct tend to work only for relatively small and simple synchronous systems, while testing methods, although increasingly more sophisticated, do not guarantee production of error-free code because exhaustive testing is not practical in most cases. Therefore, it is reasonable to investigate techniques that permit software-based systems to operate reliably and safely even when (potential) faults are present.

A way of handling unknown and unpredictable software (and hardware) failures (faults) is through fault tolerance. Over the last two decades, there has been a considerable amount of research, as well as practical software engineering, in this area. In this chapter, we introduce some elementary principles that underlie construction of fault-tolerant software based on the software diversity principle, that is, provision of fault tolerance through functional redundancy. We leave the details of advanced analyses and the details of practical implementations to other texts. The reader who wishes to implement fault tolerance in a software-based system in practice is strongly advised to consult additional texts such as [Eckh85, Voge87a, Litt89, Lapr90a, Mili90, Eckh91, Lapr92, Siew92, Lyu95a] (and references therein) which provide a *detailed* discussion of the more recent advances and problems in practical software fault tolerance, hardware–software interactions, and fault tolerance for distributed systems.

In this chapter, we first provide some background information, including an overview of major industrial and academic efforts related to fault-tolerant software. We then present the principles and terminology, and give a general overview of the more common techniques for tolerating software faults. This is followed by a discussion of more advanced techniques, and then by some techniques which can be used in modeling the behavior of fault-tolerant software. Finally, we discuss issues such as independence of failures, and issues related to development and cost of fault-tolerant software.

14.2 Present Status

Fault-tolerant software has been considered for use in a number of critical application areas. For example, in nuclear power plants [Gmei79, Bish86], in railway systems [Hage87], and in aerospace systems [Mart82, Will83, Bric84, IEEE84, Spec84, Madd84, Kapl85, Troy85, Aviz87, Aviz88, Davi93]. Overviews of the use of software diversity in computerized control systems can be found in [Vog87a, Lyu95a].

A number of systematic experimental studies of fault-tolerant software issues have been conducted over the last 20 years by both academia and industry. For example, experiments related to the use of fault-tolerant software were reported for nuclear industry applications [Bish86, Bish88, Voge87c], aerospace applications [Knig86, Shim88, Kell88, Aviz88, Bril90, Vouk90a, Eckh91, Lyu92a, Huda93], as well as in other areas [Ande85, Lee93].

It would appear that the first industrial use of fault-tolerant software, based on the software diversity principle, occurred in a railway system [Voge87b, Ster78]. A number of organizations have used the approach to either help develop, verify, or actually implement an operational railway application for deployment in Sweden, Denmark, Finland, Switzerland, Turkey and Bulgaria [Hage87], Italy [Frul84], Singapore [Davi84], and the United States [Turn87].

Use of fault-tolerant software in aerospace applications has received a lot of attention over the years. It has been considered and implemented in both military (e.g., [Mart82, Turn87]) and civilian (e.g., [Hill83, Wrig86, Will83, Youn86, Swee95]) aircraft, and in the U.S. space shuttle [Madd84, Spec84]. For example, the slat/flap control system for the civilian Airbus A310 airliner consists of two functionally identical computers with diverse hardware and software [Wrig86, Trav87]. Also, fault tolerance is an essential part of the experimental flight technology such as that found in forward-swept wing, aerodynamically unstable but very agile, aircraft [Kapl85, Davi93]; and fly-by-wire military aircraft invariably incorporate fault tolerance, although not necessarily fault-tolerant software. Another example is the NASA space shuttle. The shuttle carries a configuration of four identical flight computers, each loaded with the same software, to combat hardware failures, and a fifth computer developed by a different manufacturer and running dissimilar (but in part functionally equivalent) software, which is executed only if the software in the other four processors cannot reach consensus during critical phases of the flight [Spec84, Madd84]. Software diversity was a salient issue in all developments mentioned above. We discuss this concept in more detail below.

Practical experiences with fault-tolerant software appear to be mixed but, in our opinion, they are more positive than negative, although a number of issues remain unresolved. *The general consensus appears to be that fault-tolerant software has the capability of increasing the reliability of a computer-based system.* Open and controversial issues include items such as how much fault-tolerant software actually increases system reliability in practice [Butl93], whether fault-tolerant software should be used in critical systems at all [IEEE94], and which fault-tolerance mechanism to use and how cost-effective it is [Lapr90a, Voge87b].

The primary reason for these doubts about redundancy-based software methods is the potential for common-cause faults and correlated coincident failures among the software elements that provide the redundancy. Unlike hardware failures, software faults are for the most part the result of software specification and design errors, and thus simple replication of software components does not provide reasonable protection. This dictates the need to strive for designs and development methods that encourage the use of diverse algorithms in redundant components and to minimize the potential for common-cause faults. Many experiments with fault-tolerant software have reported failure correlation among software versions used to provide redundancy (e.g., [Scot84a, Scot84b, Vouk85, Knig86, Vouk86a, Bish91, Eckh91, Gers91]), but the origins and the extent of that correlation in practical systems is still not well understood. It is conjectured, however, that failure correlation is a strong function of, among other things, software process and methods employed in version development [Lyu92b, Lyu93a]. Improving this development process thus can effectively increase overall system reliability.

14.3 Principles and Terminology

A principal way of introducing fault-tolerant software into an application is to provide a method to dynamically determine if the software is producing correct output, that is, a self-checking or *oracle* capability [Yau75]. This is often accomplished through a combination of different, but *functionally equivalent,* software *alternates, components, versions,* or *variants* and run-time comparisons among their results. However, other techniques, ranging from mathematical consistency checking to coding, are also useful [Ande81, Lin83, Mili90, Lapr90a, Lapr92a, Adam93] as are methods which use data diversity [Amma87, Chri94] (see Probs. 14.1 and 14.2).

When software execution encounters a software fault or defect, very often the system will make a transition into an erroneous (internal) state, that is, an unexpected internal result will be created. If this erroneous result propagates and is eventually observed by the user of the system, we say that we have observed a system failure [Aviz84]. Once an erroneous state has been identified, error *recovery* can be initiated. It may involve *backward recovery,* that is, system states are saved at predetermined *recovery points,* and on detection of an erroneous state the system is rolled back or restored to a previously saved recovery point and then restarted from that state. An alternative approach is *forward recovery.* Forward recovery may be implemented as a transition into a new system state in which the software can operate (often in a degraded mode), or by *error compensation* based on an algorithm that uses redundancy built into the system to derive the correct answer. A special case of the latter is permanent *fault masking* where compensation takes place regardless of whether an error is detected or not (e.g., certain forms of voting) [Lapr90a]. Combinations of forward and backward recovery are also used.

An important factor in determining how to detect and handle errors is whether the erroneous state results from algorithmic or implementational *memory,* or not. An algorithm or a program is said to be "memoryless" if it uses only the data received or generated after the last time it has delivered a result. An example of a memoryless algorithm is process monitoring where tasks begin based on current sensor data and do not use data from previous processing [Lapr90a].

Important criteria for judging suitability of a fault-tolerance scheme are the processing overhead required to implement fault tolerance, nature of the error detection mechanism, whether correctness of the result is determined in an absolute or relative manner (e.g., with respect to specifications, or another version), whether the scheme is sequential or parallel, whether error control involves suspension of the service or not, whether results are presented within time constraints, and how many errors can be tolerated and at what cost [Lapr90a].

14.3.1 Result verification

14.3.1.1 Acceptance testing. The most basic approach to self-checking is through an (internal) *acceptance test.* An acceptance test is a programmer-provided, program-specific, error-detection mechanism, that provides a check on the results of program execution. An acceptance test might only consist of bounds or simple tests to determine acceptability. For instance, it is much easier to develop software that determines if a list is sorted than it is to develop software that performs the sorting. However, in general an acceptance test can be complex and as costly to develop as the full problem solution. An important characteristic of an acceptance test is that it uses only the data that are also available to the program at run time.

An interesting example is the following implicit specification of the square root function [Fair85], SQRT, which can serve as an acceptance test:

$$\text{for } (0 \le x \le y) \qquad (\text{ABS}((\text{SQRT}(x)*\text{SQRT}(x)) - x) < E) \tag{14.1}$$

where E is the permissible error range, and x and y are real numbers. If E is computed for the actual code generated for the SQRT program, and machine specifications are known to the program, then Eq. (14.1) can serve as a full self-checking (acceptance) test. If E is known only to the programmer (or tester), and at run time the program does not have access to machine specifications or the information about the allowable error propagation within the program, then the test is either partial or cannot be executed by the program at general run time at all.

Acceptance tests that are specifically tailored to an algorithm are sometimes called *algorithmic* [Abra87, Huda93]. For example, provision of checksums for rows and columns of a matrix can facilitate detection of problems and recovery [Huan84]. Similarly, use of redundant links in linked lists can help combat partial loss of list items [Tayl80].

14.3.1.2 External consistency. An *external consistency check* is an extended error-detection mechanism. It may be used to judge the correctness of the results of program execution, but only with some outside intervention. It is a way of providing an oracle for off-line and development testing of the software, as well as for run-time *exception handling*. In situations where the exact answer is difficult to compute beforehand, it may be the most cost-effective way of validating components of a fault-tolerant system, or checking on run-time results.

A consistency check may use *all* information, including information that may not be available to the program in operation, but which may be available to an outside agent. Examples are watchdog processes that monitor the execution of software-based systems and use information that may not be available to software, such as timing, to detect and resolve problems [Upad86, Huda93]. Another example is periodic entry (manual or automatic) of location coordinates to a navigation system. Yet another example is an exception signal raised by the computer hardware or operating system when floating-point or integer overflow and divide-by-zero are detected.

The interrupt signal, or exception, that abnormal events occurring in a computer system generate represents a particularly useful and prevalent resource for external consistency checking. Often, these signals can be detected and trapped in software and the exceptions can be handled to provide a form of failure tolerance. For example, many modern programming languages* allow trapping of floating-point exceptions, divide-by-zero exceptions, or IEEE arithmetic signals (such as NANs†) [IEEE85, IEEE87a], and invocation of appropriate exception handlers that provide an alternative computation or other action, and thus shield the users from this type of run-time error. A good example of applied exception handling in FORTRAN is found in [Hull94].

Consistency checking may include comparisons against exact results, but more often it involves use of knowledge about the exact nature of the input data and conditions, combined with the knowledge of the transformation (relationship) between the input data and the output data. The consistency relationship must be sufficient to assert correctness.

For example, suppose that navigational software of an aircraft samples accelerometer readings, and from that computes its estimate of the aircraft acceleration [Eckh91]. Let an acceleration vector estimate, $\hat{\mathbf{x}}$, be given by the least squares approximation

$$\hat{\mathbf{x}} = [\mathbf{C}^T\mathbf{C}]^{-1}\mathbf{C}^T\mathbf{y} \tag{14.2}$$

The matrix $\mathbf{C}$ is the transformation matrix from the instrument frame to the navigation frame of reference, $\mathbf{C}^T$ is its transpose, -1 denotes matrix inverse, and the sensor measurements are related to the true acceleration vector $\mathbf{x}$ by

$$\mathbf{y} = \mathbf{C}\mathbf{x} + \tilde{\mathbf{y}} \tag{14.3}$$

where $\tilde{\mathbf{y}}$ is the sensor inaccuracy caused by noise, misalignment, and quantization. Then,

$$\mathbf{C}^T\mathbf{C}(\hat{\mathbf{x}} - \mathbf{x}) = \mathbf{C}^T\tilde{\mathbf{y}} \tag{14.4}$$

is a criterion to assert correctness for acceleration estimates. Note that $\mathbf{x}$ and $\tilde{\mathbf{y}}$ are not normally available to the navigation software. How-

* For example, UNIX signals can be trapped in C (e.g., see standard "man" pages for "signal(3)" system calls).

† NAN is an acronym for not-a-number, used to describe arithmetic exception events that do not result in numbers.

ever, if we supply all information, including that pertaining to the environment, we can control **x** and $\tilde{\mathbf{y}}$ and detect problems with algorithms without having advance knowledge of the correct answer. This can provide oracle capabilities during the off-line testing when the environment is completely under control. Of course, such a test cannot be employed during operational use of software unless an accurate environment status is provided independently.

On the contrary, hardware and operating system *exceptions,* such as overflow and underflow, *can and should* be handled at run time, and appropriate exception handling algorithms should be part of any software system that strives to provide a measure of failure tolerance.

14.3.1.3 Automatic verification of numerical results. A rather special set of techniques for dynamic detection and control of numerical failures* is *automatic verification of numerical precision.* This type of verification treats errors resulting from algorithmic micromemory, that is, error propagation within a numerical algorithm, and possibly numerical algorithm instability. The essence of the problem is that verification of a numerical algorithm does not guarantee in any way its numerical correctness unless its numerical properties are explicitly verified.

Floating-point arithmetic is a very fast and very commonly used approach to scientific and engineering calculations. As a rule, *individual* floating-point operations made available in modern computers are maximally accurate, and yet it is quite possible for the reliability of numerical software to be abysmally poor because a series of consecutive floating-point operations delivers completely wrong results due to rounding errors and because large numbers swamp small ones. To illustrate the issue we consider the following example from [Kuli93, Adam93].

Let **x** and **y** be two vectors with six components, $\mathbf{x} = (10^{20}, 1223, 10^{24}, 10^{18}, 3, -10^{21})$, and $\mathbf{y} = (10^{30}, 2, -10^{26}, 10^{22}, 2111, 10^{19})$. The scalar product of these two vectors is defined as

$$\mathbf{x} \cdot \mathbf{y} = \sum_{i=1}^{6} x_i \cdot y_i \tag{14.5}$$

The correct answer is 8779. However, implementation of this expression on practically every platform available today will return zero unless special precautions are taken. The reason is the rounding coupled with

* An example of a numerical software-associated life-critical failure is the tragic death of a number of American service personnel during the 1991 Gulf War due to a failure of a Patriot antimissile missile to destroy an incoming enemy surface-to-surface missile because of a numerical error [GAO92].

the large difference in the order of magnitude of the summands. This happens despite the fact that each individual number can be quite comfortably represented within the floating-point format of all platforms.

It is possible to construct more subtle and more complex examples which show that simple numerical algorithms, such as Newton's method, can become very unstable if ordinary floating-point arithmetic is used without explicit error propagation control [Kuli93]. The arithmetic error propagation problem can become very acute in applications such as simulation and mathematical modeling, and it is exacerbated by modern high-speed computers.

A solution proposed in [Kuli81, Klat91, Klat92, Adam93, Kuli93] relies on the computation of the optimal dot product using fixed-point accumulation to *guarantee* maximal computational accuracy [Kuli81] on interval arithmetic (which implies certain rounding rules) to compute accurate upper and lower bounds on the result and on automatic differentiation methods [Grie92, Adam93]. If the computed result cannot be verified to be correct (for example, the computed bounds are too large), the user can be given the option of providing alternatives to the algorithms and methods, or the option of changing to higher-precision arithmetic followed by reverification of results and a decision regarding the acceptability of the results. This approach dynamically tolerates and controls this type of failure. Other solutions are available. Anyone involved with design of critical systems that use numerical software is strongly advised to consult relevant literature (e.g., [Cart83, Grie92, Adam93]).

14.3.2 Redundancy

The technique of using redundant software modules as a protection against residual software faults was inherited from hardware. Hardware faults are usually random (e.g., due to component aging). Therefore using identical backup units, or redundant spare units, with automatic replacement of failed components at run time, is a sensible approach (e.g., [Triv82, Nels87, Siew92]). However, replication of a software version to provide backup redundancy has limited effectiveness since software faults are almost exclusively design- and implementation-related and therefore would also be replicated. The net effect would be that excitation of a replicated fault would result in a simultaneous failure of all versions and there would be no fault tolerance. This does not include timing or transient faults, which often occur because of complex hardware/software/operating system interaction. Such failures (called *Heisenbugs* in [Gray90]) can rarely be duplicated or diagnosed. A common solution is to reexecute the software in the hope that the transient disturbance is over.

A solution proposed specifically for software was to have independent manufacturers produce functionally equivalent software components* [Rand75, Aviz77]. It was conjectured that different manufacturers would use different algorithms and implementation details, and that the residual faults from one independent software manufacturer would be different from those made by another; therefore when one version failed, its backup or spare would *not* fail for the same input data and conditions and would become the primary module, or at least could force a signal of the disagreement. The goal is to make the modules as diverse as possible. The overall philosophy is to enhance the probability that the modules fail on *disjoint* subsets of the input space, and thus have at any time at least one correctly functioning software component.

Specifications used in this process may themselves be diverse as long as final functional equivalency of the products is preserved. The specification indicates certain critical outputs which must be presented to an adjudication program to determine if the system is operating correctly. Each developer creates a software module or version which implements the specification and provides the outputs indicated by the specification.

Redundancy requires the ability to judge acceptability of the outputs of several modules either by direct evaluation or by comparison. The algorithm that compares or evaluates outputs is called an *adjudicator*. Such a program can be very simple or very complex depending on the application, and therefore can also be a source of errors. An adjudication program may use the outputs from redundant versions to determine which, if any, are correct or safe to pass on to the next phase of the software. The decision may be based on several different algorithms. There are several adjudication techniques which have been proposed. This includes voting, selection of the median value, and acceptance testing, as well as more complex decision making. In all situations, of course, problems arise if failures are coincidental, correlated, or similar.

14.3.3 Failures and faults

We use the terms *coincident, correlated,* and *dependent* failures (faults) as follows. When two or more functionally equivalent software components fail on the *same* input case, we say that a *coincident* failure has occurred. Failure of k components raises a k-fold coincident failure. When two or more versions give the same incorrect response (to a given tolerance) we say that an *identical-and-wrong* (IAW) answer was

* We use the terms *component(s)*, *alternate(s)*, *version(s)*, *variant(s)*, and *module(s)* interchangeably in this chapter.

obtained. If the measured probability of the coincident failures is significantly different from what would be expected by random chance, usually based on the measured failure probabilities of the participating components, then we say that the observed coincident failures are *correlated.* Note that two events can be correlated because they *directly depend* on each other, or because they both depend on some other, but same, event(s) (*indirect dependence*), or both.

Let $P\{\ \}$ denote probability. Then

$$P\{\text{ version}(i)\text{ fails } \mid \text{ version}(j)\text{ fails }\} \neq P\{\text{ version}(i)\text{ fails }\} \qquad (14.6)$$

means that the conditional probability that version i fails given that version j has failed is different from the probability that version i, considered on its own, fails on the same inputs. If this relationship is true, we do not have failure independence [Triv82].

We shall say that several components contain the *same* or *similar fault* or *common-cause fault* if the fault's nature, and the variables and function(s) it affects, are the same for all the involved components. The result (answer) of execution of common-cause faults may be identical (IAW to within tolerance), or may be different. It is also possible that different faults result in a coincident failure by chance, giving either different answers or IAW answers.

Possible failure events are illustrated in Fig. 14.1. The Venn diagram shown in the figure represents the overlaps in the failure space of three functionally equivalent software units (or a 3-*tuple* of variants). Unshaded areas are regions where one of the three components (programs p_1, p_2, p_3) fails for an input. Lightly shaded areas show the regions where two out of three components fail coincidentally, while the darkly shaded area in the middle is the region where all three

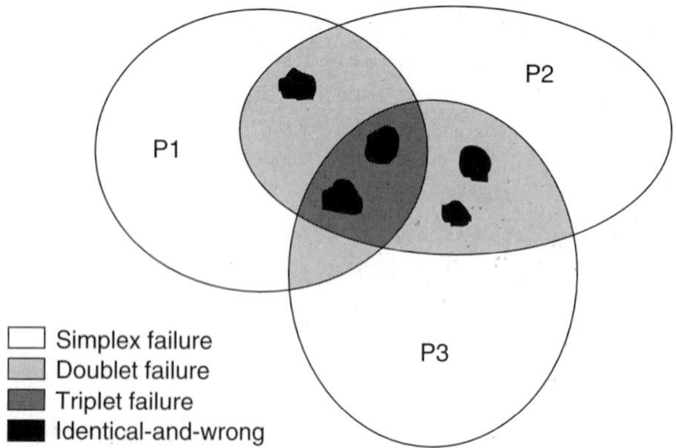

Figure 14.1 Illustration of failure space for three functionally equivalent programs.

components fail coincidentally. Of special interest are regions marked in black, which represent events where components produce IAW responses.

14.3.4 Adjudication by voting

A common adjudication algorithm is voting. There are many variants of voting algorithms (e.g., [Lorc89, McAl90, Vouk90b, Gers91, Lyu95a]). A voter compares results from two or more functionally equivalent software components and decides which, if any, of the answers provided by these components is correct.

14.3.4.1 Majority voting. In an m-out-of-N fault-tolerant software system, the number of versions is N (an N-tuple), and m is the *agreement number,* or the number of matching outputs which the adjudication algorithm (such as voting) requires for system success [Eckh85, Triv82, Siew92]. The value of N is rarely larger than 3. In general, in *majority voting,* $m = \lceil (N + 1)/2 \rceil$, where $\lceil \ \rceil$ denotes the ceiling function.

14.3.4.2 Two-out-of-*N* voting. It is shown in [Scot87] that, if the output space is large, and true statistical independence of variant failures can be assumed, there is no need to choose m larger than 2, regardless of the size of N. We use the term *2-out-of-N voting* for the case where agreement number is $m = 2$.

There is obviously a distinct difference between *agreement* and *correctness.* For example, a majority voter assumes that if a majority of the module outputs agree, then the majority output must be the correct output. This, however, can lead to fallacious results, particularly in the extreme case when the number of possible module outputs is very small. For example, suppose that the output of each module is a single variable that assumes the values of either 0 or 1. This means that all incorrect outputs automatically agree and it is very likely, if modules have faults, that there may be a majority of IAW outputs.

In general, there will be multiple output variables, each one assuming a number of values. The total number of allowed combinations of output variables and their values defines the number ρ of program output states, or the cardinality of the output space. If there are multiple correct outputs, then a simple voter is useless. Hence, when voting, we will assume that there is only one correct output for each input. From this it follows that, given output cardinality of ρ, we have one correct output state, and $\rho - 1$ error states.

In that context, mid-value selection (or simple *median voting*) is an interesting and simple adjudication alternative where the median of all output values is selected as the correct answer. The philosophy behind the approach is that, in addition to being fast, the algorithm can handle multiple correct answers (and for small samples is less biased than averaging, or mean value voting), and it is likely to pick a value that is at least in the correct range. This technique has been applied successfully in aerospace applications.

14.3.4.3 Consensus voting. A generalization of majority voting is *consensus voting* described in [McAl90]. In consensus voting the voter uses the following algorithm to select the *correct* answer:

- If there is a majority agreement ($m \geq \lceil (N+1)/2 \rceil$, $N > 1$), then this answer is chosen as the correct answer.
- Otherwise, if there is a unique maximum agreement, but this number of agreeing versions is less than $\lceil (N+1)/2 \rceil$, then this answer is chosen as the correct one.
- Otherwise, if there is a tie in the maximum agreement number from several output groups, then

  If consensus voting is used in N-version programming, one group is chosen at random and the answer associated with this group is chosen as the correct one.

  Else if consensus voting is used in consensus recovery block, all groups are subjected to an acceptance test, which is then used to choose the correct output.

The consensus voting strategy is particularly effective in small output spaces because it automatically adjusts the voting to the changes in the effective output space cardinality. It can be shown that, for $m \geq 2$, majority voting provides an upper bound on the probability of failing the system using consensus voting, and 2-out-of-N provides a lower bound [McAl90]. When the output space cardinality is 2, the strategy is equivalent to majority voting, and to 2-out-of-N voting when the output space cardinality tends to infinity, provided the agreement number is not less than 2. We provide experimental comparison of consensus and majority voting strategies in Sec. 14.7.

14.3.5 Tolerance

Closely related to voting is the issue of tolerance to which comparisons are made. Let TOL be the comparison tolerance, and consider an N-tuple of versions. The following two mutually exclusive events do *not* depend on whether the answers are correct.

- All N components agree on an answer. In this case we have an AGREEMENT event.

- There is at least one disagreement among the C_2^N comparisons of alternate outputs, where C_2^N denotes the number of combinations of N objects taken two at a time (2-tuples). We will call this case a CONFLICT event. All 2-tuples need to be evaluated because agreement may not be transitive, that is, $|a - b| \leq$ TOL and $|b - c| \leq$ TOL does not always imply that $|a - c| \leq$ TOL (see Fig. 14.2).

It is very important to realize that use of an inappropriate tolerance value, TOL, may either completely mask failure events (that is, too large a tolerance will always return AGREEMENT events) or cause an avalanche of CONFLICT events (the tolerance is too small and therefore many answer pairs fail the tolerance test). Assume that we have an oracle, so that we can tell the correctness of an answer. Note an oracle can take the form of an external consistency check (see Sec. 14.3.1.2). The following mutually exclusive events *depend on* the knowledge of the correctness of the output, or agreement with the correct answer:

- All N components agree with the *correct* (call it *golden*) answer. Then a NO_FAILURE event occurs.
- One or more of the versions disagree with the *correct* answer. Then a FAILURE event occurs.

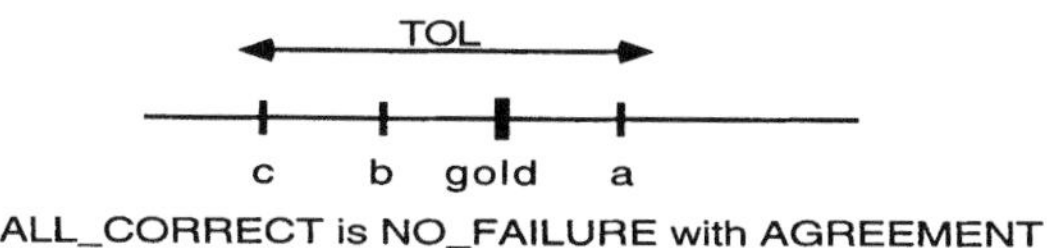

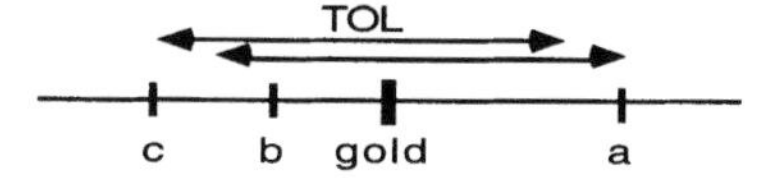

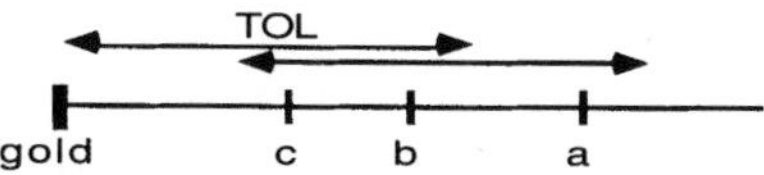

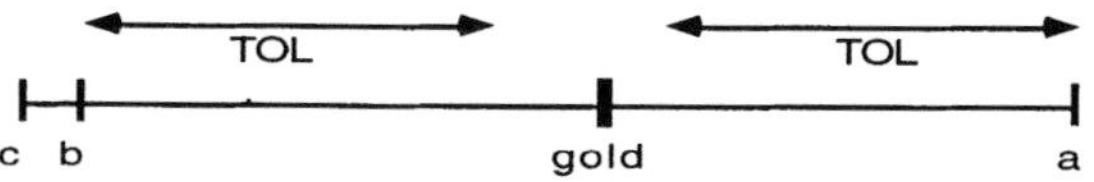

Figure 14.2 Illustration of comparison events.

Combinations of the above elementary events produce the following mutually exclusive and collectively exhaustive multiversion comparison events:

- *ALL_CORRECT event.* A NO_FAILURE occurs with an AGREEMENT.
- *FALSE_ALARM event.* A NO_FAILURE occurs with a CONFLICT. Comparison signals an error when one is not present, which may or may not lead to a failure of the adjudication algorithm. Recall that agreement is not transitive, so FALSE_ALARM events are not inconsistent.
- *DETECTED_FAILURE event.* A FAILURE occurs together with a CONFLICT. Comparison correctly detects a failure (fault).
- *UN_DETECTED_FAILURE event.* A FAILURE event occurs simultaneously with an AGREEMENT. This is the most significant event. A potential failure exists but is not detected by comparison.

Consider again Fig. 14.1, which shows responses from a hypothetical three-version system. A simplex failure occurs when only one of the three versions fails (unshaded regions). A doublet failure (2-tuple) occurs when two components fail coincidentally (light shading). A triplet failure, or 3-tuple failure, occurs when all three components fail coincidentally (dark shading). If the probability that any of the *shaded* areas exceed or do not achieve the probability of overlap expected by random chance, then the assumption of independence is violated [Triv82]. That is,

$$P\{\mathrm{p}_i \text{ fails } \textit{and } \mathrm{p}_j \text{ fails}\} \neq P\{\mathrm{p}_i \text{ fails}\}\, P\{\mathrm{p}_j \text{ fails}\} \qquad (i \neq j) \qquad (14.7)$$

or

$$P\{\mathrm{p}_1 \text{ fails } \textit{and } \mathrm{p}_2 \text{ fails } \textit{and } \mathrm{p}_3 \text{ fails}\} \neq P\{\mathrm{p}_1 \text{ fails}\}\, P\{\mathrm{p}_2 \text{ fails}\}\, P\{\mathrm{p}_3 \text{ fails}\} \qquad (14.8)$$

where p_i is the ith software variant. The most undesirable state of the system, UN_DETECTED_FAILURE, occurs when the responses from three coincidentally failing versions are identical, in which case mutual comparison of these answers does not signal that a failure has occurred.

Figure 14.2 provides an illustration of the events that may result from comparison to tolerance TOL of floating-point outputs a, b, and c, from hypothetical programs p_1, p_2, and p_3, respectively. Additional examples are found in Prob. 14.5.

It is important to remember that excessively small tolerances may produce an excessive incidence of FALSE_ALARM events which may increase testing costs [Vouk88], while in operation this may result in degraded system operation or even a critical system failure.

14.4 Basic Techniques

Two common fault-tolerant software schemes are the N-version programming [Aviz77, Aviz85] and the recovery block [Rand75]. Both schemes are based on software component redundancy and the assumption that coincident failures of components are rare, and when they do occur responses are sufficiently dissimilar that the mechanism for deciding answer correctness is not ambiguous.

Fault-tolerant software mechanisms based on redundancy are particularly well suited for parallel processing environments where concurrent execution of redundant components may drastically improve sometimes prohibitive costs associated with their serial execution [Vouk90b, Bell90, Lapr90a]. Some hybrid techniques, such as consensus recovery block [Scot83, Scot87], checkpoints [Aviz77], community error recovery [Tso86, Tso87], N-version programming variants [Lapr90a, Tai93], and some partial fault-tolerance approaches are also available [Hech79, Stri85, Mili90].

14.4.1 Recovery blocks

One of the earliest fault-tolerant software schemes that used the multiversion software approach is the *recovery block* (RB) [Rand75, Deb86]. The adjudication module is an *acceptance test* (AT). The process begins when the output of the first module is tested for acceptability. If the acceptance test determines that the output of the first module is not acceptable, it restores, recovers, or "rolls back" the state of the system before the first or primary module was executed. It then allows the second module to execute and evaluates its output, etc. If all modules execute and none produce acceptable outputs, then the system fails. Figure 14.3 illustrates the technique.

One problem with this strategy in a uniprocessor environment is the sequential nature of the execution of versions [Lapr90a, Bell91], although in a distributed environment the modules and the acceptance tests can be executed in parallel. Distributed recovery block is discussed in detail in [Kim89, Lyu95a]. Another potential problem is finding a simple and highly reliable acceptance test which does not involve the development of an additional software version.

The form of acceptance test depends on the application. As suggested in Fig. 14.3, there may be a different acceptance test for each module,

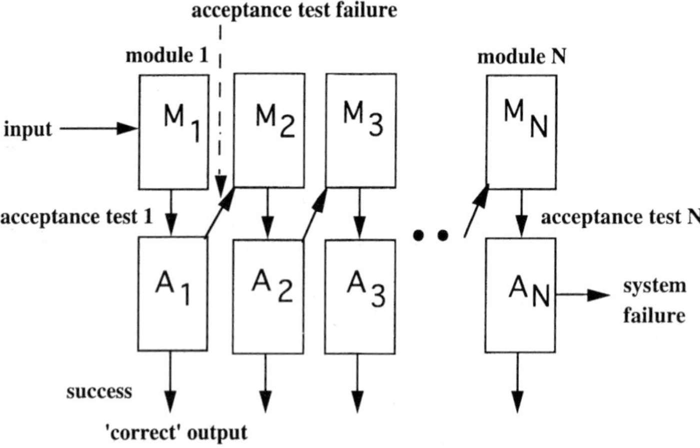

Figure 14.3 Recovery blocks.

but in practice only one is usually used. An extreme case of an acceptance test is another complete module, and the acceptance test would then consist of a comparison of a given module output with the one computed by the acceptance test. This would be equivalent to a staged two-version programming scheme (see the following section) where one of the outputs in each stage was always from the same version (the acceptance test).

14.4.2 N-version programming

N-version programming (NVP) [Aviz77, Chen78, Aviz85] proposes parallel execution of N independently developed functionally equivalent versions with adjudication of their outputs by a voter. N-version programming or multiversion programming (MVP) is a software generalization of the N-modular-redundancy (NMR) approach used in hardware fault tolerance [Nels87]. The N versions produce outputs to the adjudicator, which in this case is a *voter.* The voter accepts all N outputs as inputs and uses these to determine the correct, or best, output if one exists. There is usually no need to interrupt the service while the voting takes place. Figure 14.4 illustrates the technique. We note that the approach can also be used to help during testing to debug the versions. This method, called *back-to-back testing,* is discussed further in Sec. 14.8.2.

Over the years simple majority-voting-based N-version fault-tolerant software has been investigated by a number of researchers, both theoretically [Aviz77, Grna80, Eckh85, Scot87, Deb88, Litt89, Voge87a, Kano93a, Lyu95a] and experimentally [Scot84a, Scot84b, Bish86,

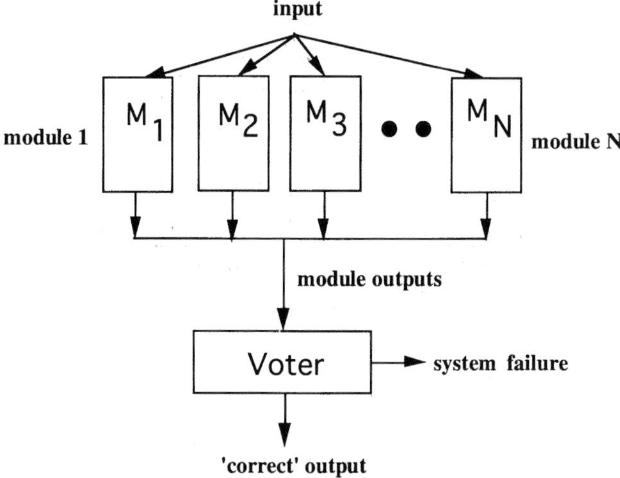

Figure 14.4 N-version programming.

Knig86, Shim88, Eckh91, Lyu93a, Duga93b, Vouk93a]. A reasonable alternative to majority voting could be to use consensus voting, described earlier. Another simple variation is *median voting.*

There are variants of the above architecture for distributed systems, some of which are further discussed in Chap. 15. One such variant is the *N self-checking programming* (NSCP), discussed below.

14.5 Advanced Techniques

There are ways to combine the preceding simple techniques to create hybrid techniques. Studies of more advanced models such as consensus recovery block [Bell90, Scot87, Deb88, Scot84a], consensus voting [McAl90], or acceptance voting [Bell90, Atha89, Gant91, Gers91] are less frequent and mostly theoretical in nature.

14.5.1 Consensus recovery block

In [Scot83] and [Scot87] a hybrid system called *consensus recovery block* (CRB) was suggested. It combines NVP and RB in that order. If NVP fails the system reverts to RB using the same modules (the same module results can be used, or modules may be rerun if a transient failure is suspected). Only in the case that NVP and RB both fail does the system fail. A system block diagram is given in Fig. 14.5 where the block RB means that an acceptance test is applied to the outputs of the variants in the NVP block. CRB was originally proposed to treat

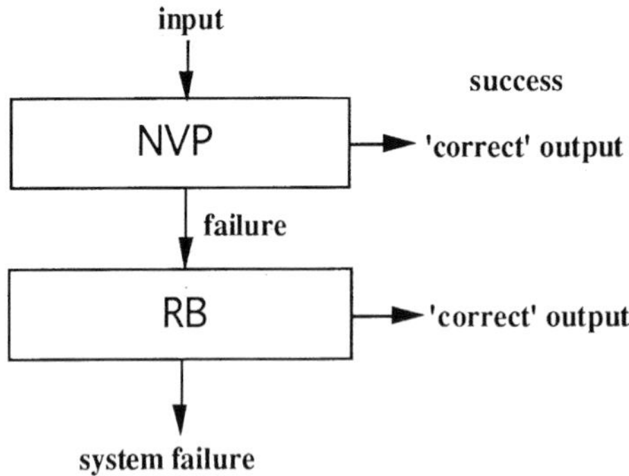

Figure 14.5 Consensus recovery block.

the case of multiple correct outputs, since appropriate acceptance testing can avoid that issue.

14.5.2 Acceptance voting

The converse of the above CRB hybrid scheme, which we call *acceptance voting* (AV), was proposed by [Atha89, Gant91, Bell91]. As in NVP, all modules can execute in parallel. The output of each module is then presented to an acceptance test. If the acceptance test accepts the output it is then passed to a voter. The system is shown in Fig. 14.6.

The voter sees only those outputs which have been passed by the acceptance test. This implies that the voter may not process the same number of outputs at each invocation and hence the voting algorithm must be dynamic. The system fails if no outputs are submitted to the voter. If only one output is submitted, the voter must assume it to be correct, and therefore passes it to the next stage. Only if two or more outputs agree can the voter be used to make a decision. We then apply dynamic majority voting (DMV) or dynamic consensus voting (DCV). The difference between DMV and MV is that even if a small number of results are passed to the voter, dynamic voting will try to find the majority among them. The concept is similar for DCV and CV.

14.5.3 N self-checking programming

A variant of the N-version programming with recovery, that is, N self-checking programming, is used in the Airbus A310 system [Lapr90a, Duga93b]. In NSCP, N modules are executed in pairs (for an even N) [Lapr90a]. The outputs from the modules can be compared, or can be assessed for correctness in some other manner. Let us assume that comparison is used. Then the outputs of each pair are tested and if they do not agree with each other, the response of the pair is dis-

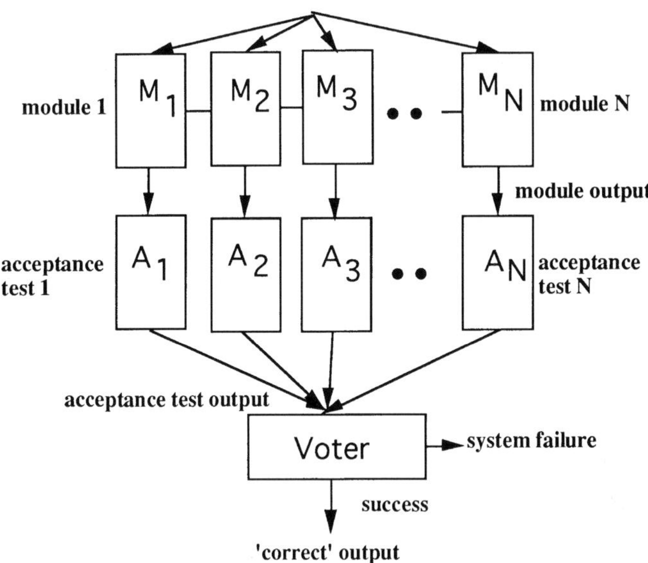

Figure 14.6 Acceptance voting.

carded. If the outputs of both pairs agree, then these outputs are compared again. Failure occurs if both pairs disagree, or the pairs agree but produce different outputs. The technique is shown in Fig. 14.7 for $N = 4$.

If a comparison of the outputs of the first pair of modules, M_1 and M_2, is successful, then the output is passed to the next phase of the computation and the system is successful. If these two outputs disagree, then a comparison of the outputs of the second pair of modules, M_3 and M_4, is made. If the outputs of the second pair agree, then the output is passed to the next phase. Otherwise the system fails. There is no attempt to compare the four outputs simultaneously. We leave an analysis of the reliability of the system as exercise.

14.6 Reliability Modeling

Although existing fault-tolerant software (FTS) techniques can achieve a significant improvement over non-fault-tolerant software, they may not be sufficient for ensuring adequate reliability of critical systems. For example, experiments show that incidence of correlated failures of FTS system components may not be negligible in the context of current software development and testing techniques, and this may result in a disaster [Scot84a, Vouk85, Eckh85, Knig86, Kell86, Kell88, Eckh91]. Obviously, it is important to detect and eliminate faults causing dependent failures as early as possible in the FTS life cycle and to develop

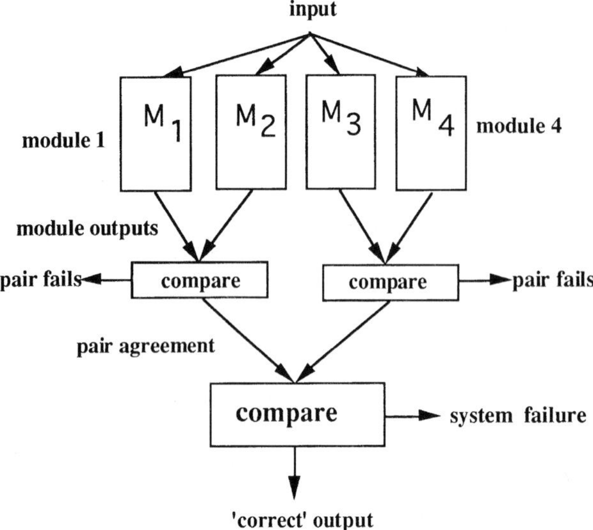

Figure 14.7 NSCP for $N = 4$.

FTS mechanisms that can adequately cope with any remaining faults. Modeling of different FTS mechanisms gives insight into their behavior and allows quantification of their relative merits.

14.6.1 Diversity and dependence of failures

Intuition suggests that the modules which are used to compose a multiversion fault-tolerant system should be as diverse as possible. Software reliability cannot be improved by using similar versions in a multiversion system. The issue is how to quantify diversity in versions and which techniques can be used to encourage the diversity [Lyu94a].

We first distinguish between specific inputs and programs versus randomly chosen inputs and programs. Hence, suppose a countable collection of program versions PV = $\{p_1, p_2, \ldots\}$ have been independently developed, and assume, for generality, that the probability of selecting one of the programs from PV is governed by the random variable Π with density function S. That is, $S(\mathrm{p})$ is the probability that p is chosen from PV or that $\Pi = \mathrm{p}$. Also assume that the possible set of inputs is $\mathbf{X} = \{x_1, x_2, x_3, x_4, \ldots\}$ and that the probability that an arbitrarily chosen input $X = x$ is the value of the density function Q, $Q(x)$. Let υ be the bivariate *score* function υ defined by

$$\upsilon(\mathrm{p}_i, x_j) = 1 \qquad \text{if program } \mathrm{p}_i \text{ fails on input } x_j \tag{14.9}$$
$$= 0 \qquad \text{otherwise}$$

The value $\upsilon(\mathrm{p}_i, x_j)$ is the probability that the specific program p_i fails on the specific input x_j. Let us first calculate the probability that an arbitrary program Π fails on a given input x:

$$P\{\Pi \text{ fails on } x\} = \sum_{\mathrm{PV}} \upsilon(\mathrm{p},x)P\{\Pi = \mathrm{p}\}$$

$$= \sum_{\mathrm{PV}} \upsilon(\mathrm{p},x)S(\mathrm{p}) \qquad (14.10)$$

$$=: \theta(x)$$

The function θ is the *intensity function* defined in [Eckh85]. Similarly, we can define the probability that a specific program p fails on an arbitrary input X [Litt89]:

$$P\{\mathrm{p} \text{ fails on } X\} = \sum_{X} \upsilon(\mathrm{p},x)P\{X = x\}$$

$$= \sum_{X} \upsilon(\mathrm{p},x)Q(x) \qquad (14.11)$$

$$= \phi(\mathrm{p})$$

Correspondingly, we can also define the probability that an arbitrary program Π fails on an arbitrary input X. Because of the duality of the previous two probabilities we can define the random variable $\theta(X) = \Theta$, or the random variable $\phi(\Pi) = \Phi$ and take their expected values ($E[\,]$) over the appropriate domain:

$$P\{\Pi \text{ fails on } X\} = E[\Theta] = E[\Phi]$$

$$= \sum_{\mathrm{PV}} \sum_{X} \upsilon(\mathrm{p},x)S(\mathrm{p})Q(x) \qquad (14.12)$$

We now wish to compute the probability that *two* randomly chosen programs fail on a single randomly chosen input X. This probability becomes

$$P\{\Pi_1 \text{ fails on } X \text{ and } \Pi_2 \text{ fails on } X\}$$

$$= \sum_{X} \sum_{\mathrm{PV}} \sum_{\mathrm{PV}} \upsilon(\mathrm{p}_1,x)\upsilon(\mathrm{p}_2,x)S(\mathrm{p}_1)S(\mathrm{p}_2)Q(x)$$

$$= \sum_{X} (\theta(x))^2 Q(x) = E[\Theta^2] \qquad (14.13)$$

$$= \sigma_{\Theta}^{\ 2} + E^2[\Theta]$$

where σ_Θ^2 is the variance of the random variable Θ. The variance is zero if and only if $\theta(x)$ is equal to its expected value for all x, that is, θ must be a constant for two random programs to fail independently on a random input!

However, we are interested in specific programs failing on random inputs. The probability that two specific programs, p_1 and p_2, fail on an arbitrary input X (i.e., the probability that p_1 and p_2 have coincident failures) is

$$P\{p_1 \text{ fails on } X \text{ and } p_2 \text{ fails on } X\} = \sum_X v(p_1,x)v(p_2,x)Q(x) \qquad (14.14)$$

If the failures were independent then this product should be equal to $P\{p_1 \text{ fails on } X\}P\{p_2 \text{ fails on } X\}$. We leave it as an exercise to show that the latter product can underestimate *or* overestimate joint failure depending on the amount of overlap of the input failure sets of the two programs p_1 and p_2. As you would expect, in practice, we wish for the failure input sets to be disjoint to minimize the probability of coincident failures. If this is the case, the independence assumption overestimates the probability of joint failure.

Scott and his colleagues [Scot84b] were first to show, using an experiment, that programs may not fail independently, and they developed models to treat this case. Their results were later corroborated by other experimenters. Unfortunately, the models developed to treat the general case become quite complicated and intractable as the number of versions increases, since joint failure probabilities must be estimated. A set of experimental data related to failure correlation is discussed later in this chapter. For a more general treatment of the correlation issue, you should consult the works by [Scot84a, Eckh85, Litt89].

Originally, the definition of reliability involved the behavior of hardware over time. We are also interested in software behavior over time as faults are identified and repaired. In critical systems, however, we are interested also in the behavior of redundant modules for each input and we wish to know the probability that a software-fault-tolerant system will produce the correct answer. This motivates the approach called *data-domain reliability modeling* [Ande81]. We can then use this and other information, as well as techniques such as Markov modeling and Petri nets, to determine such standard parameters as mean time to failure, etc. The latter is part of the time-domain analysis. Time-domain analysis is concerned with the behavior of FTS systems over a mission (or time period) within which reliability of individual components may or may not change. It is discussed very briefly later in this section and, for example, in [Kano93a].

The *reliability* of a module is the probability it will produce the correct output (assuming the input is correct) where inputs are taken from the operational input domain with density function Q. Since Q is rarely known, it is usually assumed to be uniformly distributed or random. Normally, the *reliability* of a module is estimated from testing and is a function of the number of test cases that have been presented.

Let f_i denote the probability that module p_i fails (on an arbitrary input):

$$f_i = P\{\text{module } \mathrm{p}_i \text{ fails}\} = \sum v(\mathrm{p}_i, x)Q(x) \tag{14.15}$$

An estimate of the failure probability, $\hat{f}_i$, is the number of failures observed in presenting random inputs to a module based on the operational input distribution. That is, if k is the number of failures in n random inputs, then

$$\hat{f}_i = \frac{k}{n} \tag{14.16}$$

We leave it to the reader to estimate the variance of this estimate. We will assume that we have a nonzero value for $\hat{f}_i$ in the discussion below. In the independent case, the reliability of module i, that is, the probability that it will not fail, is estimated as

$$\hat{r}_i = 1 - P\{\text{module } i \text{ fails}\} = 1 - \hat{f}_i \tag{14.17}$$

14.6.2 Data-domain modeling

The following data-domain analysis examples are intended to illustrate two things: (1) how to construct models by first defining *events* of interest and the associated probabilities, and then combining them into a reliability estimate, and (2) provide insight into the relative merits of different fault-tolerance strategies.

For tractability, the analyses are made using the *assumption* that intervariant failure events are independent, i.e., the failures of specific programs on random inputs are independent of each other. Although this abstraction simplifies the modeling and provides insight into the relative behavior of different FTS strategies, it does not always provide a realistic result for real-life situations where common-cause faults and correlated coincident failures are present. For analyses that incorporate different interversion failure correlation assumptions, the reader is directed to works of [Eckh85, Litt89, Nico90, Tai93, Kano93a, Tome93, Duga94c, Duga95, Lyu95a].

We restrict our examples to $N = 3$, and we leave it as exercises to analyze the systems for other values of N. We also leave it to the reader to construct solutions for more complex mechanisms (e.g., AV and CRB, see Probs. 14.18 and 14.19). In this context, let r_1, r_2, and r_3 be the reliabilities of each version of a three-version fault-tolerant system. Let B be the reliability of the acceptance test in RB; let R_V be the reliability of the voter in NVP; and let S denote the system reliability.

Recovery block. In RB, to simplify analysis, we assume that the (conditional) probability, β, of rejecting a correct answer is equal to the probability of accepting an incorrect one, that is $\beta = (1 - B)$. Then the system success depends on at least one module producing correct output and the acceptance test recognizing that it is correct. We can partition the event space by the number of the module which produces the correct output that is also accepted by the AT. We will assume that the state of the system is always recovered without error. Let the three-version RB be denoted by RB3.

1. The first event is that the primary module is correct and the AT accepts the output. The probability of this event is r_1B.
2. The second event is that the output of the first module is rejected and the output of the second module is correct and accepted. This event has two possible outcomes: the first module can be incorrect and the AT appropriately rejects it, or the first module can be correct but the output is rejected by the AT. Hence, the probability of the second event is $(1 - r_1)\,B\,r_2\,B + r_1\,(1 - B)\,r_2\,B$.
3. Similarly, for the third event, if the third module produces the correct output, then the output of modules 1 and 2 were rejected by the AT. This can happen in one of four ways:
   a. Module 1 output is incorrect and the AT correctly rejects it, module 2 output is incorrect and the AT correctly rejects it, and module 3 is correct and the AT accepts it.
   b. Module 1 output is correct but the AT rejects it, module 2 output is incorrect and the AT correctly rejects it, and module 3 output is correct and the AT correctly accepts it.
   Cases *c* and *d* are similar.

Rearranging and simplifying the sum of these probabilities yields a system reliability of

$$S_{\text{RB3}}(r_1, r_2, r_3, B) = B(r_1 + r_1r_2 + r_1r_2r_3 + r_2B - 2r_1r_2B + r_1r_3B + r_2r_3B - 4r_1r_2r_3B + r_3B^2 - 2r_1r_3B^2 - 2r_2r_3B^2 + 4r_1r_2r_3B^2 \tag{14.18}$$

If we assume that all versions have the same reliability, r, we have

$$S_{\text{RB3}}(r, r, r, B) = B\,r\,(1 + B + B^2 + r + r^2 - 4r^2B - 4rB^2 + 4r^2B^2) \tag{14.19}$$

If, in addition, we assume $B = 1$, that is, ideal operation of the acceptance testing algorithm, Eq. (14.19) reduces to

$$S_{\mathrm{RB3}}(r, r, r, 1) = 3\, r\, (1 - r) + r^3 \tag{14.20}$$

The surface plot of RB3 system reliability as a function of B and r is shown in Fig. 14.8.

N-version programming. The reliability of a three-version NVP system is the probability that at least two modules produce correct output and that the voter is correct. The probability that at least two modules are correct is the probability that modules 1 and 2 are correct and module 3 fails, or modules 1 and 3 are correct and module 2 fails, or modules 2 and 3 are correct and module 1 fails, or that all three are correct. Under our assumptions, this probability is

$$r_1 r_2(1 - r_3) + r_1 r_3(1 - r_2) + r_2 r_3(1 - r_1) + r_1 r_2 r_3 \tag{14.21}$$

Hence, if we assume voter failure is also independent of module failure, the system reliability $S_{\mathrm{NVP3}}(r_1, r_2, r_3, R_V)$, of a three-version NVP fault-tolerant system becomes

$$S_{\mathrm{NVP3}}(r_1, r_2, r_3, R_V) = R_V\,(r_1 r_2 + r_1 r_3 + r_2 r_3 - 2 r_1 r_2 r_3) \tag{14.22}$$

In practice we would expect that all units that comprise an FTS system will have been tested to the point where there are *no known* residual faults. This may or may not mean that they have very similar reliability, but it may be a reasonable assumption. Hence, an interesting special case is the one where all functionally equivalent versions are assumed to have equal, and very high, lower bounds on their relia-

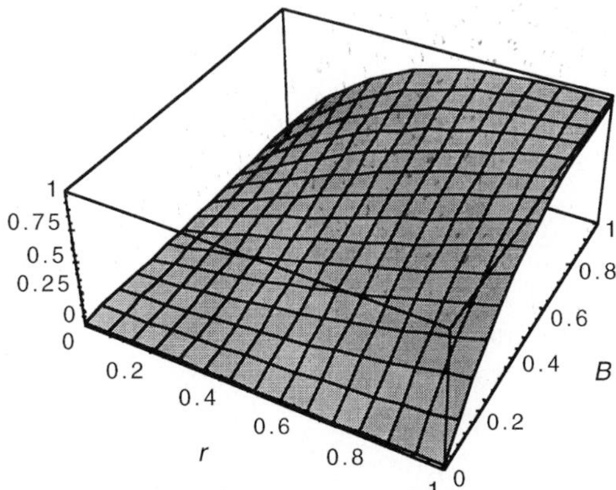

Figure 14.8 S_{RB3} as functions of r and B.

bility. Individual version reliability estimates must be obtained independently using, for example, appropriate reliability growth models.

Let all versions have the same estimated reliability r. Then the probability that an NVP system will operate successfully (assuming a perfect voter) under majority voting strategy is given by the following expression (e.g., [Grna80, Triv82, Nels87]):

$$S_{\mathrm{NVP3}}(r_1 = r_2 = \ldots = r_n = r, R_V) = R_V \sum_{i=m}^{n} C_i^n r^i (1-r)^{n-i} \tag{14.23}$$

where summation starts with the lower bound on required agreement number.

Equation (14.23) can be used to show that majority voting increases reliability over a single version only if the reliability of the versions is larger than 0.5 and the voter is perfect. If the output space has cardinality ρ, then N-version programming will result in a system that is more reliable than a single component only if $r > 1/\rho$ [McAl90].* We call this value the *boundary version reliability*. It is the generalization of the classical N-modular redundancy rule for a binary output space where $r > 0.5$, and it applies in the case of consensus voting. Note that, when a version fails and we let the probability of occurrence of any incorrect output be q, then, in the simplest situation, $q = (1 - r)/(\rho - 1)$.

In Fig. 14.9 we show the classical majority voting approach with a binary output space (boundary version reliability of $1/\rho = 0.5$). We see that the version reliability must be larger than the boundary version reliability in order to improve the performance of the system when more versions are added.

Figure 14.10 shows the effect of version reliability and the number of versions under consensus voting strategy. The minimal agreement number is $m = \lfloor (n + \rho - 1)/\rho \rfloor = \lfloor (n + 2)/3 \rfloor$, where $\lfloor \ \rfloor$ denotes the floor function. The average boundary reliability of the versions is $1/\rho = 1/3$. All versions are assumed to have the same reliability, and all failure states ($j = 2,3$) the same probability $(1 - q)/(1 - \rho) = (1 - q)/2$ of being excited.

If all versions have the same reliability we have

$$S_{\mathrm{NVP3}}(r, r, r, R_V) = R_V(3r^2 - 2r^3) \tag{14.24}$$

We note that S_{NVP3} is bounded by R_V. Hence, if $R_V \leq r$, then one should opt to invest software development time on a single version rather than develop a three-version NVP system.

* Additional assumptions: all components fail independently; they have the same reliability r; correct outputs are unique; and the voter is perfect.

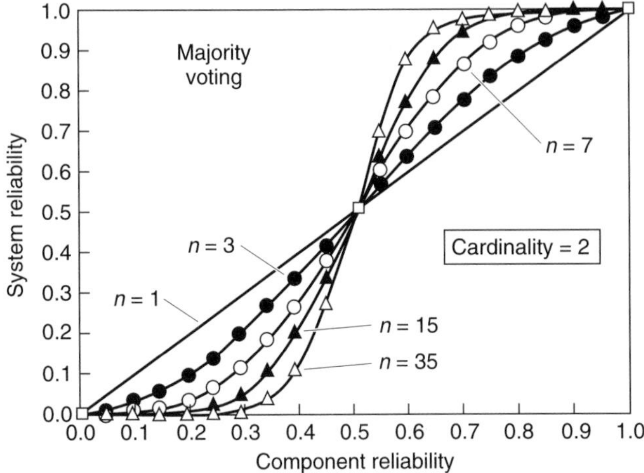

Figure 14.9 System reliability versus component reliability for majority voting strategy. Number of components used for voting is n, the agreement number is m, $\rho = 2$, and boundary version reliability is $1/\rho = 0.5$.

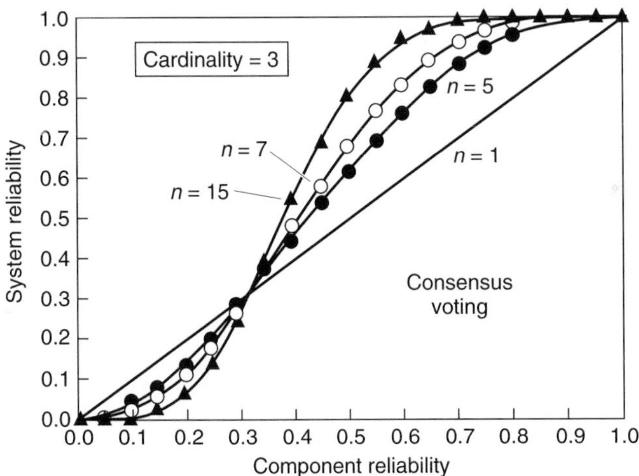

Figure 14.10 System reliability versus component reliability for the consensus voting strategy. The number of voting components is n, all are equally reliable, the agreement number is m, $\rho = 3$, and the boundary version reliability is $1/\rho = 0.3333$.

It is interesting to compare an RB3 with perfect acceptance test to an NVP3 system with perfect voter. This is done in Fig. 14.11. We see that under the assumption of failure independence, the RB system is a better solution than a majority-voting three-version system. However, note that it may be far easier to ensure very high reliability of the voting software than to devise and implement an acceptance test with no faults.

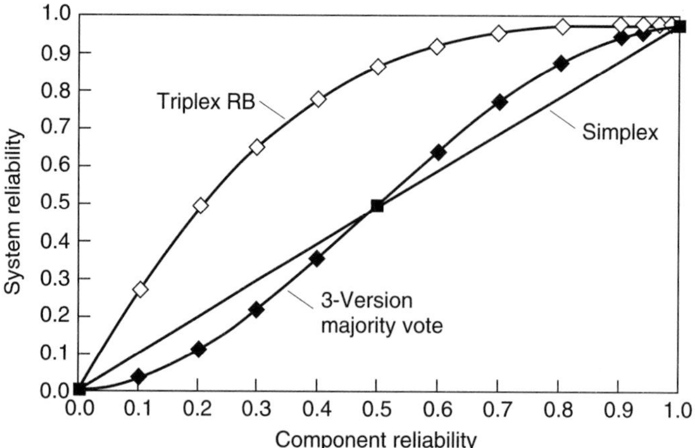

Figure 14.11 Comparison of N-version and recovery block schemes for $n = 3$. Both voter and acceptance test are assumed to be perfect.

This is confirmed by the work of Kanoun et al. [Kano93a]. They have shown that the impact of *independent* faults is much higher in the case of NVP than in the case of RB because the versions are run in parallel. They also concluded that the impact of common-cause faults will likely be higher in the case of RB than in the case of NVP because very reliable acceptance tests may be difficult to construct. The results shown in Sec. 14.7 confirm this. We note the more substantial impact of faults on NVP when reliability of individual components is low, and the better performance of NVP when reliability of components is higher but RB acceptance test is failure prone. In the case of RB, common-cause faults include *similar* or *related* faults among RB alternates and the acceptance test, as well as *independent faults* in the acceptance test. In the case of NVP, common-cause faults are similar or *related* faults among components and the voter, as well as *independent* faults in the voter.

14.6.3 Time-domain modeling

Time-domain analysis is concerned with the behavior of system reliability over time. For example, during software debugging and testing we would expect the reliability of the components (e.g., [Musa87]) and the system (e.g., [Kano93a]) to grow. On the other hand, during operation without repair, the reliability of a component remains constant. In the time-domain, reliability can be defined as the probability that a system will complete its mission, or operate through a certain period of time, without failing.

The simplest time-dependent failure model assumes that failures arrive randomly with interarrival times exponentially distributed with expected value λ. Hence, the probability that a module will produce the correct output decreases over time since it receives a larger number of inputs, and we have

$$r(t) = e^{-\lambda t} \tag{14.25}$$

During operation it is often assumed that the *failure* or *hazard rate* λ is constant; however, during reliability growth or reliability decay periods the failure rate is itself a function of time, and then the expression that describes r becomes more complex (e.g., [Musa87, Kano93a]).

Time-dependent behavior of components can have significant impact on the operation of a fault-tolerant system. Therefore, it is important that practical fault-tolerant systems are analyzed not only with respect to their data-domain characteristics, but also with respect to their time-domain characteristics (e.g., [Grna80, Triv82, Deb86, Deb88, Arla90, Lapr90a, Siew92, Tai93, Kano93a]).

To illustrate, consider the following. Assuming that Eq. (14.25) holds, that λ is fixed, and that $R_V = 1$, Eq. (14.24) can be modified to yield

$$S_{\text{NVP3}}(r, r, r, 1, t) = 3e^{-2\lambda t} - 2e^{-3\lambda t} \tag{14.26}$$

This system has an interesting property. If we plot $S_{\text{NVP3}}(r, r, r, 1, t)$ and $r(t)$ against time, we find that the two curves cross when $t = t_0 = \ln 2/\lambda \approx 0.7/\lambda$ [Triv82, Siew92]. For $t \le t_0$ the system is more reliable than a single version, but during longer missions, $t > t_0$, NVP3 fault tolerance may actually degrade reliability.

Of course, the above is just an illustration of a very special case. Usually, the problem is far more complex, and a complete analysis, including failure correlation effects and hardware issues, is essential (see Chap. 15 and [Grna80, Tome93, Kim89, Lyu95a, Duga95]). For example, Tomek et al. have modeled RB with failure correlation and have analyzed the time-dependent behavior of RB reliability in considerable detail [Tome93]. Another example is the work of Kanoun et al. [Kano93a], who have modeled reliability growth of individual components using the hyperexponential model [Lapr90b], and have analyzed the impact this has on reliability of NVP and RB models. As mentioned earlier, they have found that NVP is far more sensitive to the removal of independent faults than RB because of the parallel nature of the NVP execution and decision making (voting).

On the other hand, if similar or related faults are present they are likely to have a larger impact on RB performance because acceptance tests tend to be more complex and more correlated to the actual application-specific nature of the components than simple voting comparisons. Hence, removal of similar or related faults and faults in decision nodes will probably produce more substantial reliability gains in the case of RB than in the case of NVP.

14.7 Reliability in the Presence of Interversion Failure Correlation

Experiments have shown that interversion failure dependence among independently developed functionally equivalent versions may not be negligible in the context of current software development and testing strategies [Scot84a, Scot84b, Vouk85, Knig86, Eckh91, Gers91]. There are theoretical models of FTS reliability which incorporate interversion failure dependence in different ways (e.g., [Eckh85, Litt89, Nico90, Tai93, Duga94c]). Coincident failures can be treated as resulting from statistically correlated faults (e.g., [Eckh85, Nico90]) or as deriving from *related* or *similar* faults that cause IAW results, and from unrelated or independent software faults that cause *dissimilar* but wrong results (e.g., [Lapr90a, Duga94c]). Furthermore, the related and unrelated software faults can be assumed to behave in a statistically independent [Duga94c], mutually exclusive [Lapr90a], or some other manner. However, many models assume interversion failure independence as well as failure independence of acceptance tests and voters with respect to versions and each other.

In this section we illustrate the effects that can be observed in an FTS systems under severe failure correlation conditions. We compare several experimental implementations of consensus recovery block and consensus voting with more traditional schemes, such as N-version programming with majority voting. The data derived from the experimental study is described in [Vouk93a].

14.7.1 An experiment

Experimental results based on a pool of functionally equivalent programs developed in a large-scale multiversion software experiment are described in several papers [Kell88, Vouk90a, Eckh91, Vouk93a]. Twenty versions of an avionics application were developed by 20 two-member development teams working independently at four universities. The versions were written in Pascal and ranged in size between 2000 and 5000 lines of code.

The results discussed here are for the program versions in the state they were in immediately after the unit development phase, but *before* they underwent an independent validation phase (in real situations, versions would be rigorously validated before operation). This was done (1) to keep the failure probabilities of individual versions relatively high and easier to observe and (2) to retain a considerable number of faults that exhibit mutual failure correlation in order to highlight correlation-based effects. The nature of the faults found in the versions is discussed in detail in two papers [Vouk90a, Eckh91].

Two subsets of N programs (called *N-tuples*) were generated: those with similar average* N-tuple reliability and those that have reliability within a particular range. The average N-tuple reliability is used to focus on the behavior of a particular N-tuple instead of the population (pool) from which it was drawn.

In the experiment a number of input profiles, different combinations of versions, and different output variables were considered. Failure probability estimates, based on the three most critical output variables (out of 63 monitored), are shown in Table 14.1. The variables are of type *real,* and each has a very large output space.

Two test suites, each containing 500 uniform random-input test cases, were used in all estimates. The sample size is sufficient for the version and N-tuple reliability ranges reported here. One suite, called Estimate I, was used to (1) estimate individual version failure probabilities, (2) N-tuple reliability, (3) select acceptance test versions, (4) select sample N-tuple combinations, and (5) compute expected independent model response. The other test suite, Estimate II, was used to investigate the actual behavior of N-tuple systems, based on different voting and fault-tolerance strategies.

For recovery block and consensus recovery block, one version was used as an acceptance test. This provided correlation not only among versions, but also between the acceptance test and the versions. Acceptance test versions were selected first, then N-tuples were drawn from the subpool of remaining versions. The voter (comparator) was assumed to be perfect.

The fault-tolerant algorithms of interest were invoked for each test case. The outcome was compared with the correct answer obtained

---

* Average N-tuple reliability estimate is defined as

$$\bar{p} = \sum_{i=1}^{N} \frac{\hat{p}_i}{N}$$

and the corresponding estimate of the standard deviation of the sample as

$$\hat{\sigma} = \sqrt{\sum_{i=1}^{N} \frac{(\bar{p} - \hat{p}_i)^2}{N-1}}$$

where

$$\hat{p}_i = \sum_{j=1}^{k} \frac{s_i(j)}{k}$$

is estimated reliability of version i over the test suite composed of k test cases, $s_i(j)$ is a score function equal to 1 when version i succeeds and 0 when it fails on test case j, and $1 - \hat{p}_i$ is the estimated version failure probability.

TABLE 14.1 Estimated Version Failure Probabilities ($\hat{f}_i$)

Version	Failure rate*	
	Estimate I	Estimate II
1	0.58	0.59
2	0.07	0.07
3	0.13	0.11
4	0.07	0.06
5	0.11	0.10
6	0.63	0.64
7	0.07	0.06
8	0.35	0.36
9	0.40	0.39
10	0.004	0.000
11	0.09	0.10
12	0.58	0.59
13	0.12	0.12
14	0.37	0.38
15	0.58	0.59
16	0.58	0.59
17	0.10	0.09
18	0.004	0.006
19	0.58	0.59
20	0.34	0.33

* Based on three most important output variables. Each column was obtained on the basis of a separate set of 500 random test cases.

from a "golden" program [Aviz77, Vouk90a], and the frequency of successes and failures for each strategy was recorded.

14.7.2 Failure correlation

The failure correlation properties of the versions can be deduced from their joint coincident failure profiles, and from the corresponding *identical-and-wrong* response profiles. For example, Tables 14.2 and 14.3 show the profiles for a 17-version subset (three versions selected to act as acceptance tests are not in the set). In Table 14.2 we show the number of versions that fail coincidentally, and the corresponding number of occurrences of the event over the 500 samples. Also shown is the expected number of occurrences for the model based on independent failures, or the binomial model [Triv82].

For instance, inspection of Table 14.2 shows that the number of occurrences of the event where nine versions fail coincidentally is expected to be about 8. In reality, we observed about 100 such events. Table 14.3 summarizes the corresponding occurrences of *identical-and-wrong* coincident responses. For example, in 500 tries there were 15 events where eight versions coincidentally returned an answer which

TABLE 14.2 Frequency Data for a 17-Version Set

No. of versions that failed together	0	1	2	3	4	5	6	7	8	9	10	11	12	13	14	15	16	17
Frequency	168	13	28	0	0	0	75	31	14	105	15	17	0	18	15	1	0	0
Model	0	4	18	52	96	121	106	65	28	8	2	0	0	0	0	0	0	0

TABLE 14.3 Frequency of Empirical IAW Events Over 500 Test Cases for a 17-Version Set

No. of versions that coincidentally returned an IAW answer	1	2	3	4	5	6	7	8	9	10	11	12	13	14	15	16	17
Frequency	2049	164	1	16	1	1	2	15	0	0	0	0	0	0	0	0	0

was wrong yet identical within the tolerance used to compare the three most critical (real) variables. These results are strong indicators of a high degree of interversion failure dependence in this version set.

14.7.3 Consensus voting

Figures 14.12 and 14.13 illustrate the observed relationship between N-version programming with consensus voting and with majority voting. The figures show success frequency for three-version and seven-version systems over a range of average N-tuple reliability assuming perfect voting. The ragged look of the experimental traces is partly due to the small sample (500 test cases), and partly due to the presence of very highly correlated failures. The experimental behavior is in good agreement with the trends indicated by the theoretical consensus voting model based on failure independence [McAl90, Vouk93a].

For instance, we see that for $N = 3$ and low average N-tuple reliability, N-version programming has difficulty competing with the best version. Note that the *best version* was not preselected based on Estimate I data. Instead, it is the N-tuple version which exhibits the smallest number of failures during the actual evaluation run (Estimate II). The reason N-version programming has difficulty competing with the best version is that the selected N-tuples of low average reliability are composed of versions which are not balanced, that is, their reliability is very different, and therefore variance of the average N-tuple reliability is large. As average N-tuple reliability increases, N-version programming performance approaches or exceeds that of the best version. In part, this is because N-tuples become more balanced, since the number of higher-reliability versions in the subpool from which versions are

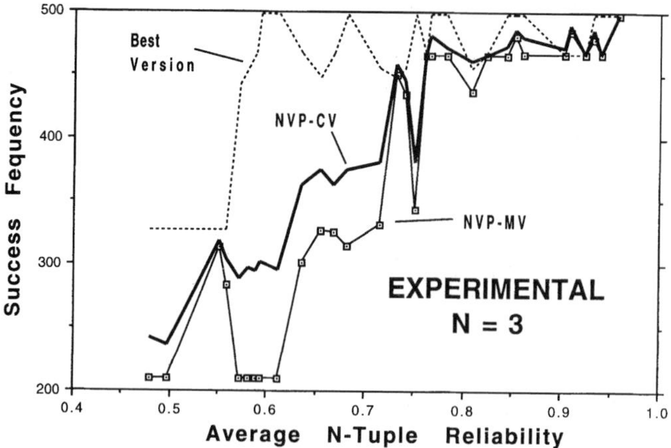

Figure 14.12 System reliability by voting ($N = 3$).

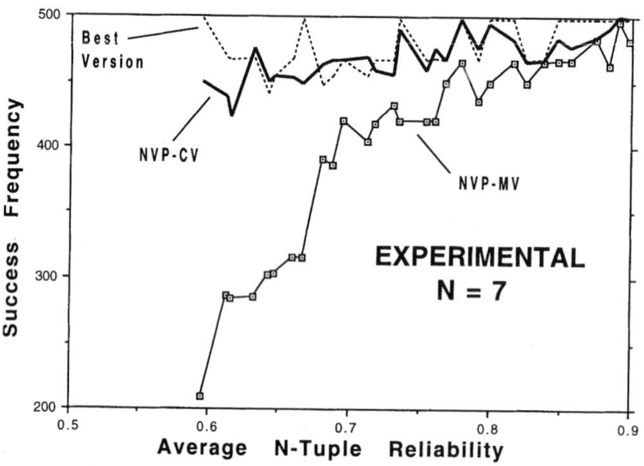

Figure 14.13 System reliability by voting ($N = 7$).

selected is limited. We also see that $N > 3$ improves performance of consensus voting more than it does that of majority voting. This is to a large extent because, for $N > 3$, *plurality* decisions become possible, that is, in situations where there is a unique maximum of identical outputs, the output corresponding to this maximum is selected as the correct answer even though it is not in the majority.

The advantage of consensus voting is that it is more stable than majority voting. It always offers reliability at least equivalent to majority voting, and it performs better than majority voting when average N-tuple reliability is low, or the average decision space in which voters work is not binary. A practical disadvantage of consensus voting may be the added complexity of the voting algorithm, since the strategy requires multiple comparisons and random number generation.

14.7.4 Consensus recovery block

In the case of version failure independence and zero probability for identical-and-wrong responses, consensus recovery block is always superior to N-version programming (given the same version reliability and the same voting strategy), or to recovery block (given the same version and acceptance test reliability) [Scot87, Bell90]. However, given the same voting strategy, and very high interversion failure correlation, we would expect consensus recovery block to do better than N-version programming only in situations where coincidentally failing versions return different results. We would not expect the consensus recovery block to be superior to N-version programming in situations where the probability of identical-and-wrong answers is very high, since then many decisions are made in a very small voting space, and the consensus recovery block acceptance test is invoked very infrequently.

Figures 14.14 and 14.15 show the number of times the result provided by a fault-tolerance strategy was correct, plotted against the average N-tuple reliability. The same acceptance test version was used by consensus recovery block and recovery block. From Fig. 14.14 we see that for $N = 3$, consensus recovery block with majority voting provided reliability *always* equal to or better than the reliability by N-version programming with majority voting (using the same versions). The behavior of a five-version system using consensus voting, instead of majority voting, is shown in Fig. 14.15. From the figure we see that, at lower N-tuple reliability, N-version programming with consensus voting becomes almost as good as consensus recovery block. Consensus recovery block with consensus voting is quite successful in competing with the best version. However, it must be noted that, given a sufficiently reliable acceptance test, or binary output space, or very high interversion failure correlation, all schemes that vote may have difficulty competing with recovery block.

Consensus recovery block with consensus voting is a more advanced strategy than N-version programming with consensus voting, and most of the time it is more reliable than N-version programming with consensus voting. However, there are situations where the reverse is true. Consensus recovery block with consensus voting employs the acceptance test to resolve situations where there is no plurality. N-version programming with consensus voting uses random tie-breaking. N-version programming with consensus voting may be marginally more reliable than consensus recovery block with consensus voting

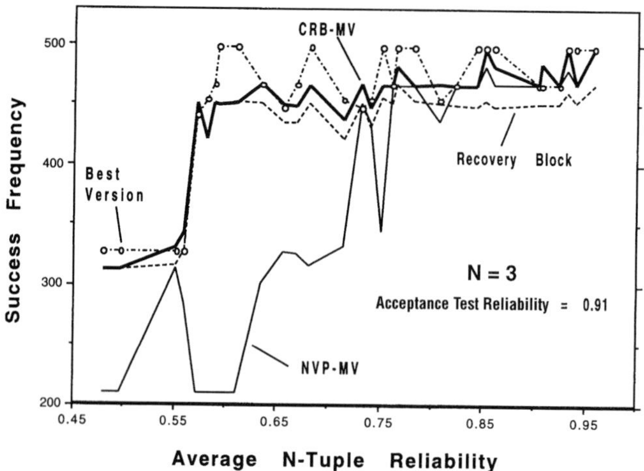

Figure 14.14 Consensus recovery block system reliability with majority voting.

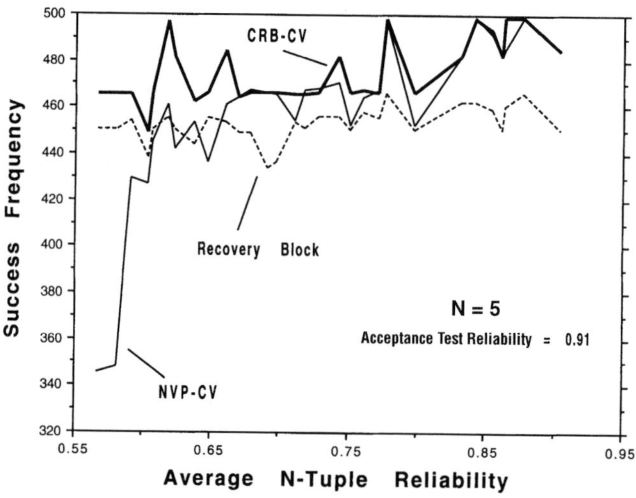

Figure 14.15 Consensus recovery block with consensus voting compared with N-version programming with consensus voting and recovery block.

when the acceptance test reliability is low, or when acceptance test and program failures are identical and wrong.

Similarly, consensus recovery block with consensus voting is usually more reliable than consensus recovery block with majority voting. However, if the number of agreeing versions is less than the majority, the reverse may be true. For instance, if there is no majority, then majority voting will fail and the decision will pass to the acceptance test (which may succeed), while consensus voting will vote, and, if the plurality is incorrect because of identical-and-wrong answers, consensus voting may return an incorrect answer.

Both events described in the previous two paragraphs have been observed [Vouk93a]. In our experience, neither event is very frequent. A more general conclusion is that the consensus recovery block strategy appears to be quite robust in the presence of high interversion correlation, and that the behavior is in good agreement with analytical considerations based on models that make the assumption of failure independence. Of course, the exact behavior of a particular system is more difficult to predict, since correlation effects are not part of the models.

An advantage of consensus recovery block with majority voting is that the algorithm is far more stable, and is at least as reliable as N-version programming with majority voting. However, the advantage of using a more sophisticated voting strategy such as consensus voting may be marginal in high-correlation situations where the acceptance test is of poor quality. In addition, consensus recovery block will perform poorly in all situations where the voter is likely to select a set of identical-and-wrong responses as the correct answer (e.g., a binary output space). Instead, we could either use a different mechanism, such as the acceptance voting algorithm discussed below, or an even more complex hybrid mechanism that would run consensus recovery block and acceptance voting in parallel, and adjudicate series-averaged responses from the two [BelJ90, Atha89]. A general disadvantage of all hybrid strategies is an increased complexity of the fault-tolerance mechanism, although this does not necessarily imply an increase in costs [McAl91].

14.7.5 Acceptance voting

Acceptance voting is very dependent on the reliability of the acceptance test (AT). In some situations AV performs better than CRB, or any other voting-based approach. For example, AV reliability performance can be superior when there is a large probability that the CRB voter would return a wrong answer, and at the same time the AT is sufficiently reliable so that it can eliminate most of the incorrect responses before the voting. This may happen when effective output space is small (that is, voter decision space is small; see Prob. 14.6*b*). If AT is sufficiently reliable, AV can perform better than RB. In general, however, AV systems will be less reliable than CRB systems. Figure 14.16 illustrates experimental results for $N = 3$.

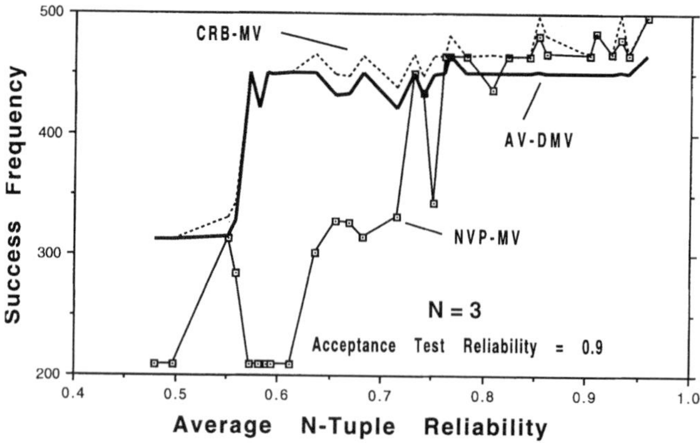

Figure 14.16 A comparison of CRB and AV, $N = 3$.

14.8 Development and Testing of Multiversion Fault-Tolerant Software

As we have seen, fault-tolerant software mechanisms often rely on the functional redundancy of components. This means that significant intercomponent dependence of failures may seriously endanger the effectiveness of these mechanisms. Hence, it is important to detect and eliminate faults that can cause correlated failures as early as possible. Unfortunately, current software production approaches are generally not geared toward early detection and classification of faults that can cause coincident and correlated software failures; neither is there a clear understanding of how this class of errors is generated. The FTS development issues are discussed in some detail in, for example, [Cris85, Kell86, Vouk86b, Voge87a, Kell88, Vouk88, Lapr90a, Lyu92b, Lyu93a].

Appropriate specification, design, coding, and testing approaches are essential, and in this context of special interest is practical use of formal methods, prototyping, reliability growth modeling, and methods for early detection of coincident failures.

A successful FTS development strategy for multiversion software should ensure the following:

- A small probability that the components participating in failure detection and correction decisions fail coincidentally. This includes independent as well as correlated coincident failures.
- High individual component reliability.
- High reliability of adjudication algorithms and their implementations, if adjudication is used, as well as low probability that the adjudication algorithm failures are related to those of the components.

- High accuracy and reliability of acceptance tests, if acceptance testing is used, as well as low probability that the acceptance test failures are related to those of the components.

14.8.1 Requirements and design

Two areas where FTS development must differ from single-component development, and where special attention should be focused, are software requirements and design. These phases are the potential source of a large number of correlated errors [Vouk90a].

Of course, we should use independent and isolated teams for development of multiple software versions or variants. But equally important is that the requirements are specified and analyzed using formal methods suitable for the problem being considered [IEEE94]. Risk analysis should be part of the approach (e.g., [Boeh86, Fran88]). Specification documents must be debugged and stabilized prior to being used for the development of the components. This can be achieved by developing prototypes (pilot code) of the final code. However, one must be wary of excessive coupling of the detailed prototype solutions with the specifications. This could eliminate beneficial fault-randomizing diversity usually provided by the detailed software design and implementation solutions.

Two decisions need to be made relatively early in the process: how many versions will be developed and which fault-tolerance strategy to use. Apart from economic considerations (see Sec. 14.8.3) the key questions in both cases are (1) how many faults need to be tolerated and (2) what level of fault-tolerance is expected.

In general, the larger the number of versions, the more faults can be tolerated. For example, two components are usually not capable of correcting for a failure of one of them. On the other hand, three versions tolerate one fault, four versions can tolerate up to two faults, etc. The real problem is whether or not an increase in the number of versions affects the number of correlated faults and its impact on the effectiveness of the selected fault-tolerance algorithm [Lapr90a].

The size of components is also an issue. A decomposition of a software problem into smaller components helps in making more precise decisions and effects better error control, but it adds processing overhead and also reduces diversity through a larger number of decision points, which require at least some amount of execution synchronization [Lapr90a, Vouk90b]. The choice of the fault-tolerance technique will be driven by trade-off analysis (modeling) of (1) the reliability gains, (2) performance requirements, and (3) cost, resource, and schedule constraints [Lapr90a].

During all phases of the development of multiversion software, it is necessary to follow a carefully designed and enforced protocol for problem reporting and resolution. Such a protocol must have provisions for ensuring independence of the development efforts and avoidance of more common sources of correlated faults—for example, communication errors and common knowledge gaps [Vouk90a] or casual exchanges of information among development teams [Lyu93].

14.8.2 Verification, validation, and testing

Verification, validation, and testing should be formalized and should strive to provide evidence of diversity, as well as evidence that individual components have high reliability and that there are no correlated failures either among the components or between the components and the decision algorithms (e.g., voting, acceptance test). With a process that includes careful inspection and testing of specifications, designs, and code, fault-tolerant software becomes a viable option for increasing reliability of a software-based system [Thev91].

A testing technique that, under the right conditions, may provide some help is back-to-back testing [Sagl86, Vouk90c, Lapr90a]. Back-to-back testing technique involves pairwise comparison of the responses from all functionally equivalent components developed for the FTS system. Whenever a difference is observed among responses, the problem is thoroughly investigated for all test cases where even one component answer differs. Of course, IAW responses are still a problem and need to be addressed separately through inspections and testing [Vouk90a]. However, excessive reliance on back-to-back testing can be counterproductive and can result in an overestimation of the component and system reliability [Bril87, Vouk90c].

As an illustration of the error-detecting power of back-to-back testing, consider an approximate bound on the effectiveness of this testing strategy assuming negligible intercomponent failure correlation. It is reasonable to assume that in practice an attempt will be made not to release software versions with any known faults, and that the versions will be tested to approximately the same level of reliability. Therefore we shall assume that all components have failure probability equal to f. The probability that n independent versions fail simultaneously on a test case is f^n. If the output space is binary, back-to-back testing will not detect a failure when all components fail, i.e., all answers are identical and wrong.

Hence, the probability that a failure will be detected is

$$P\{\text{failure is detected by back-to-back testing}\} \geq 1 - f^n - (1 - f)^n \tag{14.27}$$

If we measure the efficiency of the processes through the probability that a failure is detected by a test case, we see that it depends on the program failure probability f and the number of versions involved.

The process of adding more components in order to increase failure-detection efficiency is one of diminishing returns under the assumption of independent failures. Let us assume that the probability of IAW responses is zero. Then, ideally, the fractional gain in failures detected by increasing n-tuple size from $n - 1$ to n is

$$F(n) = \frac{1 - (1 - f)^n}{1 - (1 - f)^{n-1}} \tag{14.28}$$

It can be shown that for small f this fraction reduces to $F(N) = N/(N - 1)$, that is, to the series 2/1, 3/2, 4/3, . . . ,1. This is illustrated in Fig. 14.17.

The fraction is plotted against the size of the larger tuple. Each point compares the efficiency of a k-tuple with that of the tuple one component smaller. We see that the incremental contribution to the efficiency of failure detection is considerably reduced for N-tuple sizes larger than 4 or 5. The line marked with $\hat{f} = 0.113$ shows experimental data obtained from a large multiversion experiment [Kell88, Vouk90c]. Note that the theoretical calculations are based on an interaction model that assumes failure independence, while in the experiment the interversion failure correlation was in excess of what would be expected if the failures were independent.

14.8.3 Cost of fault-tolerant software

Cost-effectiveness of fault-tolerant software is an open issue, although there is evidence that in some cases the approach is cost-effective.

For example, the experience of the Ericsson company is that diversity is cost-effective [Hage87]. Ericsson found that the costs of develop-

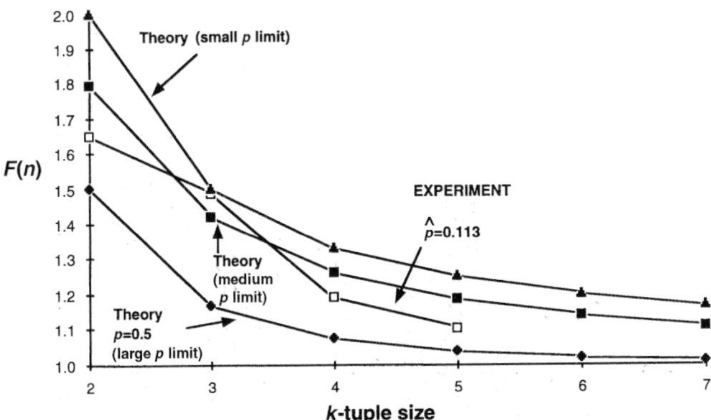

Figure 14.17 Illustration of the diminishing returns from successively larger k-tuples. The theoretical calculations are based on a failure model that assumes failure independence. Experimental data exhibited some positive failure correlation.

ing two functionally equivalent software versions is not double the cost of a single one for at least two reasons. First, not all parts of the system are critical, and therefore only the critical parts require additional work. Second, while the cost of program specification (design), coding, and testing is doubled, the cost of requirement specification, system specification, test specification, and system test execution is not doubled. There is also evidence that back-to-back testing is effective in discovering faults not detected by other testing techniques, and that it improves the quality of testing. There are other examples.

Panzl [Panz81] has found that dual-program development (with back-to-back testing) increased the initial development cost by 77 percent (not factor 2), but reduced the number of residual errors from 69 to 2.

[Voge87c] described several experiments related to the use of diverse programming and comparison testing. In one experiment 14 percent of the total number of detected faults were detected by back-to-back testing of three code versions *after* extensive individual testing of the versions was completed. It is also noted that dual programming was good not only for detection of implementation faults, but for detection of specification faults.

In the PODS experiment [Bish86, Bish88], again *after* extensive application of more traditional techniques, nine faults were detected by back-to-back testing, three of which were classified by the authors as "fail-danger" or critical faults. The cost of traditional testing was about 0.4 person-hours per test case, while the cost of back-to-back testing was about 0.4 person-hours per 250 test cases. It is also found that the cost of single-version development compared with threefold diversity (without back-to-back testing costs) was about 997 versus 2258 person-hours, i.e., an increase of about 126 percent, not a factor of 3.

Similarly, in [Shim88] authors report that 107 faults discovered by back-to-back testing were *not* detected by any other testing technique they used. However, they also note that the other testing found about 150 faults *not* detected by back-to-back testing they applied *after* the conventional testing.

Laprie et al. [Lapr90a] have analyzed the cost of a number of FTS approaches. They consider a number of sources of increased costs, such as the overhead due to decision-point synchronization, failure detection, and adjudication. They also consider a number of factors that reduce the cost per version, such as back-to-back testing, common test-harness development, and common test suites. Their findings are that in a multiversion setting a typical component cost is about 75 to 80 percent of single-version costs. This supports empirical results mentioned in the previous paragraphs.

The cost of FTS has been modeled by a number of researchers. The cost models are closely tied to reliability modeling and the underlying assumptions. The actual models are beyond the scope of this book, and the interested reader is directed to [Bhar81, McAl85, Sagl86, Vouk90c, Lapr90a, McAl91, Lyu95a] and references therein.

14.9 Summary

A way of handling unknown and unpredictable software failures (faults) is through fault tolerance. In this chapter we introduced some techniques that can be used to develop fault-tolerant software. We focused our attention on methods that are based on redundancy through functionally equivalent software components.

The basic *idea* is that the required functionality is provided through a set of functionally equivalent software modules developed by diverse and independent production teams. In operation, all modules are given the same inputs. If one module fails, another can provide the correct answer. The underlying *assumption* is that it is possible to distinguish between incorrect and correct answers and continue system operation using the correct output. The basic *problem* is that it is conceivable that all modules will harbor the same fault. In operation, this may prevent distinction between incorrect and correct responses and a critical system failure may occur. The frequency of occurrence of such events in real-life software is still an open issue.

We have described some common and some advanced FTS techniques. For example, consensus voting is a generalization of N-version programming with majority voting. It provides adaptation of the voting strategy to varying component reliability, failure correlation, and output space characteristics. Since failure correlation among versions effectively changes the cardinality of the space in which voters make decisions, consensus voting is usually preferable to simple majority voting in any fault-tolerant system since it may provide some degree of protection from correlated failures.

Consensus recovery block is a hybrid technique that usually outperforms N-version programming. It also competes very successfully with recovery block in situations where the acceptance test is not of the highest quality. Consensus recovery block is surprisingly robust even in the presence of failure correlation. Acceptance voting is, under special circumstances, more reliable than both consensus recovery block and recovery block. However, in general, acceptance voting offers lower reliability than the other techniques.

We briefly discussed time-dependent issues and the need for such modeling, and FTS development and cost issues.

Problems

14.1 *a.* What is forward recovery and what is backward recovery? Give an example of each approach.

b. Using papers and books mentioned in Sec. 14.3, write a two- to three-page paper describing how error coding (e.g., convolutional coding) can provide information for fault tolerance (give at least one explicit example).

14.2 *a.* What is the difference between an acceptance test and an external consistency check? Construct a valid acceptance test for an algorithm that inverts matrices (include a list of assumptions and limitations).

b. Using papers and books mentioned in Sec. 14.3, write a two- to three-page paper describing how mathematical consistency checking and automatic verification of numerical computations can provide fault tolerance (give at least one explicit example).

c. Using papers and books mentioned in Sec. 14.3, write a two- to three-page paper describing how data diversity can provide fault tolerance (give at least one explicit example).

14.3 *a.* Use your calculator to compute the expression given in Eq. (14.5), and then repeat the calculation by hand. Explain, step by step, how the accuracy loss occurs.

b. Consider a floating-point system with base 10 and 5-digit arithmetic (that is, a mantissa of length 5 digits), the usual double-precision multiplication (10-digit arithmetic in this case), and rounding after every floating-point operation. You are given the following two numbers:

$$x = 0.10005 \times 10^5 \qquad \text{and } y = 0.99973 \times 10^4$$

Compute by hand the difference $x - y$.

c. Now assume that x and y are, in fact, the result of two previous multiplications and that the unrounded products that yield x and y are

$$x = \mathrm{x1} \times \mathrm{x2} = 0.1000548241 \times 10^5$$

$$y = \mathrm{y1} \times \mathrm{y2} = 0.9997342213 \times 10^4$$

Normalize and round to five places and then compute $x1 \times x2 - y1 \times y2$. The result should be 0.81402×10^1. It differs in every digit from the result obtained in item *b*.

Which is the correct result? Explain the anomaly.

14.4 You are given a recovery block system composed of N (diverse) versions of equal reliability and a perfect acceptance test. Derive the equation that describes its reliability.

14.5 Read Sec. 14.3.5 and consider the following. The following table shows responses of three programs to TOL = 0.1. The correct or "golden" value is 3.5 ± 0.1. The first column identifies the comparison event, the second one the actual event, and the last one the multiversion event. Although the numbers given in this table are hypothetical, all events have been observed in multiversion experiments described in [Kell88, Vouk90a].

p_1 p_2 p_3	Events (TOL = 0.1, correct response = 3.5 ± 0.1)		
	Comparison	Actual	Multiversion
3.4 3.5 3.4	Agreement	NO_FAILURE	ALL_CORRECT
3.5 3.5 3.5	Agreement	NO_FAILURE	ALL_CORRECT
3.4 3.5 3.6	Conflict	NO_FAILURE	FALSE_ALARM
3.4 3.5 3.7	Conflict	1_FAILURE	DETECTED_FAILURE
3.3 3.3 3.7	Conflict	3_FAILURE	DETECTED_FAILURE
3.3 3.3 3.3	Agreement	3_FAILURE	UN_DETECTED_FAILURE
3.3 3.3 3.2	Agreement	3_FAILURE	UN_DETECTED_FAILURE
3.3 3.4 3.4	Agreement	1_FAILURE	UN_DETECTED_FAILURE

An increase in the tolerance from 0.1 to 0.4 yields AGREEMENT for all comparisons. This eliminates the FALSE_ALARM event shown in the table, but also produces two new UN_DETECTED_FAILURE events. On the other hand, had the tolerance been made very small, most comparisons would have resulted in a CONFLICT increasing the incidence of FALSE_ALARM events, but also eliminating all but one UN_DETECTED_FAILURE event.

a. What is the difference between AGREEMENT and NO_FAILURE comparison events?

b. Construct a table comparable to the above given that in addition to version p_1, p_2, and p_3 we have version p_4 column with values as follows (3.4, 3.3, 3.5, 3.5, 3.5, 3.5, 3.3, 3.3).

c. Add majority voter and consensus voter columns (assuming perfect voters) to your table, and put in results of the decisions by these voters (use ACCEPT and REJECT as the two alternatives).

14.6 *a.* What is the minimum number of versions, and what is the smallest output space cardinality (assuming unique correct state) for which consensus voting makes sense (give an example).

b. Average conditional voter decision space (CD space) is defined as the average size of the space (i.e., the number of available unique answers) in which the voter makes decisions given that at least one of the versions has failed. We use CD space to focus on the behavior of the voters when failures *are* present. Of course, the maximum voter decision space for a single test case is *N*.

Add a column to the table generated in Prob. 14.5*b* that you will call "Decision space." The column should contain the number of *actual* answer categories (determined by tolerance) which are presented in each case to CV to make a decision.

14.7 Assume that version p_4 acts as an acceptance test, and that p_1, p_2, and p_3 form a voting 3-tuple. Repeat Prob. 14.5 using CRB3 and AV3 strategies.

14.8 *a.* Find the variance in the estimate for $\hat{f}_i$ (Eq. (14.16)).

b. What is the variance for the estimate for $\hat{r}_i$?

14.9 Let all versions in an NVP system have the same reliability. Let the voter be perfect. Then NVP with majority voting increases reliability over a single version only if the reliability of the versions is larger than 0.5.

a. Prove the above statement for $N = 3$.

b. Prove the above statement for any N.

14.10 Suppose N modules fail independently and have the same probability of failure f. Find the probability that exactly M modules of the N fail on a random input.

14.11 Compare the reliabilities of each of the redundant fault-tolerant techniques of Secs. 14.4 and 14.5 for two version systems. Assume that voting fails if the two versions do not agree. Assume the failure probabilities are identical for all components and that failures are independent.

14.12 Show that two randomly chosen programs p_1 and p_2 fail independently on a given input x with probability $\theta(x)^2$. What can you say about a specific program p failing on two randomly chosen inputs X_1 and X_2?

14.13 Construct an example of the function $v(p,x)$ over five programs and five inputs. Assume that the probability of selection of a program or an input is the same (1/5). Compute the functions $\theta(x)$ and $\phi(p)$. Find the probability that two randomly chosen programs will fail on a randomly chosen input.

14.14 Show that it is possible that random programs can fail on the same inputs yet still fail independently. Show that it is possible for random programs to fail on disjoint subsets of the input space yet fail independently.

14.15 Suppose we have independently developed N programs to solve a given problem. Exhaustive testing is impossible so we test the programs on a proper subset of the input space, repair them, and retest until they have no known errors. Is it possible that the corrected programs fail independently? Are the resulting programs randomly selected from the set of all programs?

14.16 Assume independence of module failures and analyze the reliability of the Airbus A310 system described in Sec. 14.5. Then assume equal module reliabilities and plot the system reliability as a function of module reliability.

14.17 Assume that specific software modules p_1 and p_2 have the same probability of failure. What can you say about the maximum difference $\{P[p_1 \text{ fails}, p_2 \text{ fails}] - P[p_1 \text{ fails}]\, P[p_2 \text{ fails}]\}$?

14.18 *a.* Derive the reliability polynomials for RB, CRB, and AV for the case that $r_1 = r_2 = r_3 = V = B = r$ in [0,1] and the faults are independent (do the derivation from first principles). Graph and compare reliability for each of the systems. Show that AV is inferior to all of the other systems in this case.

b. Perform sensitivity analysis for all three systems to independent faults in the decision nodes, that is, in the voter and acceptance tests.

For example, perform the analysis for the situation where the voter and acceptance test are perfect, where both have reliability of 0.99, 0.9, 0.85, 0.8, 0.7, etc.

c. Obtain and read reference [Kano93]. How do the results you obtained in item *b* compare with those obtained by Kanoun et al.? Explain.

14.19 *a.* Derive Eq. (14.23).

b. Use the Estimate II data in Table 14.1 to construct an independent-failures model. Give detail and explain your modeling work. Tabulate results.

c. The frequencies shown in Table 14.3 sum up to 500. Why is it that the sum of frequencies shown in Table 14.2 does not? Explain, using examples.

d. Compare the model in item *b* with experimental data given in Table 14.3 using the chi-squared test to comment on whether there is enough evidence to claim statistically significant departures between your model and the actual data for

Three or more failures

Majority

Twelve or more failures

e. Repeat the chi-squared test using Estimate I and Table 14.3 data. Are the test results different from those obtained in item *c*? Explain.

14.20 *a.* Write a two- to three-page paper discussing and justifying advantages and disadvantages of the following: (1) the desirable feature of a fault-tolerant software is *failure independence* among software variants and between software variants and adjudication algorithms; (2) the desirable feature of a fault-tolerant software is that software variants and adjudication algorithms have *disjoint failure sets.* Is either of the statements realistic?

b. Show mathematically that the assumption of module failure independence can be an overestimate or an underestimate of the probability of joint failure of two specific programs. What about two arbitrary programs?

14.21 Given three arbitrary functionally equivalent programs, the corresponding score functions, and density functions S and Q,

a. Derive an expression that states that at least two of the programs fail on an arbitrary input X.

b. Repeat item *a* but assume that the three programs are specific programs on an arbitrary input X.

c. How do the above expressions simplify if we assume the input space is finite and Q is a constant?

14.22 Suppose we are given a population of seven programs and three possible inputs. A table of the score functions for each program is given below: Assume that S and Q are constant.

v	x_1	x_2	x_3
p_1	1	0	0
p_2	0	1	0
p_3	0	0	1
p_4	0	1	1
p_5	1	0	1
p_6	1	1	0
p_7	1	1	1

a. Find $\theta(x_j)$ for each j.
b. Find $\phi(p_i)$ for each i.
c. Find $E(\Theta)$ and $E(\Theta^2)$ and variance squared of Θ.
d. Determine if two randomly chosen programs fail independently.
e. Compute the probability that p_i and p_j fail jointly.

14.23 Construct a table that has the following columns: *Method* (the name of the FTS method, e.g., RB, NSCP, NVP), *Failure detection mechanism* (e.g., by acceptance test, by comparison), *Failure tolerance mechanism* (e.g., rollback, reexecution, majority vote), *Number of functionally equivalent versions required to tolerate X independent failures* (e.g., $X + 1$ for RB).
a. Put into the table entries for RB, NVP-MV, NVP-CV, NSCP-MV, and NSCP-CV (MV—majority vote, CV—consensus vote).
b. Put into the table entries for CRB-MV, CRB-CV, AV-MV, and AV-CV.

14.24 Consider material in Sec. 14.8.2
a. Compare Eq. (14.27) with the RB reliability given in Eq. (14.20), and with NVP reliability given in Eqs. (14.23) and (14.24). What is the implication of Eq. (14.27), if any, on operational fault tolerance of these strategies? Is there an inconsistency? Explain.
b. Derive Eq. (14.28).
c. What is the implication of Eq. (14.28), if any, on the number of versions one chooses for a fault-tolerant system?

14.25 Show that if two programs fail independently on an input space of cardinality 2, then one program must always fail or never fail. Is this the case for an input space of cardinality 3?

14.26 *a.* What is back-to-back testing?
b. Read [Bril87, Vouk90c, Thev91] and write a two- to three-page discussion about the advantages and disadvantages of back-to-back testing as an aid in developing fault-tolerant software (include a discussion on why some authors believe that extended back-to-back testing may compromise N-version programming principles, and suggest some alternatives).

Chapter

15

Software System Analysis Using Fault Trees

Joanne Bechta Dugan
University of Virginia

15.1 Introduction

This chapter will introduce you to the use of fault trees for the analysis of software systems. Fault trees provide a graphical and logical framework for analyzing the failure modes of systems. Their use helps the analyst to assess the impact of software failures on an overall system, or to prove that certain failure modes cannot occur (or occur with negligible probability). Fault tree models provide a conceptually simple modeling framework that can be used to compare different design alternatives or architectures for fault tolerance.

After introducing the fault tree modeling technique, we briefly discuss both qualitative and quantitative analysis techniques. We then describe two uses of fault trees as a design aid for software systems. Fault tree models can help the designer to efficiently combine off-line and on-line tests to prevent or detect software failures. Software safety validation uses software fault trees to qualitatively examine safety-critical software on a fine-grain (statement-by-statement) basis. On a coarser scale, fault trees can be used to qualitatively and quantitatively analyze fault-tolerant software systems. We consider both a qualitative and quantitative analysis of software-fault-tolerant systems, with respect to both reliability and safety. The need for parameter values for the software part of the models provides a case study for parameter estimation from experimental data.

15.2 Fault Tree Modeling

A fault tree model is a graphical representation of logical relationships between events (usually failure events). Fault trees were first developed in the 1960s to facilitate analysis of the Minuteman missile system, and have been supported by a rich body of research since their inception. Initially, a fault tree was defined as a tree (in the graph theoretic sense), but as fault tree analysis techniques evolved, more general connections were permitted. In the current usage, fault tree nodes (gates and basic events) can have more than one parent node, and thus a fault tree is no longer a tree.

Fault tree models have long been used for the qualitative and quantitative analysis of the failure modes of critical systems. A fault tree provides a mathematical and graphical representation of the combinations of events that can lead to system failure. The construction of a fault tree model can provide insight into the system by illuminating potential weaknesses with respect to reliability or safety. A fault tree can help with the diagnosis of failure symptoms by illustrating which combinations of events could lead to the observed failure symptoms. The quantitative analysis of a fault tree is used to determine the probability of system failure, given the probability of occurrence for failure events.

The construction of a fault tree, if performed manually, provides a systematic method for analyzing and documenting the potential causes of system failure. The analyst begins with the failure scenario being considered, and decomposes the failure symptom into its possible causes. Each possible cause is then investigated and further refined until the basic causes of the failure are understood. From a system design perspective, the fault tree analysis provides a logical framework for understanding the ways in which a system can fail, which is often as important as understanding how a system can succeed.

A fault tree consists of the undesired top event (system or subsystem failure) linked to more basic events by logic gates. The top event is resolved into its constituent causes, connected by *AND, OR,* and *M-out-of-N* logic gates, which are then further resolved until basic events are identified. The basic events represent basic causes for the failure, and represent the limit of resolution of the fault tree. Fault trees do not generally use the *NOT* gate, because the inclusion of inversion may lead to a noncoherent fault tree [Henl82], which complicates analysis. It is quite rare to have need for complementation in a fault tree, so this limitation is acceptable for the analysis of practical systems.

As an example, consider the fault tree shown in Fig. 15.1, which provides a simple analysis of a washing machine that overflows. The cause of the overflow can be attributed to one of two causes: either the shutoff valve is stuck open, or the machine stayed in "fill" mode too long. The first cause, failure of the shutoff valve, is not considered further, as it is considered a basic event. When the washing machine is filling, either of two events can cause the filling to stop. First, there is a timer, which prevents the machine from filling indefinitely. This timer was designed into the system to help avoid a flood in case of a leak in the tub. Second, there is a sensor which determines when the tub is full. Both the timer and the sensor must fail for the machine to be unable to stop filling.

15.2.1 Cutset generation

Analysis of a fault tree begins with an enumeration of the *minimal cutsets,* the minimal sets of component failures which cause system failure. A cutset is a set of basic events whose occurrence causes the top event, system failure. A minimal cutset is a cutset with no redundant elements; that is, if any event is removed from a minimal cutset then it ceases to be a cutset.

A top-down algorithm for determining the cutsets of a fault tree starts at the top event of the tree and constructs the set of cutsets by considering the gates at each lower level. A set of cutsets is expanded at each lower level of the tree until the set of basic events is reached. If the gate being considered is an *AND* gate, then all the inputs must occur to enable the gate, so a gate is replaced at the lower level by a listing of all its inputs. If the gate being considered is an *OR* gate, then the cutset being built is split into several cutsets, one containing each input to the *OR* gate.

Figure 15.2 shows an example fault tree whose cutset generation is shown in Fig. 15.3. The undesired top event occurs when either subevents G2 or G3 occur, which are themselves *AND* combinations of

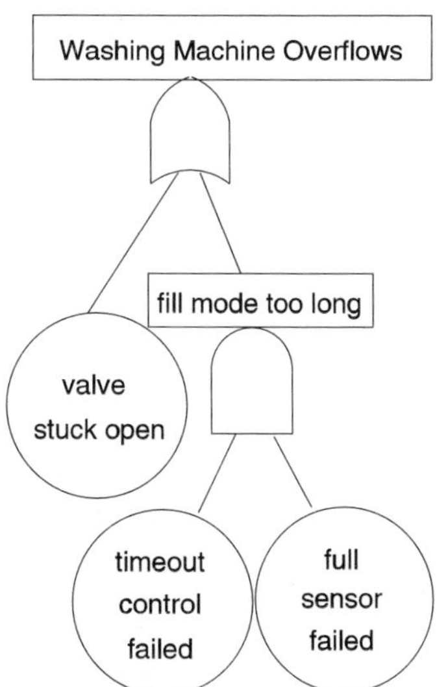

Figure 15.1 A simple fault tree model.

other subevents or basic events. There are five basic events in the fault tree, labeled A1 through A5, which are all statistically independent. One basic event, A4, can contribute to system failure along two paths.

The top-down algorithm starts with the top gate, G1. Since G1 is an *OR* gate, it is replaced in the expansion by its inputs, G2 and G3. G3 is an *AND* gate, and is replaced in the expansion by the basic events {A4, A5}, a cutset for this tree. G2 is expanded into {G4, G5}, since both must occur to activate it. Expanding the G4 term splits the set into two, since it is a two-input *OR* gate: {A1, G5} and {A2, G5}. Finally, the expansion of G5 splits both sets in two, yielding {A1, A3}, {A1, A4}, {A2, A3}, and {A2, A4}, as the remaining minimal cutsets for the tree.

If a gate being expanded is a *k-out-of-n* gate, then its expansion is a combination of the *OR* and *AND* expansions. The *k-out-of-n* gate is expanded into the $\binom{n}{k}$ combinations of input events that can cause the gate to occur. For example, consider a cutset with a gate Gx that is a *3-out-of-4* gate, with inputs *I*1, *I*2, *I*3, and *I*4. Gate Gx gets split into four cutsets, replacing Gx with the four possibilities for selecting three of the inputs, namely, {*I*1, *I*2, *I*3}, {*I*1, *I*3, *I*4}, {*I*1, *I*2, *I*4}, and {*I*2, *I*3, *I*4}.

When using such an algorithm for generating cutsets, some reduction might be necessary. If a cutset contains the same basic event more

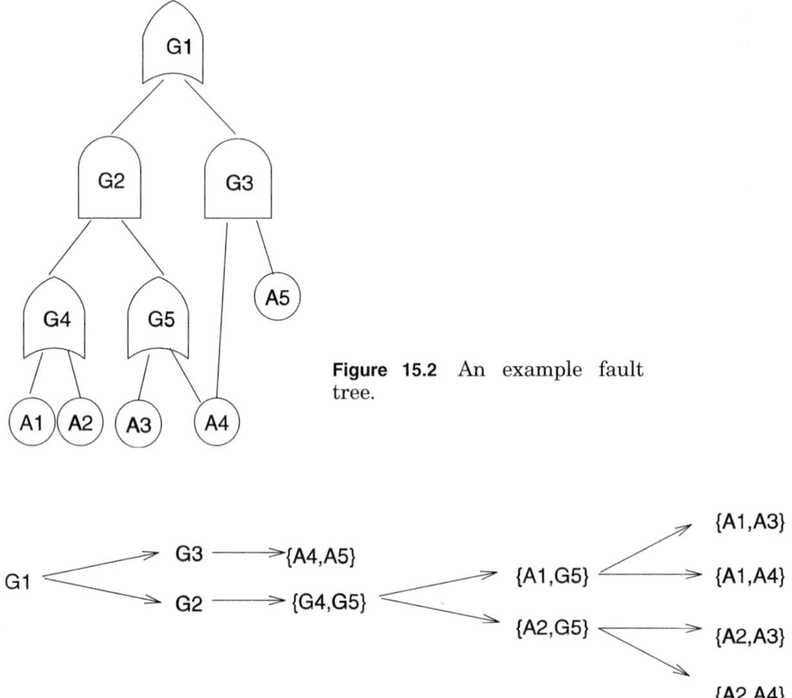

Figure 15.2 An example fault tree.

Figure 15.3 Cutset generation for a fault tree.

than once, then the redundant entries can be eliminated. If one cutset is a subset of another, the latter can be removed from further consideration, since it is not a minimal cutset. For example, the set of cutsets { {A1, A2, A1, A3}, {A3, A4}, {A2, A3, A4} } can be reduced to { {A1, A2, A3}, {A3, A4} }.

15.2.2 Fault tree analysis

Qualitative analysis of the fault tree usually consists of studying the minimal cutsets; for example, to determine if any single points of failure exist. A single point of failure is any component whose failure (by itself) can cause system failure. Single points of failure are identified by cutsets with only a single element. For the example fault tree of Fig. 15.2, all cutsets had cardinality two, so there are no single points of failure. Cutsets can help to identify system hazards which might lead to unsafe or failure states so that appropriate preventive measures can be taken or reactive measures planned. If the top event corresponds to an unsafe condition (rather than system failure), the cutsets can help determine which combinations of events lead to the unsafe condition, and can thus help to identify the need for interlocks. Vulnerabilities resulting from particular component failures can be identified by considering cutsets which contain the component of interest. For the example system, once A4 fails, the system is vulnerable to a failure of either A1, A2, or A5.

Quantitative analysis is used to determine the probability of occurrence of the top event, given the (estimated or measured) probability of occurrence for the basic events. The probability of occurrence for the top event of the tree can be determined from the set of minimal cutsets. The set of cutsets represents all the ways in which the system will fail, and so the probability of system failure is simply the probability that all of the basic events in one or more cutsets will occur.

$$P\{\text{system failure}\} = P\{\bigcup_i C_i\} \qquad (15.1)$$

where C_i are the minimal cutsets for the system. Since the cutsets are not generally disjoint, the probability of the union is not equal to the sum of the probability of the individual cutsets. If the individual probabilities of the cutsets are simply added together, probability of system failure would be overestimated because the intersection of the events would be counted more than once.

Several methods exist for the evaluation of Eq. (15.1) [Henl82, Shoo90], the simplest of which is termed *inclusion/exclusion*. The inclusion-exclusion method is a generalization of the rule for calculating the probability of the union of two events:

$$P\{A \cup B\} = P\{A\} + P\{B\} - P\{A \cap B\} \tag{15.2}$$

and is given by

$$\begin{aligned} P\{\bigcup_{i=1}^{n} C_i\} = {} & \sum_{i=1}^{n} P\{C_i\} \\ & - \sum_{i<j} P\{C_i \cap C_j\} \\ & + \sum_{i<j<k} P\{C_i \cap C_j \cap C_k\} \\ & \mp \cdots \\ & \pm P\{\bigcap_{i=1}^{n} C_i\} \end{aligned} \tag{15.3}$$

That is, the sum of the probabilities of the cutsets taken one at a time, minus the sum of the probabilities of the intersection of the cutsets taken two at a time, plus the sum of the probabilities of the intersection of cutsets taken three at a time, etc.

Equation (15.3) calculates the probability of system failure exactly. As each successive summation term is calculated and added to the running sum, the result alternatively overestimates (if the term is added) or underestimates (if the term is subtracted) the desired probability. Thus, bounds on the probability of system failure can be determined by using only a portion of the terms in Eq. (15.3).

Consider the example fault tree shown in Fig. 15.2, whose cutsets are

$$C_1 = \{A_4, A_5\}$$

$$C_2 = \{A_1, A_3\}$$

$$C_3 = \{A_1, A_4\}$$

$$C_4 = \{A_2, A_3\}$$

$$C_5 = \{A_2, A_4\}$$

Assuming that the probability of occurrence for each of the basic events is

$$P\{A_1\} = P_{A1} = 0.05$$

$$P\{A_2\} = P_{A2} = 0.10$$

$$P\{A_3\} = P_{A3} = 0.15$$

$$P\{A_4\} = P_{A4} = 0.20$$

$$P\{A_5\} = P_{A5} = 0.25$$

then the probability of occurrence for each of the cutsets is

$$P\{C_1\} = P_{A4} \times P_{A5} = 0.05$$

$$P\{C_2\} = 0.0075$$

$$P\{C_3\} = 0.01$$

$$P\{C_4\} = 0.015$$

$$P\{C_5\} = 0.02$$

The sum of the probabilities for the singular cutsets, 0.1025, is an upper bound on the unreliability of the system.

$$0 \leq \text{unreliability} \leq 0.1025$$

The second term of Eq. (15.3) is the sum of the probability of occurrence for all the possible combinations of two cutsets; for the current example this is 0.015175. Subtracting this from the first term yields a lower bound on the unreliability of the system, 0.087325:

$$0.087325 \leq \text{unreliability} \leq 0.1025$$

Adding the third term, 0.0020875, the sum of the probabilities for all possible combinations of three cutsets yields a better upper bound:

$$0.087325 \leq \text{unreliability} \leq 0.0894125$$

Subtracting the fourth term, 0.0003, the sum of the probabilities for all the possible combinations of four cutsets yields a tighter lower bound:

$$0.0891125 \leq \text{unreliability} \leq 0.0894125$$

If we are interested in three decimal places of accuracy, the expansion can stop here, with a known unreliability of 0.089. Adding the final term, the probability that all five cutsets will occur (0.0000375) results in the exact unreliability:

$$\text{unreliability} = 0.08915$$

15.3 Fault Trees as a Design Aid for Software Systems

Although fault trees have traditionally been used to analyze hardware systems, they can provide a useful qualitative design aid for software systems as well [Hech86]. When designing robust software, fault trees can help the designer determine a good set of on-line reasonableness checks and off-line validation tests to cover a class of potential faults. In some sense, a fault tree analysis of a software system is complementary to a formal design review. A formal design review helps to ensure that a software system *does* what it *should* do. A fault tree analysis helps to ensure that a software system *does not do* what it *should not* do.

For each major function that a software system is expected to perform, there is an associated list of potential failures. For each potential failure with appreciable consequences, a fault tree model depicting the possible causes of the failure can be developed. In analyzing a software system, possible causes can include combinations of software faults, inputs, and operating modes. As in the analysis of a mechanical or hardware system, the undesired event is decomposed into its constituent causes, which become the basic events of the fault tree. In the analysis of hardware systems, the basic events are usually associated with physical component failures. In a software system, the basic events represent software modules which might produce an incorrect result or accept an invalid input. Or a basic event can represent the incorrect setting of an initialization parameter by a user or a buffer overflow.

A fault tree for a mechanical system is used to gain an understanding of how unavoidable events (component failures) can impact the system. If a system is determined to be particularly vulnerable to a certain failure mode, then the design is altered so as to reduce this vulnerability. Design alternatives might include choosing a more reliable substitute component, shielding the component from fault-inducing situations or environments, and enhancing redundancy.

How then are fault tree models applicable to software systems? A software component does not experience physical wearout or age degradation like a hardware component does. However, the sheer size and complexity of software systems currently being designed virtually guarantees that sometime in the lifetime of the system a software failure will occur. A fault tree analysis can help uncover the vulnerabilities of the system to particular classes of software failures, and can guide the designer in choosing preventive or protective measures. The basic events of a software fault tree analysis can be software modules which are decomposed to the point where they are either exhaustively testable or reliable failure detection and recovery mechanisms can be written. If a module is small enough to be exhaustively testable, then after testing, the analyst can be reasonably assured that a software failure in that module will not occur. If, on the other hand, exhaustive testing is infeasible, it may be reasonable to define a detection and recovery routine to handle the potential failure.

The logical structure of the fault tree helps to determine where such tests or routines are best placed [Hech86]. If an undesired event in a fault tree is the output of an *OR* gate, then each input to the *OR* gate must be covered by exhaustive testing or detection/recovery routines in order to prevent the undesired outcome. If, however, the undesired event is the output from an *AND* gate, then the protection of *one* of the inputs will prevent the undesired event. At lower levels of the tree, testing and/or exception handling can be used to prevent intermediate events which ultimately can lead to the undesired top event. Testing or exception handling close to the top event in a fault tree has the greatest impact, and can sometimes provide a low-cost solution to satisfy the reliability requirements of less critical applications.

Consider again the fault tree shown in Fig. 15.2. Suppose that the basic events in the fault tree represent software modules whose failures combine to cause system failure as depicted by the fault tree. Module A4 inputs to the *AND* gate labeled G3; if module A4 does not fail, then the output of gate G3 will not occur. So, we can protect the system from one of its two major failure modes (labeled G2 and G3) by exhaustively testing module A4. But, even though we have protected G3, the output event for gate G2 could still occur. Since gate G2 is an *AND* gate also, its occurrence can be prevented by exhaustively testing A3 (in addition to A4). Alternatively, one could provide a detection and recovery routine for the gates G2 or G4. The system can be protected from software failure by exhaustively testing only two of the five modules, or by testing one and providing a single point of detection and recovery. Of course, the particulars of the software system dictate whether exhaustive testing of a module is feasible, or whether it is reasonable to insert an exception handler at the point represented by a gate in the fault tree.

The fault tree model depicting the failure modes in a software system explicitly enumerates the failure modes being considered, as well as those being ignored or overlooked. A later analysis of the system might well ask whether some particular failure mode was considered; the fault tree model can provide the answer. If the mode has been considered, it will appear in the fault tree; if not, it will be absent.

15.4 Safety Validation Using Fault Trees

In the previous section, we saw that the manual construction of a fault tree model can help a designer or analyst understand the potential failure modes of a software system, and it provides a logical structure for the placement of exception tests. In this section we will see how the formal structure of the fault tree can provide the basis for automated tools to aid in safety validation.

Computer systems are often used to monitor or control a critical system where failure can have life-threatening or other severe consequences. Safety analysis of a critical system begins by identifying and classifying a set of hazards within the context of the operational environment. A *hazard* is a set of conditions (a state) that can lead to an accident, given certain environmental conditions, and can be classified as *critical* or *catastrophic,* depending on the potential outcome [Leve86, Leve91a]. A critical hazard is one that can lead to severe injury, severe occupational illness, or major system damage. A catastrophic hazard is one that can lead to death or system loss.

Once a set of critical or catastrophic system hazards is identified, fault tree analysis is used to identify the combinations of events which can lead to each hazard. The root of the fault tree is the hazard, and the causes of the hazard are resolved to the point where the critical software interfaces are identified. The critical behavior of the software (usually involving output values or missing or untimely outputs) is then analyzed using software fault trees [Leve86, Leve91a]. The goal of software fault tree analysis is to either find paths through the code from particular inputs to the hazardous outputs, or prove that such paths do not exist.

Software fault tree analysis uses failure templates for program structures to generate a fault tree model of the software. In each template, it is assumed that the execution of the statement causes the critical event, and the statement result is broken down into its constituent causes. This is similar to the approach used in formal axiomatic verification, where the weakest preconditions necessary to satisfy the given postconditions are derived. In fact, software fault tree analysis is a graphical application of axiomatic verification where the postconditions describe the hazardous conditions rather than the correctness conditions [Leve91a]. If the fault tree analysis leads to a contradiction (a false weakest precondition), then the analysis on this branch can be halted. If the fault tree analysis leads back to an input statement without reaching a contradiction, then the code must be redesigned to avoid the hazard.

Figures 15.4 and 15.5 [Leve91a] show example templates for the Assignment and If-Then-Else statements. The assignment statement fault tree shows that an assignment statement can fail because of an unsafe value or because of unsuccessful execution. The If-Then-Else statement can fail because of the condition evaluation, the “If” part or the “Then” part of the statement. The body of the Else and Then parts of the statements are replaced by the templates associated with the statement body.

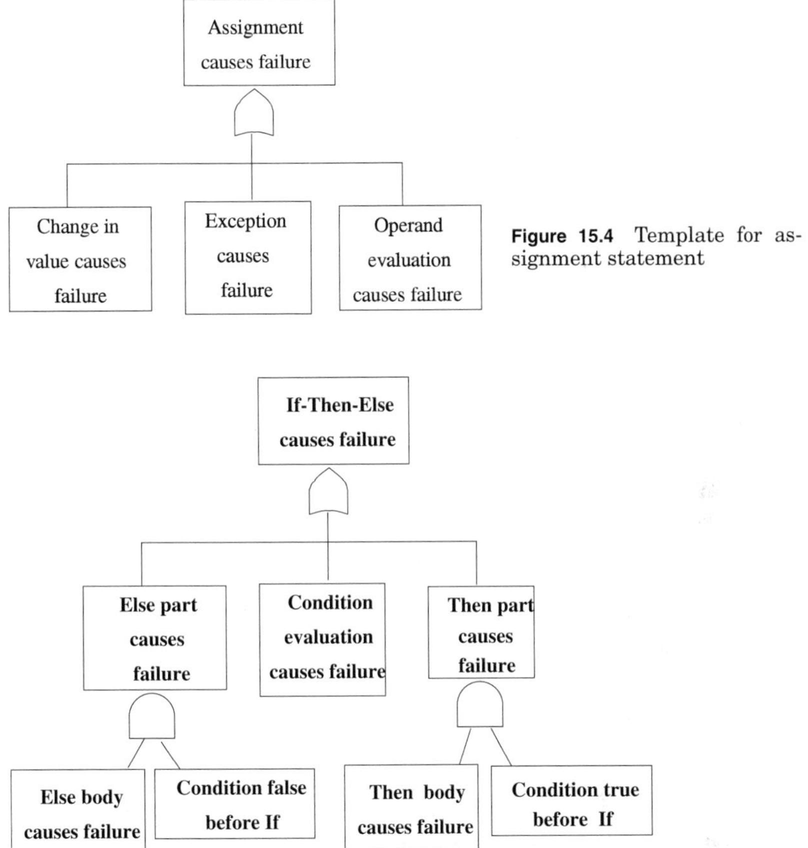

Figure 15.4 Template for assignment statement

Figure 15.5 Template for If-Then-Else statement.

Consider the simple example of a program segment shown in Fig. 15.6, and suppose that the system fails if $x > 14$. The software fault tree model for this program segment is shown in Fig. 15.7. The software fault tree can be derived automatically from the program segment [Frie93], and can then be analyzed and reduced by the (human) analyst. Each of the "Then" and "Else" parts of the statement reduce to an AND condition. The software fault tree then reduces to that shown in Fig. 15.8. Each of the conditions at the lowest level of the fault tree in Fig. 15.8 can be further decomposed until either a contradiction is reached (which then proves that the hazard cannot occur) or until it is determined that a software repair is needed.

While software fault tree analysis has been applied to relatively small, industrial software at a reasonable cost, the practicality of its use has not been demonstrated on large-scale software [Leve91a]. However,

```
If y<6
   then x := z + y
   else
      begin
         q := 3
         x := (y+1)*q;
      end
```

Figure 15.6 A simple example program statement used for software fault tree analysis.

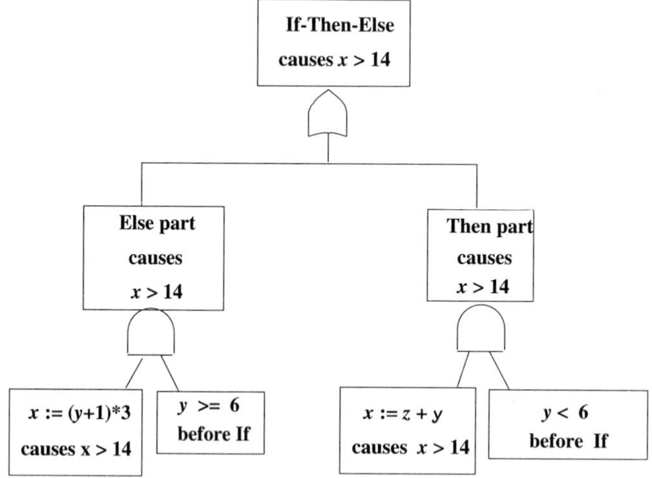

Figure 15.7 Software fault tree for program segment.

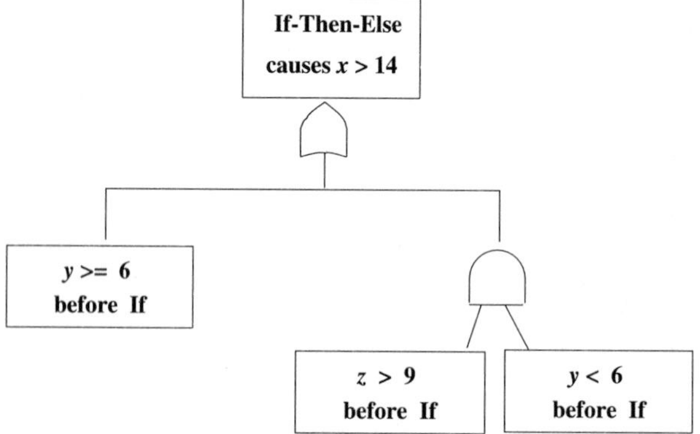

Figure 15.8 Reduced software fault tree for program segment.

since the software fault tree analysis is limited to identified hazards, if the error containment and isolation are satisfactory, only a small percentage of the code may need to be analyzed in detail. Also, the fault tree analysis can be stopped before reaching a contradiction if a run-time assertions or exception conditions are included in the code. The software fault tree provides the necessary information regarding content and placement of effective run-time assertions. Because run-time assertions are expensive, the guidance provided by software fault trees is useful from a practical consideration.

15.5 Analysis of Fault-Tolerant Software Systems

In addition to the detailed analysis of single-version critical software, fault tree models are useful for analyzing the failure modes associated with fault-tolerant software applications. Software fault trees for safety verification operate at a very fine granularity, considering each internal statement of the code. System analysis of fault-tolerant software, on the other hand, considers fault activation scenarios as basic events, and analyzes system-level failures. We will present fault tree models of three popular architectures for tolerating software faults: distributed recovery blocks, N-version programming, and N self-checking programming.

Figure 15.9 shows the hardware and error confinement areas [Lapr90] associated with the three architectures being considered. The systems are defined by the number of software variants, the number of hardware replications, and the decision algorithm. The hardware error confinement area (HECA) is the lightly shaded region; the software error confinement area (SECA) is the darkly shaded region. The HECA or SECA covers the region of the system affected by faults in that component. For example, the HECA covers the software component since the software component will fail if that hardware experiences a fault.

We make the following assumptions for this analysis.

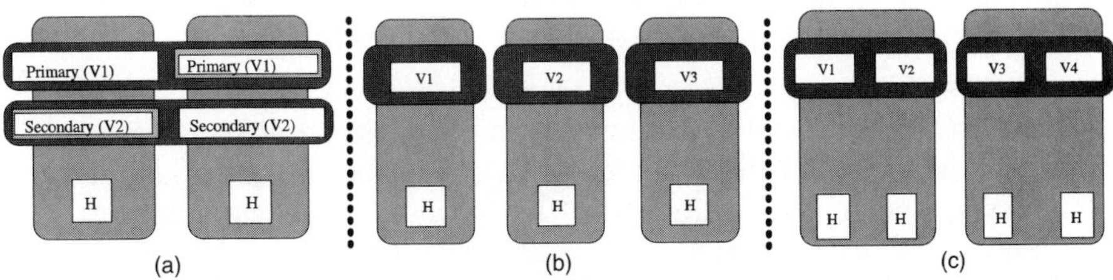

Figure 15.9 Structure of (*a*) distributed recovery block (DRB); (*b*) N-version programming (NVP); (*c*) N self-checking programming (NSCP).

Task computation. The computation being performed is a task (or set of tasks) which is repeated periodically. A set of sensor inputs is gathered and analyzed and a set of actuations are produced. Each repetition of a task is independent. The goal of the analysis is the probability that a task will succeed in producing an acceptable output, despite the possibility of hardware or software faults. More interesting task computation processes could be considered using techniques described in [Lapr92] and [Wei91]. We do not address timing or performance issues in this model. See [Tai93] for a performability analysis of fault-tolerant software techniques.

Software failure probability. Software faults exist in the code despite rigorous testing. A fault may be activated by some random input, thus producing an erroneous result. Each instantiation of a task receives a different set of inputs which are independent. Thus, a software task has a fixed probability of failure when executed, and each iteration is assumed to be statistically independent. Since we do not assign a failure rate to the software, we do not consider reliability growth models.

Coincident software failures in different versions. If two different software versions fail on the same input, they will produce either similar or different results. In this work, we use the Arlat/Kanoun/Laprie [Arla90] model for software failures and assume that similar erroneous results are caused by *related* software faults, and that different erroneous results that are simultaneously activated are caused by *unrelated* (called *independent* in their terminology) software faults. There is one difference between our model and that of Arlat/Kanoun/Laprie: our model assumes that related and unrelated software faults are statistically independent, while their's assumes that related and unrelated faults are mutually exclusive. Further, this treatment of *unrelated* and *related* faults differs considerably from models for correlated failures [Eckh85, Litt89, Nico90], in which unrelated and related software failures are not differentiated. Rather, software faults are considered to be statistically correlated and models for correlation are considered and proposed. A more detailed comparison of the two approaches is given in [Duga94a].

Transient hardware faults. A transient hardware fault is assumed to upset the software running on the processor and to produce an erroneous result that is indistinguishable from an input-activated software error. We assume that the lifetime of transient hardware faults is short compared to the length of a task computation, and thus we assign a fixed probability to the occurrence of a transient hardware fault during a single computation. Permanent hardware faults are considered separately, in Sec. 15.7.

Fault tree models will be used to describe the combinations of failure events (hardware and software) which can combine to produce an unacceptable output. This analysis will ignore failures of the common platform services (communication network, operating system, device drivers, etc.) and will concentrate on the fault tolerance of the application software instead.

Each of the fault tree models will use the following notation for basic events.

V# (where # is an integer between 1 and 4) For (up to) four versions of software, the input for a single computation activates an unrelated fault.

D An independent fault in the decider (acceptance test, majority voter, comparator, adjudicator).

RV## (where each # is an integer between 1 and 4) The input for a single computation activates a related fault between two versions. A related fault is one that occurs in two different versions, causing both to produce the same erroneous result.

RALL A related fault affects all versions as well as the decider, caused by imperfect specifications.

H# (where # is an integer between 1 and 4) A hardware fault affects the task computation.

15.5.1 Fault tree model for recovery block system

There are at least two different ways to combine hardware redundancy with the recovery block approach to software fault tolerance. In [Lapr90a], the RB/1/1 architecture duplicates the recovery block on two hardware components. Both hardware components execute the same variant, and hardware faults are detected by a comparison of the acceptance test and computation results. The distributed recovery block (DRB) advocated by Kim and Welch [Kim89] executes different alternates on the different hardware components in order to improve performance in case an error is detected. In the DRB system, one processor executes the primary alternate, while the other executes the secondary. If an error is detected in the primary results, the results from the secondary are immediately available. The fault tree model of both systems is identical.

The fault tree model of DRB is shown in Fig. 15.10. A single task computation will produce unacceptable results if one of three events occur. First, if both the primary and secondary fail on the same input because of two unrelated faults or a single related fault. Second, if both hardware components experience faults, then the computations being hosted will be upset and be unable to produce correct results. Third, if the decider fails to either detect unacceptable results or to accept correct results, then the computation fails.

The fault tree model provides a compact format for describing the effects of both software and hardware faults. Even without generating the cutsets for the DRB system, one can easily visualize the effects of a decider failure or a related fault between the versions. There are five minimal cutsets for the DRB system. Three of these cutsets have a single element, those being *RV, RALL,* and *D,* as a related fault and a decider fault are single points of failure. The other two cutsets have two members, one for both versions failing, one for both hardware hosts failing. The probability that an unacceptable result is produced during a single task iteration is given by

$$P_{RV} + Q_{RV}P_D + Q_{RV}P_{RALL}Q_D + Q_{RV}Q_{RALL}Q_DP_H^2 + P_V^2Q_{RV}Q_{RALL}Q_D(1 - P_H^2) \tag{15.4}$$

where P_X is the probability that event X occurs, and $Q_X = 1 - P_X$.

15.5.2 Fault tree model for N-version programming system

The example NVP system consists of three identical hardware components, each running a distinct software version. It is a direct mapping of the NVP method onto hardware. If any of the hardware components experiences a fault, it causes the software version running on that

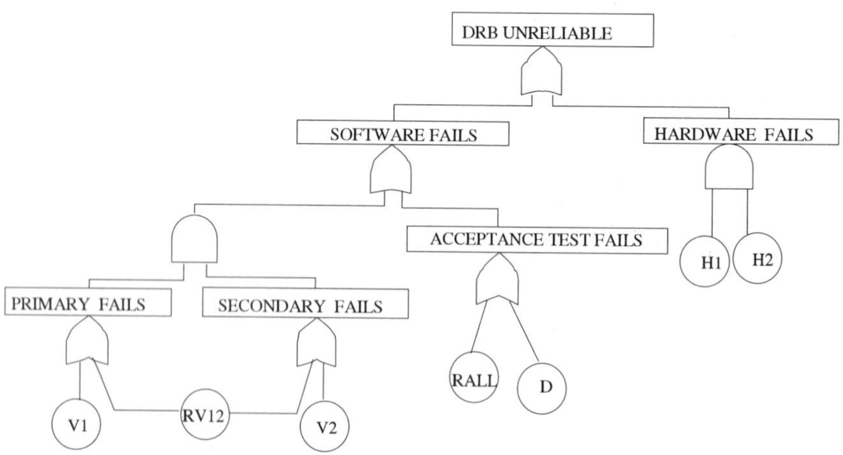

Figure 15.10 Reliability model of DRB.

hardware to produce inaccurate results. If all of the other hardware and software modules are functioning properly, the system will still produce a correct result, since two out of the three versions, a majority, are correct. If two software or hardware components have faults, the system will fail, since there will be only one correct result. The system will also fail if at least one hardware component and one software component fail, but only if the faulty hardware does not host the faulty software version.

Figure 15.11 shows the fault tree model of NVP. With three software versions running on three separate processors, several different failure scenarios must be considered, including coincident unrelated faults as well as related software faults, and combinations of hardware and software faults. A single task iteration can fail from several causes: first, if two of the three versions activate unrelated faults, or if any related fault between two versions is activated; second, if the input activates a fault which affects all three versions or a fault in the decider; third, if two of the three processors experience faults during the same task; finally, if a hardware host fails and one of the software components on another host also fails (via an unrelated or related fault).

The NVP fault tree has 20 minimal cutsets, of which 5 have a single member (*RV*12, *RV*13, *RV*23, *RALL*, and *D*). The remaining cutsets enumerate the 15 ways in which software and/or hardware components combine to fail two of the three versions. The solution of the NVP fault tree model is given by

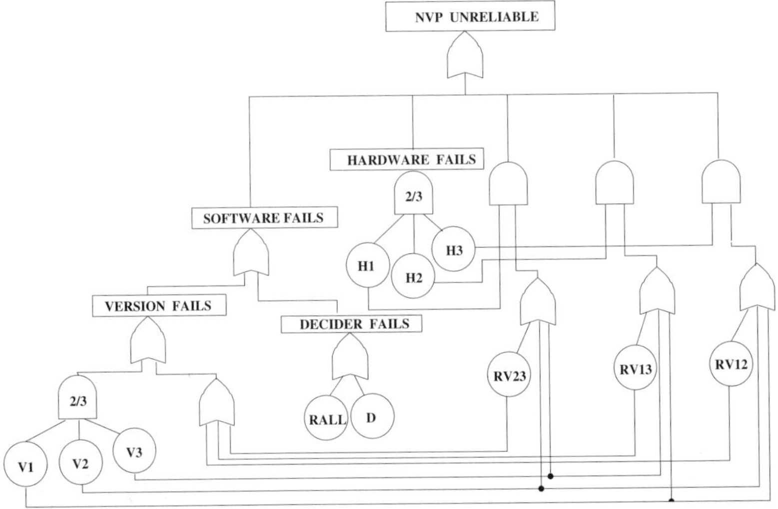

Figure 15.11 Reliability model of NVP.

$$
\begin{aligned}
&P_{RV} + \\
&Q_{RV}P_{RV} + \\
&Q_{RV}^2P_{RV} + \\
&Q_{RV}^3P_D + \\
&Q_{RV}^3P_{RALL}Q_D + \\
&P_V^2Q_{RV}^3Q_{RALL}Q_D + \\
&P_V^2Q_VQ_{RV}^3Q_{RALL}Q_D + \\
&P_V^2Q_VQ_{RV}^3Q_{RALL}Q_D + \\
&Q_VP_VQ_{RV}^3Q_{RALL}Q_DP_H^2Q_H(1 - P_V) + \\
&Q_{RV}^3Q_{RALL}Q_DP_H^2Q_H(1 - P_V)(1 - P_V^2) + \\
&Q_VP_VQ_{RV}^3Q_{RALL}Q_DP_H^2Q_H(1 - P_V) + \qquad (15.5) \\
&Q_{RV}^3Q_{RALL}Q_DP_H^2Q_H(1 - P_V)(1 - P_V^2) + \\
&Q_VP_VQ_{RV}^3Q_{RALL}Q_DP_H^2Q_H(1 - P_V) + \\
&Q_{RV}^3Q_{RALL}Q_DP_H^2Q_H(1 - P_V)(1 - P_V^2) + \\
&Q_VP_VQ_VQ_{RV}^3Q_{RALL}Q_DP_HQ_H(1 - P_H) + \\
&Q_V^2P_VQ_{RV}^3Q_{RALL}Q_DP_HQ_H(1 - P_H) + \\
&P_VQ_VQ_{RV}^3Q_{RALL}Q_DQ_H^2P_H(1 - P_V) + \\
&Q_V^2P_VQ_{RV}^3Q_{RALL}Q_DQ_H^2P_H + \\
&P_VQ_VQ_{RV}^3Q_{RALL}Q_DQ_H^2P_H(1 - P_V) + \\
&Q_VP_VQ_VQ_{RV}^3Q_{RALL}Q_DQ_H^2P_H
\end{aligned}
$$

15.5.3 Fault tree model for N self-checking programming system

The example NSCP architecture is comprised of four software versions and four hardware components, each grouped in two pairs, essentially dividing the system into two halves. The hardware pairs operate in hot

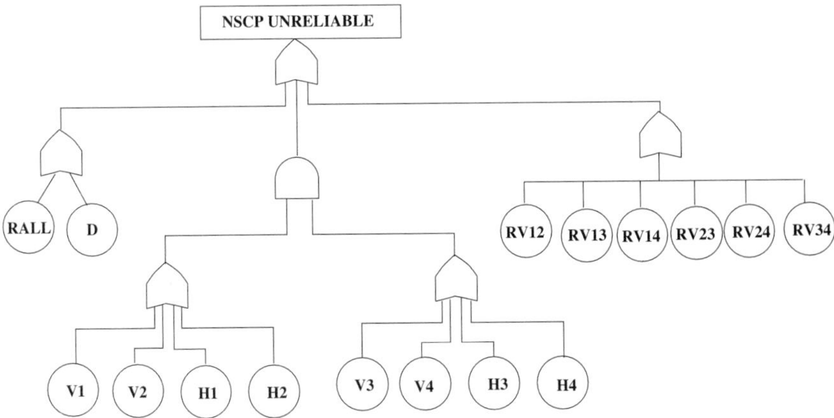

Figure 15.12 Reliability model of NSCP.

standby redundancy with each hardware component supporting one software version. The version pairs form self-checking software components. A self-checking software component consists of either two versions and a comparison algorithm or a version and an acceptance test. In this case, error detection is done by comparison. The four software versions are executed and the results of V1 and V2 are compared against each other, as are the results of V3 and V4. If either pair of results do not match, they are discarded and only the remaining two are used. If the results do match, the results of the two pairs are then compared. A hardware fault causes the software version running on it to produce incorrect results, as would a fault in the software version itself. This results in a discrepancy in the output of the two versions, causing that pair to be ignored.

The fault tree model of the NSCP system (Fig. 15.12) shows that the system is vulnerable to related faults, whether they involve versions in the same error confinement area or not. (To allow later comparison with the NVP and DRB systems, we have ignored the possibility of a related fault affecting three versions.) There are 24 cutsets for the NSCP system. Six singleton cutsets enumerate the related faults affecting two versions, and two singleton cutsets reflect the single points of failure in the decider and in a related fault affecting all versions (*RALL*). There are also 16 cutsets with two elements, enumerating all combinations of version and/or hardware failures affecting one version in each error confinement area. The solution of the model is given by

$$
\begin{aligned}
&P_{RV} + \\
&Q_{RV}P_{RV} + \\
&Q_{RV}^2P_{RV} + \\
&Q_{RV}^3P_{RV} + \\
&Q_{RV}^4P_{RV} + \\
&Q_{RV}^5P_{RV} + \\
&Q_{RV}^6P_{RALL} + \\
&Q_{RV}^6P_DQ_{RALL} + \\
&P_V^2Q_{RV}^6Q_DQ_{RALL} + \\
&P_V^2Q_VQ_{RV}^6Q_DQ_{RALL} + \\
&P_VQ_V^2Q_{RV}^6Q_DQ_{RALL}P_H + \\
&P_VQ_V^2Q_{RV}^6Q_DQ_{RALL}Q_HP_H + \\
&Q_VP_V^2Q_{RV}^6Q_DQ_{RALL} + \qquad (15.6) \\
&P_V^2Q_VQ_{RV}^6Q_DQ_{RALL}(1 - P_V) + \\
&P_VQ_V^2Q_{RV}^6Q_DQ_{RALL}P_H(1 - P_V) + \\
&P_VQ_V^2Q_{RV}^6Q_DQ_{RALL}Q_HP_H(1 - P_V) + \\
&Q_V^2P_VQ_{RV}^6Q_DQ_{RALL}P_H + \\
&Q_VP_VQ_{RV}^6Q_DQ_{RALL}P_H(1 - P_V)^2 + \\
&Q_V^2Q_{RV}^6Q_DQ_{RALL}P_H^2(1 - P_V)^2 + \\
&Q_V^2Q_{RV}^6Q_DQ_{RALL}P_H^2Q_H(1 - P_V)^2 + \\
&Q_V^2P_VQ_{RV}^6Q_DQ_{RALL}Q_HP_H + \\
&Q_VP_VQ_{RV}^6Q_DQ_{RALL}P_H(1 - P_V)^2(1 - P_H) + \\
&Q_V^2Q_{RV}^6Q_DQ_{RALL}P_H^2(1 - P_V)^2(1 - P_H) + \\
&Q_V^2Q_{RV}^6Q_DQ_{RALL}P_H^2Q_H(1 - P_V)^2(1 - P_H)
\end{aligned}
$$

15.6 Quantitative Analysis of Fault-Tolerant Software

The qualitative analysis of the fault-tolerant software systems described in the previous section was useful for understanding system structure and behavior. However, it is difficult to compare the systems unless the probabilities associated with the basic events are known. The fact that one system has more cutsets (or even more singleton cutsets) does not necessarily mean that it is less reliable. A quantitative assessment of the probability of failure using a common set of assumptions and parameter values provides a clearer comparison.

15.6.1 Methodology for parameter estimation from experimental data

Given the probability of occurrence for the basic events, the determination of the probability of system failure is relatively straightforward, using well-known methods [Henl82, Shoo90]. The estimation of parameters provides a more difficult problem. The estimation of failure probabilities for hardware components has been considered for a number of years, and reasonable estimates exist for generic components (such as a processor). However, the estimation of software version failure probability is less accessible, and the estimation of the probability of related faults is more difficult still. In this section we will describe the methodology for estimating model parameter values from experimental data, followed by a case study using a set of experimental data.

Several experiments in multiversion programming have been performed, as described in Chap. 14. Among other measures, most experiments provide some estimate of the number of times different versions fail coincidentally. For example, the NASA Langley Research Center study involving 20 programs from four universities [Eckh91] provides a table listing how many instances of coincident failures were detected. The Knight-Leveson study of 28 versions [Knig86] provides an estimated probability of coincident failures. The Lyu-He study [Lyu93a] considered three- and five-version configurations formed from 12 different versions. These sets of experimental data can be used to estimate the probabilities for the basic events in a fault tree model of a fault tolerant software system.

Coincident failures in different versions can arise from two distinct causes. First, two (or more) versions may both experience unrelated faults that are activated by the same input. If two programs fail independently, there is always a finite probability that they will fail coincidentally, else the programs would not be independent. A coincident failure does not necessarily imply that a related fault has been activated. Second, the input may activate a fault that is related between the two versions. In order to estimate the probabilities of unrelated and related faults, we will determine the (theoretical) probability of failure by unrelated faults. To the extent that the observed frequency of coincident faults exceeds this value, we will attribute the excess to related faults.

The experimental data are necessarily coarse. As it is infeasible to exhaustively test a single version; it is more difficult to exhaustively observe every possible instance of coincident failures in multiple versions. The sampling techniques used to gather the experimental data provide an estimate of the probabilities of coincident failures rather than the exact value. Considering the coarseness of the experimental data, we will limit ourselves to the estimation of three parameter values: P_V, the probability of an unrelated fault in a single version; P_{RV}, the probability of a related fault between two versions; and P_{RALL}, the probability of a related fault in all versions. To attempt to estimate more (for example, the probability of a related fault that affects exactly three versions or exactly four versions) seems unreasonable. Notice that we will assume that the versions are all statistically identical, and we do not attempt to estimate different probabilities of failure for each individual version or for each individual case of two simultaneous versions.

The following notation will be used throughout the remainder of this section.

N	The number of different versions involved in the experiment
P_V	The estimated probability (for each version) that an unrelated fault is activated in a single version
P_{RV}	The estimated probability (for each pair of versions) that a related fault affects two versions
P_{RALL}	The estimated probability that a related fault affects all versions
F_i	The observed frequency that i of the N versions fail coincidentally

The first parameter that we estimate is P_V, the probability that a single version fails unrelated. The estimate for P_V comes from considering F_0 (the observed frequency of no failures in the N versions) and F_1 (the observed frequency of exactly one failure in the N versions). When considering N different versions processing the same input, the probability that there are no failures is set equal to the observed frequency of no failures.

$$F_0 = (1 - P_V)^N (1 - P_{RV})^{\binom{N}{2}} (1 - P_{RALL}) \qquad (15.7)$$

Then, considering the case where only a single failure occurs, we observe that a single failure can occur in any of the N programs, which implies that a related fault does not occur (else more than one version would be affected). This is then set equal to the observed frequency of a single failure of the N versions.

$$F_1 = N(1 - P_V)^{(N-1)} P_V (1 - P_{RV})^{\binom{N}{2}} (1 - P_{RALL}) \tag{15.8}$$

Dividing Eq. (15.7) by Eq. (15.8) yields an estimate for P_V.

$$P_V = \frac{F_1}{NF_0 + F_1} \tag{15.9}$$

Estimating the probability of a related fault between two versions, P_{RV}, is more involved, but follows the same basic procedure. First, consider the case where exactly two versions are observed to fail coincidentally. This event can be caused by one of three events:

- The simultaneous activation of two unrelated faults
- The activation of a related fault between two versions
- Both (the activation of two unrelated and a related fault between the two versions)

The probabilities of each of these events will be determined separately. The probability that unrelated faults are simultaneously activated in two versions (and no related faults are activated) is

$$\binom{N}{2} P_V^2 (1 - P_V)^{(N-2)} (1 - P_{RV})^{\binom{N}{2}} (1 - P_{RALL}) \tag{15.10}$$

The probability that a single related fault (and no unrelated fault) is activated is given by

$$\binom{N}{2} (1 - P_V)^N P_{RV} (1 - P_{RV})^{(\binom{N}{2} - 1)} (1 - P_{RALL}) \tag{15.11}$$

Finally, the probability that both an unrelated fault and two related faults are simultaneously activated is given by

$$\binom{N}{2} P_V^2 P_{RV} (1 - P_V)^{(N-2)} (1 - P_{RV})^{(\binom{N}{2} - 1)} (1 - P_{RALL}) \tag{15.12}$$

Because the three events are disjoint, we can sum their probabilities and set the sum equal to F_2, the observed frequency of two coincident errors.

$$F_2 = \binom{N}{2} (P_V^2 + P_{RV} - P_V^2 P_{RV})(1 - P_V)^{(N-2)} (1 - P_{RV})^{(\binom{N}{2} - 1)} (1 - P_{RALL}) \tag{15.13}$$

Dividing Eq. (15.13) by Eq. (15.8) and performing some algebraic manipulations yields an estimate for P_{RV} which depends on the experimental data and the previously derived estimate for P_V.

$$P_{RV} = \frac{2F_2P_V(1-P_V) - (N-1)F_1P_V^2}{2F_2P_V(1-P_V) + (N-1)F_1(1-P_V^2)} \tag{15.14}$$

The estimate for P_{RALL} is more involved, as there are many ways in which all versions can fail. There may be a related fault between all versions that is activated by the input, or all versions might simultaneously fail from a combination of unrelated and related faults. Consider the case where there are three versions. In addition to the possibility of a single fault affecting all three versions, all three versions could experience a simultaneous activation of unrelated faults, or one of three combinations of an unrelated and related fault affecting different versions may be activated. The fault tree in Fig. 15.13 illustrates the combinations of events that can cause all three versions to fail coincidentally. A simple methodology for estimating P_{RALL} could use the previously determined estimates for P_V and P_{RV} and repeated guessing for P_{RALL} in the solution of the fault tree in Fig. 15.13, until the fault tree solution for the probability of simultaneous errors approximates the observed frequency of all versions failing simultaneously.

The fault tree model for three versions can easily be generalized to the case where there are N versions. The top event of the fault tree is an *OR* gate with two inputs, an *AND* gate showing all versions failing, and a basic event, representing a related fault that affects all versions

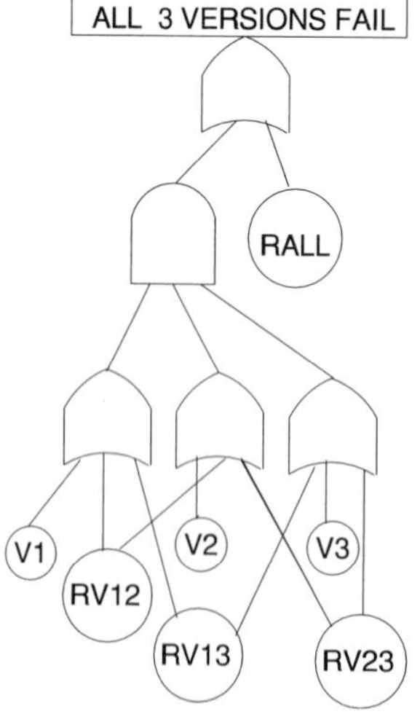

Figure 15.13 Fault tree model used to estimate P_{RALL} for a 3-version system.

simultaneously. The *AND* gate has N inputs, one for each version. Each of the N inputs to the *AND* gate is itself an *OR* gate with N inputs, all basic events. Each *OR* gate has one input representing an unrelated fault in the version, and $N - 1$ inputs representing related faults with each other possible version.

As an example parameter calculation, consider an experimental data set from an early implementation of a three-version system [Chen78, Hech86]. From a sample set of seven versions, twelve different three-version configurations were constructed. Each three-version configuration was subjected to 32 test cases, with the results as tabulated in Table 15.1. For this data set, we can estimate $P_V = 0.0109$.

$$P_V = \frac{F_1}{3F_0 + F_1} = 0.075$$

The estimate for P_{RV} is then

$$P_{RV} = \frac{2F_2P_V(1 - P_V) - (2)F_1P_V^2}{2F_2P_V(1 - P_V) + (2)F_1(1 - P_V^2)} = 1.185 \times 10^{-2}$$

The fault tree shown in Fig. 15.13 is used to estimate $P_{RALL} = 9.7 \times 10^{-3}$.

15.6.2 A case study in parameter estimation

In this section we will use the data from the Lyu-He study [Lyu93a] to determine parameter values for models of three example fault-tolerant software systems (Fig. 15.9). The systems being considered are DRB (distributed recovery block, Fig. 15.10), NVP (N-version programming, three versions, Fig. 15.11), and NSCP (N self-checking programming, Fig. 15.12).

For the Lyu-He data, two levels of granularity were used to define software execution errors and coincident errors: by case or by frame. The first level was defined based on test cases (1000 in total). If a version failed at any time in a test case, it was considered failed for the

TABLE 15.1 Experimental Results from Three-Version Programming

Number of failures	Number of test cases	Observed frequency
0	290	$F_0 = 0.755$
1	71	$F_1 = 0.185$
2	18	$F_2 = 0.047$
3	5	$F_3 = 0.013$

whole case. If two or more versions failed in the same test case (no matter at the same time or not), they were said to have coincident errors for that test case. The second level of granularity was defined based on execution time frames (5,280,920 in total). Errors were counted only at the time frame upon which they manifested themselves, and coincident errors were defined to be the multiple program versions failing at the same time frame in the same test case (with or without the same variables and values).

The 12 programs accepted in the Lyu-He experiment were configured in pairs, whose outputs were compared for each test case. Table 15.2 shows the number of times that 0, 1, and 2 errors were observed in the two-version configurations. The data from Table 15.2 yield an estimate of $P_V = 0.095$ for the probability of activation of an unrelated fault in a two-version configuration, and an estimate of $P_{RV} = 0.0167$ for the probability of a related fault for the by-case data. The by-frame data in Table 15.2 produces $P_V = 0.000026$ and $P_{RV} = 1.3 \times 10^{-7}$ as estimates.

Next, the 12 versions were configured in sets of three programs. Table 15.3 shows the number of times that 0, 1, 2, and 3 errors were observed in the three-version configurations. The data from Table 15.3 yield an estimate of $P_V = 0.0958$ for the probability of activation of an unrelated fault in a three-version configuration. Table 15.4 compares the probability of activation of 1, 2, and 3 faults as predicted by a model, assuming independence between versions, with the observed values. The observed frequency of two simultaneous errors is lower than predicted by the independent model; thus there is no support in the data for related faults affecting two versions, and P_{RV} is estimated to be zero. The observed frequency of three simultaneous errors is higher than predicted by the independent model, so we derive an estimate for P_{RALL}, based on the $P_{RV} = 0$ assumption.

Using the assumption that $P_{RV} = 0$, the probability that three simultaneous errors are activated is given by

$$F_3 = P_V^3 + P_{RALL} - P_V^3 P_{RALL} \tag{15.15}$$

yielding an estimate of $P_{RALL} = 0.0003$ for the by-case data.

TABLE 15.2 Error Characteristics for Two-Version Configurations

	By case		By frame	
Category	Number of cases	Frequency	Number of cases	Frequency
F_0 (no errors)	53,150	0.8053	348,522,546	0.99994786
F_1 (single error)	11,160	0.1691	18,128	0.00005201
F_2 (two coincident)	1,690	0.0256	46	0.00000013
Total	66,000	1.0000	348,540,720	1.00000000

TABLE 15.3 Error Characteristics for Three-Version Configurations

	By case		By frame	
Category	Number of cases	Frequency	Number of cases	Frequency
F_0 (no errors)	163,370	0.7426	1,161,707,015	0.99991790
F_1 (single error)	51,930	0.2360	94,835	0.00008163
F_2 (two coincident)	4,440	0.0202	550	0.00000047
F_4 (three coincident)	260	0.0012	0	0.00000000
Total	220,000	1.0000	1,161,802,400	1.00000000

TABLE 15.4 Comparison of Independent Model with Observed Data for Three Versions, By Case

No. errors activated	Independent model	Observed frequency
0	0.7393	0.7426
1	0.2350	0.2360
2	0.0249	0.0202
3	0.0009	0.0012

The by-frame data in Table 15.3 produces $P_V = 0.000027$ as an estimate. For this by-frame data, when the failure probabilities that are predicted by the independent model are compared to the actual data (Table 15.5), the observed frequency of two errors is two orders of magnitude higher than the predicted probability. There were no cases for which all three programs produced erroneous results. Thus, we will estimate $P_{RALL} = 0$ and derive an estimate for $P_{RV} = 1.57 \times 10^{-7}$.

The same 12 programs which passed the acceptance testing phase of the software development process were analyzed in combinations of four programs; the results are shown in Table 15.6. The by-case data from Table 15.6 yields an estimate of $P_V = 0.106$ for the probability of activation of an unrelated fault in a four-version configuration. Table 15.7 compares the probability of activation of 1, 2, 3, and 4 faults as predicted by a model, assuming independence between versions, with the observed values. The observed frequency of two simultaneous

TABLE 15.5 Comparison of Independent Model with Observed Data for Three Versions, By Frame

No. errors activated	Independent model	Observed frequency
0	0.999919	0.999918
1	0.000081	0.0000816
2	2×10^{-9}	5×10^{-7}
3	2×10^{-14}	0.0

errors is lower than predicted by the independent model, while the observed frequency of three simultaneous errors is higher than predicted. For this set of data we will assume that $P_{RV} = 0$. The observed frequency of four simultaneous failures is also lower than predicted by the independent model, so we will also assume that $P_{RALL} = 0$. The by-frame data in Table 15.6 produces $P_V = 0.000026$ and $P_{RALL} = 1.3 \times 10^{-7}$ as estimates.

15.6.3 Comparative analysis of three software-fault-tolerant systems

Table 15.8 summarizes the parameters estimated from the Lyu-He data. The parameter values for the three systems were applied to the fault tree models shown in Fig. 15.14, using both the by-case and by-frame data. The fault tree models in Figure 15.14 represent systems that use simple comparison of results for error detection, and thus do not directly relate to the DRB, NVP, and NSCP models. The predicted failure probability using the derived parameters in the fault tree models agrees quite well with the observed data, as listed in Table 15.8. The observed failure frequency for the four-version configuration is difficult to estimate because of the possibility of a 2–2 split vote. The data for

TABLE 15.6 Error Characteristics for Four-Version Configurations

	By case		By frame	
Category	Number of cases	Frequency	Number of cases	Frequency
F_0 (no errors)	322010	0.65052	2,613,781,410	0.99989519
F_1 (single error)	152900	0.30889	271,920	0.00010402
F_2 (two coincident)	16350	0.03303	2,070	0.00000079
F_3 (three coincident)	3700	0.00747	0	0.00000000
F_4 (four coincident)	40	0.00008	0	0.00000000
Total	495000	1.00000	2,614,055,400	1.00000000

TABLE 15.7 Comparison of Independent Model with Observed Data for Four Versions, By Case

No. errors activated	Independent model	Observed frequency
0	0.63878	0.65052
1	0.30296	0.30889
2	0.05388	0.03303
3	0.00426	0.00747
4	0.00013	0.00008

the occurrences of such a split are not available. Thus the observed failure frequency in Table 15.8 is a lower bound (it is the sum of the observed cases of three or four coincident failures). If the data on a 2–2 split were available, then the probability of a 2–2 split would be added to the observed frequency values listed in Table 8. For the by-frame data, for example, if 5 percent of the two-coincident failures produced similar wrong results, then the model and the observed data would agree quite well.

TABLE 15.8 Summary of Parameter Values Derived from Lyu-He Data

2-version model	3-version model	4-version model
	By-Case Data	
$P_V = 0.095$ $P_{RV} = 0.0167$	$P_V = 0.0958$ $P_{RV} = 0$ $P_{RALL} = 0.0003$	$P_V = 0.106$ $P_{RV} = 0$ $P_{RALL} = 0$
Predicted failure probability (from the model)		
0.0265	0.0262	0.0044
Observed failure probability (from the data)		
0.0256	0.0214	0.0076
	By-Frame Data	
$P_V = 0.000026$ $P_{RV} = 1.3 \times 10^{-7}$	$P_V = 0.000027$ $P_{RV} = 1.57 \times 10^{-7}$ $P_{RALL} = 0$	$P_V = 0.000026$ $P_{RV} = 1.3 \times 10^{-7}$ $P_{RALL} = 0$
Predicted failure probability (from the model)		
1.31×10^{-7}	4.73×10^{-7}	7.8×10^{-7}
Observed failure probability (from the data)		
1.32×10^{-7}	4.73×10^{-7}	0

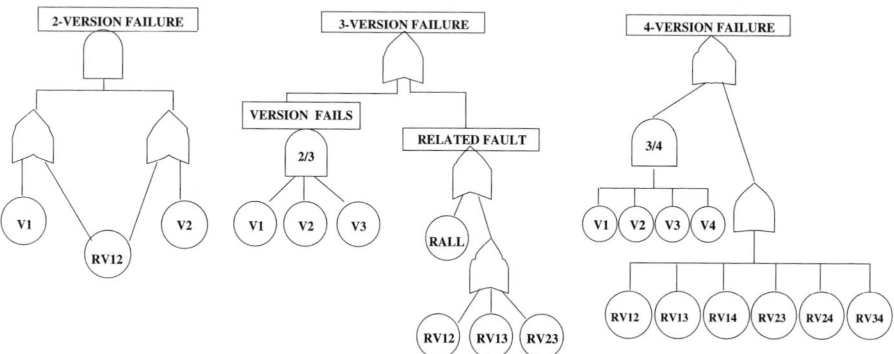

Figure 15.14 Fault tree models for two-, three-, and four-version systems.

These parameters are derived from a single experimental implementation and so may not be generally applicable. Similar analysis of other experimental data will help to establish a set of reasonable parameters that can be used in models that are developed during the design phase of a fault-tolerant system.

The first observation that we can make from Table 15.8 is that there is good agreement between the model and the experimental data. Second, we note that for the by-case data the individual versions were not highly reliable (failure probabilities on the order of 0.1) and yet the fault-tolerant software systems achieved respectable levels of reliability.

The difference in reliability between the by-case and by-frame data is striking. The increased reliability associated with the by-frame data suggests a strong advantage associated with frequent error-checking, since forward-error recovery may be possible. A more complete analysis would also reveal any disadvantages, and would allow a useful trade-off analysis. For example, more frequent comparisons could introduce more overhead for synchronization and message passing, which might jeopardize a hard deadline.

A more complete analysis of the fault-tolerant systems for a single task computation includes the effects of both hardware faults and decider failures and is shown in Table 15.9. For the hardware faults, we assume a fairly typical failure rate of 10^{-4} per hour. In the by-case scenario, a typical test case contained 5280 time frames, each time frame being 50 ms, so a typical computation executed for 264 seconds. Assuming that hardware faults occur at a rate $(10^{-4}/3600)$ *per second,* we see that the probability that a hardware fault occurs during a typical test case is

$$1 - e^{-10^{-4}/3600 \times 264 \text{ seconds}} = 7.333 \times 10^{-6} \tag{15.16}$$

We conservatively assume that a hardware fault that occurs anywhere during the execution of a task disrupts the entire computation running on the host. For the by-frame data, the probability that a hardware fault occurs during a time frame is

$$1 - e^{-10^{-4}/3600 \times 0.05 \text{ seconds}} = 1.4 \times 10^{-9} \tag{15.17}$$

If we further assume that the lifetime of a hardware fault is 1 second, then it can affect as many as 20 time frames. We thus take the probability of a hardware fault to be 20 times the value calculated in Eq. (15.17), or 2.8×10^{-8}.

Since no decider failures were observed during the experimental implementation, it is difficult to estimate this probability. The decider used for the recovery block system is an acceptance test, and for this application is likely to be significantly more complex than the comparator used for the NVP and NSCP systems. For the sake of comparison, for the by-case data we will assume that the comparator used in the NVP and NSCP systems has a failure probability of only 0.0001 and that the acceptance test used for the DRB system has a failure probability of 0.001. For the by-frame data, the decider is considered to be extremely reliable, with a failure probability of 10^{-7} for all three systems. If the decider were any less reliable, then its failure probability would dominate the system analysis, and the results would be far less interesting.

15.7 System-Level Analysis of Hardware and Software System

Computer systems that are used for critical applications are designed to tolerate both hardware and software faults by executing multiple software versions on redundant hardware and by actively reconfiguring the system in response to a permanent failure of a hardware component. In the previous section, the impact of hardware failures was limited to the analysis of a single task; a more complete analysis considers the dynamic reconfiguration of the system configuration in response to hard permanent faults.

Sophisticated techniques exist for the separate analysis of fault-tolerant hardware [Geis90, John88] and software [Lapr84, Scot87,

TABLE 15.9 Comparison of Base Case with More General Case

RB model	NVP model	NSCP model
	By-case data	
Probability of decider failure used for system analysis		
0.001	0.0001	0.0001
Predicted failure probability (perfect decider, no HW faults)		
0.0256	0.0261	0.0403
Predicted failure probability (imperfect decider, HW faults)		
0.0266	0.0262	0.0404
	By-frame data	
Probability of decider failure used for system analysis		
1×10^{-7}	1×10^{-7}	1×10^{-7}
Predicted failure probability (perfect decider, no HW faults)		
1×10^{-6}	2.07×10^{-6}	1.23×10^{-5}
Predicted failure probability (imperfect decider, HW faults)		
1.1×10^{-6}	2.17×10^{-6}	1.24×10^{-5}

Shin84], and a few authors have considered their combined analysis [Lapr84, Star87, Lapr92b]. We will combine the fault tree analysis of a single repetitive task with a Markov model representing the evolution of the hardware configuration as permanent faults occur. The fault tree model captures the effects of software bugs and transient hardware faults which can affect a single task computation, while the Markov model describes how the system on which the software is running can change with time.

A reliability model of an integrated fault-tolerant system must include at least three different factors: computation errors, system structure, and coverage modeling. The fault tree models for the fault-tolerant software systems which we have already considered will describe the computation error process. In these fault tree models, we have deliberately remained vague as to the hardware faults being considered. Here, let us be more precise. In the computation error model, we consider only transient hardware faults that affect the computation but cause no permanent hardware damage. A transient hardware fault is assumed to upset the software running on the processor and produce an erroneous result that is indistinguishable from an input-activated software error. Permanent hardware faults, which require automatic system reconfiguration, are included in the Markov model of system structure.

The longer-term system behavior is affected by permanent faults and component repair, which require system reconfiguration to a different mode of operation. The system structure is modeled by a Markov chain, where the Markov states and transitions model the long-term behavior of the system as hardware and software components are reconfigured in and out of the system. Each state in the Markov chain represents a particular configuration of hardware and software components and thus a different level of redundancy.

The short-term behavior of the computation process and the long-term behavior of the system structure are combined as follows. For each state in the Markov chain, there is a different combination of hardware transients and software faults that can cause a computation error. The fault tree model solution produces, for each state i in the Markov model, the probability q_i that an output error occurs during a single task computation while the state is in state i. The Markov model solution produces $P_i(t)$, the probability that the system is in state i at time t. These two measures are combined to produce $Q(t)$, the probability that an unacceptable result is produced at time t:

$$Q(t) = \sum_{i=1}^{n} q_i P_i(t)$$

The models of the three systems being analyzed (DRB, NVP, and NSCP; see Fig. 15.9) will consist of two fault trees and one Markov model. Since each of the systems can tolerate one permanent hardware fault, there are two operational states in the Markov chain. The initial state in each of the Markov chains represents the full operational structure, and an intermediate state represents the system structure after successful automatic reconfiguration to handle a single permanent hardware fault. (For the sake of simplifying the comparisons, we assume that the systems are not repairable. Repair can easily be considered in the Markov model of the system structure.) There is a single failure state which is reached when the second permanent hardware fault is activated or when a coverage failure occurs.

A coverage failure occurs when the system is unable to detect and recover from the activation of a permanent hardware fault. The probability that the system can correctly detect, isolate, and reconfigure in response to a permanent hardware fault is the parameter c in the Markov models. If the fault is not covered, then a coverage failure is said to occur, which leads to immediate system failure. The coverage parameter (c) can be determined from a coverage model that considers such effects as physical fault behavior, error and fault detection, and recovery and reconfiguration mechanisms. Coverage modeling is described in more detail in [Duga89a, Duga93a].

The safety models for the three systems are similar to the reliability models in that they consist of a Markov model and two associated fault trees. The major difference between a reliability and safety analysis is in the definition of failure. In the reliability models, any unacceptable result (whether or not it is detected) is considered a failure. In a safety model, a detected error is assumed to be handled by the system in a fail-safe manner, so an unsafe result occurs only if an undetected error is produced.

In the Markov part of the safety models, two failure states are defined. The fail-safe state is reached when the second covered permanent hardware fault is activated. The fail-unsafe state is reached when any uncovered hardware fault occurs. The system is considered safe when in the absorbing fail-safe state. This illustrates a key difference between a reliability analysis and a safety analysis. A system which is shut down safely (and thus is not operational) is inherently safe, although it is certainly not reliable.

15.7.1 System reliability and safety model for DRB

The Markov model for the long-term behavior of the DRB system is shown in Fig. 15.15. The Markov model details the initial state configuration, where the recovery block structure is executed on redundant hardware, and the reconfigured state, after the activation of a permanent hardware fault. There are two processors available in the initial state. On one processor, the primary is executed first and the secondary remains idle until needed, while the other processor executes the secondary software module first. The idle software component is shaded.

In the initial configuration of the DRB system, there are two active processors, which can fail independently at rate λ. If the system can properly respond to the failure of one of the processors (with probability c), then the system is reconfigured to a single processor; thus the rate $2\lambda c$ from the initial state to the intermediate state and the rate $2\lambda(1-c)$ for an uncovered failure. When a single processor remains, the system survives until that processor fails.

The fault tree model for the computation process associated with the initial state was analyzed previously (see Fig. 15.10). The fault tree model for the computation process in the reconfiguration state is derived from that for the initial state and is shown in Fig. 15.16. In the reconfiguration state, a single recovery block structure executes on the single remaining processor.

The safety model of DRB, shown in Fig. 15.17, shows that an acceptance test failure is the only software cause of an unsafe result. As long as the acceptance test does not accept an incorrect result, then a safe output is assumed to be produced. The hardware redundancy does not increase the safety of the system, as the system is vulnerable to the acceptance test in both states. The hardware redundancy can actually decrease the safety of the system, since the system is perfectly safe when in the fail-safe state, and the hardware redundancy delays absorption into this state.

15.7.2 System reliability and safety model for NVP

The Markov model for the long-term behavior of the NVP system is shown in Fig. 15.18. In the initial state there are three active processors,

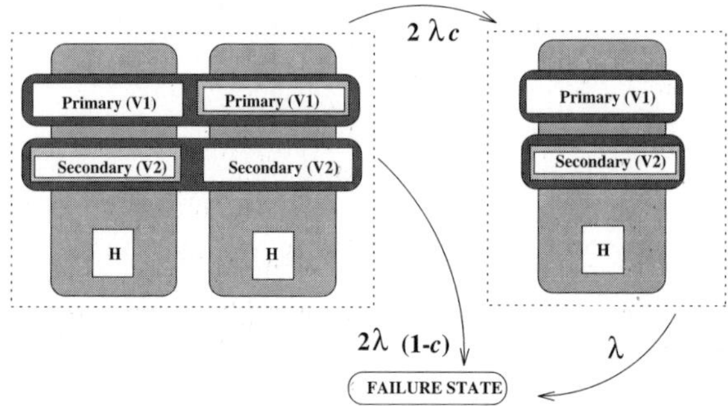

Figure 15.15 Markov reliability model of DRB.

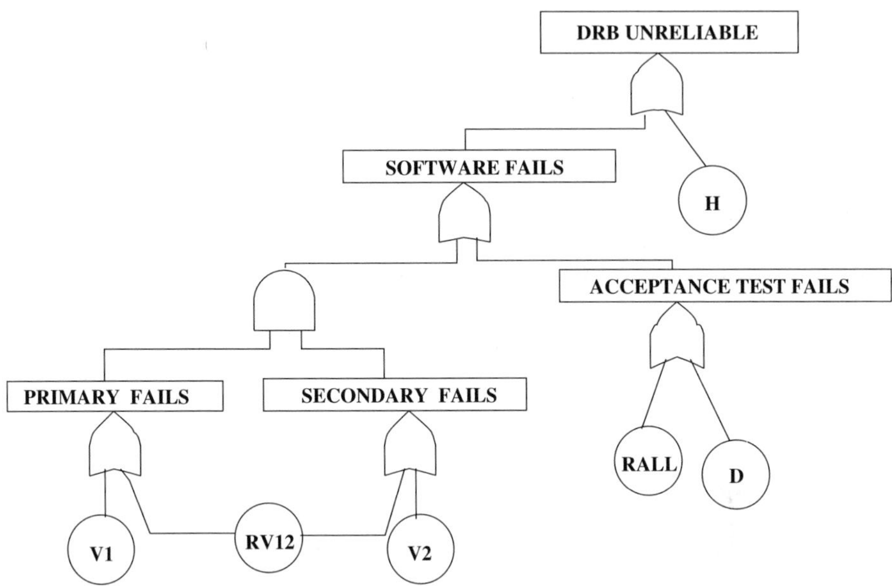

Figure 15.16 Fault tree model of computation process in DRB reconfiguration state.

so the transition rate to the reconfiguration state is $3\lambda c$ and the transition rate to the failure state caused by an uncovered failure is $3\lambda(1-c)$. We assume that the system is reconfigured to simplex mode after the first permanent hardware fault. (See [Doyl95] for a discussion of the TMR-simplex reconfiguration scheme). In the reconfigured state, an unreliable result is caused by either a hardware-transient or a software-

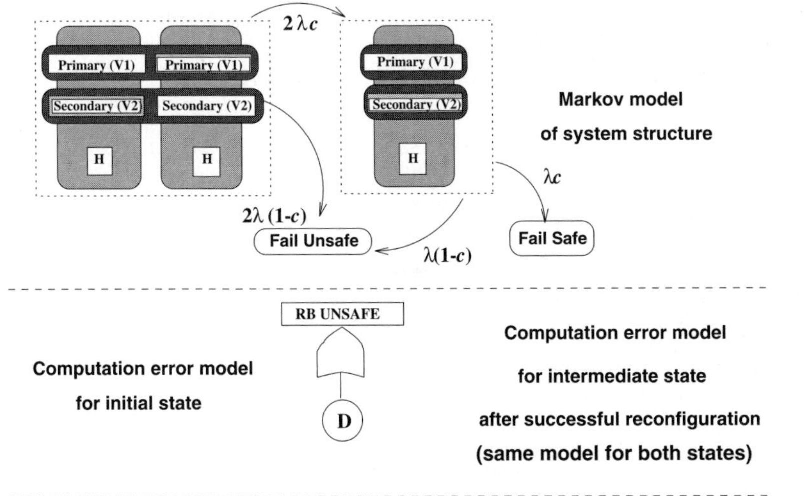

Figure 15.17 Safety model of DRB.

fault activation, as shown in the fault tree of Fig. 15.19. The system fails when the single remaining processor fails; thus the transition rate λ from the reconfiguration state to the failure state.

The NVP safety model (Fig. 15.20) shows that the safety of the NVP system is vulnerable to related faults as well as decider faults. In the Markov model, we assume that the reconfigured state uses two versions (rather than one, as was assumed for the reliability model) so as to increase the opportunity for comparisons between alternatives and thus increase error detectability.

15.7.3 System reliability and safety model for NSCP

The Markov model for the long-term behavior of the NSCP system is shown in Fig. 15.21, while the fault tree model for the reconfiguration state is shown in Fig. 15.22.

The NSCP safety model (Fig. 15.23) shows the same vulnerability of the NSCP system to related faults. When the system is fully operational, all two-way related faults will be detected by the self-checking arrangements, leaving the system vulnerable only to a decider fault, and a fault affecting all versions similarly. After reconfiguration, a related fault affecting both remaining versions could also produce an undetected error.

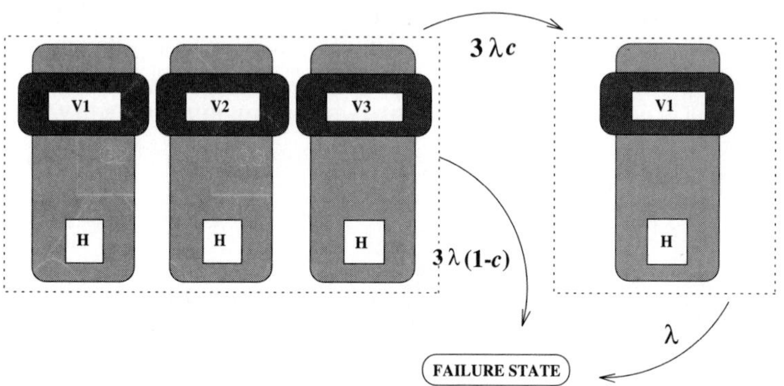

Figure 15.18 Markov reliability model of NVP.

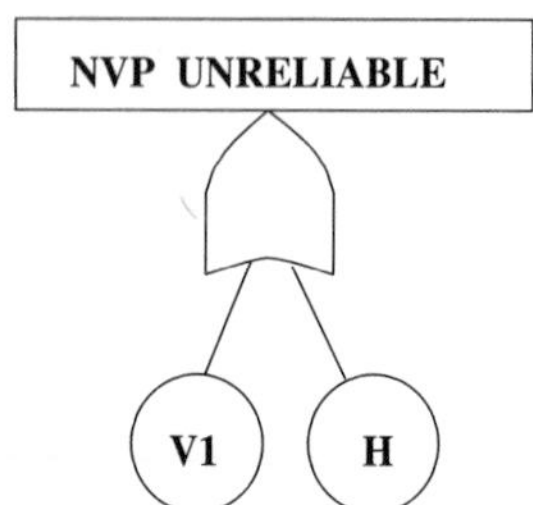

Figure 15.19 Fault tree model of computation process in NVP reconfiguration state.

15.7.4 A case study in system-level analysis

This section contains a quantitative analysis of the system-level reliability and safety models for the DRB, NVP, and NSCP systems. The software parameter values used in this study are those derived earlier from the Lyu-He data. Typical permanent failure rates for processors range in the 10^{-5} *per hour* range, with transients perhaps an order of magnitude larger. Thus we will use $\lambda_p = 10^{-5}$ per hour for the Markov model. The fault and error recovery process is captured in the coverage parameters used in the Markov chain [Duga89a]. We assume a commonly used value for the coverage parameter in the Markov model, $c = 0.999$.

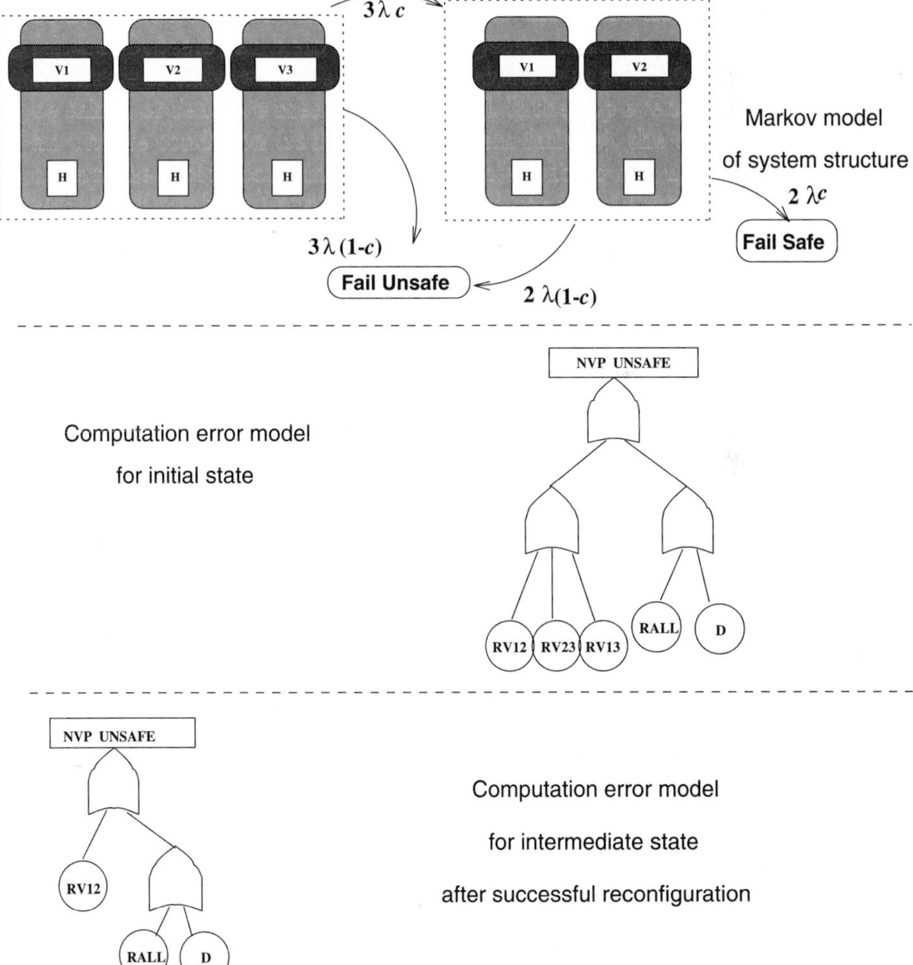

Figure 15.20 Safety model of NVP.

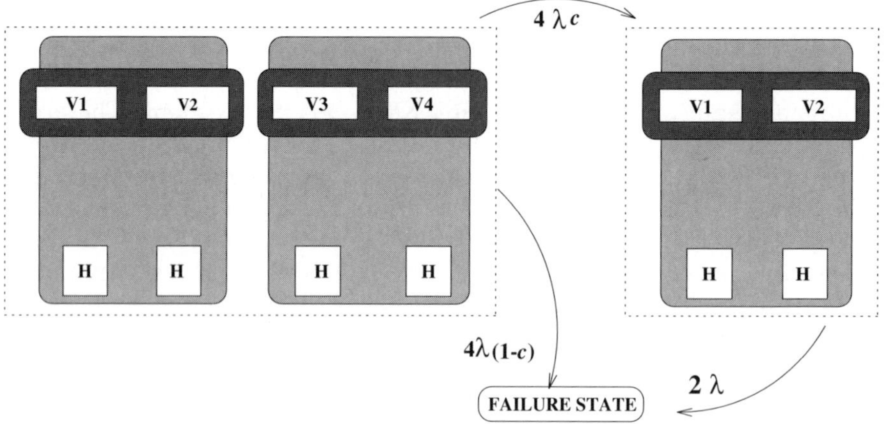

Figure 15.21 Markov reliability model of NSCP.

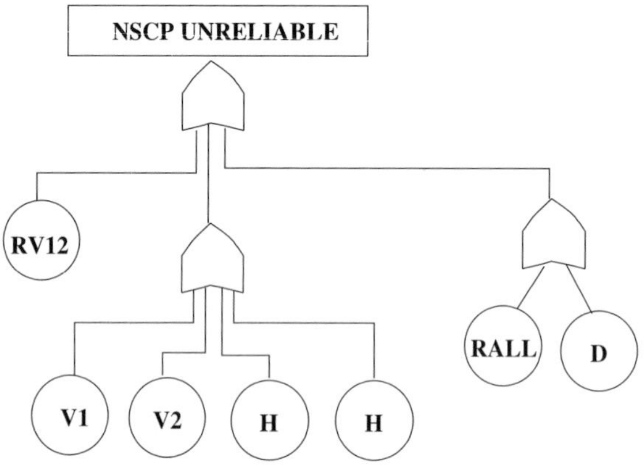

Figure 15.22 Fault tree model of computation process in NSCP reconfiguration state.

Figure 15.24 compares the predicted reliability of the three systems. Under both the by-case and by-frame scenarios, the recovery block system is most able to produce a correct result, followed by NVP. NSCP is the least reliable of the three. Of course, these comparisons are dependent on the experimental data used and assumptions made. More experimental data and analysis are needed to enable a more conclusive comparison.

Figure 15.25 gives a closer look at the comparisons between the NVP and DRB systems during the first 200 hours. The by-case data show a crossover point where NVP is initially more reliable but is later less reliable than DRB. Using the by-frame data, there is no crossover point, but the estimates are so small that the differences may not be statistically significant.

Figure 15.26 compares the predicted safety of the three systems. Under the by-case scenario, NSCP is the most likely to produce a safe result, and DRB is an order of magnitude less safe than NVP or NSCP. This difference is caused by the difference in assumed failure probability associated with the decider. Interestingly, the opposite ordering results from the by-frame data. Using the by-frame data to parameterize the models, DRB is predicted to be the safest, while NSCP is the least safe. The reversal of ordering between the by-case and by-frame parameterizations is caused by the relationship between the probabilities of related failure and decider failure. The by-case data parameter values resulted in related fault probabilities that were generally lower than the decider failure probabilities, while the by-frame data resulted in related fault probabilities that were relatively high. In the safety models, since there were fewer events that lead to an unsafe result, this relationship between related faults and decider faults becomes significant.

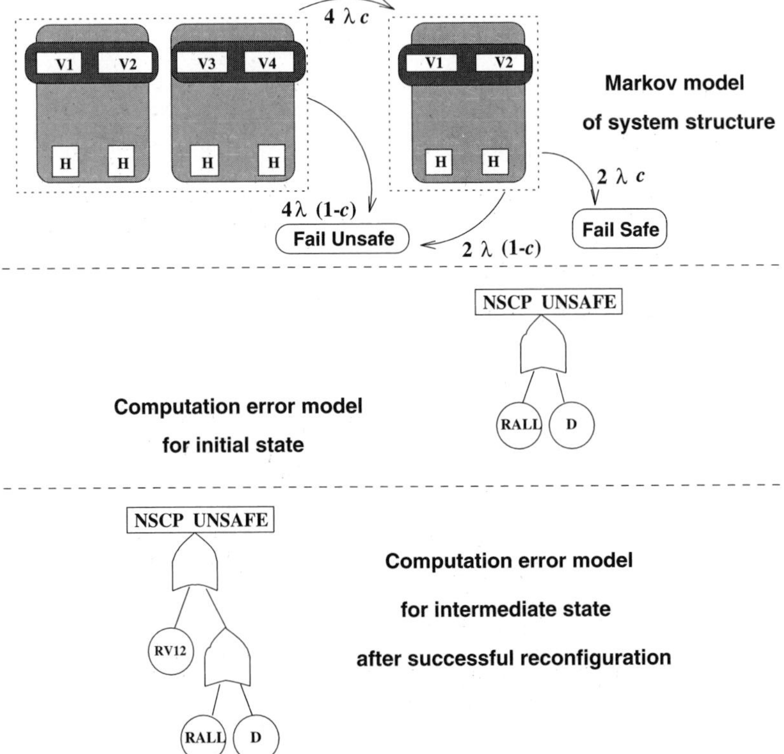

Figure 15.23 Safety model of NSCP.

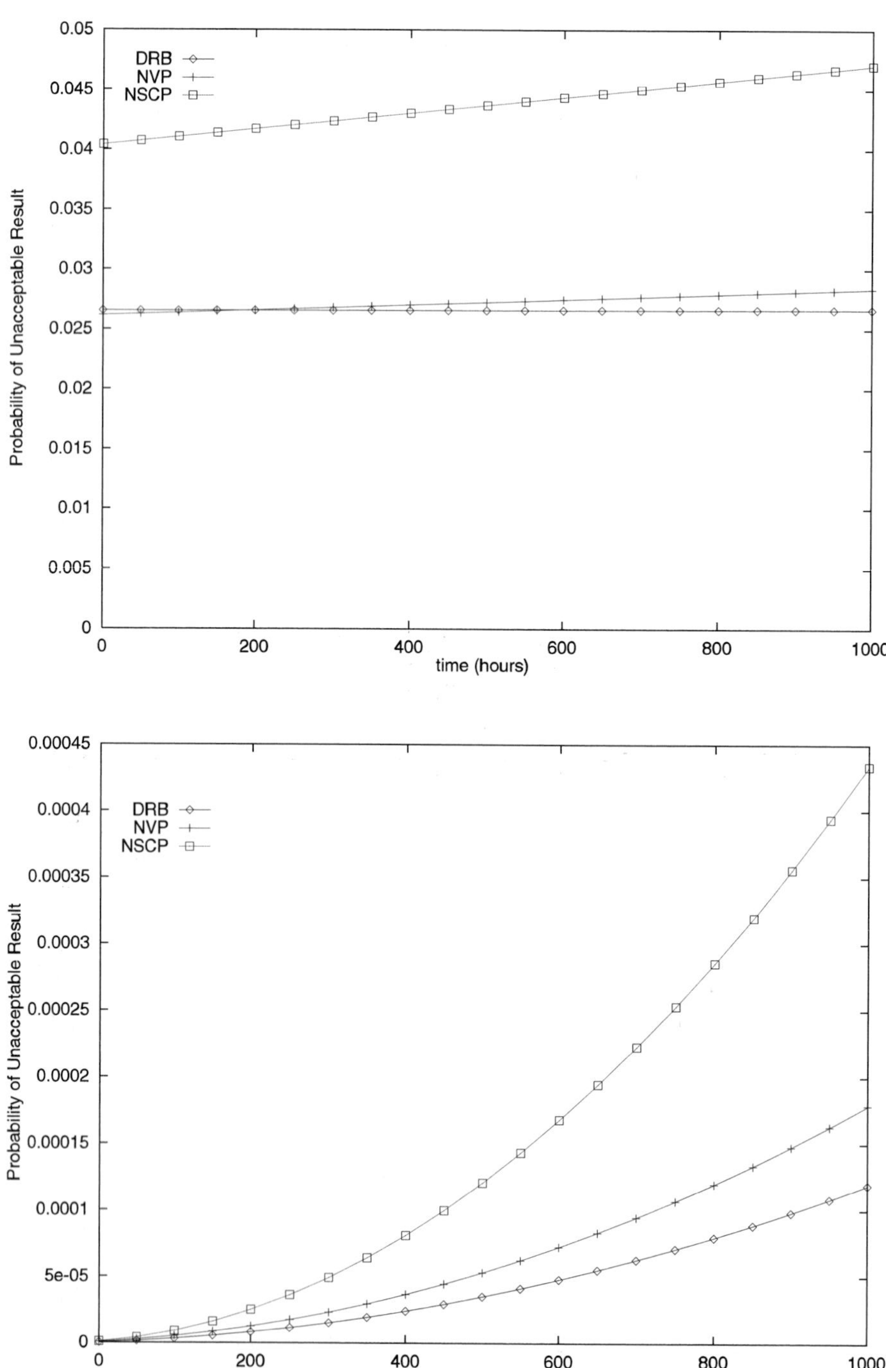

Figure 15.24 Predicted reliability, by-case data (top) and by-frame data (bottom).

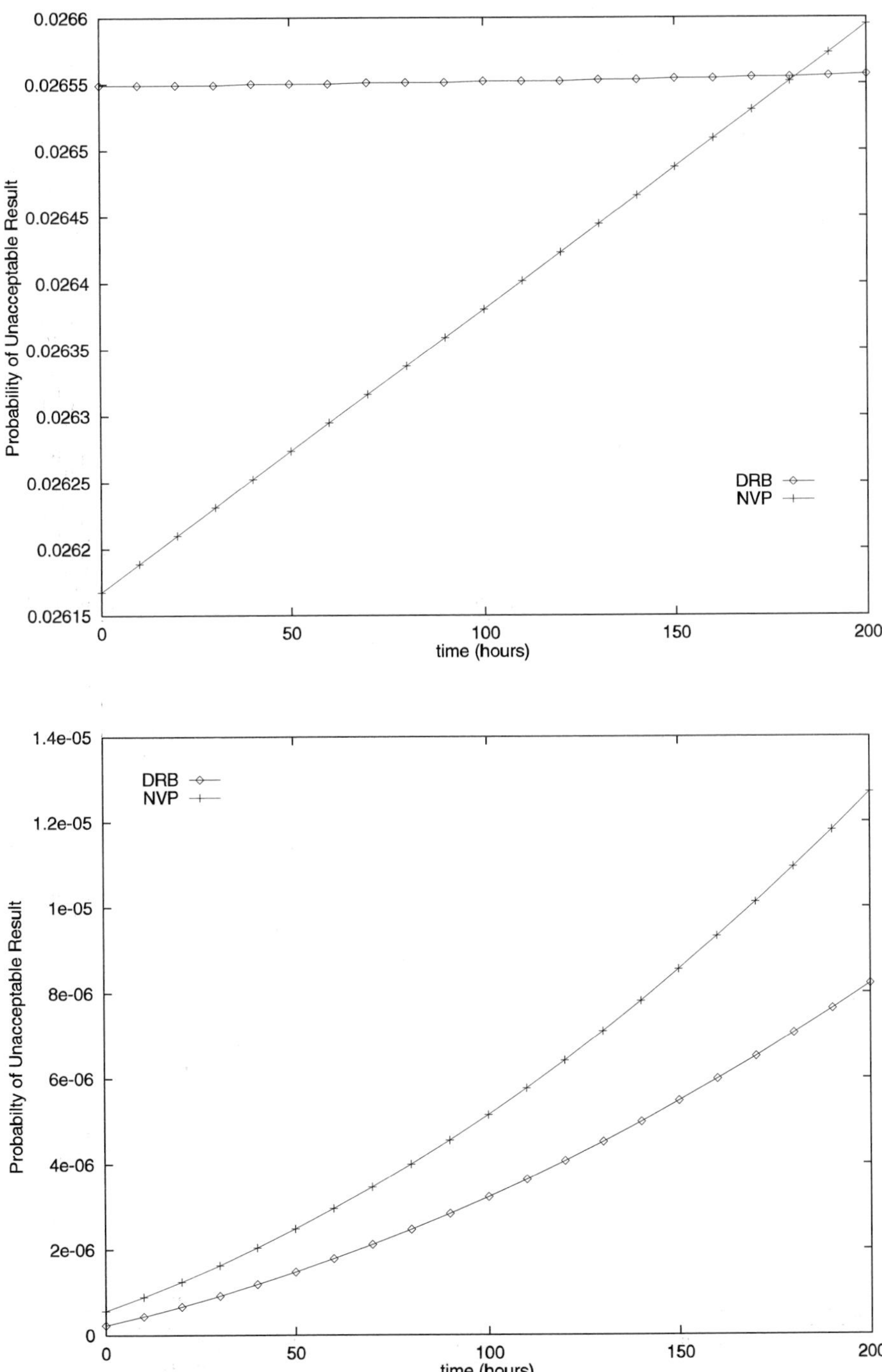

Figure 15.25 Predicted reliability, by-case data (top) and by-frame data (bottom).

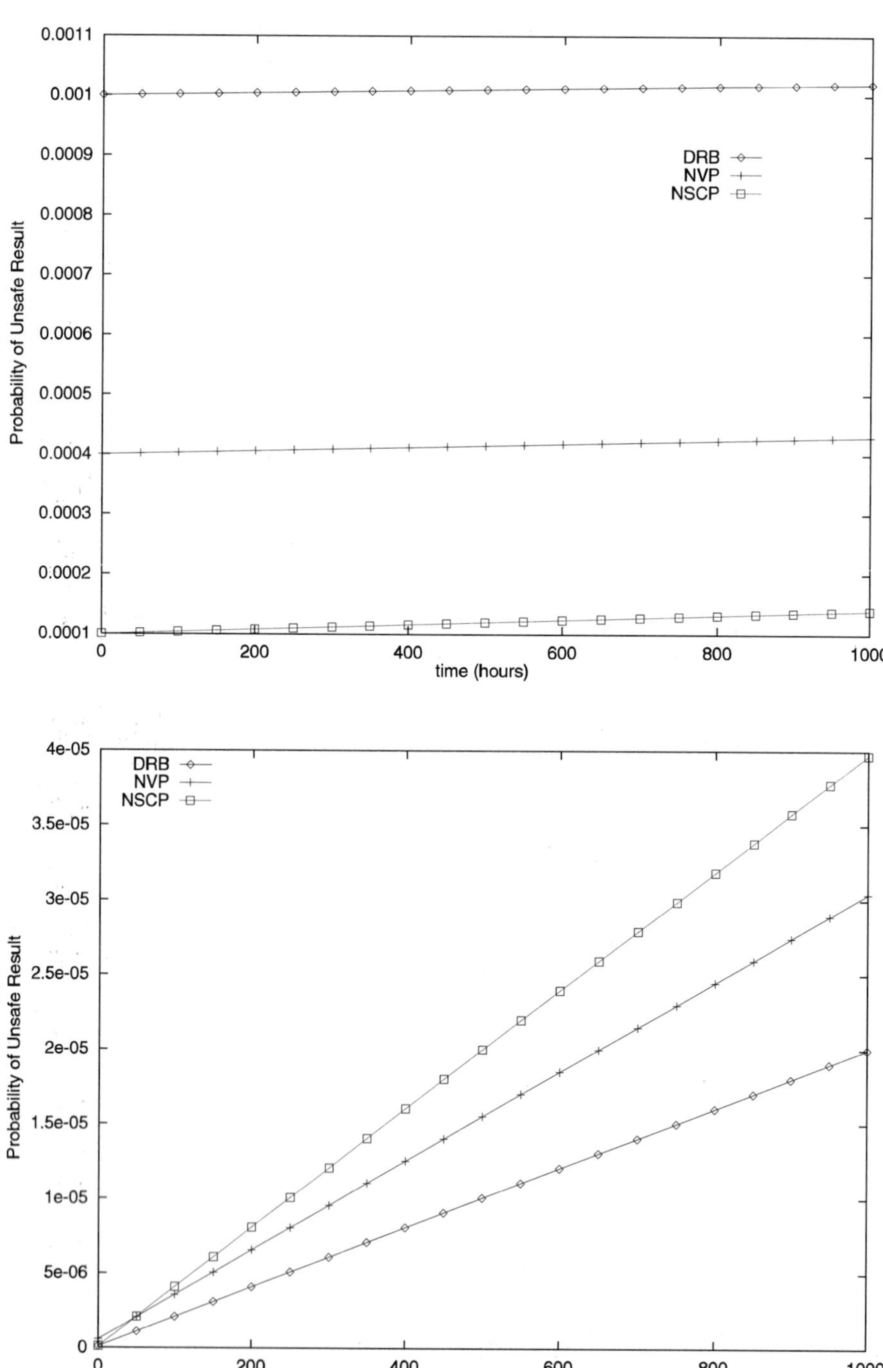

Figure 15.26 Predicted safety, by-case data (top) and by-frame data (bottom).

A more complete comparative analysis of these three systems, including a sensitivity analysis and an assessment of the impact of the decider failure probability, appear in [Duga95]. A major disadvantage associated with fault trees is the exponential solution time, but fault trees share this disadvantage with every other comparable modeling technique. Approaches to this problem include the development of good approximate solution techniques [Duga89b] and the recent use of binary decision diagrams (BDD) for quantitative analysis [Coud93, Rauz93]. A second disadvantage associated with fault tree modeling is the inability to model sequence-dependent failures. Fault trees are a *combinatorial* model (as are reliability block diagrams) that represent combinations of events which lead to system failure. As such, combinatorial models cannot capture information concerning the *order* in which failures have occurred. As an approach to this problem, a dynamic fault tree has been defined, which used a Markov chain for solution [Duga92].

15.8 Summary

Fault tree models, which have traditionally been used for the analysis of hardware systems, are well suited to the analysis of software. Fault trees can serve as a design aid to help determine the effective use of on-line and off-line testing. Software safety validation is aided by the use of software fault trees, where the code is analyzed on a statement-by-statement basis. At the systems level, where a software program or a processor are each considered as basic components, fault trees combine well with Markov models to predict overall system reliability and safety. Such system models may be parameterized using experimental data if field experience is insufficient.

The advantages associated with the use of fault trees are the graphical and mathematical foundations, which give rise to good qualitative and quantitative solution methods. Since fault trees are applicable to many different systems, they can provide a common framework for comparative analysis.

Problems

15.1 What are the minimal cutsets for the fault tree in Fig. 15.1? What is the probability of occurrence of the top event in the tree, given the probabilities of occurrence for the basic events: P_{valve}, P_{timeout}, and P_{full}?

15.2 For the fault tree shown in Fig. 15.2, suppose that we know that event $A4$ has already occurred. Given this information, what is now the set of minimal cutsets, and what is the probability of occurrence for the top event in the tree? (Define P_{Ai} to be the probability of occurrence for the basic event A_i).

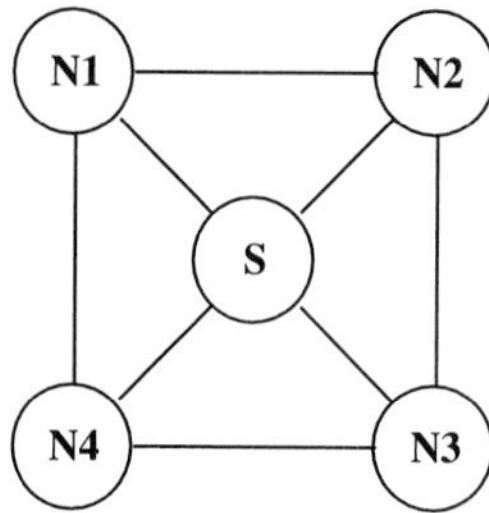

Figure 15.27

15.3 For Probs. 15.3 to 15.5, consider the system shown in Fig. 15.27. The circles in the figure represent processing nodes and the lines represent bidirectional links between the nodes. The nodes labeled $N1$, $N2$, $N3$, and $N4$ are active nodes, while node S is a spare node. Active and spare nodes have the same probability of failure p_N, while links fail with probability p_l.

Assume that links do not fail, and that the system is operational as long as four operational nodes can communicate. A failed node disables the attached nodes. Draw the fault tree model for the system and list the minimal cutsets.

15.4 For the fault tree derived in Prob. 15.3, suppose that the probability of node failure is $p_N = 0.05$. What is the probability that four nodes are connected?

15.5 Assume that both the nodes and links can fail. When a node fails, it can still relay messages on unfailed links. So the system fails when two of the five nodes either fail or are disconnected from the rest of the network. Draw a fault tree model for the system.

15.6 Figure 15.8 showed part of a fault tree used for safety validation. Normally, we would continue expanding each of the cases. Suppose instead that we try to detect a potential hazard on the fly, and take some corrective or preventive action. Suppose during run time that we could detect whether $y > 0$ and whether $z > 0$ at any point in the program. How would that help?

15.7 Consider the consensus recovery block (CRB) [Scot87] described in Chap. 14. Determine a fault tree model to analyze the reliability of CRB (similar to the fault tree models derived in Sec. 15.5).

15.8 Develop a fault tree model for reliability and safety analysis of a two-version NVP system.

15.9 Develop a fault tree model for reliability and safety analysis of a three-version DRB system.

15.10 Develop a fault tree model for reliability and safety analysis of a four-version NVP system.

15.11 Consider an experimental implementation of a multiversion programming system that resulted in 27 versions [Knig86]. Testing with more than a million test cases revealed the failure behavior shown in Table 15.10. If a 2-version system that used comparison matching were formed by randomly selecting 2 of the 27 versions, what would be the expected reliability of the software

TABLE 15.10

Number of failed versions	Observed frequency
0	0.983539
1	0.15206e-1
2	0.551e-3
3	0.343e-3
4	0.242e-3
5	0.73e-4
6	0.32e-4
7	0.12e-4
8	0.2e-5
More than 8	0

system? (Assume that the system fails if it is unable to produce a correct result. Thus a mismatch results in a failure.)

15.12 For the same system described in Prob. 15.7, what would be the expected safety of a similarly constructed two-version system? (The system fails when an incorrect result is delivered.)

Chapter

16

Software Reliability Simulation

Robert C. Tausworthe
Jet Propulsion Laboratory

Michael R. Lyu
AT&T Bell Laboratories

16.1 Introduction

Previous chapters discuss the opportunities and benefits of SRE throughout the entire life cycle, from requirements determination through design, implementation, testing, delivery, and operations. Properly applied, SRE is an important positive influence on the ultimate quality of all life-cycle products. The set of life-cycle activities and artifacts, together with their attributes and interrelationships, that are related to reliability* comprise what we here refer to as the *reliability process.* The artifacts of the software life cycle include documents, reports, manuals, plans, code, configuration data, test data, ancillary data, and all other tangible products.

Software reliability is dynamic and stochastic. In a new or upgraded product, it begins at a low figure with respect to its new intended usage and ultimately reaches a figure near unity in maturity. The exact value of product reliability, however, is never precisely known at any point in its lifetime.

The software reliability models described in Chap. 3 attempt to assess expected reliability or future operability using observed failure data and statistical inference techniques. Most of these treat only the exposure and handling of failures during testing or operations. They are restricted in their life-cycle scope and adaptability to general use

* Suitable extensions of the concepts of this chapter may also apply to simulation of other quality profiles, such as availability.

for a number of reasons, including their foundation on oversimplified assumptions and their primary focus on testing and operations phases.

Modelers have traditionally imposed certain simplifying assumptions in order to obtain closed-form, idealized approximations of software reliability. Some modelers may have relaxed an assumption here or there in attempts to provide more generality, but as models become more and more realistic, the likelihood of obtaining simple analytic solutions plunges to impossibility.

This situation is not a roadblock to software reliability modeling, but perhaps a boon, in that it forces us to apply modern technology to the problem. Computer models are not subject to the oversimplifications required to obtain closed-form results. Numerical methods can cope with models having very realistic and complex representations of project processes, software artifacts, and the development and operational environments.

Reliability models attempt to capture the structure and interrelationships among artifacts, activities, resources, quality, and time. However, this chapter is mainly about computational techniques for modeling reliability behavior. It does not present a tool for operational situations that you may immediately apply off-the-shelf. It does present concepts for generalized tools that mirror reliability processes. We hope that the material presented will demonstrate the power, flexibility, and potential benefits that simulation techniques offer, together with methods for representing artifacts, activities, and events of the process, and techniques for computation.

16.2 Reliability Simulation

A simulation model describes a system being characterized in terms of its artifacts, events, interrelationships, and interactions in such a way that one may perform experiments on the model, rather than on the system itself, ideally with indistinguishable results.

Simulation presents a particularly attractive computational alternative for investigating software reliability because it averts the need for overly restrictive assumptions and because it can model a wider range of reliability phenomena than mathematical analyses can cope with. Simulation does not require that test coverage be uniform, or that a particular fault-to-failure relationship exist, or that failures occur independently, if these are not actually the case.

But power and generality are ineffective where ignorance reigns. Scientific philosophy teaches us to seek the simplest models that explain poorly understood phenomena. For example, when we do not understand how fault attributes relate to consequent failures, we may as well simplify the model by assuming that faults produce independent failures, at least until our experiments prove otherwise.

But objective validation of even a simple reliability model may be problematic, because controlled experiments, while easy to simulate, will be impossible to conduct in practice. However, if we can build an overall model upon simple and plausible submodels that together integrate cleanly to simulate the phenomenon under study, then we may gain some aggregate trust from the combined levels of confidence we may have in the constituent submodels.

16.2.1 The need for dynamic simulation

Reliability modeling ultimately requires good data. But software projects do not always collect data sets that are comprehensive, complete, or consistent enough for effective modeling research or model application. Additionally, industrial organizations are reluctant to release their reliability data for use by outside parties. Further, data required for software reliability modeling in general, and execution time models in particular, seem to be even more difficult to collect than other types of software engineering data. Even when data are available, they are rarely suitable for isolation of individual reliability drivers.

In practicality, isolating the effects of various driving factors in the life cycle requires exploring a variety of scenarios "with other factors being the same." But no real software project can afford to do the same project several times while varying the factors of interest. Even if it could, control and repeatability of factors would, at best, be questionable. A project may attempt, of course, to utilize data from past experiences, "properly adjusted" to appear as if earlier realizations of the current project were available. However, in view of the current scarcity of good, consistent data, this may not be realistic.

Reliability modelers thus never have the real opportunity to observe several realizations of the same software project. Nor are they provided with data that faithfully match the assumptions of their models. Nor are they able to probe into the underlying error and failure mechanisms in a controlled way. Rather, they are faced not only with the problem of guessing the form and particulars of the underlying random processes from the scant, uncertain data they possess, but also with the problem of best forecasting future reliability using those data.

Since good data sets are so scarce, one purpose of simulation is to supply carefully controlled, homogeneous data or software artifacts having known characteristics for use in evaluating the various assumptions upon which existing reliability models have been built. Since actual software artifacts (such as faults in computer programs) and processes (such as failure and fault removal) often violate the assumptions of analytic software reliability models, simulation can perhaps provide a better understanding of such assumptions and may even lead to a better explanation of why some analytic models work well in spite of such violations.

But while simulation may be useful for creating data sets for studying other, more conventional reliability models, it cannot provide the necessary attributes of the phenomena being modeled without real information derived from real data collected from real projects, past and present.

A second use of simulation, then, is in forecasting the driving influences of a real project. Models that can faithfully portray the relative* consequences of various proposed alternatives can potentially assess the relative advantages of the candidates. Once a project sufficiently characterizes its processes, artifacts, and utilization of resources, then trade-offs can indicate the best hopes for project success.

Simulation can mimic key characteristics of the processes that create, validate, and revise documents and code. It can mimic faulty observation of a failure when one has, in fact, occurred, and, additionally, can mimic system outages due to failures. Furthermore, simulation can distinguish faults that have been removed from those that have not, and thus can readily reproduce multiple failures due to the same as-yet unrepaired fault. Some reliability subprocesses may be sensitive to the passage of execution time (e.g., operational failures), while others may depend on wall-clock, or calendar, time (e.g., project phases); still others may depend on the amount of human effort expended (e.g., fault repair) or on the number of test cases applied. A simulator can relate model-pertinent resource dependencies to a common base via resource schedules, such as workforce loading and computer utilization profiles.

16.2.2 Dynamic simulation approaches

Simulation in this chapter refers to the technique of imitating the character of an object or process in a way that permits one to make quantified inferences about the real object or process. A *dynamic* simulation is one whose inputs and observables are events and parameter values, either continuous or discrete, that vary over time. The formal characterization of the object or process is the *model* under study.

When the form of the model changes over time, adapting to actual data from an evolving project, the simulation is *trace-driven*. If parameters and interrelationships are static, without trace data, the simulation is *self-driven*.

* Absolute accuracy is not required for many trade-off studies. Factors which remain the same for all alternative choices do not affect the relative advantage analyses.

The observables of interest in reliability engineering are usually discrete integer-valued quantities (e.g., counts of errors, defects, faults, failures, lines of code) that occur, or are present, as time progresses. Studies of reliability in this context belong to the general field of discrete-event process simulation. Readers wishing to learn more about discrete-event simulation methods may consult [Kreu86].

One approach to simulation produces actual physical artifacts and portions of the environment according to factors and influences believed to typify these entities within a given context. The artifacts and environment are allowed to interact naturally, whereupon we observe the actual flow of occurrences of activities and events. We refer to this approach as *artifact-based* process simulation, and discuss it in detail in Sec. 16.4.

The other reliability simulation approach [Taus94, Taus96] produces time-line imitations of reliability-related activities and events. No artifacts are actually created, but are modeled parametrically over time. The key to this approach is a *rate-based* architecture, in which phenomena occur naturally over time as controlled by their frequencies of occurrence, which depend on driving factors such as numbers of faults so far exposed or yet remaining, failure criticality, workforce level, test intensity, and execution time.

Rate-based event simulation is a form of modeling called *system dynamics,* with the distinction that the observables are discrete events randomly occurring in time. Systems dynamics simulations are traditionally nonstochastic and nondiscrete. But, as will be shown, extension to a discrete stochastic architecture is not difficult. For more information on the systems dynamics technique, see [Robe83].

The use of simulation in the study of software reliability is still formative, experimental, speculative, controversial, and in the proof-of-concept stage. Although simulation models conceptually seem to hold high promise both for creating data to validate conventional models and for generating more realistic forecasts than do analytic models, the evidence to support these hypotheses is currently rather scant and arguable. There are some favorable indications of potential, however, to be discussed.

16.3 The Reliability Process

Because of the lack of good data, past efforts in modeling the reliability process have perhaps been, to some, daunting tasks with uncertain benefits. However, as projects are now becoming increasingly better instrumented, data availability will eventually make this modeling entirely feasible and accurate. Some simulations of portions of the reliability process where measurements are routinely taken are practical.

The reliability process, in generic terms, is a *model* of the reliability-oriented aspects of software development, operations, and maintenance. Since every project is different, describing an "average" case requires characterizing behavior typical of a class, with variations according to product, situation, environmental, and human factors. In this section, we shall attempt to describe some of the more qualitative aspects of the software reliability process. Quantitative profiles will then follow in subsequent sections.

16.3.1 The nature of the process

Quantities of interest in a project reliability profile include artifacts, errors, inspections, defects, corrections, faults, tests, failures, outages, repairs, validations, retests, and expenditures of resources such as CPU time, staff effort, and schedule time.

A number of factors hold varying degrees of influence over these interrelated elements. Influences include relatively static entities, such as product requirements, as well as other, more dynamic factors, such as the order and concurrency among activities in the process. One would hope to quantify trends, correlations, and perhaps causal factors from data gathered from previous similar projects that would be of current use. Even when formal data are not available, project personnel may often be able to apply their experiences to estimate many of the parameters of the reliability profile needed for modeling.

We will aggregate activities relating to reliability into typical classes of work, such as

1. *Construction* generates new documentation and code artifacts, while human mistakes inject defects into them. Activities divide into separate documentation and coding subphases, and perhaps further divide into separate work packages for constructed components.

2. *Integration* combines reusable documentation and code components with new documentation and code components, while human mistakes may create further defects. Integration activities divide into separate documentation and code integration subphases, and perhaps further divide into separate work packages according to the build architecture.

3. *Inspection* detects defects through static analyses of software artifacts. Inspections also divide into separate document and code subphases mirroring construction. Inspections may fail to recognize defects when encountered.

4. *Correction* analyzes and removes defects, again in document and code correction subphases. Corrections may be ineffective, and may inject new defects.

5. *Preparation* generates test plans and test cases, and readies them for execution.
6. *Testing* executes test cases, whereupon failures occur. Some failures may escape observation, while others may initiate system outages. Failure criticality determinations are made.
7. *Identification* makes failure-to-fault correspondences and fault category assignments. Each fault may be new or previously encountered. Identification may erroneously identify the cause of a failure.
8. *Repair* removes faults (not necessarily perfectly) and possibly introduces new faults.
9. *Validation* performs inspections and static checks to affirm that repairs are effective, but may err in doing so; it may also detect that certain repairs were ineffective (i.e., the corresponding faults were not totally removed), and may also detect other faults.
10. *Retest* executes test cases to verify whether specified repairs are complete. If not, the defective repair is marked for re-repair. New test cases may be needed. Retests may err in qualifying a fault as repaired.

16.3.2 Structures and flows

Work in a project generally flows in the logical precedence of tasks listed above. But some activities may take place concurrently and repeatedly, especially in rapid prototyping, concurrent engineering, and spiral models of development. Models of behavior cannot ignore project paradigms, but must adapt to them.

Events occur and activities take place through the application of resources over intervals of time. No progress in the life cycle results unless activities consume resources. As examples, a code component of 500 lines of code (LOC) may require an average of W_c work hours and H_c CPU hours per LOC to develop, to be expended between the schedule times t_1 and t_2; testing the component may require W_t work hours to generate and apply test cases and H_t CPU hours per test case to execute, scheduled for the time interval between t_3 and t_4; and a repair activity may require W_r work hours and H_r CPU hours to complete, during the interval between times t_5 and t_6.

The project resource schedule is essential for managing the reliability process. It defines the project activities, products, flow of work, and allocation of resources. It thus reflects the planned development methodology, management and engineering decisions, and environment constraints.

Projects may, of course, measure failure profiles and other reliability data without recording the schedule and resource of actual performance details. However, they will not be able to extract quantitative relationships among reliability and management parameters without these details.

The data essential to a process schedule define the resources and resource levels that are applied throughout the project duration. Schedule items may, for example, appear as tuples, such as

$$(resource,\ event\_process,\ rate,\ units,\ t_{begin},\ t_{end})$$

Together, the items relate the utilization of all resources at each instant of time throughout the process. The tuple specifies that the named *event_process* activity uses the designated *resource* at the given application *rate* during the designated time interval (t_{begin}, t_{end}), not to exceed the allocated *units* limit.

The *rate* defines the amount of *resource* consumed per *dt* of the *event_process.* If *dt* is calendar time and the resource is human effort, the rate is staff level; if the resource is CPU and *dt* is in CPU hours, the rate is CPU hours per calendar day. When an *event_process* expends its allocated *units,* the effective *rate* becomes zero.

Projects typically express schedule information in units of calendar time. If a project includes weekends, holidays, and vacations, then the schedule must either exclude these as inactive periods or else provide compensating rate factors between resource days and calendar time. For example, if a project is idle for two weeks during the winter holiday season, the schedule should not allocate any resources during this time. If a project works only 5 days a week, the resource utilization rate should allocate only 5/7ths of a workday per calendar day. (However, if the project allocates time and resources in weeks, then 5 days is a normal work week, and no rate adjustment is necessary in this case.)

16.3.3 Interdependencies among elements

Causal relationships exist between a project's input reliability drivers and its resulting reliability profile, in that all development subprocesses consume resources and are driven, perhaps randomly, by other factors of influence.

Quantification of relationships is tantamount to modeling, and is required for simulation. As examples, the degree to which code and documents are inspected correlates with the number and seriousness of faults discovered in testing; the correctness of specifications relates to the correctness of ensuing code; and the seriousness of failures influences when a project will schedule the causal faults for repair.

Some relationships may be generic, while others may be unique to a given project. Some interrelationships may be subtle, while others may seem more axiomatic. Some of the typical axiomatic generic relationships among reliability profile parameters are:

1. All activities (including outages) consume resources.
2. Code written to missing, incorrect, or volatile specifications will be more faulty than code written to correct, complete, and stable specifications.
3. Tests rely on the existence of test cases. Old test cases rarely expose new faults.
4. The number of faults removed will be less than the number attempted. The attempted removal activity may also create new faults.
5. The number of validated fault removals will not exceed the number of attempts. Validation may erroneously report a fault removed.
6. Retesting usually encounters only failures due to bad fixes.

16.3.4 Software environment characteristics

Software in a test environment performs differently than it will in an operational environment. There are many reasons, more adequately addressed in Chap. 13, why this is the case. Principal reasons among them, however, are differences in configuration, execution purpose, execution scenarios, attitudes toward failures, and orientation of personnel. In brief, testing and operations are different environmentally.

Reliability profiles during test and operations depend on the environments themselves, not just on the test case execution scenarios and values of environment parameters. Although testing may attempt to emulate real operations in certain particulars, we must recognize that the characters of testing and operations are apt to differ significantly.

Predicting failures in differing environments requires, at the least, adaptability of the reliability model to fit configuration, scenario, and previous failure data. Such adaptations must accommodate for differences in hardware, test strategies, loading, database volume, and user training.

16.4 Artifact-Based Simulation

Software developers have long questioned the nature of relationships between software failures and program structure, programming error characteristics, and test strategies. Von Mayrhauser et al. [Mayr91, Mayr92, Mayr93] have performed experiments to investigate such questions, arguing that the extent to which reliability depends merely on these factors can be measured by generating random programs having the given characteristics, and then observing their failure statistics. It is not important, in this respect, that the programs actually execute to perform useful functions, but merely that they possess the hypothesized properties that "real" programs would have in a given environment.

If the hypothesis is true, then the effects of the various controlled elements under study would be readily discovered. For example, by adjusting code structural characteristics (e.g., size, ratio of branching decisions to loop decisions, and fault distribution) in a controlled set of experiments, we may observe the contributory effects to failure behavior. We may also learn something about the sensitivities of reliability models to their founding assumptions. Such studies would lead practitioners to the best model(s) to use in given situations.

To explore the conjecture, they identified program properties and test strategies to be investigated. Then they performed experiments using automatically generated programs having the given properties, subjected these to the selected test strategies, and measured the reliability results.

Their investigations proceeded using only single-module programs (i.e., ones with no procedure calls), assumed that faults are of only a single type and severity, distributed uniformly throughout the program, and considered only a constant likelihood that a failure results when execution encounters a statement containing a fault.

There is no fundamental limitation in the artifact simulation technique that excludes procedure calls, multiple fault types, and time-dependent statistics. They were excluded in these early experiments to establish basic relationships. Their architecture will support multiple subprograms; faults of various types, severities, and distributions; and time-varying parameters at the later stages of experimentation.

16.4.1 Simulator architecture

The reported simulation covers the coding, testing, and debugging portions of the software life cycle. The simulator consists of the following components (see Fig. 16.1).

The *code generator* uses program design and/or code structural and error characteristics to produce executable code with faults. Code generation is discussed more fully later (Sec. 16.4.1.2). The faults injected into the program cause actual execution failures during testing to occur in such a manner as to be detected by the *test harness* module, discussed below.

The *compiler* is an ordinary compiler, the same as an actual project would use. The compiler generates executable code from the generated code and from updates following each of the fault repairs.

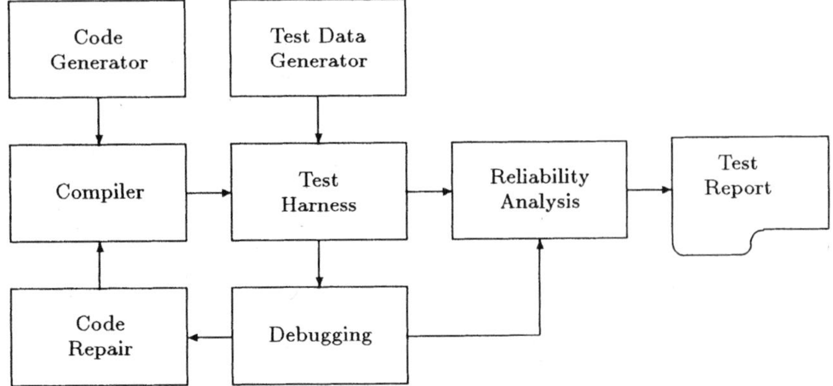

Figure 16.1 Artifact-based software process simulator program.

The *test data generator* uses the generated code, together with parameters that select testing strategy, testing criteria, and phase (unit test, integration test, system test, etc.) to produce test input data and testing procedure parameters.

The *test harness* module applies test data to the simulated system in accordance with the selected test procedures, then detects each failure as it occurs, and categorizes it according to predetermined fault exposure and severity criteria.

The *debugger* and *code repair* functions of the simulation locate and repair faults recognized by the test harness, and then reschedule the program for compilation and retesting. The debugger may fail to locate the fault and may either completely or incompletely remove the fault, when located. It may, at times, even introduce new faults. The debugger parameters include inputs to control locatability, severity, completeness, and fault detectability.

Reliability analysis combines the failure data output by the test harness with the residual fault data from the debugger (undetected errors and incorrect repairs) to assess the reliability of the simulated code. This assessment compares failure results with the output of a conventional software reliability model.

16.4.1.1 Simulation inputs. Artifact simulation experiments can vary many aspects of program construction and testing to investigate the effect of static properties on dynamic behavior. Inputs may include those which characterize code structure, coding errors, test input data, test conduct, failure characteristics, debugging effectiveness, and computing environment.

The investigated code structure parameters pertained to control flow, data declaration, structural nesting, and number and size of subprograms. Statement type frequencies represented the structural dependencies of a program. The experiments assumed four types of program statements: assignments, looping statements, if statements, and subprogram calls. Data structure declaration characteristics were not simulated because faults in such structures tend to be caught by the compiler, and because the effects of faults in such statements would be included among those of the four chosen types.

Type, distribution, density, and fault-to-failure relationship parameters influenced the insertion of coding errors. The generator used type information to select the kinds of statements composing the program. Distribution information controlled where faults were located, either clustered in specified functions or scattered randomly throughout the program. Fault-to-failure relationships defined the frequency of failures when faults are encountered at run time.

Test input data depend on the testing environment, operational scenario, testing strategies, test phase, desired coverage, and resources available for testing. In the simulations reported, resource considerations were not addressed. Provisions for test strategies included features for random, directed, functional, mutation, sequencing, and feature testing. Test coverage selection included parameters designating node, branch, and data flow modes.

Projects classify failure attributes by type, severity, and detection status. Investigations so far have treated only failures of a single type and severity.

Debugging effectiveness depended on parameters associated with fault detection, identification, severity, and repair. Each of these, except severity, has correctness and resource dimensions. For example, identification establishes a fault-to-failure correspondence and the time required to make that correspondence.

Computing-environment parameters included all the data required to run the test harness and analyze the failure data. The experiment environment data included machine, language, and workload parameters.

16.4.1.2 Simulated code generation. A code generator may produce simulated code using measured parameters of the actual project (trace-driven), or from generic data taken from a wide variety of project histories (self-driven).

Figure 16.2 illustrates a self-driven code generator architecture. The reported code simulator operates approximately as follows: Given the number of modules and the set of module sizes, the generator creates statements of the specified types according to their given occurrence frequencies, sometimes followed by code that represents a fault of a specified character.

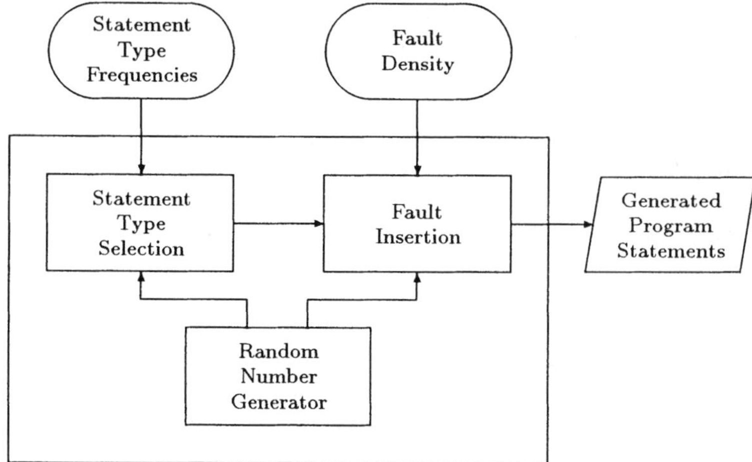

Figure 16.2 Self-driven artifact simulation of the coding phase.

The means for invoking multiple modules and for controlling the depth and length of nested structures were not explicitly revealed in the source references. If you wish to duplicate the simulator for your own experiments you will have to decide upon appropriate models for these characteristics.

It is not necessarily assumed that real faults are uniformly distributed over the program; rather, the program generator can seed faults on either a function-by-function or statement-by-statement basis, according to a distribution by statement type and nesting level. Further, the fault-exposure ratios of each fault need not be the same.

The presence of a real fault in a normal program corresponds to an ersatz element within the simulated program that can cause a failure contingent on a supposed failure characteristic. As the simulated program executes, a statement containing a fault will, with a given probability (the fault-exposure ratio), cause a failure.

But the ersatz failure, when it occurs, is not meant to duplicate the appearance of the real failure; only its occurrence and location are of importance. The injected fault thus needs to raise an exception with information that will identify where, when, and what type of failure has occurred. The reported simulator used a divide-by-zero expression to trigger the fault, which was then trapped by the execution harness via the signal capability of C.

An important step toward extending the utility of the simulation technique would be to make it trace-driven, or adaptive to project measurements as they emerge dynamically, rather than using only the static historic data of the self-driven simulation described above. Figure 16.3 illustrates how trace data would replace the random selection of statements during program execution.

16.4.1.3 Execution harness. The reported execution harness contains a test driver program that creates an interface between the generated program and its test data, spawns a child process to execute the generated program, and collects execution-time data on the child process separately from that of its ancillary functions, which may not have the same structural characteristics. The returned value of the child process indicated whether the test resulted in failure or terminated naturally.

Simulated faults in the generated program could have been represented in any of a number of ways. The reported experiments used arithmetic overflow. Having detected the failure, the test harness enters the returned information into the failure log for use in locating and removing the fault. The updated program then recompiles and reexecutes.

16.4.1.4 Reliability assessment. The output log provides the execution time of each test run and indicates which runs experienced failures; it also identifies which fault caused the failure. Tools, such as those described in App. A, can use these data to generate tabular and graph-

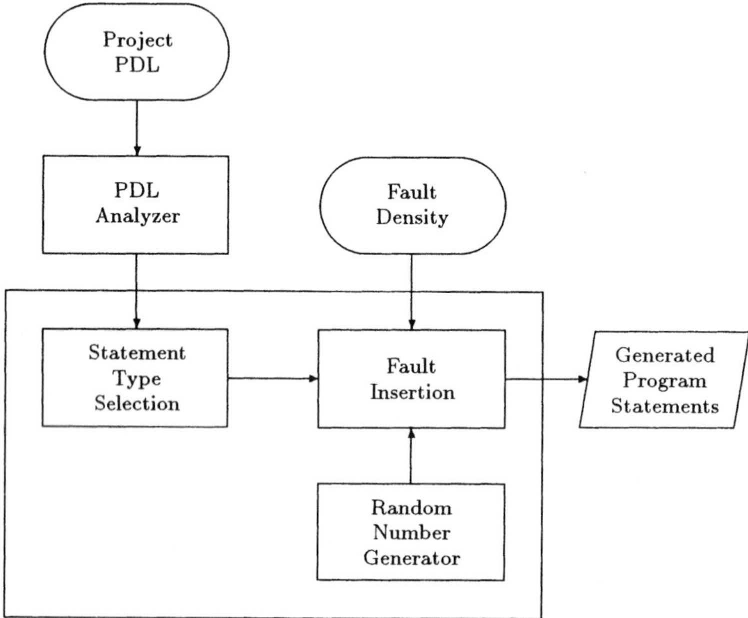

Figure 16.3 Trace-driven artifact simulation of the coding phase.

ical analyses of the failures. Such analyses may include application of any of a number of reliability growth models, maximum likelihood estimates and confidence limits for model parameters, and visual plots of important reliability attributes, such as cumulative failures or present failure intensity versus time.

The reliability assessment function also has available to it the output of the debugging function, which tells which faults were correctly, incorrectly, or incompletely made. At any time, then, the status of remaining faults in the generated program is visible.

16.4.2 Results

Reliability investigations using artifact simulation are currently in their formative stage. The fundamental, first-order validations of the equivalence hypotheses are yet in progress. Consequently, the process of evolution has imposed some limitations that will disappear, with time. The fundamental question has been: Do simulated programs in simulated environments exhibit reliability profiles representative of real programs in real environments that have the same parameters?

A software artifact simulation study, [Mayr91], compared (Fig. 16.4) the results of testing a 5000-line C program with the predicted performance using the basic execution time model. These experiments

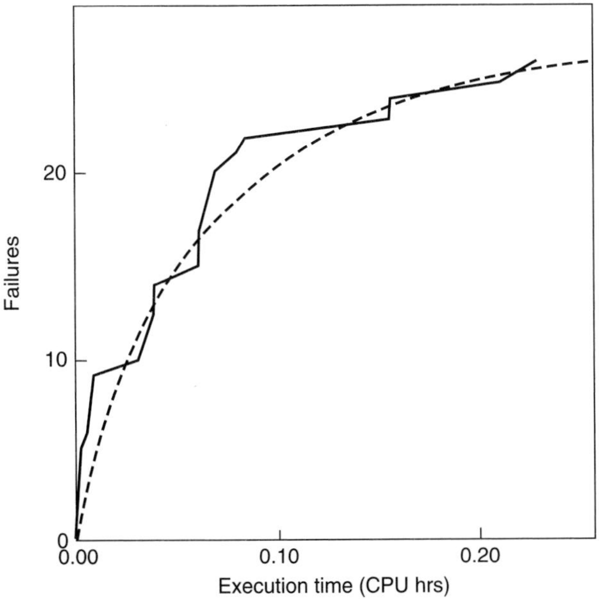

Figure 16.4 Simulated code experimental cumulative failures (from [Mayr91]).

demonstrated that the order in which failures occurred among statements containing faults closely matched the execution counts for those statements, and that the failure counts correlated with the types of program structures surrounding the faults.

These and other early results tend to confirm that static measures of program structure, error characteristics, and test strategies influence the reliability profiles of simulated and real programs in the same ways.

Artifact simulation studies of the future will continue to quantify the extent to which static parameters relate to reliability dynamics. As the software simulation art evolves, the effects of size, multiple-procedure program structures, multiple failure types, nonuniform fault distributions, and nonstationary parameters on reliability will increasingly become known.

16.5 Rate-Based Simulation Algorithms

The fundamental basis of rate-controlled event process simulation is the representation of a stochastic phenomenon of interest by a time series $x(t)$ whose behavior depends only on a rate function, call it $\beta(t)$, where $\beta(t)\,dt$ acts as the conditional probability that a specified event occurs in the infinitesimal interval $(t, t + dt)$.

A number of the analytic reliability growth models discussed in Chap. 3 echo this assumption and further assume that events in nonoverlapping time intervals are independent. The processes modeled are thereby Markov processes [Papo65], or nonhomogeneous Poisson processes (NHPP), which are also Markov processes. These include the models proposed by Jelinski and Moranda ([Jeli72]), Goel and Okumoto ([Goel79]), Musa and Okumoto ([Musa84]), Duane ([Duan64]), Littlewood and Verrall ([Litt73]), and Yamada ([Yama83]). Rate functions for these appear in Sec. 16.6.1.

The algorithms described here not only apply to simulating Markov processes, but are capable of simulating processes having time-dependent event-count dependencies and irregular rate functions. These algorithms can simulate a much more general and realistic reliability process than has ever been hypothesized for any analytic model.

The mathematics presented in this section treats general statistical event processes and rate-driven event processes, not merely those believed to describe software failures. As in the analytic models mentioned above, it is only the form of the rate functions and interpretation of parameters that set these models apart as pertaining to software. We begin this specialization formally in the next section and continue it through Sec. 16.7. First, however, we derive the forms of the simulation algorithms.

16.5.1 Event process statistics

If S_0 and S_1 denote the states of an event $\mathcal{E}$, S_0 in effect before the event and S_1 after its occurrence, then a particular member of the stochastic time series defined by $\{\beta_0(t), S_0, S_1\}$ beginning at time $t = 0$ is a *sample function,* or *realization,* of the general rate-based discrete-event stochastic process. The zero subscript on $\beta_0(t)$ signifies the S_0, or zero occurrences, starting state.

The statistical behavior of this process is well known: the probability that event $\mathcal{E}$ will not have occurred prior to a given time t is given by the expression

$$P_0(t) = e^{-\lambda_0(t,\, 0)} \tag{16.1}$$

where

$$\lambda_0(t, t_0) = \int_{t_0}^{t} \beta_0(\tau)\, d\tau \tag{16.2}$$

The form of $\beta_0(t)$ is unrestricted, but generally must satisfy

$$\beta_0(t) \geq 0 \qquad \text{and} \qquad \lambda_0(\infty, 0) = \infty \tag{16.3}$$

The first of these prevents the event from occurring at a negative rate, and the second stipulates that the event must eventually occur. If the second condition is violated, there will be a finite probability that the event will never occur.

When the events of interest are failures, $\beta_0(t)$ is often referred to as the process *hazard function* and $\lambda_0(t, 0)$ is the *total hazard.* The cumulative distribution function and probability density function for the time of an occurrence are then

$$F_1(t) = 1 - P_0(t) \tag{16.4}$$

$$f_1(t) = \beta_0(t) e^{-\lambda_0(t,\, 0)} \tag{16.5}$$

The mean time of occurrence is

$$E(t) = \int_0^{\infty} t\beta_0(t) e^{-\lambda_0(t,\, 0)}\, dt \tag{16.6}$$

If $\lambda_0(t, 0)$ is known in closed form, we may sometimes be able to write down and analyze the event probability and mean time of occurrence functions directly. In all but the simplest cases, however, we will require the assistance of a computer. When we cannot express the integrals in closed form, we can still evaluate them using straightforward numerical analysis.

16.5.2 Single-event process simulation

It is rather easy and straightforward to simulate the rate-based single-discrete-event process, as illustrated in the following computer algorithm (expressed in the C programming language) which returns the occurrence time:

```
double single_event(double t, double dt, double (*beta)(double))
{
        int event = 0;

        while (event == 0)
        {       if (occurs(beta(t) * dt))
                        event++;
                t += dt;
        }
        return t;
}
```

Above, the C language syntax defines a function named `single_event()` that will eventually return a double-precision floating-point value of the time of event occurrence. Starting at time `t`, and continuing as long as the `event` value remains 0, the function monitors the event status; at the occurrence, `event` increases by 1, as signified by the ++ operation, which stops the iteration. Time augments by `dt` units each iteration, denoted by the "+=" operation.

In the following we have programmed the `occurs(x)` operation as a macro that compares a `random()` value over [0, 1) with the formal parameter `x`, which must be less than unity, thus attaining the specified conditional probability function. (The `extern double` designation declares that `random()` is in an external library that returns a double-precision floating-point value.) You may wish to consult [Knut70] for a discussion of random-number-generation techniques.

```
extern double random(void);
#define occurs(x) (random() < x)
```

The particular application determines the form of the user-supplied rate function `beta(t)`. Any required initialization takes place in the `main()` program prior to invocation of the `single_event()` function. Figure 16.5 depicts the basic data flow of the overall program.

We must choose the dt in simulations to satisfy all the following conditions:

1. dt is smaller than the desired time-granularity of the reliability profile.
2. Variation in $\beta(t)$ over the incremental time intervals $(t, t + dt)$ is negligible.

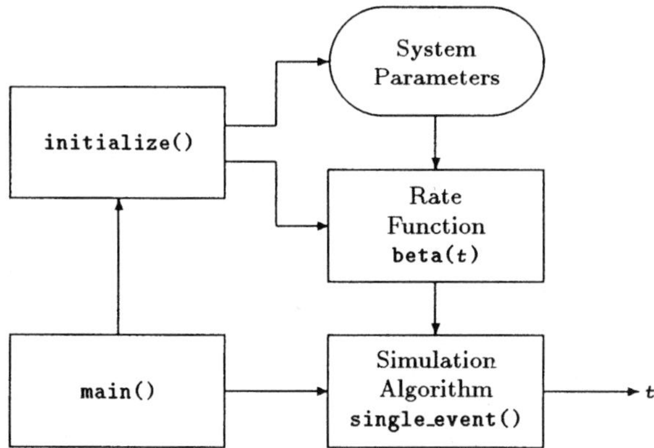

Figure 16.5 Simulation program structure for a single event occurrence.

3. The chance of multiple event occurrences within a dt interval is negligible.
4. The magnitude of $\beta(t)\,dt$ is less than unity at each t in the interval of interest.

The time complexity of the algorithm is $O(\beta t/dt)$, where the β component represents the maximum complexity of computing $\beta(t)$.

We may also simulate the behavior of a nonstochastic* rate-based single-event process merely by altering the algorithm for `occurs()`. If $\beta(t)$ represents the occurrence rate, then the event occurs when its integral reaches unity.

```
double accumulated_rate;
#define occurs(x) (if ((accumulated_rate += x) < 1.) \
    then FALSE else TRUE)
```

The construction above increments `accumulated_rate` by `x` prior to checking its value; the expression then switches from a false to a true state when the value reaches unity. (The "\" at the end of the line signifies continuation on the next line of the macro.)

16.5.3 Recurrent event statistics

If we permitted the iteration in the previous algorithm to continue throughout a given time interval $(0, t)$, then the simulated event could occur a random number of times, which could be counted. We may com-

* This technique also approximates the calculation of the mean occurrence behavior of a stochastic process; however, the method is exact only for the constant-hazard case.

pute the cumulative distribution function $F_n(t)$ that the nth occurrence lies in the interval $(0, t)$ as follows: if t_{n-1} has just been observed as the $(n-1)$st event occurrence, then we may treat the interval immediately after t_{n-1} as a new experiment. Translating Eq. (16.1) to the nth occurrence interval produces the occurrence distribution function conditioned on t_{n-1},

$$P_{n-1}(t \mid t_{n-1}) = e^{-\lambda_{n-1}(t, t_{n-1})} \tag{16.7}$$

$$F_n(t \mid t_{n-1}) = 1 - P_{n-1}(t \mid t_{n-1}) \tag{16.8}$$

$$\lambda_k(t, t_k) = \int_{t_k}^{t} \beta_k(\tau)\, d\tau \tag{16.9}$$

The time dependency retained in Eq. (16.9) reflects the possible nonstationary nature of the event process. Each of the $\beta_k(t)$ functions is subject to the restrictions given in Eq. (16.3); otherwise $F_n(t \mid t_{n-1})$ above must be divided by $1 - P_{n-1}(\infty \mid t_{n-1}) = 1 - e^{-\lambda(\infty, t_{n-1})}$. We shall assume these requirements in the remainder of this chapter.

The nth occurrence probability densities then follow from differentiation of Eq. (16.8),

$$f_n(t \mid t_{n-1}) = \beta_{n-1}(t) e^{-\lambda_{n-1}(t, t_{n-1})} \tag{16.10}$$

$$f_n(t) = \beta_{n-1}(t) \int_0^t e^{-\lambda_{n-1}(t, \tau)} f_{n-1}(\tau)\, d\tau \tag{16.11}$$

the latter being recursively defined, with t_0 for the $n = 1$ case defined as 0. The conditional probability displays the same type of statistical behavior seen in Eq. (16.5) for the single-occurrence case above, but operates piecewise on successive intervals between occurrences.

Finally, $F_n(t)$ follows by integration,

$$F_n(t) = \int_0^t f_n(\tau)\, d\tau \tag{16.12}$$

When events are modeled as Markov occurrences, the probability $P_n(t)$ that exactly n occurrences appear in the interval $(0, t)$ is known [Taus91] to be of the form

$$P_0(t) = e^{-\lambda_0(t, 0)} \tag{16.13}$$

$$P_n(t) = \int_0^t \beta_{n-1} P_{n-1} e^{-\lambda_n(t, \tau)}\, d\tau \tag{16.14}$$

Mathematically closed-form solutions for these probability functions are rarely* known. General solutions thus require simple, but perhaps

* Closed-form solutions for $P_n(t)$ and $f_n(t)$ are known to exist when the process is of the nonhomogeneous Poisson variety, namely, $P_n(t) = \lambda^n(t, 0) \exp[-\lambda(t, 0)]/n!$ and $f_n(t) = \beta(t)\lambda^{n-1}(t, 0) \exp[-\lambda(t, 0)]/(n-1)!$.

time-consuming, recursive numerical methods: the time complexity of $f_n(t \mid t_{n-1})$ is of order $O(\beta(t - t_{n-1})/dt)$; $f_n(t)$ and $P_n(t)$ are of order $O(\beta nt/dt)$, and $F_n(t)$ is also of order $O(\beta nt/dt)$. The space complexities of these measures are, respectively, $O(1)$, $O(t/dt)$, and $O(t/dt)$.

The expected time of the nth occurrence follows directly from Eq. (16.11) as a recursive expression,

$$\bar{t}_n = \int_0^\infty t\beta_{n-1}(t) \int_0^t e^{-\lambda_{n-1}(t,\tau)} f_{n-1}(\tau)\, d\tau \qquad (16.15)$$

with time complexity $O(\beta n t_\infty / dt)$ and space complexity $O(t_\infty / dt)$.

16.5.4 Recurrent event simulation

Simulation offers a relatively economical alternative in the evaluation of rate-based performance over the more complex numeric integrations of the previous section. The recurrent events algorithm below is a simple extension of the single-occurrence event code that returns the number of occurrences over the time interval (t_a, t). Its computational complexity to the nth occurrence is only $O(\beta t_n/dt)$, in constant space:

```
void recurrent_event(double ta, double t, double dt,
                     double (*beta)(int, double), int *events)
{
    while (ta < t)
    {   if (occurs(beta(events, ta) * dt))
            ++*events;
        ta += dt;
    }
}
```

The calling program must initialize the `events` parameter to the actual number of occurrences prior to time t_a; `events` will contain the new count after the function returns. (Note that we renamed `events` in the plural to acknowledge that multiple occurrences are being counted.) Figure 16.6 depicts the program data flow structure.

Mathematically, $\beta_n(t)$ is valid only in the interval $t_n \le t < t_{n+1}$ and signifies that n occurrences of the event have occurred prior to t. The use of `beta(events, t)` in the algorithm acknowledges that the event may recur from time to time and that the occurrence rate function may not only change over time, but also may be sensitive to the number of event occurrences (as well as possibly other influences). The simulation algorithm observes the event occurrence times and may change the `beta()` function as required by the application.

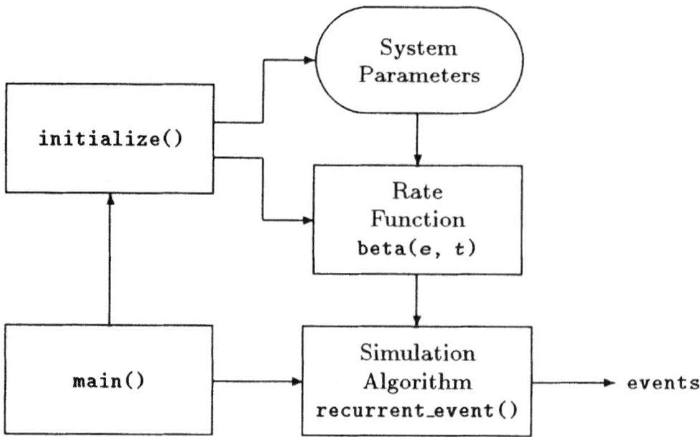

Figure 16.6 Simulation program for recurrent events.

We may also simulate nonstochastic rate-based recurrent-event processes* by making the single-occurrence `occurs()` function recognize unit crossings of the rate accumulator, as follows:

```
#define occurs(x) (if ((accumulated_rate += x) < 1.) \
                then FALSE else (accumulated_rate -= 1., TRUE))
```

Note that `accumulated_rate` decrements by unity at each occurrence, signified by the "−=" operation.

16.5.5 Secondary event simulation

Another type of event process of interest is when a primary event triggers the occurrence of a secondary event of a different type. For example, producing a unit of code may create a fault in the code.

Notationally, if p_i denotes the probability that the ith occurrence of the primary event causes the occurrence of the secondary event, then we may express the probability $P_m^{(2)}(t)$ that m such secondary events have occurred in the interval $(0, t)$ as

$$P_m^{(2)}(t) = \sum_{n=m}^{\infty} p_{m|n}(t) P_n(t) \tag{16.16}$$

* This technique, as before, approximates the average occurrence behavior of stochastic recurrent-event processes.

with

$$p_{m|n} = P\{m \text{ secondary events} \mid n \text{ primary events in } (0, t)\} \tag{16.17}$$

$$= \sum_{\boldsymbol{i} \in \mathcal{I}} p_{i_1} \cdots p_{i_m}(1 - p_{i_{m+1}}) \cdots (1 - p_{i_n}) \tag{16.18}$$

where the index vector $\boldsymbol{i} = (i_1, i_2, \ldots, i_n)$ is a permutation of $(1, 2, \ldots, n)$ such that $(i_1, \ldots, i_m)$ extends over all combinations of m out of n primary events, a set $\mathcal{I}$ of size $\binom{n}{m}$. The computational complexity of $P_m^{(2)}(t)$ is thus of combinatorial order, and not practical to evaluate in general cases of practical interest. In the special case that $p_i = p$ is constant, $p_{m|n}$ reduces to the binomial function,

$$p_{m|n} = \binom{m}{n} p^m (1 - p)^{n-m} \tag{16.19}$$

The simulation algorithm for a dependent secondary event process, however, can remain quite general; one merely adds a mapping array `secondary_event` that relates the primary event to its secondary event and a function `p(i, events, t)` that returns the probability that the primary event triggers the secondary event:

```
if (occurs(beta(i, events, ta) * dt))
{   ++events[i];
    if ((j = secondary_event[i]) && occurs(p(j, events, t)))
    {   ++events[j];
    }
}
```

We may similarly treat multiple secondary events emanating from a single primary event at only a moderate increase in algorithm complexity.

16.5.6 Limited growth simulation

When the final number N of occurrences that an event process may reach is prespecified, the normal growth of the event count over time must stop after the Nth occurrence. For example, if there are N faults to repair, and repairs proceed reasonably, then effort ceases after the last one is fixed.

Simulating this behavior is simple, but must include steps to prevent the event count from overshooting N when multiple occurrences occasionally take place within a `dt` interval. This may be done by altering the event-counting functions, not to exceed prespecified maxima `max_events`, as follows:

```
if (events[i] < max_events[i])
    ++events[i];
```

16.5.7 The general simulation algorithm

You may have already guessed the form of a general rate-based discrete-event process simulator. It is merely the recurrent-event algorithm augmented to accommodate multiple simultaneous events, multiple event categories, secondary events, and growth limits.

The general algorithm below incorporates all of these features. It simulates `f` event processes over a time interval `ta` to `t` using time slices of duration `dt`; an initialized input array `events` counts the occurrences, which may not exceed corresponding values in the `max_events` array; an array `event_category` contains the mapping of event occurrences into `categories`, which counts occurrences up to the maxima specified in the `max_categories` array; and a `secondary_event` array and `p()` function control secondary occurrences, as described in Sec. 16.5.5. For readability, the control function name `beta()` becomes `rate()`. We also add `action()` and `display()` functions, described below.

```
void simulate(int f, double ta, double t, double dt,
              double (*rate)(int, int *, double),
              int events[], int max_events[],
              int categories[], int max_categories[],
              int event_category[],
              int secondary_event[], double (*p)(int, int *, double),
              void (*action)(int *, double),
              void (*display)(int *, double))
{
    int i, j, k;

    while (ta < t)
    {   for (i = 0; i < f; i++)
        {   if (occurs(rate(i, events, ta) * dt))
            {   if (events[i] < max_events[i])
                {   ++events[i];
                    k = event_category[i];
                    if (categories[k] < max_categories[k])
                        ++categories[k];
                }
                if ((j = secondary_event[i]) && occurs(p(j, events, ta))
                {   if (events[j] < max_events[j])
                    {   ++events[j];
                        k = event_category[j];
                        if (categories[k] < max_categories[k])
                            ++categories[k];
                    }
                }
                action(events, ta);
```

```
            }
        }
        ta += dt;
        display(events, ta);
    }
}
```

The `action()` function specifies what takes place when an event occurs. For example, if one category of events represents identified faults and another represents repairs, then `action()` may compute an unrepaired fault parameter for `display()`, or it may recompute appropriate `max_events` or `max_categories` bounds. The `action()` functions may well also pass additional parameters, such as `i`, `j`, `k`, and `m`, should these local values be needed to effect the proper change in state.

The `display()` function outputs the simulation status monitors as a profile in time. It may publish only certain parameters of interest, or it may detail the entire reliability state at each `dt`, depending on the time-line information desired by the user. Figure 16.7 shows the overall simulation program data flow.

We must choose the `dt` for the simulation experiments simultaneously to satisfy earlier-stated constraints imposed by each of the event rates. As a consequence, execution may be very slow. Alternatively, we could speed up the algorithm by choosing larger values of `dt` and computing the numbers of multiple events that may occur during each of the larger intervals, as determined by the probability functions of primary and secondary events. It is known, when event occurrences in nonoverlapping intervals are independent (see, e.g., [Taus91]), that primary events are Poisson distributed and secondary events are binomi-

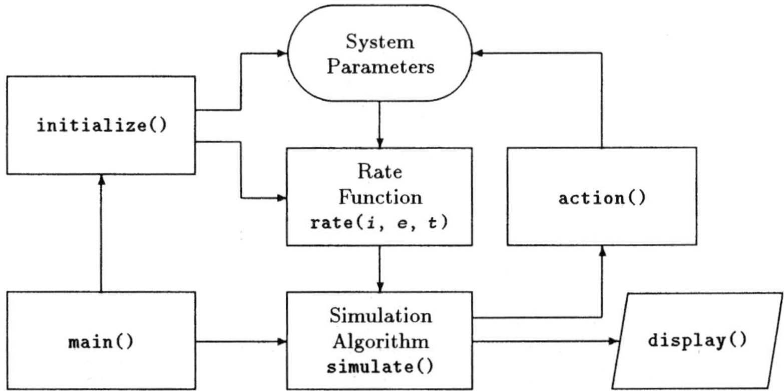

Figure 16.7 General rate-controlled process simulator program.

ally distributed. Generally, however, the probability functions are unknown, even when the rate functions are fairly simple.

But if these probability functions were known, there would be only slight changes required in the algorithm above: `occurs(rate() * dt)` would be replaced by a `primary(rate() * dt)` function that counts the random number `n` of primary event occurrences in the `dt` interval; `occurs(p())` gets replaced by `secondary(n, p())`, which counts the number `m` of occurrences of secondary events; and `events[]` augments by `n` and `m`, rather than unity, respectively.

If we desire, for execution-time reasons, a value of `dt` that is too large for use in the general algorithm above, but is yet small enough that primary and secondary event statistics over `dt` intervals are approximately Poisson and binomially distributed, respectively, then the modified algorithm can be applied. We refer to this configuration as the *piecewise-Poisson* approximate simulation. Piecewise-Poisson simulations, of course, are valid for all the usual NHPP models, because no approximations are actually made. We have not yet studied the validity of the approximation applied to other processes.

16.6 Rate-Based Reliability Simulation

Rate-based reliability simulation is a natural extension of techniques for analyzing conventional models, because many of these are also rate (or hazard) based. The underlying processes assumed by these models are thus the same.

Because of algorithmic simplicity, simulation serves as a powerful tool not only for analyzing the behaviors of processes assumed to have complex rate functions, but also for investigating whether the stochastic nature of a project's measured failure data is typical of that obtained by simulation. We may vary the modeling assumptions until profiles reach a satisfactory alignment.

The challenge in life-cycle simulation is finding rate functions that satisfactorily describe *all* of the activities, not just testing. Such a model enables optimum planning through trade-offs among allocated resources, test strategies, etc.

16.6.1 Rate functions of conventional models

Several published analytic models treat (or approximate) the overall growth in reliability during the test and fault-removal phases as nonhomogeneous Poisson processes in execution time, while others focus on Markov execution-time interval statistics. While these may differ significantly in their assumptions about underlying failure mechanisms, they differ mathematically only in the forms of their rate functions. Some examples are the following:

1. The *Jelinski-Moranda* model [Jeli72] describes statistics of failure time intervals under the presumption that $\beta_n(t) = \beta_0(1 - n/n_0)$, where n_0 is the estimated (unknown) number of initial software faults and β_0 is initial failure rate.
2. The *Goel-Okumoto* model [Goel79] treats an overall reliability growth process with $\beta(t) = n_0\phi e^{-\phi t}$, where n_0 and ϕ are input parameters, $n_0\phi$ being the initial failure rate, and ϕ the rate decay factor. Strictly speaking, this rate function violates the conditions on $\lambda(t, 0)$ imposed in Eq. (16.3), because $\lambda_0(\infty, 0) = n_0$ and $P_0(\infty) = e^{-n_0}$. In practicality, n_0 is usually fairly large, so the consequences may be negligible.
3. The *Musa-Okumoto* model [Musa84] posits an overall reliability growth process in which $\beta(t) = \beta_0/(1 + \theta t)$, where β_0 is the initial failure rate and θ is a rate decay factor. Both β_0 and θ are input parameters.
4. The *Duane* model [Duan64] deals with another overall reliability growth model, with $\beta(t) = kbt^{b-1}$, where k and b are input parameters. Equation (16.3) requires that $0 < \beta < 1$.
5. The *Littlewood-Verrall inverse linear* model [Litt73] is an overall reliability growth model with $\beta(t) = \beta_0/\sqrt{1 + \theta t}$ where β_0 is the initial failure rate and θ is a rate decay factor.
6. The *Yamada delayed S-shape* model [Yama83] represents still another overall reliability growth model, with $\beta(t) = \phi\gamma te^{1-\gamma t}$, where ϕ (the maximum failure rate) and γ are input parameters. This rate function, too, violates condition (16.3), as $\lambda_0(\infty, 0) = e\phi/\gamma$ and $P_0(\infty) = e^{-e\phi/\gamma}$; again, when the number of faults is large, the effect is negligible.

You may find further discussions of these models in Chap. 3.

16.6.2 Simulator architecture

We have already discussed the algorithm for rate-based simulation. The remaining architectural considerations are characterized by input parameters, event rate functions, event response actions, and output displays. The scope of user requirements should set the level of detail being simulated.

A reliability process simulator should be able to respond to schedules and work plans and to report the performance of subprocesses under the plan. By viewing simulated results, users may then replan as necessary. The simulator described here therefore does not assume specific relationships involving staff, resource, or schedules, but expects these as inputs in the form described in Sec. 16.3.2.

Simulations should also embody interrelationships among project elements. For example, defective specifications should lead to faults in the code unless defects are corrected before coding takes place; missing specifications should introduce even more coding errors; testing should not take place without test cases to consume; repair activity should follow fault identification and isolation; and so on.

A more comprehensive simulation model ([Taus91]) of the reliability process uses about 70 input parameters describing the software project and development environment, together with a project plan of arbitrary length containing activities, resources allocated, and application schedules. This simulator, SoftRel, displays time-line profiles of almost 50 measures of project reliability status and the resources consumed, by activity. The SoftRel tool is included in the Data and Tool Disk.

We shall illustrate the principles of reliability process simulation in a somewhat more simplified example—only 25 input parameters and a project resource schedule are required. You should not regard this example necessarily as an illustration ready for industrial use, but as a framework and means for experimentation, learning, and extension.

In the example (see Sec. 16.7), we simulate only a single category of events for each reliability subprocess. Further, simulations produce only two types of failure events, namely, defects in specification documents and faults in code, all considered to be in the same severity category.

We also simplify the example reliability process not to include document and code reuse and integration, test preparations and the dependencies between testing and test-case availability, outages due to test failures, repair validation, and retesting.

Other, more detailed, simplifications appear in the discussions below.

16.6.2.1 Environment considerations. We know that characteristics of the programming, inspection, test, and operational environments can influence the rates at which activities take place. For simplicity, however, we have eliminated as many of these from the example simulator as seemed reasonable to our goals here. A more refined tool for general-purpose industrial use would, of course, probably include more definitive environmental inputs.

Events, of themselves, carry no intrinsic hazard values. The rates at which events occur depend on a number of environmental and other factors, including the nature of the events themselves. The model must treat event hazards differently in different situations.

Some faults may be easier to discover by inspection than by testing, while for others the opposite may be true. The fault discovery rate in testing normally depends on such parameters as the CPU instruction execution rate, the language expansion factor, the failure-to-fault relationship, and the scheduled CPU hours per calendar day that are applied. During inspections, on the other hand, fault discovery depends on the discovery-to-fault relationship, the fault density, the inspection rate, and applied effort.

A fault is independent of its means of discovery. The model must therefore realize different hazard-per-fault rates in differing discovery environments, rather than merely assign a specific hazard rate to the fault itself.

16.6.2.2 Subprocess representation. In the example simulator, each activity produces occurrences of one or more uncategorized event types, either primary or secondary. Table 16.1 lists the simulated primary events. Except for test failures, all are goal-oriented processes with limiting values, as shown. Test failures are limited by the current fault hazard function.

Table 16.2 defines the secondary events that occur with a primary event, controlled by an occurrence probability that may depend on a number of combined factors. For example, the number of defects or faults recognized during inspections will not only depend on the inspection efficiency (the fraction of defects recognized when inspected), but also on the density of defects in the material being inspected. All secondary event occurrences are naturally limited in number to the occurrences of their primary events; no other limits are imposed.

16.6.3 Display of results

Internally, a process simulator carries very detailed, fine-grained information on the activities and events under study, of types that are both visible and latent in real projects. In the spirit of simulation, the profiles viewed by humans should appear as if taken from reality.

However, a simulation user may well desire visibility into latent values, such as the numbers of unfound defects and faults, in order to make decisions on subsequent actions. When real project profiles match their corresponding simulation profiles, then the user probably

TABLE 16.1 Reliability Process Primary Events and Limits

Primary event	Rate control	Limit
Doc unit created	Build workforce	Doc size
Doc unit inspected	Document insp workforce	Doc insp goal
Doc defect treated	Document corr workforce	Defects recognized
Code unit created	Coding workforce	Code size
Code unit inspected	Code insp workforce	Code insp goal
Code fault treated	Code corr workforce	Faults created
Test failure	Size, faults, cpu, exposure	∞
Failure analyzed	Analysis workforce	Test failures
Fault repair attempt	Repair workforce	Faults found

TABLE 16.2 Reliability Process Secondary Events, Correspondences, and Controls

Secondary event	Primary event	Rate control
Defect created	Doc unit created	Defect density
Defect recognized	Doc unit inspected	Latent defects, efficiency
Defect corrected	Defect treated	Correction efficiency
Fault created	Code unit created	Fault density, missing/faulty doc
Fault recognized	Code unit inspected	Latent fault density, efficiency
Fault corrected	Fault treated	Fault correction efficiency
	Test failure	
Fault identified	Failure analyzed	Id efficiency, fault density
Fault repaired	Repair attempt	Repair efficiency

expects that the latent behaviors will also agree. But we must not expect latent, model-internal behaviors to be accurate, because they can never be matched with reality.

To some extent, real profiles depend on how projects instrument and organize themselves for reliability measurement. They may record the status of documents and development code only at certain milestones. Other parameters, such as failures, may be logged automatically by the operating system, if detected, or by humans on a daily or weekly basis.

Visible project parameters include (1) the input facts (or assumptions) that define the environment and (2) the measured profiles, such as pages of documentation, lines of code, defects and faults found by inspections, failures, test faults identified, repairs, resources expended, and schedule time.

16.7 The Galileo Project Application

This section describes simulating a real-world project based on data and parameters taken from a subsystem of the Galileo project at the Jet Propulsion Laboratory ([Lyu91a]).

Galileo is an outer planet spacecraft project that began at the start of fiscal year 1977, a mission that was originally entitled "Jupiter Orbiter and Probe," or JOP. Unlike previous outer solar system missions, the Galileo orbiter was intended to remain in Jovian orbit for an extended interval of time. This would allow observations of variations in planetary and satellite features over time to augment the information obtained by single-observation opportunities afforded by previous fly-by missions. Galileo was launched in October of 1989 and reached the Jovian system in 1995.

There are two major on-board flight computers in the Galileo spacecraft: the Attitude and Articulation Control Subsystem (AACS), and the Command and Data System (CDS). A significant portion of each of these systems is embodied in software. This case study focuses on the CDS software reliability profile.

The CDS performs such critical functions as command and control of the spacecraft and the acquisition and transmission of flight data. CDS software selects among the many available telemetry rates and modes, and commands and controls all on-board experiments involving instruments.

The CDS flight software is characterized as a real-time embedded subsystem having high reliability requirements in a project where the mission design was redone* several times. The software consists of about 17,000 lines of assembly language code, with about 1400 pages of documentation, produced over a period of approximately 300 calendar weeks. The project spent 1200 days (in 5-day workweeks) in pretest activities and 420 days (in 7-day workweeks) in test preparation, tests, and rework, for a total of 1620 total days. The actual test period lasted only 280 of the 420 days; the project recorded the failure profile only during this 280-day subsystem software testing period.

16.7.1 Simulation experiments and results

Some of the CDS project parameters needed for simulation were calculated from project records; other values were estimated by project personnel; we chose the remaining values as probably typical of this project, but for which we had no immediately available data. We assigned believed-typical values, for example, to parameters relating to the injection and removal of defects and faults. Thus, even though only a few verifiable parameters were available outside the software testing phase, we nevertheless formed an entire plausible hypothetical model in order to illustrate an end-to-end reliability process.

For lack of better development life-cycle information, we presumed that all CDS events occurred at uniform rates per event, that all activities took place without resource and schedule variations, and that testing required applied CPU resources according to the basic execution-time model.

Observing experiments using the simulator described in [Taus91] led to regressive adjustments of the estimated project rate input parameters. Each experiment profiled the status of defects and faults as random streams; the final parameter values resulted in event profiles typified by those shown in Figs. 16.8 and 16.9. The figures depict the results of a single experiment in simulating defect and fault profiles of the CDS software, sampled at 2-week intervals.

Note the smoothness that appears in the rise of some curves in these figures is due to the regularity of the schedule, not randomness in per-

* Redesigns were necessitated by launch delays due to congressional actions and the Space Shuttle Challenger disaster.

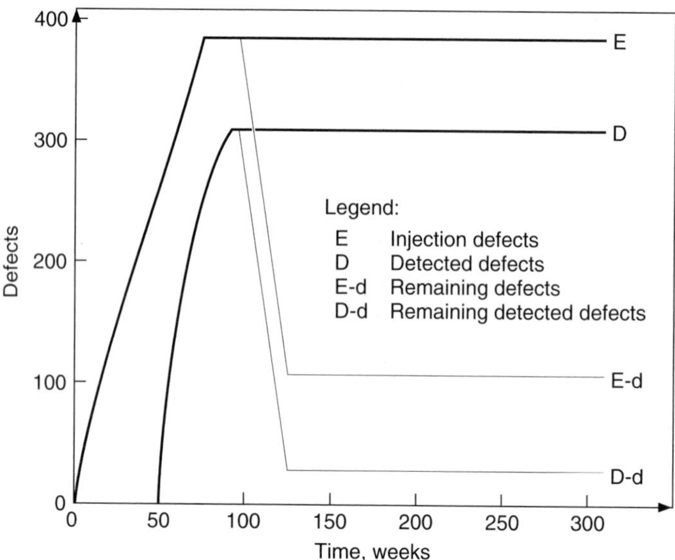

Figure 16.8 Simulated Galileo CDS defects status profile.

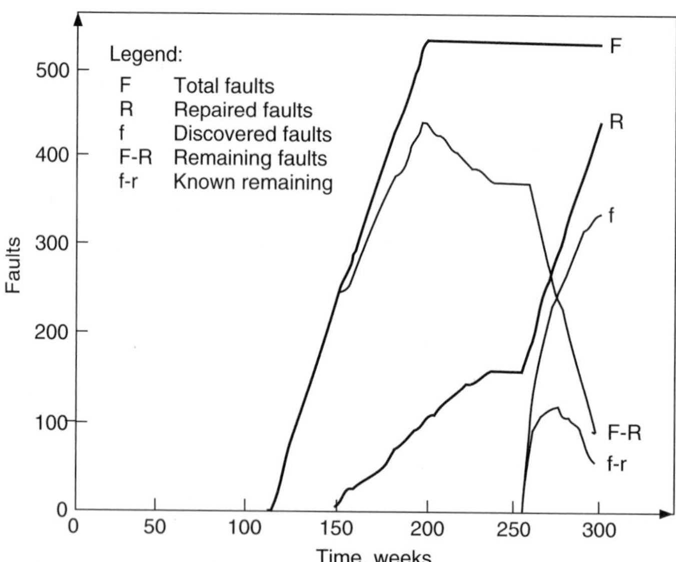

Figure 16.9 Simulated Galileo CDS fault status profile.

formance. Performance deviations seem invisible not because they are small, but because they are *relatively* small, as a result of the law of large numbers.* Although we have no CDS data to refute this behavior, we doubt that the assumed constant resource levels reflect reality. A more realistic extension to the case study would have been to introduce irregular schedules, since we know that people rarely dedicate their time exclusively to one single activity at a time. If actual CDS schedule information had been available, we could have input this data into the simulation, whereupon the process statistics would probably have appeared more irregular.

Figure 16.8 displays the experimental defect behavior: injected document errors (`E`), detected defects (`D`), remaining defects (`E-d`); and remaining detected defects `D-d`. These profiles appear a little more irregular than do those of documentation and code production, but not much. The documentation appears to contain a sizable number of latent defects; even many of the detected defects appear to have been left uncorrected. Experimental rms deviation in the final defect counts was about 25.

Figure 16.9 shows the experimental fault activity. These profiles exhibit visible randomness, only partially masked by the law of large numbers. The rise in total faults (`F`) during the code construction activity appears almost linear, again a consequence of a constant-effort schedule. We chose project parameters that prevented the creation of faults by imperfect corrections and repairs.

Correction of faults found in inspections began in week 150 and continued until week 240, removing 162 of them. The plateau in total repaired faults (`R`) and in total remaining faults (`F-R`) between weeks 240 and 260 occurred due to staff preparations for testing. At week 260, the test phase began, and failures (`f`) rose to 341 by week 300. Of these, 284 were repaired (`r`).

By the end of the 300-week simulated project, almost 10 faults per kiloline of code had been found in inspections and corrected, and another 20 faults per kiloline of code had been uncovered by testing and removed. The latent fault density was about 2 faults per kiloline of code.

Standard deviations computed after conducting many such experiments were about 22 in fault count (`F`), 30 in faults remaining (`F-R`), 32 in discovered faults (`f`), and 25 in remaining discovered faults (`f-r`).

If the simulation parameters were typical of the CDS project, and had the real CDS project been conducted a number of times, these same ranges of variations in the final status of the CDS artifacts would

* The law of large numbers governs the rate at which the sample mean of an experiment converges to the distribution mean. For many processes, this is of order $O(1/\sqrt{n})$.

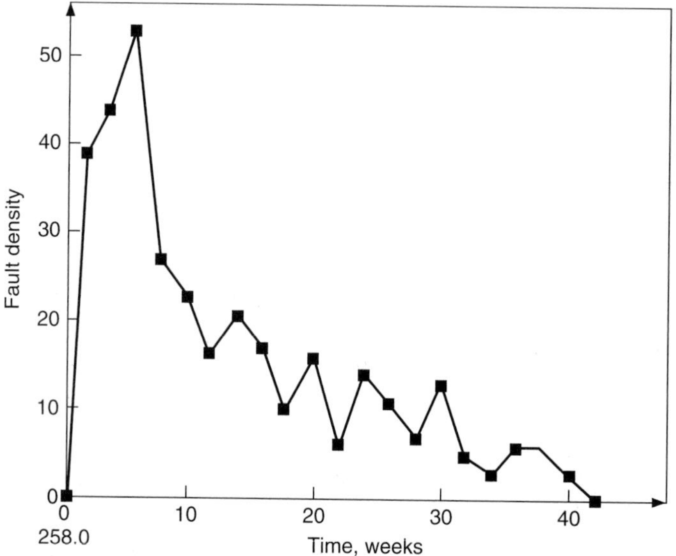

Figure 16.10 Simulated Galileo CDS testing fault density profile (newly discovered faults per two-week interval), constant CPU resource.

have been observed. The simulation did not replicate the CDS project behavior, but mirrored the behavior of a CDS-type project.

Although the final fault discovery count seems typical of a CDS-type project, the time profile of the simulation results shown in Fig. 16.10 does not quite seem to match the character of the actual project data. The failure rate seems too high during early tests and too low during the later tests. The actual test resource schedule was certainly not as simple as that used in the simulation.

On the basis of these experiments, it appears that realistic simulation of the general reliability process will require that detailed resource and schedule information will have to be provided to the model. It is important to remember that an actual project will probably not proceed as smoothly as its simulation. Consequently, projects will have to plan and measure their achievements as carefully for simulation as they will for the actual production.

16.7.2 Comparisons with other software reliability models

Figure 16.11 compares the actual CDS subsystem failure data with that obtained from a constant-test-hazard-per-fault simulation. We detailed the testing phase into five subactivities with constant staffing, but having irregular CPU and schedule allocations, as shown in Table 16.3. We obtained these schedule parameters using "eyeball regression" of the

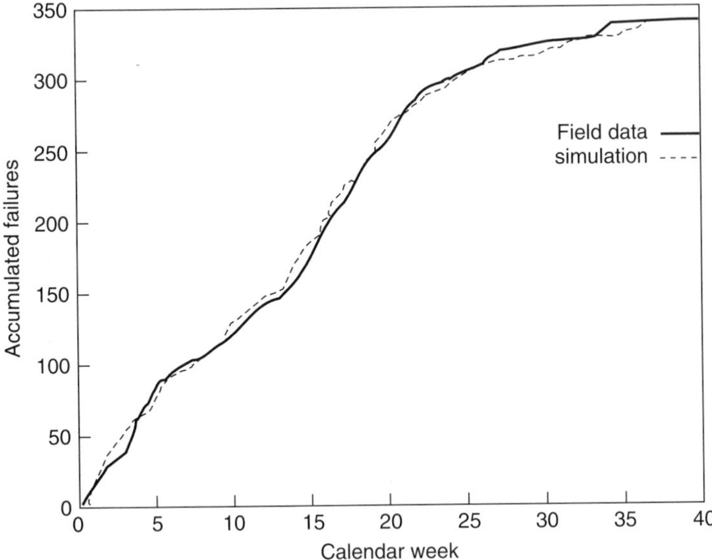

Figure 16.11 Cumulative failure data for Galileo CDS.

simulator output against the project data (see `CDS.DAT` on the Data Disk). The fit appears adequate to describe the underlying nature of the failure process (we did not expect an exact fit).

A comparison of failure profile simulation results with predictions of three other models, Jelinski-Moranda (JM), Musa-Okumoto (MO), and Littlewood-Verrall (LV), appears in Fig. 16.12. For better amplification of model differences, the figure displays failures per week, rather than cumulatively. The JM, MO, and LV statistics are one-week-ahead predictions, in which all failure data up to a given week are used to predict the number of failures for the next week.

The figure shows that the CDS simulation behavior is very similar to the noisy actual profile in variability and trends; the simulation could have been used for assessing the CDS reliability status and trends during the entire testing phase. The simulated profile could even have been calculated well prior to the start of testing from schedule and

TABLE 16.3 Simulator Schedule for CDS Testing Phase

Activity	Accumulated failures	Begin week	End week	Staffing	CPU rate
1. Functional test	90	0	5	2.0	0.4
2. Feature test	150	5	13	2.0	0.4
3. Operation test 1	300	13	23	2.0	1.2
4. Operation test 2	325	23	33	2.0	1.0
5. Operation test 3	341	33	40	2.0	2.0

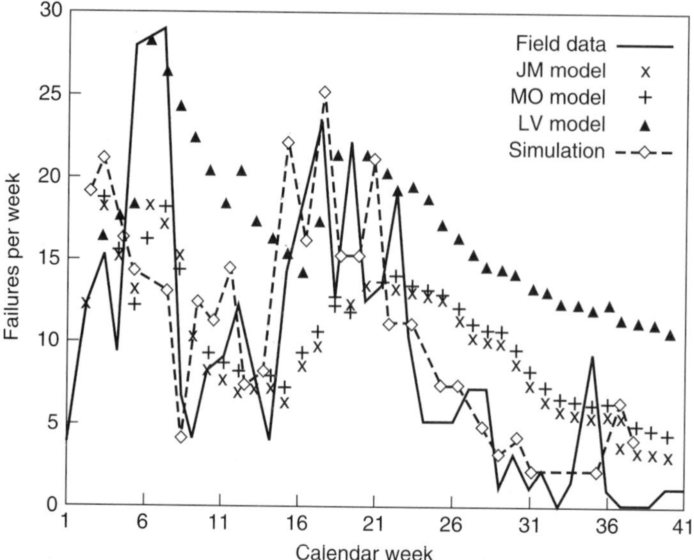

Figure 16.12 Comparison of actual, model-predicted, and simulated (variable CPU resource) Galileo CDS test fault densities.

resource plans. The preceding models could not adequately predict even one week ahead.

16.8 Summary

In many ways, the methods for software reliability assessment reported in this chapter are very satisfying, and in other ways, most frustrating. The techniques provide quantitative measures of software quality that can be used by management to guide progress of a project. The frustration is that progress unveils the depth of our ignorance about system reliability and the dearth of experimental reliability data. We have neither addressed the means for obtaining the best simulation structures nor the number of past examples needed to validate them. Nor have we addressed means for forecasting parameter values for a project from historical data. But ignorance, frustration, and the challenge they inspire are potent motivations for research.

The modeling assumptions required by the two simulation approaches addressed in this chapter are certainly less restrictive, but perhaps more demanding, than those underlying analytic models. Simulation solves software reliability prediction problems by producing programs and data conforming precisely to reliability process assumptions. If simulation profiles differ from actual performance, then the user can adjust the simulation model until an acceptable match with reality obtains. Simulation thus enables investigations of questions too difficult to be answered analytically.

Tools and environments supporting simulations may offer significant assistance and insight to researchers and practitioners in understanding the effects of various software reliability drivers in evaluating sensitivities of behavior to various modeling assumptions and in forecasting software project status profiles, such as time lines of work products and the progress of testing, fault isolation, repair, validation, and retest efforts.

Attempts to reproduce reliability signatures of real-world projects using simulation have, so far, been encouraging. The results tend to coincide intuitively with how real programs behave, and strengthen the hope that such methods in the future will enable fuller investigations into the relationships between static measures and dynamic performance. Such relationships foretell reliability profiles of programs not yet written.

Problems

16.1 Sketch a C program for the self-driven simulated code generator of Sec. 16.4.1.2. Which method did you use to represent the injected faults?

16.2 Use Eq. (16.10) to derive a closed-form expression for the conditional mean occurrence times $\hat{t}_n$ when the rate function is independent of time, but depends on the number n of events (that is, $\beta_n(t) = \beta_n$).

16.3 Write a program to calculate the mean by Eq. (16.15) and conditional mean occurrence profiles for the simple, rate-driven recurrent event process in Prob. 16.2.

16.4 Develop a formula for calculating the variance $\sigma_n^2 = E[(t_n - \bar{t}_n)^2]$ of a rate-driven process. Extend the program in Prob. 16.3 to compute the standard deviation, σ_n.

16.5 Use the program of Prob. 16.4 to analyze the behavior of a Jelinski-Moranda rate function $\beta_n = 1 - n/25$. Run the program and compare the conditional mean profile with the true mean occurrence time. Is there a significant difference? Plot the mean profiles and ± 1-σ_n event envelopes. Is the expected deviation from the mean significant?

16.6 Write a program to simulate the event process in Prob. 16.5. Plot several simulated random-event profiles. How significant are the differences among the profiles?

16.7 Rewrite the rate function of the program in Probs. 16.5 and 16.6 to analyze the performance of the Musa-Okumoto model. How significant are the differences between the output profiles? How do these results compare with those of Probs. 16.5 and 16.6?

16.8 Gather environmental and project data (including the resource schedule) of a simple reliability process in your organization (such as software failures) and simulate it. Compare simulated and measured results. Was it possible to make the two appear as sample functions of the same random process? What changes in the simulator inputs were required?

16.9 Based on comparisons of simulated and actual project profiles, what conclusions can be made on the accuracy of simulation experiments?

16.10 Write the C code for the `rate(process,events,t)` function of the example simulator from the descriptions given in the discussions of reliability subprocess architectures. The formal parameters are `process`, the integer index of the event; `events`, a pointer to the integer array of event counts; and `t`, the time of the simulation. Indicate how the program consumes staff and computer resources as activities unfold.

Chapter

17

Neural Networks for Software Reliability Engineering

Nachimuthu Karunanithi
Bellcore

Yashwant K. Malaiya
Colorado State University

17.1 Introduction

Artificial neural networks (or simply *neural networks*) are a computational metaphor inspired by studies of the brain and nervous systems in biological organisms. They are highly idealized mathematical models of the essence of our present understanding of how simple nervous systems work. Neural networks operate on the principle of learning from examples; no model is specified a priori. Neural networks are likened to nonparametric models in the statistical literature. Recent development in neural networks has shown that they can be applied in a variety of problem domains. For example, neural networks are used to solve complex nonlinear function approximation problems, difficult linearly inseparable pattern classification problems, speech recognition and control problems, and complex time-series modeling problems. Though the neural network technology has been applied in various fields, its utility in software engineering has not been completely explored.

The purpose of this chapter is to introduce how this newly emerging technology can be used in software reliability engineering applications. In particular, we demonstrate the utility of neural networks models for solving two problems in the area of software reliability engineering. In the first example, we illustrate how a neural network can be used as a general reliability growth model. We validate the utility of this general model by learning to predict the cumulative faults for several software projects. Our results suggest that neural network models can provide a better predictive accuracy than some of the analytic models. In the second example, we illustrate how a neural network can be used as a classifier to identify fault-prone (or change-prone) software modules from their static complexity metrics. We demonstrate the applicability of this approach using metrics data from a Medical Imaging System software. Our results suggest that the neural network classifier may provide an edge over simple classifiers in certain categories.

17.2 Neural Networks

Neural networks are computational systems based on mathematical idealization of our present understanding of biological nervous systems. However, the present neural network models do not take into consideration all scientific knowledge about biological nervous systems; rather they model only a few rudimentary characteristics that can be expressed in simple mathematical equations. In general, neural networks can be characterized in terms of the following three entities [Karu92d]:

- Models of *neurons,* i.e., characteristics of the processing unit
- Models of *interconnection structure,* i.e., the topology of the architecture and the strength of the connections that encode the knowledge
- A *learning algorithm,* i.e., the steps involved in adjusting connection weights

The neural network research community has introduced a variety of models for these entities. Consequently, there exists a variety of neural network models and learning algorithms. We review here some of the relevant neural network models and their characteristics.

17.2.1 Processing unit

There exist many mathematical idealizations for the processing unit (or artificial neuron). A typical processing unit is described in terms of: (1) a distinct set of *fan-in connections,* which specifies a set of weighted connections through which the unit receives input either from other units in the network or the external world; (2) a distinct set of *fan-out connections,* which specifies a set of weighted connections through which the unit sends its output either to other units in the network or to the external world; (3) a *fan-in function,* which integrates inputs to produce a net input to the processing unit; and (4) an *activation function,* which acts on the current net input to produce an output. A typical processing unit is illustrated in Fig. 17.1.

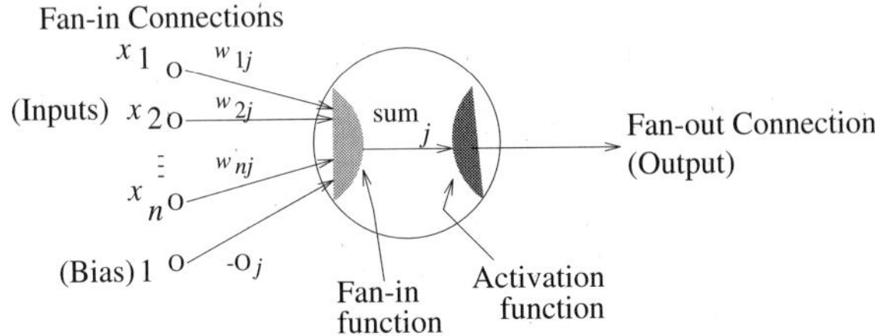

Figure 17.1 A typical processing unit.

Fan-in function. The purpose of the fan-in function is to integrate inputs received from other units or the external world, and then produce a net input to the processing unit. One of the most widely used fan-in functions is the dot-product function. Assume that w_{ij} is the fan-in weight vector of unit j from unit i, sum_j is the net input to the unit, and x_i is the input from unit i, $1 \leq i \leq n$. Then the dot-product function is expressed as

$$\text{sum}_j = \sum_{i=1}^{n} w_{ij} x_i - \theta_j \tag{17.1}$$

where $-\theta_j$ represents the threshold, which is usually created by an adjustable weight from a special unit called *bias* unit whose output is always 1.

Activation function. The purpose of the activation function is to produce an activation value a_j for the unit j from the net input sum_j. The general form of an activation function is expressed as

$$a_j = F(\text{sum}_j) \tag{17.2}$$

The activation function can be linear or nonlinear. However, neural network models often employ a nonlinear activation function. There are several nonlinear functions that can be used in a neural network. We give a brief overview of some of the commonly used functions here.

The simplest function is the *linear threshold function.* The output response of the linear threshold function is defined as

$$F(\text{sum}_j) = \begin{cases} 0 & \text{if } \text{sum}_j \leq 0 \\ C \cdot \text{sum}_j & \text{if } 0 < \text{sum}_j < L \\ 1 & \text{if } \text{sum}_j \geq L \end{cases} \tag{17.3}$$

where $C > 0$ is the slope constant and L, the threshold. Figure 17.2*a* depicts a linear threshold function with $L = 1$.

Another simplest nonlinear function is the *hard-limiting threshold function.* The hard-limiting threshold function is given by

$$F(\text{sum}_j) = \begin{cases} 1 & \text{if } \text{sum}_j \geq 0 \\ 0 & \text{otherwise} \end{cases} \tag{17.4}$$

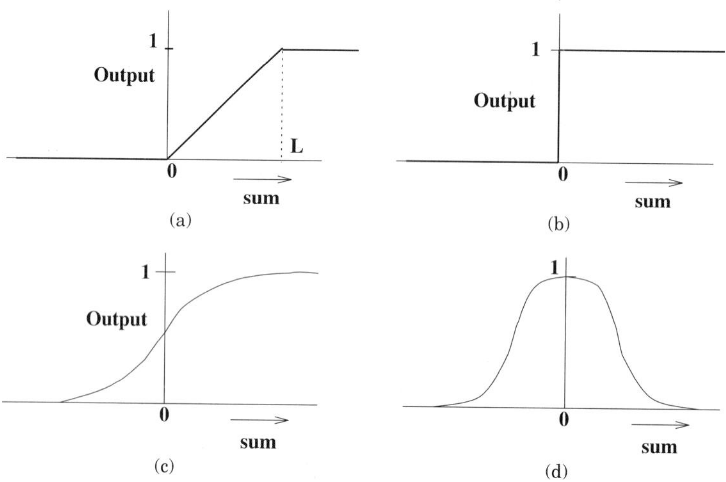

Figure 17.2 Output of typical activation functions.

The output behavior of this function is given in Fig. 17.2*b*.

The most widely used nonlinear activation function is the *logistic function*. The logistic function is defined as

$$F(\text{sum}_j) = 1/(1 + e^{-\text{sum}_j/T}) \tag{17.5}$$

where T is the so-called temperature coefficient, which controls the slope of the sigmoidal characteristics. The inverse of T is usually known as the *gain factor* of the activation function. The response of a sigmoid function is shown in Fig. 17.2*c*. One of the interesting features of the logistic function is that it produces a continuous output. A processing unit that incorporates a logistic activation function is often referred to as *sigmoidal unit*. The output of the sigmoidal unit is bounded between 0.0 and 1.0.

Another widely used nonlinear activation function is the *gaussian function*. A gaussian function with unit normalization is defined as

$$F_g(\text{sum}_j) = e^{[-(\text{sum}_j/\sigma)2]} \tag{17.6}$$

where σ is a parameter which can be used to control the width of the bell-shaped response curve. The output of a typical gaussian function is illustrated in Fig. 17.2*d*.

17.2.2 Architecture

We can characterize the architecture of a neural network in terms of two attributes: (1) number of layers in the network and (2) the type of network topology used.

Number of layers. The units that act as an interface between the external input and the network constitute the *input layer.* Typically, the input layer is not involved in any useful computation; rather, each unit in the input layer acts as a distribution point for the external inputs. The units that output the network's response to the external world constitute the *output layer.* The layers that do not have direct communication with the external world are called *hidden layers.* The number of layers in a network may vary from a lower limit of two (one input and one output layer) to any higher positive integer. In the neural network literature, some authors do not consider the input units as a layer. Thus, a network is often called a *single-layer network* if it does not have a hidden layer. On the other hand, networks with one or more hidden layers are called *multilayer networks.* Hidden layers of a multilayer network allow the network to develop its own internal representation of the problem. Each hidden layer produces an internal representation from the input it receives. The number of hidden units in a hidden layer represents the dimensionality of the internal representation space. Thus, by controlling the number of hidden units in a hidden layer, we can expand or shrink the internal representation of a problem.

Type of connectivity. Based on the connectivity and the direction in which links propagate activation values, we can classify a multilayer network into one of two well-known classes of models: *feed-forward networks* and *recurrent networks.*

If a network employs only forward-feeding connections then it is called a *feed-forward network.* A feed-forward network can be either single layer or multilayer. Historically, a single-layer network with a hard-limiting threshold output is known as a *perceptron.* However, a single-layer network with sigmoidal unit is also commonly referred to as a *perceptron.* Perceptrons have limited applicability because they are capable of solving only linearly separable classification problems. Multilayer networks, on the other hand, are highly suited for problems that require nonlinear function mappings and linearly inseparable classification boundaries. A three-layer feed-forward network is shown in Fig. 17.3*a*. This feed-forward network has one unit each in the input and output layers, and three (hidden) units in the hidden layer. An additional unit, called the *bias unit,* is always used to supply threshold values (using adjustable links) to all hidden and output units in the network. For simplicity we have not included the bias unit in Fig. 17.3*a*. For a given problem, the number of units required for the input and the output layers are dictated by the dimensionality of the problem space. For example, if a problem has two independent variables and a dependent variable, then the network will have two input units and one output unit. However, for a given problem, both the number of hidden layers needed in the network and the number of units needed within each hidden layer of the network are dictated by its complexity and size.

In addition to feed-forward connections, we can also use recurrent connections to feed the previous time-step output values (i.e., the states of the units corresponding to the previous input pattern or the time step) of units either to the units in preceding layer(s) or back to the units themselves. Multilayer networks that employ feedback connections are referred to as *recurrent networks.* Based on how recurrent connections are established, we can classify a recurrent network into one of three categories: (1) *simple recurrent networks* proposed by Elman [Elma90], (2) *semirecurrent networks* proposed by Jordan [Jord86], and (3) *fully recurrent networks* [Will89]. In a fully recurrent network every unit receives input from all other the units in the network. In the simple recurrent network (or Elman network), the recurrent connections originate from the hidden units. In a standard semirecurrent network (also known as Jordan network) there is one-to-one feedback from the output units to "state units," and all these feedback links have a fixed weight of 1.0. Apart from the output feedback, each state unit receives self-feedback through a learnable link. Thus, the activation of a state unit is a function of the output of the network as well as its own activation at the previous time step. The state units, like the input units, propagate their activations in the forward direction to all the hidden units. For illustration, we show a modified Jordan-style recurrent network without self-feedback links of the state units in Figure 17.3*b*. Our experience shows that both feed-forward networks and the modified Jordan-style recurrent network are useful in software reliability engineering applications.

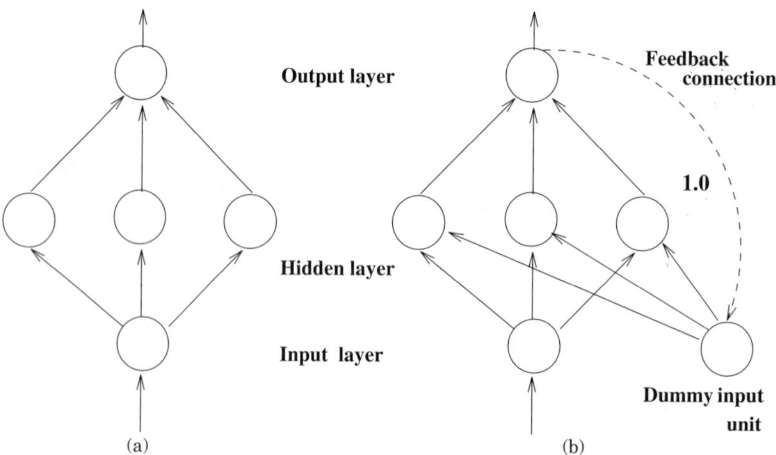

Figure 17.3 (*a*) A standard feed-forward network and (*b*) a modified Jordan network.

17.2.3 Learning algorithms

To solve a problem using a neural network, the network must first be taught solutions using a set of typical instances of input-output pairs known as the *training set.* The procedure by which the network is taught is known as the *learning algorithm.* During the training (or learning) phase, the strength of the interconnection links of the network are adjusted to reduce the residual error resulting from the training set. A variety of algorithms exist for training multilayer networks. Among them, the *back-propagation algorithm* is the most widely used. The back-propagation algorithm was proposed independently by several researchers [Werb74, Park82, Rume86]. In the mid-eighties, Rumelhart, Hinton, and Williams [Rume86] popularized the back-propagation algorithm by training multilayer networks to solve several interesting problems. Thus, the back-propagation algorithm has become one of the main driving forces behind the recent surge both in multilayer neural networks research and development of several variants of multilayer neural network training algorithms. A brief review of the back-propagation algorithm can be a valuable first step toward understanding other training algorithms and neural network models. Hence, we provide an overview of the back-propagation algorithm in the next section.

17.2.4 Back-propagation learning algorithm

The back-propagation learning algorithm is a class of supervised learning* algorithms in which the network weights are iteratively adapted using errors propagated back from the output layer. For the purpose of illustration, let us consider a simple three-layer feed-forward network constructed using sigmoidal units and trace how the back-propagation algorithm works.

Algorithm. (1) To start with, initialize the network weights with a set of random values. This step is called the *initialization phase.* Typically, a set of random values drawn from a small interval (for example, between –1.0 and 1.0) is used. However, one can also initialize the network weights with a set of values from a known distribution. (2) Next, in the *weight adjustment phase,* adjust the network weights incrementally over several iterations. In each iteration, adjust the weights in the direction of steepest decreasing gradient of the error surface (i.e., the surface formed by the sum of the square of the error between the desired output and the actual output for all patterns in the training

* A training algorithm is "supervised learning" if it requires actual outputs for each input pattern in the training set.

set). This iterative adjustment continues until either a minimum is reached in which the error is less than a prespecified tolerance limit, or until a set number of iterations has been reached. During each iteration, the sum of squared errors is calculated as follows:

$$E = \frac{1}{2} \sum_{p=1}^{P} \sum_{j=1}^{M} (y_j^p - o_j^p)^2 \tag{17.7}$$

where y^p is the desired output for the input vector in_p, o^p is the actual output of the network, M is the number of output units, and P is the number of patterns in the training set. This error is propagated back through the network to adjust weights using a gradient descent procedure. The gradient descent procedure changes the weights by an amount proportional to the partial derivative of the error with respect to each weight w_{ij}. Thus, the change in the weight of a link from unit i to unit j at the tth iteration is given by

$$\Delta w_{ij}(t) = \eta \cdot \delta_j \cdot in_i + \alpha \cdot \Delta w_{ij}(t-1) \tag{17.8}$$

where η, a proportionality constant called the *learning rate,* α, the momentum term, $\Delta w_{ij}(t-1)$, weight change during the previous iteration, in_i, the output activation of the unit i, and δ_j, partial derivative of the error with respect to the net input (sum_j) to the unit j. The error derivative δ_j for the jth unit in the output layer is given by

$$\delta_j = o_j(1 - o_j)(y_j - o_j) \tag{17.9}$$

and for the kth unit in the hidden layer is given by

$$\delta_k = h_k(1 - h_k) \sum_{j=1}^{M} (\delta_j \cdot w_{kj}) \tag{17.10}$$

where h_k is its activation.

Though the back-propagation algorithm can be used to train any multilayer network, one must be aware of several practical issues that could affect its efficiency. Since the back-propagation algorithm is a gradient descent optimization procedure, it is vulnerable to the problem of premature convergence. Premature convergence occurs whenever the algorithm gets stuck in a local minimum and the value of E is still higher than the allowed tolerance limit. Though several solutions have been proposed to improve/avoid premature convergence of the back-propagation algorithm [Jaco88], none of the solutions have been proved to work consistently across all error surfaces.

The second issue is specifying an optimum network architecture for a given problem. A network architecture is considered optimum if it has the minimum number of hidden units (and hence the minimum number of interconnection links) with which it can successfully learn the training set. If the network architecture is too small, then it may not be able to learn the entire training set. On the other hand, if the network architecture is too large, it may have too many degrees of freedom (weight or parameters) to learn the training set. Thus, if the network has too many weights, then it will memorize the training set rather than generalize it. Furthermore, an inappropriate network may consume an unreasonable amount of simulation resources. The back-propagation algorithm is applied to train the network with the assumption that the architecture of the network is specified either ahead of time by the user, or experimentally determined by trial and error. In the trial-and-error approach, the user may waste time experimenting with different architectures to find an appropriate architecture.

To address the limitations of the standard back-propagation algorithm, Scott Fahlman and colleagues [Fahl90] developed an efficient constructive training algorithm known as *cascade-correlation learning architecture* for feed-forward networks. We demonstrate the use of neural networks for software reliability applications using this algorithm. To understand how this algorithm works, we provide an overview of the algorithm in the following section.

17.2.5 Cascade-correlation learning architecture

The cascade-correlation algorithm combines two important ideas in its learning method: the *cascade architecture,* to add hidden units one at a time, and a *learning algorithm* (typically, Fahlman's "quickpropagation" [Fahl88]) to create, train, and install new hidden units. The cascade-correlation algorithm in effect grows a neural network. In the first stage of learning, the cascade-correlation uses no hidden units; this means that initially the net applies a simple perceptron-type network to learn as many training patterns as possible. When the algorithm can no longer reduce the error, a potential candidate hidden unit, which is separately optimized to maximize the correlation between its outputs and the residual error of the network over the entire training set, is added. When hidden units are trained, the weights connecting the output units are kept unchanged. After the hidden unit is connected to the output, training updates all the weights that directly go to the output layer. Once installed, each hidden unit becomes a new hidden layer in the network, and its incoming weights remain frozen for the rest of the training period. When subsequent hidden units are added, the outputs of the previously added hidden units become as additional inputs to the new hidden unit. This dynamic expansion of network architecture continues until the problem is solved.

The cascade-correlation algorithm consists of the following steps.

1. *Initialize the network.* Create a network architecture consisting of only input and output layers. Establish links from the input layer to the output layer and initialize them with random values.
2. *Train output layer.* Adjust weights feeding the output units. If the learning is complete (i.e., the error is below a preset limit) then stop; else if the error has not been reduced significantly for a certain number of consecutive epochs, or the maximum number of epochs allowed has been reached, then go to the next step.
3. *Initialize a candidate unit.* Create and initialize a candidate unit with random weights from all input units and all preexisting hidden units.
4. *Train the candidate unit.* Adjust candidate unit's weight to maximize the correlation between activation, v_c, of the candidate unit c and the residual error e_j at each output unit j.
   a. Compute correlation. The correlation is computed in terms of covariance,

$$\text{cor}_c = \sum_{j=1}^{M} \left| \sum_{p=1}^{P} (v_c^p - \bar{V})(e_j^p - \bar{E}_j) \right| \tag{17.11}$$

   where $\bar{V} = \Sigma_{p=1}^{P} v_c^p / P$ and $\bar{E}_j = \Sigma_{p=1}^{P} e_j^p / P$
   b. Update candidate unit's weights using gradient ascent to maximize cor_c,

$$\Delta w_{ci} = \alpha \cdot \frac{\partial \text{cor}_c}{\partial w_{ci}} \cdot i_i \tag{17.12}$$

   c. If the correlation at the current epoch is not significantly better than the previous epoch, then go to step 5; otherwise go back to step 4.*a*.
5. *Install the candidate unit.* Install the candidate unit as a hidden unit by establishing weights to output units and initializing them with the negative of the correlation values. Now freeze the incoming weights of the candidate unit and go to step 2.

The cascade-correlation learning algorithm has many advantages over the standard back-propagation algorithm. Three of the major advantages are: (1) the user need not specify the architecture; rather it is evolved automatically; (2) its learning speed is one or two orders of magnitude faster than the standard back-propagation algorithm; and (3) it is highly consistent in converging during training. Because of these advantages and our experience with the back-propagation algorithm, we use the cascade-correlation algorithm for all example demonstrations in this chapter.

17.3 Application of Neural Networks for Software Reliability

The problem of developing reliable software at a low cost still remains as an open challenge. To develop a reliable software system, we must address several issues. These include specifications for reliable software, reliable development methodologies, testing methods for reliability, reliability growth prediction modeling, and accurate estimation of reliability. Two of the problem areas in which the neural network is applicable are developing a general-purpose reliability growth model, and identifying change/fault-prone software modules early during the development cycle. This section reviews some of the limitations of the traditional modeling approaches used to solve these problems and argues that we can try the neural network approach as an alternative.

17.3.1 Dynamic reliability growth modeling

In current software-reliability research, one of the concerns is how to develop general prediction models. Existing models typically rely on a priori assumptions about the nature of failures and the probability of individual failures occurring. Furthermore, these models, referred to as *parametric models,* attempt to capture in two or three explicit parameters all the assumptions made about the software development process and environment. Because all of these assumptions must be made before the project begins, and because many projects are unique, the best that one can hope for is statistical techniques that predict failure on the basis of failure data from similar project histories. Though there is evidence to suggest that certain analytic models are better suited to certain types of software projects than other models, the issue of finding a common model for all possible software projects is yet to be solved.

Selection of a particular model is very important in software reliability growth prediction because both the release date and the resource allocation decision can be affected by the accuracy of predictions. Several solutions have been proposed to address the issue of model selection. For example, in Chap. 4 we suggest two alternatives: (1) try several software reliability growth models and select the one that gives highest confidence and (2) use a recalibration method to compensate for the bias of a model. The second alternative can be used either alone or in combination with the first solution. Alternatively, in Chap. 7 we propose a linear (or a weighted linear) combination of prediction results from models with opposite bias. Li and Malaiya [Li93] show that an adaptive prediction combined with preprocessing can enhance the predictive capability of the analytic models. All these solutions can broadly be termed *postprocessing* methods. Nevertheless, the issue of generalization of prediction models still remains open. An alternate approach is to use an adaptive model-building system that can develop its own model of the failure process from the actual characteristics of the given data set. In this chapter we demonstrate that such a general-purpose reliability growth model can be developed using the neural network approach.

17.3.2 Identifying fault-prone modules

Another concern in software reliability engineering is to identify potentially fault-/change-prone modules early during the development cycle. This concern is motivated by the developers' need to improve the overall reliability of the product by allocating more test efforts to potentially troublesome modules. Intrinsic complexity of the program texts, measured in terms of static complexity metrics, is often used as an indicator of troublesomeness of program modules. By controlling the complexity of software program modules during development, we can produce software systems that are easier to maintain and enhance (because simple modules are easier to understand). As seen in Chap. 12, static complexity metrics are measured from the passive program texts early during the development cycle and can be used as valuable indicators for allocating resources in future development efforts.

Several statistical regression and classification models have been suggested to predict the fault-proneness of software modules [Craw85, Shen85, Rodr87, Muns92, Lyu95b]. However, existing statistical models make simple assumptions that are often violated in practical measures. Furthermore, there are numerous metrics that are either redundant or that have some linear (or nonlinear) dependence among other metrics. High redundancy in the metric space and multiply-related metric dimensions may often result in unreliable predictive models. In this chapter, we demonstrate that neural networks can also be used as a classifier for identifying fault-prone software modules.

17.4 Software Reliability Growth Modeling

In this section we illustrate how neural networks can be used for predicting software reliability growth process. As pointed out earlier, the predictive capability of a neural network can be affected by which neural network model is used to model the failure data, how the input and output variables are represented to it, the order in which the input and output values are presented during training, and the complexity of the network. We address these issues in this section, and empirically show that neural networks can give accurate predictions across different software projects. Furthermore, we also perform an analysis to show that neural networks are capable of adapting their complexity to match the complexity of the training data set.

To illustrate how neural networks can be used as a prediction system, the following definitions are introduced [Karu91, Karu92a, Karu92b].

Definition 1

Sequential prediction: Given a sequence of inputs ($(i_1, \ldots, i_t) \in I$) and a corresponding sequence of outputs ($(o_1, \ldots, o_t) \in O$) up to the present time t and an input ($i_{t+d} \in I$) belonging to a future instant $t + d$, predict the output ($o_{t+d} \in O$).

For $d = 1$ the prediction is called the *next-step prediction* (or *short-term prediction*) and for $d = n(\geq 2)$ consecutive intervals it is known as the *n-step-ahead prediction* (or *long-term prediction*). A special case of long-term prediction is *end-point prediction,* which involves predicting an output for some future fixed point in time. In end-point prediction, the prediction horizon becomes shorter as the fixed point of interest is approached.

We can represent a neural network as a mapping $\mathcal{NN}: I \mapsto O$ where I is an n dimensional input space and O is the corresponding M dimensional output space. Generally this mapping is accomplished using a multilayer network. The training procedure is a mapping operation $\mathcal{T}$: $I_k \mapsto O_k$ where $(I_k, O_k) = \{(i, o) \mid i \in I \textit{ and } o \in O\}$ is a subset of k input-output pairs sampled from the actual problem space (I, O). The function $\mathcal{T}$ represents an instance of $\mathcal{NN}$ that has learned to compute (or approximate) the actual mapping of the problem.

Definition 2

Neural network mapping: Sequential prediction can be formulated as a neural network mapping

$$\mathcal{P}: ((I_t, O_t), i_{t+d}) \mapsto o_{t+d}$$

in which (I_t, O_t) represents a sequence of t consecutive samples used for training and o_{t+d} the predicted output corresponding to a future input i_{t+d}.

Definition 3

Neural network software reliability growth model: Software reliability growth prediction can be expressed in terms of a neural network mapping as

$$\mathcal{P}: \{(T_k, F_k), t_{k+h}\} \mapsto \mu_{k+h}$$

where T_k is a sequence of cumulative execution time $(t_1, \ldots, t_k)$, F_k is the corresponding observed accumulated failures $(\mu_1, \ldots, \mu_k)$ up to the present time t_k used to train the network, $t_{k+h} = t_k + \Delta$ is the cumulative execution time at the end of a future test session $k+h$ and μ_{k+h} is the prediction of the network.

In the above definition $\Delta = \Sigma_{j=k+1}^{k+h} \Delta_j$ represents the cumulative execution time of h consecutive future test sessions. Note that each test session Δ_j can be either a fixed duration or a random interval.

17.4.1 Training regimes

A neural network's predictive ability can be affected by what it learns and in which sequence it learns. The notion of a training regime is introduced to distinguish the order in which data are presented during training. Two training regimes can be used in software reliability prediction: *generalization training* and *prediction training.* Figure 17.4 illustrates these training regimes.

Generalization training is the standard way of training feed-forward networks. During training, each input i_t at time t is associated with the corresponding output o_t. Thus the network learns to model the actual functionality between the independent and the dependent variables.

Prediction training, on the other hand, is an approach often employed in training recurrent networks. Under this training, the value of the input variable i_t at time t is associated with the actual value of the output variable at time $t + 1$. Here the network learns to predict outputs anticipated at the next time step.

If we combine these two training regimes with the feed-forward network (FFN) and the modified Jordan network (JN), we get four neural network prediction models. Let us denote these models as *FFN-generalization, FFN-prediction, JN-generalization* and *JN-prediction.*

17.4.2 Data representation issue

The issue of data representation is concerned with the format used to represent the input-output variables of the problem to the neural net-

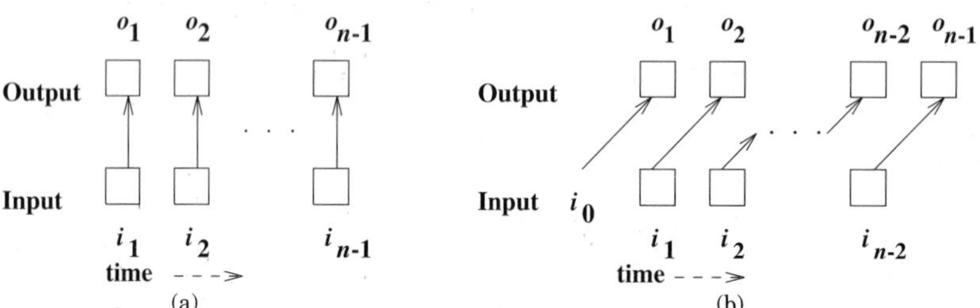

Figure 17.4 Two network-training regimes: (*a*) generalization training and (*b*) prediction training.

work. If a sigmoidal unit is used as the output unit, then its output response will be bounded between 0.0 and 1.0. Since the output variable of the software reliability growth model may vary over a large numerical value, it is necessary to scale the output variable to a range that conforms within the operational range of the output units. A simple representation is to use a direct scaling, which scales cumulative faults from 0.0 to 1.0. On the other hand, the input variables, in theory, need not be scaled to this range because the weights feeding the hidden units from the input layer can scale them appropriately. But, for practical reasons, it is a reasonable heuristic to scale also the input variables to an appropriate range. For the purpose of our illustration, we scaled both cumulative faults and cumulative execution time from 0.1 to 0.9 because our experience shows that (1) the network is less accurate in discriminating inputs whose scaled values are close to the boundary values 1.0 or 0.0, and (2) the sigmoidal unit's error derivative, which affects the rate of weight adaptation during training, becomes inconsequential when its output is close to 1.0 or 0.0. To scale the data, however, it is necessary to guess the appropriate maximum values for both the cumulative faults and the cumulative execution time [Karu92c].

17.4.3 A prediction experiment

To illustrate the predictive accuracy of neural network models, five well-known analytic software reliability growth models and failure history data sets from several different software projects were considered. These models include the *exponential* model proposed by Moranda [Mora75b], the *logarithmic* model proposed by Musa and Okumoto [Musa87], the *delayed S-shaped* model proposed by Yamada et al. [Yama83], the *inverse-polynomial* model proposed by Littlewood and Verrall [Litt74], and the *power* model proposed by Crow [Crow74]. All these models have two parameters and are nonhomogeneous Poisson process except for the *inverse-polynomial* model. Details of these models appear in Chap. 3.

The data sets used for illustration were collected from several different software systems, including 14 data sets (see the Data Disk). These data sets represent the observed failure history of those systems. Each data point within a set consists of two observations: the cumulative execution time and the corresponding accumulated number of defects disclosed.

17.4.3.1 Measures for evaluating predictability. In order to compare the predictive accuracy of different models, we have to use some meaningful quantitative measures. The software reliability research community uses a variety of metrics for comparison of models. We review three distinct approaches that are very common in software reliability research [Mala90a, Mala90b] and point out which one is relevant for our comparison.

Let the data be grouped into n points (t_i, D_i), $i = 1$ to n, where D_i is the cumulative number of defects found at time t_i, and t_i is the accumulated execution time (i.e., the time spent for testing the software) in disclosing D_i defects. Let μ_i be the projected number of defects at time t_i by a model.

1. *Goodness-of-fit.* In this approach, first a curve corresponding to a selected model is fitted to all the data points $\{t_i, \mu_i\}$, $i = 0, 1, \ldots, n$; then the deviation between the observed and the fitted values is evaluated by using the chi-square test or Kolmogorov-Smirnov test.
2. *Next-step predictability.* In this approach a partial data set corresponding to, say, $\{t_i, D_i\}$, $i = 1, \ldots, (l-1)$ is used to predict the value of μ_l (cumulative number of defects after lth test interval). The predicted and the observed values of cumulative defects are then compared.
3. *Variable-term predictability.* In actual practice, the need to predict the behavior at a distant future of the test phase using present failure history is very important. This approach, used by Musa et al. [Musa87], makes projections of the final value of μ_n using a partial data set $\{t_i, D_i\}$, $i = 0, \ldots, l$, where $l < n$. The percentage prediction error in these projections can then be plotted against time.

A *two-component predictability measure* consisting of *average error* (AE) and *average bias* (AB) was used by Malaiya et al. [Mala90a, Mala92] to compare predictive capabilities of parametric models at different fault-density ranges. These measures are as follows. For a specific model m, let μ_{ij}^m be the projected total number of the defects to be detected at a future time t_j, where $j = i + d$. Using the projected value at each point i, we can calculate the model's prediction error $(\mu_{ij}^m - D_j)/D_j$, $i = 1$ to $n - 1$. Then predictability measures for a given data set s are given by

$$AE_s^m = \frac{1}{n-1} \sum_{i=1}^{n-1} \left| \frac{\mu_{ij}^m - D_j}{D_j} \right| \tag{17.13}$$

$$AB_s^m = \frac{1}{n-1} \sum_{i=1}^{n-1} \frac{\mu_{ij}^m - D_j}{D_j} \tag{17.14}$$

Two extreme prediction horizons of interest are: $j = i + d = i + 1$, the *next-step prediction*, and $j = i + d = n$, the *end-point prediction*. AE is a measure of how well a model predicts throughout the test phase, and

AB is the general bias of the model. AB can be either positive or negative depending on whether the model is prone to overestimation or underestimation. Note that the above AE measure can be used to compare the predictive accuracy of models within a single data set only. However, what we need is a normalized AE measure (normalized within each data set) with which competing models can be ranked across different software projects.

Let $m \quad m_{\max}$ be the competing model that has the maximum average error measure for the data set s. Let $AE_s^{m\,\max}$ be its average error measure. Then the normalized AE measure is given by

$$NAE_s^m = \frac{AE_s^m}{AE_s^{m\,\max}} \tag{17.15}$$

Thus $NAE_s^m = 1.0$ when $m = m_{\max}$ (i.e, for the model which has the highest prediction error) and $0.0 < NAE_s^m < 1.0$ for $m \neq m_{\max}$. Note that more than one model may have the same value if their AE_s^m values are equal.

Let γ_s be the weighting (importance) factor of a data set s. Now an overall rank metric of the model m can be calculated as

$$R_m = \sum_{s=1}^{ND} \gamma_s \cdot NAE_s^m \tag{17.16}$$

where ND is the number of data sets used in comparing models. If we give equal weight to all data sets, then the above rank metric reduces to a simple sum

$$R_m = \sum_{s=1}^{ND} NAE_s^m \tag{17.17}$$

We can apply these metrics for both end-point predictions and next-step predictions.

17.4.3.2 Prediction results. We trained neural networks with the execution time as the input and the observed fault count as the target output. The training ensemble at time t_i consists of the complete failure history of the system since $t_{i=0}$ (i.e., since the beginning of testing). Any prediction of a neural network without proper training is equivalent to the network making a random guess. So we took care to see that the neural network was trained with at least some initial portion of the failure history. In all the experiments, we set the minimum size of the training set so it would contain at least the first three observed data points. We then increased the training set in steps of one point from this minimum set to all but the last point in the data set. At the end of each training, the network was fed with future inputs to measure its prediction of the total number of defects.

Table 17.1 summarizes the predictive accuracy of models in terms of the rank metric R_m defined earlier. This metric provides simple summary statistics. In order to find their relative accuracies, we also calculated the average and the standard deviation of R_m. The R_m values for end-point predictions of neural networks are well below the overall average of 6.10. This suggests that neural networks are better suited for end-point predictions than are analytic models. Jordan nets have R_m values 2.09 and 2.23, which are one standard deviation below that of the overall average of 6.10. The results suggest that the Jordan net models are better at end-point predictions than are all other models. One reason the Jordan nets exhibit such a low end-point prediction error may be that they are able to capture the correlation among points that are in the immediate past. In comparison, the analytic models have R_m values that are well above the average. This suggests that analytic models are either too pessimistic or too optimistic. Numbers in the "Rank" column represent the rank of these models based on their overall prediction accuracy.

Note that, except for the JN-prediction model, all models seem to have almost similar next-step prediction accuracy. This observation is further supported by the fact that all other models have R_m values that are bounded between one standard deviation above and below the average. The JN-prediction model has $R_m = 8.00$, which is one standard deviation below the overall average of 9.82, and suggests that this model has better next-step predictive accuracy than the other models compared.

In order to check whether the above observations have statistical significance, we performed further analysis using the analysis of variance (ANOVA) approach. In this approach we viewed the AE measures as outcomes of randomized block experiments in which the projects (or

TABLE 17.1 Summary of Normalized AE Measure

	End-point predictions		Next-step predictions	
Model	R_m	Rank	R_m	Rank
FFN-generalization	2.86	4	11.79	9
FFN-prediction	2.64	3	10.09	7
JN-generalization	2.09	1	9.81	5
JN-prediction	2.23	2	8.00	1
Logarithmic	6.29	5	8.78	2
Inverse polynomial	7.60	6	9.54	4
Exponential	8.20	7	8.96	3
Power	11.39	8	11.43	8
Delayed S-shape	11.59	9	9.95	6
Average	6.10		9.82	
Std	3.85		1.21	

data sets) were randomly selected and software reliability growth prediction models as "treatments" applied to each of the projects. Note that this approach accounts for the data set peculiarities that could affect performance of these competing models.

The overall average of AE values (i.e., the average of AE measures over all 14 data sets) are shown in Table 17.2. These values represent the predictive accuracy of models across different projects. The resulting F-statistics for projects and models are highly significant at the 1 percent level, and show that models have significantly different predictive accuracy. Since the models have significant F-statistics, we can use the least significant difference (LSD) procedure to differentiate among them in terms of their overall AE measure. Under LSD, two competing models are considered *significantly different* if their means in Table 17.2 differ by an amount equal to or greater than the value given by the LSD procedure. On the other hand, if the difference is less than the value given by the LSD procedure, then we can interpret that two models have similar predictive accuracy across all projects. Thus if a model X has an AE which is significantly lower than that of another model Y, then we can interpret, using > to denote significantly better, that {X} > {Y}.

The resulting LSD for the end-point prediction is 4.52 ($T_{5\%,104} = 1.98$). Thus, based on the averages in Table 17.2 we can conclude that {FFN-generalization, FFN-prediction, JN-generalization, JN-prediction} > {logarithmic, inv. polynomial, exponential} > {power, delayed S-shape}. Thus our analysis suggests that the neural network models are significantly better than analytic models in predicting end points.

The corresponding LSD value for the next-step prediction is 1.39 ($T_{5\%,104} = 1.98$). Based on this LSD value and the overall average of AE in Table 17.2, we can interpret that {JN-prediction, logarithmic, exponential} > {FFN-generalization, power}. Since the remaining four models do not show any significant difference in the next-step prediction accuracy, we can conclude that neither of these two competing approaches (neural network models versus analytic models) taken

TABLE 17.2 Overall Average of AE Measure

Model	End-point predictions	Next-step predictions
FFN-generalization	6.67	6.62
FFN-prediction	6.12	5.38
JN-generalization	4.75	5.47
JN-prediction	4.94	4.46
Logarithmic	14.23	5.04
Inverse polynomial	17.93	5.64
Exponential	18.45	5.19
Power	26.42	7.44
Delayed S-shape	25.61	5.80

alone have a distinct advantage. However, it should be noted that the JN-prediction model has a higher next-step prediction accuracy than all other models.

Since we used two different network architectures, we performed an additional ANOVA analysis to find out whether there is any significant difference among neural network models. The resulting LSD values (with a critical value of $T = 2.02$) are 1.16 for end-point predictions and 1.11 for next-step predictions, respectively. The LSD of 1.16 and the overall averages in Table 17.2 suggest that the Jordan network models are significantly better end-point predictors than the feed-forward network models. Furthermore, based on the LSD value of 1.11 for next-step predictions we conclude that the JN-prediction model is a better next-step predictor than the other neural network models. Thus, the Jordan network models are better predictors than the feed-forward network models.

In summary, our statistical analyses show that (1) on the average, neural networks models have better end-point prediction accuracy than analytic models, and (2) the type of neural network architecture can influence the predictive accuracy.

17.4.4 Analysis of neural network models

So far we have seen how we can use neural networks constructed using the cascade-correlation algorithm to accurately predict cumulative faults. As pointed out earlier, the number of hidden units added to the final network by the cascade-correlation algorithm may vary as the size and the complexity of the training set are changed. This is especially true in our reliability growth modeling problem because the number of points in the training set increased according to the time horizon that we took into consideration. Also, the number of hidden units varied from one data set to another because of their inherent peculiarity. Thus, most of the time the networks were constructed with zero, one, or two hidden units and occasionally with three or four hidden units. Thus, the models developed by the neural network approach are more complex than most analytic models that have two or three parameters.

17.5 Identification of Fault-Prone Software Modules

In this section, we demonstrate how neural networks can be used as a pattern classifier to identify fault-prone software modules early during the development cycle. There are two reasons for this demonstration: (1) to show that neural network classifiers can be developed as a complement to existing statistical classifiers and (2) to demonstrate that classifiers can be developed without the usual assumptions about the input metrics. The idea of using a neural network for classifying fault-prone software modules was first demonstrated by Koshgoftaar et al. [Kosh93c], using a multilayer network trained using a standard back-propagation algorithm. Here, we expand and evaluate the neural network approach using a perceptron network and a multilayer feed-forward network developed using a modified cascade-correlation algorithm [Karu93b, Karu93c]. We also address other issues such as selection of proper training samples and representation of software metrics.

17.5.1 Identification of fault-prone modules using software metrics

We can relate static complexity measures of program texts with faults found (or program changes made) during testing using two broad modeling approaches. In the *estimative approach,* regressions models are used to predict the actual number of faults that will be disclosed during testing [Craw85, Shen85, Khos90, Muns92, Lyu95b]. Regression models assume that the metrics that constitute the input variables are independent and identically distributed normals. However, most practical measures often violate the normality assumption. This in turn results in poor fit of the regression models and inconsistent predictions.

In the *classification approach,* software modules are categorized into two or more fault-prone classes. A special case of the classification approach is to categorize software modules into either low-fault (simple) or high-fault (complex) classes. The main rationale behind the two-class classification approach is that software managers are more often interested in getting an approximate classification from this type of model than an accurate prediction of the residual faults. Existing two-class categorization models are based on the linear discriminant principle [Rodr87, Muns92]. Linear discriminant models assume that the metrics are orthogonal and that they follow a normal distribution. However, it is often true that some of the real metrics are variants of an existing metric, and they tend to exhibit strong collinearity among themselves. We can reduce multicollinearity among metrics using either principal component analysis or some other dimensionality reduction techniques. However, the reduced metrics may not explain all the variability if the original metrics have nonlinear relationship.

17.5.2 Data set used

The metrics data used in this section were obtained from [Lind89] for Medical Imaging System software. As described in Sec. 12.4.2, the complete system consists of approximately 4500 modules amounting to about 400,000 lines of code written in Pascal, FORTRAN, and PL/M assembly language. From this set, a random sample of 390 high-level language routines was selected for the analysis. For each module in the sample, program changes were recorded as an indication of software fault. The number of changes in the program modules varied from zero to 98. In addition to changes, 11 software complexity metrics were extracted from each module. These metrics include [Lind89]: (1) total number of lines (code, comments, and declarations inclusive); (2) number of executable lines (comments and declarations excluded); (3) total number of characters; (4) number of comments; (5) number of comment characters; (6) number of code characters; (7) Halstead's length measure, which counts the total number of operators and operands; (8) Halstead's estimated length measure (calculated from an equation derived using the number of unique operands and operators); (9) Jensen's estimated length measure (calculated using the number of unique operands and operators); (10) McCabe's cyclomatic complexity (counts the number of paths through the code); and (11) Belady's bandwidth measure (computes the average nesting level of instructions).

For the purpose of our classification study, these metrics represent 11 input (both real and integer) variables of the classifier. We consider a software module as a low-fault-prone module (category I) if there is zero or one change and as a high-fault-prone module (category II) if there are 10 or more changes. We consider the remaining modules to be a medium-fault category. For the purpose of this study we consider only the low- and high-fault-prone modules. Our extreme categorization and deliberate discarding of program modules is similar to the approach used in other studies [Rodr87, Muns92]. After discarding medium-fault-prone modules, there are 203 modules left in the data set. Of 203 modules, 114 modules belong to the low-fault-prone category while the remaining 89 modules belong to the high-fault-prone category.

17.5.3 Classifiers compared

We demonstrate the utility of both statistical and neural network classifiers. We consider different classifiers because it could be useful in evaluating their relative merits and limitations. We use a simple gaussian classifier from the traditional statistical family, and both a perceptron and a multilayer feed-forward network from the neural network family. The perceptron classifier represents the simplest model of the neural network family, while the feed-forward network is a typical realization of a complex nonlinear classifier. Since we are interested in assigning modules into two extreme categories, we can use two output units in our neural nets corresponding to these categories. Thus, a given arbitrary vector **X** is assigned to category I if the value of the output unit 1 is greater than the output of unit 2, and to category II otherwise.

17.5.3.1 A perceptron classifier. A perceptron with a hard-limiting threshold can be considered as a realization of a simple nonparametric linear discriminant classifier. If we use a sigmoidal unit, then the continuous valued output of the perceptron can be interpreted as a likelihood or probability with which inputs are assigned to different classes. To train a perceptron network we can use back-propagation or quick-propagation procedures, or a simple optimization procedure. We chose the quick-propagation procedure, which is part of the cascade-correlation algorithm, as our training algorithm. In almost all our experiments, the perceptron learned about only 75 to 80 percent of the training set. This implies that the rest of the training samples may not be linearly separable.

17.5.3.2 A multilayer network classifier. To evaluate whether a multilayer network can perform better than the other two classifiers, we repeated the same set of experiments using feed-forward networks constructed using the cascade-correlation algorithm [Fahl90]. Our initial results suggested that the multilayer networks constructed by the cascade-correlation algorithm are not capable of producing a better classification accuracy than the other two classifiers. An analysis at the end of the training suggested that the resulting networks have too many free variables (i.e., due to too many hidden units). A further analysis of the rate of decrease in the residual error versus the number of hidden units added to the networks revealed that the cascade-correlation algorithm is capable of adding more hidden units to learn individual training patterns at the later stages of the training phase than in the earlier stages. This happens if the training set contains patterns that are interspersed across different decision regions, or what might be called *border patterns* [Ahme89]. Such an unrestricted growth of the network can be a disadvantage in certain applications. The larger the size of the network the less likely that the network will be able to generalize. Thus it is necessary to constrain the growth of the network during training.

17.5.3.3 Minimal network growth using cross-validation. One standard approach used in statistical model fitting is to incorporate a cross-validation during parameter estimation. (See Stone [Ston74] and Efron [Efro79] for the basic theory and details.) The idea of using cross-validation to construct minimal networks has been extended to neural networks by several researchers within the context of the standard back-propagation algorithms [Morg89, Weig90]. Here, we demonstrate the utility of cross-validation within the context of the cascade-correlation algorithm. The modified cascade-correlation algorithm incorporates the cross-validation check during the output layer training phase to constrain the growth of the size of the network. The specific method that we employ is to divide each training set S into two sets: (1) a *training set,* used both to add hidden units and to determine weights and (2) a *cross-validation set,* which is used to decide when to stop the algorithm. To stop the network construction, the performance on the cross-validation set is monitored during the output training phase. We stop training as soon as the residual error of the cross-validation set stops decreasing from the residual error at the end of the previous output layer training phase. Another issue that needs to be addressed in using cross-validation is selecting an appropriate cross-validation set. As a rule of thumb, for each training set of size S, we randomly pick one-third for cross-validation and the remaining two-thirds for training. The resulting network learned about 95 percent of the training patterns. As shown in Sec. 17.5.7, the cross-validated construction considerably improves the classification performance of the networks on the test set.

17.5.3.4 A minimum distance classifier. In order to compare neural network classifiers with statistical linear discriminant classifiers we also implemented a simple minimum distance based a two-class gaussian classifier of the form [Nils90]:

$$|\mathbf{X} - \mathbf{C}_i| \triangleq ((\mathbf{X} - \mathbf{C}_i)(\mathbf{X} - \mathbf{C}_i)^t)^{1/2} \tag{17.35}$$

where $\mathbf{C}_i$, $i = 1, 2$ represent the prototype points for categories I and II, $\mathbf{X}$ is an 11-dimensional-metrics vector, and t is the transpose operator. The prototype points $\mathbf{C}_1$ and $\mathbf{C}_2$ are calculated from the training set based on the normality assumption. In this approach a given arbitrary input vector $\mathbf{X}$ is placed in category I if $|\mathbf{X} - \mathbf{C}_1| < |\mathbf{X} - \mathbf{C}_2|$ and in category II otherwise.

17.5.4 Data representation

All raw component metrics had distributions that are asymmetric with a positive skew (i.e., long tail to the right), and they had different numerical ranges. Note that asymmetric distributions do not conform to the normality assumption of a typical gaussian classifier. First, we transformed each metric using a natural logarithmic base to remove the extreme asymmetry of the original distribution of the individual metric. Next, we divided each metric by its standard deviation of the training set to mask the influence of the individual component metric on the distance score, These transformations considerably improved the performance of the gaussian classifier. To be consistent in our comparison, we used the same (log) transformation and scaling of inputs for other classifiers.

17.5.5 Training data selection

We had two objectives in selecting training data: (1) to evaluate how well a neural network classifier will perform across different-sized training sets and (2) to select the training data that are as unbiased as possible. The first objective was motivated by the need to evaluate whether a neural network classifier can be used early in the software development cycle. Thus, the classification experiments were conducted using training sets of increasing size $S = 1/4, 1/3, 1/2, 2/3, 3/4, 9/10$ fraction of 203 samples belonging to categories I and II. The remaining $(1 - S)$ fraction of the samples was used for testing the classifiers. In order to avoid bias in the training data, we randomly selected 10 different training samples for each fraction **S.** This resulted in 60 (that is, 6×10) different training and test sets.

17.5.6 Experimental approach

Since a neural network's performance can be affected by the weight vector used to initialize the network, we repeated the training experiment 25 times with different initial weight vectors for each training set. This resulted in a total of 250 training trials for each value of S. The results reported here for the neural network classifiers represent a summary of statistics for 250 experiments. The performance of the classifiers is reported in terms of classification errors. There are two types of classification errors that a classifier can make: a type I error occurs when the classifier identifies a low-fault-prone (category I) module as a high-fault-prone (category II) module; a type II error is produced when a high-fault-prone module is identified as a low-fault-prone module. From a software manager's point of view, these classification errors will have different implications. Type I misclassification will result in waste of test resources (because modules that are less fault-prone may be tested longer than what is normally required). On the other hand, type II misclassification will result in releasing products that are of inferior quality. From reliability point of view, a type II error is a more serious error than a type I error.

17.5.7 Results

First, we provide a comparison between the multilayer networks developed with and without cross-validation. Table 17.3 compares the complexity and the performance of the multilayer networks developed with and without cross-validation. Columns 2 through 7 represent the size and the performance of the networks developed by the cascade-correlation without cross-validation. The remaining six columns correspond to the networks constructed with cross-validation. Hidden unit statistics for the networks suggest that the growth of the network can be considerably constrained by adding cross-validation during the output layer training. With cross-validation, the rate of growth of the network is not severely affected by the increase in the size of the training set. Networks without cross-validation, on the other hand, may grow linearly depending on the size and the nature of the classification boundary of the training set. The corresponding error statistics for both the type I and type II errors suggest that an improvement in classification accuracy can be achieved by cross-validating the size of the networks. Another side benefit with cross-validation is that the training time of the cascade-correlation algorithm can be reduced significantly (because the algorithm adds only a few hidden units).

Next, we compare the classification accuracy of classifiers in terms of type I and type II errors. Table 17.4 illustrates the comparative results for type I error. The first three columns in Table 17.4 represents the size of the training set in terms of S as a percentage of all patterns, the size of the training set in terms of number of patterns and the size of the test set, respectively. Column 4 represents the number of test patterns belonging to category I. The remaining six columns represent the type I error for the three classifiers in terms of percentage mean error and standard deviation. The percentages of errors were obtained by dividing the number of misclassifications by the total number of test patterns belonging to category I. These results show that the gaussian and the perceptron classifiers may provide better classification than multilayer networks at the early stages of the software development cycle. However, the difference in performance of the gaussian classifier is not consistent across all values of S. For example, the gaussian clas-

TABLE 17.3 A Comparison of Nets With and Without Cross-Validation

Training set size	Without cross-validation						With cross-validation					
	Hidden units		Type I error		Type II error		Hidden units		Type I error		Type II error	
S (%)	Mean	Std.	Mean	Std.	Mean	Std.	Mean	Std.	Mean	Std.	Mean	Std.
25	5.1	1.5	24.64	7.2	16.38	6.4	1.9	1.3	20.19	5.4	12.11	4.7
33	6.2	1.8	20.24	8.4	17.27	5.5	2.2	1.0	18.24	5.5	12.40	4.1
50	7.4	1.8	18.30	7.4	18.65	6.4	2.0	0.9	17.41	5.6	15.04	5.2
67	9.7	1.7	15.78	6.5	18.05	7.1	2.7	1.1	14.32	5.8	14.08	5.5
75	10.4	1.8	14.54	7.6	16.85	7.3	2.7	1.3	13.27	7.0	13.84	5.4
90	11.2	1.6	10.33	7.2	17.73	8.3	2.9	1.2	9.77	9.4	15.47	5.1

sifier did not improve its accuracy when $S = 90\%$. The neural network classifiers, on the other hand, seem to improve their performance with an increase in the size of the training set. Among neural networks, the perceptron classifier seems to do better classifications than a multilayer net.

Table 17.5 illustrates the comparative results for type II errors. Column 4 represents the number of category II patterns in the test set. The remaining six columns represent the error statistics for type II errors. The mean values of the error statistics suggest that a multilayer network classifier, on the average, may provide a better classification of category II modules than the other two classifiers. This is an important result from the reliability perspective. Furthermore, the difference in performance between the multilayer network and the other two classifiers is consistent across all training sets. Unlike in category I classification, both the neural networks and the gaussian classifiers seem not to improve their classification accuracy as the training set size is increased. This may partly be attributed to the fact that the number of test inputs for category II is lower than for category I.

In summary, the multilayer neural network classifiers may provide better classification of category II modules than other classifiers, and the perceptron (or the gaussian) classifier may be a useful candidate for classifying category I modules.

TABLE 17.4 A Summary of Type I Error

	No. of patterns		Test patterns	Error statistics					
				Gaussian		Perceptron		Multilayer nets	
S	Training set	Test set	Category I (%)	Mean	Std.	Mean	Std.	Mean	Std.
25	50	153	86	13.16	4.7	16.17	5.5	20.19	5.4
33	66	137	77	11.44	4.0	11.74	3.9	18.24	5.5
50	101	102	57	12.45	3.2	11.58	3.2	17.41	5.6
67	136	67	37	9.46	4.1	10.14	3.9	14.32	5.8
75	152	51	28	8.57	5.4	9.15	5.8	13.27	7.0
90	182	21	12	14.17	7.9	4.03	4.3	9.77	9.4

TABLE 17.5 A Summary of Type II Error

	No. of patterns		Test patterns	Error statistics					
				Gaussian		Perceptron		Multilayer nets	
S	Training set	Test set	Category II (%)	Mean	Std.	Mean	Std.	Mean	Std.
25	50	153	67	15.61	4.2	15.98	7.8	12.11	4.7
33	66	137	60	15.46	4.6	15.78	6.6	12.40	4.1
50	101	102	45	16.01	5.1	16.97	6.8	15.04	5.2
67	136	67	30	16.00	5.4	16.11	7.6	14.08	5.5
75	152	51	23	17.39	5.8	18.39	6.3	13.84	5.4
90	182	21	9	21.11	6.3	19.11	5.6	15.47	5.1

17.6 Summary

We demonstrated the applicability of neural networks for modeling software reliability growth and to classify error-prone software modules. In both applications, the neural network offers an alternative to conventional analytic models that are obtained using empirical methods or developed using some a priori assumptions.

Though we have demonstrated the application of neural nets in the context of two problems related to software reliability engineering, their applicability need not be restricted to only these problems in software reliability engineering. With the availability of public-domain and commercial neural network software, the neural network approach may be used as a tool in other software engineering problems, such as identification of software reuse components, document understanding, test-case generation, and partitioning of test cases.

Problems

17.1 Obtain the public domain cascade-correlation algorithm simulator from the following Internet ftp address.

`pt.cs.cmu.edu (128.2.254.155)`, *login:* `anonymous`, *password:* `your address`, and *directory:* `/afs/cs/project/connect/code/supported`

Get the shell archive file "`cascor-v1.2.shar`" or the latest version. Familiarize yourself with the simulator by running the example XOR problem (File name: `xor.data`) that comes with the simulator. Also observe how the training and test data are represented, how the initial network is specified, the important parameters of the simulator, and how various parameters are set.

17.2 Obtain the data set Data2 in the Data Disk, scale it, and construct a training set for the generalization training regime (refer to Fig. 17.4) with the entire data set. Train a neural network using the cascade-correlation simulator and answer the following.

a. How many hidden units did the simulator add to successfully train the network?

b. What is the number of weights in the network?

c. What are the values of the final weight vector?

(*Hint:* To scale the data, first separate the cumulative execution time and cumulative faults, and then scale them between 0.1 and 0.9 such that the highest value corresponds to 0.9 while the lowest value corresponds to 0.1.)

17.3 For the trained network in Prob. 17.2, use the training set as the test set and record the network outputs. Rescale the recorded outputs back to the original scale and plot a fitness curve with execution time on the x axis and cumulative faults on the y axis. Now plot a similar curve with the original data. Visually observe the deviation between these two curves.

17.4 For the data set Data2 in Prob. 17.2, construct a training set for the *prediction training* regime (refer to Fig. 17.4 for details). Repeat the experiments of Probs. 17.2 and 17.3 with this training set.

17.5 In Prob. 17.3, a feed-forward neural network was trained using Data2. In this exercise, use the same procedure, data set, and the steps outlined below to test the next-step prediction accuracy of the FFN-generalization model. First, construct a training set with the first three pairs of Data2. The corresponding test set will contain one input representing the execution time of the fourth observation. After training the network, test the network by feeding the fourth execution time as input. Record the network output. Next, construct another training set by including the fourth pair of the data into the previous training set. The corresponding test will consist of the fifth observation of the execution time. Again train and test a network. Repeat this step by incrementally adding all but the last observation to the training set. Thus, there will be $n - 3$ predicted values (where n is the number of points in Data2). Finally, evaluate the predictive accuracy of the network using:

a. A graph similar to the one in Prob. 17.3.

b. The average error (AE) and the average bias (AB).

17.6 Repeat the steps used in Prob. 17.5 and evaluate the end-point prediction accuracy of the FFN-generalization model using Data2. Note that the training set will have to be expanded as in Prob. 17.5, while the test set will always contain the last observation of the data set.

17.7 Consider the data set Data2 and evaluate the predictive accuracy of the JN-generalization model. Note that the training set for the JN-generalization model has to be changed to accommodate an additional input corresponding to the output of the network from the previous time step (i.e., the previous input). A special case of training the JN-generalization model, known as *teacher forced training,* is to use the actual output from the data set rather than the output of the network corresponding to the previous time step. Thus, each point in the training set will consist of two inputs, corresponding to the current execution time and the cumulative fault of the previous time step, and an output for the current cumulative fault. Evaluate both the next-step and the end-point prediction accuracies.

17.8 Repeat the steps used in Prob. 17.6 and evaluate the JN-prediction model using the data set Data2.

17.9 Collect software complexity metrics data from a project in your organization and the associated failure history.

17.10 Use the data set obtained in Prob. 17.9 and conduct a two-class classification experiment as performed in Sec. 17.5.

17.11 Use the data set obtained in Prob. 17.9 and conduct a three-class classification experiment by including the medium-fault category that we have omitted in Sec. 17.5. Observe the following:

a. Classification accuracy of the network

b. Increase/decrease in complexity of the network

17.12 Multilayer neural network models solve problems by creating an internal representation of the input variables. It is a useful exercise to analyze their internal representations and understand how such internal representations can be related to external inputs. For example, in our application involving identification of fault-prone software modules, it was not obvious what type of associations the neural network classifier created among the input metrics. Provide an analysis of the internal representation of the neural network in terms of

a. Its association with inputs metrics

b. The final weight vector of the network

c. Its association with the output categories

17.13 We used neural network models to associate static complexity metrics with the number of faults (and hence fault-prone categories). Instead, develop models to associate

a. Software complexity metrics to maintenance metrics

b. Design metrics with quality and maintainability objectives

Appendix

Software Reliability Tools

George Stark
Mitre Corporation

A.1 Introduction

In studying the SRE estimation examples in Parts 1 and 2 of this book, you will notice several features needed to execute most applications of SRE. They include the following:

1. Collecting failure and test time information
2. Calculating estimates of model parameters using the information
3. Testing the fit of a model against the collected information
4. Selecting a model to make predictions of remaining faults, time to test, or other items of interest
5. Applying the model

It is the commonality of these and other features that leads to the development of special-purpose SRE measurement tools. This appendix provides a summary description of several of these tools. It does not consider early prediction tools, as they are generally less mature and not as readily available to the software engineering community.

Section A.2 discusses the relative merits of using an SRE tool rather than a general-purpose application like a spreadsheet or statistical package for conducting an SRE analysis. Section A.3 lists criteria for consideration when deciding which tool to purchase or use for a particular SRE project. These criteria should be kept in mind while reading Secs. A.4 through A.9, which summarize some widely used tools with an example execution of each tool. Finally, Sec. A.10 provides additional details on the features of the highlighted tools as well as some additional tools in tabular format.

A.2 Comparison of Commercially Available Tools with General-Purpose Languages and Applications

One of the many important decisions a reliability modeler or analyst must make in performing an SRE study is the choice of a tool. An inappropriate choice may in itself kill an SRE project if it cannot be completed in time, does not handle the type of data collected for the project, or does not have a robust set of models that may fit the project to make accurate predictions of important information. Engineers may choose to implement one of the myriad of software reliability models using a general-purpose application program such as a spreadsheet or a statistical package such as SAS or SPSS. They may also choose to develop their own models using a general-purpose programming language such FORTRAN or C. The following are some advantages of using a commercially available tool rather than a general-purpose application or developing your own program.

1. Commercially available tools provide most (if not all) of the features needed in executing a software reliability analysis, resulting in a decrease of programming time that can often be significant.
2. Comparing multiple models on the same failure data and changing the analysis to use a different model's predictions is generally easier to accomplish using a commercially available tool.
3. The tools provide better error detection because many potential types of errors have been identified and are checked for automatically. Since no code must be written, the chance of making a mistake in a calculation or formula is very small.
4. The tools provide a general framework for reliability estimation and prediction. Their basic structure is from the theories developed by researchers and uses the terminology of those models.

On the other hand, programming your own tool or using a general-purpose application such as a spreadsheet or statistical package to analyze the failure data offers several advantages. For example:

1. Most modelers already know a general-purpose application or language and have access to these items on a computer that the analyst wants to use. This is often not the case with a commercially available tool.
2. An efficiently written program in a general-purpose language may take less time than using a commercially available tool. This is

because commercial tools are designed to handle a wide variety of situations within their expected input types, whereas a FORTRAN program can be tailored to a particular environment.

3. General-purpose tools and languages allow greater flexibility than other tools. For example, using a general-purpose package the analyst is able to use models that are not part of a commercial tool. Also, tailoring a program to a particular project may allow the analyst to accommodate factors (e.g., workload, complexity, fault tolerance) that are not relevant to some models implemented in a tool. Using a spreadsheet or statistical package allows the analyst to look at the reliability data in a number of ways that may not be available in a commercial tool.

Although there are clearly advantages to using either approach, in general an analyst should give serious consideration to the use of a commercially available tool. If such a decision is made, the criteria discussed in Sec. A.3 may be helpful in deciding which particular tool to use.

A.3 Criteria for Selecting a Software Reliability Estimation Tool

Almost all software reliability tools use one of two basic types of input data: time-domain data (i.e., time-between-failures data) or interval-domain data (i.e., failure-count data). These types of data, defined in Chap. 1, are also used by modelers using general-purpose applications or languages. We assume in this section that a decision has been made to use a software reliability tool rather than a general-purpose program or programming language, and we present criteria which may be useful in selecting a tool. There are two levels at which a decision with regard to reliability tools must be made. At the highest level, an organization must decide which tools to purchase or lease for its general use. You should not necessarily feel that a single tool must be chosen, but it does help management if results are displayed consistently across projects for comparisons of processes and software engineering technologies. At the lower level, an analyst must decide which tool to use for a particular project or study.

The following are some of the criteria that should be considered in selecting a tool for an organization [Sarg79]:

1. Availability of the tool for the company's computer system(s)
2. Cost of installing and maintaining the program
3. Number of studies likely to be done

4. Types of systems to be studied
5. Quality of the tool documentation and support
6. Ease of learning the tool
7. Flexibility and power of the tool

When an analyst must pick a tool for a particular application, many of the above criteria are still relevant. In addition, however, the following factors are important:

1. Availability of tools, either in-house or on a network
2. Goals and questions to be answered by the study
3. Models and statistical techniques understood by the analyst
4. Schedule for the project and type of data collected
5. Tool's ability to communicate the nature of the model and the results to a person other than the analyst (e.g., the end user or a manager).

The following sections overview several widely used tools and present a sample execution of each tool using failure data from an operational system. Section A.10 provides additional details on the tools in tabular format for easy comparison.

A.4 AT&T Software Reliability Engineering Toolkit

The AT&T Software Reliability Engineering Toolkit is a command-line-driven system that executes the Musa basic and Musa/Okumoto logarithmic Poisson execution time software reliability models. These models are described in Chap. 3. After having been developed by AT&T in 1977, the toolkit evolved through a couple of versions; the latest and most comprehensive version is available through a three-day AT&T software reliability training course offered throughout the year, and its MS/DOS version is included in the Data and Tool Disk. The toolkit is available for any platform running MS/DOS or UNIX® operating systems that support the C language. References for the AT&T Toolkit include the Program Reference Guide [ATT90, Musa77a, Musa77b, Star91].

The simplicity and intuitive nature of the Musa model parameters coupled with the toolkit support for both time domain and interval domain failure data as input has wide appeal. The outputs from this

```
                         SOFTWARE RELIABILITY ESTIMATION
                           EXPONENTIAL (BASIC) MODEL
                              HANDBOOK DATA SET

BASED ON A SAMPLE OF                129 TEST FAILURES
TEST EXECUTION TIME IS              20 CPU-HR
FAILURE INTENSITY OBJECTIVE IS      2.4 FAILURES/1000-CPU-HR
CURRENT DATE IN TEST                900419
TIME FROM START OF TEST IS          37 DAYS
                          CONF. LIMITS            MOST            CONF. LIMITS
                   95%     90%     75%     50%    LIKELY     50%     75%     90%     95%
TOTAL FAILURES     134     134     135     137     139       142     144     148     151
       ***********  FAILURE INTENSITIES (FAILURES/1000-CPU-HR) ***********
INITIAL 1463       1521    1614    1705    1837    1972      2070    2172    2238
PRESENT 78.69      85.49   97.25   109.9   130.3   154.0     172.8   194.5   209.4
      *** ADDITIONAL REQUIREMENTS TO MEET FAILURE INTENSITY OBJECTIVE ***
FAILURES              5       5       6       7      10        13      15      19      21
TEST EXEC. TIME    20.85   22.09   24.21   26.49   30.19     34.61   38.29   42.73   45.98
WORK DAYS          6.52    7.05    8.02    9.13    11.08     13.60   15.85   18.73   20.91
COMPLETION DATE    900430  900501  900502  900503  900507    900509  900511  900516  900518
```

Figure A.1 Tabular output from AT&T Toolkit.

tool are easy to understand. Summary estimates for such reliability measures as total failures (for the basic model), the initial failure rate (the toolkit and Musa use the term *failure intensity* instead of *failure rate*), and the present failure rate of the program under test are shown in both tabular and graphical fashion. Figure A.1 shows a sample output from the AT&T Toolkit. Because the toolkit is estimating the parameters of the model from collected data, the tool also reports confidence intervals around the estimated (or most likely) value. Thus, in our example session, although total failures are reported as 139 (the "most likely" value), we can say with 90 percent confidence that total failures are between 134 and 148.

Other plots from the toolkit help you to see how well the model fits the actual data, the trend in the initial and current failure rate for the program, and predict the completion date of the project. In addition to the estimation model (est and plot), the AT&T SRE Toolkit also includes (1) a prediction model that calculates model-based predictions of cost and schedule for a range of failure-rate objectives and (2) a reliability demonstration model that helps an engineer develop a reliability demonstration chart to demonstrate the reliability of acquired software for a given operational profile.

A.5 Statistical Modeling and Estimation of Reliability Functions for Software (SMERFS)

SMERFS is a menu-driven tool that is suited particularly well for a newcomer to software reliability modeling. Originally developed in 1983 by the U.S. Naval Surface Warfare Center in Dahlgren, Virginia, this public domain tool has evolved through several versions, the latest being SMERFS V. Historically, SMERFS has been the most popular tool because it offers flexibility in data collection and provides multiple time-domain (i.e., Littlewood and Verrall, Musa basic execution time, Musa/Okumoto logarithmic Poisson, Jelinski-Moranda, geometric, and nonhomogeneous Poisson) and interval-domain (i.e., Schneidewind, Brooks and Motley, nonhomogeneous Poisson, Yamada S-shaped, and generalized Poisson) models. This makes it useful for modelers who are not ready to settle on a single model for their software debugging process.

The program is written in a subset of ANSI FORTRAN '77, making it portable to a wide range of hardware platforms. SMERFS is designed as a driver program and a series of model libraries. Because the source code and software design documentation are provided with SMERFS, users can add new SRE models or delete models that are no longer in favor as they wish. The design also allows users to construct their own driver and develop a tailored user interface. A more detailed description of SMERFS, with examples, can be found in the SMERFS User's Guide [Farr93a] and in [Farr88].

SMERFS V both implements a database concept to data entry and allows ASCII file input of the data. In the database input, the user enters the failure data using the SMERFS data input module. Thus, the user does not need to know or understand the format of the input file, although it can be time-consuming. The ASCII file format is similar to that of the AT&T Toolkit. SMERFS allows the analyst to choose the model parameter estimation method: either maximum likelihood or least squares. SMERFS also provides basic statistics calculated from the data and the ability to analyze the residuals from the model analysis.

SMERFS allows the user to enter data, edit and/or transform the data if necessary, plot the data, select an appropriate model to fit the data, determine the fit of the model using both statistical and graphical techniques, make various reliability predictions based upon the fitted model, and try different models if the initial model proves inadequate. For model selection SMERFS provides the prequential likelihood statistic (see Chap. 4) as well as u-plots, y-plots, and measure of noise. Among the various reliability indicators provided by the different models are the following: expected time-to-next-failure occurrence, an estimate of the reliability for a specified operational time, the number of faults remaining in the software, an estimate of the time it will take to trigger the remaining failures, and the expected number of failures in the next session of a given duration. Figure A.2 shows SMERFS menus and sample model executions.

```
THE AVAILABLE MAIN MODULE OPTIONS ARE:
    1 DATA INPUT              6 PLOT(S) OF THE RAW DATA
    2 DATA EDIT               7 MODEL APPLICABILITY ANALYSES
    3 UNIT CONVERSIONS        8 EXECUTIONS OF THE MODELS
    4 DATA TRANSFORMATIONS    9 STOP EXECUTION OF SMERFS
    5 DATA STATISTICS
   ENTER MAIN MODULE OPTION.
          5
                          INTERVAL DATA WITH EQUAL LENGTHS
                           WITH FAULT COUNTS TOTALING TO         129
                          ******************************************
   MEDIAN OF THE DATA     *            .50000000E+01                *
   LOWER & UPPER HINGES   *   .20000000E+01     .85000000E+01       *
   MINIMUM AND MAXIMUM    *   .00000000E+00     .27000000E+02       *
   NUMBER OF ENTRIES      *                20                       *
   AVERAGE OF THE DATA    *            .64500000E+01                *
   STD. DEV. & VARIANCE   *   .63451183E+01     .40260526E+02       *
   SKEWNESS & KURTOSIS    *   .18568731E+01     .35976645E+01       *
                          ******************************************

   ENTER MAIN MODULE OPTION, OR ZERO FOR A LIST.
          0
   THE AVAILABLE MAIN MODULE OPTIONS ARE:
    1 DATA INPUT              6 PLOT(S) OF THE RAW DATA
    2 DATA EDIT               7 MODEL APPLICABILITY ANALYSES
    3 UNIT CONVERSIONS        8 EXECUTIONS OF THE MODELS
    4 DATA TRANSFORMATIONS    9 STOP EXECUTION OF SMERFS
    5 DATA STATISTICS
   ENTER MAIN MODULE OPTION.
8
ENTER COUNT MODEL OPTION, OR ZERO FOR A LIST.
          0
   THE AVAILABLE FAULT COUNT MODELS ARE:
    1 THE BROOKS AND MOTLEY MODEL
    2 THE GENERALIZED POISSON MODEL
    3 THE NON-HOMOGENEOUS POISSON MODEL
    4 THE SCHNEIDEWIND MODEL
    5 THE S-SHAPED RELIABILITY GROWTH MODEL
    6 RETURN TO THE MAIN PROGRAM
   ENTER MODEL OPTION.
          3
   ENTER ONE FOR NHPP MODEL DESCRIPTION; ELSE ZERO.
          0
   ENTER ONE FOR  MAXIMUM LIKELIHOOD METHOD,  TWO FOR LEAST SQUARES
   METHOD, OR THREE TO TERMINATE MODEL EXECUTION.
          1
   ML MODEL ESTIMATES ARE:
   (THE APPROXIMATE 95% CONFIDENCE INTERVALS APPEAR IN PARENTHESES)
    PROPORTIONALITY CONSTANT    .13230E+00 (  .9738E-01,  .1672E+00)
    TOTAL NUMBER OF FAULTS      .13885E+03 (  .1290E+03,  .1638E+03)
    # OF FAULTS REMAINING       .98495E+01 (  .0000E+00,  .3481E+02)

   THE AVAILABLE FUTURE PREDICTIONS ARE:
    1) THE NUMBER OF FAULTS EXPECTED IN THE NEXT TESTING PERIOD
    2) THE NUMBER OF PERIODS NEEDED TO DISCOVER THE NEXT M FAULTS
   ENTER PREDICTION OPTION, OR ZERO TO END PREDICTIONS.
          1
    ENTER PROJECTED LENGTH OF THE PERIOD, OR ZERO TO END.
       1.000000000000000
    # OF FAULTS EXPECTED        .12206E+01
```

Figure A.2 SMERFS main menu and sample model executions.

A.6 Statistical Modeling and Reliability Program (SRMP)

The Statistical Modeling and Reliability Program (SRMP) was developed by the Reliability and Statistical Consultants, Limited, of the United Kingdom in 1988. SRMP is a command-line-oriented tool developed for an IBM PC/AT with 500K of memory, and requires a math coprocessor to be installed. It also runs on UNIX®-based workstations. SRMP contains nine models: Musa/Okumoto, Duane, Jelinski-Moranda, Goel/Okumoto, Bayesian Jelinski-Moranda, Littlewood/Verrall, Littlewood, Keiller/Littlewood, and Littlewood nonhomogeneous Poisson. SRMP uses the maximum likelihood estimation technique to compute the model parameters, and provides the following reliability indicators: reliability function, failure rate, mean time to failure, median time to failure (as well as the 25 and 75 percent values), and the model parameters for each model. It expects time domain input data and does not execute on interval domain data. This tool was the first to provide a user with the ability to analyze model goodness-of-fit using the analytical techniques of prequential likelihood, u-plots, y-plots, and several measures of noise. These techniques have become a standard part of the analyst's toolkit and are considered necessary for most tools today.

SRMP requires an ASCII data file as input. The file contains the name (or other identification) of the project for which reliability calculations are being performed, the number of failures involved in the reliability analysis, and the interfailure times of all the failures. The input file also specifies the initial sample size (the initial portion of the total number of failures) chosen by the analyst and used by SRMP for the initial fitting of each reliability model to the data. The remaining failures are used by SRMP to calculate the prequential likelihood and other measures for assessing a reliability model's prediction accuracy. Furthermore, the input file contains certain mathematical parameters, chosen by the analyst, which are needed to initiate and control the SRMP algorithm's search for a convergent solution. Obviously, analysts must be knowledgeable in setting up the data file, as many parameters are at their discretion and the user manual does not provide an example file that can be copied. The input file allows flexibility in the analysis, such as partitioning the data set or scaling the data, and gives the analyst a choice of executing one model at a time or all models on a particular data set. To format the results from an SRMP run for review, the analyst must execute a second program, called OUTPUT. If the results are sent to the screen, the analyst must control the scrolling from the keyboard. The results may be printed to a file for later viewing or hard-copy printing.

More detail on SRMP is available in the User's Guide [SRMP88]. A sample SRMP output file is shown in Fig. A.3.

```
                          *** JELINSKI & MORANDA MODEL ***

                              PARAMETER ESTIMATION

  I        T(I+1)         NHAT          FI            LOGF          FAIL        NUM
 35          65.            47    0.251152D-03  -.208315D+03         0          11
 36         176.            51    0.222643D-03  -.214248D+03         0          10
 37          58.            54    0.204387D-03  -.220518D+03         0           9
--------

--------
133        1160.           140    0.361335D-04  -.946668D+03         0           9
134        1864.           141    0.355285D-04  -.955210D+03         0           8
135        4116.           142    0.348906D-04  -.963945d+03         0           8

                             RELIABILITY PREDICTIONS

  I    T(I+1)       MEAN          LOWQ         MEDIAN            UPQ          ROCOF
 35      65.   0.33180D+03   0.95454D+02   0.22999D+03     0.45998D+03   0.30138D-02
 36     176.   0.29943D+03   0.86142D+02   0.20755D+03     0.41510D+03   0.33396D-02
 37      58.   0.28780D+03   0.82796D+02   0.19949D+03     0.39898D+03   0.34746D-02
--------

--------
133    1160.   0.39536D+04   0.11374D+04   0.27404D+04     0.54808D+04   0.25293D-03
134    1864.   0.40209D+04   0.11567D+04   0.27871D+04     0.55742D+04   0.24870D-03
1354116.   0.40944D+04       0.11779D+04   0.28380D+04     0.56761D+04   0.24423D-03

                         ANALYSIS OF PREDICTIVE QUALITY

  I   T(I+1)       U(I+1)          P(I+1)          SLOGP
 35      65.   0.177904D+00   0.247765D-02   -.600045D+01
 36     176.   0.444439D+00   0.185537D-02   -.122901D+02
 37      58.   0.182517D+00   0.284041D-02   -.181539D+02
--------

--------
133    1160.   0.254279D+00   0.188618D-03   -.752167D+03
134    1864.   0.370970D+00   0.156439D-03   -.760930D+03
135    4116.   0.634054D+00   0.893767D-04   -.770253D+03

                                SUM OF DEVIANCE OF
                        ROCOF          LOWQ           MEDIAN          UPQ
ABSOLUTE     :     0.118622D-01   0.337083D+04    0.812175D+04   0.162435D+05
NORMALISED   :     0.823370D+01   0.940515D+01    0.940515D+01   0.940515D+01
```

Figure A.3 SRMP tabular output.

A.7 Software Reliability Program (SoRel)

SoRel is a Macintosh-based software reliability measurement tool that was developed by LAAS, a lab of the National Center for Scientific Research in Toulouse, France, in 1991. It runs on a Macintosh II or later computer with a math coprocessor. The program was written in Pascal and requires about 200K of memory. SoRel is composed of two parts. The first part allows several reliability trend tests: the arithmetical test, the Laplace test, Kendall test, and Spearman test. These tests allow an analyst to identify whether the reliability function is increasing or decreasing so that an appropriate model can be applied (see Chap. 10). The second part allows reliability growth model application and contains four models. The Goel-Okumoto model and the Yamada S-shaped model is available for interval domain data, the Littlewood/Verrall model for time domain, whereas the hyperexponential model operates on both time and interval domain data. The chosen model can then be validated using SoRel's three criteria: Kolmogorov-Smirnov distance, prequential likelihood, and *residue.* Residue is the residual value (observed – expected) from the model fit.

SoRel uses ASCII input files that are created using a spreadsheet. Numerical results are displayed on the screen during execution; the user can also request plots of the data. SoRel uses the maximum likelihood parameter estimation technique and provides the following reliability indicators: mean time to failure, cumulative number of failures, failure intensity, as well as the model parameters to evaluate other reliability functions. While only one model is executed at a time, the results are automatically saved to ASCII files which can be imported into spreadsheets or other applications for model comparisons. SoRel also allows the analyst to partition the data set for anal-

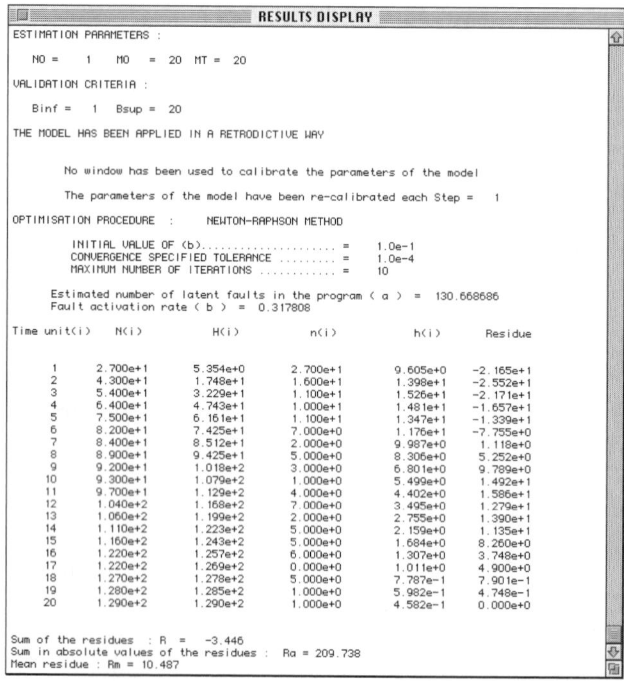

RESULTS DISPLAY

ESTIMATION PARAMETERS :

NO = 1 MO = 20 MT = 20

VALIDATION CRITERIA :

Binf = 1 Bsup = 20

THE MODEL HAS BEEN APPLIED IN A RETRODICTIVE WAY

No window has been used to calibrate the parameters of the model

The parameters of the model have been re-calibrated each Step = 1

OPTIMISATION PROCEDURE : NEWTON-RAPHSON METHOD

INITIAL VALUE OF (b)...................... = 1.0e-1
CONVERGENCE SPECIFIED TOLERANCE .... = 1.0e-4
MAXIMUM NUMBER OF ITERATIONS .... = 10

Estimated number of latent faults in the program (a) = 130.668686
Fault activation rate (b) = 0.317808

Time unit(i)	N(i)	H(i)	n(i)	h(i)	Residue
1	2.700e+1	5.354e+0	2.700e+1	9.605e+0	-2.165e+1
2	4.300e+1	1.748e+1	1.600e+1	1.398e+1	-2.552e+1
3	5.400e+1	3.229e+1	1.100e+1	1.526e+1	-2.171e+1
4	6.400e+1	4.743e+1	1.000e+1	1.481e+1	-1.657e+1
5	7.500e+1	6.161e+1	1.100e+1	1.347e+1	-1.339e+1
6	8.200e+1	7.425e+1	7.000e+0	1.176e+1	-7.755e+0
7	8.400e+1	8.512e+1	2.000e+0	9.987e+0	1.118e+0
8	8.900e+1	9.425e+1	5.000e+0	8.306e+0	5.252e+0
9	9.200e+1	1.018e+2	3.000e+0	6.801e+0	9.789e+0
10	9.300e+1	1.079e+2	1.000e+0	5.499e+0	1.492e+1
11	9.700e+1	1.129e+2	4.000e+0	4.402e+0	1.586e+1
12	1.040e+2	1.168e+2	7.000e+0	3.495e+0	1.279e+1
13	1.060e+2	1.199e+2	2.000e+0	2.755e+0	1.390e+1
14	1.110e+2	1.223e+2	5.000e+0	2.159e+0	1.135e+1
15	1.160e+2	1.243e+2	5.000e+0	1.684e+0	8.260e+0
16	1.220e+2	1.257e+2	6.000e+0	1.307e+0	3.748e+0
17	1.220e+2	1.269e+2	0.000e+0	1.011e+0	4.900e+0
18	1.270e+2	1.278e+2	5.000e+0	7.787e-1	7.901e-1
19	1.280e+2	1.285e+2	1.000e+0	5.982e-1	4.748e-1
20	1.290e+2	1.290e+2	1.000e+0	4.582e-1	0.000e+0

Sum of the residues : R = -3.446
Sum in absolute values of the residues : Ra = 209.738
Mean residue : Rm = 10.487

Figure A.4 Sorel output: S-shaped model application result.

ysis and establish intervals for validation criteria evaluation. More detail on SoRel can be found in [Kano92]. An example SoRel session is shown in Fig. A.4.

A.8 Computer-Aided Software Reliability Estimation (CASRE) Tool

CASRE is a PC-based tool that was developed in 1993 by the Jet Propulsion Laboratories for the Air Force to address the ease-of-use issues of other tools. CASRE requires the WINDOWS™ operating environment. It has a pull-down, menu-driven user interface and uses the same model library as the SMERFS tool (see Sec. A.5) with the additional feature of allowing linear combinations of models to create new ones at the user's discretion. Four combined models are permanently available in CASRE. These are constructed using the nonhomogeneous Poisson process, the Musa/Okumoto, and the Littlewood/Verrall models for time domain data. A more detailed description of CASRE, with examples, can be found in the CASRE User's Guide [Niko93] and in [Lyu92d, Lyu93b].

CASRE allows an analyst to invoke a preferred text editor, word processor, or other application from within CASRE to create the ASCII input data set. The input data set contains fields for the test interval number, the number of failures observed in the interval, the length of the test interval, the fraction of the program tested, and the severity of the failure. Once the data is entered, CASRE automatically provides the analyst with a raw data plot.

CASRE provides the analyst with the ability to convert from time-domain data to interval-domain data and vice versa. Model parameters can be estimated using either maximum likelihood or least squares as determined by the analyst. After the application of several models to a data set, multiple model results can be displayed in the graphical display window for analysis. CASRE uses the SMERFS library routines to calculate the prequential likelihood statistic for interval-domain models as well as u-plots, y-plots, and measures of noise for time-domain models. Figure A.5 shows sample CASRE models' execution results.

CASRE also provides operations to transform or smooth the failure data to remove noise from the data or change the shape and position of the data; the user can select and/or define models for application to the data and make various reliability predictions based upon the best model. Because multiple models may be executed, compared, and combined at the same time, the CASRE tool offers modeling flexibility not offered in the other tools.

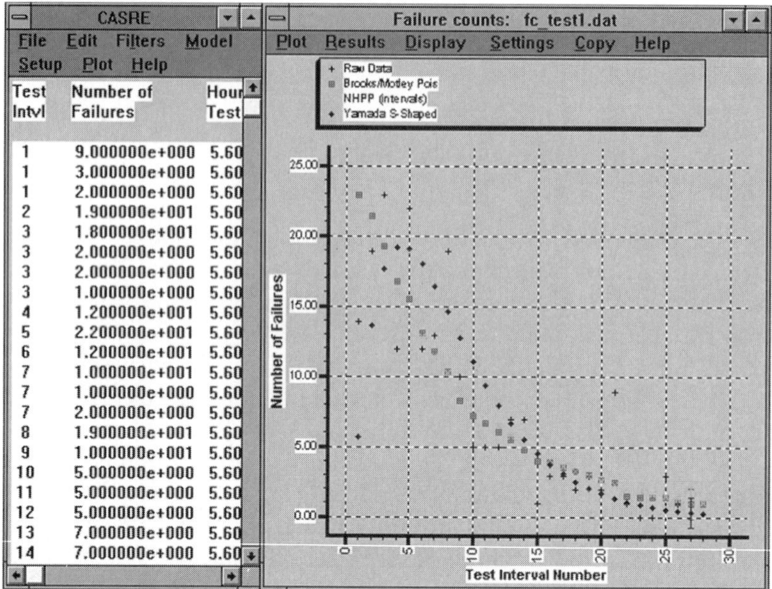

Figure A.5 CASRE model results display.

A.9 Economic Stop Testing Model (ESTM) Tool

The Bellcore ESTM System is a command-line-driven system that can be used to help decide when to stop testing a large software system. The package determines the optimal stopping time using a birth-death model for the introduction of faults, and an economic model to measure the trade-off between shipping and further testing. Unlike other packages, the ESTM System assumes that the system under test changes over time. A measure of this change, usually the number of NCNCSL (new or changed noncommentary source lines) is part of the input to the model.

The methodology implemented by the ESTM System is described in [Dala90, Dala92, Dala94]. The package runs on any platform that runs the UNIX® operating system and supports the C and PostScript™ languages.

The authors of the ESTM System suggest that a time metric other than calendar days be used to measure testing effort; their recommendation is to use the number of staff days spent by the testing team. Some (Bourne) shell scripts and an X-Window System™ program are provided to assist in collecting the extra data (staff time and NCNCSL). (The ESTM System has been used with other metrics measuring effort like the number of transactions processed by the system.)

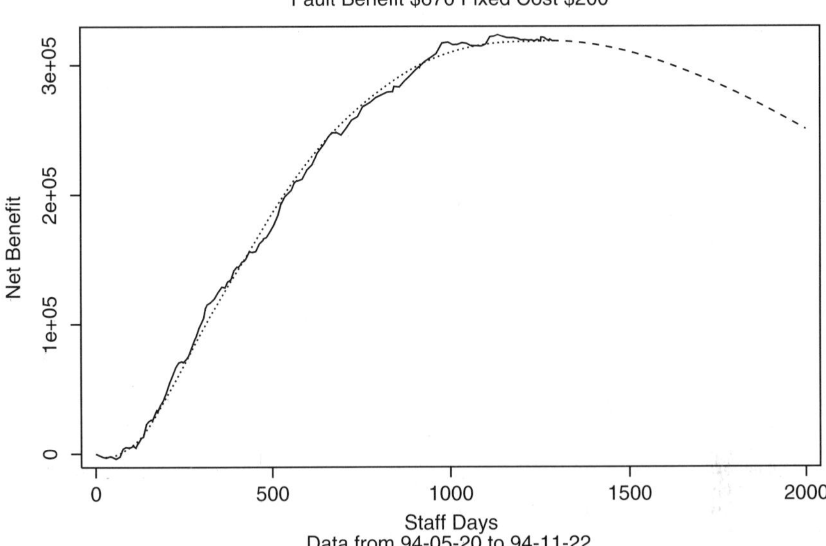

Figure A.6 Sample ESTM output.

The program that fits the model requires four columns of interval-domain data as input: the date, the number of staff days spent testing on that date, the number of faults found on that date, and the cumulative number of NCNCSL added to the system as of that date. Provision is made for adding historical data from other relevant systems (usually previous releases of the same system) to improve the accuracy of predictions.

The main output of the ESTM System is a series of plots, written in the PostScript language. The plots are intended to help assess the fit of the model, as well as help decide when to stop testing. A sample plot of ESTM output is shown in Fig. A.6.

A.10 Tool Comparisons

Several additional tools are available to the software reliability engineer, although most can be replaced by the tools highlighted in this chapter. For example, the GOEL tool [Vinn87] which is distributed through the U.S. Data and Analysis Center for Software (DACS) provides only parameter estimation for the Goel-Okumoto model, which is a basic NHPP model that is implemented in all of the above tools.

Besides the tools highlighted in this chapter, other tools are available to the software reliability engineer and new ones are becoming available every year. Tables A.1 and A.2 provide an overall comparison

TABLE A.1 Information About Current Software Reliability Estimation Tools

Tool name	Supplier	Contact	Models	Hardware	Minimum operating system
Statistical modeling and estimation of reliability functions for software (SMERFS)	Naval Surface Warfare Center (NSWC)	Dr. William Farr NSWCDD-B10 17320 Dahlgren Rd., Dahlgren, VA 22448 (540) 653-8388	Littlewood/Verrall Musa Basic Musa/Okumoto Jelinski-Moranda Geometric Execution Time NHPP Generalized Poisson NHPP Brooks/Motley Schneidewind S-Shaped	Cyber 170/760, DEC VAX, IBM PC	DEC VMS, MS DOS 3.0, Cyber Operating System
Software Reliability Modeling Programs (SRMP)	Reliability and Statistical Consultants, Ltd.	Dr. Bev Littlewood Center for Software Reliability Northampton Square London EC1V0HB, England (+44)-71-477-8420	Musa/Okumoto Duane Jelinski/Moranda (JM) Goel/Okumoto Bayesian JM Littlewood/Verrall Littlewood Keiller/Littlewood Littlewood NHPP	IBM PC	MS DOS 3.0
GOEL	Data & Analysis Center for Software (DACS)	DACS P.O. Box 120 Utica, NY 13503 (315) 734-3696	Goel/Okumoto	IBM PC	MS DOS 2.11
ESTM	Bell Communications Research	Dr. Sid Dalal Bellcore 445 South Street Morristown, NJ 07960 (201) 829-4292	Goel/Okumoto with economic testing criteria	Sun, HP, Dec Workstations	UNIX® System
AT&T SRE Toolkit	AT&T Bell Laboratories	Dr. Michael Lyu AT&T Bell Laboratories 600 Mountain Ave. Murray Hill, NJ 07974 (908) 582-5366	Musa Basic Musa/Okumoto	Any platform running UNIX® System V or MS/DOS	see above
SoRel	LAAS-CNRS	Dr. Karama Kanoun LAAS-CNRS 7, avenue du Colonel Roche 31077 Toulouse Cedex France (+33) 61 33 6235	Goel/Okumoto Littlewood/Verrall Hyperexponential Yamada S-shaped	Macintosh II with a math coprocessor	Macintosh
CASRE	NASA COSMIC	Ms. Karen Newcomb COSMIC The University of Georgia 382 East Broad Street Athens, GA 30602 (706) 542-7265	Littlewood/Verrall Musa Basic Musa/Okumoto Jelinski-Moranda Geometric Execution Time NHPP Generalized Poisson NHPP Brooks/Motley Schneidewind S-Shaped	IBM PC	MS-DOS 5.0 or higher with Windows 3.1 Windows NT Windows 95

TABLE A.1 Information About Current Software Reliability Estimation Tools (*Continued*)

	Release data					Program developed for		Program structure				
Minimum memory	Current version	Current release	Original release	Distributed copies	Development language	Commercial use	Project-specific use	Menu-driven	Command-driven	Integrated system	Stand-alone tool	Cost ($)
256K	5.0	Oct-93	Oct-83	More than 200	FORTRAN 77	X		X		X		$59.95 (free with this book)
500K	1.0	May-88	May-88	Unknown	FORTRAN	X			X	X		$5,000
256K	1.0	Nov-87	Nov-87	68	Unknown	X		X			X	$50
—	1.0	Jun-93	1987	Unknown	C	X				X	X	Call Bellcore
120K	1.0	May-91	May-91	> 200	C	X			X		X	Free with this book
200K	1.0	May-91	May-91	Unknown	Pascal	X (all documentation in French)		X	X		X (needs Excel™ for plotting)	Free
8 MB	1.3	1994	1995	Unknown	FORTRAN	X		X		X		$100 for software (free with this book) $36 for documentation

TABLE A.2 Comparisons Among Available Software Reliability Estimation Tools (Part 1)

	Available models			Parameter estimation		Inputs			Performance measures and confidence intervals		
Tool name	Time domain	Interval domain	Total	Max. likeli-hood	Least squares	Time between failure	Failure counts and interval length	Resource parameters	Current relia-bility or failure rate	Expect total failure	Expect faults remain-ing
AT&T	2	2	2	X		X	X	X	X	X	X
SMERFS	6	6	12	X	X	X	X	X	X	X	X
SRMP	9	0	9	X		X			X		
SoRel	3	3	4	X	X	X	X		X	X	
CASRE	10	6	16*	X	X	X	X	X	X	X	X
GOEL	1	1	1	X		X	X	X	X	X	X
ESTM	0	2	2	X			X	X	X	X	X

* NOTE: CASRE has the capability to combine models to create new ones

TABLE A.2 Comparisons Among Available Software Reliability Estimation Tools (Part 2)

	Data manipulation					User interface					
Tool name	Storage retrieval	Transfor-mations	Editing	Can use externally created data	Handles missing values	On-line help available	Off-line support	Interactive processing	Batch processing	Error messages	High-resolution graphics
AT&T				X			X		X	X	X
SMERFS	X	X	X	X		X	X	X		X	
SRMP				X					X	X	
SoRel		X	X	X		X	X	X		X	X
CASRE	X	X	X	X		X	X	X	X	X	X
GOEL				X		X		X		X	
ESTM	X			X					X	X	X

of the tools highlighted in this chapter as well as some additional tools. Table A.1 provides an organization-level look at the tools; Table A.2 provides the analyst view. The list of criteria used in the tables is not exhaustive. In particular, we have chosen not to include computer time efficiency, computer storage requirements, or ease of learning the tool, since we believe these depend heavily on the computer used, the analyst's skill, and personal bias.

At the publication of this book a new tool, M-elopee, is also made available. M-elopee is implemented for Windows™ environment, integrating software reliability models and relational databases. Interested readers may contact Mathix, 19 rue du Banquier, 75013 Paris France. Tel: 33(1)43-37-76-00, FAX 33(1)43-37-00-73.

Performance measures and confidence intervals			Model estimates and analytical tools								
Time-to-next-failure dist.	Time-to-*K*th-failure dist.	Schedule or cost estimate	Parameter estimate	Variance of estimates	Model goodness-of-fit	*u*-plot	*y*-plot	Noise	Residue	Basic statistics	Residual plots
		X	X								
X	X		X		X	X	X	X		X	X
X	X		X		X	X	X	X			
X			X	X	X	X			X		X
X	X		X		X	X	X	X		X	
X	X	X	X	X	X					X	
		X	X		X						X

Output formatting options selectable						Documentation					Product support		
Line printer graphs	Table output	Page size	Fonts	Titles	Color	Explain model theory	Explain tool usage	Sample run	Explain error messages	Aids result interpretation	Full support	No support	Support no commitment
	X			X			X	X			X		
X	X			X		X	X	X		X			X
X	X					X	X	X		X			X
	X					X	X	X	X	X			X
	X	X	X	X	X	X	X	X	X	X			X
X	X					X	X	X		X		X	
				X		X	X	X	X	X			X

A.11 Summary

We highlight several software reliability tools currently available in the market. For each tool we briefly describe its functionality, capability, and user interface. Sample execution or output of each tool is also provided. Note that AT&T SRE Toolkit, SMERFS, CASRE, and SoftRel (the software reliability simulation tool described in Chap. 16) are included in the Data and Tool Disk.

Appendix

B

Review of Reliability Theory, Analytical Techniques, and Basic Statistics

This appendix reviews the reliability theory, analytical modeling techniques, and statistical techniques commonly used in software reliability engineering studies. Reliability theory establishes a foundation for the application of reliability concepts and reliability-related quantities to a system. Analytical modeling provides frameworks for abstracting the information obtained from measurement-based studies. Statistical techniques allow us to extract reliability measures from data, analyze the structure of data, and test hypotheses. These techniques are useful in every phase of the empirical evaluation of software reliability. The reliability theory reviewed in this appendix includes reliability definitions, underlying mathematics, and failure rate functions. The analytical methods consist of combinatorial models, Markov models, Markov reward analysis, birth-death processes, and Poisson processes. The statistical techniques cover parameter estimation, characterization of empirical distribution, and multivariate analysis. Our discussion is not intended to be comprehensive. For a comprehensive study of the techniques, you are encouraged to read [Dani79, DeGr86, Dill84, Hogg83, Howa71, John82, Kend77, Mood74, Shoo83, Triv82].

B.1 Notation and Terminology

This section gives notation, terminology, and several important distributions that are referred to throughout App. B. The set of all possible outcomes of an experiment is called a *sample space*. A sample space can be made up of all kinds of things. For example, conducting an experiment may consist of tossing a coin two times and observing the face of each toss. The sample space may be represented by S = {(head,head),(head,tail),(tail,head),(tail,tail)}. Another example is to draw a ball from an urn containing blue, green, and red balls and record their color; in this case the sample space is S = {blue, green, red}. In order to develop mathematical models for describing the probabilities of the occurrence of outcomes (events) in a sample space, it is convenient to define a function that maps each outcome in the sample space to a single numerical value. Such a function is called a random variable. Therefore, we define a *random variable* to be the following: a random variable, say X, is a function defined over a sample space, S, which associates a real number, $X(e) = x$, with each possible outcome e in S. There are two types of random variables. If the set of all possible values of a random variable is finite or countably infinite, we call it a *discrete random variable.* On the other hand, if a random variable is capable of attaining any value in some interval and not just discrete points, then we call it a *continuous random variable.* Random variables are usually denoted by capital letters, such as X, Y, and Z, while the possible values that the corresponding random variables can attain are denoted by the lowercase letters x, y, and z.

B.1.1 Discrete random variables

For a discrete random variable X, the sample space is countable. Therefore, the values that X can assume are countable as well. The probability of the event such that $X(e) = x$ is given by $P(e : X(e) = x, e \in S)$, it is usually denoted by $p(x)$. We call $p(x)$ the *probability density function* (pdf) or *density function* of X if and only if $p(x_i) \geq 0$ and $\Sigma_{x_i} p(x_i) = 1$ where x_i's are the possible values of X. The *cumulative distribution function* (cdf) or simply *distribution function,* $P\{X \leq x\} = \Sigma_{x_i \leq x} p(x_i)$, is the probability that X is less then or equal to the fixed value x. Associated with random variable X are two important characteristics of its distribution—the *mean* (or *expected value*) and the *variance.* The *expected value* of X is defined to be

$$E[X] = \sum_x xp(x) \tag{B.1}$$

where the sum is taken over all possible values of X. $E[X]$ is a weighted average used to measure the center of the associated distribution. The following variance, however, measures the dispersion of the associated distribution:

$$Var(X) = E[(X - E[X])^2] = \sum_x x^2p(x) - \left(\sum_x xp(x)\right)^2 \tag{B.2}$$

Several important discrete pdf's and their corresponding mean and variance are given in Table B.1.

B.1.2 Continuous random variables

For each terminology we used for the discrete random variables, there is a parallel analogy for the continuous ones. We denote the pdf of a *continuous random variable* X by $f(x)$. The function $f(x)$ must satisfy the following two conditions: (1) $f(x) \geq 0$, $\forall x$; and (2) $\int_{-\infty}^{\infty} f(x)dx = 1$. Recall from the discrete case that the cdf of X at x is the probability that X is less than or equal to the point x. Unlike what we have for the discrete case, instead of summing over all $\{x_i : x_i \leq x\}$ we integrate the pdf over this subset to obtain the cdf. That is,

$$F(x) = P\{X \leq x\} = \int_{-\infty}^{x} f(y)dy \tag{B.3}$$

The mean of a continuous random variable X is defined to be

$$E[X] = \int_{-\infty}^{\infty} xf(x)dx \tag{B.4}$$

and the variance is

$$Var(X) = E[(X - E[X])^2] = \int_{-\infty}^{\infty} x^2 f(x)dx - \left(\int_{-\infty}^{\infty} xf(x)dx\right)^2 \tag{B.5}$$

Table B.2 summarizes some of the important continuous pdf's and their corresponding mean and variance.

B.1.3 Conditional probabilities and conditional probability density functions

In some random experiments, we are interested in only those outcomes that are elements of a subset C_1 of the sample space S. This means that the sample space is essentially the subset C_1. The problem is, how do we define probability functions with C_1 being the "new" sample space?

TABLE B.1 Pdf, Mean, and Variance of Important Discrete Distributions

	Bernoulli	Binomial	Poisson
Parameters	$0 < p < 1, q = 1 - p$	$0 < p < 1, q = 1 - p$	$0 < \lambda$
pdf	$p^x q^{1-x}, x = 0, 1$	$\binom{n}{x} p^x q^{1-x}, x = 0, 1, \cdots, n$	$\frac{e^{-\lambda}\lambda^x}{x!}, x = 0, 1, \cdots$
Mean	p	np	λ
Variance	pq	npq	λ

TABLE B.2 Pdf, Mean, and Variance of Important Continuous Distributions

	Normal	Exponential	Gamma	Chi-square
Parameters	$-\infty < \mu < \infty$	$0 < \lambda$	$0 < \lambda,\ 0 < \alpha$	$v = 1,2,\cdots$
pdf	$\frac{1}{\sqrt{2\pi}\sigma} e^{-[(x-\mu)/\sigma]^2/2}$,	$\lambda e^{-\lambda x}$,	$\frac{\lambda^\alpha}{\Gamma(\alpha)} x^{\alpha-1} e^{-\lambda x}$,	$\frac{1}{2^{v/2}\Gamma(v/2)} x^{v/2} e^{-x/2}$
	$-\infty < x < \infty$	$0 < x$	$0 < x$	$0 < x$
Mean	μ	$1/\lambda$	α/λ	v
Variance	σ^2	$1/\lambda^2$	α/λ^2	$2v$

Let $P(C_1)$ be a probability function defined on the sample space S such that $P(C_1) > 0$, and let C_2 be another subset of S. Then the probability of the event C_2 relative to the new sample space C_1 or the conditional probability of C_2 given C_1, denoted by $P(C_2 \mid C_1)$, is defined to be $P(C_1 \cap C_2)/P(C_1)$.

A similar concept is carried through for the conditional pdf of a discrete random variable. Let X_1 and X_2 be two discrete random variables having $p_1(x_1)$ and $p_2(x_2)$, respectively, as their marginal pdf's and $p(x_1, x_2)$ as their joint pdf. Note that we can obtain the marginal pdf for X_1 by summing the joint pdf over all possible values of X_2, that is, $p_1(x_1) = \Sigma_{\forall x_2}\, p(x_1, x_2)$, and vice versa for X_2. Then the conditional pdf of X_i given X_j for $i, j \in \{1,2\}$ is given by

$$p(x_i \mid x_j) \equiv P(X_i = x_i \mid X_j = x_j) = \frac{P(X_i = x_i, X_j = x_j)}{P(X_j = x_j)}$$

$$\equiv \frac{p(x_i, x_j)}{p_j(x_j)} \qquad p_j(x_j) > 0 \tag{B.6}$$

Analogously, for continuous random variables we define the conditional pdf of X_i given X_j to be

$$f(x_i \mid x_j) = \frac{f(x_i, x_j)}{f_j(x_j)} \qquad f_j(x_j) > 0 \tag{B.7}$$

for $i,j \in \{1,2\}$, where $f_j(x_j) = \int_{-\infty}^{\infty} f(x_i, x_j)dx_i$ is the marginal pdf of X_j.

B.1.4 Stochastic processes

A stochastic process is a collection of random variables X_t or $X(t)$ where t belongs to a suitable index set. The index t can be a discrete time unit, then the index set is $T = \{0,1,2,3,4,\cdots,\}$; or it can be a point in a continuous time interval, then the index set is equal to $T = [0, \infty)$. An example of a discrete time stochastic process is the outcomes at successive tosses of a coin. In this case, outcomes can be observed only at a discrete time unit, i.e., toss 1, 2, 3, etc. Conversely, the number of births in a population is an example of a continuous time stochastic process, since a birth can happen at any time in a day and any day in a year. Stochastic processes are classified by their *state space,* or the range of their possible values, by their index set, and by the dependence structure among random variables $X(t)$ that make up the entire process. We will discuss different types of stochastic processes in the subsequent sections.

B.2 Reliability Theory

Reliability theory is essentially the application of probability theory to the modeling of failures and the prediction of success probability. This section summarizes some of the key points in reliability theory. It is assumed that the reader has an introductory knowledge of probability theory [Shoo83].

B.2.1 Reliability definitions and mathematics

Modern probability theory bases many of its results on the concept of a random variable, its pdf's, and the cdf's. In the case of reliability, the random variable of interest is the time to failure, T. We develop the basic relationships needed by focusing on the probability that the time to failure T is in some interval $(t, t + \Delta t)$

$$P(t \leq T \leq t + \Delta t) \equiv \text{probability that } t \leq T \leq t + \Delta t$$

The above probability can be related to the density and distribution functions, and the results are

$$P(t \leq T \leq t + \Delta t) = f(t)\Delta t = F(t + \Delta t) - F(t) \tag{B.8}$$

where $F(t)$ and $f(t)$ are the cdf and pdf (or the failure density function), respectively.

If we divide by Δt in Eq. (B.8) and let $\Delta t \to 0$, we obtain from the fundamental definition of the derivative the fact that the density function is the derivative of the distribution function:

$$f(t) = \frac{dF(t)}{dt} \tag{B.9}$$

Clearly, the distribution function is then the integral of the density function

$$F(t) = \int_0^t f(x)dx \tag{B.10}$$

Note this function is equivalent to the probability of failure by time t. Since the random variable T is defined only for the interval 0 to $+\infty$ (negative time has no meaning), from Eq. (B.8) we can derive

$$F(t) = P(0 \le T \le t) = \int_0^t f(x)dx \tag{B.11}$$

One can also define the probability of success at time t, $R(t)$, as the probability that the time to failure is larger than t (that is, $T > t$):

$$R(t) = P(T > t) = 1 - F(t) = \int_t^\infty f(x)dx \tag{B.12}$$

where $R(t)$ is the *reliability function.*

Mathematically, Eq. (B.12) summarizes most of what we need to know about reliability theory. However, when we start to study failure data for various items, we find that the density function $f(t)$ is not very useful. Instead, the failure rate function (hazard function) is derived.

B.2.2 Failure rate

A useful concept in reliability theory to describe failures in a system and its components is the *failure rate.* It is defined as the probability that a failure per unit time occurs in the interval, say, $[t, t + \Delta t]$, given that a failure has not occurred before t. In other words, the failure rate is the rate at which failures occur in $[t, t + \Delta t]$. That is,

$$\text{Failure rate} \equiv \frac{P(t \le T < t + \Delta t \mid T > t)}{\Delta t} = \frac{P(t \le T < t + \Delta t)}{\Delta t P(T > t)} = \frac{F(t + \Delta t) - F(t)}{\Delta t R(t)}$$

The *hazard rate* is defined as the limit of the failure rate as the interval approaches zero, that is, $\Delta t \to 0$. Thus, we obtain the hazard rate at time t as

$$z(t) = \lim_{\Delta t \to 0} \frac{F(t + \Delta t) - F(t)}{\Delta t R(t)} = \frac{f(t)}{R(t)} \tag{B.13}$$

The hazard rate is an instantaneous rate of failure at time t, given that the system survives up to t. In particular, the quantity $z(t)dt$ represents the probability that a system of age t will fail in the small interval t to $t + dt$. Note that although there is a slight difference in the definitions of hazard rate and failure rate, they are used interchangeably in this book.

The functions $f(t)$, $F(t)$, $R(t)$, and $z(t)$ could be transformed with one another. For example, combining Eq. (B.9) with Eq. (B.13) for any time t yields

$$z(t) = \frac{dF(t)}{dt}\frac{1}{R(t)} \tag{B.14}$$

From Eq. (B.12), we observe that $dF(t)/dt = -dR(t)/dt$, and substitution in Eq. (B.14) yields

$$\frac{dR(t)}{R(t)} = -z(t)dt \tag{B.15}$$

Integrating both sides with respect to t, we obtain

$$\ln R(t) = -\int_0^t z(x)dx + c$$

Since the system is initially good and the initial condition $R(0) = 1$, c must be 0. Exponentiating both sides results in

$$R(t) = \exp\left[-\int_0^t z(x)dx\right] \tag{B.16}$$

Note Eq. (B.16) is the fundamental equation relating reliability to failure rate.

Differentiating both sides of Eq. (B.16), $f(t)$ is given in terms of $z(t)$ by

$$f(t) = z(t)\exp\left[-\int_0^t z(x)dx\right] \tag{B.17}$$

Note all of the above relationships hold for the corresponding conditional functions as well. One simply replaces the hazard, reliability, cumulative distribution, or probability density functions for a "single" failure by the associated conditional functions. For example, suppose the system has not failed at time t_i, then the conditional hazard rate function is denoted as $z(t\,|\,t_i)$, where $t \geq t_i$ and $z(t\,|\,t_i) = f(t\,|\,t_i)/[1 - F(t\,|\,t_i)] = f(t\,|\,t_i)/R(t\,|\,t_i)$.

The hazard rate will change over the lifetime of a system. The hazard rate curve depicted in Fig. B.1 exhibits the characteristics of many systems or components. The shape is often referred to as a *bathtub curve* and can generally be divided into three distinct regions.

Region I, known by various names such as the *debugging phase* or *infant mortality,* represents early failures because of material or manufacturing defects or improper design. Quality control and initial product testing usually eliminate many substandard devices and thus

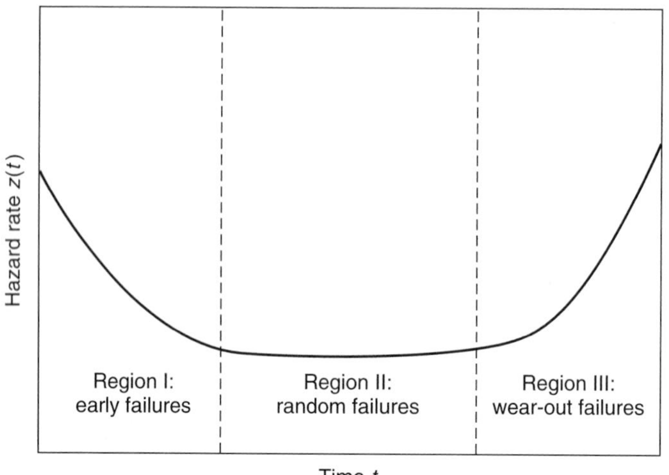

Figure B.1 Typical hazard rate of a system or component.

avoid this higher initial hazard rate. In this region, the hazard rate tends to decrease as a function of time.

Region II is known as the useful life period or normal operating phase and represents chance failures caused by sudden stress or extreme conditions. This is the only region in which the exponential distribution is valid: since the hazard remains constant, $f(t)$ is roughly the density of an exponential distribution.

Region III represents the wear-out or fatigue failures and is characterized by a rapid increase in the hazard rate. In the case of software, there is no software wear-out failure mode. As a result, this region does not apply to software. However, there is a different set of failure modes for software: incorrect specification, misunderstood specifications, algorithmic error, input data error, program logic error, etc. The complexity of these software failure modes rivals or surpasses the difficulties in analyzing hardware failures.

Example B.1 (Constant Hazard) If a constant-hazard rate $z(t) = \lambda$ is assumed, the time integral is given by $\int_0^t \lambda dx = \lambda t$, resulting in

$$z(t) = \lambda \tag{B.18}$$

$$f(t) = \lambda e^{-\lambda t} \tag{B.19}$$

$$R(t) = e^{-\lambda t} = 1 - F(t) \tag{B.20}$$

The four functions $z(t)$, $f(t)$, $F(t)$, and $R(t)$ are drawn in Fig. B.2. A constant-hazard rate implies an exponential density function and an exponential reliability function.

Example B.2 (Linearly Increasing Hazard) When wear or deterioration is present, the hazard will increase as time passes. The simplest increasing-hazard model

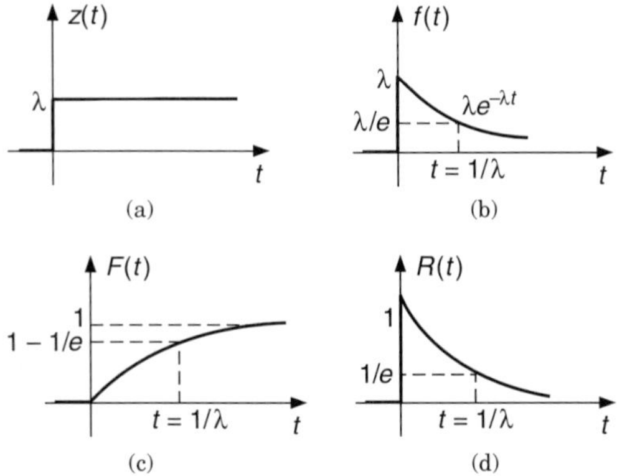

Figure B.2 Constant-hazard model: (*a*) constant hazard; (*b*) decaying exponential density function; (*c*) rising exponential distribution function; (*d*) decaying exponential reliability function.

that can be postulated is one in which the hazard increases linearly with time. Assuming that $z(t) = Kt$ for $t \geq 0$ yields

$$z(t) = Kt \tag{B.21}$$

$$f(t) = Kte^{-Kt^2/2} \tag{B.22}$$

$$R(t) = e^{-Kt^2/2} \tag{B.23}$$

These functions are sketched in Fig. B.3. The density function of Eq. (B.22) is a Rayleigh density function.

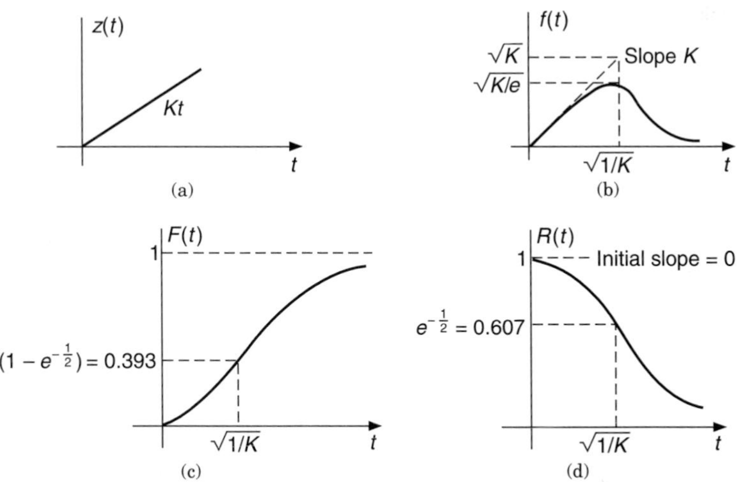

Figure B.3 Linearly increasing hazard: (*a*) linearly increasing hazard; (*b*) Rayleigh density function; (*c*) Rayleigh distribution function; (*d*) Rayleigh reliability function.

Example B.3 (The Weibull Model) In many cases, the $z(t)$ curve cannot be approximated by a straight line, and the previously discussed models fail. In order to fit various $z(t)$ curves, it is useful to investigate a hazard model of the form that is known as a Weibull model [Weib51]:

$$z(t) = Kt^m \text{ for } m > -1 \tag{B.24}$$

$$f(t) = Kt^m e^{-Kt^{m+1}/(m+1)} \tag{B.25}$$

$$R(t) = e^{-Kt^{m+1}/(m+1)} \tag{B.26}$$

By appropriate choice of the two parameters K and m, a wide range of hazard curves can be approximated. The various functions obtained for typical values of m are shown in Fig. B.4. For fixed values of m, a change in the parameter K merely changes the vertical amplitude of the $z(t)$ curve; thus, $z(t)/K$ is plotted versus time. Changing K produces a time-scale effect on the $R(t)$ function; therefore, time is normalized so that $\tau^{m+1} = [K/(m+1)]t^{m+1}$. Note the curves $m = 0$ and $m = 1$ are constant-hazard and linearly increasing–hazard models, respectively.

B.2.3 Mean time to failure

It is often convenient to characterize a failure model or a set of failure data by a single parameter. We generally use the mean time to failure (MTTF) for this purpose. This is the *expected life,* or the expected time during which the system will function successfully without mainte-

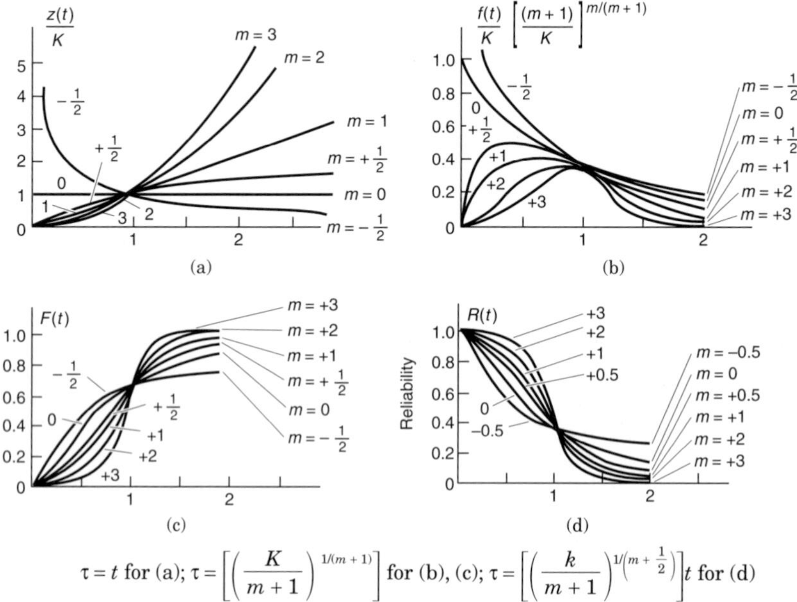

$$\tau = t \text{ for (a)}; \ \tau = \left[\left(\frac{K}{m+1}\right)^{1/(m+1)}\right] \text{ for (b), (c)}; \ \tau = \left[\left(\frac{k}{m+1}\right)^{1/\left(m+\frac{1}{2}\right)}\right] t \text{ for (d)}$$

Figure B.4 Reliability functions for the Weibull model: (*a*) hazard function; (*b*) density function; (*c*) distribution function; (*d*) reliability function.

nance or repair. For a hazard model with density function $f(t)$ over time t, it is defined as

$$\text{MTTF} = E[T] = \int_0^\infty tf(t)dt \tag{B.27}$$

Another convenient method for determining MTTF is given in terms of reliability function by

$$\text{MTTF} = \int_0^\infty R(t)dt \tag{B.28}$$

Several examples of Eq. (B.28) for different hazards are computed for MTTF. For constant hazard

$$\text{MTTF} = \int_0^\infty e^{-\lambda t}\, dt = \left.\frac{e^{-\lambda t}}{-\lambda}\right|_0^\infty = \frac{1}{\lambda} \tag{B.29}$$

For a linearly increasing hazard

$$\text{MTTF} = \int_0^\infty e^{-Kt^2/2}dt = \frac{\Gamma\left(\frac{1}{2}\right)}{2\sqrt{K/2}} = \sqrt{\frac{\pi}{2K}} \tag{B.30}$$

For a Weibull distribution

$$\text{MTTF} = \int_0^\infty e^{-Kt^{(m+1)}/(m+1)}dt = \frac{\Gamma[(m+2)/(m+1)]}{[k/(m+1)]^{1/(m+1)}} \tag{B.31}$$

B.2.4 Failure intensity

The last important functions that we consider are the failure intensity function and the mean value function for the cumulative number of failures. We denote the failure intensity function as $\lambda(t)$. This is the instantaneous rate of change of the expected number of failures with respect to time. Suppose we let $M(t)$ be the random process denoting the cumulative number of failures by time t and we denote $\mu(t)$ as its mean value function, i.e.,

$$\mu(t) = E[M(t)] \tag{B.32}$$

The failure intensity function is then obtained from $\mu(t)$ as its derivative, i.e.,

$$\lambda(t) = \frac{d\mu(t)}{dt} = \frac{d}{dt}(E[M(t)]) \tag{B.33}$$

In order to have reliability growth we should have $d\lambda(t)/dt < 0\ \forall t \geq t_0$ for some t_0. The failure intensity function may also exhibit a zigzag-type behavior, but it must still be decreasing to achieve reliability growth.

B.3 Analytical Methods

B.3.1 Combinatorial models

A logical approach to deal with a complex system is to decompose the system into functional entities consisting of units or subsystems. We model characteristics of each entity and then connect these models according to the system structure. We compute the system reliability in terms of the subdivision reliabilities. Combinatorial models are useful for modeling hardware reliability. It is usually difficult to model software as a combination of units because of the logical complexity of software and possible hidden interactions between units. Also, software faults are design faults, and therefore obtaining the characteristics of software units is not straightforward. Fault tree analysis, a combinatorial modeling technique, has been used to model software safety and reliability. In a fault tree analysis, we deduce various failure modes that can contribute to a specified undesirable event. We then display all the events graphically: the top undesired events are identified and plotted, followed by the secondary undesired events, and so on, until the basic events are reached.

B.3.2 Markov models

A powerful technique for analyzing complex probabilistic systems, based on the notion of state and transitions between states, is Markov modeling [Howa71, Triv82]. To formulate a Markov model, system behavior is abstracted into a set of mutually exclusive system states. For example, the states of a system can be the set of all distinct combinations of working and failed modules in a reliability model. A set of equations describing the probabilistic transitions from one state to another state and an initial probability distribution in the state of the process uniquely determine a Markov model. One of the most important features of a Markov model is that the transition from state i to another state depends only on the current state. That is, the way in which the entire past history affects the future of the process is completely summarized in the current state of the process.

If the state space is discrete, either finite or countably infinite, then the model is called a *discrete-space Markov model*, and the Markov process is referred to as a *Markov chain;* otherwise, the model is called a *continuous-space Markov model.* If the model allows transitions between states at any time, the model is called a *continuous-time*

Markov model. In a *discrete-time Markov model,* all state transitions occur at fixed time intervals. We only consider the discrete-space Markov model.

In the case of a continuous-time model, the state transition equation has the form

$$\frac{dP_j(t)}{dt} = \left[\sum_{i \neq j} P_i(t) r_{ij}(t) \right] - P_j(t) r_j(t) \tag{B.34}$$

where $P_j(t) = P\{X(t) = j\}$, $r_{ij}(t)$ = transition rate from state i to state j at time t, and $r_j(t)$ = total transition rate out of state j at time t. A Markov process is called *homogeneous* (or *stationary*) when $P\{X(t + s) = j \mid X(s) = i\} = P_{ij}(t)$, $\forall s \geq 0$. If $P\{X(t + s) = j \mid X(s) = i\}$ depends on s, it becomes a *nonhomogeneous* (or *nonstationary*) process.

Example B.4 Figure B.5 shows a simple continuous-time Markov model representing the operating system reliability for a seven-machine VAXcluster system. S_i represents that i machines are down because of software. So S_0 represents a normal state, and S_7 represents that all seven machines are down because of software. In each state, error generation and recovery occur in all machines. In the case that the transition rates between states are time-invariant, the transition rate from state S_i to state S_j is estimated from the data:

$$r_{ij} = \frac{\text{total number of transitions from } S_i \text{ to } S_j}{\text{cumulated time the system was in } S_i} \tag{B.35}$$

The set of states and the transition rates capture all relevant reliability characteristics of the system at the modeled level of abstraction.

B.3.3 Markov reward analysis

Markov reward analysis combines Markov modeling and reward analysis. Each state in a Markov model is associated with a reward rate. Markov reward analysis has been used to evaluate performance-related reliability of computer systems [Meye92, Triv92]. In such an analysis, the states in a model capture all possible combinations of failures in major system components, and reward for each state represents the performance level of the system in the state. The relative perfor-

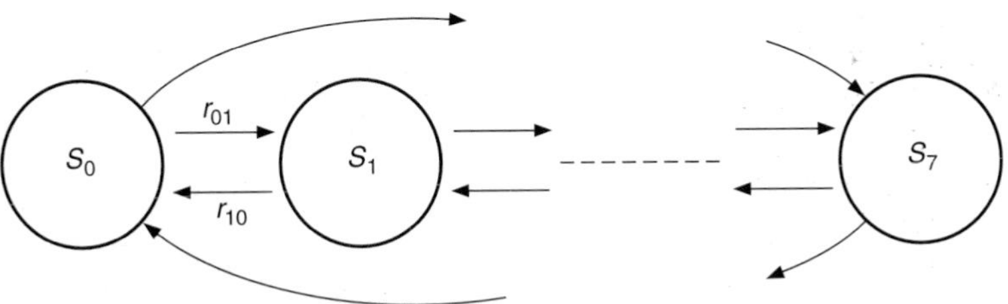

Figure B.5 Simple operating system reliability model for 7-machine VAXcluster.

mance the system delivers at time t is given by

$$E[X(t)] = \sum_i r_i p_i(t) \tag{B.36}$$

where $p_i(t)$ is the probability of the system being in state i at time t, and r_i is the reward rate for state i. The quantity $E[X(t)]$ is the expected instantaneous reward rate at time t [Goya87]. $E[X(t)]$ is a measure of the instantaneous capacity of system performance assuming 100 percent capacity at time 0. If r_i is 1 in a nonfailure state and 0 in a failure state and the model does not allow a repair of system failure, $E[X(t)]$ equates to reliability.

The expected time-averaged accumulated reward over the time period $(0,t)$, i.e., the expected interval reward rate [Goya87], $Y(t)$, can be calculated by

$$E[Y(t)] = \frac{1}{t}\int_0^t \sum_i r_i p_i(x)dx \tag{B.37}$$

$E[Y(t)]$ is a measure of the time-averaged accumulated service provided by the system. This quantity has been used to evaluate the probability of task completion or mission success in the presence of system degradation, when a repair of system failure is not allowed. The expected reward rate at the steady-state (i.e., when the states stabilize and no rate changes occur), Y, can be estimated by

$$Y = \sum_i r_i p_i \tag{B.38}$$

where p_i is the probability of the system being in state i in steady state.

Example B.5 The key step is to define a reward function that characterizes the performance loss in each degraded state. Here we illustrate Markov reward analysis using the seven-machine VAXcluster model shown in Fig. B.5. Given a time interval ΔT (random variable), a reward rate for a machine in the VAXcluster system in ΔT is determined by

$$r(\Delta T) = W(\Delta T) / \Delta T \tag{B.39}$$

where $W(\Delta T)$ denotes the useful work done by the system in ΔT and is calculated by

$$W(\Delta T) = \begin{cases} \Delta T & \text{in normal state} \\ \Delta T - n\tau & \text{in error state} \\ 0 & \text{in failure state} \end{cases} \tag{B.40}$$

where n is the number of raw errors (error entries in the log) in ΔT, and τ is the mean recovery time for a single error. Thus, one unit of reward is given for each unit of time when a machine is in the normal state. In an error state, the penalty paid depends on the time the machine spends on recovery in that state, which is determined by the linear function $\Delta T - n\tau$ (normally, $\Delta T > n\tau$; if $\Delta T < n\tau$, $W(\Delta T)$ is set to 0). In a failure state, $W(\Delta T)$ is by definition zero.

Applying Eq. (B.40) to the seven-machine VAXcluster, the reward rate formula has the following form:

$$r(\Delta T) = \sum_{j=1}^{7} W_j(\Delta T) / (7 \times \Delta T) \tag{B.41}$$

where $W_j(\Delta T)$ denotes the useful work done by machine j in time ΔT. Here, all machines are assumed to contribute an equal amount of reward to the system. For example, if three machines fail, the reward rate is 4/7.

The expected steady-state reward rate, Y, can be estimated by

$$Y = \frac{1}{T} \sum_{\Delta t_j \in T} r(\Delta t_j)\Delta t_j \tag{B.42}$$

where T is the summation of all Δt_j's (particular values of ΔT) in consideration. If we substitute r from Eq. (B.41) and let ΔT represent the holding time of each state in the error model, Y becomes the steady-state reward rate of the VAXcluster, which is also an estimate of software availability (performance-related availability). Since the model is an empirical one based on the error event data (of which the failure event data are a subset), the information about errors and failures of all machines for each particular Δt_j can be obtained from the data.

In Eq. (B.42), if we substitute r from Eq. (B.41) and let ΔT represent the time span of the error event for a particular type of error, Y becomes the steady-state reward rate of the system during the event intervals of the specified error. Thus, $(1 - Y)$ measures the loss in performance during the specified error event. Examples B.6 and B.7 are continuations of Example B.5.

Example B.6 The steady-state reward rate for the VAXcluster in Example B.5 was computed with τ being 0.1, 1, 10, and 100 ms. The results are given in Table B.3. The table shows that the reward rate is not sensitive to τ. This is because the overall recovery time is dominated by the failure recovery time, i.e., the major contributors to the performance loss are failures, not nonfailure errors. In the range of these τ values, the VAXcluster availability is estimated to be 0.995.

Example B.7 Table B.4 shows the steady-state reward rate for each error type (τ = 1 ms) for the VAXcluster. These numbers quantify the loss of performance incurred by the recovery from each type of error. For example, during the recov-

TABLE B.3 Steady-State Reward Rate for the VAXcluster

τ	0.1 ms	1 ms	10 ms	100 ms
Y	0.995078	0.995077	0.995067	0.994971

TABLE B.4 Steady-State Reward Rate for Each Error Type in the VAXcluster

Error type	CPU	Memory	Disk	Tape	Network	Software
Y	0.14950	0.99994	0.61314	0.89845	0.56841	0.00008

ery from CPU errors, the system can be expected to deliver approximately 15 percent of its full performance. During disk error recovery, the average system performance degrades to nearly 61 percent of its capacity. Since software errors have the lowest reward rate (0.00008), the loss of work during the recovery from software errors is the most significant.

B.3.4 Birth-death processes

A birth-death process is the special case of a Markov process in which transitions from state j are permitted only to neighboring states $j + 1$, j, and $j - 1$. This restriction allows us to carry the solution much further for Markov processes in many cases. Our main interest will focus on (continuous-time) birth-death processes with discrete state space. When the process is said to be in state j, we will let this denote the fact that the *population* at that time is of size j. Moreover, a transition from j to $j + 1$ will signify a "birth" within the population, whereas a transition from j to $j - 1$ will denote a "death" in the population.

Regarding the nature of births and deaths, we introduce the notion of a *birth rate* λ_j, which describes the rate at which births occur when the population is of size j. Similarly, we define a *death rate* μ_j, which is the rate at which deaths occur when the population is of size j. Note that these birth and death rates are independent of time and depend only on state j; thus we have a continuous-time homogeneous Markov of the birth-death type.

To be more explicit, the assumptions we need for the birth-death process are that it is a homogeneous Markov chain $X(t)$ on the states 0, 1, 2, . . . , that births and deaths are independent (this follows directly from the Markov property), *and*

B_1: P[exactly 1 birth in $(t,t + \Delta t)$ | current population size is j] $= \lambda_j \Delta t + o(\Delta t)$

D_1: P[exactly 1 death in $(t,t + \Delta t)$ | current population size is j] $= \mu_j \Delta t + o(\Delta t)$

B_2: P[exactly 0 birth in $(t,t + \Delta t)$ | current population size is j] $= 1 - \lambda_j \Delta t + o(\Delta t)$

D_2: P[exactly 0 death in $(t,t + \Delta t)$ | current population size is j] $= 1 - \mu_j \Delta t + o(\Delta t)$

From these assumptions we see that multiple births, multiple deaths, or in fact both a birth and a death in a small time interval are prohibited in the sense that the probabilities of such events are of order $o(\Delta t)$, where $o(\Delta t)$ denotes an unspecified function satisfying

$$\lim_{\Delta t \to 0} \frac{o(\Delta t)}{\Delta t} = 0$$

We wish to solve for the probability that the population size is j at time t. We denote the probability by

$$P_j(t) \equiv P[X(t) = j] \tag{B.43}$$

We begin by expressing the Chapman-Kolmogorov dynamics. We focus on the possible motions of the number of members in our population during an interval $(t,t + \Delta t)$. We will find ourselves in state j at time $t + \Delta t$ if one of the three following mutually exclusive and exhaustive events occurred:

1. The population size was j at time t and no state changes occurred.
2. The population size was $j - 1$ at time t and we had a birth during the interval $(t,t + \Delta t)$.
3. The population size was $j + 1$ at time t and we had one death during the interval $(t,t + \Delta t)$.

The probability for the first of these possibilities is merely $P_j(t)$ times the probability that we moved from state j to state j during the next Δt time period; this is represented by the first term on the right-hand side of Eq. (B.44). The second and third terms on the right-hand side of that equation correspond, respectively, to the second and third cases listed above. The probability of any event other than the ones mentioned above is included in $o(\Delta t)$. Thus we may write, assuming B_1, D_1, B_2, and D_2,

$$\begin{aligned} P_j(t + \Delta t) = P_j(t)[1 - \lambda_j\Delta t + o(\Delta t)][1 - \mu_j\Delta t + o(\Delta t)] + P_{j-1}(t) \\ [\lambda_{j-1}\Delta t + o(\Delta t)] + P_{j+1}(t)[\mu_{j+1}\Delta t + o(\Delta t)] + o(\Delta t) \qquad j \geq 1 \end{aligned} \tag{B.44}$$

$$\begin{aligned} P_0(t + \Delta t) = P_0(t)[1 - \lambda_0\Delta t + o(\Delta t)] + P_1(t)[\mu_1\Delta t + o(\Delta t)] \\ + o(\Delta t) \qquad j = 0 \end{aligned} \tag{B.45}$$

In Eq. (B.45) we have used the assumption that it is impossible to have a death when the population is of size 0 and the assumption that one can indeed have a birth when the population size is 0. Expanding the right-hand side of Eqs. (B.44) and (B.45), and rearranging the terms, we have the following:

$$\frac{P_j(t+\Delta t)-P_j(t)}{\Delta t} = -(\lambda_j+\mu_j)P_j(t)+\lambda_{j-1}P_{j-1}(t)+\mu_{j+1}P_{j+1}(t) + \frac{o(\Delta t)}{\Delta t} \qquad j \geq 1 \tag{B.46}$$

$$\frac{P_0(t+\Delta t)-P_0(t)}{\Delta t} = -\lambda_0 P_0(t)+\mu_1 P_1(t)+\frac{o(\Delta t)}{\Delta t} \qquad j = 0 \tag{B.47}$$

Taking the limit as Δt approaches 0, we see that the left-hand sides of Eqs. (B.46) and (B.47) represent the formal derivative of $P_j(t)$ with respect to t and also that the term $o(\Delta t)/\Delta t$ goes to 0. Consequently, we have the resulting equations:

$$\frac{dP_j(t)}{dt} = -(\lambda_j+\mu_j)P_j(t)+\lambda_{j-1}P_{j-1}(t)+\mu_{j+1}P_{j+1}(t) \qquad j \geq 1$$

$$\text{and} \qquad \frac{dP_0(t)}{dt} = -\lambda_0 P_0(t)+\mu_1 P_1(t) \qquad j = 0 \tag{B.48}$$

The set of equations given by Eq. (B.48) is clearly a set of *differential-difference* equations and represents the dynamics of our probability system. The solution to the differential equations describing the behavior of $P_j(t)$ is found in [Cohe69]. The differential-difference equations displayed by Eq. (B.48) could be summarized by a *state-transition-rate diagram.* In such a diagram the state j is represented by an oval surrounding the number j. Each nonzero infinitesimal rate r_{ij} is represented in the state-transition-rate diagram by a directed branch pointing from i to j and labeled with the value r_{ij}. Furthermore, we do not include the self-loop from j back to j, since it contains no new information. Thus the state-transition-rate diagram for the general birth-death process is as shown in Fig. B.6.

Concentrating on state j, we observe that we may enter it only from state $j-1$ or from state $j+1$ and, similarly, we leave state j only by entering state $j-1$ or state $j+1$. We also observe that the rate at which probability that the process "flows" into state j at time t is given by

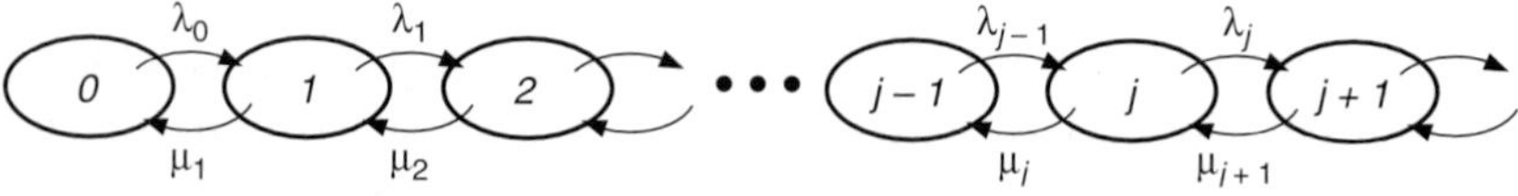

Figure B.6 State-transition-rate diagram for the birth-death process.

$\lambda_{j-1}P_{j-1}(t) + \mu_{j+1}P_{j+1}(t)$, whereas the flow rate out of the state j at time t is given by $(\lambda_j + \mu_j)P_j(t)$.

B.3.5 Poisson processes

The simplest birth-death process to consider is a *pure birth* system in which $\mu_j = 0\ \forall j$ and $\lambda_j = \lambda\ \forall j$. Substituting this into our Eq. (B.48), we have

$$\frac{dP_j(t)}{dt} = -\lambda P_j(t) + \lambda P_{j-1}(t) \qquad j \geq 1$$

$$\frac{dP_0(t)}{dt} = -\lambda P_0(t) \qquad j = 0 \tag{B.49}$$

For simplicity we assume that the system begins at time 0 with 0 members, that is,

$$P_j(0) = \begin{cases} 1 & j = 0 \\ 0 & j \neq 0 \end{cases} \tag{B.50}$$

Solving for $P_0(t)$ we have immediately

$$P_0(t) = e^{-\lambda t}$$

Inserting this last into Eq. (B.49) for $j = 1$ results in

$$\frac{dP_1(t)}{dt} = -\lambda P_1(t) + \lambda e^{-\lambda t}$$

The solution to this differential equation is clearly

$$P_1(t) = \lambda t e^{-\lambda t}$$

Continuing by induction, then, we finally have as a solution to Eq. (B.49)

$$P_j(t) = \frac{(\lambda t)^j}{j!} e^{-\lambda t} \qquad j \geq 0, t \geq 0 \tag{B.51}$$

This is the celebrated *Poisson distribution*. It is a pure birth process with constant birth rate λ giving rise to a sequence of birth epochs that constitute a *Poisson process*.

With the initial condition in Eq. (B.50), $P_j(t)$ gives the probability that j arrivals occur during the time interval $(0,t)$. It is intuitively clear, since the average arrival rate is λ, that the average number of arrivals in an interval of length t must be λt. In fact both the *mean* and the *variance* of a Poisson process are equal to λt.

B.4 Statistical Techniques

B.4.1 Parameter estimation

Among the most important characteristics of a random variable are its probability distribution, mean, and variance. In practice, means and variances are usually unknown parameters. This subsection discusses how to estimate these parameters from data [Hogg83, Mood74].

B.4.1.1 Point estimation. *Point estimation* is often used in reliability analysis. Examples include the estimation of the detection coverage from fault injections and the estimation of mean time to failures (MTTF) from field data. Each fault injection and each failure occurrence can be treated as a sample, which is assumed to be independent of other samples.

Given a collection of n sampling outcomes, $x_1, x_2, \ldots, x_n$, of a random variable X, each x_i can be considered as a realization of the random variable X_i. These X_i's are independent of each other and identically distributed as X. The set $\{X_1, X_2, \ldots, X_n\}$ is called a *random sample* of X. Our purpose is to estimate the value of some parameter θ (θ could be $E[X]$ or $Var(X)$) of X using a function of $X_1, X_2, \ldots, X_n$. The function used to estimate θ, $\hat{\theta} = \hat{\theta}(X_1, X_2, \ldots, X_n)$, is called an *estimator* of θ, and $\hat{\theta}(x_1, x_2, \ldots, x_n)$ is said to be a *point estimate* of θ.

An estimator $\hat{\theta}$ is called an *unbiased estimator* of θ, if $E[\hat{\theta}] = \theta$. The unbiased estimator that has the minimum variance, i.e., that minimizes $Var(\hat{\theta}) = E[(\hat{\theta} - \theta)^2]$ among all unbiased estimators $\hat{\theta}$'s, is said to be the *unbiased minimum-variance estimator.* It can be shown that the sample mean

$$\bar{X} = \frac{1}{n} \sum_{i=1}^{n} X_i \tag{B.52}$$

is the unbiased minimum-variance linear estimator of the population mean μ, and the sample variance

$$S^2 = \frac{1}{n-1} \sum_{i=1}^{n} (X_i - \bar{X})^2 \tag{B.53}$$

is, under some mild conditions, an unbiased minimum-variance quadratic estimator of the population variance $Var(X)$. If an estimator $\hat{\theta}$ converges in probability to θ, that is,

$$\lim_{n \to \infty} P(|\hat{\theta}(X_1, X_2, \ldots, X_n) - \theta| \geq \varepsilon) = 0 \tag{B.54}$$

where ε is any small positive number, it is said to be *consistent.*

Method of maximum likelihood. If the functional form of the pdf of the variable is known, the *method of maximum likelihood* is a good approach to parameter estimation. In many cases, approximate functional forms of empirical distributions can be obtained. In such cases, the maximum likelihood method can be used to determine distribution parameters.

The maximum likelihood method is to choose an estimator such that the observed sample is the most likely to occur among all possible samples. The method usually produces estimators that have minimum-variance and consistency properties. But if the sample size is small, the estimator may be biased.

Assuming X has a pdf $f(x \mid \theta)$, where θ is an unknown parameter, the joint pdf of the sample $\{X_1, X_2, \ldots, X_n\}$,

$$L(\theta) = \prod_{i=1}^{n} f(x_i \mid \theta) \tag{B.55}$$

is called the *likelihood function* of θ. If $\hat{\theta}(x_1, x_2, \ldots, x_n)$ is the point estimate of θ that maximizes $L(\theta)$, then $\hat{\theta}(X_1, X_2, \ldots, X_n)$ is said to be the *maximum likelihood estimator* of θ. The following example illustrates the method.

Example B.8 Let X denote the random variable time between failures in a computer system. Assuming X is exponentially distributed with an arrival rate λ, we wish to estimate λ from a random sample $\{X_1, X_2, \ldots, X_n\}$. By Eq. (B.55),

$$L(\lambda) = \prod_{i=1}^{n} \lambda e^{-\lambda x_i} = \lambda^n e^{-\lambda \sum_{i=1}^{n} x_i}$$

How do we choose an estimator such that the estimated λ maximizes $L(\lambda)$? An easier way is to find the λ value that maximizes $\ln L(\lambda)$ instead of $L(\lambda)$. This is because the λ that maximizes $L(\lambda)$ also maximizes $\ln L(\lambda)$, and $\ln L(\lambda)$ is easier to handle. In this case we have

$$\ln L(\lambda) = n \ln(\lambda) - \lambda \sum_{i=1}^{n} x_i$$

To find the maximum, consider the first derivative

$$\frac{d[\ln L(\lambda)]}{d\lambda} = \frac{n}{\lambda} - \sum_{i=1}^{n} x_i$$

The solution of this equation at zero,

$$\hat{\lambda} = \frac{n}{\sum_{i=1}^{n} x_i}$$

is the maximum likelihood estimator for λ.

Method of moments. Sometimes it is difficult to find maximum likelihood estimators in closed form. One example is the pdf of the gamma distribution $G(\alpha,\theta)$

$$g(x) = \frac{1}{\Gamma(\alpha)\theta^{\alpha}} x^{\alpha-1} e^{-x/\theta} \qquad x > 0$$

The estimation of α and θ is complicated by the existence of the gamma function $\Gamma(\alpha)$. The gamma distribution, however, is useful for characterizing arrival times in the real world. In such cases, the *method of moments* can be used if an analytical relationship is found between the moments of the variable and the parameters to be estimated.

To explain the method of moments, we introduce the simple concepts of *sample moment* and *population moment*. The kth ($k = 1, 2, \ldots$) sample moment of the random variable X is defined as

$$m_k = \frac{1}{n} \sum_{i=1}^{n} X_i^k \tag{B.56}$$

where $X_1, X_2, \ldots, X_n$ are a sample of X. The kth population moment of X is just $E[X^k]$.

Suppose there are k parameters to be estimated. The method of moments sets the first k sample moments equal to the first k population moments, which are expressed as the unknown parameters, and then solves these k equations for the unknown parameters. The method usually gives simple and consistent estimators. However, some estimators may not have unbiased and minimum-variance properties. The following example shows details of the method.

Example B.9 We wish to estimate α and λ based on a sample $\{X_1, X_2, \ldots, X_n\}$ from a gamma distribution. Since $X \sim G(\alpha, \lambda)$, we know

$$E[x] = \frac{\alpha}{\lambda} \qquad E[x^2] = \frac{\alpha}{\lambda^2} + \frac{\alpha^2}{\lambda^2}$$

The first two sample moments, by definition, are given by

$$m_1 = \frac{1}{n} \sum_{i=1}^{n} x_i = \bar{X} \qquad m_2 = \frac{1}{n} \sum_{i=1}^{n} x_i^2 \approx S^2 + \bar{X}^2$$

Setting $m_1 = E(X)$ and $m_2 = E(X^2)$ and solving for α and λ, we obtain

$$\hat{\alpha} = \frac{\bar{X}^2}{S^2} \qquad \hat{\lambda} = \frac{\bar{X}}{S^2}$$

These are the estimators for α and λ from the method of moments.

Least-squares estimates. The least-squares estimation technique is commonly applied in engineering and mathematics problems. We assume that a linear law relates two variables, the independent variable x and the dependent variable y:

$$y = ax + b$$

The true data relating y and x are a set of n pairs of points: (x_1, y_1), $(x_2, y_2), \ldots, (x_n, y_n)$. The error between the true value of the dependent variable and the best fit of a linear function is

$$\text{error}_i = y_i - (ax_i + b)$$

The error measure for the accuracy of fit is given by the sum of the squared errors (SSE):

$$\text{SSE} = \sum_{i=1}^{n} (\text{error}_i)^2 = \sum_{i=1}^{n} (y_i - ax_i - b)^2$$

The best estimates of a and b are the values of a and b that minimize the sum of the squared errors, which is achieved by

$$\partial\text{SSE}/\partial a = 0 \qquad \partial\text{SSE}/\partial b = 0$$

Solving for the resulting values of a and b yields

$$\hat{a} = \frac{\Sigma_{i=1}^{n} (y_i - \bar{y})(x_i - \bar{x})}{\Sigma_{i=1}^{n} (x_i - \bar{x})^2} \tag{B.57}$$

and

$$\hat{b} = \bar{y} - \hat{a}\,\bar{x} \tag{B.58}$$

where

$$\bar{x} = \frac{1}{n}\sum_{i=1}^{n} x_i \qquad \bar{y} = \frac{1}{n}\sum_{i=1}^{n} y_i$$

The symbols $\hat{a}$ and $\hat{b}$ stand for the least-squares estimates of a and b, respectively. Note that we can also perform least-squares estimation in a similar manner with other nonlinear functional relationships between y and x.

B.4.1.2 Interval estimation. So far, our discussion has been limited to the point estimation of unknown parameters. The estimate may deviate from the actual parameter value. To obtain an estimate with a high confidence, it is necessary to construct an interval estimate such that the interval includes the actual parameter value with a high probability. Given an estimator $\hat{\theta}$, if

$$P(\hat{\theta} - e_1 < \theta < \hat{\theta} + e_2) = \beta \tag{B.59}$$

the random interval $(\hat{\theta} - e_1, \hat{\theta} + e_2)$ is said to be $100 \times \beta$ percent *confidence interval* for θ, and β is called the *confidence coefficient* (the probability that the confidence interval contains θ).

Confidence intervals for means. In the following discussion, the sample mean $\bar{X}$ is used as the estimator for the population mean. As mentioned in Sec. B.4.1.1, it is the unbiased minimum variance linear estimator for μ. Let's first consider the case in which the sample size is large. By the central limit theorem, $\overline{X}$ is asymptotically normally distributed, no matter what the population distribution is. Thus, when the sample size n is reasonably large (usually 30 or above, sometimes 50 or more if the population distribution is badly skewed with occasional outliers), $Z = (\overline{X} - \mu)/(S/\sqrt{n})$ can be approximately treated as a standard normal variable. To obtain a 100 β percent confidence interval for μ, we can find a number $z_{\alpha/2}$ from the normal distribution $N(0, 1)$ table such that $P(Z > z_{\alpha/2}) = \alpha/2$, where $\alpha = 1 - \beta$. Then we have

$$P(-z_{\alpha/2} < \frac{\overline{X} - \mu}{S/\sqrt{n}} < z_{\alpha/2}) = 1 - \alpha$$

Thus, the $100(1 - \alpha)$ percent confidence interval for μ is approximately

$$\overline{X} - z_{\alpha/2}\frac{S}{\sqrt{n}} < \mu < \overline{X} + z_{\alpha/2}\frac{S}{\sqrt{n}} \tag{B.60}$$

If the sample size is small (considerably smaller than 30), the above approximation can be poor. In this case, we consider two commonly used distributions: normal and exponential. If the population distribution is normal, the random variable $T = (\overline{X} - \mu)/(S/\sqrt{n})$ has a Student's t-distribution with $n - 1$ degrees of freedom. By repeating the same approach performed above with a t-distribution table, the following $100(1 - \alpha)$ percent confidence interval for μ can be obtained:

$$\overline{X} - t_{n-1;\alpha/2}\frac{S}{\sqrt{n}} < \mu < \overline{X} + t_{n-1;\alpha/2}\frac{S}{\sqrt{n}} \tag{B.61}$$

where $t_{n-1;\alpha/2}$ is a number such that $P(T > t_{n-1;\alpha/2}) = \alpha/2$. Theoretically, Eq. (B.61) requires X to have a normal distribution. However, this estimator is not very sensitive to the distribution of X when the sample size is reasonably large.

If the population distribution is exponential, it can be shown that $\chi^2 = 2n\overline{X}/\mu$ has a chi-square distribution with $2n$ degrees of freedom. Thus, we can use the chi-square distribution table. Because the chi-square distribution is not symmetrical about the origin, we need to find two numbers, $x^2_{2n;1-\alpha/2}$ and $x^2_{2n;\alpha/2}$, such that $P(\chi^2 < x^2_{2n;1-\alpha/2}) = \alpha/2$ and $P(\chi^2 > x^2_{2n;\alpha/2}) = \alpha/2$. The obtained $100(1 - \alpha)$ percent confidence interval for μ is

$$\frac{2n\overline{X}}{x^2_{2n;\alpha/2}} < \mu < \frac{2n\overline{X}}{x^2_{2n;1-\alpha/2}} \tag{B.62}$$

Confidence intervals for variances. Our discussion focuses on the two commonly used distributions: normal and exponential. If X is normally distributed, the sample variance S^2 can be used to construct the confidence interval. It is known that the random variable $(n - 1)S^2/\sigma^2$ has a chi-square distribution with $n - 1$ degrees of freedom. To determine a $100(1 - \alpha)$ percent confidence interval for σ^2, we follow the procedure for constructing Eq. (B.62) to find the numbers $x^2_{n-1;1-\alpha/2}$ and $x^2_{n-1;\alpha/2}$ from the chi-square distribution table. The confidence interval is then given by

$$\frac{(n-1)S^2}{x^2_{n-1;\alpha/2}} < \sigma^2 < \frac{(n-1)S^2}{x^2_{n-1;1-\alpha/2}} \tag{B.63}$$

Our experience shows that this equation, like Eq. (B.61), is not restricted to the normal distribution when the sample size is reasonably large (15 or more).

If X is exponentially distributed, we can use Eq. (B.62) to estimate the confidence interval for $Var(X)$, because of the exponential random variable, $Var(X)$ equals μ^2. Since all terms in Eq. (B.62) are positive, we can square them. The result gives a $100(1 - \alpha)$ percent confidence interval for $Var(X)$:

$$\left(\frac{2n\overline{X}}{x^2_{2n;\alpha/2}}\right)^2 < Var(X) < \left(\frac{2n\overline{X}}{x^2_{2n;1-\alpha/2}}\right)^2 \tag{B.64}$$

Confidence intervals for proportions. Often, we need to estimate the confidence interval for a proportion or percentage whose underlying distribution is unknown. For example, we may want to estimate the confidence interval for the detection coverage after fault injection experiments. In general, given n Bernoulli trials with the probability of success on each trial being p and the number of successes being Y, how do we find a confidence interval for p? If n is large (particularly when $np \geq 5$ and $n(1 - p) \geq 5$ [Hogg83]), Y/n has an approximately normal distribution, $N(\mu,\sigma^2)$, with $\mu = p$ and $\sigma^2 = p(1 - p)/n$. Note that Y/n is the sample mean, which is an estimator of μ or p. By Eq. (B.60), the $100(1 - \alpha)$ percent confidence interval for p is

$$\frac{Y}{n} \pm z_{\alpha/2}\sqrt{p(1-p)/n} \tag{B.65}$$

Example B.10 We would like to determine the number of injections required to achieve a given confidence interval for an estimated fault detection coverage. Let n represent the number of fault injections and Y the number of faults detected in the n injections. Assume that all faults have the same detection coverage, which is approximately p. Now we wish to estimate p with the $100(1 - \alpha)$ percent confidence interval being e. By Eq. (B.65), we have

$$e = z_{\alpha/2}\sqrt{p(1-p)/n} \tag{B.66}$$

Solving the equation for n gives us

$$n = \frac{z_{\alpha/2}{}^2 p(1-p)}{e^2} \tag{B.67}$$

where n is the number of injections required to achieve the desired confidence interval in estimating p.

For example, assume detection coverage $p = 0.6$, confidence interval $e = 0.05$, and confidence coefficient $1 - \alpha = 90$ percent. Then the required number of injections is

$$n = \frac{1.645^2 \times 0.6 \times 0.4}{0.05^2} = 260$$

B.4.2 Distribution characterization

While mean and variance are important parameters that summarize data by single numbers, probability distribution provides further information about the data. Analysis of distributions can help us understand the data in detail and arrive at conclusions regarding the underlying models. For example, if the time to failure and the recovery time for a system are all exponential, then the model is a Markov model; otherwise, it could be one of the other types of models.

B.4.2.1 Empirical distribution. Given a sample of X, the simplest way to obtain an empirical distribution of X is to plot a histogram of the observations, shown in Fig. B.7. The range of the sample space is divided into a number of subranges called *buckets*. The lengths of the buckets are usually the same, although this is not essential. Assume that we have k

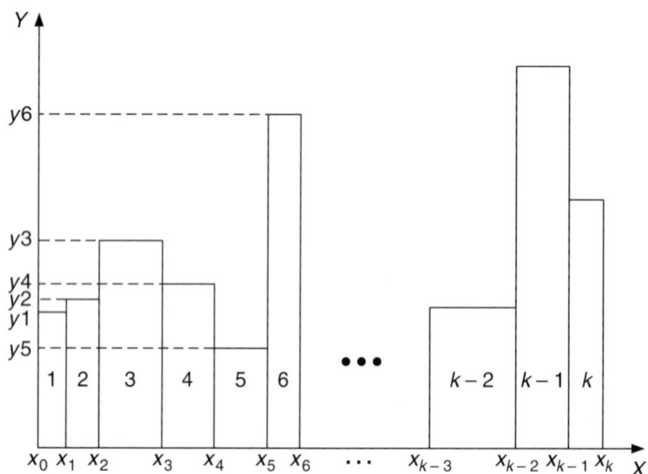

Figure B.7 Histogram for the pdf of X.

buckets, separated by $x_0, x_1, \ldots, x_k$, for the given sample of size n. In each bucket, there are y_i instances. Clearly, the sample size n is $\Sigma_{i=1}^{k} y_i$. Then, y_i/n is an estimation of the probability that X takes a value in bucket i. The histogram is an *empirical pdf* of X. An empirical cdf can be constructed from the histogram (shown in Fig. B.8):

$$F_k(x) = \begin{cases} 0 & x < x_0 \\ \sum_{l=1}^{i} \frac{y_l}{n} & x_{i-1} \leq x < x_i \\ 1 & x_k \leq x \end{cases} \tag{B.68}$$

The key issue in plotting histograms is to determine the bucket size. A small size may lead to such a large variation among buckets that the distribution cannot easily be characterized. On the other hand, a large size may lose details of the distribution. Given a data set, it is possible to obtain very different distribution shapes by using different bucket sizes. One guideline is that if any bucket has less than five instances, the bucket size should be increased or a variable bucket size should be used. Normally 10 or more buckets are sufficient in most cases, depending on the sample size.

B.4.2.2 Distribution function fitting. Analytical distribution functions are useful in analytical modeling and simulations. Thus, it is often desirable to fit an analytical function to a given empirical distribution. Function fitting relies on knowledge of statistical distribution functions. Given an empirical distribution, step 1 is to make a good guess of the closest distribution function(s) based on the shape of the empirical

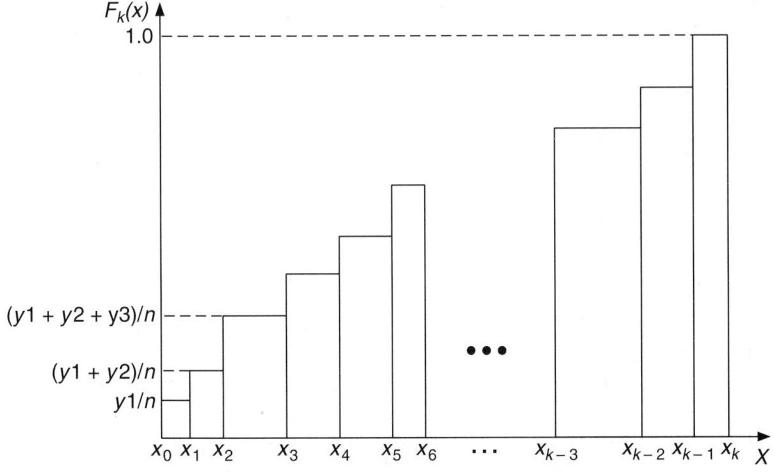

Figure B.8 Histogram for the cdf of X.

distribution, prior knowledge, and intuition. Step 2 is to use a statistical package to obtain the parameters for a guessed function by trying to fit it to the empirical distribution. Step 3 is to test the goodness-of-fit to see if the fitted function is acceptable. If the function is not acceptable, we go to step 1 to try a different function.

Let's look at step 3—the significance test. Assume that the given empirical cdf is F_k, defined in Eq. (B.68), and the hypothesized cdf is $F(x)$, obtained from step 2. Our task is to test the hypothesis

$$H_0 : F_k(x) = F(x)$$

Two commonly used goodness-of-fit test methods are the *chi-square test* and the *Kolmogorov-Smirnov test.* We now briefly introduce these two methods [Dani90].

B.4.2.3 Chi-square test. The chi-square test assumes the distribution under consideration can be approximated by a multinomial distribution. Assume X comes from the distribution $F(x)$. Let

$$p_i = F(x_i) - F(x_{i-1}) \qquad i = 1, \ldots, k$$

where p_i is the probability that an instance falls into bucket i (that is, the interval $[x_{i-1}, x_i]$). For a random sample of size n, $X_1, X_2, \ldots, X_n$, we form a new random variable to count the number of instances in each bucket:

$$Y_i = \sum_{j=1}^{n} I_{[x_{i-1} \leq X_j \leq x_i]} \qquad i = 1, \ldots, k \tag{B.69}$$

where

$$I_{[x_{i-1} \leq X \leq x_i]} = \begin{cases} 1 & x_{i-1} \leq X \leq x_i \\ 0 & \text{otherwise} \end{cases}$$

Y_i has a joint multinomial distribution, where the expected instances falling into bucket i is np_i. Furthermore, the sum of error squares divided by the expected numbers

$$q_{k-1} = \sum_{i=1}^{k} \frac{(y_i - np_i)^2}{np_i} \tag{B.70}$$

is a measure of the closeness of the observed number of instances, y_i, to the expected number of instances, np_i, in bucket i. If q_{k-1} is small, we tend to accept H_0. This can be measured in terms of statistical significance if we treat q_{k-1} as a particular value of the random variable Q_{k-1}. It can be shown that if n is large ($np_i \geq 1$), the distribution of Q_{k-1} is approximately a chi-square distribution with $k - 1$ degrees of freedom,

$\chi^2(k-1)$. If H_0 is true, we expect q_{k-1} to fall into an acceptable range of Q_{k-1}, so that the event is likely to occur. The boundary value, or critical value, of the acceptable range, $\chi^2_\alpha(k-1)$ is chosen such that

$$P[Q_{k-1} > \chi^2_\alpha(k-1)] = \alpha$$

where α is called the *significance level* of the test. Thus, we should reject H_0 if $q_{k-1} > \chi^2_\alpha(k-1)$. Usually, α is chosen to be 0.05 or 0.1.

Example B.11 Mendelian theory indicates that the shape and color of a certain variety of pea ought to be grouped into four groups, "round and yellow," "round and green," "angular and yellow," and "angular and green," according to the ratios 9/3/3/1. For $n = 1600$ peas, the following were observed (the last column gives the expected number):

Round and yellow	948	900
Round and green	279	300
Angular and yellow	284	300
Angular and green	89	100

A 0.05 significance level test of the null hypothesis H_0: $p_1 = 9/16$, $p_2 = 3/16$, $p_3 = 3/16$, and $p_4 = 1/16$ is given by the following: reject H_0 if and only if $q_3 = \Sigma_1^4 (y_i - np_i)^2/np_i$ exceeds $\chi^2_{1-\alpha}(k) = \chi^2_{.95}(3) = 7.81$. The observed q_3 is

$$\frac{(948-900)^2}{900} + \frac{(279-300)^2}{300} + \frac{(284-300)^2}{300} + \frac{(89-100)^2}{100} \approx 6.09$$

and so there is good agreement with the null hypothesis; that is, there is a good fit between the data and the model.

B.4.2.4 Kolmogorov-Smirnov test. The Kolmogorov-Smirnov test is another nonparametric method in that it assumes no particular distribution for the variable in consideration. The method uses the empirical cdf, instead of the empirical pdf, to perform the test, which is more stringent than the chi-square test. It can be shown that $F_k(x)$ in Eq. (B.68) has an asymptotic normal distribution. Namely, $\sqrt{k}[F_k(x) - F(x)]$ has a limiting normal distribution with mean 0 and variance $F(x)[1 - F(x)]$. The Kolmogorov-Smirnov statistic is thus defined by

$$D_k = \sup_x \mid F_k(x) - F(x) \mid \qquad \text{(B.71)}$$

where $\sup_x$ represents the least upper bound of all pointwise differences $\mid F_k(x) - F(x) \mid$. In calculation, we can choose the midpoint between x_{i-1} and x_i, for $i = 1, \ldots, k$, to obtain the maximum value of $\mid F_k(x) - F(x) \mid$. It is seen that D_k is a measure of the closeness of the empirical and hypothesized distribution functions. It can be derived that D_k follows a distribution whose cdf values are given by the table of Kolmogorov-Smirnov acceptance limits [Hand66]. Thus, given a significance level α, we can find the critical value d_k from the table such that

$$P[D_k > d_k] = \alpha$$

The hypothesis H_0 is rejected if the calculated value of D_k is greater than the critical value d_k. Otherwise, we accept H_0.

Example B.12 A hospital is interested in knowing whether the times of birth are uniformly distributed over the hours of the day. For 37 consecutive births in the hospital, the following times were observed: 1:53 P.M., 3:06 P.M., 6:45 P.M., 6:26 A.M., 8:12 A.M., 10:45 A.M., 2:02 P.M., 11:46 P.M., 12:26 A.M., 5:49 A.M., 8:40 A.M., 2:17 P.M., 4:09 P.M., 4:44 P.M., 7:02 P.M., 11:08 P.M., 11:45 P.M., 3:56 A.M., 5:08 A.M., 9:06 A.M., 11:19 A.M., 12:25 P.M., 1:30 P.M., 3:57 P.M., 2:28 A.M., 6:32 A.M., 7:40 A.M., 8:25 A.M., 12:40 P.M., 12:55 P.M., 3:22 P.M., 4:31 P.M., 7:46 P.M., 1:24 A.M., 3:02 A.M., 10:06 A.M., 10:07 A.M. Both the hypothesized uniform cdf and the sample cdf are sketched in Fig. B.9.

One can calculate $\sup_x \mid F_k(x) - F(x) \mid = \mid (31/37) - (1004/1440) \mid \approx 0.1406$.

The critical value for significance $\alpha = 0.10$ is greater than 0.2; so, according to the Kolmogorov-Smirnov goodness-of-fit test, the data do not indicate that the hypothesis that times of birth are uniformly distributed throughout the hours of the day should be rejected. (That is, there is a good fit of the data.)

B.4.3 Multivariate analysis

In reality, measurements usually consist of realizations from multiple variables. For example, a computer workload measurement may in-

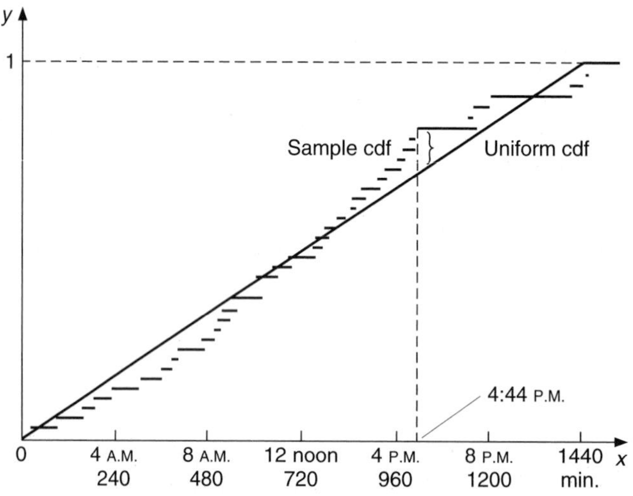

Figure B.9 Uniform cdf and sample cdf of the birth data.

clude usages on the CPU, memory, disk, and network. A computer failure measurement may collect data on multiple components. Multivariate analysis is the application of methods that deal with multiple variables [Dill84, Kend77, John82]. These methods, including cluster analysis, correlation analysis, and factor analysis, identify and quantify relationships among multiple variables.

B.4.3.1 Correlation analysis. The correlation coefficient, $Cor(X_1, X_2)$, between two random variables X_1 and X_2 is defined as

$$Cor(X_1, X_2) = \frac{E[(X_1 - \mu_1)(X_2 - \mu_2)]}{\sigma_1 \sigma_2} \tag{B.72}$$

where μ_1 and μ_2 are the means of X_1 and X_2 and σ_1 and σ_2 are the standard deviations of X_1 and X_2, respectively. If we use ρ to denote the correlation coefficient of X_1 and X_2, then ρ satisfies $-1 \le \rho \le 1$. The correlation coefficient is a measure of the linear relationship between two variables. When $|\rho| = 1$, we have $X_1 = aX_2 + b$, where $a > 0$ if $\rho = 1$, and $a < 0$ if $\rho = -1$. In these extreme cases, there is an exact linear relationship between X_1 and X_2. When $|\rho| \ne 1$, there is no exact linear relationship between X_1 and X_2. In this case, ρ measures the goodness of the linear relationship $X_1 = aX_2 + b$ between X_1 and X_2.

If a random variable, X, is defined on time series, the correlation coefficient can be used to quantify the time serial dependence in the sample data of X. Given a time window $\Delta t > 0$, the *autocorrelation coefficient* of X on the time series t is defined as

$$Autocor(X, \Delta t) = Cor(X(t), X(t + \Delta t)) \tag{B.73}$$

where t is defined on the discrete values $(\Delta t, 2\Delta t, 3\Delta t, \ldots)$. In this case, we treat $X(t)$ and $X(t + \Delta t)$ as two different random variables, and the autocorrelation coefficient is actually the correlation coefficient between the two variables. That is, $Autocor(X,\Delta t)$ measures the time serial correlation of X with a window Δt.

B.4.3.2 Factor analysis. The limitation of correlation analysis is that the correlation coefficient can only quantify a dependency between two variables. However, dependencies may exist within a group of more than two variables or even among all variables. The correlation coefficient cannot provide information about such multiway dependencies. *Factor analysis* is a statistical technique to quantify multiway dependencies among variables. The method attempts to find a set of unobserved common factors that link together the observed variables. Consequently, it provides insights into the underlying structure of the data. For example, in a distributed system, a disk crash can account for failures on those machines whose operations depend on a set of critical data on the disk. The disk state can be considered to be a common factor for failures on these machines.

Let $\mathbf{X} = (X_1, \ldots, X_p)^{\mathrm{T}}$ be a normalized random vector. We say that the k-factor model holds for $\boldsymbol{X}$ if $\boldsymbol{X}$ can be written in the form

$$\mathbf{X} = \Lambda\mathbf{F} + \mathbf{E} \tag{B.74}$$

where $\Lambda = (\lambda_{ij})$ $(i = 1, \ldots, p; j = 1, \ldots, k)$ is a matrix of constants called *factor loadings,* and $\mathbf{F} = (f_1, \ldots, f_k)^T$ and $\mathbf{E} = (e_1, \ldots, e_p)^T$ are random vectors. The elements of $\mathbf{F}$ are called *common factors,* and the elements of $\mathbf{E}$ are called *unique factors* (error terms). These factors are unobservable variables. It is assumed that all factors (both common factors and unique factors) are independent of each other and that the common factors are normalized.

Each variable x_i $(i = 1, \ldots, p)$ can then be expressed as

$$x_i = \sum_{j=1}^{k} \lambda_{ij} f_j + e_i$$

and its variance can be written as

$$\sigma_i^2 = \sum_{j=1}^{k} \lambda_{ij}^2 + \psi_i$$

where ψ_i is the variance of e_i. Thus, the variance of x_i can be split into two parts. The first part

$$h_i^2 = \sum_{j=1}^{k} \lambda_{ij}^2$$

is called the *communality.* It represents the variance of x_i that is shared with the other variables via the common factors. In particular $\lambda_{ij} = Cor(x_i, f_j)$ represents the extent to which x_i depends on the jth common factor. The second part, ψ_i, is called the *unique variance.* It is due to the unique factor e_i and explains the variability in x_i not shared with the other variables.

B.4.3.3 Cluster analysis. *Cluster analysis* is helpful in identifying patterns in data. More specifically, it helps in reading a large number of points plotted in an n-dimensional space into a few identifiable states called *clusters.* For example, it can be used for characterizing workload states in computer systems by identifying the points in a resource usage plot that are similar by some measure and grouping them into a cluster. Assume we have a sample of p workload variables. We call each instance in the sample a *point* characterized by p values. Let $\mathbf{x}_i = (x_{i1},$

$x_{i2}, \ldots, x_{ip}$) denote the ith point of the sample. The Euclidean distance between points i and j,

$$d_{ij} = |\mathbf{x}_i - \mathbf{x}_j| = \left(\sum_{l=1}^{p} (x_{il} - x_{jl})^2 \right)^{1/2}$$

is usually used as a similarity measure between points i and j.

There are several different clustering algorithms. The goal of these algorithms is to achieve small *within-cluster* variation relative to the *between-cluster* variation. A commonly used clustering algorithm is the *k-means* algorithm. The algorithm partitions a sample with p dimensions and n points into k clusters, $\mathbf{C}_1, \mathbf{C}_2, \ldots, \mathbf{C}_k$. The mean, or centroid of the $\mathbf{C}_j$ is denoted by $\overline{\mathbf{x}}_j$. The error component of the partition is defined as

$$\tilde{E} = \sum_{j=1}^{k} \sum_{\mathbf{x}_i \in C_j} |\mathbf{x}_i - \overline{\mathbf{x}}_j|^2 \qquad \text{(B.75)}$$

The goal of the k-means algorithm is to find a partition that minimizes $\tilde{E}$

The clustering procedure starts with k groups, each of which consists of a single point. Each new point is added to the group with the closest centroid. After a point is added to a group, the mean of that group is adjusted to take into account the new point. After a partition is formed, the procedure searches for another partition with smaller $\tilde{E}$ by moving points from one cluster to another cluster until no transfer of a point results in a reduction in $\tilde{E}$ [Spat80].

The presence of outliers in the sample is a problem associated with the clustering algorithms. Outliers can be an order of magnitude greater than most (usually more than 95 percent) of the other points of the sample and can be scattered over the sample space. As a result, the generated clusters may not characterize the features of the sample well. For example, most generated clusters may contain only one or two outliers, with all other points groupable into only a few clusters. One way to deal with this problem is to specify in the algorithm the minimum number of points to form a cluster, typically 0.5 percent of the sample size. Another way is to define an upper bound for the radius (maximum distance between the centroid and any point in a cluster) of any generated cluster. A recommended range for the upper bound is 1.0 to 1.5 standard deviations of the sample [Arti86].

References

[Abde86a] Abdel-Ghaly, A.A., "Analysis of Predictive Quality of Software Reliability Models," Ph.D. dissertation, City University, London, 1986.

[Abde86b] Abdel-Ghaly, A.A., Chan, P.Y., and Littlewood, B., "Evaluation of Competing Software Reliability Predictions," *IEEE Transactions on Software Engineering,* vol. SE-12, no. 9, September 1986, pp. 950–967.

[Abra87] Abraham, J.A., Metze, G., Iyer, R.K., and Patel, J.H., "The Evolution of Fault-Tolerant Computing at the University of Illinois," *The Evolution of Fault-Tolerant Computing,* vol. 1 of *Dependable Computing and Fault-Tolerant Systems,* A. Avižienis, H. Kopetz, and J.-C. Laprie (eds.), Springer-Verlag, Wien and New York, 1987, pp. 271–311.

[Abra92] Abramson, S.R., et al., "Customer Satisfaction-Based Product Development," *Proceedings International Switching Symposium,* vol. 2, Inst. Electronics, Information, Communications Engineers, Yokohama, Japan, 1992, pp. 65–69.

[Adam84] Adams, E.N., "Optimizing Preventive Service of Software Products," *IBM Journal of Research and Development,* vol. 28, no. 1, January 1984, pp. 2–14.

[Adam93] Adams, E., and Kulisch, U. (eds.), *Scientific Computing with Automatic Result Verification,* Academic Press, New York, 1993.

[Agre92] Agresti, W.W., and Evanco, W.M., "Projecting Software Defects From Analyzing Ada Designs," *IEEE Transactions on Software Engineering,* vol. 18, no. 11, November 1992, pp. 988–997.

[Ahme89] Ahmed, S., and Tesauro, G., "Scaling and Generalization in Neural Networks: A Case Study," *Advances in Neural Information Processing Systems 1,* D. Touretzky (ed.), Morgan Kaufmann, San Francisco, 1989, pp. 160–168.

[AIAA93] American Institute of Aeronautic and Astronautics, *Recommended Practice for Software Reliability,* ANSI/AIAA R-013-1992, February 1993.

[Akai74] Akaike, H., "A New Look at Statistical Model Identification," *IEEE Transactions on Automatic Control,* AC-19, 1974, pp. 716–723.

[Amma87] Ammann, P.E., and Knight, J.C., "Data Diversity: An Approach to Software Fault Tolerance," *Proceedings of the 17th International Symposium on Fault-Tolerant Computing* (FTCS-17), IEEE Computer Society Press, Pittsburgh, Pennsylvania, 1987, pp. 122–126.

[Ande81] Anderson, T., and Lee, P.A., *Fault Tolerance—Principles and Practice,* Prentice-Hall, 1981.

[Ande85] Anderson, T., Barrett, P.A., Halliwell, D.N., and Moulding, M.R., "Software Fault-Tolerance: An Evaluation," *IEEE Transactions on Software Engineering,* vol. SE-11 (12), 1985, pp. 1502–1510.

[Angu82] Angus, J.E., and James, L.E., "Combined Hardware/Software Reliability Models," *Proceedings of the Annual Reliability and Maintainability Symposium,* 1982, pp. 176–181.

[Anna80] Anna-Mary, B., "A Study of the Musa Reliability Model," M.S. thesis, Computer Science Department, University of Maryland, 1980.

[ANSI86] ANSI/IEEE Std. 1012, "ANSI/IEEE Standard for Software Verification and Validation Plans," *Software Engineering Standards,* 3d ed., 1986.

[ANSI91] ANSI/IEEE, "Standard Glossary of Software Engineering Terminology," STD-729-1991, ANSI/IEEE, 1991.

[Arla90] Arlat, J., Kanoun, K., and Laprie, J.-C., "Dependability Evaluation of Software Fault-Tolerance," *Proceedings of the 18th IEEE International Symposium on Fault-Tolerant Computing* (FTCS-18), Tokyo, June 1988, pp. 142–147; also in *IEEE Transactions on Computers,* vol. 39, no. 4, April 1990, pp. 504–513.

[Arno73] Arnold, T.F., "The Concept of Coverage and Its Effect on the Reliability Model of Repairable Systems," *IEEE Transactions on Computers,* vol. C-22, June 1973, pp. 251–254.

[Arti86] Artis, H.P., "Workload Characterization Using SAS PROC FASTCLUS," *Workload Characterization of Computer Systems and Computer Networks,* G. Serazzi (ed.), Elsevier Science Publishers, 1986.

[Asch84] Ascher, H., and Feingold, H., *Repairable Systems Reliability: Modeling, Inference, Misconceptions and Their Causes,* lecture notes in statistics, vol. 7, Dekker, New York and Basel, 1984.

[Atha89] Athavale, A., "Performance Evaluation of Hybrid Voting Schemes," M.S. thesis, North Carolina State University, Department of Computer Science, December 1989.

[ATT90] AT&T Bell Laboratories, "Draft Software Reliability Engineering: Reliability Estimation Tools Reference Guide Version 3.7," August 1990.

[Avey80] Aveyard, R.L., and Man, F.T., "A Study on the Reliability of the Circuit Maintenance System 1-B," *Bell System Technical Journal,* vol. 59, October 1980, pp. 1317–1332.

[Aviz77] Avižienis, A., and Chen, L., "On the Implementation of N-Version Programming for Software Fault-Tolerance during Program Execution," in *Proceedings COMPSAC 77,* 1977, pp. 149–155.

[Aviz78] Avižienis, A., "Fault-Tolerance: The Survival Attribute of Digital Systems," *Proceedings of the IEEE,* vol. 66, no. 10, October 1978, pp. 1109–1125.

[Aviz86] Avižienis, A., and Laprie, J.-C., "Dependable Computing: From Concepts to Design Diversity," *Proceedings of the IEEE,* vol. 74, no. 5, May 1986, pp. 629–638.

[Aviz84] Avižienis, A. and Kelly, J.P.J., "Fault Tolerance by Design Diversity: Concepts and Experiments," *IEEE Computer,* August 1984, pp. 67–80.

[Aviz85] Avižienis, A., "The N-Version Approach to Fault-Tolerant Software," *IEEE Transactions on Software Engineering,* vol. SE-11, no. 12, December 1985, pp. 1491–1501.

[Aviz87] Avižienis, A., and Ball, D.E., "On the Achievement of a Highly Dependable and Fault-Tolerant Air Traffic Control System," *IEEE Computer,* vol. 20, no. 2, 1987, pp. 84–90.

[Aviz88] Avižienis, A., Lyu, M.R., and Schütz, W., "In Search of Effective Diversity: A Six-Language Study of Fault-Tolerant Flight Control Software," *Proceedings of the 18th International Symposium on Fault Tolerant Computing,* Tokyo, Japan, June 1988, pp. 15–22.

[Barl75] Barlow, R.E., and Proschan, F., *Statistical Theory of Reliability and Life Testing,* Holt, New York, 1975.

[Basi84a] Basili, V.R., and Perricone, B.T., "Software Errors and Complexity: An Empirical Investigation," *Communications of the ACM,* vol. 22, no. 1, January 1984, pp. 42–52.

[Basi84b] Basili, V., and Weiss, D., "A Methodology for Collecting Valid Software Engineering Data," *IEEE Transactions on Software Engineering,* vol. SE-10, no. 6, 1984, pp. 728–738.

[Basi88] Basili, V.R., and Rombach, H.D., "The TAME Project: Towards Improvement Oriented Software Environments," *IEEE Transactions on Software Engineering,* vol. 14, no. 6, June 1988, pp.758–773.

[Bass94] Bassin, K., "The Butterfly Model. A Proven Approach to Software Quality Improvement," IBM Technical Report, Glendale Programming Lab., vol. 752-5582, January 1994.

[Baue85] Bauer, H.A., Croxall, L.M., and Davis, E.A., "The 5ESS Switching System: System Test, First-Office Application, and Early Field Experience," *AT&T Technical Journal,* vol. 64, no. 6, 1985, pp. 1503–1522.

[Beck90] Becker, G., and Camarinopoulos, L., "A Bayesian Estimation Method for the Failure Rate of a Possibly Correct Program," *IEEE Transactions on Software Engineering,* vol. 16, no. 11, November 1990, pp. 1307–1310.

[Beiz90] Beizer, B., *Software Testing Techniques,* 2d ed., Van Nostrand, 1990.

[BELL89] BELLCORE, *Network Switching Element Outage Performance Monitoring Procedures,* SR-TSY-000963, issue 1, April 1989.

[BELL90a] BELLCORE, *The Analysis and Use of Software Reliability and Quality Data,* SR-TSY-001547, issue 1, January 1990.

[BELL90b] BELLCORE, *Reliability and Quality Measurements for Telecommunications Systems (RQMS),* TR-TSY-000929, issue 1, June 1990.

[BELL90c] BELLCORE, "Reliability Section 12, Issue 3," in *LSSGR—LATA (Local Access and Transport Area) Switching Systems Generic Requirements,* Bellcore, February 1990.

[Bell90] Belli, F., and Jedrzejowicz, P., "Fault-Tolerant Programs and Their Reliability," *IEEE Transactions Rel.,* vol. 29(2), 1990, pp. 184–192.

[Bell91] Belli, F., and Jedrzejowicz, P., "Comparative Analysis of Concurrent Fault-Tolerance Techniques for Real-Time Applications," *Proceedings of the Second International Symposium on Software Reliability Engineering,* Austin, Texas, 1991.

[Benn92] Bennett, J., Denoncourt, M., and Healy, J.D., "Software Reliability Prediction for Telecommunication Systems," *Proceedings of the Second Bellcore/Purdue Symposium on Issues in Software Reliability Estimation,* October 1992, pp. 85–102.

[Berg89] Bergen, L.A., "A Practical Application of Software Reliability to a Large Scale Switching System," *IEEE International Workshop: Measurement of Quality During the Life Cycle,* Val David, Quebec, Canada, April 25–27, 1989.

[Beya81] Beyaert, B., Florin, G., Lonc, P., and Natkin, S., "Evaluation of Computer Systems Dependability Using Stochastic Petri Nets," *Proceedings of the 11th IEEE International Symposium Fault-Tolerant Computing* (FTCS-11), Portland, Maine, June 1981, pp. 79–81.

[Bhan94] Bhandari, I., Halliday, M.J., Chaar, J., Chillarege, R., Jones, K., Atkinson, J.S., Lepori-Costello, C., Jasper, P.Y., Tarver, E.D., Lewis, C.C., and Yonezawa, M., "In-Process Improvements Through Defect Data Interpretation," *IBM Systems Journal,* vol. 33, no. 1, 1994, pp. 182–214.

[Bhar81] Bhargava, B., and Hua, C., "Cost Analysis of Recovery Block Scheme and Its Implementation Issues," *International Journal of Computer and Information Sciences,* vol. 10, no. 6, 1981, pp. 359–382.

[Biro74] Birolini, A., "Some Applications of Regenerative Stochastic Processes to Reliability Theory—Part One: Tutorial Introduction," *IEEE Transactions on Reliability,* vol. R-23, no. 3, August 1974, pp. 186–194.

[Bish86] Bishop, P.G., Esp, D.G., Barnes, M., Humphreys, P., Dahl, G., and Lahti, J., "PODS—A Project on Diverse Software," *IEEE Transactions on Software Engineering,* vol. SE-12, no. 9, 1986, pp. 929–940.

[Bish88] Bishop, P.G., and Pullen, F.D., "PODS Revisited—A Study of Software Failure Behavior," *Proceedings of the 18th International Symposium on Fault-Tolerant Computing,* Tokyo, Japan, 1988, pp. 2–8.

[Bish91] Bishop, P.G., and Pullen, F.D., "Error Masking: A Source of Failure Dependency in Multi-Version Programs," in *Dependable Computing for Critical Applications,* J.-C. Laprie and A. Avižienis (eds.), Springer-Verlag, Vienna, Austria, 1991, pp. 53–73.

[Biya95] Biyani, Shriram, "A Graphical Display for Categorical Data Series," *IBM Research Report,* 1995.

[Bobb86] Bobbio, A., and Trivedi, K.S., "An Aggregation Technique for the Transient Analysis of Stiff Markov Chains," *IEEE Transactions on Computers,* vol. C-35, September 1986, pp. 803–814.

[Boeh79] Boehm, B.W., "Guidelines for Verifying and Validating Software Requirements and Design Specifications," in *Proceedings EURO IFIP'79,* London, September 1979, pp. 711–719.

[Boeh81] Boehm, B.W., *Software Engineering Economics,* Prentice-Hall, Englewood Cliffs, New York, 1981.

[Boeh86] Boehm, B.W., "A Spiral Model of Software Development and Enhancement," *ACM SIGSOFT Software Engineering Notes,* vol. 11, no. 4, 1986, pp. 14–24.

[Boeh89] Boehm, B.W., *Tutorial: Software Risk Management,* IEEE CS Press, 1989.

[Boeh91] Boehm, B.W., "Software Risk Management: Principles and Practices," *IEEE Software*, January 1991, pp. 32–41.

[Bour69] Bouricius, W.G., Carter, W.C., Schneider, P.R., "Reliability Modeling Techniques for Self-Repairing Computer Systems," *Proceedings of the 24th ACM National Conference,* 1969, pp. 295–309.

[Bria92] Briand, L.C., Basili, V.R., and Hetmanski, C.J., "Providing an Empirical Basis for Optimizing the Verification and Testing Phases of Software Development," *Proceedings of the Third International Symposium on Software Reliability Engineering,* Research Triangle Park, North Carolina, October 1992, pp. 329–338.

[Bria93] Briand, L.C., Thomas, W.M., and Hetsmanski, C.J., "Modeling and Managing Risk Early in Software Development," *Proceedings of the 15th International Conference on Software Engineering,* 1993, pp. 55–65.

[Bric84] Brick, D.B., Draper, J.S., and Caulfield, H.J., "Computers in the Military and Space Sciences," *Computer,* vol. 17, no. 10, 1984, pp. 250–262.

[Bril87] Brilliant, S.S., Knight, J.C., and Leveson, N.G., "The Consistent Comparison Problem in N-Version Software," *ACM SIGSOFT Software Engineering Notes,* vol. 12, no. 1, 1987, pp. 29–34.

[Bril90] Brilliant, S.S., Knight, J.C., and Leveson, N.G., "Analysis of Faults in an N-Version Software Experiment," *IEEE Transactions on Software Engineering,* vol. 16, no. 2, 1990, pp. 238–247.

[Broc87] Brocklehurst, S., "On the Effectiveness of Adaptive Software Reliability Modelling," Technical Report, Centre for Software Reliability, City University, London, 1987.

[Broc90] Brocklehurst, S., Chan, P.Y., Littlewood, B., and Snell, J., "Recalibrating Software Reliability Models," *IEEE Transactions on Software Engineering,* vol. SE-16, no. 4, April 1990, pp. 458–470.

[Broc92] Brocklehurst, S., and Littlewood, B., "New Ways to Get Accurate Reliability Measures," *IEEE Software,* vol. 9, no. 4, July 1992, pp. 34–42.

[Broo80] Brooks, W.D., and Motley, R.W., *Analysis of Discrete Software Reliability Models,* Rome Air Development Center Technical Report, RADC-TR-80-84, April 1980.

[BStd86] British Standard 5760, "Reliability of Constructed or Manufactured Products, Systems, Equipments and Components, Part 4: Guide to Specification Clauses to the Achievement and Development of Reliability in New and Existing Items," British Standard Institution, 1986.

[Budd80] Budd, T.A., "Mutation Analysis of Program Test Data," Ph.D. dissertation, Yale University, May, 1980.

[Burk46] Burks, A.W., Goldstine, H.H., and von Neumann, J., *Preliminary Discussion of the Logical Design of an Electronic Computing Instrument,* U.S. Army Ordnance Department, 1946.

[Bush90] Bush, M., "Improving Software Quality: The Use of Formal Inspections at the Jet Propulsion Laboratory," *Proceedings of the 12th International Conference on Software Engineering (ICSE12),* Nice, France, March 26–28, 1990, pp. 196–199.

[Butl91] Butler, R.W., and Finelli, G.B., "The Infeasibility of Experimental Quantification of Life-Critical Software Reliability," *Proceedings of ACM SIGSOFT'91 Conference on Software for Critical Systems,* New Orleans, Louisana, December 1991, pp. 66–76.

[Butl93] Butler, R.W., and Finelli, G.B., "The Infeasibility of Quantifying the Reliability of Life-Critical Real-Time Software," *IEEE Transactions on Software Engineering,* vol. SE-19, January 1993, pp. 3–12.

[Carm95] Carman, D.W., Dolinsky, A.A., Lyu, M.R., and Yu, J.S., "Software Reliability Engineering Study of a Large-Scale Telecommunications Software System," *Proceedings 1995 International Symposium on Software Reliability Engineering,* Toulouse, France, October 1995.

[Cart70] Carter, W.C., Jessep, D.C., Bourricius, W.G., Wadia, A.B., McCarthy, C.E., and Milligan, F.G., "Design Techniques for Modular Architectures for Reliable Computer Systems," IBM T.J. Watson Report No. 70.208.0002, 1970.

[Cart83] Carter, W.C., "Architectural Considerations for Detecting Run-Time Errors in Programs," *Proceedings of the 13th International Symposium on Fault-Tolerant Computing (FTCS-13)*, IEEE Computer Society Press, Milano, Italy, 1983, pp. 249–256.

[Cast81] Castillo, X., and Siewiorek, D.P., "Workload, Performance, and Reliability of Digital Computing Systems," *Proceedings of the 11th IEEE International Symposium on Fault-Tolerant Computing (FTCS-11)*, Portland, Maine, June 1981, pp. 84–89.

[Cast82] Castillo, X., and Siewiorek, D.P., "A Workload Dependent Software Reliability Prediction Model," *Proceedings of the 12th International Symposium on Fault-Tolerant Computing*, June 1982, pp. 279–286.

[Chaa93] Chaar, J., Halliday, M., Bhandari, I., and Chillarege, R., "In-Process Evaluation for Software Inspection and Test," *IEEE Transactions on Software Engineering*, 19, no. 11, November 1993.

[Chan92] Chan, F., Dasiewicz, P., and Seviora, R., "Metrics for Evaluation of Software Reliability Growth Models," *Proceedings of the Second International Symposium on Software Reliability Engineering*, Austin, Texas, May 1991, pp. 163–167.

[Char89] Charette, R.N., *Software Engineering Risk Analysis & Management*, McGraw-Hill, New York, 1989.

[Chen78] Chen, L., and Avižienis, A., "N-Version Programming: A Fault-Tolerance Approach to Reliability of Software Operation," *Proceedings of the 8th International Symposium on Fault-Tolerant Computing*, Toulouse, France, 1978, pp. 3–9.

[Chen92a] Chen, M., Horgan, J.R., Mathur, A.P., and Rego, V.J., "A Time/Structure Based Model for Estimating Software Reliability," Technical Report SERC-TR-117-P, Software Engineering Research Center, Department of Computer Science, Purdue University, W. Lafayette, Ind., 1992.

[Chen92b] Chen, M., Mathur, A.P., and Rego, V.J., "Effect of Testing Techniques on Software Reliability Estimates Obtained Using Time Domain Models," *Proceedings of the 10th Annual Software Reliability Symposium*, IEEE Reliability Society, Denver, Colo., June 25–26, 1992, pp. 116–123; also in *IEEE Transactions on Reliability*, vol. 44, no. 1, March 1995, pp. 97–103.

[Chen93] Chen, M.H., Jones, M.K., Mathur, A.P., and Rego, V.J., "Terse: A Tool for Evaluating Software Reliability Models," *Proceedings of the 4th International Symposium on Software Reliability Estimation*, Denver, Colo., November 1993, pp. 274–283.

[Chen94a] Chen, M., "Tools and Techniques for Testing Based Reliability Estimation," Ph.D. dissertation, Purdue University, 1994.

[Chen94b] Chen, M., Mathur, A.P., and Rego, V.J., "A Case Study to Investigate Sensitivity of Reliability Estimates to Errors in Operational Profiles," *Proceedings of the Fifth International Symposium on Software Reliability Engineering*, Monterey, Calif., November 6–9, 1994.

[Cheu80] Cheung, R.C., "A User-Oriented Software Reliability Model," *IEEE Transactions on Software Engineering*, vol. SE-6, March 1980, pp. 118–125.

[Chil90] Chillarege, R., and Siewiorek, D.P., "Experimental Evaluation of Computer Systems Reliability," *IEEE Transactions on Reliability*, vol. 39, no. 4, October 1990.

[Chil91] Chillarege, R., Kao, W.-L., and Condit, R.G., "Defect Type and Its Impact on the Growth Curve," *Proceedings of the 13th International Conference on Software Engineering,* 1991.

[Chil92] Chillarege, R., Bhandari, I.S., Chaar, J.K., Halliday, M.J., Moebus, D.S., Ray, B.K., and Wong, M.-Y., "Orthogonal Defect Classification—A Concept for In-Process Measurements," *IEEE Transactions on Software Engineering,* vol. 18, no. 11, November 1992, pp. 943–956.

[Chil95] Chillarege, R., and Bassin, K., "Software Triggers and Their Characteristics—A Case Study on Field Failures from an Operating Systems Product," *Fifth IFIP Working Conference on Dependable Computing for Critical Applications,* September 1995.

[Choi89] Choi, B.J., DeMillo, R.A., Krauser, E.W., Mathur, A.P., Martin, R.J., Offutt, A.J., Pan, H., and Spafford, E.H., "The Mothra Toolset," *Proceedings of Hawaii International Conference on System Sciences,* HI, January 3–6, 1989.

[Chri88] Christenson, D.A., "Using Software Reliability Models to Predict Field Failure Rates in Electronic Switching Systems," *Proceedings of the Fourth Annual National Joint Conference on Software Quality and Productivity,* Washington, D.C., 1988.

[Chri90] Christenson, D.A., Huang, S.T., and Lamperez, A.J., "Statistical Quality Control Applied to Code Inspections," *IEEE Journal on Selected Areas in Communications,* vol. 8, no. 2, 1990, pp. 196–200.

[Chri94] Christmansson, J., Kalbarczyk, Z., and Torin, J., "Dependable Flight Control System Using Data Diversity with Error Recovery," *Journal of Computer Systems Science Engineering,* 1994.

[Clar89] Clarke, L.A., Podgruski, A., Richardson, D.J., and Zeil, S., "A Formal Evaluation of Data Flow Path Selection Criteria," *IEEE Transactions on Software Engineering,* vol. 15, no. 11, November 1989, pp. 1318–1332.

[Clev93] Cleveland, W., *Visualizing Data,* AT&T Bell Laboratories and Hobard Press, 1993.

[Clem87] Clement, G.F., and Giloth, P.K., "Evolution of Fault Tolerant Switching Systems in AT&T," in *The Evolution of Fault-Tolerant Computing,* A. Avižienis, H. Kopetz, J.-C. Laprie (eds.), Springer-Verlag, Wien, Austria, 1987, pp. 37–54.

[Cohe69] Cohen, J., *The Single Server Queue,* North Holland, Amsterdam, 1969.

[Cost78] Costes, A., Landrault, C., and Laprie, J.-C., "Reliability and Availability Models for Maintained Systems Featuring Hardware Failures and Design Faults," *IEEE Transactions on Computers,* vol. C-27, June 1978, pp. 548–560.

[Cote88] Cote, V., et al., "Software Metrics: An Overview of Recent Results," *Journal of Systems and Software,* vol. 8, 1988, pp. 121–131.

[Coud93] Coudert, O., and Madre, J.C., "Fault Tree Analysis: 10^{20} Prime Implicants and Beyond, *Proceedings of the Reliability and Maintainability Symposium,* January 1993, pp. 240–245.

[Cour77] Courtois, P.J., *Decomposability: Queuing and Computer System Application,* Academic, New York, 1977.

[Cout73] Coutinho, J. de S., "Software Reliability Growth," *IEEE Symposium on Computer Software Reliability,* 1973.

[Cox62] Cox, D.R., *Renewal Theory,* Muthuen, London, U.K., 1962.

[Cox66] Cox, D.R., and Lewis, P.A.W., *The Statistical Analysis of a Series of Events,* Methuen, London, 1966.

[Cox78] Cox, D.R., and Lewis, P.A.W., *The Statistical Analysis of a Series of Events,* Wiley & Sons, New York, 1978.

[Cram92] Cramp, R., Vouk, M.A., and Jones, W., "On Operational Availability of a Large Software-Based Telecommunications System," *Proceedings of the Third International Symposium on Software Reliability Engineering,* IEEE Computer Society, 1992, pp. 358–366.

[Craw85] Crawford, S., McIntosh, A., and Pregibon, D., "An Analysis of Static Metrics and Faults in C Software," *The Journal of Systems and Software,* vol. 5, 1985, pp. 37–48.

[Cris82] Cristian, F., "Exception Handling and Software Fault Tolerance," *IEEE Transactions on Computers,* vol. C-31, no. 6, June 1982, pp. 531–540.

[Cris85] Cristian, F., "A Rigorous Approach to Fault-Tolerant Programming," *IEEE Transactions on Software Engineering,* vol. SE-11, 1985, pp. 23–31.

[Crow74] Crow, L.H., "Reliability Analysis for Complex Repairable Systems," *Reliability and Biometry,* F. Proshan and R.J. Serfling (eds.), SIAM, Philadelphia, pp. 379–410.

[Crow77] Crow, L.H., "Confidence Interval Procedures for Reliability Growth Analysis," tech. report 1977, U.S. Army Material System Analysis Activity, Aberdeen, Md., 1977.

[Csen90] Csenki, A., "Bayes Predictive Analysis of a Fundamental Software Reliability Model," *IEEE Transactions on Reliability,* vol. R-39, 1990, pp. 177–183.

[Curr86] Currit, P.A., Dyer, M., and Mills, H.D., "Certifying the Reliability of Software," *IEEE Transactions on Software Engineering,* vol. SE-12, no. 1, January 1986, pp. 3–11.

[Cusu95] Cusumano, M., and Selby, R., *Microsoft Secrets: How the World's Most Powerful Software Company Creates Technology, Shapes Markets, and Manages People,* Free Press, Simon & Schuster, New York, 1995.

[Dala88] Dalal, S.R., and Mallows, C.L., "When Should One Stop Testing Software," *Journal of the American Statistical Association,* vol. 83, no. 403, September 1988, pp. 872–879.

[Dala90] Dalal, S.R., and Mallows, C.L., "Some Graphical Aids for Deciding When to Stop Testing Software," *IEEE Journal on Selected Areas in Communications,* vol. 8, no. 2, February 1990, pp. 169–175.

[Dala92] Dalal, S.R., and Mallows, C.L., "Buying with Exact Confidence," *The Annuals of Applied Probability,* vol. 2, no. 3, 1992, pp. 752–765.

[Dala93] Dalal, S.R., Horgan, J.R., and Kettenring, J.R., "Reliable Software and Communication: Software Quality, Reliability, and Safety," *Proceedings of the 15th International Conference on Software Engineering,* Baltimore, Md., May 1993.

[Dala94] Dalal, S.R., and McIntosh, A.A., "When to Stop Testing for Large Software Systems with Changing Code," *IEEE Transactions on Software Engineering,* vol. 20, no. 4, April 1994, pp. 318–323.

[Dani78] Daniel, W.W., *Applied Nonparametric Statistics,* PWS-KENT Pub., Boston, Mass., 1978.

[Davi84] Davies, P.A., "The Latest Developments in Automatic Train Control," in *Proceedings of the International Conference on Railway Safety Control and Automation Towards 21st Century,* London, U.K., September 1984, pp. 272–279.

[Davi93] Davis, G.J., Earls, M.R., and Patterson-Hine, F.A., "Reliability Analysis of the X-29A Flight Control System Software," *Journal of Computer and Software Engineering,* vol. 1, no. 4, 1993, pp. 325–348.

[Dawi84] Dawid, A.P., "Statistical Theory: The Prequential Approach," *Journal Royal Statistical Society,* series A, vol. 147, 1984, pp. 278–292.

[Deb86] Deb, A.K., and Goel, A.L., "Model for Execution Time Behavior of a Recovery Block," *Proceedings COMPSAC 86,* 1986, 497–502.

[Deb88] Deb, A.K., "Stochastic Modelling for Execution Time and Reliability of Fault-Tolerant Programs Using Recovery Block and N-Version Schemes," Ph.D. thesis, Syracuse University, 1988.

[DeGr86] DeGroot, M.H., *Probability and Statistics,* Series in Statistics, Addison-Wesley, Reading, Mass., 1986.

[DeMi91] DeMillo, R.A., and Mathur, A.P., "On the Use of Software Artifacts to Evaluate the Effectiveness of Mutation Analysis for Detecting Errors in Production Software," Technical Report SERC-TR-42-P, Software Engineering, Research Center, Purdue University, W. Lafayette, Ind., 1991.

[Dill84] Dillon, W.R., and Goldstein, M., *Multivariate Analysis,* John Wiley & Sons, 1984.

[DiMa91] DiMario, M.J., "Measuring Software Product Quality That Includes Customer Perception," *QAMC/IEEE International Workshop,* Val David, Quebec, Canada, April 24, 1991.

[Doyl95] Doyle, S.A., and Mackey, J.L., "Comparative Analysis of N-Version Programming (NVP) Architectures, *Proceedings of the Reliability and Maintainability Symposium,* January, 1995.

[Drap86] Draper, D., and Smith, H., *Applied Regression Analysis,* 2d ed., Wiley, New York, 1986.

[Duan64] Duane, J.T., "Learning Curve Approach to Reliability Monitoring," *IEEE Transactions on Aerospace,* vol. 2, 1964, pp. 563–566.

[Duga89a] Dugan, J.B., and Trivedi, K.S., "Coverage Modeling for Dependability Analysis of Fault-Tolerant Systems," *IEEE Transactions on Computers,* vol. 38, no. 6, 1989, pp. 775–787.

[Duga89b] Dugan, J.B., Veeraraghavan, M., Boyd, M., and Mittal, N., "Bounded Approximate Reliability Models for Fault Tolerant Distributed Systems," *Proceedings of the 8th Symposium on Reliable Distributed Systems,* 1989, pp. 137–147.

[Duga91] Dugan, J.B., "Correlated Hardware Failures in Redundant Systems," *Proceedings of the 2nd IFIP Working Conference Dependable Computing for Critical Applications,* Tucson, Arizona, February 1991.

[Duga92] Dugan, J.B., Bavuso, S., and Boyd, M., "Dynamic Fault Tree Models for Fault Tolerant Computer Systems," *IEEE Transactions on Reliability,* September 1992.

[Duga93a] Dugan, J.B., Bavuso, S., and Boyd, M., "Fault Trees and Markov Models for Reliability Analysis of Fault Tolerant Systems," *Journal of Reliability Engineering and System Safety,* vol. 39, 1993, pp. 291–307.

[Duga93b] Dugan, J.B., and Van Buren, R., "Reliability Evaluation of Fly-by-Wire Computer Systems," *Journal of Systems and Safety,* June, 1993.

[Duga94a] Dugan, J.B., "Experimental Analysis of Models for Correlation in Multiversion Software," *Proceedings of the International Symposium on Software Reliability Engineering,* 1994.

[Duga94b] Dugan, J.B., and Lyu, M.R., "System-Level Reliability and Sensitivity Analysis for Three Fault-Tolerant System Architectures," *4th IFIP International Working Conference on Dependable Computing for Critical Applications (DCCA4),* San Diego, Calif., January 1994, pp. 295–307.

[Duga94c] Dugan, J.B., and Lyu, M.R., "System Reliability Analysis of an N-Version Programming Application," *IEEE Transactions on Reliability,* December 1994, pp. 513–519; also in *Proceedings ISSRE'93,* 1993, pp. 103–111.

[Duga95] Dugan, J.B., and Lyu, M.R., "Dependability Modeling for Fault-Tolerant Software and Systems," chapter 5 in *Software Fault Tolerance,* M. Lyu (ed.), John Wiley & Sons, Chichester, U.K., 1995.

[Dura84] Duran, J.W., and Ntafos, S.C., "An Evaluation of Random Testing," *IEEE Transactions on Software Engineering,* vol. SE-10, 1984, pp. 438–444.

[Eckh85] Eckhardt, D.E., and Lee, L.D., "A Theoretical Basis for the Analysis of Multi-version Software Subject to Coincident Errors," *IEEE Transactions on Software Engineering,* vol. SE-11, no. 12, 1985, pp. 1511–1517.

[Eckh91] Eckhardt, D.E., Caglayan, A.K., Kelly, J.P.J., Knight, J.C., Lee, L.D., McAllister, D.F., and Vouk, M.A., "An Experimental Evaluation of Software Redundancy as a Strategy for Improving Reliability," *IEEE Transactions on Software Engineering,* vol. 17, no. 12, 1991, pp. 692–702.

[EEC91] *Information Technology Security Evaluation Criteria, Provisional Harmonised Criteria,* Office for Official Publications of the European Communities, June 1991.

[Efro79] Efron, B., "Computers and the Theory of Statistics: Thinking the Unthinkable," *SIAM Review,* vol. 21, no. 4, October 1979, pp. 460–480.

[Ehre83] Ehrenberger, W., "Safety, Availability and Cost Questions About Diversity," *4th IFAC/IFIP/IFORS International Conference on Control in Transportation Systems,* Baden-Baden, Germany, April 1983.

[Ehre85] Ehrenberger, W., "Statistical Testing of Real Time Software," *Verification and Validation of Real Time Software,* W.J. Quirk (ed.), Springer-Verlag, New York, 1985, pp. 147–178.

[Ehrl90] Ehrlich, W.K., Lee, K., and Molisani, R.H., "Applying Reliability Measurements: A Case Study," *IEEE Software,* March 1990.

[Ehrl90a] Ehrlich, W.K., Stampfel, J.P., and Wu, J.R., "Application of Software Reliability Modeling to Product Quality and Test Process," *Proceedings of the 12th International Conference on Software Engineering,* Nice, France, March 1990.

[Ehrl93] Ehrlich, W.K., Prasanna, B., Stampfel, J.P., and Wu, J.R., "Determining the Cost of a Stop-Test Decision," *IEEE Software,* March 1993, pp. 33–42.

[Eick92] Eick, S.G., Steffen, J.L., and Sumner, E.E., "SeeSoft—A Tool for Visualizing Line-Oriented Software Statistics," *IEEE Transactions on Software Engineering,* vol. 18, no. 11, 1992, pp. 957–968.

[Eick94] Eick, S.G., and Lucas, P.J., "Visualizing Run-Time Errors in Program Code," *Proceedings of the 5th International Symposium on Software Reliability Engineering,* Industrial Track, 1994.

[Elma90] Elman, J., "Finding Structure in Time," *Cognitive Science,* no. 14, 1990, pp. 179–211.

[Endr75] Endres, A., "An Analysis of Errors and Their Causes in System Programs," *Proceedings of the International Conference on Software Engineering,* April 1975, pp. 327–336.

[ESA88] European Space Agency, "Software Reliability Modeling Study," Invitation to tender AO/1-2039/87/NL/IW, February 1988.

[Ever90] Everett, W.W., Furlong, R.J., Klinger, D.J., Tortorella, L.M., and Vanderbei, K.S., *Reliability by Design,* Customer Information Center Code 010-810-105, Chap. 4, November 1990.

[Ever92] Everett, W.W., "An 'Extended Execution Time' Software Reliability Model," *Proceedings of the Third International Symposium on Software Reliability Engineering,* IEEE Computer Press, 1992, pp. 14–22.

[Ever93] Everett, W.W., and Musa, J.D., "A Software-Reliability Engineering Practice," *IEEE Computer,* vol. 26, no. 3, 1993, pp. 77–79.

[Faga76] Fagan, M.E., "Design and Code Inspections to Reduce Errors in Program Development," *IBM Systems Journal,* vol. 15, no. 3, 1976, pp. 219–248.

[Faga86] Fagan, M.E., "Advances in Software Inspections," *IEEE Transactions on Software Engineering,* July 1986, pp. 744–751.

[Fahl88] Fahlman, S., "Faster-Learning Variations on Back-Propagation: An Empirical Study," *Proceedings of the Connectionist Models Summer School,* D. Touretzky, G. Hinton, and T. Sejnowski (eds.), Morgan Kaufmann, San Francisco, Calif., 1988, pp. 38–51.

[Fahl90] Fahlman, S., and Lebiere, C., "The Cascaded-Correlation Learning Architecture," *Advances in Neural Information Processing Systems 2,* D. Touretzky (ed.), Morgan Kaufmann, San Francisco, Calif., 1990, pp. 524–532.

[Fair85] Fairley, R., *Software Engineering Concepts,* McGraw-Hill, N.Y., 1985.

[Farr83] Farr, W.H., *A Survey of Software Reliability Modeling and Estimation,* NSWC TR-171, Naval Surface Warfare Center, September 1983.

[Farr88] Farr, W.H., and Smith, O.D., "Statistical Modeling and Estimation of Reliability Functions for Software (SMERFS) User's Guide," TR 84-373, Revision 1, NSWC, December 1988.

[Farr93a] Farr, W.H., and Smith O., *Statistical Modeling and Estimation of Reliability Functions for Software (SMERFS) User's Guide,* NSWCDD TR 84-373, Revision 3, Naval Surface Warfare Center Dahlgren Division, September, 1993.

[Farr93b] Farr, W.H., and Smith O., *Statistical Modeling and Estimation of Reliability Functions for Software (SMERFS) Access Guide,* NSWC TR 84-371, Revision 3, Naval Surface Warfare Center Dahlgren Division, September, 1993.

[FCC92] Federal Communications Commission, "Notification by Common Carriers of Service Disruptions," 47 CFR Part 63, Federal Register, vol. 57, no. 44, March 5, 1992, pp. 7883–7885.

[Fent91] Fenton, N.E., *Software Metrics: A Rigorous Approach,* Chapman and Hall, New York, 1991.

[Fran88] Frankel, E.G., *Systems Reliability and Risk Analysis,* second revised edition, Kluwer Academic Publishers, 1988.

[Fran93] Franklin, P.H., "Software-Reliability Prediction in a Multiple-Processor Environment," *Proceedings of the 1993 Reliability and Maintainability Symposium,* Atlanta, Georgia, January 1993.

[Frie91] Fries, R.C., *Reliability Assurance for Medical Devices, Equipment and Software,* Interpharm Press, Inc., Buffalo Grove, Ill., 1991.

[Frie93] Friedman, M.A., "Automated Software Fault-Tree Analysis of Pascal Programs," *Proceedings of the 1993 Reliability and Maintainability Symposium,* Atlanta, Georgia, January, 1993, pp. 458–461.

[Frul84] Frullini, R., and Lazzari, A., "Use of Microprocessor in Fail-Safe on Board Equipment," *Proceedings of the International Conference on Railway Safety Control and Automation Towards 21st Century,* London, U.K., September 1984, pp. 292–299.

[Gaff88] Gaffney, J.E., and Davis, C.F., "An Approach to Estimating Software Errors and Availability," SPC-TR-88-007, version 1.0, March 1988, *Proceedings of the Eleventh Minnowbrook Workshop on Software Reliability,* July 1988.

[Gaff90] Gaffney, J.E., and Pietrolewicz, J., "An Automated Model for Software Early Error Prediction (SWEEP)," *Proceedings of the 13th Minnowbrook Workshop on Software Reliability,* July 1990.

[Gant91] Gantenbein, R.E., Shin, S.Y., and Cowles, J.R., "Evaluation of Combined Approaches to Distributed Software-Based Fault Tolerance," *Pacific Rim International Symposium on Fault Tolerant Systems,* 1991, pp. 70–75.

[GAO92] United States General Accounting Office, *Patriot Missile Defense,* GAO, IMTEC 92–26, February 1992.

[Gaud90] Gaudoin, O., "Statistical Tools for Software Reliability Evaluation," Ph.D. thesis, Joseph Fournier Univ. Grenoble I, December 1990; in French.

[Geis90] Geist, R., and Trivedi, K., "Reliability Estimation of Fault-Tolerant Systems: Tools and Techniques," *IEEE Computer,* July 1990, pp. 52–61.

[Geph78] Gephart, L.S., Greenwald, C.M., Hoffman, M.M., and Osterfeld, D.H., *Software Reliability: Determination and Prediction,* Air Force Flight Dynamics Laboratory Technical Report, AFFDL-TR-78-77, June 1978.

[Gers91] Gersting, J., Nist, R.L., Roberts, D.R., Van Valkenburg, R.L., "A Comparison of Voting Algorithms for N-Version Programming," *Proceedings of the 24th Annual Hawaii International Conference on System Sciences,* vol. II, 1991, pp. 253–262. Reprinted in *Fault-Tolerant Software Systems: Techniques and Applications,* Hoang Pham (ed.), IEEE Computer Society Press, 1992, pp. 62–71.

[Gert94] Gertman, D., and Blackman, H.S., *Human Reliability and Safety Analysis Data Handbook,* John Wiley & Sons, Inc., New York, 1994.

[Ghez91] Ghezzi, C., Jazayeri, M., and Mandrioli, D., *Fundamentals of Software Engineering,* Prentice-Hall, Englewood Cliffs, New Jersey, 1991.

[Gibb94] Gibbs, W.W., "Software's Chronic Crisis," in *Scientific American,* vol. 271, September 1994, pp. 86–95.

[Girg86] Girgis, M.R., and Woodward, M.R., "An Experimental Comparison of the Error Exposing Ability of Program Testing Criteria," *Proceedings of the Workshop on Software Testing, Validation, and Analysis,* Banff, Canada, July 15–17, 1986.

[Gmei79] Gmeiner, L., and Voges, U., "Software Diversity in Reactor Protection Systems: An Experiment," *Proceedings of the IFAC Workshop SAFECOMP'79,* 1979, pp. 75–79.

[Gned69] Gnedenko, B.V., Belyayev, Y.K., and Solovyev, A.D., *Mathematical Methods of Reliability Theory,* Academic Press, New York, 1969.

[GNU93] GNU, TkGnats Package, Free Software Foundation Inc., 1993.

[Goel85] Goel, A.L., "Software Reliability Models: Assumptions, Limitations, and Applicability," *IEEE Transactions on Software Engineering,* vol. 11, no. 12, 1985, pp. 1411–1423.

[Goel79] Goel, A.L., and Okumoto, K., "Time-Dependent Error-Detection Rate Model for Software and Other Performance Measures," *IEEE Transactions on Reliability,* vol. R-28, no. 3, August 1979, pp. 206–211.

[Goya87] Goyal, A., Lavenberg, S.S., and Trivedi, K.S., "Probabilistic Modeling of Computer System Availability," *Annals of Operations Research,* no. 8, March 1987, pp. 285–306.

[Grad86] Graden, M.E., Horsley, P.S., and Pingel, T.C., "The Effects of Software Inspections on a Major Telecommunications Project," *AT&T Technical Journal,* vol. 65, issue 3, 1986, pp. 32–40.

[Grad87] Grady, R.B., and Caswell, D.L., *Software Metrics: Establishing A Company-Wide Program,* Prentice-Hall, Englewood Cliffs, New Jersey, 1987.

[Grad92] Grady, R.B., *Practical Software Metrics for Project Management and Process Improvement,* Prentice-Hall, Englewood Cliffs, New Jersey, 1992.

[Gray85] Gray, J., "Why Do Computers Stop and What Can We Do about It?" Tandem Technical Report 85.7, June 1985.

[Gray86] Gray, J.N., "Why Do Computers Stop and What Can Be Done About It?" *Proceedings of the 5th Symposium on Reliability in Distributed Software and Database Systems,* Los Angeles, January 1986, pp. 3–12.

[Gray90] Gray, J., "A Census of Tandem System Availability Between 1985 and 1990," *IEEE Transactions on Reliability,* vol. 39, no. 4, October 1990, pp. 409–418.

[Grie92] Griewank, A., and Corliss, G.F. (eds.), *Automatic Differentiation of Algorithms—Theory, Implementation and Application,* SIAM, Philadelphia, 1992.

[Grna80] Grnarov, A., Arlat, J., and Avižienis, A., "On the Performance of Software Fault Tolerance Strategies," *Proceedings of the 10th IEEE International Symposium on Fault-Tolerant Computing (FTCS-10),* Kyoto, Japan, October 1980, pp. 251–253.

[Gros84] Gross, D., and Miller, D.R., "The Randomization Technique as a Modeling Tool and Solution Procedure for Transient Markov Processes," *Operations Research,* vol. 32, no. 2, 1984, pp. 343–361.

[Hage87] Hagelin, G., "ERICSSON Safety System for Railway Control," in [Vog87a], 1987, pp. 11–21.

[Hals77] Halstead, M.H., *Elements of Software Science,* Elsevier North-Holland, New York, 1977.

[Hami78] Hamilton, P.A., and Musa, J.D., "Measuring Reliability of Computation Center Software," *Proceedings of the Third International Conference on Software Engineering,* 1978, pp. 29–36.

[Haml90] Hamlet, D., and Taylor, R., "Partition Testing Does Not Inspire Confidence," *IEEE Transactions on Software Engineering,* vol. SE-16, no. 12, 1990, pp. 1402–1411.

[Haml93] Hamlet, D., and Voas, J., "Faults on Its Sleeve: Amplifying Software Reliability Testing," *Proceedings of the 1993 International Symposium on Software Testing and Analysis,* Cambridge, Mass., June 1993, pp. 89–98.

[Hand66] *Handbook of Tables for Probability and Statistics,* Chemical Rubber Company, Cleveland, 1966.

[Hans92] Hansen, J.P., and Siewiorek, D.P., "Models for Time Coalescence in Event Logs," *Proceedings of the 22nd International Symposium on Fault-Tolerant Computing,* July 1992, pp. 221–227.

[Harr90] Harrington, P.V., "Applying Customer-Oriented Quality Metrics," *IEEE Software,* November 1989.

[Hech79] Hecht, H., "Fault-Tolerant Software," *IEEE Transactions on Reliability,* vol. R-28, August 1979, pp. 227–232.

[Hech86] Hecht, H., and Hecht, M., "Fault-Tolerant Software," *Fault-Tolerant Computing: Theory and Techniques,* D.K. Pradhan (ed.), vol. 2, Prentice-Hall, Englewood Cliffs, New Jersey, 1986, pp. 658–696.

[Hech87] Hecht, H., and Fiorentino, E., "Reliability Assessment of Spacecraft Electronics," *Proceedings of the Annual Reliability and Maintainability Symposium,* 1987, pp. 341–346.

[Henl82] Henley, E.J., and Kumamoto, H., *Probabilistic Risk Assessment,* IEEE Press, New York, 1982.

[Henr91] Henry, S.M., and Wake, S., "Predicting Maintainability with Software Quality Metrics," *Software Maintenance: Research and Practice,* vol. 3, 1991, pp. 129–143.

[Hill83] Hills, A.D., "A310 Slat and Flap Control System Management and Experience," *Proceedings 5th DASC,* November 1983.

[Hoad81] Hoadely, B., "Quality Measurement Plan (QMP)," *Bell Systems Technical Journal,* vol. 60, no. 2, 1981, pp. 215–273.

[Hoad86] Hoadely, B., "Quality Measurement Plan (QMP)," *Encyclopedia of Statistical Sciences,* Kotz, Johnson, and Read (eds.), John Wiley & Sons, Inc., New York, 1986, pp. 393–398.

[Hogg83] Hogg, R.V., and Tanis, E.A., *Probability and Statistical Inference,* 2d ed., Macmillan Publishing Co., Inc., 1983.

[Holl74] Hollander, M., and Proschan, F., "A Test for Superadditivity for the Mean Value Function of a Non-Homogeneous Poisson Process," *Stochastic Procedure and Their Applications,* vol. 2, 1974, pp. 195–209.

[Holl78] Hollander, M., "Testing Whether More Failures Occur Later," *Proceedings of the Annual Reliability and Maintainability Symposium,* 1978, pp. 103–106.

[Hopf86] Hopfield, J., and Tank, D., "Computing with Neural Circuits: A Model," *Science,* vol. 23, August 1986, pp. 625–633.

[Horg91] Horgan, J.R., and London, S.A., "Dataflow Coverage and the C Language," *Proceedings of the Fourth Annual Symposium on Testing, Analysis, and Verification,* Victoria, British Columbia, Canada, October 1991, pp. 87–97.

[Horg92] Horgan, J.R., and Mathur, A.P., "Assessing Tools in Research and Education," *IEEE Software,* May 1992, pp. 61–69.

[Horg94] Horgan, J.R., London, S.A., and Lyu, M.R., "Achieving Software Quality with Testing Coverage Measures," *IEEE Computer*, vol. 27, no. 9, September 1994, pp. 60–69.

[Howa71] Howard, R.A., *Dynamic Probabilistic Systems,* John Wiley & Sons, Inc., New York, 1971.

[Howd80] Howden, W.E., "Functional Testing," *IEEE Transactions on Software Engineering,* vol. SE-6, no. 2, March 1980, pp. 162–169.

[Hsue87] Hsueh, M.C., and Iyer, R.K., "A Measurement-Based Model of Software Reliability in a Production Environment," *Proceedings of the 11th Annual International Computer Software & Applications Conference,* October 1987, pp. 354–360.

[Hsue88] Hsueh, M.C., Iyer, R.K., and Trivedi, K.S., "Performability Modeling Based on Real Data: A Case Study," *IEEE Transactions on Computers,* vol. 37, no. 4, April 1988, pp. 478–484.

[Huan84] Huang, K-H., and Abraham, J.A., "Algorithms-Based Fault-Tolerance for Matrix Operations," *IEEE Transactions on Computers,* vol. C-33, 1984, pp. 518–528.

[Huan93] Huang, Y., and Kintala, C., "Software Implemented Fault Tolerance: Technologies and Experience," *Proceedings of the 23rd International Symposium on Fault-Tolerant Computing,* June 1993, pp. 2–9.

[Huda93] Hudak, J., Suh, B., Siewiorek, D., and Segall, Z., "Evaluation and Comparison of Fault-Tolerant Software Techniques," *IEEE Transactions on Reliability,* vol. 42, no. 2, June 1993, pp. 190–204.

[Hude92] Hudepohl, J., Snipes, W., Jones, W.D., and Hollack, T., "A Methodology to Improve Switching System Software Service Quality and Reliability," *Proceedings of the IEEE Global Telecommunications Conference (GLOBCOM),* December 1992.

[Hull94] Hull, T.E., Fairgrieve, T.F., Tang, P.T.P., "Implementing Complex Elementary Functions Using Exception Handling," *ACM Transactions on Mathematical Software,* vol. 20, no. 2, June 1994.

[Hump89] Humphrey, W.S., *Managing the Software Process,* Addison-Wesley Publishing Company, Reading, Mass., 1989.

[Ibe92] Ibe, O.C., and Wein, A.S., "Availability of Systems with Partially Observable Failures," *IEEE Transactions on Reliability,* IEEE, vol. 41, no. 1, March 1992, pp. 92–96.

[IBM90] IBM MHVPL PTM Work Group, *Requirements for Program Trouble Memorandas,* IBM Mid Hudson Valley Programming Lab, Myers Corners Road, Wappingers Falls, N.Y., 1990.

[IBM95] IBM, "ODC Data Requirements and Definitions," working document, ODC Project, IBM Watson Research, 1995.

[IEEE84] IEEE *Computer,* "Special issue on fault-tolerant computing," vol. 17, no. 8, 1984.

[IEEE85] American National Standards Institute/Institute of Electrical and Electronics Engineers, *A Standard for Binary Floating-Point Arithmetic,* ANSI/IEEE Std. 754-1985, New York, 1985 (reprinted in SIGPLAN vol. 22, no. 2, 1987, pp. 9–25).

[IEEE86] IEEE Std. 1012-1986, IEEE Standard, *Software Verification and Validation Plans,* IEEE 1986.

[IEEE87a] American National Standards Institute/Institute of Electrical and Electronics Engineers, *A Standard for Radix-Independent Floating-Point Arithmetic,* ANSI/IEEE Std. 854-1987, New York, 1987.

[IEEE87b] IEEE Standard, "A Standard Classification of Software Errors, Faults and Failures," *Technical Committee on Software Engineering, Standard P-1044/D3,* December 1987.

[IEEE88a] IEEE Standard, *Dictionary of Measures to Produce Reliable Software* (ANSI), IEEE Std-982.1-1988, IEEE, New York, 1988.

[IEEE88b] IEEE, *Guide for the Use of IEEE Standard Dictionary of Measures to Produce Reliable Software* (ANSI), IEEE Std-982.2-1988, IEEE, New York, 1988.

[IEEE90] IEEE Standard, *Glossary of Software Engineering Terminology* (ANSI) IEEE Std-610.12-1990, IEEE, New York, 1990.

[IEEE90a] IEEE, "Theme Articles: Metrics," *IEEE Software,* vol. 7, no. 2, March 1990.

[IEEE90b] IEEE Standards, "Standard for Software Quality Metrics Methodology," *Software Engineering Standards Committee, Standard P-1061/D21,* April 1990.

[IEEE91] Institute of Electrical and Electronics Engineers, *ANSI/IEEE Standard Glossary of Software Engineering Terminology,* IEEE Std. 729-1991, 1991.

[IEEE94] IEEE, "Special Issue on Safety-Critical Systems," *IEEE Software,* J. Knight and B. Littlewood (eds.), January 1994.

[IEEE95] IEEE, *Charter and Organization of the Software Reliability Engineering Committee,* 1995.

[Ishi91] Ishikawa, K., *Introduction to Quality Control,* 3A Corporation, Tokyo, 1991.

[ISO87] ISO, "International Standard ISO 9001: Quality Systems—Model for Quality Assurance in Design/Development, Production, Installation and Servicing," *ISO 9001,* Switzerland, 1987.

[ISO91] ISO, "Quality Management and Quality Assurance Standards—Part 3: Guidelines for the Application of ISO 9001 to the Development, Supply and Maintenance of Software," *ISO 9000-3,* Switzerland, June 1991.

[Iyer82a] Iyer, R.K., and Rossetti, D.J., "A Statistical Load Dependency Model for CPU Errors at SLAC," *Proceedings of the 12th International Symposium on Fault-Tolerant Computing,* June 1982, pp. 363–372.

[Iyer82b] Iyer, R.K., Butner, S.E., and McCluskey, E.J., "A Statistical Failure/Load Relationship: Results of a Multi-Computer Study," *IEEE Transactions on Computers,* vol. C-31, July 1982, pp. 697–706.

[Iyer85a] Iyer, R.K., and Velardi, P., "Hardware-Related Software Errors: Measurement and Analysis," *IEEE Transactions on Software Engineering,* vol. SE-11, no. 2, February 1985, pp. 223–231.

[Iyer85b] Iyer, R.K., and Rossetti, D.J., "Effect of System Workload on Operating System Reliability: A Study on IBM 3081," *IEEE Transactions on Software Engineering,* vol. SE-11, no. 12, December 1985, pp. 1438–1448.

[Iyer86] Iyer, R.K., Rossetti, D.J., and Hsueh, M.C., "Measurement and Modeling of Computer Reliability as Affected by System Activity," *ACM Transactions on Computer Systems,* vol. 4, no. 3, August 1986, pp. 214–237.

[Iyer90] Iyer, R.K., Young, L.T., and Iyer, P.V.K., "Automatic Recognition of Intermittent Failures: An Experimental Study of Field Data," *IEEE Transactions on Computers,* vol. 39, no. 4, April 1990, pp. 525–537.

[Jaco88] Jacobs, R., "Increased Rates of Convergence Through Learning Rate Adaptation," *Neural Networks,* vol. 1, 1988, pp. 295–307.

[Jaco91] Jacob, J., "The Basic Integrity Theorem," *Proceedings of the IEEE International Symposium on Security and Privacy,* Oakland, Calif., May 1991, pp. 89–97.

[Jeli72] Jelinski, Z., and Moranda, P.B.: "Software Reliability Research," *Proceedings of the Statistical Methods for the Evaluation of Computer System Performance,* Academic Press, 1972, pp. 465–484.

[Jewe85] Jewell, W.S., "Bayesian Extensions to a Basic Model of Software Reliability," *IEEE Transactions on Software Engineering,* SE-11, 1985, pp. 1465–1471.

[JohK82] Johnson, N., and Kotz, S. (eds.), *Encyclopedia of Statistical Sciences,* Wiley & Sons, Inc., New York, 1982.

[John82] Johnson, R.A., and Wichern, D.W., *Applied Multivariate Statistical Analysis,* Prentice-Hall, Englewood Cliffs, New Jersey, 1982.

[John88] Johnson, A.M., and Malek, M., "Survey of Software Tools for Evaluating Reliability, Availability, and Serviceability," *ACM Computing Surveys,* vol. 20, no. 4, pp. 227–269, December 1988.

[Jone91] Jones, W.D., "Reliability Modeling for Large Software Systems in Industry," *Proceedings of the Second International Symposium on Software Reliability Engineering,* May 1991, pp. 35–42.

[Jone92] Jones, W.D., "Reliability of Telecommunications Software: Assessing Sensitivity of Least Squares Reliability Estimates," *Proceedings of TRICOM,* February 1992.

[Jone93] Jones, W.D., and Gregory, D., "Infinite Failure Models for a Finite World: A Simulation of the Fault Discovery Process," *Proceedings of the Fourth International Symposium on Software Reliability Engineering,* November 1993, pp. 284–293.

[Jord86] Jordan, M., "Attractor Dynamics and Parallelism in a Connectionist Sequential Machine," *Proceedings of the 8th Annual Conference of the Cognitive Science,* 1986, pp. 531–546.

[JPL91] *Handbook For Software Reliability Measurement,* Software Product Assurance Section, Jet Propulsion Laboratory, JPL D-8672, June 20, 1991.

[Juhl92a] Juhlin, B.D., "Implementing Operational Profiles to Measure System Reliability," *Proceedings of the 3rd International Symposium on Software Reliability Engineering,* Research Triangle Park, North Carolina, October 7–10, 1992, pp. 286–295.

[Juhl92b] Juhlin, B.D., "Applying Software Reliability Engineering to International PBX Testing." Presentations at the *9th International Conference on Testing Computer Software,* Washington, D.C., June 16–18, 1992, pp. 165–176.

[Juhl93] Juhlin, B.D., "Software Reliability Engineering in the System Test Process," presentations at the *10th International Conference on Testing Computer Software,* Washington, D.C., June 14–17, 1993, pp. 97–115.

[Kan91] Kan, S.H., "Modeling and Software Development Quality," *IBM Systems Journal,* vol. 30, no. 3, 1991, pp. 351–362.

[Kana95] Kanawati, A., Kanawati, N., and Abraham, J., "FERRARI: A Flexible Software-Based Fault and Error Injection System," *IEEE Transactions on Computer,* vol. 44, no. 2, February 1995.

[Kano87] Kanoun, K., and Sabourin, T., "Software Dependability of a Telephone Switching System," *Proceedings of the 17th IEEE International Symposium on Fault-Tolerant Computing (FTCS-17),* Pittsburgh, June 1987, pp. 236–241.

[Kano88] Kanoun, K., Laprie, J.-C., and Sabourin, T., "A Method for Software Reliability Growth Analysis and Assessment," *Proceedings of the 1st Interna-*

tional Workshop on Software Engineering and Its Applications, Toulouse, Dec. 1988, pp. 859–878.

[Kano89] Kanoun, K., "Software Dependability Growth—Characterization, Modeling, Evaluation," Doctor ès-Sciences thesis, Toulouse Polytechnic National Institute, September 89, LAAS Report no. 89.320; in French.

[Kano91a] Kanoun, K., Bastos Martini, M., and Moreira De Souza, J., "A Method for Software Reliability Analysis and Prediction—Application to the TROPICO-R Switching System," *IEEE Transactions on Software Engineering,* April 1991, pp. 334–344.

[Kano91b] Kanoun, K., and Laprie, J.-C., "The Role of Trend Analysis in Software Development and Validation," *Proceedings IFAC International Conference on Safety, Security and Reliability (SAFECOMP'91),* 30 October–1 November, 1991, Trondheim, Norway.

[Kano92] Kanoun, K., Kaâniche, M., Laprie, J.-C., and Metge, S., "SoRel: A Tool for Reliability Growth Analysis and Prediction from Statistical Failure Data," Centre National de la Recherche Scientifique, LAAS Report 92.468, December 1992. Also in *FTCS-23 Proceedings,* Toulouse, France, June 1993, pp. 654–659.

[Kano93a] Kanoun, K., Kaâniche, M., Béounes, C., Laprie, J.-C., and Arlat, J., "Reliability Growth of Fault-Tolerant Software," *IEEE Transactions on Reliability,* vol. 42, no. 2, June 1993, pp. 205–219.

[Kano93b] Kanoun, K., Kaâniche, M., and Laprie, J.-C., "Experience in Software Reliability: From Data Collection to Quantitative Evaluation," *Proceedings of the Fourth International Symposium on Software Reliability Engineering, (ISSRE'93),* Denver, Colo., November 1993, pp. 234–246.

[Kao93] Kao, W., Iyer, R., and Tang, D., "FINE: A Fault Injection and Monitoring Environment of Tracing the UNIX System Behavior under Faults, *IEEE Transactions on Software Engineering,* vol. 19, no. 11, November 1993, pp. 1105–1118.

[Kapl85] Kaplan, G., "The X-25: Is It Coming or Going?," *IEEE Spectrum,* vol. 22, no. 6, 1985, pp. 54–60.

[Kare90] Kareer, N., Kapur, P.K., and Grover, P.S., "An S-Shaped Software Reliability Growth Model with Two Types of Errors," *Microelectronics and Reliability,* vol. 30, no. 6, 1990, pp. 1085–1090.

[Karu91] Karunanithi, N., Malaiya, Y.K., and Whitley, D., "Prediction of Software Reliability Using Neural Networks," *Proceedings of the 2nd International Symposium on Software Reliability Engineering,* IEEE Computer Society Press, May 1991, pp. 124–130.

[Karu92a] Karunanithi, N., Whitley, D., and Malaiya, Y.K., "Prediction of Software Reliability Using Connectionist Approachs," *IEEE Transactions on Software Engineering,* vol. 18, no. 7, July 1992, pp. 563–574.

[Karu92b] Karunanithi, N., Whitley, D., and Malaiya, Y.K., "Using Neural Networks in Reliability Prediction," *IEEE Software,* vol. 9, no. 4, July 1992, pp. 53–59.

[Karu92c] Karunanithi, N., and Malaiya, Y.K., "The Scaling Problem in Neural Network for Software Reliability Prediction," *Proceedings of the Third International Symposium on Software Reliability Engineering,* IEEE Computer Society Press, October 1992, pp. 76–82.

[Karu92d] Karunanithi, N., "Generalization in the Cascade-Correlation Architecture: Some Experiments and Applications," Ph.D. dissertation, Computer Science Department, Colorado State University, Fort Collins, Colo., December 1992.

[Karu93a] Karunanithi, N., "A Neural Networks Approach for Software Reliability Growth Modeling in the Presence of Code Churn," *Proceedings of the 4th International Symposium on Software Reliability Engineering,* Denver, Colo., November 3–6, 1993, pp. 310–317.

[Karu93b] Karunanithi, N., "Identifying Fault-Prone Software Modules Using Connectionist Networks," *Proceedings of the International Workshop on Applications of Neural Networks to Telecommunications,* (IWANNT'93), October 18–20, 1993, pp. 266–272.

[Karu93c] Karunanithi, N., "Identifying Fault-Prone Software Modules Using Feed-Forward Networks: A Case Study," *Advances in Neural Information Processing Systems 6,* J. Cowan, G. Tesaruo, and J. Alspector (eds.), Morgan Kaufmann, San Francisco, Calif., 1993, pp. 793–800.

[Keen92] Keene, S., and Chris, L., "Combining Software and Hardware Aspects of Reliability," *Quality and Reliability Engineering International,* vol. 8, no. 4, 1992, pp. 419–426.

[Keil83] Keiller, P.A., Littlewood, B., Miller, D.R., and Sofer, A., "Comparison of Software Reliability Predictions," *Proceedings of the 13th IEEE International Symposium on Fault-Tolerant Computing (FTCS-13),* Milano, Italy, June 1983, pp. 128–134.

[Kell86] Kelly, J.P.J., Avižienis, A., Ulery, B.T., Swain, B.J., Lyu, R.T., Tai, A.T., and Tso, K.S., "Multiversion Software Development," *Proceedings IFAC Workshop SAFECOMP'86,* Sarlat, France, October 1986, pp. 43–49.

[Kell88] Kelly, J., Eckhardt, D., Caglayan, A., Knight, J., McAllister, D., and Vouk, M.,"A Large Scale Second Generation Experiment in Multi-Version Software: Description and Early Results," *Proceedings of the 18th International Symposium on Fault-Tolerant Computing,* Tokyo, Japan, June 1988, pp. 9–14.

[Kend77] Kendall, M.G., *The Advanced Theory of Statistics,* Oxford University Press, 1977.

[Kenn92] Kenney, G.Q., and Vouk, M.A., "Measuring the Field Quality of Wide-Distribution Commercial Software," *Proceedings of the 3rd IEEE International Symposium on Software Reliability Engineering (ISSRE'92),* Research Triangle Park, North Carolina, October 1992, pp. 351–357.

[Kenn93a] Kenney, G.Q., "Estimating Defects in Commercial Software During Operational Use," *IEEE Transactions on Reliability,* vol. 42, no. 1, 1993, pp. 107–115.

[Kenn93b] Kenney, G.Q., "The Next Release Effect in the Field Defect Model for Commercial Software," Ph.D. dissertation, North Carolina State University, Department of Computer Science, 1993.

[Khos89] Khoshgoftaar, T.M., and Woodcock, T.G., "A Simulation Study of the Performance of the Akaike Information Criterion for the Selection of Software Reliability Growth Models," *Proceedings of the 27th Annual South East Region ACM Conference,* April 1989, pp. 419–423.

[Khos90] Khoshgoftaar, T.M., and Munson J.C., "Predicting Software Development Errors Using Software Complexity Metrics," *IEEE Journal on Selected Areas in Communications,* vol. 8, no. 2, February 1990, pp. 253–261.

[Khos91] Khoshgoftaar, T.M., and Woodcock, T.G., "Software Reliability Model Selection: A Case Study," *Proceedings of the Second International Symposium on Software Reliability Engineering,* May 1991, pp. 183–191.

[Khos92a] Khoshgoftaar, T.M., and Munson, J.C., "A Measure of Software System Complexity and Its Relationship to Faults," *Proceedings of the 1992 International Simulation Technology Conference,* Houston, Texas, November 1992, pp. 267–272.

[Khos92b] Khoshgoftaar, T.M., and Munson, J.C., "Applications of a Relative Complexity Metric for Predicting Source Code Complexity at the Design Phase," *Proceedings of the Second Software Engineering Research Forum,* Melbourne, Florida, November 1992, pp. 191–198.

[Khos92c] Khoshgoftaar, T.M., Munson, J.C., Bhattacharya, B.B., and Richardon, G., "Predictive Modeling Techniques of Software Quality from Software Measures," *IEEE Transactions on Software Engineering,* vol. 18, no. 11, November 1992, pp. 979–987.

[Khos92d] Khoshgoftaar, T.M., Pandya, A.S., and More, H.B., "A Neural Network Approach for Predicting Software Development Faults," *Proceedings of the Third International Symposium on Software Reliability Engineering,* IEEE Computer Society Press, October 1992, pp. 83–89.

[Khos93a] Khoshgoftaar, T.M., Munson, J.C., and Lanning, D.L., "Dynamic System Complexity," *Proceedings of the IEEE-CS International Software Metrics Symposium,* Baltimore, Md., May 1993, pp. 129–140.

[Khos93b] Khoshgoftaar, T.M., Munson, J.C., and Lanning, D.L., "A Comparative Study of Predictive Models for Program Changes During System Testing and Maintenance," *Proceedings of the Conference on Software Maintenance,* Montreal, Quebec, Canada, September 1993, pp. 72–79.

[Khos93c] Khoshgoftaar, T.M., Lanning, D.L., and Pandya, A.S., "A Neural Network Modeling Methodology for the Detection of High-Risk Programs," *Proceedings of the Fourth International Symposium on Software Reliability Engineering,* Denver, Colo., November 1993, pp. 302–309.

[Khos94a] Khoshgoftaar, T.M., Lanning, D.L., and Pandya, A.S., "A Comparative Study of Pattern Recognition Techniques for Quality Evaluation of Telecommunications Software," *IEEE Journal on Selected Areas in Communications,* vol. 12, no. 2, February 1994, pp. 279–291.

[Khos94b] Khoshgoftaar, T.M., Munson, J.C., and Lanning, D.L., "Alternative Approaches for the Use of Metrics to Order Programs by Complexity," *Journal of Systems and Software,* vol. 24, no. 3, March 1994, pp. 211–221.

[Kim89] Kim, K.H., and Welch, H.O., "Distributed Execution of Recovery Blocks: An Approach for Uniform Treatment of Hardware and Software Faults in Real-Time Applications," *IEEE Transactions on Computers,* vol. 38, no. 5, May 1989, pp. 626–636.

[Kits93] Kitson, D., and Masters, S., "An Analysis of SEI Software Process Results: 1987–1991," *Proceedings of the Fifteenth International Conference on Software Engineering,* IEEE Computer Society Press, 1993, pp. 68–77.

[Klat91] Klatte, R., Kulisch, U., Neaga, M., Ratz, D., and Ullrich, C., *PASCAL-XSC—Language Description with Examples,* Springer-Verlag, New York, 1991.

[Klat92] Klatte, R., Kulisch, U., Lawo, C., Rauch, M., and Wiethoff, A., *C-XSC,* Springer-Verlag, New York, 1992.

[Knaf92] Knafl, G., "Overview of the Software Reliability Models, Estimation Procedures, and Predictive Performance Measures," lecture notes for Tutorial Track 2a for the *Third International Symposium on Software Reliability Engineering,* October 1992.

[Knig86] Knight, J.C., and Leveson, N.G., "An Experimental Evaluation of the Assumption of Independence in Multiversion Programming," *IEEE Transactions on Software Engineering,* vol. SE-12, no. 1, 1986, pp. 96–109.

[Knut70] Knuth, D., *The Art of Computer Programming: Semi-Numerical Algorithms,* Addison-Wesley Book Company, Reading, Mass., 1970, pp. 550–554.

[Knut84] Knuth, D.E., "A Torture Test for TEX," Technical Report No. STAN-CS-84-1027, Department of Computer Science, Stanford University, Stanford, Calif., 1984.

[Knut86] Knuth, D.E., *TEX: The Program,* Addison-Wesley, Reading, Mass., 1986.

[Knut89] Knuth, D.E., "The Errors of TEX," *Software Practice and Experience,* vol. 19, no. 7, July 1989, pp. 607–685.

[Kozl70] Kozlov, B.A., and Ushakov, U.A., *Reliability Handbook,* L.H. Koopmans and J. Rosenblat (eds.), Holt Rinehart and Winston, 1970.

[Kreu86] Kreutzer, W., *System Simulation: Programming Styles and Languages,* International Computer Science Series, Addison-Wesley Publishing Company, Menlo Park, Calif., 1986.

[Krug88] Kruger, G., "Project Management Using Software Reliability Growth Models," *Hewlett-Packard Journal,* June, 1988, pp. 30–35.

[Kuli81] Kulisch, U., and Miranker, W.L., *Computer Arithmetic in Theory and Practice,* Academic Press, New York, 1981.

[Kuli93] Kulisch, U., private communication, 1993.

[Kypa84] Kyparisis, J., and Singpurwalla, N.D., "Bayesian Inference for the Weibull Process with Applications to Assessing Software Reliability Growth and Predicting Software Failures," *Computer Science and Statistics,* 16th Symposium Interface, Atlanta, Georgia, 1984, pp. 57–64.

[Lang85] Langberg, N., and Singpurwalla, N.D., "A Unification of Some Software Reliability Models," *SIAM Journal of Scientific and Statistical Computation,* vol. 6, no. 3, 1985, pp. 781–790.

[Lapr84a] Laprie, J.-C., "Dependability Modeling and Evaluation of Hardware-and-Software Systems," *Proceedings of the 2nd GI/NTG/GMR Conference on Fault-Tolerant Computing,* Bonn, Germany, September 1984, pp. 202–215.

[Lapr84b] Laprie, J.-C., "Dependability Evaluation of Software Systems in Operation," *IEEE Transactions on Software Engineering,* vol. SE-10, no. 6, November 1984, pp. 701–714.

[Lapr85] Laprie, J.-C., "Dependable Computing and Fault Tolerance: Concepts and Terminology," *Proceedings of the 15th International Symposium on Fault-Tolerant Computing (FTCS-15),* Ann Arbor, Michigan, 1985, pp. 2–11.

[Lapr87] Laprie, J.-C., Arlat, J., Béounes, C., Kanoun, K., and Hourtolle, C., "Hardware and Software Fault-Tolerance: Definition and Analysis of Architectural Solutions," *Proceedings of the 17th International Symposium on Fault-Tolerant Computing (FTCS-17),* Pittsburgh, Pennsylvania, 1987, pp. 116–121.

[Lapr89] Laprie, J.-C., "Hardware-and-Software Dependability Evaluation," *Proceedings of the IFIP 11th World Congress,* San Francisco, Calif., August 1989, pp. 109–114.

[Lapr90a] Laprie, J.-C., Arlat, J., Béounes, C., and Kanoun, K., "Definition and Analysis of Hardware- and Software-Fault-Tolerant Architectures," *IEEE Computer,* vol. 23, no. 7, July 1990, pp. 39–51. Reprinted in *Fault-Tolerant Software Systems: Techniques and Applications,* Hoang Pham (ed.), IEEE Computer Society Press, 1992, pp. 5–17.

[Lapr90b] Laprie, J.-C., Béounes, C., Kaâniche, M., and Kanoun, K., "The Transformation Approach to the Modeling and Evaluation of the Reliability and Availability Growth," *Proceedings 20th IEEE International Symposium on Fault-Tolerant Computing, (FTCS-20),* IEEE Computer Society, 1990, pp. 364–371.

[Lapr91] Laprie, J.-C., Kanoun, K., Béounes, C., and Kaâniche, M., "The KAT (Knowledge-Action-Transformation) Approach to the Modeling and Evaluation of Reliability and Availability Growth," *IEEE Transactions on Software Engineering* vol. 17, no. 4, April 1991, pp. 370–382.

[Lapr92a] Laprie, J.-C., *Dependability: Basic Concepts and Terminology, Dependable Computing and Fault-Tolerant Systems,* vol. 5, J.-C. Laprie (ed.), Springer-Verlag, Wien, New York, 1992.

[Lapr92b] Laprie, J.-C., and Kanoun, K., "X-Ware Reliability and Availability Modeling," *IEEE Transactions on Software Engineering* vol. 18, no. 2, February 1992, pp. 130–147.

[Lapr92c] Laprie, J.-C., "For a Product-in-a-Process Approach to Software Reliability Evaluation," *Proceedings of the 3rd International Symposium on Software Reliability Engineering, ISSRE'92,* Research Triangle Park, North Carolina, October 1992, pp. 134–139.

[Lapr93] Laprie, J.-C., "Dependability: From Concepts to Limits," *Proceedings SAFECOMP'93,* Springer-Verlag, Poznan, Poland, 1993, pp. 157–168.

[Lee90] Lee, P.A., and Anderson, T., *Fault Tolerance: Principles and Practices,* Springer-Verlag, New York, 1990.

[Lee91] Lee, I., Iyer, R.K., and Tang, D., "Error/Failure Analysis Using Event Logs from Fault Tolerant Systems," *Proceedings 21st International Symposium on Fault-Tolerant Computing,* June 1991, pp. 10–17.

[Lee92] Lee, I., and Iyer, R.K., "Analysis of Software Halts in Tandem System," *Proceedings of the 3rd International Symposium on Software Reliability Engineering,* October 1992, pp. 227–236.

[Lee92a] Lee, L., *The Day the Phones Stopped: How People Get Hurt When Computers Go Wrong,* Donald I. Fine, Inc., New York, 1992.

[Lee93a] Lee, I., Tang, D., Iyer, R.K., and Hsueh, M.C., "Measurement-Based Evaluation of Operating System Fault Tolerance," *IEEE Transactions on Reliability,* vol. 42, no. 2, June 1993, pp. 238–249.

[Lee93b] Lee, I., and Iyer, R.K., "Faults, Symptoms, and Software Fault Tolerance in the Tandem GUARDIAN90 Operating System," *Proceedings of the 23rd International Symposium on Fault-Tolerant Computing,* Toulouse, France, June 1993, pp. 20–29.

[Lee94a] Lee, I., and Iyer, R.K., "Identifying Software Problems Using Symptoms," *Proceedings of the 24th International Symposium on Fault-Tolerant Computing,* San Antonio, Texas, June 1994, pp. 320–329.

[Lee94b] Lee, I., "Software Dependability in the Operational Phase," Ph.D. dissertation, Department of Electrical and Computer Engineering, University of Illinois at Urbana-Champaign, October 1994.

[Lee95] Lee, I., and Iyer, R.K., "Software Dependability in the Tandem GUARDIAN System," *IEEE Transactions on Software Engineering,* vol. 21, no. 5, May 1995, pp. 455–467.

[LeGa90] LeGall, G., Adam, M.F., Derriennic, H., Moreau, B., and Valette, N., "Studies on Measuring Software," *IEEE Journal of Selected Areas in Communications,* vol. 8, no. 2, 1990, pp. 234–245.

[Leve86] Leveson, N., "Software Safety: What, Why and How," *ACM Computing Surveys,* June 1986, pp. 125–164.

[Leve87] Levendel, Y., "Quality and Reliability Estimation for Large Software Projects Using a Time-Dependent Model," *Proceedings of COMPSAC 87,* Tokyo, Japan, October 1987, pp. 340–346.

[Leve89] Levendel, Y., "Defects and Reliability Analysis of Large Software Systems: Field Experience," *Proceedings of the 19th IEEE International Symposium on Fault-Tolerant Computing (FTCS-19),* Chicago, June 1989, pp. 238–244.

[Leve90] Levendel, Y., "Reliability Analysis of Large Software Systems: Defect Data Modeling," *IEEE Transactions on Software Engineering,* vol. SE-16, no. 2, February 1990, pp. 141–152.

[Leve91] Levendel, Y., "Software Quality Improvement Process: When to Stop Testing," *Proceedings Software Engineering & Its Applications,* Toulouse, France, December 1991, pp. 729–749.

[Leve91a] Leveson, N.G., "Safety Verification of Ada Programs Using Software Fault Trees," *IEEE Software,* July 1991, pp. 48–59.

[Leve93] Levendel, Y., "Fault-Tolerance Cost Effectiveness," *Proceedings of the Third Workshop on Issues in Software Reliability Workshop Program,* U.S. West Advanced Technologies, Boulder, Colorado, November 1–2, 1993.

[Leve95] Levendel, Y., "The Cost Effectiveness of Telecommunication Service Dependability," *Software Fault Tolerance,* Lyu, M.R. (ed.), Wiley & Sons, Inc., January 1995, pp. 279–314.

[Lewi64] Lewis, P.A., "A Branching Poisson Process Model for the Analysis of Computer Failure Patterns," *Journal of Royal Statistical Society,* series B, vol. 26, no. 3, 1964, pp. 398–456.

[Li93] Li, N., and Malaiya, Y., "Enhancing Accuracy of Software Reliability Prediction," *Proceedings of the 4th International Symposium on Software Reliability Engineering,* November 4–6, 1993, pp. 71–79.

[Lin83] Lin, J., and Costello, Jr., D.J., *Error Control Coding—Fundamentals and Applications,* Prentice-Hall, Englewood Cliffs, New Jersey, 1983.

[Lin90] Lin, T.T., and Siewiorek, D.P., "Error Log Analysis: Statistical Modeling and Heuristic Trend Analysis," *IEEE Transactions on Reliability,* vol. 39, no. 4, October 1990, pp. 419–432.

[Lind89] Lind, R., and Vairavan, K., "An Experimental Investigation of Software Metrics and Their Relationship to Software Development Effort," *IEEE Transactions on Software Engineering,* vol. 15, no. 5, May 1989, pp. 649–653.

[Litt73] Littlewood, B. and Verrall, J., "A Bayesian Reliability Growth Model for Computer Software," *Journal of the Royal Statistical Society,* series C, vol. 22, no. 3, 1973, pp. 332–346.

[Litt74] Littlewood, B., and Verrall, V., "A Bayesian Reliability Model with a Stochastically Monotone Failure Rate," *IEEE Transactions on Reliability,* vol. R-23, no. 2, 1974, pp. 108–114.

[Litt78] Littlewood, B., "Validation of a Software Model," Software Life Cycle Management Workshop, Atlanta, Georgia, 1978, published by the International Business Services, Inc., pp. 146–152.

[Litt79a] Littlewood, B., "How to Measure Software Reliability and How Not To," *IEEE Transactions on Reliability,* vol. R-28, no. 2, June 1979, pp. 103–110.

[Litt79b] Littlewood, B., "A Software Reliability Model for Modular Program Structure," *IEEE Transactions on Reliability,* vol. R-28, no. 2, June 1979, pp. 241–246.

[Litt80a] Littlewood, B., "The Littlewood-Verrall Model for Software Reliability Compared with Some Rivals," *Journal of Systems and Software,* vol. 1, no. 3, 1980, pp. 251–258.

[Litt80b] Littlewood, B., "Theory of Software Reliability: How Good Are They and How Can They Be Improved?," *IEEE Transactions on Software Engineering,* vol. SE-6, 1980, pp. 489–500.

[Litt80c] Littlewood, B., "A Bayesian Differential Debugging Model for Software Reliability," *Proceedings of the International Computer Software Applications Conference,* IEEE Computer Society, 1980, pp. 511–519.

[Litt81] Littlewood, B., "Stochastic Reliability Growth: A Model for Fault-Removal in Computer Programs and Hardware Designs," *IEEE Transactions on Reliability,* vol. R-30, no. 4, October 1981, pp. 313–320.

[Litt86] Littlewood, B., Abdel-Ghaly, A.A., and Chan, P.Y., "Tools for the Analysis of the Accuracy of Software Reliability Predictions," *Software System Design Methods,* Springer-Verlag, Heidelberg, 1986, pp. 299–335.

[Litt87] Littlewood, B., and Miller, D.R., "A Conceptual Model of Multi-Version Software," *Proceedings of the 17th International Symposium on Fault-Tolerant Computing,* IEEE Computer Society Press, July 1987, pp. 150–155.

[Litt87a] Littlewood, B., *Software Reliability: Achievement and Assessment,* Blackwell, Oxford, 1987.

[Litt87b] Littlewood, B., "How Good are Software Reliability Predictions?" *Software Reliability: Achievement and Assessment,* Blackwell, Oxford, 1987, pp. 172–191.

[Litt87c] Littlewood, B., and Sofer, A., "A Bayesian Modification to the Jelinski-Moranda Software Reliability Growth Model," *Journal of Software Engineering,* no. 2, 1987, pp. 30–41.

[Litt88] Littlewood, B., "Forecasting Software Reliability," *Software Reliability Modeling and Identification,* S. Bittanti (ed.), Springer-Verlag, Berlin, 1988, pp. 140–209.

[Litt89] Littlewood, B., and Miller, D.R., "Conceptual Modeling of Coincident Failures in Multiversion Software," *IEEE Transactions on Software Engineering,* vol. 15, no. 12, 1989, pp. 1596–1614.

[Litt91] Littlewood, B., "Limits to Evaluation of Software Dependability," in *Software Reliability and Metrics,* B. Littlewood and N. Fenton (eds.), Elsevier, Amsterdam, 1991.

[Litt93] Littlewood, B., and Strigini, L., "Validation of Ultra-High Dependability for Software-Based Systems," *Communications of the ACM,* vol. 36, no. 11, November 1993.

[Liu87] Liu, G., "A Bayesian Assessing Method of Software Reliability Growth," *Reliability Theory and Applications,* S. Osaki and J. Cao (eds.), World Scientific, 1987, pp. 237–244.

[Lorc89] Lorczak, P.R., Caglayan, A.K., and Eckhardt, D.E., "A Theoretical Investigation of Generalized Voters for Redundant Systems," *Proceedings 19th Annual International Symposium on Fault-Tolerant Computing (FTCS-19),* 1989, pp. 444–451.

[Lu92] Lu, M., Brocklehurst, S., and Littlewood, B., "Combinations of Predictions Obtained from Different Software Reliability Growth Models," *Proceedings 10th Annual Software Reliability Symposium,* 1992, pp. 24–33.

[Lyu89] Lyu, M.R., and Kinlaw, J., "ASAS Software Reliability Prediction: Methodology and Result," in *Proceedings ATT/HP/JPL Software Reliability Measurement Technical Exchange Meeting,* Pasadena, Calif., June 1989.

[Lyu91a] Lyu, M.R., and Nikora, A.P., "Software Reliability Measurements Through Combination Models: Approaches, Results, and a Case Tool," *Proceedings of the 15th Annual International Computer Software and Applications Conference (COMPSAC'91),* Tokyo, Japan, September 1991, pp. 577–584.

[Lyu91b] Lyu, M.R., "Measuring Reliability of Embedded Software: An Empirical Study with JPL Project Data," *Proceedings of the International Conference on Probabilistic Safety Assessment and Management,* Beverly Hills, Calif., February 1991, pp. 493–500.

[Lyu91c] Lyu, M.R., and Nikora, A.P., "A Heuristic Approach for Software Reliability Prediction: The Equally Weighted Linear Combination Model," *Proceedings of the 1991 International Symposium on Software Reliability Engineering,* IEEE Computer Society Press, May 1991, pp. 172–181.

[Lyu92a] Lyu, M.R., "Software Reliability Measurements in N-Version Software Execution Environment," *Proceedings of the 1992 International Symposium on Software Reliability Engineering,* Raleigh, North Carolina, 1992, pp. 254–263.

[Lyu92b] Lyu, M.R., and Avižienis, A., "Assuring Design Diversity in N-Version Software: A Design paradigm for N-Version Programming," *Dependable Computing and Fault-Tolerant Systems,* J.F. Meyer and R.D. Schichting (eds.), Springer-Verlag, Wien, Austria, 1992, pp. 197–218.

[Lyu92c] Lyu, M.R., and Nikora, A.P., "Using Software Reliability Models More Effectively," *IEEE Software,* July 1992, pp. 43–52.

[Lyu92d] Lyu, M.R., and Nikora, A.P., "CASRE—A Computer-Aided Software Reliability Estimation Tool," *CASE 92 Proceedings,* Montreal, Canada, July 1992, pp. 264–275.

[Lyu93a] Lyu, M.R., and He, Y., "Improving the N-Version Programming Process Through the Evolution of Design Paradigm," *IEEE Transactions on Reliability,* vol. 42, no. 2, 1993, pp. 179–189.

[Lyu93b] Lyu, M.R., Nikora, A.P., and Farr, W.H., "A Systematic and Comprehensive Tool for Software Reliability Modeling and Measurement," *Proceedings of the 23rd International Symposium on Fault-Tolerant Computing (FTCS-23),* Toulouse, France, June 1993, pp. 648–653.

[Lyu94a] Lyu, M.R., Chen, J., and Avižienis, A., "Experience in Metrics and Measurements for N-Version Programming," *International Journal of Reliability, Quality and Safety Engineering,* vol. 1, no. 1, 1994, pp. 41–62.

[Lyu94b] Lyu, M.R., Horgan, J.R., and London, S., "A Coverage Analysis Tool for the Effectiveness of Software Testing," *IEEE Transactions on Reliability,* December 1994, pp. 527–535.

[Lyu95a] Lyu, M.R. (ed.), *Software Fault Tolerance,* John Wiley & Sons, Chichester, U.K., January 1995.

[Lyu95b] Lyu, M.R., Yu, J., Keramidas, E., and Dalal, S., "ARMOR: Analyzer for Reducing Module Operational Risk," *Proceedings of the 25th International Symposium on Fault Tolerant Computing (FTCS-25),* Pasadena, Calif., June 1995, pp. 137–142.

[Madd84] Madden, W.A., and Rone, K.Y., "Design, Development, Integration: Space Shuttle Primary Flight Software System," *Communications of the ACM,* vol. 27, no. 8, 1984, pp. 902–913.

[Mala90a] Malaiya, Y.K., Karunanithi, N., and Verma, P., "Predictability Measures for Software Reliability Models," *Proceedings of the 14th IEEE International Computer Software and Applications Conference (COMPSAC 90),* October 1990, pp. 7–12.

[Mala90b] Malaiya, Y.K., and Srimani, P.K. (eds.), *Software Reliability Models: Theoretical Developments, Evaluation and Applications,* IEEE Computer Society Press, 1990.

[Mala92] Malaiya, Y.K., Karunanithi, S., and Verma, P., "Predictability of Software-Reliability Models," *IEEE Transactions on Reliability,* vol. R-41, December 1992, pp. 539–546.

[Mart82] Martin, D.J., "Dissimilar Software in High Integrity Applications in Flight Controls," *Proceedings AGARD-CP 330,* September 1982, pp. 36.1–36.13.

[Mart90] Martini, M.R., Kanoun, K., and de Souza, J.M., "Software Reliability Evaluation of the TROPICO-R Switching System," *IEEE Transactions on Reliability,* vol. 33, no. 3, 1990, pp. 369–379.

[Mart91] Martini, M.R., and de Souza, J.M., "Reliability Assessment of Computer Systems Design," *Microelectronics Reliability,* vol. 31, no. 2/3, 1991, pp. 237–244.

[Math91] Mathur, A.P., "On the Relative Strengths of Data Flow and Mutation Testing," *Proceedings of the Ninth Annual Pacific Northwest Software Quality Conference,* October 7–8, Portland, Oreg., 1991.

[Mats88] Matsumoto, K., Inoue, K., Kikuno, T., and Torii, K., "Experimental Evaluation of Software Reliability Growth Models," *Proceedings of the 18th International Symposium on Fault-Tolerant Computing,* Tokyo Japan, June 1988, pp. 148–153.

[Mayr91] von Mayrhauser, A., and Keables, J., "A Data Collection Environment for Software Reliability Research," *Proceedings of the 2nd International Symposium on Software Reliability Engineering,* IEEE Computer Society Press, 1991.

[Mayr92] von Mayrhauser, A., and Keables, J., "A Simulation Environment for Early Life Cycle Software Reliability Research Prediction," *Proceedings of the International Test Conference,* IEEE Computer Society Press, 1992.

[Mayr93] von Mayrhauser, A., Malaiya, Y.K., Keables, J., and Srimani, P.K., "On the Need for Simulation for Better Characterization of Software Reliability," *Proceedings of the 4th International Symposium on Software Reliability Engineering,* Denver, Colo., 1993.

[Mays90] Mays, R., Jones, C., Holloway, G., and Studinski, D., "Experiences with Defect Prevention," *IBM Systems Journal,* vol. 29, no. 1, 1990.

[Mazz88] Mazzuchi, T.A., and Soyer, T., "A Bayes Empirical-Bayes Model for Software Reliability," *IEEE Transactions on Reliability,* vol. R-37, pp. 248–254.

[McAl85] McAllister, D.F., "Some Observations on Costs and Reliability in Software Fault-Tolerant Techniques," *Proceedings TIMS-ORSA Conference,* Boston, Mass., April 1985.

[McAl90] McAllister, D.F., Sun, C.E., and Vouk, M.A., "Reliability of Voting in Fault-Tolerant Software Systems for Small Output Spaces," *IEEE Transactions on Reliability,* vol. 39, no. 5, 1990, pp. 524–534.

[McAl91] McAllister, D.F., and Scott, R.K., "Cost Models for Fault-Tolerant Software," *Journal of Information and Software Technology,* vol. 33, no. 8, October 1991, pp. 594–603.

[McCa76] McCabe, T.J., "A Complexity Metric," *IEEE Transactions on Software Engineering,* vol. 2, no. 4, December 1976, pp. 308–320.

[McCo79] McConnell, S.R., Siewiorek, D.P., and Tsao, M.M., "The Measurement and Analysis of Transient Errors in Digital Computer Systems," *Proceedings of the 9th International Symposium on Fault-Tolerant Computing (FTCS-9),* Madison, Wisconsin, June 1979, pp. 67–70.

[Mell93] Mellor, P., "Failures, Faults, and Changes in Dependability Measurement," *Information and Software Technology,* vol. 34, no. 10, October, 1992, pp. 640–654.

[Merc94] Mercer, "Product Advisor Survey," Trouble Reports, Mercer Analysis, 1994.

[Meye78] Meyer, J.F., "On Evaluating the Performability of Degradable Computing Systems," *Proceedings of the 8th IEEE International Symposium on Fault-Tolerant Computing (FTCS-8),* Toulouse, France, June 1978, pp. 44–49.

[Meye88] Meyer, J.F., and Wei, L., "Analysis of Workload Influence on Dependability," *Proceedings of the 18th International Symposium on Fault-Tolerant Computing (FTCS-18),* Tokyo, June 1988, pp. 84–89.

[Meye92] Meyer, J.F., "Performability: A Retrospective and Some Pointers to the Future," *Performance Evaluation,* vol. 14, February 1992, pp. 139–156.

[Mili90] Mili, A., *An Introduction to Program Fault-Tolerance—A Structured Programming Approach,* Prentice-Hall International Ltd., U.K., 1990.

[Mill86] Miller, D.R., "Exponential Order Statistic Models of Software Reliability Growth," *IEEE Transactions on Software Engineering,* vol. SE-12, no. 1, January 1986, pp. 12–24.

[Mill90] Miller, G., "The Magic Number Seven," *Psychological Review,* vol. 63, 1990.

[Mill92] Miller, K.W., Morell, L.J., Noonan, R.E., Park, S.K., Nicol, D.M., Murrill, B.W., and Voas, J.M., "Estimating the Probability of Failure When Testing Reveals No Failures," *IEEE Transactions on Software Engineering,* vol. 18, no. 1, 1992, pp. 33–43.

[Mood74] Mood, A., Graybill, F., and Boes, D., *Introduction to the Theory of Statistics,* 3d ed., McGraw-Hill, Inc., New York, 1974.

[Mora72] Moranda, P.L., and Jelinski, Z., *Final Report on Software Reliability Study,* McDonnell Douglas Astronautics Company, MADC Report Number 63921, 1972.

[Mora75a] Moranda, P.B., "Software Reliability Predictions," *Proceedings of the Sixth Triennial World Congress of the International Federation of Automatic Control,* 1975, pp. 34.2–34.7.

[Mora75b] Moranda, P.B., "Predictions of Software Reliability During Debugging," *Proceedings of the Annual Reliability and Maintainability Symposium,* Washington, D.C., 1975, pp. 327–332.

[Mora79] Moranda, P.B., "Event-Altered Rate Models for General Reliability Analysis," *IEEE Transactions on Reliability,* vol. R-28, no. 5, 1979, pp. 376–381.

[Morg89] Morgan, N., and Bourlard, H., "Generalization and Parameter Estimation in Feedforward Nets: Some Experiments," *Advances in Neural Information Processing Systems 2,* D. Touretzky (ed.), Morgan Kaufman, San Francisco, 1989, pp. 630–637.

[Mosl94] Mosleh, A., *Reliability Data Collection and Analysis System (REDCAS),* Center for Reliability Engineering, University of Maryland, College Park, Md., 1994.

[Mour87] Mourad, S., and Andrews, D., "On the Reliability of the IBM MVS/XA Operating System," *IEEE Transactions on Software Engineering,* vol. SE-13, no. 10, October 1987, pp. 1135–1139.

[Muns89] Munson, J.C., and Khoshgoftaar, T.M., "The Dimensionality of Program Complexity," *Proceedings of the 11th Annual International Conference on Software Engineering,* Pittsburgh, May 1989, pp. 245–253.

[Muns90a] Munson, J.C., and Khoshgoftaar, T.M., "Regression Modeling of Software Quality: Empirical Investigation," *Journal of Information and Software Technology,* vol. 32, no. 2, March 1990, pp. 105–114.

[Muns90b] Munson, J.C., and Khoshgoftaar, T.M., "Applications of a Relative Complexity Metric for Software Project Management," *Journal of Systems and Software,* vol. 12, no. 3, 1990, pp. 283–291.

[Muns90c] Munson, J.C., and Khoshgoftaar, T.M., "The Relative Software Complexity Metric: A Validation Study," *Proceedings of the Software Engineering 1990 Conference,* London, 1990, pp. 89–102.

[Muns91] Munson, J.C., and Khoshgoftaar, T.M., "The Use of Software Complexity Metrics in Software Reliability Modeling," *Proceedings of the International Symposium on Software Reliability Engineering,* Austin, Texas, May 1991, pp. 2–11.

[Muns92] Munson, J.C., and Khoshgoftaar, T.M., "The Detection of Fault-Prone Programs," *IEEE Transactions on Software Engineering,* vol. 18, no. 5, 1992, pp. 423–433.

[Muns93] Munson, J.C., and Khoshgoftaar, T.M., "Measurement of Data Structure Complexity," *Journal of Systems and Software,* vol. 12, no. 3, March 1993, pp. 217–225.

[Musa75] Musa, J.D., "A Theory of Software Reliability and Its Applications," *IEEE Transactions on Software Engineering,* vol. SE-1, no. 3, 1975, pp. 312–327.

[Musa77a] Musa, J.D., "Program for Software Reliability and System Test Schedule Estimation—User's Guide," Bell Telephone Laboratories, Inc., 1977.

[Musa77b] Musa, J.D., and Hamilton, P.A., "Program for Software Reliability and System Test Schedule Estimation—Program Documentation," Bell Telephone Laboratories, Inc., 1977.

[Musa78] Musa, J.D., "Progress in Software Reliability Measurement," *Second Software Life Cycle Management Workshop,* published by the IEEE, New York, 1978, pp. 153–155.

[Musa79] Musa, J.D., "Software Reliability Data," Technical Report, Data and Analysis Center for Software, Rome Air Development Center, Griffins AFB, New York, 1979.

[Musa79a] Musa, J.D., "Validity of Execution—Time Theory of Software Reliability," *IEEE Transactions on Reliability,* vol. R-28, no. 3, 1979, pp. 181–191.

[Musa79b] Musa, J.D., "Software Reliability Measures Applied to System Engineering," *Proceedings of the National Computer Conference,* 1979, pp. 941–946.

[Musa80] Musa, J.D., "The Measurement and Management of Software Reliability," *Proceedings of the IEEE,* vol. 68, no. 9, 1980, pp. 1131–1143.

[Musa83] Musa, John D., and Okumoto, K., "Software Reliability Models: Concepts, Classification, Comparisons, and Practice," *Electronic Systems Effectiveness and Life Cycle Costing,* J.K. Skwirzynski (ed.), NATO ASI Series, F3, Springer-Verlag, Heidelberg, pp. 395–424.

[Musa84] Musa, J.D., and Okumoto, K. "A Logarithmic Poisson Execution Time Model for Software Reliability Measurement," *Proceedings Seventh International Conference on Software Engineering,* Orlando, Florida, pp. 230–238.

[Musa84a] Musa, J.D., "Software Reliability," *Handbook of Software Engineering,* C.R. Vick and C.V. Ramamoorthy (eds.), Van Nostrand Reinhold, New York, 1984, pp. 392–412.

[Musa87] Musa, J.D., Iannino, A., and Okumoto, K., *Software Reliability—Measurement, Prediction, Application,* McGraw-Hill, New York, 1987.

[Musa90] Musa, J.D., and Everett, W.W., "Software-Reliability Engineering: Technology for the 1990s," *IEEE Software,* vol. 7, November 1990, pp. 36–43.

[Musa91a] Musa, J.D., "Reduced Operation Software," *ACM Software Engineering Notes,* vol. 16, no. 3, July 1991, p. 78.

[Musa91b] Musa, J.D., "Rationale for Fault Exposure Ratio K," *ACM Software Engineering Notes,* vol. 16, no. 3, July 1991, p. 99.

[Musa93] Musa, J.D., "Operational Profiles in Software Reliability Engineering, *IEEE Software,* vol. 10, no. 2, March 1993, pp. 14–32.

[Musa94] Musa, J.D., "Sensitivity of Field Failure Intensity to Operational Profile Errors," *Proceedings of the 5th International Symposium on Software Reliability Engineering,* Monterey, Calif., November 6–9, 1994, pp. 334–337.

[Myer90] Myers, R.H., *Classical and Modern Regression with Applications,* Duxbury Press, Boston, Mass., 1990.

[Nage82] Nagel, P.M., and Skrivan, J.A., "Software Reliability: Repetitive Run Experimentation and Modeling," Report NASA CR-165836, February 1982.

[Naka92] Nakamura, K. (ed.), *Ayumi: Continuous Improvement of Software Quality Is Key at Fujitsu in Japan,* JUSE Press, 1992.

[Navl87] Navlakha, J.K., "Measuring the Effect of External and Internal Interface on Software Development," *Proceedings of the 20th Annual Hawaii International Conference on System Sciences,* 1987, pp. 127–136.

[Nels87] Nelson, V.P., and Carroll, B.D. (eds.), *Tutorial: Fault-Tolerant Computing,* IEEE Computer Society Press, 1987.

[Neuf93] Neufelder, A.M., *Ensuring Software Reliability,* Marcel Dekker, Inc., New York, 1993.

[Nico90] Nicola, V.F., and Goyal, A., "Modeling of Correlated Failures and Community Error Recovery in Multi-Version Software," *IEEE Transactions on Software Engineering,* vol. 16, no. 3, 1990.

[Niko92] Nikora, A.P., Lyu, M.R., and Antczak, T.M., "A Linear Combination Software Reliability Modeling Tool with a Graphically Oriented User Interface," *Proceedings of Symposium on Assessment of Quality Software Development Tools,* New Orleans, Louisana, May 1992, pp. 21–31.

[Niko93] Nikora, A.P., "CASRE User's Guide," Jet Propulsion Laboratories, August 1993.

[Nils90] Nilsson, J.N., *The Mathematical Foundations of Learning Machines,* Morgan Kaufmann, San Francisco, 1990, chapters 2 and 3.

[Ohba84] Ohba, M., "Software Reliability Analysis Models," *IBM Journal of Research and Development,* vol. 21, no. 4, July 1984, pp. 428–443.

[Ohte90] Ohtera, H., and Yamada, S., "Optimum Software-Release Time Considering an Error Detection Phenomenon During Operation," *IEEE Transactions on Reliability,* vol. R-39, 1990, pp. 596–599.

[Okum80] Okumoto, K., and Goel, A., "Optimum Release Time for Software Systems Based on Reliability and Other Performance Measures," *The Journal of Systems and Software,* vol. 1, no. 4, 1980, pp. 315–318.

[Onom93] Onoma, A.K., and Yamaura, T., "Practical Quantitative Methods of Improving Software Quality: Based on Decades of Experience," *NRC Workshop on Statistics in Software Engineering,* NRC, Washington, D.C., October 1993.

[Onom95] Onoma, A.K., and Yamaura, T., "Practical Steps Toward Quality Development," *IEEE Software,* vol. 12, no. 5, September 1995, pp. 68–77.

[Page80] Pages, A., and Gondran, M., *System Reliability,* Eyrolles, Paris, 1980; in French.

[Pant91] Pant, H., "Tracking Quality from Verification to Customer," *Software Quality from the Customer Viewpoint,* Globcom, Phoenix, Ariz., December 2–5, 1991.

[Panz81] Panzl, D.J., "A Method for Evaluating Software Development Techniques," *The Journal of Systems Software,* vol. 2, 1981, pp. 133–137.

[Papo65] Papoulis, A., *Probability, Random Variables, and Stochastic Processes,* McGraw-Hill Book Company, New York, N.Y., 1965, pp. 534–551.

[Park82] Parker, D., "Learning Logic," *Invention Record S81-64,* File 1, Stanford University, Stanford, Calif., 1982.

[Parn74] Parnas, D.L., "On a 'Buzzword': Hierarchical Structure," in *Proceedings of the 1974 IFIP Congress,* pp. 336–339.

[Paul93] Paulk, M.C., Curtis, B., Chrissis, M.B., and Weber, C.V., "Capability Maturity Model, Version 1.1," *IEEE Software,* July 1993, pp. 18–27.

[Pign88] Pignal, P.I., "An Analysis of Hardware and Software Availability Exemplified on the IBM 3725 Communication Controller," *IBM Journal of Research and Development,* vol. 32, no. 2, March 1988, pp. 268–278.

[Prue95] Pruett, W.R., *Personal Communication and Data Clarification Report,* NASA, January 26, 1995.

[RADC87] RADC, *Methodology for Software Reliability Prediction and Assessment,* RADC Technical Report TR-87-171, Rome Air Development Center, 1987. Revised in [RL92].

[Rama82] Ramamoorthy, C.V., and Bastani, F.B.: "Software Reliability—Status and Perspectives," *IEEE Transactions on Software Engineering,* vol. SE-8, no. 4, July 1982, pp. 354–371.

[Rand75] Randell, B., "System Structure for Software Fault Tolerance," *IEEE Transactions on Software Engineering,* vol. SE-1, no. 2, June 1975, pp. 220–232.

[Rapp90] Rapp, B., "Application of Software Reliability Models in Medical Imaging Systems," *Proceedings of the 1990 International Symposium on Software Reliability Engineering,* Washington, D.C., April 1990.

[Rauz93] Rauzy, A., "New Algorithms for Fault Tree Analysis," *Reliability Engineering and System Safety,* vol. 40, 1993, pp. 203–211.

[Robe83] Roberts, N., et al., *Introduction to Computer Simulation,* Addison-Wesley Book Company, Reading, Mass., 1983.

[Rodr87] Rodriguez, V., and Tsai, W., "A Tool for Discriminant Analysis and Classification of Software Metrics," *Information and Software Technology,* vol. 29, no. 3, April 1987, pp. 137–149.

[Rohn72] Rohn, W.B., and Arnold, T.F., "Design for Low Expected Downtime Control Systems," *Proceedings of the 4th International Conference on Computer Communications,* Philadelphia, Pennsylvania, June 1972, pp. 16–25.

[RL92] Rome Laboratory (RL), *Methodology for Software Reliability Prediction and Assessment,* Technical Report RL-TR-92-52, volumes 1 and 2, 1992.

[Ross89] Ross, N., "The Collection and Use of Data for Monitoring Software Projects," *Measurement for Software Control and Assurance,* B.A. Kitchenham and B. Littlewood (eds.), Elsevier Applied Science, London and New York, 1989, pp. 125–154.

[Roy69] Roy, B., *Modern Algebra and Graph Theory,* Dunod, Paris, 1969; in French.

[Rudi85] Rudin, H., "An Informal Overview of Formal Protocol Specification," *IEEE Communications Magazine,* vol. 23, no. 3, March 1985, pp. 46–52.

[Rume86] Rumelhart, D., Hinton, G., and Williams, R., "Learning Internal Representations by Error Propagation," *Parallel Distributed Processing,* vol. I, MIT Press, 1986, pp. 318–362.

[SAE90] SAE RMS Guidebook, *Reliability, Maintainability, Supportability Guidebook,* Society of Automotive Engineers (SAE) G-12 RMS Committee. To order, call (412) 776-4970 using #M-102.

[Sagl86] Saglietti, F., and Ehrenberger, W., "Software Diversity—Some Considerations about Benefits and Its Limitations," *Proceedings IFAC SAFECOMP'86,* 1986, pp. 27–34.

[Sahi92] Sahinoglu, M., "Compound-Poisson Software Reliability Model," *IEEE Transactions on Software Engineering,* SE-18, no. 7, 1992, pp. 624–630.

[Sahn87] Sahner, R.A., and Trivedi, K.S., "Reliability Modeling Using SHARPE," *IEEE Transactions on Reliability,* vol. R-36, no. 2, June 1987, pp. 186–193.

[Sahn95] Sahner, R.A., Trivedi, K.S., and Puliafito, A., *Performance and Reliability Analysis of Computer Systems: An Example-Based Approach Using the SHARPE Software Package,* Kluwer Academic Publishers, Boston, Mass., 1995.

[Sand63] Sandler, G.H., *Systems Reliability Engineering,* Prentice-Hall, Englewood Cliffs, New Jersey, 1963.

[Sarg79] Sargent, R.G., "An Introduction to the Selection and Use of Simulation Languages," Syracuse University, TR-79-1, Department of Industrial Engineering.

[SAS85] *SAS User's Guide: Basics,* SAS Institute, 1985.

[Saye90] Sayet, C., and Pilaud, E., "An Experience of a Critical Software Development," *Proceedings of the 20th IEEE International Symposium on Fault-Tolerant Computing (FTCS-20),* Newcastle, U.K., July 1990, pp. 36–45.

[Schi73] Schick, G.J., and Wolverton, R.W., "Assessment of Software Reliability," *Proceedings of the Operations Research,* Physica-Verlag, Wurzburg-Wien, 1973, pp. 395–422.

[Schn75] Schneidewind, N.F., "Analysis of Error Processes in Computer Software," *Sigplan Note,* vol. 10, no. 6, 1975, pp. 337–346.

[Schn92a] Schneidewind, N.F., "Methodology for Validating Software Metrics," *IEEE Transactions on Software Engineering,* vol. 18, no. 5, May 1992, pp. 410–421.

[Schn92b] Schneidewind, N.F., and Keller, T.W., "Application of Reliability Models to the Space Shuttle," *IEEE Software,* July 1992, pp. 28–33.

[Schn92c] Schneidewind, N.F., "Minimizing Risk in Applying Metrics on Multiple Projects," *Proceedings of the Third International Software Reliability Engineering,* Research Triangle Park, North Carolina, October 1992, pp. 173–182.

[Schn93a] Schneidewind, N.F., "Software Reliability Model with Optimal Selection of Failure Data," *Proceedings of the 1993 Annual Oregon Workshop on Software Metrics,* March 23, 1993.

[Schn93b] Schneidewind, N.F., "Optimal Selection of Failure Data for Predicting Failure Counts," *Proceedings of the 1993 Complex Systems Engineering Synthesis and Assessment Technology Workshop (CSESAW '93),* Naval Surface Warfare Center Dahlgren Division, July 20–22, 1993, pp. 141–157.

[Schn93c] Schneidewind, N.F., "Software Reliability Model with Optimal Selection of Failure Data," *IEEE Transactions on Software Engineering,* vol. 19, no. 11, November, 1993, pp. 1095–1104.

[Schn93d] Schneidewind, N.F., "Optimal Selection of Failure Data for Predicting Failure Counts," *Proceedings of the Fourth International Symposium on Software Reliability Engineering,* November, 1993, pp. 142–149.

[Scot83] Scott, R.K., Gault, J.W., and McAllister, D.F., "The Consensus Recovery Block," *Proceedings of the Total Systems Reliability Symposium,* 1983, pp. 3–9.

[Scot84a] Scott, R.K., Gault, J.W., McAllister, D.F., and Wiggs, J., "Investigating Version Dependence in Fault-Tolerant Software," *AGARD 361,* 1984, pp. 21.1–21.10.

[Scot84b] Scott, R.K., Gault, J.W., McAllister, D.F., and Wiggs, J., "Experimental Validation of Six Fault-Tolerant Software Reliability Models," *Proceedings of the IEEE 14th Fault-Tolerant Computing Symposium,* 1984, pp. 102–107.

[Scot87] Scott, R.K., Gault, J.W., and McAllister, D.F., "Fault-Tolerant Reliability Modeling," *IEEE Transactions on Software Engineering,* vol. SE-13, no. 5, 1987, pp. 582–592.

[Shen85] Shen, V., Yu, T., Thebaut, S., and Paulsen, L., "Identifying Error-Prone Software: An Empirical Study," *IEEE Transactions on Software Engineering,* vol. SE-11, no. 4, April 1985, pp. 317–323.

[Shim88] Shimeall, T.J., and Leveson, N.G., "An Empirical Comparison of Software Fault-Tolerance and Fault Elimination," *Proceedings of the 2nd Workshop on Software Testing, Verification and Analysis,* Banff, IEEE Computer Society, July 1988, pp. 180–187.

[Shin84] Shin, K.G., and Lee, Y.-H., "Evaluation of Error Recovery Blocks Used for Cooperating Processes," *IEEE Transactions on Software Engineering,* vol. SE-10, no. 6, November 1984, pp. 692–700.

[Shoo72] Shooman, M.L., "Probabilistic Models for Software Reliability Prediction," *Statistical Computer Performance Evaluation,* Academic Press, New York, June 1972, pp. 485–502.

[Shoo73] Shooman, M.L., "Operational Testing and Software Reliability Estimation During Program Developments," *Record of 1973 IEEE Symposium on Computer Software Reliability,* IEEE Computer Society, New York, 1973, pp. 51–57.

[Shoo76] Shooman, M.L., "Structural Models for Software Reliability Prediction," *Proceedings of the 2nd International Conference on Software Engineering,* IEEE Computer Society, New York, October 1976.

[Shoo77a] Shooman, M.L., "Spectre of Software Reliability and Its Exorcism," *Proceedings of the 1977 Joint Automatic Control Conference,* IEEE, New York, 1977, pp. 225–231.

[Shoo77b] Shooman, M.L., and Naturaja, S., *Effect of Manpower Deployment and Bug Generation on Software Error Models,* Rome Air Development Center Technical Report, RADC-TR-76-400, 1977.

[Shoo83] Shooman, M.L., *Software Engineering,* McGraw-Hill, New York, 1983.

[Shoo90] Shooman, M.L., *Probabilistic Reliability: An Engineering Approach,* McGraw-Hill, New York, 2d ed., 1990.

[Siew82] Siewiorek, D.P., and Swarz, R.S., *The Theory and Practice of Reliable System Design,* Digital Press, Bedford, Mass., 1982.

[Siew92] Siewiorek, D.P., and Swarz, R.S., *Reliable Computer Systems—Design and Evaluation,* 2d ed., Digital Press, Bedford, Mass., 1992.

[Siew93] Siewiorek, D., Hudak, J.J., Suh, B., and Segall, Z., "Development of a Benchmark to Measure System Robustness," *Proceedings of the 23rd International Symposium on Fault-Tolerant Computing,* 1993, pp. 88–97.

[Sing85] Singpurwalla, N.D., and Soyer, R., "Assessing (Software) Reliability Growth Using a Random Coefficient Autoregressive Process and Its Ramifications," *IEEE Transactions on Software Engineering,* vol. SE-11, no. 12, December 1985, pp. 1456–1464.

[Sing91] Singpurwalla, N.D., "Determining an Optimal Time Interval for Testing and Debugging Software," *IEEE Transactions on Software Engineering,* vol. 17, no. 4, 1991, pp. 313–319.

[Sing92] Singpurwalla, N.D., and Soyer, R., "Nonhomogenous Auto-Regressive Process for Tracking (Software) Reliability Growth, and Their Bayesian Analysis," *Journal of the Royal Statistical Society,* series B, vol. 54, 1992, pp. 145–156.

[Smit88] Smith, R.M., Trivedi, K.S., and Ramesh, A.V., "Performability Analysis: Measures, an Algorithm, and a Case Study," *IEEE Transactions on Computers,* vol. 37, no. 4, April 1988, pp. 406–417.

[Smit93] Smith, W., "Software and Switching System Reliability: Cause, Cure, or Both?" *Proceedings of Network Reliability: A Report to the Nation,* Symposium of the National Engineering Consortium, Washington, D.C., June 10–11, 1993.

[Soft93] Software Edge, *Defect Control System for Windows,* The Software Edge, Inc., Colorado Springs, Colo., 1993.

[Spat80] Spath, H., *Cluster Analysis Algorithms,* Ellis Horwood, West Sussex, U.K., 1990.

[Spec84] Spector, A., and Gifford, D., "The Space Shuttle Primary Computer System," *Communications of the ACM,* vol. 27, no. 8, 1984, pp. 874–900.

[SRMP88] *Software Reliability Modeling Programs,* Reliability and Statistical Consultants Ltd., Version 1.0, May 1988.

[Stam93] Stamen, J.P., "Structuring Data for Analysis," *IEEE Spectrum,* October 1993, pp. 55–58.

[Star87] Stark, G.E., "Dependability Evaluation of Integrated Hardware/Software Systems," *IEEE Transactions on Reliability,* vol. R-36, no. 4, 1987, pp. 440–444.

[Star91] Stark, G.E., "A Survey of Software Reliability Measurement Tools," *Proceedings of the International Symposium on Software Reliability Engineering,* Austin, Texas, May 1991, pp. 90–97.

[Ster78] Sterner, B.J., "Computerized Interlocking System—A Multidimensional Structure in the Pursuit of Safety," *IMechE Railway Engineer International,* November/December 1978, pp. 29–30.

[Ston74] Stone, M., "Cross-Validatory Choice and Assessment of Statistical Predictions," *Journal of the Royal Statistical Society,* series B, vol. 36, no. 2, 1974, pp. 111–147.

[Stri85] Strigini, L., and Avižienis, A., "Software Fault-Tolerance and Design Diversity: Past Experience and Future Evolution," *Proceedings IFAC SAFECOMP'85,* 1985, pp. 167–172.

[Suke76] Sukert, A., *A Software Reliability Modeling Study,* Rome Air Development Center Technical Report, RADC-TR-76-247, 1976.

[Suke80] Sukert, A., and Goel, A., "A Guidebook for Software Reliability Assessment," *1980 Proceedings of the Annual Reliability and Maintainability Symposium,* 1980, pp. 186–190.

[Sull91] Sullivan, M.S., and Chillarege, R., "Software Defects and Their Impact on System Availability—A Study of Field Failures in Operating Systems," *Proceedings of the 21st International Symposium Fault-Tolerant Computing,* June 1991, pp. 2–9.

[Swee95] Sweet, W., "The Glass Cockpit," *IEEE Spectrum,* September 1995, pp. 30–38.

[SWTR93] SWTRHA, *Report of the Inquiry into the London Ambulance Service,* South West Thames Regional Health Authority, February 1993.

[Tai93] Tai, A.T., Meyer, J.F., and Avižienis, A., "Performability Enhancement of Fault-Tolerant Software," *IEEE Transactions on Reliability,* vol. 42, no. 2, June 1993, pp. 227–237.

[Take86] Takeda, M., and Goodman, J., "Neural Networks for Computation: Number Representations and Programming Complexity," *Applied Optics,* vol. 25, no. 18, September 1986, pp. 3033–3045.

[TAND85] Tandem Computers Inc., *Product Reporting System User's Guide,* June 1985.

[TAND89] Tandem Computers Inc., *Tandem Maintenance and Diagnostic System Reference Manual,* March 1989.

[Tang90] Tang, D., Iyer, R.K., and Subramani, S., "Failure Analysis and Modeling of a VAXcluster System," *Proceedings of the 20th International Symposium on Fault-Tolerant Computing,* June 1990, pp. 244–251.

[Tang91] Tang, D., and Iyer, R.K., "Impact of Correlated Failures on Dependability in a VAXcluster System," *Proceedings of the 2nd IFIP Working Conference on Dependable Computing for Critical Applications,* Tucson, Arizona, February 1991.

[Tang92a] Tang, D., and Iyer, R.K., "Analysis and Modeling of Correlated Failures in Multicomputer Systems," *IEEE Transactions on Computers,* vol. 41, no. 5, May 1992, pp. 567–577.

[Tang92b] Tang, D., and Iyer, R.K., "Analysis of the VAX/VMS Error Logs in Multicomputer Environments—A Case Study of Software Dependability," *Proceedings of the Third International Symposium Software Reliability Engineering,* Research Triangle Park, North Carolina, October 1992, pp. 216–226.

[Tang92c] Tang, D., "Measurement-Based Dependability Analysis and Modeling for Multicomputer Systems," Ph.D. thesis, Department of Computer Science, University of Illinois at Urbana-Champaign, 1992.

[Tang93a] Tang, D., and Iyer, R.K., "Dependability Measurement and Modeling of a Multicomputer Systems," *IEEE Transactions on Computers,* vol. 42, no. 1, January 1993, pp. 62–75.

[Tang93b] Tang, D., and Iyer, R.K., "MEASURE+—A Measurement-Based Dependability Analysis Package," *Proceedings of the ACM SIGMETRICS Conference on Measurement and Modeling of Computer Systems,* Santa Clara, Calif., May 1993, pp. 110–121.

[Taus91] Tausworthe, R.C., "A General Software Reliability Process Simulation Technique," Technical Report 91-7, Jet Propulsion Laboratory, Pasadena, Calif., March 1991.

[Taus94] Tausworthe, R.C., and Lyu, M.R., "A Generalized Software Reliability Process Simulation Technique and Tool," *Proceedings of the 5th International Symposium on Software Reliability Engineering,* Monterey, Calif., November 1994.

[Taus96] Tausworthe, R.C., and Lyu, M.R., "A Generalized Technique for Simulating Software Reliability," *IEEE Software,* March 1996.

[Tayl80] Taylor, D.J., Morgan, D.E., and Black, J.P., "Redundancy in Data Structures: Improving Software Fault-Tolerance," *IEEE Transactions on Software Engineering,* vol. SE-6, 1980, pp. 585–594.

[Thay78] Thayer, T.A., Lipow, M., and Nelson, E.C., *Software Reliability,* North-Holland Publishing Company, New York, New York, 1978.

[Thev91] Thévenod-Fosse, P., "Software Validation by Means of Statistical Testing: Retrospect and Future Direction," *Dependable Computing and Fault-Tolerant Systems, Vol. 4,* A. Avižienis and J.-C. Laprie (eds.), Springer-Verlag, Wien, Austria and New York, 1991, pp. 25–48.

[Thom80] Thompson, W.E., and Chelson, P.O., "On the Specification and Testing of Software Reliability," *Proceedings of the 1980 Annual Reliability and Maintainability Symposium,* IEEE, New York, 1980, pp. 379–383.

[Tian93a] Tian, J., and Lu, P., "Measuring and Modeling Software Reliability: Data, Models, Tools, and a Support Environment," Technical Report, TR-74.117, IBM Canada Laboratory, March 1993.

[Tian93b] Tian, J., and Lu, P., "Software Reliability Measurement and Modeling for Multiple Releases of Commercial Software," *Proceedings of the Fourth International Symposium on Software Reliability Engineering,* Denver, Colo., November 3–6, 1993, pp. 253–260.

[Tohm89] Tohma, Y., Tokunaga, K., Nagase, S., and Murata, Y., "Structural Approach to the Estimation of the Number of Residual Faults Based on the Hyper-Geometric Distribution," *IEEE Transactions on Software Engineering,* vol. SE-15, no. 3, March 1989, pp. 345–355.

[Tohm89a] Tohma, Y., Jacoby, R., Murata, Y., and Yamamoto, M., "Hyper-Geometric Distribution Model to Estimate the Number of Residual Software Faults," *Proceedings COMPSAC 89,* IEEE CS Press, 1989, pp. 610–617.

[Tohm91] Tohma, Y., Yamano, H., Ohba, M., and Jacoby, R., "Parameter Estimation of the Hyper-Geometric Distribution Model for Real Test/Debug Data," *Proceedings of the 1991 IEEE International Symposium on Software Reliability Engineering,* May 1991, pp. 28–34.

[Tome93] Tomek, L.A., Muppala, J.K., and Trivedi, K.S., "Modeling Correlation in Software Recovery Blocks," *IEEE Transactions on Software Engineering,* vol. 19, no. 11, 1993, pp. 1071–1086.

[Toy85] Toy, W.N., "Modular Redundancy Concept, Problems and Solutions," *EPRI Seminar: Digital Control and Fault-Tolerant Computer Technology,* Scottsdale, Arizona, April 1985.

[Trac90] Trachtenberg, M., "A General Theory of Software Reliability Modeling," *IEEE Transactions on Reliability,* R-39, no. 1, 1990, pp. 92–96.

[Trav87] Traverse, P., "AIRBUS and ATR System Architecture and Specification," in [Voge87a], 1987, pp. 95–104.

[Triv75] Trivedi, A.K., "Computer Software Reliability: Many-State Markov Modeling Techniques," Ph.D. dissertation, Polytechnic Institute of Brooklyn, June, 1975.

[Triv82] Trivedi, K.S., *Probability and Statistics with Reliability, Queuing, and Computer Science Applications,* Prentice-Hall, Englewood Cliffs, New Jersey, 1982.

[Triv92] Trivedi, K.S., Muppala, J.K., Woolet, S.P., and Haverkort, B.R., "Composite Performance and Dependability Analysis," *Performance Evaluation,* vol. 14, February 1992, pp. 197–215.

[Troy85] Troy, R., and Baluteau, C., "Assessment of Software Quality for the Airbus A310 Automatic Pilot," *Proceedings of the 15th International Symposium on Fault-Tolerant Computing,* Ann Arbor, Mich., IEEE CS Press, June 1985, 438–443.

[Tsao83] Tsao, M.M., and Siewiorek, D.P., "Trend Analysis on System Error Files," *Proceedings of the 13th International Symposium on Fault-Tolerant Computing,* June 1983, pp. 116–119.

[Tso86] Tso, K.S., Avižienis, A., and Kelly, J.P.J., "Error Recovery in Multi-Version Software," *Proceedings IFAC SAFECOMP'86,* Sarlat, France, 1986, pp. 35–41.

[Tso87] Tso, K.S., and Avižienis, A., "Community Error Recovery in N-Version Software: A Design Study with Experimentation," *Proceedings of the 17th Fault-Tolerant Computing Symposium,* 1987, pp. 127–133.

[Tuke77] Tukey, J.W., *Exploratory Data Analysis,* Addison-Wesley, Reading, Mass., 1977.

[Turn87] Turner, D.B., Burns, R.D., and Hecht, H., "Designing Micro-Based Systems for Fail-Safe Travel," *IEEE Spectrum,* vol. 24, no. 2, February 1987, pp. 58–63.

[Uemu90] Uemura, M., Yamada, S., and Fujino, K., "Software Reliability Method: Application of Delayed S-Shaped NHPP Model and Other Related Models," *International Symposium on Reliability and Maintainability,* Tokyo, 1990, pp. 467–472.

[Upad86] Upadhyaya, S., and Saluja, K., "A Watchdog Processor Based General Rollback Technique with Multiple Retries," *IEEE Transactions on Software Engineering,* vol. SE-12, 1986, pp. 87–95.

[USAT93] *USA Today,* April 15, 1993, pp. 6B–7B.

[Vale88] Valette, V., "An Environment for Software Reliability Evaluation," *Proceedings of Software Engineering & Its Applications,* Toulouse, France, December 1988, pp. 879–897.

[Vale92] Valette, V., and Vallee, F., "Software Quality Metrics in Space Systems," *Proceedings of the Third International Symposium on Software Reliability Engineering,* Research Triangle Park, North Carolina, October 1992, pp. 296–302.

[Vela84] Velardi, P., and Iyer, R.K., "A Study of Software Failures and Recovery in the MVS Operating System," *IEEE Transactions on Computers,* vol. C-33, no. 6, June 1984, pp. 564–568.

[Vinn87] Vinneau, R., *User's Guide to a Computerized Implementation of the Goel-Okumoto Non-Homogeneous Poisson Process Software Reliability Model,* IIT Research Institute, Data Analysis Center for Software (DACS) report 90-0027, November 1987.

[Voge87a] Voges, U. (ed.), *Software Diversity in Computerized Control Systems,* vol. 2 of *Dependable Computing and Fault-Tolerant Systems,* A. Avižienis, H. Kopetz, and J.-C. Laprie (eds.), Springer-Verlag, Wien and New York, 1987.

[Voge87b] Voges, U., "Flight Applications," in [Voge87a], 1987, pp. 87–93.

[Voge87c] Voges, U., "Use of Diversity in Experimental Reactor Safety Systems," in [Voge87a], 1987, pp. 29–49.

[Vouk85] Vouk, M.A., McAllister, D.F., and Tai, K.C., "Identification of Correlated Failures of Fault-Tolerant Software Systems," in *Proceedings COMPSAC 85,* 1985, pp. 437–444.

[Vouk86a] Vouk, M.A., McAllister, D.F., and Tai, K.C., "An Experimental Evaluation of the Effectiveness of Random Testing of Fault-Tolerant Software," *Proceedings of the Workshop on Software Testing,* Banff, Canada, IEEE CS Press, July 1986, pp. 74–81.

[Vouk86b] Vouk, M.A., Helsabeck, M.L., Tai, K.C., and McAllister, D.F., "On Testing of Functionally Equivalent Components of Fault-Tolerant Software," *Proceedings COMPSAC 86,* 1986, pp. 414–419.

[Vouk88] Vouk, M.A., "On Engineering of Fault-Tolerant Software," *10th International Symposium,* "Computer at the University," Cavtat 88, Cavtat, Croatia, 1988.

[Vouk90a] Vouk, M.A., Caglayan, A., Eckhardt, D.E., Kelly, J., Knight, J., McAllister, D., and Walker, L., "Analysis of Faults Detected in a Large-Scale Multiversion Software Development Experiment," *Proceedings DASC'90,* 1990, pp. 378–385.

[Vouk90b] Vouk, M.A., Paradkar, A., and McAllister, D., "Modeling Execution Time of Multistage N-Version Fault-Tolerant Software," *Proceedings COMPSAC '90,* October 1990, pp. 505–511. Reprinted in *Fault-Tolerant Software Systems: Techniques and Applications,* Hoang Pham (ed.), IEEE Computer Society Press, 1992, pp. 55–61.

[Vouk90c] Vouk, M.A., "Back-to-Back Testing," *Information and Software Technology,* vol. 32, no. 1, 1990, pp. 34–45.

[Vouk92] Vouk, M.A., "Using Reliability Models During Testing with Non-Operational Profiles," *Proceedings Second Workshop on Issues in Software Reliability Estimation,* October 12–13, 1992, Bellcore, Livingston, N.J.

[Vouk93a] Vouk, M.A., McAllister, D.F., Eckhardt, D.E., and Kim, K., "An Empirical Evaluation of Consensus Voting and Consensus Recovery Block Reliability in the Presence of Failure Correlation," *Journal of Computer and Software Engineering,* vol. 1, no. 4, 1993, pp. 367–388.

[Vouk93b] Vouk, M.A., and Tai, K.C., "Some Issues in Multi-Phase Software Reliability Modeling," *Proceedings CASCON '93,* October 1993.

[Wago73] Wagoner, W., *The Final Report on a Software Reliability Measurement Study,* The Aerospace Corp., El Segundo, Calif., Report No. TOR-0074 (4112)-1, August 15, 1973.

[Wall84] Wallace, J.J., and Barnes, W.W., "Designing for Ultrahigh Availability: The Unix RTR Operating System," *IEEE Computer,* August 1984, pp. 31–39.

[Wals85] Walsh, P.J., "A Measure of Test Case Completeness," Ph.D. dissertation, State University of New York, Binghamton, N.Y., 1985.

[Wang93] Wang, Y.M., Huang, Y., and Fuchs, W.K., "Progressive Retry for Software Error Recovery in Distributed Systems," *Proceedings of the 23rd International Symposium on Fault-Tolerant Computing,* June 1993, pp. 138–144.

[Wats91] Watson, G.F., "Service Disrupted in Cities: Bell Companies, Manufacturers Join to Cure Phone Outages," *The Institute,* IEEE Press, September 1991, pp. 1 and 7.

[Weer94] Weerahandi, S., and Hausman, R.E., "Software Quality Measurement Based on Fault-Detection Data," *IEEE Transactions Software Engineering,* September 1994, pp. 665–676.

[Wei91] Wei, L., "A Model Based Study of Workload Influence on Computing System Dependability," Ph.D. thesis, University of Michigan, 1991.

[Weib51] Weibull, W., "A Statistical Distribution Function of Wide Application," *J. Appl. Mech.,* vol. 18, 1951, pp. 293–297.

[Weig90] Weigend, A., Huberman, B., and Rumelhart, D., "Predicting the Future: A Connectionist Approach," Stanford University, TR Stanford-PDP-90-01, April 1990.

[Wein90] Wein, A.S., and Sathaye, A., "Validating Complex Computer System Availability Models," *IEEE Transactions on Reliability,* vol. 39, no. 4, October 1990, pp. 468–479.

[Weis88] Weiss, S.N., and Weyuker, E.J., "An Extended Domain-Based Model of Software Reliability," *IEEE Transactions on Software Engineering,* SE-14, no. 12, 1988, pp. 1512–1524.

[Werb74] Werbos, P., "Beyond Regression: New Tools for Prediction and Analysis in the Behavioral Sciences," Ph.D. thesis, Harvard University, Cambridge, Mass., 1974.

[Will83] Williams, J.F., Yount, L.J., and Flanningan, J.B., "Advanced Autopilot Flight Director System Computer Architecture for Boeing 737-300 Aircraft," *Proceedings of the 5th Digital Avionics Systems Conference,* Seattle, Wash., 1983.

[Will89] Williams, R., and Zipser, D., "A Learning Algorithm for Continually Running Fully Recurrent Neural Networks," *Neural Computation,* vol. 1, no. 2, 1989, pp. 270–280.

[Wong93] Wong, W.E., "On Mutation and Data Flow," dissertation, available as Technical Report SERC-TR-149-P, Software Engineering Research Center, Purdue University, W. Lafayette, Ind., 1993.

[Wrig86] Wright, N.C.J., "Dissimilar Software," *Workshop on Design Diversity in Action,* Baden, Austria, June 1986, see summary in [Voge87b].

[Wrig88] Wright, D.R., "A Modified u-Plot Applied to Failure Count Prediction," Technical Report, Centre for Software Reliability, City University, London, 1988.

[Wrig93] Wright, D.R., *Recalibrated Prediction of Some Software Failure-Count Sequences,* PDCS2 Project (ESPRIT Project 6362) First Year Report, chap. 4, part 4.1, Centre for Software Reliability, City University, London, 1993.

[Xie91a] Xie, M., *Software Reliability Modeling,* World Scientific Publishing Company, 1991.

[Xie91b] Xie, M., and Zhao, M., *On Some Reliability Growth Models with Simple Graphical Interpretations,* Institute of Technology, Linkoeping, Sweden, ISSN 0281-5001, 1991.

[Xie93a] Xie, M., "Software Reliability Models—A Selected Bibliography," *Journal of Software Testing, Verification and Reliability,* no. 3, 1993, pp. 3–28.

[Xie93b] Xie, M., and Zhao, M., "On Some Reliability Growth Models with Simple Graphical Interpretations," *Microelectronics and Reliability,* vol. 33, no. 2, 1993, pp. 149–167.

[Yama83] Yamada, S., Ohba, M., and Osaki, S., "S-Shaped Reliability Growth Modeling for Software Error Detection," *IEEE Transactions on Reliability,* vol. R-32, no. 5, December 1983, pp. 475–478.

[Yama85] Yamada, S., and Osaki, S., "Software Reliability Growth Modeling: Models and Assumptions," *IEEE Transactions on Software Engineering,* vol. SE-11, no. 12, December 1985, pp. 1431–1437.

[Yama86] Yamada, S., Ohtera, H., and Narihisa, H., "A Testing-Effort Dependent Reliability Model for Computer Programs," *The Transactions of the IECE of Japan,* vol. E 69, no. 11, pp. 1217–1224, 1986.

[Yama91] Yamada, S., Tanio, Y., and Osaki, S., "Software Reliability Measurement and Assessment Methods during Operational Phase and Their Comparisons," *Transactions Inst. Electronic Inf. Communication Engineering*, vol. J74-DI, March 1991, pp. 240–248; in Japanese.

[Yau75] Yau, S.S., and Cheung, R.C., "Design of Self-Checking Software," *Proceedings of the 1975 International Conference on Reliable Software,* 1975, pp. 450–457.

[Youn86] Yount, L.J., "Use of Diversity in Boeing Airplanes," *Workshop on Design Diversity in Action,* Baden, Austria, June 1986, see summary in [Voge87b].

[Your89] Yourdon, E., *Modern Structured Analysis,* Prentice-Hall, Englewood Cliffs, New Jersey, 1989.

[Zave93] Zave, P., "Feature Interactions and Formal Specifications in Telecommunications," *IEEE Computer,* August 1993, pp. 20–29.

[Zinn90a] Zinnel, K.C., "Using Software Reliability Growth Models to Guide Release Decisions," *Proceedings of the 1990 International Symposium on Software Reliability Engineering,* Washington, D.C., April 1990.

[Zuse91] Zuse, H., *Software Complexity: Measures and Methods,* Walter De Gruyter, New York, 1991.

Index

ABOUT THE EDITOR

Michael R. Lyu is currently a Member of the Technical Staff at AT&T Bell Laboratories, Murray Hill, focusing on software reliability engineering, software fault tolerance, and distributed systems. He has published fifty papers in these fields. He is also the editor of *Software Fault Tolerance* (Wiley, 1995). Dr. Lyu received his B.S. in Electrical Engineering from National Taiwan University in 1981, M.S. in Electrical and Computer Engineering from University of California, Santa Barbara, in 1984, and Ph.D. in Computer Science from UCLA in 1988. He previously worked at JPL, Bellcore, and taught at the University of Iowa.